BALTIMORE

in

WORLD WAR II

BALTIMORE in WORLD WAR II

Copyright © 1993 by Historical Briefs, Inc.
All rights reserved

No part of this publication may be reproduced, stored in a retrieval system, or transmitted in any form or by any means, electronic, mechanical, photocopying, recording, or otherwise, without the prior permission of the publisher.

Developed under agreement with **Historical Briefs, Inc.**, Box 629, Sixth Street & Madalyn Ave., Verplanck, NY 10596.

Printed by:
Monument Printers & Lithographer, Inc.
Sixth Street & Madalyn Ave., Verplanck, NY 10596

Foreword

The events of World War II as viewed by historians and the people of the world, in general, is of interest to everyone who would be interested for scholarly or other reasons.

But the events of World War II as seen through the eyes of Baltimorians is best viewed from the vantage point of the local newspaper of the day in Baltimore, the News Post. After all we who lived in Baltimore at the time had our own special interests. Sure we were interested in world events as they affected different people in different places, but we were most interested in the things that were happening in our town.

That's what this book is all about. It's a look back at the way we were, and the way Baltimore was during the World War. This is nostalgia mixed with history mixed with our personal feelings.

The Editors

Come now for a journey through the
"Pages of Time-Gone-By"
from the greatest natural repository of history
The Newspapers that recorded it all
for posterity.

POPE PLEADS FOR WORLD PEACE

THE WEATHER
Weather Forecast on Page 2, Col. 1.

The Only Newspaper in Maryland with both the Associated Press and International News Service.

THE BALTIMORE NEWS-POST
AN INDEPENDENT NEWSPAPER
The Largest Daily Circulation in the Entire South

COMPLETE MARKETS

VOL. CXXXIV.—NO. 102 C

Entered as second-class matter at Baltimore Postoffice.
Copyright, 1939, by Hearst Consolidated Publications, Inc.
SATURDAY, MARCH 4, 1939

PRICE 2 CENTS

Army Expansion Bill Passed By House

New Pontiff Making World Plea For Peace

In an eloquent plea for peace, Pope Pius XII., shown above as he broadcast from the Sistine Chapel, asked for justice, charity and concord among the nations of the world, just after receiving formal acknowledgment of his powers from College of Cardinals. The picture was telephoned to London, radioed to New York and telephoned to Baltimore. International News Service Radiophoto.

Bill Directs U. S. To Cut Expenses

Pope In Plea For World Peace

Text of Pope Pius XII.'s radio broadcast will be found on Page 2.

VATICAN CITY, March 3—(I. N. S.).—Newly elected Pope Pius XII. may soon appoint another Cardinal—perhaps two—for the United States, one to be a successor to the late Patrick Cardinal Hayes as Archbishop of New York, it was indicated today.

The Most Rev. Stephen J. Donahue of the New York Diocese is an outstanding probability. A fifth cardinal for the United States, possibly one living on the Pacific coast, also was considered.

By FRANK GERVASI
International News Service Staff Correspondent.

VATICAN CITY, March 3.—Pope Pius XII. struck the keynote of his reign as Supreme Pontiff of the Roman Catholic Church today with an impassioned plea for peace on earth and charity among men.

Losing no time in making his views known, the newly elected Pope, in a short radio address, invoked the aid of the Holy Spirit to pacify mankind and bring concord between nations.

VIBRANT VOICE

His vibrant Roman voice, youthful and full of energy, His Holiness imparted with the clarity of rounded Latin phrases a stirring address which he delivered just after receiving formal acknowledgment of his powers from the Senators.

Earlier, all 61 members of the College of Cardinals had taken their third oath of fealty to the Pontiff whom they elected yester day to the throne of St. Peter. He

Continued on Page 8, Column 1.

House O.K.'s 499 Million Army Bill

WASHINGTON, March 3—(I. N. S.).—In an unprecedented move, the House today passed the $499,000,000 Army supply bill with less than a half hour action.

There was no recorded vote. The measure now goes to the Senate.

784 PLANES PROVIDED

The bill carried funds for the acquisition of 784 additional planes for the Army, 565 of which would be built as a part of the new expansion program.

CITES PRECEDENT

There was only one minor amendment.

Representative Snyder (Democrat) of Pennsylvania, chairman of the House Appropriations Subcommittee on military establishments told the Chamber that it was the first time in the 150 years' history of this country the House had approved a regular military supply bill without noteworthy change.

The measure also provided for a $6,756,378 expansion program for the air and coast defenses in Hawaii and the Panama Canal.

Other major provisions of the bill include:

For the pay of the Army—$170,208,385, an increase of $24,000,000 over 1938. A sum of $46,840,62 for the Ordnance Department (munitions and supplies), and increase of $8,608,586 over last year.

SEACOAST DEFENSES

For seacoast defenses—$7,250,523, an increase of a half million dollars. For the National Guard—$44,803,305, an increase of $2,700,000.

For organized reserves—$12,802,557, an increase of $1,000,000. For citizens' military training—$7,109,742, an increase of $500,000.

Loses Son

Count Kurt Haugwitz-Reventlow has obtained custody of his son, Lance, on a court order. He is estranged from the Countess (above), the former Barbara Hutton.

Story on Page 2.

War On Crows On Poplar Is.

EASTON, March 3—(A. P.).—Poplar Island is going to be the scene Monday of a pitched battle on crows, enemies of mainland farmers, whose fields they ravage daily.

About 100 sportsmen have declared a one-day war on the pests, and fixed Monday as the day. The sportsmen, armed with shotguns, will take a special boat to the island, about three miles out in the bay, and lie in wait for the crows, which return to roost late in the day.

Harvey Samis of Easton, will be the "general" of the offensive forces.

40-Ton Airliner Ends Maiden Hop

HONGKONG, March 3—(A. P.). Pan American Airways' new 40-ton, 74-passenger clipper today completed her maiden trans-Pacific flight, alighting here on the final leg from Manila. She carried mail, express and 28 persons, all members of the staffs of Pan-American airways or the Boeing and Wright companies.

HUGE PLANT REOPENS

MANNINGTON, W. Va., March 3 (A. P.).—The Mannington Sanitary Pottery, one of the largest plants of its kind in the world, resumed operations today after four months of idleness.

House Asks Curbs On Roosevelt

Latest developments in the national program to cut Government costs were:

1. New reorganization bill directs President to reduce Federal expenditures.

2. Congress asks Secretary Morgenthau to submit a plan to eliminate taxes on business.

By WILLIAM S. NEAL
International News Service Staff Correspondent.

WASHINGTON, March 3.—President Roosevelt today was directed in the new Government reorganization bill to "reduce" Federal expenditures to the fullest extent possible consistent with efficient operation of Government as the measure was formally reported to the House.

The report, filed with the House by Representative Cochran (Democrat) of Missouri, chairman of the special committee on Government reorganization, directed the President to carry out the reorganization program with the following standards in view:

1. "Reduce expenditure to the fullest extent possible consistent with the efficient operation of Government.

INCREASE EFFICIENCY

2. "Increase efficiency of operations of Government to the fullest extent practicable within revenues.

3. "Group, co-ordinate and con-

Continued on Page 3, Column 3.

Fight Court Union In Caroline Co.

DENTON, March 3—(A. P.).—Opposition to centralization of county police courts in Caroline County was expressed at a county-wide meeting called by Elmer T. Orme, chairman of the County's Democratic State Central Committee.

Orme, Allison H. Covey of Federalsburg, and Thomas L. Truce of Preston, were named to present the group's opposition to the Legislature.

Under a proposed bill reorganis the magistrate system, the county would have one justice, to be paid $1,200 annually, instead of a magistrate in every town.

A Real-Life Horror Story Poe Might Have Written. Psychologist explains how oss of memory and sleep-walking can change a worthy citizen into somebody entirely different. Illustrated feature in the American Weekly, with next Sunday's Baltimore American.—Adv.

Pope Felicitated By Roosevelt

CHARLESTON, S. C., March 3 (A. P.).—President Roosevelt cabled felicitations today to the new Pope at the Vatican. The text of his message to the former Eugenio Cardinal Pacelli, who visited the President at Hyde Park, N. Y., last fall:

"His Holiness Pope Pius XII. the Vatican City.

"It is with true happiness that I learned of your selection as supreme Pontiff. Recalling with pleasure our meeting on the occasion of your recent visit to the United States, I wish to take this occasion to send you a personal message of felicitation and good wishes.

(Signed) "Roosevelt."

Naval Radio Gets Ship's SOS Call

PEIPING, China, March 3—(U. P.).—The Naval radio intercepted an S O S call today from the steamer Gemlock in Techila Gulf north of Shantung Peninsula, saying it was aground on the rocks and that the crew was taking to the boats.

$1,000,000 Asked For Savage Dam

CUMBERLAND, Md., March 3—(A. P.).—The first official step toward obtaining $1,000,000 to help finance [illegible] earth dam across the Savage river was taken today by the Allegany County Commissioners.

They approved and sent to the Legislature bill to permit them to issue bonds for the $1,000,000 or borrow it from a Federal agency.

The dam is designed to control the flow of water into the Potomac. It would keep the Potomac at a constant level during drought periods, for the benefit of industrial plants along the stream, and prevent floods during spring rain and thaw.

BETTER SANITATION

Proponents say it also will improve sanitary conditions in Allegany and Garrett counties by providing greater dilution of sewage dumped into Western Maryland streams by small towns and unincorporated communities.

The commissioners are directed under the projected law to give the proceeds of the bond issue or loan over to the Savage River Dam project, excepting incidental costs incurred by the Upper Potomac River Commission.

EMERGENCY CLAUSE

The act contains an emergency clause which would it effective upon passage.

The $1,000,000 which would be supplied by the county if the act passes and the commissioners decide to float the bonds or obtain the loan, would be augmented by $1,452,000 from the Works Progress Administration.

The $2,452,000 dam, plans for which already have been drawn, would be almost a quarter of a mile long and 185 feet high. It would be built across the Savage river in Garrett county near the river's confluence with Crabtree creek.

15 Burmese Dead In Religious Riots

RANGOON, Burma, March 3—(A. P.).—Fifteen persons have been killed and 200 injured in a fresh wave of Hindu-Moslem rioting starting yesterday. Police and military patrols clashed several times with demonstrators.

18 In Santa Anita Handicap

MIAMI, Fla., March 3—(U. P.).—Headed by H. Maxwell Howard's Stagehand, a field of nine was entered today for the fourth running of the $50,000 added Widener Challenge Cup at Hialeah Park tomorrow. Other entries were: Teddy Weed, Sir Damion, Warlaine, Mythical King, Pasteurized, Francesco, Bull Lea and Xavier.

ARCADIA, Cal., March 3—(U. P.).—A field of eighteen was entered today for the $100,000 added Santa Anita Handicap, world's

Continued on Page 37, Column 7.

Accuse Undertaker In 50 Safe Thefts

DETROIT, March 3—(I. N. S.).—Climaxing a two-year mystery of safes stolen during robberies, Undertaker Herbert Harbin, thirty-five, today was under arrest, charged with being the leader of a gang of safecrackers who used his hearse to cart safes away from the scene of the crimes—more than 50 in number—netting $50,000.

The LIFE Of The New 'Pope Of Peace'

The Story of His Holiness, PIUS XII.

(The News-Post herewith presents the first chapter of a remarkable life-story of the new Pope, Pius XII., written by Thomas B. Morgan, author of "Reporter at the Papal Court." Mr. Morgan, during his many years at Vatican City, came into direct contact with the new Pope while the latter, as Cardinal Pacelli, was serving as Papal Secretary of State.

This up-to-the-minute biography of the new Pontiff of the Roman Catholic Church will tell in dramatic detail the story of Cardinal Pacelli's life and career.)

CHAPTER I.
By THOMAS B. MORGAN
AUTHOR OF "REPORTER AT THE PAPAL COURT"

(World copyright, 1939, by King Features Syndicate, Inc. All rights reserved. Reproduction in whole or part strictly prohibited.)

With him who was to become Pius XII. I stood on the terrace of the Villa Falconara overlooking the blue waters of the Mediterranean at Civitavecchia, forty miles from

Continued on Page 2, Column 1.

W. R. Hearst To Speak Tonight On Prosperity

Mr. William Randolph Hearst will speak from California over the coast-to-coast Red network of the National Broadcasting Company tonight at 6.45 o'clock, Pacific Coast time (9.45 P. M., E. S. T.) on "A Plea For Prosperity." Mr. Hearst will broadcast from Station KFI, N B. C. studio in Los Angeles, and will be heard here over WFBR.

THE BALTIMORE NEWS-POST, SATURDAY, MARCH 4, 1939   9

Feelin' low, are you?

What you need is a **BOND CAMERON WORSTED**

New herringbones for tall men

New cluster stripes for short men

New tick weaves for portly men

Shake off that Winter "hangover". A change is all you need—a change to a fresh new suit. *A Bond Cameron Worsted!* Give your spirit a lift, with a dash of new Spring color. Put pep in your step with a smooth Cameron herringbone, a new cluster stripe. Shoulder into a flattering new double-breasted. You'll feel like a different man. ★ Hundreds of crisp Cameron Worsteds are ready to give you "the cure". They are the finest our tailors have ever produced. And they cost little—for they come to you direct from our own workrooms, with no middleman's profit added on. Try Bond's Cameron prescription today or tomorrow. It'll work wonders for you.

$25
with two trousers

Complete Outfitters to Men

BOND CLOTHES
27-31 W. Baltimore St. at Hanover
Open Daily 9 to 6   Saturday 9 to 9
Two-Hour Parking at Fayette Auto Parking

Charge It the Bond way. Pay weekly or twice a month. It costs nothing extra.

Nicaragua Now A Fast Friend Of Uncle Sam

President Somoza Urges Construction Of New Lock Canal

By H. R. KNICKERBOCKER
International News Service Staff Correspondent
(Copyright 1939 by International News Service. Reproduction in whole or part strictly prohibited.)

MANAGUA, March 3 — War threats loom large in American thinking at home, but every step nearer to the Panama canal the potential menace grows more vivid, and today in Nicaragua the problem of our national defense is as acutely regarded as though this country were a part of the United States.

The rise of the totalitarian and imperialist powers and their aggressions against weak nations have put the Monroe Doctrine in a new light for the little countries of Central America.

The fate of Manchukuo, China, Abyssinia, Austria and Czechoslovakia is the background and the good neighbor policy is the foreground of the international picture as viewed today in this part of the world.

OLD COLOSSUS DEAD.

America is no longer the colossus of the North, to be suspected and feared. In the eyes of these small nations the United States has now assumed the role of a necessary protector against the predatory ambitions of European and Asiatic powers.

The good neighbor policy, religiously practiced as it has been for the last seven years, often to the financial disadvantage of Americans, has finally convinced the majority public opinion of these countries that the United States should now be trusted.

YOUNGEST PRESIDENT

No head of a state south of the Rio Grande has keener appreciation of what the United States means for his country than Anastasio Somoza, elected president of Nicaragua in 1936 at the age of 40, and still the youngest president in Central America.

Seated in a railroad train he remarked:

"As long as the United States protects our freedom and sovereignty we will remain free and independent, but as soon as the United States withdraws or is unable to continue this protection, we will become the likely victims of European or Asiatic powers.

"That's the common sense about the Monroe Doctrine, and that's why we have as great an interest in your national defense as you have. They talk about U. S. aggression in Nicaragua but your marines never came here except at the request of Nicaraguan governments."

COMMANDED TROOPS

Somoza, before becoming president, was commander of the national guard, now a force of 2,500 men, said to be the best army for its size in Central America. In their flat steel helmets, their immaculate khaki, they look like U. S. marines.

The most gratifying thing to learn in Nicaragua is that the "invading" marines, far from being remembered unfavorably, were the most popular visitors ever to come to the country. Their persons as well as their payroll are wistfully recollected by the Nicaraguan people.

President Somoza waxed enthusiastic on the one subject that preoccupies every Nicaraguan's life. Every second citizen of the country is said to have acquired land in hopes will multiply in value when their canal dream comes true.

BACKS UNITED STATES

The president asserted:

"You really have only one alternative to the Nicaraguan canal. That is to build another fleet the size of your present navy. The extra set of locks at Panama won't provide the necessary security. Figure out how much it would cost to duplicate your navy and then compare the cost of maintenance of the Nicaraguan canal with the cost of maintaining another navy."

President Somoza concluded by saying:

"Whether you build the canal here or not, Nicaragua is behind the United States 100 per cent, in peace or war. You can count every soldier our country can raise for the defense of the continent. Your defense is our defense not only on Nicaraguan sympathy and affection for the United States, but you can count on fense."

Forest Park High To Hold Jubilee

Preparations are under way at the Forest Park Junior High School for the annual student presentation, the Jolly Junior Jubilee, on the nights of March 10 and 11.

The event, which combines entertainment and a bazar, is one of the chief means of raising funds for extra-curricular activities with all proceeds turned over to the board of student activities. The "jubilee" is in three parts—gym show, auditorium show and dance.

All of the scenery, costumes, advertising posters and other materials are made by the students and nearly 100 will participate in the entertainment. Hugh Roper and Julius Robinson will act as masters of ceremonies.

JULIUS GUTMAN & CO.
Downstairs
LEXINGTON STREET AT PARK AVENUE

New for Spring!
THRIFT COATS
Dress Coats! Tweed Coats! Reefer Coats! Toppers!

- Smart, Nuby Eponge!
- Smart Striped Worsted!
- All Occasion Tweeds!
- Sizes 12 to 20, 38 to 52
- Checks!   • Stripes!
- Black!   • Navy!

$9.74

A little cash price for lots of style and quality! Such variety, you'll think you're seeing a *fashion show* of the new coats! So smart you can just about pick with your eyes closed! Whatever type of coat is most becoming to *you*—you'll find it tomorrow in the Thrift Department!

New Swing Skirt. Sizes 12 to 20.

Spring Coat Group! Cash Priced
Toppers and reefers! Suede cloth, eponge, tweeds, diagonal twill effect! Fine worsteds in navy and black! Sizes 12 to 20, 38 to 44 in this amazing group!
$6.66

Boxy Tweed, Sizes 12 to 20, 38 to 44.   *Eponge Reefer, Sizes 12 to 20.*

Huge Variety!
Thrift Dresses
$1.88

- Smart Spun Rayon Prints!
- Popular Rayon Cynara Crepe!
- High Fashion Polka Dots!
- Bright Rayon French Crepe Prints!
- Sizes 12 to 20, 38 to 52!

Help yourself to armfuls of bright, smart refreshing frocks tomorrow! You'll be thrilled with the variety; each as appealing as the next! You'll be impressed with the LARGE cash saving! They're the very dresses you want RIGHT NOW and for all spring—ready for a smart future!

Backless Pump, Patent, Blue, Japonica   *Barge Oxford, Brown, Camel, Black*   *Saddle Oxford, Brown and White, Camel and Brown*

Toeless Oxford, Patent, Japonica   *Congo Sandal, Patent, Blue, Japonica*   *Patent Pump, Drape Effect*

Just 6 Of Our 67 New Spring Styles
IN OUR NEW DOWNSTAIRS SHOE DEPARTMENT   **$1.59**

Smart Novelties! Sport Styles! Comfortable Arch and Nurse Shoes! A complete department of popular and desirable women's shoes—priced LOWER for CASH! Sorry, No Mail or C. O. D. Orders!

Event!
Crisp New Cotton Frocks
97c

Dozens to choose from. TAILORED STYLES with such details as long zippers, button-down-the-front coats, crisply trimmed collars or chic collarless ones! FLUFFY STYLES with vestees, frills! Handy pockets! Sizes 14 to 52.

★ Gutman's buy and sell for cash only. The constant savings resulting from our doing business in this way are passed on to you. Get the Cash Store habit and you'll be pleased at the savings accumulated over a period of months.

POLICE SERGEANT SHOT IN GUN BATTLE ON N. GILMOR STREET

THE BALTIMORE NEWS-POST

The Largest Daily Circulation in the Entire South

THE WEATHER
Weather Forecast on Page 2, Col. 1.

MEAN TEMPERATURES YESTERDAY.
Baltimore	47	Chicago	47
xAtlanta	55	xOmaha	57
xBoston	42	Los Angeles	66
New York	45	xSalt Lake City	55
Portland, Maine	40	Seattle	50
xWashington	46	New Orleans	68

xObservations taken at airport.

VOL. CXXXIV.—NO. 127   SATURDAY EVENING, APRIL 1, 1939   PRICE 2 CENTS

NIGHT RACE SPECIAL

Nazis Seek New Conquests--Knickerbocker
HITLER TO ANSWER BRITAIN

Police Sergeant Shot In Gun Battle On North Gilmor Street

Sergt. John H. Schmidt was shot below the heart today during a gun battle between police and a Negro on the pavement in the 1600 block North Gilmor street.

The Negro, identified as Clarence Brown, eighteen, was shot three times.

Seriously wounded, Sergeant Schmidt was taken to West Baltimore General Hospital and was taken immediately to the operating room for an emergency operation.

ORDERED TO HOME

Patrolman Thomas Higgins, who took part in the gun duel with Brawn, said he and Sergeant Schmidt had been ordered to go to Brown's home and arrest him as a suspect in a shooting affray last night.

Higgins said:

"As we approached Brown's home in the 1600 block North Gilmor street we saw Brown on the pavement in front of the house. I have known Brown for several years.

"Brown saw us at about the same time.

BREAKS AWAY

"He started to run and we grabbed him. He broke away and tried to run but we seized him again.

"Then he drew a pistol from his waist and put it against Sergeant Schmidt's back. I drew my gun and ran around him, trying to get in position to fire at Brown.

"He fired once at me. I could see the Sergeant trying to get his own gun out of the holster.

"I fired three times at Brown

Continued on Page 2, Column 2.

Roosevelt Keeping Watch On Europe

WARM SPRINGS, Ga., April 1—(A. P.)—Concerned over fresh threats to world peace, President Roosevelt kept close by his mountain cottage telephone again today, receiving a play-by-play account of the latest moves on the European diplomatic checkerboard.

Temperatures
Midnight	42	6 A. M.	43
1 A. M.	42	7 A. M.	45
2 A. M.	41	8 A. M.	45
3 A. M.	42	9 A. M.	46
4 A. M.	42	10 A. M.	47
5 A. M.	43	11 A. M.	52

Race entries, scratches, comment, will be found on Sport Pages today

---

In Battle

SERGT. JOHN SCHMIDT

PATROLMAN THOMAS HIGGINS

Sergt. John H. Schmidt, Northwestern district, was shot and dangerously wounded today in a gun battle he and Patrolman Thomas Higgins fought on the street in the 1600 block North Gilmor street today, with a Negro, Clarence Brown, who also was wounded. Higgins escaped injury. Pictures copyright, 1939, by The Baltimore News-Post. All rights reserved.

Louis Baker Is Victim Of Fatal Beating

PITTSBURGH, April 1—(A. P.)—Friends of the famous chocolate-making family last night identified the victim of a fatal beating in Y. M. C. A. dormitory as Louis Marshall Baker, forty-seven, one-time host to royalty and boyhood friend of Rear Admiral Richard Evelyn Byrd.

The man who once was a civic leader at his ancestral house at Winchester, Va., a philanthropist, the owner of theatres and a baseball club, died a WPA recreation supervisor, tight-lipped about his past and declining to the death to name his assailant.

He died in a hospital at noon yesterday, six days after detectives learned he was beaten in his Y. M. C. A. room.

BODY TO WINCHESTER

The coroner's office reported the body had been released to a Pittsburgh undertaker, who said he would send it to Winchester tomorrow. A brother in Winchester

Continued on Page 2, Column 6.

No Tags

The first arrest of a motorist for not having 1939 license tags took place early today in the shadow of police headquarters.

The victim was Private Walter Bell of Fort George G. Meade. Patrolman James A. Lennon, Central district, made the arrest.

Taken before Lieut. John Spites, Bell said, "he forgot" to get the new tags. He had to deposit $10.50 for a hearing April 26.

Preposterous "April Fool" Jokes That Made History. Read about some of the pranks that the world won't forget in The American Weekly, distributed with tomorrow's Baltimore Sunday American.—Adv.

U. S. Debt Passes 40-Billion Mark

WASHINGTON, April 1—(A. P.)—The Treasury's debt passed the $40,000,000,000 mark today, coming within $5,000,000,000 of the statutory limit. The debt now is equivalent to approximately $305 per person. A year ago the $37,556,302,000 debt equalled $289.17 per capita.

Says Reich Seeks New Conquests

Breathing Spell To Be Brief, Says Knickerbocker

By H. R. KNICKERBOCKER
International News Service Staff Correspondent.
(Copyright, 1939.)

PARIS, April 1—British Prime Minister Neville Chamberlain may have stopped Chancellor Hitler for a few days, but news reached Paris from Berlin today that Der Fuehrer, whose figure now towers over Europe like no one since Napoleon, has told German Foreign Minister Joachim von Ribbentrop:

"I must finish my program this year."

TIME IS SHORT

The time is short. The program is vast. There may be room for a breathing spell for a week or two, but that is all Europe hopes for now.

According to Hitler's book, "Mein Kampf," the Reichsfuehrer does not propose to cease conquering until there is space for 200,000,000 Germans in Europe.

"GLOOMY SATURDAY"

This day, therefore, despite the Anglo-French declaration of sup-

Continued on Page 2, Column 7.

France To Seek Russia's Help

PARIS, April 1—(A. P.)—France worked today to co-ordinate her military effectiveness—in line with the new anti-Hitler bloc created by the British-French pledge of aid to preserve Polish independence.

In French eyes, Poland and Rumania are the outlying "alarm" States—ready to sound the call if Germany endeavored to acquire new territory.

Soviet Russia, diplomatic circles said, would be urged by the French to promise Poland or Rumania she would rush planes, tanks and motorized equipment to aid, when and if either asked for them.

By agreement with London, Paris was reported to be handling negotiations with Russia under the French-Russian mutual assistance treaty.

Torch Singer Bride

Libby Holman (above), the Broadway torch singer, whose first husband, Smith Reynolds, tobacco heir, died a violent death, is a bride again. The new husband is Ralph Holmes, twenty-three, Washington, an actor and the son of the veteran stage star, Taylor Holmes. Picture from International News Photograph Service.

Poles Continue War Preparations

WARSAW, April 1—(A. P.)—Poland, promised full French-British military assistance in the event of German attack, calmly awaited Chancellor Hitler's speech today as the key to the next Nazi move.

Although Poles generally expressed belief that "nothing will happen now," the government continued preparations for a possible war.

One official said:

"The Fuehrer's speech is sure to be full of sparks. Maybe they'll set fire to something."

It also was reported that a defensive alliance between Poland and Lithuania, which ceded Memel to Germany, had been under discussion and now was being hastened to a conclusion.

EXCHANGE DATA

Poland was reportedly reliably already exchanging military information with Britain and France to implement the new Anglo-French guarantee to help assure Polish independence, announced yesterday by Premier Chamberlain.

Scratches At Bowie

First Race—Eagle's Wonder.
Second—Idle Bill, Kermay, Golden Vein.
Early Times, Jax Breaker, New Deal.
Third—Francipessa, Bounding Count, High Betsy.
Seventh—Princepessa, Bounding Count.
Weather clear; track slow.

Thousands Gather At Battleship Launching To Hear Reichsfuehrer

BERLIN, April 1—(A. P.)—Adolf Hitler's speech at Wilhelmshaven, in which he is expected today to answer Prime Minister Chamberlain's pledge of British aid to defend Polish independence, will not be broadcast, Propaganda Ministry officials announced, unless there is a last-minute change in plans.

WILHELMSHAVEN, Germany, April 1—(A. P.)—Germany's new 35,000-ton battleship Von Tirpitz was launched in the presence of Chancellor Hitler today amid thunderous shouts of "Sieg Heil!" (Hail Victory!) from thousands of Nazis, who expected him to reply later to the British pledge of aid to preserve Polish independence.

The battleship slid majestically into the estuary of the North sea—called Jadebusen—at 11.30 A. M. (5.30 A. M., Eastern standard time). It bore the name of Von Tirpitz in honor of the man who never spoke of the British except as "that old pirate nation" and who was famous in the World War for advocating submarine warfare.

LOOKS ON PROUDLY

Hitler looked on proudly, his hand raised in the Nazi salute, as the ship left the ways. He appeared pale, tense and somewhat preoccupied.

Admiral von Tirpitz's daughter, wife of the former Ambassador to Rome, Ulrich von Hassell, seemed deeply moved as she broke the traditional bottle of champagne.

CHRISTENS SHIP

She said:

"On the orders of the Fuehrer and supreme commander of the armed forces, I christen thee Tirpitz."

She wore a dark blue tailored

Continued on Page 2, Column 5.

Little States Want Britain As Protector

LONDON, April 1—(A. P.)—The little States of Eastern Europe who have feared expanding Germany welcomed the new British foreign policy today in the hope they might get the same protection as that promised to Poland.

General relief was apparent both here and in the Balkans and other countries as a result of Premier Chamberlain's declaration to Parliament yesterday—that Britain and France would fight "at once" beside Poland if she were attacked during negotiations for a broad anti-aggression understanding.

AWAITS ANSWER

Europe, nevertheless, anxiously awaited an answer to this from the

FACTORIES BUSY

Armaments factories worked throughout the night. The supply of gas masks was increased for Warsaw citizens.

Turn Over.

Europe At A Glance

Latest developments in the European situation:

WILHELMSHAVEN, Germany—Adolf Hitler attends launching of new battleship; thousands gather to hear Fuehrer's reply to Britain's pledge of aid to preserve Polish independence.

LONDON—Little states of Eastern Europe hope Britain will give them same protection promised to Poland.

PARIS—Strives to co-ordinate military effectiveness; wants aid of Russia if Poland is attacked; H. R. Knickerbocker, noted American correspondent, says Germany seeks new conquest.

WARSAW—Continues preparations for war.

NAPLES—Premier Mussolini tells crowd at Capua "somebody will have to provide" land they lack for their families.

'Joe & Asbestos'

Ken Kling's popular comic strip of the racing world will be found in the Sports Section

---

What Every Woman Wants to Know About Charm----New Feature in Tomorrow's American

THE BALTIMORE NEWS-POST, SATURDAY, APRIL 1, 1939

NITE LIFE :- By LOU CALVERT

Brilliant night-life entertainment abounds in most every one of our town's after-dark show places, and to try and acquaint you and you with what's in store for you on your "night out," come along with us to the Dutch Mill Supper Club, where Sam Vinci, the "quince" of comedy, will provide you with a very pleasant nonsensical evening, assisted by Eddie, the singing waiter, and several other outstanding artists.

TRIO PROVIDES 'JAM'

'nerally speaking, babies and ren look for "jam," but you s can find plenty of jam when Statesmen Trio "swings out" Sweeney's and the lovely Gale Jolly sings her songs.

Marty Aument in his sixth week at the Green Villa and seems to be going stronger than ever, with the present show one of the best that has been seen at this spot so far this season, so give yourself a treat and drop down to see Marty first chance you get.

Flash! Did you know that Winter's Lounge features continuous entertainment every night, with Lou Ruley's orchestra, Joan Hutson and Eddie ("Curley") Brown to entertain you, and those inimitable "mixologists," Scotty and Elmer, to concoct your favorite drinks?

John Matusky's night club is really stepping along as a "hot" spot for dancing, because of the great rhythms of Gus Weibe and his "Knights," who positively "burn up" swinging out those new and old dance tunes.

Always one of the best liked places in town, Sam's Rail Inn continues to delight patrons week after week with the delightful dancepations of the "Bandsmen" orchestra, plus the swellegant vocalizing by Miss Dorothy Lee.

Max Cohen, genial owner of the Oasis Cabaret, was among the passengers on the new Yankee Clipper that left here Tuesday for Bermuda. When Max returns on Sunday he will have an interesting story about the new plane and it's performance, but there's a few spots in town that can "top" the performance of lovely Fifi Dinning, excellent dance artist appearing at the Oasis. In addition, there are 12 other dancing debutantes (year of 1909) and Willie Gray, affable master of ceremonies, now in his thirteenth straight year.

C. AND L. PACKED

The very charming atmosphere created by indirect lighting and new, modernistic furniture, plus the serving of excellent foods, keeps the management of the C. & L. delicatessen busy these nights catering to the wishes of their many patrons, all of whom are turned into fast friends after one visit.

One of the most entertaining burlesk shows ever to be presented in a night club is the present offering at the Esquire Club, which features these names: Elcie Patterson, Mickey Cannon, Walter Budd, Smoky Burns, Mac Barron, Eddie Miller, the original "hitch-hiker"; Lillian Byron, Bee Baxter, Betty Louden, Ann Davis and Jean Linda. Quite a cast, if you ask us, and all talented, too!

TRIPLE ATTRACTION

DeLuca's delightful cafe in Dundalk features a triple attraction, in that you can enjoy a swell floor show, dance to the grand rhythms of the Jack Weber Trio and eat some delicious spaghetti, prepared personally by Mrs. Rose DeLuca, whose reputation is State-wide for excellent Italian cooking.

For you Bowie fans who appreciate good food as well as good horses, try almost any dish at Nates and Leons, particularly their broiled steaks and chops cooked to your order. M...m...m... Are they good!

Kathleen's has a bright new show on tap that features Bonnie Lee, versatile and talented dance star, who has just completed a successful engagement in Miami, Fla.

Also in the cast is Alma Carson, Sharon and Marshall and his Starlight Serenaders, with the genial Al King on hand to welcome you personally.

Hearty laughs are heard this week at Carl's Night Club, where Leo Bateman, the "dean" of the emcees, holds forth as the headliner of a floor show that stars "Coke" Homan, the 300-pound dancer; Nell Deacon, the swingstress, and Patti Karlan, the dancing sensation.

A completely new show is being presented from the merry-go-round center of the octagonal musical bar at the Blue Mirror Cocktail Lounge, which features the Three M's, a new vocal and instrumental trio who come here direct from an entire season on Broadway, New York.

AT BIB'S CLUB

Bib's Nite Club features the swing rhythms by Freddy Creager's orchestra and the "top" warbling of Miss Kay Crandall, plus several other well-known acts, with a special party given every Tuesday night from 9 to midnight, at which a lot of fun is had by everyone present.

Miss Virginia Lee Marchant, whose dance studios have turned out some excellent professional dance stars, will give another recital some time in June.

If our memory serves us right, her last recital was the "talk of the town," with a display of real talent that left nothing in the art of dancing to be desired.

Note: Tonight marks the beginning of the third year as master of ceremonies of Bob Bruce at Ivan Frank's cabaret-restaurant. As a sort of extra honus, Frank, of slander, the genial manager, has decided to allow Bob to have three dinners a night as salary, instead of the customary two. Wow, Bob! the meals must be good!

The Flying Deals, another successful team of roller skaters sponsored by Willie Biehl of the Washington Roller Rink, are kept so busy with engagements that they have hardly a night to themselves.

The Dutchman's Cafe features a swellegant floor show tonight and tomorrow night, with many added attractions, and the dance music of Charles Danza and his Avalon orchestra.

As the Blue Danube Cafe every Wednesday night is "peanut night," with the peanuts served on the "house."

Two grand dance bands alternate playing at this attractive spot, and prices are most moderate, with a policy of no cover or minimum charge at any time.

At Aversa's Swing Club, Johnny Stevens, versatile emcee, has been held over for a fourth week, with Miss Hilda Walton, dancing star, and a sensational new comedian to complete the show.

WONDER BAR PLANS

There are plans in the offing for a new addition to the Wonder Bar and also for a general redecoration scheme that will make this already attrctive room one of the most beautiful dine and dance spots in Baltimore.

Mr. Louis has remodeled his Tavern on East Cross street, so that it is now the most modern and up-to-date spot in South Baltimore, with a swell band for dancing and a policy of no cover or minimum, with a slogan of "an uptown place but downtown prices."

Cuban Orchestra Now At El Patio

Quite a change from the usual awaits you on your visit to the El Patio, where dreamy rhythms, plus the sensational rhythms of the Caballeros, the only authentic Cuban band in Baltimore, will both quicken your senses and quiet your nerves.

This unique band has played many successful engagements in leading night clubs throughout the country, having just come from El Chico Club in New York City.

SAM VINCI
Comic Emcee at The Dutch Mill

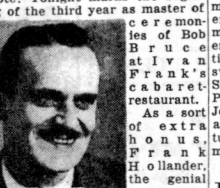

BOB BRUCE
Now in Third Year at Ivan Frank's

FIFI DENNING
Dance Star at Oasis Cabaret

'Top' Dance Team At 2 O'Clock Club

Springing a surprise, as usual, Sam Lampe has brought two of the finest dancers in the show business to his Two O'clock Club in the person of McDonald and Ross, whose lightning tap-dance routines will cause you to applaud, so perfect are their execution and grace.

Miss Mimi Rollins, a "swellegant" rhythm singer, delights with some sensational songs, and Freddie LaMont shows why he is regarded as one of New York's better singing masters of ceremonies.

Penthouse Show Is 'Topnotch'

The Penthouse's new revue staged by Tom Barry is easily the best show that has been presented at this smart spot in many a season. Not only does Tom sing and emcee, but he has enthused the members of the cast to such an extent that the spontaneous merriment is appreciated by the audience. Featuring Nina Futia, sensational dance star; "Ginger" Mason, swing songstress; Alma and Flo Sullivan, sister dance team; the Pearl Magley girl ensemble and Johnny Piccard, that suave singing accordionist, plus the danceable tunes of Bernie Lipsch and his music, the show is a "smash hit."

Earle Club Has 'Laff A Minute'

A floor show that is different in manner is presetned this week at the Earle Club, using as its theme "A laff-a-minute," and the patrons are flocking in droves to this gay spot.

Featuring the nit-wit and clever comedian, Lenny Ross, whose wacky antics keep the audience in a continuous state of merriment, the show also boasts such stellar performers as Dolores Fowble, tap dance star; Bobby O'Connor, songstress; Litt Maris, rotund comedienne; Marlyn Lane, ballad singer, and by popular demand a return engagement of that little "bundle of pep," Beanie Bean.

Club Subway Has Laugh Show

"Laugh and the world laughs with you" is the bye-word at the Club Subway this week, for if any one can refrain from laughing at the mad antics of Rogers and Morris, then there is something radically wrong with their sense of humor.

These two have really studied just what it takes to make the patrons merry, and from start to finish, their show is one "gag" after another.

Continuous Fete At Club Bar Lounge

The Club Bar Lounge is featuring a policy of continuous entertainment, with the Sol Lurie Trio, Sol Lurie and his electric violin; Bill Horn and his grand piano playing; Joanne Price, "blonde" bombshell; Pauline, the singing hat check girl and several others.

Cavalcade Of Stars In Night Life

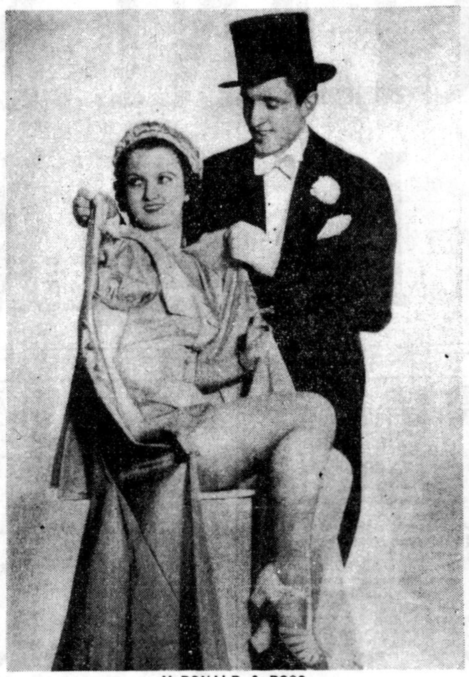

MARY SENNA

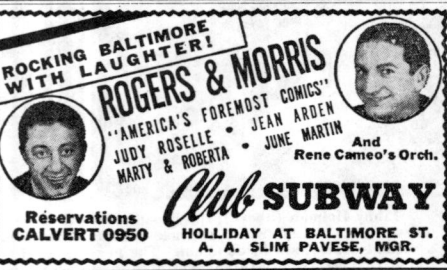

McDONALD & ROSS

ROBERTA

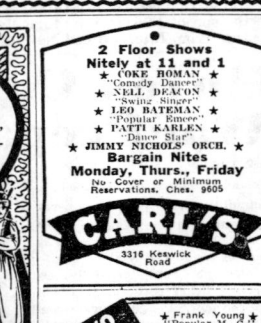 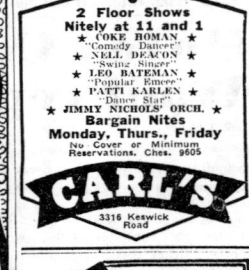

DOLORES FOWBLE   ALBERTO BETTINI   GRACE O'HARA

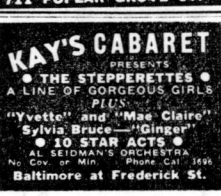

McDonald & Ross, sensational tap-dancing team, stopping shows nightly at the Two O'Clock Club. Mary Senna, entertaining nightly at the Blue Mirror. Alberto Bettini, whose Cuban Cabalerros are playing at the El Patio. Roberta, dance star at the Club Subway. Dolores Fowble, dainty dance star at the Earle Club. Grace O'Hara, whose swingaroo singing is heard at Getz's Supper Club.

ROCKING BALTIMORE WITH LAUGHTER!
ROGERS & MORRIS
"AMERICA'S FOREMOST COMICS"
JUDY ROSELLE · JEAN ARDEN
MARTY & ROBERTA · JUNE MARTIN
And Rene Cameo's Orch.
Reservations CALVERT 0950
Club SUBWAY
HOLLIDAY AT BALTIMORE ST.
A. A. SLIM PAVESE, MGR.

NOW! New Easter Review!
SAM LAMPE PROUDLY PRESENTS
MIMI ROLLINS "EMPRESS OF SONG"
FREDDIE LA MONT "Singing Master-of-Ceremonies"
McDONALD AND ROSS
MURIEL BAKER · NAN WOODS
THE 2 O'CLOCK ENSEMBLE
MILTON LYONS & HIS ORCH.
Reservations CALvert 0704
6 Gorgeous Dancing Girls Cast of 20
No Cover Charge At Any Time
THE 2 O'CLOCK CLUB

CLUB ASTORIA
1309-11-13 EDMONDSON AVE.
Featuring a New Spring Show With Internationally Famous Sepia Stars
Dance To Swing At Its Best
In The Nite Spot Sensation of Baltimore
Never a Cover or Minimum Charge
Reservations Gilmor 2362

Mt. Royal's New Room Big 'Hit'

The Mount Royal Hotel's newest contribution to night life, the "Algerian Room," seems to be just the thing that staid Baltimoreans have been looking for, because since its opening patronage has steadily increased, with visitors stating that it was "delightful."

It's styled in an intimate manner, with beautiful wall murals of Algerian steeds and their gorgeous trappings, indirect lights, soft carpets and the jilting, romantic modern music of Maurice and his orchestra.

Singer Stars At Getz's

Miss Grace O'Hara, a sensational rhythm singer, is the "hit" attraction of Getz's new floor show, and if "stopping" the show two or three times nightly means anything, then Pel Schmidt has a great find in this very pleasant, blonde songstress.

Coming to Getz's by way of a seven-month engagement at the Viking Club in Philadelphia, Miss O'Hara's singing is just about "tops" in her line.

Kibby's To Have New Dollar Party

Known to many Baltimoreans as their favorite spot to wine and dance, Kibby's popular night club will stage another of their famous dollar parties Tuesday night, April 4, with favors, fun and surprises galore. Heading the floor show will be Frank Young as emcee, with Kavanaugh & Ramon, dance stars; Vivi Gallo, acro dancer; Elaine Fay, radio songstress, and Bill Wortham's orchestra.

Headliners

HELAINE & DONALDSON

NELL DEACON

Helaine & Donaldson, famous society dance team, appearing in the Pearl Magley Revue at the Penthouse. Nell Deacon, vivacious rhythm singer, headlining the floor show at Carl's.

HIT THE DAILY DOUBLE
Here is Double Your Money's Worth of Fun!
Greatest Comedy Show in Baltimore
Atlantic City's Favorite Comic M. C.
LENNY ROSS NEW REVUE
FEATURING AN ALL-STAR CAST WITH Beanie Bean · Litt Maris · Marilyn Lane · Bobby Rycznor · & His Orchestra Chrisy Williams and Floor Show from 3 to 7 Sunday Matinee and Floor Show
THE EARLE Club
Reservations · ORIGINAL · 12 S. PATTERSON PARK AVE.

Getz's SUPPER CLUB
BALTIMORE'S NITE CLUB SHOW
Presenting
FLOOR SHOWS NITELY at 10:30 and 12:30
Featuring
★ GRACE O'HARA "Mistress of Swing"
★ Jack & Honey WILSON "International Dance Stars"
★ TERESE ROSE "Accordionist"
★ MARIANNA BRIDGES "Sensational Dancer"
★ Pel Schmidt's Orch.
Enjoy Your Favorite Drink at Our New Cocktail Bar!
We Cater to Organisations and Private Parties
Ask Us For Menu
PEL SCHMIDT, Manager
3150 FREDERICK AVE.
No Cover or Minimum Week-Days
Regular 75c Dinner from 6 to 9 P. M.

Penthouse
"ATOP THE STANLEY"
3 Floor Shows Nitely
No Cover or Minimum Week-Days
Regular 75c Dinner from 6 to 9 P.M.
Tom BARRY
Broadway Singing Star
Bernie Lipsch and His Orch.
and Pearl Magley Dancing Revue
Reservations Ver. 7720
Ample Protected Parking

Ivan Frank's
American - Alpine Cabaret Restaurant
THE BRADY SISTERS
"Dance of the Drums"
BOB BRUCE
And the "Open Mike"
Plus an ALL-STAR REVUE
TACKA'S ALL-GIRL SWING BAND
$1.00 SIX COURSE DINNER $1.00
110 N. Liberty St. · PL. 2385

ALL TYPES of DANCING for PROFESSIONALS TEACHERS AMATEURS
Special Dances Arranged
Virginia Lee Marchant
136 W. Fayette St. · CAlvert 3288

COMMERCE CLUB
The Town's Most Intimate Rendezvous
MUSIC NITELY BY JOE HASSAN'S JE-RY KAYE, Vocalist
Our Food is Famous!
Made Every Saturday Afternoon 4 to 5
105 Mercer St., near Water
Chef, Tina's Former Location

Aloha! means carefree enjoyment!
Just 10 minutes drive from Charles and Baltimore Streets brings you to the Waikiki Hideaway, where native Hawaiians greet you with their cheery Aloha, and Okolehao Punch served in coconut shells removes your every care. An evening here is a transposition into a different world, and there's no cover or minimum either. Reservations Wolfe 10302.

Bert Sherry Says to Mickey Strauss:
Folks That That Cast Their Bread on the Water This Week Will Get Mutzoh's Back

WAIKIKI HIDEAWAY · 2500 N. Rowley's Lane (East at 4300 Block Belair Road)

THE HA-HA CLUB
932 N. BROADWAY · WOLFE 6811
Cocktails Sunday 3 to 7 with Floor Show

MAN BITES DOG!
That's supposed to be news. But when a night club runs for twelve years and keeps packing them in nightly ... that calls for a headline! That's our record and we're proud of it. It's been built on the simple idea of providing fun, fast and furious, and whoopee unadorned at prices that don't send you out to hock the family folks ... Of course, there's no cover or min., and you're in for the time of your life.
It's time for a visit.
OASIS CABARET
Baltimore Street at Frederick

WINE — DINE — DANCE "MIDST AN ATMOSPHERE OF REFINEMENT"
CHICKEN AND STEAK DINNERS
GREEN SPRING INN
CARROLL KELLY'S ORCHESTRA FALLS AND VALLEY ROADS
Cocktail Dancing Sundays 2:30 to 6:30 TOWSON 104

Cuban Gayety IN BALTIMORE!
HEAR THOSE FASCINATING RHUMBAS AND TANGOS as played by
THE CABALLEROS
Only Authentic Cuban Band in Town
PLUS LARRY LONDON'S SWING ORCHESTRA
DELICIOUS CUBAN DRINKS: CUBA LIBRAS, CARIOCA COOLERS, BACARDIS, etc. — Or Your Favorite Cocktail or Highball.
No Advance In Prices
No Cover, No Minimum
EL PATIO
ST. PAUL at MADISON STS. · Ver. 6555

BLUE MIRROR
ALL NEW Show Distinguished for Its Excellence
Smart ... sophisticated entertainment from New York's best clubs.
THE THREE M's Instrumental & vocal hits
TONY & MARY SENNA Piano and Songs
MARIE BELL Smartest Mistress of Songs Cocktail Hour Daily 3.30-6.30 P.M.
929 N. CHARLES ST.
"Where it's smart to be seen!"

BURLESK AT THE SQUIRE CLUB
Esquire still going El Dumpo sensation was created by Senorita Mickey, 340½ lbs. of joy, when she challenged all other heavyweight singers in the world singing "Cheese Creepers."
CLUB ESQUIRE
FAYETTE at HANOVER · CAL. 1077

There's Nothing Like It In Or Around Baltimore!
"The ALGERIAN ROOM"
"Morocco Brought to You"
Featuring the languid, romantic modern music of
MAURICE and his ORCHESTRA
DANCING NITELY FROM 9 P.M.
No cover or minimum charge
COCKTAILS AND MIXED DRINKS FROM 25c
MOUNT ROYAL HOTEL
MT. ROYAL AVE. at CALVERT
No Cover, No Minimum

"You'll Be Satisfied Here!"
SAM VINCI — "Comic M.C."
EDDIE — "Singing Waiter"
3—Other Outstanding Acts—3
TWO FLOOR SHOWS NITELY
HARRY DOBB'S ORCHESTRA
No Cover or Minimum Charge
THE DUTCH MILL
6615 HARFORD ROAD

CARL'S
2 Floor Shows Nitely at 11 and 1
"COKE" HOMAN "Comedy Dancer"
NELL DEACON "Swing Singer"
LEO BATEMAN "Popular Emcee"
PATTI KARLEN "Dance Star"
JIMMY NICHOLS' ORCH.
Bargain Nites Monday, Thurs., Friday
No Cover or Minimum Reservations, Ches. 9605
3316 Keswick Road

The CLUB BAR
BALTIMORE'S POPULAR COCKTAIL LOUNGE
Continuous Entertainment
SOL LURIE TRIO "Versatile Musical Artists"
PAULINE "Singing Hat Check Girl"
JOANNE PRICE "Singing Guitarist"
COCKTAILS 25c
NEVER A COVER OR MINIMUM
SPECIAL COCKTAIL SESSION 2-4 SATURDAYS & SUNDAYS
BIB'S NITE CLUB
115 N. GREENE ST.
2—FLOOR SHOWS NITELY—2
KAY CRANDALL "MISTRESS-OF-CEREMONIES"
FREDDY CREAGER'S ORCH.
50c Party Every Tues. Nite

KIBBY'S 711 POPLAR GROVE ST.
TWO FLOOR SHOWS NITELY
★ Frank Young "Popular M. C."
★ Elaine Fay "Radio Songstress"
★ Kavanaugh & Ramon "Dance Stars"
★ Bill Wortham's Orchestra
No Cover or Minimum Big Dollar Party Tues. Nite, April 4.

KAY'S CABARET
PRESENTS
★ THE STEPPERETTES ★
A LINE OF GORGEOUS GIRLS
★ PLUS ★
★ "Yvette" and "Mae Claire" ★
Sylvia Bruce — "Ginger"
★ 10 STAR ACTS ★
AL. SEIDMAN'S ORCHESTRA
115 W. McCLELLAN PLACE
Baltimore at Frederick St.

Food · Fun · Frivolity

Aversa's	SWING CLUB, 3303 Philadelphia Ave. Continuous entertainment. 2 Floor Shows Nitely. No Cover or Minimum Charge. Johnny Stevens, MC. · Our Spaghetti is the Best in Town!
BEARD'S CAFE	Choice Wines — Liquors — Beers. Best Food in Town. Meet the "Boys" Here. N. E. Cor. Baltimore & Holliday Sts.
Benkert's Park	Wine, Dine, Dance Every Fri., Sat., Sun. Nite. Walter Hubbell Orch. Large dance floor. Low prices. No cov. or min. Balto., Hilton, Caton Ave. Gil 1511
Blue Danube Cafe	Dance Wed. & Sun. to Gordon Wharran's Swinging Strings; Fri. & Sat. Melody Playboys. No cov. or min. · 2306 Boston St.
C & L Delicatessen	Air Conditioned. Capacity 170. Sandwiches—Luncheons—Dinners. 3908 Liberty Heights Ave. Phone Liberty 6012.
DE LUCA'S	4010 Willow Spring Road—Dundalk 117. The Best of Foods, The Best Floor Show, with Jack Weber and His Orchestra. No cover or minimum ever.
Dutchman's Cafe	Enjoy the music of the "Avalon Orchestra." We Cater to Special Parties. Reasonable prices. Floor Show & Dancing. 3126 Greenmount Ave.
4 Corners Corral	All roads lead to Jacksonville, Md. from Towson, Baltimore, Md., etc. Nites, Hi Nod and His Orch. Never a cover or min., ever.
Green Villa Nite Club	Dancing and 2 Floor Shows Nightly. Marty Aument, comic M. C. and a Great Show. 5423 O'Donnell Street.
KATHLEEN'S	2 BIG FLOOR SHOWS NITELY. NO COVER OR MINIMUM. 4612 EAST BALTIMORE ST.
LOUIE'S TAVERN	7 E. CROSS ST. Continuous Entertainment. WINE—DINE—DANCE. Everything New But the Name. Visit us & Save Money. Open Sundays. No cov., Min.
MATUSKY'S	SUPPER CLUB, RIVIERA BEACH, MD. Dance to Gus Weibe and his "Knights of Rhythm" Orch. Sat. and Sun. No cover or min. Reasonable prices.
NATE & LEON'S	2630 W. NORTH AVE. Dancing Fri., Sat., Sun. Nites. "THE BANDSMEN" Swing Orchestra, with DOROTHY LEE, Vocalist. No cov. or minimum.
Sam's Rail Inn	DELICATESSEN. Stop in After the Show for Midnight Snack. Delicious Sandwiches. OPEN ALL NIGHT! 850 WEST NORTH AVE.
Sweeney's	3128 GREENMOUNT AVE. Amateur Nite Thursday. Dance to Statesman's Swing Trio. BUDDY MONROE, Vocalist. Floor Shows Sat. & Sun. Harold Sietharpil, Mgr.
WASHINGTON	Roller Rink. Open Nitely from 7 to 11 P. M., Children, Ladies, Mon. to Thurs., 13c; Gents, 25c. Mon. always, 1303 N. Washington St.
WINTER'S	Cocktail Bar—Restaurant. Continuous entertainment—Moderate Prices—Never a Cover or Minimum Charge. DINNER SERVED, starting at Preston St.
Wonder Bar—New Howard Hotel	GOOD TIME ALWAYS

Hitler, Duce Discussed War Alliance, Berlin Hears

THE BALTIMORE NEWS-POST

An Independent Newspaper

The Largest Daily Circulation in the Entire South

VOL. CXXXVI—NO. 114 — MONDAY EVENING, MARCH 18, 1940 — PRICE 3 CENTS

★★★★★ 8 ★★★★★

THE WEATHER
Baltimore and vicinity—Overcast, with rain tonight and Tuesday, with lowest temperature around 45 degrees. Colder Tuesday afternoon and night. Moderate easterly winds. Detailed Weather Report on Page 24.

MEAN TEMPERATURES YESTERDAY

Baltimore	42	New York	36
Atlanta	58	Omaha	52
Boston	34	Portland, Maine	32
Chicago	31	Salt Lake City	47
Jacksonville	72	San Antonio	72
Los Angeles	61	Seattle	49
Miami	66	Tampa	72
New Orleans	62	Washington	46

Definer Takes 2d Race At Tropical ★

GIRL, 2 MEN QUIZZED IN SLAYING

Hitler, Duce Discussed War Alliance That May Include Moscow, Report

LONDON, March 18—(I. N. S.)—An Exchange Telegraph dispatch from Rome today said it was rumored in the Italian capital that French Premier Edouard Daladier was en route to Genoa for a conference with Premier Mussolini tomorrow.

ROME, March 18—(I. N. S.)—Reports persisted today that in his conversation with Hitler at the Brenner Pass, Mussolini produced a new Anglo-French peace proposal brought by American Under Secretary of State Sumner Welles.

This proposal, it was reported, suggested a conference of Germany, Great Britain and France to compromise on Poland, Czechoslovakia, the Balkans, and the Near East.

In addition, the reports said, Britain would agree to return of Germany's war-lost colonies in exchange for "modification" of the Reich's friendly attitude toward Soviet Russia.

PARIS, March 18—(A. P.)—If the Hitler-Mussolini conference is the first act of an Easter week peace offensive, the play is doomed to failure, the French say. Government sources said today the Allies could not accept an immediate compromise peace, but would fight on until they had won victory and guarantees of security. London echoed this view.

BERLIN, March 18—(A. P.)—Extension of the Rome-Berlin axis to Moscow and possible eventual participation of Italy in the European war on Germany's side were cited today by excellently informed Berlin circles as the main apparent results of today's historic Brenner Pass meeting between Hitler and Premier Mussolini.

The two statesmen appeared to have worked on plans for a complete reorganization of Europe, with Soviet Russia as their partner.

MOLOTOFF PARLEY SEEN

Berlin was filled with rumors that German Foreign Minister Joachim von Ribbentrop would confer with Russian Premier-Foreign Commissar Vyacheslaff Molotoff as soon as possible, either in Berlin or Moscow.

Hitler and Mussolini were said to have agreed on possible ultimate participation of Italy in the European war on Germany's side if and when such a course should be deemed preferable to the present

Continued on Page 2, Column 7.

VERY LATEST NEWS
(Race Results From Howard Sports Daily, Inc.)

DEFINER WINS SECOND AT TROPICAL PARK
Second—Definer, $9.80, $5.90, $4.20; Cendrillon, $17, $7.70; Trimmed, $3.40.
Daily Double—Patricia A. and Definer paid $336.10.

WOMAN, 49, PLUNGES TO DEATH IN WASHINGTON
WASHINGTON, March 18—(A. P.)—Mrs. Myrtle L. Haiman, forty-nine-year-old clerk in the Veterans Administration, plunged to her death today from the tenth story of the Transportation Building near Seventeenth and H streets, N. W.

SAYS DIVINE TO REFUSE $5,900 REFUND ORDER
NEW YORK, March 18—(A. P.)—Edward Potter, who described himself as attorney for Father Divine, said today the Harlem evangelist would refuse to recognize a Supreme Court order directing him to refund $5,900 to a disgruntled former "angel."

Hitler, Duce Meet At Border

A surprise move in the diplomatic by-play that now overshadows the military action in the European war was the meeting of German Fuehrer Adolf Hitler and Italy's Duce, Benito Mussolini, in the little Italian frontier town of Brennero, in the Brenner Pass. The two dictators are shown above as they met last during Mussolini's visit to Munich. The nature of their conversation was a mystery, but most observers believed the meeting was an attempt by Hitler to pave the way for a new axis "peace offensive" or to persuade Mussolini to support a joint Nazi-Soviet policy in the Balkans.

Baby Survives 110° Fever
Picture on Page 3.

SPOKANE, Wash., March 18—(A. P.)—An infant girl was reported improving today after surviving a temperature of at least 110 degrees.

The child, daughter of Mr. and Mrs. James Yount, was brought to Spokane Friday night. The father, and A. A. Shuler kept the baby alive with artificial respiration while Mrs. Shuler drove the 55 miles from Ritzville, Wash.

Dr. E. J. Barnett said the baby's temperature Friday night was "at least 110—our thermometers won't go any higher." Later the temperature dropped to 99.

Dr. Barnett ascribed the child's condition to a "disturbance in the heat regulating center of the brain."

TROPICAL PARK RESULTS
FIRST RACE—Purse $800; for maiden fillies, two-year-olds; four furlongs. Off at 2.09. Time, :48 2-5.

Patricia A., 116 (Snider)	$66.90	$23.20	$10.30
Subura, 116 (Wright)		4.40	3.00
dHaste Back, 116 (Steffen)			2.60
dLady Jaffa, 116 (Schmidl)			
Total mutuels			$114.90

Also Ran—Unending, Sweet Refrain, Miss Beeville, Naghleh, Ambo, On the Beam, aDarby Dame, a Tact also ran. d—Dead heat for third. a—Darby Dan Farm-Elebred Farm entry.

Holds Girl In Mid-Air, Balks Leap

An attempt by a young woman to plunge from the Dulaney Valley road bridge, 60 feet above the Loch Raven reservoir, was balked today by Patrolman William Powers, who reported the girl hung suspended in mid-air in his grasp for several minutes.

Finally, Powers said, he was able to grip the iron bridge railing with his knees, and with the leverage thus afforded was able to hoist the girl to the bridge level.

TAKEN TO STATION

She was taken to the Towson Police Station, along with a man who, Patrolman Powers said, had been on the bridge with her.

Police said the man gave his name as Loring Stevenson, twenty-nine, of Cockeysville. The girl, according to Lieut. William B. Dorsey, was Stevenson's wife, Mrs.

Continued on Page 2, Column 6.

Magda Lupescu Flees Rumania

LONDON, March 18—(I. N. S.)—Fearing for her safety, Mme. Magda Lupescu, titian-haired companion of King Carol, left Bucharest two days before the Rumanian monarch lifted the ban on the anti-Semitic Iron Guard organization, the London Daily Herald reported today.

The paper said it was believed she was en route to England and later would go to the United States.

U. S. Ship Test At Gibraltar Speeded

WASHINGTON, March 18—(A. P.)—Examination of American ships by British authorities at Gibraltar has been speeded up in March, the State Department announced today.

Nazis Renew Drive For Rumanian Oil

BUCHAREST, March 18—(A. P.)—Germany's renewed spring drive for more Rumanian oil and other products opened today with the arrival of Dr. Karl Clodius, top Nazi trade negotiator.

BOO KING, 4 FINED

LONDONDERRY, Northern Ireland, March 18—(A. P.)—Booing a newsreel in which King George and Queen Elizabeth appeared today cost four youths fines of 40 shillings (about $8) each.

Temperatures

Midnight	43	7 A. M.	39
1 A. M.	42	8 A. M.	39
2 A. M.	41	9 A. M.	42
3 A. M.	40	10 A. M.	44
4 A. M.	38	11 A. M.	45
5 A. M.	39	12 Noon	47
6 A. M.	39	1 P. M.	50

Woman Companion Of Victim Views 2 Suspects; Guns Are Found In Auto

Two men and a woman, from whom police said they seized a .32-caliber automatic pistol and a .22-caliber rifle, were being questioned by police today in connection with the "Lovers' Lane" hold-up murder.

The trio was arrested after a traffic dispute with a taxi driver. That argument was brought to police attention, according to arresting officers, when the cabbie told them one of the men assertedly bared a .32-caliber revolver.

VIEWS TWO MEN

After questioning under the direction of Lieutenant Harry Fischer and Inspector Hamilton R. Atkinson, the two men were placed in a room with seven other men and Miss Phyllis Taylor—who was slugged with a pistol butt by the men who slew her escort — was brought into the room.

Lieutenant Fischer made no statement on her reaction at seeing the two men.

Meanwhile, the woman who was arrested with them, was taken by police to her rooming house for search, officers stated.

ALL THREE HELD

All three were held on charges of investigation, after their automobile was brought to the Northwestern District station.

Arresting Policeman Harold Borman, who was cruising with Sergeant Frank Weslowski at the time of the arrest, said that the two men locked the car and refused to open it.

TWO GUNS FOUND

Police said they towed the machine to the station house and there opened it with keys which they found in searching the men. Inside, officers said, they found the two guns and welding equipment. The men explained the lat-

Continued on Page 2, Column 4.

10 Seized In 'Pay As Slay' Murder Ring

NEW YORK, March 18—(A. P.)—A murder-to-order combine which killed by contract for "big shot" racketeers was said today by a Brooklyn prosecutor to have been responsible for at least a dozen—possibly 20—gangland slayings.

Brooklyn District Attorney William F. O'Dwyer said 10 men were under arrest in connection with the crimes. He said the gang was implicated in seven murders and two attempted slayings in Brooklyn and three killings in Sullivan county in up-State New York.

RACKETEERS ACCUSED

Youthful gunmen did the trigger work under agreements with such racket overlords as Lucky Luciano, imprisoned Manhattan vice king, Louis ("Lepke") Buchalter and Jacob ("Gurrah") Shapiro, O'Dwyer said.

The prosecutor quoted one in

Continued on Page 2, Column 4.

U. S. Ship Reported Aground Off Japan

TOKYO, March 18—(A. P.)—Domei, Japanese news agency, today reported the American freighter Cripple Creek aground off the port of Yokosuka, on the Japanese Southern coast. The ship, carrying scrap iron from San Pedro, Cal., was not damaged and was expected to be refloated at high tide.

'Helping Mother,' But Put Baby In Hospital

NEW YORK, March 18—(A. P.)—Three-year-old Martin Neville and his little sister tried to "help mama" while she was at Palm Sunday services, and as a result their three-months-old sister is in the hospital with serious burns and a possible fractured skull.

Martin and his sister, Evelyn, eighteen months old, decided to give the baby a bath. As their father, a night engineer, slept a few feet away, they lifted the baby out of her crib, dragged her across the floor to the bathroom, and awakened the father.

Martin said:

"Daddy, we're giving the baby a bath—we're helping

'WHEN I LOVED YOU'—New Serial by Hazel Livingston—Starts in TOMORROW'S NEWS-

Wallace Beery Is Union Army Man In Century's Film

By NORMAN CLARK

LOOKS AS IF "Gone With the Wind" might have started our Civil War all over again. However, the two biggest money-makers in the history of screendom—"G. W. T. W." and "Birth of a Nation"—had to do with the boys of the Blue and the Grey, so it is only to be expected that Hollywood should begin thinking of Richmond, Gettysburg and such historic spots.

DOLORES DEL RIO

Sergeant Barstow, a tough Indian scout from the Dakotas now in the Union Army, and his superior officer, Lieut. Oliver Clark, a nice young man from Boston, escape from the vile Confederate prison camp, euphoniously called Belle Isle. They head back for the Northern lines, very eager to tell General Grant about some things that Johnny Rebs hope to accomplish.

Barstow is a grumbler who thinks largely of finding food to fill his spacious innards, but he certainly can see, hear and smell his way through woods, fields and streams. Quite a time of it do the fugitives have on their jaunt. They come upon a lovely lady as she shoots a Confederate officer who didn't act as a gent should. It may surprise you a bit to learn that Jenny is a Russian, and so is the Confederate officer she put a bullet through. However, it's mighty fortunate that Jenny is a Russ, as the all-important map Barstow and Clark find on the corpse is in Russian.

Well, sir, we now have three persons sneaking toward the Union lines—Barstow, Clark and Jenny. Do they meet with excitement! They get into a house full of axes and dead people, they encounter a crazy Union soldier who is murdering right and left, they are arrested by some Campbellites and accused of slaying a couple of women. Anyway you take it, war is a helluva mess.

"The Man From Dakota" shaps up as a so-so melodrama. The role of Barstow has been cut to the measure of Wallace Beery and he struts around in it with huge relish. Dolores Del Rio is pleasant eye-wash and John Howard a manly officer.

"Man From Dakota"

"THE MAN FROM DAKOTA," starring Wallace Beery. Screen play by Laurence Stallings. Based on the novel, "Arouse and Beware," by MacKinlay Kantor. Directed by Leslie Fenton. A Metro-Goldwyn-Mayer Picture, presented at Loew's Century.

THE CAST

Sergt. Barstow	Wallace Beery
Oliver Clark	John Howard
Jenny	Dolores De Rio
Vestry	Donald Meek
Parson Summers	Robert Barratt
Provost Marshal	Addison Richards
Campbellite	Frederick Burton
Union Soldier	William Haade
Mr. Carpenter	John Wray

Walter Winchell On Broadway

Man About Town

Director George Stevens, linked often (by the paragraphers) with Ginger Rogers, has reconciled with his wife . . . Mrs. Jack Dempsey (Hannah Williams) has definitely decided to resume her stage career. She will not use the champ's name in the act she's rehearsing now . . . Robert Ripley's niece, Louise, becomes Mrs. George Dickerson in June. He is chief inspector for the Pratt-Whitney airplane plant . . . The youngest of the Rockefeller clan, David, wishes Will Rogers' daughter, Mary, would say the word . . . Watch for another New York court scandal. It concerns a man who was given a suspended sentence, who was not in court when he was tried. He was in a Queens cell at the time! . . . Editors overlooking Franchot Tone's real romance are muffing a beaut. She is Anne Falvo, due the 23rd at the St. Moritz, a 20-year-old version of Hedy Lamarr.

Jac Lewis, scion of one of Philly's First Families, and Audrey Palmer of the "DuBarry" show, are on fire, but his tribe is trying to extinguish it. Jac works as a staff designer for Eaves, the theatrical costumers. Watch the smoke, his family will battle it . . . The Boro President Palmas of Richmond have exploded . . . Langdon Post, the former N. Y. Housing Commish, and Margaret Solomon, a home girl, will announce their betrothal soon . . . Two of the "DuBarry" chorus men slugged it out backstage while the show was on the other night.

Aimee Semple MacPherson's daughter, Roberta, will marry H. Salter of the Hobby Lobby program in the spring . . . Ed Wynn's second wife, Frieda Mierse, and M. Mayer, who designed Grace Moore's film costumes, are a new duet . . . Jack Lynch was rushed to Philly from Miami very ill . . . Damon Runyon is bedded again . . . A prominent deb will be named co-respondent in the divorce action against a German broker . . . Victor Moore's next role in "Louisiana Purchase" will be a travesty on Governor Dickinson of Michigan!

Two former child stars, now husband and wife, have been living in a small furnished room with only doughnuts to eat. They are Peggy Montgomery Ayres (once the famous Baby Peggy, who earned almost $250,000 before retirement) and Gordon Ayres, one of the original members of the "Our Gang" comedies. The other day we confused her with Baby Marie Osborne, who once banked 5 Gs week-y. It's the Osborne girl, not Baby Peggy, who is a stand-in now for Moran at RKO . . . Robert Cullen Young, an actor last in "The American Way," recently hitchhiked to Hollywood. He bought the Ayres couple breakfast with his last dollar. Mr. Ayres just landed a bartender job which restocks their cupboard, while Baby Peggy and Young look for screen jobs . . . Surely the Hollywood casters will do something about these people??????

Babs Hutton's ex, Count von Reventlow, is comforting Mrs. Max Ausschnitt, wife of the sentenced Rumanian munitions king—on the Riviera . . . Richard Haydn and Brenda Forbes, of "Two for the Show," are ignited . . . A number of prominent New York lawyers have grouped to suggest legislation (for the first time) to protect anything original. What! And put a lotta colyumers outta work . . . Jim Reynolds, of the Coq Rouge crew, and Jean Moorehead of "DuBarry" will be riveted around the time the N. Y. Yanks are winning the Worlds Series again . . . Mrs. Crater's lawyer is readying a ten million stockholders' action against a famed steel company . . . M. Berle is spending coin freely for long distance calls to Lorraine Lloyd of the Royal Palm show at Miami . . . The E. Holtz crew starts at the Stork Club early in April.

The lowdown from Havana is that Batista is shelving the Commys and lining up with General Menocal bears no love for Batista, hero of the Upper Classes . . . Meno cal bears no love for Batista, however, and may be making the move to weaken his chances . . . Howard Johnson, the restaurant man (he has 134) will open fifty new ones in and around New York within 18 months . . . Firms which moved up town in the boom days to get away from Wall Street's high rents, are moving back there since rentals are lower than in midtown .

Producer and songwriter Lew Brown did marry his nurse. In New Jersey on November 24th . . . Dewey's secret murder case (being withheld until just before election) is an underworld mess, the suspected murderer already being in the lockup—for life!

The Feminine Voice Of Old Broadway

By DOROTHY KILGALLEN

Excerpts From Miss Midnight's Diary

LAST week on Broadway was enlivened by Walter Huston's return to the stage as a dyed-in-the-greasepaint villain, the sight of pretty girls riding hobby horses in the gilded kindergarten of El Morocco, and the selection of a sort of subway Brenda Frazier as "Miss Cafeteria Society 1940."

I will not attempt to explain why the girls were riding horses in El Morocco, because when I came in things were at such a pitch you couldn't tell whether it was being done for $100 bills, the Finnish Relief, or just the heck of it—but there they were.

I did observe that some of the girls were very shy about riding the horses Western style in very short or very skimpy skirts, excepting Patricia "Honeychile" Wilder, who got no complaints from the gallery when she revealed her knees.

The other lassies all took their horses and their blushes into the back room and rocked away, having a wonderful time, while the grown-ups rhumba'd.

JOHN GARFIELD, who once called Bill's Gay Nineties "a shrine to the theatre," dropped back again Monday night, to the temporary delight of his feminine admirers, who all send over post cards and menus to be autographed. But apparently John thinks a shrine is no place for an autograph hound, for he returned all the post-cards without his signature.

Tuesday evening seemed to be Food night, with all the celebs storing away steaks, chops and truffles. Crosby Gaige, the epicure, was storing it away in Colbert's, the Jimmy Walkers were busy with the knife and fork a few tables away, and three glamour girls famous for their figures — Margot Graham, Lily Pons, and Sylvia Sidney — were all behaving as if they had never heard of a calorie.

THE TAVERN, on the same evening, looked like Honeymoon Island, what with the Ernest Westmores (Peggy Kent) at one table, and Oscar Levant and June Gale at another. The Levants were chaperoned by young Alfred Gwynne Vanderbilt, who appeared to be doing most of the quipping, and, unless it is treason to say so, getting most of the laughs. But Oscar came through in the end; when things began looking a little dull, he gave himself a hot foot.

Over at le Coq Rouge, Conde Nast and Peppy D'Albrew and Dwight Fiske bent their sophisticated ears to Betty Bryant singing Hoagy Carmichael's "I Walk with Music," and Thomas Mitchell got positively sentimental listening to it. Mr. Mitchell, the Oscar-winning No. 1 supporting player, attracted a great deal of movie-tan attention.

La Conga really bulged Wednesday night when the merrymakers celebrated the return of Desi Arnaz to the floor show. Willie Moore, the restaurant fellow, made matters more crowded by bringing in a crowd of 30, including Ann Graham, Geraldine Spreckles, Betty Allen, Benny Baker and Lois Andrews.

WALTER HUSTON'S audience for the premiere of "A Passenger to Bali" was, I am unhappy to report, more enthusiastic than chic, or even famous. A few items saved the evening, from the purely rubberneck standpoint. They were: (a) George Jessel's arrival with Elinor Troy, who wore six feet of white fox, from chin to toes, a pink lace dress, and a black bow. (b) Tommy Manville's appearance without Elinor Troy. (c) Valentina's appearance in a black lace helmet which revealed only a small portion of her nose, mouth and eyes.

In Times Square at the Fiesta Danceteria, I helped choose "Miss Cafeteria-Society" while several hundred customers craned their necks, whistled, stood on chairs to see, and applauded the prettiest.

The prize—$100—went to Miss Muriel Klushin, an eighteen-year-old stenographer who is prettier and better-mannered than most debutantes and certainly walks better than any I see around the Stork Club. She was, I think it is not tattling to tell, the judges' unanimous choice.

THEY LOVE SCHOOL

Fredric March's two adopted children, Penelope and Anthony, will remain in school in New York while the star is in Hollywood teaming with Joan Crawford in "Susan and God." The two youngsters like their school so much that it seemed a shame to transfer them, March said.

GAYETY
EXTRA! EXTRA! NOW PLAYING
The Sensation of the West Coast
DIANA LOGAN
BILLY (CHEESE 'N' CRACKERS) HAGAN
THE FUNNIEST OF ALL FUNNY MEN
COLEMAN & BENTLEY
CAST OF 40 STARS—A GREAT EASTER WEEK SHOW
MATS. CONT. 12 TO 5 - - - 35c
NITES 8.30 RES. CAL. 2669
THE ONLY BURLESK SHOW IN TOWN

She's A Charmer

MURIEL ANGELUS

Miss Angelus, a newcomer to Hollywood, plays the part of the "other woman" in "The Way of All Flesh" and makes a bum out of Akim Tamiroff, a trusted cashier.

MOVIE CLOCK

FEATURE PHOTOPLAYS in Baltimore's leading picture theatres today and their starting times are as follows:

HIPPODROME
"RENO"
11.30 A. M., 1.55, 4.40, 7.25, 10.10 P. M.

CENTURY
"MAN FROM DAKOTA"
11.40 A. M., 1.40, 3.45, 5.50, 7.50, 9.55 P. M.

STANLEY
"INVISIBLE STRIPES"
11.20, A. M., 1.25, 3.30, 5.35, 7.40, 9.45 P. M.

KEITHS
"CASTLE ON HUDSON"
10.46 A. M., 12.37, 2.29, 4.21, 6.13, 8.05, 9.59 P. M.

NEW
"GRAPES OF WRATH"
10.10 A. M., 12.28, 2.46, 5.04, 7.22, 9.40 P. M.

LITTLE
"SECRET AGENT"
11.30 A. M., 1.35, 3.40, 5.45, 7.50, 9.55 P. M.

TIMES
"MR. DEEDS GOES TO TOWN"
1.34, 4.23, 7.12, 10.01 P. M.

PARKWAY
"LIGHT THAT FAILED"
1.30, 3.35, 5.35, 7.35, 9.35 P. M.

VALENCIA
"GONE WITH THE WIND"
10 A. M., 2.30, 8 P. M.

MUSICAL CONCERT ON TIMES' SCREEN

An innovation in motion picture entertainment by Paramount, a musical concert, will be offered by the Times theatre for one week beginning March 27. A departure in its field, "The Distinguished Film Concert" is presented by the National Philharmonic Orchestra of one hundred and twenty-four men accompanied by a chorus of forty male voices. With Frederick Feher conducting, the National Philharmonic Orchestra will present Tannhauser, Schubert's Unfinished Symphony and Viennese Waltzes.

CHARLIE McCARTHY IN CENTRE'S FILM

Charlie McCarthy will be seen as a crime-solving sleuth in Universal's "Charlie McCarthy, Detective," which plays from today through Wednesday at the Centre.

In the principal supporting roles will be seen Robert Cummings, Constance Moore, John Sutton, Louis Calhern, Edgar Kennedy, Harold Huber, Samuel S. Hinds and Warren Hymer.

GEORGE RAFT JANE BRYAN WM. HOLDEN in "INVISIBLE STRIPES"
25c to 1 P.M.
STARTS SATURDAY ERROL FLYNN Miriam Hopkins in "VIRGINIA CITY"
WARNER BROS. STANLEY

KEITHS
"TOGETHER... They're Torrid! Terrific! T.N.T."
25¢ TO 12:30
12:30 TO 6-21&35
NIGHTS .40
SUN. MATS. .35
CHILDREN .15
JOHN GARFIELD · ANN SHERIDAN
PAT O'BRIEN
"CASTLE on the HUDSON"
BURGESS MEREDITH
Starting Friday at 10 A. M.
DEANNA DURBIN in "IT'S A DATE"

HIPPODROME NOW
ON OUR STAGE
AMERICA'S DISTINCTIVE STYLIST OF RHYTHM
IN PERSON! EDDY DUCHIN and his ORCHESTRA AND "TOP HAT" Revue
25—ENTERTAINERS—25
ON SCREEN
EXPOSE OF THE DIVORCE RACKET
"RENO"
WITH GAIL PATRICK ANITA LOUISE RICHARD DIX PAUL CAVANAGH LAURA CREWS
EXTRA LATEST ISSUE OF "INFORMATION PLEASE"
FRI. SCREEN—WALT DISNEY'S Latest Full Length Feature "PINOCCHIO" in MULTIPLANE TECHNICOLOR ★★ Plus—A BIG STAGE SHOW

Loew's Century
Till 6 P. M. Ex. Sun. & Hol. 25c · Any Nite 40c
"The MAN From DAKOTA"
M-G-M. Hit Starring WALLACE BEERY
FRIDAY · CLARK GABLE · JOAN CRAWFORD · STRANGE CARGO ·
Parkway
RONALD COLMAN · WALTER HUSTON
"The LIGHT THAT FAILED"

NEW THEATRE
THE GRAPES OF WRATH by John Steinbeck
with HENRY FONDA

LITTLE
HITCHCOCK'S 'SECRET AGENT' Madeleine Carroll Peter Lorre
Also: 30 minutes of old time fun Doug Fairbanks "MANHATTAN MADNESS"

John Garfield Priscilla Lane
Linden
"DUST BE MY DESTINY"

RIVOLI
J. EDGAR HOOVER'S
"PAROLE FIXER"

Keeping Track Of Hollywood Activities

By HARRISON CARROLL

King Features Syndicate Writer.

HOLLYWOOD, March 18.—Florida's reception to Rosalind Russell was not so nice.

On the first night that the star and her sisterd were in Palm Beach, Rosalind's jewels are said to have been burgled.

Haven't seen anything about it, but the story must be true, cause Rosalind communicated with representatives in Hollywood asking them to check on the valuation of the gems.

Fifi Dorsay's South American admirer, George Bolini, has given her until the end of the week to make up her mind. She probably won't wed him now or later, however, because she doesn't want to live in Argentine and, more important, because she doesn't want to sacrifice her American citizenship.

The makeup of Virginia Brissac in "The Ghost Breakers," they say, will almost match the horror of Charles Laughton's Quasimode. The character actress, a handsome woman in real life, portrays an ancient and half mad Caribbean Negress. Seventeen layers of paper-thin rubber are used on her face to give her the appearance of being incredibly wrinkled. Some of her teeth are blackened out and she has a stubby mustache on her upper lip.

The effect is so guresome that there were complaints when she ate in the commissary. Studio Manager George Bagnall has arranged for her meals to be served in her dressing-room.

The Governor of Sonora, Mexico, threw a dinner for Gary Cooper and presented him with an expensive shotgun. So what happened? So Sam Goldwyn called the star back for retakes on "The Westerner" and Gary had to leave without firing one shot.

You probably could have gotten odds of 100 to 1 that Edward Arnold wouldn't be hurt in 1940 riding a bicycle built for three. But it happened on the "Lillian Russell" set. Arnold, Alice Faye and Warren William took a spill. Eddie was the only one injured. They had to take two stitches in a cut on his knee and he will be out of the picture for a couple of days.

In case Mickey Rooney has forgotten, the first autograph he ever signed using his present screen name was to Andy Devine. It happened in the office of Publicity Man John Leroy Johnson on the day that Mickey's name was changed from McGuire to Rooney.

Andy still has the autographed picture and he tells me he will give it to Mickey for his souvenirs.

What do you think Freddie Bartholomew is getting on his sixteenth birthday? A complete set of trap drums.

Zanuck Signs Dean Jagger To Play Role Of 'Brigham Young'

By LOUELLA O. PARSONS

Motion Picture Editor International News Service.

HOLLYWOOD, March 18.—May I present Dean Jagger, whose name you are going to hear many times within the next few months? He has been signed to play "Brigham Young," and so quietly was the signing done that no one even knew Jagger was under consideration. He was flown out here from New York by plane, and, after a series of extensive tests, Darryl Zanuck put his okay on the selection and arranged with George Abbott to borrow him for this important 20th Century-Fox movie.

MARLENE DIETRICH

The stage history of Jagger, who is six feet two and a strapping lad of thirty-two, includes an appearance with Ethel Barrymore and a star role in "The Unconquered." He was here two years ago at "Para" for movies, but, like many another, was never given a chance. Well, "Brigham Young," which Henry Hathaway directs next month, ought to provide the path to stardom if Jagger has what it takes.

If Franchot Tone gets back from his Broadway play in time, he's going to find a job right at his front door ready and waiting for him. Joe Pasternak, who picks them and knows what he wants, has his eyes on Franchot for the male lead opposite Marlene Dietrich in "Seven Sinners." He would like to cast Franchot as a naval officer—in the male lead of course. So Franchot, if you read this, maybe you'd like the job. I couldn't help but watch Marlene dancing at Ciro's. She looked radiant. A year ago she was despondent and blue. Now, with success at hand, her whole outlook has changed.

Wesley Ruggles has at last found a hero for "Arizona" to play opposite Jean Arthur. After hunting the highways and byways for a "tall, dark and handsome," he has handed the part to William Holden. Not since they were tracking down Scarlett O'Hara has there been such a manhunt. Gary Cooper, Randy Scott and Joel McCrea were all up for the role—not to mention 25 tests made of unknowns. In case it has slipped your mind "Arizona" is the two million dollar picture for which Columbia erected a whole town just outside Tucson—and then postponed production until the box office looked up.

Snapshots of Hollywood collected at random: Congratulations are being sent to Dora Joyce and Charles Morrison who were married November 11th; Perc Westmore, makeup specialist, and Juliette Novas, so-o-o pretty, interesting twosome at the Brown Derby; Cary Grant at Ciro's supping with Elizabeth Inglis; Liz Whitney was with a party—Bruce Cabot and three others. She seemed in great spirits and danced every dance—but then, who can resist that Emil Coleman music at Ciro's? Our first stop was at the Cocoanut Grove, and the whole town was literally there for the gambol and the entertainment which was of many hours duration; Norma Shearer and George Raft, with Rocky and Gary Cooper, were early arrivals. Talked with Dolores Costello Barrymore and her bridegroom, Dr. John Vruwink. She looks radiant; Queenie Vassar and her bridegroom of forty some years, Joseph Cawthorn, held court; Marjorie Rambeau and her husband in the same party; Claudette Colbert, Joan Bennett, Edna Best and their favorite escorts with the William Goetzes; Bette Davis stopped at our table to chat, and she and Orry Kelly had a lot of laughs. Betty wore a fascinating old lace collar on a black dress. Arthur Farnsworth, Bob Taplinger and others in her party. Virginia O'Brien from "Meet the People" stole the show. I could listen to her sing with that curious intonation for hours and hours.

That's all for today. See you tomorrow!

CAPRA MONTH! LAST 2 DAYS!
MR. DEEDS GOES TO TOWN
Also SONS of LIBERTY Both Academy Winners!
TIMES Full Show Latest NEWSREELS
Wed.—Errol Flynn, "GREEN LIGHT"

Today's Movie Calendar

Theatres advertised in this column belong to the Motion Picture Theatre Owners of Maryland.

Alpha Catonsville — Robert Montgomery in "EARL OF CHICAGO" Comedy.

Ambassador 4604 Liberty Heights — Edgar Bergen in "Charlie McCarthy, Detective" "March of Time," No. 6.

Apollo 1500 Harford Ave. — Ann Sothern in "CONGO MAISIE" "Bandits and Ballads."

Arcade Harford Rd. & Hamilton Ave. — Ann Sothern in "CONGO MAISIE" "Fashion Forecasts."

Astor Poplar Grove at Edmondson — Lew Ayres in "SECRET OF DR. KILDARE" "March of Time."

Aurora 7 East North Ave. — Paul Muni in "SCARFACE" "Rocking Thru the Rockies."

Avalon 4300 Park Heights Ave. — Ronald Colman in "THE LIGHT THAT FAILED" "The Mouse Exterminator."

Avenue Milton Ave. & Hoffman St. — Lew Ayres in "SECRET OF DR. KILDARE" "Peace on Earth."

Avon 3019 Hamilton Ave. — Lillian Gish in "BIRTH OF A NATION" "Presto Chango."

Belnord 2700 Philadelphia Ave. — Ann Sothern in "CONGO MAISIE" "Bow and Arrows."

Boulevard 33rd at Greenmount — Ann Sothern in "CONGO MAISIE" "March of Time."

Bridge Edmondson Ave. & Pulaski St. — Ronald Colman in "THE LIGHT THAT FAILED" Comedy.

Broadway 509 S. Broadway — Ann Sothern in "CONGO MAISIE" "Three Stooges."

Cameo 4706 Harford Road — Don Ameche in "SWANEE RIVER" "Three Stooges."

Capitol 1518 W. Baltimore St. — Ann Sothern in "CONGO MAISIE" "Chicken Feed."

Casino 1118 Light St. — Craig Reynolds in 'GENTLEMAN FROM ARIZONA' "Green Hornet."

Cluster 303 S. Broadway — Richard Dix in "THE MARINES FLY HIGH" "The Republic of Finland."

Columbia 709 Washington Blvd. — Ann Sothern in "CONGO MAISIE" "Monkeys Is the Craziest People."

Earle Belair Rd. at Woodlea Ave. — Edgar Bergen in "Charlie McCarthy, Detective" "Little Lambkin."

Edgewood Edmondson & Edgewood — Ronald Colman in "THE LIGHT THAT FAILED" "Where Turf Meets Surf."

Forest Garrison & Liberty Heights — Ronald Colman in "THE LIGHT THAT FAILED" "Threads of a Nation."

Fulton Fulton Ave. at Baker St. — James Cagney in "ROARING TWENTIES" "Time Out for Lessons."

Garden Charles at Cross — Jane Withers in "SHOOTING HIGH" "Early Bird Gets the Worm."

Glen Glen Burnie — W. C. Fields in "MY LITTLE CHICKADEE" Musical Comedy.

Grand 511 S. Conkling St. — Richard Dix in "THE MARINES FLY HIGH" "One for the Book."

Gwynn 4609 Liberty Heights Ave. — Lew Ayres in "SECRET OF DR. KILDARE" "The Teacher's Pest."

Hampden 911 W. 36th St. — Ronald Colman in "THE LIGHT THAT FAILED" Comedy.

Harford 2616 Harford Ave. — James Stewart in "DESTRY RIDES AGAIN" Comedy and News.

Hippodrome Eutaw at Balto. St. — Richard Dix in "RENO" Eddy Duchin and His Orchestra.

Horn 2014 West Pratt St. — Ronald Colman in "THE LIGHT THAT FAILED" "Hook, Line and Sinker."

Howard 115 N. Howard St. — Jean Hersholt in "MEET DR. CHRISTIAN" "Bandits and Ballads."

Ideal 903 W. Thirty-sixth St. — Ann Sothern in "CONGO MAISIE" Comedy.

Irvington 4113 Frederick Ave. — Jeanette MacDonald in "SWEETHEARTS" "Andy Pandy Goes Fishing."

Leader 248 S. Broadway — Dennis Moore in "EAST SIDE KIDS" "Springtime in the Movies."

Lexway 31 W. Lexington St. — Leslie Howard in "INTERMEZZO" Comedy.

Linwood 908 S. Linwood Ave. — Lon Chaney, Jr., in "OF MICE AND MEN" Comedy.

Little 523 North Howard St. — Madeleine Carroll in "SECRET AGENT" with Robert Young.

Lord Baltimore 1110 West Baltimore St. — Ronald Colman in "THE LIGHT THAT FAILED" Comedy.

Lord Calvert 2444 Wash. Blvd. — Wm. Gargan in "ISLE OF DESTINY" Russ Morgan and Orchestra.

Lyceum Sparrows Point, Md. — Marlene Dietrich in "DESTRY RIDES AGAIN" Comedy.

McHenry 1037 Light St. — Ann Sothern in "CONGO MAISIE" "March of Time."

Met Pennsylvania & North Aves. — Ronald Colman in "THE LIGHT THAT FAILED" Latest News.

New Reisterstown, Md. — Robert Montgomery in "THE EARL OF CHICAGO" "The Fishing Bear."

Northway Harford & North. Pky. — Allan Jones in "GREAT VICTOR HERBERT" "Sniffles and the Bookworm."

Overlea Belair Rd. End of Car Line. — Cary Grant in "HIS GIRL FRIDAY" "Miracle of Lourdes."

Palace Gay and Hoffman Sts. — Richard Dix in "MARINES FLY HIGH" "Rhumba Land."

Patterson Eastern and East Aves. — Ronald Colman in "THE LIGHT THAT FAILED" "Night Descends on Treasure Island."

Pikes Pikesville, Md. — The Lane Sisters in "FOUR WIVES" "Puss Gets the Boot."

Pimlico Park Heights & Belvedere — Ann Sothern in "CONGO MAISIE" "Teacher's Pest."

Preston 1108 East Preston St. — Allan Jones in "GREAT VICTOR HERBERT" "Hunting Hounds."

Red Wing 2241 E. Monument St. — Lon Chaney, Jr., in "OF MICE AND MEN" "Porky's Hotel."

Rex 4600 York Rd. — Lew Ayres in "SECRET OF DR. KILDARE" Comedy.

Rialto 846 W. North Ave. — Edgar Bergen in "Charlie McCarthy, Detective" Latest News.

Ritz 1607 N. Washington St. — Ronald Colman in "THE LIGHT THAT FAILED" "Pete Smith Specialty."

Senator 5904 York Road — Ronald Colman in "THE LIGHT THAT FAILED" Comedy and News.

State Monument and Castle Sts. — Ann Sothern in "CONGO MAISIE" Vaudeville.

Strand Dundalk, Md. — Gene Autry in "SHOOTING HIGH" "Information, Please."

Towson Towson, Md. — Basil Rathbone in "TOWER OF LONDON" Comedy.

Vilma Belair Rd. and Mayfield Ave. — Ronald Colman in "THE LIGHT THAT FAILED" "Merrie Melody."

Walbrook 3100 W. North Ave. — Ronald Colman in "THE LIGHT THAT FAILED" Comedy and News.

Waverly Greenmount at Gorsuch — Richard Dix in "MARINES FLY HIGH" "Threads of a Nation."

Westway Aldershot at Edmondson — Burgess Meredith in "OF MICE AND MEN" "Musical Bandits and Ballads."

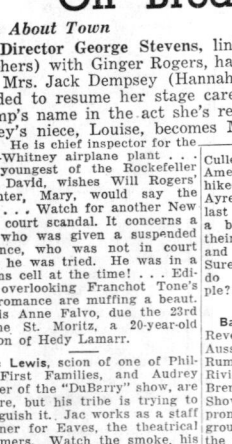

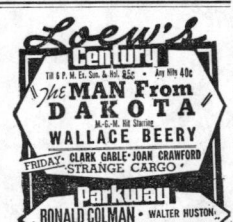

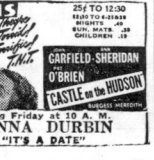

McGowan To Return For Final Operation

THE BALTIMORE NEWS-POST SPORTS

12 MONDAY EVENING, MARCH 18, 1940

Rodger H. Pippen *Sports Editor* Says:

AIKEN, South Carolina, March 18.

Take it from Clark Griffith, venerable owner and president of the Washington Baseball Club, the Orioles have secured two valuable players in Lamar Ashby Newsome, shortstop, and William Taylor Nagel, third sacker.

RODGER H. PIPPEN

Griff says Newsome will be the best defensive shortstop in the International League. As Clark sees him, the Birds haven't had such a fine fielder since Joe Boley was sold to the Athletics. Nagel, according to Griff, will find the short leftfield fence at Oriole Park very much to his liking. Bucky Harris, manager of the Senators, agrees with him.

Speaking of Griffith, he is a most remarkable fellow. Seventy-one years old his next birthday, he has more pep and enthusiasm than most of the ball players now in training in major and minor camps all over the country.

I sat with him near the Washington players' bench in Orlando, Fla., during the first game with the New York Giants. His keen eyes followed every move and he was the first to shout a vigorous protest to the umpire when Lefty Melton, former Oriole hurling for New York, got away with what appeared a balk in throwing to first base in an effort to nail a runner. He talked to his players as they moved in and out between innings and reminded several that they were not displaying much ginger.

Just before the game got under way, Griff and his coach, Nick Altrock, engaged in a little horse play at the plate after the Mayor of Orlando had tossed the first ball to the Washington owner. The toss, by the way, was bad, but Griff judged the bounce and caught it.

More active than most men of fifty, Griff goes to the office every day and not a move in the conduct of the organization is made without his knowledge or approval. That, of course, does not apply to Bucky Harris in his duties as fielder leader.

* * *

Griff and His Golfing Feat

Now for that part of the story which inspired the statement in the opening paragraphs about Griff being a most remarkable fellow.

Clark performed a golfing feat at Orlando the other day which is worth a feature story in every magazine in the country.

Playing over the difficult links of the Dubsdread Golf and Country Club, he shot the back nine in 37, or two over par; he made a birdie on the three-par 140-yard twelfth, and on the sixteenth he smacked a low ball straight down the fairway for 235 yards.

How many men of seventy in this country could match that performance? Not one in a thousand.

Griff's first nine wasn't so hot. He was topping his drives and his poor work off the tee influenced the rest of his game, particularly his putting. On the back nine, however, he recovered his drive and his putting touch, and it was mainly through his fine playing that he and his partner, Billy Smith, were able to take the second nine and the match from William M. Baskervill of the Baltimore Country Club, and the writer. The Baltimoreans won the first nine, but lost the match on the last hole when Griff came through with a par five on a 505-yard hole.

Clark started the last nine with a par four on the 395-yard tenth. This is a dog leg to the left and requires two accurate shots of about two hundred yards each for a man of Griff's power and ability. His second was just in front of the green and his pitch was close to the pin. He was on with a wood and an iron in the 320-yard eleventh. The twelfth is a 140-yard par three, with a lake in front of the green. Clarks four-iron carried the ball right for the pin and the sphere settled ten feet beyond. His putt was in all the way.

The baseball magnate went one over the thirteenth, fourteenth and seventeenth, all par fours.

Using a wood, he drove the 186-yard, par-three fifteenth. He made a par four on the 412-yard sixteenth, and a very difficult par it is for anybody except a long driver. This was the hole on which he made his long drive.

He went one over on the seventeenth and then won the match with his par on the long last hole.

Dizzy Signs Pact For $10,000

LOS ANGELES, March 18 — (A. P.).—Jerome Herman Dean, who isn't as talkative as he once was, is back in the fold.

Diz signed a contract last night to pitch this season for the Chicago Cubs. He will receive $10,000—just half of what he drew last year. The end of his holdout siege was as unexciting as that. The great one simply capitulated.

CHILLY RECEPTION

Chronologically, his Sabbath went something like this:

12.30 P. M.—Stepped off a train from Dallas, five hours late. Hopped into a cab for Wrigley Field, where the Cubs were billed in an exhibition against Connie Mack's Philadelphia Athletics.

1.10 P. M.—Walked into the Cub dressing room, to a few not too enthusiastic "hi ya's". The reception was definitely chilly.

1.28 P. M. — Found Clarence (Pants) Rowland, Cub executive, and started a conference.

1.37 P. M.—Rowland announced "We're deadlocked. Dean knows the terms of his contract and it is up to him."

1.38 P. M.—Dean remarks, "If I'd known this was the way it would be I wouldn't have come out at all."

WATCHES GAME

1.48 P. M.—Settles himself wearily and alone in a left field box to watch the game, observing "It looks like I'll be catching the train back to Dallas. I got to get back to my farm and get to farming."

3.40 P. M.—Comments "That was all right" anent the Cubs' 4-2 victory, enters a cab and drives away.

4.15 P. M.—Walks into Rowland's hotel room.

5.45 P. M.—Walks out again, arm in arm with the Cub official, bound for a party at Charlie Root's house. "He signed for $10,000," Rowland smiles. "That's right,' Diz adds, "I'm in great shape. Down to 195 pounds and ready to go. Last year I weighed 210 at this time."

NO BONUS CLAUSE

The contract, it was announced, contains no bonus clause, but it was believed Diz would be eligible for one if he earned it

Last year, for his $20,000, he won six and lost four. Some of his teammates, who worked a lot harder for a lot less, were openly resentful. At spring training camp, the attitude of everyone concerned was noticeably indifferent to the great one's published statements that he'd sign for $15,000—no less.

How soon Diz will get a chance on the mound was problematical. Observers anticipated that he'd be assigned to test out the arm which has given him so much trouble within a few days.

New Oriole Gives A Sample

LAMAR NEWSOME

LOOKS GOOD—But can he throw from there? Anyhow, it appears that, if the stunt above is a sample of Lamar (Skeeter) Newsome's wares, the fans can expect some acrobatic fielding around the Oriole shortstop position. If you want an expert opinion on the bloke, why, Rodger H. Pippen, Sports Editor, quotes Clark Griffith in his column today as declaring that Skeeter will be the best defensive shortstop in the International League. Newsome is shown in action at the Aiken, S. C., field, where the Birds are training. Picture copyright, 1940, by The Baltimore News-Post. All rights reserved.

Ankle Fails To Limber Properly

By HUGH TRADER, JR.

AIKEN, S. C., March 18.—Failing to observe much, if any, improvement in his ailing left ankle, Frank McGowan revealed today that he expects to quit the Orioles' camp here within the next few days and return to Baltimore for a final operation.

Mac is satisfied that, once his ankle is mended, he can help the club in olden form.

"As it is, I'm not helping either the club or myself," says Frank, "because I can't run hard without pain in my left ankle. Otherwise, I feel fine and believe I can put in a good season when I have that adhesion removed. My other ankle, operated on last year, is strong and I can still hit that 'apple.' The Doc told me to come down here for a week to try and work out the trouble, but even he felt that I'd need another operation."

Skipper Thomas agrees with McGowan's decision and also shares Mac's optimism for a grand comeback a month hence.

Meanwhile, Bob Hamilton and Norman Deweese, both rookies battling for the right field job, have displayed promise but done nothing outstanding as yet.

However, Thomas found much solace in the Birds' second-straight 5-to-3 defeat yesterday by Atlanta in the pitching finesse of rookies Ken Trinkle and Lloyd Gross. Of the two, Trinkle was more impressive. In fact, the kid pitched the best ball of any hurler in the two games at Savannah over the weekend

REAL SPEED

Working three innings, and fanning five while allowing only one run, Trinkle showed real speed and a sharp-breaking curve that you could hang your hat on. Gross didn't display as much "stuff," but uncorked a fast ball that was "taking off" during his three-inning stretch in which he allowed only two bingles.

"What I liked most, though," says Thomas, "is that both were pouring that ball in there. From what they've shown so far, each has a real chance to stick and win, especially Trinkle. Of course, I'm anxious to see them under fire for six or seven innings now, but I'm encouraged."

Other features yesterday included the slugging of Skinny Graham and Red Howell and the fielding gem supplied by Skeeter Newsome who scampered behind second for a hard drive and completed a dazzling play. Graham and Howell are hitting much better than they did in camp last spring.

Considering that the club is far behind in its conditioning, due the recent rainy spell, the Birds made a creditable showing in Savannah. The hitters need more batting practice and the infield is ragged yet, though the diamond at Savannah was very poor.

PITCHING SITUATION

Of course, exactly how strong the pitching is remains to be seen when the chuckers begin toiling the entire route.

When Bill Nagel swings into action, the attack undoubtedly will function faster and Gene Corbett will move into second base. However, Ed Vandergrift impressed Thomas against Atlanta in the opening game last Saturday, though he bobbled a couple. Due to a blistered heel, he didn't play yesterday.

Cunningham In Two-Mile Test

KANSAS CITY, March 18—(A. P.).—Glenn Cunningham, outstanding miler of the past decade, steps up the dinstance to two miles tonight against Taisto Maki, Walter Mehl and probably Archie San Romani in the Missouri Valley A. A. U. indoor meet, a Finnish benefit affair.

Paavo Nurmi, the "Phantom Finn" of 15 years ago, will appear in a half mile feature.

RED ISN'T RED

Red Barber, the Brooklyn baseball broadcaster, isn't red at all but a platinum blond.

All-Star Ball Tilt Proves Nothing

By WHITNEY MARTIN

TAMPA, Fla., March 18—(A. P.).—The long-abused National Leaguers today strutted the streets in broad daylight, and if pressed, very lightly, would say casually:

"Oh yes, the American League. We had their stars over for a practice game yesterday. Beat them, 2 to 1, with our reserves."

Which, in essence, is true. The National League All-Stars did win an exhibition game, which more than 13,000 spectators contributed approximately $20,000 to the Finnish Relief Fund to see. And three substitutes did blend their talents to score the winning run in the ninth inning.

NOTHING PROVED

But, in reality, the game proved nothing, except that the pitchers are far ahead of the batters in spring training, and that a lineup of sluggers is just another lineup when the fast ones, and not the hurlers, are snapping.

However, the victory was greeted gleefully by the senior circuit. It was St. Patrick's Day to the rest of the country, but it was groundhog day to the National Leaguers, who popped out of the holes in which they had been hiding since the last World Series to yelp defiance.

FIVE SINGLES

For a spring exhibition it was a corking ball game, with the big surprise the inability of the row on row of siege guns in the American lineup to get much more than a loud foul. They were held to five hits, Bill Dickey and Frank Crosetti getting two each and Jimmy Foxx one, and none was better than a single.

The National Leaguers collected six blows, all singles, putting two of them together in the ninth for the ball game. As the heavy-hitters on boh teams were stymied, the parade of pitchers marched serenely along.

The Americans took the lead in the second inning when DiMaggio walked, went to second on Dickey's single and went home on Crosetti's first hit.

The Nationals tied it up in the fourth when Ott walked, advanced when Harry Danning was hit by Buck Newsom, and scored on Demaree's single to right, beating a fine throw by Williams by inches.

FELLER WILD

Bob Feller started the eighth inning for the Americans. He had plenty of stuff, but was wild. A double play pulled him out of a hole in that inning, but in the ninth Al Lopez, Boston Bee catcher and the pride of Tampa, sent a slashing single to center, went to second when Hal Trosky, Cleveland first baseman, dropped Rollie Hemsley's throw on Terry Moore's sacrifice, and scored the winning run on Pete Coscarart's single through short.

Bill McKenchnie, Red manager in charge of the National team, started Paul Derringer and followed with Kirby Higbe, Luke Hamlin, Bucky Walters and Harry Gumbert, with Gumbert the winning pitcher. Joe McCarthy, American pilot who started seven of his Yankees, sent Red Ruffing to the mound, and followed him with Newsom, Dutch Leonard and Feller.

The game was replete with good plays, including a neat catch by Hank Greenberg, Detroit's reformed first baseman, in left field, and five fast double killings.

Exhibition Baseball

At Tampa, Fla. — National League All-Stars, 2; American League All-Stars, 1.

At St. Petersburg, Fla.—St. Louis (N.), 4; New York (A.) 2.

At Sarasota, Fla.—Brooklyn (N.), 9; Boston (A.), 2.

At Miami Beach, Fla.—Boston (N.), 12; Philadelphia (N.), 1.

At Fort Myers, Fla.—Cleveland (A.), 2; Rochester (I.), 1.

At Orlando, Fla.—Detroit (A.), 9; Washington (A.), 7.

At San Diego, Cal.—San Diego (P. C.), 7; Pittsburgh (N.), 4.

At San Antonio, Texas—St. Louis (A.), 12; Tulsa (T. L.), 4.

At Los Angeles, Cal.—Chicago (N.), 4; Philadelphia (A.), 2.

At Hollywood, Cal.—Chicago (A.), 6; Hollywood (P. C.). 5.

TODAY'S SCHEDULE

At St. Petersbzurg — St. Louis (N.) vs. Detroit (A.).

At Fort Myers—Philadelphia (N.) vs. Cleveland (A.).

At Anaheim, Cal—Philadelphia (A.) vs. Chicago (A.).

At Bradenton, Fla. — Boston (N.) vs. New York (N.).

At Sebring, Fla.—Boston (A.) vs Newark (I.).

At San Bernardino, Cal. — Pittsburgh (N.) vs. Hollywood (P. C.).

At Ontario, Cal.—Chicago (N.) vs. Los Angeles (P. C.).

Hassett Out For 2 Weeks

BRADENTON, Fla., March 18—(A. P.).—Buddy Hassett of the Boston Bees is sidelined for probably two weeks with an ankle injury suffered in a game against Rochester. Carvell Rowell will fill in for him in right field.

ALLOWS ONE HIT

CLEARWATER, Fla., March 18—(A. P.).—Hopes that Hugh Casey would have a good year with the Brooklyn Dodgers were bolstered by his performance against the Boston Red Sox yesterday. He allowed only one hit in five innings and set down his first 11 foes in order.

FULL SQUAD

SAN BERNARDINO, Cal., March 18—(A. P.).—Frankie Frisch plans to carry a full crew of Pittsburgh Pirates almost up to May 15, when major league squads must be cut to 25 players. His idea is to get a good look at the rookies under fire. After the cut the squad will number 10 pitchers, three catchers, six infielders and six outfielders.

SEEKS OFFICE

Buck Grundy, the old Lehigh swimming star, is to run for constable at the May elections in Miami.

As N. L. Stars Won

HEADS FOR HOME WITH THE BACON—Al Lopez, Boston Bee catcher, is shown sliding safely into third base on his march toward home with the winning run in the major league all-star game at Tampa, Florida.

On the next play Lopez scored on a grounder by Pete Coscarat of the Brooklyn Dodgers and the National Leaguers took a 2-1 game from the American League, believe it or not.

Tribe Unbeaten In Citrus Loop

By JUDSON BAILEY
Associated Press Sports Writer

If baseball's spring squirt, the Grapefruit League, has proved anything to date, it is that the Cincinnati Reds and St. Louis Cardinals are about to have a great two-club race—for last place in the Grapefruit League.

Playing about the same brand of opponents (the New York Yankees and each other), the Cardinals have managed to take the lowest crouch in the cellar by losing seven out of nine games, but the Reds have dropped six out of eight to make a stout fight.

INDIANS UNBEATEN

The Cleveland Indians, on the other hand, have won four and lost none of their exhibition games and the Detroit Tigers have triumphed in six and dropped one.

It just goes to show that the spring struggles are all in fun, or at least futility. In the early innings of the Grapefruit grind a year ago, the Cardinals were setting a hot pace for all the major league clubs and the Indians were't even threatened as cellar champions.

Standings:

Club.	Intra League.	Intra League.	All Games.
Cleveland Indians	0-0	1-0	4-0
Detroit Tigers	5-1	1-0	6-1
Boston Red Sox	4-1	0-0	4-1
Chicago White Sox	2-1	0-0	3-1
Phil. Phillies	0-0	0-1	3-1
Phil. Athletics	1-2	0-0	10-4
New York Yankees	5-3	0-0	5-3
New York Giants	2-2	1-0	3-2
Chicago Cubs	2-2	0-0	2-2
Boston Bees	0-1	2-0	2-2
Pitts. Pirates	1-1	0-0	2-2
St. Louis Browns	0-0	0-0	1-1
Brooklyn Dodgers	2-5	2-0	4-5
Wash. Senators	1-1	0-2	1-3
Cincinnati Reds	0-4	2-2	2-6
St. Louis Cardinals	2-3	0-4	2-7

Golf 'Assistant'

MRS. JOHNNY BASS

Not only is Mrs. Johnny Bass the wife of the Clifton Park golf professional but also sort of an assist[illegible] in his golf work. While Mrs. Bass doesn't [illegible] sons, she maintains an attractive shop [illegible] and is quite apt at making and mending

10,000 FAMILIES HOMELESS IN PENNA. FLOODED AREAS★

THE BALTIMORE NEWS-POST

AN INDEPENDENT NEWSPAPER

The Largest Daily Circulation in the Entire South

Entered as second-class matter at Baltimore Postoffice.

Copyright, 1940, by Hearst Consolidated Publications, Inc.

VOL. CXXXVI.—NO. 126 | MONDAY EVENING, APRIL 1, 1940 | PRICE 3 CENTS

7 HOME FINAL

IN THE NEWS

ASKED by the newsmen if there was any "particular reason" for the complete secrecy regarding Welles' observations abroad, Mr. Early, the President's secretary, replied:

"Is there any reason why there shouldn't be? Did the President send Welles to Europe to come back and to report to you (the press)?"

Is not that answer of Mr. Early's a bit of impertinence—a bit of insolence, in fact?

Is not his supercilious statement rather a like master like man pose—a like leader like lackey attitude?

The newsmen are not asking for information for themselves.

They do not care about Mr. Early or Mr. Welles or Mr. Roosevelt personally.

These political gentlemen are only important in so far as they represent the American people.

And the newsmen are merely inquiring about the publication of data for the edification of the American people.

Are not the American people supposed to take an interest in what their representatives are doing to get them into foreign wars which they, the people, will have to fight, and which they, the politicians, will carefully avoid?

Is Government a public matter or a private matter in this alleged republic?

The newsmen in no way suggested a report from Mr. Welles to themselves. But a report to the people might be in order by Mr. Welles explaining on what authority he went poking his political nose into foreign affairs and relating what powers he possessed to act or investigate with regard to the conflict abroad, and stating what he did over there to get himself called a joke in Italy, a nuisance in France, and a meddler in England.

It was in the latter country that the London Daily Mirror said of Mr. Welles:

"We are struggling for our lives. We do not like to be impeded even by charming people in that task."

And again it was in England that the London Daily Mail, on its first page, linked Mr. Welles' mission to President Roosevelt's personal political future in the light of the third-term controversy in America.

Surely it is not presumptuous on the part of the American people and their news purveyors to take a modest interest in their Government, even if it is getting to be an arbitary and absolute one.

SENATOR CONNALLY of Texas last week attacked Thomas E. Dewey for his criticism of the New Deal's foreign policy.

Said Senator Connally:

"Dewey thinks he is a candidate, but he isn't."

And continued Senator Conally:

"The best answer to Mr. Dewey is that we (members and supporters of the Administration) have kept the nation out of war."

But, Senator, it is not you New Dealers who have kept the nation out of war.

YOU passed the unneutrality bill to sell implements of slaughter to the embattled nations, possibly for the benefit of the du Ponts and other American manufacturers of war materials.

You appropriated the public monies for partisan loans to one side or the other among the warring nations to satisfy your personal preferences.

You withdrew your Ambassador from Germany, a country you do not like, but not from Russia, your political partner and preceptor.

You have instructed your Ambassadors in this or that foreign country to favor this or that foreign policy in which we have no actual interest and no rightful participation.

You have sent special emissaries of the New Deal Administration milling around Europe to meddle secretly in matters which do not properly concern them or us.

You have allowed our diplomatic representatives to take partisan sides and make silly public expression of their personal half-baked opinion.

You have denounced, for no reason, America's valuable trade treaty with imperialist Japan, whose Government you do not approve of, and have sent millions of the American people's dollars to Communist China,

Continued on Page 2, Column 8.

Throngs Await Bowie Opening

Rising Waters Lap At Syracuse Flood Relief Center

Spring floods struck widely separated sections of the nation and took a toll of ten lives over the week-end. Northern California, Central and Eastern Pennsylvania and South-Central New York all reported heavy damage as rains and melting snow caused rivers and streams to rise. Here is an air view of a section of Syracuse, N. Y., where the swelling waters of Onondaga creek, which inundated a large part of the city, were no respecters of authority. They lapped impudently (in the photo above) at the driveway of a fire house which is serving as a flood relief center. Note the rescue boats "parked" by the building.

Leaking Gas Tank Perils Refugees In Flight

Governor James Set To Fly To Disaster Center

By International News Service.

The National Headquarters of the Red Cross announced today at Washington that preliminary reports from field workers on the Susquehanna watershed indicated that approximately 10,000 families in 50 Pennsylvania communities—5,000 in Wilkes-Barre alone—had been forced to leave their homes by rising flood waters.

The situation in the Wilkes-Barre area, where the Susquehanna river had risen to a dangerously high stage, became more acute when a leaking gasoline storage tank and a broken dike at nearby Kingston threw thousands into a panic.

SPREAD ON WATER

The inflammable contents of the tank spread over the swollen river. Wilkes-Barre hotels were crowded with people who fled from their homes. Many stores were closed.

The river stage was believed to have approached its crest shortly before 10 A. M., when flood waters rose to 31.45 feet above low-water mark, compared with a record crest of 33.6 in 1936.

John Mirmak, official river observer, who reported the reading, said that the stream had remained stationary for nearly two hours.

If no additional snow melts on the upper watershed a further rise is unlikely, he said. Choppy condition of the stream was viewed as a favorable sign.

SIX FEET DEEP

The Covert street section of Kingston was reported to be under six feet of water. Residents who believed themselves safe found their homes surrounded by water within 10 minutes. Farm lands also were inundated.

At Harrisburg, Gov. Arthur H. James asked the WPA to provide $2,000,000 immediately for emergency flood relief.

The Governor made preparations

Continued on Page 2, Column 1.

Vanderbilt Shaken Up In Crash

Alfred Gwynne Vanderbilt, president of the Maryland Jockey Club, escaped injury today when the automobile in which he was riding and a heavy truck collided at Maryland and Mount Royal avenues.

When the crash occurred Mr. Vanderbilt was en route from his breeding and training farm, Sagamore Stables, in the Worthington Valley, to the Maryland Club, where he was to pick up some friends and take them to Bowie for the opening the racing season.

Although considerably shaken up, he continued to the club in a taxicab and said that he would go to the track with his friends. The automobile in which he was riding was driven by his chauffeur, Michael McGrath.

According to police, the Vanderbilt machine was bound south on Maryland avenue and the truck, driven by Russell Boyce, 700 block Cumberland street, was bound north. Police said that the truck, attempting to make a left turn into Mount Royal avenue, struck the rear of the automobile.

Police charged Boyce with reckless driving. No charge was placed against the Vanderbilt chauffeur.

Wm. Horlick, Jr., Succumbs at 65

RACINE, Wis., April 1—(I.N.S.). William Horlick, Jr., sixty-five, treasurer and chairman of the board of the Horlick Malted Milk Corporation which his father founded, died today after a heart attack.

SEVERE QUAKE RECORDED

NEW YORK, April 1—(A. P.).—Fordham University's seismograph recorded a "severe" tremor at 6.21.52 A. M., New York time, today. The distance of the movement was estimated at 8,050 miles from New York in the general direction of the Philippines.

Nazis Make New Neutral Charge

By PIERRE J. HUSS
International News Service Staff Correspondent.

BERLIN, April 1.—Threatening to let the American Congress decide for itself the authenticity of its white paper accusing the United States of fostering Europe's war, Germany today charged that the American Government has been violating its own neutrality laws.

Diplomatic Correspondence, organ of the German Foreign Office, carried the dispute between Berlin and Washington a step further by commenting:

"The surprising and even monstrous fact must be noted that representatives of a power, in principle strongly opposed to interference with other continents since the days of Washington and Monroe, is now engaged in aggravating the conflict's danger to third powers.

'AMATEUR DIPLOMATS'

"These amateur diplomats are even more inconceivable because

Continued on Page 2, Column 1.

Jap Troops Claim 37-Mile Advance

HONGKONG, April 1—(A. P.).—Japanese today reported rapid progress in an offensive in Southern Kwangsi province toward the French Indo-China border, apparently aimed at closing Chinese overland supply routes. They said they had captured Szelo, 37 miles from the frontier.

VERY LATEST NEWS

GARMENT WORKERS VOTE DOWN REDS

NEW YORK, April 1—(A. P.).—An "overwhelming" defeat of Communist candidates for office in the International Ladies Garment Workers Union was announced today by President David Dubinsky.

CALIFORNIA A. F. OF L. URGES END TO WPA

LOS ANGELES, April 1—(A. P.).—Abolition of the WPA and re-election of Sen. Hiram W. Johnson were advocated today by the California State Federation of Labor's Executive Committee.

10,000 Expected As Bowie Track Opens

By GABY

BOWIE, Md., April 1.—The spacious Bowie parking lot began filling early and indications pointed to a crowd of approximately 10,000 being present to usher in the new 1940 racing season here today.

The weather, cold earlier in the day, was comfortable by noon. Scattered clouds were in the sky, but there seemed to be little chance of rain. The track, wet yesterday, was drying rapidly under a warm sun and wind and it appeared the going would be good by the first race.

SCRATCH ROUGH PASS

Only one horse, Yancey Christmas' Kentucky Derby candidate, Rough Pass, was scratched out of

Continued on Page 10, Column 3.

The Man Who Made Time Stand Still for 60 years. From the days of Queen Victoria until his recent death, he refused to admit that the world was changing. Read about his strange existence in the American Weekly, the magazine with next Sunday's Baltimore American.—Adv.

350 Rescued At City Hospitals Fire

The possibility that the sprawling, three-story, seventy-five-year-old infirmary at City Hospitals may be replaced was considered today as firemen probed the six-alarm blaze that yesterday routed 590 patients.

What hospital authorities and firemen have dreaded for years, a major fire in the old building, struck shortly after 7 A. M. yesterday.

Three-hundred and fifty patients, trapped by flames, were rescued by firemen and hospital attendants who risked their lives time and again to enter the building. Six hundred others were ordered from the building as a precautionary measure.

TERROR-STRICKEN

Firemen breaking their way into the west wing of the building containing the women's wards found scores of smoke-blinded patients stumbling about, falling over beds or huddling, helpless with terror, on the floors.

Ladders were raised and 13 of the patients were carried down by the firemen. Others were led or carried through the smoke-filled passages to the center wing and out of the main door to safety.

SOUNDS ALARM

The fire started in the first-floor locker room and spread rapidly.

Continued on Page 2, Column 1.

Temperatures

12 Midn'ht	57	7 A. M.,	43
1 A. M.,	53	8 A. M.,	44
2 A. M.,	50	9 A. M.,	47
3 A. M.,	47	10 A. M.,	50
4 A. M.,	45	11 A. M.,	52
5 A. M.,	43	12 Noon,	53
6 A. M.,	42	1 P. M.,	55

THE WEATHER

Partly cloudy and slightly colder tonight, with lowest temperature around 32 degrees in the suburbs and 38 degrees in center of city. Tuesday increasing cloudiness, followed by rain Tuesday night. Moderate northerly winds, shifting to easterly on Tuesday.

Detailed Weather Report on Page 22

MEAN TEMPERATURES YESTERDAY.

Baltimore	58	New York	52
Atlanta	62	Omaha	56
Boston	50	Portland, Maine	48
Chicago	51	Salt Lake City	60
Jacksonville	64	San Antonio	76
Los Angeles	58	Seattle	50
Miami	81	Tampa	76
New Orleans	66	Washington	58

THE Baltimore NEWS-POST

The Largest Daily Circulation in the Entire South

VOL. CXXXVI—NO. 134 — WEDNESDAY EVENING, APRIL 10, 1940 — PRICE 3 CENTS

BATTLE IN NORTH SEA DESTROYS 6 WARSHIPS OF ALLIED, NAZI FLEETS

IN THE NEWS

THE creation of a war lord in the English Cabinet by Mr. Chamberlain is an important step in the right direction.

Whether creating Mr. Churchill that war lord, by making him director of all the nation's wartime services is the RIGHT step in the right direction is a large question.

Mr. Chamberlain may be in the right church but in the wrong pew.

Mrs. Florence Bayard Hilles, daughter of Thomas F. Bayard, famous Ambassador to England under Cleveland, and herself a distinguished lady much admired because of her wit and intellectual attainments, once told of a very aristocratic and exclusive daughter of one of Washington's first families who strode down the aisle of her church to the historic family pew one Sunday and found a strange lady seated in it.

The aristocratic dame drew herself up to her full haughty height and said witheringly:

"Madame, with your permission, I would like to occupy my own pew."

Perhaps Mr. Chamberlain should occupy his own pew.

If a dictator is necessary in time of war—and certainly concentrated authority is absolutely essential—the Prime Minister himself should occupy the pew and be the dictator, and not someone who has less the confidence of the country and perhaps less the qualifications necessary for the exercise of arbitrary authority.

Mr. Churchill is a very brilliant orator and writer.

His books are extremely interesting and valuable.

His speeches are among the most effective political utterances in the British Parliament.

But he has never demonstrated any outstanding executive or organizing ability.

In fact, he has displayed a notable lack of such qualities, especially in military matters.

Everybody knows that there was a disastrous Gallipoli campaign to force the Dardanelles in the last war.

Everybody knows that Mr. Churchill was the inspiring and directing figure behind that Gallipoli campaign.

But few realize how disastrous that campaign was.

Mr. Churchill has stated that if the army had co-operated properly with the navy, the campaign need not have failed—but the campaign did fail, and utterly unprejudiced sources place the blame heavily on the British forces and their direction — or rather misdirection.

The International Encyclopedia, a standard publication which, if biased at all, would be so on the side of America and the Allies, says in describing the naval action at Gallipoli:

"About the middle of February the combined British and French fleets began their fruitless attempt to force a passage of the Dardanelles.

"NO OPERATIONS IN THE WHOLE COURSE OF THE WAR WERE SO POORLY CONCEIVED AND SO INEFFICIENTLY CARRIED OUT.

"It is hard to understand the folly of the British Government in embarking upon such an expedition.

"If there is one thing that is well understood in naval war it is the absurdity of attacking strong forts by ships, especially without adequate military support."

According to the record of the encyclopedia, the five great British battleships OCEAN and IRRESISTIBLE and GOLIATH and TRIUMPH and MAJESTIC were sunk.

The French battleship BOUVET was sunk, and the British battle cruiser INFLEXIBLE badly injured by gunfire.

The troopship ROYAL EDWARD was sent to the bottom with the loss of 800 lives, and the sinking of the troopships ROMANZON (English) and MARQUETTE (French) were disasters almost as great.

The encyclopedia continues:

"The Dardanelles operations were now admitted to be a failure, and the British began to transfer their troops to Saloniki."

In regard to the land campaign the encyclopedia says:

"It resulted in failure, for although the troops got ashore,

Continued on Page 2, Column 8.

Norwegians, Germans In Battle

Planes Used In New Encounter Near Swedish Border

STOCKHOLM, April 10—(A. P.).—Travelers from Norway today reported that a battle was in progress this morning between German troops, supported by planes, and Norwegian infantry at Elverum, 75 miles northeast of Oslo, where the Norwegian royal family and the Government took refuge yesterday.

Elverum is only 25 miles from the border of neutral Sweden, which might provide another refuge for the Government if Norwegian troops are unable to stem the German advance.

PLANES AID

German forces were transported to the battle zone by bus yesterday. Aerial reinforcements were brought up later.

All frontier communication lines were broken so that nothing further could be learned in Sweden about the fighting or where the royal family was today.

Almost helpless, shorn of the chance of active aid from Sweden, Norway's only real hope of fighting German invasion lay in Allied promises which were in turn contingent upon a struggle for control of the approaches to her shores.

UP TO SWEDEN

Under pressure of a demarche from Germany, Sweden promised Adolf Hitler strict neutrality but reserved full freedom to take measures deemed necessary for maintenance of that neutrality.

Sweden is Norway's next-door neighbor, linked to her by 1,000 miles of land frontier and long collaboration in foreign policy.

Swedish Foreign Minister Per Al-

Continued on Page 2, Column 3.

Half Of Nazi Fleet Ready For Battle

Combined Navies Of Britain, France Await Meeting

PARIS, April 10—(I. N. S.).—Germany has massed 600 heavy bombing planes at Oslo and Bergen to combat the French and British navies, it was reported in Paris today. German aerial transports were reported landing additional troops at Narvik.

By KENNETH DOWNS
International News Service Staff Correspondent.

PARIS, April 10—(I. N. S.).—Nazi Germany has now exposed half of her high seas fleet to the combined navies of Great Britain and France and the latter "will live up to their great traditions," Premier Paul Reynaud told the French Senate today. He said:

"According to our information half of the German fleet which hitherto refused to come out of harbor is at present exposed to the Allied fleet.

"Let British and French sailors feel assured that we are following them in their battle with all our hearts and with full unanimity."

FIGHT TO FINISH

Expressing the Allies' firm determination to fight Germany to a finish, Reynaud characterized the Reich's Scandinavian invasion as a failure.

He declared that "not a single ton" of Swedish iron ore would henceforth reach Germany from Narvik, one of the German-occupied ports in Norway.

TELLS OF SAILORS

Reynaud described the Scandinavian invasion in considerable detail, stating again that Germany had sent sailors described as merchant seamen into Norway.

The Franco-British blockade can no justification for the invasion, he declared.

Nazi Accord With Norway Seen Due

LONDON, April 10—(A. P.).—Foreign Secretary Lord Halifax told a luncheon audience today the Allies would regard any Norwegian negotiations with Germany as "action taken under duress."

BERLIN, April 10—(A. P.).—Informed quarters this afternoon announced that a complete and "mutually satisfactory" agreement with Norway over conditions of German military occupation would be reached within a few hours.

It was also stated that Germany was instructed to determine whether the new or old Cabinet was in charge of the Norwegian Government and the sole power to designate the Prime Minister.

At the same time an official announcement said that the German Minister to Norway had sought and obtained an audience with King Haakon to clarify the situation there and determine who is the authority for governing Norway.

The German Minister was instructed to determine whether the new or old Cabinet was in charge of the Norwegian Government and the King, who, by the constitution, has the sole power to designate the Prime Minister.

Don Ameche Faces Suit For $170,000

HOLLYWOOD, April 10—(I. N. S.).—Don Ameche, film and radio star, today faced a suit for $170,000 damages, filed in Federal Court here by Paramount Studios. The studio alleged Ameche had been borrowed from Twentieth Century-Fox for the picture "The Night of January 16," but that when everything was in readiness for production, Ameche refused to appear on the Paramount lot.

War Rages On Land And Sea

In its new northern theatre, Europe's war raged with a fury that has been foreign to the "waiting war" on the western front. Along 1,000 miles of Norway's coast British and German sea and air forces battled. The ship symbols on the map indicate loss of British destroyers Hunter and Hardy in an engagement at Narvik, and of the German cruisers Bluecher and Karlsruhe in the Skagerrak. The swastikas indicate areas Germany has taken in her Scandinavian invasion and approximate air line distances showing Germany's advantages in her new bases, are indicated. On land, a battle between Norwegians and Germans raged at Elverum, a town near the Swedish border, close to Hamar, Norway's temporary capital since the fall of Oslo.

BULLETINS

STOCKHOLM, April 10—(I. N. S.).—The German steamer Curityba sent out an SOS from Oslofjord today, stating she was sinking as the result of heavy fire from Norwegian coastal batteries.

NEW YORK, April 10—(I. N. S.).—Two German warships have anchored at an unnamed Swedish port, the British National Broadcasting Company reported today. The Broadcasting Company's short-wave station, the British announcement added that British ships all over the world have been ordered not to sail from ports.

LONDON, April 10—(A. P.).—A British announcement said units of the Royal Air Force were busy all this afternoon along the Norwegian coast and "several aircraft were engaged by enemy machines."

COPENHAGEN, April 10—(I. N. S.).—Danish Premier Thorvald Stauning, speaking before a special Reichstag (Par-

Continued on Page 2, Column 6.

Temperatures

Midnight, 44	7 A. M., 43
1 A. M., 43	8 A. M., 47
2 A. M., 42	9 A. M., 50
3 A. M., 42	10 A. M., 52
4 A. M., 41	11 A. M., 55
5 A. M., 40	12 Noon, 57
6 A. M., 39	1 P. M., 58

By Associated Press.

Naval warfare off the Norwegian coast today exacted a heavy toll of ships and men from the British, German and Norwegian navies fighting for control of invaded Norway.

Acknowledged as lost were the German cruisers Bluecher and Karlsruhe and the British destroyers Hardy and Hunter.

British dispatches also said Norway's two biggest warships had been torpedoed and sunk by German vessels at Narvik with the loss of more than 500 men.

The Germans said they had scored hits on the following: Four battleships, two battle cruisers, two heavy cruisers and two transports.

Britain reported five German cruisers had been hit, at least one of them sunk.

BERLIN, April 10—(I. N. S.).—Admitting loss of two of her own crack cruisers, Germany today claimed eleven Allied warships, including the 26,500-ton French battleship Dunkerque, were damaged by Nazi air bombs in the North sea yesterday.

The German cruisers Bluecher and Karlsruhe were sunk by Norwegian mines and coastal shells, a communique by the High Command admitted. But, the statement asserted, four Allied battleships, two battle cruisers, three heavy cruisers and two armed transports were struck and badly damaged by German bombs.

LONDON, April 10—(A. P.).—Norway's two biggest warships, the Norge and Eidsvold, each 4,166 tons, were reported by Reuters news agency today to have been torpedoed and sunk by German vessels at Narvik, Norway. Only 20 of the crews of 560 men were saved, the British agency said, attributing its report to the Swedish newpaper Social Demokraten.

LONDON, April 10—(A. P.).—The British and German navies, struggling for mastery of Scandinavia, fought the biggest naval battle of the war off Norway's northwestern coast at dawn today.

Five British destroyers engaged six German destroyers off the Port of Narvik, occupied by the Germans yesterday, and before the guns were silenced Britain had lost two destroyers and suffered damage to two, and she claimed to have sunk one of the German craft and left three "heavily hit and burning."

SUPPLY SHIP BLOWN UP

LONDON, April 10—(I. N. S.).—Royal Air Force planes are making steady reconnaissance flights over virtually all of Norway and have had several encounters with German aircraft, it was announced in London tonight.

BERLIN, April 10—(A. P.).—German air squadrons are engaging in battles with the British Navy "at several points" in the northern part of the North sea, DNB, the official German news agency, reported today.

The agency said German scouting

Continued on Page 2, Column 4.

Nazi Airmen Fight British Naval Forces

LONDON, April 10—(I. N. S.).—Prime Minister Chamberlain presented a story of the battle to cheering House of Commons. He presented it as a British victory, stating six merchant ships believed to be carrying supplies for the Germans were sunk and that the German ammunition ship Ravensfeldt was blown up.

The German force, which Chamberlain said was composed of six of the "latest and largest type," was

Continued on Page 2, Column 7.

VERY LATEST NEWS

BRITISH MARINES LANDED IN NORWAY, REPORT

LONDON, April 10—(A. P.).—A usually reliable neutral source said it had been learned that a British naval flotilla returned to Narvik after the unsuccessful dawn raid today, forced an entrance to the Fjord and began landing marines. There was no British or other confirmation of this report.

U. S. COURT RULES AGAINST NLRB

RICHMOND, Va., April 10—(A. P.).—The United States Fourth Circuit Court of Appeals today ruled against the practice of of the National Labor Relations Board in requiring the posting of "clean and desist" promises.

★ MONTGOMERY WARD ★ RETAIL STORE ★ MONTGOMERY WARD ★ RETAIL STORE ★ MONTGOMERY WARD ★ RETAIL STORE

The PERFECT Washing Machine COVER

YOURS ... without extra cost with the purchase of any Ward Electric Washer priced at $41.95 or more!

The perfect washing machine cover sells everywhere at $2.19! It fits any Ward Electric Washer, and is made of 8-oz. stone-colored covert cloth. It's washable, and goes on and off in a jiffy...

Protects Washers from Dust and Dirt!

You won't see any better washers anywhere ... at any price! Choose the one that suits your needs ... the one that fits your pocketbook!

Each model is a streamlined beauty! Nothing has been spared in up-to-the-minute styling, mechanical perfection, in usable features!

And when you purchase any of these washers at $41.95 or more you get the Perfect Washer Cover at no extra cost. This offer is for a limited time only—get yours tomorrow!

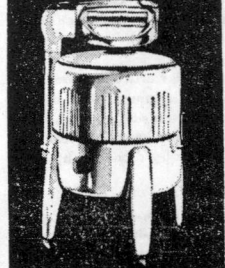

DE LUXE 23 GALLON
$4 Monthly **41.95**

Outstanding in its price class! Lovell wringer with Pressure Selector! All white! With pump $5 more!
No. R-08500—Tel. Gil. 8100 Ext. 87

SPECIAL 20 GALLON
$4 Monthly **29.95**

Economy model! A great value! Worth about $45 elsewhere! Finished in green!
No. R-08501—Tel. Gil. 8100 Ext. 87

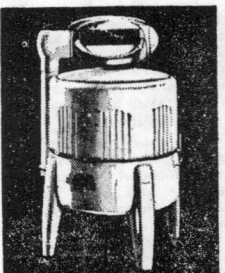 

DE LUXE 24 GALLON
$4 Monthly **48.95**

Compare with $80 values! Big, beautifully styled! All white! Features of higher-priced models! With pump $5 more!
No. R-08502—Tel. Gil. 8100

STANDARD 20 GAL.
$4 Monthly **36.95**

A $60 value! Fast! Efficient! All white! Lovell wringer. Adjustable wringing pressure! With pump $5 more!
No. R-08503—Tel. Gil. 8100

WARDS WONDER VALUES!

7 TUBE CONSOLE SENSATION!
Record Smashing Value!

TRADE IN YOUR OLD RADIO ON ANY CONSOLE MODEL AND GET EUROPE DIRECT!

31.95 $5 MONTHLY, Down Payment, Carrying Charge

• Built-in loop aerial! Television and phono plug-in!
• Has tone control ... automatic tuning ... tuning eye!

Now ... save more than ever! This big 7-tube is comparable to other makes at $59.95! And Wards liberal trade-in at this low price actually assures you a DOUBLE SAVING! You get improved superheterodyne circuit ... full-vision edge-lighted dial ... giant 12-inch Projectotone! See this radio TODAY at its special reduced price!
No. R-06200—Telephone Gilmor 8100

7-TUBE SUPER-HET MANTEL HAS ACTUAL $30 FEATURES

19.95 $4 MONTHLY, Down Payment, Carrying Charge

• Gets Europe! Has Television and phono plug!
• Built-in loop aerial! Personal tone control!
• Big super-dynamic speaker! Automatic tuning!

Now ... at this low price ... you get a mantel set with the features of the console above! See it! Tune it! Hear it! Compare anywhere!
No. R-06201—Telephone Gilmor 8100

PLAYS ANYWHERE!

17.95 $4 MONTHLY, Down Payment, Carrying Charge

• 6-tube super-het complete with batteries!
• Alloy dynamic speaker! Built-in loop aerial!
• Approved by Underwriters! Air-luggage case!

Here's the portable for you! Take it anywhere!
No. R-06202—Telephone Gilmor 8100

FINEST 4-TUBE PORTABLE WITH BUILT-IN LOOP!

13.95 $2 MONTHLY, Down Payment, Carrying Charge

• Complete with 200-hour batteries
• Has 5-inch alloy dynamic speaker

Carry your radio wherever you go! See this amazing value superheterodyne ... and compare Wards price and performance with any other make! See it TODAY!
No. R-06203—Telephone Gilmor 8100

SALE! RADIO "B" BATTERIES 98c

Wards 45-volt Hy-Watt Factory construction ... sealed ... dated and guaranteed! Plug-in type!
No. R-06205

4-Tube SUPERHETERODYNE BEST OF ALL THE MIDGETS!

6.45

• Approved by Fire Underwriters!
• Walnut plastic! Built-in aerial!
• 4-inch super-dynamic speaker!

Unsurpassed in its price class ... in power, selectivity and downright value! Plug it in anywhere and play!
Ivory Finish, $1 more!
No. R-06204—Telephone Gilmor 8100

Wards New Gas Rangette

26.95 $3 DOWN, $4 Monthly (Plus Carrying Charge)

Compact ... ideal size for small kitchens! Modern cabinet in gleaming, easy-to-clean porcelain. 3 fast round burners. Porcelained fast-heating oven.

★ Fully Insulated Oven
★ Roomy Storage Compartment
★ Approved by the A. G. A.
No. R-06800—Telephone Gilmor 8100

Streamlined Portable Oil

6.25

2 range-size wickless burners! Adjusto-Flame valves! 2½-qt. fuel tank! Cast-iron grates! Silicon steel inner chimneys!
3-Burner Size **7.90**
No. R-06801—Tel. Gil. 8100

Two-Burner Portable Oil

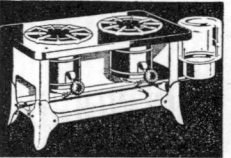

3.55

Two powerful range-size wickless burners. Extra roomy cooktop, cast-iron grates. 14 inches high.
3-Burner Size **4.55**
No. R-06802—Tel. Gil. 8100

Double Picket Lawn Fence

Combining beauty with strength! All wire hot-dip galvanized copper-steel resists strain and lasts longer! Strong and rigid! 36 inches high!

Double Picket Heavy Weight **12c** Running Foot
Single Picket Heavy Weight **8½c** Running Foot
No. R-08700—Telephone Gilmor 8100

2-Year-Old .. Field-Grown ROSE BUSHES

8 in Bundle!

Regular $1.59 Value! **97c** BUNDLE

Choose from this extensive variety: Paul's Scarlet (red), Etoile de Hollande (red), Golden Ophelia (yellow), Editor McFarland (pink), R. A. Victor (white), Margaret McGredy (red-yellow), Red Radiance, President Hoover (2-tone pink). Quantities limited—hurry!
No. R-08700—Tel. Gil. 8100

Bundle of 5 Shrubs 69c

GRASS SEED

Standard Quality	Select Quality
5 pounds **1.15**	5 pounds **1.58**
25c pound	35c pound
No. R-08701—Tel. Gil. 8100	No. R-08702—Tel. Gil. 8100

MONTHLY PAYMENT PLAN may be used on any purchases totaling $10 or more! Buy NOW...pay LATER!

MONTGOMERY WARD

CATALOG ORDER SERVICE saves you money on thousands of items we haven't room to stock in our store!

RETAIL STORE ● SOUTH MONROE ST. at WASHINGTON BLVD. ● HOURS: Daily 9 A.M. to 5 P.M.----Saturdays 9 A.M. to 5.30 P.M. ● Telephone Gilmor 8100

Last At Pimlico Goes To Charles F.

THE WEATHER
Clear to partly cloudy and continued cool tonight, Saturday, clear and continued cool, followed by light rains.

MEAN TEMPERATURES YESTERDAY.
Baltimore.... 60 New York.... 59
Atlanta...... 76 Omaha....... 61
Boston....... 53 Portland, Maine. 48
Jacksonville. 77 Salt Lake City. 62
Chicago...... 54 San Antonio.. 69
Los Angeles.. 80 Seattle...... 66
Miami........ 77 Tampa........ 76
New Orleans.. 74 Washington... 60

THE BALTIMORE NEWS-POST
AN INDEPENDENT NEWSPAPER

The Largest Daily Circulation in the Entire South

VOL. CXXXVII.—NO. 5 — Entered as second-class matter at Baltimore Postoffice. Copyright, 1940, by Hearst-Consolidated Publications, Inc. — FRIDAY EVENING, MAY 10, 1940 — PRICE 3 CENTS

Chamberlain Succeeded By Churchill

ALLIED FORCES BATTLE NAZIS

Warn Britain Of Nazi 'Chute Troops

PARIS, May 10—(A. P.).—French military authorities reported tonight that Allied and German advance guards had entered into contact along the French-Luxembourg frontier. The Germans, preceded by motorcycle troops and motorized infantry, pushed into Luxembourg without interference, a military commentator told a press conference. At the same time, the Allied war machine was rumbling north and east, the spokesman declared. He said contact was established.

WITH THE BRITISH EXPEDITIONARY FORCE IN BELGIUM, May 10—(A. P.).—British troops crossed the Belgium frontier today and are pressing forward to a new battle front. The columns have been moving smoothly and steadily toward the east. French troops also are marching into Belgium. Crowds of civilians pelted the singing soldiers with flowers and ran beside troop-filled lorries offering bottles of beer.

LONDON, May 10—(A. P.).—The Government tonight warned every Briton to be on the lookout for German troops landing by parachute in Britain.

AMSTERDAM, May 10—(A. P.).—The Commander-in-Chief of The Netherlands armed forces tonight declared Germany's surprise attack on Holland a failure.

Belgians Halt Germans, King Leopold Assumes Full Command Of Army

BERLIN, May 10—(A. P.).—The German High Command announced tonight that German troops had broken border resistance on the Belgian-Netherlands-Luxembourg front.

BRUSSELS, May 10—(A. P.).—The German land forces have been stopped within a few hundred yards of the frontier after entering Belgium as part of Adolf Hitler's "Blitzkrieg" against the low countries, the Foreign Ministry announced today.

Defense Minister General Henri Denis told the Chamber of Deputies that, at noon, the Germans were halted everywhere on the Belgian defensive lines. He said he was "con-

Continued on Page B, Column 2.

VERY LATEST NEWS
(Race Results From Howard Sports Daily, Inc.)

CHARLES F. WINS EIGHTH RACE AT PIMLICO
Eighth—Charles F., $29.60, $10.90, $7.10; Burner, $5.00, $3.60; Flying Centaur, $5.80.

AT CHURCHILL DOWNS
Fifth—Epidor, $3.60, $3.00, $2.80; Little Tramp, $7.40, $4.20; Ballinderry, $3.60.
Sixth—Jennie May, won; Love Quest, 2; White Feathers, 3

ARMY PLANE CRASHES IN IDAHO
MOSCOW, Idaho, May 10—(A. P.).—A low-wing Army airplane, believed to be a pursuit bomber, crashed in the Moscow business district and burst into flames today.

UNION INDICTED UNDER ANTI-TRUST LAW
NEW YORK, May 10—(A.P.).—A Federal grand jury today indicted Local 46 of the Wood, Wire and Metal Lathers' International Union and several of its officers and business agents for violation of the anti-trust laws.

HOURLY TEMPERATURES
2 A. M., 54   6 A. M., 52   10 A. M., 65   2 P. M., 67
3 A. M., 53   7 A. M., 56   11 A. M., 66   3 P. M., 68
4 A. M., 52   8 A. M., 59   12 Noon, 67   4 P. M., 6?
5 A. M., 52   9 A. M., 62   1 P. M., 68   5 P. M., 67

Allies Order 2,000 More U. S. Planes

WASHINGTON, May 10—(A.P.).—Aviation authorities said today that the British and French Governments have ordered 2,000 or more additional American-made warplanes in the last few days.

The new contracts, for the latest type fighting planes and bombers developed for the United States Army Air Corps, were said to have boosted the Allies' purchases with in the last month to 4,000 or more military aircraft.

At the same time it was disclosed that the War Department intends to recommend to President Roosevelt that Congress be asked for funds immediately to build 200 long-range, four-motor bombers to reinforce Western Hemisphere defenses.

The additional bombers would be a part of the 6,000-plane quota which Congress authorized for the Air Corps last year. Fifty-two of the big bombers, which cost about $400,000 each, are in service and 200 others are on order.

The Baltimore News-Post today is printed in
3 Sections
Be sure you get the complete newspaper.

BERLIN, May 10—(A. P., by Radio).—An official announcement tonight said almost 100 "enemy" airplanes either had been shot down in aerial battles or destroyed on the ground. Seven German airplanes were reported missing, in addition to two known to have made forced landings, it said.

ROTTERDAM, The Netherlands, May 10—(A. P.).—Germany's plane and parachute troops, attempting to fight their way through Rotterdam, were driven back into a dangerous position late today by the attacks of reinforced Dutch troops and the pounding of Dutch artillery.

Strong detachments of Netherlands marines made repeated rushes into the enemy positions on the River Nieuwe Maas and the fighting was fierce.

Dutch incendiary shells set fire to the large Maas Hotel from which the Germans were operating on the left bank of the stream, which divides Rotterdam.

The fire spread rapidly, threatening the thin German lines.

One German transport plane, alighting on the river, was damaged badly when it hit a boat.

A communique by General Henri Gerard Winkelman, commander-in-chief of the Netherlands armed forces, said:

"Netherlands border troops offered bitter resistance to the Germans on the Ijssel and Maas Rivers.

"Notwithstanding strong German attacks, our troops maintain themselves in Delfzijl.

"Four German armored trains

have been disposed of; one was blown to pieces on the railroad bridge near Venlo.

"At least 70 German planes have been shot down on air fields or when they tried to make landings in the interior of the country.

"German troops landed by parachute in the interior tried to maintain themselves, but they

Continued on Page 3, Column 4.

No Change As Regards U.S. —Roosevelt

WASHINGTON, May 10—(A.P.).—John Cudahy, American Ambassador at Brussels, informed the State Department just before noon today that German forces had overrun the whole of Luxembourg and all of Limberg, a province of Holland.

WASHINGTON, May 10—(A.P.).—President Roosevelt said today he saw no change with respect to the possibilities of the United States keeping out of Europe's war.

At a press conference he told reporters who crowded his office that the walls that there was not much he could say about the situation

Continued on Page 2, Column 6.

LONDON, May 10—(A. P.).—Winston Churchill, belligerent First Lord of the Admiralty and longtime target of Adolf Hitler's wrath, tonight became Britain's man of destiny, succeeding Neville Chamberlain as Prime Minister as war surged over Western Europe.

The Government announced:

"The Right Honorable Neville Chamberlain resigned the office of Prime Minister and First Lord of the Treasury this evening and the Right Honorable Winston Churchill accepted His Majesty's invitation to fill the position.

"The Prime Minister desires that all ministers should remain at their posts and discharge their functions with full freedom and responsibility while the necessary arrangements for the formation of a new administration are made."

Chamberlain, the apostle of appeasement who saw his policy fail and when war came expressed the hope he could

Continued on Page 3, Column 1.

How the Horses Finished At Pimlico

Daily Double (Sun Ginger / Tiny Trick) Paid $28.90

Copyright, 1940, by Cecilia Co. (Daily Racing Form)
TRACK FAST.
FIRST RACE—FOUR AND ONE-HALF FURLONGS. FOR TWO-YEAR-OLDS. Purse $1,000. Value to winner $700, second $150, third $100, fourth $50. Went to post at 7.22. Off at 2:25½. Start good from gate. Won driving, place same. Winner, F. DWYER. Time .23 3-5, .48 1-5, .54 3-5. Owned by MILLSDALE STABLE. Trained by P.

Sun Ginger 117 4   3   1½   1½   1n   R. Neves $1.50
aHy Happy   113 12 4   4   3   2½   J. Wagner   9.75

Long Lane   113 3 2   4   3½   3n   M. Berg   5.10
Bright Arc   106 2 1   3½   5   4½   N. Wall   9.55
Meadow Dew   110 1 5   2½   4   5   L. Dupps   20.55
bKantar Run 112 8 10   6½   6½   6   G. Smith   13.55
Masthead   110 5 8   7   7   7   H. Mora   17.05
Duces Wild   106 7 9   10   8   8   H. Dabson   36.25
Rough Wild   113½ 9 12   12   11   9½   F. A. Smith   9.75
aCathode   107 11 11   11   9   10½   H. Lemmons   32.45
bKsi Patrol 109 10 6   8½   10   11   K. Wholey   32.45
Miss Identify 6
aBreckinridge Long and H. G. Bedwell entry. bHirsch and Augustus entry.

$2 Mutuels Paid—Sun Ginger, $5.00 straight, $3.70 place, $2.70 show. Hy Happy, $7.40 place, $4.50 show. Long Lane, $3.60 show. Total mutuels... $26.90
Sun Ginger was rated along, responded when roused in the stretch and held her

Continued on Page 31, Column 5.

THE BALTIMORE NEWS-POST, FRIDAY, MAY 10, 1940

ALL THE MOST ADVANCED SUMMER HAT FASHIONS AT

A New Low Price 79¢

Why pay a fortune for a perishable Summer hat? See Wards marvelous new low-priced styles! Big brims! Bretons! Sailors! Rayon crepe turbans! Pastels, white, wheat and natural in simulated rough straws and felt! Headsizes for everyone!
No. R-01200—Tel. Gil. 8100

Montgomery Ward
RETAIL STORE
S. Monroe St. at Washington Blvd.

Save Up to 50% More in Wards BARGAIN ANNEX

Children's Footwear

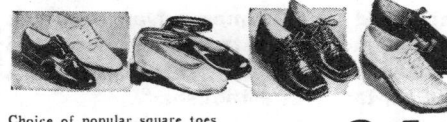

Choice of popular square toes dainty oxfords, Mary Janes and Dutchies! Leather uppers, insoles and soles and rubber heels—some have rubber soles. Every pair a real bargain!
Values to $1.19! 64¢
No. R-03800—Telephone Gilmor 8100

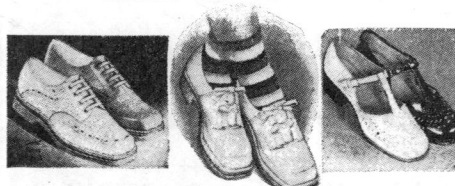

Your choice of these three popular models. Smooth leather uppers, grain leather insoles. Goodyear stitchdowns, and crepe rubber or composition rubber soles and heels.
Values to $1.35! 94¢
No. R-03801—Telephone Gilmor 8100

A Large Selection of Women's and Men's **Wrist Watches** Values To $12.95! **5.97** Popular makes — guaranteed time pieces! Others 7.27 to 19.97 values to 29.95! No. R-03802—Tel. Gil. 8100	Reg. 9.95 Split Cowhide **Wardrobe Suitcases 4.97** Black or Brown Reg. 14.95 Full Grain **Wardrobe Suitcases 6.97** Black or Brown No. R-03803—Tel. Gil. 8100

Men's Reg. $5.95 Summer Suits 3.47
Coat and trousers; sanforized single and double breasted models in grayish blue and grayish green. Sizes 34 to 42. (No alterations.)
No. R-03804—Telephone Gilmor 8100

Men's Reg. $1.69 Summer Slacks 1.17
Pleated fronts, tapered bottoms, stripes and solid colors. Sizes 28 to 42.
No. R-03805—Telephone Gilmor 8100

Percale House Dresses 57¢
In an extensive selection of new patterns.
Values to $1!
No. R-03806—Telephone Gilmor 8100

NO PHONE or MAIL ORDERS!

MONTGOMERY WARD'S BARGAIN ANNEX
RETAIL STORE ★ S. Monroe St. at Washington Blvd.

WARDS SALE FOR INFANTS AND TOTS

Infants' Dresses 29¢
Hand embroidery on fine American cotton! Buy 2 for every baby you know and save extra! 6 mo.-1 yr.
No. R-03100. Tel. Gilmor 8100.

Tots' Crepe Sleepers 69¢
Two jiffy-change button-on pants for youngsters. 1-3. Cotton crinkle. No ironing. Pink or blue. 3 pieces!
No. R-03101—Tel. Gil. 8100

Infants' 49c Creepers 39¢
Hand made and hand embroidered! Tubfast broadcloth with tiny belts or pockets. Pastels. 6 mos. to 2 years.
No. R-03102—Tel. Gil. 8100

27" Birdseye Diapers 44¢
Soft and comfy—and hemmed, ready for use! Extra absorbent! Cellophane wrapped! (Pkg. of 6)
No. R-03103—Tel. Gil. 8100

SALE! Tots' Gowns, Wrappers, Gertrudes 5 for $1
Regularly 25c each! Fine cotton flannels. Individually cellophane wrapped! A Ward buy!
No. R-03105
Infants' Rayon Silk Training Pants Values at 10¢ pr.

Look at These Values, too!
Training Pants! Double Crotch 9c
Infants' Fine White High Shoes. 1 to 4.47c
Fluffy Tubfast Crib Blankets, 36x50 ...49c
Fancy Rayon Plaited Anklets, 4 to 6 ...8c
25c Handmade Batiste Gertrudes to 1 yr. 21c
No. R-03104—Tel. Gil. 8100
For youngsters just out of diapers. Elastic waist. 1 to 3.

Wards Regular $24.95 Hand-Tailored Suits

★ Finer Fabrics!
★ Smart Tailoring!
★ Newest Styles!

19.96 Pay Monthly!

Today and Saturday Only!

Slip into one of these fine suits! Watch the way the jacket drapes, the way it broadens your shoulders, and nips in your waist. Notice how roomy and comfortable the trousers are. See how smart and new every pattern is. And save $4.99!
No. R-03900—Tel. Gil. 8100.

SUMMER HATS
WERE NEVER SMARTER!
WARDS PRICES WERE NEVER LOWER!

1.59 Worth of Smart Style! You Pay Only 98¢

They're lighter! They're smarter! They've blossomed out in a dozen new shapes. Sporty styles, bright bands. Straw sailors. "Panama" shapes.
No. R-03500—Tel. Gil. 8100.

Wards Save You 23% on these 1.95 Values! 1.49

"20 degrees cooler inside!" The manufacturer's magic makes these hats champions in the featherweight class! New weaves, new shapes, new bands!
No. R-03501—Tel. Gil. 8100.

Montgomery Ward
RETAIL STORE
South Monroe St. at Washington Blvd.

MORE SPEED AND POWER PER DOLLAR WITH MONTGOMERY WARDS 1940 Sea King OUTBOARD MOTORS

Best Buy in America! Sea King Special SINGLE
2.8 horsepower
37.88
No other motor in America has as much speed, for as much horsepower per dollar as this Sea King Special Single. It's a completely new and streamlined motor. Weedless aluminum propeller; automatic self-pilot; extra quiet underwater exhaust! See it today!
No. R-06000—Tel. Gil. 8100

Weighs Only 15 lbs.! Sea King MIDGET SINGLE
Wards low price
28.95
Twice as powerful as nationally advertised motors at the same price! 1 N.O.A. Certified H.P. at 3750 R.P.M.! Easier to carry than a pair of oars, and drives average boat faster than a man can row! See this little giant!
1.8 H.P. Sea King Streamlined Single 47.95
No. R-06001—Tel. Gil. 8100

New Sea King De Luxe LIGHT TWIN
74.95
The last word in outboards! 3 N.O.A. Certified H.P. at 3500 R.P.M.! Has beautiful new streamlined hood; easy-pull starter; rubber clutch to protect gears and propeller; all the latest features!
Sea King Standard Large Twin, 5 N.O.A. certified horsepower 79.95
No. R-06002—Tel. Gil. 8100

MONTHLY PAYMENT PLAN
Enjoy your boat and outboard motor while you're paying monthly for them. A small down payment, convenient monthly payments, plus a reasonable carrying charge.

Sea King Runabout
Pay Only $7 a Month Down Payment and Carrying Charges
89.95 Delivered
Compare with $110 to $140 boats! Handles any outboard. Dry at high speeds. 14-ft. length. With 54-Semi-"V" bottom.
14-ft. Hooper Is. Skiff, 49.95 (Delivered)
No. R-06003—Telephone Gilmor 8100

Sea King Steel Boat
Pay Only $5 a Month Down Payment and Carrying Charge
25.95
Made of rust-resisting copper-bearing steel; Double air chambers — absolutely can not sink! 10-Ft. Length Delivered
12-ft. 29.45
14-ft. 33.95
16-ft. 38.95
No. R-06004—Tel. Gil. 8100

SALE FOR Fishermen!

89c Oil Silk Flyline............39c	Snelled Wet Trout Flies.........6c
55c OTISCO Vacuol Silk Fly Line.............35c	Eyed Dry Trout Flies............9c Bass Ketcher Plugs............17c
$4 Automatic Fly Reel........2.69	Gudgeon, Perch or Pike Lines............15c to 69c
$7 Thorobred Fly Rod..........3.49	3-Pc. Bamboo Gudgeon Poles ft. 15c
$2 English-type Fly Reel......1.29	3-Pc. Bamboo Poles......12 ft. 39c
$2.25 Level Wind Casting Reel 1.39	Tom Loving's New Trout
$4 Steel Casting Rod..........2.59	and Bass Flies......19c to 65c
$4 Special Bay or Boat Rod...2.79	75c Bill DeWitt Pocket Fly Box............45c
$6.50 Star Drag S. W. Reel....4.29	Sample Tube FIENOLUBE
Trout Hooks tied on Nylon, pkg.23c	FREE with Every Reel!
No. R-06005—Telephone Gilmor 8100

Completely Equipped 1940 HAWTHORNE for Girls'—Boys'
★ Electric Headlight
★ White Sidewall Balloon Tires!
★ Luggage Carrier!
★ New Departure Coaster Brake!
★ Chain Guard!

22.95 $3 DOWN $4 Monthly (Small Carrying Charge)

Full size, strong double-bar model, chrome-plated truss rods. Choice of 10 different color combinations!

FREE WITH THIS BIKE
With the purchase of this bike for girl or boy you get a DeLuxe Rear Vision Mirror!
Other Full-Size Hawthorne Double-Bar Bikes Reg. **18.88**
No. R-06006—Telephone Gilmor 8100

WARDS Sale FOR LAWN and GARDEN

Rubber Tire Mower
Compare With $9 Mowers
4.89
Ball-bearing construction and 4 self-sharpening blades. Finished aluminum color, with blue trim. 10-inch rubber-tired wheels. 14-inch cut.
No. R-08400—Tel. Gil. 8100

5-BLADE MOWER
$12 quality, 16-inch cut. Semi-pneumatic tires. Ball bearings at 4 points, for extra smoothness.
8.95 10-inch Reg. 8.95
No. R-08401—Tel. Gil. 8100

2-Yr. Guarantee Hose
25-foot Non-kinking
94¢
A layer of strong braided cotton, vulcanized between two heavy layers of rubber, means added strength ... longer wear. Bends easily without cracking. Tested to 350 pounds pressure per square inch. Black rubber.
No. R-08402—Tel. Gil. 8100

Guaranteed 4 Yrs.
3.40
Stronger construction. Has layer of double-braided cord. Tested to 400 lbs. pressure 50 foot. Red rubber.
No. R-08403—Tel. Gil. 8100

Lawn and Garden Accessories
Reg. 25c Grass Shear...19c
49c blade frame tool steel.
Reg. 45c Grass Hook...38c
Curved blade, polished tool steel.
Reg. 55c Grass Scythe...47c
Five smooth 12 to 16 in. sizes.
75c Hose Nozzle......45c
Cast Brass. Adjustable spray.
Reg. 79c Sprinkler......66c
Spray range 15 to 60 ft. circle.
No. R-08404—Tel. Gil. 8100

Service Your Car and Save More at ★ Wards Service Station! ★

Complete Oil Change

DRAIN SERVICE—Now ... at Wards ... you can cut your oil bill from ⅓ to ¼! Simply drive in and let Wards change your oil and fill with Supremely Quality 100% Pure Pennsylvania Motor Oil, refined from the finest Bradford Alleghany crude! No charge for crankcase service.
90¢ 5 Qts.

.. with Gulflube
MOTOR OIL ... 1.25 5 Qts. Tax Inc.

.. with Gulfpride
MOTOR OIL ... 1.75 5 Qts. Tax Inc.

Complete Lubrication Service
Using Gulf Lubricants, including spraying springs.
75¢
Brake Re-Lining 7.95
Brake Adjusting 75c
Car Washing 75c

TRACTOR DEMONSTRATION
Field on Washington Blvd.—Rear Ward Building
TOMORROW — 10 A.M. to 4 P.M.

See Wards complete selection of Garden Tractors for every purpose and every farm need. Fill your needs and use Wards convenient Monthly Payment Plan! See this interesting demonstration tomorrow!

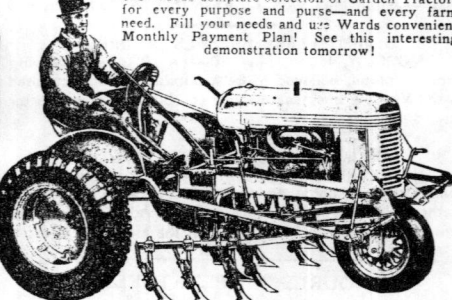

MONTGOMERY WARD ★ RETAIL STORE
South Monroe St. at Washington Blvd.

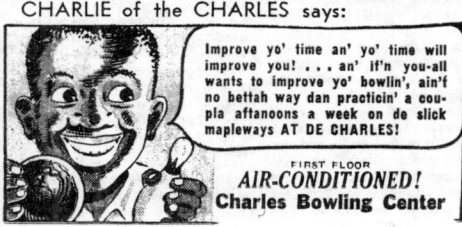

ITALY TAKES FRENCH SOIL

Declaration Of War Made Before Throngs

By PERCY WINNER
International News Service Staff Correspondent.

ROME, June 10.—Italy has declared war on Great Britain and France, Premier Benito Mussolini announced today. The electrifying announcement that Italy has thrown her "eight million bayonets" against the armies of England and France was made by Il Duce from the balcony of the Palazzo Venezia while thousands, gathered in the square below, cheered him to the echo.

Mussolini cried:

"Combatants on land, sea and in the air! Blackshirts of the Revolution and of the Legion! Men and women of Italy, of the Empire and of the Kingdom of Albania!

"Listen:

"The hour of destiny is ticking in the skies of our country.

"A declaration of war has been handed to the Ambassadors of Great Britain and France."

(In Washington, the White House announced that U. S. Ambassador to France, William C. Bullitt, had informed President Roosevelt at 11.53 (E. S. T.) that Italy had declared war on France and Great Britain.)

"The decision is irrevocable.

"We shall descend into the battlefield against the plutocracies and the reactionary democracies of the west which, for all time, have obstructed the march of the Italian people.

"Promises, menaces and threats have been made to us or against us.

"Our conscience is absolutely tranquil.

"STANDS AS TESTAMENT"

"The whole world stands as a testament that Italy has done whatever was humanly possible to avoid the storm that is overhanging Europe.

"The Allies should not have re-
Continued on Page 2, Column 7.

THE BALTIMORE NEWS-POST

AN INDEPENDENT NEWSPAPER

The Largest Daily Circulation in the Entire South

Entered as second-class matter at Baltimore Postoffice. Copyright, 1940, by Hearst Consolidated Publications, Inc.

7 HOME FINAL

VOL. CXXXVII.—NO. 31   MONDAY EVENING, JUNE 10, 1940   PRICE **3** CENTS

IN THE NEWS

THE Hearst papers have earnestly advocated for this country the Swiss system of universal compulsory military training as a democratic system which in no way endangers the institutions of a democratic nation.

The Swiss system supports no standing army of professional soldiers whatever.

According to the authorized description "the defense of the republic rests with its citizens."

Yet with this unburdensome and comparatively inexpensive system the Swiss nation of approximately 4,000,000 total population is enabled to put in the field as initial mobilization 260,000 fully armed and equipped forces.

While behind this fully effective force is the landsturm reserve of another 260,000 men—all of which latter are competently trained as soldiers and about half of whom are armed.

The armament of the Swiss citizen soldiery is perfectly modern and perfectly suited to their terrain.

Modifications might naturally have to be made to suit our vast territories.

But when it is said that the Swiss soldiers are thoroughly trained, that means that they have been trained in military knowledge and discipline from the time that they are fourteen years of age and that they have been active in the citizen army from the time that they are twenty years of age.

This training, while entirely effective, is not as engrossing or expensive as it would seem.

THE military training of youth is part of the school and college curriculum.

When the students reach the age of twenty, they are graduated as scholars and graduated as soldiers too.

Henceforward the actual military maneuvers occupy but three months of the FIRST year, and only fourteen days each year thereafter.

The citizens merely keep in trim and in training, a good thing for any men to do, be they civilians or soldiers.

If the United States should follow the universal military service system of Switzerland, we would be able to put 5,000,000 men into our initial mobilization first line, all fully and effectively armed.

And we would be able to support that first line with another 5,000,000 of reserves, all fully trained as soldiers. That is an army which no nation on the face of the earth would dare attack—a democracy which no dictator, no matter how dangerous, would either disparage or defy.

The question before the country, therefore, is merely whether we, the citizenry, want to subscribe the SERVICE to create and CONSTITUTE this impregnable defense.

There is no question about the cost. If the system were very costly in proportion to population and resources, comparatively impoverished Switzerland could not afford it.

AS far as our country is concerned, our political remnants and ravelings which we call Government waste more money on indiscriminate squander mania than we could possibly expend honestly on legitimate national protection.

If we cannot count on honest and intelligent expenditure, then we had better change our Government. If we can count on honesty and intelligence, then we have money now in plenty for democratic defense without extravagant taxation.

The cost of military training in the schools is comparatively trifling. Thus the youth of the country would become trained soldiers at graduate age, without any material addition to the school budget.

Switzerland actually pays its citizen army only while in the field, the which, after the first years of training, is but fourteen days a year.

But it takes care of any families which might be in genuine need during the absence of the family head.

In our liberal country, employers would doubtless continue salary for those two weeks, and consider the fourteen days spent in Army maneuvers a part of service not only to the State, but to the private institutions which

Continued on Page 4, Column 1.

Italian Legions March Into French Territory Through The Riviera

BERLIN, June 10—(A. P.)—Italian forces marched into French territory through the Riviera at approximately 6.30 P. M. tonight (11.30 A. M., E. S. T.). This information was given reporters by authorized sources at a conference at the Berlin Foreign Office called by Foreign Minister Joachim von Ribbentrop.

Information concerning Italian invasion of France was given out before a statement by Von Ribbentrop.

The Foreign Minister declared all Germany was "filled with jubilant enthusiasm" over Italy's intervention and said Nazi and Fascist forces would fight shoulder-to-shoulder until "the rulers of England and France are ready to respect the vital rights of both our nations."

Place Paris In State Of Defense

LONDON, June 10—(A. P.)—Reuters, British news agency, reported tonight that Paris had been placed in a state of defense.

PARIS, June 10.—(A. P.)—Trading was suspended on world-famous Paris Bourse today, and there

Continued on Page 2, Column 1.

Nazis Claim Allies In Retreat

By PIERRE J. HUSS
International News Service Staff Correspondent.

BERLIN, June 10.—After five days of the big German push, the possibility that Nazi troops have succeeded in precipitating another French retreat was made evident by German quarters today.

Despite official German reserve, there seems to be every indication that the German advance has piled up a tremendous mileage and that tanks and air force again hammered

Continued on Page 2, Column 4.

THE WEATHER

Cloudy, with occasional light showers tonight. Lowest temperature around 68 degrees. Tuesday partly cloudy and warmer, followed by local showers and thunderstorms in the afternoon. Moderate east and southeast winds.

"New England Kitchen Memories." Interesting and instructive article for every one interested in cooking. Unusual feature distributed with next Sunday's Baltimore American.—*Adv.*

MEAN TEMPERATURES YESTERDAY.

Baltimore	78	Chicago	74
Atlanta	76	Omaha	74
Boston	64	Los Angeles	66
Jacksonville	82	Salt Lake City	59
New York	72	San Antonio	74
Miami	81	Seattle	63
Portland, Maine	56	Tampa	78
Washington	78	New Orleans	80

Mexican Leader Sees Reich Revolt

JUAREZ, Chihuahua, Mexico, June 10—(A. P.)—Gen. Juan Andreu Almazan, denouncing the Hitler regime, today predicted that the German people would tire of "oppression" and would overthrow the Nazis.

Almazan called for a united front by Mexico and the United States against both Nazi and Communist elements.

Buying Sets In After Stock Sag

NEW YORK, June 10—(A. P.)—Italy's declaration of war on the Allies brought a momentary selloff in the Stock Exchange today, quickly followed by a short-lived buying wave in steels.

The market was erratic, however, with many leaders off $1 to $3 or more a share near the start of the last hour of trading.

Commodities strengthened, with wheat up 2 to 3 cents a bushel, and rubber and hides bounding upward in futures dealings. Cotton, however, was sluggish.

Temperatures

Midnight	74	7 A. M.	73
1 A. M.	73	8 A. M.	72
2 A. M.	72	9 A. M.	70
3 A. M.	72	10 A. M.	68
4 A. M.	71	11 A. M.	66
5 A. M.	71	12 Noon	66
6 A. M.	72	1 P. M.	66

VERY LATEST NEWS
(Race Results From Howard Sports Daily, Inc.)

AT SUFFOLK DOWNS

First — Special Racket, $14.60, $7.60, $4.60; Filandro, $4.80, $3.40; Whooper, $6.00.

AT AQUEDUCT

First—Hoof Heart, $9.20, $5.80, $4.30; Maevic, $16.30, $9.00; Cavu, $5.90.

WOMAN, 48, PLUNGES 2 STORIES TO DEATH

WASHINGTON, June 10—(A. P.) — Mrs. Esther Schwartzman, forty-eight, Brooklyn, N. Y., plunged to her death today from the second story of the home of a sister, with whom she had been staying. The coroner said he would issue a certificate of suicide.

THE BALTIMORE NEWS-POST, MONDAY, JUNE 10, 1940 3

Wiegand Says Hitler Moves To Hit Dover

Biggest Long-Range Guns Set At Calais

By KARL H. VON WIEGAND

Chief Foreign Correspondent for the Hearst Sunday Newspapers and for 28 Years Outstanding American Political Observer in Europe and the Far East.

BERLIN, June 10.—Adolf Hitler says the war must and will end this year — with a German victory.

This is a promise to the German people and a prophecy to the world.

To make good on both and to clear the way to Hitler's "revolutionary concept of at least a hundred years European peace," the Austro-German Napoleon has ordered a terrific drive of Germany's famous "Panzer" divisions, armored and mechanized forces, masses of infantry and motorized artillery, supported by bombardment air squadrons — to break through General Maxime Weygand's lines and take Paris.

ENGLAND AS TARGET

Soon the Germans may begin what may indeed be the greatest and most terrific air attacks in history, to hammer England into a frame of mind to sue for peace.

German preparations to follow the British to England by air and sea are approaching their peak.

The British withdrawal from Norway was a miniature "Gallipoli." The "Gallipoli" of Dunkirk, on the coast of Flanders, was a national tragedy of strategical and tactical blunders.

It was relieved only by acts of heroism few of which will be recorded but that lift it up above those blunders which recall so vividly to old war correspondents like myself, the sacrifice of more than 200,000 Australians, New Zealanders and Canadians on the peninsula of Gallipoli in the World War.

UNDER CHURCHILL

It may not be significant but it is interesting to note that all three "Gallipolis" took place under Winston Churchill.

Also that the strategical and tactical mistakes in the three withdrawal-retreats, were somewhat analagous and that each was marked by deeds of valor that one expects only in Hollywood films.

The Germans are placing their heaviest long-range guns at strategic points nearest to Dover and Folkestone, especially in the region of Calais.

COULD POUND DOVER

Others of these long-barreled monsters with their enormous 11-inch shells of special construction, are being moved up.

They can from their emplacements pound Dover and Folkestone and the surrounding region should a German invasion be planned at those points.

Women and children have already been evacuated from Dover.

The plan of attack on England is, of course, a tightly kept secret of the German general staff.

U. S. NAVY COPIED

In the main, at least in the opening stage, it would seem to be limited to incessant attacks of the dreaded German "Stukas" with their 550, 1,100 and 2,200 pound high-explosive bombs, and squadrons of Heinkel and Dornier bombardment planes.

"Those are fine Stukas you have made out of our '*hell divers*' of the American naval air arm,"

I remarked to one of the most famous of German general of fliers:

of the American naval air arm."

His reply was:

"It was open to the others to take up the American idea as well as it was to us. If they did not do so they can blame only themselves."

AFTER R. A. F.

As in France and Belgium, where the Germans heavily bombed 65 military airdromes and air bases with their hangars, shops and gasoline depots the first day, destroying many warplanes, so the Germans will concentrate on the air bases of the British Royal Air force in England

Not unless and until Field Marshal Goering feels he is master of the air over England is there likely to be any attempt at an invasion from across the Channel.

The dropping of parachutists on a large scale would be the signal for an invasion by air and from the coast of Belgium and France by sea.

NAVY NOT ENOUGH

Whether such an invasion is really planned is a matter of lively speculation and discussion among foreign military and air attaches here.

The ports, harbors, docks and military establishments in England are expected to come in for terrific hammering from the air. It is logical that an attempt at invading England will depend mainly if not wholly upon the degree of success of the German assaults from the air.

The British Navy alone can no longer protect England. That will now largely fall upon the Royal Air Force and the ground defense system of anti-aircraft artillery.

Whether the hand that holds the the "German sword" has the power and the strength to wield it simultaneously in two directions—against England and against Paris—will be revealed shortly.

ANCIENT WATER

Great Salt Lake is the remnant of an immense ancient body of water known to science as Lake Bonneville.

Mercy Ship Docks

BRINGS WAR REFUGEES HOME

NOTABLES ON PASSENGER LIST

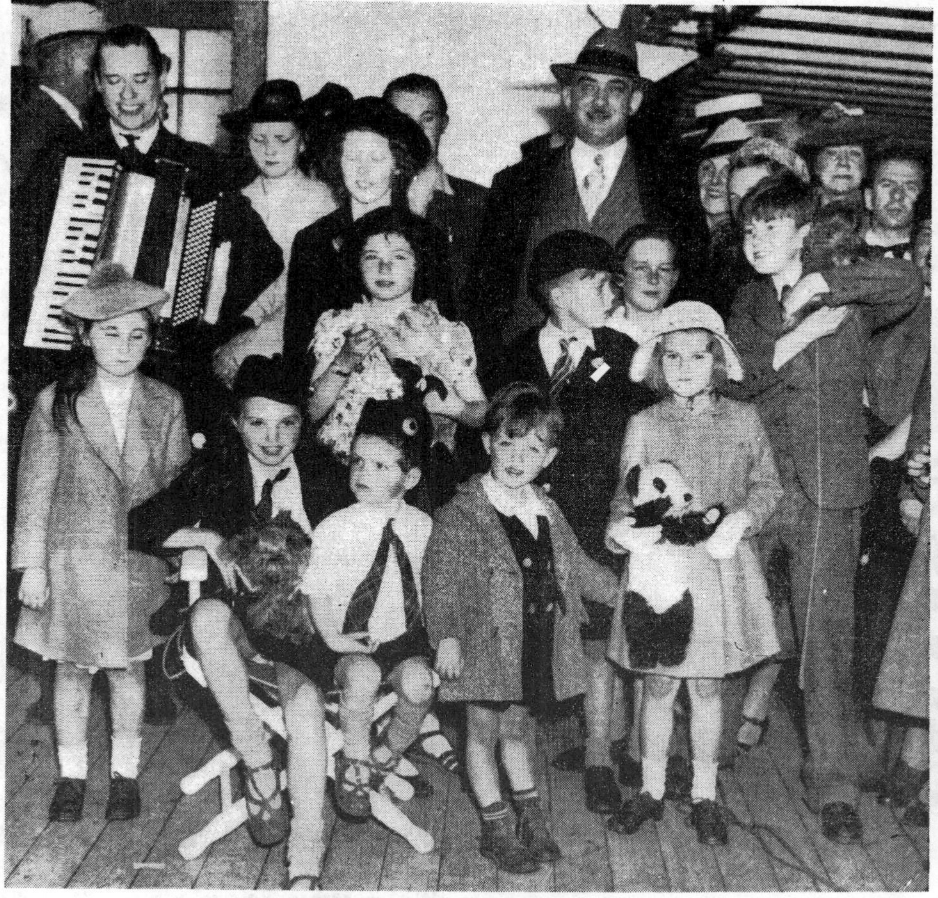

HAPPY OVER SAFE ARRIVAL FROM WAR ZONE

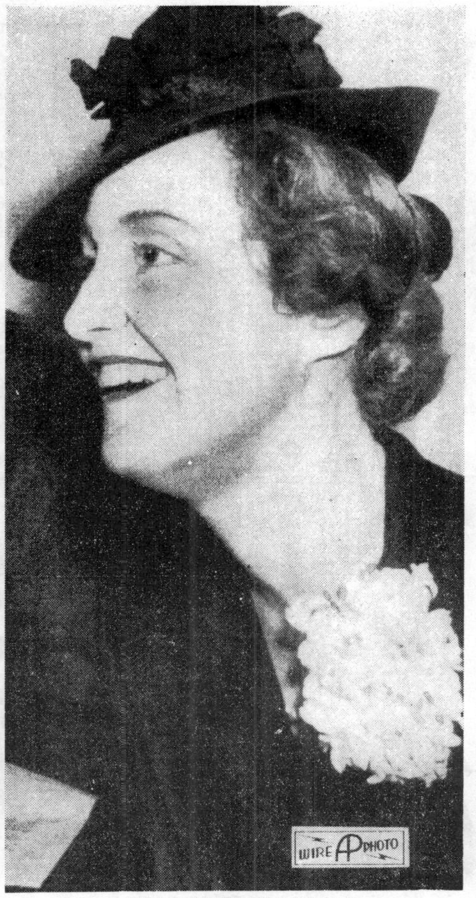
WIRE AP PHOTO

MRS. KERMIT ROOSEVELT

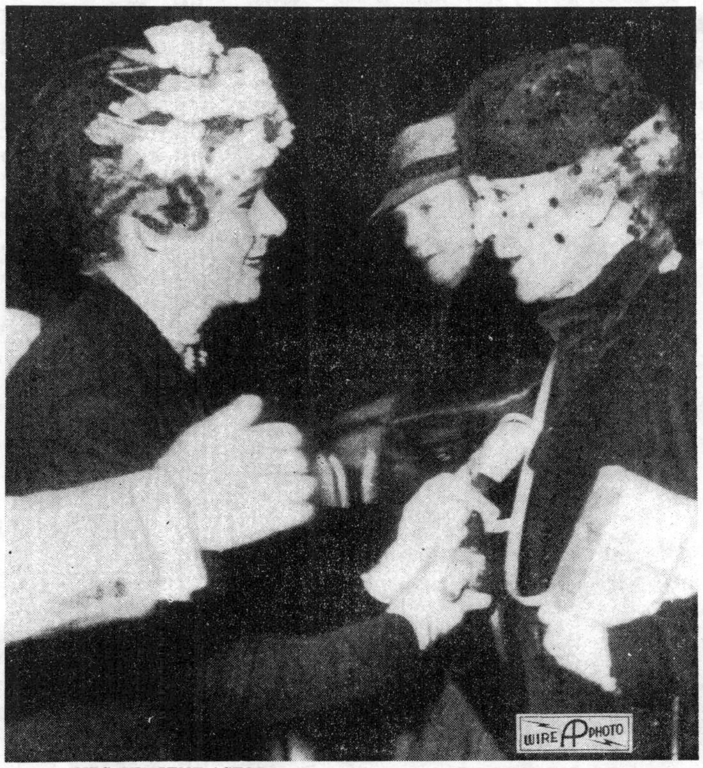
WIRE AP PHOTO

MRS. VINCENT ASTOR — LADY RIBBLESDALE

These pictures were taken as the United States liner President Roosevelt arrived in New York from Galway, Ireland, with 700 American children and adults—refugees from the invasion-menaced British Isles. Mrs. Roosevelt was one of the passengers. Her husband is serving as a major in the British Army and was last reported with the forces at Narvik, Norway, which the Allies have now abandoned. Mrs. Astor greeted her husband's mother, Lady Ribblesdale, on her arrival.

Ford Studies Plane; Mass-Output, Aim

Seeks To Learn 1,000-A-Day Possibility

DETROIT, June 10—(A. P.).—Henry Ford, genius of mass production, who periodically startles the industrial world with some undertaking seemingly impossible of achievement, expected to learn tod: precisely what may be involved in placing airplane manufacture on a volume output basis.

Ford, seventy-six, offering his aid to the Government in its defensive armament program, has said that under certain conditions, he could get airplane production up to 1,000 units a day within six months after receiving an order.

Today Ford and a group of his engineers planned to examine the type of pursuit plane the War Department believes would be most n ded "in an emergency."

Advance word regarding the plane indicated it is one of the latest models, known as the P-38 interceptor type, capable of a speed in excess of 400 miles an hour and powered with two 1,100-horse power liquid-cooled engines.

1 OUT OF 8 IN ARMY

One out of every eight Swiss citizens are in the army. One out of every eight Swiss marry foreigners. One out of every eight Swiss go abroad to live.

Billy Mitchell Is Skeleton In The Military Closet

By ARTHUR ("BNGS") BAER

The skeleton in the military closet has epaulets on its collar bones. It's the old moss-back that court-martialed Billy Mitchell.

Fifteen years ago Bill proved an airplane could sink a battleship. And fifteen years ago the moss-backs sank Bill.

Fifteen years have gone into the chopper and have been as wasted as fish-heads in a butcher shop.

The old moss-backs run the Army like a private club until war start. Then the public is invited in.

Refugees Reach U. S., More Due

NEW YORK, June 10—(A. P.).—The Statue of Liberty became a sentinel of safety and peace today to new hundreds of American and alien refugees fleeing the widening holocaust of European war.

Steaming through fog and rain, the commissioned United States liner President Roosevelt, a "floating nursery" with 150 children among its 723 passengers, docked last night after a nightmare voyage of storm and terror from Galway, Ireland.

FIRST OF THREE HOME

It was the first of three United States liners racing home with Americans stranded in the path of spreading battle zones.

The Manhattan, scheduled to arrive late today, will bring 1,904 refugees from Genoa, Italy. Hundreds of clamoring passengers who "missed the boat" at Galway will be picked up later in the week by the United States liner Washington, which sailed from a French port Saturday.

FEEL WATER SHORTAGE

Rough weather and shortages of fresh water and diapers added to the troubles of passengers aboard the President Roosevelt, which was jammed with hundreds of extra cots and lifebelts.

Half of the refugees were women, many of them wives of American business men who remained in England. At least two had husbands in the British Royal Air Force. Among the children were 33 babies, whose mothers were forced to launder for them in sea water.

There were also fourteen Rhodes scholars, who agreed the British were confident "they'll win in the long run."

SCORES SEASICK

Scores of passengers were so seasick they remained below decks for days. Describing a storm that struck the ship the third day after they left Galway on June 2, Mrs. Paul H. Sullivan, wife of a Goodyear Rubber Company official, said:

"Everyone thought the ship had broken in two. There was a terrible noise and the motors shut down. We were told later that the propeller came out of the water, the ship pitched so."

Other passengers included Mrs. Robert Montgomery, whose movie star husband became a volunteer ambulance driver in France, and Mrs. Kermit Roosevelt.

Mrs. Roosevelt said that her husband, fighting as a major in the British Army, had retained his American citizenship.

2 Shot After Cult Refuses Flag Salute

KENNEBUNK. Me., June 10—(I. N. S.).—Six alleged Jehovah's Witnesses members were in jail today, two men they allegedly shot were in hospitals, and the sect's headquarters was charred debris from citizen fury.

Police said that a search of the Jehovah's Witnesses' building after 2,500 persons had twice set it afire and ransacked it, revealed two rifles and six shotguns, pictures of Hitler and Stalin, and maps on which were allegedly marked locations of industrial plants, railroad lines, and bridges in Maine cities and towns.

Victims of the shooting were Dwight Robinson, shipyard worker and Fred McDonald.

Trouble originally flared at Sanford Saturday night when two men were beaten by a crowd of 1,000 persons after they refused to salute the American flag.

Leaders Aver G. O. P. Race Still Wide Open

By WILLIAM K. HUTCHINSON

International News Service Staff Correspondent.

WASHINGTON, June 10.—Although their Presidential convention assembles in Philadelphia in two weeks, Republican leaders in Congress today asserted the race for the 1940 G. O. P. nomination is still wide open.

FEW PREDICT VICTORY

Capitol Hill Republicans believe Ohio Senator Robert A. Taft will lead on the first ballot, with New York Racket-Buster Thomas E. Dewey in close pursuit and Michigan Senator Arthur H. Vandenberg in third place.

But few Capitol politicos are predicting the nomination of either Taft or Dewey, even while contending that Taft has gained and Dewey has lost strength since the German invasion of the low countries.

Followers of Taft claim he will have between 300 and 400 of the 1,000 delegates on the first ballot. Dewey's managers make like claims.

SEE TAFT ON TOP

If these claims prove to be true, many Capitol Republicans predict that the ticket will be Taft and Dewey, one way or the other, but with Taft more likely to be on top due to his greater experience in public affairs.

Canada To Build 2 New War Plants

OTTAWA, June 10 — (A. P.). — Canada, in assissination with the British and French Governments, will begin construction immediately on two munitions plants costing approximately $20,000,000, Munitions Minister Charles Howe announced today.

One will be a shell filling plant costing $8,000,000 and the other, costing $12,000,000, will produce nitro-cellulose explosives.

These plants will be additional to the explosives plant now nearing completion in Northwestern Ontario.

Use Of Ultra Violet To Aid Army Studied

NEW YORK, June 10—(A. P.).—Ultra-violet light, something never before used in war, is under consideration to protect the health of fighting men in the United States Army and Navy and the British Army.

This new step in war medicine was described briefly today for the American Medical Association by W. F. Wells, director of the laboratories for study of air borne diseases of the University of Pennsylvania.

He said inquiries had come from all three services. In the United States Army it is proposed to use mild ultra-violet lights in barracks to prevent spread of contagion. The United States Navy wants to try them in ships.

The British inquiry is for their use in hospitals crowded with wounded to prevent spread of air-borne infections which in the past have killed many wounded who would have recovered from their military injuries.

The light used, Mr. Wells said, is a form of ultra-violet which does not appear in sunshine. It is much milder to the human skin, taking several hours to do as much burning as three minutes of direct summer sun.

Eleventh Hour 'At Hand,' Gen Weygand Warns

PARIS, June 10—(A. P.). In proclaiming in his order of the day to his troops yesterday that "the last quarter hour has come," Allied Generalissimo Maxime Weygand was using the French equivalent of the English expression, "eleventh hour."

It means the close approach of the supreme test from which either victory or defeat will result.

Seeks Cause For Battleship 'Leak'

PORTLAND, Oregon, June 10—(A. P.).—Police examined the battleship Oregon today to learn if saboteurs or juvenile visitors opened the seacock that let 600 tons of water into the ship at her anchorage here. Mayor Joseph K. Carson believed someone attempted to sink the Oregon, though she has no combat value.

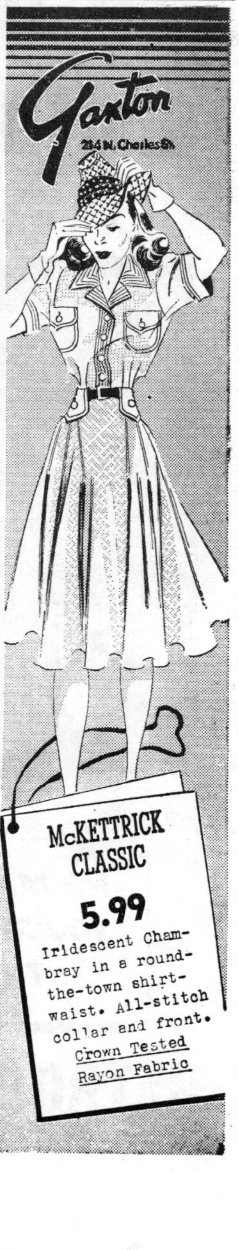
Gaxton
214 N. Charles St.
McKETTRICK CLASSIC
5.99
Iridescent Chambray in a round-the-town shirtwaist. All-stitch collar and front.
Crown Tested Rayon Fabric

BALTIMORE NEWS-POST, MONDAY, JUNE 10, 1940

Child Needs Cod Liver Oil In Summer--Dafoe

By ALLAN ROY DAFOE, M. D.
Personal Physician to the Dionne Quintuplets

I've had several dozen letters recently from persons remembering I'm a strong advocate of cod liver oil in winter, asking if I think the oil is needed by children in summer also.

DR. DAFOE

My opinion is, in general, yes, although the answer in a specific case is dependent upon the climate in which the individual lives and upon the child's state of health.

Most persons probably believe that it is only necessary to give oil when there isn't plenty of sunshine. However, the child may be in the sun a number of hours a day and still not be getting enough of the vital Vitamin D.

DOUBLY SURE

The Dionne Quintuplets take cod liver oil morning and evening, in summer as well as winter. Because up here in Callander we are rather far north and the sunshine doesn't have as much ultra-violet ray power as it has further south. So we make doubly sure that Marie, Emilie, Yvonne, Annette and Cecile get adequate quantities of Vitamin D by giving cod liver oil.

Of course, we don't give the same dosage in summer as in winter. We moderate them, for naturally there isn't as great an ultra-violet ray deficiency to make up for in summer.

Callander's latitude places it only a few miles north of St. Paul, Superior, Wis., and Duluth Minn., are north of us. We are about on a line with the northern boundary of South Dakota. So I would say that the need for summer cod liver oil in those northerly States is about the same as here in Callander.

By the way, a great many persons do not realize that some of Canada is south of some of the United States. On visits to the States I've run into some arguments about this. One man from North Dakota accused me of using a trick map to show him up as a more northerner than I am.

Regardless of climate, I don't see why parents should want to cut off the cod liver oil dosage in summer. Children get used to taking it regularly. It isn't as nauseating to them as to adults who can't start in taking it young. Neither is it so very expensive, considering its great value.

TELLS OF ARGUMENTS

Long studies have led experts to estimate that if 100 modern babies chosen at random were given no cod liver oil whatever, at least 50 would develop rickets.

(Copyright, 1940, King Features Syndicate, Incorporated.)

Hindsight and Foresight
By HOLGAR J. JOHNSON
President, Institute of Life Insurance

NO MATTER why it happens, a man hates to drop his life insurance. And your insurance company doesn't like it, either.

The company, when it takes in a new policyholder who doesn't stick, is in much the same position as a landlord who makes improvements for his tenants—only to have them move out soon afterwards.

On the other hand, some tenants have good reasons for moving. And so do some policyholders have good reasons for dropping their life insurance.

* * *

For instance, a man may buy insurance to protect his aged mother. If the mother dies, he may want to drop the policy. In most cases, however, he would be much better off if he kept it—refitting it to meet his present or prospective needs.

Or, a man may take out a policy because he is taking financial risks in his business. But if he stops taking these risks he may no longer want that protection. So he allows the policy to lapse.

Many lapses are caused by unavoidable misfortune such as losing a job or a temporary financial setback. And some occur because the policyholder was not entirely convinced in the first place.

After 20 years of experience in dealing with people, however, I am of the opinion that one of the causes of lapse goes right back to human nature. We start lots of things—from correspondence courses to savings-bank accounts—and then fail to keep them up.

HERE are some suggestions that may help you avoid lapse. It's a good idea to review, once in a while, what your insurance program will do, so as to remind you that it's worth fighting for. And your agent or your company should always be notified well in advance if you can foresee a possible lapse.

You'll find that your company, like all others, has several different means of helping to tide over the man who has a run of hard luck and good agents do not spare themselves in trying to keep even the smallest policy from lapsing.

NOTE: In this regular Monday column, paid for at advertising rates, the Institute of Life Insurance has asked its president to discuss questions of interest to life insurance policyholders. Inquiries may be addressed to 60 East 42nd Street, New York City.

JUNE IS Food Fair SELF SERVICE MARKETS
STOCK UP! BUY NOW! SAVE MONEY!

MONTH OF VALUES!

Our second big week! and the second Big Event in our June Month of Values!... A Huge Stock-Up Sale!... Stock Up your pantry, your cottage or country place now at substantial savings!

What a Month!...What a Sale! and what Savings!!... Just look at these for real value! Of course we couldn't list all of the many, many specials now effective but these few will give you an idea!

Beginning "Our Great Stock-Up SALE!"

HUNDREDS OF VALUES LIKE THESE EFFECTIVE **Monday, Tuesday and Wednesday**

801-7 W. BALTIMORE STREET
25TH AND GREENMOUNT AVENUE
743-47 FREDERICK ROAD
2140 N. FULTON AVENUE
FLEET AND HAVEN STREETS
405 N. FRANKLINTOWN ROAD
631 S. BROADWAY
3901-25 BELVEDERE AVENUE
2720 W. NORTH AVENUE
2515 E. MONUMENT STREET
449 NORTH GAY STREET
1000-10 S. CHARLES STREET

BAKED BEANS FYNE-TASTE with Pork & Tomato Sauce	2 No. 2½ cans	15c
Chicken OF THE Sea TUNA GRATED STYLE	No. 1 can	21c
Chase AND Sanborn COFFEE	2 1-lb. bags	43c
Del Monte Coffee Drip Or Regular	1-lb. can	22c
Fyne-Taste Coffee	2 1-lb. bags	25c
Del Monte DE LUXE Plums	2 No. 2½ cans	23c
Del Monte Pineapple CRUSHED	2 No. 2 cans	25c
Tomato Catsup FYNE-TASTE	2 12-oz. bottles	19c
Thomson Raisins SEEDLESS	2 1-lb. bag	11c
Maine Sardines OIL OR MUSTARD	3 No. ¼ cans	14c
Tomato Paste CONTADINA	3 6-oz. cans	13c
Fancy Rice BLUE ROSE RADIO BRAND	2 1-lb. bags	9c

FANCY QUALITY RED RIPE TOMATOES No. 2 can **5c**

FYNE-TASTE SPAGHETTI 1s1½-oz. can **5c**

Come Into Our Garden Of FRESH FRUITS & VEGETABLES

Words can't describe it!... You must see our Huge Displays of Fruits and Vegetables to fully appreciate the clean, Crisp freshness, the uniform quality! The Variety! and the exceptionally low prices!

GOLDEN RIPE BANANAS	DOZ.	15c AND 19c None Priced Higher
FINEST QUALITY ARIZONA CANTALOUPES	2 FOR	25c
FANCY QUALITY FRESH STRINGLESS BEANS	2 lbs.	11c
FRESH CALIF. SWEET GREEN PEAS	2 lbs.	19c
FRESH SOUTHERN GREEN CABBAGE	4 lbs.	9c
NEW POTATOES MED. SIZE	15-lb. peck	21c

PROTECTED, SELECTED and GUARANTEED MEATS
They Must Please You or Your Money Refunded!

SUGAR CURED BONELESS SMOKED NECKS	lb.	21c
MILK FED VEAL CHOPS RIB AND LOIN	lb.	25c
LEAN SUGAR CURED SLICED BACON	½-lb. cello pkg.	8c
FRESH GROUND HAMBURG	lb.	15c
FRESH KILLED, YOUNG TENDER FRYING CHICKENS	lb.	25c

Fresh Seafoods

FRESH LIVE SOFT CRABS doz. 55c

Nearby Country **EGGS** 2 doz. in cartons **37c**

WISCONSIN FULL CREAM MILD **CHEESE** lb. **19c**

FRESH MADE HAM BOLOGNA pound sliced **21c**

WAFER SLICED **DRIED BEEF** ¼ lb. **10c**

✓ 6 BIG ADVANTAGES— the rest can't match!

Why take less than the best? Why guess which is best? Check facts on the "All 3 Group" for 1940 and here's what you find!

COMPARE PERFORMANCE! Here's the only 8-cylinder engine! Fastest, smoothest—action no "6" can match!

COMPARE ECONOMY! Here's the best gas mileage, officially proved. And the car that owners themselves report needs no oil added between 2000-mile changes!

COMPARE COMFORT! Here's the longest springbase, greatest kneeroom, steadiest-riding car of the lot!

COMPARE BRAKES! Here are the biggest hydraulics ever used on a low-price car. Only ones with 12" drums!

COMPARE FEATURES! Only Ford has full Torque-Tube Drive, semi-centrifugal clutch, engine that needs no "breaking in," valves that don't need periodic adjusting!

COMPARE EQUIPMENT! Here's extra equipment, included in the price, that the others charge extra for!

NO MATTER WHAT YOU'RE DRIVING NOW... THIS YEAR TRY FORD!

FORD V·8
METROPOLITAN BALTIMORE FORD DEALERS

DEALER ADVERTISEMENT

Charities Group Honors Blaustein

President, Retiring After Four Years Of Service, Guest Of Honor At Dinner

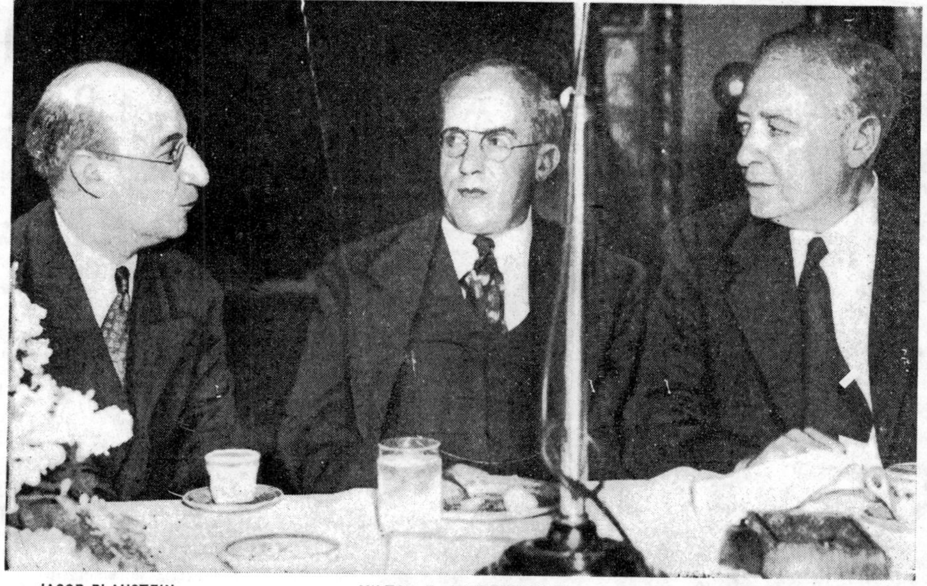

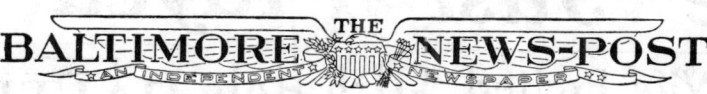

JACOB BLAUSTEIN — MILTON E. GUNDERSHEIMER — L. EDWIN GOLDMAN

Approximately 500 persons attended a banquet in the Lord Baltimore Hotel last night given in honor of Jacob Blaustein (left), retiring as president of the Associated Jewish Charities after four years service. Milton E. Gundersheimer (center), newly elected first vice-president of the organization, was toastmaster, and L. Edwin Goldman (right) was elected president of the A. J. C. to take the place left vacant by Mr. Blaustein's retirement. Picture copyright, 1940, by The Baltimore News-Post. All rights reserved.

The Baltimore News-Post Has the Largest Circulation of Any Newspaper in the South

THE BALTIMORE NEWS-POST — AN INDEPENDENT NEWSPAPER

2ND FRONT PAGE — NEWS-POST HAS TWO FRONT PAGES DAILY

MONDAY EVENING, JUNE 10, 1940

Courts To Get Flags Today

Supreme Bench To Accept U. S. Banners From City

By ALDINE R. BIRD

The American flag, emblematic of the Constitutional form of Government, today will take an honored position in the courtrooms of Baltimore.

On the steps of the Calvert street entrance to the Courthouse, and in a setting unique in patriotic impressiveness, a score of flags will be presented by the city and accepted by the Supreme Bench of Baltimore for daily tribute and recognition.

FETE BEGINS AT 4 O'CLOCK

The ceremonies will begin at 4 P. M., and will be featured by the appearance of the full membership of the judicial body in their official robes.

In case of rain, the ceremonies will be held in one of the larger court rooms, it was announced.

Each member of the City Council will hold one of the flags, and one by one they will be presented by Richard C. O'Connell, arrangements chairman, to Mayor Jackson, and, in turn, to Chief Judge Samuel K. Dennis for delivery to the individual jurists.

The St. Mary's Industrial School Band, under direction of Brother Edward Joseph, will provide the patriotic musical background for the program.

The flags were purchased by the Board of Estimates, and include emblems not only for the Suprem Bench but for the Juvenile and People's Courts and the City Council.

MARCH TO CITY HALL

An hour later the band and the official group will march to the City Hall, where Mayor Jackson will present the City Council's flag in the Council chambers. President O'Connell will accept it on behalf of the legislative body.

After today, each session of the courts and Council is expected to begin with a standing salute to the flag, a practice which has recently spread throughout the country.

The ceremonies were arranged as a feature of the city's observance of National Flag Week, which Mayor Jackson proclaimed for Baltimore to include the period of June 8 to 14.

TO DEDICATE FLAGS

Tomorrow night the new, silk flag of the National Legion of Mothers of America, Maryland Council, will be dedicated in ceremonies to be held in the Lord Baltimore Hotel. The Legion is a nation-wide organization of wom-

Continued on Page 14, Column 4.

Three Killed In Week-End Auto Accidents

Baltimore Man Dies As Car Overturns In Marsh

Three persons were dead today and several injured as a result of automobile accidents on Maryland roads over the week-end,as thousands sought nearby watering-places for relief from the heat.

The dead:

Roland I. Koller, twenty-one, 600 block of East Clement street, killed when a car plunged into a marsh.

HITCH-HIKER STRUCK

Warren B. Cox, seventy-one, a hitch-hiker of New London, Conn., killed on Philadelphia road near Bush river.

Edward L. Smith, twenty-nine, Cambridge, killed in a head-on collision on Route 16.

The accident in which Koller lost his life took place near Prince Frederick, and Eugene McDonough and Carl Frederick, fellow Naval Reservists of Baltimore, were injured.

RIDING ON OUTSIDE

The three were riding on the running-board when the car struck a roadside post and overturned in four feet of water, pinning them under the car.

George H. Whims of Aberdeen, according to State police, was the driver of the car which fatally struck Cox.

Smith, State police said, was trying to pass a car on a curve near Cambridge and ran head-on into another machine.

Off For Shrine Meet

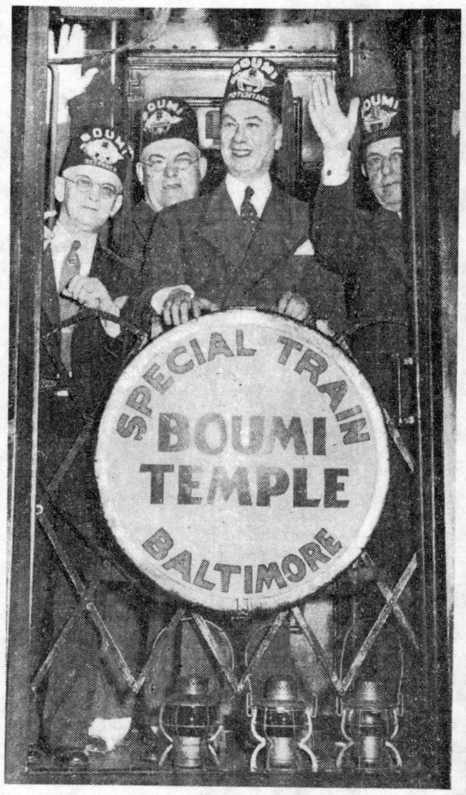

Shriners, members of Boumi Temple, Baltimore, were on their way today to Memphis, Tenn., for the annual Shrine convention. Some of the leaders are shown above in the rear vestibule of the special train. They are (left to right): F. Warren Hammerslough, J. Purnell Johnson, Potentate E. Elmer Langrall and George M. Armor.

Goucher Grads Warned Of Reds

The evil spirit of vulgarity is attacking the dignity and decency of the American way of life, the Rev. Dr. Albert Joseph McCartney of Washington told Goucher graduates in his baccalaureate address yesterday.

This was the third in a series of five days of graduation exercises which will culminate in the commencement tomorrow. Dr. McCartney also spoke of the menace of Communism in the United States, and said:

"The real question at issue is whether we can improve things by discarding our democratic principles based, we believe, on the Christian philosophy and by smashing what we have.

"One thing to remember is that wherever these schemes and theories of life have established themselves, they have become the avowed enemies of religion."

Foto Friends Club To Hear Physicist

How to make "multiflash one-millionth-second" photographs will be explained to members of the newly-formed Foto Friends Club tonight at a meeting to be held at 924 St. Paul street. The speaker will be Regis B. Winslow, S. J., physicist at Loyola College, and he will be aided by Louis A. Scholz, director of the club. The meeting will be held at 8 P. M. in the clubrooms of Montfaucon Post, American Legion.

Beat And Rob Man In Clifton Park

Police today pressed their search for two youthful thugs who beat sixty-year-old George F. Webster unconscious in Clifton Park early yesterday and escaped with $11.

Webster told police that the attack occurred near the bandstand in the park. After recovering consciousness he made his way to his home in the 2800 block Roselawn avenue, and was later sent to St. Joseph's Hospital for first-aid treatment.

TODAY'S TIDES

High tide	9.50 A. M.	10.26 A. M.
Low tide	3.36 A. M.	4.53 P. M.

Warns Of 5th Column, Of Poverty, Disease

A warning against the "Fifth Column of poverty, disease and hunger" was coupled with a plea for national defense last night by Jacob Blaustein in his final address as president of the Associated Jewish Charities.

Speaking before a group of 500 professional workers, trustees and laymen associated with the Jewish Charities in Baltimore, attending a dinner in the Lord Baltimore Hotel marking his retirement after four years as president of the group, Mr. Blaustein said:

"To the extent that our local charities are outflanked will our enemies on the outside be joined by the forces of poverty, disease and crime to lay waste to our land."

REFERS BY INTERENCE

Referring only by inference to the international situation, Mr. Blaustein declared:

"There is a man who started out first as an enemy only of our own people, but who now has developed into the enemy of all democracy, all things that are decent, just and good. The slogan of our national defense must be preparedness, but we must look to our welfare defenses as well."

OWE DUTY, VIEW

The speaker said that we owe a duty to the unfortunate people in other countries, and added:

"We must remember that here in America is our first line of defense, the beloved country in which we live."

New officers were elected before the opening of the banquet, and L. Edwin Goldman, formerly first vice-president, was elevated to the presidency of the Associated Jewish Charities.

OTHERS ELECTED

Other officers elected were Milton E. Gundersheimer, toastmaster at the dinner, first vice-president; Lester S. Levy, second vice-president; Dr. Alvin Thalheimer, treasurer, and L. Manuel Hendler, assistant treasurer.

Elected to the board of directors were Hugo Dalsheimer, Jr.; Morris Eisen, Samuel H. Hoffberger, Sidney Hollander, Walter Hollander, Ephraim Macht, Abraham Marcis and Morris A. Rome.

Mayor Jackson made a brief address, and Gov. Herbert R. O'Conor sent a letter expressing his regrets at being unable to attend the dinner.

OUTLINES NEEDS

Harry Greenstein, executive director of the organization, spoke briefly, outlining the current need of Jewish charities in Baltimore. He stressed the need of Sinai Hospital for new maternity facilities; urged more aid for aged and chronically ill Jews and advocated an expansion of educational facilities for youth.

During the dinner Mr. Blaustein was presented with an illuminated parchment, commemorating his services to the Associated Jewish Charities during the four years he served as president.

Trolleys To Bisect The Circle

Within a few weeks street cars will pass straight through Park Circle, the grass-plotted area in front of Carlin's Park.

Workmen of the Baltimore Transit Company began today to dig up portions of the circle so trolley tracks could be laid through it. Autos will not go through, however. They will continue to use the circle, as at present.

George Carter, city highways engineer, said:

"Street cars will not take on or discharge passengers in the circle. The loading and unloading platforms will be at the outside of the circle.

"It is felt the new arrangement will aid materially in clearing up a rather difficult traffic situation at that location. After the work is completed, autos will go around the circle without the hindrance of street cars in front of them."

Patterson Park Graduation Tonight

Diplomas will be awarded by Mayor Jackson to 173 seniors of Patterson Park High School at graduation exercises to be held tonight at 8.15 o'clock in the school auditorium. Dr. David L. Weglein, superintendent of schools, and Norman L. Clark, principal of the school, will preside.

U. Of B. Gift Goes To Roosevelt

Ediors of the yearbook of the University of Baltimore were in Washington today to present a copy of the volume to President Roosevelt, to whom it is dedicated.

The staff voted President Roosevelt the "greatest living American" and used a photograph of him in the book, with a statement about him, and a statement which the President sent to the editors.

The presentation was to take place at the White House today.

Victim

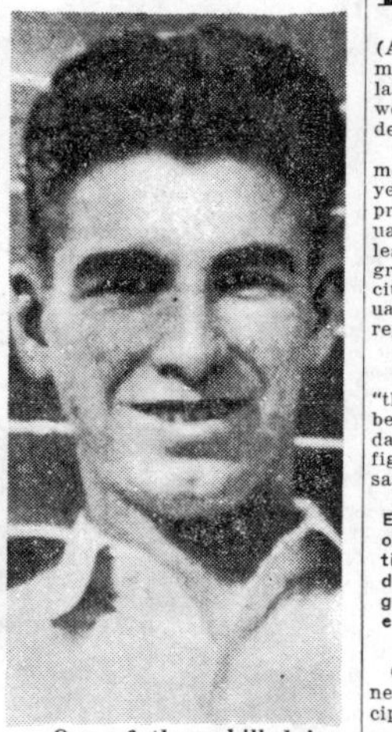

One of three killed in Maryland auto crashes over the week-end was Roland I. Koller, twenty-one (above), a Naval reservist, 600 block of East Clement street, who lost his life when a car carrying six persons plunged into a marsh near Prince Frederick, Md.

Governor Addresses Elks Group

CUMBERLAND, Md., June 10—(A. P.).—The American flag soon may be "the emblem marking the last frontier of democracy in the world," Gov. Herbert R. O'Conor declared here.

Speaking at the Flag Day ceremony of Cumberland Elks Lodge yesterday, the Governor said war preparations are limiting individual rights in England and France, leaving this nation as "the one great power of the world whose citizens still may go their individual ways unhampered by restrictive regulations and legislation.

SOUNDS WARNING

He cautioned against belief that "this grand flag of ours could not be torn down," asserting that today "democracy is on the defensive, fighting for its very existence." He said:

"This tragic war now raging in Europe is more than simply another war between Europe's nations. It is a war between two diametrically opposed systems of government, two basically different modes of thought."

URGES PREPAREDNESS

O'Conor urged national preparedness and loyalty to American principles.

POETS PLAN PROGRAM

Under auspices of the Society of American Poets a musical program will be presented Wednesday night in the Peabody Concert Hall, a feature of the evening to be a presentation of Lizette Woodworth Reese's poem, "Miracle," sung by Miss Doris Wright. Miss Wright set the poem to music. Mrs. Eleanor Wilson Shugerman is in charge of arranging the program.

Red Cross May Have Task Here

Where to Make Donations

Persons wishing to make a donation to the Baltimore Chapter of the American Red Cross, to aid the war stricken in Europe, can do so in any bank in the city, or in Baltimore and Howard counties.

Announcement to this effect was made at Red Cross Headquarters, 202 Guilford avenue.

When cash is presented at banks, a receipt will be given. In addition, an extra receipt will be forwarded by the Red Cross as soon as the donation reaches headquarters.

The American Red Cross war relief fund may soon have work to do in Baltimore, Miss Cristine Limbert, executive secretary of the Baltimore chapter, said today.

A special committee has been revived and made ready for action whose duty will be to aid American refugees from the war zones who might be landed in Baltimore, she said.

Charles H. Robson, Jr., is chairman of the committee, which includes Maurice B. Carlin, A. R. Archibald and Albert Schram.

Two ships bearing war refugees have been met in New York by Red Cross committees, and it is possible that freighters soon to dock in Baltimore may have others aboard, Miss Limbert explained.

Arrest 2 Youths In Stolen Auto

Arrest of two youths in a stolen auto led Northeastern district police today to believe that they have solved a series of more than 30 recent auto larcenies and thefts from parked cars. Most of the robberies took place in the neighborhood of Johns Hopkins, Sinai and St. Joseph's Hospitals and Church Home and Infirmary. Sergt. Leo McDonough said two physicians' satchels containing surgical instruments were found in the car in which the youths were arrested.

ELKS PLAN FLAG DAY FETE

A Flag Day celebration will be held next Sunday at 8.30 P. M. by the Baltimore Lodge of Elks, the program to be staged in front of the War Memorial Building. Police Inspector Thomas J. Mooney, exalted ruler of the lodge, said the Elks will march from their clubhouse to the War Memorial plaza.

NEW SHOP FOR ABERDEEN

Bids are to be opened July 9 for a new shop building for the ordnance school at the Aberdeen Proving Grounds, Army officials announced today.

Sneeze Causes Crash

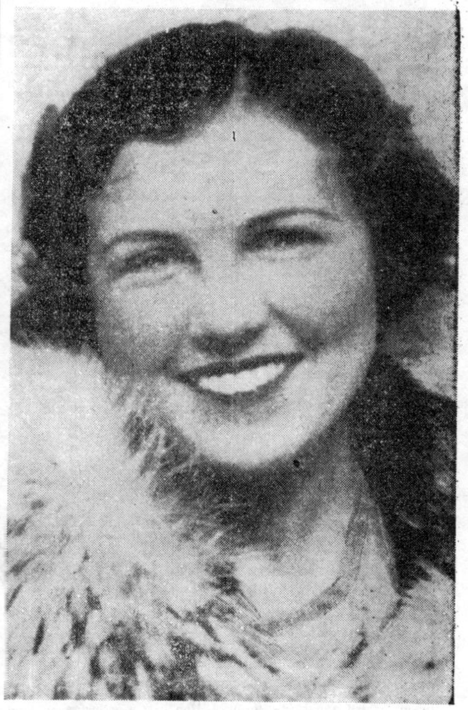

Her sneeze caused an auto accident. At least that's what the police say, quoting John R. Mueller, whose auto smacked into the rear of Representative Thomas D'Alesandro's car at Pratt and Light streets. Mueller said the young woman, Miss Dorothy Kreiger, twenty-five, 1700 block East Fayette street, his companion in the car, sneezed and distracted his attention from driving for a moment. It was then that the crash occurred. Mueller and Miss Kreiger were injured slightly, Representative D'Alesandro and members of his family not at all. Photograph copyright, 1940, by The Baltimore News-Post. All rights reserved.

Win Cash For News Tips And Amateur Photographs

Do you want money for being alert? The Baltimore News-Post and Sunday American are offering cash prizes each week for news tips and amateur photographs. Total awards of $50 are distributed weekly for news tips, $25 for the best, $10 for the next best and $1 prizes for the next fifteen. For each amateur photograph published, $3 will be paid, with special bonuses for outstanding pictures. Spot-news pictures are preferred, but candid camera shots that pull at the heart-strings are acceptable. Avoid pictures of ordinary scenes. Telephone The News-Tip Editor at Lexington 0100 (Lexington 4165 from midnight to 6.30 A. M.) for news tips and rush spot-news photographs in to the Picture Editor.

SKIPPY — By Percy Crosby

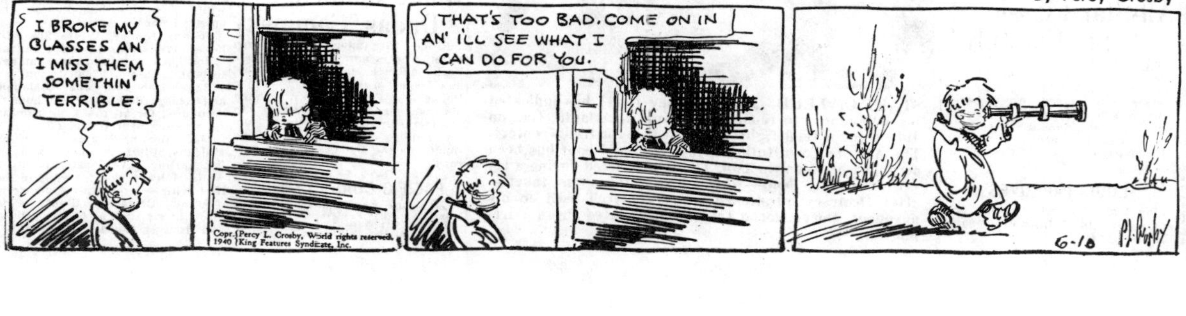

Little Just Played Better Golf---Sarazen

THE BALTIMORE NEWS-POST SPORTS
MONDAY EVENING, JUNE 10, 1940 19

Little's Wife Excited

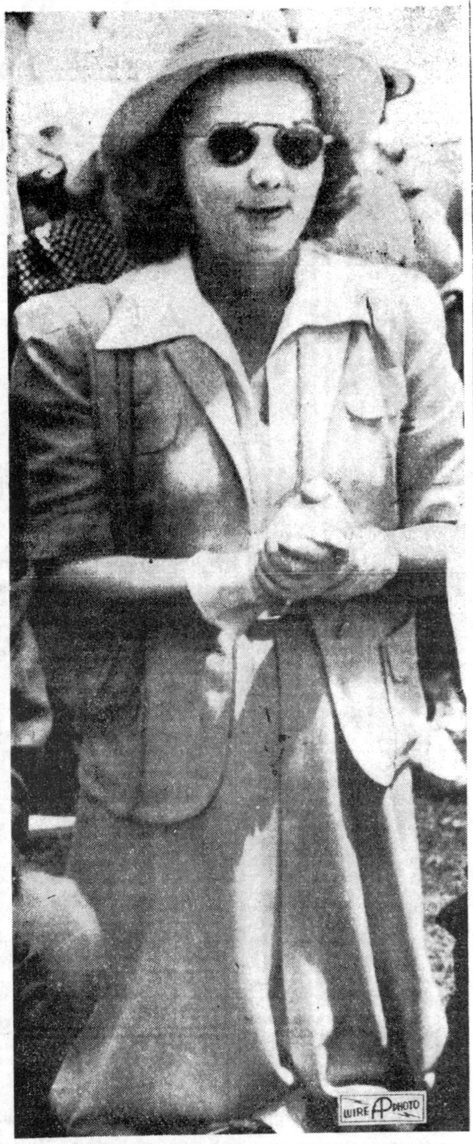

"HE'S WON, MY HUSBAND'S WON!"—That's the thought that curled the corners of Mrs. Lawson Little's lips as Little's putt dropped on the eighteenth at Canterbury Golf Club, Cleveland. The putt gave Little the National Open golf title. While waiting for the putt, Mrs. Little nervously donned her dark glasses. It meant something for her husband to win—about $50,000, the golf writers say. Associated Press Wirephoto.

Rodger H. Pippen *Sports Editor* Says:

The ghosts of Ned Hanlon's old Orioles, famed for their fire, fight and resourcefulness, hovered over the local ball yard yesterday as one of the oldest members of the present Orioles proved to the satisfaction of five thousand sweltering fans that he is young as any in spirit.

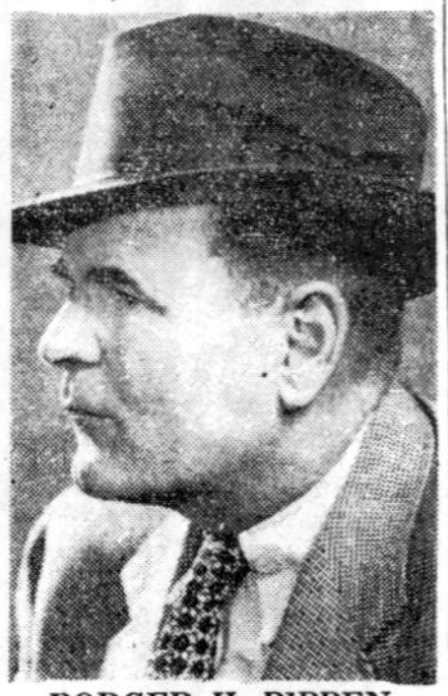

RODGER H. PIPPEN

Jack Redmond, born in Florence, Arizona, September 3, 1910, came to the bat for Baltimore in the eighth inning of the first game. Much to the surprise of the Buffalo infield, and particularly Third Baseman Danny Carnevale, Redmond dropped a peach of a bunt toward third and beat it out without half trying. That was reminiscent of Wee Willie Keeler, of the aforementioned old Orioles.

Collier, the next batsman, grounded toward first and Les Scarsella tried for a force out at second. Dashing to second, Redmond, who played football for the University of Arizona, found Jimmy Outlaw right in his path. Jack, well within his rights, crashed into the visiting infielder with a feet first slide. The shock knocked the ball from Jim's hands and Redmond was safe. That brought memories of the late John McGraw, Hanlon's famous third sacker.

Eddie Collins, attempting to sacrifice, dropped a bunt which the pitcher fielded and threw to third. The ball was just a split second ahead of Redmond, as he steamed from second and the umpire waved him out. But wait—once more Redmond hit the dirt and the visiting third sacker, who happened to be the same Carnevale who was dozing or thinking of other matters when Redmond had caught him flat footed with his bunt, was bowled over. The ball popped out once more and for the second time the Oriole was called safe. The decision was right and Redmond's bit of football was likewise perfectly proper. Carnevale, a youngster from the Buffalo sandlots, was in front of the bag and directly in the path of the base runner. If he doesn't learn better, he's likely to lose a leg. This incident revived more Oriole memories

Continued on Page 20, Column 3.

Fifth Hole Clinched Title

(Editor's Note: Herewith Is the last article of a series by Gene Sarazen, former United States and British Open golf champion, who tied for the former title again last week.)

By GENE SARAZEN
(Former U. S. and British Open Golf Champion.)

WARRENSVILLE, Ohio, June 10—(I. N. S.).—The best, simplest and truest explanation that I can give today for my defeat in the National Open championship play-off with Lawson Little as that he played the better golf.

I never was more confident in my life before a match than I was yesterday before we started out, and I wasn't even troubled too much after I had dropped strokes on the first two holes. But after the fifth I knew it would be tougr, for on this hole Little gained two strokes instead of losing one, as you would have expected him to do.

TURNING POINT

That was the turning point of the match, when I had a good drive and Little was bunkered and he still took a three to my five. That break more than anything else deprived me of winning my third Open championship, but that's golf for you.

It was a tough week for most of us, and especially for Little and me, and I'm glad it's over, although I hope to be right back in there again next year still trying. I may win another one yet, if I keep coming close enough.

In so far as this tournament was concerned, it was great from start to finish and as wide open as I predicted. With Sam Snead, Ben Hogan and some of the other boys favored, the odds against Little and me getting in a play-off would have been 1,000 to 1, especially in a tournament of this kind, where there are so many fine players.

PREDICTED TIE

I also flatly predicted a tie and play-off, although I had no idea at the time that I would be one of the players involved, and I said the long hitters had the best chance without knowing that I would be the one to lose finally to the long-hitting winners. Little had the power.

And to show you how very important sometimes seemingly small things can be, I'd like to mention that I lost five strokes to par in the five rounds, including the play-off, on the last two holes. I lost four of those strokes in the championship proper and another one yesterday. One of those strokes would have won the title for me. But that's golf, too.

And next year will be another year.

Little's $200 'Fee' Means College For His Caddy

CLEVELAND, June 10—(A. P.). It'll be college next fall for eighteen-year-old Henry Eickhoff who carried Lawson Little to his national open golf championship.

The youth received $200 of the $1,000 purse Little captured along with the title—enough to pay a year's tuition at Fenn College where he will study metallurgy.

"You're the swellest guy I know," he said soberly as the new champion handed him two crisp $100 bills. "I wouldn't be going to school if it wasn't for this."

Little thought his caddy was "pretty swell," too.

"I asked and followed his advice on a lot of shots in this tournament and he didn't let me down once...He won the title for me."

Little, strangely, was seventeenth choice among the caddies who selected players for whom they worked according to numbers based on seniority.

"I was holding my breath 'till they got down to my number," Caddy Eickhoff said, "and a lot of them laughed when I picked Little. I've got a laugh on them now."

PRINCETON SPORTS

At Princeton University last winter a total of 1,575 students took part in university class and club tournaments in basketball, bowling, boxing, hockey, squash, racquets, swimming, wrestling, polo, gymnastics and billiards.

Runs For Week

AMERICAN LEAGUE

Teams	S.	M.	T.	W.	T.	F.	S.	T'l
Philadelp'a	9	..	..	..	..	..	..	9
Boston	..	..	..	..	..	..	..	..
Chicago	4	..	..	..	..	..	..	4
Cleveland	3	..	..	..	..	..	..	3
Detroit	..	..	..	..	..	..	..	..
New York	4	..	..	..	..	..	..	4
St. Louis	12	..	..	..	..	..	..	12
Washington	3	..	..	..	..	..	..	3

NATIONAL LEAGUE

Teams	S.	M	T.	W.	T.	F.	S.	T'l
Boston	9	..	..	..	..	..	..	9
Brooklyn	11	..	..	..	..	..	..	11
Chicago	22	..	..	..	..	..	..	22
Cincinnati	7	..	..	..	..	..	..	7
New York	18	..	..	..	..	..	..	18
Philadelp'a	11	..	..	..	..	..	..	11
Pittsburgh	12	..	..	..	..	..	..	12
St. Louis	13	..	..	..	..	..	..	13

INTERNATIONAL LEAGUE

Teams	S.	M.	T.	W.	T.	F.	S.	T'l
Baltimore	24	..	..	..	..	..	..	24
Buffalo	10	..	..	..	..	..	..	10
Jersey City	8	..	..	..	..	..	..	8
Montreal	4	..	..	..	..	..	..	4
Newark	7	..	..	..	..	..	..	7
Rochester	5	..	..	..	..	..	..	5
Syracuse	3	..	..	..	..	..	..	3
Toronto	4	..	..	..	..	..	..	4

This Play Almost Caused A Fight

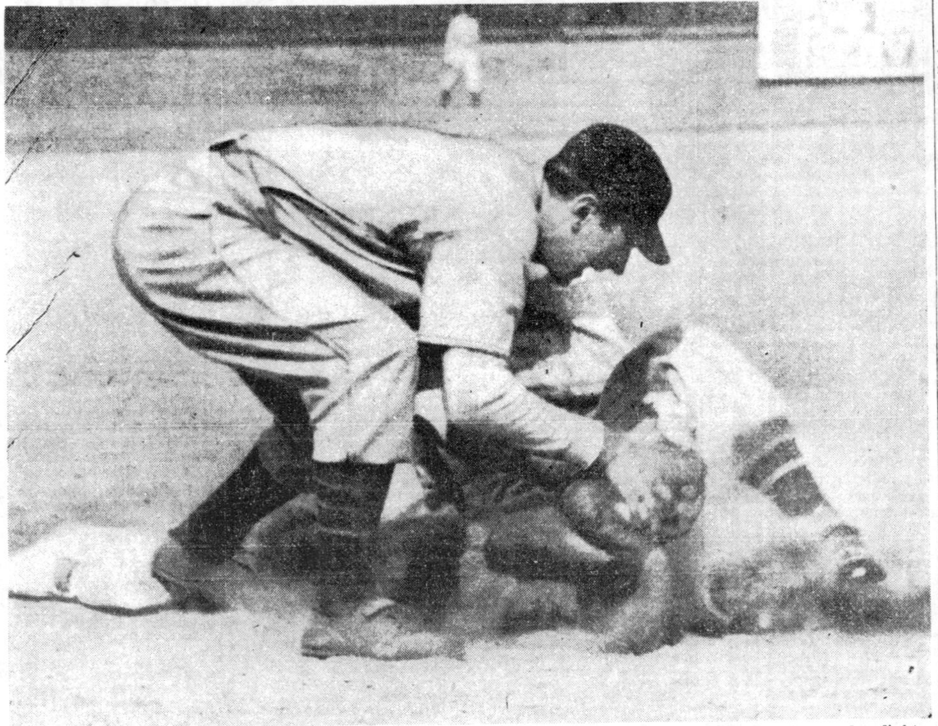

BOWLED HIM OVER A SECOND LATER—Storming into third base a split second after Danny Carnevale had taken the throw for a force play, Jack Redmond, Oriole catcher, crashed into the Buffalo infielder and bounced him three feet into the air, the latter dropping the ball as he hit the ground with a thud. The play, which occurred in the eighth inning of the first game yesterday at Oriole Park, almost caused a fight as Carnevale and Redmond exchanged words and the players of both clubs milled around. Previously, Redmond had "taken out" Jimmy Outlaw at second on a similar play. Anyhow, the Orioles captured a double-header, 12 to 6 and 12 to 4, to hod third place in the race. Picture copyright, 1940, by The Baltimore News-Post. All rights reserved.

Little Proves Right To Open Golf Title

By EARL HILLIGAN

CLEVELAND, June 10—(A. P.). There was little room today for questioning burly Lawson Little's rank as one of the great golfers of the day, Gene Sarazen's right to a place in the game's hall of fame, and the forty-fourth National Open championship's rating as the most dramatic and hectic in the event's history.

The thirty-year-old Little, professional at Bretton Woods, N. H., owned the Open crown by virtue of a 70-73 play-off victory yesterday over the doughty Sarazan at Canterbury Golf Club.

But back of Little's play-off victory lay a Saturday which will be long remembered. It was a day climaxed by Sarazen's amazing stretch finish for a deadlock at 287 over 72 holes as a twenty-three-year-old youth sat heartbroken in the clubhouse — himself possessor of a 287 score and a message from tournament officials that he had been disqualified for starting ahead of schedule.

The youth was Ed (Porky) Oliver of Hornell, N. Y. He had a fine one-under-par 71 on his final round, thrown out as he and five other overanxious competitors were disqualified.

Little meanwhile was battling his way gamely to a fourth-round 73, going one over par on the eighteenth hole to take what appeared to be a stranglehold on the championship. Then Sarazen, "the Knickerbocker Knight" whose plus fours have been a colorful part of golf during a great career which saw him first win the Open in 1922 and repeat as champion a decade later, started his remarkable rush.

Little had the upper hand in the play-off, however, and showed as much heart winning the crown as Sarazen had displayed in tying for the lead Saturday. Little went out in 34 and came home in 36 for a two-under-par 70 as Sarazen took a 37-36—73.

All-Star Classic Set For July 9

ST. LOUIS, June 10—(I. N. S.).—The All-Star baseball game between American and National League stars will be played July 9, beginning at 1.30 P. M. (C. S. T.), in St. Louis, it was announced today. If postponement, is necessary, it will be played at 9 A. M. the following day.

LOUIS IMPROVES

Joe Louis has whittled his golf score down to 77 from over 100 in the past year.

Reese, Watching Game, Nearly Hurt Again

CHICAGO, June 10—(A. P.).—Harold (Peewee) Reese, Brooklyn shortstop who was felled by a pitched ball June 1, planned to leave tonight to rejoin his teammates in Pittsburgh.

Reese has been in a hospital since he was struck on the head by a ball pitched by Jake Mooty, rookie pi•her of the Chicago Cubs. The twenty-year-old shortstop said he expected it would be a week or more before he would get into uniform.

He saw the Cubs trample the Boston Bees twice yesterday during which he almost was injured again. A foul drive from the bat of Dominic Dallessandro, Cub outfielder, struck his nurse on the arm. She was seated next to Reese in a third-base-line box.

Dempsey Coming Back?

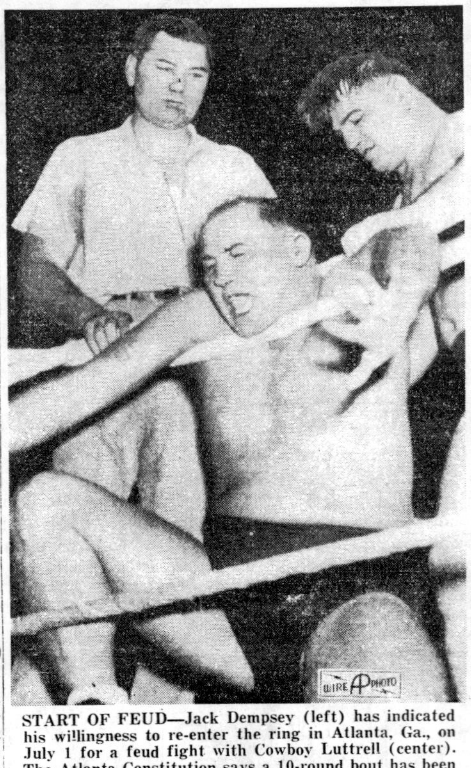

START OF FEUD—Jack Dempsey (left) has indicated his willingness to re-enter the ring in Atlanta, Ga., on July 1 for a feud fight with Cowboy Luttrell (center). The Atlanta Constitution says a 10-round bout has been arranged between the two. The feud started during a recent wrestling bout—when this picture was taken—after Dempsey questioned tactics Luttrell used on his opponent, Dorve Roche (right). Associated Press Wirephoto.

Diz Dean Wins First Sidearm Effort

By BOB McCALL

TULSA, June 10—(A. P.).—They gave old Diz an old-fashioned home-coming to the Texas League and he gave Tulsa fans a story-book finish. He scored the winning run.

The one-time fireballer coaxed his lame right arm with sidewise pitching yesterday, but he batted straightaway in the pinch to lick the Fort Worth Cats, 5 to 4.

DEAN SINGLES

Two Oilers were out and the score was tied when Jerome Herman singled in the ninth inning. Two successive errors moved him home and he won for the stomping, cheering crowd of about 7,500.

It was hot and sticky, the kind of weather Diz hopes will cure his wing and his major-league lapse. He sidearmed a full nine innings for the first time, allowing six hits, including two home runs.

"How does your arm feel?" was the post-game question.

"Pretty good," said the sweat-wet Dean. "It got a little tired, but it felt all right for six or seven innings."

His pitches weren't those of his heyday, but neither were they "nothing" balls. He showed more speed than had been expected, edged the corners inside and out and kept good control all the way. His only walk was intentional. He struck out four.

SIDEARM PITCHING

Diz indicated he thought the sidearm throwing would do, once he perfected it. This was only his second nine innings this season and his first 100 per cent. sidewinding.

"It throws you off balance," he said. "That's the reason I was 3-and-2 on so many. The other way you throw the ball more."

Blake Challenges Dudas, Cominsky

Bruce Alexander, local Negro boxer, who is now fighting in New York under the name of Al Blake, has issued a challenge to Steve Dudas and Pat Cominsky through his manager, Pete Jagadzinski. In his last start Blake stopped Tommy Phillips of Cleveland in two rounds on the Buddy Baer-Campolo card.

PACIFIC COAST LEAGUE

Los Angeles, 5-9; Sacramento, 3-10.
San Diego, 3-1; San Francisco, 2-2.
Oakland, 4-1; Seattle, 1-2.
Hollywood, 3-8; Portland, 2-2.

Birds' 'Big Three' In Hot Race

By HUGH TRADER, JR.

Strictly a "daytime" ball club, with a record of 26 won and 14 lost for a .650 percentage through the afternoon games (which means they've lost nine out of eleven games at night!) your Orioles are still snugly intrenched in the International League's first division after a recovery as complete as the slump into which they fell a week ago today.

Having lost five straight night games to Montreal and Buffalo, to start the experts wagging "I told you so!" our heroes regained their batting eyes to such an extent that they not only bagged three out of four over the week-end from Buffalo, climaxed by yesterday's double win, 12 to 6 and 12 to 4, but even little Skeeter Newsome swatted his first home run of the season and the tenth in his eleven-year baseball career.

While it was gratifying to M'sieur Tommy Thomas to see both Orlin Collier and Roy Bruner go the pitching distance yesterday, the victories were hauled in through the simple but elegant expedient of 22 base hits, including six home runs.

Four of these circuit clouts were drilled by Messrs. Red Howell and Nick Etten, each bopping a pair, and it is immediately noted that the Orioles' "Big Three"—Howell, Etten and Nagel—stepped up the pace to such a gait over the week-end that they're not only involved in a lively local fight for honors but also dominate the league.

DRIVES IN SEVEN RUNS

In the two games yesterday, Howell served notice that he's on the way back from his slump by whacking his ninth and tenth homers and driving in seven runs.

Etten, who has been hitting the ball hard right along, though he recently dropped to .280, forged ahead of 'em all yesterday and assumed command of the league's individual slugging race when he exploded homers Nos. 13 and 14 and chased five runs across the plate thereby.

Nagel, not so fortunate in the matter of base hits yesterday, nonetheless came through in the clutch in the second game with a 385-foot double while the sacks were loaded to drive in three runs.

It's a swell three-cornered race, apparently destined to wage warm all season, and here's how they compare:

	AB.	H.	2B.	3b.	HR.	RBI.	Pct.
Howell	189	67	10	1	10	41	.354
Etten	175	56	11	0	14	46	.320
Nagel	184	55	9	0	13	45	.299

REDMOND FEATURES

But that wasn't all the slugging. The Skeeter, having played a grand game at shortstop all through the home stand which concluded yesterday, finally got himself some base knocks, including his aforesaid homer, and Jack Redmond, who has taken over the No. 1 catching job, crashed his seventh round-tripper. Redmond is doing a splendid all-around job, and his 19 hits for the year have driven in 23 runs.

Indeed, Redmond supplied the fireworks yesterday as he spilled Danny Carnevale storming into third. The latter, blazing mad, began "popping off" and the players of both clubs milled around for "action." Nothing resulted, which would seem to Carnevale's advantage.

Still gallantly holding their third place spot in the race, despite their slump and the inconsistency of their pitchers, the Orioles move out tonight and into Rochester to open a five-day trip tomorrow against the loop-leading Red Wings. The series is all-important to the Birds, who'll open on the hill with Italo Chelini.

PRESS BOX PATTER—Only 164 homers were hit in Oriole Park all last year by both the Orioles and the opposition . . . This season, in just 30 games, exactly 105 clouts have been parked outside . . . The opposition hit 68 in 1939 and already has hit 54 in 1940, with less than half the campaign completed! . . . Nagel is in hot pursuit of Joe Hauser's strikeout record, having whiffed 41 times . . . On the other hand, Etten tops the club in walks, with 38, and in runs scored with 50 . . . Did you know that the Orioles top the league in stolen bases and are only a step behind the leaders with 48 d. p.'s?

YESTERDAY'S STARS

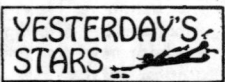

By Associated Press.

Roy Cullenbine, John Bernadino and Walt Judnich, Browns—A homer a niece by the first two gave the Brownies a nightcap victory while Judnich's homer won the opener from the Athletics.

Johnny Rigney, White Sox—Relieved Ted Lyons in ninth and allowed but two hits in three innings to beat Senators, 4-3, in 11 innings.

Babe Dahlgren, Joe DiMaggio and George Selkirk—Their homers accounted for all the Yank runs in 4-3 triumph over Cleveland.

Mace Brown, Pirates, and Hugh Mulcahy, Phils—Former's fine relief hurling gave Pirates nightcap while Mulcahy won for Phils in the first with seven-hit performance.

Frank Demaree, Giants — He drove in six runs as Giants copped two from St. Louis.

BRITAIN THROWS ALL RESOURCES INTO BATTLE

THE BALTIMORE NEWS-POST
AN INDEPENDENT NEWSPAPER
The Largest Daily Circulation in the Entire South
VOL. CXXXVII.—NO. 35
Entered as second-class matter at Baltimore Postoffice.
Copyright, 1940, by Hearst Consolidated Publications, Inc.
FRIDAY EVENING, JUNE 14, 1940
PRICE 3 CENTS
10

THE WEATHER

Mostly clear and slightly cooler with lowest temperature between 65 and 70 degrees. Saturday partly cloudy and slightly warmer. *Detailed Weather Report on Page 14*

MEAN TEMPERATURES YESTERDAY.

Baltimore	82	New York	80
Atlanta	79	Omaha	72
Boston	76	Portland, Maine	70
Chicago	67	Salt Lake City	78
Jacksonville	82	San Antonio	79
Los Angeles	68	Seattle	64
Miami	84	Tampa	82
New Orleans	74	Washington	82

IN THE NEWS

YOU may not approve of the American citizen who goes abroad to fight for some alien theory or some foreign land.

You might not have applauded the action of those misguided American youths who went to Spain to fight for Communism.

You might not have understood their amazing willingness to surrender their solid American advantages and opportunities for the unsound principles of Red radicalism.

But at least you realized that they had some commendable quality.

They were willing to make material sacrifices for their spiritual convictions.

Say what you would, and say it as sincerely and as severely as you please, yet there was in your heart some reserve of admiration.

These mistaken enthusiasts were yielding THEIR OWN LIVES in support of THEIR OWN IDEALS.

Gentle reader, you undoubtedly are a very true and loyal American.

You require from yourself the first and best of your devotion for your own dear country.

You measure others by their loyalty to their native land.

You set that high standard as the test of their patriotic merit and devotion.

But you certainly have respect for a man who is willing to give up his life for a cause—be it your cause or his cause—be it a righteous cause or even a mistaken cause.

Those Americans who wish to go to France to fight for the success of France have your respect and your honest admiration.

You may not wish your country to be involved in the unending wars of Europe, but if individual Americans, out of spiritual conviction, want to sacrifice their own lives for other ideals than ours, the act is heroic.

It compels our respect. It challenges our admiration.

But what do you think of the American who prospers in this land, and prospers from it, but owes no obligation to it or to another?

He does not want to go abroad to fight in foreign lands. He does not want to risk there or here his own thick hide.

He does not wish to make personal sacrifice of blood, or even of comfort.

Yet he is willing to send somebody else abroad to do the fighting—eager to entrust somone else with the duty of suffering and dying while he—tender heart and sympathetic soul—sits ensconced in his easy chair and reads the casualty lists in the newspapers.

We can all respect the views of a man who is willing to back them up with his life.

We will all go down to the ship and cheer the departure of the man who is willing to prove the sincerity of his sentiments by sacrifice.

But what can we say or think of the man who wants to send our children to be immolated as burnt offering on the fiery altars of war, while he reposes in security by his own fireside?

Must mothers feed their babes to Moloch to satisfy his safe sentiments?

Americans are inspired by ideals. They are not aroused by sordid and selfish advocacies. They are not led by laggards.

Senator Rush D. Holt (Democrat) of West Virginia, says of these vicarious heroes:

"If the danger is what they say, and the cause is what they preach, they should have the courage to offer THEIR lives."

Certainly it is no evidence of courage, or even of sincerity, to offer, no matter how liberally, the lives of others.

THE poll of Congress by the Hearst papers on the best coordinated plan for the defense of the United States has developed interesting suggestions.

The decision, however, will undoubtedly be made by the President.

Almost everything in Government is decided by the President nowadays.

To use preparedness phraseology, the President is the drill sergeant. The Congress is but the company of raw recruits going

Continued on Page 4, Column 1.

Makes Microbes Help Scientists Fight Diseases. The men who work magic in test tubes have just brought about a major miracle. Read this up-to-date science story in the American Weekly, the magazine distributed with next Sunday's Baltimore American.—Adv.

ARMY OF PARIS IN FIGHTING RETREAT

Weary Poilus Counter-Attack With Fury; Maginot Line Assault Repulsed

BERLIN, June 14—(A. P.).—The conquering German army marched into Paris today, jubilantly declared the French to be collapsing on the whole northern front, and loosed a frontal assault on France's Maginot Line from the region of the Saar.

Simultaneously, other German divisions moved from the rear against that mighty chain of fortresses—defended by more than a million Frenchmen—and appeared to be slowly turning it.

Montmedy, the line's northern anchor, fell to them and they also claimed to have stormed through the southern fringe of the Argonne Forest behind the defenses in that area.

The Germans were advancing on Verdun, a key northern fortification in the Maginot system.

PARIS TAKEN

In this fiercest of all offensives, the old French capital, undefended Paris—was taken without bombardment, and the Nazi high command announced:

"The third phase—pursuit of the enemy until final destruction—now has begun."

Hitler declared a three-day holiday. Bands played. Crowds cheered hoarsely in Berlin.

From the sea to Sedan, about 25 miles northwest of Montmedy, French resistance was declared to be crumbling.

With German troops marching in Paris for the first time since 1871, German authorities denied a report that U. S. Ambassador William C. Bullitt, who remained there until the end, was in the protective custody of the invaders.

PREDICT COLLAPSE

German authorities said exultantly that the fall of Paris meant the "beginning of the general collapse of France," and they described as "a cry of despair" the appeal for American aid made by Premier Paul Reynaud of France to President Roosevelt.

"The complete defeat of France is now only a question of time," the authoritative commentary service Dienst Aus Deutschland declared.

"With the loss of the capital, the heart of France has been struck. France has been stripped of the main part of its armament industries.

"Communications with England

Continued on Page 2, Column 1.

VERY LATEST NEWS

(Race Results From Howard Sports Daily, Inc.)

BROWN KNIGHT WINS SEVENTH AT DELAWARE

Sixth—Grey Wolf, $5.00, $3.50, $2.60; Stagefright, $5.00 $3.30; Gold Teddy, $3.40.

Seventh — Brown Knight, $7.00, $3.90, $3.20; Autumnquest, $5.50, $3.70; Royal Teddy, $4.80.

AT SUFFOLK DOWNS

Eighth—Sue Harpen, $445.20, $146.40, $61.00; Reminding, $33.60, $16.00; Pepper Patch, $7.20.

AT LINCOLN FIELDS

Sixth—Torch Gleam, $5.60, $3.40, $2.60; Chigre, $14.00, $6.20; Beau Do, $3.60.

AT CHARLES TOWN

Fifth — Autumn Echo, $5.40, $3.40, $2.60; Sundrops, $4.60, $3.20; Miss Poole, $5.80.

Sixth—Quick Vine, 1; Ravenhurst, 2; Royal Marriage, 3.

LATEST BASEBALL SCORES

(A) At Cleveland—Cleveland, 8; Philadelphia, 0; final.

(A) At Detroit—Detroit, 10; Washington, 1; end 6th.

BRITAIN THROWS ALL RESOURCES INTO NAZI BATTLE

LONDON, June 14—(A. P.).—Britain tonight opened full wide the war chest treasured against the now-abandoned conception of a "long war" and ordered the immediate wholesale purchase of every tool of battle available in America.

In the momentous decision that the tide must be turned in France within weeks at most, the British made clear they were going "all out" to obtain post-haste guns and ammunition, even of World War vintage, to supply Tommies streaming back into the continent on "return tickets" from the disaster of Flanders.

STAKE EVERYTHING

At the expense of sorely needed home defenses, the British coupled all their stored-up economic resources with manpower, staking everything on a fight in France far below the abandoned city of Paris.

The British decision is a sudden turn from the long war plan aimed at starving out Germany—as was done in 1918—and it comes in the face of Nazi claims that the British blockade of the seas has been broken by the Allied setbacks in Scandinavia, the low countries and Flanders.

Government forces disclosed that war funds allocated for years now are released for spending in weeks.

In effect it is an economic Blitzkrieg to meet the piled-up Nazi war stores and men pressing ever deeper into France and to offset, as best it can, the loss of 75 to 80 per cent. of France's steel producing plants, now in German-occupied territory.

STILL HOLD PLANTS

Most French ammunition plants, however, are in the south and thus still in Allied hands.

The Government now is more concerned with obtaining war materials already fabricated in the United States rather than in pressing for new manufactures.

Obsolete though they may be, the

Continued on Page 2, Column 3.

Two Defense Steps Told By Roosevelt

WASHINGTON, June 14—(I. N. S.).—Speedy passage of the bill setting up a home defense guard of 1,000,000 men was predicted today by Representative Anderson (Republican) of California, who disclosed that the War Department is studying the measure carefully.

WASHINGTON, June 14—(A.P.). President Roosevelt repeated today that all possible help was being extended to the Allies and pointed to Hitler's record in response to a report that the German Chancellor had said invasion of the Western Hemisphere was grotesque.

Mr. Roosevelt was told at a press conference that Hitler had called the possibility of German invasion

Continued on Page 2, Column 8.

LACROSSE LINE-UPS

	SOUTH		NORTH	
11	Kelly, Maryland	G	Turner, Princeton	1
15	Tolson, Johns Hopkins	P	Swift, Army	11
10	Mulitz, Maryland	C.P.	Lynn, Princeton	2
20	Shawn, Johns Hopkins	F.D.	Case, Dartmouth	17
14	J. Mueller, Maryland	S.D.	Potter, Williams	14
4	Brown, Duke	C	Naylor, Princeton	5
16	Donnelly, Swarthmore	S.A.	Buser, Penn State	10
13	Nevares, Maryland	F.A.	Ferris, Hobart	3
12	Thomas, Johns Hopkins	O.H.	Brennan, Cornell	12
1	Parkinson, Virginia	I.H.	Dell, Yale	9

Substitutes—South: 6, Litz, Loyola; 3, Enders, Johns Hopkins; 19, Passano, Johns Hopkins; 9, Wolfe, Swarthmore; 18, L. Mueller, Maryland; 5, Luce, Lehigh; 8, Cole, Maryland; 7, Bond, Baryland; 2, Finkel, North Carolina; 17, Walker, Loyola.

North: 4, Stewart, Princeton; 5, Naylor, Princeton; 6, Guigert, Union; 7, Brooks, Yale; 8, King, Princeton; 13, Rich, Syracuse; 15, Evans, Rutgers; 16, Gillespie, Syracuse; 18, Ritter, Penn State; 19, De John, Syracuse; 20, Dobbin, Hobart; 21, Fairlamb, Army.

Time of game, 8.30 P. M.

The Baltimore News-Post today is printed in

3 Sections

Be sure you get the complete newspaper.

'Americas To Americans' ---Hitler

By KARL H. VON WIEGAND

Chief Foreign Correspondent of the Hearst Newspapers and for 28 Years Outstanding American Political Observer in Europe and the Far East.

Copyright, 1940, by the Hearst Newspapers. Reproduction in Whole or in Part Forbidden

WITH THE GERMAN ARMIES NEARING PARIS, June 14.—**"The Americas to Americans, Europe to the Europeans."**

This reciprocal basic Monroe Doctrine, mutually observed, declared Adolf Hitler to me today, not only would insure peace for all times between the Old and the New Worlds, but would be a most ideal foundation for peace throughout the whole world.

In caustic language, with scorn and indignation, he denounced "the lies" that he has or ever had in "dream or thought" played with the faintest idea of interfering in the Western Hemisphere by only manner or means.

'STUPID, FANTASTIC'

He characterized America's fears of him or Germany as most flattering, but "childish and grotesque," and the whole idea of the possibility of the invasion of the United States from Europe by sea, air, or the "mythical 'Fifth Column'" as "stupid and fantastic."

With his great German war machine, whose amazing perfection of organization, strength, strategical and tactical leadership has startled the world, now on the edge of Paris, Hitler told me he had no intention of attacking the beautiful French capital if it "remains an open city like Brussels."

Vehemently, the Fuehrer denied he ever had or even now has as a

Continued on Page 22, Column 1.

CAIRO, June 14 – (I. N. S.) – Allied naval units have been searching the Eastern Mediterranean since the outbreak of the war with Italy but have yet to sight a Fascist warship at sea, a spokesman for the British naval forces declared today.

BERLIN, June 14 — (I. N. S.). — Both the German High Command and the Nazi Foreign Office tonight emphatically denied reports published in the United States that Ambassador William C. Bullitt has been taken into "protective custody" in Paris. "Nothing is known about Mr. Bullitt being taken into custody," authoritative spokesmen for both branches of the government told International News Service.

TOURS, France, June 14—(A. P.).—The main armies of France fell back tonight far below abandoned, German-invaded Paris in a fighting retreat that may be their last movement of the war.

Other forces far to the east were declared to have thrown back, with "tremenodus losses," a German head-on attack against the Maginot line.

All but broken under the mightiest assault ever thrown agains men, the Poilus who fought the main battle of France counter-attacked with a desperate fury as they retired under the Nazi pressure.

They did not even know whether their command could continue the struggle.

Paris, from which the Government long since had fled, was gone—occupied by the Germans and ringed by their armored units and infantrymen.

Tours, the new emergency seat of the ministers from which Premier Reynaud sent a "last appeal" to President Roosevelt last night for American aid, was being abandoned for yet another refuge—presumably the far southern seaport of Bordeaux.

Both naval and aerial attacks on Italy were announced. The high

TELL COUNTER ATTACKS

command said French warships fired on industrial establishments and a railway line along the Italian coast, while planes set fire to fuel reservoirs near Venice.

The night French communique said:

From the sea to the Argonne the

Continued on Page 2, Column 6.

Temperatures

12 Midn'ht	76	8 A. M.	78
1 A. M.	75	9 A. M.	80
2 A. M.	75	10 A. M.	81
3 A. M.	74	11 A. M.	81
4 A. M.	73	12 Noon	81
5 A. M.	73	1 A. M.	82
6 A. M.	76	2 P. M.	84
7 A. M.	77	3 P. M.	86

Delaware Results

FIRST RACE—Five furlongs. Off at 2.04½. Time 1.01 2-5.

Jerrisa, 108 (R. Wholey)	$48.30	$14.10	$6.30
Cheetah, 115 (R. Donoso)		4.60	2.90
Sunington, 114 (J. Wagner)			3.10

Also Ran—Bright Harvest, On The Beam, First Course, Nutmeg Lass, Druidesse II., Meer Khan, Merwick, Kelly's Lad and Solo Dash.

SECOND RACE—Six furlongs. Off at 2.37½. Time, 1.13 4-5.

My Lawyer, 119 (E. Decamillas).)	$20.40	$9.20	$4.90
Phara Belle, 107 (J. Boyle)		5.30	3.00

Continued on Page 32, Column 3.

THE BALTIMORE NEWS-POST, FRIDAY, JUNE 14, 1940

Raisin Custard Pie As Alkaline

Raisin pie has been given the distinction of being the single example of an alkaline pie. It means the enjoyment of a well-beloved dessert by many who avoid other pastry which is definitely of an acid-forming nature.

RAISIN CORNSTARCH-CUSTARD PIE
- 1 cup seedless raisins.
- 2½ cups milk.
- 4 tablespoons cornstarch.
- ½ cup granulated sugar.
- ¼ teaspoon salt.
- 1 teaspoon vanilla extract.
- 1 teaspoon lemon extract.
- 3 eggs.
- Baked pastry shell (9-inch, deep type).
- Meringue (basis 3 egg whites).

Rinse and drain raisins. Combine with 2 cups milk in top of double boiler. Heat to just below boiling point. Combine remaining ½ cup milk, cornstarch, sugar, salt, flavoring and egg yolks, and beat until well blended. Stir into hot milk and raisins. Cook and stir until thick. Pour into pastry shell. Cover with meringue and bake in a slow oven (300 to 325 degrees F.) 25 to 30 minutes. Cool before cutting. Serves 6 to 8.

Chopped Nuts On Loaf Cake

Warm weather calls for dishes made in a jiffy so the next time you prepare a sheet or loaf cake sprinkle chopped nuts and shaved sweet chocolate over the top after the batter has been poured into the baking pan. When baked the cake comes out already frosted.

WAFFLE TOPPER

Strained honey and orange juice, in equal portions, makes a grand topper for hot waffles or pancakes. Mix it up in a pitcher and pour as needed.

Grandmother's Cook Book

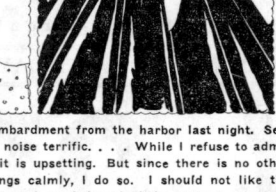

CARAMEL CAKE
- 2 cups sugar
- 1 cup milk and cream
- 3 eggs
- 1 cup butter
- 2 teasps. baking powder
- 3½ cups flour
- 1 tbsp. molasses
- 1 teasp. vanilla

Mix ingredients in order named and stir over hot fire until its consistency is like molasses. Then put in saucepan in hot water until cake is ready to be iced.

Cream butter and sugar. Beat in yolks, then flour, mild, and last the egg white. Beats to a froth. Bake in cake tins in a quick oven (450 degrees).

Ingredients for icing:
- 3 tblsps. butter
- 3 tblsps. milk
- 3 tbsps. water
- 1 lb. brown sugar

NOVEL CONTAINER

A scooped out cabbage makes a novel container for crisp vegetable salad. Carefully remove the center of a firm young cabbage. Chop the removed cabbage and mix in some seasonings and salad dressing. Roughly refill the cabbage with the salad. Sprinkle the top with chopped parsley and grated raw carrots.

"... A frightful bombardment from the harbor last night. Several houses afire and the noise terrific.... While I refuse to admit fear, I will confess that it is upsetting. But since there is no other course but to accept things calmly, I do so. I should not like the children to feel alarmed and so I heard their prayers as usual and told them a story so that they would see that I regarded the noise and fire as a matter of course...."—From Caroline Jenkins' Diary, June 12, 1864. (Copyright, N. J. Bond.)

Vinegar Water Cleans Sprouts

Soak cauliflower, whole lettuce heads, artichokes and brussels sprouts for 30 minutes in 4 cups of water with a tablespoon of vinegar in it to remove dirt and draw out insects. Rinse the vegetables in cold water and cook as desired. Use warm water to loosen the dirt and sand from spinach, broccoli and asparagus. Then rinse thoroughly in cold water to freshen.

For your eyes' sake, remember ... only an eye physician can both treat and examine eyes. See Dr. Barenburg now! Free consultation... liberal terms.

Dr. Barenburg (M. D.)
★ TWO EYE CLINICS
Park & Fayette • 3316 Eastern Ave.
Eastern Ave. Clinic Open Nights 'til 9

BUY ON CREDIT ★ THE AMERICAN WAY

ROSENTHAL'S
EUTAW AT SARATOGA ★ Furniture—312 N. EUTAW
BALTIMORE'S BIG DOWNTOWN CREDIT DEPARTMENT STORE

DRESSES To Give You "Man-Power"
$3.99
50c A WEEK BUYS THEM

STYLES HAND-PICKED TO APPEAL TO YOUR MAN—AND MAKE YOU MORE APPEALING! CHOOSE YOUR WARDROBE HERE—AND GET YOUR MAN!

SIZES 9 TO 17, 12 TO 20, 38 TO 52, 18½ TO 24½

MERIT FOOD STORES
SPECIALS FOR FRIDAY & SATURDAY, JUNE 14th & 15th

Tonight's the Night!
TO HAVE OLD-FASHIONED STRAWBERRY SHORTCAKE
Made With the New
BISQUICK large size **29c**

SOFTASILK WINS AGAIN!
See Our Display for MICROSCOPE PROOF!
44-Oz. Pkg.
SOFTASILK CAKE FLOUR 25c

NATIONAL BISCUIT CO.
Old-Fashion lb. **17c**
Assortment
RITZ ½-lb pkg. **14c**

TORSCH'S
Crushed Corn 2 cans 23c
Shoe Peg Corn 2 cans 25c
Fresh Lima Beans can 10c

McCORMICK'S
TEA HOUSE TEA full pound **79c**
Individual Tea Bags... 25 for 23c

BIG CASH PRIZES
LB. CAN **18c**
CRISCO 3-LB. CAN **50c**
FREE RECIPE

BRILLO CLEANS ALUMINUM QUICKLY 2 EASY WAYS
CLEANSER PADS & SOAP SEPARATE 5 **15c** or SOAP PADS SOAP-FILLED PADS 5 2 pkgs. **15c**

OAKITE 2 pkgs. **21c**
OLD DUTCH CLEANSER 2 for **15c**

A GOOD SOAP
OCTAGON SOAP 4 bars **14c**
Save Octagon Coupons for Free Gifts

OCTAGON Toilet Soap 3 FOR **13c**
OCTAGON Granulated LARGE SIZE PKG. **20c**

PURE IVORY SOAP FLAKES
IVORY FLAKES lge. pkg. **21c** med. pkg. 2 for **19c**
High-Test **OXYDOL** med. pkg. 2 for **19c** lge. pkg. **20c**

SweetHeart TOILET SOAP
"THE SOAP THAT AGREES WITH YOUR SKIN"
An extra bar for 1c with purchase of 3 bars **18c**

FREE! SILVER PLATED SPOON WITH PURCHASE OF **KIRKMAN'S** GRANULATED SOAP pkg. 20c
KIRKMAN'S BORAX SOAP 4 bars 14c
Valuable Premium Coupons On All Kirkman's

FRUIT COCKTAIL 2 tall cans **25c**
BARTLETT PEARS 2 tall cans **25c**

DAZZLE You will recognize the Label as an old friend with a New Name.
Pints... **10c** Quarts... **15c**

DETHOL ½ pint **23c** pint **39c**

KAYS HELP YOU REMEMBER DAD
FATHER'S DAY June 16th

KAY'S COAST TO COAST

Kay's help you by offering a complete display of fine gifts...Kay's also help by offering easy credit terms

Use Your Credit

REMINGTON DUAL SHAVER
Shave in 90 seconds with this dual head shaver.
$15.75
50c A WEEK

Dad will appreciate this—
NAME KEY CHAIN $1.50
Three initials or name linked into this ruggedly good-looking chain gift. A personalized gift that is sure to please Dad.
Additional letters 25c each
OPEN AN ACCOUNT

Man's Swank Set
Massively designed in the new trend
$2.50
50c A WEEK

Parker Deluxe PEN SET
The "Parkette"—a smart, practical gift.
$2.95
50c A WEEK

Ronson Lighter
Engraved chrome case with diamond shaped panel for initials.
$3.75
50c A WEEK

Onyx Initial Ring
10K natural gold. Choice of initial settings.
$8.95
50c A WEEK

YOUR PROMISE TO PAY IS GOOD WITH KAY

26th YEAR OF SERVICE TO AMERICA
KAY KAY JEWELRY CO.
7 W. Lexington St.
3420 Eastern Ave.

No Charge for EASY CREDIT

BUY ON CREDIT ★ THE AMERICAN WAY

ROSENTHAL'S
EUTAW AT SARATOGA ★ Furniture—312 N. EUTAW
BALTIMORE'S BIG DOWNTOWN CREDIT DEPARTMENT STORE

FATHER'S DAY Sunday, June 16th

"Baby Snooks" SAYS:
"I'M ASHAMED HOW BAD I'VE BEEN TO MY DADDY—SO I'M GIVING HIM SOMP'N EXTRA-SPECIAL THIS DADDY'S DAY!"

Follow "Snooks's" suggestion, and give Dad something really swell from Rosenthal's, something that will put a smile on his face, a twinkle in his eye?

You'll find these "extra-special" things at Rosenthal's at "extra-special" prices! They're hand-picked by our own staff, fellows who know what men like!

50c a Week Pays the Bill AT ROSENTHAL'S
"Buy on Credit—The American Way"

★ Hear Snooks and Daddy on "Good News of 1940," Thursday, WFBR.

MAKE DAD GLAD--FATHER'S DAY, JUNE 16th

SPORT ENSEMBLES
He'll wear this breezy outfit all summer for sports and lounging, and he'll thank you every time he slips into it.
1.98

NEW STYLED SHIRTS
Fashion decrees the wide-spread collar which resists wrinkles, looks neater on sultry summer days.
1.55

B.V.D. SHIRTS, SHORTS
What Dad needs most for summer, a new supply of cool underwear. A practical gift for proud Dads!
35c 3 for $1

COCONUT STRAWS
A sporty straw to make Dad young again and a gift of real comfort and style.
1.95

GAY SPLASH TIES
Cheerful, refreshing summer shades in hand-tailored silk and novelty ties.
55c 2 for $1

Norwegian Moccasins
These smart moccasins will make Dad happy every time he wears them.
1.95

"Charge It" AT ROSENTHAL'S

Light From Star Gets Bette Davis Picture Under Way

By NORMAN CLARK

THE THINGS these Hollywood publicity men think up!

Not a mere President, Governor or Mayor pressed a button to start things a-going at the premiere in Hollywood of Bette Davis' new picture, "All This and Heaven, Too."

No, sirree!

The projection machine that sent the images flashing to the screen of the Cathay Circle Theatre was started by Pollux. Who is Pollux? Well, if you are not an astronomer, you might be forgiven for asking that question. Pollux is a star, dearly beloved, that twinkles far away in the distant skies.

It is Miss Davis' guiding star, we are informed. Anyhow, the light from Pollux, which takes 31 years to reach the earth, furnished the impulse which set off a series of photo-electric cell rays harnessed to an electric circuit.

Miss Davis simply pressed a button, Pollux got 31 years of light to impulsing, so to speak, and "All This and Heaven, Too" was under way.

Arrangements for the scientific inauguration of the picture's run at the Carthay were completed with Dr. Dinsmore Alter, head of the Cathay Park Observatory. The Pollux rays which reached Hollywood in time for the premiere started from the sky at the hour Miss Davis was born 31 years ago.

What? Well, it's a change from news, anyway.

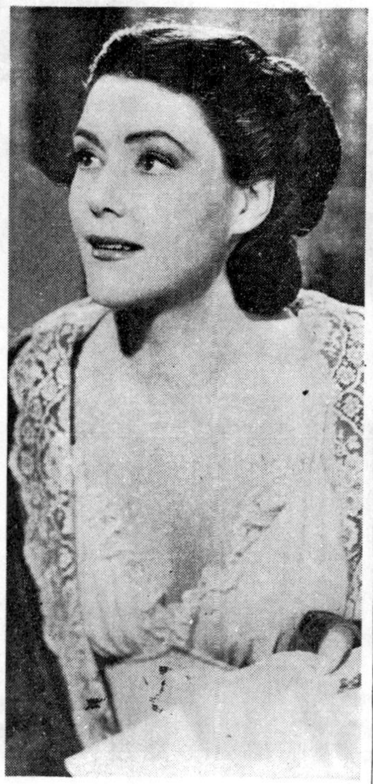

BARBARA O'NEIL

Speaking of "All This and Heaven, Too," one of the principals is about to be married. She is Barbara O'Neil, who plays the role of the Duchess de Praslin. Her husband-to-be is known to quite a few Baltimoreans. He is Joshua Lockwood Logan, Jr., and he was quite active with the University Players at the Maryland Theatre a few years ago. Mr. Logan is now a successful director of stage plays.

Fred Niblo, once a famous Hollywood movie director, has resumed active work in motion pictures as an actor. Today he is portraying Jackie Cooper's father in Paramount's "The Aldrich Family in Life With Henry," which stars Cooper.

And therein lies a story.

For Mrs. Fred Niblo (Enid Bennett) portrayed Cooper's mother in "Skippy," Jackie's first big film success, in 1932.

And Fred Niblo directed "Donovan's Boy," one of Cooper's best pictures.

"And now I'm portraying Jackie's father," comments Niblo. "Given enough time, I'm wondering what next the Niblo's will have to do with Jackie."

Behind Scenes In Hollywood Studios

By HARRISON CARROLL
King Features Syndicate Writer.

HOLLYWOOD, June 14.—Nobody expects movie heavies to be that way off screen, but Hollywood is amused at the latest exploit of Albert Dekker. The actor, who played a tough guy in "Strange Cargo" and who repeats in "Rangers of Fortune," has just invented, of all things, a new kind of baby's bed.

With a two-and-one-half-year-old daughter and with another youngster expected soon, Dekker decided that something ought to be done about children's beds which are too high for the convenience of mothers and too wide to be moved through many doors.

So Dekker has up and designed a bed that will correct both these faults. He's willing to let any furniture company use the plans free.

There was much snickering at Chasen's the other night over the discomfiture of Peter Lorre. Peter has been trimming everybody at table tennis and has been getting pretty chesty about it. So the gang imported a Hungarian champion and matched him against Lorre without warning the star what he was up against.

Peter was trimmed to a fare-you-well. In fact, the champ finally wound up playing the star while sitting in a chair.

The Joshua Logan, Jr., who marries Barbara O'Neil soon, is Jimmie Stewart's old pal. They had bachelor quarters together in Hollywood.

Hear from Camerman Hal Mohr that James Cruze has been ill for two months but has made use of the time to write a novel called "Land of the Golden Apples." The scene is New York and Hollywood.

Paul Whiteman certainly crossed up the plans of his pals. They had a 50-piece band to greet the orchestra leader at the airport. But when the plane came in there was no Whiteman.

Without telling anybody, he had stopped off in Davenport, Iowa, to put a wreath on the grave of Dix Biedendeck, who used to be one of the greatest of trumpet players.

As you probably know, Whiteman's trip to Hollywood is to do a stint in M-G-M's "Strike Up the Band."

Strange guy, George Raft. He has a big house but never entertains, a fancy bar but never drinks, a swimming pool but never swims.

There are pictures of Norma Shearer and her children in almost every room in the house.

Sonja Henie is off for a month's trip to Chicago and New York. Her mother goes along and probably Millionaire Topping, who still refuses to take no for an answer. Report is that the Norwegian star will conclude arrangements for another skating tour.

Bette Davis, Boyer To Co-Star Again In Film, 'The Gambler'

By HARRIET PARSONS
International News Service.

HOLLYWOOD, June 14.—Warners must be completely sold on the combination of Bette Davis and Charles Boyer. Without even waiting to see how the public takes to the team in "All This And Heaven, Too," the studio is going ahead with plans to co-star them again in Dostoevsky's famed "The Gambler" Milton Krims is making the adaptation and Anatole Litvak will again direct Bette and Charles. There'll be a fat part for Albert Basserman as the old Russian general. Background of the story is Paris and a funny twist is the fact that Boyer plays a tutor. Taking over the school books from Bette, who is a governess in "Ataht."

Boyer has a commitment to fill at Paramount before he reports at Warners for "The Gambler," which probably means that Bette will do "Calamity Jane" first. And by the way, doesn't this plan to reunite Bette and Charles seem to give the lie to those rumors about icicles on the "Ataht" set?

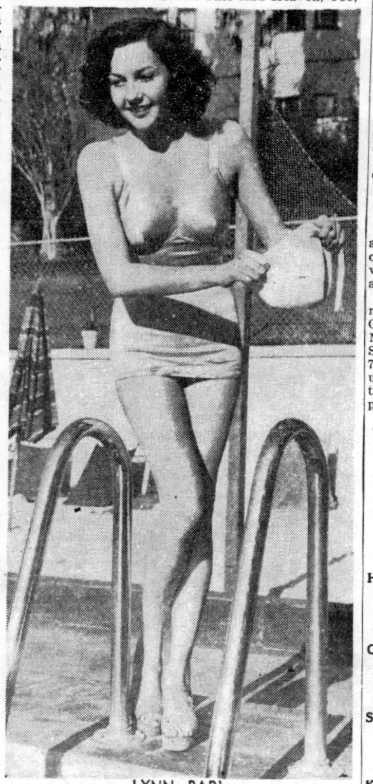

LYNN BARI

Lynn Bari, who's been on loan-out to Edward Small for "Kit Carson" returns to the home lot to play the lead in "Charter Pilot," an original by Lester Ciffren It's about a romantic flyer who ferries matrimonial-minded couples to and from an elopement center, probably Yuma, Ariz. Picture goes into production at Twentieth Century-Fox around July 15. Lynn's idol, House Peters, by Universal, the studio which first starred her dad. She goes into "Junior G-Men." Roland Drew getting a repeat bid from Paramount. They liked him in "Mystery Sea Raider," so he'll have a role in Cliff Reid's 'Wild Cat Bus."

Snapshots of Hollywood Collected at Random: The whole town is primping and preparing to preen itself at the premiere this evening of "All This and Heaven Too." Bette just back from location at Cayenta, Ariz., where the Navajo Indians made her a princess and tagged her "Shining Star." You don't suppose studio praisers helped them think up that moniker, do you? Anyway, we hope it's propetic for Lynn and that she becomes a star even before she becomes a mama, which will bein about seven months.

PRUNE HITLER 'HEILS'

BERLIN, June 14—(A. P.).—Germans have cut the official greeting, "Heil Hitler," down to its barest essentials. A few still say both words strongly. Others have trimmed it simply to "Hitler." But the bulk of casual greetings are simply: " 'tler."

Milton Berle's Revue At Hipp

The headliner, beginning today, at the Hippodrome Theatre is Milton Berle, comedy star of stage, screen and radio.

Berle is presenting his Broadway "Laff" Revue. Vivacious Lillian Carmen clowns with the star, then puts over a group of songs which were the vogue some time ago, and are coming back with favor.

Another highlight of the program is the Stuart Morgan dancers, an adagio quartet. The Four Step Brothers are a group of sepia steppers. Mrs. Sara Berle, Milton's mother, makes her first professional stage appearance in a comedy assignment.

'NEWS OF DAY' ON SCREEN AT TIMES

"News of the Day" current film at the Time Theatre, bring scenes of Italy's entry into Europe's total war. News from other war fronts also is pictured.

Other topics: Fifty Navy planes released to Allies . . National Guard gets new armored cars . . . Midshipmen off on Navy cruise . . . Steamship Roosevelt arrives with 723 refugees . . . General Pershing urges aid to Allies . . Lawson Little wins National Open golf championship.

MOVIE CLOCK

FEATURE PHOTOPLAYS

in Baltimore's leading picture theatres today and their starting times are as follows:

HIPPODROME . . .
"THE SAINT TAKES OVER"
11.30 A. M., 2.10, 4.50, 7.30, 10.15 P. M.

CENTURY . . .
"MORTAL STORM"
10.30 A. M., 12 40, 2.55, 5.15, 7.30, 9.45 P. M.

STANLEY . . .
"TORRID ZONE"
10.45 A. M., 12.55, 3.10, 5.24, 7.35, 9.50 P. M.

KEITHS . . .
"SAFARI"
10.01 A. M., 12.02, 2.04, 4.05, 6.07, 8.08, 10.10 P. M.

NEW . . .
"FOUR SONS"
10 A. M., 12, 2, 4, 6, 8, 10 P. M.

LITTLE . . .
"PRISONER OF ZENDA"
11 A. M., 12.45, 2.35, 4.25, 6.10, 8.11, 9.45 P. M.

TIMES . . .
"DARK VICTORY"
2.19, 4.57, 7.35, 10.13 P. M.

PARKWAY . . .
"WATERLOO BRIDGE"
12.40, 2.50, 5.05, 7.20, 9.35 P. M.

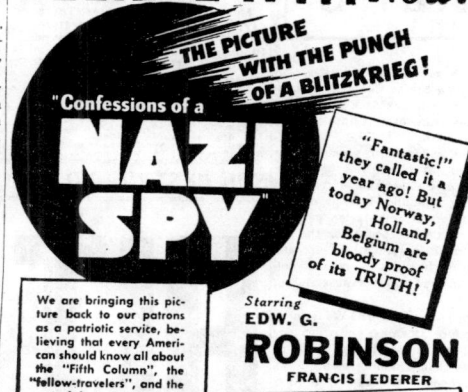

WILL AMERICA BELIEVE IT . . . Now!
THE PICTURE WITH THE PUNCH OF A BLITZKRIEG!
"Confessions of a NAZI SPY"
"Fantastic!" they called it a year ago! But today Norway, Holland, Belgium are bloody proof of its TRUTH!
We are bringing this picture back to our patrons as a patriotic service, believing that every American should know all about the "Fifth Column", the "fellow-travelers", and the rest of the traitorous crew!
The Management
Starring EDW. G. ROBINSON
FRANCIS LEDERER
LAST DAY "TORRID ZONE"
WARNER BROS. STANLEY • TOMORROW

KEITHS
Now Playing!
A thrilling love story told against the flaming background of men's lust wilderness . . . the roaring depths of the African jungle!
DOUGLAS FAIRBANKS, JR.
MADELEINE CARROLL
SAFARI
25¢ TO 12:30
12:30 TO 6-25&35
NIGHTS .40
SUN. MATS. .35
CHILDREN .15
A Paramount Picture with
TULLIO CARMINATI
MURIEL ANGELUS
LYNNE OVERMAN
BILLY GILBERT
Directed by Edward H. Griffith

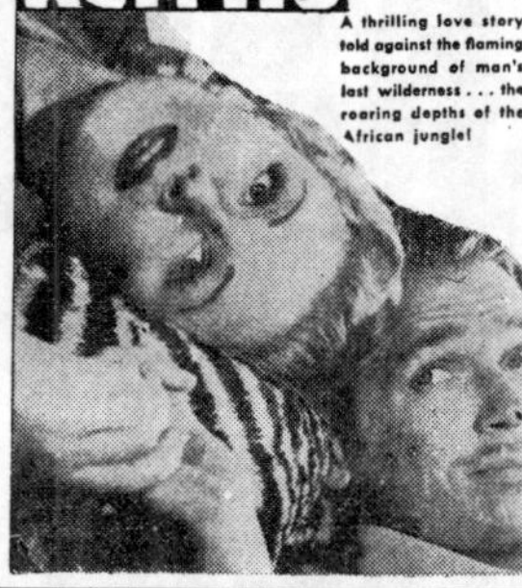

HOWARD and FRANKLIN LITTLE • AIR CONDITIONED
Starts Tomorrow
Old Time Movie Week!
The 1923 Sensation...
THE COVERED WAGON
also... THE RACE for LIFE with MABEL NORMAND MACK SENNETT BARNEY OLDFIELD The KEYSTONE COPS
and NEWSREEL of GREAT EVENTS from 1895... including FASHIONS of 1900....
NEW SUMMER PRICES
25c TO 6 P. M. 40c EVERY NIGHT
Last Day: "Prisoner of Zenda"

"It is one of the most sensitive and haunting pictures of the year."
—N. Y. TIMES.
BETTE DAVIS
"DARK VICTORY"
Arrived Today! Complete Show
LATEST NEWSREELS
Also: "WHILE AMERICA SLEEPS"
TIMES
Expose! Fifth Column in U. S. A.

RIVOLI
LON CHANEY, JR.
"ONE MILLION, B. C."

OPEN AIR THEATRE
GOV. RITCHIE HIGHWAY 3 MI. SOUTH OF BALTIMORE
NIGHTLY CONTINUOUS 8 TO 12
2 FEATURES 2
J. Stewart M. Dietrich in 'Destry Rides Again'
PLUS
Ralph Bellamy Ann Dvorak in "BLIND ALLEY"
Children Cars FREE ADULTS 30¢
SIT IN YOUR CAR

The Voice Of Broadway

By Dorothy Kilgallen

Gossip in Gotham

NORMA TALMADGE, the ex-Mrs. George Jessel, will waltz down the aisle any day now with her long-time beau, a doctor—if she hasn't secretly, already! . . . The Arthur Teachers (he's the cinema Jeeves) are knitting tiny garments . . . Thomas E. Dewey's next big clean-up campaign will be directed against a New Jersey gang reported to be collecting a half million dollars a month in New York, via the money-lending racket. The leader is a very dangerous fellow . . . The Sam Levene-Elspeth Eric romance, backstage at "Margin for Error" all season, has frost on it now . . Grace Poggi, once Joe Schenck's dream girl, has secretly married her dancing partner, Igor . . . The Duke of Windsor is due for a new set of headlines—biggest he's ever had . . . Watch for two impending Hollywood divorces—both the husbands are movie executives, both the wives are actresses recently on Broadway.

LEILA GAYNES, of the Club 18 floor show, was awarded $11,000 for injuries she received in an accident last year . . . Leon Janney, the "juvenile" star, and Wilma Frances, his bride, have parted—but she won't go to Reno while he's enacting the part of a 17-year-old boy on a radio show, because what would the sponsors say to their 'adolescent' actor getting his second divorce?

Bill Grady, the casting director, is out at M-G-M . . . What's this feud between Barbara Hutton and Liz Whitney? It's keeping the Hollywood telephone wires humming with chatter . . . Vic Mature, the Hollywood beau, and Hal Roach's daughter, Margaret, are yum, yum.

Felix Knight, the singer, and Tommy Riggs, the radio star, both shed their tonsils this week . . . George Raft has Norma's permission to fly to New York this week-end for a fortnight's vacation.

Gold Stars

TO Charles Boyer and Bette Davis, and the best acting of the year, in "All This and Heaven Too' . . . Erskine Hawkins' Bluebird platter of "Midnight Stroll" —in a class with "Tuxedo Junction" . . . The Cook and Brown team in the new Kit Kat show—very funny.

Raye and Naldi's entrancing dancing at Ben Mardin's Riviera . . . Jerry Livingston's smooth band, now that he's revamped the style . . . The gay atmosphere of the Brevoort sidewalk cafe—like Paris, 1939 . . . Tony Martin singing, "Only Fools Fall In Love" at the Versailles, lighting torches all around the room.

Petrita's hot rumba rhythms at Colbert's . . Loretta Young's clever nonsense in Columbia's "The Doctor Takes a Wife."

Action Shots

JOAN CRAWFORD, in her Summer furs, pausing under the archway to the main room at Monte Carlo—glamor on wheels . . . Major Bowes ordering Gai Choy Gong—what's that, Maje? from a waiter at the Beachcomber—Ilka Chase fluttering inch-long eyelashes at her companion in the Waldorf lobby.

George S. Kaufman and Bob Benchley, of the wit department chuckling at Kitty Carlisle's quips in the tavern. They should know . . . Hannah Williams, the ex-Mrs. Champion, sparring at Goodwin's Gym.

Luis Beebe, whose passion is fashion, plucking at his sombre cravat in the lobby of the Madison . . . Eugenie Leontovich making her celery crackle at Theodore's . . . Tallulah Bankhead mooning over a portrait of the Giants baseball team in a Fifth avenue sports shop window.

Local Items

ONLY thing holding up the Frances Farmer-Leif Erickson divorce is the property and money settlement. Her demands are too high . . . La Conga is dickering with Dolores Del Rio to make her night club debut on Broadway this Fall.

STARTS TODAY
HIPPODROME
Back Again BY POPULAR DEMAND!
Baltimore's Favorite Comedian!
WITH A SHOW THAT'S 10 TIMES FUNNIER THAN EVER!
Hilarious Comedy STAR of STAGE, SCREEN & RADIO!
In Person!
MILTON BERLE
and his ALL NEW Broadway "LAFF" REVUE
WITH LILLIAN CARMEN
The Lovely Singing Star of Stage and Radio
STUART MORGAN DANCERS ● THE 4 STEP BROTHERS
FIRST TIME ON ANY STAGE
Extra Added! Mrs. SARA BERLE MILTON'S FAMOUS MOTHER
Extra! THE MOST IMPORTANT ISSUE THIS YEAR! THE NEW MARCH OF TIME SHOWS The U. S. NAVY—1940 See The Navy's Role in America's New Plans For Our National Defense!
FICTION'S MIGHTY MAN OF MYSTERY..
THE NEWEST AND BEST OF ALL THE SAINT STORIES
THE SAINT TAKES OVER
GEORGE SANDERS
WENDY BARRIE

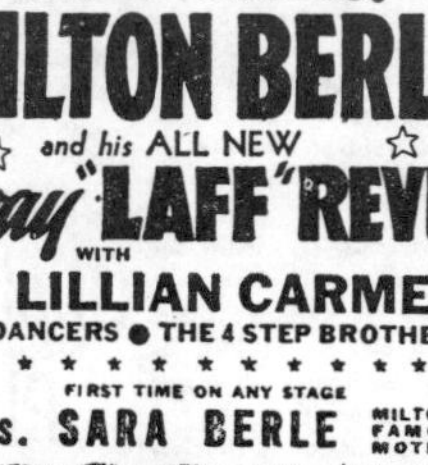

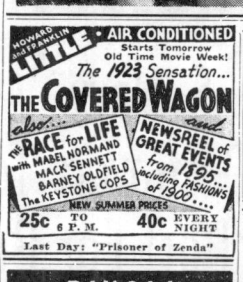

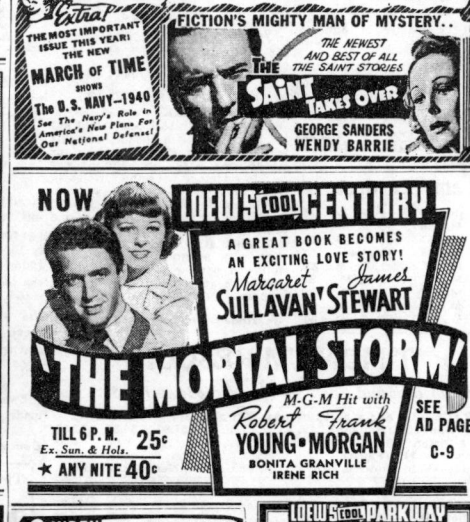

Announcement Extraordinaire
REGARDING AN EXTRAORDINARY PICTURE!
The manner in which audiences receive "4 SONS" is something never before witnessed in the presentation of any film. The force of its timely drama affects men and women alike! Particularly the women—it's a picture they'll virtually rush their men to see!
STARTS TOMORROW NEW THEATRE
FOUR SONS
Don Ameche • Eugenie Leontovich
Mary Beth Hughes • Alan Curtis
George Ernest • Robert Lowery
Lionel Royce • Sig Rumann
CENTRE THEATRE Today and Tomorrow ★ Sidney Toler Majorie Weaver in "Charlie Chan's Murder Cruise" ★

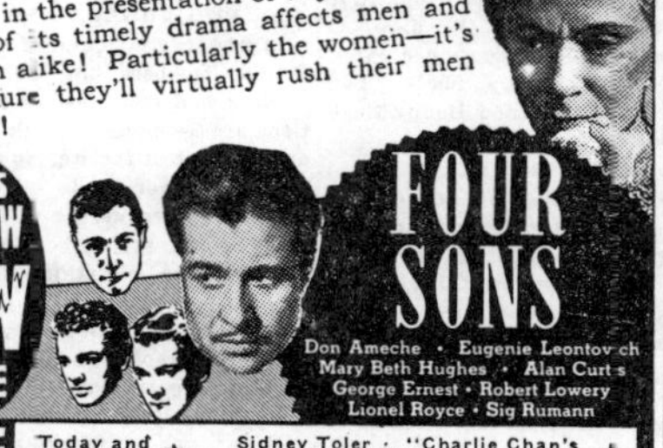

NOW
LOEW'S COOL CENTURY
A GREAT BOOK BECOMES AN EXCITING LOVE STORY!
Margaret SULLAVAN James STEWART
'THE MORTAL STORM'
M-G-M Hit with Robert YOUNG • Frank MORGAN
BONITA GRANVILLE
IRENE RICH
TILL 6 P. M. 25c Ex. Sun. & Hols.
★ ANY NITE 40c
SEE AD PAGE C-9

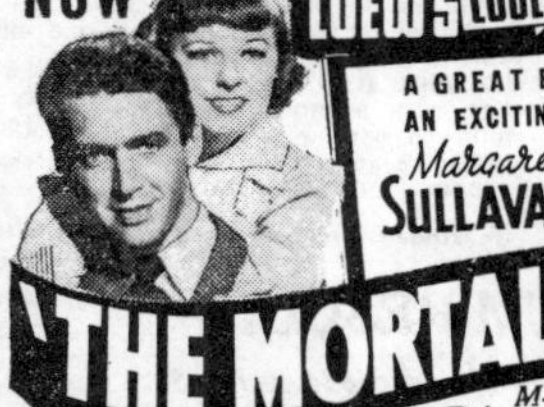

COOL • LEXWAY • 15¢ to 6 P.M.
TODAY AND TOMORROW
GINGER ROGERS—JOEL McCREA
"PRIMROSE PATH"
LATEST NEWSREELS DAILY

MONROE 1924-26 W. Pratt St. (Near Monroe)
Charles BOYER Jean ARTHUR
"History Is Made At Night"

LINDEN Geo. Raft—Joan Bennett
"HOUSE ACROSS THE BAY"

LOEW'S COOL PARKWAY
VIVIEN LEIGH • ROBT. TAYLOR
"WATERLOO BRIDGE"

Today's Movie Calendar

Theatres advertised in this column belong to the Motion Picture Theatre Owners of Maryland.

Alpha Catonsville
Jack Benny in
"BUCK BENNY RIDES AGAIN"
Comedy.

Ambassador 4604 Liberty Heights
Anna Neagle in
"IRENE"
"Tomorrow's Stars."

Apollo 1500 Harford Ave.
Wallace Beery in
"20-MULE TEAM"
"Big Premiere."

Arcade Harford Rd. & Hamilton Ave.
Wallace Beery in
"20-MULE TEAM"
"Big Premiere."

Astor Poplar Grove at Edmondson
Anna Neagle in
"IRENE"
"Home on the Range."

Aurora 7 East North Ave.
Anna Neagle in
"IRENE"
News.

Avalon 4300 Park Heights Ave.
Jack Benny in
"BUCK BENNY RIDES AGAIN"
Our Gang Comedy.

Avenue Milton Ave. & Hoffman St.
Mickey Rooney in
"YOUNG TOM EDISON"
Color Cartoon

Avon 3019 Hamilton Ave.
Carole Landis in
"ONE MILLION B. C."
"Tomorrow's Stars."

Belnord 2700 Philadelphia Ave.
Wallace Beery in
"20-MULE TEAM"
'Slightly at Sea."

Boulevard 33rd at Greenmount
Anna Neagle in
"IRENE"
"Rainy Day."

Bridge Edmondson Ave. & Pulaski St.
Russell Hayden in
"LIGHT OF WESTERN STARS"
Comedy.

Broadway 509 S. Broadway
Boris Karloff in
"MAN WITH NINE LIVES"
"Dizzy Doctors."

Cameo 4706 Harford Road
Rochelle Hudson in
"ISLAND OF DOOMED MEN"
"Mollie Cures a Cowboy."

Capitol 1518 W. Baltimore St.
Anna Neagle in
"IRENE"
"The Hidden Master."

Casino 1118 Light St.
Vincent Price in
"INVISIBLE MAN RETURNS"
"Terry and the Pirates."

Cluster 303 S. Broadway
Anna Neagle in
"IRENE"
"Confederate Honey."

Columbia 709 Washington Blvd.
Wallace Beery in
"20-MULE TEAM"
"Domineering Male."

Earle Belair Rd. at Woodlea Ave.
Ann Sheridan in
"IT ALL CAME TRUE"
"Ants in the Plants."

Edgewood Edmondson & Edgewood
Sidney Toler in
"Charlie Chan's Murder Cruise"
"Double or Nothing."

Forest Garrison & Liberty Heights
Wallace Beery in
"20-MULE TEAM"
"Greyhound and the Rabbit."

Fulton Fulton Ave. at Baker St.
Tyrone Power in
"JOHNNY APOLLO"
"The Croquettes."

Garden Charles at Cross
Dennis Morgan in
"TEAR GAS SQUAD"
Carl Hoff and Band.

Glen Glen Burnie
Dorothy Lamour in
"TYPHOON"
Comedy.

Grand 511 S. Conkling St.
Cesar Romero in
"VIVA CISCO KID"
"The Right Way."

Gwynn 4609 Liberty Heights Ave.
Frank Morgan in
"THE GHOST COMES HOME"
"Cross-Country Detours."

Hampden 911 W. 36th St.
Boris Karloff in
"MAN THEY COULDN'T HANG"
Comedy.

Harford 2616 Harford Ave.
Priscilla Lane in
"Three Cheers for the Irish"
"Home on the Range."

Hippodrome Eutaw at Baltimore Street
Wendy Barrie in
"SAINT TAKES OVER"
On Stage: Milton Berle and His Revue.

Horn 2014 West Pratt St.
Martha Raye in
"THE FARMER'S DAUGHTER"
"Double or Nothing."

Howard 115 N. Howard St.
Jack Benny in
"BUCK BENNY RIDES AGAIN"
Comedy.

Ideal 903 W. Thirty-sixth St.
Joe Penner in
"MILLIONAIRE PLAYBOY"
Comedy.

Irvington 4113 Frederick Ave.
Jack Benny in
"BUCK BENNY RIDES AGAIN"
Comedy and News.

Leader 248 S. Broadway
Tex Ritter in
"PALS OF THE PURPLE SAGE"
"Once Over Lightly."

Lexway 31 W. Lexington St.
Ginger Rogers in
"PRIMROSE PATH"
With Joel McCrea.

Linwood 908 S. Linwood Ave.
Albert Dekker in
"DR. CYCLOPS"
"Going Places."

Little 523 North Howard St.
Ronald Colman in
"PRISONER OF ZENDA"
with Madeleine Carroll.

Lord Baltimore 1110 West Baltimore St.
Florence Rice in
"GIRL IN 313"
"Flying Stewardess."

Lord Calvert 2444 Wash. Blvd.
Vera Zorina in
"I WAS AN ADVENTURESS"
"Bows and Arrows."

Lyceum Sparrows Point, Md.
Madeleine Carroll in
"MY SON, MY SON"
Comedy.

McHenry 1037 Light St.
Anna Neagle in
"IRENE"
Artie Shaw and Band.

Met Pennsylvania & North Aves.
Jack Benny in
"BUCK BENNY RIDES AGAIN"
Latest News.

New Reisterstown, Md.
Joan Bennett in
"HOUSE ACROSS THE BAY"
"Spots Before Your Eyes."

Northway Harford & North. Pky.
Penny Singleton in
"BLONDIE ON A BUDGET"
"XXX Medico."

Overlea Belair Rd., End of Car Line
Tyrone Power in
"JOHNNY APOLLO"
Comedy.

Palace Gay and Hoffman Sts.
Boris Karloff in
"The Man With Nine Lives"
"One For the Book."

Patterson Eastern and East Aves.
Jack Benny in
"BUCK BENNY RIDES AGAIN"
"Pilgrim Porky."

Pikes Pikesville, Md.
Lew Ayres in
"Dr. Kildare's Strange Case"
"Ants in the Plants."

Pimlico Park Heights & Belvedere
Carole Landis in
"ONE MILLION B. C."
"Zorro's Fighting Legion."

Preston 1108 East Preston St.
All-Star Cast in
"LAW BEYOND THE RANGE"
Comedy.

Red Wing 2241 E. Monument St.
Albert Dekker in
"DR. CYCLOPS"
"Sky Game."

Rex 4600 York Rd.
Boris Karloff in
"BLACK FRIDAY"
Walt Disney Cartoons.

Rialto 846 W. North Ave.
Vera Zorina in
"I WAS AN ADVENTURESS"
Latest News.

Ritz 1607 N. Washington St.
Jack Benny in
"BUCK BENNY RIDES AGAIN"
"Early Worm Gets the Bird."

Senator 5904 York Road
Jack Benny in
"BUCK BENNY RIDES AGAIN"
"March of Time."

State Monument and Castle Sts.
Vera Zorina in
"I WAS AN ADVENTURESS"
Vaudeville.

Strand Dundalk, Md.
Raymond Massey in
"ABE LINCOLN IN ILLINOIS"
Fox News.

Towson Towson, Md.
Wallace Beery in
"20-MULE TEAM"
Comedy.

Vilma Belair Rd. and Mayfield Ave.
Jack Benny in
"BUCK BENNY RIDES AGAIN"
"Slap Happy Pappy."

Walbrook 3100 W. North Ave.
Jack Benny in
"BUCK BENNY RIDES AGAIN"
"Silly Season."

Waverly Greenmount at Gorsuch
George Brent in
"ADVENTURE IN DIAMONDS"
Comedy.

Westway Aldershot at Edmondson
Jean Arthur in
"TOO MANY HUSBANDS"
Comedy.

Timonium Fifth To Balkanese

THE WEATHER
Mostly clear tonight and Thursday; little change in temperature. Lowest temperature tonight around 60 degrees. Gentle winds.
Detailed Weather Report on Page 28

MEAN TEMPERATURES YESTERDAY

Baltimore	75	New York	74
Atlanta	80	Omaha	76
Boston	74	Portland, Maine	70
Chicago	70	Salt Lake City	70
Jacksonville	80	San Antonio	85
Los Angeles	70	Seattle	64
Miami	81	Tampa	80
New Orleans	86	Washington	74

THE BALTIMORE NEWS-POST
AN INDEPENDENT NEWSPAPER
The Largest Daily Circulation in the Entire South

VOL. CXXXVII.—NO. 105 | Entered as second-class matter at Baltimore Postoffice. | WEDNESDAY EVENING, SEPTEMBER 4, 1940 | PRICE 3 CENTS

Copyright, 1940, by Hearst Consolidated Publications, Inc.

10

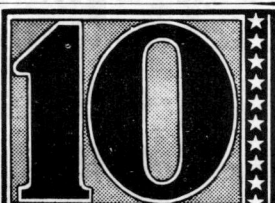

HITLER THROWS AIR MIGHT OVER LONDON

Raid Follows Fuehrer's Threat

IN THE NEWS

Citizens!

Let us make one last appeal to the United States Congress to continue this country as a democracy and not transform it into a militaristic state.

Let us endeavor to persuade the Congress to adopt the defensive system of Switzerland, a true and enduring republic, instead of the systems of the totalitarian powers.

Let us try to secure for the defense and perpetuation of our American liberties a citizen soldiery, instead of a great standing army.

The present Burke-Wadsworth bill before Congress provides for continuous service in the army of not less than a million men.

It proposes to take a million young Americans from productive and acceptable employment, and by compulsion to make professional soldiers of them for a period not to exceed five years.

The number of men under arms and at the command of the Executive may at any time be increased, however, by subsequent measures, when the principle of a great standing Army is established.

The force necessary to compel acquiescence with such a demand, or any other demand of an autocratic Government, is fully provided, once a great standing army under the control of the Government is created.

Democracy is not necessarily a permanent form of government.

From the time of ancient Greece and Rome we have seen democracies disappear and tyrannies take their places.

All that we can say of democracy is that it is the noblest form of government—the happiest form of government—the freest form of government.

But to PRESERVE democracy a people must DESERVE democracy.

They themselves must be noble and worthy of the liberties they enjoy.

They must appreciate their happiness, rejoice in their freedom, and realize that the price of liberty is eternal vigilance.

They must certainly have the simple intelligence and the common knowledge to know that militarism is the most usual means of corrupting and destroying democracy, and that universal citizen service, in defense of a free country, by a free people, is the surest and safest way of preserving democracy.

What system, then, of citizen soldiery — what plan of providing protective military service while retaining a free and unenslaved citizenry—is the best and most effective means of both defending and preserving the republic?

What system has been in operation in a free republic for the longest period of time, and with the greatest measure of success?

What system now operates with the highest success in a republic most nearly like our own free land?

What system is amply proven effective protection for a free people in their rights and liberties, and is so popular with the people that enrollment in it is sought as an honor and benefit as well as a civil duty?

There is only one answer—the Swiss system of universal popular military service.

What is it?

First, we must remember that Switzerland is a republic exceedingly similar to our own, that it has a free government like our own, and that it is divided into cantons or states, each with a measure of self-government like our own.

Second, we should remember that Switzerland is inhabited by a virile people like our own, who cherish freedom and who have fought for it, secured it and preserved it.

Third, that Switzerland, in the midst of the clash of arms which continually surrounds it on every side, has so remained free—and neutral—that its national emblem has become the insignia of peace and neutrality and freedom throughout the world.

The complete analogy between the Swiss people and nation and government and our own having been established, the appropriate application to us of the military system they have found most desirable to defend such a people, nation and government, becomes both practicable and advisable.

In the Swiss system, every citizen is a potential soldier; but no soldier ever ceases to be a free and productive citizen, residing in his own home and pursuing his chosen occupation.

A limited but adequate military training is merely a part of his life and his duty—his pursuit and his pleasure.

At the age of fourteen, a reason-

Continued on Page 4, Column 6.

U. S. Navy Will Take Destroyers To Canada Port For British Use

WASHINGTON, Sept. 4—(I. N. S.).—Despite protests that it might precipitate war with Germany, the Navy prepared today to use American crews to deliver the first of the 50 destroyers traded to Great Britain at an unnamed Canadian port Friday.

Senator Clark (Democrat) of Idaho charged that it would be "dangerous" for America to deliver the destroyers to the English. He insisted:

"If any of these ships should be destroyed by Germany while still in the possession of American crews it might precipitate this country into war."

However, naval experts pointed out the United States would retain title to the ships up until they arrived at Canadian ports.

House Republicans unleashed a barrage of criticism at President Roosevelt for the deal with Great Britain as the Chief Executive himself took steps to allay Congressional opposition.

Shortly after Mr. Roosevelt had summoned his legislative leaders to the White House for a forenoon conference the House heard a warning that the exchange of 50 United States destroyers for base rights on eight British Western Hemisphere possessions was "clearly an act of war and it is merely a question of whether Germany and Italy will strike back now or later."

The warning came from Representative Smith (Republican) of Ohio, who charged that the deal violated both American law and the 1907 Hague Convention against unneutral acts.

USURPING POWER

He was joined by another Ohio Congressman, Representative Bender (Republican) of Cleveland, who claimed that Mr. Roosevelt's step was an usurpation of the powers of Congress. Declared Bender:

"The President took the law into his own hands."

Representative Rich (Republican) of Pennsylvania declared that in no sense could Congress be

Continued on Page 2, Column 1.

Warns U. S. Dictators Threaten

By WILLIAM S. NEAL
International News Service Staff Correspondent

WASHINGTON, Sept. 4.—In an impassioned plea for conscription, Rep. James W. Wadsworth, Republican of New York, co-author of the compulsory military training bill, today told the House that the safety of the United States and the Monroe Doctrine are threatened by dictator nations.

As he took the floor during debate on the measure, he was roundly hissed by gallery spectators, but was generously applauded by both Democratic and Republican members supporting the legislation. Wadsworth said:

"We cannot afford to adopt a 'wait and see' policy. Others have done it and perished.

"What about the safety of the United States when we read the literature of the Nazis and Fascists, outspoken and brutally frank, that their next field of exploitation shall be Central and South America?

"We need troops—I mean soldiers organized and trained as units—as quickly as we can get them. I hate to let a day go by. At the present rate of enlistment it would take two years to do it.

"The thing I plead for is that we shall fashion our defense so that we shall be master of our own destiny."

Rep. Sweeney (Democrat) of Ohio told the House that he rose from a sick bed to oppose the measure which leaders say will be passed

Continued on Page 2, Column 4.

Use Anti-Aircraft Guns To Battle Big Plane Armada

LONDON, Sept. 4—(A. P.).—London's anti-aircraft opened up tonight with the heaviest barrage yet lifted above this city, beating at a strong German air raid loosed upon London just a few hours after Adolf Hitler had thundered his threat: "I'm coming!"

It appeared that there were more planes aloft than ever had been sent against London in a night raid.

Half a hundred searchlights threw up their bears, ilndicating that the attack was moving in from several directions simultaneously.

Distant explosions could be heard.

'ARCHIES' REPLY

The "Archies"—anti-aircraft guns—were throwing shells at the rate of one every two seconds.

The alarm was the third of the day.

The Nazis came in from high—apparently above 25,000 feet—and now and again sharp bursts of machine-gun fire from British planes could be heard from aloft.

Flares from the German planes lit up wide areas.

More than half an hour after the assault was begun, anti-aircraft fire still was gathering fury, first in one direction and then in another, and it seemed clear that the Nazis were coming over in waves.

The official British score card for daylight aerial engagements, which themselves were very heavy, meanwhile was upped to 45 German planes shot down; 11 British planes lost.

The official British score card by late Wednesday claimed 41 German and 5 British planes lost.

The biggest Nazi formation of 200 planes crossed the Kent coast about noon, beating against terrific British anti-aircraft barrages and British fighting planes.

Several formations were admit-

Continued on Page 2, Column 7.

Promises Thousands Of Tons Of Bombs Will Rain Nightly On Foe

BERLIN, Sept. 4—(A. P.).—Hundreds of thousands of pounds of bombs will drop from the sky on England nightly hereafter in retaliation for British night raids on Germany, Adolf Hitler announced tonight amid enthusiastic cries of his followers.

The Fuehrer, with a triumphant year of war behind him and an unpredictable winter ahead, spoke out to his British foes with fury and jeers—and a threat that the bombers of Germany will "erase" English cities to avenge the night raids of the R. A. F.

There was no indication when Hitler expected the war to end but he observed that when the war started and Prime Minister Neville Chamberlain spoke of a three-year conflict he "told Goering to prepare for five years."

Addressing 25,000 workers for the eighth winter relief campaign at the Sports Palace, the Fuehrer said:

"For three months I have waited for the British to cease the nuisance of nightly, planless bomb-throwing. Now we will give the answer night after night."

(The German radio quoted the Fuehrer as declaring that "I know only one date as the date of English collapse. If it is said in England, 'Why does it not come?' then I say, be sure it will come.")

"If the British throw two or three thousand kilograms (of bombs)," said Hitler, "we will unload 150,000, 180,000, yes 200,000 . . ."

Apparently Hitler intended to continue with this progression of figures, but he was stopped by the shouts of his audience. (A kilogram is 2.2 pounds.)

"If they attack our cities we will simply erase theirs," Hitler declared. "We will call a halt to these night pirates. The hour will come when one of us two will crack up—and it will not be Nazi Germany.

"Whatever may come, England will collapse."

It was his first speech since July 19, when he addressed what he called "one more appeal to reason" to the British and warned them that their empire would be destroyed if they kept on fighting.

In the early hours of the day, British bombers and German defenders had met west of Berlin in Central Germany's mightiest air engagement of the war so far.

The Fuehrer made fun of the English for wondering when Hitler would come, saying he always has prepared for everything thoroughly.

"If they ask, *'Why doesn't he come?'* my reply is: Just be quiet, He's coming all right."

Hilarious laughter greeted this.

Hitler was in a facetious mood throughout. He poked fun at England at several points, first speaking of "General Revolution" as the chief British ally, then General Winter and General Hunger and roared:

"They ought to make General Bluff their Reichs Marshal.

"Against these generals of the British army we pose the General Deed."

Later referring to the winter re-

Continued on Page 2, Column 7.

Ever Feel Like Kicking Yourself? Then read about the automatic self-kicker, and how it is filling a great human need. An amusingly illustrated feature in The American Weekly, the magazine distributed with next Sunday's Baltimore American.—Adv.

Only one more day on which Baltimore voters, who have failed to take advantage of previous opportunities, may register in their precincts, so that they may vote in the election, November 5.

The final day for precinct registration is—
NEXT SATURDAY.
Registration hours:
From noon till 10 P. M.

VERY LATEST NEWS

(Race Results From Howard Sports Daily, Inc.)

VICTORY LIGHT WINS SIXTH RACE AT TIMONIUM

Sixth — Victory Light, $13.70, $5.40, $3.60; Bellthorn, $3.90, $2.80; Furr Buckle, $3.30.

AT NARRAGANSETT PARK

Eighth—Sun Breeze, $10.00, $6.40, $4.80; Chancemaker $32.00, $19.80; Mobcap, $11.20.

AT HAWTHORNE

Fifth — Dissension Sir, $27.20, $8.60, $4.80; De Kalb, $3.00, $2.60; Town Miss, $3.80.

Sixth—Court Dance, $24.20, $10.00, $6.00; Busy Morn, $13.40, $7.00; Morcarine, $11.40.

LATEST BASEBALL SCORES

(I) At Oriole Park—Syracuse, 3; Balto., 1; end 4th, 2d g.
(A) At Washington—Wash., 6; New York, 5; final.
(A) At Chicago—St. Louis, 4; Chicago, 1; final.
(A) At Boston—Philadelphia, 1; Boston, 1; end 6th.
(A) At Detroit—Detroit, 4; Cleveland, 2; end 6th.

COAST ARMY MEN SENT TO ALASKA

WASHINGTON, Sept. 4—(I. N. S.).—The War Department announced today that 2,400 officers and enlisted men were being sent from West Coast Army posts to the new Army base and air field at Anchorage, Alaska.

Temperatures

Midnight	70	9 A. M.	74
1 A. M.	68	10 A. M.	76
2 A. M.	67	11 A. M.	80
3 A. M.	66	12 Noon	82
4 A. M.	66	1 P. M.	83
5 A. M.	67	2 P. M.	82
6 A. M.	66	3 P. M.	83
7 A. M.	68	4 P. M.	81
8 A. M.	70	5 P. M.	80

Orioles Lose 1st, Play Nightcap

SECOND GAME
Syracuse.. 2 1
Baltimore 0
(Other Scores on Sport Page)

By HUGH TRADER, JR.

ORIOLE PARK, Sept. 4.—Syracuse snatched a ball game right out of Baltimore's hip pocket here this afternoon, the Chiefs rallying for three runs in the ninth inning and a 5-to-4 victory over the Orioles in the first game of the wind-up double-header between the clubs.

Traling by two runs and with one oue in the ninth, Syracuse got a life when Italo Chelini nipped Jeulich with a pitched ball. Kahny followed with a double and Nagel tossed in an error which let in the winning run as Leip singled to

Continued on Page 23, Column 3.

Timonium Feature To Balkanese

By GABY

TIMONIUM, Sept. 4.—Balkanese, owned by Mrs. E. C. Moyer and ridden by Apprentice D. Hamer, won the six-and-a-half-furlong Springfield Farm Purse, feature here today.

Balkanese worked his way up steadily, took the lead from Riotous, which had set the pace, on the final turn, and continued gamely to beat Riotous a length. Bell Chimes was third and Happy Hostess fourth.

Bell Chimes went into the air at the start, losing her chance to make good for favorite players among the estimated crowd of 6,000. Balkanese paid $17.20 and the running time was 1:22.4.

Ewart Johnston's Delhi Dan made every post a winning one in

Continued on Page 23, Column 7

The Baltimore News-Post today is printed in
3 Sections
Be sure you get the complete newspaper.

TIMONIUM RESULTS

Delhi Dan and Pack Saddle paid $44.50 for $2.

FIRST RACE—Six and a half furlongs. Off at 2.06½. Time 1.23 1-5.

Delhi Dan, 120 (Holland)	$7.80	$4.30	$2.80
Top's Sister, 115 (Martinez)		4.00	3.10
Erin's Girl, 112 (Faust)			4.50

Also Ran—Baby Mowlee, Glitter Girl, Sun Scene, Neutral, Corlander.

SECOND—Six and a half furlongs. Off at 2.37. Time 1.23.

Pack Saddle, 113 (Faust)	$8.90	$4.70	$3.20
Scarlet Flame, 104 (Claggett)		5.70	3.90
Kelley Pot, 113 (W. Kirk)			7.50

Also Ran—Miss Chicro, Lady Timarole, Stars Above, Mac's Cantor, Sail By.

Continued on Page 23, Column 6.

DEMOCRATS SWEEP MD.

THE WEATHER
Somewhat colder and mostly clear tonight, with the lowest temperature between 35 and 40 degrees. Thursday clear and moderately cold.
Detailed Weather Report on Page 30

MEAN TEMPERATURES YESTERDAY.

Baltimore	63	Omaha	36
Atlanta	62	Portland, Maine	46
Boston	60	Salt Lake City	36
Chicago	48	San Antonio	70
Jacksonville	69	Seattle	48
Los Angeles	62	Tampa	73
Miami	77	Washington	60
New York	60		

THE BALTIMORE NEWS-POST
AN INDEPENDENT NEWSPAPER
The Largest Daily Circulation in the Entire South

7

VOL. CXXXVIII.—NO. 2
Entered as second-class matter at Baltimore Postoffice.
Copyright, 1940, by Hearst Consolidated Publications, Inc.
WEDNESDAY EVENING, NOVEMBER 6, 1940
PRICE 3 CENTS

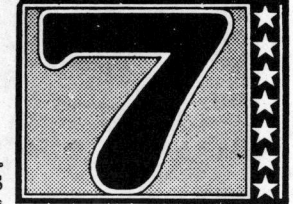

ROOSEVELT RE-ELECTED WILLKIE ADMITS DEFEAT

President Has 449 Electoral Votes

IN THE NEWS

MR. WILLKIE announced that if elected his first message to Congress would recommend a constitutional amendment limiting the time any one President might serve to eight years.

Mr. Roosevelt has declared that there will be no fourth term.

He would be satisfied to serve three terms.

Perhaps, now that he is elected, he will be satisfied to be the only President to serve three terms.

At any rate if he is sincere in his statement he should be willing to support a constitutional amendment limiting the Presidential term to eight years or twelve years.

There certainly should be some constitutional limit put upon a Presidential term of office.

THERE HAS been in the history of our country a growing tendency on the part of popular Presidents to crave a third term.

There has been a growing tendency in our Governmental practice to concentrate more and more power in the hands of the executive branch of Government and to unbalance the relation established by the founders between the executive, the legislative, and the judicial departments.

That steady development of Executive proponderance of power if unchecked can only result in one thing, and that is rule by the Executive, and the subordination to the Executive of the Congress and the courts.

That form of government can be called what you please but it is certainly not democracy.

It is certainly not the free Government to which this republic has been accustomed and under which it has grown to greatness.

It means that the power and opinion of one man has been recognized as superior to the power and opinion of the representatives of the people in Congress assembled and to the impartial judgment of the courts.

It means that this power and opinion of the Executive will soon not be challenged by the Congress or the courts,—and that necessarily means absolutism in government.

It is the end of democracy.

GIVE ANY executive the right and the power to perpetuate

Continued on Page 4, Column 1.

Lemminkainen and the women of the island. Another tale from the Kalevals, the heroic saga of Finland, told by John Erskine, famous author, and illustrated in full color by Willy Pogany, on the front page of The American Weekly, the Magazine distributed with next Sunday's Baltimore American.—(Adv.)

Democrats Sweep Md., Carry City By 87,615; Radcliffe Defeats Nice

Thanks largely to this industrial city of Baltimore, the State of Maryland, with its eight electoral votes, was today safely in the Roosevelt column as the result of the election yesterday in which party lines were beaten down by the surge of other forces.

Wendell Willkie, Republican nominee and third-term challenger, made a gallant fight against the Presidential title-holder, and in the coutnies his fight was not without result; but in the city the pro-Roosevelt tide swept him off his feet.

Latest returns from 1,260 of the State's 1,331 polling places, including Baltimore city's 471 precincts, gave the President a majority of 114,531 over the man who valiantly sought to uphold the American tradition against a third term.

The vote from these polling places was:

Roosevelt	367,223
Willkie	252,692

In Baltimore city the Roosevelt majority was 87,615, according to unofficial returns, which gave:

Roosevelt	199,861
Willkie	112,246

In the Senatorial race, former Governor Harry W. Nice sustained the most crushing defeat of his long political career, Senator George L. Radcliffe riding to re-election on the crest of a wave which gave him a majority of 113,886 in Baltimore cit yalone.

Margin Gains As Polls Report

This big margin was augmented as returns from the counties came in.

Returns from 1,233 of the State's 1,331 polling places, including the complete city vote, gave:

Radcliffe	367,798
Nice	189,356

On the face of returns, complete in Baltimore city and nearing completion in the counties, the Democratic Congressional candidates rode to success in all six districts.

CONGRESSMEN'S RACE

The five Democratic incumbents—David J. Ward (First district); William P. Cole (Second district); Thomas D'Alesandro (Third district); Lansdale G. Sasscer (Fifth district) and William D. Byron (Sixth district) were apparently re-elected over their Republican challengers—former Judge Robert F. Duer, Theodore F. Brown, John A. Janetzke, Jr., John N. Torvestad, and Walter P. Johnson (the Big Train of baseball fame), respectively.

Owing to Representative Ambrose J. Kennedy' defeat in the

Continued on Page B Column 3.

IN THE NEWS-POST TODAY

Assigns Md. Quotas In Draft

Special to The News-Post.

ANNAPOLIS, Nov. 6.—Governor O'Conor today announced the number of men to be drafted from each of the State's 66 local selective service districts in order to fill Maryland's quota of 157 men for the nation's first peace-time draft army.

Baltimore city will be called upon ta furnish 73 men, the counties providing the remaining 84 men.

BALTIMORE'S QUOTA

No board in the State will be called upon to furnish more than four men, while several counties will furnish one each. The breakdown for Baltimore's 26 boards follows:

No. 1, three men; No. 2, two men; No. 3, three men; No. 4, three men; No. 5, three men; No. 6, there men; No. 7, two men; No. 8, two men; No. 9, three men; No. 10, three men; No. 11, three men; No. 12, three men; No. 13, four men.

No. 14, three men; No. 15, three men; No. 16, three men; No. 17, three men; No. 18, four men; No. 19, two men; No. 20, two men; No. 21, three men; No. 22, four men; No. 23, two men; No. 24, two men; No. 25, two men; No. 26, three men.

COUNTY LISTINGS

Tse following quotas were fixed for the county draft boards:

Allegany County — No. 1, two men; No. 2, two men; No. 3, two men; No. 4, three men.

Anne Arundel County—No. 1, two men; No. 2, three men.

Baltimore County — No. 1, three men; No. 2, two men; No.. 3, one man; No. 4, two men; No. 5, five men.

Continued on Page 19, Column 7.

Five Are Hurt As Train Jumps Rails

SALT LAKE CITY, Nov. 6—(A. P.).—Conductor L. T. Newlin sustained a broken leg and four passengers were injured when a Union Pacific passenger train left the rails four miles north of Brigham City last night. Railroad sources here said eight cars of the 15-car passenger train were derailed. The cause of the accident was not determined.

Temperatures

Midnight,	62	7 A. M.,	49
1 A. M.,	61	8 A. M.,	52
2 A. M.,	60	9 A. M.,	52
3 A. M.,	55	10 A. M.,	53
4 A. M.,	53	11 A. M.,	53
5 A. M.,	51	12 Noon...	53
6 A. M.,	50	1 P. M.,	54

Popular Electoral Vote Return

At 9 A. M. (Eastern Standard Time)
By Associated Press.

State	Voting Units	Units Reporting	Popular Vote Roosevelt	Popular Vote Willkie	Indicated Electoral Vote Rvlt	Indicated Electoral Vote Wlke
Alabama.	2,300	1,206	155,253	23,376	11	..
Arizona..	430	311	48,306	25,567	3	..
Arkansas..	2,169	807	54,292	12,105	9	..
California	13,692	10,756	1,205,063	862,707	22	..
Colorado.	1,610	725	93,992	104,043	..	6
Connecticut.	169	169	417,858	361,869	8	..
Delaware.	249	217	57,233	45,404	3	..
Florida...	1,428	964	256,633	99,952	7	..
Georgia..	1,720	1,410	196,657	29,046	12	..
Idaho....	792	502	68,383	56,830	4	..
Illinois...	8,378	7,299	1,837,107	1,719,952	29	..
Indiana...	3,898	2,957	700,805	714,443	..	14
Iowa.....	2,453	1,809	426,369	457,678	..	11
Kansas...	2,734	1,997	228,752	322,956	..	9
Kentucky.	4,343	2,292	304,477	198,704	11	..
Louisiana.	1,712	518	143,977	23,852	10	..
Maine....	629	623	154,732	153,782	..	5
Maryland.	1,331	1,221	358,365	245,888	8	..
Massach'ts	1,810	1,550	892,150	797,884	17	..
Michigan..	3,632	2,216	546,285	621,796	..	19
Minnesota	3,696	1,410	333,351	296,117	11	..
Mississippi	1,668	635	87,190	4,179	9	..
Missouri..	4,479	3,792	773,961	676,304	15	..
Montana.	1,495	638	85,143	55,674	4	..
Nebraska.	2,043	1,543	181,283	253,999	..	7
Nevada...	260	203	19,396	14,096	3	..
N. Ha'pshire	294	293	177,330	104,912	4	..
New Jersey	3,631	3,225	887,521	859,787	16	..
New Mexico	919	442	61,598	41,795	3	..
New York.	9,319	9,293	3,256,726	3,021,421	47	..
N. Carolina	1,916	1,688	562,213	176,171	13	..
N. Dakota.	2,261	719	44,385	51,050	..	4
Ohio.....	8,675	8,019	1,544,931	1,433,163	26	..
Oklahoma	3,613	2,715	337,045	229,748	11	..
Oregon...	1,693	1,046	104,994	102,739	5	..
Pennsy'nia	8,118	7,968	2,070,778	1,8[illegible]7,522	36	..
Rhode Island	259	259	181,881	138,432	4	..
S. Carolina	1,277	953	81,867	4,144	8	..
S. Dakota.	1,963	1,414	85,047	1[illegible]9,401	..	4
Tennessee.	2,300	2,073	303,206	139,751	11	..
Texas....	254	224	504,430	1[illegible]8,198	23	..
Utah.....	831	457	84,511	52,100	4	..
Vermont..	246	246	64,244	78,335	..	3
Virginia..	1,716	1,649	231,739	106,088	11	..
Washing'n	3,018	1,558	212,278	137,842	8	..
W. Virginia	2,389	1,242	273,005	195,309	8	..
Wisconsin.	3,038	2,722	619,453	608,492	12	..
Wyoming.	697	575	46,403	42,113	3	..
Totals.	127,245	96,550	21,302,601	17,766,716	449	82

Democrats Keep Rule In Congress

WASHINGTON, Nov. 6—(A. P.).—The Democrats, riding a tide of votes with President Roosevelt, kept control of both House and Senate in Tuesday's election.

An official tabulation showed they had won 227 House seats, for more than a majority, to 110 for the Republicans. In addition, one incumbent American Laborite was re-elected. A majority is 218.

MAY BOLSTER MARGIN

Contrary to Republican predictions that they would gain from 50 to 80 seats, the returns indicated that the Democrats might win a few more than their present House strength of 258.

The Democrats have held control of the House since John N. Garner, now Vice-President, was chosen speaker in 1931, and of the Senate since victors in the first Roosevelt landslide of 1932 took office on March 4, 1933.

WIN 16 OUT OF 25

The majority in the new Senate, convening next January 3, was hardly in danger, but any vestige of doubt was eliminated when the tabulation showed they had won at

Continued on Page A Column 3.

NEW YORK, Nov. 6—(A. P.).—Wendell L. Willkie today telegraphed President Roosevelt congratulations on his re-election in these words:

"Congratulations on your re-election as President of the United States. I know that we are both gratified that so many American citizens participated in the election. I wish you all personal health and happiness.

"Cordially,

"Wendell L. Willkie."

By WILLIAM K. HUTCHINSON
International News Service Staff Correspondent.

NEW YORK, Nov. 6.—President Roosevelt today was swept into the White House for a precedent-shattering third successive term on the crest of a tidal wave of ballots that swamped the vigorous effort made by Wendell Willkie to oust the New Deal from office.

By mid-morning late returns had given the President such a resounding vote of confidence that the Republican nominee, after hours of apparent disbelief, conceded he had been vanquished and dispatched a telegram of congratulation to Mr. Roosevelt.

WILLKIE SURE OF ONLY 7 STATES

Meanwhile, as States considered doubtful overnight swung into line, the Roosevelt victory became hourly more impressive. The President definitely had taken 38 States with a total electoral vote of 449, wresting an early lead in New Jersey from Willkie and was bidding tenaciously for North Dakota where Willkie's lead still held.

Actually, Willkie was assured the definite support of only seven States. These, with a total of 45 electoral votes, were rock-ribbed Maine and Vermont, Colorado, Iowa, Kansas, Nebraska and South Dakota.

TREMENDOUS PROTEST VOTE

The President won magnificently, but Willkie captured a tremendous protest vote against the Administration. In addition, the President ran far ahead of local tickets in many States in which the Republican elected Governors and United States Senators.

On the whole, the American people apparently placed their faith in the President's pledges to keep the nation out of war, to achieve unity in the nation and to solve domestic problems.

Mr. Roosevelt won the greatest "vote of confidence" ever given an American by his countrymen in over 150 years of our democracy. He responded by calling on the country to present a "united front" against the menace of the world's dictatorships.

Senator Charles L. McNary, G. O. P. Vice-Presidential nominee and Republican leader of the Senate congratulated both the President and the new Vice-President-elect, Henry A. Wallace of Iowa. McNary telegraphed

Continued on Page B Column 7.

Democrats Hail Party Triumph

AS BALTIMORE piled up Democratic majorities for the entire ticket, Representative Tommy D'Alesandro, Jr. (left), Mrs. John A. Rutherford and U. S. Senator Radcliffe registered satisfaction as they listened to returns in headquarters. Mr. D'Alesandro defeated John A. Janetzke, Jr., for the Third District Congressional seat; Senator Radcliffe stood off the challenge of former Governor Nice.

"HAPPY DAYS Are Here Again," and "A Hot Time in the Old Town Tonight" were among the old campaign songs that echoed throughout Baltimore early today wherever Democrats gathered to celebrate their victory. The group of girls pictured singing here in the Emerson Headquarters are, from left to right, Misses Marjorie Free, Marjorie Mann, Catherine Keene, Elainse Holbroow, Jean Breitung and Jane Ratigan.

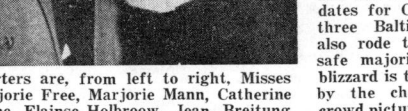

DEMOCRATIC HEADQUARTERS in the Emerson Hotel was the gayest spot in Baltimore last night as the city gave President Roosevelt a majority of 87,615, according to unofficial returns. Senator Radcliffe and the Democratic candidates for Congress in the three Baltimore districts also rode to victory with safe majorities. A paper blizzard is tossed in the air by the cheering, milling crowd pictured above in the Emerson.

MORE THAN 1000,00 persons jammed their way into Times Square, New York City, last night and lingered on throughout the early morning hours to watch returns flashed from all sections of the country in what may prove to be the most significant Presidential election in the history of the country. A part of the crowd is pictured above as it appeared to a photographer posted at 45th street, looking south on Broadway. Partisans cheered as the battle ebbed and flowed.

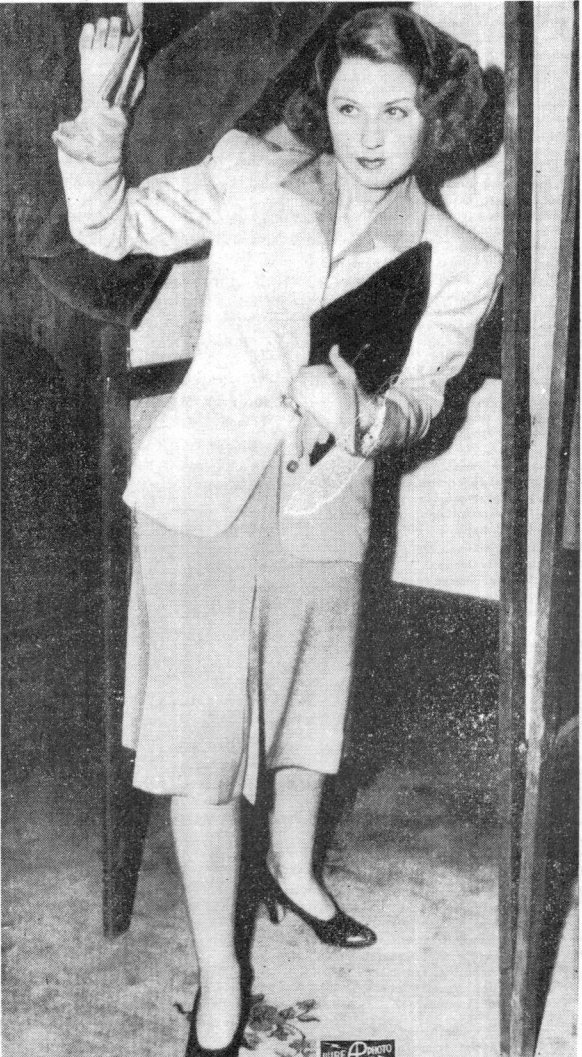

THE ONLY time that lovely Norma Shearer cannot exercise the feminine prerogative of changing her mind is after pulling the lever in a voting machine. Miss Shearer is pictured leaving the voting booth in Santa Monica, Cal.

Girl Asks About Going With Man Who Is Married

Annette Advises Her Against Such Dates

By ANNETTE

She fancies herself in love with married man.

DEAR ANNETTE: About a year ago I went with a crowd of boys and girls who were all a couple of years older. In the crowd was a married couple and I will call the man R. When going to parties and different places I was always picked to be R's girl. I was fond of him at first, but after awhile I found that I really loved him. Some time ago he and his wife were separated and he asked me to go out with him. I went every time he asked me, but I always had to meet him on corners, as my mother wouldn't have allowed me to go with a married man. He told me he loved me, but some time ago he started breaking dates. I didn't hear from him for over a month; then he called one night, asking me to go out, and said he would explain why he hadn't called before. I said I couldn't and hung up. Now I am worried that he won't talk to me when he sees me. Should I call him or write him a letter telling him that I am sorry I couldn't go out with him? I am seventeen years old.

SOMEBODY TOLD ME HE LOVED ME.

hardly think he would stop speaking to you because of this, and if he did. I don't think it would be a great loss. A married man, even though he is separated from his wife, isn't the sort of a beau a seventeen-year-old girl should have, and you will certainly be risking your good name if you make a practice of meeting young men outside your home, and particularly a married man. Don't do it, my dear. There are too many nice single lads for you to waste your time on one who is already involved.

DEAR ANNETTE: I am eighteen and in love with a boy of twenty. I have been keeping company with him for two months. Several weeks age he met A, whom he likes also. He asked me to go steady, but he is going with her, too. Should I keep going with him or stop seeing him?

BLACKIE.

If you like the boy and enjoy going with him, there is no reason why the fact that he goes with another girl should interfere with your dates. But don't agree to drop your other friends for him. Make other dates as well.

SPEAKING ON ENGLAND

Miss Letitia Stockett, Baltimore author, teacher and lecturer, will speak on "The History of England in Sixty Minutes" at a lecture for the benefit of the Sisters of the Holy Nativity at 8.30 P. M. in the Central Library, Cathedral and Franklin streets.

Daily Fashion

B
A
4608

by Anne Adams

Pattern 4608 is available in sizes small (32-34), medium (36-38) and large (40-42). Small size, apron A, takes 2⅛ yards 35-inch fabric and 3 yards ric-rac; apron B, 2⅛ yards 35-inch fabric and 2 yards ruffing.

Send FIFTEEN CENTS for this pattern to Pattern Department, The Baltimore News-Post, 243 West Seventeenth street, New York, N. Y. Additional TEN CENTS will bring you latest Pattern Book.

YOUR FIGURE, MADAME!

By Ida Jean Kain

IT'S HAPPINESS — NOT CARROTS—THAT MAKES JULIE HAYDON'S HAIR CURL!

Feminine competition in the lovely make-believe world of the theatre is so fierce that fibbing about one's age is an accepted form of self-preservation.

And Julie Haydon—whose Alice-in-Wonderland freshness would enable her to pass for twenty in the merciless light of the noonday sun—upsets what amounts to a conviction when she insists that she is all of thirty-one!

But that just goes to show what kind of a girl Miss Haydon is.

And if there is any truth in the saying that what we fear is sure to overtake us, we can reason backward to find an explanation for her extremely youthful appearance in this frank indifference to birthdays.

HAS YOUTHFUL FIGURE

In addition, she has what science is pleased to label "the characteristics of youth"—a slim, lithe figure, the quick, lilting walk of a carefree child and a fine, fresh complexion.

Her measurements are: Bust, 33 inches; waist, 22½ inches; hips, 34 inches. Yes, she exercises!

A talented dancing sister with a strong will power insisted on teaching her a "set of leaps and bounds that were never intended for the confines of a hotel room, but which keep one in excellent condition." And, obviously, in fine form!

Then, there's the matter of posture. As you are probably aware, posture is a paramount consideration in the theatre. It is also the way an actor or actress gauges age!

It's almost a commonplace, Miss Haydon tells me, to hear:

"You can tell Miss So-and-So is getting along—just look at her hunching her shoulders!"

And knowing that poor posture is supposed to be a sign of age is enough to make any woman straighten up.

CARES FOR OWN HAIR

That "nice child" complexion is apparently the result of heredity and soap-and-water cleanliness. And the sheen of her simple coiffure?

Just good, vigorous application of the hair brush—not so many strokes, but until the arms are too weary to lift the brush for another stroke!

Julie Haydon takes care of her own hair washing and brushing. She doesn't bother with having it set, "because it won't set!"

All these usually fundamental things in beauty, however, seem superficial when a sincere attempt is made to analyze the Haydon charm. Certainly, one of the "secrets" is her keen interest in other people.

IT'S ONE SECRET OF CHARM

Whether it's deliberate or a natural gift, this fascinating actress is adept in the art of encouraging people to talk about themselves—even when she is supposed to be the topic of conversation!

Any woman who can lead people on and convince them that she is enjoying her role of a good listener is in full possession of one secret of charm!

And she doesn't have to worry very much about seeming young. It's generally taken for granted that anyone who likes to listen IS young.

But here are two more Haydonisms which, I'll warrant, will pique your interest. She believes that beauty is a state of mind, and declares that when she is happy her hair curls!

And she doesn't hold with the theory that women shouldn't worry. "Why, worry is part of living," she says, "and it makes you want to work harder!"

If you didn't have a sister to stand over you and make you exercise, send a stamped return envelope for Ida Jean Kain's leaflet, "Streamline the Midsection."

(Copyright, 1940, King Features Syndicate, Incorporated.)

Mission Rally Set Tomorrow

Sponsors of the National Christian Mission, headed by Mayor Jackson and Dr. J. M. T. Finney, honorary chairman, and Dr. J. H. Mason, Knox, general chairman, will hold a "mobilization rally" in First Methodist Church, St. Paul and Twenty-second streets, a 8 P. M. tomorrow.

The meeting has been called by Latimer S. Stewart, chairman of the executive committee, and the Rev. John W. Harms, executive secretary of the Council of Churches, to map out final details of the mission, which will be held here during the week of November 24.

Baltimore will be the tenth city to be visited by the mission, which is headed by 30 Christian leaders of international fame.

The program for the city includes daily morning Bible forums, afternoon seminars and a mass-meeting each night in the Fifth Regiment Armory.

Various youth organizations will be in charge of the meetings on Saturday, November 30, terminating that evening in a mass service in the armory at which a chorus of 500 young people will sing under the direction of J. Edward Moyer, choir director at Mt. Vernon Place Church.

Advertisement.

FLUSH KIDNEYS OF POISONS AND STOP GETTING UP NIGHTS

Live a Healthier, Happier, Life

Thousands of men and women wonder why backache bothers them—why they have to visit the bathroom often at night—why flow is scanty and sometimes smarts and burns.

Any one of these symptoms may mean that your kidneys and bladder need attention now before these minor symptoms may develop into serious trouble.

To flush out excess waste poisons and acid from kidneys, soothe your irritated bladder and put more healthy activity into them, get a 35 cent package of GOLD MEDAL Haarlem Capsules and take as directed.

This tried and true medicine should make you feel better in a few days — it's an effective diuretic and kidney stimulant that relieves the pains caused by gouty phases of sciatica, neuritis and rheumatic joint agony when irritated by excess uric acid.

Don't be an EASY MARK and accept a substitute—Get Gold Medal Haarlem Oil Capsules — the original and genuine. Look for the Gold Medal on the box — 25 cents.

10% OFF During November

ON ALL VENETIAN BLINDS AND WINDOW SHADES

Tremendous buying resources to supply new building program gives us surplus stock which we can sacrifice at this genuine reduction. An amazing reduction at the height of season.

Phone MUlberry 2010

STURDIFOLD AWNINGS & SHADE CO. 15 W. Preston St.

Kryptok Seamless BIFOCALS Complete

Eye Physician In Attendance

Latest style glasses with famous Kryptok white lenses for both near and far vision in one pair of glasses.

YOU SAVE MONEY WHEN YOU BUY YOUR GLASSES AT GUTMAN'S

We offer the people of this community a complete eye service with single vision glasses as low as $3.84. Newest styles, all popular prices. Satisfaction assured.

Optical Dept., Street Floor.

PRICE INCLUDES EYE TEST, PRESCRIPTION and GLASSES

$5.94 Eye Test Included

GUTMAN'S Lexington & Park

EXTRA!

TRADE

When you take Smith Brothers Cough Drops, you get Vitamin A at no extra cost. Smith Brothers—Black or Menthol—still cost only 5¢.

Smith Bros. Cough Drops are the only drops containing VITAMIN A

Vitamin A (Carotene) raises the resistance of mucous membranes of nose and throat to cold infections, when lack of resistance is due to Vitamin A deficiency.

MARK

Watch for Adolph's Ad Every Wednesday!

THURS., FRI., SAT. SPECIAL

CLIP THIS AD

ADOLPH BEAUTY SHOPS 5 Convenient Locations

205 N. LIBERTY ST. 3 doors from Lexington CALVERT 5158
2126 E. MONUMENT ST. Cor. Collington Ave. BDWY. 9634
3 E. NORTH AVE. 2 doors from Charles VERNON 6871
3220 GREENMOUNT AVE. At Gorsuch Ave. CHES. 9841
5500 HARFORD RD. Over Purdum's Drug Store HA. 9755

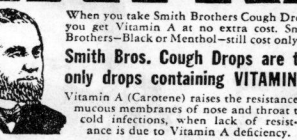

THIS AD IS WORTH $1 ON ANY WAVE OF $2.50 OR MORE

(CLIP THIS AD)
REG. $5.00 STAY-SET PERMANENT
Without Ad $2.50
WITH THIS AD
$1.50 With Shampoo and Set.

NP 11-6-40

OPEN MON., WED. & FRI. EVES. TILL 9

You need never have gray hair
Let us restore it to its natural shade. Choice of any tint.
$2.50
Free Consultation on Any Hair Problem

Reg. $6.50 OIL-OF-PINE $3.50—With Ad $2.50
Reg. $7.50 DUART $5.00—With Ad $4.00
Reg. $10 PARK AVE. Machineless $5.95—With Ad $4.95

You'd Expect Cloth Coats at This Low Price
But Never FUR COATS of such Gorgeous Furs!

Unclaimed Mink-Dyed Marmot
VALUES to $79!
$39
Some were left for storage; others for repairs. All sold as-is.

Choose also:
NATURAL MUSKRAT $39
CARACUL LAMB (black or grey) 39
SILVER BELLY MUSKRAT 39
BLACK OR BROWN PONY 39
BEAVER-DYED CONEY 39
S. AMERICAN SPOTTED CAT 39

TRADE IN Your Old Fur Or Cloth Coat
EASY BUDGET TERMS Pay While Wearing

Unclaimed JACKETS
Values to $49!
Year-Round Flattery!
$19
Fisher Dyed Opossum! Sable Striped Coney! Lynx-Dyed Wolf! Grey Kidskin! Mouton Lamb!

Genuine Silver Fox SCARFS $10 A SKIN, sold as-is
Genuine Silver Fox TAIL CAPES $5
Fur-Trimmed CLOTH COATS $5
Illustrated Catalog Sent on Request

Fur Outlet Co.
318 N. HOWARD STREET

OPEN MONDAYS and FRIDAYS till 9 P. M.

Did you buy YOUR car on "Millinery"?

YOU hear it said often nowadays that it's *millinery* that sells automobiles.

All right—let's put it up to one who knows. Did you buy *your* car on nick-nacks, trick devices, novelties?

We don't think so.

We believe that while considering style, and room, and comfort—*you really picked your car on what it would do on the road!*

Now, we take our hats off to no car for being *smarter*-looking than Buick. We'll match our product against any for room, for appointments, for fine finish, for the comfort of its all-coil springing and the safety of its Body by Fisher.

But beyond all that, we challenge the whole field to equal Buick on its downright all-round performance *ability.*

On its power—on its pull—on its pickup—on its easy handling (*including freedom from shifting*)—yes, and on its thrift.

Nowhere will you find a car that *does so much so well and so frugally*—and we invite you to find that out for yourself.

You'll find novelties in the new Buicks of course, but they're not the *chief* attraction. Instead you'll see the *two big basic engineering developments of the year*—FIREBALL design and Compound Carburetion.

They give you an automobile that packs a real thrill—and if that means more to you than superficialities, better come in and learn more about it.

BUICK PRICES BEGIN AT $935 for the Business Coupe
delivered at Flint, Mich. State tax, optional equipment and accessories—extra. Prices subject to change without notice.

WHEN BETTER AUTOMOBILES ARE BUILT
BUICK WILL BUILD THEM
"Best Buick Yet"
EXEMPLAR OF GENERAL MOTORS VALUE

BROOKS-PRICE CO.
1370-72-74 West North Ave.
MADISON 9300

KELLY-BUICK SALES CORP.
Charles and Mt. Royal Avenue
VERNON 2800

The Baltimore News-Post Has the Largest Circulation of Any Evening Newspaper in the South

THE BALTIMORE NEWS-POST
AN INDEPENDENT NEWSPAPER

WEDNESDAY EVENING, NOVEMBER 6, 1940

2ND FRONT PAGE
NEWS-POST HAS TWO FRONT PAGES DAILY

Winners

Democrats Take Maryland's Six Seats In House Contests

City Voters Reject Daylight Saving

Hawaii-Bound

DORIS DUKE CROMWELL ON TRIP

HUSBAND LOSING SENATE CAMPAIGN

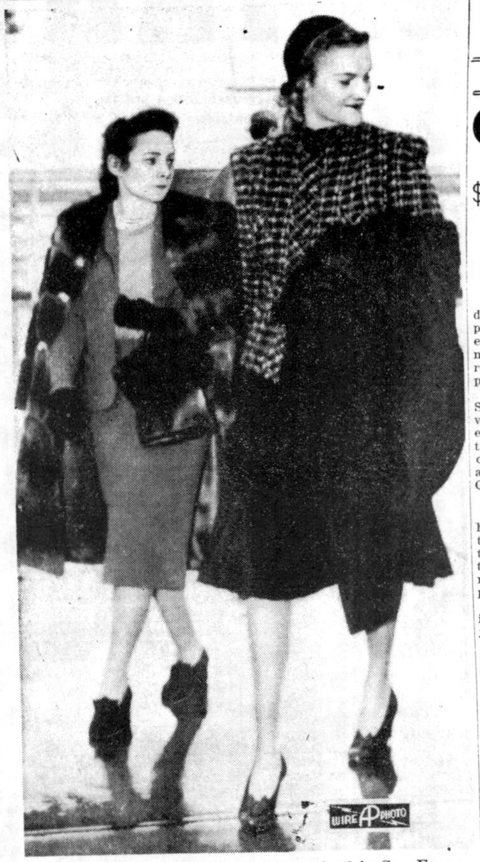

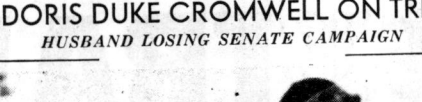

Doris Duke Cromwell (right) arrived in San Francisco yesterday by plane from New York and was seeking passage on the China Clipper scheduled to depart today for Hawaii. Mrs. Cromwell is shown leaving airport. Woman at left is unidentified. While Mrs. Cromwell was arranging flight to Hawaii her husband, James H. R. Cromwell, appeared to be losing race as candidate for United States Senate in New Jersey.

$5,000,000 Paving Loan Is Also Defeated

Daylight saving went down to defeat and so did the $5,000,000 paving loan, but the $5,000,000 sewer loan was approved by Baltimore voters, according to complete returns today from the city's 471 polling places.

Incomplete returns from the State as a whole showed that the voters of Maryland had registered emphatic disapproval of Constitutional amendments designed to increase the salaries of legislators and to limit the tenure of office of Governors to one term.

COURT IS VICTORIOUS

The People's Court amendment, however, scored an outstanding victory. By a ratio of something like three to one the voters approved the amendment which would remove the "poor man's court" from partisan political influences.

Voters of the State were strongly in favor of taxing salaries of judges, decisively disapproved the proposal for creating a Fisheries Commission to replace the existing Conservation Commission, and favored revising the setup of the State Industrial Accident Commission.

The latter two measures were referenda, not involving any change in the State Constitution.

Seven other measures voted on yesterday, however, provided for amendments to the Constitution. In addition, Baltimore voters—but not those of the counties—voted on four other measures.

CLOSEST VOTE

One of these, the daylight saving amendment to the City Charter, brought the closest vote. The final score stood 94,961 against this amendment to 82,952 for it.

The $5,000,000 paving loan, too, was slapped down—and by a vote of more than two to one. A total of 91,038 ballots were cast against this measure, to 36,937 in favor of it.

SEWER LOAN WINS

But the $5,000,000 sewer loan was passed by a vote of 81,845 to 53,342 against.

One more city measure, an amendment providing for the printing or engrossing of ordinances before City Council for third reading, passed by a vote of 69,882 to 30,632.

VOTE ON COURT

Of the State-wide measures the People's Court amendment was clearly the people's favorite. It scored 121,579 votes in favor of it, to only 40,247 votes in opposition. Another amendment, providing that the Court of Appeals shall appoint its clerk hereafter, was passed by a vote of 76,449 to 34,786. In the past the voters have balloted on the choice of this State official.

An amendment providing for an additional judge in the Seventh Circuit (Prince George's, Calvert, Charles and St. Mary's counties) was passed, 77,618 to 37,050. But the voters turned down the amendment to increase legislators' salaries, scoring 92,882 votes against it to 37,272 for.

GOVERNOR'S TERM

The amendment providing that two judges of the Third Circuit shall be residents of Baltimore county and one judge a resident of Harford county was passed, but by the rather slender margin of 59,842 votes for to 52,328 against.

Another amendment limiting Governors to one term was decisively defeated, 110,855 to 52,590 for. A final amendment, providing judges and other public officials shall not be exempted from paying State income taxes, was passed, 83,852 for to 34,762 against.

CARD PARTY TONIGHT

The Rho Province of Sigma Phi Gamma Sorority will hold a charity bazar and card party at Pythian Hall tonight at 8 o'clock. The Children's Mountain School will benefit from the proceeds of the affair.

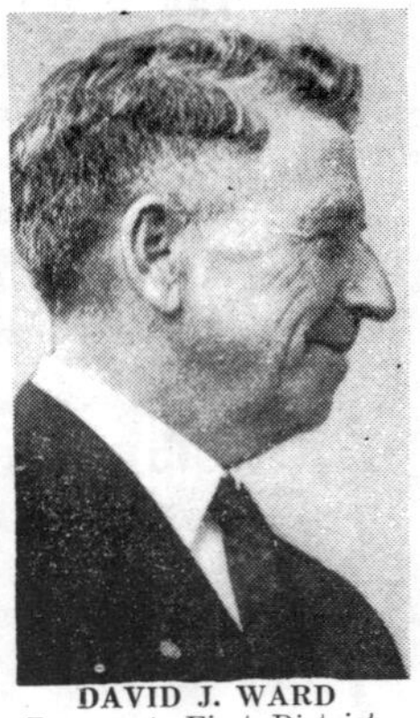

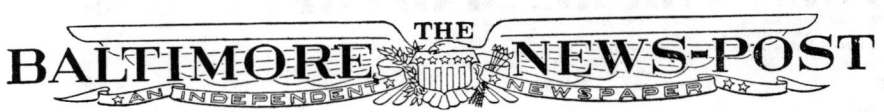

DAVID J. WARD
Democrat, First District

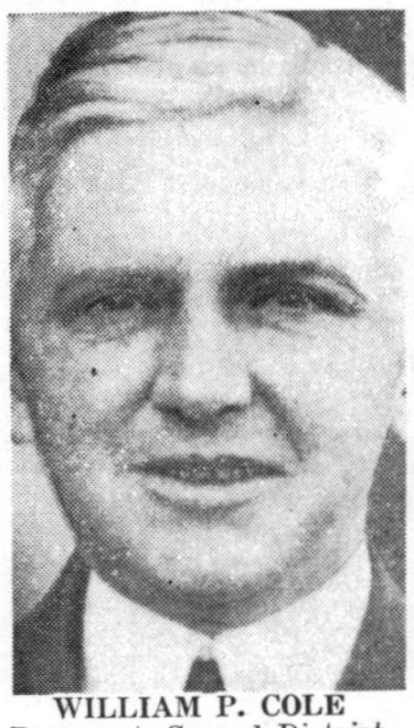

WILLIAM P. COLE
Democrat, Second District

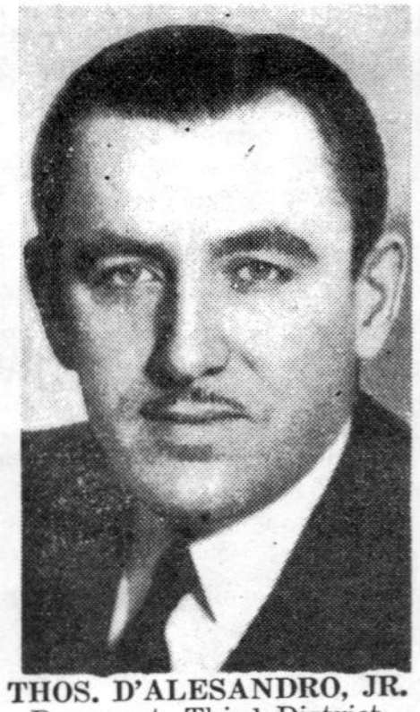

THOS. D'ALESANDRO, JR.
Democrat, Third District

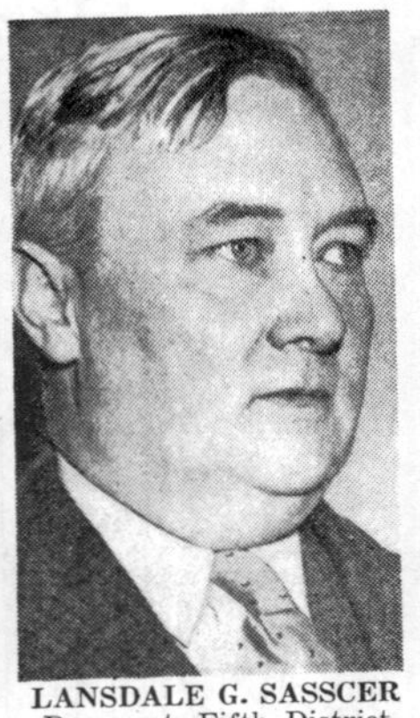

LANSDALE G. SASSCER
Democrat, Fifth District

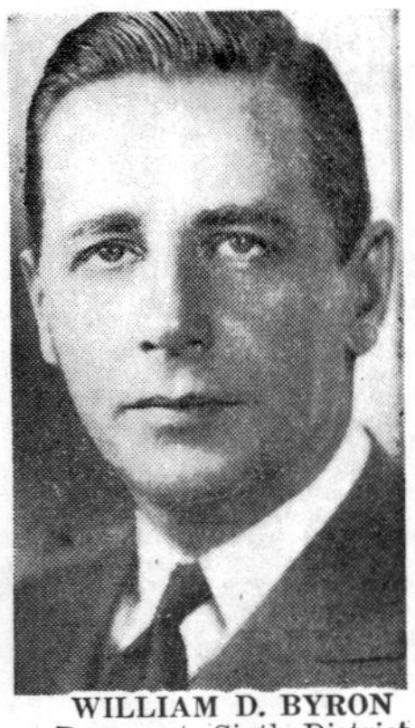

WILLIAM D. BYRON
Democrat, Sixth District

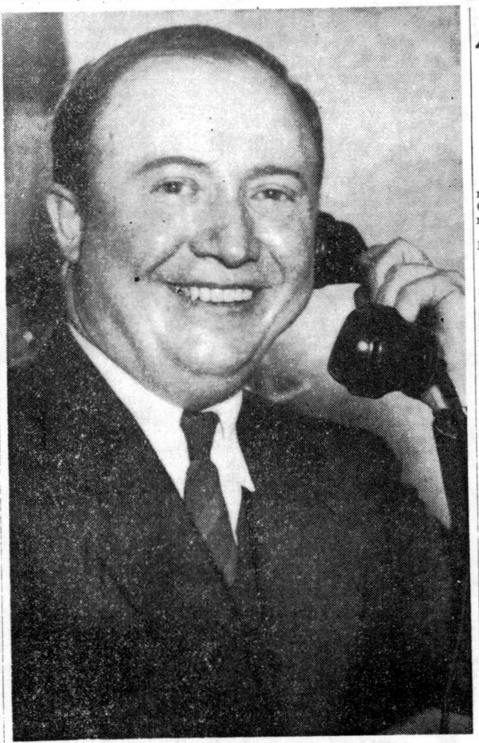

REPRESENTATIVE JOHN A. MEYER

Maryland's Congressional delegation is pictured above on a basis of nearly complete returns from throughout the State. The only "freshman" member of the delegation is Representative Meyer, who won a hard-fought battle in the Fourth district against City Councilman Daniel Ellison, the Republican aspirant. The other five Congressmen were re-elected. Photographs copyright, 1940, by The Baltimore News-Post. All rights reserved.

Archduke Otto Will Talk At J. H. U. Today

The Archduke Otto von Hapsburg, pretender to the Austrian throne and sworn enemy of Adolf Hitler, will deliver the first of four lectures in Baltimore today at Johns Hopkins University, where he will speak at 5 P. M., on "The Battle of Austria."

The twenty-seven-year-old nobleman will be the guest of Theodore Marburg at his home on Mount Vernon place during his Baltimore visit. The second lecture at Hopkins will be given in Latrobe Hall at 5 P. M. Friday.

WILL TALK AT GOUCHER

Tomorrow night at 8 o'clock he will speak in Catherine Hooper Hall, Goucher College, taking as his topic "The Actual European Situation and Central Europe." He will conclude his Baltimore series with a second lecture at Goucher on Monday.

Now a resident of New York, Archduke Otto paid his first visit to Baltimore last March when he flew here on one of the Atlantic clippers.

TOLD VIEWS

At that time he declared that the restoration of a free Austria was the keystone of peace in Europe after the present war. He declared that such a nation, even larger than the pre-World War Austria, would be able to checkmate any dictator like Hitler who might arise in the future.

City Seaman Reported Hurt

Transferred at sea from his four-masted schooner to a Coast Guard cutter, Oscar N. Tate, East Baltimore seaman aboard the Albert F. Paul, today is in a Gloucester Hospital suffering from injuries received while en route to Portland, Maine.

An Associated Press dispatch from Boston sated Tate had a broken arm with possible blood-poison complications, but details of how the injuries were sustained were lacking.

The schooner, Baltimore-owned, sailed from Jacksonville, Fla., to Portland with a full cargo of lumber. Commanded by Capt. Robert O. Jones, the vessel was in Baltimore a month ago with logwood picked up in Haiti for a Canton chemical firm.

Hold 2 In Election Day Beer Charge

Charged with selling beer on election day and also without a license, a man an woman docketed as Leo J. Kraus, 1500 block Malster avenue, a plumber, and Miss Rose A. Dailey, 1900 block Tuttle street, were to be given a hearing today in Northern district police court.

They were arrested late last night by Sergeant Alexander Emerson and members of the police vice squad who said they found them in the kitchen of a house in the 1900 block of Tuttle street. Miss Dailey was reported to have a saloon license for another location in the neighborhood.

Fund Workers To Make First Report

Culminating three months of preliminary effort, volunteer workers in the fifteenth annual Community Fund campaign for a goal of $1,189,739 are scheduled to make the first report of their progress at 12.15 P. M. today in the ballroom of the Lord Baltimore Hotel.

John C. Legg, Jr., campaign chairman, will preside and call for reports from division heads.

Reports are expected from all divisions in the trade and industry grouping, with partial returns from the men's sales army.

WOMEN OPENING DRIVE

Also at noon today women workers will open their campaign with a luncheon in Hotel Emerson.

Vincent Sheean, author and foreign correspondent, will speak on "Freedom's Cause and the Dictators." Mrs. J. A. Dushane Penniman, women's division chairman, will preside.

Yesterday afternoon 175 school teachers representing more than 4,000 city teachers and public school employes opened their campaign after talks by Legg and Charles H. Roloson, Jr., former fund president and campaign chairman.

END DRIVE BY NOV. 18.

They hope to conclude solicitation by November 18.

Five more general campaign report meetings will be held on November 8, 12, 14, 18 and 20. Funds pledged will go to insure the continuance of Baltimore welfare work by the 35 member agencies of the Community Fund.

Two new agencies, the Young Men's Christian Association and the Baltimore League for the Hard of Hearing, have been admitted to the fund.

Campaign heads estimate that approximately $60,000 in "new money" is needed to care for the needs of the two new agencies and for certain losses from contributors who have died or moved from the city.

This means, they said, increased giving on every hand in order to meet the goal.

DE MOLAY UNIT TO MEET

The Mothers' Club of Belvidere Chapter, Order of DeMolay, will hold a meeting Friday night in the home of Mrs. Roy E. McCurdy, 2337 West Lexington street.

Arrange Benefit Party For Church

A card party for the benefit of Our Lady of the Sea Church, Solomons, Md., will be held Wednesday at 8.15 P. M. in Monastery Hall, Irvington, sponsored by the Brother Isidore Veteran Unit of the Catholic Students' Mission Crusade. Miss Elizabeth Barlow is in charge of arrangements. The Rev. Maurice B. Alexander is pastor of the church.

Archbishop To Preside At Mass

Archbishop Michael J. Curley will preside at solemn mass in honor of St. Martin which will be offered at 11 A. M., November 17, in celebration of the diamond jubilee of St. Martin's Catholic Church.

Assisting the archbishop will be the Rev. Dr. John J. Russell, pastor of St. Ursula's Church, Parkville, a former assistant of St. Martin's, who will preach. The Rev. Msgr. Louis O'Donovan, pastor of the church, will be celebrant of the mass.

Others participating in the celebration will be the Rev. E. Jerome Winter and the Rev. Richard J. Barron, deacon and subdeacon, respectively, the Very Rev. F. Joseph Manns, archpriest, and the Rev. Leo L. Otterbein and the Rev. Henry D. Collins, who will be deacons of honor to the archbishop.

Hit By Car, Man Has Broken Leg, Arm

Struck by an automobile while crossing Harford avenue, near Biddle street last night, John Watkins, fifty, 1200 block East Chase street, was given treatment in St. Joseph's Hospital for a broken arm and leg and held for observation today.

He was taken to the hospital by Robert Bailey, twenty-six, 900 block East Preston street, operator of the car, who was charged by police with reckless driving.

Assign Md. Quotas In Draft

Continued from Page 1.

Calvert County—One board, one man.
Caroline County—One board, one man.
Carroll County—No. 1, one man; No. 2, two men.

ONE FOR CECIL

Cecil County—One board, two men.
Charles County—One board, two men.
Dorchester County—One board, two men.
Frederick County—No. 1, three men; No. 2, two men.
Garrett County—No. 1, three men.
Harford County—No. 1, two men; No. 2, two men.
Howard County—One board, two men.
Kent County—One board, one man.

7 IN MONTGOMERY

Montgomery County—No. 1, two men; No. 2, three men; No. 3, two men.
Prince Georges County—No. 1, three men; No. 2, three men; No. 3, three men.
Queen Anne County—One board, one man.
St. Mary's County—One board, one man.
Talbot County—One board, one man.
Washington County—No. 1, three men; No. 2, three men.
Wicomico County—No. 1, one man; No. 2, one man.
Worcester County—No. 1, two men.

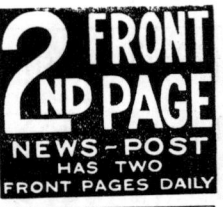

Caveat to Broening Will Is Dropped

A caveat filed to the will of the late Henry J. Broening, attorney, by his son, H. Lyman Broening, was dismissed in Orphans' Court today at the request of the son's attorneys, Harry O. Levin and Daniel S. Sullivan.

Under a will dated October 21, 1937, the Broening estate, estimated at $35,375, was left to his second wife, Mrs. Althea E. Broening. Mr. Broening, brother of former Mayor William F. Broening, died last May. His widow lives in the 3600 block Hillsdalye road.

Hostess

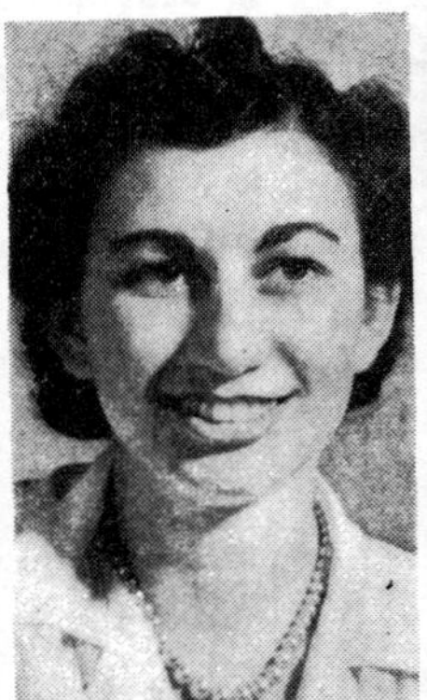

Hostess of Phi Delta Tau's dance at Cadoa Hall next Sunday evening will be Miss Frances Klein (above), 3300 block Gwynn's Falls Parkway. The affair is in celebration of Armistice Day.

Pick Jury In 2nd Red Fraud Trial

Jury to try Richard D. Broune, 1600 block John street, on charges of perjury in connection with the Maryland Communist Party's nominating petition, was selected in Criminal Court today.

Broune is charged with falsely swearing that he knew each of 11 signers of one petition was a registered voter and also that he personally saw the signatures affixed. Judge Edwin T. Dickerson overruled technical motion offered by Leo M. Alpert, defense attorney.

Next Monday Sophie Kaplan and Benjamin Davis will face similar charges, and the last of the defendants, Paul J. Jervis and Minnie Stambler are slated for trial on the 25th.

Mrs. Dorothy Rose Blumberg, wife of Dr. Albert E. Blumberg, secretary of the Communist party in Maryland, the first of the defendants brought to trial, was found guilty several weeks ago. Sentence was deferred following a motion for a new trial.

Despite the indictments, efforts to bar the Communist party from the ballot in Maryland failed following the collapse of a court action in Anne Arundel county.

Gamblers Draw $17,403 In Fines

Statement by Judge Eugene O'Dunne recently that he had adopted a policy of "taking the profit out of the gambling industry" was followed today with official information that in the last few weeks, when that jurist presided in a special session of Criminal Court, the State collected $17,403.11 in fines imposed against convicted gamblers.

The figures establish some kind of record in Baltimore city, according to best informed attaches.

Judge O'Dunne volunteered his services to help in relieving congestion of Criminal Court dockets when he found his own docket in the equity courts slowing up.

Among 361 cases tried by him, there were 145 pleas of guilty, 111 convictions and 103 acquittals. Two charges were stetted by the prosecution.

Picked For Bermuda Run

A clipper ship used on the Alaskan run during the past summer will be brought here within a few weeks to resume Baltimore-Bermuda service by Pan American Airways, it was announced today.

The service was temporarily halted two weeks ago when the Sikorsky flying boat used on the Bermuda run suffered damage in making a landing.

The Alaskan plane, the original Bermuda Clipper, familiarly known as Betsy, is in Seattle. A clipper captain is on the way to Seattle to supervise the transfer flight.

Win Cash For News Tips And Amateur Photographs

Do you want money for being alert? The Baltimore News-Post and Sunday American are offering cash prizes each week for news tips and amateur photographs. Total awards of $50 are distributed weekly for news tips, $25 for the best, $10 for the next best and $1 prizes for the next fifteen. For each amateur photograph published, $3 will be paid, with special bonuses for outstanding pictures. Spot-news pictures are preferred, but candid camera shots that pull at the heart-strings are acceptable. Avoid pictures of ordinary scenes. Telephone The News-Tip Editor at Lexington 0100 (Lexington 4165 from midnight to 6.30 A. M.) for news tips and rush spot-news photographs in to the Picture Editor.

SKIPPY — By Percy Crosby

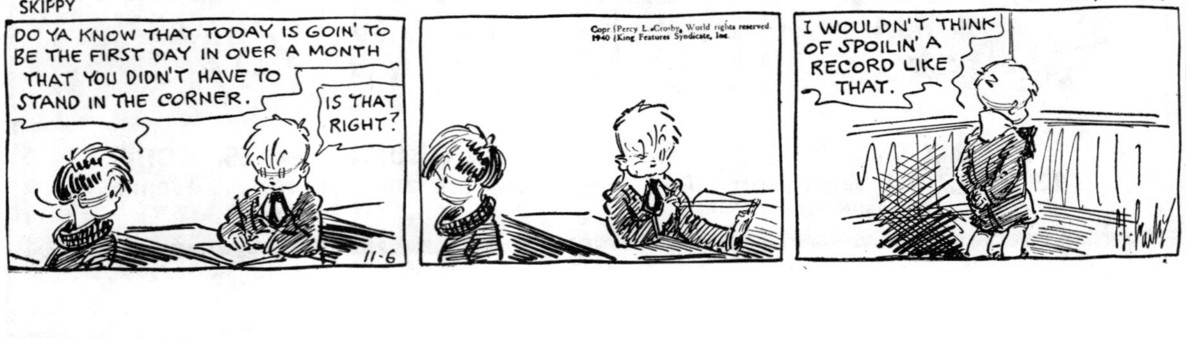

RACING AT PIMLICO
DAILY TO NOVEMBER 15
A Stake Race Every Day
THE BATTLESHIP STEEPLECHASE 'CAP
FIRST RACE 1.15 P. M.
DAILY DOUBLE CLOSES 1 P. M.
Admission (with tax) $1.65

DANCE TONIGHT
Chas. Vincent's Music
ALCAZAR
Ladies 25c, Gentlemen 40c

You Positively Can't Afford To Miss:
HINDA WASSAU
Now! GAYETY THEATRE

Nazis Drop 95,920,000 Lbs. Of Bombs On Britain

THE BALTIMORE NEWS-POST
AN INDEPENDENT NEWSPAPER
The Largest Evening Circulation in the Entire South

VOL. CXXXVIII.—NO. 50 · THURSDAY EVENING, JANUARY 2, 1941 · PRICE 3 CENTS

7 HOME FINAL

Entered as second-class matter at Baltimore Postoffice.
Copyright, 1941, by Hearst Consolidated Publications, Inc.

THE WEATHER

Rain this afternoon and tonight, ending Friday morning, and followed by partly cloudy to clear weather. Colder Friday.

Detailed Weather Report on Page 26

MEAN TEMPERATURES YESTERDAY.

Baltimore	42	New York	41
Atlanta	52	Omaha	39
Boston	36	Portland, Maine	33
Chicago	38	Salt Lake City	22
Jacksonville	58	San Antonio	70
Los Angeles	58	Seattle	42
Miami	74	Tampa	42
New Orleans	68	Washington	45

HERO FATHER, 2 GIRLS PERISH IN FIRE HERE

IN THE NEWS

YOUR columnist is in deep water. He is confronted with a problem which he is unable to solve.

He naturally has respect for the views of the President of the United States, who is a great and good man.

Your columnist also has a high respect for the opinions of the late British Ambassador to the United States, who was a very high-minded, sincere, and able British statesman.

Both President Roosevelt and Lord Lothian have been very ardent supporters of Great Britain's democratic ideals and imperial purposes.

Lord Lothian's ability and sincerity were recognized by England to such a degree that the English Government made him their official representative as Ambassador to Washington.

That post is considered by the British Government the most important diplomatic place in the world.

Lord Lothian was believed by the British Government to be the best fitted man to fill that great post.

The British Government kept Lord Lothian in that post and never removed him. He was only removed by death.

Therefore, Lord Lothian's opinions are of exceptional importance.

They are frank opinions, advanced opinions, liberal opinions.

Perhaps we will consider them too liberal, but they are the opinions of a devoted Englishman.

Lord Lothian left them in clear and permanent printed form for the perusal of posterity.

They are particularly interesting because they freely tell conditions which existed, and accurately foretell the results which have since occurred.

They are interesting, too, because they differ somewhat from the opinions forcefully expressed by President Roosevelt in his recent speech, although both Lord Lothian and the President are equally devoted to the English cause—Lord Lothian as an Englishman, President Roosevelt as an American.

Your columnist would not assume to take any personal attitude in the presentation of the views of these great men.

It would seem a sort of sacrilege to interrupt the free flow of elevated thought and of careful and conscientious recommendation from these authoritative sources by the intrusion of minor opinion.

President Roosevelt's views were printed in extenso Monday.

It is not necessary nor desirable to give Lord Lothian's at such length, but verbatim extracts from his writings are printed herewith:

"The Treaty of Versailles imposed two things upon her (Germany). First, a great reduction in territory, a loss of colonies and heavy reparations. Second, 'defenselessness' against her neighbours through the unilateral disarmament clauses of Part V. of the treaty. Since 1918 this 'inequality' for Germany has, in fact, been France's 'security.'

"It is, then, 'inequality' that Germany is absolutely determined to get rid of today. It involved liability to the Ruhr invasion and to incidents like the present Memel situation. It meant that, in practice, the neighbours of Germany could consult about European problems, while Germany was kept outside the door, and then ask her to 'sign on the dotted line.' They could afford to do this because Germany, normally one of the great powers of the world, could not, in the last resort, resist. National Socialism, which among other things is a movement of individual and national self-respect, came into being largely to end the abasement of Germany."

(From "Germany and France," in the London Times, January 31 and February 1, 1935.)

"If Danzig, which is a German city, wants to rejoin Germany, now that Poland has got Gdynia, it is not worth a war to prevent it. It would be wise for Poland to make some permanent arrangement for enabling Germany to have

Continued on Page 4, Column 1.

95,920,000 Lbs. Of Bombs Dropped On Britain, Nazis Claim

BERLIN, Jan. 2—(A. P.).—The German air force has dropped 25 pounds of bombs on England for every pound loosed on Germany, the German High Command reported today, giving its own total since August 8 at 92,400,000 pounds of high explosive bombs and 3,520,000 pounds of incendiaries.

ROME, Jan. 2—(A. P.).—The Rome radio announced today German air forces had come to Italy to fight with the Italians and also disclosed that Italian air units, which had been aiding the Nazi fliers in the bombardment of Great Britain, had returned home.

ROME, Jan. 2—(U. P.).—Germany is sending air squadrons to Italy and several hundred Fascist war planes are being rushed home from bases at the English Channel, it was revealed today, in order to bolster Italian air strength in Albania and North Africa and attack British supply lines and sea power in the Mediterranean.

Announcement of the move was made by Gen. Francesco Pricolo, Italian Under Secretary for Air, who said the Nazi planes would come to Italy for duty in the Mediterranean basin.

Afternoon newspapers, commenting on Pricolo's announcement said that the German and Italian High Commands had decided jointly to entrust to veteran German air units "special action" in the Mediterranean. The newspapers said also that the returning Italian air squadrons would be used in the Mediterranean.

COMPLETE FORCES

Well-informed sources said the German reinforcements would be complete with ground crews, machine shops and repair facilities, but that they would operate under the Italian High Command.

MAY OPERATE IN AFRICA

The German planes also may operate in North Africa and Albania, it was said, but those theatres are the destination of the several hundred Italian planes being brought back from Channel bases, where they have co-operated with the Luftwaffe in the attack on Britain.

JOSEPH MORDECAI DIES

LONDON, Jan. 2—(U. P.).—Joseph Mordecai, eighty-nine, portrait painter, died Tuesday, it was announced today. Mordecai painted portraits of King Edward VII., King George V. and the Duke of Windsor.

IN 500TH DAY OF SLEEP

ALBANY, Jan. 2—(U. P.).—Doreen Shook, six-year-old sleeping sickness victim, began her 500th day of slumber today and physicians said there was "no change" in her condition.

NOW! ALL THREE GREAT
WIRE SERVICES
Only in The Baltimore News-Post and Baltimore Sunday American will you find ALL THREE great wire services:
INTERNATIONAL NEWS SERVICE
ASSOCIATED PRESS---UNITED PRESS
For all the News from Everywhere you Must Read
THE BALTIMORE NEWS-POST AND SUNDAY AMERICAN

Found Dead In Fire-Swept Home

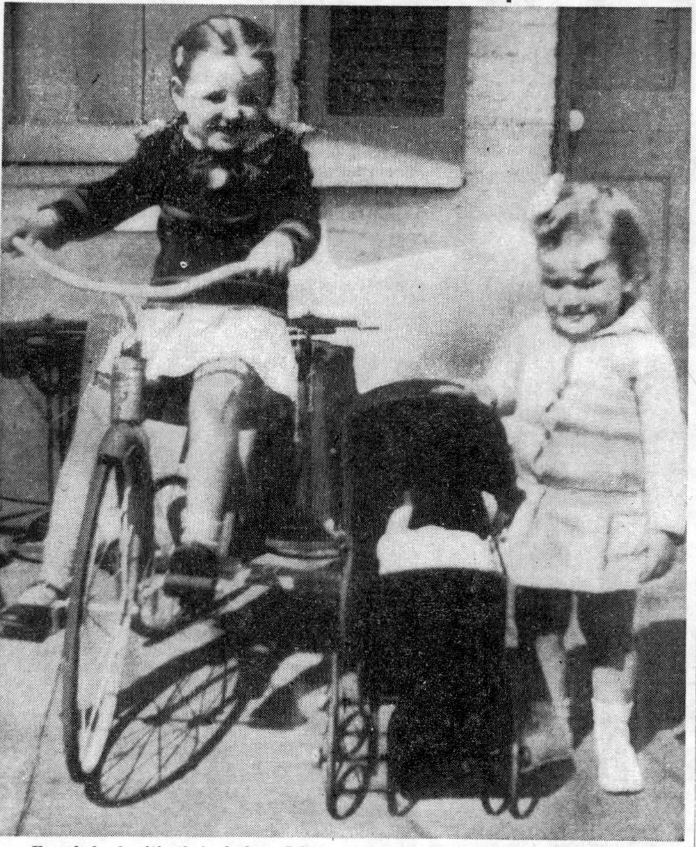

Found dead with their father, John A. Healy, thirty-two, in the bedroom of their fire-swept home at 1423 North Milton avenue were the two little girls pictured above. Mary Elizabeth, four, is on the tricycle, while her little sister, Kathleen, two, stands beside the doll carriage Santa brought her. *Other Pictures on Page 3.*

Mother's Life Saved When She Is Thrown From 2d-Floor Window

Two little girls died in their cribs, and their father met death trying to reach their side early today when a two-alarm fire swept their home at 1423 North Milton avenue.

Firemen found John A. Healy, thirty-two, dead on the floor between the cribs occupied by the children, Mary Elizabeth, four, and Kathleen, two years old.

Their mother, Mrs. Kathryn Healy, thirty-one, was saved when thrown from a second-story rear window by her brother, John Ellwood, a fireman off duty, who boarded in the home.

Ellwood leaped to safety after flames cut him off from the room in which the father and daughters were trapped.

Mrs. Healy, semi-hysterical, suffering from burns, shock and a possible fracture of the ankle in her fifteen-foot fall from the window told the following story in St. Joseph's Hospital:

"I was awakened by the shouts of people outside and found the room filled with smoke. I called to my husband and then ran to the rear bedroom, where my brother, John Ellwood, a fireman, was asleep. I left my husband with the little girls in the front room."

At South Baltimore General Hospital, where Ellwood was taken in a Fire Department ambulance, he told how he had dropped his sister fifteen feet from a rear window and then tried to reach the

Continued on Page 2, Column 7.

See Gas Bombs As Invasion Prelude

By KENNETH DOWNS
International News Service Staff Correspondent.

WASHINGTON, Jan. 2. — When thousands of poison gas bombs begin dropping on England, laying their dread blankets of garlic-like fumes, you can bet the hour of invasion is finally at hand, according to the latest and best information in Washington today.

For, on the basis of confidential reports here, it is expected the heaviest gas attack that can be launched from the air will precede the German move on England, when and if it comes.

SPECIFIC OBJECTIVES

The attacks would be limited to a restricted number of specific objectives, principally air bases, it is said.

Mass gassing of civilians trapped in large metropolitan centers and similar horrors conjured up by the

Continued on Page 2, Column 6.

Temperatures

12 Midn't,	44	7 A. M.,	38
1 A. M.,	43	8 A. M.,	38
2 A. M.,	41	9 A. M.,	38
3 A. M.,	40	10 A. M.,	38
4 A. M.,	39	11 A. M.,	37
5 A. M.,	38	12 Noon,	37
6 A. M.,	38	1 P. M.,	38

Tells Hitler's Invasion Plan

Germany is expected to attempt an invasion of England any day now. Sensational details of how the invasion may be carried out are revealed herein by Sir Philip Gibbs, who enjoys the confidence of leading members of the British Government and is in position to write with authority.

By SIR PHILIP GIBBS
International News Service Special Correspondent.

LONDON, Jan. 2.—Is a German invasion of Britain about to begin?

One of the odd results of President Roosevelt's fireside talk in the minds of many English people is their belief that it will hurry up Adolf Hitler's invasion plan.

There is no overwhelming evidence that Germany has decided to stake her fate upon the perilous gamble of invasion.

It is, of course, in Hitler's mind, and thousands of his subjects are being trained as parachute troops. His army is practicing embarkations and landings.

INVASION FEARED

Just before Christmas there was a general feeling that invasion was imminent.

The army was standing to along the coasts of Britain from Land's End to John O'Groats. The bell-ringers were ready to sound the tocsin from the church towers of every town and village.

The Royal Air Force was tuned up for an instant attack by troop-carrying planes.

Christmas has gone and the new year has come—a year of terrific destiny for all mankind.

Most people I meet have the fixed idea that it will not be many days

Continued on Page 2, Column 1.

Make Us Invisible In War. Best Brains of the nation among architects, artists, philosophers, engineers and other technicians being trained to turn out new tricks hiding America from an enemy. Don't miss this illustrated feature in The American Weekly, the magazine with next Sunday's Baltimore American.—Adv.

VERY LATEST NEWS

(Race Results From Howard Sports Daily, Inc.)

CONVICT 17, ENDS LIFE IN CELL BLOCK

RALEIGH, N. C., Jan. 2—(U. P.).—A seventeen-year-old North Carolina convict committed suicide in the main cell block of Central State Prison here today by jumping from the fifth cell tier to the concrete floor below.

ARMY TO DRAFT 100,000 IN JANUARY

WASHINGTON, Jan. 2—(A. P.).—The Army's draft schedule was reported today to call for induction of approximately 100,000 selective service trainees in January.

THE BALTIMORE NEWS-POST

AN INDEPENDENT NEWSPAPER

The Largest Evening Circulation in the Entire South

VOL. CXXXVIII.—NO. 65

Entered as second-class matter at Baltimore Postoffice.

Copyright, 1941, by Hearst Consolidated Publications, Inc.

MONDAY EVENING, JANUARY 20, 1941

PRICE 3 CENTS

WALL ST. CLOSE 9

THE WEATHER

Clear and continued cold tonight. Tomorrow mostly clear with slowly rising temperature; moderate northwest winds, becoming gentle variable tomorrow.

MEAN TEMPERATURES YESTERDAY

Baltimore	33	New York	29
Atlanta	34	Omaha	42
Boston	32	Portland, Me.	30
Chicago	8	Salt Lake City	19
Jacksonville	44	San Antonio	44
Los Angeles	63	Seattle	46
Miami	58	Tampa	50
New Orleans	40	Washington	30

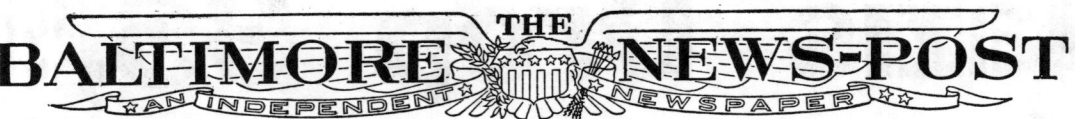

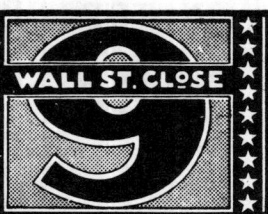

ROOSEVELT TAKES OATH OF OFFICE

Asks American People To Perpetuate Democracy In His Inaugural Address

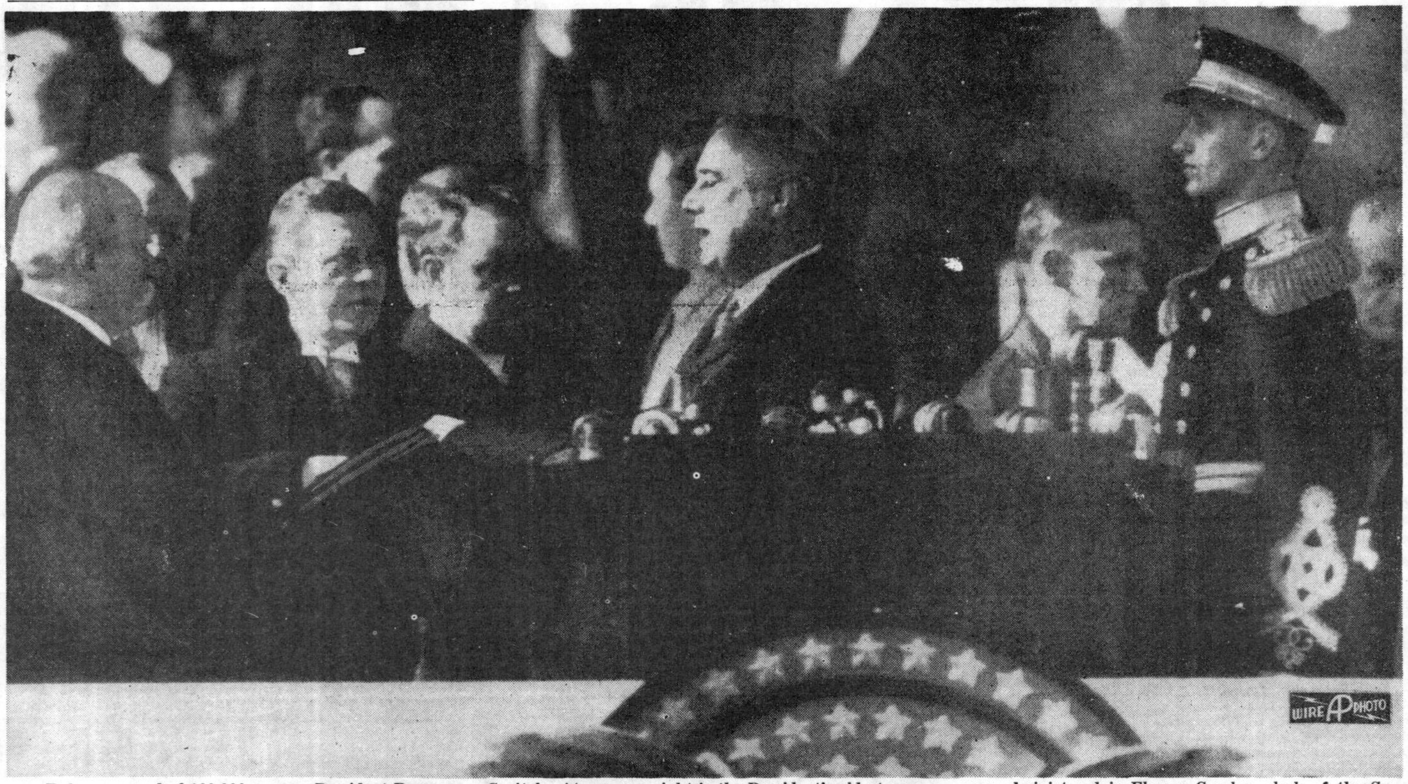

Before a crowd of 100,000 persons President Roosevelt took the oath of office for his history-making third term from Chief Justice Charles Evans Hughes at the Capitol. At extreme right is the President's oldest son, James, in full-dress uniform of a captain of the Marine Corps Reserves. Holding the Bible on which the oath was administered is Elmore Cropley, clerk of the Supreme Court.

(Other pictures on Pages 2, 3, A and B)

Axis Officials Hear Pledge For Liberty

1,000,000 Line Capital Streets to Cheer President

Text of Address on Page A.

By WILLIAM K. HUTCHINSON
International News Service Staff Correspondent

WASHINGTON, Jan. 20.—Franklin Delano Roosevelt entered American history today as the nation's first third-term President and immediately dedicated his future to perpetuating the "integrity of democracy" and to preserving its institutions against tyranny and slavery.

With representatives of the Axis powers sitting behind him, amid an inaugural crowd of 100,000 on the Capitol plaza, the President called on the American people to act "quickly, boldly and decisively" to preserve the "sacred fire of liberty and the destiny of the republican form of government."

Clear, but sub-freezing weather bathed his third-term inauguration in sunshine—a happy augur to New Dealers, after his blustery, rain-swept inaugurations of 1933 and 1937.

1,000,000 CHEER

The President rode to the Capitol down historic Pennsylvania avenue, through shivering crowds numbering nearly 1,000,000 who stood in curbstone lines for hours to cheer him.

The crowds were still there an hour later as he returned to the White House, sworn to execute faithfully the office of President for another four years.

Mr. Roosevelt keynoted his third term with a simple inaugural speech, after Chief Justice Charles Evans Hughes administered the Presidential oath to him for the third time.

His chief appeal was to the American people to "muster the spirit of America and the faith of America" to uphold their sacred democracy.

DEPARTS FROM TEXT

The President departed from his text once—and then perhaps inadvertently. In the text, he asked his countrymen to "take stock" in

Continued on Page A Column 1.

IN THE NEWS

MR. LOUIS LURIE wants a relief from American history, but not, we are sure, from historic American policy.

We strive to please.

THIS country always has had, and always should have an opposition party.

The Republican party is not an opposition party.

As a matter of fact, there is no opposition party in the United States today.

As a further matter of fact, there is no Republican party.

There is a cuckoo party which has invaded the nest and taken the name—in vain—of the Republican party.

But it nominated an ex-Democrat as its national leader who loudly and vigorously supported the regular Democratic candidate and the Democratic party in all its most important policies.

There are Republicans in the United States, but there is no national Republican party to represent them.

There are citizens opposed to the incumbent party and its policies.

But there is no party to represent THEM.

There are many citizens of the United States who do not believe in participating in every foreign war on the face of the earth.

But there is no party to represent THEM.

There are many citizens of the United States who have no faith in Mr. Roosevelt's pre-election pledges to keep America out of foreign wars.

And who have just as little faith in Mr. Willkie's promises to keep this independent nation out of every European and Asiatic mess.

There are many, and maybe a majority, of the American citizenry who now feel (to paraphrase the words of Saint Paul) that Mr. Roosevelt's promises are but the tinkling of cymbals, and Mr. Willkie's echo of them but the sounding of brass.

THERE are many loyal Americans who believe that America should mind its own American business and pursue its own free and independent American policies and keep alive its own fine and free American youth, even if all the misguided nations of Europe and Asia want to stew and strive and destroy themselves in the juice of their own greed and hatred and envy and jealousy and commercial rivalry.

These loyal American citizens, be they few or many—be they a majority or even a minute fraction of the population—are entitled to representation on this vital question in the two-party system of the United States, and they have none.

The so-called Democratic party gives them no representation.

And the so-called Republican party gives them no representation.

Mr. Roosevelt, leader of the phoney Democratic party, and Mr. Willkie, leader of the phoney Republican party, are engaged in a headlong race to see which will get this American nation into foreign war first and farthest.

Mr. Roosevelt and Mr. Willkie are vying with each other in their interest in foreign activities and affairs, and in their lack of interest in the activities and affairs of their own free and independent America.

MAYBE America ought to be in every foreign war that breaks out anywhere, between the Chinese and the Japanese, the Indo-Chinese and the Siamese, the Italians and the Greeks, the Germans and the English, the Russians and the Finns, the Senegalese and the Abyssinians—or maybe it should not.

Maybe the New World should keep aloof from the greeds and jealousies and the continual conflicts of the Old World—or maybe it should not.

Maybe the United States should conserve its resources for the defense of its own liberties—or maybe it should not.

Maybe it should dissipate its wealth and destroy its youth in the support of alien principles and policies with which it has no actual interest or association—or maybe it should not.

Maybe there should be a free and independent United States of America—or maybe there should not.

These are not the sole questions under discussion.

The questions now before the House are whether or not a large proportion, and maybe a majority, of the citizenry of the United States who are opposed to the nation's involvement in foreign wars are entitled to representation in the historic two-party system of this nation—or whether they are not?

Whether there is a party of op-

Continued on Page 4, Column 1.

Gen. Berganzoli Reported Suicide

LONDON, Jan. 20—(I. N. S.).—Gen. Anniballe Berganzoli, Italian commander-in-chief of the captured Libyan fortress of Bardia, is believed to have committed suicide in the North African desert, the London Daily Express reported today in a dispatch from British headquarters at Bardia.

Hitler, Duce Fear British Eire Move

ROME, Jan. 20—(I. N. S.).—An official communique late today announced that Premier Benito Mussolini and Reichsfuehrer Hitler had held a conference and that their meeting was "most cordial."

By PIERRE J. HUSS
International News Service Staff Correspondent.

BERLIN, Jan. 20.—Reichsfuehrer Adolf Hitler and Premier Benito Mussolini met today for their "last conference before the war's climax" as informed German quarters predicted early British occupation of Eire.

(BACKGROUND NOTE: This was the first time Berlin had spoken openly of any such planned coup by Britain. Germany justified her invasions of Denmark, Norway and the Lowlands on the grounds Britain had planned similar violations of neutrality to strike at the Reich.)

The influential Nazi newspaper Vreme of Belgrade today termed

Continued on Page 2, Column 1.

VERY LATEST NEWS

(Race Results From Howard Sports Daily, Inc.)

LATE PASS WINS FOURTH AT HIALEAH

AT HIALEAH PARK

Third—Royal Master, $40.60, $15.80, $8.20; Foxworth, $4.60, $3.80; Ceepeetee, $3.90. Tot. muts., $76.90.

Fourth—Late Pass, $22.50, $9.50, $7.50; Gallant Stroke, $6.00, $4.70; Clean Swept, $12.40.

GREEKS DESTROY ENEMY SUBMARINE

ATHENS, Jan. 20 — (A. P.). — Destruction of an enemy submarine by "our anti-submarine organization" was reported tonight by the Greek Ministry of Marine.

NEW YORK STOCK EXCHANGE TOTAL SALES

NEW YORK, Jan. 20—(A. P.).—Total sales on the New York Stock Exchange today were 377,280 shares.

Temperatures

Midnight,	25	8 A. M.,	26
1 A. M.,	26	9 A. M.,	28
2 A. M.,	26	10 A. M.,	30
3 A. M.,	25	11 A. M.,	30
4 A. M.,	25	12 Noon,	31
5 A. M.,	25	1 P. M.,	32
6 A. M.,	25	2 P. M.,	33
7 A. M.,	25	3 P. M.,	34

Armed Man Seized Near White House

WASHINGTON, Jan. 20 — (I. N. S.).—Secret Service agents seized a man in front of the White House today bearing a loaded gun.

They said he was dressed in a war veteran's uniform and was discovered in the "Court of Freedom" directly in front of the Executive Mansion.

He was immediately rushed into the office of the District of Columbia police for questioning. The incident occurred while Mr. Roosevelt was at the Capitol taking his oath of office.

Police declined to make the man's name public pending further inquiry. They described the weapon as a "pistol" and asserted it was fully loaded.

Later it was announced the man had besn taken to Gallinger Hospital for examination by psychiatrists.

Prize Winning Norwegian Recipes. You'll find them in the Housewife's Food Almanack; also a gastronomical calendar for February, and a number of odd and unusual facts about food. All in The American Weekly, the magazine with next Sunday's Baltimore American.—Adv.

280 Warplanes Roar Over Capitol

By EDWARD B. LOCKETT
International News Service Staff Correspondent.

WASHINGTON, Jan. 20.—Aerial might, displayed on an unprecedented scale, today touched off celebration of President Roosevelt's triumphant inaugural for a third term in the White House.

With a tremendous roar, 280 of the Navy's and Army's finest planes —scores of four-motored and twin-motored bombers, with groups of lightening-like pursuit ships above them—swept overhead shortly after the President's return to the Executive Mansion.

Traffic was jammed for miles, as motorists stopped their cars dead in the streets to leap out and peer upward at the most unique aerial armada ever to fly over the Capitol dome.

Back and forth across the sky for 15 minutes they swept as a prelude to the inaugural parade down Pennsylvania avenue.

HIALEAH RESULTS

FIRST RACE—Purse $1,200; maiden two-year-olds; three furlongs out of chute. Off at 2.04. Time .33 3-5.

Fade, 118 (Arcaro)	$5.00	$3.00	$2.60
True Heart, 118 (Gilbert)		4.80	3.50
Fate, 118 (Young)			10.50
Total mutuels			$29.40

Also Ran—Brown Dancer, Lustrous, Rations, Manella, Sampler, Bonnie Golos, Portable, Sallymar, fTower Maid, fBlossom Lane. fField.

SECOND—Purse $1,200; claiming; three-year-olds; seven furlongs out of chute. Off at 2.34. Time 1.26 3-5.

Our Florence, 104 (McCreary)	$5.90	$4.20	$3.30
Bit O Green, 104 (Meade)		12.10	8.00
Stop Loss, 104 (Lemmons)			15.10
Total mutuels			$48.60

Also Ran—Babs, Wallace E., Rest Awhile, Battle Won, Lewiston, Rusty Gold, Arabesque, Mexicana.

Daily Double—Fade In & Our Florence paid $19.20 for $2

THE BALTIMORE NEWS-POST
AN INDEPENDENT NEWSPAPER
The Largest Evening Circulation in the Entire South
VOL. CXXXIX.—NO. 8 Entered as second-class matter at Baltimore Postoffice. TUESDAY EVENING, MAY 13, 1941 PRICE 3 CENTS

NIGHT
RACE SPECIAL

6 HESS AIDES SEIZED ON ORDERS OF HITLER

No. 3 Nazi Who Fled To Scotland Called Sane

IN THE NEWS

EX-PRESIDENT Hoover's speech was a fine American utterance and did much to restore his prestige and position as a leader of American opinion.

Let us hope that it also did much to bring sober and unprejudiced thought to the American people.

On American Week, at any rate, we ought to bring careful consideration to the best interests of our own America and decid- calmly and dispassionately whether or not it is for the present or future advantage of this country to project our people into this foreign conflict.

Mr. Hoover, according to the dispatches, stated that although our relations with the Axis Powers are strained, we are still not in the war.

But, he declared, we would be in the war the moment our Navy goes into action.

"And," continued the Ex-President, *"it is now proposed that we should put the American Navy into action.*

"THAT," said Mr. Hoover, *"is a straightforward, understandable proposal which boldly makes clear the meaning of words like convoys and patrols.*

"THAT is joining in this war once and for all.

"From here the steps are automatic.

"Our Navy must attack German submarines, ships and planes if it is to be of any use.

"To make it effective, then, we must expand naval and air bases abroad.

"We must equip these bases with expeditionary forces.

"And that is WAR FOR LONG YEARS TO COME."

THAT the war will be prolonged for *"years to come"* is evidenced not only by Ex-President Hoover's temperate statement but by the inadvertent words regarding our war activities uttered by Winston Churchill and Lloyd George in the recent vote of confidence debate in the British House of Commons.

Said Mr. Churchill, the Prime Minister, in discussing England's war chances for 1941 and 1942 and 1943:

"It may be that 1943, if we have to endure it as a year of war, will present easier problems.

"The United States patrol announced by President Roosevelt" (not merely proposed, mind you, but announced by President Roosevelt), *"and on which the American Navy and air force ARE ALREADY ENGAGED, takes a considerable part of the Atlantic in a certain degree off our hands, but we need A GOOD DEAL MORE HELP.*

"I expect we shall get a good deal more help.

"In fact, it has been declared we are to have ALL HELP NECESSARY."

So we see from Mr. Churchill's speech that the war we are entering into so heedlessly is expected to endure, as Mr. Hoover says, *"for long years to come,"* in spite of our entry and, indeed, because of our entry.

Without our encouragement to war and without the commitments of our President—secretly entered into and undisclosed to the American people—the war would be over now—would have been over long ago.

And England would have accepted the terms of the Axis, guaranteeing the integrity of the British Empire and merely demanding that England keep her intrusive fingers out of Europe—that England allow European nations to form their own treaties and unions—and that England do not set one European nation against another and destroy both in order to maintain her own hegemony on the Continent.

It is clear from Mr. Churchill's remarks not only that our country has been committed by our autocratic President to war, and that the United States Navy and air force are *"already engaged"* in *"the patrol announced by President Roosevelt,"* but also that the war, in spite of the con-

Continued on Page 4, Column 1.

Ship Seizure Bill Is Potential Act Of War, Senate Foes Charge

WASHINGTON, May 13—(U. P.).—President Roosevelt's goal of 2,000,000 tons of emergency shipping for immediate service to Great Britain will be reached by mid-June, informed officials said today.

By WILLIAM S. NEAL
International News Service Staff Correspondent.

WASHINGTON, May 13.—The Senate headed into a violent controversy today over the Administration's bill authorizing requisition of all foreign ships in U. S. harbors as Senatorial foes charged that the measure goes beyond the Lease-Lend Law policy and embraces a potential act of war.

Senator Bailey (Democrat) of North Carolina, chairman of the Commerce Committee, which approved the bill by a 11-to-4 vote, plans to formally report the legislation to the Senate today. He hopes to call it up tomorrow.

TWO EXPLOSIVE ISSUES

Two explosive issues are to be raised, which may plunge the Senate into its most extended debate in weeks over American foreign policy and possible American entrance into the world war. They are:

1. Proposal of Senator Tobey (Republican) of New Hampshire to write in an amendment prohibiting convoys.

2. Amendment of Senators Vandenberg (Republican) of Michigan and Clark (Democrat) of Missouri to prohibit President Roosevelt from transferring 30 seized German and Italian merchant vessels to Great Britain.

The trend of the battle over Tobey's proposal was uncertain. While he insisted that he would offer the "rider" some non-interventionists hoped to persuade him to abandon the effort in the ship bill fight, and seek a clear-cut decision on a motion to consider his measure alone.

Senator Burton (Republican) of Ohio, who supported the lease-lend bill, split with the Administration on the ship seizure measure. He declared that while the lease-lend bill was designed to assure peace, transfer of vessels of one warring nation to another invites the danger of war.

British Reduce Shipping Losses

BERLIN, May 13—(A. P.).—The German High Command announced today that Nazi submarines had sunk nine merchants ships, totaling 56,248 tons, "during a persistent attack lasting several days on a convoy strongly protected by destroyers."

LONDON, May 13—(A. P.).—British merchant shipping losses in the battle of the Atlantic in April, 301,070 tons out of a total of 488,124 tons sunk in all theatres of the war during the month, were the lowers in 11 months, it was announced today.

The month's total previously was included in an announcement Saturday, which placed losses in the year since the Nazi invasion of the low countries at 1,098 ships totalling 4,734,407 tons.

The sharply reduced sinkings in the Atlantic, authoritative quarters asserted, indicated the effectiveness of counter-measures against Adolf Hitler's air, surface and undersea weapons. An informant said:

"There are no signs that the results of the great efforts the enemy is making will enable him to attain the quick victory he needs."

The losses in the battle of the Atlantic, plus 187,054 tons of ships lost in the removal of troops from Greece and in other areas of the Mediterranean, made up the April total.

A Night At Maxim's Now. M. Jacques Lerminat, well-known French journalist, describes life in conquered Paris and tells how the world-famous cafe has become the "Black Bourse." Read his startling revelations in The American Weekly, the magazine distributed with next Sunday's Baltimore American.—Adv.

Hess Known As Hitler's 'Shadow'

By Associated Press.

In Adolf Hitler's climb to power, probably no single individual was longer or more closely associated with his every political plan and action than Rudolf Hess.

Germans referred to him as Hitler's "shadow."

MET IN WAR

They met on the battlefields of France in the World War. After the war Hess threw his lot with Hitler and for two decades they worked in apparent harmony before his dramatic flight from the Reich.

As recently as nine days ago Hess and Hitler sat side by side at a meeting of the Reichstag.

When Hitler celebrated his fifty-second birthday anniversary, April 20, Hess was with the Fuehrer at his military headquarters on the Balkan front and greeted him:

"Your spirit and your will brought a new people and a new soldier to protect them. Trust in you is unlimited. God protect our Fuehrer."

Since 1933 Hess had acted as Hitler's personal representative in all matters concerning the National Socialist Party.

DEVOTED TO HITLER

His devotion to his leader and zeal in carrying out his orders

Continued on Page 2, Column 7.

N. Y. Leaders Seek Willkie As Mayor

NEW YORK, May 13—(I. N. S.). Local Republican leaders today proposed that Wendell L. Willkie, 1940 G. O. P. presidential candidate, seek the New York city mayoralty post. To date, Mayor F. H. LaGuardia has not indicated whether he intends to seek renomination.

Cotton Futures Rise $2.30 A Bale

NEW YORK, May 13—(A. P.).—Cotton futures opened as much as $2.30 a bale higher today after the unanimous approval of an 85 per cent. parity loan by House and Senate conferees on the Fulmer bill.

Temperatures

12 Midn't,	56	6 A. M.,	53
1 A. M.,	53	7 A. M.,	56
2 A. M.,	51	8 A. M.,	59
3 A. M.,	50	9 A. M.,	62
4 A. M.,	50	10 A. M.,	64
5 A. M.,	48	11 A. M.,	66

BERLIN, May 13.—Six adjutants who were believed to have had knowledge the fugitive Rudolph Hess had resumed flying contrary to Hitler's orders have been arrested. A spokesman denies that Hess's wife and baby son, stunned by the flight, are in custody. (Background Note: London, however, has reports that many friends and aides of Hess are now in custody in Germany.)

Hitler's Aide Flees

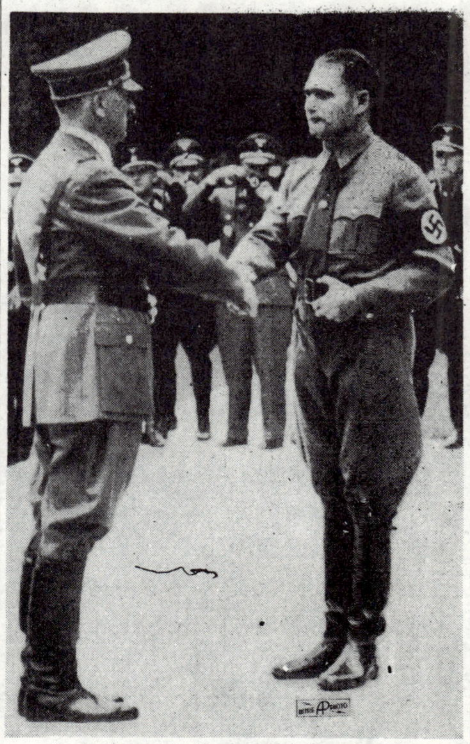

Rudolf Hess (right), second in succession to Adolf Hitler (left) as ruler of the Nazi Reich, and one of the Fuehrer's closest friends, was in British hands today at an unrevealed place in the British Isles after an unexplained airplane flight from Germany. The picture above was made on the occasion of a Nazi party rally at Nurnberg, Germany.

LONDON, May 13 — (A. P.). — Photographs of the wreckage of the Messerschmitt fighting plane from which Rudolf Hess is said to have bailed out show the tail punctured by a number of machine-gun bullets. British sources took this as an indication that pursuers—either German or British—tried to bring down the plane.

LONDON, May 13—(U. P.).—Reports spread through London today that Rudolf Hess was ready to disclose to the Government teh secrets of Germany's war plans and internal situation. These reports were unconfirmed; officials were close-lipped.

LONDON, May 13—(A. P.).—An authoritative source said today that Rudolf Hess' flight from Germany was the voluntary act of a sane man and was carried out in defiance of German authority.

This source declared that Hess brought no peace terms and that his coming to Scotland could not be described as a special mission.

This informant added that Hess knew that if he had gone to a neutral country instead of parachuting onto a Scottish moor, as he did last Saturday night while his Messerschmitt crashed, he would have been in imminent danger of being "bumped off" by Nazi agents.

Hess has been seen by doctors, who found him sane and healthy, this source said. He was identified by Ivan Krikpatrick, former British Charge d'Affaires in Berlin.

PRISONER OF WAR

The former No. 2 heir apparent to Adolf Hitler is being treated as a prisoner of war.

Despite the official statement in London that Hess brought no special message, the rumor flood at Glasgow included one that Hess had asserted he possessed certain important information about the German air force which he wanted to communicate to the British.

Authoritative sources here quick-

Continued on Page 2, Column 1.

Painful Tragedy, Is Berlin View

By PIERRE J. HUSS
International News Service Staff Correspondent.

BERLIN, May 13.—A "fixed obsession" that by personal contact with British friends he could bring about an Anglo-German understanding was blamed today for Deputy Nazi Leader Rudolf Hess' astonishing flight to Scotland.

The official German radio gave this explanation for Hess' action in the first definite German admission that Reichsfuehrer Adolf Hitler's Number 3 Nazi actually is a prisoner of war in British hands.

The broadcaster gave the impression that Hess for some time had been obsessed with the idea of swinging a single-handed peace that would benefit Nazi Germany and at the same time end war in the world.

Earlier, authoritative German circles conceded that Hess' dissapearance from the Reich constitutes an "extraordinarily painful tragedy."

At the same time, they emphasized that his sudden departure will have no effect upon Germany's war or foreign policies or the basic structure of Nazism.

Frequent consultations with stargazers, fortune-tellers and quack doctors were sited as evidence of Hess' gradual breakdown. A friend said:

"The obsession which haunted

Continued on Page 2. Column 7.

Peru, Ecuador To Arbitrate Dispute

LIMA, Peru, May 13—(A. P.).—Peru accepted early today with qualifications the offer by the United States, Argentina and Brazil of their good offices to help settle the 110-year-old dispute between Peru and Ecuador over a rich expanse of land near the headwaters of the Amazon river.

Earl Of Suffolk, 6 Soldiers Killed

LONDON, May 13—(U. P.).—The Earl of Suffolk and six soldiers were killed yesterday by the explosion of a bomb, it was disclosed today.

THE WEATHER

Mostly clear today, tonight and Wednesday. Slightly warmer today, with highest temperature around 74 degrees. Moderately cool tonight, followed by warmer Wednesday. Gentle, variable winds, mostly southerly.

RACE ENTRIES, COMMENTS WILL BE FOUND ON PAGES 21-22-23

THE BALTIMORE NEWS-POST, TUESDAY, MAY 13, 1941 7

MURDER BY RADIO ✦ ✦ ✦ *By Sanford Jarrell* ✦ ✦ ✦ A Short Story

ATLANTIC CITY, N. J.
THE SHELBURNE On the Boardwalk European Plan

THE CAST OF CHARACTERS IN "MURDER BY RADIO"

CHARLES CIRCLEVILLE, murder mystery addict, whose "eminent namesake" gives him an idea that

MARY, his perfect wife, thinks will help her get that cottage.

With a feeling of supreme contentment, Charles Circleville arose from the dinner table in the corner of the living-room of his West Pico apartment. And why should he not feel complacent, even smug? He had a steady job as head mechanic in a garage out on Sunset boulevard, money in the bank, a nice car.

He and Mary had been happily married since he got back from France in 1919, and their two lovely daughters were good and popular students at U. C. L. A. Furthermore, added contentment came from a full stomach. Nobody in Los Angeles, not even at some of those high-toned eateries on Wilshire, could cook a roast like Mary did, and her apple pie would win (and had) the appreciation of any honest trencherman.

Mr. Circleville took his evening paper to his favorite chair by the radio, a chair of gargantuan proportions that spelled easy comfort. He twiddled with the dial until he got a light musical program and then set about the task of reading the news of the war, on which he was a recognized authority at McGrew's garage and the cafe around the corner where he lunched. Mary, meanwhile, busied herself with the humdrum chore of clearing off the gateleg table and washing the dishes. She was an ideal housekeeper and wife. The girls were out somewhere, a school banquet or pep meeting or something.

COMMENTS ON NEWS

Every once in a while Mr. Circleville would summon Mary in from the kitchen to comment sagely on some phase of the foreign dispatches, to which she would listen attentively and then agree that her husband had exactly the right slant on things. After the kitchen had been rendered as clean and spotless as a hospital corridor, she returned to the living room and the prosaic job of mending her stockings and those of her daughters. At 7.59, by the electric clock over the bookcase filled to overflowing with detective novels, her husband turned the dial again with the remark, "Time for the 'Prosecuting Attorney' program." Mary nodded,

ANCHORS AWEIGH — Hold That Oar!

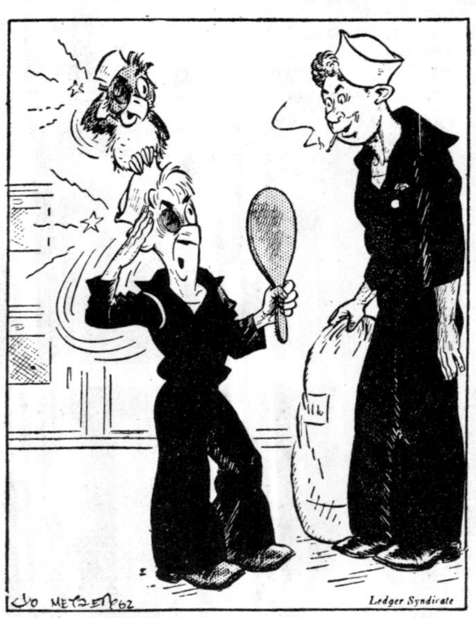
Ledger Syndicate

"That was a slip—but boy, with a little more practice I'll have the snappiest salute in the Navy!"

kept on with her needlework, and Mr. Circleville laid aside his paper, carefully folded to the comics.

It was not until after the announcer with a soft voice thick with hidden romance had extolled a hair tonic that both Mr. and Mrs. Circleville sat up straight in their chairs. For the producer of the series was saying: "The scene is in the lecture hall of a great university and a famous criminologist and psychology authority is speaking. He is Professor Charles Circleville . . ."

A somewhat cracked and irritating voice with an upper bracket pitch seemingly was in the middle of a discourse on the mental processes back of a few of our more stimulating homicides. Suddenly he choked, painful gasps came over the air waves, the loud thump of a falling body. Excited voices, then someone said, "Professor Circleville is dead!" Strains of music followed briefly, and the eager listeners in their West Pico flat next heard the famed Prosecuting Attorney and his ace detective discussing the death of the professor. "Yes," said the P. A., "he was murdered all right. He took enough poison to kill an elephant. But how? And why?"

CIRCLEVILLE SMILES

Mr. Circleville, the crack auto mechanic, grinned at his wife. "Gaze at the body, Mary." She smiled and said, "I'm so thrilled, Charlie." The story then went on; it was a beauty. Said a student, being grilled by the P. A.: "Yes, sir, I hated Professor Circleville. He was an elongated termite. He kept me from passing last semester. But I didn't kill him, I didn't, I didn't." Most suspicious was the late criminologist's assistant, who was to gain the most by Charles Circleville's death. He didn't like the old fellow either. It appeared that no one did. True to the rigid code of murder mysteries, the author made the victim an unprepossessing, unfair and unpopular man, whose passing was not mourned save perhaps in a disconnected way by the world of science where he cut the most ice. Action was enforced in the radio drama by a blow on the head in the dark of Professor Circleville's laboratory assistant, night prowlers and the like.

The Prosecuting Attorney discovered that the dead man for years had vanished mysteriously over each week-end and thus was the butt of a ribald student song, "Oh where, oh where, does Charlie go every Saturday afternoon?" By this means he traced the professor's wife. Everybody had thought she was single, but she could add little light on the motive for the murder. It developed that poison was transmitted by means of the manuscript he was reading. He had the habit of wetting his fingers with his tongue as he flipped the pages, and this led to his unholy doom. It turned out that the professor's wife was insane and had done the job herself.

Charles Circleville, the mechanic, enjoyed every minute of the thriller.

"I wonder," said Mr. Circleville, "if any of our friends listened in?"

"Sure they did," said Mary. "This is one of the most popular programs on the air."

MOCK SURPRISE

Spike McGrew expressed mock surprise when Mr. Circleville showed up for work the next day. He shouted into his office, so all could hear. "Cancel that order for flowers for Charlie Circleville's funeral, Miss Harris. The darned fool ain't dead a-tall."

At Rosy's Cafe that noon, pretty Jenny Warfield, the waitress, greeted him tartly. "They finally caught up with you. I see, you bald-headed old termite. First time in my life I've ever had to serve steak and potatoes to a ghost."

Mary told him that night how Mrs. Babson, in the apartment across the hall, and Mr. Apolli, the grocer down at the corner, had kidded her, too. The girls had heard about it all over the U. C. L. A. campus, she said, though they hadn't listened to the program. "We're famous," she said.

"I wonder how they got hold of my name?" said Mr. Circleville. "After all, it isn't a common one. I never met any other Circleville except my Cousin Joe, back in Grand Island."

"Maybe one of those movie writer fellows who have their work done in the garage wrote it," she suggested.

"I'd like to find out," he said.

It was Patsy Miller, his sidekick at the garage, who put the idea first into Charlie Circleville's head that he might make some easy money.

SUGGESTS SUIT

"You and Mary've got plenty of grounds to sue them people," he said. "Making you out a termite and she a crazy murderess. Why don't you see my brother Pete, down on Spring street. He's a lawyer and a good one, too I'll bet he can make them people cough up a couple of grand."

A couple of thousand dollars, Mr. Circleville reflected, plus an equal sum drawn from his saving account, would buy that cottage they were looking at the other day in Arcadia, without any payments and interest to meet in the future. He talked it over with Mary and she said Mr. Apolli, the grocer, had made a similar suggestion. So he telephoned Mr. Vincent Miller, Patsy's brother, and made an appointment with him. Mary went with him, and they told the lawyer about the program they had heard over the air.

"Unquestionably," said the lawyer, "you must have suffered much mental anguish because of this."

Mr. Circleville was dubious, but said maybe that was right.

"I'll dictate a letter for you to sign, Mr. Circleville, and you, too, Mrs. Circleville," said the man of law. "They may pay without us going to the trouble to sue. My charge will be only $25, but if we have to go to court, of course, it will be more. I never take a case on a contingent basis."

WRITES CHECK

Mr. Circleville wrote out a check for $25, and half an hour later he and Mary had posted the letter to the broadcasting network, with a copy to the sponsors of the program. They drove out a way and once went by the little Cape Cod cottage in Arcadia. Mary planned how she would arrange the furniture after they received the money from New York and bought the place.

"Just think," she said, "the Santa Anita race track is only two miles from us."

"You know I don't play the ponies," said Mr. Circleville.

"I know you don't," she said, "but we can go once in a while just to see Bing Crosby and Hedy Lamarr and all those other stars. They must go there every day. I see their pictures in the paper with field glasses in their hands."

The boys at the garage all wished Charlie Circleville luck, but Spike McGrew didn't think he had a chance. "You know that hair-tonic crowd didn't murder you for spite," he said. "I'll bet they've got an out."

Finally an important looking letter came to the West Pico address, but Mary didn't dare open it until her husband came home. Perhaps it contained that check. Instead, it was a friendly letter from the advertising agency which handled the hair-tonic program.

"Obviously," the letter stated, "we must prepare against lawsuits, so we employ a very simple method which affords us great leeway, yet legal protection as well. In order to obtain last names we use cities from the atlas. Thus if we need a Greek name, a French one, or whatever nationality we need, we simply pick a town from the atlas and then ascribe any given name that sounds well when coupled with the town or city picked.

"For example, we wanted an important sounding name for the professor in the story you heard. We went to the atlas, State of Kansas, and found Circleville. This had what we wanted as a last name and we happened to pick Charles. Putting the two together, we had Charles Circleville for our eminent professor and authority on crime. Little did we know that there existed an eminent person with an identical name. This method of name selection has been upheld by the courts . . ."

"There," said Mary sadly, "goes our cottage in Arcadia."

Charles Circleville put his arm about her.

"No, Mary," he said. "We'll buy that house, anyhow, with the money we've earned and saved and not with any phony lawsuit dough. But," he added, "I'd like to paste that lawyer one. He just took us——"

"Like Grant took Richmond," beamed his wife, "Oh, Charlie, I'm so happy."

(Copyright, 1941, by News-Syndicate, Co., Inc.)

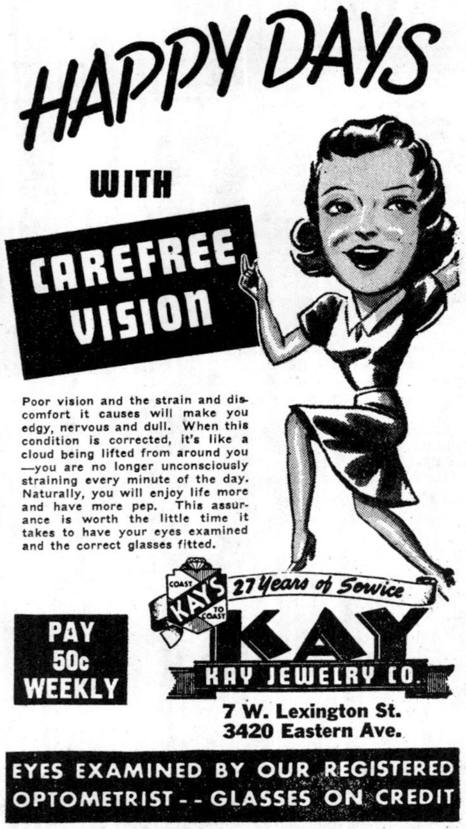
HAPPY DAYS
WITH
CAREFREE VISION
Poor vision and the strain and discomfort it causes will make you edgy, nervous and dull. When this condition is corrected, it's like a cloud being lifted from around you—you are no longer unconsciously straining every minute of the day. Naturally, you will enjoy life more and have more pep. This assurance is worth the little time it takes to have your eyes examined and the correct glasses fitted.
PAY 50c WEEKLY
COAST KAYS TO COAST
27 Years of Service
KAY
KAY JEWELRY CO.
7 W. Lexington St.
3420 Eastern Ave.
EYES EXAMINED BY OUR REGISTERED OPTOMETRIST -- GLASSES ON CREDIT

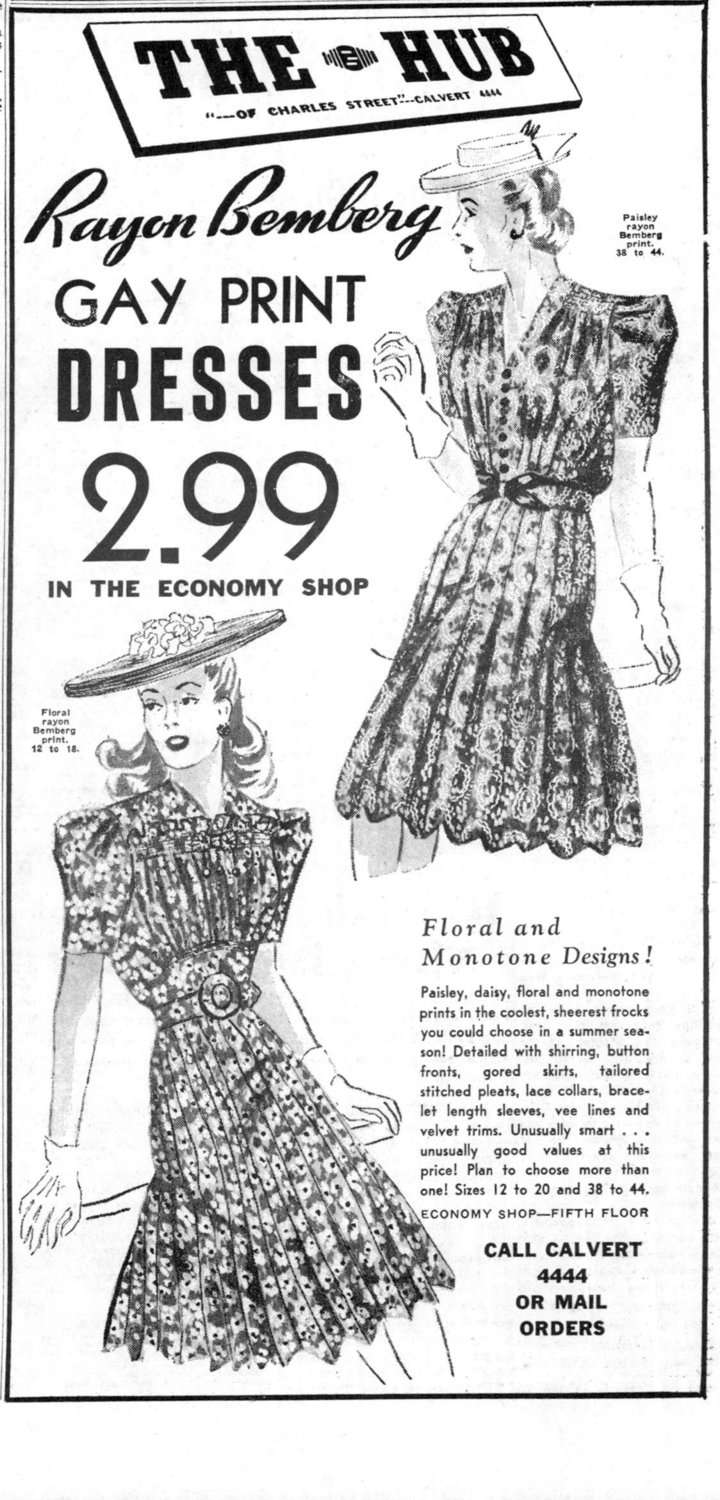
THE HUB
"---OF CHARLES STREET"--CALVERT 4444
Rayon Bemberg
GAY PRINT
DRESSES
2.99
IN THE ECONOMY SHOP
Paisley rayon Bemberg print. 38 to 44.
Floral rayon Bemberg print. 12 to 18.
Floral and Monotone Designs!
Paisley, daisy, floral and monotone prints in the coolest, sheerest frocks you could choose in a summer season! Detailed with shirring, button fronts, gored skirts, tailored stitched pleats, lace collars, bracelet length sleeves, vee lines and velvet trims. Unusually smart . . . unusually good values at this price! Plan to choose more than one! Sizes 12 to 20 and 38 to 44.
ECONOMY SHOP—FIFTH FLOOR
CALL CALVERT 4444 OR MAIL ORDERS

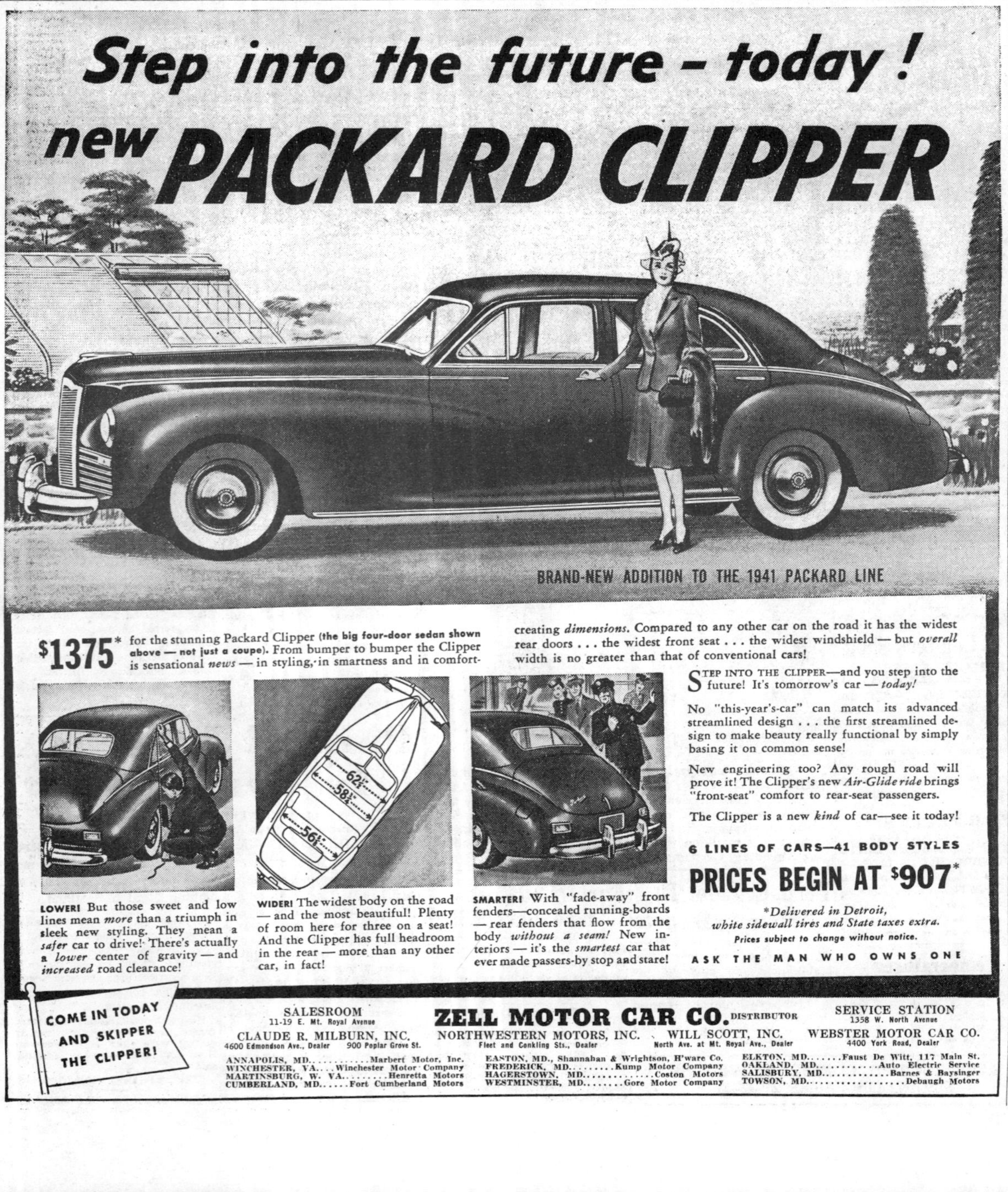
Step into the future - today!
new PACKARD CLIPPER
BRAND-NEW ADDITION TO THE 1941 PACKARD LINE
$1375* for the stunning Packard Clipper (the big four-door sedan shown above — not just a coupe). From bumper to bumper the Clipper is sensational news — in styling, in smartness and in comfort-creating dimensions. Compared to any other car on the road it has the widest rear doors . . . the widest front seat . . . the widest windshield — but overall width is no greater than that of conventional cars!
62½" 58¼" 56¼"
LOWER! But those sweet and low lines mean more than a triumph in sleek new styling. They mean a safer car to drive! There's actually a lower center of gravity — and increased road clearance!
WIDER! The widest body on the road — and the most beautiful! Plenty of room here for three on a seat! And the Clipper has full headroom in the rear — more than any other car, in fact!
SMARTER! With "fade-away" front fenders—concealed running-boards — rear fenders that flow from the body without a seam! New interiors — it's the smartest car that ever made passers-by stop and stare!
STEP INTO THE CLIPPER—and you step into the future! It's tomorrow's car — today!
No "this-year's-car" can match its advanced streamlined design . . . the first streamlined design to make beauty really functional by simply basing it on common sense!
New engineering too? Any rough road will prove it! The Clipper's new Air-Glide ride brings "front-seat" comfort to rear-seat passengers.
The Clipper is a new kind of car—see it today!
6 LINES OF CARS—41 BODY STYLES
PRICES BEGIN AT $907*
*Delivered in Detroit, white sidewall tires and State taxes extra.
Prices subject to change without notice.
ASK THE MAN WHO OWNS ONE
COME IN TODAY AND SKIPPER THE CLIPPER!
SALESROOM 11-19 E. Mt. Royal Avenue
ZELL MOTOR CAR CO. DISTRIBUTOR
SERVICE STATION 1358 W. North Avenue
CLAUDE R. MILBURN, INC. 4600 Edmondson Ave., Dealer 900 Poplar Grove St.
NORTHWESTERN MOTORS, INC. Fleet and Conkling Sts., Dealer
WILL SCOTT, INC. North Ave. at Mt. Royal Ave., Dealer
WEBSTER MOTOR CAR CO. 4400 York Road, Dealer
ANNAPOLIS, MD. . . . . Marbert Motor, Inc.
WINCHESTER, VA. . . . Winchester Motor Company
MARTINSBURG, W. VA. . . . Henretta Motors
CUMBERLAND, MD. . . . Fort Cumberland Motors
EASTON, MD., Shannahan & Wrightson, H'ware Co.
FREDERICK, MD. . . . Kump Motor Company
HAGERSTOWN, MD. . . . Coston Motors
WESTMINSTER, MD. . . . Gore Motor Company
ELKTON, MD. . . . Faust De Witt, 117 Main St.
OAKLAND, MD. . . . Auto Electric Service
SALISBURY, MD. . . . Barnes & Baysinger
TOWSON, MD. . . . Debaugh Motors

Baer Given Chance By Nova's Manager

THE BALTIMORE NEWS-POST SPORTS

TUESDAY EVENING, MAY 13, 1941

HAAS REINSTATED

By Associated Press.

Leon (Buddy) Haas has received word from the Maryland State Racing Commission that it has considered his case and his suspension was lifted. The Pimlico stewards suspended him and referred the case to the commission after his mount, Black Raider, had carried out Equipet in the Pimlico Nursery Stakes. Testimony was given the commission that the colt was sore and had borne out in similar fashion in his last previous effort in Kentucky.

Happy Birthday!

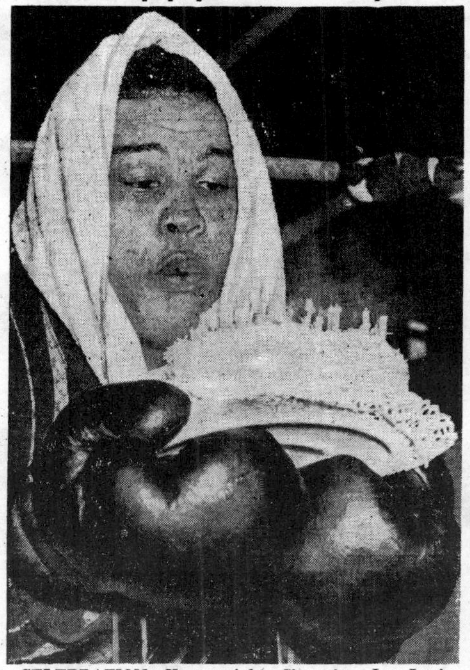

CELEBRATION—Heavyweight Champion Joe Louis takes time out from training for his title bout with Buddy Baer at Washington to douse the candles on his birthday cake. The champ is twenty-seven years old today. International News Photo.

Rodger H. Pippen

Sports Editor *Says*

RINGSIDE, WASHINGTON, D. C.

Referee Eddie LaFond cast his ballot for Harry Jeffra as the Baltimorean lost his feather crown to Joey Archibald before 1,800 customers in Griffith Stadium, Washington, last night. The referee was right.

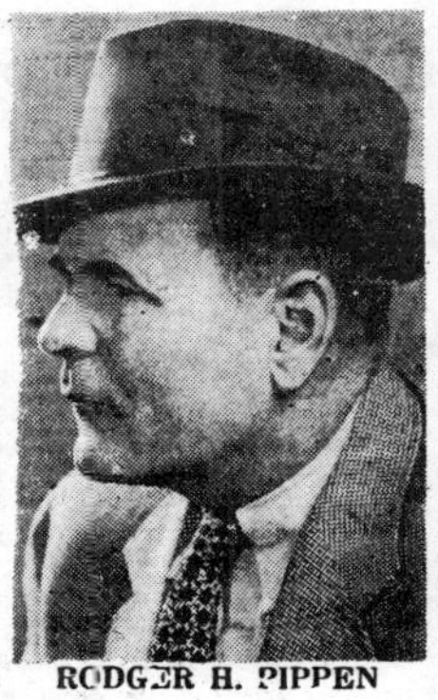

RODGER H. PIPPEN

The two judges—Jim Sullivan and Bob Eller—voted for the challenger. They were wrong.

Harry not only won the fight, but won it easily. He was the aggressor from start to finish, landed the most damaging punches and twice had Archibald on unsteady legs from rights to the chin.

Joey spent most of the evening skipping merrily backwards and waiting until the pursuing Jeffra caught up to him. Every once in a while he would throw a long left hook and when it landed the crowd, pulling for Joey, would scream with delight. Those yelps must have influenced the judges, it being very evident that their hearing was better than their vision.

When these some battlers fought in Washington a year ago, Jeffra's handlers claimed that he had been robbed of the verdict. I could not agree with that. Las night, Max Waxman, manager of Jeffra, and his trainer, Heinie Blaustein, were bitter in their recriminations over the decision. They had a right to be indignant. And Waxman should be put in an insane hospital if he ever takes another Baltimore fighter to Washington.

* * *

Harry Weeps

If the New York writers thought that Ken Overlin was given the works when he fought and lost to Billy Socse last week, they should have been in the town where the whacky New Dealers are squandering our money. Jeffra was so sure he had won and was so aroused when Archibald's hand was raised, he sat down on his stool and cried like a baby. An hour later, in the dressing room, he was still weeping.

The fight, as I saw it, wasn't close. I gave Archibald only three rounds. Two were even. And Jeffra won ten without any question. Harry's rights equaled Joey's left hooks and during the infighting the Baltimorean piled up a big margin of points by giving him fifty rights to the back and sde.

* * *

Lost By Single Point

Unofficially, it was reported after the fight that one judge gave the fight to Archibald by a single point. If that is true, it shows how really ridiculous was the decision. No championship should change hands on such a narrow margin.

Dick O'Brien, in the Washington Herald verifies the above with the statement in this morning's paper that Jeffra lost the fight, so far as Judge Bob Eller's score card was concerned, when he let go two punches after Joey had slipped to the floor in the thirteenth session. The low blow cost Harry two points, according to boxing rules in the District. On Jimmy Sullivan's card it made no difference. Sullivan had Archibald on top by five points at the finish.

* * *

Guilty Of One Foul

During the fight, Harry was charged with two fouls and Joey with one. The first charge of foul brought a wail of protest from Harry and his handlers. Harry, as truthful a fighter as ever lived, said he wasn't guilty and leaned over the ropes to tell me that he felt he was due for another unfair decision. Plainly upset by having points taken away from him, Harry lost his temper and with it his timing and judgment of distance. For a round or two, he was so mad he couldn't co-ordinate properly.

As to the second foul, he was guilty. Thinking he had floored Archibald, he leaped in and him him twice while the Providence lad was on one knee. It was overeagerness and not dirty fighting. The punches didn't do any damage.

* * *

Jeffra Wasn't At His Best

In saying that Harry should still be the champion today, I can't say that he fought one of his best fights. He didn't use his left

Continued on Page 23, Column 1.

MANAGER THOMAS TRYING TO STRENGTHEN LOCAL NINE

Orioles Seek Hank Majeski

Baer Is Given Chance By Nova's Pilot

By JACK MAHON

NEW YORK, May 13—(I. N. S.). The citizens who think big Buddy Baer can whip Champion Joe Louis down in Washington, D. C., May 23, are as scarce as ideas on how to stop Hitler—but we ran into one gentleman of authority today who said Buddy can knock Louis out. The prophet is Mr. Ray Carlen, one of the more conservative fight managers and current guardian of Lou Nova, another of Brother Louis' persistent suitors.

We caught Carlen dashing madly to escape the health-giving sunlight which beat down on the cement sands of Jacobs' Beach. "Mind you I'm not picking Baer to win," said Ray, "but I do think he can knock out Joe."

Since Mr. Carlen is not given to popping off about fighters other than Nova and is one of the more fair-minded members of the fistic fraternity, he was asked to elaborate.

BAER HAS PUNCH

"Baer has all the equipment to beat Louis," says Ray "He's always had that beautiful physique and punch. He's never had the will to fight before, but he may be coming into his own."

"All along Buddy has played second fiddle to his brother Max. It was always Max they chased for the autographs; Max in the spotlight and to Max, Buddy was always 'the kid brother.' That's what I think has been wrong with Buddy all along.

"Louis will have to be knocked out to lose his title and Buddy has the punch to do it. Those 245 pounds and his six feet six inches give him plenty of power. I really think the kid may be out to make a name on his own now, and if I'm right, Louis is taking a great risk."

PRAISES LOUIS

Carlen does not agree with many of the experts of the press and his own clique, that Louis has gone back. "I think Joe is a more polished fighter. He proved that in the second Godoy fight. He had trouble with Arturo in their first meeting and handled him perfectly in the return to knock him out."

Ray thinks Billy Conn has everything necessary to beat Joe except punch and doesn't give Abe Simon, whom Joe is to face in July a "ghost of a chance."

The manager also explained why he has sat so placidly while Promoter Jacobs shoved the Baer cub in and contracted for a Simon-Louis return before giving Nova his chance.

"Before I saw the Baer-Louis thing in black and white I wanted Louis in June," he explained. "I do not intend to have Nova termed one of those "bums of the month" so we're perfectly willing to wait till September. Nova will get Louis after a two months' layoff and the fight will command the respect it deserves."

Carlen and Nova have been chewing their fingernails down to the bone in recent months as they watched Louis fight Red Burman, Gus Dorazio and Tony Musto. They're really worried about Louis hurting himself or possibly blowing his title before Nova can get to him.

Scratches At Charles Town

First Race—John's Buddy, Miss Rippon, Sun Maker, Lit Up, Pete's Gold, Clifton's Dawn.
Second — Rebellious, Web Foot, Uulu Khayyam, Balkanese, Miss Hildur, Clocks.
Third—Vantryst, Trostar, Bud's King, Part One, Simmer, Lafitoff.
Fourth — Mystic Man, Brazen Hussy, Tavern, Fernbrake, Bullet B., Autumn Echo.
Fifth—Smart Lad, Wenuit, Sun Scene, Jalaine, Grist, Bill K.
Sixth—Reigh Tetrarch, Kingoo, Flagetta, Georgetown, Toast, Dashing Doe.
Eighth—Smables, Mariyah, Agnes Knight, Easter Holiday, Beau Bon, Emda.
Sub—Declared off.
Weather, clear; track, fast.

Scratches At Belmont

First Race—Budos.
Fourth—Shadows Pass.
Sixth—Waller.
Weather clear; track fast.

Scratches At Suffolk

Fourth—Swing Band, Jane Vito.
Weather clear; track fast.

BI-STATE LEAGUE

Martinsville, 8-5; Mount Airy, 4-7.
Mayodan, 5; Sanford, 0.
Leaksville, 13; Danville, 3.

Baltimore Battler Becomes Ex-Champion

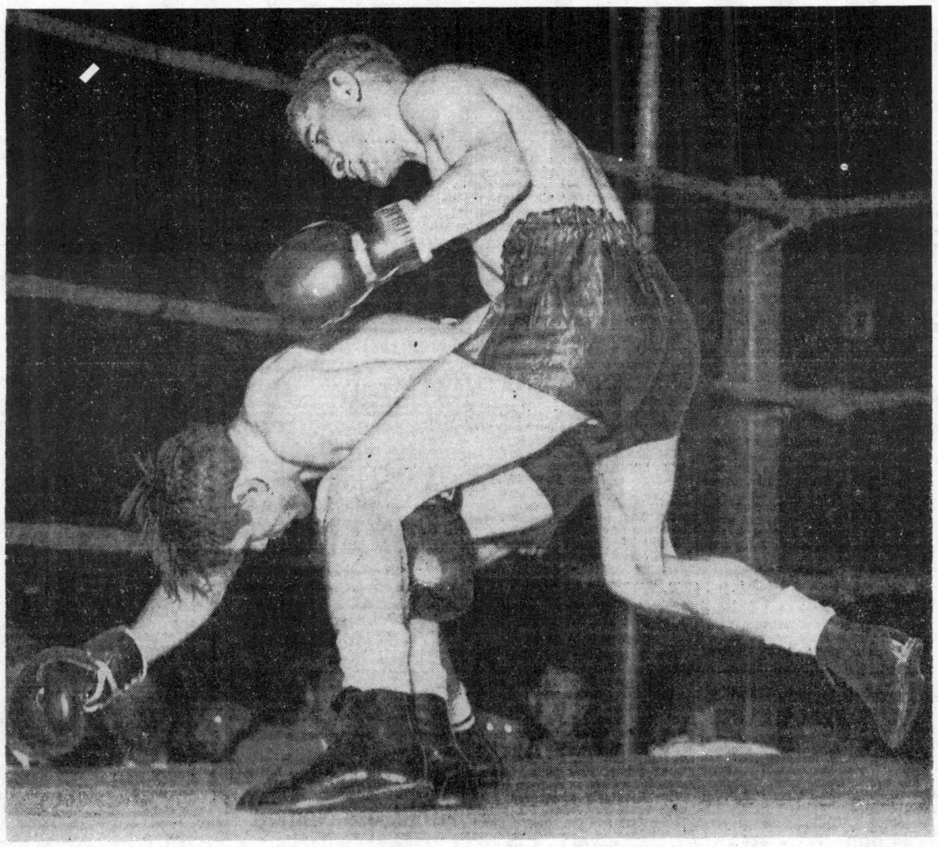

ARCHIBALD SLIPS—This slip cost Baltimore's Harry Jeffra 2 points, possibly enough to have swayed the two judges who voted against him, as he dropped the featherweight crown to Joey Archibald last night at Griffith Stadium, Washington. As the Providence battler slipped to one knee in the thirteenth round, Harry unthinkingly continued to pummel Joey with punches and, consequently, drew the 2-point penalty. The two judges voted for Archibald while the referee cast his ballot for the Baltimorean at the end of the 15 rounds. Only a few points separated the fighters when the figures were totaled. Associated Press Photo.

Jeffra Loses Title On Split Decision

WASHINGTON, May 13—(U. P.).—Joey Archibald regained an old possession today—the featherweight championship.

The pint-sized Providence (R. I.) puncher moved back into the throne room (New York State style) by belting out a 15-round victory over Harry Jeffra of Baltimore, the man who captured the crown from him a year ago.

The title transfer, consummated about 11.30 P. M. last night, was witnessed by scarcely a quorum of fans huddled around Griffith Stadium's home plate.

$2,700 GATE

The 1,800 spectators, who contributed a meager gate of $2,700, likewise witnessed the perpetuation of one of the most unusual winning streaks in sports. It was the twenty-first consecutive victory Archibald has scored in a Washington ring. He never has lost a fight here. Today, they're calling that "Washington luck."

But it was a combination of shrewdness, courage and a pile-driving left hook that enabled Archibald to recover the crown.

Joey entered the ring an 8-to-5 underdog. And for the better part of the first eight rounds, the odds seemed justified. But when it appeared that Archibald's comeback was doomed to failure, the jumping-jack New Englander turned on the heat.

SPLIT DECISION

He withstood a desperate last-round attack by Jeffra who had nailed him with a crashing left to the jaw. And when the firing ceased, Joey was proclaimed the winner on a split decision, with the referee voting for Jeffra and the two judges for Archibald. The United Press score sheet gave Archibald six rounds, Jeffra five and called four even.

Program Selections

AT CHARLES TOWN

First race—Coq A Lane, Myrtle M., Prison Ship.

Second—Small Change, Brainchild, Pleasant Lady.

Third—War Rumor, Windsor Chief, Last Scamp.

Fourth—Scullery Maid, Stumming, Time Scout.

Fifth — Undependable, Fusionette, Commandress.

Sixth—Schley Al, Wale Signal, Doctor's Nurse.

Seventh—Centervill, Forest Ranger, Briar Blue.

Eighth—Worthowing, Artist, Singing Steel.

Ty Cobb Sued-- For 15 Cents

PALO ALTO, Cal., May 13—(I. N. S.).—Ty Cobb, who achieved baseball immortality through his fighting heart, found himself in the middle of a different kind of battle today—a lawsuit filed against him for 15 cents.

It was Arnold "Parky" Sharkey, former prizefighterf, who brought the action in Palo Alto small claims court on a charge that Cobb drove out of his parking station without paying the fee. It cost the former pugilist $1.50 to file the 15-cent suit.

Overlin Before Ring Body Today

NEW YORK, May 13—(I. N. S.). The New York Boxing Commission today planned to study the protested decision in which Billy Soose lifted the world (New York variety) middleweight championship from Ken Overlin last Friday night.

Overlin and his manager, Chris Dundee, were scheduled to appear before the Commission for a discussion of their protest. Also summoned before the ring officials were Referee Arthur Donovan, Billy Healey and Marty Munroe, the judges, who awarded Soose a verdict that pitched Madison Square Garden into a pandemonium of booing.

Al Flair Is Playing Fine Ball

By HUGH TRADER, JR.

MONTREAL, Quebec, May 13.—Groping at any chance, any price, to grab a hitter with some power, but keeping a level head in this storm as his Orioles sink deeper in the International League cellar, Tommy Thomas told the writer today that he's on the trail of Hank Majeski, clouting infielder of the Boston Bees, who smacked .323 with Newark last season.

But the manager added that the war draft, in particular, and injuries are causing many clubs to sit tight on possible trades or sales.

"I've contacted a number of clubs already," says Thomas, "and most of them are afraid to make a move on account of the draft claiming players into the Army. Injuries have balked us, too. I was all set to make a deal with Syracuse when Secory broke his leg and Longacre was caught in the draft to report next week. Both are outfielders and our chances now of grabbing Rosen are mighty slim, I guess.

DEAL WITH ROYALS

"Montreal also was ready to deal and then Gilbert and Ross got hurt and, of course, we've got Sea... Hafey, Graham, Hamilton, Richmond, Midkiff and Niller all ailing and that stops us. I might have made a deal on Graham, but he can't throw now."

There's nothing definite on Baltimore's chances of acquiring Majeski, except that the Bees do intend to keep him, but there's no doubt Hank would help immeasurably. If Majeski joined the Birds right now he'd go to third base for Tom Hafey is on the shelf for a week or two, and when Hafey returned, then Majeski could play second base or perhaps the outfield. He's a right-hand hitter with real power, walloping 17 homers with the Bears last summer.

The one consolation for Thomas at the moment is the fact that this trip has been a financial success for the Birds, in spite of their road record of four wins and nine defeats. The Baltimore Club got paid off for an 8,000 crowd in Toronto the opening day and 3,500 two days later. In Buffalo the Birds drew 5,500 for a Sunday game and here in Montreal a near-full house of 16,500 paid customers watched last Sunday's double-header. That constitutes a successful trip at the gate in itself.

TRINKLE HURLS WELL

It was a pretty slim audience for yesterday's game, however, and whoever remained at home didn't miss anything, as the Birds were shut out by a 4-to-0 score. Krafty Ken Trinkle pitched a swell ball game for the Flock, opposed to the now-famous Ed Head, and allowed only two earned runs, but our heroes got only one extra-base hit, a triple by Kracher, and five singles off Head. It was a corking good effort by Trinkle, who also got a couple of tough breaks, such as Pitcher Head bouncing a hit off home plate with the bases loaded in the sixth. But the best Trinkle could have hoped for was a tie, for lack of power has the Birds in a deep, deep rut, and only the ac-

Continued on Page 23, Column 2.

Siebert Out On Attempted Steal

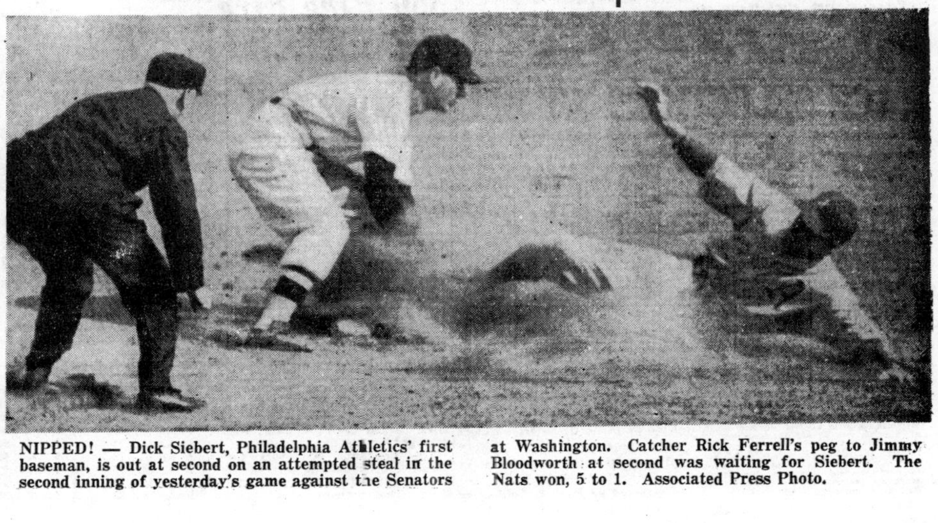

NIPPED! — Dick Siebert, Philadelphia Athletics' first baseman, is out at second on an attempted steal in the second inning of yesterday's game against the Senators at Washington. Catcher Rick Ferrell's peg to Jimmy Bloodworth at second was waiting for Siebert. The Nats won, 5 to 1. Associated Press Photo.

THE WEATHER
Clear to partly cloudy and continued warm tonight and Wednesday. Showers Wednesday afternoon.
Detailed Weather Report on Page 30

MEAN TEMPERATURES YESTERDAY

Baltimore	70	New York	68
Atlanta	76	Omaha	78
Boston	68	Portland, Maine	60
Chicago	72	Salt Lake City	62
Jacksonville	76	San Antonio	77
Los Angeles	72	Seattle	53
Miami	78	Tampa	80
New Orleans	79	Washington	70

THE BALTIMORE NEWS-POST
AN INDEPENDENT NEWSPAPER
The Largest Evening Circulation in the Entire South

10

VOL. CXXXIX.—NO. 20 Entered as second-class matter at Baltimore Postoffice. TUESDAY EVENING, MAY 27, 1941 PRICE 3 CENTS

BRITISH CRUISER'S TORPEDO FINISHED BISMARCK--LONDON

IN THE NEWS

THE Mediterranean sea is full of islands.

That is one of the main reasons why this sea became an early center of civilization.

If folks are paddling around a big body of water in a rowboat—and even a mighty trireme with its three banks of oars was a rowboat—they like to have a nearby harbor to duck into in case a storm arises.

Otherwise they are sunk, not only figuratively but factually.

The many islands of the Mediterranean afforded the near and frequent harbors, made communication possible in those ancient days, and aided in the spread of civilization from its sources and centers in Egypt and Mesopotamia.

The whole of the northeast arm of the Mediterranean, called the Aegean sea,—together with the waters bordering the coasts of Greece and of Asia Minor,—are actually spattered with islands,—sown thick with them,—so much so that it would almost seem possible for an extra tall man with extra long legs to step across from one island to another.

WHAT a spot for rowboats, and what wonder that sea power had its birth there.

Crete, the largest of these Aegean islands, was the cradle of sea power.

The idea evolved from the brain of King Minos of Crete some 3,000 years before the time of Christ.

Still sea power, or *"thallocracy,"* as the Greeks called it, was a natural development for Crete—as natural as self-defense—as natural as aggression.

The ships of Crete enabled it to contact the civilization of Egypt and Assyria, and to exchange its products with the products of these lands.

Thus the island kingdom of Crete grew rich and powerful, as did in later days the island kingdom of England and the island kingdom of Japan.

The Phoenician and Carian pirates preyed upon the ships of Crete.

Warships were built to defend Crete's commerce.

Trade followed the flag then, as it does now, and the flag followed trade.

The Cretans defeated the Carians and took their islands.

And then the Cretans took other islands and made them dominions.

And finally the flood of Cretan conquest apparently overflowed the mainland of Greece in the early Mycenaean age.

EVERYTHING in these early periods, however, is seen through the glass of tradition darkly.

Most of the *"history"* of these prehistoric days comes to us by means of myths and fables.

But the myths always have an element of truth as their bases and beginnings, and some of the initial facts with relation to Crete have been verified by the scientific excavations which have been conducted in Crete and in Greece by expeditions from the English and American colleges.

Tradition says that King Minos ruled over Crete proper himself, and gave his sons dominion over the conquered islands of the Carian: and the subjugated peoples of the mainland.

From Greece King Minos exacted tribute not only of money but of men and maidens.

All of this power and wealth and tribute Crete secured and maintained by means of its ships—its dominion of the seas.

Small seas they were—but all that early civilization knew.

When at last, after many centuries, the Cretan sea power waned, the Greeks threw off the Cretan yoke.

About 1300 B. C. Crete, it would seem, was invaded from the mainland by the Greeks in their turn.

Its cities were taken and largely destroyed.

And so the Cretan civilization ended,—and the Greek civilization began.

THE saga of this Greek liberation is told in the story of Theseus.

It is a romance, a myth, but has its elements of basic fact.

Troy was supposed to be a myth, and Homer's Iliad a poetic fable, until a little American groceryman named Schlieman dug Troy from its ruins and made it live again.

Myths are, as a rule, but ele-

Continued on Page 4, Column 1.

I Watched The Old World Crumble. Memoirs of One of the Former Leaders of Russian and French Aristocracy, Who Paints an Intimate Picture of the Trivialities, Tragedies, and Comedies of European Courts. Don't Miss the Opening Chapter in The American Weekly, the Magazine Distributed With Next Sunday's Baltimore American.—Adv.

Nazi Battleship Bismarck Sunk By British Navy

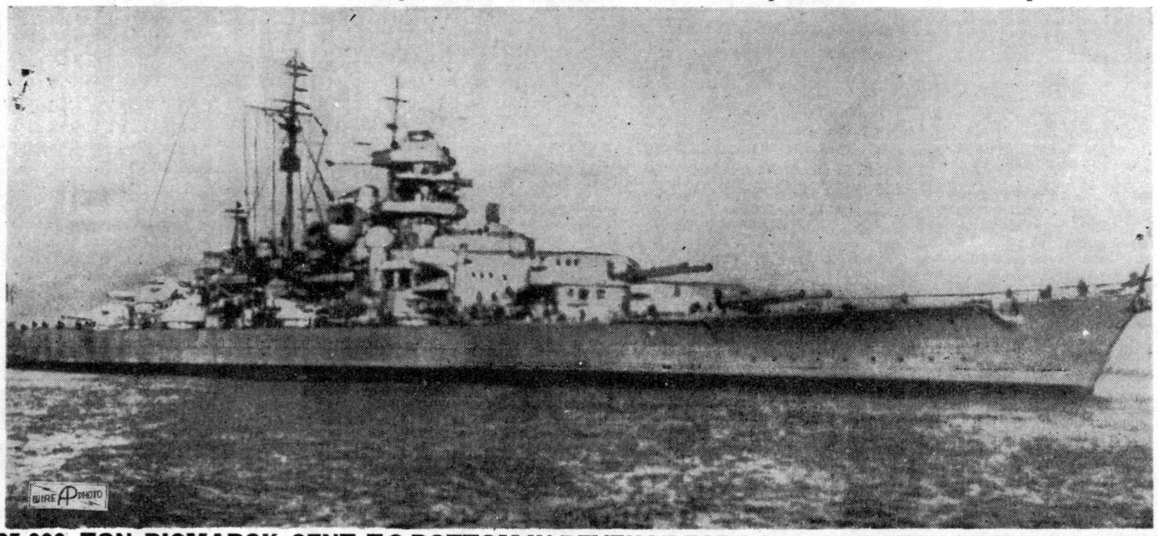

35,000-TON BISMARCK SENT TO BOTTOM IN REVENGE FOR LOSS OF BATTLE CRUISER HOOD
Other Pictures on Pages 2, 3 and 10

U. S. Made Plane 'Spots' Enemy As English Navy Sinks Pride Of Nazi Fleet

WASHINGTON, May 27—(A. P.).—Secretary Hull, commenting on the sinking of the German battleship Bismarck, said today he supposed the law of retribution arose to some extent at least.

LONDON, May 27 — (A. P.). — The might of Britain's fleet and air arm, converging from points as distant as Gibraltar and Newfoundland, pounced in terrible revenge today upon the German battleship Bismarck, destroyer of the Hood, and sent her to the bottom of the sea.

At least 11 battleships, aircraft carriers, battle-cruisers and cruisers, with the vital help of destroyers and torpedo planes, came at 11.01 A. M. British time to the end of a 1,750 mile chase, some 400 miles west of Brest.

There they sank the 35,000-ton Bismarck—three days and a few hours after the Hood, mightiest warship in the world, had been blown to bits by a hit in the magazine from one of the Bismarck's 15-inch shells.

Torpedoes from the cruiser Dorsetshire finished her off, but already, torpedoes from planes and destroyers alike had had her reeling in wild circles.

1,300 NAZIS LOST

Down with her went some 1,300 men, a great German admiral, Guenther Luetjens, and about one-fourth of Germany's known capital ship strength.

Participating in the kill were the torpedo planes of the fleet air arm, based on the aircraft carrier Ark Royal, and the new 35,000-ton battleship Prince of Wales.

But it was an American-made Catalina that hunted down the quarry Monday and led the killers to her, so torpedo after torpedo might be shot into her vitals from the air.

Prime Minister Winston Churchill and First Lord of the Admiralty, A. V. Alexander, gave the nation the story of the Bismarck's destruction—but they disclosed, too, the loss of two cruisers, the Gloucester and Fiji; the sinking of four destroyers and the damaging of two battleships and several other cruisers of the Mediterranean fleet in the raging battle for Crete.

SAFEGUARD CRETE

Yet they were able to say that the fleet, even so pounded, has thus far prevented sea-borne German forces from reaching Crete and has covered the safe arrival of reinforcements for the British-Greek defenders of the island.

For the nation the sinking of the Bismarck, however, was the real news.

Churchill intervened in the House proceedings to make the dramatic announcement of the Bismarck's

Continued on Page 2, Column 1.

Roosevelt Asks 13,000 New Planes

WASHINGTON, May 27—(A. P.).—In the midst of preparing a momentous pronouncement of Government policy, President Roosevelt asked Congress today for $3,319,000,000 in appropriations for more airplanes.

The Army would get the bulk of the money and, an informed source said, it would use $2,506,868,000 of it to provide 13,000 war planes. Of the total, $2,790,00,000 would be for the Army and $529,000,000 for the Navy.

By GEORGE DURNO
International News Service Staff Correspondent.

WASHINGTON, May 27.—The White House today promised that by tomorrow morning the world will know definitely where Uncle Sam stands in the grim and war-fraught international stiuation.

Presidential Secretary Stephen T. Early, speaking of President Roosevelt's momentous fireside chat tonight, told reporters:

"I think you can say that by Wednesday morning there can be no longer any doubt as to what the national policy of this Government is."

As the Chief Executive continued his labor on the address for which the major capitals of the world have been anxiously waiting, the White House requested the radio chains to give Mr. Roosevelt 15 minutes additional time. He will go on the air at 9.30 P. M. (E. S. T.) and speak until 10.15 P. M.

CONFERENCE OFF

So immersed was the President in completion of the document which will place the United States Government on final record, that he booked no engagements and cancelled his customary Tuesday afternoon press conference.

Secretary Early said the final draft probably would not be completed until shortly before 6 o'clock this evening.

The presidential spokesman ex-

Continued on Page 2, Column 4.

350 Flee Fire In Ellicott City Plant

About 350 employes of the Doughnut Machine Corporation of America, Ellicott City, were forced to flee this afternoon when fire, starting in a two-story frame warehouse, ignited the main mill of the plant.

As the blaze spread, it was feared that the heat would cause the explosion of nine concrete elevators, each 100 feet high, in which grain is stored.

Lard, said to have been stored in the warehouse, was held the cause of huge clouds of smoke which billowed from the building, and which hung like a pall over Ellicott City.

At the first alarm, three fire engines from Ellicott City responded, and additional apparatus was summoned from Towson and Catonsville.

Some of the employes' automobiles, parked near the plant, were damaged by the fire.

The Doughnut Machinery Corporation occupies the site of the old Ellicott's Mills, later Gambrill's Mills. The company,

Baseball Scores

International League

Baltimore at Newark, night game.
Jersey City at Syracuse, night game.
Toronto at Montreal, night game.
Only games scheduled.

American League

At Boston— FIRST GAME

		R.	H.	E.
Phila.	000 001 010	2	7	1
Boston	111 020 00x	5	7	0

Batteries—Hadley and Hayes; Wagner and Pytlak.

At Boston— SECOND GAME

		R.	H.	E.
Phila.	001 400 6			
Boston	000 000 1			

Batteries—Marchildon and Hayes; H. Newsome and Peacock.

At Chicago—

		R.	H.	E.
St. Louis	003 002 0			
Chicago	010 000			

Batteries—Muncrief and Ferrell; Rigney and Tresh.

At Cleveland—

		R.	H.	E.
Detroit	111 010 5			
Cleveland	110 002			

Batteries—Rowe and Tebbetts; Milnar and Hemsley.

At Washington—

		R.	H.	E.
New York	101 412			
Wash.	001 00			

Batteries—Ruffing and Rosar; Chase and Early.

National League

At Philadelphia—

		R.	H.	E.
Brooklyn	102 003 000	6	8	0
Phila.	000 000 000	0	7	1

Batteries—Casey and Phelps; Podgajny and Warren.

Boston at New York, night game.
Chicago at St. Louis, night game.
Only games scheduled.

Temperatures

12 Midn't	71	9 A. M.	85
1 A. M.	71	10 A. M.	88
2 A. M.	70	11 A. M.	88
3 A. M.	69	12 Noon	89
4 A. M.	71	1 P. M.	90
5 A. M.	75	2 P. M.	92
6 A. M.	75	3 P. M.	93
7 A. M.	79	4 P. M.	92
8 A. M.	82	5 P. M.	93

Pilot Describes Bismarck Hunt

(Picture on Page 10)

LONDON, May 27—(A. P.).—"It was the hottest fire I've ever been under," said the pilot of one of the United States-built Catalina long-range flying boats which shadowed the 35,000-ton German battleship Bismarck to her fatal rendezvous with the British fleet today.

The pilot looked thoughtfully tonight at the several holes in the hull of his boat—holes put there by the terrific salvos from the Bismarck during the brief interval that the plane slipped from one cloud to another.

Even so, the plane continued her dogged pursuit for ten hours after an overall flight of 24 hours, the Air Ministry's news bulletin said.

SPOTTED BY HUDSONS

The Catalina planes relieved British Sunderland flying boats in the chase which originated when other American-built planes, Hudsons, spotted the mighty Bismarck in a Norwegian fjord.

"There was lots of cloudy weather and a misty haze," related the Catalina's pilot. "We had ducked into a cloud and were trying to edge around the Bismarck.

"Suddenly we came to the end of our cloud and found ourselves bang over the ship which was only 400 yards away.

"I thought they had us. The Bismarck put up the worst barrage I've ever seen. She seemed one big flash from box to stern and must have been turning loose on us everything she had.

"The Bismarck apparently thought we were going to bomb her because she turned a full 90 degrees off course when we ran out of the clouds and opened fire as she turned.

"I really don't know how we managed to dodge all the stuff she threw up.

TICKLISH MOMENT.

"It was a ticklish moment and we were lucky to get back into a cloud, but the Catalina went on flying despite the holes the Bismarck put in her hull.

"I had several members of the

Continued on Page 3, Column 4.

BELMONT PARK RESULTS

FIRST RACE—Purse, $1,500; claiming; maiden 3-year-olds; seven furlongs. Off at 1.22. Time, 1.25⅘.

Resolute II., 126 (P. Ryan)	$16.10	$9.80	$5.50
Bardy, 108 (J. Skelly)		20.20	10.30
Cinder Maid, 108 (J. Harrell)			4.50

lso Ran—Dancetty, Demonax, Sergeant Bob, Grand Acclaim, Persian Queen, Six Shooter, Sun Nimbus, Daily Dublin.

SECOND—Purse $1,500; claiming; three-year-olds and up; mile and an eighth. Off at 1.50½. Time 1.52 1-5.

Cee Joe, 109 (Oliver)	$8.00	$4.10	$3.20
Oddesa's Pride, 118 (C. McCreary)		7.90	5.50
Attracting, 112 (N. Wall)			6.90

Also Ran—Irish Lancer, Love Mark, Shansi, Gay Troubadour, Battle Won.

Daily Double—Resolute II. and Cee Joe paid $60.60 for $2

THIRD—Purse 1,$500; claiming; three-year-olds; mile and one-sixteenth. Off at 2.21. Time 1.45 1-5.

Rancho's Boy, 113 (F. A. Smith)	$7.60	$2.90	$2.40
Chorus, 108 (D. Madden)		2.40	2.10

Continued on Page 24, Column 7.

VERY LATEST NEWS

(Race Results From Howard Sports Daily, Inc.)

GEN. L. WINS EIGHTH RACE AT BELMONT

Eighth—Gen. L., $11, $5.90, $4.30; Red Mars, $10.20, $5.40; High Blame, $3.80.

AT SUFFOLK DOWNS

Eighth—Fore Isus, won; Franco Saxon, 2; Ess Jay Tee, 3.

AT CHARLES TOWN

Fifth—Schley Goree, $6.40, $3.20, $2.60; Waugh Scout, $3.40, $2.80; Wale Signal, $4.60.

AT LINCOLN FIELDS

Sixth—Prairie Dog, $4.20, $2.60, $2.20; Leading Article, $2.80, $2.40; Mattie J., $2.60.

LATEST BASEBALL SCORES

(A) At Boston—Phila., 11; Boston, 1; end 8th.
(A) At Chicago—St. Louis, 5; Chicago, 1; end 7½.
(A) At Cleveland—Detroit, 9; Cleve., 6; end 7th.

APPROVES $31,115,000 FOR NAVY WORKS

WASHINGTON, May 27—(U. P.).—The House Naval Affairs Committee today approved a bill authorizing the Navy to spend $31,115,000 on public works at its shore establishments.

Where There Is No Unemployment

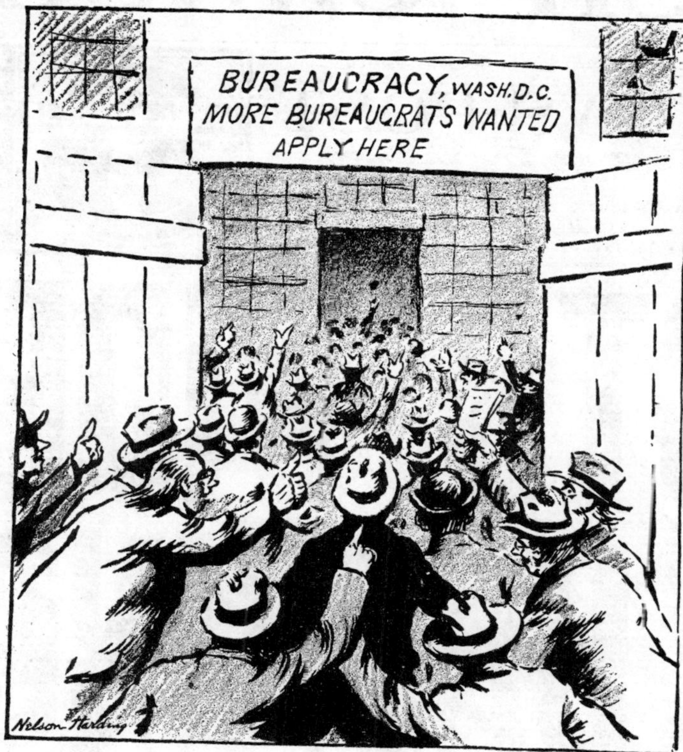

Let's Help The Police

BALTIMORE is in the midst of a crime wave. Nothing serious, to be sure, but a crime wave nevertheless.

In his report made public yesterday Police Commissioner Robert F. Stanton noted that crime in Baltimore increased 71 per cent. in April over the corresponding month of 1940.

Contributing factors to this jump, Commissioner Stanton revealed, were bicycle thefts, pocketbook snatching and the theft of articles from parked automobiles.

Hold-ups decreased 26.6 per cent. and burglaries were down 75.4 per cent. Which shows that the increase in crime is attributable in the main to petty larcenies.

Which is where Mr. and Mrs. Public can aid the police in quelling this outburst of small but irritating larcenies.

If you are the owner of a bicycle be sure that you don't leave it on the street unattended. If you must leave it on the street, be sure to lock it, that makes it quite a bit more difficult to steal.

If you have been shopping don't leave the articles in your parked car while you go to a movie. You may lock your car, but that doesn't make the articles safe. Car windows can be jimmied and there are numerous other ways that resourceful thieves can get in your car.

Let's help the police in stopping this wave of petty thieveries. Watch your bicycle, don't allow articles to remain in your parked car and hang on to your pocketbooks.

M. P.'s In Baltimore

AT LEAST, for an experimental period, military police will be in Baltimore during week-ends, helping the Baltimore city police.

The M. P.'s will have no authority over civilians. They will look out for boys on leave from the camps who may get a bit too boisterous or otherwise run afoul of the laws.

The decision to assign a military patrol here for week-ends is undoubtedly the result of proper caution.

Baltimore police have enough on their hands with normal police activities. It is good co-operation for military officials to try to relieve them of extra activities which might result from the weekly influx of soldiers.

So far, however, it is pleasant to report that the decision is based on apprehensions about what might happen, rather than experience of the recent past.

The great number of soldiers who have thronged Baltimore each week-end during the past few months have not aggravated police troubles in Baltimore, except, perhaps, because they have created more traffic.

The conduct of the boys has been, on the whole, impressively good.

It is a tribute, not only to camp training but also to the boys themselves.

We are glad to have the military police here. But we hope they won't have much to do—and present indications are that this hope will be fulfilled.

Text For Today—"He that dwelleth in the secret of the Most High shall abide under the shadow of the Almighty."
I will say of the Lord, "He is my refuge and fortress; my God, in Him will I trust." Psalm XCI: 1, 2.
O. C. S. Wallace, D. D., pastor emeritus of the Eutaw Place Baptist Church.

THE HUMAN SIDE OF THE NEWS

—By Edwin C. Hill

When the British let Harry St. John Philby out of jail several weeks ago and put him in circulation in the Middle East, the events of both his arrest a year ago and his unexplained release were put down by our newspapers as a "mystery." He is, indeed, a cryptic sort of personage, a natural lure for mystery addicts, oozing around through Islam for many years, wearing native dress, joining the Wahibi sect, making intimate friendships with desert chieftains, visiting the lost cities of Magan and Urbar, which no European ever saw before.

But there isn't so much of a mystery about him as one might think, if one reads the British newspapers. The cause of his arrest and his recent release has been reported faithfully. Mr. Philby was incarcerated when appeasement ended and the Churchill government came in, because, for many years, he had been a friend and ally of the Nazi and Fascist elements of England, who had stalled armament and defense and helped build up Adolf Hitler. He also had been the friend and ally of these forces throughout Islam and had done much to incline 80,000,000 Moslems toward the Fascist orbit.

TURNED LOOSE

He was turned loose when the Nazis lunged down toward the Middle East as the one man who could bat effectively for England in the crucial war of wits and nerves now going on in the desert which lies on the road to India. As the word comes from England, his meditation in jail brought a change of heart, and he will now squat on his heels with the desert sheiks and swear by Aldebaron that he was all wrong the first time, and the best thing the Arabs can do is to string with old England.

All in all, in the light of Mr. Philby's record of past performance, it is one of the most fantastic episodes of the war. Mr. Philby was a friend of Lawrence of Arabia and, like Lawrence, gained great influence in the Moslem world and made commitments, which he expected to be fulfilled, to make all Islam a safe and satisfied ally of the empire.

INTO REVERSE

Can he and will he go into reverse and hold Islam for Britain. Those 80,000,000 Moslems are a tremendous stake in this war. As we get the picture from informed Englishmen and other Europeans who know the Middle East, the British muddling in this long encounter has been due to an unfortunate confusion of policies and personnel which has prevented any clear and realistic policy from emerging.

First, there is the Colonial Office, which complacently follows traditional policies without regard to new demands. Then the Foreign Office devises policies frequently in conflict with the Colonial Office and relies too complacently on moss-grown foreign service officers who have more or less taken root in some remote spot and have forgotten for whom they are working.

That is exactly the story of Palestine—the building up of the tough Grand Mufti of Jerusalem, who later was to duck to Iraq and start the current trouble there; shadow-boxing with the cunning Emir Abdullah of Jerusalem, who still wants to be king of the dual state of Transjordon and rough up the Jews; going a block or two with young King Farouk of Egypt in his ambition to be Caliph of all the Moslem world, and then pulling back; tolerating King Saud's permanent war with Iman Yahia on the theory that it's best to keep them divided; tossing a bone once in a while to the cantankerous Syrian Arabs. That's the story you get from loyal Englishmen. They wonder dubiously whether the adaptable and reversible Mr. Philby will help much.

(Copyright, 1941, King Features Syndicate, Incorporated.)

LISTEN, WORLD!

—By Elsie Robinson

A BOOK THAT MAKES AMERICA REAL

These are bewildering days for most of us. We know that frightful things are happening. We know we should be alarmed about them . . . should do something about them. But we can't. For, somehow, in spite of all the terrible headlines, it doesn't seem real.

The taxes mount. The strikes increase. Junior goes marching off with the draft. We worry. We weep. We complain. And yet it doesn't actually seem real. The war doesn't seem real. The strikes don't seem real. America, itself, doesn't seem real. The whole affair doesn't get through to where we live.

This isn't because we're a stupid people or a bad people or a disloyal people. It's simply because we've been a comfortable and complacent people for too long. We've taken ourselves and country and our good fortune for granted, for too long. Other countries and their varied misfortunes have been like bad dreams to us...bad dreams that could never happen to us.

Only lately, slowly and reluctantly, are we awakening to the fact that these things may happen to us; that we are made of the same stuff as other nationals; that our high principles will not save us unless we make them a living issue.

In short, we Americans have been indulging in a beautiful pipe dream...and will end in a pile of ashes unless something awakens us in time. Something REAL, that will make us realize what we mean, and what our country means. A simple but terrific jolt of truth.

That's why I want to tell you about a certain book today...Dorsha Hayes' "THE AMERICAN PRIMER." For it's what we all need to jolt us out of that pipe dream of complacency and content.

There's nothing new about "THE AMERICAN PRIMER." It's simply a fresh and vigorous statement of the principles on which America was based . . . and for which it should still stand. But, reading it, one realizes, perhaps for the first time, how much those principles mean and what a terrible price they may cost.

We know, theoretically, what those principles cost one hundred and fifty years ago. But we have forgotten that principles go on costing, that their price is never really paid. It was not enough that America won her freedom once—she must go on winning it. It was not enough that we defied tyranny and injustice once—we must go on defying them. Even if all the proud plans of our hearts are crumbled into dust.

FOR THAT IS WHAT IT MEANS TO BE AN AMERICAN!

"What it means to be an American," that is the gist of Dorsha Hayes' brief book. It may not seem very profound . . . it's as simple as a First Reader in its construction. But it is the best medicine I've found to move the profound inertia . . . the deadly ignorance . . . the diseased complacency of the modern American.

For, whether we know it or not, we are already invaded. We are invaded by our own stupidity . . . our own vanity . . . our own intolerance . . . our own ghastly self-satisfaction. Unless we change, these things will destroy us far more speedily and horribly than an enemy's hordes.

Read Dorsha Hayes' book. Bring it home tonight with your loaf of bread and pound of round steak . . . spread it out on the table so your children may listen to its simple words. Let it tell them how great your heritage was once, and may still be. Let it make them feel to what cheapness they have reduced that inheritance.

MAKE AMERICA REAL ONCE MORE . . . BRING IT BACK INTO YOUR HOME.

(Copyright, 1941, King Features Syndicate, Incorporated.)

ONE WORD LED TO ANOTHER

By Bugs Baer

FACTS NOT WORTH KNOWING

Facts Not Worth Knowing: 1—A full-rigged ship of 50 years ago had 37 sails set when it started going places and doing things. 2—The Hottentots were so named by the Dutch Africans because they hotted and totted or stammered and stuttered. 3—A gleyde is an old sway-backed hoss of the glue factory type. 4—Dextroversion is a bit of ogling toward the lady on the right.

Learn One Thing Each Day: If you are frondivorous you should certainly like saald.

Dibs and Dabs: 1—Jack Drum's reception is to be booted out of doors. 2—Embonpoint means in good condition. 3—An ekka is a native one-hoss carriage bumping along outside of Bombay. 4—Well, here's something about an Ephebus who was a Spartan lad about eighteen doing his year in the conscript army. 5—If you are a bit embrangled about all this, do not consult your doctor or your dentist for it means you are a bit confused.

Daily Double: 1—Dhyana is the higher contemplation in Yoga and could mean a paperhanger figuring out a daily double at Churchill Downs. 2—While we are talking about paperhangers we will get right down to generals, admirals and hodcarriers, for the original epaulet was a pad on the shoulder to ease the weight of the hod. Soldiers took the idea and wore a pad to take the weight of the musket while marching. Somebody added a gold fringe and there's your epaulet.

Explanation of the Above: That's your home work.

Irritating Items: 1—The vine of the morning glory twines from the left to the right. 2—The Dhole is an Indian dog that will attack tigers and beat them. 3—To flaffer is to flutter. 4—Drinking will make your nose drupaceous or fluffy. Ask me or Bill Fields.

Flash: A synclinorium is a compound flexure of the earth's surface. Unflash.

Postponed Postscripts: 1—Bottomtry is a loan on a boat. 2—Smart muggs like you and me would describe over-lapping roof tiling as imbricated. 3—Frottage is a bit of polishing like a monocle. 4—And if that gloppens you temporarily you are astonished.

(Distributed by King Features Syndicate, Incorporated.)

Gen. Hugh S. Johnson Says:

Freedom Of Seas 'False Phantom'

Only Echo Of Real Slogan: 'Britannia Rules Waves'

By GENERAL HUGH S. JOHNSON

(Distributed by King Features Syndicate, Inc. Reproduction in whole or in part strictly prohibited.)

WASHINGTON, May 27.—We passed the neutrality act to keep us out of foreign wars, Now, unless all signs fail, we are going to repeal or evade it. Why? Obviously for the reverse of the purpose of its passage, namely, to get into foreign wars.

As this is written the President has not yet spoken, but the two more strident endmen of the Washington minstrel show have spoken plenty—War Ministers Stimson and Knox.

It is an astonishing situation when, with 80 per cent. of our people so clearly opposed to war, there can be such complacency about every Governmental step that makes war inevitable.

TWO FACTORS CITED

Is it public ignorance about what is going on, or a sort of national fatalism that contents itself with believing that our President has gathered to himself so many of the powers of Government that no wish of the people can stop him?

In traveling up and down and around this country trying to get the "feel" of this intangible thing called public opinion, one gathers an impression that it is partly both.

This is very strange even in this strange new world because neither ignorance nor resignation is any part of the American character.

SEA LINKED TO WARS

When the principle of the Neutrality Act was first suggested, though not urged, by B. M. Baruch, this column said:

"Something about the sea helped to get us into every one of our foreign wars except the war with Mexico."

Economic causes are responsible for most wars. Our Revolution was partly against the force of British sea power to dominate and exploit these colonies—Boston tea-party, et cetera.

We engaged in an undeclared naval war with France and a second naval war with Britain in protest against interference with our shipping. During the Civil War, England came within inches of declaring war on us for doing what she has always claimed the right to do.

We stopped a British ship and took off two Confederate enemies of the United States. That war was averted by our apology and restitution because Lincoln said, "one war at a time is enough."

Our war with Spain was made possible by public indignation over sinking the battleship Maine in Havana harbor.

In the World War, we had as much legal cause for fighting England as for fighting Germany over interferences by both Governments with our "freedom of the seas."

The British practically blockaded our Atlantic coast, intercepted our mails, interfered with our commerce and violated all our concepts of international law.

DIFFERENCE NOTED

The deciding difference was that German submarine interference destroyed American lives. The British only destroyed American commerce.

We said that we went to war to vindicate our "freedom of the seas." That was a principle one of Mr. Wilson's "fourteen points." It was dropped overboard and, without explanation until later, sunk without trace at his first contact with the British architects of the Treaty of Versailles.

The "freedom of the seas" slogan fooled us into one war. Now it is fooling us into another.

We have no freedom of the seas today where British interests are involved. You can't, for example, write an air-mail letter to Venezuela via Bermuda that will not be opened and censored—and we stand for it. "Freedom of the seas" is a phantom—an echo of the real words, which is, and always has beeen, "Britannia rules the waves."

O. K. This is not even protesting that. It is only protesting a second eagle-screaming misuse of "freedom of the seas" to get us into war.

"FALSE PHANTOM"

The Neutrality Act does need revision, but, if the purpose of the revision is to force American vessels through actual blockades and to make war for us inevitable if one is sunk—in vindication of a right never before claimed by any non-belligerent nation—then, it would be far more forthright now to present to Congress the issue of a war declaration and stop fooling our people with any such legalistic skullduggery or sloganeering them with any such false phantom as "freedom of the seas."

On The Side

By E. V. DURLING

What is the voice of strange command
Calling you still as friend calls friend,
With love that cannot brook delay,
To rise and follow the ways that wend
Over the hills and far away.
—W. E. Henley.

Sprang out of bed yesterday morning at the crack of nine-thirty and after a light breakfast of orange juice, a little cereal, a few stacks of hot cakes, several boiled eggs, a slice of ham and a couple of pots of coffee, boarded the Santa Fe's elegant streamliner for Chicago and New York. Have traveled from coast to coast by bus, automobile, boat, train and plane, but this is the first time I ever brought a dog along. This pup has never been anywhere but for a ride to the drug store, the veterinarian's or the butcher shop. When he started he figured he was going to one of these three places and no doubt was hoping it was the butcher shop, where he enjoys looking at the steaks. Now on the train he seems to think it is a house, but is bewildered by the fact that every time he is taken out the door the back yard is different. At the moment he is peering intently at a herd of cattle with an expression on his face indicating he is in about the same state of mind as Alice was in Wonderland when she said:

"Things get curioser and curioser."

Passed through Arcadia, Cal., famous for the Santa Anita race track, a statue of Seabiscuit and its 98 per cent. pure mountain water. A town with water like that should have a brewery. Good pure mountain water does much in the making of good beer. Going through Glendora, Cal., always makes me think of Frank Chance, the peerless leader of the Chicago Cubs. He lived there and also had in Glendora a place of business known as the Cubs' drug store. Claremont, Cal., is where Robert Taylor's alma mater, Pomona College, is situated. While at college Taylor had no great reputation as a heart-breaker.

We breezed by Fontana, Cal., at which place the Folder of Fancy Facts the porter gave me says is "the largest hog farm in the world." This statement leaves me a little in the dark as it doesn't say how many hogs they have at this farm. I like figures with my fancy facts. We came to the Calico mountains, from which, the folder says, "have been taken over eighty millions of dollars' worth of silver." I wish there were more silver dollars in circulation. I used to like to clang them on the counter. We stopped at Trinidad, Col., which has a $75,000 opera house, a million-dollar courthouse and jail, a statue of Kit Carson and a fine place to walk a dog near the station. The pup is running me ragged on this walk proposition. Every time the train doesn't stop at a station he gives me a reproachful look. He is also a little sore because I won't stop the train and let him out to bark at the cattle. If you want to forget the war news, all you have to do, sir, is to take a two-year-old pup that has never been on a train on a three-thousand-mile trip.

Being a member of the society opposed to calling Pullman porters George, I asked our porter his name, and he said it was Solomon Simpson. That's quite an experience, having a porter named Solomon Simpson, but not quite equal to the last trip, when we had a porter with a mustache. A Pullman porter with a mustache is as rare as a traffic cop with a beard. You don't see as many people playing cards on trains as formerly. Most of them seem to be reading non-fiction best sellers. I played some gin-rummy with my girl friend, and she won some of my hard-earned money. But I'll tempt her into a pinochle game and get it back before this trip is over.

"Bar rails for men only" is what a legislator states he is for in proposing a law be passed requiring women being served drinks to sit at tables. I think if the women enjoy sitting on high stools at the cocktail bars, or even standing at same, they should be permitted to do so. Let the girls have their fun, says I . . . Paulette Goddard is pictured wearing something called "evening shorts." Seems to be an evening dress made like a tennis costume or a bathing suit. Might be popular with women possessed of unusual symmetry of limb. Women with good-looking limbs are always very unhappy when wearing something that conceals their legs . . . Note a number of missionaries on the way to Africa were aboard a steamer sunk by a German raider. Missionaries on their way to civilize the savages should avoid places where men enjoying the benefits of civilization are occupied in murdering each other and slaughtering women and children.

(Distributed by King Features Syndicate, Incorporated.)

THE POLITICAL PARADE

—By George Rothwell Brown

Special to The News-Post.

WASHINGTON, May 27.—There is every sign in Washington today, as the nation waits a momentous fireside chat, that Mr. Roosevelt's period of procrastination is at an end, and his time for action at hand.

The national mind has been prepared for this contemplated action, by all the devices of the vast Washington bureaucracy.

What else could that contemplated act be but one of such a character as to be a euphremism for war?

This writer does not pretend to have an inkling of what the President proposes to tell the American people as they sit, breathless, expectant, and with troubled minds, at their radios.

But the ground-work has been done for sweeping aside the neutrality acts, of 1935, and as finally amended in 1939. Knox and Stimson have demanded it. The President has declared himself to be a champion of the old American tradition of "the freedom of the seas."

FREEDOM OF SEAS

This notwithstanding he signed the laws which sacrificed freedom of the seas, temporarily, in a war-mad world, to sane freedom from war for America.

Chairman Bloom of the House Foreign Affairs Committee, who put through the neutrality legislation in his branch of Congress, has announced he is ready to take up the fight for repeal of neutrality if the President gives his signal.

But, as this is written, Chairman George of the Senate Foreign Relations Committee, makes it known that he has been given no intimation of any desire on the President's part for repeal of the Neutrality Act of 1939.

Any attempt to repeal the neutrality law would meet such stubborn resistance at the Senate that the debate and argument might drag on for weeks.

But the inference is clear in the warlike utterances of members of the President's Cabinet and other responsible officials, that the time for action is NOW.

RADIO AUDIENCE

Without presenting to know what is in the President's mind to say to the radio audience, it is permissable to venture a guess. It would be this:

There being no time for repeal of neutrality, the President will make known to the people his intention to avail himself of his vast power under the lend-lease law, to sweep aside the neutrality law, which clearly today stands in the way of rendering to Britain that aid which the President has pledged and which Congress has financed to the extent of $8,300,000,000.

The lend-lease law, Clause A, Section 3, authorizes the President to do a great many things "NOTWITHSTANDING THE PROVISIONS OF ANY OTHER LAW."

It is true that Clauses D and E of Section 4 of the law provide "that nothing in this act" shall be construed to authorize convoying by naval vessels, or to authorize the entry of American vessels in combat areas, in violation of Section 3 of the Neutrality Act of 1939.

NEGATIVE RESTRICTIONS

But a reading of these prohibitions discloses that these are negative restrictions on the President's powers. They are not mandatory restrictions.

Is not, then, the broad power of the President, under Section 3 of the lend-lease law, sufficient to enable him to set aside the Neutrality Act of 1939, by executive order, on the ground that this law interferes with the carrying out of the all-aid for Britain? I think it is. At least, it can be argued that this power is sufficient.

If the President did not foresee the time when he would need this power, why did he insist upon its grant to him?

Are we on the brink of war—a war not declared by Congress, as the Constitution requires, but a war precipitated by executive order?

Well, we are on a brink and you may lay to that!

You are on your way, though you may not know where you are going.

You will probably know after tonight's radio pep talk.

If the naval battle in the Arctic occurred off the coast of Greenland, as the British claim, then by coming into the Western Hemisphere Hitler may have given the President the signal he has needed.

Happigrams

By ERICH BRANDEIS

A minister admonished the naturalized citizens of his flock to keep silent on the world crisis.

Does that minister realize what he said? Does he realize that to foreign-born citizens America is an ideal realized?

To the immigrant his citizenship paper is his Bill of Rights.

To him, America is the land of fulfillment, the church in which he may worship freely, the tree that grows in the soil of liberty and on which grows the fruit of happiness and contentment.

There may be exceptions. But the average naturalized American will defend America to the last drop of his blood!

He cherishes freedom most who has known tyranny!

(Distributed by King Features Syndicate, Incorporated.)

IN THE NEWS

MD. FLIER, 21 OTHERS DIE IN BRITISH CRASH

THE BALTIMORE NEWS-POST

AN INDEPENDENT NEWSPAPER

The Largest Evening Circulation in the Entire South

WALL ST. CLOSE 9

VOL. CXXXIX.—NO. 88 Entered as second-class matter at Baltimore Postoffice. FRIDAY EVENING, AUGUST 15, 1941 PRICE 3 CENTS

THE WEATHER

Cloudy and somewhat warmer, with occasional rain and brief thundershowers tonight and Saturday. Cooler Saturday night.

Detailed Weather Report on Page 38

MEAN TEMPERATURES YESTERDAY

Baltimore	70	New York	69
Atlanta	74	Omaha	80
Boston	64	Portland, Maine	62
Chicago	66	Salt Lake City	69
Jacksonville	80	San Antonio	85
Los Angeles	78	Seattle	66
Miami	85	Tampa	88
New Orleans	86	Washington	68

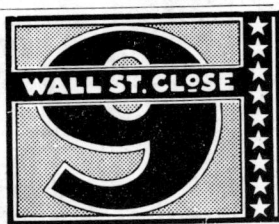

U. S. EXPECTS WIDE PEACE AIM BACKING

WELL, friends and fellow citizens, our New Deal Administration has finally succeeded, after great and constant effort, in antagonizing almost every nation on the face of the earth.

We have antagonized them entirely unnecessarily.

We have antagonized them usually not to satisfy the sentiments of our genuine Americans but to gratify the revenges of the hordes of refugees who are overrunning our country and taking control of it.

We have antagonized those various nations in Europe and Asia and Africa, not to protect our own American liberties, but to inflict upon them and permanently impose upon them the crackpot New Deal theories and practices which have proved such expensive and such disastrous failures in our own land.

THE latest nation which we have antagonized by attempting to dictate its national and international policies is France.

We know nothing about actual conditions prevailing in France and in Europe and in the French colonies in Africa, but that makes no difference to our New Deal Administration.

It operates the most freely and offends the most effectively when it is entirely devoid of any factual knowledge of actual conditions.

And it generally is as empty of useful knowledge and bare of beneficial experience as a dried bone.

So now we have arrayed against us Germany and Italy and Hungary and Rumania and Finland and Latvia, Lithuania and Estonia and France.

And we will surely soon have Japan and Spain and Portugal, and very possibly all the Scandinavian countries and all the Balkan peninsula.

NONE of these countries wants to bother the United States, but our New Deal Administration INSISTS upon bothering and BEING BOTHERED.

Of course, sooner or later we are going to be accommodated with the trouble we are continually inviting if we keep on meddling with matters which do not concern us and attempting to run the other independent nations of the world as unsuccessfully as our New Deal Government has run our own.

We would probably be exceeding the duties and functions of the United States were we trying to AMERICANIZE the world.

But the New Deal is NOT trying to Americanize the world.

It is trying to COMMUNIZE the world.

It is not trying to sow the seeds of American individualism and constitutional liberty, and freedom of thought and speech and publication, and equality before the law, and opportunity for all men throughout the world.

MOST assuredly NOT, since the New Deal has discarded these essential and elemental freedoms here at home.

Have not our most distinguished New Deal leaders repudiated the Constitution as belonging to the ox-cart era?

Have they not rejected the Bill of Rights as an outmoded survival of the horse and buggy period?

Have they not substituted for American independence

Continued on Page 4, Column 1.

Britain Winning Battle Of Atlantic, Claim; Russ Admit Ukraine Retreat

LONDON, Aug. 15—(A. P.).—Britain's position in the battle of the Atlantic is "very much better" because of widening operations against German submarines and "most valuable" United States assistance, authoritative sources declared today. The Axis, simultaneously, has "suffered very heavily" in the Mediterranean, they added.

HELSINKI, Aug. 15—(A. P.).—The drive on Leningrad was reported launched in earnest from the north today with powerful Soviet defenses on the Karelian Isthmus smashed, the towns of Kirvu and Elisenvaara captured, and the Red Army in retreat.

MOSCOW, Aug. 15—(U. P.).—Russia, admitting a German advance of more than 60 miles into the Ukraine, asserted that the army of Marshal Semyon Budenny was retreating deliberately and orderly, in line with the strategic plans of the High Command to make the Germans pay dearly for every mile of ground gained.

(BACKGROUND NOTE: London dispatches said the Rusian Army of the Ukraine is engaged in a grim and historic retreat, leveling fields and wrecking factories in its wake, for a finish fight against the German forces on the Dnieper river line.

The day's first war communique admitted the Russians had given up the cities of Kirovograd and Pervomaisk, and it was plain that the Germans were striking close to the great industrial district in the bend of the Dnieper river.

(BACKGROUND NOTE: Kirovograd is 90 miles east of Uman, scene of fierce fighting for days on

Continued on Page 2, Column 3.

BASEBALL, RACING RESULTS—PAGE 35

Crash Kills Marylander, British Chief

(Picture on Page 3)

MONTREAL, Aug. 15—(U. P.).—Arthur B. Purvis, chief of the British Purchasing Commission to the United States; 12 Americans, one a Marylander; Capt. P. F. Lee, Jr., of Frederick; eight Canadians and one other Briton were killed in the crash of an airplane taking off from Great Britain for the United States, it was announced today.

The Royal Air Force Ferry Command said that among the American victims was Joseph C. Mackey of Kansas, pilot of the bomber in which Sir Frederick Banting, codiscoverer of insulin, was killed when it crashed in Newfoundland last winter.

Other Americans killed were Flying Officer E. W. Watson, Torrence, Cal.; Flight Engineer R. F. Davis, Huntingdon, W. Va.; Capt. M. D. Dilley, Kansas City; Capt. J. J. Kerwin, Oakland, Cal.; Capt. E. B. Anding, Merrick, N. Y.; Flying Officer W. L. Trimble, Fort Worth, Texas; Capt. M. J. Wetzel, Jamesburg, N. Y.; Capt. G. Hull, Royal Oak, Mich.; Capt. E. Hamel, Baintree, Mass.; Capt. P. F. Lee, Jr., Frederick, Md.

Maryland Flier Son Of U. S. F. & G. Chief

Capt. P. F. Lee, Jr., one of 22 persons killed when an airliner crashed in taking off from Britain for the United States, was a son of P. F. Lee, vice-president of the United States Fidelity and Guaranty Company.

Captain Lee joined the Canadian Air Corps last year and had been engaged in ferrying bombers to Britain from Canada.

He was a brother of J. Tyson Lee, member of the Maryland House of Delegates. Other survivors include his widow, a five-year-old daughter, a brother, Augustus W. Lee, Pittsburg, and a sister, Miss Georgine Lee, Urbana, Md.

Captain Lee worked for the U. S. Fidelity and Guaranty Company before going to Canada, and lived with his parents at their home near Urbana, Frederick county.

In 1932 Captain Lee was so anxious to get to the Olympic Games in Los Angeles, Cal., that he bought an airplane to take him there. At the time he lived in the 1100 block North Calvert street. He had been flying for 10 years.

Temperatures

12 Midn't.	68	8 A. M.	72
1 A. M.	67	9 A. M.	73
2 A. M.	67	10 A. M.	76
3 A. M.	66	11 A. M.	77
4 A. M.	66	12 Noon	78
5 A. M.	67	1 P. M.	80
6 A. M.	68	2 P. M.	81
7 A. M.	69	3 P. M.	81

Choicest Recipes of a Famous Organization. For the First Time In Its 208-Year-Old History the "Schuylkill Fishing Company" Social Organization Reveals Its Recipes. Get Them With the Housewife's Food Almanack, in The American Weekly, the Magazine Distributed With Next Sunday's Baltimore American.—Adv.

VERY LATEST NEWS

(Race Results From Howard Sports Daily, Inc.)

HIALEAH WINS FIFTH AT SARATOGA

Fourth — Speed To Spare, $4.50, $2.90, $2.40; Mary Schulz, $3.10, $2.80; Scotch Trap, $3.40.

Fifth — Hialeah, $3.30, $2.70, $2.20; Put In, $5.60, $3.60; Espero, $3.30.

AT NARRAGANSETT PARK

Fifth—Beamy, $6.00, $3.70, $3.40; Patrol Flight, $5.00, $4.00; Volpone, $6.10.

AT WASHINGTON PARK

Third—Commission, $10.80, $5.40, $2.80; Darby Dallas, $6.20, $2.80; Epiget, $2.40. Total mutuels, $30.40.

Fourth—Unity, won; After School, 2d; Drollon, 3d.

LATEST BASEBALL SCORES

(A) At Washington—Boston, 2; Washington, 0; end 2d.

(N) At Cincinnati—Chicago, 1; Cincinnati, 0; end 2d.

VOTE $244,929,800 NAVAL SHORE FUNDS

WASHINGTON, Aug. 15—(A. P.).—The House completed Congressional action today on legislation authorizing $244,929,800 worth of naval shore facilities.

'Mere Screen,' Says Tinkham Of U. S., British Statement

By GEORGE HOLDEN TINKHAM

Representative in Congress from Massachusetts. Member of House Foreign Affairs Committee. Special to The News-Post.

WASHINGTON, Aug. 15.—The statement issued by President Roosevelt and Prime Minister Winston Churchill contains many words and no information and no new ideas. It was merely a screen to conceal vital commitments and engagements.

Their alleged peace aims seem to be to disentomb and to attempt to reanimate the defunct League of Nations, the creation of which had much to do with promoting the present wars.

Their fantastic suggestions in relation to disarmament will not mislead the world. To them disarmament means what it meant to the League of Nations, the disarmament of their foes, and nothing more.

Their declaration concerning freedom of the seas merely means the perpetuation of the navalism of Great Britain pooled with the navalism of the United States. This pooling of naval powers was announced to Parliament by Mr. Churchill in March of 1938. President Roosevelt had no moral or legal right to make such an agreement.

The moral bankruptcy of their statement is most apparent in their formal announcement of the alliance of the United States and Great Britain with homicidal, Communistic Soviet Russia.

Undoubtedly there was discussed at the conference between President Roosevelt and Prime Minister Churchill the formation of another American Expeditionary Force. British manpower is not sufficient to win the present wars.

Let Mr. Churchill take notice, however, that the vote cast by the House of Representatives two days ago in relation to the extension of service of America's conscript Army will bar for many months such a betrayal of American manhood.

One-Way Censorship;

British There, But No U. S. Reporters At Sea Parley

The following dispatch is based on a story appearing yesterday in the London Daily Mail. It emphasizes a fact made clear with release of news and pictures: That the ship on which President Roosevelt and Mr. Churchill met had an ample supply of English reporters, correspondents and cameramen, but that censorship was imposed on the American press and no American reporters, correspondents or cameramen were allowed.

LONDON, Aug. 14—(A. P.).—A constantly moving circle of destroyers, patrol boats and other small warships formed a precautionary defensive ring around the Roosevelt-Churchill conference ship, and American planes droned overhead, the Daily Mail said today in a dispatch from its correspondent "somewhere on the American Atlantic coast."

Correspondent Walter Farr said President Roosevelt and Prime Minister Churchill sat on the sunlit deck of the ship "with seagulls wheeling around."

'TAKING NO CHANCE'

Farr said:

"Occasionally the drone of a big American flying boat patrolling the skies was heard. The Navy was taking no chance."

From these descriptions the British concluded the conferences took place close to the American shore.

Farr quoted a high American official who took part in the conversations as saying:

"The President is the happiest looking man on earth today. At the conferences it was hard to tell

Continued on Page 2, Column 6.

Hull Hopes World's Nations Will Rally To American-British Plan

(Sidelights and comments on historic "Peace-aim" pact on Page 6.)

WASHINGTON, Aug. 15—(U. P.).—Secretary of State Cordell Hull said today that he hoped all civilized nations of the World, including Soviet Russia, will rally round the Roosevelt-Churchill program for destruction of Nazi tyranny and a new world order.

LONDON, Aug. 15—(A. P.).—President Roosevelt and Prime Minister Churchill were reported today to be planning to send a communication to Josef Stalin proposing a meeting in Moscow between Stalin and his war chiefs on one hand and high British and American officials on the other.

By GRIFFING BANCROFT

International News Service Staff Correspondent.

WASHINGTON, Aug. 15.—Congressional reaction to President Roosevelt's dramatic meeting with British Prime Minister Churchill, and the eight-point declaration of the democracies which developed from it, crystalized today into two main trends:

1. A general feeling, varying from chagrin to anger, against the fact that Congress was kept in the dark about the whole thing, which promoted a strong bi-partisan group to demand an explanation from the Administration.

2. A sigh of relief grounded on the general belief that the United States really is no closer to war as a result of the high seas conference, coupled with the allaying of real fears that President Roosevelt himself may have been in personal danger during the meeting.

(BACKGROUND NOTE: Belief is growing in Washington that the President and British Prime Minister have sent a special message to Premier Joseph Stalin of Soviet Russia. It is assumed the message was in the nature of encouragement to Russia to continue to resist the German military onslaught, and probably included a promise of increased aid from both Great Britain and the United States. There is reason to believe that the United States and Great Britain would like to have Stalin indorse the Anglo-American eight-point program for a new world era based on peace and happiness after this war is over.)

OTHER VIEWS

Behind the formal statements issued by Congressmen and Senators

Continued on Page 2, Column 1.

Roosevelt Ban On U. S. Press Scored

WASHINGTON, Aug. 15—(I. N. S.).—Reports that two British newspapermen were present at the high seas meeting of President Roosevelt and Prime Minister Churchill while the American press was barred, brought a storm of criticism today from journalist members of Congress.

Representative Knutson (Republican) of Minnesota, publisher of Wadena (Minn.) Pioneer-Journal, charged that the incident "was part of the whole plot of secrecy." He declared:

"There is only one inference to be drawn from it.

"President Roosevelt does not want the American people to know what transpired at that meeting."

Later, Knutson made a speech to the House in which he declared that the American people "don't want to be treated like children." He said:

"Naturally, those Americans who yet do their own thinking and have a regard for the future of their own country are asking why the British press was permitted to get the big-

Continued on Page 2, Column 7.

Curtis Creek Coast Guard Trains 4,000

Yard Is Humming With Activity On Defense Plans

By EARLE R. POORBAUGH
News-Post Staff Correspondent

U. S. COAST GUARD YARD, CURTIS CREEK, Md., Aug. 15.—Here at the United States Coast Guard Yard, on the southern edge of Baltimore, Uncle Sam has trained more than 4,000 of his efficient seagoing police force since national defense became the prime motivating force of the nation.

Charged with the enforcement of all laws of the United States, by act of Congress, the Coast Guard also has the dual function of life-saving in time of peace and of fighting as part of the Navy in time of war.

THREE FUNCTIONS

To fulfill the three functions, the Coast Guard maintains five training stations similar to the Baltimore depot, where young men from the plains and mountains are turned into apprentice seamen within three months of their enlistment.

Quiet mannered, soft spoken Captain LeRoy Reinburg, U. S. C. G., who graduated from the Coast Guard Academy when it was located right here on Curtis Creek, commands the Yard, which is humming with activity in connection with the defense program.

A veteran of more than 29 years service, Captain Reinburg heads the yard's activities, which at present include training a corps of recruits, repairing all small arms of the service, training a force of 175 radio operators and keeping the radio equipment of the Coast Guard vessels and shore stations in repair.

IN SPARE TIME

In his spare time, Captain Reinburg sees to it that Coast Guard and Naval vessels are repaired, that life boats for the services are built, supplies issued, and as a sort of spare time activity, plays the part of "service father" to the 1200 service men and 1500 civilian employees of the yard.

Early this fall, the yard will begin the building of sea-going ships, in addition to its already expanded activities. Shipways for the construction of the vessels have already been installed, as has a dry dock which will accommodate vessels up to 350 feet in length.

22 MARYLANDERS

At present, 22 Marylanders are training at the Recruit Training Center of the yard, hoping to be assigned to a ship or shore station, where they may become second-class seamen, first step up the ladder to a Chief Warrant Officer's rating, and a salary of $300 a month.

Today's Coast Guard, with a Rear Admiral at its head, numbers 26,000 men and officers, and maintains more than 400 vessels, many of which are stationed in far distant parts of the world, as liaison units in Uncle Sam's force to keep tabs upon his nationals.

IN TIME OF WAR

Operating in time of peace under the Treasury Department, charged with the maintenance of all lighthouses and vessels, with patrolling thousands of miles of beaches and maintaining life saving stations, the Coast Guard in time of war becomes an integral part of the Naval establishment, since, by act of Congress, its primary duty is as an arm of the national defense.

Baltimore's Coast Guard station has already made an important contribution to the national defense program through the training of recruits who have already been assigned to active service, and, Captain Reinburg says, it will continue at an accelerated pace until the present emergency is past.

Smith To Address Cumberland C. I. O.

CUMBERLAND, Aug. 15—(A. P.) Members of Allegany county C. I. O. unions will hear Edwin S. Smith, a member of the National Labor Relations Board, at their Labor Day meeting September 1. Smith notified local labor leaders that he had postponed his vacation in order to appear at the celebration.

SCHOOL ENROLLMENT OFF

CAMBRIDGE, Aug. 15—(A. P.)—Enrollment of beginners in Dorchester county public schools this term will find 272 new white students and 134 newcomers in the Negro schools, officials reported today. Total enrollment is 88 less than last year.

Your Finest Day or Evening

9 every morning, all-day cruise to SEASIDE PARK. Picnic groves, rides, salt water bathing, 75c. children 40c. Nightly, 8.30, moonlight cruise. Joe Dowling dancing music, 55c. Salt air, Moonlite 30c. Light St. children 20c. Nightly, Light St. and trips at 2.30 P.M. to Seaside.

Thursdays only, boat trips at 2.30 P.M. to Seaside.

Wilson Line's New BAY BELLE

The Feminine Voice ❖ Of Broadway

By DOROTHY KILGALLEN

Gossip In Gotham

Mrs. Victor Mature (Martha Kemp) is in Good Samaritan Hospital, Hollywood, with an internal ailment. Too ill to come to New York, as she planned ... Leon Janney, the juvenile, and Elaine Ellis, also a thespian, are a heartillery barrage.

Errol Flynn and Lili Damita will keep their divorce friendly, in view of his generous settlement ... Prince and Princess Ibrahim (he was "the Tommy Manville of Europe") will lullaby in Paris.

It was Mayor LaGuardia's personal intervention that got Merle Oberon out of trouble with the local immigration authorities, proving that chivalry isn't dead around City Hall ... Kaarene Verne, of the "King's Row" cast, will shed her husband, now in England.

Bette Davis' discovery, Richard Travis, has discovered Gail Patrick ... Jimmy Walker is writing his long-awaited biography at a spot twenty-five miles north of Saratoga ... Tommy Manville's mother is gravely ill at Doctors Hospital. Producer Edward Grainger and Model Jinx Falkenburg, are cooing ... Alice Marble looks set for a radio spot as sports commentator ... This happens to somebody every season: When Mimi Barrie, the Conover pretty, sings at a night club, starting next week, her mother will occupy a table near the bandstand every night to keep the wolves away. Because Mimi's only seventeen.

Douglas Fairbanks, Jr., may get a permanent post as ambassador to one of the South American countries.

Louise King, the Hit Parade singer, eloped to Chicago over the week-end with Jimmy Both, a musician ... Fred Astaire is slated to play the lead, "Pal Joey," in the cinema ... Tommy Suffern Tailer, the golfer-socialite-cinemact, has proposed to pretty Patricia Foss ... High jinks department: At Phil Amidown's birthday party the merry-makers dunked Orrin Lehman in the swimming pool—but he was wearing one Amidown's suits!

The phone company made a mint on Alice Faye and Phil Harris before she joined him here. They called each other twice a day for lengthy coo-talk.

The new papa, Bob Topping, leaves in a fortnight for Pensacola to join the flying corps. He'll bunk with Winnie Gardiner.

GOLD STARS: Maxine Sullivan's platter, "Who Is Sylvia" backed by "If I Had A Ribbon Bow" ... Billy Vine's comedy number, "Wedding Bells," at the Hurricane ... Count Basie's platter of Milt Ebbins' killer-diller, "Tune Town Shuffle" ...

Jay Eddy, the youth who gave up the local social whirl to work in a rhumba troupe, is the hit of Chicago—does his act with a 500-pound lass, a rhumba that literally "shakes down the house."

Hollywood will make "Arsenic and Old Lace" with the principals from the play—a breathless innovation from that sector.

Broadway Rose has a crush on Nick Arno, of Ames and Arno, the Strand comedy duo. Brings him home-made cake.

Warner Bros. have snapped up the Maxwell Theatre interests in England for a paltry $3,600,000 right under a competitor's nose.

Now that Rosemary Lane is initially, it'll take plenty to top Buddy town you can reconcile yourself to Westmore in Rosemary's affections.

... the romance items—but, confident...

BEFORE TRAIN TIME

STEP INTO THE Savarin PENNSYLVANIA STATION

What's better than a Bon Voyage "send-off" over a delicious Savarin luncheon? Waiter will call you at train time. Air-Conditioned.

Today's Savarin Luncheon Surprise Crab Imperial with Julienne Potatoes, Bavarian Cole Slaw, Choice of Appetizers, Soup or Dessert. **65¢**

Ann Lewis
208 W. LEXINGTON

16.98

Your First Fall Love ...
Velveteen with Lace Trim!

Of course we have it for the smart young junior-miss who likes her clothes to have a certain air of distinctiveness! Button-up tie-back in black, rose, royal, beige and wine. 9 to 15.

EDWARD G. **ROBINSON!** MARLENE **DIETRICH!** GEORGE **RAFT!**

(He's mad about Dietrich!) (She's mad about Raft!) (He's mad about the whole thing!)

All Together! "MANPOWER"

Filmdom's most dynamic threesome put all their power into

See it Folks—and see it TOMORROW! It'll be ages—before there'll be another picture this exciting!

A WARNER BROS. HIT with Alan HALE • Frank McHUGH • Directed by Raoul Walsh
Original Screen Play by Richard Macaulay & Jerry Wald

STANLEY THEATRE

Last Day—"UNDERGROUND" with Jeffrey Lynn • Philip Dorn • Kaaren Verne • Mona Maris

---

Sears Is Open Tonight 9:30
Saturday and Monday 'til

BUY NOW!
AT TODAY'S Known LOW PRICE

6½-Cu. Ft. All-Steel Coldspot!

Study The Picture

Tested and Approved Good Housekeeping Institute

Immediate Delivery!

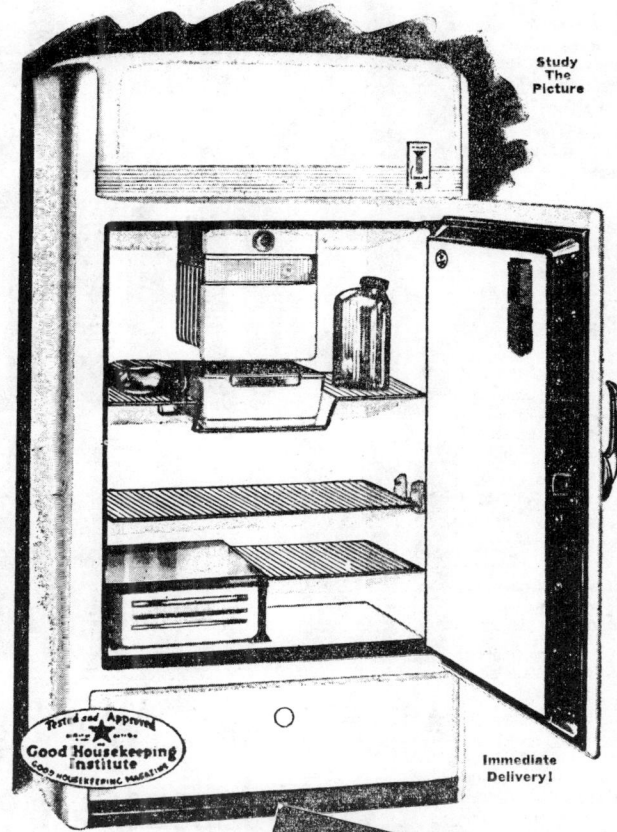

41's Big Buy! *Sumptuously Equipped.*

—You'll go a long way to find a greater refrigerator value than this one! Not only is it the big 6.5 cu. ft. size ... but it's equipped! That's something you don't find every day at 119.88.

$119.88
$4.00 Down

- Foodex Vegetable Drawer
- Roll-Out Handi-Bin Drawer
- Automatic Reset Defrost
- 9-Lb. Capacity Meat Saver
- 9-Point Cold Control
- Sliding Adjustable Shelf
- Stainless Freezer for Frozen Foods

Here's The "4 Star" Beauty!

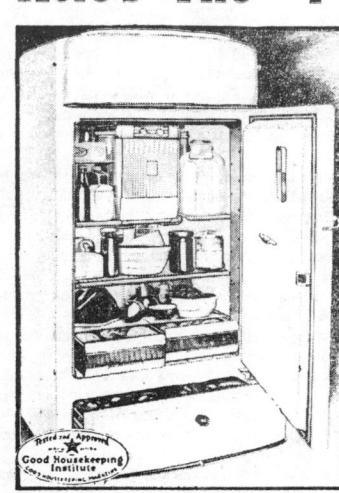

6.5 Cubic Foot 1941 Model

COLDSPOT
139.95

$4 Down Delivers It!
Balance Monthly, Plus Carrying Charge

—By far and wide the greatest electric refrigerator in America at $139.95! It has to be to carry Sears "4 Star" emblem. Completely deluxe ... it has all those extra conveniences you'd look for in $180 boxes.

- 2-Dial Thermostat! 9-Point Cold!
- Roll-Out Handi-Bin Holds Bushel
- 10-Lb. Frozen Packaged Food
- 2 Glass Covered Foodex Drawers
- 10-Lb. Capacity Meat Saver Tray
- Automatic Reset Defrosting.

Tested and Approved Good Housekeeping Institute

SEARS, ROEBUCK AND CO.

Retail Store — North Ave. at Harford Rd. — UNiversity 3970

THE WEATHER

Cloudy and somewhat warmer tonight with lowest temperature around 33 degrees in the suburbs. Tuesday colder and mostly cloudy.

Detailed Weather Report on Page 32

MEAN TEMPERATURES YESTERDAY

Baltimore	38	New York	32
Atlanta	43	Omaha	43
Boston	30	Portland, Maine	30
Chicago	31	Salt Lake City	38
Jacksonville	50	San Antonio	46
Los Angeles	68	Seattle	42
Miami	69	Tampa	58
New Orleans	46	Washington	38

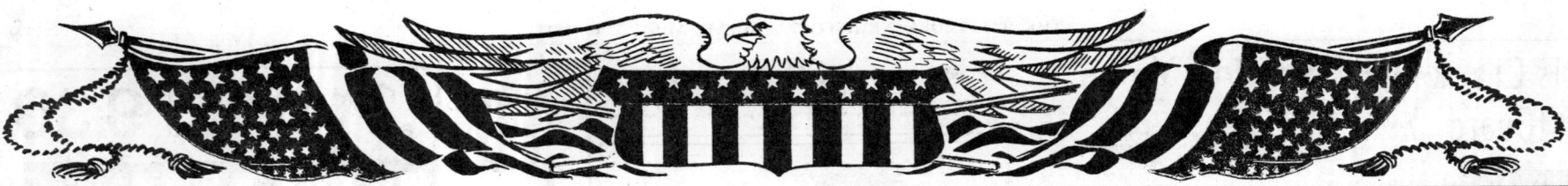

THE BALTIMORE NEWS-POST

AN INDEPENDENT NEWSPAPER

The Largest Evening Circulation in the Entire South

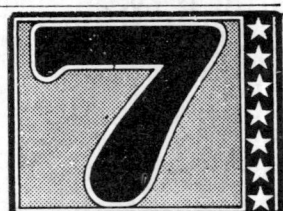

7

VOL. CXL.—NO. 29 Entered as second-class matter at Baltimore Postoffice. MONDAY EVENING, DECEMBER 8, 1941 PRICE 3 CENTS

BATTLESHIP WRECKED 3,000 CASUALTIES IN HAWAII BOMBING

IN THE NEWS

By WILLIAM RANDOLPH HEARST

WELL, fellow Americans, we are in the war and we have got to win it.

There may have been some difference of opinion among good Americans about getting into the war, but there is no difference about how we should come out of it.

We must come out victorious and with the largest V in the alphabet.

We are not completely prepared for war.

We have not got a Swiss system of universal service that we will have to have some day, since the lands are full of robbers and sea of pirates.

But we will get better and stronger every day, and we will not have to get very good and very strong to knock the everlasting daylights out of Japan.

We may have some small reverses at first, but do not let that worry you—if it happens.

It is not who wins the first round but who wins the last one that counts for victory.

And there is no doubt about the victory, folks—none whatever.

The worst thing about the war with Japan is that it will divide our efforts and prevent us from rendering the all-out aid to England that we were doing and planning further to do.

But we will still manage to keep Britain going with our right hand while we poke Japan in the nose with our left.

Japan has been wanting war for a long time.

It has been swaggering around Asia, murdering a lot of unarmed Chinamen.

Now it is going to get a war and a real one.

Fortunately, we are well on our way towards a dominating and determining two-ocean navy and an all-skies aeroplane fleet.

Fortunately we can manufacture ten ships to Japan's one, and ten aeroplanes to Japan's one.

Naturally we can fly the planes better and fight the ships better.

And that means that as soon as we swing into action we will wash up the war.

Japan's attack on Hawaii is probably with the idea of keeping us on defense at home.

But we will not stay at home and we will not stay on defense.

Before the war is over we will have burned up all the paper houses in Japan and sunk most of their scrap iron battleships and put this bunch of Oriental marauders back on the right little, tight little, out-of-sight little island where they belong.

And we will have fenced them in there.

Then maybe we will let them have a little oil—coal

Continued on Page 4, Column 1.

Allied Planes, Warships Locked With Japanese Fleet In Pacific

BANGKOK, Dec. 8—(I. N. S.).—The Thailand Government today announced cessation of all resistance to Japanese invasion. Japanese troops presumably will be permitted to travel unmolested through Thailand, cutting the land bridge between Singapore and Southern China.

By RICHARD HALLER
International News Service Staff Correspondent.

HONOLULU, Dec. 8—Warships and planes of America, Britain and Australia were locked in far-flung naval war today with Japanese forces, as dawn broke over the Pacific.

Honolulu emerged from a total blackout this morning with U. S. Army and Navy planes filling the skies from which "suicide" squadrons of Jap warplanes rained death and destruction yesterday morning in history's first aerial assault on American soil.

Details of action were lacking in the naval battle which was presumed to stretch across 5,000 miles of ocean, from the Philippines to the Eastern Pacific off the California coast.

VENGEANCE BATTLE IS UNDERWAY

Rumors flew thick and fast. There was no immediate confirmation of reports that vengeance-bent U. S. warcraft had sunk six Japanese submarines as well as one of the aircraft carriers from which the Honolulu attack was launched—or of Japanese claims that to date they have sunk American battleships.

There was no panic in bomb-torn Honolulu. Rather, the savage Japanese attack served to fire the civilian population with a fierce determination to justify Hawaii's key position as the spearhead of America's Pacific defense.

What seemed to be heavy cannonading was heard at sea off Barber's Point, a promontory jutting out from the Pearl Harbor entrance. There were rumors four enemy ships had been sighted.

The Navy moved swiftly to exact retribution for the devastating raids of Japanese bombers yesterday in which upwards of 350 soldiers and civilians may have been killed and in which the U. S. S. Oklahoma was reported set afire, and two other U. S. warships sunk, one of them the West Virginia and the other understood to be the aircraft carrier Lexington.

Bent on vengeance and retaliation, the grim, gray warcraft of the mighty United States fleet, concentrated in Hawaiian waters for more than two years, slid out of Pearl Harbor seeking the aircraft carriers from which the death-dealing Jap planes were launched.

It was presumed that at least a small fleet of other

Continued on Page 2, Column 4.

State Air-Raid Observers Called

Between 2,000 and 3,000 air-raid observers in Maryland were called out today to man the State's 250 spotter stations as Mayor Jackson, in a telegram to Governor O'Conor, demanded military protection for city water supply stations, sewerage plants and the Municipal Airport.

Mayor Jackson, in his telegram to the Governor, asked that 250 to 300 members of the Maryland State Guard be mobilized to prevent possible sabotage of municipal utilities.

TELEGRAM TO O'CONOR

In his telegram the Mayor said:

"Dear Governor O'Conor: Some weeks ago Brigadier General Dwight L. Mohr attended a conference with Chief Engineer George Cobb, Water Engineer Leon Small and Sewerage Engineer George Fink in my office, in reference to protection for the water supply, sewage disposal, the airport and waterfront.

"Mr. Cobb talked again yesterday with General Mohr, and he now recommends, and I request, military protection for the following: Loch Raven dam, Prettyboy dam, eleven Bureau of Water automatic stations and reservoirs, Back River disposal plant, Patapsco Sewage Treatment Works and the Municipal Airport.

"Mr. Cobb estimates that adequate protection will require 250 to 300 men for active duty.

"Howard W. Jackson, Mayor."

ARMORY GUARDED

Earlier in the day officers of the Maryland State Guard flung a pro-

Continued on Page 17, Column 6.

Temperatures

12 Midn't,	35	7 A. M.,	35
1 A. M.,	35	8 A. M.,	38
2 A. M.,	34	9 A. M.,	39
3 A. M.,	35	10 A. M.,	40
4 A. M.,	32	11 A. M.,	44
5 A. M.,	34	12 Noon,	46
6 A. M.,	33	1 P. M.,	47

British Join War On Japs

LONDON, Dec. (A. P.).—Great Britain declared war on Japan today, allying herself with the United States. Prime Minister Churchill summoned a special session of Commons to hear his declaration. He said:

"I spoke to President Roosevelt on the Atlantic telephone last night with a view to arranging the time of our respective declaration.

"Instructions were sent to our Ambassador at Tokyo and a communication was dispatched to the Japanese Charge D'Affaires stating that in view of Japan's wanton acts of unprovoked aggression, the British Government informed them that a state of war existed between the two countries."

Armed Guard Bars Doors Of Capitol

WASHINGTON, Dec. 8—(A.P.).—Heavily guarded doors barred entrance to the Capitol today to all but members of Congress, their staffs and other persons regularly assigned to the building.

Three sets of Capitol police identified each person who entered the House side; corridors were barricaded and streets about the Capitol were cleared of automobiles. Barriers went up at entrances to the grounds.

Representative Hoffman (Republican) of Michigan was stopped by a guard at the main House entrance at 9.15 A. M. Good-humoredly he told the uniformed policeman that he did not have a card to the building "and I don't need any."

Hoffman brushed by and swung through a revolving door, with the officer in close pursuit. Once inside, other guards quickly identified the Michigan member.

Galleries in the House, usually open to the public, were locked. Marines with fixed bayonets stood guard inside Capitol doors.

The Wizard of Lake Chibougamau. The deadly bullet borne by "powers" of the wild and other "sorceries" of an ancient wisdom, witnessed by an anthropologist, who describes what he saw in a double-page illustrated feature in The American Weekly, the magazine distributed with next Sunday's Baltimore American.—Adv.

White House Says Nearly 1,500 Were Killed In Attack; Planes Wrecked

U. S. Awaits Roosevelt Message

WASHINGTON, Dec. 8—(A. P.). A united Congress, vested with powers to declare war, anxiously read Japanese boasts of smashing blows at the United States Pacific fleet today while President Roosevelt drafted his message to be delivered personally to a closely-guarded joint session at 12.30 P. M.

Tokyo's claim was sweeping—an aircraft carrier sent to the bottom by a submarine off Honolulu, two American battleships sunk, four others damaged and four heavy cruisers damaged in the unprovoked Sunday morning bombing attack that exploded war throughout the Pacific. The announcement said no Japanese losses had occurred.

Official sources here ignored the Japanese claims in silence, but the communique issued by the naval section of the Japanese Imperial Headquarters was the grimmest sort of news to a city that was at peace only yesterday.

SOME HARD BLOWS

The nation had been bracing itself for bad tidings. It was known the Navy had taken some hard blows, and the White House warned last night that the fleet's losses undoubtedly would prove heavy. The Tokyo claims heightened the grimness.

No one seemed to question that,

Continued on Page 2, Column 1.

Finn Ship Taken By U. S. In Texas

GALVESTON, Texas, Dec. 8—(A. P.).—Some hours after the United States acted against Finnish ships in American ports, Coast Guardsmen took charge of the Panamanian freighter Delaware at her dock here and sent her crew of 23 Finns to jail.

Maritime records show that until last summer the vessel flew the Finnish flag. Her registry was changed to Panamanian.

WASHINGTON, Dec. 8—(A. P.).—The White House announced today that the Japanese attack on Hawaii had resulted in the capsizing of an old battleship, the destruction of a destroyer, damage to other vessels and destruction of a relatively large number of planes.

An official White House statement, the first authentic Government appraisal of the attack yesterday, said that casualties were expected to mount to about 3,000, nearly half of them fatalities.

It added that several Japanese planes and submarines had been accounted for.

This was announced as a war resolution was drafted for immediate introduction in the Congress which President Roosevelt was addressing personally on the Far Eastern situation at a momentous joint session at 12.30 P. M.

Chairman Connally (Democrat) of Texas prepared the war resolution, saying he acted on his own initiative without knowing what the President would say.

It was disclosed that active resistance was "still continuing" against the Japanese attacking force in the vicinity of Hawaii. Reinforcements of planes are being rushed to the islands, the White House said, and repair work is under way on ships, planes and ground facilities.

ISLANDS ATTACKED

The White House said that Wake and Midway Islands, in addition to the Island of Guam and Hongkong, China, had been attacked but details were lacking.

Asked whether there was any official information why Japan was

Continued on Page 2, Column 3.

Tokyo Claims Control Of Sea

TOKYO, Tuesday, Dec. 9—Official radio picked up by A. P.).—The Japanese asserted tdoay they had won naval supremacy over the United States in the Pacific, claiming by official or unofficial reports the destruction of two American battleships and an aircraft carrier and the damaging of six cruisers.

These, declared the Japanese, were the principal results of the first shock of their air-naval offensive.

The claim to supremacy appeared in a commentary-resume broadcast by Domei, which said that any force the United States now could muster "would be regarded as utterly inadequate to accomplish any successful outcome in an encounter with the thus far intact Japanese fleet."

The headquarters announcement said many men

Continued on Page 2, Column 7.

| 24 | WANT ADS—Lexington 0100 | THE BALTIMORE NEWS-POST, MONDAY, DECEMBER 8, 1941 | WANT ADS—Lexington 0100 |

FORECAST — Baltimore and vicinity—Most all radio sets tuned to WBAL.

WBAL NEWS

"The richest man cannot buy for himself what the poorest man gets free by radio."

VOL. III. NO. 12. BALTIMORE MONDAY, DECEMBER 8, 1941 ★★★★★

FIRST 13 MOST POPULAR HALF-HOUR PROGRAMS--ALL ON WBAL

We knew when we gave you Red Network programs that we were giving you the best in the nation over your favorite local station --- a combination that's hard to beat.

The latest nation-wide survey of radio listeners shows that N. B. C. RED is more than ever "the network most people listen to most." Every one of the 13 leading half-hour evening programs are N. B. C. RED network programs, broadcast in Maryland only by WBAL.

You can always be sure that when you are tuned to WBAL you are in tune with America's first and finest radio programs whether it be music, news, drama, humor or sports.

They're dressed up and have gone places—to first place, in fact, among evening half-hour programs. Each Sunday at 8.00 P. M. Edgar Bergen and Charlie McCarthy join with Abbott and Costello and other guests for radio's most popular program.

Back on the air less than eight weeks and already way up in second place! Jack Benny and Mary Livingston look highly pleased. With plenty of other stars they broadcast over WBAL each Sunday evening at 7.00.

Fibber (Jim Jordan) McGee is a man who never knows when he's beaten—particularly at the game of trying to foist some of those fables of his on Molly (Marian Jordan). And Molly is equally bound and determined to apply a shaker full of salt to any and all of Fibber's declamations. The inimitable pair are going strong (number three) on the "Fibber McGee and Molly" series, heard at 9.30 P. M. on Tuesdays over WBAL.

The hat is a helmet to prevent surprise attacks. Accessory equipment included one periscope, one direction finder tree (moss on north side), one gas catching "whoofis canary," one rear guard action mirror, one windmill to keep home fires burning. It is the invention of WBAL-N. B. C. RED Network's "George Burns and Gracie Allen." Occupying number eleven place in popularity, they're heard each Tuesday at 7.30 P. M.

The Great Profile (otherwise John Barrymore) and Rudy Vallee seem to be happy about their script writers. Well they might for their Thursday doings at 10.00 P. M. are now rated twelfth among the half-hour evening shows.

Here is "The Aldrich Family," all together for once. Left to right are Mary, Mr. and Mrs. Aldrich and Henry, played by Charita Bauer, House Jameson, Katherine Raht and Ezra Stone, respectively. "The Aldrich Family" is heard on Station WBAL at 8.30 P. M. on Thursdays. They're number four in popularity.

It takes concentration (and how!) to reach the number five spot in program rating and that's where the Bob Hope program is. With Jerry Colona and a big cast, Hope's program is broadcast each Tuesday at 10.00 P. M.

Ralph Edwards is master of ceremonies of the sensational "Truth or Consequence" program heard Saturdays on WBAL at 8.30 P. M. The program is thirteenth in popularity.

Red Skelton has been on the air but a few weeks (Tuesday at 10.30 P. M.) and is already in fifteenth place. He knows Santa (Ozzie Nelson) and songbird Harriet Hilliard will help bring his program rating up higher before many weeks roll around.

Tobe Reed is master of ceremonies of the "Band Wagon" program, which features famous bands over WBAL each Sunday at 7.30 P. M. Listeners have placed the program eighth in popularity.

"The Barbours pose for a family picture. WBAL's famous "One Man's Family" spend the day at author Carlton E. Morse's Hollywood home and gather round for a family group picture. Standing from left to right are Cliff, Claudia, Nicky, Hazel and Jack. Seated on arm of chair is Betty, Father Barbour, Mother Barbour and Paul. Seated on grass is Teddy and Joan. They're on WBAL each Sunday at 8.30 P. M., the seventh most popular program.

Baby Snooks (Fanny Brice) seems to be measuring Daddy (Hanley Stafford) this time for a sweater. They and Frank Morgan are stars of "Coffee Time" each Thursday evening at 8.00. The program ranks sixth in the latest survey.

Eddie Cantor is dusting off the microphone for his "Time to Smile" broadcast on WBAL (Wednesday at 9.00 P. M.). Eddie's showmanship and capable cast have landed his program in the number ten spot in the latest listener survey.

Resourceful and relentless foe of criminals and racketeers is Jay Jostyn, who plays the title role in N. B. C.'s radio drama, "Mr. District Attorney." A product of Marquette University and the University of Wisconsin Dramatic School, Jostyn made his professional debut in Milwaukee at the age of nineteen. "Mr. District Attorney" is broadcast over WBAL each Wednesday at 9.30 P. M. and occupies the number nine spot in popularity.

Defend America--Buy Defense Stamps, Bonds

RUSSIANS RECAPTURE KEY CITY OF MOZHAISK

DEFEND AMERICA BUY A BOMBER

THE BALTIMORE NEWS-POST
AN INDEPENDENT NEWSPAPER
The Largest Evening Circulation in the Entire South

10

VOL. CXL.—NO. 66 Entered as second-class matter at Baltimore Postoffice. TUESDAY EVENING, JANUARY 20, 1942 PRICE 3 CENTS

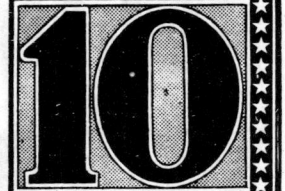

U. S. ARMY PLANES SINK JAP CRUISER

IN THE NEWS

"LONDON,
January 17, 1942.
"William Randolph Hearst,
"Wyntoon, California.

"THIS leader appears in Lord Beaverbrook's Evening Standard Monday, as a result of your stirring editorial.

"Will you write our editorial Tuesday, 500 words cable collect?

"Frank Owen, Editor.

"Thank you Mr. Hearst.

"Mr. William Randolph Hearst has never been a personal friend of this country and we must add the feeling has been mutual, for up till a few weeks ago he has not showed much sympathy with this war.

"Mr. Hearst is a big, bold, and some would say bad, American with a few vehement principles and a host of violent prejudices.

"His chief principle was that he loved his idea of America and his chief prejudice was that he hated his idea of Britain.

"This was the Mr. Hearst of November, 1941.

"January, 1942, has brought a change.

"He has written an article which breathes all the thunder, fire, energy and hardihood which made America great.

"He minimizes none of the dangers which his country must face, but his faith in America's power to rise and conquer is shining and absolute.

"Mr. Hearst was an isolationist in the days of peace, but he wants his country to fight no limited war.

"Fortunately, he says, we can manufacture ten ships to Japan's one and ten airplanes to Japan's one.

"Naturally, we can fly the airplanes better and fight the ships better.

"America is not going to stay at home. The Japs are to be put back on the right little, tight little, out of sight little island where they belong.

"But America is not to be deflected from her purpose of washing up the biggest enemy of mankind.

"It is good that somebody has said it in the strong, loud voice which the situation demands.

"According to the popular gibe, America was caught with her pants down, but she is putting her boots on now. She will stride far before she takes them off.

"America is a young nation, her founders were Pilgrims, pioneers and pirates, all of them men of daring.

"Her earliest statesmen first pronounced truths which old Europe dared not utter and which in turn helped to make Europe young again.

"The sons of these great fathers discovered a new continent on this planet by their own brawn and will. They subdued forest and lakes and rivers to the service of man.

"This empire was not conquered by a dull, unthinking horde.

"Through all these years of achievement tempestuous ar-

Continued on Page 4, Column 1.

Mozhaisk Is Recaptured By Russ

LONDON, Jan. 20—(A. P.).—The Russian High Command tonight announced capture of Mozhaisk.

This was the first word on the situation in Mozhaisk, 57 miles west of Moscow, since the army newspaper Red Star announced Monday that Red troops were fighting the Germans in the streets and that the city was in flames.

Some 100,000 crack German troops have been reported in the Mozhaisk salient, with three divisions defending the city itself.

(BACKGROUND NOTE: Russian troops, fighting in the intense cold of 25 below zero, have captured Mozhaisk and opened the way for a drive westward toward Vyazma and Smolensk, the Moscow radio announced today.)

The Russian communique said:

"On January 20 our troops made further advances and drove the German troops back to the west, inflicting heavy losses upon them.

"Our units captured Mozhaisk.

"On January 19, 16 German planes destroyed.

Our losses were five planes."

Izvestia, Government newspaper, said three German divisions—the Twenty-third, the One Hundred and Sixth Infantry and the Fifth Tank—were smashed in the Red Army assault across the Lama, which, it was stated, carried the Russians from Volokolamsk through Latoshino.

The Twenty-third Division alone was estimated to have lost 1,500 men killed, it said.

Russian heavy artillery preparation, followed by a Cossack attack, broke a wide gap through the Germans' strongly fortified positions, it explained.

Blasted By Torpedo From Axis Submarine

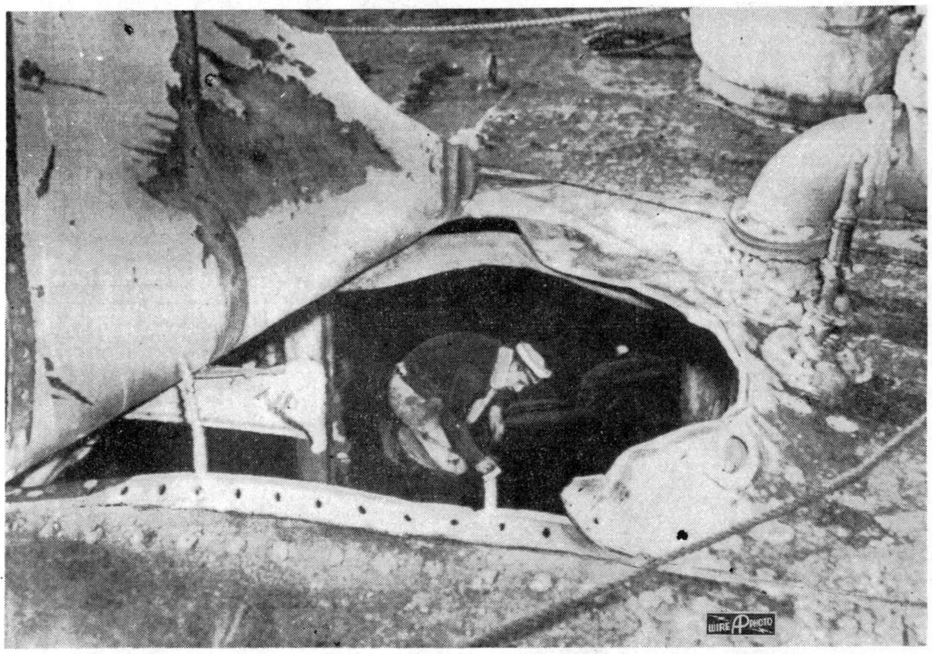

An officer aboard the U. S. tanker Malay, skippered by Captain John M. Dodge of Baltimore, inspects damage caused by an exploding torpedo from an Axis submarine during an hour's engagement off the Carolina coast. The deck plates were forced apart by the concussion. The U-boat attack killed one man and injured three others. Four men are missing. (Other pictures on Page Three).

Fliers Also Score Direct Hit And Set Tanker Afire; 3 Enemy Planes Downed

WASHINGTON, Jan. 20—(A. P.).—The War Department said today American bombers sank a Japanese cruiser and scored direct hits on a tanker, leaving the latter in flames, 100 miles off Jolo in the Southern Philippines.

Three enemy airplanes were shot down as the Japanese renewed their attack on General Douglas MacArthur's forces on Bataan peninsula on the Island of Luzon, the Department's communique also said.

At the same time, the first indication for many days that the Japanese were still opposed by American forces on the Island of Mindanao came in a report from MacArthur that sharp fighting was in progress between Philippine troops and a Japanese force about 35 miles north of Davao, which is on the southern end of Mindanao.

The attack on the Japanese cruiser and tanker was carried out by six Army bombers.

(BACKGROUND NOTE: Although there was no identification of the cruiser sunk, the blow was obviously a heavy one to the Japanese Navy. Because of the enemy's vastly overextended lines of communication in the Far East, cruisers are of tremendous importance, due to their long range, as well as fighting ability.

RANGE OF SHIPS

(Jap cruisers range from 10-year-old first-class ships, such as the 9,850-ton Atago, Takao, Tyokai and Maya, all the way down to 26-year-old 3,230-ton ships such as the Tatuta. The first-class cruisers, however, are among the world's best fighting ships, mounting 10 eight-inch guns, 12 anti-aircraft guns, eight machine-guns and eight torpedo tubes.)

Sinking of the cruiser raised to 40 the total of Japanese war craft and other vessels sunk by United States military and naval action.

The Navy previously had reported the sinking of 29 vessels, including a light cruiser destroyed by the marines at Wake island, and also four destroyers, four submarines, eight transports, five cargo vessels, three merchantmen and one each of the following—gunboat, mine sweeper, supply vessel and liner.

The Army had announced the destruction of the battleship Haruna,

Continued on Page 2, Column 4.

Von Bock Named To Reichenau Post

BUENOS AIRES, Jan. 20—(U. P.).—Field Marshal Fedor Von Bock has been appointed to succeed the late Field Marshal Walter Fon Reichenau on the southern Russian front, the newspaper La Prensa reported today in a Berlin dispatch.

BUY BONDS FOR BOMBERS

Can You Find a White Marigold? Here's a Search That Might Be Very Profitable. All Lovers of Flowers Will Want to Read This Interesting Article and See the Illustrations in The American Weekly, the Magazine Distributed With Next Sunday's Baltimore American.—Adv.

Torpedoed Ship Reaches Port

Capt. John M. Dodge, skipper of the torpedoed and shelled tanker Malay, lives at 5900 Bellona avenue, Baltimore, and has been a deep-sea sailor for more than half a century. He is a native of Maine, according to his wife.

Mrs. Dodge said the first word she received of her husband's adventure was a telegram last night from Norfolk which read: "Arrived Newport News. Am safe. Don't worry."

Captain Dodge has been skipper of the Malay for 13 years, his wife said. He is sixty-nine years old and started his maritime career at thirteen, sailing on old-time windjammers. During World War I. a cargo ship he commanded joined with four other ships in rescuing 1,100 men from a torpedoed transport.

By S. G. DEBNAM
International News Service Staff Correspondent.

NEWPORT NEWS, Va., Jan. 20.—With Nazi submarines reported as "thick as catfish" in the Western Atlantic, survivors of the damaged U. S. tanker Malay, skippered by Capt. John M. Dodge of Baltimore, limped into port here today to disclose a story of undergoing an hour's attack by an enemy U-boat off the Carolina coast.

The U-boat attack killed one crew member and injured three others, while four crewmen of the 8,206-ton U. S. Marine Transport Line tanker are missing. The other 26 members of the crew reached port safely.

The fatality was Addams J. Hay, second cook, of Burlington, N. J.

U. S. naval patrols, meanwhile, ranged the coastline on an intensified search for enemy undersea raiders, who have taken a toll of four ships in Western Atlantic waters in the last seven days.

Extent of American successes against the Nazi invasion of Ameri-

Continued on Page 2, Column 1.

Carriers Sell 133,664 Stamps

By ALDINE R. BIRD

With pledges and cash sales for stamps and bonds beyond the two-million mark for the first week of Baltimore's "Buy-A-Bomber" campaign, carriers of The Baltimore News-Post and Sunday American today reported sales of 133,664 ten-cent defense savings stamps last week as their contribution toward the fund.

Under the day-by-day plan of the Treasury Department for stamps and bonds for bombers here, Monday of each of the four weeks has been set aside for newspaper and radio employes to sponsor the sales, and the carriers turned in the record report of $13.366.40 for their part.

CARRIERS LAUDED

This brought the total amount of stamps sold by the carriers to $42,512.90 since the beginning of the sales campaign and immediately brought commendations from officials of the Treasury Department in Washington.

As a means of further stimulating interest in selling defense

Continued on Page 14, Column 1.

VERY LATEST NEWS

(Race Results From Howard Sports Daily, Inc.)

BELLE POISE WINS SIXTH RACE AT HIALEAH

Sixth—Belle Poise, $8.30, $4.50, $3.50; One Jest, $3.40, $3.00; Pet, $3.70.

Seventh—Greedan, won; Robert E. Lee, 2d; Run By, 3d.

AT FAIR GROUNDS

Third—Roziante, $16.60, $9.20, $6.20; Takeaway, $4.60 $3.40; Blue Northern, $6.40.

ROOSEVELT REASSURES CHINA, AUSTRALIA

WASHINGTON, Jan. 20—(A. P.).—President Roosevelt assured a press conference today that the United States was contributing to the war against the Axis in almost every part of the globe. The remarks gave reassurance to China and Australia, where some uneasiness has been reported over the possibility that American supplies might go more into the battle against Hitler than into the fight against Japan.

Temperatures

Midnight,	45	9 A. M.,	42
1 A. M.,	45	10 A. M.,	43
2 A. M.,	45	11 A. M.,	45
3 A. M.,	44	12 Noon,	42
4 A. M.,	43	1 P. M.,	44
5 A. M.,	42	2 P. M.,	46
6 A. M.,	42	3 P. M.,	48
7 A. M.,	42	4 P. M.,	44
8 A. M.,	42	5 P. M.,	43

THE WEATHER

Baltimore and vicinity, no precipitation and colder tonight. Lowest temperatures slightly below freezing in the northern and western suburbs and around freezing in the center of the city. Diminishing winds.

Detailed Weather Report on Page 22

HIALEAH RESULTS

FIRST RACE—Three furlongs (chute). Off at 2.02. Time, 0:34.

Ample Reward, 118 (M. Peters)	$14.20	$6.30	$4.50
aWise Bob, 118 (B. James)		3.40	2.80
Orpheum, 118 (J. Gilbert)			6.60
Total Mutuels			$37.80

Also Ran—Tower Captain, aFlying John, War Arrow, Diggie, Blue Swords, Leo's Brandy, Alacyon, Color Week, aKing's Gambit, fWater Pearl and fFin Try.
aBryson and Babylon entry. fField.

SECOND—Seven furlongs (chute). Off 2.34. Time, 1.27.

High Plaid, 114 (K. McCombs)	$37.40	$24.60	$9.80
Stimuli, 112 (B. James)		12.10	6.80
Challante, 108 (N. Coule)			4.00
Total mutuels			$94.70

Also Ran—Peter Argo, Vingt Et Un, Sherron Ann, Our Chuckie, Bold Turk, Gay American, Morning Mail, Highscope, Yellow Mask.

Daily Double—Ample Reward, High Plaid, $688.10 for $2

Continued on Page 18, Column 6.

Wake Hero's Kin

News Cheers The Cunninghams
LEARN COMMANDER IS IN YOKOHAMA

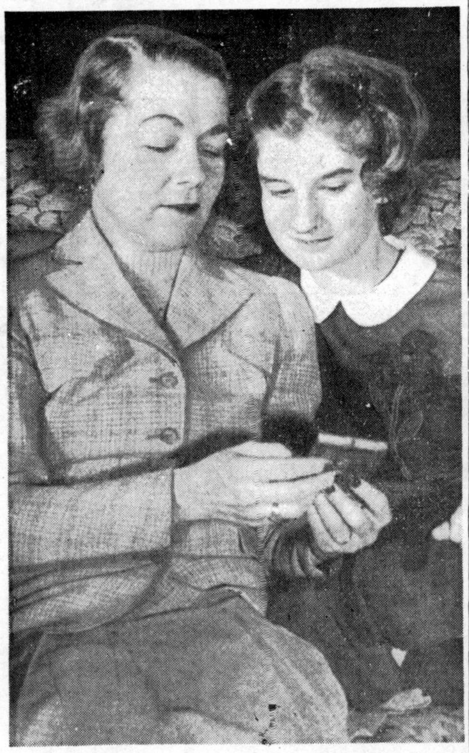

Confidence that her husband, Commander Winfield Scott Cunningham, in charge during the Japanese raids on Wake Island, will not "crack up under the strain of being a prisoner of war in Yokohama" was expressed today at Annapolis by his wife. Mrs. Cunningham and their daughter, Valerie, nine, are shown in their Annapolis apartment looking at a photograph of the commander.

The Baltimore News-Post Has the Largest Circulation of Any Evening Newspaper in the South

THE BALTIMORE NEWS-POST — AN INDEPENDENT NEWSPAPER

2ND FRONT PAGE — NEWS-POST HAS TWO FRONT PAGES DAILY

TUESDAY EVENING, JANUARY 20, 1942 13

Back Drive For Plane

Post Office Men Get Behind Buy-A-Bomber Campaign

Air Raid Whistle Tests Thursday

36 City Factories To Take Part In 'Alarm'

At exactly 12.15 P. M. Thursday, whistles in thirty-six Baltimore factories and institutions will sound an air-raid alarm in a test to determine how far the blasts will carry.

In announcing the test, Adrian Hughes, chairman of planning for the Baltimore Committee on Civilian Defense, emphasized the sound is not expected to reach all sections of the city. The devices are being tried out in an effort to find out what additional equipment must be put into use to make the alarm system adequate, he explained.

FIVE-SECOND BLASTS

The official warning will consist of a series of short blasts, each lasting about five seconds, with an interval of three seconds of silence, and continuing for two minutes.

Two minutes later, or at 12.19 P. M., the "all clear" signal will be given. It is a long blast lasting for two minutes.

The tests will be repeated exactly five minutes after the first "all clear", the second "alarm" due for 12.26 P. M.

Effectiveness of the whistles will be checked by means of post cards to be distributed by police to persons living in scattered sections. The "listeners" are asked to indicate whether the signal was heard indoors or out, and how distinctly.

Reports from the population as a whole will be welcomed by the committee, Mr. Hughes said, but he added a plea that such reports not be made by telephone. Such a procedure would clog the lines, he explained, and the committee staff is not large enough to record each report.

PLAN IN DETAIL

Explaining the plan in detail, Mr. Hughes said:

"It is in accordance with approced OCD procedure to make use of all possible existing noise-making devices in setting up an alarm system.

"Only after we have determined the effectiveness of what we already have can we add anything necessary.

"Through the co-operation of the police, we have listed 200 factories and institutions with whistles and sirens.

"We want to keep the number of whistles to a minimum, because each whistle means a telephone call which must be made in time of an actual raid. However, others may be added to the list of those to be tried out Thursday.

"All praise is due the owners of equipment which we will test this week. They have agreed to man the whistles twenty-four-hours a day, and in many cases have installed special telephone for this use only.

PURCHASED OWN DEVICES

"Some even have purchased the noise devices, when their older equipment seemed inadequate. All this without any cost to the taxpayer and in a spirit of wholehearted co-operation."

Mr. Hughes said that fifteen of the whistles have been available for use since January 12, when the warning center first went into full-time service. It is from the warning center that instructions to sound an alarm will come if the city ever actually is bombed.

BUY BONDS FOR BOMBERS

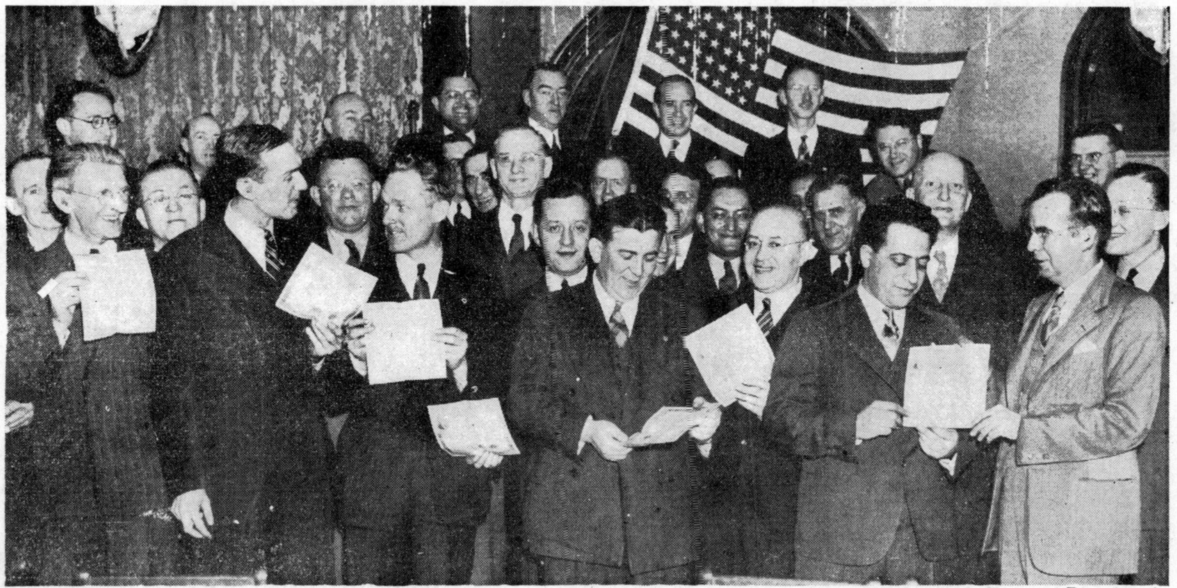

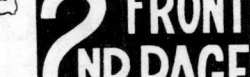

Members of the National Federation of Post Office Clerks, Baltimore Local 181, not only sell stamps and bonds every day to the public but have joined the ranks of "customers" and are contributing their share to the Buy-a-Bomber campaign here. Shown at a meeting of their local, they announced purchases of $600 in bonds and pledged $500 more during the four-week Treasury Department campaign. Harry G. Millison, president, is shown at right receiving bonds from Joseph F. O'Conor (in light suit), treasurer.

Men At Meade Hail Drive For Red Cross

By EARLE POORBAUGH
News-Post Staff Correspondent.

FORT MEADE, Jan. 20.—"The **program of the American Red Cross contributes materially to the comfort and welfare of the patients of this hospital."**

Col. Daniel P. Card, commanding officer of the station hospital here, is the speaker, and behind his simple statement is a wealth of experience, for the Colonel has seen 35 years' service in the Army Medical Corps, including service with the A. E. F.

Backing up the Colonel and lauding the Red Cross organization are some six hundred ill and injured soldier patients, beneficiaries of the humanitarian efforts of the great mercy organization.

200 CARTONS OF CIGARETS

Corp. William Hart of the Medical detachment, who plays an important role in the Red Cross program here, modestly admits he has dispensed more than 200 cartons of cigarets to his hospitalized comrades this week. And adds:

"About 100 safety razors, more than 200 tooth brushes, 300 tubes of tooth paste, 200 packages of razor blades, a hundred bars of soap, nearly 100 combs, 150 tubes of shaving cream and 15 canes. Might be about the total of assistance given needy soldier patients here this week."

Private Edwin Schmidt, 2609 Pennsylvania avenue, Baltimore, who volunteered for foreign service in January, and had the bad luck to fall and break his hand a few days later, volunteered again today.

From among the crowd of soldiers about the booth Schmidt stepped forward and he said:

"Help the American Red Cross raise the money, it needs to help us here. It is doing a fine job."

All about the recreation hall today convalescent patients were reading, playing ping-pong, checkers and other games, or listening to the radio and phonograph installed by the Red Cross.

IS ON THE JOB

Throughout the entire armed forces of the nation today, as during the stirring days of World War One. The American Red Cross is on the job, caring for the physical needs of the men and relieving mental burdens by assistance to them and their families.

Death in the Army is an all too frequent occurrence, even in times of peace, and to ai dthe widows and dependents of service men, the Red Cross maintains a field director with each service unit.

Pension forms, copies of marriage, birth and death certificates Government insurance forms are filed for widows and children. Food and shelter are provided until Government benefits arrive.

Western High Girls Hold Air-Raid Drill

By MARJORIE MATHIS

Through the quiet corridors of Western High School a bell rang in a prolonged peal, was silent—pealed again.

Instantly 1,650 young girls and their teacners were on the move, proceeding in absolute silence and quick precision with an air-raid drill which had every girl seated in her alloted place on the corridor floors within four minutes.

Without a word the girls poured from their classrooms. The first student to leave each room fastened the door back against the wall, minimizing danger of shattered glass in the upper panels.

WALK QUICKLY

None ran, but everyone walked very quickly, each girl going directly to her locker to obtain her coat, according to instructions. Books were left on the desks where they had been at the time of the alarm, but each student carried her pocketbook.

At the side of ten handicapped students in the school two other girls appeared, to assist their crippled fellows to the hospital room.

Once the girls had their coats, they moved on to places in the corridors of the four floors of the school, each girl taking a place alongside her "home" room but well away from the opened doors.

AISLE LEFT

A spacious aisle was left in the middle of the corridor. Teachers who are wardens counted their charges as they arrived. Girls who had been in the gymnasium and in gymnasium costumes were last to arrive, for they had had to change into ordinary clothing.

Still no one spoke. Young faces were serious and intent. Heels clicked sharply along the stone floors.

Wardens for each floor then reported to Miss Mildred Coughlin, principal, that each girl was accounted for. Miss Coughlin raised her hand. All the girls sat down close together, pressed as closely as possible against the walls.

The silence continued for a few moments until another bell sounded through the building. It was the all-clear signal, and the young people scrambled to their feet and started back to their classrooms.

The drill was over. The girls chatted a little as they went back to regular routine.

Miss Coughlin explained that the corridors have been adjudged the safest places in the building, which is, itself, unusually strongly built to resist a raid.

FIRE WARDENS

The precaution system included eleven fire wardens, all members of the janitors and custodian's staff, under Dr. Frank R. Blake, professor of modern languages.

It is the duty of the fire wardens to go to the roof in case of an attack and dispose of any incendiary bombs which may fall.

'Toy-Gun Bandit' Jailed

Daniel Karwacki, twenty-two, father of two hcildren, who used a toy pistol as a short cut to fortune, was sentenced to two years in the Maryland House of Correction today by Judge W. Conwell Smith for a $240 hold-up.

The "toy-gun bandit" was convicted of entering a store at Elliott and Clinton streets, holding up a clerk, and escaping with $241.59. He was arrested later in a bus terminal and all of the money recovered except the cost of a ticket to New York.

Judge Smith was told that Karwacki had committed an "act of desperation" because a physical defect made it impossible for him to get a job. The case was prosecuted by Assistant State's Attorney Bernard Peter.

DOCTORS TO SPEAK

Dr. Walter E. Dandy, Dr. Thomas P. Sprunt and Dr. Charles W. Maxson will be the speakers at a meeting of the Maryland Academy of Medicine and Surgery, to be held tonight in the Hotel Belvedere.

Schaeffer To Speak At Dinner Tonight

Edwin H. Schaeffer, supervisor of standards, Bayonne, N. J., will be guest speaker at a dinner meeting of Baltimore Chapter, National Association of Cost Accountants, at 6.30 P. M. today in the Emerson Hotel. Mr. Schaeffer will discuss "Ratios for Defense Industries." William T. Winand, president of Baltimore Chapter, will preside.

Sees Elevated Road Traffic Solution

Baltimore's "terrific traffic congestion" problem may some day be solved by the construction of elevated highways through the city's business district, members of the Rotary Club were told today by V. G. Iden, secretary of the American Institute of Steel Construction.

Mr. Iden pointed out that Detroit is planning an elevated highway to span the city's congested center, and Chicago and Washington are working on similar programs.

PLAYED PART

In his discussion of steel spans Mr. Iden brought out the fact, not hitherto widely known, that J. E. Greiner of Baltimore played a part in the construction or alteration of all four of the bridges which span the Susquehanna river between Havre de Grace and Perryville.

Back in 1884, Mr. Iden said, the first Baltimore and Ohio Railroad bridge over the Susquehanna was designed by Edwin Thatcher, chief engineer for the Keystone Bridge Works of Pittsburgh, and his young assistant, Mr. Greiner, then only a few years out of college.

In 1908 Mr. Greiner redesigned the same bridge to carry double tracks. In 1922 the State of Maryland purchased the old P., B. & W. Railroad bridge at Havre de Grace and converted it into a highway span, with Mr. Greiner doing the designing.

FIRM DID WORK

When the same bridge was double-decked Mr. Greiner's firm did the work. And when the new four-lane highway bridge was built in 1939-1940 Mr. Greiner was instrumental in that work, too.

Mr. Iden said:

"It is doubtful whether there is a stretch of river one mile long anywhere else where the same engineer has played an important part in the development of four separate bridge structures."

Freezing Weather Expected By Tonight

By MARTIN L. DOBLER

Colder weather with below freezing temperatures is expected here tonight.

Temperatures by mid-afternoon today should be in the high 40s.

Total rainfall here amounted to 0.79 inches in the past 24 hours—just a soaking, steady rainfall.

MOUNTAIN SNOW DEPTHS

For the benefit of winter sports fans, let's take a glance at the snow depths this morning along the Blue Ridge and Allegheny mountains.

In our Western Maryland mountains snow depth has rapidly decreased, due to the warm spell over the week-end and the soaking rains.

We find one to three inches of snow near Mount Savage summit so, for the present, no skiing is possible up there.

THREE TO FIVE INCHES

But down at Mount Mitchell, N. C., strange to say, we find three to five inches of snow.

No very low temperatures appear in the Eastern United States but temperatures here in Maryland will be somewhat lower tonight.

LOCAL NEWS IN BRIEF

Police arrested 242,321 persons here in 1941, an increase of 62,083 over the arrests made in 1940, according to a report made to Police Commissioner Robert F. Stanton today by his secretary, George J. Brennan.

An appropriation of $2,500 today was asked by the School Board at a meeting of the Board of Estimates to purchase material to protect glass in school corridors, where pupils will gather in the event of air raids.

Police reported today that Jacob Hoke Cullen, thirty-five, of Crisfield, Md., had fired a bullet into his temple last night at a boarding house in the 700 block North Monroe street, where a brother, Jack Cullen, lived. Cullen was pronounced dead at Franklin Square Hospital. He had been despondent, the police said.

Public Service Commission today signed an order approving transfer of property and assets of Youghiogheny Hydro-Electric Corporation (Garrett county) to Pennsylvania Electric Company.

A chase through streets and alleys near the 400 block Aisquith street ended today with a Negro being held at the Central Police Station as a purse-snatching suspect. The man was believed to have stolen a purse from Mrs. Mary Russo containing $7.79.

Conventions Set '41 Record Here

Delegates to 120 conventions held in Baltimore last year spent $1,047,652 in the city, a report of the convention bureau of the Association of Commerce revealed today.

The year set a new record in the number of such meetings held here and prospcts for 1942 are equally promising, the bureau announced.

Already 72 organizations have announced they would meet here this year, a number 22 per cent. greater than the conventions scheduled at the same time in 1941.

Sincerely:

We of The Belvedere hope you have as much pleasure dancing to Lang Thompson's Orchestra as we have in bringing it to you. Hear it tonite—in The Charles Room.

TOMORROW NIGHT
PAUL JONES
ALCAZAR
Joe Dowling's Music

CUTIES ·:· By E. Simms Campbell

Registered U. S. Patent Office

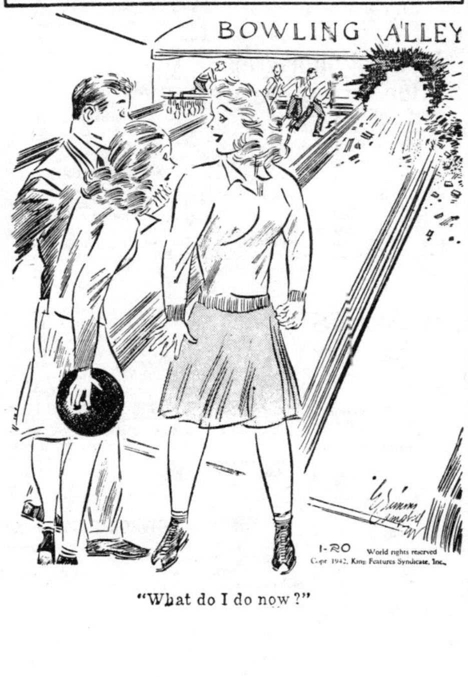

"What do I do now?"

Win Cash For News Tips And Amateur Photographs

Do you want money for being alert? The Baltimore News-Post and Sunday American are offering cash prizes each week for news tips and amateur photographs. Total awards of $50 are distributed weekly for news tips, $25 for the best, $10 for the next best and $1 prizes for the next fifteen. For each amateur photograph published $3 will be paid, with special bonuses for outstanding pictures. Spot-news pictures are preferred, but candid camera shots that pull at the heartstrings are acceptable. Avoid pictures of ordinary scenes. Telephone The News-Tip Editor at Lexington 0100 for news tips and rush spot-news photographs in to the Picture Editor.

SKIPPY — By Percy Crosby

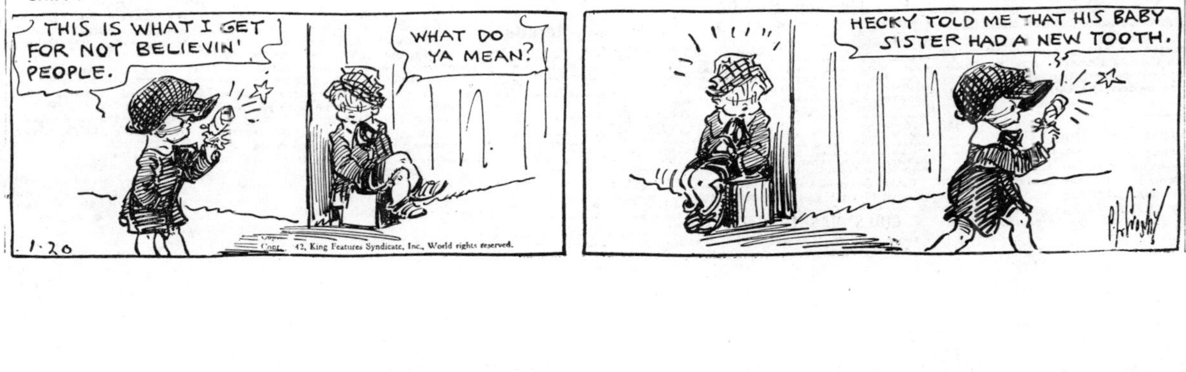

SAVE
By Ordering
CARRIER SERVICE!

Besides the convenience of having your favorite paper delivered at your door every afternoon, carrier service saves you money if you live in Baltimore or the immediate suburbs.

NEWS-POST
12c A WEEK
DELIVERED TO YOUR HOME

A Saving of $3.12 a year when you get your News-Post the Home delivery way.

Grove Changes His Mind About Retiring

THE BALTIMORE NEWS-POST SPORTS
18 TUESDAY EVENING, JANUARY 20, 1942

FORGOT GUEST

WINNIPEG, Jan. 20—(A. P.).—Canada's athletic elite gathered last night to honor Theo Dubois, champion rower, who was voted the Dominion's outstanding athlete of 1941. That is, everyone but Dubois was present. Finally he arrived, and Toastmaster Bruce Murray apologized with "I forgot to invite the guest of honor."

HORNSBY VOTED INTO BASEBALL'S HALL OF FAME

Rogers Is 14th To Be Named

Rodger H. Pippen
Sports Editor Says

KEEP YOUR CHIN UP

The baseball writers of the country finally came to their senses and voted Rogers Hornsby into Cooperstown's Hall of Fame.

This should have been done years ago.

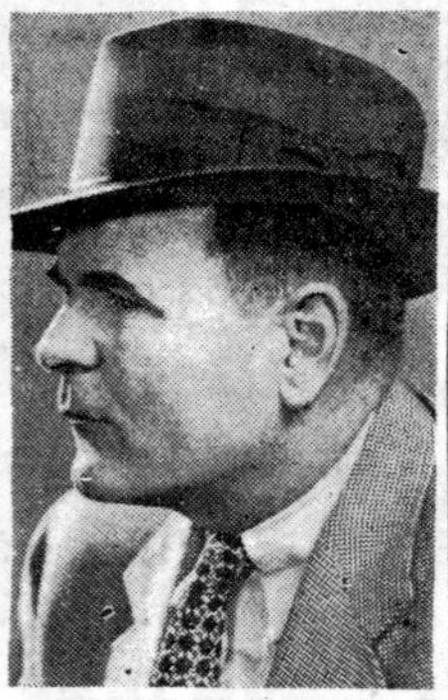

RODGER H. PIPPEN

Hornsby's great record speaks for itself. The honor he deserved was delayed because of narrow-minded personal opinions. Rogers was too outspoken to be generally popular.

Never effusive, Hornsby was plainly pleased when notified at Fort Worth, Texas, where he is wintering.

"It's quite a distinction," Hornsby said in his hotel room, where he was shaping activities of the Fort Worth Cats, Texas League Club, of which he is field and business manager.

"I certainly thank the baseball writers for voting me that distinction and I appreciate it more than I can express, but right now there's a couple of things more important:

"First, winning the war.

"Second, baseball."

The sport is Hornsby's life. "It's the only business I know," he said, "and I've been in it since I was eighteen."

Dream Of Majors

Hornsby is dreaming of returning to the majors as a manager or owner. Texas is his home and he loves it, but he can't get the big leagues out of his head.

"That's where we all want to be," he said. "I'd like to get another crack as manager in the big time or some day have a club of my own."

His Hitting Secret

He won his greatest glory as a hitter and cared little whether he was facing a righthanded or lefthanded moundsman.

"I always hit at the ball—not at the pitcher's motion. I'd wait until I saw the ball and that's honestly all that counted. I didn't care if the pitcher threw with his foot, as long as it came in the strike zone," Hornsby said. "Maybe that's how come I could hit."

Greatest Thrill

Having a plaque in baseball's Hall of Fame "gives a fellow a thrill," but the Rajah's greatest thrill came in the 1926 World Series.

That was when, as manager of the St. Louis Cardinals, he sent Grover Cleveland Alexander to the mound to fan Tony Lazzeri and win the series from the New York Yankees.

"And that team was the best the Yanks ever had," he declares.

Only Three Named First Round

Of the 763 writers who competed in the so-called "brains battle" to name the winner and the time of the knockout in the Joe Louis-Buddy Baer contest, only three ventured to predict the heavyweight contest would end in the first round.

The winner of the $100 prize offered by Frank G. Menke for the Gillette Razor Company was John Rhodes of the Evening Star of Winchester, Va. His prediction was 2.07 of the first heat. The official time, as you know, was 2.56.

Bud Cornish of the Press Herald of Portland, Maine, with .2.05, was second. Francis Hile of the Sentinel of Parkersburg, W. Va., was third, with 2.02.

Only seventeen of the 763 picked Baer to win. This shows that the Bomber was almost a 1-to-45 shot to win in the consensus opinion.

Here's how the 763 sports writers, who chose Joe Louis, thought about it so far as the final round was concerned:

1st—	3	6th—	95	11th—	12
2nd—	26	7th—	77	12th—	3
3rd—	116	8th—	56	13th—	4
4th—	174	9th—	39	14th—	2
5th—	140	10th—	4	15th—	12

All these who named the fifteenth guessed Joe to win the decision. None guessed a knockout in the round. None of the contestants thought the bout would end in a draw.

Suggest Basket Ball Series For Uncle Sam

To add to the "Buy a Bomber Fund," William M. Kennard of the Bethlehem Accounting Athletic Club suggests a series of games between the best teams of Baltimore and Maryland Basket Ball Leagues. It is his idea to have St. Stanislaus, Roberts Jewelers and Bethlehem Accounting represent the Maryland League, and Y. M. H. A., Stonewalls and Lithuanians play for the Baltimore loop.

Such a series would create a lot of interest and would surely help Uncle Sam.

Rennert Bar In New Home

Yielding to the wrecking crew, the old Hotel Rennert, famous for half a century in the annals of Maryland, is coming down. Soon the structure at Saratoga and Liberty streets will be but a memory.

But part of it—and an interesting part—will be preserved in new surroundings. The bar and the mirror have been transferred to the new refreshment room at Carlin's Iceland.

The bar, according to the historians, is not the original pre-prohibition bar but one which was later constructed along the lines of the original model. The original at the time it was outmoded by the dry era, had served for many years, and was disintegrating. It was split up and distributed as souvenirs.

Statesmen galore frequented the Rennert in the old days and not a few of them patronized the bar and the restaurant where beverages or dishes, prepared with unrivalled skill, were to be had.

For a large part of its career the Rennert was a great haunt of politicians—especially Democratic politicians. Politicians are great persons for conferring and what is a more auspicious place for a conference than a snug place at or neighboring the bar?

After the Eutaw House had waned as a center of political assemblage, the Rennert became a Mecca. Travel was not so convenient then as now and the county people who came to town for a State convention or State committee meeting, put up over night. And their favorite rendezvous was the Rennert.

During some of the prohibition years, the Rennert continued as a political center. John Mahon lived there and held court there as leader of the Baltimore city Democratic organization.

To consult with Mahon came John S. (Frank) Kelly at times when the relations between those two leaders were not too strained for the ameities of conference.

Associated with Mahon were Robert J. Padgett and colorful "Danny" Loden of Concord Club fame and of the rainbow-hued socks.

These personages were a prominent part of the old Rennert scene. Mahon would receive reports from subordinates as he sat in a big chair in the lobby.

Governor Ritchie was frequently at the Rennert and on the eve of a State convention or other occasion for congregation of Democratic leaders and workers throughout the State, he was much in evidence.

The old-time leaders have passed on now and the hotel where they foregathered is being resolved into its elements. Dust to dust . . . But the bar has been salvaged and will be perpetuated (for hte serving of the lighter beverages) in the modernistic surroundings of Carlin's.

Reports Finding Lost Dog

Mrs. Lillian Knight, 226 S. Collins avenue, Irvington, has written to this column reporting that her husband picked up a lost dog on Eastern avenue near Patterson Park, just in time to save the little fellow from being run over. The dog, according to Mrs. Knight's description is a small male, black with brown face and feet, and it limps slightly in the left foreleg. She would like to return it to its owner.

Grove Changes Mind About Retiring

By JACK CUDDY

NEW YORK, Jan. 20—(U. P.).—Robert (Lefty) Grove has a deep respect for the persuasive powers of age over the muscular potency of baseball players, particularly pitchers, but today the tall, deep-voiced gentleman from Lonaconing, Md., said that his 42 years would not prevent him from winning ten games if he rejoined the Boston Red Sox.

Grove, speaking by telephone from his Maryland home, said that despite the unconditional release he received in December, he hoped to be on the firing line for another campaign, particularly because three other Red Sox southpaws—Mickey Harris, Earl Johnson and Larry Powell—have marched away to war.

"Hunting and fishing have kept me right at my playing weight of 204 pounds," Lefty said, "and furthermore, my arm feels just fine.

"What if I will be forty-two in March? A man's as young as he feels; and I feel like I'd be sure to win about ten games for Boston this season."

WON SEVEN LAST YEAR

Last year this pitching immortal combined the canny pitching skill of years of mound experience with some of the natural wizardry left in his time-worn left arm. He won seven and lost seven, appearing in 21 games. He registered an earned run average of 4.37. His last victory was achieved on July 24, when the Sox beat the Indians, giving him the three hundredth mound triumph of his 17 years in the majors. He was the twelfth man to accomplish that feat in baseball history.

Grove, whose fire-ball made him the king pitcher of the majors and the American League's most valuable player of 1931, when he was with the Philadelphia Athletics, emphasized that he would accept no minor league offers.

BOWLING BOOMS

"If I don't get an offer to pitch or coach with the Red Sox or some other major league club," he said, "I'll just retire from baseball. And I won't have a thing to worry about either, because my bowling alley business here in Lonaconing is in full bloom. But I'd sure like to do some more pitching."

Grove figures he'll do better this season, if given the chance, for two reasons:

1—His arm is better, and,

2—With so many youngsters going into the service, the batting opposition may not be as tough.

Lefty would like to emulate Cy Young, who pitched for the Boston Braves in 1911 at the age of forty-four. "Iron Man" Joe McGinnity turned in baseball's old-age record pitching feat. Although Joe left the Giants after the 1908 season, at thirty-seven, he continued in the minors until fifty-four. At that age he won six and lost six for Dubuque. But at fifty-two, in 1923, McGinnity pitched Dubuque to its league pennant, appearing in 42 games and 206 innings, and winning 15 against 12 defeats.

Bosox Wouldn't Accept Grove, Says Collins

BOSTON, Jan. 20—(A. P.).—Eddie Collins, general manager of the Boston Red Sox, said today that an offer of Lefty Bob Grove to return to the Red Sox to compensate in a measure for loss of three left-handed pitchers through military service would not be accepted.

"While the Boston Red Sox deeply appreciate the long and faithful service that Bob Grove has given to the Boston Club and are grateful for his offer recently made to return to try to help the Sox," Collins said, "we feel that such a comeback attempt would be an anti-climax to a grand and glorious career. We think too much of Old Mose to ask him to shoulder any more pitching burdens."

Fair Grounds Results

FIRST RACE—Six furlongs. Off at 3.18. Time 1.14 1-5.

Silver Sallie, 104 (S. Parise)	$118.00	$58.80	$12.00
Shining Day, 109 (Sconza)		6.80	3.80
Bride's Best, 109 (S. Clark)			2.80

Also Ran—Loretta Rice, Bit o'Bud, Header, Green Elf, Primzo, Glacialis, Malvois.

SECOND—Mile and seventy yards. Off at 3.47. Time 1.46 2-5.

Winged Phariah, 108 (E. Guerin)	$5.80	$2.80	$2.20
Liberty Cloud, 100 (S. Parise)		3.20	2.60
Piplad, 105 (P. Milligan)			2.80

Also Ran—Bootsey Byrd, Empire Isle, Delivery, Playful Lass, Majestic, Golden Ford and Ground Clipper.

Daily Double—Silver Sallie and Winged Phariah paid $618.80 for $2.

GIRLS' BASKET BALL

Forest Park, 25: Montrose, 12.

Jack Passes The Hat For A Bomber

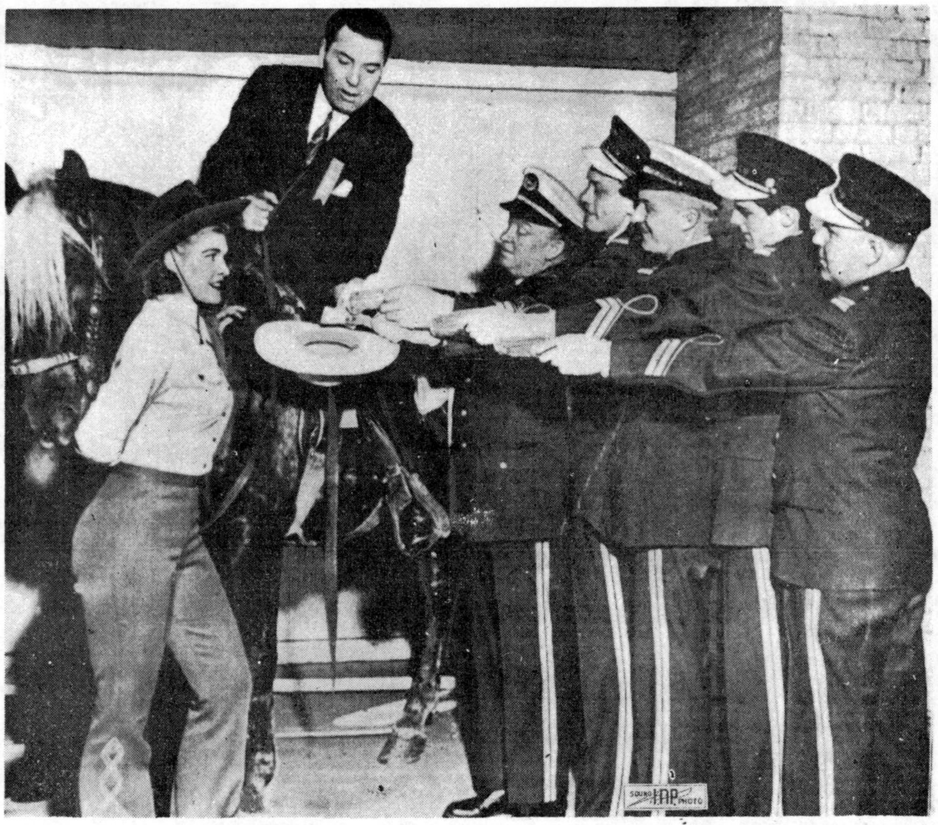

C'MON, FELLERS, BUY A BOMBER—Turned down when he tried to enlist in Uncle Sam's Army, former Heavyweight Champ Jack Dempsey manages to get in a lick at the Axis by working for the Buy-A-Bomber campaign. Mounted on a bronc named Peanuts, the Manassa Mauler is shown passing a 10-gallon hat for contributions to the Bomber fund at a rodeo in Chicago. Left to right are Peggy O'Neill, gal rider; Dempsey, Major Edward Flaming, and Pink Neilsen, Tates Johnson, Richard Ryan and Raymond Stang, ushers. International News Soundphoto.

End Qualifying Round Sunday At Recreation

With the announcement that approximately 1,000 bowlers competed over the week-end in the first-half of the qualifying round, officials estimated today that 500 more duckpinists will swing into action Saturday and Sunday in the Recreation Classified Bowling Tournament.

In other words, the 1942 tourney, annually conducted over the Recreation Centre alleys in co-operation with The News-Post and Sunday American, will draw a complete field of nearly 1,500 entrants.

Finals in the event are scheduled for January 31 and February 1. Forty of the original field in each of the seven classifications, will qualify for the finals.

The qualifying round will be completed this week-end with all classes booked for competition. On Saturday the women's Class A and the men's Class D groups will resume the firing at 2 o'clock. On Sunday at 2, 5.30 and 8.30 o'clock all classes except the women's Class A is scheduled.

Qualifying scores do not carry over into the final round. All finalists, shooting for the twenty-eight cash prizes, will start again from scratch. It's still anybody's, and everybody's, tourney.

Havana Results

FIRST RACE—Five and a half furlongs. Off at 3.02. Time 1.20.

Waka, 115 (J. Fernandez)	8-5	3-5	out
Vonnie, 115 (A. Gonzalez)		1-1	out
Bruneta, 110 (J Vina)			out

Also Ran—Balanced Budget, Lunsford, Purple Sweep and Lacee.

SECOND—Six furlongs (chute). Off at 3.36½. Time 1.25 4-5.

Shantime, 110 (J. Alfonso)	3-5	1-5	out
Eneas F?, 105 (A. Alonso)		1-1	out
Elstree, 115 (J. Vina)			out

Also Ran—Idolatry, King Preston, Bright Sox(Ayers and Merry Kin.

THIRD—Six furlongs. Off 4.05½. Time 1.26 1-5.

Army Surgeon, 119 (R. Alonso)	2-1	7-10	Out
On Wisconsin, 110 (Posada)		7-10	Out
Lady Tichner, 105 (Morejon)			Out

Also Ran—Principessa, Emvee, Lignum Vitae, Lightly, Courtney's Pet.

Belle Poise Captures Hialeah Park Feature

HIALEAH PARK, Fla., Jan. 20. — The Blenheim's Farm's Belle Poise, with Don Meade up, today led all the way to win the one mile and an eighth Little River Purse, sixth and feature race. In a driving finish, Belle Poise lasted to beat One Jest with Pet third.

HIALEAH PARK, Fla., Jan. 20—(A. P.).—Ira Hanford, who was the first apprentice to win a Kentucky Derby (on Bold Venture) but not so busy these days, today booted Wood Robin to a popular score in the one mile of the fifth contest, restricted to three-year-old colts.

Paying $6.20 for two, Wood Robin was rated within range of the early leaders. He responded to urging through the last quarter mile and drove to the wire a length better than Five-O-Eight. Horn lost second money by another length.

The customary 14 juveniles met in the three-furlong opening number. Ample Reward, a first-time starter in the field of maiden colts and geldings, dashed to the front soon after the break, crossed over and impeded several horses a furlong after the start, and went on to score by two lengths. He returned $14.20. Wise Bob and Orpheum, both apparently bothered by the winner's swerving, were next in line, a length apart.

$688.10 DOUBLE

Completing a daily double worth $688.10 for two, High Plaid spurted just in time to win the second race by a head, paying $37.40. Stimuli followed, a length in advance of Challante, while the stoutly backed Sherron Ann could do no better than fourth in the limit field.

High Plaid lacked the early foot to keep up while Challante was showing the way. The latter shortened stride in the run home, allowing both High Plaid and Stimuli to run past her.

CLOSE FINISH

In one of those tight photo finishes which leave observers arguing for hours, Whiscendent, on the outside, received the camera verdict over John Hunnicutt in the third event. A half dozen lengths behind the pair came Michigan Sun to earn the show.

John Hunnicutt, a close second choice to the winner, could not maintain a long lead. He weakened just enough to toss it off to Whiscendent, which forced the running and paid $7.10.

BAD START

The fourth race was marred by a messy start which saw Lit Up left at the post and Courteous also deprived of a fair chance. The winner turned up in Remembering, which Paul Keiper drove home a length and a half before Layaway. White Bait missed the place by five lengths.

Layaway, which drew a strong play, set the pace but could not get clear and finally succumbed to the persistent challenge of Remembering, a $18.80-for-two shot.

Graham Named Athletic Director

WICHITA, Kan., Jan. 20—(A. P.). Ralph Graham, assistant backfield coach at Indiana U., since 1934, today stepped into a $4,000 job as athletic director at Wichita U. Graham won nine varsity letters—three each in football, basket ball and tennis—at Kansas State College and was all Big Six fullback his junior and senior years. He succeeds Al Gebert, resigned.

Don Kerr Signs Contract With Pirates

PITTSBURGH, Jan. 20—(A. P.). The Pittsburgh Pirates announced today James McDonald Kerr, right-handed pitcher drafted from the Baltimore Orioles of the International League, had sent in his signed contract for the 1942 season.

Kerr, who is six feet tall and weighs 187 pounds, appeared in 43 games last season and was credited with five victories and 13 defeats. He is 23.

Pirates' Shortstop Due To Join Army

PITTSBURGH, Pa., Jan. 20—(I. N. S.)—Shortstop Billy Cox, purchased by the Pittsburgh Pirates from Harrisburg, Pa., at the end of last season, expects to be inducted into the Army within a month and President Bill Benswanger of the Pirates has asked Commissioner Kenesaw Mountain Landis and National League president Ford Frick to place Cox's name on the National Defense list.

HIALEAH RESULTS

Continued from Page 1.

THIRD—1⅛ miles. Off 3.01½. Time, 1.55.

Whiscendent, 104 (J. Breen)	$7.10	$3.70	$3.20
John Hunnicutt, 117 (W. Day)		3.50	2.80
Michigan Sun, 114 (P. Keiper)			3.10
Total mutuels			$23.40

Also Ran—Spritewick, Oldwick, Foxcub, Here Now, Isle de Pine.

FOURTH—Six furlongs. Off 3.35½. Time, 1.13 4-5.

Remembering, 116 (P. Keiper)	$10.80	$5.10	$4.30
Layaway, 119 (J. Pollard)		4.00	3.70
White Bait, 112 (K. Greever)			9.20

Also Ran—Marny, Royal Weista, Courteous, Intruding, Buffalo, Brave Sir, Lit Up, Michigan Sweet.

FIFTH—Mile (chute) .Off 4.01½. Tune, 1.40 4-5.

Wood Robin, 116 (I. Hanford)	$6.20	$3.60	$2.70
Five-O-Eight, 110 (B. James)		8.80	4.30
Horn, 100 (W. Mehrtens)			3.00

Also Ran—Nestonian, Bayridge, On The Fence, Raisin Bread, Catcall.

Was Considered Greatest Right Hand Hitter

By JUDSON BAILEY

NEW YORK, Jan. 20—(A. P.).—The fabulous baseball career of Rogers Hornsby, the greatest right-handed hitter of all time, carried him into the Hall of Fame today.

The Rajah, who performed for five different clubs and managed four of them in a 23-year span in the majors, who batted over .400 in three seasons and twice was named the most valuable player in the National League, who earned perhaps half a million dollars from baseball and lost most of it, received .182 votes out of 233 cast by baseball writers.,

MANAGES TEXAS CLUB

As a result a bronze plaque, bearing his dimple-cheeked likeness, will soon be placed alongside those of baseball's other immortals—Cobb, Wagner, Ruth, Mathewson and the rest — in the little shrine at Cooperstown, N. Y.

Hornsby, who will be forty-six in April, now is the general manager and bench pilot of Fort Worth in the Texas League. He is a jovial, gray-haired minor league executive. But in days that a vast majority of the baseball fans can still remember he was a bright comet shooting an unpredictable course across sport's horizon.

He broke into the National League with the St. Louis Cardinals in 1915 as a shortstop. Later he played every position in the infield, tried the outfield and moved to the New York Giants, to the Boston Braves, to the Chicago Cubs, to the Cardinals again and finally to the St. Louis Browns. He managed the Cards, Braves, Cubs and Browns, reaching a salary peak of $40,000 a year with the Cubs.

He led the National League in batting for seven years, six of them in succession for the Cardinals from 1920 to 1925, inclusive. He batted .401 in 1922, in 1924 reached .424, the modern record for both major leagues, and in 1925 followed up with .403.

He also led the league in 1928 with .387 for the Braves and was voted the most valuable player in 1925 with the Cards and 1929 while with the Cubs.

Hornsby had no faults on the playing field, but the magnates found some with him off the diamond.

TRADED TO GIANTS

In 1926, at the height of his career as a player and manager, the Cardinals let him go because he could not be brought to salary terms by President Sam Breadon. He was traded to the New York Giants for Frank Frisch and served one season as captain under John McGraw, then was traded to Boston as manager of the Braves. His salary, then about $36,000, was too much for the club to carry and he was passed along to the Cubs in the biggest trade in history—Chicago giving $200,000 in cash and five players.

Hornsby's passion for betting on horse races was probably his biggest stumbling block with the club owners, however. He was in hot water with Commissioner Kenesaw M. Landis about this at one time or another and in 1927 was sued for $90,000, which a Cincinnati betting commissioner claimed was due him. Hornsby contended this was a gambling debt and not admiserable at law and a Circuit Court jury found in his favor.

MANAGED ORIOLES

The Cubs let him go unceremoniously in 1932 and the Browns dismissed him "for actions off the ball field" in 1937. Since then no major league club has ever hired him, but he has managed at Baltimore and Oklahoma City in the minors and is moving to Fort Worth this year.

Hornsby is the fourteenth player elected to the Hall of Fame. To enter he had to receive 75 per cent. of the baseball writers' vote, a qualification he narrowly missed at the last election three years ago. He follows Lou Gehrig, who was chosen last year under a suspension of the rules.

Besides Hornsby, five other former stars received more than 100 votes in the newest poll—Frank Chance, 136; Rube Waddell, 126; Ed Walsh, 113; Miller Huggins, 111; Ed Delahanty, 104.

TOWSON QUINT WINS

The Towson Catholic School basket ball team beat Bel Air, 36 to 22, yesterday as Zacharko scored 12 points. B. Greer got 15 of Bel Air's 22 points.

BATTER JAP FLEET AT BALI

Fall Of Rangoon Feared Near

THE BALTIMORE NEWS-POST

AN INDEPENDENT NEWSPAPER

The Largest Evening Circulation in the Entire South

VOL. CXL.—NO. 95 Entered as second-class matter at Baltimore Postoffice. TUESDAY, FEBRUARY 24, 1942 PRICE 3 CENTS

BUY UNITED STATES DEFENSE BONDS AND STAMPS

COMPLETE MARKETS

FREEZING OF WAGES SEEN

IN THE NEWS

THE trial of Daladier and Blum in France may be the, beginning of a new era of justice and of peace on this earth.

If we are to have a better and a happier world, it is surely time that the men responsible for the murder and misery of war should be tried and convicted and deservedly punished for the highest of all crimes against Heaven and humanity.

It is to be hoped that the guilty will be convicted in France and that their prosecution and conviction will afford an example—a precedent—which all the other outraged peoples of the world will follow.

DALADIER is accused of having projected his nation, though unprepared, into a war where hundreds of thousands of his people were slain, millions rendered destitute, millions made to mourn throughout their lives because of the loss of loved ones.

Blum is accused of being responsible for the unpreparedness which Daladier inherited.

He is blamed for coddling the Communists and the Anarchists when they were undermining the strength of France by strikes and sabotage, and every kind of obstruction to progress and production.

He is arraigned for having wasted the wealth of France in political boondoggling in compelling the payment of the preposterous increases that disloyal strikers demanded through force and violence.

He is indicted for buying political popularity at the expense of a plundered people, for hampering and even destroying the industries of France, and for having filled the public offices of France with political bureaucrats loyal to nothing but themselves and the regime which kept them in place and power.

IF BLUM did these evil things—and the dispatches of his time relate that he did—he committed treason against his country and should be prosecuted as a traitor.

But he did not involve his country in war.

He only made it impotent in war—and incompetent in peace.

Daladier, who must have known of the criminal incompetence of the Blum regime—(since he denounced it)—and of the unpreparedness of France, nevertheless did involve his nation in war and in utter disaster.

BUT the question is not merely whether Blum destroyed the wealth of France in his persistent endeavor to buy the ballots to sustain his party in power.

It is not, indeed, wholly a question of whether Daladier led his nation into war, knowing its financial weakness and its military and industrial unpreparedness.

The point that holds out a bright promise for a better future is that leaders who project their nations into war are already being prosecuted, with fair hope of punishment, for their failures in war.

The only remaining step to be taken in the interests of

Continued on Page 4, Column 1.

Draft Chief Asks Labor Control

By GRIFFING BANCROFT
International News Service Staff Correspondent.

WASHINGTON, Feb. 23.—Brigadier General Lewis B. Hershey, draft director, today warned Congress that the nation's wages may have to be frozen and that some system of labor allotment may have to be imposed because "we've got to have more control over the placement of men."

The General also declared that workers in plane factories and ship yards who expect draft deferments "may be in for a rude awakening."

REPLACED BY WOMEN

He said:

"I think these men can more easily be replaced by women than men on farms and in some other necessary occupations."

The statements were made before the House Agricultural Committee, where Hershey was called by members who contend that a serious hardship is being worked on farmers because agricultural labor is being drafted.

The General pointed out that many more men are leaving the farms for better-paying industrial jobs than for service in the Army, and assured the committee that every effort is being made to defer essential farm labor.

HITS RECRUITING

Asserting flatly that "we've got to have more control over the placement of men," Hershey again declared that he was "sorry to say" that men are still being recruited into the Army in addition to those being drafted.

Belligerent Loan Act Is Suspended

WASHINGTON, Feb. 23—(A. P.). President Roosevelt signed today legislation suspending for the duration of the war a restriction against loans or credits to belligerent nations by American citizens. The President had asked Congress to suspend this restriction of the Neutrality Act on the ground that it hampered normal trade relations with certain belligerents, especially Canada.

Honored

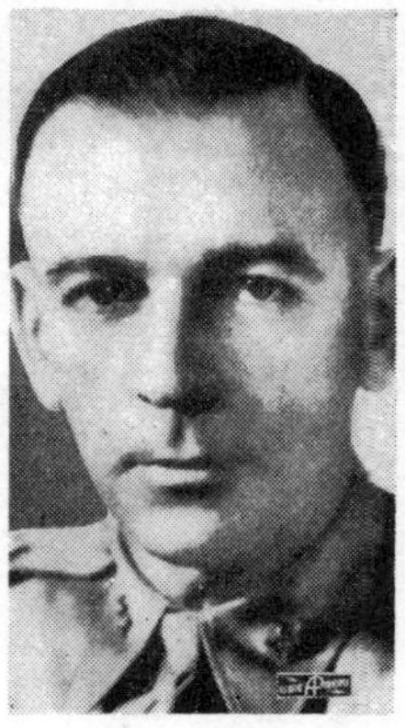

GEN. R. K. SUTHERLAND

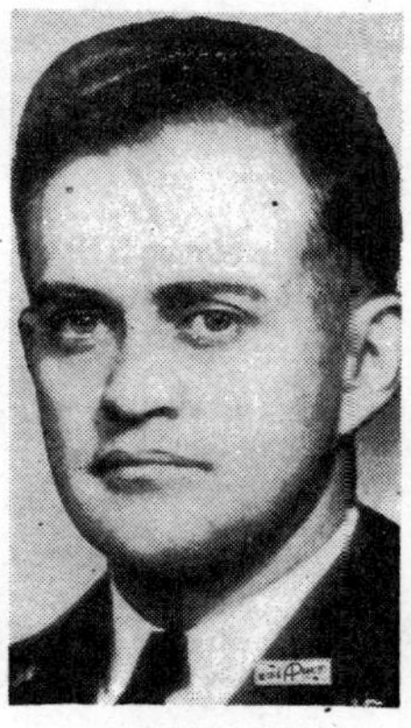

GEN. R. J. MARSHALL

Major General Sutherland, a native of Maryland and Brigadier General Marshall, a former member of the Maryland National Guard, have received the Distinguished Service Star of the Philippines on recommendation of Gen. Douglas MacArthur, the War Department announced.

(Story on Page 3)

When Happy Brides Faced Adventure and Sacrifice With a Smile. See "The Covered Wagon Girl," Another Painting by Henry Clive, Well-Known Artist, in His "Maid in America" Series With Verses, by Phyllis McGinley, in The American Weekly, the Magazine Distributed With Next Sunday's Baltimore American.—Adv.

BULLETINS

CANBERRA, Australia, Feb. 23—(A. P.).—Japanese flying boats again bombed shipping in the Sea of Timor during the week-end, the Royal Australian Air Force reported today, but said the attacks were "without results so far as known."

LONDON, Feb. 23—(U. P.).—British bombers attacked ports and other objectives in northwest Germany and the docks at Ostend during the night, the Air Ministry reported. All the raiders returned safely.

MOSCOW, Feb. 21—(A. P.).—Tass, official Soviet news agency, denied today as a "provocational fabrication" a report which it said appeared in the Japanese newspaper Nichi Nichi alleging that a representative of the Russian Embassy in Tokyo "was among foreign representatives who congratulated the Japanese on the fall of Singapore."

Probe Faulty Shells On U. S. Warship In Pacific

Yanks, Dutch Batter Jap Fleet At Bali

SYDNEY, Australia, Feb. 23—(U. P.).—The Australian Air Force heavily attacked Japanese-held Rabaul, on New Britain Island, the Press reported today. The Sydney Sun said that enemy shipping and airdromes were attacked despite extremely bad weather and that some hits were observed.

BATAVIA, N. E. I., Feb. 23—(A. P.).—A Japanese merchant ship of more than 10,000 tons was set afire and other ships were machine-gunned in a new raid by Allied dive bombers on Banka Strait off Sumatra, the United Nations headquarters announced today.

BATAVIA, N. E. I., Feb. 23—(A. P.).—Dutch and American air and naval forces destroyed and scattered the entire Japanese invasion fleet which attacked Bali last week, but some of the invaders have succeeded in getting ashore, overrunnning part of the island and seizing the airport at Denpasar, the Dutch announced today.

(BACKGROUND NOTE: At least 19 enemy ships, including five cruisers and four destroyers, were damaged or sunk, and the total may have been as high as 32, according to various communiques.)

A communique of the Netherlands Indies armed forces declared, however, that the Japanese who had landed through a hail of bombs from American and Dutch air forces were isolated now from supplies and reinforcements.

The communique said:

"Not a single warship or transport remained near Bali to give the Japanese troops support of supplies.

Big formations of American four-motored bombers, dive bombers and fighters, and Dutch and American cruisers and destroyers attacked the Japanese armada, the communique said.

A statement issued by the Netherlands Indies Government said:

"A singie ship which succeeded in escaping destruction has fled."

U. S. REPORT

The United States War Department in Washington said Saturday

Continued on Page 2, Column 1.

Chinchilla Show Held By Breeders

INGLEWOOD, Cal., Feb. 23—(A. P.).—The nation's chinchilla breeders held their first livestock show here, with 21 ranches of the United States and a few from Canada represented. Eighty dead chinchillas, comprising that many pelts in a woman's coat, received most of the "oh's" and "ah's," however. The price: $38,000.

Billion In Bonds, Stamps, A.F.L. Goal

WASHINGTON, Feb. 23—(U. P.). The American Federation of Labor today began its "Labor Invests in Victory" Week with a pledge to purchase $1,000,000,000 in defense stamps and bonds this year.

U. S. Eyes French Fleet Activities

WASHINGTON, Feb. 23—(A. P.). Sumner Welles, acting Secretary of State, said today the United States was watching closely all developments bearing on the French fleet, including the arrival of the battleship Dunkerque at Toulon.

He was asked at a press conference whether the State Department viewed with concern the reappearancs of the Dunkerque, which was badly damaged by the British at Oran, Northern Africa, shortly after the French capitulation in 1940.

In reply Welles said the United States Government frequently has made known, both to the French Government at Vichy and in public statements, the concern with which it would view any relaxation of control over the French fleet by the French Government itself or any indication that the fleet was anything but a purely French fleet.

26 Firms To Allot Pay To Buy Bonds

Twenty-six firms, employing approximately 9,500 workers, were added last week to Maryland's roll of concerns who have agreed to inaugurate payroll allotment plans for the purchase of defense bonds, it was announced today by Walter N. Ruth, director of the State defense savings staff.

TORY PARTY HEAD QUITS

LONDON, Feb. 23—(A. P.).—Sir Douglas Hacking resigned today as chairman of the dominant Conservative Party and will be succeeded March 6 by Major Thomas L. Dugdale, deputy chief Government whip since last year.

Fear Fall Of Rangoon Near

CHUNGKING, Feb. 23—(I. N. S.). Details reached Chungking tonight of a terrific air battle on the Bilin river front in Burma in which American pilots sent five Japanese planes hurtling to death in as many minutes.

LONDON, Feb. 23—(A. P.).—British hopes of holding Rangoon against superior Japanese forces were regarded by observers here tonight as considerably diminished, and with them hopes of preventing invasion of all Burma.

Very little official information on the fighting was available and some informed sources suggested that the cables from Rangoon might have been cut.

The last word was that British troops were fighting somewhere between the Bilin and Sittang rivers, the latter only 20 miles east of the Rangoon-Lashio railway which feeds the Burma road.

The view that the British soon may be forced to fall back upon India's defenses was advanced because of the speed with which the Japanese forced the Salween and Bilin river lines.

The break through the Bilin defenses, where the British were said to have constructed "a series of strong points," indicated that the invasion forces had been reinforced with troops diverted from Malaya after the fall of Singapore.

Darwin Under Military Rule

CANBERRA, Australia, Feb. 23—(A. P.).—The northern part of the northern territory of Australia, including the bomb-scarred Port Darwin, was placed under military control today, War Minister Francis Forde announced.

Towns and the territory as far south as Birdum, southern terminus of a railway from Darwin, were included, Exchange Telegraph said.

Wisconsin U. To Train Radio Men

GREAT LAKES, Ill., Feb. 23—(I. N. S.).—A new naval training school with a capacity for turning out 1,200 trained radio operators every four months will open at the University of Wisconsin, Madison, Wis., on April 1, it was announced today by Rear Admiral John Downes.

THE WEATHER

Continued cold today with slowly diminishing winds.

Rear Admiral To Testify At House Inquiry

(Full text of Agronsky broadcast on Page 2.)

WASHINGTON, Feb. 23—(I. N. S.).—The House Naval Affairs Committee today voted to launch an investigation into reports that ammunition aboard an American warship in the Far East was antiquated and only about 30 per cent. efficient.

Representative Vinson (Democrat) of Georgia, committee chairman, said the inquiry will be started tomorrow with public testimony by Rear Admiral W. H. P. Blandy, chief of the Navy's Bureau of Ordnance.

SAN FRANCISCO, Feb. 23—(I. N. S.).—A United States warship convoying American troopships to Java failed to fight off attacking Japanese bombers because of old, virtually ineffective ammunition aboard the warship.

This assertion was contained today in the full transcript of a short wave broadcast by Martin Agronsky, N. B. C. war correspondent, who escaped to Sydney before the fall of Singapore.

Agronsky at the same time revealed an ominous picture of the Allied position in the Netherlands East Indies.

Agronsky reported that Allied forces would have a "good chance" of holding Java with immediate reinforcements of 1,000 American fighter pilots and planes and half as many bombers.

Agronsky told of seeing a great quantity of war material on the Singapore naval base before he escaped from the conquered British fortress two weeks ago. He said it was "unprotected, undispersed, a perfect target for Jap bombers."

The Australian warship aboard which he left Singapore, Agronsky said, intercepted a large convoy en route to Singapore from England, carrying R. A. F. veterans of the battle of Britain to defend Singapore. Another ship carried planes that the pilots were to fly.

Agronsky asserted with some vehemence that the "Japs are not supermen," and said that Americans at home must realize "exactly what your sons and husbands are fighting against in this part of the world.

Navy To Seek Recruits On Shore

Six towns on the Eastern Shore of Maryland will be visited by a Naval Reserve recruiting party during the week of March 1. Purpose of the visits will be to enlist qualified watermen into the U. S. Naval Reserves in a new classification recently inaugurated by Secretary of the Navy Frank Knox.

The towns to be visited and the dates are: Bishops Head on March 2, Vienna on March 3, Choptank on March 4, Tilghman on March 5, Easton on March 6 and Cambridge on March 7.

Qualified watermen should be between seventeen and fifty years of age and have had experience in bay boats, both power and sail.

In addition to qualified watermen, the recruiting party will interview unmarried college graduates between the ages of nineteen and twenty-seven who would be interested in gaining a commission in the Naval Reserves.

$7,000,000,000 Tax Hearing March 3

WASHINGTON, Feb. 23—(I. N. S.).—Chairman Doughton (Democrat) of North Carolina today announced that public hearings on the long-awaited new $7,000,000,000 tax bill will start before his Ways and Means Committee Tuesday, March 3.

DIRIGIBLE PIONEER DIES

BERLIN (From Official Broadcasts), Feb. 23—(A. P.).—Major August Von Parseval, a pioneer builder of non-rigid dirigibles, died today. He was eighty-one. Many of his famous "sausages" or observation balloons were used in the first World War.

"Hero Of Bataan"—Life Story Of Gen. MacArthur Starts Today -:- See Page 6

Two Oriole Rookies Called 'Minor Gems'

THE BALTIMORE NEWS-POST SPORTS

10 TUESDAY, FEBRUARY 24, 1942

Sports by Bill Corum

Answer to Brooklyn's Rise Is Just One Man, His Name's MacPhail. | *The Baseball Moguls Were Incensed At His Temerity, It Seems.*

AN EASY WAY TO MAKE FRIENDS

NEW YORK, Feb. 23.

It is easy to root for the Brooklyn Dodgers these days. They are a colorful team. They represent perhaps the most enthusiastic baseball community in this country. But there is more to it than that. It didn't just happen that practically the entire nation followed their fortunes last summer.

They have been the Dodgers for many years. They have always played in that same hotbed of diamond fanaticism, Brooklyn. They had won pennants before, and come close to winning them on other occasions.

No, the answer to Brooklyn's pre-eminent position in baseball today is due to one man, and one man only. A man who picked them up off the flat of their backs, when they were a rag-tag, ragamuffin ball team that was the joke of baseball. A team, a club that either couldn't, or wouldn't, bother to paint the seats in their park.

The man's name, as most of you know, is Larry MacPhail.

The whole story of what MacPhail has done for baseball in Brooklyn is too long to bear recounting here. Let's just say that he has in a comparatively short time restored the prestige of the team, of the game, in that community, and, in a sense, of the borough itself.

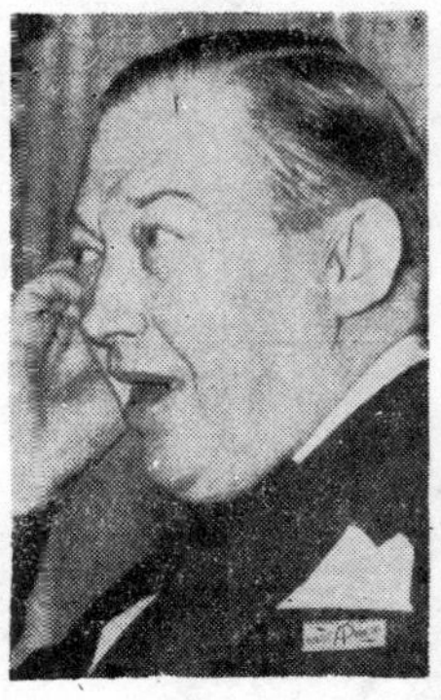

LARRY MacPHAIL

Or, to put it in an even briefer way, let's just say tnat Larry has done the biggest job in baseball since Kenesaw Mountain Landis and Babe Ruth saved the game from oblivion after the Black Sox expose.

How has this not always popular and tactful outlander from Michigan, via Cincinnati, done it?

Well, primarily, by doing something at all times. And sometimes the wrong thing. MacPhail frequently makes mistakes. But he seldom makes big mistakes. And he never makes any mistakes by being hidebound. For whatever else he may or may not be, he simply wouldn't know how to be that.

There is another reason, and one that's important. Unless I am very much in error, MacPhail is closer to his times and to what the public is thinking than any other man in baseball today.

* * *

It Sounded Sensible To Some:

He got up before the Baseball Writers' Dinner a fortnight ago and made a quiet, reasoned and well-documented appeal to the men who run the game. Not the most entertaining talk of the evening—it wasn't meant to be that—but, by every standard, the most constructive.

He spoke from notes. He didn't fly off the handle. He didn't indulge in any flights of fancy. He simply set forth some obvious and sober truths in a convincing way. At least, to some of his listeners it was convincing.

It was with no little surprise, therefore, that at the baseball meetings in the New Yorker on the following day, I heard such comments as these:

"How about that MacPhail spending other people's money!"

"Who does he think he is, Landis?"

And,

"I know at least one club that isn't going to fall for any of his crackpot ideas."

Did I say I heard those things with surprise? That isn't the word. I heard them with astonishment.

Now, I wouldn't say that the Brooklyn redhead doesn't indulge at times in flights of fancy. That he is always the ultimate in conservatism. That he can't be hard-headed and unreasonable.

But if he uttered one word, made one suggestion, in that speech that bordered on the crackpot, I can only hope that I'll always be as crazy as that. The only sins of which he could possibly have been guilty on that occasion were complete frankness and good common sense.

* * *

They Didn't Like It—Or Him:

And yet some of his baseball associates disliked him for it. Or maybe it was that they just disliked him, period.

However, the baseball people sell and the fans buy. I am often wrong and I can be wrong in this. But I am going to be sitting here a long time before I am convinced that the man who yesterday announced on behalf of the Brooklyn ball club that the Dodgers would play one home and one road game (if he could get some other N. L. club to co-operate) game for a service cause hasn't made a host of friends for his team—and for baseball.

A man who went on to add: "I wanted to have our program adopted in collaboration with the entire National League, if not both major leagues and all baseball. I tried to sell the ideas at the recent major league meetings. But since we haven't been able to go ahead on a league basis, I have decided to announce this program for the Dodgers alone."

MacPhail then did go on to announce that the Brooklyn Club would play exhibitions during the training and regular seasons with Army and Navy camp teams, donating the receipts to the camp athletic funds with no deductions for expenses.

That, of course, it would adhere to the decision of the two leagues about all individuals in the organization buying Defense Bonds and Stamps. Also the general policy of admitting service men in uniform without charge.

* * *

Farm Clubs, Too:

He also announced that all the clubs in the Brooklyn farm system would adhere to this same general policy.

I don't know what other major and minor league clubs will do in the matter. For some strange, indeed, almost inexplicable reason, it appears impossible for all baseball to get together in one dramatic and united effort for the country's cause.

But a small loaf is better than none. I still insist that it looks like a simple, even obvious, way to make friends.

When you are rooting 'em home to another pennant next summer, don't forget the name MacPhail. Not that Larry would let you if you tried.

RODGER H. PIPPEN, SPORTS EDITOR IS ON VACATION

His column will be resumed from Florida

Cards Add Arches To Shoes

ST. PETERSBURG, Fla., Feb. 23 (U. P.).—The St. Louis Cardinals, who made baseball history by using vitamin pills last spring, open spring training here today bolstered by 12,000 of the same minute medicinal aids and a flock of new air-foam arch supporters invented by the club trainer.

Manager Billy Southworth limited workouts to one a day for the 17 pitchers and three catchers at Waterfront Park until the remainder of the team arrives March 2. Southworth declared every position on the club was open.

Pitchers Murray Dickson, Harry Brecheen and Henry Novak head an unusually small holdout list. Catcher Ken O'Dea has not signed but plans to confer with Southworth soon.

Newspapermen thought Southworth was joking when he announced that all squad members would wear the new arch support invented by Dr. Harrison Weaver, the trainer. He said the arch support gives amazing buoyancy and said all Cardinal players would wear them both in baseball and civilian shoes.

The Cards play their first exhibition game in St. Petersburg March 6, when they open a nine-game series with the New York Yankees. Many experts regard it as a preview of the 1942 World Series.

Durocher Plans To Stay On Active List

HAVANA, Feb. 23—(U. P.).—Manager Leo Durocher of the Brooklyn Dodgers, weighing 190 pounds and heavier than ever in his major league career, said today that he planned to adhere to an active schedule in order to remain on the regular playing list after May 15.

Durocher was considerably heartened when Rookie First Baseman Lester Burge, up from Atlanta, announced that his draft board had given him a 1-B deferment. He was found unfit for service by his High Point (N. C.) draft board because of his right arm, broken and improperly set when he was a child. Burge, a southpaw, won the Southern Association's most valuable player award in 1941.

Yanks Start Drills Without DiMag, Keller

ST. PETERSBURG, Fla., Feb. 23 (U. P.).—Active spring conditioning work begins for the New York Yankees today and, although a good-sized squad will be on hand, a hefty holdout list will curtail the workouts.

Outfielder Joe DiMaggio, here with his wife and child, is the most prominent holdout. The others include Outfielders Charley Keller and Stan Bordagaray, Infielders Joe Gordon, Red Rolfe, Gerry Priddy and Frank Crosetti, Catcher Bill Dickey and Pitchers Marvin Breuer, Johnny Lindell, Marius Russo, Spud Chandler, Atley Donald, Red Ruffing and Johnny Murphy.

ROVERS LEAD LOOP

NEW YORK, Feb. 23.—The New York Rovers took the Eastern Hockey League lead yesterday by defeating the Washington Eagles, 6 to 3, before 13,500 fans.

Orioles' Home Games Listed

Following are the Orioles' home games for the 1942 International League baseball campaign:

April 16, 17, 18—Rochester.
April 19*, 20, 21, 22—Buffalo.
April 23, 24, 25—Toronto.
April 26*, 27, 28—Montreal.
May 17*, 18, 19—Syracuse.
May 20, 21, 22—Jersey City.
May 23, 24*, 25—Newark.
May 31*—Toronto.
June 1, 2, 3—Toronto.
June 4, 5, 6, 7*—Montreal.
June 8, 9, 10—Buffalo.
June 11, 12, 13—Rochester.
June 29, 30—Newark.
July 1—Newark.
July 2, 3, 4—Syracuse.
July 19*, 20, 21, 22—Buffalo.
July 23, 24, 25, 26*—Rochester.
August 13, 14, 15, 16*—Newark.
August 17, 18, 19—Montreal.
August 20, 21, 22, 23*—Toronto.
September 1, 2, 3, 4—Jersey City.
September 5, 6*, 7—Syracuse.
***Denotes Sunday.**

Cubs' Second Base Pair Tune Up

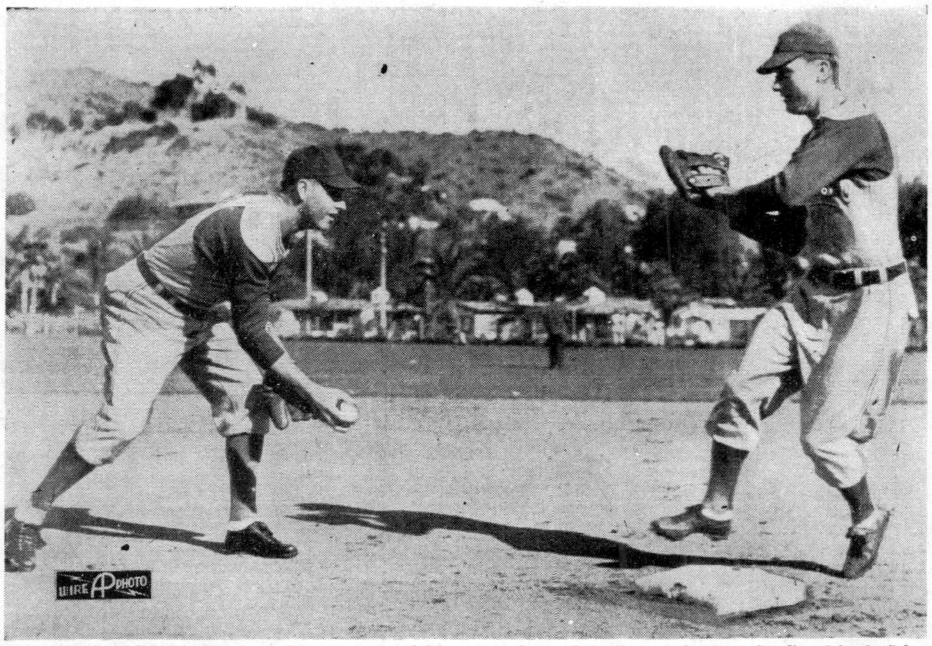

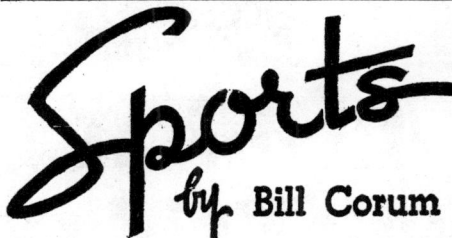

A LITTLE CREAKY—Shortstop Bob Sturgeon (left) and Second Baseman Lou Stringer of the Chicago Cubs heard quite a few creaks in their joints accumulated during the winter layoff when they stepped on the diamond for their first workout at Catalina Island, Cal. But here they are busily working to get the kinks out and build up the old smooth action around the second sack. It was the first real workout since the club's arrival at training camp. Associated Press Wirephoto.

Big Catcher May Oust Kracher

By HUGH TRADER, JR.

Poke Whalen, a baseball man for 25 years, is not an extremist. He seldom goes "overboard" on a ball player; he has to be shown not for 30 ball games but for a season. So, when Poke, who managed Tarboro last year, called up to tell me that the Orioles had two of the finest gems in the minor leagues from that club this story was practically in type.

Catcher Ray Murray of North Carolina and First Baseman Eddie Sudol of New Jersey are the players in question. Each stands over six feet tall and weighs around 200 pounds. Each hit over .300 with Tarboro last summer.

Murray, says Whalen, very likely will stick with the Orioles this year as the second-string man to Joe Becker, ousting "Jug" Kracher. The newcomer is reputed to be a powerful lad, with amazing poise behind the plate for his inexperience and possessor of a strong throwing arm.

ONE MORE YEAR

Sudol, too, will make a real bid for a regular job with the Birds, says Poke, but he probably needs another year in Class A ball. Even now Sudol is a better fielder, with a much better arm than Eddie Robinson, opines Whalen, but the jump from Class D to Double A is pretty stiff for a hitter and Poke believes the kid will profit more with a year of Class A ball under his belt.

Sudol is a line-drive type of hitter, whereas Robinson, the giant Texan who hit .290 with Elmira last summer, gets plenty of distance and figures to benefit greatly by the short fences in Oriole Park. Incidentally, Specs Toporcer insists that Robinson will "go" in Double A competition for the Birds this time. Specs saw Eddie all last summer.

Atlanta, ignorant of the fact that Baltimore had a working agreement with Tarboro, offered $2,000 for Sudol last season and planned to play the youth regularly this year, but the Orioles claimed Sudol as per their agreement to select any two players from Tarboro.

Both Murray and Sudol are right-hand hitters.

TWO OTHERS

Whalen's judgment is good enough for us. A veteran player, scout and manager, Poke picked up George Staller and Sammy Bell and placed them in professional ball and also recommended Wally Cazen to the Flock some years ago. Cazen was anything but a ball o' fire, but he had obvious ability and since has turned in a pretty good minor record. Cazen finished last season with Rochester.

Poke, by the way, is moving to Hornell (N. Y.) this season to manage that club in the Pony League. His club will train in Frederick, where Whalen played ball some 20 years ago.

Meanwhile, at Oriole Park, Prof. A. T. Thomas is up to his ears in training camp plans, contracts, and income tax reports.

"This is tougher to figure out than a batting order," sighs Alphonse.

Gen. MacArthur Is Praised At Sports Dinner

February 23.

Representing practically every sport in the world of athletics and competition, more than 200 famous figures were present last night at the first annual Old Timers' sports dinner and dance at the Emerson Hotel.

Rip Miller, Navy line coach, was toastmaster and the principal tribute of the gathering went to Gen. Douglas MacArthur, who was greatly interested in Amateur Athletic Union activities when he commanded the Third Corps Area here about a decade ago. Lieutenant Colonel James Wharton, one of the guests of honor, praised the commander of the forces at Bataan.

Speakers included Governor O'Conor, Mayor Jackson, Dr. H. C. Byrd, Merwin Jacobson, Joe Tipman, Tommy Thomas, Happy Enright, Bill Schuerholz, Bob Sindall, Dr. Mickey Whitehurst, Ed Brockman, Charley Short and Lieutenant Commander Phil Hambsch.

Governor O'Conor concluded his speech by declaring that sports will play an important role in the war.

"Success on the battlefield will be achieved from success on the baseball field, football, basket ball court and in the ring where our athletes have had their training," he said. "We are going to win this war by sportsmanship and the will to win."

Colorado Cager Eyes Second Title

DENVER, Feb. 23 — (A. P.).—Leason (Pete) McCloud, Colorado's goal shooter, seems a cinch to become the first Big Seven basket ball player to win two scoring championships in successive years.

McCloud not only has a 21-point lead over the field but needs only 22 points in three remaining league games to pass his winning total of 156 last season. He has averaged 15 per game this year.

Mioland, Market Wise Top Widener Choices

MIAMI, Fla., Feb. 23—(A. P.).—The topsy-turvy winter turf season finally has produced a couple of favorites for the $50,000 Widener Handicap March 7.

Mioland and Market Wise came through with week-end performances which stamped them as the ones to beat in the season's richest stake.

At the same time they recaptured some of the prestige lost by the group of outstanding thoroughbreds running at Hialeah Park when other champions and near-champions were badly beaten.

Choosing between the two was enough to make any handicapper scratch his head.

Starting Friday for the first time since last summer, Charles S. Howard's Mioland outfooted a small but select field in a $1,500 overnight conditioning race. Never extended, the five-year-old horse was two lengths ahead of Sir Marlboro.

Mioland, who brought his life's earnings up to $225,550, turned the mile and one-eighth in 1.51⅕—on a sloppy track.

Market Wise, the colt for which Louis Tufano laid out only $500, ran a magnificent race Saturday in whipping a classy field in the $10,000 McLennan Handicap, one of the winter's top stakes.

Running his winnings to $110,990, the "Cinderella horse" sped the mile and an eighth in 1.50⅘—on a surface considerably faster than the strip on which Mioland performed.

Dodds To Start In A. A. U. Mile

BOSTON, Feb. 23—(A. P.).—Gil Dodds, distance-running protege of Jack Ryder, Boston College track coach, said today he would enter the mile event in the National A. A. U. games at Madison Square Garden, New York, this week-end. Dodds' best time in the mile at Ashland College was 4.13.7.

SABIN TRIUMPHS

TAMPA, Fla., Feb. 23—(A. P.).—Wayne Sabin of Portland, Ore., defeated Bruce Barnes of Houston, Texas, 6—4, 6—2, 6—4, to win first Dixie Open tennis title.

Auto Races Called Off

WASHINGTON, Feb. 23—(A. P.). The American Automobile Association announced today that all official automobile racing activities under the sanction of the A. A. A. contest board would be postponed for the duration of the war.

The primary reason, the association said, was the fact that the war effort is vitally in need both of the rubber, fuel and strategic materials used in racing and of the full-time efforts of the highly-skilled young man power represented by the racing fraternity.

"The American Automobile Association will refuse its sanction for any race until world conditions permit a return to normal pursuits," the announcement said.

Pirates' Weather Flag Junked; Too Much Like Japs'

PITTSBURGH, Feb. 23—(I. N. S.).—The Pittsburgh Pirates announced today their traditional weather flag in downtown Pittsburgh would be replaced come the opening of baseball season. It looks too much like the emblem of Japan.

For years the ball club has kept local fans posted on whether a game would be played on a cold or rainy day by flying a big flag on the roof of the First National Bank building. If the flag was at the top of the pole, the game was on.

The banner's design was a red ball centered in a field of white. Too much like the emblem of the Far-Eastern sand-lotters who have been trying to break into the majors by force, decided the Pirate management. A new design will be used in future.

Mangrum's Golf Victory Nets $1,000 Check

NEW ORLEANS, Feb. 23—(A. P.).—Lloyd Mangrum stands second among the leading money winners in the National Professional Golfers Association this year, but he will need some more big winnings before he catches up with Ben Hogan, still far out in front.

Mangrum, who pocketed $1,000 yesterday by winning the New Orleans $5,000 open, now has a total of $3,108 but Hogan leads the field with $5,958, according to figures of Fred Corcoran, manager of the association.

The outstanding feature of Mangrums play in winning the New Orleans event was his chipping. On at least half a dozen occasions he blasted out of trouble and within a few feet of the pin.

"I've spent plenty of time on my chip shots the last couple of months," said the slim Oak Park (Ill.) pro after watching Snead miss a six-foot putt that would have tied him for the lead. "They used to be pretty weak—not accurate at all.

"I changed my stance a bit and practiced on them and now they all act about alike. They pulled me through here all right."

After shooting three straight eighteens of 69, three under par, Mangrum faltered to a 74 on the final round yesterday but it was enough to take first prize from Snead and Little, former national open champion, who were one point behind his 281.

25,214 Women In Bowling Tourney

CHICAGO, Feb. 23—(I. N. S.).—A total of 25,215 entrants will compete in the fourteenth annual Women's Bowling Congress tourney, starting here next Saturday, it was announced today. Detroit leads the out-of-town entries with 78 teams. Milwaukee is second with 41.

GOLFING STAR

Mike Ryba, Red Sox pitcher, is a member of the Hickory Hills C. C. at Springfield, Mo., and shoots golf in the low 80's.

BASEBALL + *Training Camp Notes*

AVALON, Cal., Feb. 23—(A. P.). The total tonnage in the camp of the Chicago Cubs probably doesn't vary much from that of last year, but there was much rejoicing when the outfielder Lou Novikoff showed up lighter and Catcher Clyde McCullough heavier.

Novikoff weighed 189 pounds when he checked in, 14 less than last year, while McCullough is heavier about the chest and shoulders.

TWO WORKOUTS

TAMPA, Fla., Feb. 23—(A. P.).—Two long workouts have been promised the Cincinnati Reds today after a vacation yesterday. Boss Bill McKechnie says he feels that the Reds lost the pennant last year because or poor preparation and isn't going to let it happen again.

ANAHEIM, Cal., Feb. 23—(A. P.). Dick Siebert, the Philadelphia Athletics' holdout first baseman, must play for the Mackmen or not at all.

"I couldn't trade him if I wanted to," Connie Mack asserted. "Sometime ago I sounded out another club, but they didn't want him. Nobody else in the league is interested either."

ROWE UNSIGNED

LAKELAND, Fla., Feb. 23 — (A. P.). — Schoolboy Rowe, who has won 104 games for Detroit since joining the Tigers in 1933, is the only unsigned player in the camp. Rowe says he shouldn't be classed a holdout, although he isn't happy over the salary offered him.

HAVANA, Feb. 23 — (A. P.). — With Don Pagett almost certain to be called up for military duty before the major league season starts, Manager Leo Durocher of the Brooklyn Dodgers is showing a lot of interest in Outfielder Augie Galan, former Chicago Cub, who was purchased from Los Angeles last season.

Galan's chronic leg injury, which hastened his dismissal by the Cubs, has not troubled him this spring.

NATS IN FIRST DRILL

ORLANDO, Fla., Feb. 23—(A. P.). One dozen members of the Washington Senators, all pitchers except Catcher Jake Early, were called together today for the team's first drill. Notably absent was the club's best flinger, Dutch Leonard, who didn't like the salary figures on his contract.

Girl, 16, Breaks U. S. Swim Mark

PORTLAND, Ore., Feb. 23—(A. P.).—Suzanne Zimmerman of Portland's Multnomah Club swimming team was clocked at 5.40.1 for a new 440-yard national junior woman's free-style record. The sixteen-year-old Oregonian, swimming in the Oregon A. A. U. meet, clipped 24.1 seconds from the record set by Rachel Knowles of Portland, Maine, two years ago.

MORGAN LOSES

In a thrilling contest Morgan State College's quintet lost to Virginia State Trojans, 49-45. The Trojans' triumph enabled them to avenge an earlier season's set-back administered by the Bears at Virginia State.

In The Dough

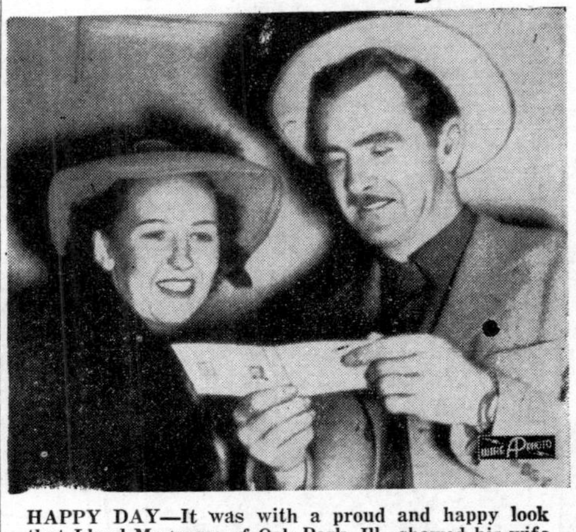

HAPPY DAY—It was with a proud and happy look that Lloyd Mangrum of Oak Park, Ill., showed his wife his score card in the $5,000 New Orleans open golf tournament, which he won for his first prize money of the winter. Mangrum finished with 281, beating out Sam Snead and Lawson Little by one stroke. Associated Press Wirephoto.

The Baltimore News-Post Has the Largest Circulation of Any Evening Newspaper in the South

THE BALTIMORE NEWS-POST
AN INDEPENDENT NEWSPAPER

2ND FRONT PAGE
NEWS-POST HAS TWO FRONT PAGES DAILY

TUESDAY, FEBRUARY 24, 1942

You Must Black Out Even If You Don't Hear Signal Friday

Will Ask Divorce

June Havoc Reported Ready TO FILE FOR DECREE

June Havoc (above) younger sister of the famous Gypsy Rose Lee, is prepared to file for her divorce very soon, Louella Parsons reports from Hollywood. Miss Havoc is married to Don Gibbs.

Youth Killed In Auto Crash

One Marylander was killed Sunday and three Baltimoreans were in hospitals here as a result of automobile accidents, according to police.

The dead person was John Ellis Martin, seventeen, of Ladiesburg, Md., who was killed when his car crashed into a culvert near Midway. He died at the Frederick City Hospital.

LEG BROKEN

Suffering from a broken leg and other bruises, George W. Hettinger, twenty-eight, 400 block East Twenty-sixth street, was at Union Memorial Hospital here. He told police he was struck by a hit-and-run driver at Greenmount avenue and Twenty-ninth street.

Harry Zarkarko, thirty-nine, 1100 block North Port street, also suffered a broken leg when he was struck by an auto which police said was driven by John D. Hoover, Jr., 2900 block Ravenwood avenue. Zarkarko was taken to Johns Hopkins Hospital.

GIRL, 17, HURT

Another casualty was Miss Virginia Blunchard, seventeen, 2400 block Llewelyn avenue, who was taken to Johns Hopkins Hospital suffering from head injuries.

According to police, Miss Blunchard was a passenger in an auto driven by Milton Pardoe, 1100 block Riverside avenue, which collided with another driven by Edgar E. Kirby, 3900 block Edmondson avenue.

Holiday Observed By Continued Work

War plants and Governmental workers in Maryland bent to their tasks here, marking the legal observance of Washington's birthday with work instead of a holiday.

Thousands of workers in industry gave up the holiday, as did employes of all State departments and agencies.

O'CONOR'S APPEAL

An appeal to honor Washington by work in this hour when "**our national situation is so critical and the need for war material so imperative,**" was made last week by Governor O'Conor. He said:

"**I think we can best honor the memory of the father of our country by putting forth redoubled efforts to preserve priceless possessions which have been ours by right of inheritance from George Washington.**"

BANKS CLOSED

Banks were closed by legal regulations that Monday be the legal holiday when the Washington's birthday anniversary falls on Sunday.

The response from industrial plants that work be continued today was wholehearted, O'Conor reported.

Residents Urged To Use Eyes In Friday's Test

Available Alarms To Sound In City, Four Counties

Depend on your eyes instead of your ears to be on time in turning out the lights for next Friday's test blackout.

This advice came today from George A. Carter, chairman of the Baltimore Committee on Civilian Defense, explaining that the test will be by the clock rather than by the signal.

All alarm devices available in Baltimore and the four adjoining counties involved will be sounded, the chairman said, but some areas will not be reached by the sound.

News of the blackout has been and will be spread by press and radio, however, he declared, and all residents are expected to abide by the blackout rules at exactly 9.45 P. M., whether or not they hear an alarm.

LACK BANDS

Although between 7,000 and 8,000 trained air-raid wardens will be on the streets in the city, they probably will not be equipped with armbands, Mr. Carter said, and will not have been assigned to their permanent posts.

Nevertheless, the committee has asked them to be active in their own neighborhoods, observing the effectiveness of the blackout, and reporting violations of the regulations, as well as offering advice.

Civilian defense leaders have no objections to residents going on the streets in an orderly fashion to observe the test, the committee chairman said.

During an actual raid all citizens are urged to stay at home or under shelter for their own protection. However, in this test quiet observation is not frowned upon.

MOTORISTS WARNED

On the other hand, motorists are warned against jamming the streets and are reminded that all cars must be pulled to the curb and all motors and lights must be turned off during the test.

Ambulances, fire engines, and other emergency equipment will be allowed to operate with lights on, Mr. Carter said. The provision does not apply to all holders of emergency cards, however, he added.

Unless there exists a real emergency, use of the cards during the blackout constitutes a violation of the regulations, he declared.

Special Policemen To Attend School

A training school for special policemen who serve in industrial and other organizations engaged in war work got under way today at the Maryland Police Training School, Pikesville. The course, which is being conducted by the State Police Department, will last three weeks and will offer instruction in first aid, criminal law, traffic direction, use of firearms and means of identification.

Sisters Of Charity Aid In War Work Course

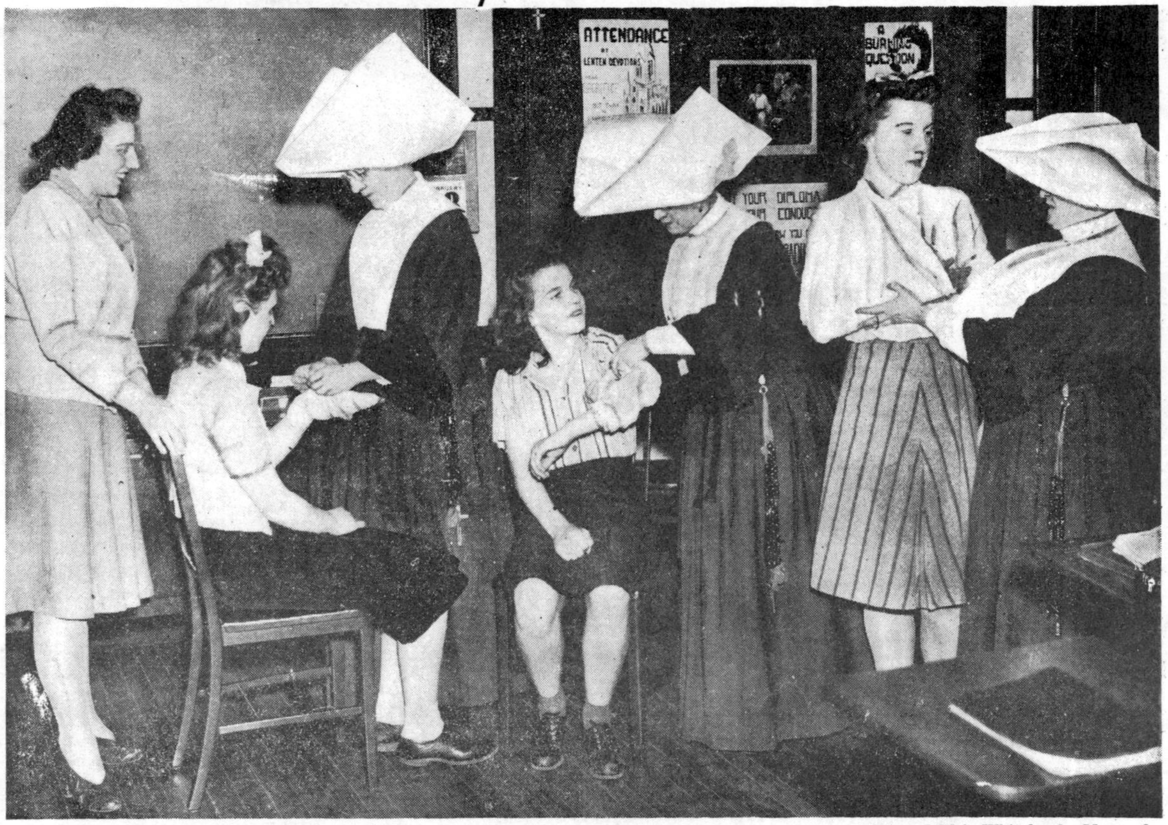

Skilled in hospital work, Sisters of Charity at Seton High School are shown aiding in a course of first-aid in national defense for students at the school under supervision of Miss Clare Willeke (extreme left), a registered nurse representing the American Red Cross. The sisters are bandaging the "victims," Misses Ann Walsky and Alice Horton (seated, left to right) and Elsie Whitehead. Many of the girls at the school are "prepping" for a career in nursing, and all of them are displaying deep interest in the first-aid course.

Over 261,000 On Fund's Aid List

The Baltimore Community Fund served the needs of more than 261,000 persons in Baltimore during 1941, according to the annual service report which had been made public here by James M. Hepbron, fund director.

The thirty-five agencies which were members of the fund last year dispensed food, shelter, clothing, hospitalization, nursing care, or special service to that number of men, women and children, the report revealed.

Among those aided were 36,555 sick children, 2,705 sick adults, 26,137 persons involved in family troubles, and 562 physically handicapped individuals who were provided with work. Jobs were found for an additional 4,483 applicants, Mr. Hepbron announced.

Direct material aid went to 168,138 persons in need, and some form of special health, recreational, welfare, or adjustment service was provided for 83,554 others.

Hatcher's Careers In 2 Services Told

By EARLE POORBAUGH
News-Post Staff Correspondent.

ORDNANCE TRAINING CENTER, Aberdeen, Feb. 23.—Brigadier General Julian S. Hatcher, commanding the Ordnance Training Center here, started out to be a sailor and wound up one of the Army's most distinguished Ordnance experts!

Between the two events is a life time of successes scored in many fields, beginning with General Hatcher's graduation from the United States Naval Academy as an honor student in 1909.

CAREER SWITCHED

Following his graduation General Hatcher served as a naval officer and navigator of a battleship, but in 1910 switched his career to the Army and has served through the successive grades to reach his present position.

Active service on the Mexican Border was followed by periods of service in various Ordnance installations.

With the outbreak of World War I. General Hatcher, then a captain, organized the Army's machine gun school, which trained hundreds of officers and soldiers as machine gun instructors.

HERE IN 1923

Service with the A. E. F. was followed by service with the War Department in Washington and 1923 General Hatcher came to Baltimore as ordnance officer for the Third Corps Area.

Since 1937 General Hatcher has been commanding officer of the Ordnance Training Center, Maryland's second largest troop concentration, and the point at which every ordnance soldier in the Army receives his basic training.

Despite his active military life, General Hatcher has found time to write small arms text books, invent ordnance, become a champion rifle and pistol shot, manage Olympic teams and act as instructor for the Federal Bureau of Investigation.

Mackenzie Gets Headquarters Post

Col. Gabriel T. Mackenzie, former Marylander, today was transferred from Davidson, N. C., to take over the post of assistant inspector general at Third Corps Area Headquarters. Colonel MacKenzie was born at Vale Summit, Md. He was honor graduate of St. John's in the class of 1916, and shortly thereafter was commissioned a second lieutenant. He served overseas with an infantry division during the first World War.

Report Gun In Hand Of Dead Autoist

Police have been investigating the death of John W. Ring, thirty-five, of Arbutus, who was found slumped on the seat of his automobile, which had been parked on Shelbourne road, near Sulphur Springs road Sunday, a bullet wound in his temple and a .38 calibre revolver in his hand, they report. Ring was pronounced dead by Dr. George S. M. Kieffer, assistant medical examiner.

Stay Off Roads In Blackout

A plea that motorists keep off State and county roads during the period of Friday night's test blackout has been made by leaders of the Baltimore County Civilian defense group.

Handling of traffic on the major highways is one of the biggest problems facing defense agencies, it was explained, and both trouble and danger may be avoided if drivers stay at home or wherever they may happen to be at 9.45 P. M.

Because the county leaders want this week's first test to be in the nature of a full-dress rehearsal for an actual raid, these additional suggestions were made:

1. Don't use your telephone during the fifteen-minute test. In an actual raid all facilities would be needed for emergency calls and unnecessary demands would jam the communication system.

2. Behave as nearly as possible as you would if there were an actual raid. Go to your refuge room in your home and stay there. It will give you valuable experience and help you in the future.

3. Give the children the blackout experience so that if an actual raid comes they will have the necessary background and will not be unnecessarily alarmed.

20 Flee Fire In Apartment House

More than twenty dwellers in a four-story apartment house at 1226 North Calvert street were forced to flee Sunday when fire swept the upper two stories. Three alarms were sounded.

One fireman was injured. Joseph Paulus, Engine Company No. 6, was cut on the hand by a piece of slate.

The fire was discovered by a passerby. Mrs. Edward Johns said that she and her daughter, Miss Peggy Johns, who is proprietor of the building, were in the living room on the first floor when a pedestrian called to them that the upper floors were afire.

Aged Man Burns To Death

An elderly man burned to death here when his clothing caught fire as he was burning brush on a lot in the rear of his home in the 5500 block Greenfield avenue.

Police said the victim, John Krach, eighty-six, started running toward his home when he discovered his clothing ablaze and that he collapsed near the yard.

Mrs. Adelaide Krach, a niece, who was ill in bed in the house was attracted by screams of her two children when they saw their grand-uncle's plight.

She ran to the kitchen, filled a bucket with water and extinguished the flames.

A neighborhood physician pronounced Mr. Krach dead.

Speed

When you need a cook, a maid or a laundress don't hesitate—

Call The News-Post and Sunday American Classified at once and insert an ad covering your needs.

This ad brought results the first day.

A-1 EXPERIENCED cook, general helper; references necessary; two in family apartment; small laundry; washing machine. $12.00. Tuxedo 6276.

Phone LExington 0100

Win Cash For News Tips And Amateur Photographs

Do you want money for being alert? The Baltimore News-Post and Sunday American are offering cash prizes each week for news tips and amateur photographs. Total awards of $50 are distributed weekly for news tips, $25 for the best, $10 for the next best and $1 prizes for the next fifteen. For each amateur photograph published $3 will be paid, with special bonuses for outstanding pictures. Spot-news pictures are preferred, but candid camera shots that pull at the heartstrings are acceptable. Avoid pictures of ordinary scenes. Telephone The News-Tip Editor at Lexington 0100 for news tips and rush spot-news photographs in to the Picture Editor.

SKIPPY

By Percy Crosby

2 U. S. WARSHIPS LOST
DEATH TOLL IS HEAVY

BUY DEFENSE STAMPS BONDS

KEEP 'EM FLYING

THE BALTIMORE NEWS-POST

AN INDEPENDENT NEWSPAPER

The Largest Evening Circulation in the Entire South

Entered as second-class matter at Baltimore Postoffice.

NIGHT

Wall St. Opening

VOL. CXL.—NO. 96 | TUESDAY EVENING, FEBRUARY 24, 1942 | PRICE 3 CENTS

JAP SUB SHELLS OIL PLANT IN CALIFORNIA

IN THE NEWS

A Mandate From The People

ALFRED M. LANDON of Kansas, in a recent address at Washington, gave expression to the wartime aspirations of a united nation.

Decrying narrow partisan bickering at this critical time, the former Governor of Kansas declared:

"The first interest of the American people is winning this war as quickly as possible. Woe to the man or group of men that gets in the way of that objective!"

Making it crystal-clear that amidst total war competence in government, rather than party labels, was the issue, Mr. Landon candidly remarked that *"in a time of national emergency such as war, the kind of politics that, because of party, defends incompetence is treason."*

Those are strong words, but these are heroic and critical times, and the need for utter candor cannot be overstated.

While men are risking their lives in outlying posts in the Pacific and on ships and in the air, it is obviously no time for politics as usual.

Now more than ever it is time for our public officials to recall Grover Cleveland's dictum that *"A public office is a public trust."*

A Blueprint For Economy

PRESIDENT ROOSEVELT put squarely up to Congress the task of cutting down the non-military expenditures of the Federal Government.

Congress should accept the challenge and immediately go to work along these lines in accordance with the blueprint drawn up by the Byrd Committee On Non-Essential Expenditures.

In thus coming to the relief of harassed taxpayers, politicians seeking re-election next November will doubtless discover that in 1942—in the slogan of a New York merchant—*"It's smart to be thrifty."*

As Plato once remarked: *"Economy is a source of great revenue."*

In regard to the President's passing the issue to Congress, Senator Byrd aptly remarked that the specific recommendations of his committee would save $1,400,000,000 a year.

Moreover, the Senator from Virginia also directed attention to the fact that an important member of the President's official family, namely, Secretary Henry Morgenthau, Jr., as a member of the Byrd committee, had signed the report which recommended abolition of the National Youth Administration, the Civilian Conservation Corps, reduction of relief and road expenditures and other economies.

If we are to show our maximum strength in this war against the Axis, there must be no boondoggling as usual.

Americanism During An Emergency

SENATOR ARTHUR CAPPER (Republican) of Kansas, in an article contributed to the Hearst newspapers concerning his political credo in a national emergency, makes

Continued on Page 4, Column 1.

Bulletin

WASHINGTON, Feb. 24—(U. P.).—The destroyer Truxton and the naval cargo ship Pollux were lost with heavy loss of life after running aground in a raging gale off the Newfoundland coast, the Navy announced today in a communique.

Roosevelt Warns Of Jap Invasion

(Full text of Roosevelt's warning to America on Page 2.)

WASHINGTON, Feb. 24—(U. P.).—President Roosevelt put Americans on warning today that the United Nations must win the war in the Southwest Pacific or the United States must expect to fight Japanese invaders on California, Oregon and Washington beaches.

As he spoke an Axis submarine was shelling a Goleta (Cal.) refinery.

VISIONS ALASKA ATTACK

On Alaska, too, he said the attack could come if Dutch, Australian and New Zealand bastions fall thousands of miles away.

It was an all-out war alert. But he promised that supplies would keep moving to all United Nations Allies and that the United States would take the offensive—"continue increasingly the policy of carrying the war to the enemy in distant lands and distant waters—as far as possible from our own home grounds."

The President spoke last night to the world with a summons not only for unity at home and among the United Nations, but with a pledge that American men, women and machines will do their part in the common effort to destroy German and Japanese militarism.

AMERICANS IN ORIENT

He revealed for the first time that thousands of American ground troops and fliers today are fighting on the Netherlands East Indies battleground lying between the Pacific Ocean and the China sea on the north and the Indian ocean on the south.

Mr. Roosevelt laid down a three-point program for Americans:

1. No strikes.
2. No special gains, privileges or advantages for any group or occupation.

M'Arthur Troops Open Plane Fund

TOKYO (From Japanese Broadcasts), Feb. 24—(A. P.).—Japanese army bombers caused widespread damage in a series of assaults against United States positions in the Samat mountains of Bataan peninsula during the last two days, Domei reported today in a dispatch from a Japanese Philippine base.

By CLARK LEE

WITH GENERAL MacARTHUR ON THE BATAAN PENINSULA, Feb. 20—(Delayed)—(A. P.).—A "bomber for Bataan" fund has been started among the American-Filipino troops fighting the Japanese on the Bataan peninsula and from Corregidor and other fortified Manila bay islands.

The movement to raise funds to obtain at least one bomber from the United States started spontaneously after the troops had heard a broadcast reporting that production of airplanes by Ford and other American producers was running to astronomical figures.

This slogan was adopted:

"Better buy one bomber than be buried on Bataan."

The campaign still is in its beginning stages but organizers believe that inasmuch as many soldiers have indicated a willingness to contribute up to one month's pay it will be possible also to raise funds for a ship to bring the bomber here plus high war bonuses for the ship's crew and to purchase gasoline and bombs.

Plenty of aviators already are here to fly the bomber.

BRITISH SHIPPING LOSS INCREASED-CHURCHILL

Says Enemy Has 'Waning' Command Of Sea And Air

By CHARLES A. SMITH
International News Service Staff Correspondent.

LONDON, Feb. 24.—Great Britain has suffered "a most serious increase" in shipping losses in the past two months, the enemy has a "waning" command of the sea and air and the empire's margin of safety in the Far East has been "notably" affected, Prime Minister Winston Churchill reported to the House of Commons today.

But, he added, in the course of a long review again defending his captaincy of the war with a new and streamlined Cabinet:

"We have a right to look forward across a good many months of sorrow and suffering to a happy and reasonable prospect of complete and final victory."

NO ROSY PICTURE

Initiating another "full dress" debate at the end of which another vote of confidence in his regime will probably be asked, Churchill made no attempt to paint a rosy picture.

He did, however, intimate closer co-ordination in the Far Eastern theatre by announcing that Chinese Generalissimo Chiang Kai-Shek has accepted an invitation to join the Pacific War Council. Chiang already has been appointed commander of all United Nations forces operating in China.

MAIN POINTS

Here are the main points of his address:

1. Admission that Britain has suffered a heavy increase in shipping losses and that the enemy has temporary but waning command of the sea and air in the Far East.

2. Announcement of Chiang Kai-Shek's participation in the War Council.

3. Disclosure that the Japanese have 26 divisions in the American-British-Dutch-Australian area.

STILL TO COME

4. A warning that "heavy and repeated" blows are still to come, along with "many hard and adverse experiences."

5. A prediction that Germany may go under "in the fourth or fifth year of the war," even though some Nazi-conquered territories still lie under Hitler's thrall.

How Popular Are You? If You Are in Doubt, You Can Find Out Once and For All by Answering a New Questionnaire by Judith T. Chase, Well-Known Quiz Expert, in The American Weekly, the Magazine Distributed With Next Sunday's Baltimore American.—Adv.

Oil Worker Tells How Submarine Shelled Refinery

SANTA BARBARA, Cal., Feb. 24—(I. N. S.).—An eye-witness who saw the enemy submarine rise from the sea and open fire on a shore-line oil field and refinery near Santa Barbara said today that the undersea craft was larger than any United States submarine he had ever seen.

G. O. Brown, oil field worker, told authorities:

"It was so big I thought it might be a destroyer or cruiser.

"I have seen many submarines and this was larger than any of those in the United States Navy that I have seen."

Brown's description of the undersea craft prompted the belief that the vessel might have been one of Japan's giant long-range submarine cruisers.

FEW FIND MARK

The oil field worker said that the submarine shelled the refinery for 20 minutes with few shells finding their mark. Most of the shells exploded against the cliffs, the beach and on open fields.

Several missiles burst in a nearby pasture, Brown said, and two horses in the field raced about in mad frenzy.

Dozens of other persons witnessed the attack from shore. All agreed that the vessel was "as large as any we've seen in pictures."

Lawrence Wheeler reported that

Continued on Page 3, Column 5.

Hours Dispute Slows Ship Work

SAN PEDRO, Cal., Feb. 24—(A. P.).—The day shift, 3,500 members of the C. I. O. Shipyard Workers' Union of America, walked off the job of building $81,000,000 worth of destroyers for the United States Navy after eight hours yesterday. They said Bethlehem Steel Company demanded that they work 10-hour shifts.

Whether 1,500 fellow employes quit the night shift after eight hours or worked 10 was not reported.

Union spokesmen were not available.

Earlier union spokesmen said that the workers were not striking.

They said the men were refusing to work a 10-hour schedule inaugurated two weeks ago by the company. Spokesmen said they would return at their regular times, 7 A. M. and 7 P. M. and work eight hours.

Company officials declined to comment.

WASHINGTON, Feb. 24—(A. P.). War production officials have decided on a promotion campaign to speed America's arms output by making workers feel their importance and responsibility in the war.

It was learned that the program awaits only the nod from President Roosevelt.

It was understood the program has received aproval of high labor quarters.

The Baltimore News-Post today is printed in

3 Sections

Be sure you get the complete newspaper.

Temperatures

12 Midn't,	33	6 A. M.,	28
1 A. M.,	33	7 A. M.,	28
2 A. M.,	32	8 A. M.,	28
3 A. M.,	31	9 A. M.,	28
4 A. M.,	30	10 A. M.,	29
5 A. M.,	29	11 A. M.,	30

THE WEATHER

Moderate cold followed by snow or rain today and early tonight. Moderate to fresh winds.

No Casualties, Damage Slight; Army And Navy Hunting Enemy Craft

WASHINGTON, Feb. 24—(A. P.).—The War Department announced today that Army and Navy aircraft and surface vessels have started a search for the enemy submarine which shelled the Bankline oil refinery near Santa Barbara, Cal., last night.

The Department's communiqued sai damage from the shelling was slight and no casualties were reported. The submarine, apparently Japanese, fired 25 rounds of five-inch shells at the refinery, the Department said.

In the Philippine fighting, the Department said, there was no ground activity on either side in the last 24 hours, but enemy aircraft dropped a number of incendiary bombs.

SANTA BARBARA, Cal., Feb. 14—(I. N. S.).—For the first time since World War I. continental United States had felt the impact of enemy gunfire today.

A huge Axis submarine rose a mile off shore at the very instant President Roosevelt was speaking to the nation last night and poured approximately 15 shells from a four or five-inch deck gun at oil fields, refineries and storage tanks at Goleta, seven miles north of Santa Barbara.

Obviously timed to coincide with the President's talk, the shelling did little damage and caused no casualties.

Only one of the shots took effect, and an eye-witness account issued by the Navy indicated that the effect was slight. It hit a derrick and, according to F. W. Borden, superintendent of the oil field, caused only minor damage to the pumping equipment and derrick.

Reports of flashing lights offshore and in the hills behind Montecito indicated possible fifth column

Continued on Page 2, Column 7.

Jap Planes Raid Wide Java Area

ALLIED HEADQUARTERS, Java, Feb. 24—(U. P.). Japanese planes attacked savagely over a wide area of Java today, hurling demolition bombs on key objectives and machine-gunning the streets of towns, but Allied planes shot down at least one of the enemy craft and damaged others.

Ten enemy planes attacked an airport near Bandoeng, in the interior, and an air base near Malang, toward the eastern end of the island, which is an acute danger spot because Japanese invasion forces were consolidating position in Bali, only one mile from Java across a shallow strait.

MACHINE-GUN STREETS

A Netherlands Indies High Command communique, announcing the Japanese attacks, said that some of the Japanese planes swept down to machine-gun streets of Bandoeng, but succeeded only in damaging a few automobiles and wounding some civilians.

Dutch anti-aircraft guns roared in a heavy fire against the Japanese planes and Allied aircraft, rising to the attack, sent them fleeing as one crashed to earth.

As the Japanese intensified their aerial attacks, Netherlands East Indies officials received orders to stick to their posts in any emergency.

PREPARE FOR ATTACK

This key island of the Netherlands Indies was prepared at any hour for a direct attack by Japanese invasion forces which were driving through Sumatra and Bali to west and east.

"Hero Of Bataan"—Life Story Of Gen. Douglas MacArthur -:- -:- See Page 6

GEN. M'ARTHUR IN AUSTRALIA

Placed In Supreme Allied Command

By JOSEPH A. BORS, International News Service Staff Correspondent.

WASHINGTON, March 17.——In the most electrifying news of the war, the War Department announced today that the redoubtable Gen. Douglas MacArthur has arrived in Australia from the Philippines to become supreme commander in that area for the forces of the United Nations. He was accompanied by Mrs. MacArthur and son, by his chief of staff, Maj. Gen. Richard K Sutherland, Brigadier General Harold H. George of the Air Corps and several other staff officers. Although he was ordered by President Roosevelt to transfer his headquarters from the Philippines o February 22, the War Department sai that the American general, at his own r quest, delayed the move until he cou perfect arrangements for his successo on Bataan peninsula.

Announcement was made by the War De partment in a communique. It followed by les than twelve hours official disclosure of the land ing of an American expeditionary force in Aus tralia.

The War Department declared that the A. E. F. that arrived there was a force of "considerable" size, composed both of air and ground units.

The movement of American troops to the land Down Under followed reports that the United Nations are preparing to launch an offensive against Japan from that continent. After more than three months of reverses in the Pacific, it was apparent that Mac Arthur has now been called upon to turn the tide.

No details were offered beyond the fact that the hero of Bataan and his aides arrived at an undisclosed Australian point by plane.

The communique said:

"He will be the supreme commander in that region, including the Philippine Islands, in accordance with the request of the Australian Government."

SMASHED JAP MOTOR CONVOY

The announcement explained, in part, the lack of news from the Philippine area during the past 10 days.

Although the War Department was silent as to the name of the man who will now be in active com mand of the American-Filipino forces on Bataan, it was noted that yesterday, on the occasion of the one hundred and fortieth anniversary of the founding of West Point, the greeting which the Philippine Army cabled to officials at the U. S. Military Academy was signed by Major General Jonathan M. Wainwright of MacArthur's staff.

There has been no news from Bataan since MacArthu

Continued on Page 2, Column 1.

IN THE NEWS

THIS is not an article of criticism or complaint.

It is an article calling for calm and unbiased consideration of a national emergency—consideration free from all prejudice or partisanship.

Apparently our Government is engaged in piling up catastrophe upon catastrophe in this war.

The reason for these disasters should be determined as early and as clearly as possible, and the fault, whatever it is, should be corrected as promptly as possible.

The plight that the United States is in is made manifest by the naval battle of Java.

We had ships in that battle, but in insufficient numbers to be effective; so nothing of benefit was accomplished.

Our ships were destroyed, along with the Dutch ships—our Navy further weakened and nothing gained.

THE Java situation is but an example of our universal naval and military condition.

We have ships scattered in every section of the globe—everywhere subject to attack and destruction—nowhere in sufficient numbers to constitute an effective striking force.

Our armies are as scattered as our ships.

The dispatches bring news of an American army landing in Ireland—of American forces freezing in Iceland—of American troops parading in London—of American forces arriving in Australia, and of 10,000 North American troops being sent from Rio de Janeiro on the Queen Mary transport, apparently headed for Africa.

The publication of these facts and others like them has been allowed by the war censors, so the information is presumably accurate.

THEN we are informed from official sources, which must be reliable, that our ships at Java were under the command at sea of the Dutch Rear Admiral Deoorman and under the supreme command of the Dutch Vice-Admiral Helfrich.

These Dutch commanders led our ships, together with their own, into a trap—a bottleneck—between the islands of Borneo on the north and Java on the south, where the Allied war vessels were torpedoed by submarines if they remained stationary and destroyed by gunfire if they attempted to escape.

The following significant paragraphs from the official joint British-American report of the battle summarizes the concluding events of the engagement vividly:

"WITH the enemy in command of sea and air north of Java in overwhelming force, the Allied command was faced with the problem of extricating the remaining Allied ships from a very dangerous situation.

"The way to Australia was barred by the 600-mile-long Island of Java with the straits at either end of it under enemy control.

"During the night a report from H. M. A. S. Perth was received which indicated that she and U. S. S. Houston had

Continued on Page 4, Column 1.

British Open Drive On Foe At Rhodes

LONDON, March 1—(U. P.)—A big-scale surprise attack by British naval and air forces on the Eastern Mediterranean Island of Rhodes was believed today to have disrupted Axis plans for a possible spring offensive in the Near East.

Heavy damage was inflicted on the big Rhodes Island base, off the Turkish coast, during the perfectly timed and co-ordinated air and sea bombardment which dispatches said lit up the target "like a Christmas tree" as hundreds of shells and bombs found their mark.

ACKNOWLEDGE ATTACKS

(BACKGROUND NOTE: Axis propaganda broadcasts, acknowledging the attacks, said also that the British planes had bombed Turkish Asia Minor, including the town of Milas, and that the Turkish Government ordered an inquiry.)

The importance of the British attack on Rhodes was emphasized by recent reports from the Middle East that Hitler might attempt to strike through Syria or Turkey toward the Russian Caucasus oil fields and the oil fields of the Near East in an effort to join forces with Japan in India.

STRONGLY FORTIFIED

Since the Axis seizure of Greece, Hitler has controlled all of the island chain stretching along the Turkish coast and Italian Rhodes has been one of the most logical bases for a possible push toward Cyprus and Syria, some 430 miles to the East.

The island has been strongly fortified by Italy and frequently has been attacked by the British since the war started.

REJECTED TWICE, ACCEPTED

TAPPAHANNOCK, Va., March 17—(A. P.).—Rejected once by the Army and once by the Navy, Arnold Motley now has been accepted by the Army for service.

VERY LATEST NEWS

U. S. SHIP TORPEDOED OFF ATLANTIC COAST

WASHINGTON, March 17—(A. P.).—The Navy announced today that a "medium-sized" United States merchant vessel had been torpedoed off the Atlantic coast.

Baltimore NEWS-POST

AN INDEPENDENT NEWSPAPER

The Largest Evening Circulation in the Entire South

Entered as second-class matter at Baltimore Postoffice

VOL. CXL.—NO. 114   TUESDAY EVENING, MARCH 17, 1942   PRICE 3 CENTS

HOME FINAL

Some Famous Americans Arrive 'Down Under'

GENERAL MacARTHUR — War Department communique announcing arrival of Gen. Douglas MacArthur in Australia, said the new supreme commander of the United Nations' forces in that region was accompanied on plane trip from the Philippines by Mrs. MacArthur and their four-year-old son Arthur. Mrs. MacArthur insisted on remaining in the islands when hostilities appeared imminent and other Army families returned to the United States.

MRS. DOUGLAS MacARTHUR

ARTHUR MacARTHUR

Wife, Son On Trip With MacArthur

WASHINGTON, March 17—(I. N. S.).—Sharing the perils of a soldier's life, Mrs. Douglas MacArthur and her four-year-old son arrived in Australia by plane today with the distinguished head of their family.

While details of the flight from Bataan were not disclosed the War Department's announcement that Gen. Douglas MacArthur and his family have arrived in Australia indicated that Mrs. MacArthur and their young son have been under fire since the start of the war.

The former Jean Faircloth of Murfreesboro, Tenn., married the

Continued on Page 2, Column 3.

Temperatures

12 Midn't,	41	7 A. M.,	43
1 A. M.,	42	8 A. M.,	43
2 A. M.,	42	9 A. M.,	45
3 A. M.,	42	10 A. M.,	49
4 A. M.,	42	11 A. M.,	50
5 A. M.,	42	12 Noon,	51
6 A. M.,	42	1 P. M.,	53

THE WEATHER

Baltimore and vicinity, moderate temperature tonight and no rain. Fresh winds.

Detailed Weather Report on Page 22

Mystery of the Nameless Lady and the Unknown Giant. Another Recollection of Famous Crimes that Baffled Us in the Past and Challenged Our Best Detective Genius, Written By Joseph Gollomb, for The American Weekly, the Magazine Distributed With Next Sunday's Baltimore American.—Adv.

Says Nazis May Move On Iceland

LONDON, March 17—(A. P.).—Closing by German authorities of all Norwegian ports from North Cape to Aalesund, a responsible source said today, makes "it appear ominously as though the Nazis are getting ready either for an assault on American-British supply lines to Russia or a move against Iceland."

The source cited these other German naval and military moves as indicating the likelihood of a new major campaign in the North.

Today's announcement by the Nazi High Command of intensified fighting in Lapland, extreme northern area which at the Russian frontier is only 50 miles from the Soviet Arctic supply base of Murmansk.

SEND REINFORCEMENTS

Authoritative information that the Germans have sent strong reinforcements to their Norwegian garrisons.

Massing of Nazi warships at Trondheim, including the Tirpitz, newest, biggest and most dangerous of Germany's battleships.

This source said the Germans now are believed to have "between 150,000 and 200,000 soldiers in Norway, in comparison with the 100,000 reported there last autumn.

TIRPITZ MAY BE LOOSE

Britain already had been warned that the Tirpitz now may be loose on the high seas.

The announcement by a British source that the powerful warshi "appears to have avoided" an aer torpedo attack dashed British that naval planes had knocked out of the war, at least for a while, near the Norwegian port of Narv eight days ago.

He said he had no informatic about the present whereabouts the Tirpitz, sistership of the toug Bismarck which sank the Britis battle cruiser Hood single-hande and, in turn, was sunk when heav British air and sea forces cornere her and pounded her to pieces la May 27.

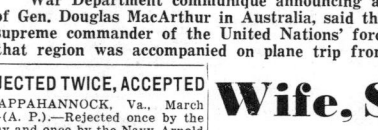

WAR SHADOW FAILS TO DIM BRILLIANCE OF OPERA AUDIENCE

MISS MARY RAMSEY   **MRS. W. W. LANAHAN**   **MISS PEGGY McCORMACK**   **MISS MARTHA CROSS**   **MISS THELMA MORELES**   **ENSIGN RALPH POPE**   **MRS. GEORGE CARTER**

Shadow of war, which may make this Baltimore's last Metropolitan Opera season until peace is achieved, failed to dim last night's brilliant audience at the Lyric, where Mozart's "The Magic Flute" was sung. There were fewer top hats and tails and more khaki and blue uniforms, but the spirit of the operagoers soared to meet the challenge of the music. Besides the leaders in Baltimore's social life, many guests from out of town were in the boxes. Miss Martha Cross, for instance, seated in the box with Miss McCormack in the picture above, is from New York, and Miss Moreles' home is in Panama. Tonight the Lyric will ring with the notes of Bizet's "Carmen," and the season will close tomorrow night with Verdi's "La Traviata."

Call By May Looms For Those In 3d Draft

No Calls, Please!

Officials at Selective Service Headquarters today requested registrants in the new draft not to telephone local boards in order to learn serial numbers. If a registrant desires to obtain his number he should go to his local board, it was advised.

Eligible Marylanders in the third draft whose numbers are among the first drawn in the lottery tonight in Washington may be called for duty in the armed forces by the latter part of May.

This was revealed today at Selective Service Headquarters in the Fifth Regiment Armory, where it was explained the list of A-1 men at several boards is at a low figure.

On the other hand quite a few of the boards still have a "fairly good supply" of 1-A men, according to Lieut.-Col. Henry C. Stanwood, State Director of Selective Service.

FACE DUTY CALL

Men for the 20-44 age group who registered in February will be called for duty as soon as the supply of 1-A men from the first two registrations is exhausted in the various board areas.

It has been estimated that between 140,000 and 145,000 Marylanders registered in the third draft.

FOR OLDER MEN

Men in the new lottery will receive questionnaires about May 15.

Local boards have been crowded for the past few days with men seeking to learn their serial numbers, which are to be contained in the capsules drawn tonight to establish order numbers.

National Selective Service Headquarters announced that thousands of men would be inducted through the new draft.

Older men will be assigned to jobs making less physical demand than those to which young men will be given if was explained.

The Army's new rehabilitation program is expected to make a number of men in the first two drafts eligible for service.

These men were formerly disqualified for physical reasons.

BALTIMORE — THE NEWS-POST

The News-Post Has the Largest Circulation of Any Evening Newspaper in the South

2ND FRONT PAGE — NEWS-POST HAS TWO FRONT PAGES DAILY

TUESDAY EVENING, MARCH 17, 1942   13

Council Studies Night Parking

Right Of Way For Ferry Offered

An offer by William Labrot to deed to the State a right of way through his property near Sandy Point, Anne Arundel county, was announced today by W. T. Emory, who for years has been an advocate of the short route to the Eastern Shore.

Not only will Mr. Labrot permit the State to build a highway through his property, but in addition he will give 1,400 feet of bay front for construction of a Western Shore terminal for the ferry boats, Mr. Emory said.

PROPERTY OWNER

Mr. Emory, who owns the Log Inn property near Sandy Point, said:

"I believe the State is making a mistake in locating the Western

Continued on Page 14, Column 2

Proposed Route

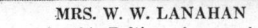

This map of that portion of Chesapeake bay between Sandy Point and Kent Island shows the so-called "short route" which has been urged for the bay ferry line, and the route proposed by the State. William Labrot, owner of the property in the St. Margaret's area of Anne Arundel county, has offered a right of way over his property if the State will establish the "short route."

Seek To Prevent Gas Ration Cards

Gasoline dealers of Baltimore were to hold a meeting tonight as the first step in a move designed to stave off the need for issuing fuel ration cards for motorists.

The meeting, to be held in the Sears Community Hall, North avenue and Harford road, at 8 P. M., was called by the Retail Gasoline Dealers' Association of Baltimore.

It was expected that virtually all of the 800 retail outlets for gasoline in the city will be represented at the meeting.

VOLUNTARY MOVE

Explaining the purposes of the meeting, Lawrence Saffner, secretary of the association, said today:

"As we understand it, Washington is planning to limit gasoline sales to seven gallons per week for the average user. To establish such a limit, ration cards would be needed, and are under consideration.

"Now, we feel that ration cards are a headache to everyone.

"They would involve a lot of bookkeeping and red tape for the retail dealer, the distributor, the wholesaler and for all involved, including the motorist. If the dealers can sell the consumer on the idea of voluntary rationing—that is, on the idea of using less gasoline—we will be avoiding a lot of trouble and bookkeeping for everybody involved."

SUNDAY CLOSING

The matter of all-day closing on Sunday for all dealers will be discussed, also the matter of night closing—from 7 P. M. to 7 A. M.—Mr. Saffner said.

Speakers at the meeting will include Wallace L. Braun, traffic consultant of the Police Department; W. G. Ewald of the Baltimore Association of Commerce, and a representative of the Department of the Interior, John Abbott, president of the Gasoline Dealers' Association, will preside.

TODAY'S TIDES
High tide.......7.54 A. M., 8.22 P. M.
Low tide........2.03 A. M., 2.29 P. M.

Fire Department, Police Protest Measure

Proposed amendments to an ordinance which would permit night parking of automobiles on the city streets will be studied in a meeting of the police and jail committee of the City Council at 2 P. M. next Monday.

The amendments were suggested after the committee yesterday heard protests against passage of the ordinance by the Police and Fire Departments, civic groups and garage owners.

Wallace L. Braun, traffic consultant of the Police Department, told the committee that night parking would increase accidents, facilitate car and accessory theft, and in some instances block streets so that fire and other emergency apparatus could not move.

VIEW SUPPORTED

These views were supported by Capt. Henry C. Kaste, head of the Police Traffic Department; George T. Evans, president of the Board of

Continued on Page 14, Column 2

Gala Throng Hears Metropolitan At Lyric

(A REVIEW OF "THE MAGIC FLUTE" APPEARS ON PAGE 14.)

By Billy Bachelor

Last night we were very proud of our fellow-citizen definitely. Not only did fine feathers make fine birds, to the physical eye, in the true sense of the proverb, but according to the perceptive ear, everyone seemed to understand what "the Magic Flute" was all about.

Which proved that some home work had been accomplished, aside from a pleasing concentration on chiffons, silks and laces—on broadcloth and fine linen, which was liberally contrasted with the impressive insignia of the services.

"They" are saying that white tie and tails are no longer obligatory for the opera, but our people are conservative, and prefer "correct form," regardless of passing fancies. And the distaff side did more than credit to their escorts.

Glitter and glamour were synonymous. Mrs. Alexander Duncan wore white crepe studded with rhinestones with a slim skirt slit for walking and lined with a touch of scarlet. Mrs. Robert Stanton in black, also stepped out in a skirt lined with scarlet and had a broad band of scarlet glittering in black sequins inserted in her bodice and sleeves.

Black also was chosen by Mrs. Alexander Gordon, who accented her costume with a tiny bandeau across her forehead, and Mrs. W. W. Abell who looked lovely in a severe crepe gown adorned by a string of pearls. Mrs. Thomas Waxter was dramatic in a full, black skirt and bodice of black and white striped velvet.

Velvet, likewise, was the material for Mrs. George Carter's gorgeous princess gown of dusty pink with off-the-shoulder large rouching of multi-colored shades of pink net.

Rosa Ponselle Jackson, Baltimore's "first lady" of the opera, allurlngly costumed in a Valentina creation of black lace and chiffon panels, was escorted by her husband, Carle Jackson and Glenn L. Martin, both in full dress and opera hats.

Mrs. Harold Randolph, guest of honor in Frederick Huber's box with Raquel Jobin, who will sing the tenor role in "Carmen" tonight, was lovely in black velvet with a scarf tied in the bodice.

With gorgeous fur cape atop a lame gown, Mrs. Howard Jackson, accompanied by the Mayor, was in full evening regalia, as were Governor and Mrs. O'Conor—she smartly turned out in an embroidered silver gray wrap over a chartreuse gown accented by an orchid corsage.

Mrs. Archibald MacBride Smart In Blue Grey Crepe Gown

Mrs. Archibald MacBride was smart in blue grey crepe embroidered in smoky pearls and glittering silver beads. Mrs. Walter Wickes also chose blue, as did Mrs. George Carey.

Mrs. S. Johnson Poe was costumed in black with a large appliqued bouquet of red roses on her bodice. Mrs. Walter C. Dorsey topped her sequin-trimmed black gown with a matching scarf.

Brilliant blue satin was the

Continued on Page 7, Column 1

PEDIGREED PEP!

Green Spring GOLDEN GUERNSEY Milk might well be called liquid pep with a pedigree. The cows from which it comes are all pure-bred Guernseys—and the superior quality of this ultra-rich milk gives it an abundance of energizing food value. Phone today for delivery tomorrow.

UNiversity 4477

GREEN SPRING DAIRY
1020 West Forty-First Street

Win Cash For News Tips And Amateur Photographs

Do you want money for being alert? The Baltimore News-Post and Sunday American are offering cash prizes each week for news tips and amateur photographs. Total awards of $50 are distributed weekly for news tips, $25 for the best, $10 for the next best and $1 prizes for the next fifteen. For each amateur photograph published $3 will be paid, with special bonuses for outstanding pictures. Spot-news pictures are preferred, but candid camera shots that pull at the heartstrings are acceptable. Avoid pictures of ordinary scenes. Telephone The News-Tip Editor at Lexington 0100 for news tips and rush spot-news photographs in to the Picture Editor.

BOOGIE WOOGIE
By Michael Berry

ICE CARNIVAL!
Cast of 100—Beautiful Girls! Comedians! Olympic Stars and National Skating Champions!
Tickets Now On Fri., Sat., Sun. Sale at Carlin's
ICELAND
MARCH 20, 21, 22
HIT SHOW

WINGS DEFEAT ORIOLES, 12-6

Devilty Takes Sixth At Havre

For VICTORY BUY UNITED STATES DEFENSE BONDS STAMPS

THE BALTIMORE NEWS-POST

AN INDEPENDENT NEWSPAPER

The Largest Evening Circulation in the Entire South

10

VOL. CXL.—NO. 140 Entered as second-class matter at Baltimore Postoffice. THURSDAY EVENING, APRIL 16, 1942 PRICE 3 CENTS

Laval Forms New Government

WOMEN IN NAVAL RESERVE

IN THE NEWS

Mr. Sigmund Janas, President, Canadian Colonial Airways, Inc.

Mr. Dear Mr. Janas:

I READ your letter to the Canadian *Financial Post* with much interest and appreciation.

You are absolutely right about my attitude towards Mr. Churchill.

I do not dislike him at all personally. On the contrary, I like him very much.

He has visited at my house at San Simeon for weeks. I have visited him in England.

I have always found him a genial and most agreeable gentleman, with a keen sense of humor and many other delightful qualities.

I only hope that he retains half the happy remembrance of me that I have of him.

I also think that Mr. Churchill is a very pleasing and persuasive speaker and a very able writer.

All this I have repeatedly said and sincerely mean.

What I do not admire are the things that Mr. Churchill is doing, or rather not doing, as Premier of England, to win this war, or rather not to win this war.

I could keep quiet about this vital matter, but should I do so? Mr. Churchill is a public man, legitimately open (in regard to his acts) to public comment and criticism.

I am an editor of a public press supposed in the honest exercise of my journalistic functions to discuss public questions and comment upon the public acts of public men.

Would I be behaving honorably if I subordinated my public duty to my personal attachments and my social contacts?

Should I not be, indeed, especially alert to the public interest and non-personal in my attitude in this time of national danger?

I certainly have never exceeded the limitations of strict parliamentary privilege and procedure in my comment upon Mr. Churchill's war acts.

I could properly have said as much on the floor of the House of Commons if I had the honor to be a member of the British Parliament.

And as much and more has

Continued on Page 4, Column 1.

Laval Takes Over, Unrest Flares

VICHY, France, April 16—(A. P.).—The present cabinet will have its "last" meeting tomorrow just before the new Government headed by Pierre Laval takes over, it was announced officially tonight.

BERN, Switzerland, April 16—(A. P.).—Pierre Laval, advocate of aid to the Axis, took over actual rule of beaten France tonight as "chief of the Government" while reports of rising unrest and violence filtered in from Paris, the German-held capital.

Reports of Paris demonstrations ag[illegible] the trend of events of the past few days were associated with word of a train wreck near Normandie in which 35 German soldiers were killed.

Authoritative advices from Vichy said that Laval, foremost French exponent of co-operation with Adolf Hitler completed formation of a new Government there tonight, himself becoming "chief of the Government." Under the aged Marshal Petain as Chief of State.

French Ambassador To Pay 'Visit' In D. C.

WASHINGTON, April 16—(A. P.) French Ambassador Henry-Haye arranged today to call at the State Department (at 6 P. M., E. W. T.), and speculation about his purpose included the thought that he might be bringing a declaration of Vichy France solidarity with Hitler's "new order."

Already United States relations

Continued on Page 2, Column 6.

Rochester Beats Birds, 12 To 6

At Baltimore—		R.	H.	E.
Rochester	271 002 000	12	14	0
Baltimore.	111 003 000	6	12	0

Batteries—Hutchinson and Narron; Roche and Becker.

By HUGH TRADER, JR.

ORIOLE PARK, April 16.—Although featuring a triple play started by Bob Lemon and two home-run smashes by Hank Edwards, the Orioles were trailing Rochester by a 10-to-3 score at the end of five innings of their 1942 International League inaugural here this afternoon.

A crowd of about 7,500 fans, in-

Continued on Page 36, Column 3.

Baseball

American League

At Washington—		R.	H.	E.
New York	001 229 0			
Wash. . . .	111 101			

Batteries—Gomez and Dickey; Wilson and Evans.

At Boston—		R.	H.	E.
Phila. . . .	010 000 300	4	7	1
Boston. . .	201 234 25x	19	21	1

Batteries—Caligiuri and Hayes; Wagner and Conroy.

At Detroit—		R.	H.	E.
Cleveland.	101 001 100	4	8	1
Detroit . .	020 020 01x	5	0	3

Batteries—Milnar and Denning; Bridges and Tebbetts.

At Chicago—		R.	H.	E.
St. Louis.	220 11			
Chicago . .	030 0			

Batteries—Galehouse and Ferrell; Dietrich and Tresh.

National League

At New York—		R.	H.	E.
Brooklyn.	100 010 00			
New York	100 009 10			

Batteries — Head and Owen; Koslo and Danning.

At Cincinnati—		R.	H.	E.
Pittsburgh	030 400			
Cincinnati	032 010			

Batteries—Hamlin and Lopez; Thompson and Hemsley.

At Philadelphia—		R.	H.	E.
Boston. . .	010 000 0001	2	5	1
Phila. . . .	000 000 0010	1	6	0

Batteries—Earley and Lombardi; Hughes and Livingston.

At St. Louis—		R.	H.	E.
Chicago . .	041			
St. Louis.	22			

Batteries—Erickson and McCullough; White and W. Cooper.

International League

At Newark—		R.	H.	E.
Buffalo . .	000 001 12			
Newark. .	100 001 10			

Batteries — Roscoe and Garbark; Gerheauser and Padden.

At Jersey City—		R.	H.	E.
Montreal.	001 100			
Jer. City. .	000 000			

Batteries—Macon and Franks; Coombs and Poland.

At Syracuse—		R.	H.	E.
Toronto. .	102 000 010	4	7	1
Syracuse.	101 200 10x	5	8	0

Batteries—Drake and Fernandes; Barrett and Hartje.

LILLARD HITS HOMER FOR ROCHESTER

Gene Lillard, third baseman of the Red Wings, is shown just after he crashed out a homer in the first inning of the Rochester-Oriole game at Oriole Park. Gene is being congratulated on his feat. Rabe scored ahead of the hard-hitting visitor as the Wings took an early lead never to relinquish it in the season's opener.

Periscope Of Submarine Shot Off

WASHINGTON, April 16—(A.P.). Legislation to create a women's auxiliary reserve in the Navy to release thousands of men for sea-going service was passed today by the House on voice vote. Under the terms of the bill, the "petticoat branch" of the Navy would be open to any woman over the age of twenty. The House previously passed a bill, now in the Senate, to establish a woman's Army auxiliary corps.

(Picture on Page 3)

Special to The News-Post.

NEW YORK, April 16.—Three Baltimore seamen today told how the machine-gun crew aboard a United States merchantman shot off one of the periscopes of an attacking submarine before the ship was sunk by two torpedoes from the undersea craft.

The Baltimoreans were Richard Bennett, thirty-four; William Olson, forty-four, and John K. Shauck, forty. They described the ship's sinking at the Third Naval District Headquarters.

Olson, who was chief engineer on the vessel, lives in the 100 block Eleventh avenue, Brooklyn Park. He holds a commission of ensign in the Naval reserves. During the first World War he

Continued on Page 2, Column 5.

Dutch Accept Gen. MacArthur

LONDON, April 16—(U. P.).—The Netherlands Government of Queen Wilhelmina has formally accepted Gen. Douglas MacArthur as United Nations commander in chief in the Southwest Pacific, it was announced officially tonight.

Daily Double (La Reigh / Free Double) Paid $47.80

HAVRE DE GRACE CHARTS

Copyright, 1942, by Triangle Publications, Inc. (Daily Racing Form.)

TRACK FAST.

FIRST RACE—FOUR AND ONE-HALF FURLONGS. FOR TWO-YEAR-OLDS. Maidens. Fillies. Special Weights. Purse $1,200. Value to winner $850, second $200, third $100, fourth $50. Went to post at 2.31. Off at 2.31½. Start good from gate. Won driving, place same. Winner ch f 2, by Count Gallahad-Risque Reigh. Owned by A. PELLETERI. Trained by W. BOOTH. Time 23 3-5, 47 3-5, 53 4-5.

	Wt.	Post	St.	¼	Str.	Fin.	Jockeys	Odds
La Reigh	116	2	3	6^{1}	2^{1}½	1^{1}½	L. Haas	$2.70
Milk Chocolate	116	4	1	1^{4}	1^{2}	2^{5}	P. Roberts	6.25
Can Time	116	10	6	3½	4^{1}½	3^{1}½	K. McCombs	30.55
Sticky Kitty	116	7	9	2^{h}	3^{1}	4^{4}	J. Harrell	3.60
Puritan Maid	116	11	11	4^{h}	5^{1}	5^{h}	J. Deering	14.25
Spanish Sun	116	9	10	9^{2}	7½	6^{h}	A. Shelhamer	2.65
Glowing Rose	116	8	8	10^{2}	8^{h}	7^{2}	A. Schmidl	19.40
Kievres	116	5	5	8^{h}	10^{1}	8^{2}	R. Merritt	38.70
Gay Jewel	116	6	4	5^{1}	6^{1}	9^{2}	R. Eccard	53.75
Lady Tennie	116	1	2	11	11	10^{1}½	M. Berg	63.65
Penny Package	116	3	7	7^{1}	9½	11	H. Claggett	69.00

$2 Mutuels Paid—La Reigh, $7.40 straight, $5.30 place, $4.40 show. Milk Chocolate, $7.40 place, $5.50 show. Can Time, $13.80 show. Total mutuels...... $43.80

La Reigh was sent up fast on the outside entering the stretch, responded to urging and wore down Milk Chocolate in the final drive. The latter quick to begin, drew away into a safe lead and then faltered. Can Time showed a good effort all the way. Sticky Kitty closed resolutely on the outside. Puritan Maid closed with determination. Spanish Sun was in close quarters shortly after the break. Glowing Rose raced greenly throughout. Kievres was never a dangerous factor. Gay Jewel could not keep up. Lady Tennie was shuffled back after the break. Penny Package was never a factor.

SECOND—SIX FURLONGS. CHUTE. FOR THREE-YEAR-OLDS. CLAIMING. Purse $1,200. Value to winner $850, second $200, third $100, fourth $50. Went to post at 3.00. Off at 3.01. Start good from gate. Won ridden out, place driving. Winner ch g 3, by Bold Venture-Mary On. Owned by BRANDYWINE STABLE. Trained by W. W. RAINES. Time 23 2-5, 47 2-5, 1.13 4-5.

	Wt.	Post	St.	¼	½	Str.	Fin.	Jockeys	Odds
Free Double	111	4	4	1^{2}	1^{4}	1^{3}	1^{2}¼	K. McCombs	$3.40
Isle de Pine	101	7	10	9^{h}	7¼	3^{1}	2^{1}½	E. Campbell	3.50
Flying Reigh	111	9	3	3^{n}	2½	2^{h}	3½	A. Schmidl	2.60
Wheat	116	8	12	10^{3}	11^{1}	6^{1}½	4^{1}	F. DeCamillis	7.05
aBaby Boy	104½	5	7	7^{2}	4^{h}	5^{1}	5^{1}	[illegible]. Remerscheid	27.50
Teco Tack	108	10	2	2^{h}	5^{h}	7^{h}	6^{n}	[illegible]. Trent	10.55
Voucher	111	12	1	6^{h}	6^{1}	8^{1}	7^{1}	W. Canning	13.30
Valdina Weidel	111	1	6	4^{h}	3½	4^{1}	8^{h}	[illegible]. Mower	72.15
aSir Jerome	108	6	5	8^{2}	9^{4}	9^{h}	9^{2}	R. Eccard	27.50
Brogee	103	3	9	11^{4}	10^{4}	11^{1}	10^{2}	J. Dattilo	41.35
Hedda Gab	105	11	8	5^{n}	8^{h}	10^{4}	11^{4}	P. Roberts	51.70
Hyead	106	2	11	12	12	12	12	J. Deering	56.35

aMrs. E. R. Mitchell-C. Lowe entry.

$2 Mutuels Paid—Free Double, $8.80 straight, $4.60 place, $3.80 show. Isle de Pine, $[illegible] place, $3.30 show. Flying Reigh, $3.00 [illegible] Total mutuels...... $28.00

Free Double outran his field from the start, drew away into a safe lead, but

Continued on Page 36, Column 5.

Maj. Houston, 6 Others Die In Air Crash

Maj. James H. C. Houston of Baltimore, a member of the Army Air Corps, was one of two officers and five enlisted men killed when a plane taking off at MacDill Field, Fla., crashed today.

Major Houston was commissioned a second lieutenant in July, 1936, after having won his wings by completing a year's intensive flight training in schools at Randolph Field and Kelly Field, Texas, and later with the Air Corps units to which he was assigned.

At that time his local residence was 2908 Whitney avenue.

In December, 1938, he married

Continued on Page 2, Column 8.

THE WEATHER

Continued rather warm tonight, with gentle to moderate winds and no rain.

Detailed Weather Report on Page 16

On A Diet? Maybe You Don't Need It. All Depends On What Type Of Body You Have. To Find Out What Type You Are and What To Do Read the Authoritative Article By Robert D. Potter in The American Weekly, the Magazine Distributed With Next Sunday's Baltimore American—Adv.

Temperatures

12 Midn't.,	66	9 A. M.,	67
1 A. M.,	66	10 A. M.,	72
2 A. M.,	65	11 A. M.,	79
3 A. M.,	63	12 Noon,	82
4 A. M.,	61	1 P. M.,	84
5 A. M.,	60	2 P. M.,	85
6 A. M.,	58	3 P. M.,	85
7 A. M.,	59	4 P. M.,	85
8 A. M.,	61	5 P. M.,	83

VICHY--

Fresh wave of terrorism breaks out as Laval forms new government.

WASHINGTON--

U. S.-Vichy crisis mounts, all Americans urged to leave France.

AUSTRALIA--

U. S. fliers dumped 110 tons of bombs on Japs in raid on Philippines.

PAGE 2, COLUMN 1.

PHILIPPINES--

Corregidor guns beat off 65th Jap air raid, blow up Nippon troops, munitions.

PAGE 2, COLUMN 1.

KUIBYSHEV--

Red Army repulses Germany's counter-attacks on Central front.

PAGE 3, COLUMN 7.

BURMA--

Japs pouring five and a half more divisions into campaign.

PAGE 2, COLUMN 3.

VERY LATEST NEWS

(Race Results From Howard Sports Daily, Inc.)

DEVILTRY WINS SIXTH AT HAVRE DE GRACE

Sixth—Deviltry, $7.70, $4.60, $3.70; Free Trader, $4.80, $3.80; Zorro, $4.50.

AT JAMAICA

Seventh — Inconceivable, $12.60, $6.70, $4.20; General Jack, $8.90, $6.00; Shaun G., $6.10.

AT NARRAGANSETT

Seventh — Catomar, $6.80, $3.80, $2.70; Ships Bells, $6.80, $3.60; Clarion Call, $3.00.

AT KEENELAND

Fourth — Lord Vatout, $16.60, $8.20, $5.20; Aureole, $15.60, $6.40; Wise Dean, $3.80.

LATEST BASEBALL SCORES

(I) At Oriole Park—Rochester, 12; Orioles, 6; final.
(I) At Jersey City—Montreal, 2; Jersey City, 0; end 7th.
(N) At Cinn.—Pittsburgh, 7; Cinn., 6; end 7th.
(N) At New York—Brooklyn, 4; New York, 2; final.
(N) At St. Louis—Chicago, 5; St. Louis, 5; end 3½.
(A) At Washington—New York, 5; Wash., 5; end 7th.
(A) At Chicago—St. Louis, 6; Chicago, 3; end 5th.

Hospital Units Feted On Eve Of Leaving For Camp

THESE NURSES, members of the University Hospital units which have been organized as General Hospitals 42 and 142 and will entrain for an Army camp shortly were feted last night at the Hotel Belvedere by members of the University Hospital staff. The group includes Naomi Gearhart, Helen Waddington, Margaretta Cockey, Elizabeth Hand, Rebecca Schmidt, Katherine Schmidt, Regina Donohue, Grace Dick, Lillian Francis, Sarah Wahab, La Vern Davis, Frances Gehman, Catherine Matthews, Miriam Reiter, Mary Ramsburg, Sarah Pattillo, Virginia Twigg, Lieut. Louise Hollister, Lieut. Ruth Frothingham, Lieut. Esther Weller, Lieut. Dorothy Toom, Rachel Skiles, Anne Hoffman, Marina Norris, Jane Ewing, Laura G. Pember, Elizabeth Granofsky, Margaret C. Turner, Nina S. Claiborne, Beatrice O'Connor, Ida Deuse, Virginia Myles, Frances Sappington, Evelyn Crew, Flora Streett, Lolah Marshall, Elizabeth Gunby, Frances Belknap, Eleanor Mudge, Edna Zoaralek, Velma Dohme, Florence Hubbard, Louise Coard, Anne Llewellyn, Nancy McGlamery, Ivy Albaugh, Anna Alt and Wilhelmina McCann.

THESE MEMBERS of the medical profession recruited from the University Hospital staff will soon go overseas as members of Army General Hospitals 42 and 142. They will leave Baltimore shortly for a training base in the Middle West. They are (from left to right), first row (seated): Major Walter F. Merkel, Major H. Vernon Langeluttig, Major Monte Edwards, Lieut. Col. Maurice C. Pincoffs, Major Geo. H. Yeager, Major Lewis P. Gundry and Major Walter L. Kilby. Second row from bottom: Major Robert B. Mitchell, Jr., Major Murry M. Copeland, Major Henry F. Ullrich, Major Samuel T. Helms, Major Harry C. Hull, Major H. Whitman Newell, Major Thomas J. Coonan, Major Simon Brager, Major Howard B. Mays and Lieut. C. C. Fitzpatrick. Third row: Lieut. James Karns, Lieut. Edwin F. Dare, Capt. Samuel Bryant, Capt. A. G. Siwinski, Capt. Lauriston L. Keown, Capt. Harry C. Bowie, Capt. James Greiner, Major Brice M. Dorsey, Lieut. Douglas A. Browning, Lieut. John Cronin, Capt. Wallace Inman, Capt. Theodore A. Schwartz and Lieut. Benjamin Allen. Fourth row: Capt. Frederick W. Wakntz, Lieut. Carl A. Bailey, Lieut. Everett S. Diggs, Capt. Francis G. Dickey, Capt. W. Kennedy Waller, Capt. William G. Hellfrich, Capt. Walter F. Karfgin, Capt. Robert C. Crawford, Capt. Stuart Coughlin, Capt. George H. Brouillet, Capt. Edward F. Cotter, Lieut. Edward J. Streidl, Lieut. S. Edwin Muller and Lieut. E. T. Lisansky. Top row: Lieut. Frederick J. Vollmer, Lieut. Robert B. Mearns, Capt. William B. Long, Lieut. J. King B. E. Seegar, Jr., Lieut. Henry Rigdon and Lieut. George F. Pollack.

Story on Page 27)

George Jessel's "High Kickers" At Ford's Next Week

LUCILLE CASEY

By NORMAN CLARK

MUSICAL COMEDIES are so scarce these days that when one sets sail for Baltimore, a fellow gets more or less stirred up. Especially one called "High Kickers." 'Twill be at Ford's all next week with Georgie Jessel and Sophie Tucker in the star parts. Those old-timers, Chick York and Rose King, are also listed among the funmakers. It seems to us we read somewhere that Chick and Rose have been living down in Texas for some years getting rich out of an oil well—but they just had to come back to Broadway for another whirl at the stage.

We understand that "High Kickers" is a sort of high-class burlesque show—y'know where the girls wear long skirts once in a while and some times show one bare leg instead of two. It comes to us after a run in Manhattan.

Rumor hath it that Miss Tucker, besides doing a lot of song-singing, also presents her version of a strip tease.

There are some grand lookers in "High Kickers," such as Betty Bruce, Imogen Carpenter and the American Beauty Octette.

Speaking of that Beauty Octette it has been responsible for the most marriages out of one show since the palmy days of the Floradora Sextet.

To hear Zac Freedman, press representative for Mr. Jessel, tell it, when Dan Cupid shot down pretty Bonnie Edwards back in November, last, she certainly started the wedding bells to tinkling for the beauties in "High Kickers."

In one short week that unpredictable love-kid mowed down six of the Jessel lovelies — and the present members of the American Beauty Octette so plainly and pleasantly visible on the stage of the Shubert, represent the replacements.

It was Tommy (Wotta) Manville who started it all by annexing in marriage Bonnie Edwards, twenty-two, blonde and ravishing. The fact that Tommy, forty - eight - year - old heir to asbestos millions, had actually taken unto himself a bride for the fifth time meant Page 1 to every editor in New York.

The couple eloped to Ridgefield, Conn., one morning.

Only a few days after Press Agent Freedman had pasted up the last newspaper clipping on the Manville affair, Al Bloomingdale, scion of the New York Department store fortune and part-owner of the show, depleted the American Beauty line still further by eloping with the beautiful Barbara Brewster.

When Joyce Matthews, only a few performances later, asked Mr. Jessel for "a leave of absence" so she could visit her pa and ma in Florida—Dan Cupid was lurking in the wings. After visiting pa and ma, Joyce headed straight for Yuma, Ariz., and into the arms of Comedian Milton Berle.

Of the original Octette, the following are still in the line: Eleanor Hall, former New York secretary and model; Lucille Casey, conventreared Newark (N. J.) girl, who, it is reliably reported, is the betrothed of Georgie Hale, producer and dance director, and Rose Teed, a gusty bit of loveliness from Chicago.

OLD GAGS

The Abbott and Costello life story, soon to begin in a national weekly, will be called, "The Older the Gag, the Louder They Laugh."

Morros And Eagle Plan Movie Based On Noted Russian's Life

Cast To Include Operatic And Concert Stars

By LOUELLA O. PARSONS
Motion Picture Editor International News Service

HOLLYWOOD, April 16.—That amazing duo—Boris Morros and S. P. Eagle, the lads who corralled all the top stars for "Tales of Manhattan"—have a new idea. I mean other than "The White Gown," which is temporarily shelved because most of the feminine favorites they want are unavailable.

Now it's a musical based on the life of Rimski-Korsakov, famous Russian composer, who was an ensign in the Russian Marines. Hence the musical movie will have a military flavor. Walter Reich has been borrowed from M.-G.-M. to write the script.

But you haven't heard anything. Now Messrs. Morros and Eagle plan an immediate trip to New York to find their talent at the Metropolitan and Carnegie Hall. With such top names as Ginger Rogers, Charles Boyer, Rita Hayworth, Eddie Robinson, etc., etc., in "Tales of Manhattan," their musicale will be just as imposing with operatic and concert stars.

Tomorrow morning Constance Bennett will check in at Universal for a movie. When I saw her a few days ago a deal was pending and now Universal says it is signed, sealed and delivered.

Connie is starred in "Madame Spy," a melodrama dealing with fifth columnists. She is an FBI agent, while Don Porter, the lad brought here for "Eagle Squadron," plays an American war correspondent.

Right up to the minute, this movie.

Chatter in Hollywood: The W. C. Fields sequence in "Tales of Manhattan," which the world knows was eliminated, may not be lost after all. I hear, through the grapevine route, that Bill has been offered $25,000 for his sequence, to be released as a short.

No one seems to want to say very much about what happened, but as I understand it censorship being what it is 20th didn't want to take a chance.

This may or may not be the case. The explanation given is that it was not in keeping with the tone of the rest of the sequences. But when did Bill Fields ever keep in tone with anything?

A Line or Two:

Ann Sothern had a huddle with her lawyer and it won't be long now before she starts divorce proceedings from Roger Pryor. Looks like love between her and Bob Sterling.

Esther Fernandez, the pretty Mexican actress, will make a picture in her native city. She is under contract to RKO now and the plan is for them to finance the picture.

Snapshots of Hollywood Collected At Random: Nice to see Virginia

Louella Parsons tells in her Hollywood column that Esther Fernandez (above) will make a picture in her native city Mexico.

O'Brien and Bill Orr together again at the Hollywood Tropics. The Priscilla Lane-John Barry romance is still plenty hot. Dorothy Lamour tossed a kitchen shower for Elaine Ramsey, her beauty operator, who recently married Jim Clark. Clark Gable, who has been leading a lone-wolf existence on his Encino ranch, dining at the Brown Derby with Al Monasco.

Victor McLaglen, carrying out the terms of his wife's will, has presented her hunter dogs to the Army. Elmer Rice has joined Bill Field, his bride, and will write a movie adaptation. Nancy Kelly very much in the foreground at Slapsie Maxies, where she went with one of the Hakim boys. When Vic Mature heard that he is verra, verra good in "My Gal Sal," he suggester 20th change the title to "Our Boy Victor."

George Montgomery has presented a studio chair outlined with copper pennies to Hedy Lamarr. Penny is his favorite name for her. Marguerite Chapman and Ivan Goff have discovered each other. So have Clifford Odets and Betty Grayson.

Hilda Hendrickson of Cedar Rapids, Iowa, says:

"Be thrifty, but swiftly. U. S. Defense bonds."

Hardy Family On Century Program

"THE COURTSHIP OF ANDY HARDY," the current feature at the Century, is the twelfth picture in the Hardy Family series, which was created five years ago. The series was launched with "A Family Affair," adapted from Aurania Rouverol's play, "Skidding." "You're Only Young Once" followed, and the next picture, "Judge Hardy's Children," put the Hardy name in the title, where it has remained ever since.

The picture introduces a new leading woman to the series in the person of Donna Reed, who follows in the footsteps of Lana Turner and Kathryn Grayson, both of whom received their start toward stardom in the Hardy series.

'Jungle Book' Parkway's Film

Rosemary De Camp, who was chosen by Alexander Korda to play the role of Messua, Sabu's young mother, in Rudyard Kipling's "Jungle Book," which will come to the Parkway Saturday, is one of radio's most famous actresses but she is unknown to screen audiences.

Miss De Camp was given the role after many of Hollywood's most noted character actresses were tested for the part. She was married three days before the role was offered to her—and hesitated about accepting it. Friends, however, persuaded her and she decided to postpone her honeymoon for three months.

LOEW'S CENTURY
LEXINGTON ST. near CHARLES

NOW! ANDY'S GOT A NEW DILLY... WOO! WOO!
The COURTSHIP of ANDY HARDY
M.G.M. HIT with LEWIS STONE MICKEY ROONEY AND THE HARDYS

NOW! **LOEW'S PARKWAY**
BRIAN DONLEVY MIRIAM HOPKINS PRESTON FOSTER
'Gentleman After Dark'

WARNER BROS. STANLEY
HOWARD NEAR FRANKLIN ST.
DOORS OPEN 10:30 A.M.

STARTS SATURDAY

WILLIAM HOLDEN—Bashful? He blushed even when his ship took off her battle dress!

PARAMOUNT PRESENTS
"THE FLEET'S IN"
starring DOROTHY LAMOUR · WILLIAM HOLDEN · EDDIE BRACKEN
with JIMMY DORSEY AND HIS ORCHESTRA

LAST 2 DAYS "THE MALE ANIMAL"

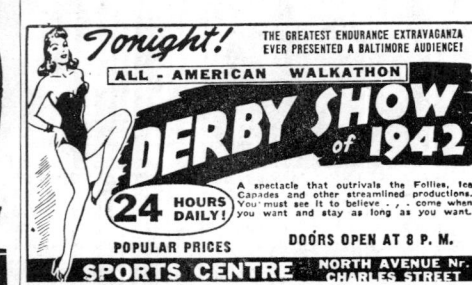

Tonight!
THE GREATEST ENDURANCE EXTRAVAGANZA EVER PRESENTED A BALTIMORE AUDIENCE!

ALL-AMERICAN WALKATHON
DERBY SHOW of 1942
24 HOURS DAILY!

A spectacle that outrivals the Follies, Ice Capades and other streamlined productions. You must see it to believe ... come when you want and stay as long as you want.

POPULAR PRICES   DOORS OPEN AT 8 P.M.
SPORTS CENTRE NORTH AVENUE Nr. CHARLES STREET

Today's Movie Calendar

Theatres advertised in this column belong to the Motion Picture Theatre Owners of Maryland.

Alpha Catonsville – Joan Carroll in "OBLIGING YOUNG LADY" Comedy.	**Garden** Charles at Gross – John Howard in "The Man Who Returned to Life" "March of Time."	**New Essex** Essex, Md. – The Fighting Anzacs in "FORTY THOUSAND HORSEMEN" With Betty Bryant.
Ambassador 4604 Liberty Heights – Carole Lombard in "TO BE OR NOT TO BE" "Hedda Hopper."	**Glen** Glen Burnie – Wallace Beery in "THE BAD MAN" Comedy.	**New Glen** Glen Burnie – Joel McCrea in "SULLIVAN'S TRAVELS" Comedy.
Apollo 508 N. Conkling St. – Bob Hope in "LOUISIANA PURCHASE" Buy Defense Bonds and Stamps.	**Grand** 511 S. Conkling St. – Una Merkel in "MAD DOCTOR OF MARKET ST." "Three Middle Mice."	**Northway** Harford & North Pky. – Gene Tierney in "THE SHANGHAI GESTURE" "Picture People."
Arcade Harford Rd. & Hamilton Ave. – Bob Hope in "LOUISIANA PURCHASE" "Information, Please."	**Gwynn** 4609 Liberty Heights – Irene Hervey in "FRISCO LIL" "Snow Trails."	**Overlea** Belair Rd., End of Car Line – Jane Withers in "YOUNG AMERICA" "Hop, Skip and Jump."
Astor Poplar Grove at Edmondson – Claudette Colbert in "REMEMBER THE DAY" Buy Defense Bonds and Stamps.	**Hampden** W. 36th St. – Tyrone Power in "SON OF FURY" With Irene Hervey.	**Palace** Gay and Fayette Sts. – Kent Taylor in "FRISCO LIL" With Irene Hervey.
Aurora 7 East North Ave. – George Sanders in "A DATE WITH THE FALCON" "Heart Burn."	**Harford** 2616 Harford Ave. – Edward G. Robinson in "UNHOLY PARTNERS" "Let Me Explain."	**Patterson** Eastern and East Aves. – Bob Hope in "LOUISIANA PURCHASE" "Superman."
Avalon 4300 Park Heights Ave. – CLOSED TEMPORARILY	**Horn** 4904 Pratt St. – Tyrone Power in "SON OF FURY" Bird Came C.O.D."	**Pikes** Pikesville, Md. – Abbott and Costello in "RIDE 'EM COWBOY" "Point of Arrows."
Avenue 2709 Philadelphia Ave. & Hoffman St. – Robert Young in "JOE SMITH, AMERICAN" Comedy and Cartoon.	**Howard** 115 N. Howard St. Special R. A. F. Cast in "SON OF FURY" With Gene Tierney.	**Pimlico** Park Heights & Belvedere – Ida Lupino in "LADY FOR A NIGHT" Comedy.
Avon 3019 Hamilton Ave. – OPEN SATURDAYS AND SUNDAYS ONLY	**Ideal** 33rd St. Special R. A. F. Cast in "TARGET FOR TONIGHT" Comedy.	**Preston** 1108 E. Preston St. – Jackie Cooper in "GLAMOUR BOY" Buy Defense Bonds and Stamps.
Belnord 2709 Philadelphia Ave. – Tyrone Power in "SON OF FURY" "Information, Please."	**Irvington** 4113 Frederick Ave. – Judy Canova in "SLEEPYTIME GAL" "Main St. on the March."	**Red Wing** 8241 E. Monument St. – Laraine Day in "A YANK ON THE BURMA ROAD" "Heart Burn."
Boulevard 33rd at Greenmount – Bob Hope in "LOUISIANA PURCHASE" "Donald's Camera."	**Lane** Dundalk, Md. – Bill Henry in "PARDON MY STRIPES" With Harriet Hilliard.	**Rex** 4600 York Road – Wallace Beery in "THE BUGLE SOUNDS" Comedy.
Bridge Edmondson Ave. & Pulaski St. – Johnny Weissmuller in "Tarzan's Secret Treasure" Comedy.	**Leader** 248 S. Broadway – All-Polish Talking Picture "DWA DNI W RAJU" Buy Defense Bonds and Stamps.	**Rialto** 846 W. North Ave. – Irene Hervey in "FRISCO LIL" Buy Defense Bonds and Stamps.
Broadway 509 S. Broadway – Conrad Veidt in "NAZI AGENT" Buy Defense Bonds and Stamps.	**Lexway** 31 W. Lexington St. – Exclusive Baltimore Showing "FORBIDDEN ADVENTURE" Not Recommended for Children.	**Ritz** 1607 N. Washington St. – Tyrone Power in "SON OF FURY" With Gene Tierney.
Cameo 4705 Harford Road – Greer Garson in "BLOSSOMS IN THE DUST" Buy Defense Bonds and Stamps.	**Linwood** 508 S. Linwood Ave. – Joan Bennett in "LADY FOR A NIGHT" "Hedda Hopper."	**Senator** York Rd. – Tyrone Power in "SON OF FURY" "Nix on Hypnotricks."
Capitol 1519 W. Baltimore St. – Gene Tierney in "THE SHANGHAI GESTURE" Buy Defense Bonds and Stamps.	**Little** 523 North Howard St. – Walt Disney's "FANTASIA" With Stokowski.	**State** Monument and Castle Sts. – Tyrone Power in "SON OF FURY" Vaudeville.
Casino 1118 Light St., Jane Frazee in "SAN ANTONIO ROSE" "Doing the Town."	**Lord Baltimore** 1110 West Baltimore St. – Bob Hope in "LOUISIANA PURCHASE" With Vera Zorina.	**Strand** Dundalk, Md. – George Sanders in "DATE WITH THE FALCON" With Wendy Barrie.
Cluster 303 S. Broadway – Special R. A. F. Cast in "TARGET FOR TONIGHT" "The Gay Parisian."	**Lord Calvert** 2444 Washington – George Montgomery in "THE LAST OF THE DUANES" Comedy.	**Towson** Towson, Md. – Bob Hope in "CONFIRM OR DENY" Comedy.
Columbia 2739 Washington Blvd. – Tyrone Power in "SON OF FURY" "Super Salesman."	**Lyceum** Sparrows Point, Md. – Robert Preston in "NIGHT OF JANUARY 16th" Comedy.	**Uptown** 5010 Park Heights – Carole Lombard in "TO BE OR NOT TO BE" "Conrad the Sailor."
Earle Belair Rd. at Woodlea Ave. – Tyrone Power in "SON OF FURY" With Gene Tierney.	**McHenry** 1037 Light St. – Bob Hope in "LOUISIANA PURCHASE" Comedy.	**Vilma** Belair Rd. and Mayfield Ave. – Bob Hope in "LOUISIANA PURCHASE" With Vera Zorina.
Edgewood Edmondson & Edgewood – Gene Tierney in "SON OF FURY" "Nix on Hypnotricks."	**Mayfair** N. Howard St. – Chester Morris in "CANAL ZONE" With Harriet Hilliard.	**Walbrook** 4100 No. Ave. – All-Star Cast in "GEORGE TAKES THE AIR" "Call of Canada."
Forest Garrison & Liberty Heights – Gene Tierney in "THE SHANGHAI GESTURE" "Information, Please."	**Met** Pennsylvania & North Ave. – Bob Hope in "LOUISIANA PURCHASE" Buy Defense Bonds and Stamps.	**Waverly** Greenmount at Gorsuch – Brod Crawford in "NORTH TO THE KLONDIKE" "Ten Pin Parade."
Fulton 614 & Baker St. – Katharine Hepburn in "WOMAN OF THE YEAR" "Under Spreading Blacksmith Shop."	**New** 210 W. Lexington St. – Conrad Veidt in "NAZI AGENT" "March of Time."	**Westport** 2205 Russell St. – Robert Young in "JOE SMITH, AMERICAN" Comedy.
		Westway 5300 Edmondson Ave. – George Sanders in "DATE WITH THE FALCON" Comedy.

3rd Week For Success At New

Betty Grable has just received her thirty-fourth military honor of the past 18 months. The charming Twentieth Century-Fox star, who is currently appearing in "Song of the Islands," which will spend the third week at the New, has been made an honorary colonel of the graduating class of the ROTC of Washington University at St. Louis, Mo.

Co-starred with Miss Grable in the technicolor musical are Vic Mature and Jack Oakie, supported by Thomas Mitchell, George Barbier, Hilo Hattie and Harry Owens and his Royal Hawaiians.

NEW THEATRE
3RD and FINAL WEEK
IN TECHNICOLOR!
BETTY GRABLE VICTOR MATURE JACK OAKIE
SONG of the ISLANDS

KEITH'S 2nd Hit Week!

A big story.. a great cast.. spectacle to match the mighty North!

REX BEACH'S
The SPOILERS
starring
MARLENE DIETRICH · RANDOLPH SCOTT · JOHN WAYNE
with Margaret LINDSAY · Harry CAREY · Richard BARTHELMESS · William FARNUM · George CLEVELAND · Samuel S. HINDS
Produced by FRANK LLOYD · Directed by RAY ENRIGHT

MAYFAIR Starts TODAY!
1st BALTO. SHOWING
Timely thrills blast the sky!
JOHN GOLDEN Presents
CLAUDIA
A Radiant Comedy by ROSE FRANKEN
With Frances Starr, Donald Cook, Dorothy McGuire, Olga Baclanova.

Ford's—Tonight 8.30
Matinees Wed. & Sat. 2.30
The Nation's Happiest Hit!
CANAL ZONE
with CHESTER MORRIS · HARRIET HILLIARD · JOHN HUBBARD

NEXT WEEK MATS. WED. & SAT.
SEATS NOW DIRECT FROM 7 MONTHS ON B'WAY
GEORGE JESSEL'S "HIGH KICKERS" SMASH MUSICAL
SOPHIE TUCKER AMERICA'S LOVELIEST SHOWGIRLS
EVES. $1.11 to $3.32, MATS. $1.11 to $2.21

LAST 3 DAYS ENDS SAT.
STRANGE LEGEND OF A STRANGE LAND!
UNBELIEVABLE PICTURES OF THE MONKEY WORSHIPPERS!
STRANGE! WOMEN! WILD BEASTS! IT'S BEYOND IMAGINATION

FORBIDDEN ADVENTURE
LEXWAY N. LEXINGTON ST.
NOT RECOMMENDED FOR CHILDREN

Gala OPENING! 23rd season
CARLIN'S AMUSEMENT PARK
2 p.m. NEXT SATURDAY
APRIL 18TH
FREE ADMISSION!

LITTLE HOWARD & FRANKLIN
WALT DISNEY'S **FANTASIA**

Today HIPPODROME
★★★ ON STAGE-IN PERSON
HERE'S ANOTHER ROUSING STAGE and SCREEN TREAT
America's Newest—The BAND you've been waiting to hear!

Les BROWN AND HIS ORCHESTRA
Featuring Betty BONNEY · Ralph YOUNG
"Butch" STONE · Bill BUTTERFIELD · Abe MOST

Hollywood's Petite Topster **LEONORE SOLA**
Comedy Star of Folies Bergere **FRED SANBORN**

Cold Lead vs. Hot Rhythm...
FREDDY MARTIN and his Orchestra refuse to play fall guys for B'way's wise guys!
SCREEN

Meet THE MAYOR of 44TH ST.
He's ROUGH! He's TOUGH!
George MURPHY · starring Anne SHIRLEY
with WILLIAM GARGAN · RICHARD BARTHELMESS · JOAN MERRILL
Freddy plays his famous "PIANO CONCERTO"

Bela LUGOSI
Black Dragons

GIGANTIC CARNIVAL OF EXCITEMENT!
FRANK BUCK'S JUNGLE CAVALCADE
ROSLYN STARTS SATURDAY

Added: CARTOON CARNIVAL
TIMES Plus BIGGEST NEWSREEL Show!

Gayety ONLY BURLESK IN BALTIMORE
NOW! IT'S SENSATIONAL **DIANE RAYE**
GEO. MURRAY—BERT CARR "The Latest in Comedy"

OPEN AIR THEATRE
TONIGHT IRENE DUNNE MAXIE ROSENBLOOM
UNFINISHED BUSINESS
PLUS JOHN PAYNE BRENDA JOYCE ROBERT LOWERY
PRIVATE NURSE

MARYLAND Com. EVES. 56c to $2.21 MATS. 56c to $1.67
COLUMBIA OPERA CO. OF N. Y.
Sun. "Trovatore." Mon. "Faust." Tue. "Otello." Wed. "Carmen." Thurs. "Tosca." Fri. "Carmen." Sat. Mat. "Hansel & Gretel." Sat. Eve. "Cavalleria" & "Pagliacci." Sun. Mat. "Martha." Sun. Eve. "Aida."
Seats at all Maryland and Maryland Theatre

RIVOLI
Ray MILLAND in **"WINGS OVER HONOLULU"** · **"HERE I COME"**
DOUBLE SHOW DAILY

MARYLAND TONIGHT AT 8.30 MATS. WED. & SAT.
MICHAEL BARTLETT & RUBY MERCER and BALTIMORE CIVIC OPERA CO. in **"THE MERRY WIDOW"**

IN THE NEWS

BUSINESS CORRESPONDENCE
Palm Beach, Fla.,
April 20, 1942.

Dear Grandpop:

THANK you for your telegram.

I liked it very much.

I went to many Easter egg hunts.

I hope you had a nice time on Easter Day.

I am supposed to be with my daddy this summer, but hope you will ask him to let me come and visit you, too.

My school ends the last of May, and I can leave after that.

I won the race at Sea Spray Beach Club this year, and I won a cup and three blue ribbons for my swimming and diving.

Love to you and every one, and I hope to see you soon.

Love,
Bunky.

April 24, 1942.
John Randolph Hearst, Esq., Jr.
c/o Mrs. Woolworth Donahue,
240 Worth avenue,
Palm Beach, Fla.

Dear Bunky:

I CERTAINLY will ask your father to let you come to Wyntoon.

In fact, I have already asked him.

I sat right down and wrote him and said:

"Please come to Wyntoon the latter part of May."

"I want to see you on business."

And I said further, "Please bring Bunky along with you. I want to see him on business, too."

I hope he will do what I ask him. He generally does—if he feels like it.

Wyntoon is lovely now. The snow has all gone.

There was lots of it at Christmas — piled up on the ground, and on the trees and on the house tops—covering the mountains until Shasta looked like a big snowman shepherding his great white flocks and herds, spread out over all the countryside.

And the clouds drifting over the top of the mountain were

Continued on Page 4, Column 1.

BULLETINS

LONDON, May 5—(A. P.).—Lord Beaverbrook, British publisher who has been in Washington on a special mission, arrived at a southwest British port this morning while members of the House of Commons were asking where he was.

BERLIN (From German Broadcasts), May 5—(A. P.).—The German radio declared today that 79 Russian warships and 145 merchants ships had been sunk in April.

BERLIN (From German Broadcasts)—May 5—(A. P.).—Fernand De Brinon, Vichy French representative in Paris, said today that French troops in Madagascar had received orders to oppose the British.

BERLIN (From German Broadcasts), May 5—(A. P.).—An attack by British motor torpedo boats on a German convoy at the entrance to the English channel was beaten off, the German High Command announced today.

ROME (From Italian Broadcasts)—May 5—(A. P.).—Axis planes bombed port installations and railway at Alexandria overnight, the Italian High Command reported today.

BAGHDAD, Iraq, May 4—(Delayed)—(A. P.).—A court martial today sentenced to death by hanging three leaders of the Rashid Ali Al Gailani's revolt of last May.

LONDON, May 5—(A. P.).—A Zurich dispatch to Exchange Telegraph said today that Adolf Hitler's Voelkischer Beobachter had called upon Germany's war industry for increased production in a last gigantic struggle and the tone of Nazi press comment was more and more grim.

Aid Asked In Sugar Registry

THE BALTIMORE NEWS-POST
AN INDEPENDENT NEWSPAPER

THE WEATHER
Somewhat cool today with gentle to moderate winds and no rain.

Read The Baltimore News-Post for complete and accurate war coverage. It is the only Baltimore newspaper possessing the three great wire services.
ASSOCIATED PRESS
INTERNATIONAL NEWS SERVICE
UNITED PRESS

The Largest Evening Circulation in the Entire South

COMPLETE FINAL

VOL. CXLI.—NO. 1   Entered as second-class matter at Baltimore Postoffice.   WEDNESDAY, MAY 6, 1942   PRICE 3 CENTS

JAPANESE LANDING ARMY ON CORREGIDOR

Assault Fort In Manila Bay

WASHINGTON, May 5—(A. P.).—The War Department announced late today that the Japanese had assaulted Corregidor fortress in Manila bay and that a landing attack was in progress there at midnight, Tuesday, Manila time.

The imminence of the collapse of this center of heroic American-Philippine resistance to the Japanese invasion was disclosed in a brief report from Lieut. Gen. Jonathan M. Wainwright that the landing attack had been started across the narrow stretch of water separating the fortified island from Bataan Peninsula.

There was no estimate of the number of troops who have been holding out against almost continuous aerial and artillery bombardment since fighting ceased on Bataan a month ago, but the force on Corregidor and the three other island forts at the entrance of Manila bay may have totalled 7,000 or more.

Text of War Department communique No. 215, as of 5 P. M. E. W. T. today:

"1. Philippine Theatre:

"General Wainwright reports that about midnight the enemy assaulted Corregidor and that a landing attack was in progress.

"Earlier today and prior to the receipt of the above message the President dispatched the following message to General Wainwright.

Jap Troops Cross China Frontier

CHUNGKING, May 5—(A. P.).—Japanese troops invaded Yunnan Province today after driving up the Burma road and crossing the shallow Wanting river, 670 miles from this capital, a military spokesman said.

Bitter fighting is in progress in the area around, the border town of Wanting, still in Chinese hands, the spokesman reported.

He declared that destruction of the Chinese section of the Burma road, which winds through sheer mountains and gaping gorges, had not yet been necessary but that the Chinese would carry out their scorched-earth policy if necessary.

(BACKGROUND NOTE — The Japanese claimed their air force already had carried the war far into Yunnan Province with a heavy raid on Yungchang, about 100 miles inside the Province, where the Burma road crosses the upper reaches of the great Mekong river. A dispatch to the Tokyo newspaper Asahi, indicating that an air base had been established there, said the raiders destroyed nine planes, seven of which were grounded. The dispatch added that the town had been left in flames.

The spokesman declared:

"The situation in Burma admittedly is serious but there is no alarm about our people or in the rank and file of the Chinese army.

"There will be no relaxation of our efforts to resist the enemy's attack.

"We owe a heavy debt to the badly outnumbered Allied forces."

Continued on Page 2, Column 6.

Mrs. Roosevelt To Address Vets

RICHMOND, Va., May 5—(A. P.).—Mrs. Franklin D. Roosevelt has accepted an invitation to address the annual convention of the Virginia Encampment, Veterans of Foreign Wars, here June 28, R. Houston Brett, commander of Richmond Post No. 1426, announced today.

She has been invited by Mrs. Cogate W. Darden, Jr., to be a guest at the Governor's Mansion during her visit here.

Governor Darden will introduce Mrs. Roosevelt. Convention headquarters will be the Jefferson Hotel. Sessions will continue through July 1.

U. S. Bombers Raid Rangoon

NEW DELHI, May 5—(A. P.).—Huge United States bombers drove through a heavy thunderstorm early today and attacked a major Japanese air base just north of Rangoon where 70 enemy aircraft had been sighted.

U.S. Navy Set For Aid At Madagascar

VICHY, France, May 5—(A. P.).—Chief of Government Laval declared tonight he had received a note from President Roosevelt demanding that France not defend Madagascar against British attack, and that the Vichy Government regarded this note as inadmissable. Laval said France under no circumstances will make the first move toward a rupture with the United States.

By KINGSBURY SMITH
International News Service Staff Correspondent.

WASHINGTON, May 5.—Secretary of State Cordell Hull this afternoon issued a new warning that American warships are ready to support the British occupation of Madagascar, vitally strategic French island outpost in the Indian ocean.

Hull said that American ships are ready to back up such actions as those which have taken place in Madagascar should it become necessary.

The Secretary of State's warning followed receipt of reports in Washington that Vichy has ordered the French forces in Madagascar to resist the British attempt to occupy the island.

DISCUSS ASSISTANCE

The question of possible American assistance to the British in Madagascar is understood to have been discussed at an important conference which Hull held this noon with high ranking Army and Navy officers.

Among those present at the conference were Vice-Admiral Frederick J. Horne, assistant chief of naval operations; Vice-Admiral Russell Willson, chief of staff to

Continued on Page 2, Column 6.

Aid Sought In Sugar Registry

So great was the jam of registrants for sugar rationing books yesterday that Louis C. Burr, State rationing and price administrator, was forced to call for volunteer assistants at the elementary schools at the request of Dr. David E. Weglein, superintendent of education.

Dr. Weglein said that teachers at the elementary schools who have been conducting the registrations were overtaxed by the vast crowds that overflowed in many cases to the sidewalks.

Volunteers were asked to communicate at once with the offices of the Board of Education, 3 East Twenty-fifth street. The telephone number is University 6300.

Approximately 190,000 Baltimoreans had obtained books up to yesterday, according to officials.

Sugar sales began yesterday at groceries and other stores after an eight-day halt—but sales are being

Continued on Page 2, Column 5.

Text Of Vichy Reply To U.S. President

VICHY, Unoccupied France, May 5—(A. P.).—Following is the text of the Vichy Government's note in reply to President Roosevelt on the British occupation of Madagascar. The text as read to correspondents by Pierre Laval, Chief of Government:

In reply to the note handed in today by the Charge d'Affaires of the United States of America, the French Government raises the most energetic protest against the aggression of which Madagascar has just been the object on the part of British forces.

It notes the assurance given that Madagascar will be returned to France some day.

REJECT U. S. WARNING

It rejects as inadmissable the pretension of the Government of the United States to forbid that France defend herself when her territory is attacked.

The French Government is the sole judge of the obligations its honor, in that manner, the defenders of Madagascar have understood correctly their duties.

They have not hesitated, despite their numerical inferiority, to carry out their duties according to the most noble tradition of the French Army.

MANIFEST HOSTILITY

England so often since the armistice has manifested hostility to France and the aggression which she had just carried out against Madagascar could not surprise the French Government.

The French Government, on the contrary, regrets to note that the Government of the United States today approves and supports the British Government and cannot but leave to President Roosevelt the part of the responsibility which will fall on him in the consequences which will result from this policy.

Posse Of 250 Seeks Armed Killer Of 5

HAMLET, N. C., May 5—(A. P.).—Police Chief J. B. Fallow and four Negroes were shot to death here today, and an armed posse of nearly 250 persons began hunting a Negro said to have done the shooting.

Police said the posse, led by sheriff's officers and State highway patrolmen, was hunting Will Dawkins, who they said was armed with a shotgun.

British Attack On Madagascar

VICHY, May 5—(A. P.).—British forces which landed on the French island of Madagascar were reported tonight to have driven to Andrakaka, less than four miles from the great naval base of Diego Suarez and six miles from their landing place on Courrier bay.

VICHY, France, May 5—(A. P.).—The British landed on Madagascar this morning, preceded by "waves of parachutists," after the governor had rejected an ultimatum with the reply: "We will defend ourselves to the very end," it was announced tonight.

LONDON, May 5—(U. P.).—British air squadrons, warships and Commando-trained assault troops using light armored units were reported hammering at the big naval base of Diego Suarez on Madagascar tonight after Vichy French commanders declared they would "fight to the end" in defense of the island.

The British forces, landing on Courier bay at the northern arrowhead tip of Madagascar, captured a French battery and reportedly sank a submarine and a small naval vessel in the opening phase of the fighting.

PLANES DOWNED

Two British planes were shot down, according to Berlin broadcasts, which also said the British used parachute troops.

The Vichy official radio said:

"Diego Suarez naval base was attacked by strong air forces.

"Attacks also were carried out by large naval forces."

It appeared that the British had taken positions on both sides of the northern tip of the island, sending commando forces ashore at Courier Bay to attack the naval base from the rear and hammering at it from the air and the sea at the same time.

REFUSES SURRENDER

An opportunity was given the French Governor General Leon An—

Continued on Page 2, Column 1.

FOLLOW VICHY

The resistance was under direct orders from Vichy, where a Government statement said the British attack was "odious aggression."

The French statement rejected the United States note warning that any warlike act against Britain would be against all of the United nations.

Acting in agreement with the United States, the British forces—

Continued on Page 2, Column 1.

Daily Double (Flying Junior / The Killer) **Paid $14.00**

PIMLICO CHARTS

Copyright, 1942, by Triangle Publications, Inc. (Daily Racing Form.)

TRACK FAST.

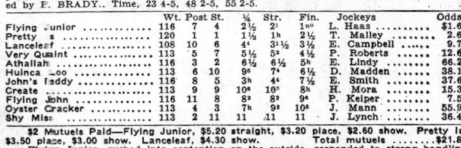

Continued on Page 28, Column 5

THE BALTIMORE NEWS-POST, WEDNESDAY, MAY 6, 1942

Sailor Tells Annette Of Problem

Receives Advice On Appreciation Of Girl

Dear Annette: I would like some advice on my love problem. I am a United States sailor, and I am worried. I went home two months ago on leave and while I was home I visited my girl friend the first night, and I didn't go back for the remainder of my leave. I love her very much, and her girl friend writes and tells me that she still loves me. I wrote and asked her to forgive me, but she answered and told me not to write to her any more. She gave me a ring for Christmas and when she told me her back the ring, well, she sent it back to me and she said she wanted me to have it. What is your advice, Annette?
A BROKEN-HEARTED SAILOR.

You must have a very nice girl, and one whose qualities you didn't begin to appreciate until this breakup occurred. It was generous of her to send you back the ring and indicates that she is a girl of principle. Well, sailor, what do you think is the best way to get her back? You had just as well learn now that worthwhile girls never will let you get away with slipshod treatment. I assume that that is the kind of girl you want. A girl who liked you well enough to give you a ring, expects a little more than indifference in return. She wants your attention when you are home on leave. She doesn't want to give the first evening to you and then have you leave without saying good-bye.

She wants you not only to tell her you prefer her company to that of others—she wants you to show it. When you stop showing it she will stop taking you seriously.

But the chances are very good that you can effect a reconciliation.

"Faint heart never won fair lady"—ask any sailor—so go after the girl again and tell her you mean it this time—if you do. Don't hash the whole thing over and over, but just laugh it off and slap on the compliments and the love stuff—thick. She'll probably take you back if you convince her she's the one.

Beer License Receipts Up $45,380

Beer, wine and liquor licenses, issued from April 13 to April 30 for the new license year which began May 1, yielded $893,425, an increase of $45,380 over the corresponding period last year, according to figures today from the office of Frank C. Robey, Clerk of the Court of Common Pleas.

Included in the total were the following major items: 348 Class A, wine and liquor licenses, off-sale, $87,000; 579 Class B, hotel and restaurant licenses, $434,250; 516 Class D, beer, wine and liquor licenses, taverns, $258,000.

Last year, among other items, 525 hotel and restaurant licenses were issued, producing $393,750; and 534 tavern licenses, producing $267,000.

The total number of licenses of all kinds issued for this year was 15,815, up 3,462 from the preceding year. Revenue total was $1,221,456.76, an increase of $140,209.01.

The 6,092 traders' licenses issued for this year brought in $136,853; 2,988 cigaret licenses, $74,631, and 845 miscellaneous licenses, $62,887.

YOUR FIGURE, MADAME! — By Ida Jean Kain

GOOD COOKING MAKES IT HARD TO DIET

The good cooks are the ones who have a hard time dieting. Their theme song is:
"Do give us any tips you can to make it easier!"

So if you qualify for help, here goes—

Let's start with dinner, for it is apt to be your undoing. Begin with your meal with a hearty salad—there is nothing like it to cut your appetite down to size.

To get the most for the fewest calories use either a very small amount of oil well diluted with vinegar or pickle juice or go the whole way and use mineral oil dressing or just a dash of lemon.

MELBA TOAST

For the second course have a clear bouillon, piping hot, and whole wheat melba toast without butter.

Next have a generous portion of lean meat. But have the meat without any gravy or fat, just a sprig of parsley.

Have two vegetables that have been cooked quickly and in the least possible quantity of water.

That preserves the flavor so you don't especially want butter or cream sauce with them.

Along with these you are entitled to a fluffy baked potato with butter. But make it only one pat, one-fourth inch thick. For the last course you can have cheese and a couple of crackers. You don't miss a course in that meal and it counts just 600 calories.

600 CALORIES LEFT

Since you are holding your calories down to 1,200 a day to reduce, you have 600 left for the other two meals.

For breakfast have half a grapefruit—which furnishes almost your entire daily requirement of Vitamin C—and if you take sugar with it, make it a single teaspoonful for 20 calories.

You can have two thin slices of whole wheat or enriched toast with one-half pat of butter. But take your coffee clear. You will get used to it and like it.

For lunch, whip up one egg plus a second egg white. This second white costs you only 18 calories and how it swells the size of the serving!

With this, have a slice of bread or toast, one-half pat of butter, sliced tomato and a glass of skim milk. Oh, you don't like skim milk! Then make it into cocoa. Use one cup of skim milk, one teaspoonful of cocoa and vanilla for flavoring.

SKIM MILK

Somewhere in the day's menu you must get in two glasses of skim milk, or one glass of milk and a serving of cheese. The milk can be in the form of soup, custard or a beverage. Just so you get it!

If you have your green salad at noon instead of at night you can have cheese with it and it will stay by you longer. American cheese, grated and sprinkled over the top, makes salad delicious. Or, you can simply have a cube of cheese. We should all use more cheese in our menus.

You can see that you do not have to give up any good cooking to diet. You just have to watch—and count—the side calories in butter, mayonnaise and the like.

If you will do that, there's only the other rule you have to follow. Never eat until you are ready to say "I can't eat another mouthful." That is what makes your appetite grow.

You will find other helpful tips on reducing in the "Reducer's Ten Commandments." Send large stamped return envelope for this leaflet.

(Copyright, 1942, King-Features Syndicate, Incorporated.)

Are you mortified by DIZZY FEELINGS
Due to the "Middle-Age" Period in a Woman's Life?

Are you nervous, weak, fretful, blue at times, perhaps suffer dizziness, hot flashes and distress of "irregularities"—due to this cause?

Then try Lydia E. Pinkham's Vegetable Compound—the best known medicine you can buy today made especially for women. Pinkham's Compound is famous to help relieve distress due to this female functional disturbance. It has thus helped thousands upon thousands of women thru trying symptoms of "middle-age." Also beneficial for younger women to help relieve distress of monthly functional disturbances. Follow label directions. Worth trying!

SURE DEATH TO ROACHES

Peterman's Roach Food is absolutely safe to use but is quick death to roaches. Results guaranteed on contact. Economical. Over 1,000,000 cans of Peterman's sold last year. Get the big economy size can at your druggist. Kills eggs, too. Effective 24 hours a day. No odor.

PETERMAN'S ROACH FOOD

3-DAY CLOSEOUT TABLE PADS $1.19 Waterproof

MEASUREMENTS BY RULER

White washable top, green back. Factory prices on all pads. Mahogany, oak, walnut, etc. Phone or write and we will call at your home to show samples and take measurements.

PLAZA 4262

Baltimore Asbestos Table Pad Co.
17 GUILFORD AVE.

100% Complete Service. We Measure, Make and Deliver Your Table Pads.

FREE! SERVICE FLAG
IF YOU HAVE A MAN IN THE SERVICE—I HAVE A FLAG FOR YOU.
JACK ROBERTS

ROBERTS
CREDIT JEWELERS
402 N. HOWARD ST.
2110 E. MONUMENT ST.

IT COSTS NOTHING TO FIND OUT
LOANS FAST SERVICE
Come in, Write or Phone

You'll like Our Service because we always try to do things YOUR way.

Loans $10 to $300

FAMILY FINANCE CORPORATION

DOWNTOWN
1 Light Street, Cor. Baltimore, 2d Floor
Thomas Building   Tel. Plaza 1730

HIGHLANDTOWN
507 South Conkling Street, next to Grand Theatre   Tel. Broadway 3020

HAMILTON
5440 Harford Road, cor. Hamilton Ave. (Entrance on Hamilton Ave.) 2d Floor
Telephone Hamilton 1424

WAVERLY
3204 Greenmount Avenue, Second Floor   Telephone UNiversity 3660

EAST BALTIMORE
2315 E. Monument St., below Patterson Park Ave.   Telephone Broadway 0877

SOUTH BALTIMORE
1037 Light Street, near Cross Street
Telephone SOuth 2640

انه مكتوب — ان الذي يقدم شرابا رديئا
لا يرضي ضيفه. لهذا اسألك يامضيفي

It is written: He who serves bad spirits, breeds bad spirits. Therefore, mine host, remember: "The very best buy is the whiskey that's dry—Paul Jones."

—From the dry sayings of the Paul Jones Camel

Paul Jones

Dryness (lack of sweetness) is a priceless quality in whiskey. Paul Jones' dryness brings out the *true* whiskey flavor and delicate aroma—for your most complete enjoyment.

A blend of straight whiskies—90 proof. Frankfort Distilleries, Inc., Louisville & Baltimore.

MUSICAL FUN! NAUTICAL JOY! POWELL AND SKELTON IN "SHIP AHOY"

What makes the wild waves wilder? You'll see when you take a care-free cruise on the fun-waves with Eleanor Powell, Red Skelton and Tommy Dorsey at the helm of M-G-M's latest smash musical comedy hit! With a merry-mad crew of sirens and music-makers! All aboard—for the time of your life! It's hilarity on the high "C's"!

"I DOOD IT!" says "RED" SKELTON

ELEANOR POWELL... dancing dynamite with all new and amazing routines!

Songs for the Hit Parade:
"Last Call For Love"
"I'll Take Tallulah"
"Poor You"
and others

With that Sentimental Gentleman of Swing
TOMMY DORSEY and His Orchestra
BERT LAHR · VIRGINIA O'BRIEN

Screen Play by Harry Clark
Directed by EDWARD BUZZELL
Produced by JACK CUMMINGS
A Metro-Goldwyn-Mayer Picture

★★ STARTS TOMORROW   Doors Open 10.30 A. M.

LOEW'S cool CENTURY
LEXINGTON ST. NEAR CHARLES

Gene Autry Will Sing Here Today At Junior Army's Giant Druid Hill Park Rally

GENE AUTRY, ROMANTIC SINGING COWBOY, WILL GREET JUNIOR VICTORY ARMY TOMORROW IN DRUID HILL PARK

By ALDINE R. BIRD

Gangway, fellows! Here comes Gene Autry!

Singing his famous theme song—"I'm Back In the Saddle Again"—the idol of American youth will visit Baltimore today to help put the Junior Victory Army solidly behind the war effort on the home front.

Accompanied by his famous "Melody Ranch" singers, all six of 'em, Autry will make his personal appearance at the huge rally in Druid Hill Park at 4 P. M.

AT MANSION HOUSE

Standing on the walk in front of the Mansion House, the "Singing Cowboys" will give thousands of boys and girls something to remember as long as they live.

Autry, who is appearing this week at the Uline Arena in Washington with his rodeo, offered to call on his young friends here who have

The Junior Victory Army did a "swell job" in collecting old phonograph records and Enoch Pratt Library announces no more are needed at present. Members should continue collections and turn records over to neighborhood retail dealers for cash, converting the money received into war stamps.

joined the Junior Victory Army and tell them just how glad he is that they are out to help Uncle Sam win this war.

Practically all of the members of the newly organized youthful army were asleep when their idol actually arrived in Baltimore.

RECEPTION AT CLUB

He reached the city shortly before midnight last night in a special car and was driven directly to the Baltimore Press Club for a reception and reunion with a young couple who previously appeared in one of his Hollywood motion pictures.

They are Vincent and Loretta Lee, brother and sister proteges of "Uncle Jack," who now are appearing with The Baltimore News-Post

Continued on Page 22, Column 3.

LORETTA AND VINCENT LEE REJOIN AUTRY

Win Cash For News Tips And Amateur Photographs

Do you want money for being alert? The Baltimore News-Post and Sunday American are offering cash prizes each week for news tips and amateur photographs. Total awards of $50 are distributed weekly for news tips, $25 for the best, $10 for the next best and $1 prizes for the next fifteen. For each amateur photograph published $3 will be paid, with special bonuses for outstanding pictures. Spot-news pictures are preferred, but candid camera shots that pull at the heartstrings are acceptable. Avoid pictures of ordinary scenes. Telephone The News-Tip Editor at Lexington 0100 for news tips and rush spot-news photographs in to the Picture Editor.

BOOGIE WOOGIE
By Michael Berry

THE BALTIMORE NEWS-POST

The Baltimore News-Post Has the Largest Circulation of Any Evening Newspaper in the South

2ND FRONT PAGE — NEWS-POST HAS TWO FRONT PAGES DAILY

WEDNESDAY, MAY 6, 1942 — 21

Mrs. Parker Unopposed In D. R. Poll

Cites Gains In Navy Officer Supply

Admiral Robinson Speaks At Ensigns' Graduation

ANNAPOLIS, May 5—(A. P.)— A high-ranking naval officer said today the Navy was launching men as swiftly as ships to keep pace with the shipbuilders creating America's two-ocean fleet far ahead of schedule.

Speaking at commissioning exercises at the United States Naval Academy for 574 reserve midshipmen who became Naval Reserve ensigns, Vice Admiral S. M. Robinson predicted that by late summer the Navy would turn out 1,080 ensigns a month to man the "ever-increasing volume of ships now beginning to pour forth from the ways."

SOLEMN CEREMONY

In a solemn ceremony, climaxing four months of intensive training, the reservists were welcomed as fellow naval officers by Admiral Robinson, Navy director of procurement and material and Rear Admiral John R. Beardall, academy superintendent.

Robinson emphasized the Navy does not regard the newly commissioned ensigns as "ersatz ensigns. You were selected with the greatest of care and discrimination. All of you came here during the seasoning of college graduates."

The present Reservists were veterans compared to Reserve Naval officers of the first World War, Admiral Robinson declared. He called cries and "tight moments" the naval officer's proving ground.

AMAZING SPEED

Admiral Robinson also told the class that shipbuilders who doubted their chances of meeting the six-year completion dates for the two-ocean Navy had amazed themselves by "far outstripping them. They have amazed us, too, although we like to tell them that we knew all along that they could do it if it had to be done."

Admiral Beardall commended the Reservists on their "singleness of purpose and devotion to duty." He said the members came to the academy in January as apprentice seamen and today "leave as commissioned officers to take up their duties in the fleet. Your predecessors here have already been in combat with the enemy and have made a substantial contribution to the Navy."

UNDER HIGH

During their stay at the Academy, the reservists were under the supervision of Lieut. Com., P. L. High, U. S. N., and were formed in a separate battalion under Reserve Midshipman Edward P. Taft, Jr., of Augusta, Ga., as battalion commander.

Company commanders in the battalion were Mark J. Brannon, Jr., Coleman, Texas; Robert A. Danse, Detroit; Harry H. Hudson, Macon, Ga.; Henry J. Marciniak, Chicago; Theobold R. Rudolf, Jr., New Orleans, and Thomas W. Ten Eyck, Denver.

CARROLL RESIGNS

Resignation of Merrill L. Carroll as executive secretary of the Advertising Club of Baltimore was announced here by William T. Childs, president of the club. Mr. Carroll has been named to a post in the sugar rationing division of the Office of Price Administration.

Maryland's War Bond Quotas

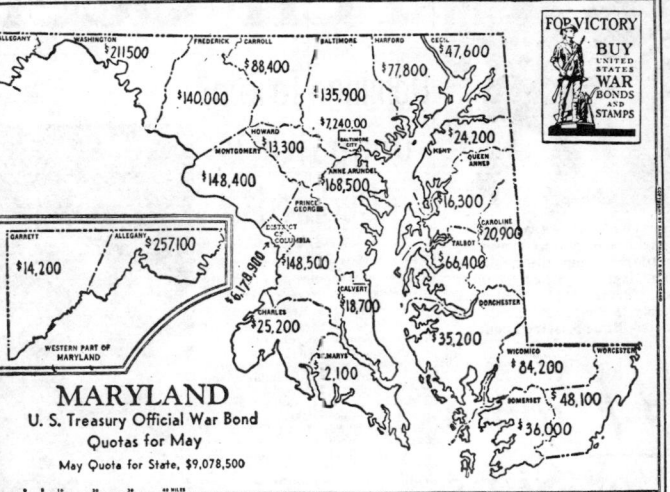

MARYLAND — U. S. Treasury Official War Bond Quotas for May — May Quota for State, $9,078,500

The above map of Maryland shows War Bond quotas, by counties, for May, 1942. Total War Bond quota for the States is $9,078,500. Every income earner in the State is expected to step-up War Bond purchases on a basis of ten per cent. or more of income. This is necessary to help America's armed forces take the offensive against the Axis powers. The American voluntary method of War Bond purchases must be successful in reaching the quotas set by the Treasury Department for every county in the nation.

Grocers Confused By Sugar Rationing

Many of Baltimore's grocers do not thoroughly understand the stamp system of sugar rationing, it was reported today by Merrill L. Carroll, manager of the sugar rationing department of the Maryland Rationing Board.

To clarify the situation, Mr. Carroll today advised grocers:

STAMP NO. 1 in sugar rationing books is good for the purchase of one pound of sugar from May 5 (today) through May 16. After May 16 the stamp is void.

STAMP NO. 2 is good for one pound of sugar from May 17 through May 30.

STAMP NO. 3 is good for one pound of sugar from May 31 through June 13.

STAMP NO. 4 is good for one pound of sugar from June 13 through June 27.

Thus, Mr. Carroll pointed out, each holder of a ration book is allowed one pound of sugar every two weeks, or one-half pound per week.

Grocers are asked to remove from the book stamps for sugar purchased in each two-week period.

So great was the confusion among grocers today, the first day of sugar sales under the rationing system, that upwards of 100 phone calls for explanation of the system were received at the sugar rationing department within the first two hours the department was open, Mr. Carroll said.

He asked that grocers clip out the instructions above and paste them on the wall in their sugar departments or on cash registers.

Dr. Bell Elected State Dental Head

Dr. Arthur I. Bell was chosen president of the Maryland State Dental Association at the fifty-ninth annual meeting of the organization in the Hotel Belvedere.

Dr. James McCarl was elected vice-president, and Dr. Meyer S. Aisenberg president-elect for 1943-44. Officers re-elected were Dr. Paul Deems, secretary; Dr. J. M. Hyson, treasurer, and Dr. Harry Levin, editor.

During the morning session a plaque was presented to Dr. B. L. Brun by the American Dental Association in recognition of his work on behalf of the association's centennial celebration held in Baltimore in 1940.

$5,000 For Main Here Approved

Board of Estimates today voted, on recommendation of Water Engineer Leon Small, approved by Chief Engineer George Cobb, $5,000 for borings preliminary to the project for constructing a 48-inch water main across the harbor to the Fairfield and Curtis Bay district, now humming with shipbuilding and other war activities.

This $1,503,600 project has been pronounced by Fred E. Schnepfe, director of the Vital Area Projects Division, as the most feasible way to meet the critical situation as regards water supply in the Fairfield area, Mr. Small stated in a letter to the board.

About a mile of the proposed main will be under water. The huge tube will be constructed as a Federal project and the Federal Works Agency will retain possession of the main, subject to an agreement to be entered into by the city and FWA, covering its use and ultimate disposition after the war emergency.

Man Held In Theft Of Cow

Andrew Daily's story before Magistrate John H. Mahle in Woodlawn Police Court today that he believed a cow he was accused of stealing was his own heifer grown up was not enough to save him from being held for county Grand Jury action on a larceny charge.

Daily told how his heifer went over the hill one day and he heard no more about her. Then he came across the cow and took her home, he said.

Witnesses, said Daily later sold the cow, whose career ended in a slaughter house. They said they identified the hide and head of the cow as property once owned by another Woodlawn farmer.

Drivers' Agent Says Cab Strike Looms

Drivers for two taxi concerns (Sun and Black and White) are becoming "restive" under what they consider unfair conditions imposed upon them and unless redress is granted a strike may result, Louis Schaffer, special business agent for the Chauffeurs' Protective Organization, said here.

Mr. Schaffer, who has filed a complaint with the Public Service Commission on behalf of the chauffeurs' group, said that so far it had been possible to keep the men in check, but that unless remedial action were had soon, he feared a strike would become inevitable.

Bandits Hold Up Altamont Hotel

Two Negro bandits carrying nickel-plated revolvers held up the night clerk and a bell boy in the Altamont Hotel, Eutaw place and Lanvale street, early yesterday and fled after taking $157 from the cash drawer, Northwestern district police reported.

William Merrill, the night clerk, told Sergt. George Dixon that he was behind the desk in the hotel lobby with Lee Tucker, bell boy, when the two men entered and produced the weapons.

One stood guard at the front door, Merrill said, while the other walked behind the desk and lined both the clerk and bell boy against a wall before opening the cash drawer and taking the money.

Before leaving, the bandits forced Merrill and Tucker down a stairway from the lobby to the basement.

Soldiers Get 4 Years In Thefts

Two young soldiers, who went AWOL shortly after their recent enlistment, were sentenced to terms of four years each by Judge J. Abner Sayler in Criminal Court after conviction on three charges of larceny involving theft of an automobile and of a delivery truck, each of which contained several thousand dollars' worth of merchandise, it was stated.

One of the youths—Dorsey Calp, seventeen—was sentenced to the House of Correction. The other—Calvin A. Jones, eighteen—was sentenced to the Penitentiary. Both are from North Baltimore.

Some of the merchandise in the truck was sold, it was charged, some being recovered. Merchandise in the truck was disposed of, but most of it was recovered, it was stated. Both youths said the automobile was taken merely for joy riding.

Large Maryland Group Attends 55th Parley

By MILDRED KAHLER GEARE

PHILADELPHIA, May 5.—With impressive patriotic ceremonies, led by Mrs. George E. Parker, Jr., of Baltimore, the fifty-first annual meeting of the national society, Daughters of the Revolution, opened here today.

Mrs. Parker, who is regent of the Maryland State Society, headed a large delegation from Maryland. Mrs. Parker has been nominated for the office of national president. The election will take place tomorrow. So far she is unopposed.

NATIONAL BOARD MEMBERS

Two members of the national board, Mrs. Charles Curlander and Mrs. Frederick Torsch of Baltimore, gave reports at this morning's session. Both Mrs. Curlander and Mrs. Torsch have been nominated to succeed themselves as members of the national board.

The national president, Miss Charlotte C. Averige of Ridgewood, N. J., presided. The invocation at the opening was given by Rear Admiral James D. MacNair, Chaplain Corps, U. S. N., retired.

ALLEGIANCE TO FLAG

Mrs. Parker's pledge of allegiance to the flag and a patriotic ceremony followed.

Reports were given by the officers and chairmen of standing committees. The banquet this evening will be the highlight of the convention, which will close tomorrow.

Vote $1,000 For Livestock Show

Despite a recently adopted policy to curtail appropriations for conventions and similar purposes, the Board of Estimates here voted the usual $1,000 for the Green Spring Livestock Show this year. The board, however, deferred action until budget-making time on a request by Robert Garrett, chairman of the Department of Public Recreation, for $604 to print 500 copies of the long-range recreation plan.

IMPORTANT NOTICE to our Milk Customers

Change in milk-delivery service necessary to comply with the Government's order to conserve war materials.

o o o

See Page 9

Western Maryland Dairy

Out She Comes!

Every day thousands of freshly washed and sterilized bottles enter the Green Spring bottling room for filling. Each one passes by a brilliant light—in front of which is an inspector. If he notices a bottle that is not in perfect condition—OUT SHE COMES! Such careful attention is another reason why Green Spring Milk is unexcelled in purity and quality.

UNiversity 4477

Green Spring Dairy
1020 West Forty-First Street

RACING AT PIMLICO

DAILY TO MAY 9

A Stake Race Daily
TODAY—THE SURVIVOR
RESERVED SEATS DAILY, $1.10
FIRST RACE 2.30 P. M. (E.W.T.)
DAILY DOUBLE CLOSES 2.15 P. M. (E.W.T.)

HELP WANTED

Experienced cook; 3 waitresses (white), and a man with restaurant experience to act as manager. Must be reliable. See Mr. Rabinowitz.
BEST WAGES PAID
HOLLYWOOD RESTAURANT
322 W. BALTIMORE ST.

Sczepkowski Tagged $50,000 Find By Shaughnessy

THE BALTIMORE NEWS-POST SPORTS

WEDNESDAY, MAY 6, 1942

THIS UMPIRE WAS A THIEF

BOISE, Idaho, May 5—(A. P.).—The Gowen Field Air Base baseball team was in a tight game at the State Penitentiary with the prison nine.

Protesting a close decision, Lieut. Carl W. Robbins screamed: "That's robbery."

"What d'ya expect," retorted an inmate, "that's what the ump is in here for."

Remember Kirby?

ONE-MAN RIOT—The photo above shows a fleet of gendarmes having the very dickens of a time removing Thomas Kirby of South Baltimore from the Stadium during the Navy-Cornell game last fall when Thomas became a trifle too boisterous. Remember? Well, he's now a corporal in the U. S. Army in South Carolina. He wrote Rodger H. Pippen, sports editor, a letter about it.

Rodger H. Pippen Sports Editor Says

KEEP YOUR CHIN UP

May 5.

Came a letter this morning from Corporal Thomas Kirby, now at Fort Jackson, South Carolina.

The name Kirby means nothing to the average reader of the sport pages. It recalls, however, a most amusing sidelight to the Navy-Cornell football game in the Baltimore Stadium last fall.

During an exciting part of the grid game, a fight started among the spectators in the East stand. Lieutenant Amhrein, assisted by five or six other policemen, were trying to eject a spectator who had done something to arouse the officer. The fan, who happened to be Kirby, was a tough nut to crack. He bowled over the cops like tenpins. One blue coat was knocked cold from a punch or a kick in the abdomen. The "law" would get Corporal Tom down and he would break loose and start battling all over again. Finally, with six holding his head, hands, body and feet, they managed to carry him out.

RODGER H. PIPPEN

Kirby really did himself proud, and from six to ten Japs will be wise if they refrain from attacking the burly boy from South Baltimore. Here's wishing Kirby good luck and telling him that his one-man show always will be a pleasant memory. He enlisted less than two months ago and has won quick promotion.

Will Fight Hard For Uncle Sam

In his letter, Corporal Kirby expressed regret for having battled the police at the Stadium. He says he is proud, however, to be serving his country and hopes soon to be a sergeant. Now that Tom is in a position to help Uncle Sam, he declares he will fight his hardest.

If all enlisted men had that commendable spirit and determination Uncle Sam would win in a hurry.

Taking Pep Out Of Baseball

Ford C. Frick, National League president, is still doing his best to take all of the scrap and pep out of baseball. He has just fined four Brooklyn players a total of $125 for arguing with his umpires.

The game is getting all too sissified, and men like Frick and Judge Landis are to blame. They should be head of a sewing circle.

Over in the International League, President Frank Shaughnessy is getting just as bad. He can't think for himself and goosesteps with Frick in deciding that managers and coaches cannot argue about balls and strikes. Why not pass a rule prohibiting all conversation during a ball game?

Howell's First Escapade

Murray Howell's trouble in Milwaukee recalls to Jimmy Powers the first escapade of the big outfielder who played for Baltimore last year. It was down at Clearwater, Florida, in '31. Howell and Van Mungo were out of the Dodger Hartford farm. Murray, stubby-legged and barrel-chested, could hit a ball a mile. Practice was rained out and a card game was decided upon in Mungo's room, with Howell, Johnny Krider and Paul Richards dividing the shuffles. A jug of corn whisky took some of the chill off the room. After losing his bankroll ($45), the well-charged Howell simply picked up the table and heaved it out of the window into Fort Harrison avenue, the town's busiest thoroughfare. Fortunately, no pedestrians were in the way.

Regarding Howell's fight with Chief Johnson last summer, Powers says that Howell held Johnson out of the window of the hotel by his ankles. And it was ten floors to the sidewalk.

Officer, Call The Padded Wagon!

Although our Orioles were in second place this morning and were being praised all around the league for their fielding and hitting and spirit, one silly local reporter continues using the hammer. If you read his dribble and didn't look at the standings, you would be sure the Birds were a hopeless last.

And, so far as the local schoolboys in the Oriole ranks are concerned, Mr. Know-It-All should blush when he reads what President Shaughnessy of the International League has to say about Ted Sczepkowski, kid infielder from Mount St. Joe. Shag tags him a $50,000 find.

Says Devil Diver Wasn't Fit

Shut Out and Devil Diver arrived here in splendid shape after a 22-hour Pullman journey from Louisville, Ky. Trainer Jack Gaver of the Greentree Stable feels that Devil Diver has a chance to reverse the result of the Derby on his stablemate.

"Devil Diver's injury at Keeneland prevented me from training him for the Derby," Gaver said.

Halsey Has Three Links Aces

Nelson Halsey, veteran public links golfer who also is known for his bowling feats, had three holes-in-one to his credit and has made two on the same hole at Mount Pleasant—the downhill sixth. He made the third ace of his career there this season.

RAMILLIES, BLUE D'OR WITHDRAWN FROM PIMLICO CLASSIC

Ten Seen In Preakness Field

Domingo To Run; Dogpatch Is Declared

By GABY

PIMLICO, May 5.—There was a change in the probable Preakness field today when word was received from Trainer Jim Healy that Walter Chrysler Jr.'s Blue D'Or and Ramilles would not fulfill their engagements in Saturday's classic.

The removal of these two pointed to ten starting in the middle cog of America's triple crown.

Pleased over his graduation race at Jamaica yesterday Trainer G. Philpot wired that Louis B. Mayer's English importation, Domingo, would start in the Preakness. Domingo won by seven lengths going a mile and seventy yards.

DOGPATCH OUT

Trainer Roy Walden wired from Louisville, Ky., that Milky Way Farm's Dogpatch would be an absentee in the Preakness field.

Domingo is due to arrive tomorrow and expected today from Jamaica is R. Sterling Clark's Colchis. The latter remained at Jamaica after his disappointing effort in the Wood Memorial. Prior to the Wood, Colchis won the Chesapeake Trial and Chesapeake Stakes at Havre de Grace.

Trainer Healey said of Ramilles that the colt at this time does not appear to be of Preakness quality and that Blue D'Or has been going sore since his good second to Requested in the Wood Memorial.

EIGHT ON GROUNDS

Eight of the 15 three-year-olds which competed in last Saturday's Kentucky Derby are now quartered here awaiting the call to the post for the Preakness.

Arriving yesterday from Louisville were the Derby winner, Shut Out, his stablemate, Devil Diver, and Apache and Fair Call. Arriving today from the Derby scene were Alsab and Valdina Orphan, second and third, respectively, in the Blue Grass classic; Fairy Manah and Requested.

SWENKE PRESENT

Arriving with Alsab were the other members of Mrs. Albert Sabath's stable. Trainer Sarge Swenke was on hand at the Mount Washington siding to supervise the unloading of Alsab.

As on every other occasion when Alsab has been beaten this year, Swenke offered no excuses for the colt last Saturday. He said Alsab ran a great race and would run another great one in the Preakness.

Question marks have been placed back of the names of three Preakness probables which did not start in the Derby. They are Sun Again, Air Current and American Wolf. The latter was one of six supplementary entries to the Preakness at a fee of $1,500 each.

Despite the fact he turned in what appeared to be a good qualifying race in the Derby Trial at Churchill Downs, Sun Again was a late scratch from the Derby. The colt arrived here yesterday along with Whirlaway, Proud One and Careless.

SUN AGAIN DOUBTFUL

Trainer Ben Jones said it may be two more days before a decision is reached as to whether Sun Again would keep his Preakness engagement. He added that while the colt looks good he has been doing none too well. If Sun Again works well and shows a fondness for the Pimlico track he will start Saturday, but no chances of knocking him out will be taken, Jones said.

Shut Out and Devil Diver will be breezed here during training hours tomorrow, according to Trainer John Gaver. From conversation gathered here and there those close to the Greentree establishment still believe Devil Diver is a better horse than the Derby winner.

A mishap interrupted Devil Diver's training for the Derby and it is no secret that the colt was not believed to be at his best last Saturday. Of the two Devil Diver is more appealing to the eye than Shut Out. With his hard Derby race under his belt there should be no excuses for Devil Diver Saturday. The slightly shorter Preakness route will be in his favor and an off track would greatly increase his chances.

D. C. TOURNEY

The District of Columbuia women's golf championship will be played at Chevy Chase, June 15.

WILL JOIN NAVY

Mac Pitt, Jr., Richmond U. athlete, will go into the Navy next month.

Don Ross Beats The Throw

HE'S SAFE—Outfielder Don Ross of Detroit is shown sliding safely into home plate in the seventh inning of the Tigers' game with the Athletics at Philadelphia. Hal Wagner, the A's catcher, desperately tries to nab him with the ball as Umpire Passarella calls the play. Ross moved around to the payoff station on Pinky Higgins' double. The Tigers won the game, 6-4. Associated Press Wirephoto.

Meade Tossed Over Colt's Head

NEW YORK, May 5—(A. P.).—Eastern racing fans, who thought they had seen Don Meade do about everything, watched him turn a new trick at Jamaica yesterday.

Meade, up on Water Pearl, was dumped neatly on the seat of his trousers at the start of a five furlong test for juveniles with the riderless colt hitting the wire first. Meade was thrown over his mount's head in the lunge out of the gate and narrowly escaped injury.

The race went to Bushel Basket, from the Greentree Stable, with Wayne Wright handling the reigns.

Will History Repeat In This Preakness?

By MASON BRUNSON

Associated Press Correspondent.

There's a striking parallel-in-reverse between Mrs. Payne Whitney's Preakness entry of Shut Out and Devil Diver and another pair of colts which made history in the race eight years ago, when a Kentucky Derby winner was beaten by his own stablemate.

This is not to predict that Shut Out, the Derby winner, will be whipped by his stablemate, Devil Diver, in the fifty-second running of the $50,000-added Preakness Saturday, but it is true that the Greentree Stable connections still feel that Devil Diver is the better of the two.

Shut Out and Devil Diver are approaching the Preakness in a situation similar in some respects to that in which Mrs. Isabel Dodge Sloane's Cavalcade and High Quest came to Pimlico back in 1934.

EASY WINNER

Cavalcade, regarded as the best horse in Mrs. Sloane's Brookmeade Stable, had won the Derby easily from Discovery and Agrarian, while High Quest, winner of the Wood Memorial, had been kept out of the Kentucky classic and saved for the Preakness.

The original plan was for Cavalcade to take a rest after his Derby triumph and for High Quest to represent Brookmeads in the Preakness. But Mrs. Sloane changed her mind and elected to win with Cavalcade and thus become the first woman to capture both the Derby and the Preakness in the same year.

She and the public wanted Cavalcade to win. But High Quest had other ideas. He led all the way and defeated Cavalcade by a nose in a terrific stretch battle to finish the mile and three-sixteenths in 1.58 1-5—a record which still stands.

What happened to Mrs. Sloane in the Preakness in 1934 happened to Mrs. Whitney in the Derby this year. Devil Diver was considered Greentree's main threat but wound up sixth in a roughly run race, while Shut Out, the stable's "ugly duckling," drove to a handsome victory.

HIGH ON DEVIL DIVER

Handlers arriving here with the Greentree horses yesterday were still "high" on Devil Diver, but not too confident about Shut Out.

Of course, the stable must figure out beating a lot of other horses, too, including Al Sabath's Alsab, Emerson F. Woodward's Valdina Orphan, second and third, respectively, in the Derby, and several others which ran out of the money in the Kentucky classic.

They'll have to reckon also with R. Sterling Clark's Colchis, which wasn't nominated for the Derby, and possibly with Warren Wright's Sun Again, which was scratched. Colchis is a certain Preakness starter, but Sun Again is doubtful.

Trainer Ben Jones wasn't at all pleased with the way Sun Again shipped from Louisville yesterday. He said glumly he felt the colt still wasn't up to his best race, and that he hadn't decided yet whether to send him out after the winner's purse that will approach $58,000.

Doubtful Starter

TARDY IN TRAINING—Calumet Farms' Sun Again, a late scratch in last Saturday's Kentucky Derby, is at Pimlico awaiting Saturday's Preakness. However, Ben Jones, Sun Again's trainer, who is shown above with the Preakness nominee, says that the colt is behind in his training and may not go to the post in the Pimlico classic.

City, Patterson Win On Diamond

May 5.

City College and Patterson Park won varsity baseball games yesterday. Fanning nine batters, Tommy Bryne pitched City to an 8-4 victory over Forest Park. He yielded only six hits. With Malone fanning eight and allowing only six safeties, Patterson blanked Southern, 7 to 0.

Bobby Doerr Outplaying Gordon

By GEORGE KIRKSEY

NEW YORK, May 5—(U. P.).—The other day baseball fans were asking if Joe Gordon, the Yankee pivot man, wasn't the greatest second baseman of all time, but today the question simply was whether Gordon is the No. 1 second sacker in the American League.

Little Bobby Doerr of the Boston Red Sox has moved up by leaps and bounds the past few days to challenge Gordon's claim to the kingpin of second basemen.

Gordon, the World Series hero, started out burning up the circuit and until he pulled a muscle in his back was clouting over .400.

SLOW START

But Gordon has slumped back to .379 and Doerr, who got a slow start because of an injured back, is now showing the way to all major league hitters with a tremendous .467. Hitting and fielding like a demon, Doerr has played havoc with the league-leading Cleveland Indians the past two days.

Yesterday he slapped out a double and two singles for a perfect "3 for 3" day at bat, drove in four runs as the Red Sox hauled down the Tribe's banner for the second straight day, 11-8. He was flawless afield, handling five chances perfectly. On Sunday Doerr hit two singles and a triple

Continued on Page 29, Column 1.

Christman Plays On Navy Ball Team

St. JOSEPH, Mo., May 5—(A. P.).—Pitching Paul Christman, All-American quarterback at Missouri in 1939, will return to action before home State fans this week—as an opponent.

Christman plays first base on Mickey Cochrane's Great Lakes Naval Training Station baseball team that has games scheduled at St. Joseph and Columbia.

BRUBAKER TO CHIEFS

SYRACUSE, N. Y., May 5—(A. P.). —Infielder Bill Brubaker was signed by Syracuse of the International League after having been made a free agent by Rochester.

CUBS SCORE

GREAT LAKES, Ill., May 5—(A. P.).—The Cubs defeated the Great Lakes Naval Training Station, 6 to 3, yesterday, after lending the Bluejackets a pitcher.

Ted Sczepkowski Tagged $50,000 Baseball Find

BUFFALO, N. Y., May 5.—The game scheduled here today between the Baltimore Orioles and the Buffalo Bisons has been postponed.

By HUGH TRADER, JR.

BUFFALO, N. Y., May 5.—Shag Shaughnessy, president of the International League, has followed the Orioles here from the start of their trip and calls young Ted Sczepkowski "the greatest seventeen-year-old ball player I have ever seen in my life."

Shaughnessy, in fact, is so "overboard" on the Baltimore youth that he even draws a laugh from Skipper Thomas who predicted a brilliant future for Ted a year ago.

CALLED $50,000 PROSPECT

"Sammy Bell will never get back in your regular line-up," Shag almost shouts. "At least, he'll never replace that kid. He's a $50,000 prospect and if anybody thinks that is the bunk, tell 'em to see me.

"You had Bell in there mainly because of his double play ability, didn't you? Well, this kid has made three double plays since he broke in at Rochester, and hasn't hurt you a bit in the field. In the meantime he has hit in some tough runs and he's a better hitter now than Bell ever was.

"Say, that kid is the greatest I have ever seen for his years. In another year or two at the most, he'll be playing with Boudreau at Cleveland instead of Mack. If I'm wrong I'll buy you a steak dinner. How's that?"

HITS OVER .300

That's a lot of praise, no doubt and whether the youthful Sczepkowski is that great will be known better at the close of this trip. Nonetheless, Ted has everything a ball player needs and his fielding and batting through the last five games have been not only good but brilliant. He's well over the .300 mark at the dish and the kid is taking it all in stride. He has nerve.

In every other respect, except pitching, the Birds are measuring up on this trip. Eddie Robinson is doing a fine job as the cleanup slugger. He's steady and sure. He doesn't lunge at any bad balls; he hasn't fanned even once this season of 18 games. He has hit .500 on the trip, smashed three homers, batted in five runs and fielded expertly.

George Staller, Bob Lemon, Hank Edwards and Jack Conway have hit hard and timely, too. And the infield defense is still as gaudy as ever. Joe Becker has been solid behind the plate.

PITCHING HELP

But the pitching is no better than it was in the opening series of the season at Baltimore and Thomas isn't going to see a fine club like this wasted on losing pitchers like, say, Clyde Smoll. He has the promise of pitching help later this week from Cleveland and when he gets it several on the staff now will be sold or traded.

He is satisfied with Naymick, Center, Trinkle, Flanigan and Niller. He wants two more consistent chuckers who can throw hard and bear down in the clutch. If the Birds get that help I won't hesitate to predict they'll run 1, 2, 3 in the pennant derby.

Thomas is tinkering with the idea of bargaining for Buffalo's George Barley, a right hand hurler, before the Birds pull out for Toronto.

Oriole Batting, Hurling Marks

BATTING

	AB.	R.	H.	2B.	3B.	HR.	RBI.	Pct.
Burkart	4	1	2	1	0	0	0	.500
McGarity	7	2	3	0	0	0	2	.429
Robinson	64	16	23	2	0	5	11	.359
Sczpk'ski	23	3	8	1	1	0	3	.348
Conway	78	15	26	8	2	2	12	.333
Becker	51	7	17	3	0	1	5	.333
Lemon	77	19	25	4	3	8	20	.325
Edwards	38	10	12	3	0	4	8	.316
Staller	67	14	21	1	0	5	15	.313
Robertson	13	3	3	1	0	1	2	.230
Sieling	40	5	9	2	0	1	5	.225
Bell	46	7	10	2	0	0	4	.217
Hamilton	29	7	5	1	0	0	5	.172
Seeds	24	1	4	1	0	0	4	.167
Flanigan	8	1	1	0	0	0	0	.125
Niller	9	0	1	0	0	0	1	.111
Naymick	12	0	1	0	0	0	2	.083
Center	7	0	0	0	0	0	0	.000
Kracher	5	0	0	0	0	0	0	.000
Smoll	5	0	0	0	0	0	0	.000
Trinkle	2	0	0	0	0	0	0	.000
Ronay	1	0	0	0	0	0	0	.000
Roche	1	0	0	0	0	0	0	.000

PITCHING

	G.	CG.	IP.	R.	H.	SO.	W.	L.
Naymick	5	2	31⅔	8	21	9	3	0
Niller	6	2	24⅓	8	21	7	2	6
Trinkle	12	0	14⅓	8	20	8	[illegible]	[illegible]
Flanigan	4	0	16⅔	14	22	5	1	1
Center	3	0	16	13	22	10	1	1
Roche	7	0	11⅓	12	18	5	1	1
Burkart	5	0	16	13	17	7	0	2
Smoll	6	0	17⅔	17	17	6	0	2
Ronay	3	0	5⅔	4	10	0	0	0
Waldt	2	0	3⅓	6	7	3	0	0

BONNIE VIEW GOLF

Mrs. C. T. Goodell won the six blind holes golf tourney at Bonnie View with a score of 23. **Mrs. S. Yewell won putting honors.**

IN THE NEWS

2-3 GALLONS SEEN GAS RATION

10 TO RUN IN PREAKNESS

THE WEATHER

Rather cool this morning, followed by mild temperatures in the afternoon; gentle to moderate winds, with no rain.

Read The Baltimore News-Post for complete accurate war coverage. It is the only Baltimore newspaper possessing the three great wire services—

ASSOCIATED PRESS
INTERNATIONAL NEWS SERVICE
UNITED PRESS

THE BALTIMORE NEWS-POST

AN INDEPENDENT NEWSPAPER

The Largest Evening Circulation in the Entire South

COMPLETE FINAL

VOL. CXLI.—NO. 4 Entered as second-class matter at Baltimore Postoffice. SATURDAY, MAY 9, 1942 PRICE 3 CENTS

SEA BATTLE FOILS AUSTRALIA ATTACK

By CHARLES S. RYCKMAN

THE Congress has learned from the President that the burden of preventing diversions from the war program is upon it and not upon him.

The President conveyed this information to Congress by urging continuance of the Civilian Conservation Corps and the National Youth Administration, at an annual cost in excess of one hundred million dollars.

If the President had seen fit to do so, he could have turned this substantial sum of money into the production of weapons; and by discontinuing the agencies he could have directed more of the nation's energies to the winning of the war.

But, of course, since the President has not done this, the burden rests upon Congress to do so if it is to be done at all.

The President thus persists in perpetuating sociological enterprise, of undoubted political value to his Administration in the past but of dubious value to the nation, without respect for the almost universal objections of the American people.

The two Federal agencies which he now proposes to continue in spite of the war represent a relatively small part of the total non-defense expenditure which could and should be eliminated.

Senator Byrd of Virginia asserts as much as two billion dollars per year could be channelled from non-essential Federal projects to vital war projects.

As the Senator points out, this is a very considerable amount of money.

The American people are sacrificing to supply the Government with it just as severely as they are sacrificing to pay war taxes and to buy war bonds.

If applied to the war program, two billion dollars saved from non-defense projects would amount to fifteen dollars for every man, woman and child in the United States.

According to the computations of Senator Byrd, it would build eight thousand fully-equipped four-motored bombing planes.

Or it would build forty-eight thousand medium tanks, or twenty-five thousand heavy tanks, or two hundred destroyers, or four hundred submarines.

The President professes belief, and strains the point se-

Continued on Page 7, Column 1.

First Sugar Book Thief Reported

BOSTON, May 8—(I. N. S.).—The first sugar rationing book thief was sought today by police. Mrs. Herbert Kinsman of Hyde Park reported the theft of six rationing books from her home. Officials said persons who have their books stolen or lost will be unable to obtain new ones until May 21.

Five More French Hostages Executed

PARIS, Occupied France, May 8. (A. P.).—The Germans announced today that five hostages had been executed and 50 others condemned to death for an attack on a member of the occupation forces May 2 in the Clichy section.

WomanFoundDead, Children Missing

CORPUS CHRISTI, Texas, May 8 (A. P.).—Mrs. George Clyde Hengy was found shot to death today in her home here. Officials said her son, George Clyde Hengy, Jr., sixteen, and her three-year-old daughter were missing.

Ten Horses Set For Preakness

$456.80

Tweendeck And Sir Kid Win Double

Devil Diver, Shut Out Entered

By GABY

PIMLICO, May 8.—Ten three-year-olds, nine colts and one gelding, have been entered overnight to compete here tomorrow in the fifty-second running of the mile-and-three-sixteenths Preakness, Maryland's outstanding horse race and one of few real American thoroughbred classics.

The approximate post time will be 4.50 P. M.

Provided there are no scratches the Preakness field will include Greentree Stable's Kentucky Derby winner, Shut Out, and his stablemate, Devil Diver; Belair Stud's Apache, Mrs. Albert Sabath's Alsab, Calumet Farm's Sun Again, R. Sterling Clark's Colchis, Louis B. Mayer's Domingo, Mill River Stable's Fair Call, Valdina Farm's Valdina Orphan and Ben F. Whitaker's Requested.

It was just a few minutes after Entry Clerk John Turner, Sr., yelled from his wicket in the race secretary's office, "Last call! Entries for tomorrow's races are closed," that Race Secretary Charles McLennan checked the Preakness en-

Continued on Page 38, Column 7.

$51.10 LONG SHOT WHIPS PICCADILLY AND MAGDALA IN FIRST RACE

SIR KID DRIVES HOME AHEAD OF JOANNY AND CLAMOR GIRL IN SECOND EVENT

U.S. Incomes In 1942 To Reach 100 Billion

WASHINGTON, May 8—(U. P.). Income payments probably will rise above the $100,000,000,000 mark in 1942 for the first time in history of the United States, the Department of Commerce predicted today.

March income payments totaled $8,654,000,000—a figure which the department said "implied" that payments for the year would reach $106,000,000,000. The March total was 21 per cent. greater than that of March, 1941, and 8 per cent. over the income of last month.

Government economists expect the national income to be between $110,000,000,000 and $120,000,000,000 this year.

Much of the March increase over February, however, was purely seasonal. The department's index of income payments rose only from 156.9 to 157.8.

The increase came mostly in salaries and wages, with other types of incomes remaining practically stable.

2 To 3 Gallons Gas Ration Predicted

WASHINGTON, May 8—(U. P.). Price Administrator Leon Henderson said today that "everybody in the war effort shudders when they see the waste of rubber and gasoline by Sunday drivers."

By WILLIAM THEIS
International News Service Staff Correspondent.

WASHINGTON, May 8—Price Administrator Leon Henderson today informed Congress that "non-essential" civilian motorists will be allowed not more than "two to three gallons a week, when gasoline rationing goes into effect next Friday in 17 Eastern seaboard States and the District of Columbia.

Appearing before the House Interstate Commerce Committee, Henderson estimated that approximate-

Continued on Page 2, Column 7.

The Baltimore News-Post today is printed in 3 Sections Be sure you get the complete newspaper.

Daily Double (Tweendeck Sir Kid) Paid $456.80

PIMLICO CHARTS

Copyright, 1942, by Triangle Publications, Inc. (Daily Racing Form.)

TRACK GOOD.

FIRST RACE—FOUR AND ONE-HALF FURLONGS. FOR TWO-YEAR-OLDS. Claiming. Purse $1,000. Value to winner $700, second $150, third $100, fourth $50. Went to post at 2.35. Off at 2.35½. Start good from gate. Won driving, place same. Winner ch c 2, by Balladier-Procne. Owned by ELOBEE FARM. Trained by V. H. WOEHLER. Time 23 3-5, 48 3-5, 55 3-5.

	Wt.	Post	St.	¼	Str.	Fin.	Jockeys	Odds
Tweendeck	110	3	5	3^{1}	3^{2}	1½	P. Keiper	$24.55
Piccadilly	120	7	4	2^{1}	1½	$2^{1½}$	L. Haas	4.00
Magdala	106	1	1	$4^{1½}$	4½	3^{2}	J. Deering	18.20
MaeJames	116	11	8	9^{4}	$5^{1½}$	4^{h}	E. Arcaro	.85
Oomph	110	2	2	1^{1}	$2^{1½}$	5^{2}	H. Trent	5.10
Captain Bart	112	8	9	6^{h}	9^{3}	6^{1}	B. Hacker	118.50
Chance Oak	110	4	3	5^{1}	6^{2}	$7^{1½}$	E. DeCamillis	36.30
Buckle Down	108	9	7	8^{2}	7½	8^{1}	P. Roberts	24.95
Cat Slip	111	6	6	7^{1}	8^{1}	9^{4}	M. N. Gonzalez	43.00
Caesar	111½	10	10	11^{h}	10^{1}	10^{3}	E. Lindy	69.30
Easy Step	112	5	11	10½	11^{2}	11^{2}	J. Mann	62.30
El Brush	103	12	12	12	12	12	F. Woodstock	235.35

$2 Mutuels Paid—Tweendeck, $51.10 straight, $20.50 place, $8.60 show. Piccadilly $5.30 place, $4.20 show. Madgala, $7.60 show. Total mutuels $97.30

Tweendeck, never far back and under steadying restraint, moved forward with a rush, wore down Piccadilly after entering the final forty yards and was drawing away at the end. Piccadilly, hustled from the start, forged to the front entering the final furlong, tired in the late stages and was unable to hold the winner. Magdala, never far back, was taken to the outside in the drive and finished strongly. Maejames began slowly and closed with a rush. Oomph had speed. Chance Oak went evenly.

SECOND—SIX FURLONGS. CHUTE. FOR THREE-YEAR-OLDS AND UP. Claiming. Purse $1,000. Value to winner $700, second $150, third $100, fourth $50. Went to post at 3.02. Off at 3.03½. Start good for all but Peace Day from gate. Won easily, place driving. Winner b g 4, by Sir Andrew-Miss Kid. Owned by J. L. FRIEDMAN. Trained by C. M. FELTNER. Time 23, 47 2-5, 1.14.

	Wt.	Post	St.	¼	½	Str.	Fin.	Jockeys	Odds
Sir Kid	111	10	9	6^{1}	3^{1}	2^{2}	1^{3}	E. DeCamillis	$3.30
Joanny	101	6	1	$2^{1½}$	2^{1}	1^{h}	2^{1}	E. Campbell	5.40
Clamor Girl	106	12	3	4^{1}	4^{1}	3^{1}	3^{1}	P. Roberts	1.55
aFred's First	109	9	11	9^{3}	10^{3}	6½	4^{h}	C. Wright	105.65
Centain Party	106	3	6	5^{1}	5^{4}	5^{4}	5½	R. D. Scott	69.15
Slugger	109	2	7	$11^{1½}$	$9^{1½}$	7^{3}	6^{1}	W. Kirk	66.00
Javert	111	4	4	1^{h}	1^{h}	4^{1}	7^{h}	J. Harrell	9.55
Post Haste	103	11	8	7^{2}	8^{2}	$8^{1½}$	8^{1}	D. Madden	10.25
Peace Day	106	5	12	12	11^{2}	9^{2}	9^{h}	W. Rudert	168.05
Berwyn	111	1	2	3^{h}	7½	10^{1}	10^{3}	P. Keiper	13.45
Running Blue	111	7	5	8^{h}	6½	11^{2}	11^{3}	J. Lynch	22.35
aDupliket	104	8	10	$10^{1½}$	12	12	12	R. Kirk	105.65

aMrs. E. R. Routt-Jerome Oxenberg entry.

$2 Mutuels Paid—Sir Kid, $8.60 straight, $4.80 place, $2.90 show. Joanny, $5.40 place, $3.30 show. Clamor Girl, $2.70 show. Total mutuels $27.70

Sir Kid, slow to begin, but quick to reach his best stride, was steadied until entering the final three-eighths, moved to the leaders with a rush and after taking command drew away swiftly to win with something left. Joanny, under strong handling from the start and on the outside of Javert, gained lead when entering the stretch, was unable to hold the winner and tired in the last stages. Clamor Girl im-

Continued on Page 38, Column 1.

Japs Fail to Save 2 Plane Carriers

ALLIED HEADQUARTERS, Australia, May 8 — (A. P.).— Naval spokesman, talking of the great sea battle raging in the Coral Sea, said today "there was a good chance that we might have been blasted out of our beds last night, if this had not happened, but we got in there and did the job."

AN ADVANCE ALLIED BASE, Australia, Saturday, May 9—(A. P.).—Desperate efforts by Japanese destroyers failed to save the aircraft carriers sunk or damaged by U. S. air and naval attack off New Guinea, and the crews had to dive overboard amid smoke and flames from the sinking ships, authorities disclosed today. Japanese personnel losses in the battle may run into the thousands.

The large Japanese concentration was spied heading in a southward direction several days ago. The U. S. forces fought them with bombers which pressed home the attack in the face of terrific anti-aircraft fire and the defense of Japanese Zero fighters.

The carriers were the main object of the initial assault. By the time this was over one carrier was sunk and one badly damaged.

Now two cruisers and two destroyers have been sunk, along with other shipping, and war and merchant ships badly damaged.

GEN. MacARTHUR'S HEADQUARTERS, Australia, May 8—(U. P.).—United States and Allied warships tonight are believed to be pressing a fight to the finish against a strong Japanese fleet after sinking 11 enemy ships and damaging six more in the greatest naval battle of the war.

The battle of the Coral sea, which may decide the whole strategy of the Southwest Pacific war, is being fought out "mercilessly" by an Allied air and naval force of "considerable strength" striking at a Japanese attempt to advance "in force," according to Allied sources.

ACTION SOUGHT

The belief was expressed that the Allied warships would make every effort to prevent breaking off the action, which United Nations forces apparently have been seeking for weeks.

The safety of Port Moresby, Allied advance base on New Guinea Island, off the northeast Australian coast and the supply line to America, probably will hinge on the outcome of the five-day sea conflict.

In two phases of the battle so far announced in Allied communiques, a total of 13 enemy warships and four transports or supply ships have been knocked out.

9 WARSHIS SUNK

Of these, 11 ships, including nine warships, were listed as sunk, among them two cruisers, two destroyers and one aircraft carrier. Eight enemy planes have been shot down.

(BACKGROUND NOTE: A Tokyo broadcast quoted the Japanese High Command as saying that the Allied losses included an American battleship of the 32,600-ton California type, a British battleship of the 37,000-ton Warspite type, the American aircraft carriers Sara-

Continued on Page 2, Column 1.

Think You Have Rheumatism? That Pain of Yours May Only Feel Like It—But Whatever the Cause. You Should Steer Clear of Quacks. So Says Dr. Leonard K. Hirshberg, In An Authoritative Article In The American Weekly, the Magazine Distributed With Next Sunday's Baltimore American.—Adv.

List Of Losses In Great Sea Battle

By United Press.

The greatest sea battle of the war, which started Monday and still was in progress today northeast of Australia, had resulted so far in these reports and claims of naval losses:

JAPANESE SHIPS SUNK (11)

One aircraft carrier

One heavy cruiser, probably of 10,000 tons.

One light cruiser, probably 6,000 tons.

Two destroyers.

Four gunboats.

One supply vessel.

One transport sunk during Allied air attack on Louisiade Islands.

JAPANESE SHIPS DAMAGED (6)

One aircraft carrier, probably a total loss.

One heavy cruiser.

One light cruiser.

One seaplane tender of 9,000 tons.

One supply ship.

One transport.

Allied losses have not yet been reported except for three airplanes announced in Thursday's communique.

AUSTRALIA--
Allied naval and air forces sink or damage 17 Jap ships in big sea battle.

TOKYO--
Claims two U. S. carriers and one battleship sunk, two British warships damaged.

BURMA--
U. S. bombers again raid Rangoon.

RUSSIA--
Russians wipe out 500 Nazi troops, capture booty.

MADAGASCAR--
British consolidate positions; French still resisting.

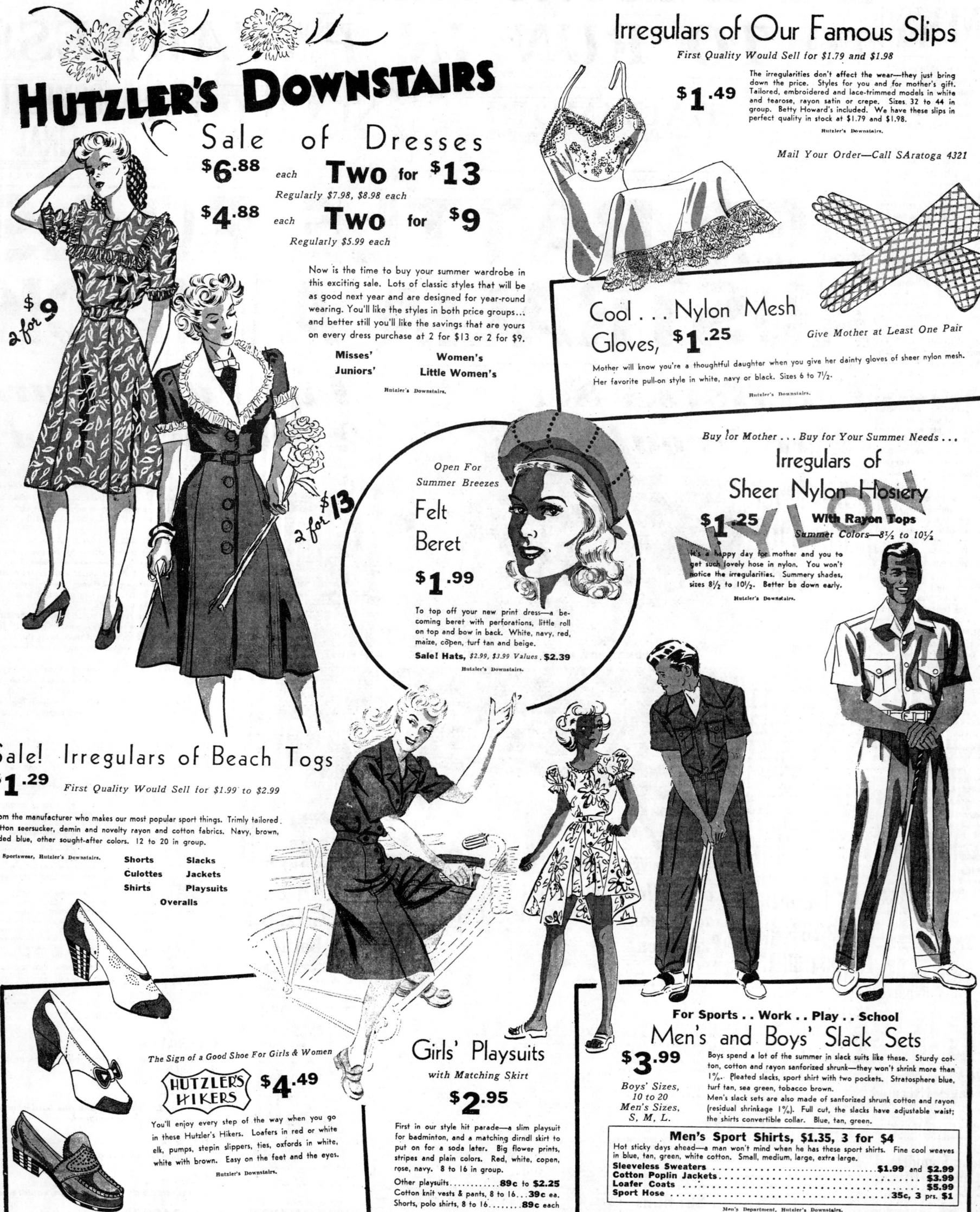

Veterans Pledge Full Support Of Jr. Victory Army

By ALDINE R. BIRD

Commanders of major Maryland veterans' organizations here came out full-force behind the organization of youth to serve on the home front as members of the Junior Victory Army.

Putting thought to action, the Jewish War Veterans—men who fought in the last World War—enrolled their children and gave them the "go sign" in helping their nation win the war.

V FOR VICTORY

On the steps of the War Memorial Building, sons and daughters of the Jewish War Veterans formed a "V" for victory line and joined in a body.

The state commanders who have endorsed the young army are the American Legion, Veterans of Foreign Wars, the Jewish War Veterans, and the Military Order of the Purple Heart.

The JVA is for boys and girls between ten and eighteen years of age, and their service will be here at home in doing many jobs which youth is well-qualified to do and is eagerly waiting an opportunity to do.

Said Philip A. Fine, Jewish War commander:

"The Maryland Free State Post of the J. W. V. is pledging its full support in the mobilization of our youth by enrolling one hundred per cent. of the sons and daughters of our entire membership.

"We feel this Junior Victory Army will help considerably in the promotion of the various phases of civilian defense and will be of great service on the home front to help win this war. We congratulate you on inaugurating such a splendid program for the youth of our city."

VICTORY ARMY

Roy L. Pyle, commander of the state Legionnaires, said:

"As Department Commander of the American Legion, I feel the urge to commend The Baltimore News-Post for the fine job being done in organizing the Junior Victory Army.

"I do not know whose thought this was, but I am sure nothing finer could be done at this time than to bring boys and girls between ten and eighteen years of age together and to afford them the opportunity to learn that their obligation is to their country and to make them feel that they are playing some part in the defeat of the enemies of democracy."

CAPABLE OF WORK

The commander of the Veterans of Foreign Wars, Adam A. Novak, had this to say:

"The mobilization of the Junior Victory Army should materially assist our plan for an all-out war effort. The collection of scrap and waste materials will give the youngsters the assignment they have long waited for.

"I am confident they will assume this responsibility with all the vigor at their youthful command, and will show they are capable of assuming responsibility.

"In the scheme of civilian defense the young element has, up to this time, not been taken into serious consideration and should be given proper recognition. May your every effort be crowned with success."

Other enthusiastic supporters of the new army included Andrew N. Segal, state commander and national junior commander of the Military Order of the Purple Heart whose members are veterans wounded in action.

COLLECT SCRAP

Among the tasks to be assigned to the JVA will be the collection of scrap metal and rubber, a constant job for them to do, building of model airplanes for the air forces schools of instruction, rendering aid to the Red Cross, and helping the sale of war stamps and bonds, fighting the Japanese beetle, helping farmers harvest their crops and thus conserve food, study of elementary first aid, fire inspection at home and many others.

Would you like to be a member of such a wide-awake American organization?

Would you like to have your son or daughter doing a real job for their country, when their services are so vitally needed?

Help them fill out the enrollment coupon and join the Junior Victory Army right away.

As soon as enrollment is completed, the army will be called into service on a series of "task assignments."

Purposes Of Jr. Victory Army

The Junior Victory Army is a patriotic organization of free children dedicated to preserving a free nation. Its ideals are those of George Washington, Abraham Lincoln and other courageous leaders who made this country great.

Its objectives will be:

To provide a role and individual responsibility in America's war effort for boys and girls ten to eighteen years with the view of encouraging them to take part in appropriate Home Front activities by all practical means.

To promote membership in various American youth organizations contributing to the national war effort.

To instruct and guide youths engaged in Home Front work through officially approved lessons and other features.

To help boys and girls build up morale, develop resourcefulness, acquire leadership and be good and useful Americans.

All boys and girls ten to eighteen years inclusive, are eligible for membership.

There are no dues.

To enroll in this patriotic organization fill in the application blank and mail to the Adjutant Junior Victory Army, P. O. Box 1795, Baltimore, Md.

If you want a beautiful Junior Victory Army pin to wear, enclose ten cents with your application.

The pin (similar to the wing-spread emblem shown at the top of the enrollment blank) is two and one-half inches wide, made of metal, and trimmed in red, white and blue enamel.

Members should wear the badge as evidence of their interest in service on the Home Front.

Children will not be asked to buy or sell anything other than to encourage the sale and purchase of war stamps and bonds.

The Junior Victory Army will not conduct any drills. Because of its juvenile nature it will not stress militarism.

It will not conflict with or infringe on the identity, character or work of other youth organizations.

Organized defense programs will be left to the various associations and schools which already have put these activities into effect.

However, the Junior Victory Army will be at the call of all official organizations engaged in Home Front work to aid in any effort where youth can be of assistance.

News and pictures of what youth is doing to help America's war effort will be printed as a matter of information and to strengthen the enthusiasm of the young army.

These plans will be announced from time to time in The Baltimore News-Post and Baltimore Sunday American.

JUNIOR Victory ARMY

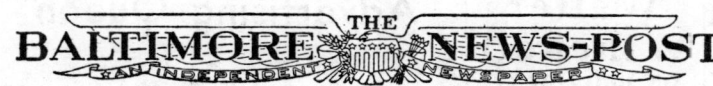

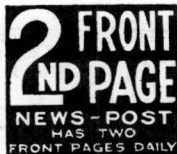

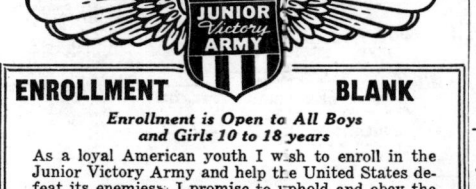

ENROLLMENT BLANK

Enrollment is Open to All Boys and Girls 10 to 18 years

As a loyal American youth I wish to enroll in the Junior Victory Army and help the United States defeat its enemies. I promise to uphold and obey the laws of my city, state and country.

Enclose ten cents (tightly wrapped) with your application if you want one of the beautiful Junior Victory Army pins, as illustrated above.

Name.......................... Age......

Print Plainly With Pencil

Address ....

City.................... State..........

If you are interested in performing any particular service during the war emergency state below:—

....

....

MAIL THIS BLANK TO ADJUTANT, JUNIOR VICTORY ARMY, P. O. BOX 1795, BALTIMORE, MD.

Join Army Of Youth

Children Of Veterans Sign Up To Do Their Part At Home

The News-Post Has the Largest Circulation of Any Evening Newspaper in the South

THE BALTIMORE NEWS-POST
AN INDEPENDENT NEWSPAPER

2ND FRONT PAGE
NEWS-POST HAS TWO FRONT PAGES DAILY

Train Hits Auto, 1 Dead, 1 Hurt

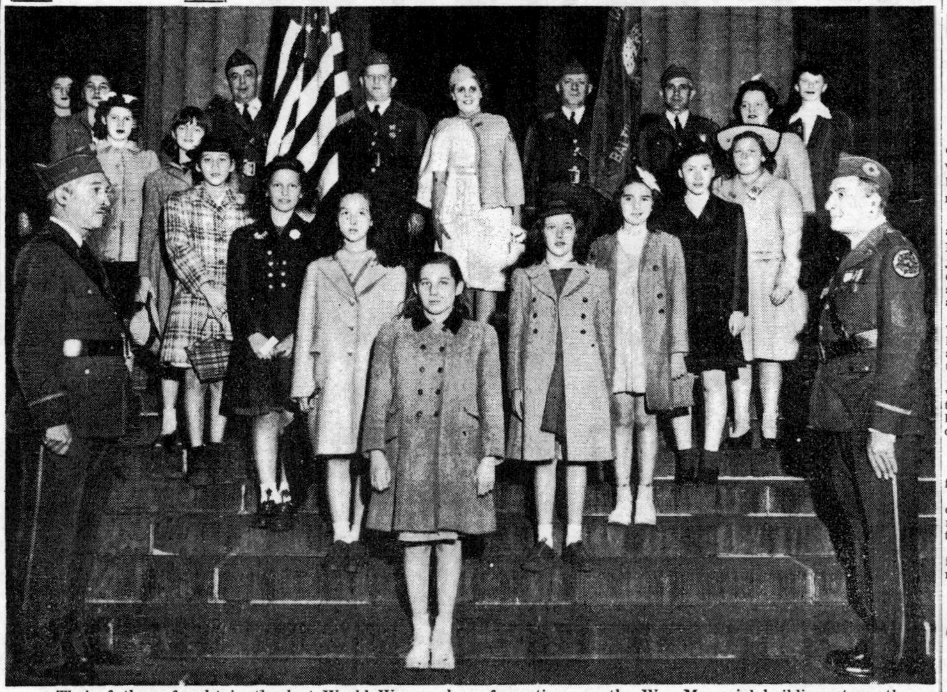

Their fathers fought in the last World War, and these boys and girls want to do their part in winning the "war of survival." They are sons and daughters of Jewish War Veterans and, forming a "V" for victory formation on the War Memorial building steps, they joined the Junior Victory Army in a body. Standing, at left, is Philip Fine, commander of the Jewish War Veterans.

Mother Slain, Her Daughter Injured

A mother was killed and her daughter critically injured here when their automobile was struck by a Western Maryland Railway mail train near Hampstead, Md.

The dead woman was identified as Mrs. Anna Rhome, fifty-five, of Hanover, Pa. Her daughter, Mrs. Joseph B. McLain, twenty-nine, also of Hanover, was brought unconscious to University Hospital in an ambulance.

According to police Mrs. McLain was on the way to Baltimore with her mother to meet her husband at a railroad depot. Mr. McLain returned from a trip North today.

A resident near the crossing, which is on the Baltimore-Hanover turnpike, said the automobile was knocked off the tracks and rolled over three times.

HURLED FROM MACHINE

The older woman was hurled from the machine by the impact.

The younger woman was extricated from the wrecked car by residents attracted by the noise of the crash.

Police said an electric bell is installed at the crossing to warn motorists of approaching trains.

Recital

Tiny Dancer To Take Part In Studio Program

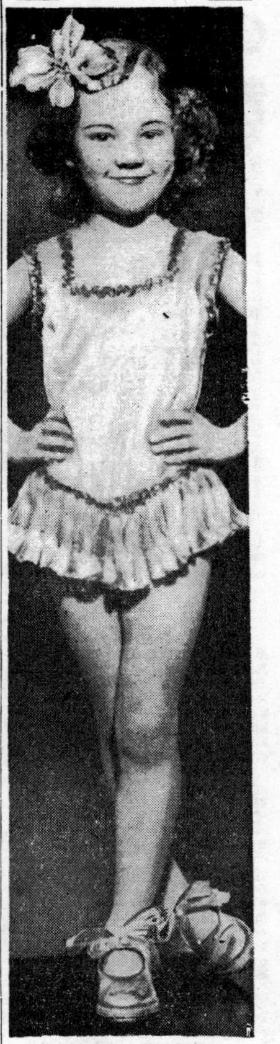

Patsy Ann Deal, above, five years old, will be one of the children of the Eloise Studio of Dancing, who will give a recital Monday night at Cadoa Hall. Patsy lives at 961 Argonne drive.

422 Get Army Motor Diplomas

Diplomas were awarded here to 422 soldiers who have completed Army transport courses at the Camp Holabird motor base.

Of the graduates 356 were from Camp Lee, Va. Other students were assigned from service units all over the United States and from Camp Holabird itself.

Most of the graduates will be assigned to posts over the nation, though 72 will be retained at Holabird for specialist training.

Wiegand Succumbs To Illness

Charles L. Wiegand, who retired a week ago from the post of Deputy Collector of Internal Revenue, died here at his home in the 2700 block Alameda, after an illness of three weeks.

Mr. Wiegand served as Deputy Collector for 12 years.

He was chief clerk to the Steamboat Inspectors for the same period of time, and prior to that was in the employ of the Postoffice for 21 years.

Survivors include his widow, Mrs. Helen H. Wiegand; two sons, Major Charles D. Wiegand and Robert Allen Wiegand, and a daughter, Miss Charlotte Wiegand.

LABOR CAREER

Mr. Wiegand had long been a factor in labor affairs in Maryland.

He was for years secretary of the Baltimore Federation of Labor and had served as national vice-president of the Federation of Federal Employes.

Early in his career he became active in politics.

He was appointed Deputy Collector by Galen L. Tait when the former Republic State chairman became Collector of Internal Revenue.

ACTIVE ELK

Mr. Wiegand was active in affairs of the Elks, and at one time held the post of grand chancellor of the Knights of Pythias.

Funeral services will be held Monday. Arrangements have not been completed.

O'CONOR TO ADDRESS GRADS

SUDLERSVILLE, Md., May 8—(A. P.).—Governor O'Conor will be principal speaker at Sudlersville High School graduation exercises Monday evening, the first of a series of exercises in Queen Anne's five high schools during the week.

Peru President In Visit To Annapolis

ANNAPOLIS, May 8—(A. P.).—A 21-gun salute roared as President Manuel Prado of Peru arrived today with Peruvian diplomats and officials to tour the United States Naval Academy.

Full military honors were accorded Dr. Prado who at President Roosevelt's invitation, is on a good-neighbor visit to this country. He is scheduled to tour several war-production centers.

Arriving by motor car from Washington, the first South American Chief Executive to visit the United States while in office, was greeted by Rear Admiral John R. Beardall, academy superintendent and former aide to President Roosevelt.

The academy band with a marine honor guard, gave four ruffles and flourishes and played the Peruvian national anthem. The flag of Peru was broken from the mast of the station ship, Reina Mercedes.

The Peruvian President, following a luncheon in his honor at the superintendent's quarters, was conducted on a tour of the academy.

TRANSFERS SOUGHT

LONDON, May 8—(A. P.).—Nearly a third of the United States troops serving with the Essex Scottish Regiment from Windsor, Ontario, have applied for transfer to American forces, Canadian sources said today.

Martin Output Rises Despite Metal Delay

Four times more bombers than last year are inching their way off the production lines of the Glenn L. Martin Company and the peak is still to come, probably in August of this year.

The production of bombing planes for Britain and America in this one plant are short many millions annually in dollar value deliveries due principally to delays in obtaining necessary aluminum stocks, Glenn L. Martin, president, told correspondents on the National Association of Manufacturers' "Production for Victory" tours of war industries. Martin said:

"Preliminary estimates of metal stocks available for airplane manufacture were not high enough and the vital aircraft manufacturing industry still has a priority rating behind battleships, trucks and tanks.

UPPED 4 TIMES IN YEAR

"We need metal, we need instruments, we need steel alloys and other essential parts to turn out bombers, but in spite of these deficiencies we have upped our production four times within a year and are on the way to peak production in August."

The correspondents on this tour saw long rows of finished bombers outside the gigantic hangars of the Martin plant, waiting for delivery. They saw dozens of additional planes moving slowly forward on assembly lines inside. They saw tens of thousands of workers—the number has been more than doubled in the last six months—turning out pieces and parts for the three types of two-engined bombers which Martin produces.

MAKES THREE TYPES

These are the B-26, 13-ton medium bombers for the United States Army, the PBM-3, nicknamed the "Mariner," a heavy bombing flying boat for the United States Navy, and the 187, the "Baltimore," a medium bomber for the British, which will soon be adapted for U. S. Army use.

The actual rate of production must remain a military secret, but not a few of these speedy, well-armed and highly maneuverable bombers are leaving the plant for action each month, Martin said.

Admitting metal is necessary in other war construction, he reaffirmed that his plants could "come up to schedule" if the priorities classification were raised, principally because he now has the workers and the tools with which to make the number of planes desired by both the American and British Governments.

NOW AUTOMATIC

Plane production has been standardized to such an extent that manufacture of hulls, gun turrets, wings, wheels and other parts has now become automatic, he said. Sixty-five per cent. of any bomber now in production is made under sub-contracts, he added.

He said his company receives only about $150,000 for a bomber whose total cost is over $250,000. The remainder is paid to the subcontractor for additional parts.

Elevator Crushes Workman To Death

Benjamin F. Waters, forty-three-year-old Negro, 400 block Myrtle avenue, was crushed to death today when he was pinned between an elevator and the floor at a furniture establishment in the first block South Howard street. Police said Waters was repairing a defective switch on the lift when the accident occurred.

1,000 To Attend Insurance Meet

About 1,000 insurance men are expected to attend the twenty-fourth annual Life Insurance Congress of the Baltimore Life Underwriters' Association, Inc., at Lord Baltimore Hotel next Friday.

Speakers at the event, forecast as the largest and most successful Congress, will include Senator Millard E. Tydings, State Insurance Commissioner John B. Gontrum and several nationally-known insurance men.

One of the most important activities of the Association during the year has been the voluntary task of introducing and explaining payroll savings for the purchase of war bonds and stamps. Door prizes will be bonds.

TODAY'S TIDES	
High tide......	2.06 A. M., 2.24 P. M.
Low tide......	8.26 A. M., 9.14 P. M.

50 Million Lose Home, States Wu

More than 50,000,000 Chinese are homeless as a result of the war, Dr. James Wu, local Chinese leader, today told members of the Civitan Club at a luncheon session in the Emerson Hotel.

The speaker told the club members he was confident the Allies would be victorious, and said many reforms are in store for China after the war.

The 300 Chinese in Baltimore contributed approximately $29,000 for China relief last year, he added.

Seaman I. T. Lind To Get Medal

A medal of valor will be presented Saturday to Second Class Seaman Irving Thomas Lind, twenty-five, of the Coast Guard, by American Legion Post No. 27 for rescuing a woman from drowning off Seal Rocks, near San Francisco, on Christmas Day, 1941.

Bar Urges Re-Election Of All Sitting Judges

The Bar Association of Baltimore here had formally recommended the re-election of all sitting judges who come up before the voters this year and went a step further, urging that they compete in both primaries, thus making the election completely non-partisan.

The judges included three on the Supreme Bench, George A. Solter, Eugene O'Dunne and Joseph N. Ulman; the chief judge of the Court of Appeals, Judge Carroll T. Bond, and Judge Joseph T. Parr of the People's Court.

The suggestion that the judges run in both primaries had been made by Joseph Sherbow in 1934 and again in 1938.

This is the first time that the association had endorsed the idea, regarded as an important step in making judicial elections completely without party action.

The judiciary committee of the association, Wendell Allen, chairman, made the recommendations to the association's executive committee, G. C. A. Anderson, president, and it was adopted unanimously.

RACING AT PIMLICO

DAILY TO MAY 9

A Stake Race Daily
TODAY—THE PIMLICO NURSERY
RESERVED SEATS DAILY, $1.10
FIRST RACE 2.30 P. M. (E.W.T.)
DAILY DOUBLE CLOSES 2.15 P. M. (E.W.T.)

SUGAR CONSERVATION

Because of the government's drastic reduction in our sugar allowance to 50%, we are compelled to restrict it's use to our patrons accordingly. Your co-operation will enable us to serve all with the least inconvenience.

Maryland Restaurant Ass'n, Inc.

FOR SALE

2—SEVEN-PASSENGER 12 AND 16 CYLINDER CADILLACS. White wall tires. Good condition. Cash. No trade. Bargain.
CALL FOR MR. KRAMER
1700 N. Gay St.

LOG INN
OPEN

Soft Crab, Chicken and Steak Dinners. Telephone Annapolis 5621 For Reservations. Drive Down Annapolis Blvd., turn left Severn River.

Win Cash For News Tips And Amateur Photographs

Do you want money for being alert? The Baltimore News-Post and Sunday American are offering cash prizes each week for news tips and amateur photographs. Total awards of $50 are distributed weekly for news tips, $25 for the best, $10 for the next best and $1 prizes for the next fifteen. For each amateur photograph published $3 will be paid, with special bonuses for outstanding pictures. Spot-news pictures are preferred, but candid camera shots that pull at the heartstrings are acceptable. Avoid pictures of ordinary scenes. Telephone The News-Tip Editor at Lexington 0100 for news tips and rush spot-news photographs in to the Picture Editor.

BOOGIE WOOGIE

By Michael Berry

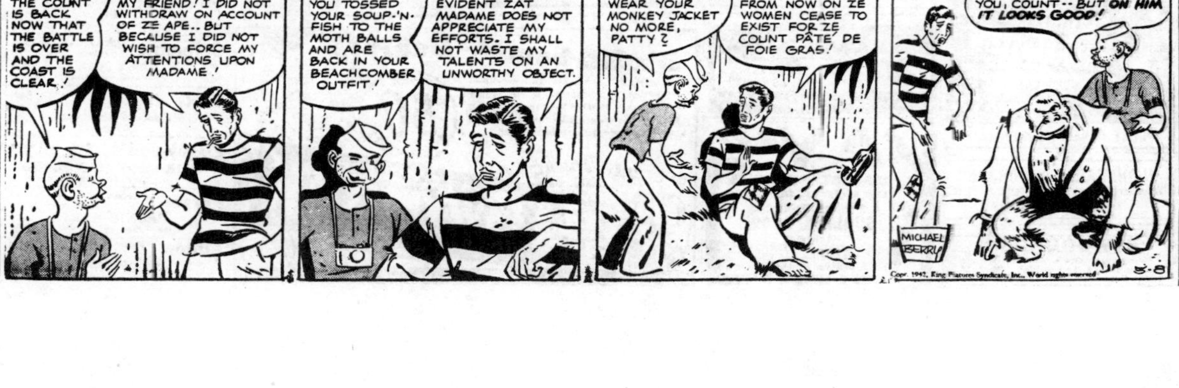

Action

describes this result story! The advertiser of this attractive News-Post & American Want Ad received dozens of replies!

BARCLAY ST., 2519—Two light housekeeping rooms. See Sunday or after 5 P. M. any weekday. No children.

Use the paper with the fast action result power

Phone LExington 0100

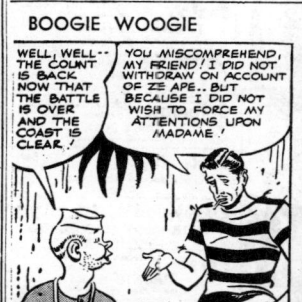

'Ship Ahoy,' With Crew Of Girls And Comics, At Century

VIRGINIA O'BRIEN—BERT LAHR

By NORMAN CLARK

THERE ARE SPIES in this musical comedy, "Ship Ahoy," with F. B. I. men on their trails, but don't get the idea that the film at Loew's Century is a serious affair.

The story hasn't been under way long before Bert Lahr bows low before dark Virginia O'Brien, kisses her hand, then keeps on kissing her arm right up to the elbow.

Apologizes Mr. Lahr:

"It's the salmon in me—running up stream."

"That'll give you an idea."

Then there is Red Skelton flitting this way and that as a hypochondriac who writes adventure stories for the pulp magazines. Added to this is Eleanor Powell, who can fling her shapely legs in more directions than an octopus could even think of; also tap her heels and toes faster than an excited woodpecker can wield his beak.

And if that isn't enough for your money, "Ship Ahoy" offers Tommy Dorsey and his orchestra, all sorts of effective dance numbers, a number of pleasant tunes and some tasty yum yums. What are yum yums? Why, peppermint sticks. Aw, you know—girls, girls, girls.

The plot is something about foreign agents who inveigle Eleanor Powell into smuggling a tiny magnetic mine into Porto Rico. These rascals make her think that she

"SHIP AHOY," starring Eleanor Powell and Red Skelton. Screen play by Harry Clork, based on a story by Matt Brooks, Bradford Ropes and Bert Kalmar. Directed by Edward N. Buzzell. A Metro-Goldwyn-Mayer Picture, presented at Loew's Century.

"THE CAST"
```
Tallulah Winters .......... Eleanor Powell
Merton K. Kibble .......... Red Skelton
"Skip" Owens .............. Bert Lahr
Fran Evans ................ Virginia O'Brien
Art Higgins ............... William Post, Jr.
"Stump" ................... James Cross
"Stamp" ................... Eddie Hartman
Pietro .................... Stuart Crawford
Dr. Farno ................. John Emery
```

is doing a job for the U. S. Government, but—oh, why gives a darn about the plot of a musical comedy. Bert Lahr is funny as the pal of Skelton and the two comedians have some rather amusing episodes together. Skelton flounders a bit when he is doing romantic scenes with Miss Powell; he is much better when engaged in rough and tumble comedy. Miss Powell, too, is much happier when she is at her nimble dancing. Virginia O'Brien is okey-doke with her dead-pan songs.

"Ship Ahoy" should prove popular with all those citizens who are seeking easy-going entertainment.

Jane Cowl Is Coming To Ford's

Having closed the doors at Ford's for the season—or so he thought—Manager John Little will reopen them next Monday night to entertain Jane Cowl and her new play, "Punch and Julia," for a stay of one week.

"Punch and Julia" is a comedy by George Donald Batson and is being tested this week in Washington. It is a Guthrie McClintic production and has been directed by him.

Miss Cowl plays the role of a renowned literary critic and radio celebrity. Others in the cast are Arthur Margetson, Frances Heflin, Gregory Peck, Viola Roche and Janet Fox.

HOT ACTING

Alexis Smith lost four and three-quarter pounds while doing her dramatic scenes in "The Constant Nymph."

Walter Winchell ON BROADWAY

Scrambled Eggs

Good to have vaudeville back in the spotlight again. But why bring back the stale stuff that helped cripple it?...Wonder why they doubled the price of score-cards in the New York ball parks?...Not only does Rita Hayworth look good in technicolor, but technicolor looks good on her...Ben Marden won a big package of Broadway cabbage at an East Side gambling spot the other night. Ben tipped the Negro waiter $1,000, and the amazed chap immediately quit and announced he was retiring for at least a year.

How come nobody ever gives medals to critics for going to so many dull shows all season? This one was so dull both the Critics Circle and Pulitzer Committee agreed no show was worth a prize ...This gives you an idea how temporary fame is. If DiMaggio doesn't get a hit one day—they boo him... Whatever happened to those people who said they had proof Hitler was dead?

I wish Hildegarde wouldn't use a uniformed sailor or soldier in the role of stooge that way...How times change! When it was first announced that Melvyn Douglas had a civilian job there was a big to-doodle in Washington. The other day he returned there to take up his duties, and nobody said anything about it.

Things to worry about: The crocodile tears spilled by the so-whatish sports writers, weeping over the possibility that night baseball games may be abolished....What's a ball game compared to the safety of some fellow out at sea?

The chorines have another wrinkle. They're wearing "Indian love bands"—an oversized wedding ring supposed to mean friendship. But the cuties wear it on the important finger, which gives the wolves the "keep away" sign.

We recently paragraphed about Miriam Lavelle, the dancer. Tried to get on Broadway for years and finally did it—but via one of those electricky signs...Agents saw her shadows on the sign, looked her up and booked her for the Strand Theatre. Then she was engaged for "Keep 'Em Laughing" and next week goes into Loew's State... That's Broadway, Roscoe!...For several years—not one job. Now for four weeks—three of them... Nick Kenny has another engaging tune: "I'll Keep the Lovelight Burning."

Russian Icons To Be Exhibited

Native settings have been arranged for an exhibition of Russian coins which will open in the Baltimore Museum of Art tonight. The speaker will be Dr. Andrey Avinoff, director of the Carnegie Museum in Pittsburgh, and once gentleman-in-waiting to the Czar.

Anatole Grosheff of the Russian Holy Trinity Church will direct a choir which will be dressed in Russian national costume.

Young Russian women in costume will sell Bublichi rolls for the Russian War Relief.

CHICKENPOX

M.-G.-M. is crossing its fingers. Raymond Severn, one of the English kids working in "Yank at Eton," has come down with the chickenpox. Mickey Rooney never has had it.

Movie CLOCK

```
CENTURY—"Ship Ahoy", 10.45 A. M.,
   12.45, 3.05, 5.20, 7.35, 9.55 P. M.
NEW—"To the Shores of Tripoli," 10 A. M.,
   12, 2, 4, 6, 8, 10 P. M.
STANLEY—"Bahama Passage," 11.35 A.
   M., 12.44, 2.36, 4.28, 6.20, 8.12, 10.04
   P. M.
KEITH'S—"Ghost of Frankenstein," 10.52
   A. M., 12.44, 2.36, 4.28, 6.20, 8.12, 10.04
   P. M.
HIPPODROME—"Tattles of Tahiti," 11
   A. M., 1.45, 4.35, 7.20, 10.07 P. M.
VALENCIA—"Gone With the Wind," 1.10,
   5.10, 9.00 P. M.
PARKWAY—"Fingers at Window," 12.45,
   2.30, 4.25, 6.15, 8.05, 9.5° P. M.
MAYFAIR—"Alias Boston Blackie," 10.18
   A. M., 12.50, 2.40, 4.30, 6.20, 8.10, 10 P. M.
TIMES—"The Strangler," 11 A. M.,
   8.46, 10.44 P. M.
ROSLYN—"In Name Only," 1.48, 3.57,
   6.06, 8.15, 10.24 P. M.
```

Advertising Queen

TRUDY MARSHALL

Because she starred in huge newspaper advertisements, on magazine covers and on billboards from one end of the nation to another, blue-eyed Miss Marshall has been signed to a Twentieth Century-Fox film contract and awarded a role in "Thunder Birds." Trudy was born in Brooklyn, where her beauty was discovered by advertising experts during her high school career.

VICTORY THEATRE TO OFFER COMEDY

The Finnish Educational Association, Inc., will present the Victory Theatre in a three-act comedy entitled "Call Me Mike," tomorrow at 8.45 P. M. The play is being staged by Miss Frieda Fleischman, director of the Victory Theatre. The play has a cast of 12.

In the cast are: Louis Vito, Nancy Drew, Ben Epstein, Sirkka Tuomi, Earl Jordon, Lorraine Dorf, Bertha Polt, John Frey, Albert Strapelli, Jeannette Bredt, Sylvia Schoenbaum, and Robert Lauren. The sets are by Don Hurley and Robert Fleischman.

A portion of the proceeds will go to the U. S. armed forces.

'ALLIANCE PLAYERS TO ACT 'THE BAT'

As the final play of their 1942 subscription series, the Alliance Players will present Mary Roberts Rinehart's, "The Bat," a comedy mystery in three acts, next Sunday and Monday at 8.30 P. M. at the Jewish Educational Alliance Auditorium, 1216 East Baltimore street.

Harry King has directed the play and designed the sets. In the cast are Milton Hamburger, Ernest Tanenbaum, Ruth Kierr, Ada Rhea Cohen, Ann Shockett, Harry Lipsitz, Joseph Kanowsky, Joseph Rosenberg, Thelma Hirsch, and Donald Hurwitz.

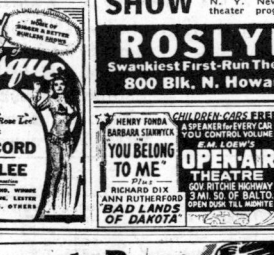

Rights To Rachel Field Story Acquired At Price Of $75,000

Paramount Deal Follows Untimely Death Of Writer

By LOUELLA O. PARSONS
Motion Picture Editor International News Service.

HOLLYWOOD, May 8.—How sad it is that Rachel Field, whose "All This and Heaven, Too" was a best-selling sensation, didn't live to know that her last story, "And Now Tomorrow," has been sold to Paramount.

I say this because few know that Miss Field began her career as a reader in the Eastern Paramount story department at a salary of $45 a week. But her friends know how happy it would have made her to know, before her untimely death six weeks ago, that the company where she started so modestly has just paid $75,000 for the rights to her last novel.

"And Now Tomorrow," now running serially in a national magazine, is a story with a New England background. In many ways it is a New England "How Green Was My Valley." It deals with two sisters, rich and powerful in an industrial town. One is of the old capitalistic school—the younger is modern and more liberal. And like most of Miss Field's works, it has a dramatic love story.

I couldn't be more interested than to hear that a deal is now cooking for Oliver Hardy and Stan Laurel to make a picture for the Azteca Film Company in Mexico City. Their attorney, Ben Shipman, flew to Mexico to make final arrangements.

I happened to be in Mexico City with Babe and Stan and you've never seen such popularity. Everywhere they went the Mexicans would shout affectionately:

"Mr. Fat and Mr. Thin!"

And that's going to be the title of the Mexican picture, or, in Spanish:

"El Gordoy el Flaco."

The boys have traveled 20,000 miles to Army camps and on good will tours this past year and they are now with the victory caravan. Their contract with Twentieth Century-Fox gives them the right to make outside pictures.

Louella Parsons, in her Hollywood column, comments on visits to the night clubs of Margaret Lindsay (above) and Woolworth Donahue.

A Line or Two: Charles Vidor, who went East to talk it over with his wife, Karen Morley, came home alone. Little doubt that the Vidors will divorce and also little doubt that Charles is, interested elsewhere.

The other eve someone put a nickel in a juke box and "Deep in the Heart of Texas" started playing. A long, lanky Marine with a Southern accent you could slice with a knife exclaimed:

"Everybody stand up, when the national anthem is played!"

Paulette Goddard is returning from New York in a few days with the latest thing in a priority wardrobe. Deanna Durbin is sick with a cold Woolworth Donahue and Margaret Lindsay are still doing the night spots. Norma Shearer and Marty Arrouge the center of all eyes at the Palladium, Susan Hayward and Jimmy McHugh keeping a luncheon date at the Paramount commissary.

Laraine Day's maid of honor will be Lewanna McAfee, switchboard operator for the M.-G.-M. publicity department. Laraine, who weds Ray Hendricks May 16, is having a crystal and silver shower given her by some of her studio friends.

Jack Harris of New York city says:

"Don't keep your bucks private—buy bonds—and watch how every buck private responds."

Today's Movie Calendar

Theatres advertised in this column belong to the Motion Picture Theatre Owners of Maryland.

Alpha Catonsville John Wayne in "THE SPOILERS" Comedy.		**Garden** Charles at 6rcaa Johnny Mack Brown in "FIGHTING BILL FAGO" "Spy Smasher."	**New Essex** Essex. Md. Lon Chaney, Jr., in "THE WOLF MAN" "Three Stooges."
Ambassador 4604 Liberty Heights Miriam Hopkins in "A GENTLEMAN AFTER DARK" "Concert in B Flat Minor."		**Glen** Glen Burnie Tim Holt in "CYCLONE ON HORSEBACK" "Spy Smasher."	**New Glen** Glen Burnie Betty Grable in "SONG OF THE ISLANDS" Comedy.
Apollo 1500 Harford Ave. Roy Rogers in "SUNSET ON THE DESERT" "Crime Doesn't Pay Story."		**Grand** 511 S. Conkling St. Roy Rogers in "SUNSET ON THE DESERT" "Spy Smasher."	**Northway** Harford & North Pky. Joel McCrea in "SULLIVAN'S TRAVELS" "Dick Tracy vs. Crime, Inc."
Arcade Harford Rd. & Hamilton Ave. Paulette Goddard in "THE LADY HAS PLANS" Comedy.		**Gwynn** 4609 Liberty Heights Ave. Bob Steele in "WEST OF CIMARRON" Comedy.	**Overlea** Belair Rd., End of Car Line Regis Toomey in "BULLET SCARS" With Edgar Kennedy.
Astor Poplar Grove at Edmondson Andrews Sisters in "WHAT'S COOKIN'" "Groom and Board."		**Hampden** 911 W. 36th St. Bill Elliott in "BULLETS FOR BANDITS" Comedy.	**Palace** Gay and Fayette Ave. John Wayne in "HOME IN WYOMING" Comedy.
Aurora 7 East North Ave. Glenn Ford in "Adventures of Martin Eden"		**Harford** 2516 Harford Ave. George Montgomery in "LAST OF THE DUANES" Comedy.	**Patterson** Eastern and East Aves. Paulette Goddard in "THE LADY HAS PLANS" "March of Time."
Avalon 4300 Park Heights Ave. Brian Donlevy in "A GENTLEMAN AFTER DARK" "Interior Decorator."		**Horn** 2014 West Pratt St. Gene Autry in "HOME IN WYOMING" "Wedding Worries."	**Pikes** Pikesville, Md. Carole Lombard in "TO BE OR NOT TO BE" Color Cartoon.
Avenue Milton Ave. & Hoffman St. Robert Montgomery in "HELL BELOW" "Captain Midnight."		**Howard** 115 N. Howard St. Brian Donlevy in "A GENTLEMAN AFTER DARK" Comedy.	**Pimlico** Park Heights & Belvedere William Holden in "TORPEDO BOAT" "Yoo Hoo General."
Avon 3019 Hamilton Ave. Jeffry Lynn in "LAW OF THE TROPICS" "Sea Raiders."		**Ideal** 903 W. Thirty-sixth St. Roy Rogers in "SUNSET ON THE DESERT" "Our Gang Comedy."	**Preston** 1108 E. Preston St. The Rough Riders in "GHOST TOWN LAW" "Dick Tracy vs. Crime, Inc."
Belnord 2700 Philadelphia Ave. Gene Autry in "HOME IN WYOMING" "Spy Smasher."		**Irvington** 4113 Frederick Ave. Marlene Dietrich in "THE SPOILERS" Comedy.	**Red Wing** 3904 North Point Rd. Bob Hope in "LOUISIANA PURCHASE" "Who's A Dummy."
Boulevard 33rd at Greenmount Paulette Goddard in "THE LADY HAS PLANS" "March of Time."		**Lane** Dundalk, Md. Johnny Mack Brown in "ARIZONA CYCLONE" Comedy.	**Rex** 846 W. North Ave. Norma Shearer in "WE WERE DANCING" Comedy.
Bridge Edmondson Ave. & Pulaski St. Richard Arlen in "TORPEDO BOAT" Comedy.		**Leader** 248 S. Broadway "ROCK RIVER RENEGADES" Buy Defense Bonds and Stamps.	**Rialto** 1607 N. Washington St. FEATURE PICTURE Also Comedy.
Broadway 509 S. Broadway Brian Donlevy in "A GENTLEMAN AFTER DARK" Buy Defense Stamps.		**Lexway** 31 W. Lexington St. Joan Fontaine in "SUSPICION" With Cary Grant.	**Ritz** 5004 York Rd. Clyde Beatty in "THE SPOILERS" "Iron Claw."
Cameo 4705 Harford Road Andrews Sisters in "WHAT'S COOKIN'" "Three Stooges."		**Linwood** 908 S. Linwood Ave. Bill Elliott in "DEVIL'S TRAIL" "Holt of the Secret Service."	**Senator** 5904 York Rd. Clyde Beatty in "THE SPOILERS" "Iron Claw."
Capitol 1518 W. Baltimore St. Andrews Sisters in "WHAT'S COOKIN'" "Three Stooges."		**Little** 523 North Howard St. Paulette Goddard in "GIRL FROM LENINGRAD" First Baltimore Showing.	**Strand** Dundalk, Md. John Wayne in "THE SPOILERS" With Marlene Dietrich.
Casino 1118 Light St. Roy Corrigan in "THUNDER RIVER FEUD" "Captain Midnight."		**Lord Baltimore** 1109 West Baltimore St. Albert Dekker in "YOKEL BOY" With Joan Davis.	**Towson** Towson, Md. Kay Kyser in "PLAYMATES" Comedy.
Cluster 303 S. Broadway Richard Arlen in "TORPEDO BOAT" "A Quiet Fourth."		**Lord Calvert** 2444 Washington Boulevard Andy Devine in "ROAD AGENT" Comedy.	**Uptown** 5010 Park Heights Marlene Dietrich in "THE SPOILERS" "March of Time."
Columbia 709 Washington Blvd. Penny Singleton in "GO WEST, YOUNG LADY" Comedy.		**Lyceum** Sparrows Point, Md. Paulette Goddard in "THE LADY HAS PLANS" "March of Time."	**Vilma** Belair Rd. and Mayfield Ave. Jean Parker in "TORPEDO BOAT" With Jean Parker.
Earle Belair Rd. at Woodlea Ave. Claude Rains in "THE WOLF MAN" Comedy.		**McHenry** 1037 Light St. Paulette Goddard in "THE LADY HAS PLANS" "March of Time."	**Walbrook** 508 N. Howard St. Ginger Rogers in "ROXIE HART" "Homework."
Edgewood Edmondson & Edgewood Paulette Goddard in "THE LADY HAS PLANS" "Spy Smasher."		**Mayfair** 508 N. Howard St. Chester Morris in "ALIAS BOSTON BLACKIE" First Baltimore Showing.	**Waverly** Greenmount at Gorsuch Bill Elliott in "ROARING FRONTIERS" "Spy Smasher."
Forest Garrison & Liberty Heights Ginger Rogers in "ROXIE HART" "Dick Tracy vs. Crime, Inc."		**Met** Pennsylvania & North Brian Donlevy in "A GENTLEMAN AFTER DARK" "Argentine Comedy."	**Westport** 2205 Russell St. Conrad Veidt in "NAZI AGENT" Comedy.
Fulton Edmondson & Baker St. Carole Lombard in "TO BE OR NOT TO BE"		**New** Brooklyn, Md. Bob Steele in "CODE OF THE OUTLAWS" "Three Blonde Mice."	**Westway** 5300 Edmondson Ave. Robert Stack in "BADLANDS OF DAKOTA" Comedy.

Behind Scenes In Hollywood Studios

By HARRISON CARROLL
King Features Syndicate Writer.

HOLLYWOOD, May 8.—Of the 10 pounds he lost on his Eastern trip, John Garfield figures at least six were dropped on a storm-tossed flight from New York to Reading, Pa. After fighting a heavy gale, the plane had to make a forced landing through fog on a bumpy field.

With the new load of fuel, it took off again, but the sky was so murky that the pilot was four hours late at Reading. He and Garfield then discovered they had flown over restricted areas and might have been the target for anti-aircraft fire.

Signing of eight-year-old Donald Davis to play in sandlot baseball scenes for "The Pride of the Yankees" represents a debt paid off by Gary Cooper.

The youngster is the son of Mrs. J. Charles Davis, who, as Marilyn Mills, the Western star, gave Cooper his first two acting jobs in the movies.

Among the 64 members of Paramount's "Wake Island" troupe who registered for the draft at the Salton sea were Jack Mulhall and John Morris Foster. Mulhall plays a lieutenant commander in the film; Foster is in charge of wardrobe.

Here's what makes it an item.

Years ago, when both were well known players at the Universal studio, Mulhall and Foster also registered together for the World War I. draft.

Several years ago, a movie troupe presented the late Carole Lombard with a new make-up kit. For years before that, Carole had carried her make-up in a little white box. She gave the box to her hairdresser, Loretta Francelle.

"If you ever see a girl you'd like to have the box," said Carole, "give it to her."

Loretta Francelle has found the girl. Carole's make-up box now is the proudest possession of Marjorie Woodworth, Hal Roach's starlet.

The farm-owning Iowa parents of Donna Reed can't stay with her at the Studio Club when they come to Hollywood, so the M.-G.-M. starlet has rented a two-room trailer and will set it up in pleasant surroundings on M.-G.-M.'s Lot 3.

Donna, who'll be working in "Random Horvest," figures this the best way for her to see the most of her parents.

KEITH'S ROOF

Keith's Roof, atop Keith's Theatre will again present two nights of dancing this week-end. Tomorrow night will find Billy Isaac on hand to play for the dancers. Sunday night brings Billy Antrim and his band, with Ann McFaul singing the songs.

Final Play

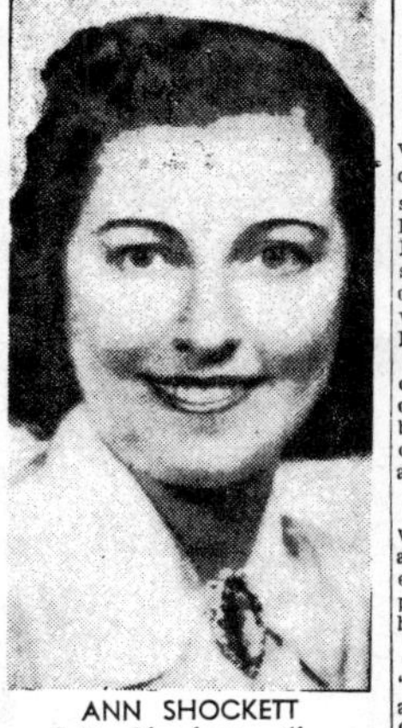

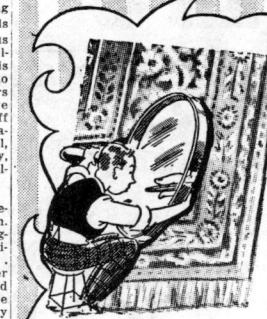

ANN SHOCKETT
Miss Shockett will appear in "The Bat," next Sunday and Monday, which closes the 1942 subscription of the Alliance Players.

Latest Report From Broadway

NEW YORK, May 8.—The Playwrights and the Theatre Guild will continue their production partnership next year with a new S. N. Behrman play co-starring Alfred Lunt and Lynn Fontanne. The script is based on an old Spanish drama called "The Pirate," which was put into English in 1916 by Ludwig Fulda.

It has a Santo Domingo setting of the early 1800s and of the cast of 40 approximately one half will be colored actors. No title has been chosen. Rehearsals in August for a September premiere here.

James Elliott, seventeen-year-old who has a part in "Junior Miss" and produced "Arlene" on his own earlier this season, has another play, a London import, which he hopes to stage in the fall.

Helen Hayes, still touring with "Candle in the Wind," has bought an untitled play by Mrs. Fremont Older which is based on the life of Harriet Beecher Stowe. It's possible that Miss Hayes will emerge as her own producer with it.

With Hollywood insisting upon the early return of Victor Moore and William Gaxton, these headliners of "Keep 'Em Laughing" may have to leave in a week or so. Clifford Fischer has been talking with Jack Durant, who was in "Pal Joey" and the films, as one possible replacement.

John Leffler, who was manager for B. G. DeSylva, will do a musical version of Avery Hopwood's old "Fair and Warmer," next season.

AT REX

"Louisiana Purchase," Paramount's celluloid edition in Technicolor of the Broadway musical hit, is the feature film today and tomorrow, at the Rex Theatre, 4600 York road. Bob Hope is at the top of his agile-witted form, Vera Zorina, is bewitching to look at and Victor Moore is superbly funny. The three stars are given excellent support by Irene Bordoni, Dona Drake, Raymond Walburn and Maxie Rosenbloom.

THE VOICE OF BROADWAY -:- By Dorothy Kilgallen

Gossip In Gotham

Anatole Litvak and Peggy Fears are putting the zing in spring . . . The reason why a big-name bandleader may have to quit for six months is tragic . . . His intimates believe that Stirling Hayden, who disappeared suddenly from Hollywood, is on active duty with the Navy . . . Jean Gabin's Manhattan romancing with Marlene Dietrich has reversed the triangle; now Ginger Rogers is carrying the torch . . . Jim Tully's son is giving him headaches again . . . Models won't be making that fabulous money any more. The new "ceiling" on wages for the beauties is $5 an hour; some of them used to pull $25 an hour . . . Frankie Hyers of the 18 Club is ailing . . . Have Ella Logan and Fred Finklehoff called it a day? . . . Dorothy Lamour, in town for a brief spell, dated Greg Bautzer on Monday, Bob Ritchie on Tuesday and Woolworth Donahue on Wednesday!

Libby Holman is scheduled to return to the night life scene soon. She'll open at a local bistro, singing folk blues to the accompaniment of Josh White's guitar . . . Lenore Lemmon is writing her memoirs (at 18!). They'll be titled "Inside the Stork Club" because she's barred from the Billingsley boite . . . Actress Katherine Locke and Norman ("This Is War") Corwin are a heart today . . . Ben Whittaker, owner of Requested, isn't taking the Derby loss too seriously —he won $500,000 when his nag breezed in at Jamaica Saturday . . . Topic of British conversation here is the report that Hitler offered to trade the five British generals captured by the Axis (two from Libya and three from Singapore) in return for Rudolf Hess . . . It's doubtful that Fefe's swank Monte Carlo will reopen this season.

Aunt Jemima and Belle Baker have also taken that technicolor pill treatment for reducing—Aunt Jemima is said to have lost 60 pounds, Belle more than 20 . . . Since Carmen Miranda missed her cue no visitors are permitted backstage at the Winter Garden during performances . . . Terrific fist fight between Abe Lyman and his personal manager, Harry Weinstein. Abe won; Harry had to be patched up by a medico . . . Dolores Del Rio has returned all the jewels her ex-swain gave her . . . Binnie Barnes looks like George Abbott's Hollywood name for his next "Beat the Band" . . . Patricia Prochnik, daughter of the former Ambassador from Austria, has switched from Tinsley Adams to Jack Bartlett . . . The Danny (Meet the People) Dares are divorcing. They're at the settlement stage now.

GOLD STARS: To The Hartmans' dance hilarities in "Keep 'Em Laughing" . . . Raymond Scott's rhythms at the Blue Gardens in Armonk . . . The new film version of "Broadway," in which George Raft, Pat O'Brien and Brod Crawford are all Grade A . . . Pierre J. Huss' exciting book on Germany: "The Foe We Face" . . . Gertrude Niesen's Decca vocals of Hoagy Carmichael's new ones, "Skylark" and "Lamplighter's Serenade" . . . Morton Downey's tenor tunes at Loew's State . . . Dorita and Velero, the Flamenco stepper at El Chico . . . Lucy Monroe's nostalgic Victor album, "Songs You Love" . . . Jay Jostyn in the ether drama "Mr. District Attorney" . . . Carol Bruce chanting "Three Little Sisters" at the Paramount.

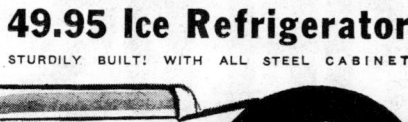

Protect Your RUGS ..Save Wool!

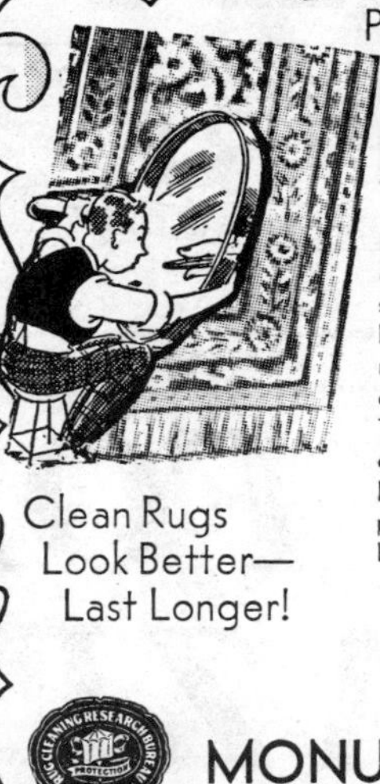

Due to changing conditions and the wool shortage, you may not be able to get new rugs for some time to come. So NOW is the TIME OF TIMES to give those you already have the very best protective care possible.

Clean Rugs Look Better— Last Longer!

SEND YOUR RUGS TO US TODAY!

YOUR GUARANTEE OF SATISFACTION

MONUMENTAL RUG CLEANERS
1915 Windsor Ave. LA. 3771

49.95 Ice Refrigerator
STURDILY BUILT! WITH ALL STEEL CABINET

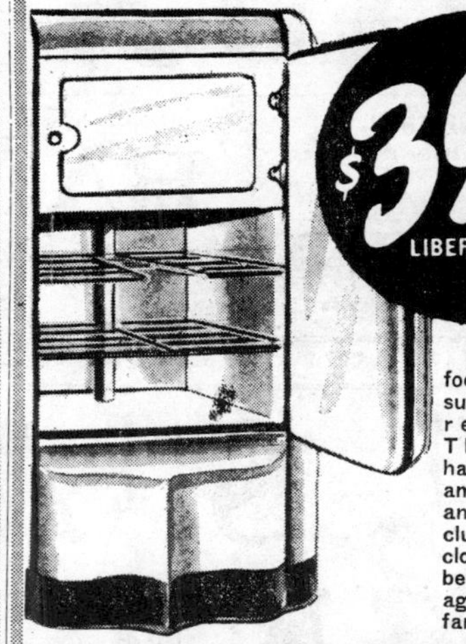

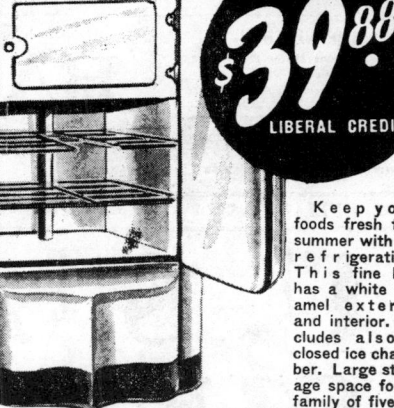

$39.88
LIBERAL CREDIT

Keep your foods fresh this summer with ice refrigeration! This fine box has a white enamel exterior and interior. Includes also a closed ice chamber. Large storage space for a family of five!

HECHT'S Broadway FURNITURE STORE
412-414 S. BROADWAY, Near Bank

★ NOTICE — HECHT'S BROADWAY FURNITURE STORE PRICES ARE IN ACCORD WITH THE NEW GOVERNMENT PRICE REGULATIONS, OUR PRICES ARE AT GOVERNMENT CEILING LEVELS OR LOWER. IF, THROUGH ERROR, ANY PRICE SHOULD BE INCORRECT WE WILL GLADLY REFUND THE DIFFERENCE.

STARTS TOMORROW
DOORS OPEN 10:30 A. M.
WARNER BROS. STANLEY
HOWARD NEAR FRANKLIN ST.

FEATURE PRESENTED AT 11.20—1.55—4.35 7.15—9.50

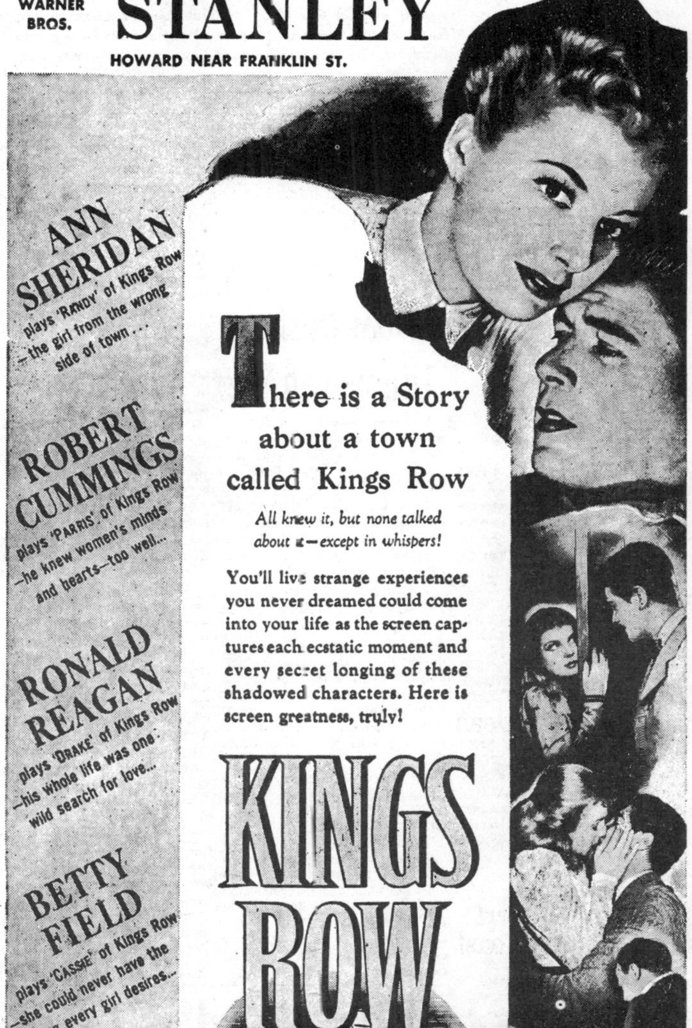
ANN SHERIDAN
plays 'RANDY' of Kings Row —the girl from the wrong side of town...
ROBERT CUMMINGS
plays 'PARRIS' of Kings Row —he knew women's minds and hearts—too well...
RONALD REAGAN
plays 'DRAKE' of Kings Row —his whole life was one wild search for love...
BETTY FIELD
plays 'CASSIE' of Kings Row —she could never have the thing every girl desires...
There is a Story about a town called Kings Row
All knew it, but none talked about it—except in whispers!
You'll live strange experiences you never dreamed could come into your life as the screen captures each ecstatic moment and every secret longing of these shadowed characters. Here is screen greatness, truly!
KINGS ROW
Where Every Heart Hid a Secret Sin
To be long remembered for the best-seller it was —for the magnificent film it is!
Directed by SAM WOOD of 'Mr. Chips' and 'Kitty Foyle' fame

WARNER BROS.' NEW SUCCESS.
with CHARLES COBURN
Claude Rains · Judith Anderson · Nancy Coleman
KAAREN VERNE · MARIA OUSPENSKAYA · HARRY DAVENPORT
The Screen Play is superbly adapted by Casey Robinson from the Celebrated Novel by Henry Bellamann; the music by Erich Wolfgang Korngold

P.B.A. GIVES 3-POINT PROTECTION TO YOU & YOUR LOVED ONES!

LIFE PROTECTION—In case of death, except from military service, of head-of-the-house, unpaid balance is cancelled. Merchandise becomes the property of your heirs. No further payments.

FIRE PROTECTION—In case of fire, except when due to act of war, in home of head-of-the-house during payment period, merchandise will be replaced if destroyed, or repaired if damaged.

CONTINUOUS CREDIT — Protect your buying power. Buy monthly, subject to Government regulation. You pay monthly. No need waiting until your account is paid up to buy more.

P. B. A. IS YOURS FOR ONLY PAYING YOUR ACCOUNT AS AGREED

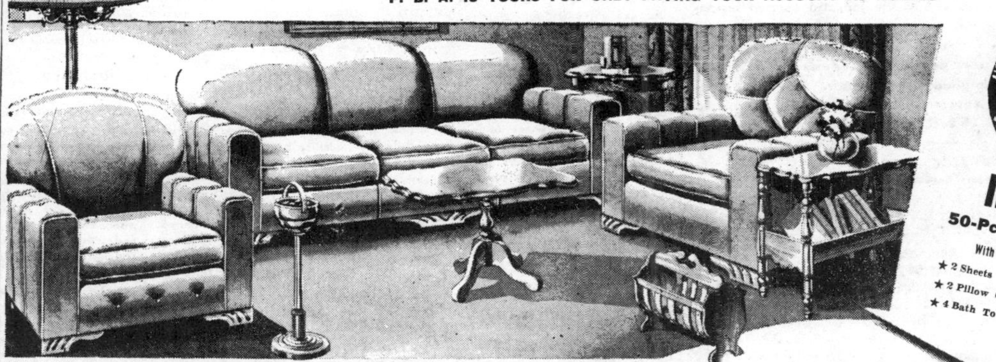

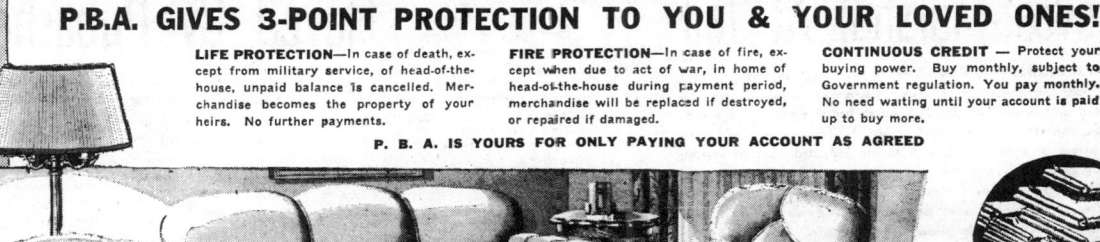

INCLUDED!
50-Pc. Linen Ensemble
With Purchase of 3-Room Outfit
* 2 Sheets * 2 Pillow Cases * 4 Bath Towels
* 12 Tea Towels * 12 Wash Cloths * 6 Dish Towels * 12 Pot Holders

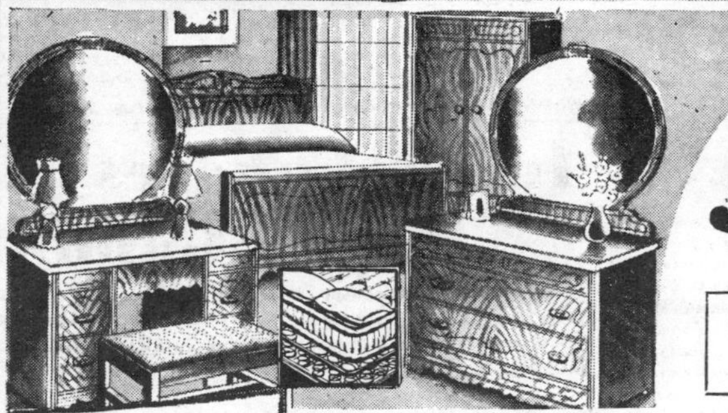

COMPLETE 3 ROOM OUTFIT
$229
CONVENIENT CREDIT
$279 VALUE!

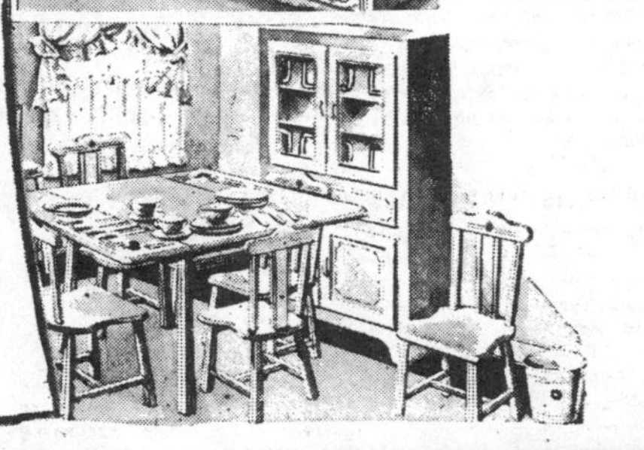

Hecht's Broadway Furniture Store Is Easy To Reach
The No. 10 Trackless Trolley passes right in front of our door. Only 14 minutes from center of town, only 8 minutes from Highlandtown. Come in tomorrow and save sensationally!

12-Pc. Bedroom Outfit	9-Piece Living Room Outfit	43-Piece Kitchen Outfit
If Bought Separately $79	If Bought Separately $99	If Bought Separately $51
Only 1.00 A Week	Only 1.25 A Week	Only 75c A Week
● Modern Bed	● Modern Sofa	● Kitchen Cabinet
● Modern Chestrobe	● Modern Arm Chair	● Table & 4 Chairs
● Dresser or Vanity	● Modern Club Chair	● Kitchen Stool
● Walnut Bench	● Coffee Table	● 32-Pc. Dinner Set
● Simmons Coil Spring	● End Table	● Step-On Can
● Mattress	● Floor Lamp and Shade	● 2 Pair Curtains
● 2 Vanity Lamps	● 2 Pair Curtains	● Waste Basket
● 2 Pillows		
● 2 Pair Curtains		

We'll Gladly Hold Your Purchases For Future Delivery!

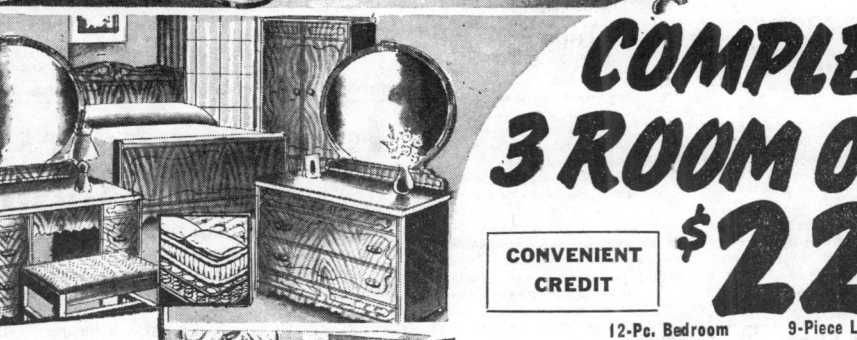

MAIL THIS COUPON
HECHT'S BROADWAY FURNITURE STORE,
412-414 South Broadway.
Please send a representative to see me about the Complete 3-Room Outfit at $229......☐
NAME ....
ADDRESS ....
ACC'T No., IF ANY N-5-8-42

ON SALE ONLY AT
HECHT'S Broadway FURNITURE STORE
412-414 S. BROADWAY—NEAR BANK

OPEN SATURDAY NIGHT TILL 9

RUSS READY TO DESTROY OIL FIELDS, NAZIS STILL ADVANCE

THE WEATHER
Moderate temperatures and moderate to fresh winds.
Detailed Weather Report on Page 13

Read The Baltimore News-Post for complete, accurate war coverage. It is the only Baltimore newspaper possessing the three great wire services—
ASSOCIATED PRESS
INTERNATIONAL NEWS SERVICE
UNITED PRESS

THE BALTIMORE NEWS-POST
AN INDEPENDENT NEWSPAPER
The Largest Evening Circulation in the Entire South

7 HOME FINAL

VOL. CXLI.—NO. 83 Entered as second-class matter at Baltimore Postoffice. SATURDAY EVENING, AUGUST 8, 1942 PRICE 3 CENTS

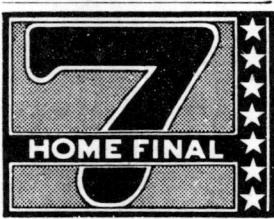

U. S. AIR FORCE BOMBERS SINK NAZI TRANSPORT

Nazi Spies Await Doom Under Strictest Guard; Provost-Marshal At Jail

WASHINGTON, Aug. 8—(A. P.).—Helmeted soldiers with fixed bayonets guarded all entrances today as tension mounted within the District Jail which holds eight Nazis awaiting the execution of sentences. At 10.16 a man known to be a priest or minister arrived at the jail and hurried inside, refusing to identify himself.

Inside the execution chambers, two dozen shiny aluminum chairs were placed in rows before the windows in the witness room which look on the plain wooden chair. The chair itself had been cleaned and covered over. It stands in the center of a room about 12 by 18 feet. The District coroner arrived.

By JACK VINCENT
International News Service Staff Correspondent.

WASHINGTON, Aug. 8.—Six of the eight Nazi saboteurs today awaited death in the electric chair at the District of Columbia Jail.

Nervously anticipating their "zero hour," the six were under heavy guard to prevent a last-minute effort to cheat justice by suicide.

PROVOST AT JAIL

Brig. Gen. Albert L. Cox, provost marshal of the Washington military district, who is in charge of the prisoners, arrived at the jail about 6.45 A. M. His arrival at this early hour was believed to indicate that the executions were near at hand.

Shortly before Cox arrived, three Army cars, carrying six Army officers, were driven into the courtyard at the jail.

The sextet—Warner Thiel, John Edward Kerlin, Heinrick Harn Heinck, Robert Quirin and Hermann Neubauer and Herbert Haupt.

TRUSTIES LOCKED UP

Prison authorities had ordered 20 trusties back from the prison laundry 45 minutes before their usual workday ends, so they could be locked in their cells before midnight.

Just before midnight a group of 15 auxiliary policemen were ordered on duty, patrolling the neighborhood of the jail. They were under instructions to remain on duty until 7 A. M. It was the first time any of them had received such orders.

HAIR CLIPPED

A prison guard said the six Nazis had their hair clipped yesterday afternoon. Another guard said two electricians were on duty in the jail all night long—for the first time in his memory.

Ray L. Huff, general superintendent of the District's penal institutions, and Alvin Green, superintendent of the jail, spent the night there. It was Huff's first overnight visit to the jail.

Claims Japs Now At War With Russ

SEATTLE, Aug. 8—(A. P.).—"Japan is already at war with Russia and it is common knowledge in Washington, D. C., that the Japs have already sunk several Russian ships in the Pacific."

Representative Warren G. Magnuson (Democrat) of Washington, a member of the Naval Affairs Committee, made the foregoing statement here in an interview.

He continued:

"The last was sunk very recently. They are justifying their action on the ground that the Russians were carrying American materials."

He said he knew only in a general way of the sinking of Russian ships by Japanese submarines. He said he had heard the name of the vessel most recently sunk in the North Pacific but had forgotten it.

ALEUTIAN SEIZURE

Magnuson told interviewers:

"War between Japan and Russia started when the Japs began strengthening their forces in Manchuria, and when they seized Attu and Kiska islands in the Aleutians.

"It is generally believed in Washington that the Japs went into Attu and Kiska for three reasons. First, they beat us to it. They knew we'd be there sooner or later

Continued on Page 2, Column 7.

An Author's Weird Adventure in Telepathy. He tuned in on a friend's mind 3,000 miles away. Once got a mental message that saved his life, and now tells how to duplicate his experiments. Read of his experiences in The American Weekly, the magazine distributed with tomorrow's Baltimore American.—Adv.

Declares Japs Menace U. S. Coastline

LOS ANGELES, Aug. 8—(U. P.).—Artemus Gates, Under Secretary of the Navy for Air, today called the Japanese occupation of two Aleutian islands a "menace to our coastline."

He said, however, that the occupation had been costly to the enemy and would continue to be.

On a tour of West Coast airplane factories and naval air bases, Gates granted an interview to reporters at the Douglas Aircraft Company plant. He said:

"In occupying the Aleutian Islands, the Japanese are just that much closer to the mainland of the United States and constitute that much more of a menace to our coastline.

"Occupancy of the islands was a part of the Midway action and outcome of that battle restricted the Jap advance to Attu and Kiska, frustrating an attempt to seize Dutch Harbor, some 600 miles closer to the continental United States."

New Axis Bomber Claimed To Be Tops In Aviation

BERLIN (from German Broadcasts), Aug. 8—(A. P.).—German newspapers published for the first time today pictures and descriptions of a new Nazi warplane—the Dornier 217—said to be the last word in dive bombers.

From press descriptions the new plane appears to be a modification of the DO-215, and the later DO-17. Adolf Hitler's newspaper Voelkischer Beobachter declared, however, that the DO-217, had a bomb-carrying capacity "several times larger" than those planes and a much greater cruising capacity.

(The DO-215, and the DO-17, are twin-engined monoplanes with a maximum bomb capacity of 2,200 pounds, a range of 750 miles, top speed of 275 miles per hour and a ceiling of 26,000 feet).

IN THE NEWS-POST TODAY

Amusements	5-16
Annette	13
"Bugs" Baer	8
Carroll Dulaney	9
Classified Ads	14-15
Comics	10
Dorothy Kilgallen	5
Editorial	8
Fashions	6
Financial	14
Gif-Ted Club	4
Horoscope	6
Local News	3-4
Louella O. Parsons	5
Louis Azrael	9
Mr. Fixit	13
Norman Clark	5
Radio	9
Rodger Pippen	11
Society	6
Sports	11-12-13

'Unreliable Handling' Of War News By U. S. Flayed By Publisher

PORTLAND, Ore., Aug. 8—(I. N. S.).—Accused of "unreliable and incomplete" handling of war news, the Federal Government last night was under criticism by Palmer Hoyt, publisher of the Portland Oregonian, for failure to obtain the complete confidence of the American people.

He said in a radio speech:

"As an editor I wouldn't hire the Government as a reporter because it does a bad job of reporting the biggest story in history to the people. I wouldn't hire the Government as a news service because its stories are too often unreliable and incomplete.

AIDING PROPAGANDA

"By its *'strange handling'* of unfavorable war news the Government has failed to gain the public's full confidence and is unwittingly building up an audience for Axis propaganda broadcasts.

"Actually, the long, dry spell of facts on the Aleutian situation from the initial phases until the Wheeler stories broke made our public dependent on Tokyo for news from the Aleutians."

(A series of eyewitness accounts of the Aleutian campaign by Keith Wheeler, Chicago newspaper man, was released for publication in the latter part of July.)

NOT JUSTIFIED

Hoyt continued:

"Too often Government failure to enlighten the people has been attributed to the necessity for military secrecy, but too often military secrecy has not justified misleading reports. No one wants to help the enemy, but none can endorse a policy of silence if it be utilized to give aid and comfort to the men responsible for our military or civil failures."

Hoyt claimed the "diffuse, nebulous and conflicting reports" on domestic shortages have created confustion in the public mind and pointed out that public confidence is "vital to a democracy in peril."

He added:

"Just as we have experienced many defeats in armed warfare, so

Continued on Page 2, Column 1.

India Congress Backs Gandhi

BOMBAY, India, Aug. 8—(A. P.).—The All-India Congress Committee in convention here today endorsed Mohandas K. Gandhi's "Britain must quit India' resolution by a large majority.

BOMBAY, Aug. 8—(A. P.).—Mohandas K. Gandhi appealed to America today to act "while there is yet time" to bring about recognition of Indian independence and permit Indians "to use their liberty in favor of the Allied cause."

Gandhi made his appeal in a letter "to American friends" before the All-India Congress convened for a session which may give the Indian leader the "go ahead sign" to launch a campaign of civil disobedience designed to end British dominion over India.

HOPES SEEN FADING

The letter, which will be published in Gandhi's newspaper tomorrow, was delivered exclusively to American correspondents today. Although Gandhi had said earlier that he would give Britain time to make further proposals before launching the campaign, little hope of such proposal was held after yesterday's meeting.

Gandhi appealed to Americans to accept as sincere his statement that the request for Britain to withdraw from power and grant freedom to India was done with the purpose of vitalizing Indian defense.

He said:

"Without this essential act of tardy justice Britain could not justify her position before world conscience, which is not vocal, but which is there nevertheless.

"Singapore, Malaya and Burma

Continued on Page 2, Column 5.

Rancher's Slayer Dies In Chair

HUNTSVILLE, Texas, Aug. 8—(A. P.).—Emiliano Benavidez, Mexican ranch worker, died in the State prison electric chair early today for the slaying of Henry Calcote, a rancher. The bodies of Calcote, his wife, infant daughter and his mother were found bullet-riddled near their home in September, 1940.

U. S. Bombers In Attack On Matruh

CAIRO, Aug. 8—(A. P.).—United States Air Force bombers destroyed a 10,000-ton transport in a large Axis convoy in the Mediterranean and made a spirited attack on another convoy, it was disclosed today by the headquarters of Maj. Gen. Lewis H. Brereton, commander of the United States Air Force in the Middle East.

Direct hits were scored on the vessel by American B-24 Consolidated bombers, said a communique covering activities of the American airmen for the past week.

The other convoy, three large transports escorted by eight destroyers, was attacked by daylight.

Two direct hits were reported by the American fliers.

A motor repair depot and other military installations at Matruh were attacked by the American Air Force in two other operations. On one of the raids R. A. F. Wellington bombers flew ahead of the Americans to drop flares over the targets.

In a raid on Tobruk B-24 bombers dropped several tons of explosives in the dock area, starting one large fire.

Nerves Strained In Air-Raid Test

LOS ANGELES, Aug. 8—(A. P.).—The Army's Civilian Protection School had an air-raid demonstration last night that was almost too much for a lot of war-tightened nerves. Flares dropped on the Occidental College football field, light explosives ripped temporary wooden structures and incindiary bombs flared as the civilian defenders rallied to their respective tasks.

Burma Premier Reported Dead

TOKYO, (From Japanese Broadcasts), Aug. 8—(A. P.).—A Miyako dispatch quoting the Italian News Agency Stefani said today that U. Saw, former premier of Burma, who was arrested by the British several months ago while en route home from England, had died in prison in Egypt.

Nazis Order Alert On Norway Coast

STOCKHOLM, Aug. 8—(A. P.).—The entire Norwegian coast is being held in a state of alert under orders of German occupation authorities and arrangements have been made to evacuate the civilian population at short notice, the newspaper Social Demokraten reported today.

Temperatures

12 Midn't.	73	6 A. M.	69
1 A. M.	72	7 A. M.	70
2 A. M.	73	8 A. M.	69
3 A. M.	71	9 A. M.	68
4 A. M.	71	10 A. M.	68
5 A. M.	70	11 A. M.	68

Russ Ready To Wreck Oil Fields As German Troops Keep Up Advance

MOSCOW, Aug. 8—(U. P.).—Red Army demolition squads stood ready today to blow up the great Maikop oil fields of the Caucasus to prevent them from falling into the hands of German forces which have broken Russian defenses at Armavir and are closing in upon Maikop from two sides.

BERLIN (From German Broadcasts), Aug. 8—(A. P.). German troops have captured Kurgannaya, Russian town 30 miles east of the Caucasian oil center of Maikop, DNB said today. Kurgannaya is half way between Armavir and Maikop.

MOSCOW, Aug. 8—(A. P.).—German columns are smashing at the approaches of the Maikop oil fields, first major goal of their Caucasus drive, from both the north and east after a major break-through in Red Army defenses, and the situation is "very tense," front-line dispatches said today.

The Army newspaper Red Star said Soviet defenders had made a heroic but unsuccessful attempt to stem the Nazi tide in the loop of the Kuban river above Maikop, in the Armavir area and east of Krasnodar.

Krasnodar is 45 miles northwest of Maikop at a point where the Kuban curves northward and Armavir is 60 miles northeast at the bottom of the river's loop.

At no place, however, have the Germans been reported here as crossing the Kuban. (The German High Command today claimed capture of Armavir, on the west bank of the Kuban, and Kurgannaya, on the Laba river 30 miles farther east, thus implying a broad crossing of the Kuban.)

The dispatches also made no mention of what the Russians intended to do should the invaders more closely approach the Maikop oil fields, but previously the Red Army has sought to destroy everything of possible value to the enemy before withdrawing from valuable positions.

Red Star itself emphasized the gravity of the situation faced by the Russian forces as German troops pounded closer to the derrick-dotted Maikop fields, which produce 7 per cent. of Russia's oil supply.

The mid-day communique said of the overnight action:

"Our troops fought the enemy in

Continued on Page 2, Column 7.

U-Boat Destroys Uruguayan Ship

For four hours under dark Atlantic skies, a sleek U-boat circled the Maldondo, a Uruguayan merchantman, whose bright lights left no doubt as to its nationality.

Then the U-boat sent a shell crashing into the ship's boiler, ignoring the flood-lit Uruguayan flag. The crew took to the boats and the submarine came alongside.

A submarine officer shouted:

"I want the captain. If not, I'll shoot."

Capt. Mario Giambruno boarded the submarine and some time later a single torpedo tore the ship in two. The submarine submerged with Captain Giambruno aboard. Captain Giambruno is a brother of the Uruguayan Minister of Education.

The Maldonado's sinking was disclosed when 13 survivors reached Bermuda. Three lifeboats containing 36 crewmen, are missing.

The announcement of this sinking yesterday, along with the disclosure of the destruction of two other merchantmen—a Norwegian and a Panamanian—increased to 418, the Associated Press tally of announced Allied and neutral ship losses in the Western Atlantic since December 7.

War At A Glance

RUSSIA—
Reds prepare to destroy oil fields; Nazis continue advance.

CAIRO—
U. S. bombers sink Nazi transport; bomb Matruh.

INDIA—
Gandhi appeals to "his American friends" to use their influence in preserving peace.

New World Map Shows Importance Of Alaska To United States -:- -:- See Tomorrow's Sunday American

The Baltimore News-Post Has the Largest Circulation of Any Evening Newspaper in the South

THE BALTIMORE NEWS-POST
AN INDEPENDENT NEWSPAPER

SATURDAY EVENING, AUGUST 8, 1942

Stanton Seeks To Decrease Pensions

Says Retired Men Accept Other Positions

Police Commissioner Robert F. Stanton acted today to lessen the number of retirements from the force.

Remarking that the Department is suffering from "pensionitis," the Commissioner said that the police surgeons will be instructed to check and double-check applicants for retirement.

TAKE WAR JOBS

The Commissioner explained that he has learned some policemen, retired on pensions, have taken jobs as special police at various industrial plants.

He took the view that if the men are fit for active jobs they should remain with the Police Department, thus decreasing pension payments and lessening the burden on the taxpayers.

Retirements and the calls of military service, to which 53 members of the force have responded, have made some inroads upon the police personnel and 60 of the applicants from the new eligible list of 241, effective in June, have already been examined.

BETTER PAY CITED.

However, Commissioner Stanton does not anticipate a situation so acute as it was in 1920, when the Department had to advertise for men.

Patrolmen now get much better pay and better working conditions than they did in the old days.

It is regarded as significant that not a man has left the active list to take a war-plant job while some accepted police applicants have given up war-time jobs to join the force, even though they were getting more pay in war work.

Gunner

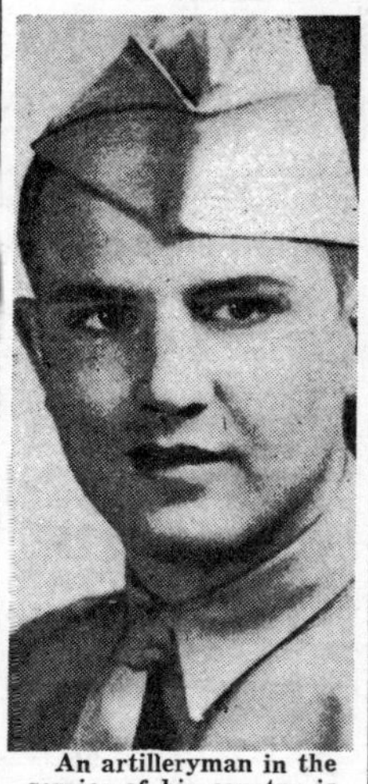

An artilleryman in the service of his country is Corporal Arthur Christ (above), whose home is in the first block South Morley street, Baltimore. He is attached to the Fourth Armored Field Artillery Battalion and now is in training at a camp in the North.

Today Dead Line For Voters To Register

Today is a double dead line with regard to the primary elections September 8.

It is the last day for Baltimore voters to get on the registration books.

It is likewise the final day for candidates to withdraw from primary contests.

PROSPECTIVE VOTERS

As in the last several days, a line of prospective voters filed past the registration desk in the Supervisors of Elections' offices in the Courthouse, being inscribed as qualified voters in this bailiwick.

The registration day began at 9 A. M. and will close at 9 P. M.

TANGLED SITUATION

Candidates in the primaries may withdraw until midnight, and in final effort to straighten out so far as possible a somewhat tangled situation on the Democratic side party leaders were busy trying to make "unblessed" contenders appreciate the desirability of graceful exits.

Even so, few possibilities for primary fights were being overlooked, and there was even a contest for nomination as candidate for city surveyor.

Waacs, Waves Will Vote In Md. Election

ANNAPOLIS, Md., Aug. 8—(A. P.).—What's good for the gander is good for the goose—at least as far as voting in Maryland goes.

State Secretary Thomas E. Jones said Maryland's absentee voters' law would give voting privileges not only to Maryland men in the service but also to Free State women in the WAACS or the WAVES.

Jones said the matter of women getting absentee ballots came up as preparations were made for mailing the ballots to the election supervisors in the various counties.

"I know it's a little early for the WAACS and the WAVES to be thinking about voting," he said, "but we want them to know they've got just as much right to cast absentee ballots as the soldiers, sailors and marines.

"If parents, relatives and sweethearts of soldiers and WAACS now in camp would write, telling them about the rules and regulations for absentee voting, I'm sure an appreciable vote would be cast by our people in the armed services."

Child 9, Injured Burning Beetles

Nine-year-old Patsy Wimpling's attempt to destroy Japanese beetles by burning them cost her severe burns on the upper part of her body, police of the Southwestern District reported today.

Patsy, who lives in the 300 block South Stricker street, had collected beetles in a paper container and had gone to the back yard to burn them, police said. The match set fire to her dress.

The child's screams brought her mother, Mrs. Marie Wimpling, who ripped off the blazing clothing and took Patsy to Franklin Square Hospital. She was treated for second-degree burns.

Kent-Cecil Cattle Shows Combined

CHESTERTOWN, Aug. 8—(A. P.).—War conditions have forced the incorporation of the annual 4-H Club Dairy Cattle Show with the Kent-Cecil Dairy Cattle Show to be held at Galena August 25. The Kent-Cecil Horse Show, which in previous years preceded the event, has been abandoned. The 4-H club show is held usually at Tolchester Beach.

Poe Contest Nearing Close

Of the many beautiful poems and bizarre stories by Edgar Allan Poe, how many of these gems can you remember? List the titles of Poe's immortal works and write a short letter describing the poem or story you enjoyed most. Your efforts might win you a war savings bond, cash or tickets to see "The Loves of Edgar Allan Poe."

The movie is showing at the New Theatre with John Shepperd and Linda Darnell in the principal roles.

In preparing your list of titles use only such poems or stories that begin with a letter in the movie title, "The Loves of Edgar Allan Poe." "The Gold Bug" is an example, the initial letter being "T."

In addition to the war bond, prizes of $5, $2 and 10 pairs of tickets for the New Theatre will be awarded.

All entries must reach the Contest Editor of The Baltimore News-Post by midnight tonight. Winners will be named next Tuesday.

RUSSIAN WAR RELIEF

Aiming at $100,000, the Russian War Relief campaign in Baltimore starts Monday with $10,000 already contributed, according to Wyman Fuller, campaign director. The drive is part of a nation-wide campaign to raise $6,000,000.

One Dead, 6 Hurt In Traffic Toll

State And City Police Report Accicents

Traffic accidents caused the death of one man in Maryland early today and resulted in the injury of six persons in Baltimore, police of the State and city reported.

The dead man—identified as Raymond G. Copenhaver, forty-two, of Providence, Cecil county — was found unconscious beside Route 280, near Elkton, and was pronounced dead at the scene by the Cecil county medical examiner.

FIVE HURT IN CRASH

Five persons were injured, city police reported, when two autos collided in the center of the Fallsway near Monument street. Victims were taken to Mercy Hospital.

Two of the injured are women, identified by police as Miss Anna Annello, seventeen, 2600 block Greenmount avenue, who received cuts on the face, and Mrs. Viola Lynch, twenty-eight, 700 block N. Appleton street, who received a possible fracture of the left knee and cuts on the hand.

They were passengers in an auto driven by Edward Wojciechowski, twenty-one, 1200 block Cooksie street, the police said.

COLLISION WITH CAB

Wojciechowski's car was in collision with a cab driven by George W. Englehardt of Catonsville, who received knee and lip injuries. Two passengers in his cab also were hurt. They identified themselves as Chalmers O. Davis, thirty-seven, 600 block South Ellwood avenue, and Robert Palmer, forty-two, of Merion Center, Pa.

Davis suffered probable fractured ribs and injuries to his shoulder, while Palmer received cuts on the chin.

MOTORCYCLE SKIDS

Miss Elizabeth T. Van Bergen, twenty-one, 1500 block Bolton street, a war worker employed at a Towson plant, was injured critically in the early hours today when her motorcycle skidded on the rain-drenched York road near Orkney road, hurling her to the street.

Witnesses gave first aid to the injured girl and called a municipal ambulance. She was taken to Union Memorial Hospital, where physicians said she had received a skull fracture and severe cuts.

Couple Celebrate 25th Anniversary

Relatives and friends of Mr. and Mrs. Milton Rosskops will join with them tomorrow in celebrating their twenty-fifth wedding anniversary. The celebration will be held at the home of Mrs. Rosskops' sister, Mrs. Lillian Berman, 4855 Reisterstown road, starting at 8.30 P. M.

Dancing Masters Re-Elect Cockey

Joshua T. Cockey, Baltimore dancing teacher and a member of the McDonogh School faculty, has been re-elected second vice-president of the Dancing Masters of America at their convention in New York city, it was announced today.

The Baltimore News-Post and Sunday American are offering weekly cash prizes for news tips and amateur photos. Best tip gets $25, the next best gets $10, and the next 15 get $1 each. For each amateur photo published $3 will be paid. Phone news-tip editor, Lexington 0100 (Lex. 4165 midnight to 6.30 A. M.). Rush news photos to picture editor.

War Comes To Pimlico

Model City Blasted At Track Before Crowd Of Preakness Size

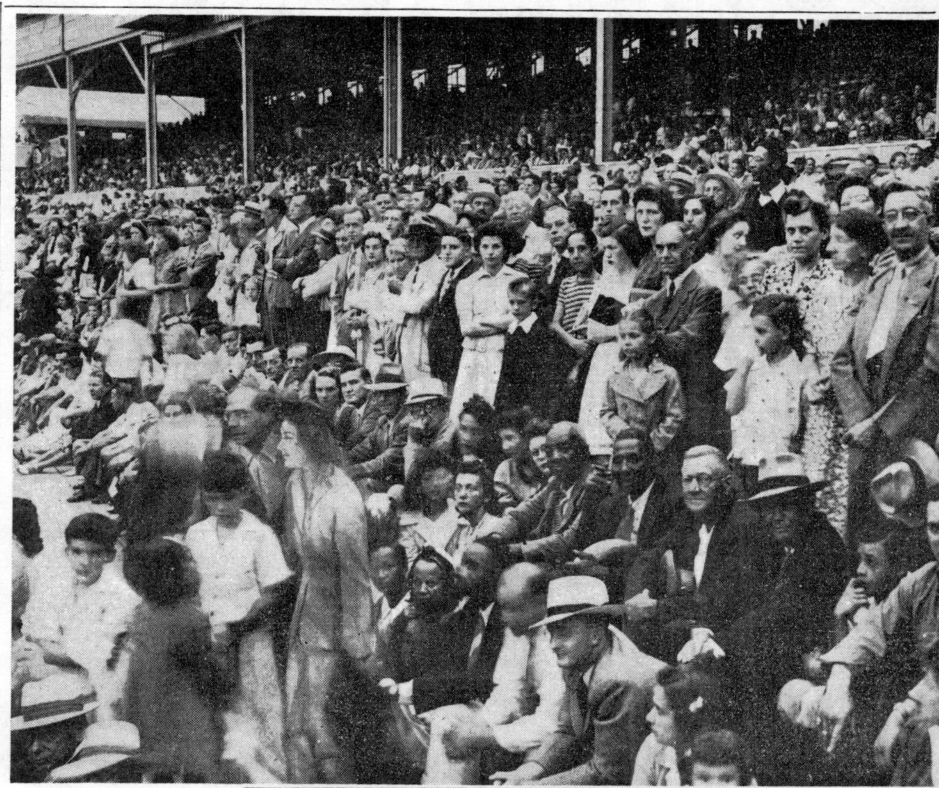

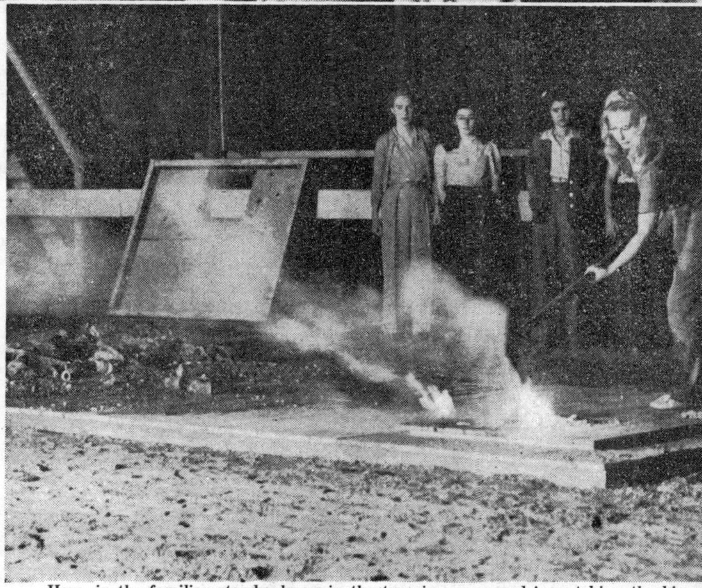

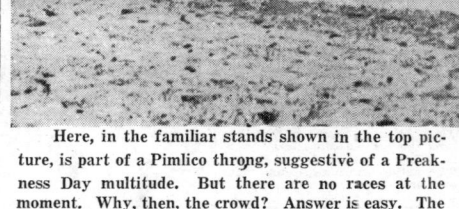

Here, in the familiar stands shown in the top picture, is part of a Pimlico throng, suggestive of a Preakness Day multitude. But there are no races at the moment. Why, then, the crowd? Answer is easy. The crowd is watching the big air-raid spectacle, staged at the former "Old Hilltop." In bottom picture Miss Wealtha Holady of Joppa and Miss Hope Veale of Woodlawn road show how an ignition bomb should be handled as several observers look intently on.

Cash For Your Baseball Thrill

What is the most exciting baseball game you ever saw?

Recount a spectacular play that gave you your greatest thrill and you may win a cash prize or a reserved seat for the initial performance of "The Pride of the Yankees," epic movie based on the career of the late Lou Gehrig.

The movie opens at the Hippodrome next Wednesday with a special show starting at 9 P. M.

To compete for a prize your story must be about a thrilling moment you enjoyed at a ball game. Keep your letter short and mail the entry to the Baseball Contest Editor of The Baltimore News-Post to reach him not later than noon on Monday. Winning letters will share in awards of $15, $5, two of $2.50 each and ten tickets to the movies.

Winners will be announced next Wednesday.

USO Fetes Former Residents Of Pa.

Former residents of Pennsylvania were guests of the Dundalk USO last night at an entertainment marking the first of a series for home-State parties. Former residents of Virginia, West Virginia, the Carolinas and New England States are to be entertained in the series.

CANAL PARTLY REOPENED

Army engineers announced today that the Chesapeake and Delaware Canal, which was blocked, July 28, when a tanker crashed into a bridge at Chesapeake City, Md., has been partly reopened to traffic.

CHILDREN TO GET AWARD

Seventy boys and girls who have completed a summer reading game will appear in their favorite book characters as they receive certificates of merit at 3 P. M. Monday in the Enoch Pratt Free Library.

Boys Make Real Effort For War

Marvin Lee Marks, six, and his chum, Stuart Jaffe, five, of the 2300 block Anoka avenue, are making a real sacrifice for their country. Today, they gathered up all of their used comic books and are busily engaged in selling them to residents of the neighborhood. At latest reports they had collected over $1 to be turned over to the American Red Cross.

Air-Raid Show Awes 40,000 Spectators

The "yellow" warning showed and the announcer at the Pimlico air-raid spectacle told the expectant multitude of 40,000 that planes were approaching.

Then came the "blue" signal.

The attacking planes were nearer.

The moment for the attack arrived.

PLANE FAILS TO APPEAR

But where were the planes, or rather, plane?

The heavens failed to reveal it.

Said the announcer:

"They seem to have been unable to find us."

But eventually the plane arrived after the bombs had been exploded and gave thrills in abundance to the air-raid demonstration, which was today called a big success on two main counts:

(1) As a pageant, it gave a thrill to the 40,000 spectators.

(2) As an object lesson, it impressed Baltimoreans with the necessity of enthusiastic and complete co-operation with their civilian defense organization.

RECKORD APPROVED SHOW

Last night's Army Incendiary Air-Raid Show was given under auspices of the War Department School for Civilian Protection and the Baltimore Committee on Civilian Defense.

The demonstration won approval of Maj. Gen. Milton A. Reckord, commanding general of the Third Service Command, who praised the soldiers who enacted the raid and congratulated B. C. C. D. Chairman George A. Carter.

Opened by an intricate drill by a Negro company, which marched onto the Pimlico race track, the show continued with a demonstration of various types of incendiary bombs—materials, extinguishing methods and their ability to do damage.

This latter was shown by actual firing of frame infield buildings.

THRILLING SPECTACLE

Flame throwers made a thrilling spectacle.

In the second part of the show came the air raid proper, none the less thrilling for delay. The alarm sounded. High in the air a plane appeared out of the darkness. Back and forth it went.

In a simulated attack buildings were set afire.

Four bombs were exploded in the infield. Ambulance and fire-fighting companies appeared; so did auxiliary police and a decontamination squad.

One of the most intent spectators was Mayor Jackson, with whom were city department heads. High military officers were interested observers of the realistic performance.

Gorman To Talk On Meat Status

Patrick Gorman, general president, Amalgamated Meat Cutters and Butcher Workmen Union (A. F. of L.), is to discuss the national meat situation at a meeting Tuesday evening in St. Paul Gardens, 800 block St. Paul street, to be attended by 2,000 members of the four local unions, it is anticipated.

Harry Cohen, president of the Baltimore Federation of Labor, will discuss the local situation.

Coming! Next Wednesday!
"Bond Bread Day"
Annual Party and Picnic at
CARLIN'S PARK
Featuring "Happy Johnny" and his Radio Stars. 100 Free Prizes given away—War Bonds, Cameras, Skates, Tennis Racquets and 50 Bond Bakers Cakes.
ASK YOUR BOND BREAD GROCER FOR FREE TICKETS TODAY!

DANCING TO HIT MUSIC
SATURDAY AND SUNDAY
HIGH UP ON KEITHS ROOF!

BOOGIE WOOGIE

By Michael Berry

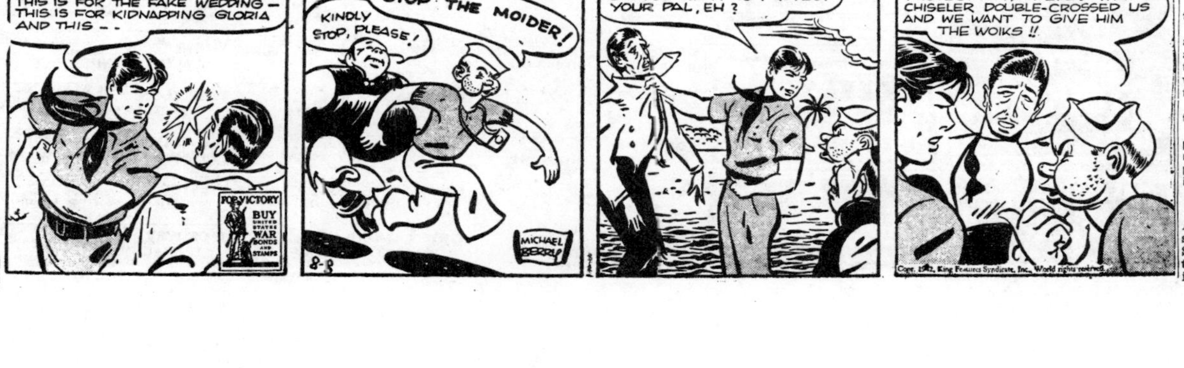

Ellery Queen In Hippodrome Film—Drama At Mayfair

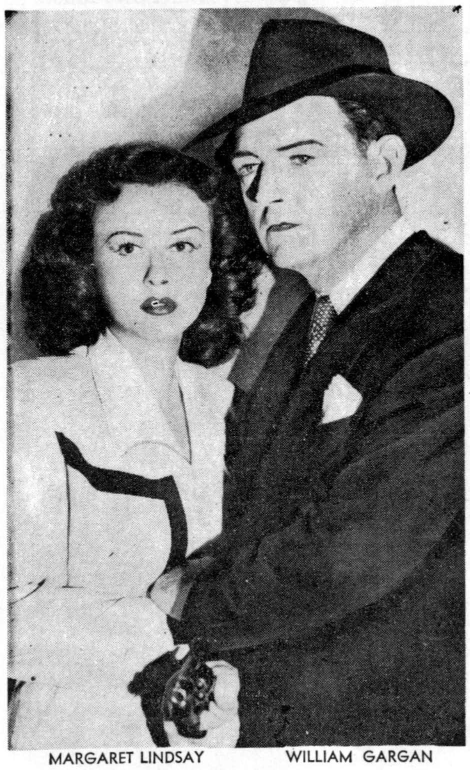

MARGARET LINDSAY WILLIAM GARGAN

By NORMAN CLARK

THESE DETECTIVES of the screen are having a busy time of it in these parlous days. Not only are they called upon to track down killers but they've got to catch up with all kinds of Nazi and Jap spies.

In "Enemy Agents Meet Ellery Queen," at the Hippodrome, Mr. Queen has it out with German agents on these shores. Of course, he puts them to rout at the proper time but not before he and his pretty secretary, Nikki, have been so close to a sudden end a couple of times—well, the undertaker is about ready to collect his tools and hop into his wagon.

Submarines, diamonds from Holland, a mummy, an art gallery, a cemetery and a night club are among the things and places which figure in "Enemy Agents Meet Ellery Queen." Sergeant Velie, as usual, wanders around in a state of fussy perplexity—and when it comes to making blunders he and Nikki run a close race. However, anybody as pretty as Nikki doesn't have to be smart. Neither does a policeman like Velie, if he has such a good friend as smart Ellery Queen.

The film at the Hippodrome keeps up the good pace set by this popular series of detective thrillers. William Gargan knows exactly what to do as Queen and how to do it. And the same goes for Margaret Lindsay, Edward Burke, Charley Grapewin, Gale Sondergaard, Gilbert Roland and Sig Rumann.

"Enemy Agents Meet Ellery Queen"

"ENEMY AGENTS MEET ELLERY QUEEN," starring William Gargan and Margaret Lindsay. Screen play by Eric Taylor from story by Ellery Queen. Directed by James Hogan. A Columbia picture, presented at the Hippodrome.

THE CAST

Ellery Queen	William Gargan
Nikki Porter	Margaret Lindsay
Inspector	Charley Grapewin
Mrs. Van Dorn	Gale Sondergaard
Paul Gillette	Gilbert Roland
Heinrich	Sig Ruman
Sergeant Velie	James Burke

AT MAYFAIR

"DR. BROADWAY," at the Mayfair. Screen play by Art Arthur from a story by Borden Chase. Directed by Anton Mann. A Paramount picture.

THE CAST

Dr. Timothy Kane	MacDonald Carey
Connie Madigan	Jean Phillips
Jack Venner	J. Carrol Naish
Vic Telli	Edward Giannelli
Patrick Doyle	Richard Lane
Margie Dove	Joan Woodbury
Maxie	Warren Hymer

DR. TIMOTHY KANE is a good-hearted guy. He'd much rather treat the lowly down-and-outers along Manhattan's Main Stem than be a big Park avenue doctor.

And when he sees a pretty girl getting ready to jump off a hotel ledge to the street below—he simply steams to the rescue. Then he does his level darnest to keep Connie Madigan from being jugged by the heartless police.

The good doctor gets into very hot water after a convict comes to see him and hands over $100,000—a legacy to be given to a long-lost daughter. The convict gets himself murdered, as it were, the cops close in on Dr. Kane, thinking he is the murderer, gangsters shanghai the worthy medico—gosh, what a fix that big-hearted man finds himself in.

"Dr. Broadway" is a cops-and-robbers action yarn. MacDonald Carey, new star, works smoothly as the harassed physician.

'SERGEANT YORK' FEATURE AT CENTRE

"Sergeant York," the picturization of the life of America's great living hero who has recently been made a major in the U. S. Army, will be the feature at the Centre from tomorrow through Thursday. Gary Cooper is starred in the title role, for which he was given the Academy Award.

Joan Leslie, Walter Brennan, George Tobias, Stanley Ridges, Margaret Wycherly and Ward Bond head the huge supporting cast.

Movie CLOCK

CENTURY—"Mrs. Miniver," 11 A. M., 1.41, 4.22, 7.00, 9.40 P. M.

NEW—"Loves of Edgar Allan Poe," 10 A. M., 12, 2, 4, 6, 8, 10 P. M.

STANLEY—"Take a Letter, Darling," 11.10 A. M., 1.15, 3.25, 5.30, 7.35, 9.40 P. M.

KEITH'S—"Pardon My Sarong," 10.01, 11.55 A. M., 1.58, 4.01, 5.54, 7.57, 10.01 P. M.

HIPPODROME—"Enemy Agents Meet Ellery Queen," 10.50 A. M., 12.45, 2.40, 4.40, 6.35, 8.30, 10.25 P. M.

VALENCIA—"Affairs of Martha," 12.40, 2.30, 4.25, 6.20, 8.15, 10.10 P. M.

PARKWAY—"True to Army," 12.30, 2.20, 4.10, 6.05, 7.55, 9.50 P. M.

MAYFAIR—"Dr. Broadway," 10.48 A. M., 12.45, 2.42, 4.39, 6.36, 8.33, 10.30 P. M.

LITTLE—"Pasha's Wives," 11 A. M., 12.50, 2.40, 4.30, 6.20, 8.10, 10 P. M.

TIMES—"Let's Get Tough," 1.30, 3.23, 5.16, 7.09, 9.02, 10.55 P. M.

ROSLYN—"Gunga Din," 12.10, 2.36, 5.02, 7.28, 9.54 P. M.

Frank Ross Gets Film Rights To Douglas Novel, 'The Robe'

Finds Encouragement In Previous Successes

By LOUELLA O. PARSONS
Motion Picture Editor International News Service

HOLLYWOOD, Aug. 8.—The new Lloyd C. Douglas novel, "The Robe," carries a spiritual message so appealing to Frank Ross that he up and bought it. He paid $100,000, and if the film version does the business that "The Magnificent Obsession" and "The Green Light"—the other two Douglas best-sellers—did at the box office, Frank has made an investment for himself.

He tells me that Jean Arthur, his wife, will not be in the picture because there is no role for her. But Frank is nothing if not ambitious. He sees Gary Cooper, Spencer Tracy or Errol Flynn as the star. Since "The Devil and Miss Jones" and "Of Mice and Men," his two previous pictures, clicked, he will probably get himself set with a major studio that will give him the talent he needs.

The posthumous fame of General Billy Mitchell, who warned that Japan was our dangerous enemy in the Pacific and pointed out the strategic importance of Alaska, has been rumored as a movie subject for months.

The first definite word comes from Samuel Bronston, Columbia producer, who has bought the official life story written by Isaac Don Levine.

William Hawks discussed the story when he was at RKO, but since he is no longer connected with that company and Bronston has paid $100,000 for the Levine book and has permission of the Mitchell family—well, this is it.

Bronston was associated with Major James Roosevelt when Jimmie was in the movie business.

One of the most attractive figures around the Beverly Hills swimming pool and at tea time is Luise Rainer, who has been here for the last few weeks. She has been in conference at Warner Brothers about a movie, but I understand it didn't materialize. However, I have the feeling Luise will really get herself a movie job this time.

Another visitor of interest at the same hotel is Lieut. Commander Wassell. I was eager to see Mrs. Wassell since the missionary doctor told me all about her when he came to see me. She seems an ideal wife and must have been very helpful in his work in China.

Snapshots of Hollywood Collected at Random: The Glenn Ford-Eleanor Powell romance, starting as a publicity stunt, has developed into the real thing. David Selznick is taking no chances with Ingrid Bergman having an unbecoming haircut. He has elected Sydney Guilaroff to do the job. Heather Angel and Andre David, friend of Charles Boyer and a French writer, a Romanoff duet.

Red Skelton is getting a new and fatter contract at M.-G.-M., due, of course, to his increasing popularity. Oscar Serlin signed eighteen-year-old Dorothy Moore, former Columbia stock actress, for his Broadway show.

John Shelton telling his troubles to Kathryn Grayson's sister, Frances Raeburn, at Mike Lyman's. Harold Lloyd's two pretty daughters guests at the wedding of Jacqueline Jones (Carlyle Jones' daughter) and John McMahan.

The New York Theatre Guild is dickering with Lilian and Dorothy Gish for the Broadway play, "Mr. Sycamore." Dorothy, according to last reports, although down to a mere ninety pounds, is much improved in health. The little child wonder, Maxine O'Brien, who is appearing in "Journey for Margaret," will ask to have her name changed to Margaret.

GUILD SEEKS HIM

Currently featured in "Submarine Alert," Nils Asther has been offered the lead opposite Helen Hayes in a Theatre Guild play on Broadway. Asther was once leading man for Garbo, Joan Crawford and most of the top actresses.

CUTIES ·:· By E. Simms Campbell

Registered U. S. Patent Office

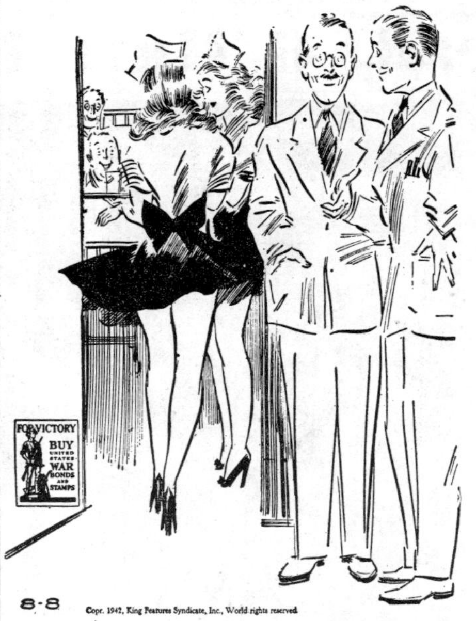

Copr. 1942, King Features Syndicate, Inc., World rights reserved

"We've found, in some cases, that substituting chorus girls for nurses does wonders for the patients!"

A Library In Miniature

1. "Not a cloud appeared on the horizon" were the famous words of what President when he took the oath of office for the second time?
2. Porker, porgy and porky should bring three different, common creatures to mind. Name them.
3. Because so many New Englanders settled within its bounds, what State is sometimes called "the New England of the West"?
4. It's easy enough to sing, but are you able to translate "auld lang syne"?
5. To have your hands cared for is to have them manicured. What name do we apply to a treatment of the feet?
6. What is your means of locomotion if you're out skijoring in the country?
7. Stentor, herald of the "Iliad," had a certain vocal characteristic which gave rise to our use of the word "stentorian." What was it?

(Distributed by King Features Syndicate, Inc.)

ANSWERS ON PAGE 13

FEMININE Voice Of BROADWAY

By DOROTHY KILGALLEN

(NOTE—If there were gossip columns in Germany, here are a few items they wouldn't print—revealed to students of the Main Stem by my friend Pierre J. Huss, International News Service war correspondent and author of "The Foe We Face."—D. K.)

PIERRE HUSS SAYS:

What Broadway over here doesn't know about Hitler's Broadway in Berlin is that the Herrenvolk are green with envy over the worldly fame of our Main Stem and have sworn to knock it cold. The super-Nordics want Berlin to become the Mecca of all tourists, and the droopy Kurfuerstendamm (cafe and theatre district of Berlin), the Broadway of the world.

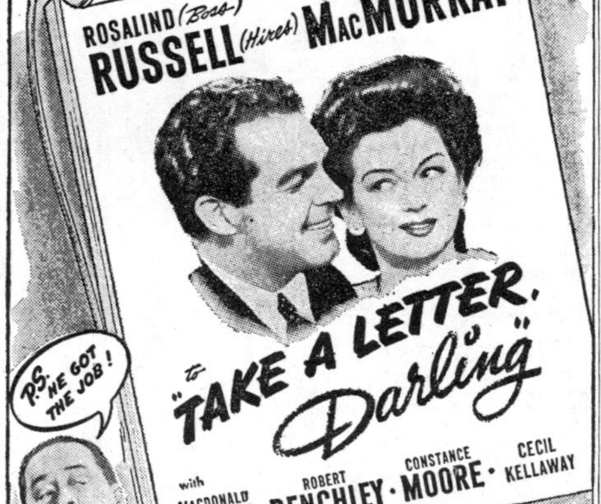

Before we rolled up our sleeves for a shooting war against Hitler and Hirohito, I saw the Nazi guntoter Baron von Killinger (once German Consul over here) and the Gestapo drunks with him get boisterous in an exclusive Berlin restaurant. Von Killinger was gleefully telling his starry-eyed gunmen what fun it would be some night to wipe out Broadway . . . "Ja, ja, dicke bomben—two or three heavy high explosive ones just when the theatres let out or maybe a couple of shells from one of our submarines—ach, himmel, what a fine panic and massacre of the Yankees on Broadway!"

Two nights later the R. A. F. dropped seven screaming 250-pounders into adjoining Tauentzien strasse and blew the plate glass out of every shop window around there.

Berlin's Broadway is longer and darker than New York's. There has been a total blackout since September, 1939, when war started.

When Dorothy Kilgallen goes columning along the Broadway hotspots she gets home in the wee small hours. In Berlin, Dorothy would be home and in bed by 10 P. M. Night life has backed up into daylight. The cabarets start at 4 P. M. The movies begin their last shows at 6 P. M. The opera starts at 4 o'clock and the wickedest night club puts the chairs bottom up at 10 P. M. The answer is the air raid. Gestapo and police make sure that nobody violates that deadline—except Gestapo and Nazi bigwigs, who will beer and wine behind locked restaurant doors until early morning.

Last American film to be shown publicly in Berlin and biggest hit of any with the krauts in early 1940 was "Broadway Melody." Eleanor Powell's dancing started a new dance fad along Berlin's dull Black Way and Una Merkel's non-stop gum-chewing set the wisecracking pace for the cabbage variety of fast humor.

Beat the Quiz Kids

The Quiz Kids are a group of bright youngsters who have amazed the country with their ability to answer correctly questions like the ones below. See if you can beat their percentages—but remember that these children are exceptional. Rate your own score to see if you can equal or beat their combined average of 84 per cent. on today's questions.

If you score 40 per cent. you have the equivalent of a public school education; 55 per cent. equals a high school education, and 70 per cent. is the rating of a college student.

QUESTIONS

1. Since 1900, six amendments have been made to the Constitution of the United States. These include amendments dealing with income taxes, the election of Senators by popular vote, the prohibition of liquor, the repeal of prohibition, nation-wide suffrage for women and a change in terms of office of the President, Vice-President and Senators and Representatives. Can you give the year in which each of these amendments were made?

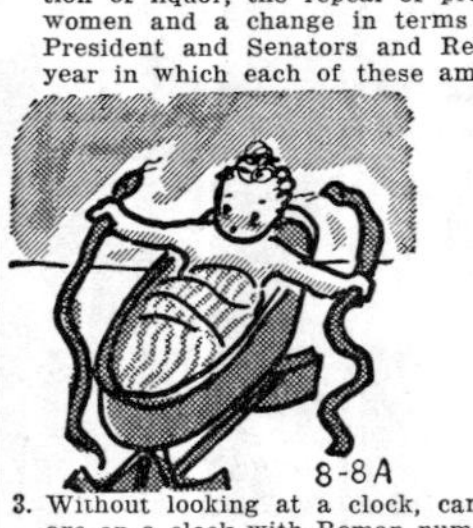

8-8A

2. In this sketch is pictured the first spectacular accomplishment of a certain mythological personage. Can you name him?
3. Without looking at a clock, can you tell us how many I's there are on a clock with Roman numerals on its face?
4. The first four lines of this poetic stanza are more frequently quoted. Can you give them after reading the second four we give here?

   For the test of the heart is trouble,
   And it always comes with the years,
   And the smile that is worth the praises of earth
   Is the smile that shines through tears.

5. Their fathers are all mentioned in the first sentence of the story, although they have little to do with the action. So, give yourself 10 points if you can remember the profession or trade of the fathers of Aladdin, Tom Thumb and Jack, the master of "Puss in Boots."
6. Maybe you know them better by another name—can you further identify Lady Korda and Mrs. William Mills?
7. Let's imagine that the police are trying to find some operatic characters and send out police calls for them. For whom is this one sent out?

   Calling all cars . . . calling all cars . . . be on lookout for glamour girl known as Violetta . . . may be found in Paris night clubs . . .

8. Have you any idea why most book critics compared Joseph Davies' "Mission to Moscow" to a twenty-some-year-old book called "My Four Years in Germany"?

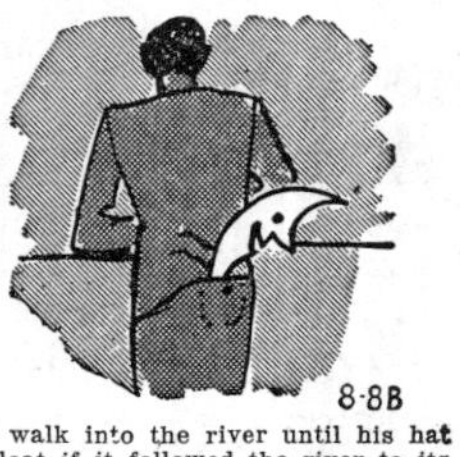

8-8B

9. If you can believe what you hear over the radio, this is surely a member of Kay Kyser's orchestra. Do you know why we think so?
10. You may have told someone to walk into the river until his hat floated. Where would his hat float if it followed the river to its outlet and he had walked into the Wabash, the Colorado, or the Rio Grande?

(Copyright, 1942, and published by permission of Louis G. Cowan. Distributed by King Features Syndicate, Inc.)

SEE ANSWERS ON PAGE 6

Today's Movie Calendar

Theatres advertised in this column belong to the Motion Picture Theatre Owners of Maryland.

Buy War Savings Bonds and Stamps At Your Favorite Theatre

Aero Middle River, Md. Bette Davis in "IN THIS OUR LIFE" Comedy.

Alpha Catonsville. Joan Bennett in "TWIN BEDS" Comedy.

Ambassador 4604 Liberty Heights. Maureen O'Hara in "Ten Gentlemen From West Point" "In the Circus."

Apollo 1500 Harford Ave. George Montgomery in "Ten Gentlemen From West Point" Buy War Stamps & Bonds

Arcade Harford Rd. & Hamilton Ave. Charles Winninger in "FRIENDLY ENEMIES" "Fleets of Strength."

Astor Poplar Grove at Edmondson. J. Anthony Hughes in "MEN OF SAN QUENTIN" "All Work & No Pay."

Aurora 7 East North Ave. Lee Bowman in "PACIFIC RENDEZVOUS" "March of Time."

Avalon 4300 Park Heights Ave. Veronica Lake in "THIS GUN FOR HIRE" "Spy Smasher."

Avenue Milton Ave. & Hoffman St. Sabu in "JUNGLE BOOK" News.

Avon 3019 Hamilton Ave. Buster Crabbe in "BILLY THE KID TRAPPED" "Winslow of the Navy."

Belnord 2700 Philadelphia Ave. Judy Canova in "TRUE TO THE ARMY" "Perils of Nyoka."

Boulevard 33rd at Greenmount. George Montgomery "Ten Gentlemen From West Point" "Donald's Snow Fight."

Bridge Edmondson Ave. & Pulaski St. Judy Canova in "TRUE TO THE ARMY" Comedy.

Broadway 509 S. Broadway. George Montgomery in "Ten Gentlemen From West Point" Buy War Stamps and Bonds.

Cameo 4705 Harford Road. Ida Lupino in "MOONTIDE" Buy War Stamps & Bonds

Capitol 1518 W. Baltimore St. Charles Winninger in "FRIENDLY ENEMIES" Buy War Bonds & Stamps.

Casino 1118 Light St. Fred Scott in "RODEO RHYTHM" "Captain Midnight."

Cluster 303 S. Broadway. Gary Cooper in "SERGEANT YORK" With Joan Leslie.

Columbia 709 Washington Blvd. Jean Rogers in "PACIFIC RENDEZVOUS" "All Work and No Pay."

Earle Belair Rd. at Woodlea Ave. Feature Cartoon "MR. BUG GOES TO TOWN" Comedy.

Edgewood Edmondson & Edgewood. Judy Canova in "TRUE TO THE ARMY" "Perils of Nyoka."

Forest Garrison & Liberty Heights. Bette Davis in "IN THIS OUR LIFE" "Spy Smasher."

Fulton Fulton Ave. & Baker St. Ida Lupino in "MOONTIDE" "Perils of Nyoka."

Garden Charles at Cross. Don Red Barry in "JESSE JAMES, JR." "Perils of Nyoka."

Glen Glen Burnie. Paul Kelly in "NOT A LADY'S MAN" "Sea Raiders."

Grand 511 S. Conkling St. Don Terry in "TOP SERGEANT" "Perils of Nyoka."

Gwynn 4609 Liberty Heights Ave. Bill Elliott in "LONE STAR VIGILANTES" "Gang Busters."

Hampden 911 W. 36th St. Milton Berle in "WHISPERING GHOST" Comedy.

Harford 2610 Harford Ave. Preston Foster in "SECRET AGENT OF JAPAN" "Puss and Toots."

Horn 2014 West Pratt St. Judy Canova in "TRUE TO THE ARMY" "Pacific Frontiers."

Howard 115 N. Howard St. Brian Donlevy in "THE REMARKABLE ANDREW" Comedy.

Ideal 903 W. Thirty-sixth St. Buck Jones in "RIDERS OF THE WEST" With Tim McCoy.

Irvington 4113 Frederick Ave. Red Skelton in "MAISIE GETS HER MAN" Comedy and Cartoon.

Lane Dundalk, Md. Bill Boyd in "TWILIGHT ON THE TRAIL" With Andy Clyde.

Leader 248 S. Broadway. Bill Elliott in "PRAIRIE GUN SMOKE" Two Serial Pictures.

Linwood 908 S. Linwood Ave. Johnny Mack Brown in "THE MASKED RIDER" "Captain Midnight."

Little 523 North Howard St. "THE PASHA'S WIVES" (Life in a Turkish Harem.)

Lord Baltimore 1110 West Baltimore St. Judy Canova in "TRUE TO THE ARMY" with Jerry Colonna.

Lord Calvert 2444 Washington Boulevard. John Kimbrough in "SUNDOWN JIM" Comedy.

Lyceum Sparrows Point, Md. Regis Toomey in "BULLET SCARS" Comedy.

McHenry 1037 Light St. Judy Canova in "TRUE TO THE ARMY" "For Common Defense."

Mayfair 508 N. Howard St. MacDonald Carey in "DR. BROADWAY" with Jean Phillips.

Met Pennsylvania & North Aves. Gary Cooper in "SERGEANT YORK" Buy War Bonds and Stamps.

New Reisterstown, Md. Roy Rogers in "SONS OF THE PIONEERS" News.

New Essex Essex, Md. Andrews Sisters in "PRIVATE BUCKAROO" Comedy.

New Glen Glen Burnie. Gary Cooper in "SERGEANT YORK" News

Northway Harford & North. Pky. Veronica Lake in "THIS GUN FOR HIRE" "Spy Smasher."

Overlea Belair Rd., End of Car Line. Laraine Day in "FINGERS AT THE WINDOW" "Perils of Nyoka."

Palace Gay and Hoffman Sts. Lionel Atwill in "STRANGE CASE OF DR. RX." Comedy.

Patterson Eastern and East Aves. Ann Sothern in "MAISIE GETS HER MAN" "Quiz Kids."

Pikes Pikesville, Md. Ann Sothern in "MAISIE GETS HER MAN" Comedy.

Pimlico Park Heights & Belvedere. Bill Boyd in "STICK TO YOUR GUNS" "In The Circus."

Preston 1108 E. Preston St. George Houston in "Lone Rider and the Bandit" Edgar Kennedy Comedy.

Red Wing 2241 E. Monument St. Bob Steele in "WESTWARD HO" "Captain Midnight."

Rex 4600 York Road. Feature Cartoon "MR. BUG GOES TO TOWN" "What Makes Lizzy Dizzy"

Rialto 846 W. North Ave. John Howard in "SUBMARINE RAIDER" Buy War Bonds and Stamps.

Ritz 1607 N. Washington St. Allan Jones in "TRUE TO THE ARMY" Comedy.

Senator 5904 York Rd. Joan Crawford in "They All Kissed the Bride" "Holt of Secret Service."

State Monument and Castle Sts. Joan Crawford in "They All Kissed The Bride" Vaudeville.

Strand Dundalk, Md. Edw. G. Robinson in "LARCENY, INC." Comedy.

Towson Towson, Md. Leslie Howard in "MISTER V" Comedy.

Uptown 5010 Park Heights Ave. Joan Crawford in "They All Kissed The Bride" Comedy.

Vilma Belair Rd. and Mayfield Ave. Lee Bowman in "PACIFIC RENDEZVOUS" Comedy.

Walbrook 3100 W. North Ave. Bette Davis in "IN THIS OUR LIFE" "Pantry Panic."

Waverly Greenmount at Gorsuch. Charles Starrett in "DOWN RIO GRANDE WAY" "Perils of Nyoka."

Westport 2205 Russell St. Ann Southern in "MAISIE GETS HER MAN" Comedy.

Westway 5300 Edmondson Ave. Marguerite Chapman in "PARACHUTE NURSE" Comedy.

WARNER BROS. COMFORTABLY COOLED
STANLEY · TODAY
HOWARD NEAR FRANKLIN STREET · DOORS OPEN 10:30 A. M.
SHE HAD HIM PUT IN A FULL DAY'S WORK... AT NIGHT!
ROSALIND (Boss) RUSSELL (Hires) FRED (Secretary) MacMURRAY
P.S. HE GOT THE JOB!
"TAKE A LETTER, Darling"
with MACDONALD CAREY · ROBERT BENCHLEY · CONSTANCE MOORE · CECIL KELLAWAY

WE SELL WAR BONDS & STAMPS!
Cool LOEW'S
CENTURY LEXINGTON NR. CHARLES
NOW! 2nd WEEK
GREER GARSON · WALTER PIDGEON, MRS. MINIVER
COMING SOON Clark GABLE Lana TURNER "Somewhere I'll Find You"
VALENCIA ATOP THE CENTURY
AFFAIRS of MARTHA Marsha HUNT Richard CARLSON
PARKWAY NORTH AT CHARLES
"TRUE TO THE ARMY" JUDY CANOVA JERRY COLONNA

Cool HIPPODROME 25c TO 12.30 PLUS TAX
In Person! On Stage
Tommy DORSEY His Trombone and HIS ORCHESTRA
"ENEMY AGENTS Meet ELLERY QUEEN"
WILLIAM GARGAN—MARGARET LINDSAY

CARY GRANT JOAN FONTAINE
PLUS GIANT NEWSREEL SHOW
ROSLYN Air-Conditioned 800 Blk. N. Howard
GUNGA DIN

"DR. BROADWAY"
MacDonald CAREY Jean PHILLIPS
J. C. Naish · Richard Lane · Edw. Ciannelli
MAYFAIR HOWARD & FRANKLIN

Special Reserve Seat Premiere
Hippodrome—All Seats Reserved—Wednesday Eve., Aug. 12, 9 P. M.
GARY COOPER IN "PRIDE OF THE YANKEES"
Buy Tickets Now—$1.10 All Seats

See THE MOST DARING ANIMAL ACT
CAPT. ROMAN PROSKE And His FEROCIOUS BENGAL TIGERS
DANCING NIGHTLY
FREE ADMISSION GWYNN OAK AMUSEMENT PARK
No. 32 Car line direct to park—1 fare

NEW WORLD PREMIERE
A strange love that will haunt you as it thrills you!
Linda DARNELL John SHEPPERD
The LOVES of EDGAR ALLAN POE
THEATRE LEX. ST. AT PARK AVE.

KEITHS Children 15¢ (Plus Tax)
BUD ABBOTT LOU COSTELLO
Pardon My Sarong
VIRGINIA BRUCE
THE SABINEA DANCING GIRLS THE FOUR INK SPOTS
YOUR TICKET TO KEITHS TONITE ALSO ADMITS TO DANCE FREE

TOM BROWN ROBT. ARMSTRONG DEAD END KIDS
FIRST RUN
'Let's Get TOUGH!'
TIMES PLUS BIG NEWSREEL SHOW 3700 N. CHARLES

Swim in the Salty Chesapeake
BAY SHORE PARK
Take No. 26 Car Direct to Park

LITTLE STARTS TODAY!
Life Behind the Walls of A Turkish Harem...
'THE PASHA'S WIVES'

OPEN-AIR
DON AMECHE · JOAN BENNETT
CONFIRM or DENY
LUCILLE BALL in TOO MANY GIRLS

RIVOLI
Milton Berle "Whispering Ghosts"
Conrad Veidt "U-Boat 29"
DOUBLE SHOW DAILY

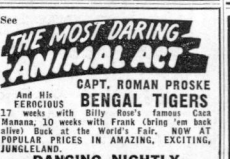

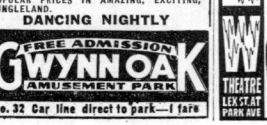

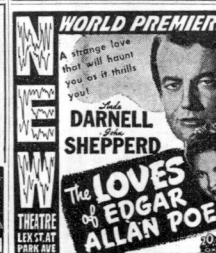

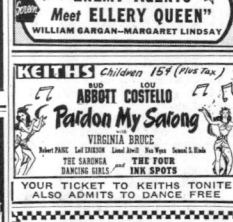

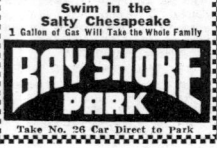

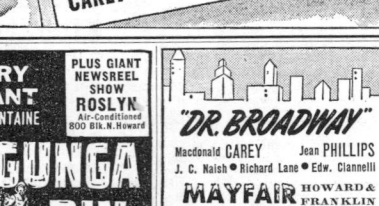

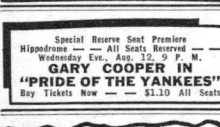

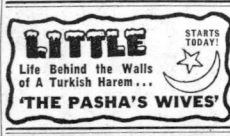

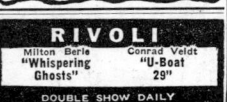

Ben Hogan Has Off-Day In Canadian Golf

Mystery Girl's Selections
AT SARATOGA

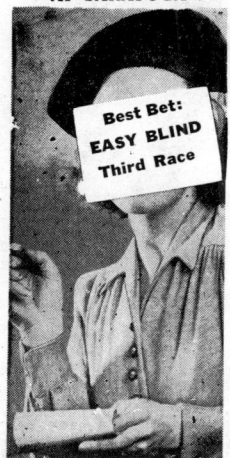

Best Bet: EASY BLIND Third Race

First Race—Tioga, Big Rebel, Castletown.
Second—Agrarist, High Hat, White Ford.
Third—Easy Blend, Rogers Boy, Kentown.
Fourth—Free Air, Noonday Sun, Twoses.
Fifth—Tip Toe, Hickory Head, Collect Call.
Sixth—Trierarch, Corydon, Sir Alfred.
Seventh—Vain Prince, Tola Rose, Porter's Cap.
Eighth—Happy Family, Over, Fair Call.

Clem McCarthy's Race Specials
SARATOGA
Fourth—Wuskenin, repeater.
Fifth—Picket, best here.
Sixth—Corydon, likely spot.
CUMBERLAND
Second—Cushlamacree, working well.
Fifth—Jello, consistent.
Seventh—Burner, well placed.
GARDEN STATE PARK
Fourth—Lord Vatout, never start.
Sixth—Foray Boop, won only start.
ROCKINGHAM
Fourth—Bellarmine, recent winner.
Sixth—Rosetown, class of field.
WASHINGTON
Second—Formal Dress, steady.
Fourth—Remembering, logical choice.
Fifth—Alsab, figures best.
Clem's Specials—Alsab and Picket.

Ed Curley's Selections
First Race—Kunawanin, Killmalock, Meeting House.
Second—Gay Flight, Querrytown, Lilson.
Third—Jorie-Mar, Querrytown, Lilson, tom.
Fourth—Flak, Polly Briar, Wuskenin.
Fifth—Jet Jello, Underdog, Halberd.
Sixth—Corydon, Olympus, Welcome Pass.
Seventh—Tola Rose, Vain Prince, Porter's Cap.
Eighth—Happy Family, Meal Flag, Great Rush.
Best Bet—Corydon in sixth race.

Scratches At Rockingham
Second—Don Pecos, Maeline.
Eighth—Panther Creek.
Ninth — Recoatna, Gossip Time, Grand Day.
Track fast.

Garden State Scratches
First Race—Grit.
Second—Bida Rita.
Fourth—Hidina.
Eighth—Allmar.
Track fast.

Cumberland Scratches
First Race—Ex Port, W. X., Bill K., Aster Lady, Braxton, Ler-Lin.
Second — Terry May, Sueqale, Market Place, Kaydeekay, Chief Teddy, Rough Amos.
Third—El Jellie.
Fourth — Arboreal, Never Home, Ida Deep Orange, Ranick's Queen.
Fifth—Alsab, Wonf Woof, Shut Eye.
Sixth—Best Seller, Starsfer, Gen'l Manager, Seventeen-Valerac, William Palmer, Mucho Gusto.
Eighth—Blind Eagle, Wicked, Gold Flag.
Ninth—Alwel, Veiled Prophet, David B. Jr.
Best Bet—Alsab.

Washington Park Scratches
First Race—Permineo, Soverton, Flemingburg, Bellevive, Richie's Charles-castleman.
Second—The Object, Marlena, Tioga.
Third—Marchon, Kanopolis, Castleman.
Fourth—Mabana.
Fifth—Speed to Spare, Jay Jay, Clyde Tolson.
Sixth—Jack S. L., Liberty Pan, Foray Song.
Seventh—Don Moss, Gentle Savage, Sunphantom.
Eighth—Flying Trick, White Front, Time Play.
Ninth (Sub.)—Declared off.
Track fast.

But He's Still In Three-Way Tie For Lead
By CHARLES B. LYNCH

TORONTO, Aug. 8—(U. P.)—Ralph Guldahl, Craig Wood and Ben Hogan led a field of 60 survivors into the final 36 holes of the Canadian Open golf championship today, with little favoritism among the trio.

Guldahl and Wood, who tied for second place in Thursday's opening round, each turned in a 69 yesterday and tied for the top spot with 36-hole totals of 135.

Hogan, in marked contrast to his record-breaking 65 on the first day, shot only a one-under-par 71 on the second 18 holes for a 36-hole total of 136. He was in trouble all day after scoring a bogey five on the first hole. He went out in 37 and came in in 34 and almost missed bettering par. A smooth 10-foot putt on the eighteenth enabled him to complete this hole in par four.

PUTTING TROUBLE

Both Wood and Guldahl had trouble with their putting. Wood went out in 36 and came back in 33 and Guldahl went out in 35 and came back in 34.

The expansive traps and lightning-fast greens of Mississauga's lengthy course played havoc with favorites, although all name players succeeded in qualifying for the final round.

Gordon Bryson, home club professional, topped the Canadians at the half-way mark. His 69 gave him 140 and sole possession of fifth place. In fourth was an amateur, Frank Stranahan of Toledo, Ohio, the best round of the day—a 67-gave him a total of 138.

Skee Reigel of Miami, Fla., another amateur, tied for sixth place with Clayton Heafner. Reigal had a 70 for a two-day total of 141.

HOT AND COLD

Heafner blew hot and cold for a 73 yesterday. His approach shots were good but his putting was off. When he missed a three-footer on the fifteenth, He slapped the ball into the hole and then picked it up and tossed it away in disgust. On the eighteenth, he was in trouble both on his drive and his approach, but holed out in par.

Gene Kunes of Philadelphia and Tony Perna of Dayton, Ohio, occupied seventh place with 142.

Second among the Canadians were Bobby Reith of Windsor; Bob Burns of Toronto and Jerry Proulx of Montreal, with 143s. They tied for ninth place in the tournament with Paul Runyan of White Plains, N. Y., and Horton Smith of Pinehurst, N. C.

CLICKING 'EM OFF

NEW YORK, Aug. 8—(A. P.)—The New York Yankees, who have completed 140 double plays in the 105 games played this season, must add 57 more two-ply killings to the total in the coming 49 games to surpass the record number they reached last season.

Louisville Times Selections
WASHINGTON PARK—Fast
First Race—Supreme's Reji, Fresh Money, Soverton.
Second—Jocaramco, Son Spinner, Former Dress.
Third—Undulator Bulleeve, Carbonate.
Fourth—Kansas City, Amazed, Don Lin II.
Fifth—Alsab, Wonf Woof, Shut Eye.
Sixth—Best Seller, Starsfer, Gen'l Manager.
Seventh-Valerac, William Palmer, Mucho Gusto.
Eighth—Blind Eagle, Wicked, Gold Flag.
Ninth—Alwel, Veiled Prophet, David B. Jr.
Best Bet—Alsab.

Race Selections
ASSOCIATED PRESS CONSENSUS
AT ROCKINGHAM—Fast Trace.
First Race—Skeeter, Baggrave, Secret Chatter.
Second—High Pointed, Victory One, Ariel Trip.
Third—Pious Display, Shasta Fiddle, Fatal Hour.
Fourth—Rough Biscuit, Bellarmine, Whisper.
Fifth—Peace Fleet, Batik, Mine.
Sixth—Rosetown, Lovedale, Wood Robin.
Seventh—Maximow, Moja, Impetuous Lad.
Eighth—Jacquar, Yankee Lad.
Ninth—Brooklandville, In Dutch, Grand Day.
Best Bet—Pious Display.

AT GARDEN STATE PARK—Track Fast.
First Race—Bryson entry, Fag Tempo, Pilatan.
Second—Bucket Shop, Chop Sticks, At Bat.
Third—Blenweed, Carman, Son o' Max.
Fourth—Sir Kic., Lord Vatout, Thorino.
Fifth—Speed to Spare, Jay Jay, Clyde Tolson.
Sixth—Jack S. L., Liberty Pan, Foray Song.
Seventh—Don Moss, Gentle Savage, Sunphantom.
Eighth—Flying Trick, White Front, Time Play.
Best Bet—King Tooth.

Joe And Asbestos
By KEN KLING

Hopeful Reward was booklet Sleeper 2 which won yesterday. Today horses 11 and 13 start. The Cumberland bet ran 2nd. Saratoga long shot scratched. Next code goes Monday. We expect to have a hot one at Saratoga as well. Today we bet $2 on PICKET at the Spa. Long shot at Detroit is Dream Boat. We bet $1 win. Cooch's Bridge lost. Bank roll $21.

Ken Kling's Parlay
SENSE—Third Race, Garden State.
MERCURY—Sixth Race, Garden State.

Riders, Odds
For Today At Saratoga
REVISED LINE

FIRST RACE—About two miles.
Big Rebel, 146, Walker 5-2
Danny Deever, 142, C. Brooks 12-1
Big Blanco II, 152, Scott 5-1
Admirality, 130, Jenning 5-1
Castletown, 149, Bellhouse 2-1
Meeting House, 148, Bland 4-1
Killmalock, 142, Cruz 8-1
Tioga, 135, Moran 20-1

SECOND—Six furlongs.
aWhite Ford, 115, Bela 5-2
bManatortume, 110, Loveridge 5-1
Sure Fire, 110, Gorman 6-1
Gay Flight, 115, Thompson 5-1
bAgrarist, 110, Renick 5-2
Austeia, 112, Longden 10-1
Lord Bart, 115, Stout 8-1
High Hat, 115, Nodarse 12-1
Kennebis, 112, McCreary 20-1
bQuerryton, 115, Robertson 4-1
Plucky Ray, 115, Woolf 20-1
aWeir entry.
bAste entry.
Scratched—Lilson, Haripp

THIRD—Seven-eighths mile.
Kentown, 113, Skelly 20-1
Misting, 108, Nodarse 12-1
Jorie-Mar, 108, McCreary 5-1
Isle De Pine, 101, Mehrtens 5-2
Austeia, 111, Lindberg 3-1
Bell Bottom, 96, Zubieta 8-1
Mythical King, 108, Cruz 20-1
Easy Blend, 116, Arcaro 3-1
bIsvads, 108, Bilbrando 30-1
Bright Camp, 111, Mehrtens 4-1
Roger's Boy, 111, Loveridge 5-1
Scratched—Parade Ground, Aquebette, Sir Lancelot.

FOURTH—Five and one-half furlongs.
Polly Briar, 113, Longden 8-1
Flak, 116, Woolf 5-2
Noonday Sun, 116, Arcaro 3-1
Dim Out, 108, Meade 20-1
Bass, 113, Skelly 12-1
Wuskenin, 113, Thompson 7-2
Mercy, 113, McCreary 5-1
Tweedy, 116, Nodarse 4-1
Jopier, 111, Garza 12-1
Gold Dan, 116, Gilbert 12-1
Great Quest, 111, Robertson 20-1
Commander, 111, Wall 20-1
Scratched—Twoses, Free Air.

FIFTH—Six furlongs.
Picket, 122, Wright 2-1
Halberd, 122, Woolf 5-1
Hickory Head, 122, Arcaro 5-1
Tip Toe, 122, Stout 4-1
Hourmont, 122, Robertson 10-1
Twoses, 122, McCreary 6-1
Collect Call, 122, Meade 4-1

SIXTH—Mile and three-sixteenths.
Sir Alfred, 110, Schmidl 4-1
Corydon, 113, Arcaro 2-1
Trierarch, 102, Loveridge 3-1
Welcome Pass, 107, McCreary 8-1
Alca-Gal, 111, Longden 8-1
Olympus, 107, Meade 6-1
Can't Wait, 118, Loveridge 4-1

SEVENTH—Seven-eighths of mile.
Porter's Cap, 110, Arcaro 5-1
Can't Wait, 114, no boy 4-1
Tola Rose, 122, no boy 3-1
Vain Prince, 110, Stout 5-2
bHartnell, 102, Wall 12-1
Solinbroke, 105, McCreary 10-1
Scratched—Sir Alfred.

EIGHT—One mile.
Happy Family, 113, McCreary 3-1
Buckskin, 118, Arcaro 3-1
Great Rush, 122, Robertson 4-1
Trierarch, 113, Stout 5-1
Over, 113, Lindberg 4-1
No. Twoses, 120, Thompson 8-1
Bardia, 111, Gorman 10-1
Scratched—Meal Flag.
Track fast.
First race, 2.30 P. M.

Busy Saturday List At Navy

ANNAPOLIS, Md., Aug. 8—(A. P.)—Navy's baseball team, tackling Georgetown this afternoon, will have its eyes on the Maryland District of Columbia League standings, but its mind will be on two games earlier this season.

In those two games Georgetown trimmed Navy and the Middies would like nothing better than to extract a measure of revenge for those lickings and improve their league position by beating Georgetown today.

The baseball game will climax one of the busiest Saturdays of the Naval Academy's summer sport season.

From Johns Hopkins will come the track and tennis squads to test the Navy's mettle and in another varsity match, the Pennsylvania golfers take on the Navy linksmen. On the polo schedule are a tennis match with the Baltimore Forest Park A. C. and a baseball game with the Baltimore Westinghouse Electric squad.

In the varsity baseball contest, a steadily improving Navy squad will try to stretch its winning streak to three games. The Navy nine topped Catholic and Maryland in its last two starts.

Calif. Youths In Net Final

CULVER, Ind., Aug. 8—(I. N. S.)—Of the all-California quartet which went into the national junior tennis semi-finals, Tom Falkenburst and Bob Falkenburg of the sensational Tom-and-Bob Falkenburg brother duo, and Edward (Budge) Patty, defending champion, were left today to fight it out for the title.

Tom Falkenburg got into the finale by scoring a stunning 9—7, 8—6 upset over Brother Bob in yesterday's play. Previously the Hollywood player had defeated Jim Brink of Seattle and Harry Likas after having apparently lost the match.

Patty wasted little time in disposing of Arthur MacDonald of San Gabriel, Cal., 6—3, 6—2.

The boys' singles championship went to Wade Herren of Birmingham, Ala., who defeated Tom Molloy of Memphis, Tenn., 6—6, 6—3. In the doubles finals in the boys' division Billy Smith of Orlando, Fla., and Molloy defeated Dean and McDonald Mathey of Princeton, N. J., 6—2, 6—2.

STEELERS BEGIN

PITTSBURGH, Aug. 8—(U. P.)—The Pittsburgh Steelers will open their summer training camp tomorrow at Hershey, Pa., where they will try to forget last year's percentages which toughening up for their tenth season in the National Pro Football League.

Major League Leaders
By Associated Press.
NATIONAL LEAGUE
Batting—Reiser, Brooklyn, .343; Lombardi, Boston, .330.
Runs—Ott, New York, 79; Reiser, Brooklyn, 71.
Runs Batted In—Mize, New York, and Medwick, Brooklyn, 75.
Hits — Medwick, Brooklyn, 129; Slaughter, St. Louis, 126.
Doubles—Hack, Chicago, 28; Reiser and Medwick, Brooklyn, 27.
Triples—Slaughter, St. Louis, 16; Nicholson, Chicago, 8.
Home Runs—Mize, New York, 19; Ott, New York, 18.
Stolen Bases—Reiser, Brooklyn, 13; Miller and Fernandez, Boston, 11.
Pitching—French, Brooklyn, 11-1; Wyatt, Brooklyn, 13-3.

AMERICAN LEAGUE
Batting—Gordon, New York, .343; Williams, Boston, .341.
Runs — Williams, Boston, 92; DiMaggio, New York, 80.
Runs Batted In—Williams, Boston, 101; DiMaggio, New York, 77.
Hits — Spence, Washington, 142; Stephens, St. Louis, 136.
Doubles—Doerr, Boston, 32; Higgins, Detroit, 31.
Triples Heath, Cleveland, 12; Vaio, Philadelphia; Spence, Washington, and DiMaggio, New York, 10.
Stolen Bases—Case, Washington, 26; Kuhel, Chicago, 18.
Pitching — Chandler, New York, 12-2; Borowy, New York, 10-2.

PACIFIC COAST LEAGUE
Sacramento, 2; San Diego, 1.
Oakland, 6; Los Angeles, 1.
Hollywood, 2; San Francisco, 1.
Portland, 1-0; Seattle, 0-6.

YESTERDAY'S STARS
By Associated Press.
NANNY FERNANDEZ, Braves — His triple in eleventh inning led to victory over Dodgers.
VINCE DiMAGGIO, Pirates — Hit two singles to drive in three runs during eight-run uprising against Cardinals, his second hit coming with bases loaded.
CARL HUBBELL, Giants— Pitched perfect ball for five innings and received credit for victory over Phils, although needing help in ninth inning.
CHET LAABS, Browns—Hit twentieth home run as contribution to triumph over Tigers.

Strictly Feminine
By ELEANOR McINTYRE

The women's club golf championship trials slated for the very near future over the Woodholme, Suburban, Baltimore Country Club, Bonnie View, Rolling Road and Country Club of Maryland courses, will draw the cream of club contenders into play.

From the looks of the link situation it is going to be another year at the helm for Mrs. Maurice Glick, thrice winner of the Woodholme stakes, and we might venture to say that it would take something like a nor'easter to blow "Lady Luck" from the throne. Mrs. Glick has sailed into the upper golf ranks within the past four years and has won her place among the State's finest golfers.

Unless a terrific upset occurs Woodholme's third-term queen has the coming championship sewed up, for not another golfer at the Pikesville course can compare with this skilled wielder of wood and iron. Runner-up berth in the Maryland State a month or so back was only the beginning for the star clubber. She's entered in the Middle Atlantic championships to be held in Washington next week and we feel certain that she's eyeing the City crown, which will go on the block here the end of the month.

Then there's Suburban's queen, Jeannette Myers, who cleaned up on about everything last year, winning the Titleholders' Tournament for the second time, the Hugh Young Trophy in competition over the nine-hole Gibson Island course, and the title event at her own club, in addition to other minor tournament prizes.

Although Miss Myers replaced Mrs. Jerome Cloman, veteran titleholder at the club, in winning the championship crown last year, the tournament was an open field with Mrs. Cloman out of competitive play. The going was far from easy but just the same Miss Myers was not worried with the spell of a defending champion at her heels.

Mrs. Sloman, however, is back in action this season and so far has been hitting the pill in championship style. Willing club championship at the Suburban final Mrs. Sloman and Miss Myers in the finals. It looks very much that way and as for the winner, your guess is as good as mine. The championship situation with take the same sort of hue this year when Mrs. Herbert Leimbach, reigning queen of the Baltimore Country Club, strokes out to defend the Roland Park course laurels. The tilt at seat, formerly held by Mrs. T. E. Schluderberg, ace of the local brigade, was vacated by that veteran last year, in order that she might participate in the Nationals at Brookline, Mass.

This year, however, the topnotch fairway star is likely to remain at home to toss her cap into the tournament ring for another crack at the crown. Mrs. Gerald P. Hopkins, runner-up for the title last year, has given up her residence in this city.

The Rolling Road club women's crown has rested untouched on the head of Mrs. C. H. Hoffforge for the past two years and the chances are that it will remain for another year. However, the unexpected may be flashed by Mrs. H. R. Stansbury, Mrs. Clinton Easton, Mrs. O. B. Coblentz, Jr., or Claire Wilson, all of whom have been performing well this season at the Catonsville Club.

Mrs. C. E. Richards is the chosen prospect to defeat Mrs. Felix A. McNally, defending titleholder at Bonnie View. Mrs. Richards, newcomer to the golfing ranks here has slipped into the top bracket of play in less time than any of us. She recently captured the Virginia Holzderber Cup tourney over the Clifton Park course and took second flight honors in the Maryland State. She has been shooting in the high eighties for several weeks in the club and association events.

Norman Tops A. A. Batsmen

CHICAGO, Aug. 8—(A. P.)—The first three places in the American Association batting averages belonged to Milwaukee teammates, in statistics computed through Wednesday, with Will Norman heading the list after vaulting to the top from eighth position a week ago.

Norman came up by collecting 15 hits in 32 trips to hike his average to .331. He was followed by the Brewers' Hall Peck and Ed Stanky, with .330 and .323, respectively; Joe Vosmik of Minneapolis, last week's leader, .322; Joe Bestudis of Indianapolis, Al Powell of St. Paul, and John Lazor of Louisville, .320 each; Heinz Becker, Milwaukee, .314; Wayne Blackburn, Indianapolis, 312, and Jim Grant, St. Paul, .308.

Norman also became the home-run leader, smacking four of them during the week to bring his total to 20. Ab Wright of Minneapolis was second with 19, but first in runs batted-in with 89. Peck had the most hits, 144; Stanky led with 39 doubles and Chuck Stevens of Toledo had poled 11 triples.

Longacre Track To Remain Open

SEATTLE, Aug. 8—(A. P.)—Longacres, only major race track operating on the West coast since the outbreak of war, will remain open "unless closed by some authority," Joseph Gottstein, president of the Washington Jockey Club, declared today after a heated conference with Gov. Arthur B. Langlie.

WOULD HALT MEET

Langlie had requested the track operators to end their racing season as soon as possible in the interest of the conservation of gasoline and rubber.

Gottstein retorted that "if the State wants to close the track they'll have to do it" after Langlie rejected his counter proposal that the season be cut 40 per cent., with the racing days reduced from five to three a week.

Informed of Gottstein's attitude, Langlie said:

"I advised Mr. Gottstein that as far as I was concerned I could stop horse racing right now I would do so."

Gottstein's legal counsel advised him against closing the plant voluntarily because of commitments which might lead to damage suits.

AID WAR EFFORT

He said he prided himself on his patriotism and that Longacres had contributed to the war effort. He pointed to the Army Relief Day Derby August 20, for which 17,000 tickets already have been sold.

Longacres, whose season began on Labor Day, has enjoyed a prosperous meeting, due largely to the idleness of the famous Santa Anita and other California tracks this year. After the war broke out these tracks did not open at the request of the Army, which contended that racing fans' automobiles would overcrowd the highways.

Main event of the track, the $10,000 Longacres mile August 30, has an impressive list of nominations.

Terp Stickmen Swamp Jay Ten

The University of Maryland's powerful lacrosse team ended its win in a row over the Johns Hopkins yesterday, defeating the Jays, 8-0, in a regular summer league game at College Park. It is the first game of the two schools' summer series the two teams are scheduled for. The Maryland team had things under complete control from the very beginning of the game. Their defense was faultless and their attack could not be halted.

Jack Hoyert, second defenseman of the Maryland team, was high scorer of the game, bagging 4 of the 8 tallies.

Maryland will wind up their summer series against the Naval Academy team next Wednesday at Annapolis.

CUMBERLAND SELECTIONS
By JACK CARPENTER
First Race—Pete's Prince, Paso Grande, Exhort.
Second—Terry May, Cushlamacree, Nyleve.
Third—Elizabeth K., Linden Girl, Big Breeze.
Fourth—Butterman, Hiblaze, Saint Pyrene.
Fifth—Begrudged, El Jelis, Herod's Plate.
Sixth—Sun Night, Star Caster, James Pat.
Seventh—Burner, Channing, Grandin.
Eighth—Some Groucher, Bar Ship, Nutmeg.
Ninth—Blue Melody, Navigation, Gibor.
Best—Begrudged.

Swim Records Fall In Meet

NEW LONDON, Conn. Aug. 8—(A. P.)—The annual revision of the record book for swimming reaches its midway point today, with two new figures already posted.

A pair of the Hawaiians, Keo Nakama and Billy Smith, Jr., started the 1942 National A. A. U. outdoor team meet off on the right tempo last night by rubbing out one world and one American record. And today Smith and Adolph Kiefer of Chicago are expected to do the record breaking.

Smith, son of a Honolulu policeman and a student at Ohio State University, sped through 220 yards of blue-green water in the Ocean Beach Park pool in 2:10.7 last night to erase the 2:13.1 mark set by Otto Jaretz of Chicago in 1940.

Nakama, now also a student at the Buckeye school, made a gloss of Jack Medica's eight-year-old figures for 880 yards, lowering the figures from 20:57.8 to 20:25.

Today Smith will focus his aim on the 440-yard freestyle standard, with Nakama as the key. Nakama will Kiefer will strive to retain his 110-yard crown. Smith is the defending champion in the quarter-mile event.

The remaining two events on the afternoon program are without defending champions because of the war. Neither Jose Balmores nor the Alexander Community House 880-yard relay team was able to make the journey from Hawaii. Balmores is the 220-yard breast stroke king.

Other champions crowned on the opening day were Sammy Lee of Pasadena, Cal., in the three-meter drive and Ohio State's 320-yard medley relay team of Mark Follansbee, Jim Counsilman and Jack Hill.

Handicappers' Score

Glen Wild set the pace for The News-Post selectors yesterday at Saratoga when four of his choices rang the bell. His winners were Lovely Night ($4.60), Vagracy ($2.60), Brittany ($14.80) and Cacodemon ($10.10). Rosewell, named as best bet by Glen Wild, finished second in the third race to pay $42.60. Jack Carpenter had four winners yesterday at Cumberland in Teco Tack, Scootie, My One and Grouchy.

Majeski, Hitting .350, Leads I. L. Batters

NEW YORK, Aug. 8—(A. P.)—Henry Majeski has been leading the International League hitters for four weeks, but the star third baseman of the Newark Bears hasn't yet reached the point where he is willing to try to coast to the batting championship.

Week by week he has been pushing his average a little higher and now has reached the .350 level, two points higher than last week.

It was just as well he did, too, because Gene Moore of Montreal rode a 15-game batting streak into second place among the hitters with .327, five points better than the second-place mark of Buffalo's Johnny Welaj last week.

ROBBIE HAS .314

Based on 250 or more times at bat before Wednesday's games the leading hitters this week were Majeski, .350; Moore, .327; Eddie Robinson, Baltimore, .314; Welaj, .312; Dutch Meyer, Buffalo, .308; Ervin Dusak, Rochester, .302; Sid Gordon, Jersey City, .298; Mike Rocco, Buffalo, .298; Bill Johnson, Newark, .294, and Frank Colman, Toronto, .294.

Majeski also retained his leadership in total hits with 150 and in runs batted in with an even 100.

56 STOLEN BASES

His roommate and renowned base-stealer, George (Snuffy) Stirnweiss, rode some of Majeski's hits home to lead the league in runs scored with 93, as well as increasing his total of stolen bases to 56. Rocco continued to top the league's home run clouters with 23, one more than Ed Robinson and two more than Montreal's Les Burge have produced.

Tommy Byrne of Newark has won 14 games and lost but two to maintain his mastery of other pitchers in the circuit.

Semi-Pro Nines Open 2d Round

The Baltimore Semi-Pro Baseball League opens its second round of play tomorrow with the Becker's Dairy nine holding a commanding lead in the race. Four twin bills are slated for action tomorrow on four separate fronts.

Becker's entertains the Canton narrow brings together the Stemmers Run Athletic Club and Gray Manor D. C. at Stemmers Run Oval. The Runners, in third place, must whip Gray Manor twice to retain any chances of catching the high flying leaders. Gray Manor can't afford to lose either as a double defeat would practically eliminate them from a playoff berth.

In the other tests tomorrow the Becker nine plays the Baltimore Bears at Becker's Oval, St. Peter's A. A. faces the Baltimore Giants at Locke Oval and Morrell Park D. C. battles the Baltimore Dolphins at Georgetown Oval.

Sandlot Baseball
SUNDAY
DOUBLE-HEADER LEAGUES
BALTIMORE MAJOR LEAGUE
(Playoff of First Round Tie)
Arbutus vs. Brooklyn, at Silents Field, 2 P. M.
NORTH BALTIMORE MAJOR LEAGUE
Rose Pleasure Club vs. Bloomingdale, Roosevelt Park.
Oak Pleasure Club vs. Pittsburger's Al-stars, Bloomingdale Oval.
Rustless at St. Ambrose.
Rogers vs. West Coast Guard at Mt. Washington.
Tri-Fit vs. Hanlon, Herring Run Park.
BALTIMORE SEMI-PRO LEAGUE
Becker's Dairy vs. Baltimore Bears, at Becker's Oval.
St. Peter's A. A. vs. Baltimore Giants, at Locke Oval.
Gray Manor D. C. vs. Stemmers Run A. C., at Stemmers Run Oval.
Morrell Park D. C. vs. Baltimore Dolphins at Georgetown Oval.
BELAIR HARFORD-ROAD LEAGUE
DeMolay at Glenn.
Belair Road A. A. vs. St. Ursula, Glen more Oval.
Gardenville vs. Overlea, Parkside Oval.
MARYLAND LEAGUE
(Playoff Series)
Catonsville vs. W. Shaivitz and Sons, Spring Grove Oval.
Local Union Number 149 vs. Ellicott City Boy's Club, Oella, Md.
SINGLE GAME LEAGUES
BALTIMORE AMATEUR LEAGUE
Homestead vs. Second District Democratic Club, Clifton No. 1, 4 P. M.
Linden Printers vs. Little Tavern, Patterson No. 2, 4 P. M.
MARYLAND AMATEUR LEAGUE
Parkside vs. Barclay, Herring Run No. 1.
St. Mary's (Govans) vs. Hampden Civic Club, Waverly No. 1.
Rosedale vs. People's Club, Patterson No. 1, 2 P. M.
MONUMENTAL LEAGUE
Spartan vs. Solley, Hanlon Park, 2 P. M.
Fay-Row vs. Glen Burnie, Carroll Park, 2 P. M.
Carneyville vs. St. Bernardine, 2 P. M.
Hartmans vs. Gwynn Oak A. A., Hanlon Park, 2 P. M.
WEST BALTIMORE INTERMEDIATE LEAGUE
Western Trojans vs. Sioux Eagles, Carroll No. 2, 2 P. M.
Walbrook Collegians vs. Arbutus Bees, Beech No. 1, 4 P. M.
Cowboys vs. Nameless, Carroll No. 4, 2 P. M.
Westchester vs. Gwynn Falls, 4 P. M.
Sentinels vs. Kenwood, Gwynn Falls, 4 P. M.
Calverton Juniors vs. Rainbows, Bloomingdale Oval, 11.30 A. M.
EAST BALTIMORE INTERMEDIATE LEAGUE
Waverly vs. Clifton, Clifton No. 1, 2 P. M.
Patterson vs. St. Elizabeth Holy Name, Patterson No. 2, 2 P. M.
EASTERN CATHOLIC INTERMEDIATE LEAGUE
St. Vincent's vs. St. James, Clifton No. 2, 4 P. M.
St. Mary's (Govans) vs. St. Elizabeth, Clifton No. 3, 4 P. M.
St. Ignatius vs. St. Francis, Clifton No. 4, 4 P. M.
St. Ambrose vs. St. Michael's, Patterson No. 3, 4 P. M.
WESTERN CATHOLIC INTERMEDIATE LEAGUE
Fourteen Holy Martyrs vs. St. Cecilia, Walbrook Oval, 4 P. M.
St. Rose of Lima vs. St. Gregory, Carroll No. 2, 2 P. M.
St. Joseph Monastery vs. St. Peter's, No. 2.
NORTHEASTERN JUNIOR LEAGUE
Rose Wildcats vs. Hamilton, 11.30 A. M.
Highland Sport Club vs. Evergreen, Patterson No. 2.
WESTERN CATHOLIC JUNIOR LEAGUE
(Games start at 11.30 A. M.)
St. Joseph Monastery vs. St. Peter's, No. 2.
St. Rose of Lima vs. Shrine of Sacred Heart.
St. Jerome's vs. St. Martin's No. 2.
St. Bernard's vs. St. Benedict's No. 1.
Holbrook vs. St. John's, Clifton No. 1.

Race Selections At Saratoga

	FIRST	SECOND	THIRD	FOURTH	FIFTH	SIXTH	SEVENTH	EIGHTH
By GLEN WILD	Killmalock Meet'g House Admiralty	G. FLIGHT Plucky Ray Aica-Gal	Rogers Boy Easy Blend	Wuskinin Noonday Sun Flak	PICKET Collect Call Halberd	Olympus Corydon Can't Wait	Tola Rose Porter's Cap	Great Rush Hap. Fam'y Fair Call
By HARRY FELDNER	P. Blanco II Lilson Castletown Meet'g House	Sure Fire Gay Flight	Rogers Boy Easy Blend Kentown	Gay Flight Guerryt'n Haripp	PICKET Halberd Collect Call	Corydon Olympus Can't Wait	TOLA ROSE Vain Prince Porter's Cap	Great Rush Buckskin Over
By TRED AVON	P. Blanco II Admiralty Tioga	Gay Flight Qua'belle Max	Mercy Jorie-Mar Qua'relle	Flak Halberd Collect Call	PICKET Trierarch Corydon	Tola Rose Vain Prince Porter's Cap	Fair Call Over Trierarch	
By JACK CARPENTER	P. Blanco II Big Rebel Meet. Ho'se	Gay Flight Guerryton Lord Bart	Roger's Boy Jorie-Mar Misting	Tweedy N'n'day Sun	CORYDON Olympus Sir Alfred	Tola Rose Porter's Cap Can't Wait	H'ppy Family Great Rush H. F. Family Buckskin	
By N. P. CLARK	Castletown P. Blanco II Tioga	Agrarist High Hat Blac. Ford	Easy Blend Jorie-Mar Misting	Wuskenin Mercy Twoses	PICKET Hickory Head Halberd Tip Toe	CORYDON Sir Alfred WelcomePass	Tola Rose Porter's Cap Vain Prince	Hap. Fam'y Hardia Great Rush
By LOUISVILLE TIMES	Big Rebel Castletown Pico Bi'co II	ROGERS BOY Jorie-Mar Bright Camp	Easy Guest Gay Flight	Wuskenin Flak Tweedy	PICKET Halberd Twoses	Corydon Olympus Jorie-Mar	Tola Rose Porter's Cap Vain Prince	H'ppy Family Meal Flag Great Rush
CONSENSUS BY A. P.	P. Blanco II Castletown Meet'g House	Roger's Boy Jorie-Mar	Easy Blend Mething	PICKET Halberd Tip Toe	CORYDON Olympus Welcome Pass	Tola Rose Porter's Cap Vain Prince	Happy Family Great Rush Over	
CONSENSUS								

NITE LIFE
By LOU and KEN CALVERT

Henny Youngman! That's about the only logical way to start our column this week, for Youngman easily ranks as one of the greatest show personalities of the day. His appearance at 21 Club beginning Wednesday should be a gala event. We for two, will be on hand to greet him.

New shows boasting new stars in a fast and furious whirl is the answer of those who hold the reins of Baltimore's nite spots to the surging influx of new faces arriving in town every day seeking new forms of diversion.

Club Charles' Georgie Price gives way on Tuesday to a complete production booked intact and featuring Eddie White and Marie Austin. Band Box adds the Three Brown Sisters, 2 O'Clock Club augments its girlie revue with new personalities, Brendel's Manor Park brings in the famous Hoosier Hot Shots on Sunday.

NEW NAMES, NEW FACES at other spots include the advent of Carl Snyder's versatile trio to DeLuca's smart Dundalk lounge.... Doc Grey, his imitations and his mpersonations at the White House Supper Club.... Phyllis DeRita at the Asner's popular Green Villa. Doris Ruby's joining the Earle Club array.... Larry Brent, the Boston baby emcee now entrenched at Strickler's.... Joe Tucker's Hawaiians at Crystal Ball Inn.

ALVINO RAY, LOOK OUT! There's a youngster named Wilson Forte... just twenty years old the twenty-third of last month ... playing steel with Marshall's boys at the Madison, and already he runs a mighty close second to you! Add note: He writes every single one of the clever arrangements used by the Madison outfit.

TO HIS MANY FRIENDS ABOUT TOWN: Bob Bruce, now in the armed forces, is on the march and moving South.... Bernie Lit came through his operation last week and in fine style and is well on the road to recovery.

CONGRATULATIONS to the Conrad Fischer's and their Woodlea Lounge on the completion this week of their first year at successfully serving folks out Belair road way. Michael Green's weekend dancing at Carlin's Forest Gardens will be well represented this week by Claude Thornhill, appearing Tuesday with his orchestra at the Roller Casino. Thornhill's orchestrations for the late Hal Kemp, for Andre Kostelanets, Skinnay Ennis and others are as popular as his own orchestra.

TO BE ENJOYED ABOUT TOWN are the comfort of the Sportsman's newly elongated bar, Jerry Kaufman's music at Sweeney's.... 5 Dukes of Rhythm at Benjamin's.... The Fielding's at Kathleen's.... The sea-food snacks and luscious dinners at Shuey's, down on Stony creek.... Eddie Cook's "Music in the Air" at Matusky's Riviera Beach spot.... The Gayety Nite Club.... Marion Dawn's perpetual charm at Club Bar.... Chago Rodrigo's troubadouring at New Hotel Broadway.... The carefree fun-full atmosphere at Golden Ring Inn, again at 4 Corners Corral.... The outdoor terrace at Joe's Airport Tavern on a warm night, or most any night. ... Abe Schaeffer's antics at the Air Port Grill.

MOST PEOPLE DON'T KNOW about the Club Bar's neon sign on Baltimore street, way up high there ... about the fine American, as well as Italian, meals at La Dicci's ... the businessmen's luncheons at Crystal Bar at Nate's and Leon's.

WE LIKE PAT'S (of Pat's Bar) story about the hillbilly who couldn't sleep on a brand-new Pullman because the "hammock" was too small! ... George Price's routine wherein he finds a thick roll of bills held together with a rubber band, throws away the bills and puts the rubber band in a safe deposit box ... Eddie Auforth's melody-making at Mueller's Victory Room ... Keystone Night Club's newly planned motif ... the meals at Teddy Reichhart's ... the congeniality at Mac's Walnut Grove ... the Saturday night dances at Sam's Rail Inn ... Bill Gordon's music at Nolan's.

Leon Lampe (of Leon's, on Park avenue) in the role of Commander Lampe, Lieut. George B. Redwood Post, V. F. W., 193, will present a finely engraved citizenship medal on behalf of his post to the News-Post carrier who has sold the most war bonds and stamps during the past two months. A fine gesture, to encourage the sale in that manner.

PRIZE GAG OF THE WEEK: Leo Bateman's of Carl's about the argument he had with his wife. Leo really told her where to get off, he says. In fact, she finally came crawling to him on her hands and knees ... screaming, "Come out from under that bed, you coward!"

Farrell Held Over At Beachcomber

Baltimore likes him, and so he stays! That's Frank Hollander's (Beachcomber impressario) attitude on the subject of Jack Farrel, and Baltimore is proving they want more and more of Farrel's cutting-up by returning time and again to enjoy his skits. Particular favorite is Farrel's blackout routines, which create a minor bedlam of laughter at every show. Shirley Dulow, local swing singer who made good ... (and better!) continues, along with Teresa Dien, Audrey Lee and the Beachcomberettes.

Merrymakers Featured In Local Nite Spots

MARIE AUSTIN
Opening Tuesday as singing star of a new Club Charles revue.

HENNY YOUNGMAN
Headline luminary slated for Baltimore and the 21 Club Wednesday.

PAUL MALLORY
His pianistic talents find favor at Doc's Lounge.

ROSE AURORA
Acrobatic artist seen in current offering at Carl's.

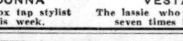
GEORGE YEATMAN
His WBAL Quartet at Blue Mirror a consistent favorite combination.

GLORIA DONNA
Adorable Band Box tap stylist "on tap" this week.

VESTA VICTORIA
The lassie who changes her costumes seven times in show at Madison.

El Patio Accent On Rhythm

If you can rhumba, if you can tango, if you can conga... Baltimore's Latin-America El Patio offers the music and atmosphere designed to make that dancing of yours doubly enjoyable. And if you haven't as yet mastered the hip-swinging motions, then El Patio's Diaz and Dolores will teach you. Between dance rhythms, this favorite rendezvous stirs up a solid array of Pan-American talent including Felicia Flores and Raymon's Rhumba Band to stage complete and colorful revues nightly.

Sisters Head Band Box Show

The Three Brown Sisters, current Band Box headliners, are riding high on the crest of Baltimore's penchant for sepia jive... an inclination which started with the Delta Rhythm Boys and carried right on down through DeLloyd McKay, 4 Peppers and Johnnie & George. The sisters boast a smoothly blended combination of voices and make good listening. Al Stone continues to pace the show with his ready wit and introduces, in addition to the Brown Sisters, Angie Belmont, Broadway songstress; Stanley Fisher, harmonica wizard; lovely Gloria Donna, tapstress.

BLUE MIRROR

Dot and Dash, delightful piano and song duo, continue on the Blue Mirror's bill of fare for another week, with George Yeatman's WBAL Quartet contributing quiet, but smart, melodies that add much to the intimacy and refinement of this smart Charles street lounge. Margie Wood's vocalizing, with the quartet, is still favorite with Blue Mirror patrons.

To Roller Casino

CLAUDE THORNHILL
Whose popular headline orchestra will play Tuesday night at Carlin's Roller Casino.

Additional news of night clubs will be found On Page 13.

OPENING WED., AUG. 12
Henny YOUNGMAN
AMERICA'S NO. 1 COMEDIAN!
CAST OF 20
NO COVER EVER MATINEE SHOW
RES. NO. 5552 4 to 6 P. M.
LARRY LONDON'S ORCH. BROADCASTING
NITELY, W-I-T-H, 10.45 P. M.
AIR CONDITIONED
21 CLUB 21 W. BALTO. ST.
NOW SHOWING!
EDDIE SCHAEFFER
Harriet Cross • REXER DANCERS

REFRESHINGLY AIR-COOLED!
Dance! Have Fun With
The THREE JAYS
JERRY, JOE and GEORGE
PLUS POPULAR
BARBARA GREY
at this smart new
NAUTICAL COCKTAIL LOUNGE
HELMS COCKTAIL LOUNGE
112-120 PATAPSCO AVE., BROOKLYN
A Breezy Ride in No. 6 Car Brings You Here in a Jiffy!
SPACIOUS PARKING

El Patio
BRENDEL'S MANOR PARK
ST. PAUL AT MADISON
10 Miles West of Baltimore
Route No. 1
"HAPPY JOHNNY'S"
Big De Luxe Stage Shows!
Tonight at 8 o'clock
Sunday Afternoon and Evening
Beginning at 1 o'clock

TONIGHT
GEORGE HORN
Baltimore's Ace Ventriloquist
PURNELL—Acrobatic Dancer
DON & LEE DALE—Comedy Magicians
DE MAYES—World's Fastest Dancers
DANCING—Pop Fisher's Barndusters—DANCING

TOMORROW—Afternoon & Evening
GREAT HOOSIER HOT SHOTS
America's Finest Attraction—Direct From
N. B. C.'s National Barn Dance
COW BOY RAY & HAND WAGON
THREE KIRKILLIES—PETER-BOARDERS
Betty Jay, Plainsmen, Happy Johnny & Boys
Broadcasting WBAL at 12.20 Daily
Admission, 35c. Children under 10, 15c

One! Two!
Three! Kick!
Lissome, Lithe, Lovely
Latin Ladies do the Rhumba!
Rhumbing Revelers in Our Pan - American Revue!
• Real 'Cuban Music by Raymon.
• 2 Shows Nightly.
• No Cover.
• Comfortably Air Conditioned.
RHUMBA! SUNDAY 4-7 P. M.
MATINEE! LEARN FREE! IT'S FUN

HEP CATS
and Daisie Mae
SENSATIONAL SEPIA QUARTET
Muriell LYNNE • Paul MALLORY
CAROLE "Cookie" STEVENS
Cocktail Hour 4 to 7 P. M.
AIR COOLED
DOC'S COCKTAIL LOUNGE
1817 N. CHARLES STREET
LEX. 6796

A Show Full of Sparkle In a Spot Full of Fun!
Vesta Victoria
America's Most Gorgeously Gowned Gal
LEE ROSS
HILARIOUS DEAD PAN COMIC
AND THAT GREAT FAVORITE ORCHESTRA
FAY MERRILL
TAPS IN THE SCOTCH MANNER
MARSHALL
His Novachorde ★ His Men of a Million Airs
MADISON
NITE CLUB • RESTAURANT • RATHSKELLER
MADISON & CHESTER
AIR COOLED
Reservations. VER. 6795

Last 3 Days!
The Inimitable
Georgie PRICE!
TUESDAY!
New Show With
EDDIE WHITE & MARIE AUSTIN
club Charles
CHARLES at PRESTON • VER. 8020-21 • AIR-CONDITIONED

Dance!
To the Music of the Country's Newest Hit Band.
MUSICAL ENTERPRISES PRESENTS:
THE AMAZING MR. CLAUDE THORNHILL
AND HIS Mammoth New Orchestra
Direct from smashing all records at famous Glen Island Casino. Only engagement in the East this year!
CARLIN'S AIR-COOLED ROLLER CASINO
One Nite Only!
TICKETS AT: Hammann's, Carlin's, Walker's, Yaeger's, Hamilton Appliance, Gorman's and Zamoiski Music Centers, Bass Radio Center, Atlantic Service Stations.
Advance Admission, $1.10
Cars No. 5, 32, 33 and Crosstown Bus. Entrance from Park & Druid Park Drive.
Aug. 11

WORRIED?
During our six successful years in the night club business we have presented for your entertainment the finest stars of stage, screen and radio... including JOHN STEELE, ANN PENNINGTON, AUNT JEMIMA, CHARLES KING, JACKIE MILES, LENNY KENT, JULIE OSHINS, CATS and the FIDDLE, DE LLOYD McKAY, JOHNNY & GEORGE, BABY ROSE MARIE, JERRY & TURK, AL STONE, MAYLA, RALPH LEWIS, AL SCHENK, SID WALKER & JANICE, FIFI D'ORSAY, SALLY KEITH, ZORITA, ROSITA ROYCE
and many others too numerous to mention.
We were the originators of bringing such stars to Baltimore. Now, with war conditions as they are and new worries arriving every day, we find that the recipe for this day and age is LAUGHTER!
We present a full one-hour show twice nightly. We have the "Priority on Fun" right here in our club. Drop down and see us. If you don't forget your troubles during the time you spend with us, the treat is on the house.
Our prices are right; drinks and service are the finest. Our past reputation speaks for itself.
2 O'CLOCK CLUB
414 E. BALTO. ST. NO COV. MIN

Top Notch Floor Shows
NIGHTLY
MIKE TRALIK'S MUSIC
Car No. 19 Goes By The Door
NO COVER CHARGE EVER
STONY CREEK TAVERN
Fun for All
SHUEY'S
CHARLEY MOORE'S MUSIC
Saturday AND Sunday
ARM. 114-R
NORTHEAST BALTO.'S OLDEST NITE CLUB
DUTCH MILL 6615 HARFORD ROAD
Cocktail Hour Sunday 4-7 P. M.

12 SOUTH PATTERSON PARK AVE.
WOLFE 9222
EARLE AIR-CONDITIONED CLUB
2 SHOWS NITELY
Cocktail Hour to 7 P. M.

DON'TS at WARREN'S
DON'T come here all decked out in the stuffy formal clothes these nights.
DON'T expect to pay a cover charge.
DON'T expect to pay a minimum.
DON'T look for Lou Sacheriti and our complete shows any place else.
SHOWS & DANCING 7 NIGHTS A WEEK!
WARREN'S UPTOWN NITE CLUB
FULTON Nr. PENNSYLVANIA AVE.

The THREE BROWN SISTERS
SEPIA SWING HARMONISTS
AL STONE M. C. COMEDIAN from West Coast
KEN NEALY PIANO & SONGS
CHARLEY FRANZ'S BAND BOX ORCH.
STANLEY FISHER HARMONICALIST
Angie BELMONT Songstress
Gloria DONNA TAP STYLIST
No Cov. No Min. Mon. Thru Thurs.
Reservations VER. 6795
BAND BOX
1309-11 N. CHARLES ST. at MT. ROYAL

RUTH GEHLERT'S ALL GIRL ORCHESTRA
SEVEN LOVELY LASSIES OF NATIONAL REPUTATION
TRY OUR DELICIOUS CHICKEN DINNER $1
UNDER THE PERSONAL MANAGEMENT OF IVAN FRANK AT THE ELECTRIC ORGAN
Mt. Royal Hotel • Mt. Royal & Calvert
ENTRANCE ON MT. ROYAL AVE.
MULBERRY 1570 AIR COOLED
Algerian Room

LAST FIVE DAYS!
JACK FARREL M. C.
"FUNNY! HE'S A SCREAM!"
SHIRLEY DULOW
TERESA DIEN • AUDREY LEE
The BEACHCOMBERETTES
NO COV. NO MIN. EXCEPT SAT.
AIR COOLED
BEACHCOMBER
110 N. LIBERTY ST. PLAZA 5049

NAT CONWAY TRIO
Coming! Thursday Nite!
Milton LYONS
and an ALL NEW ORCHESTRA
Featuring DELL HUNT
and BELLE DEANE'S Vocals
Arundel Blue Room
CHARLES & MT. ROYAL • LEX. 7640

MUSIC IN THE AIR at RIVIERA BEACH
WITH EDDIE COOK'S Orchestra
HARRY KIERNAN at the Solovox
FRI., SAT. & SUN. NIGHTS
DINNERS FROM 50c
GO TO THE END OF 26 CAR LINE TAKE BUS TO THE DOOR
MATUSKY'S Supper Club
RIVIERA BEACH, MD. CONRAD A. FISCHER
JOHN MATUSKY, ARMIGER 29-J

blue mirror
Entertainment To Fit Your Mood!
DOT & DASH
DOUBLE BARRELED DELIGHT
GEORGE YEATMAN
AND HIS WBAL QUARTET
MARGIE WOOD, Petite Songstress
Cocktail Hour Daily, 4 to 7 P. M.
AIR COOLED
929 N. CHARLES ST.

SUPER ENTERTAINERS! MASTERFUL DANCERS!
The FIELDINGS
COME IN! Dance... Sing... Enjoy good old fashioned fun to your heart's content.
312 W. FAYETTE ST. NO COV. MIN. AFTER 9 EVERY NIGHT
BENJAMIN'S BAR and LOUNGE

1st ANNIVERSARY • 1st ANNIVERSARY
Thanks!
To our many friends and well-wishers who took time out from these busy days to extend greetings and hopes for continued success on this our first anniversary. CONRAD A. FISCHER
AIR-CONDITIONED
Woodlea LOUNGE
4842 BELAIR RD. HAM. 1323

TONITE!
AND EVERY FRI., SAT. & SUN.
DANCE TO
MICHAEL GREEN'S ORCHESTRA
"PAVILION IN THE TREES"
FOREST GARDENS
At CARLIN'S PARK
45c PER PERSON

GAYETY NITE CLUB
Presents NARDIN KING — BERNIE LIPSCH
ROBERTA FRANCIS—HORACE TRENTO
SANDRA HESS—JEAN RAVEN
McCLELLAN PLACE AT BALTO. ST.
Half Block West of Lord Balto. Hotel
COMPLETE NEW FLOOR SHOW EVERY WEEK ALL STAR ACTS

CARL'S NITE CLUB
Leo Bateman • Paulette Raval • Frank Reckling • Rose Aurora
Air Cooled
COCKTAIL BAR DANCING
Jimmie NICHOL'S MUSIC
1316 KESWICK ROAD

SWINGSATIONAL!
LYNNE CORRINNES All Girl ORCHESTRA
Featuring FRANCIS QUINN
DELL MARSHALL JESSIE HAAR
LARRY BRENT, M. C.
Strickler's
RESTAURANT-BAR-LOUNGE
5209-15 HARFORD RD. HAM. 3144

Club Bar

NEW HOTEL BROADWAY
DONA FRANCIS—HAROLD WRIGHT
CHAGO RODRIGO • FRANCIS WRIGHT
CHARLEY DEGLE'S ORCHESTRA
Reservations. WOlfe 0602
BROADWAY AT ORLEANS ST.

DINING • DANCING • GAIETY

AIR PORT GRILL 6500 Riverview Ave., Dundalk. Music Fri., Sat. and Sun. Dine and Dance to Bill Yaeger and His Yanks of Rhythm— At "Abe" Shaeffer, Emcee. No cover, no minimum.

CRYSTAL BALL INN Buck Jones Orchestra Fri. & Sat. Joe Tucker's Hawaiian Trio Sunday, 8.30 to 12.30. New Philadelphia Road at Race Road.

CRYSTAL BAR 417 E. BALTO. ST. next door to EMBASSY THEATRE, featuring JOAN HUTSON and BILL TAYLOR. Continuous entertainment nitely. Delicious food and tempting drinks. No cover or minimum ever.

DE LUCA'S 62 WILLOW SPRING ROAD, DUNDALK. FEATURING CARL SNYDER'S VERSATILE TRIO WITH "MARTHA" AT THE VIBRAHARP.

4 Corners Corral Jacksonville, Md., 9 miles from Towson. Buzz out to the country and have Jacksonville's Unique Musical Combinations. Chicken and Steak Dinners.

GOLDEN RING INN Golden Ring Road and Old Phila. Road. Three Ambassadors Trio. Wed., Sat. and Sun. Delicious Food, Drinks. Never a Cov. or Min.

Green Villa Nite Club 2125 O'DONNELL ST. First Show at 9 P. M. Floor Shows Nitely. Continuous Entertainment. 3 Fine Arts plus Music, Dancing.

JOE'S AIRPORT TAVERN Rutherford Road, Windsor Mill Rd., Woodlawn. New "dressing up" for Fall! Completely redecorated! Watch for Early Reopening. Cool Suburban Hideaway Famous for Chicken Platters, 50c. Dancing Week-ends. Fine Drinks.

KATHLEEN'S 2 BIG FLOOR SHOWS NITELY. NO COVER OR MINIMUM. 612 EAST BALTO. ST.

Keystone Nite Club 2018 HOLABIRD AVE., DUNDALK.

LA RICCI RESTAURANT. 1119 N. CHARLES. SERVING THE FINEST ITALIAN AND AMERICAN LUNCHEONS, DINNERS. SPECIAL CHICKEN AND SPAGHETTI, 85c. OPEN 24 HOURS DAILY.

LEON'S MERRY-GO-ROUND BAR — BALTIMORE'S NEWEST RESTAURANT-LOUNGE—Bald. 870 PARK AVENUE. UNDER PERSONAL DIRECTION OF LEON LAMPE.

(Mac's) Walnut Grove 3612 Hanover St., Brooklyn. Featuring Delicious Fried Chicken Dinner, 60c. Music 9 to 2. Take Car No. 6. Get Off at Patapsco Avenue.

Mueller's Victory Room EDDIE AUFORTH, Singing Bartender. ILIMA ISLANDERS Dance Duo Fri. and Sat. Dinners. MUELLER FOOD & DRINK. East & Eastern Aves.

NATE & LEON'S DELICATESSEN. Stop in after the theatre. The finest Midnight Snack. Delicious Sandwiches. OPEN ALL NIGHT. 800 WEST NORTH AVENUE.

NOLAN'S NITE CLUB Wilkens & Monroe. Mixed Drinks. The Finest Food. Bill Gordon's Swing Era. Dancing. 9 P. M. TIL 2 A. M.

PAT'S BAR 116 N. LIBERTY ST. "THE MOST TALKED ABOUT PLACE IN BALTIMORE." NIGHT CLUB ATMOSPHERE. FEATURING HALF FRIED CHICKEN—60c.

SAM'S RAIL INN 2630 W. NORTH AVE. Dancing Sat. to Charlie Mitchell, piano; Harry Gardner, songs. Cocktail Hour 4-6 Sunday. Open 7 A. M. to 2 A. M. Daily. No Cov. or Min.

SPORTSMAN Cocktail Lounge & Bar. 1420 N. Charles St. Cerilla Mitchell, piano; Harry Gardner, songs. Cocktail Hour 4-6 Sunday. Open 7 A. M. to 2 A. M. Daily. No Cov. or Min.

SWEENEY'S 3128 GREENMOUNT AVE. Dance to Jerry Kaufman's Trio. Fri., Sat. and Sun. Pleasantly AIR-CONDITIONED always. Fine food & drink.

TEDDY REICHHART 2001 Annapolis Ave. Party Sunday Afternoon 3-5 and Spring Chicken Platter. Floor Shows. White House Trio featuring famous singers. No Cov. or Min.

WHITE HOUSE SUPPER CLUB

Reds In Hand-To-Hand Battle Before Stalingrad

THE BALTIMORE NEWS-POST
AN INDEPENDENT NEWSPAPER
The Largest Evening Circulation in the Entire South
Entered as second-class matter at Baltimore Postoffice.
VOL. CXLI.—NO. 96 MONDAY EVENING, AUGUST 24, 1942 PRICE 3 CENTS
7 HOME FINAL

German Tank Thrust Moves Ahead Toward City Forty Miles Away

MOSCOW, Aug. 24—(A. P.).—The Russians battle resolutely today in the narrow, flat corridor between the Don and the Volga to halt German forces which finally had consolidated a river crossing and struck out for Stalingrad probably only 40 miles away.

Another thrust at the great industrial city moved slowly ahead at terrific cost on the Kotelnikovski sector southwest of Stalingrad along a railway leading from the Black sea.

The Germans threw masses of tanks at the Russian lines northeast of Kotelnikovski and succeeded in breaking into the advance Soviet defenses as the Red Army grappled hand to hand with the enemy farther north in the bend to halt the German advance on Stalingrad, a communique said today.

NAZI TANKS THREATEN

The midday communique reported a violent struggle southeast of Kletskaya where the Germans had reached the east bank of the Don. Tanks which ferried the plains river constituted the greatest threat to Stalingrad.

The exact location of the tank crossing—established only after Russian artillery and planes had destroyed four previous pontoon bridges—was not disclosed, but Germans have been attacking heavily in the Don elbow, only 40 miles from Stalingrad and the Volga.

RUSS COUNTER-ATTACK

Russian forces remained on the west side of the river, despite the enemy breach and near Kletskaya itself were counter-attacking to relieve pressure. The lines on the outer defenses of Stalingrad appeared to be highly mobile with both armies maneuvering swiftly for position.

A Soviet tank detachment was sent against the flank of the German force northeast of Kotelnikovski and seven of the German machines were destroyed and 200 Germans killed, the midday communique said.

The struggle for Stalingrad appeared to be nearing the supreme test, Russian reports indicated, as a new crossing of the Don was forced southeast of Kletskaya by the Germans.

KILL 100 NAZIS

The Russians were fighting stubbornly to push these Germans into the river and destroy the bridgehead.

(BACKGROUND NOTE: This was the seventh day of an all-out German offensive by 800,000 to 1,000,000 Germans to break through to Stalingrad and cut the Volga from the center of the Don bend and the Kotelnikovski area. At least 500,000 of them were believed engaged in non-stop assaults in the bend of the Don. Some observers believed the battle for the approaches to Stalingrad equaled in size and ferocity the battle of Verdun.)

In another sector of the Kletskaya area, Russian troops broke into an enemy position during the night and, with bayonets and hand

Continued on Page 2, Column 1.

Nazis Claim 166 Russ Planes Lost In Day's Fighting

BERLIN (From German Broadcasts), Aug. 24—(A. P.). A total of 166 Soviet planes was destroyed by German fighters and anti-aircraft batteries yesterday, breaking all records for enemy aerial los es in a single day on the Eastern Front, Nazi military quarters reported today. German losses were put at only eight planes.

Canadians Tell Of Dieppe Raid

3 Battalions Stormed Beach, Battled Foe In City Streets

Commando soldier (nationality unknown) got a Nazi in Dieppe, and came back to tell the tale, wearing his dead enemy's helmet in place of his own. His companion, at left, brought home a hero's wound, wearing his arm in a sling, his shirt sleeve torn away. These are two of the brave lads of the battle of Dieppe. (Others pictures on Page 3.)

By ROSS MUNRO
Canadian Press War Correspondent.

SOMEWHERE IN ENGLAND, Aug. 24.—They speak with awe in Canadian Army camps of the "main beach at Dieppe," where three Canadian infantry battalions, tankmen, engineers and provost fought the longest sustained action of the raid on the old French town.

The battle of the beach was the main Canadian attack—boldly directed at the town itself. From the stories told by the men who came back this general picture has been pieced together.

SCOTS LAND FIRST

The Essex Scottish landed at about 5.20 A. M. on the eastern half of the mile-long gravel and shale beach, 75 yards wide.

The Royal Hamilton Light Infantry went in at the same time on the western half with the Calgary Tank Battalion, provost and sappers.

Les Fusiliers Mont Royal landed later as reserve.

Halfway up the beach, stretched across the Canadians' path, was barbed wire. The attackers faced a thick German fire pouring from a row of buildings looking to the beach across the broad promenade edge which was supported by a long seawall.

The defenders had field guns and the row of buildings they occupied bristiled with machine-guns and trench mortars.

SHELLED BY NAVY

The R. A. F. and the navy plastered Diepe for half an hour before the Canadians swept in from small troop-carrying craft and bigger tank-landing boats.

The first wave of Canadians met blistering machine-gun and mortar fire as they swept up the beach, cut through barbed wire and advanced to take cover behind the seawall, 10 feet high at the eastern end and lowering gradually to two feet at the western extremity.

In 10 minutes the long wall was lined with troops of the Essex Scottish and the Royal Hamilton light infantry.

Some tanks had been landed by then but were having preliminary difficulty in getting a hold hold for their treads on the shale.

CAPTURE CASINO

Heavy shelling and a torrent of small-arms fire prevented some of the troops from debarking from the tank-landing craft.

The Hamilton Battalion drove forward in force and finally captured the Dieppe Casino, a group of large buildings at the western end of the beach. Taking the Casino, which was filled with Germans, was

Continued on Page 2, Column 3.

ChineseTake Linchwan, Jap Base

CHUNGKING, Aug. 24—(A. P.). Chinese forces have captured Linchwan (Fuchow) in Central Kiangsi, second most important Japanese base in the province, the Chinese High Command announced tonight.

Linchwan, on the Fu river 60 miles southeast of Nanchang, the main enemy base in the province, has been under Chinese siege for two weeks. United States Army planes supported the Chinese ground forces in the early phases of the siege.

FELL TO JAPS

The city was captured by the Japanese in June during their drive up the Fu river toward Fukien Province. It lies south of the Chekiang-Kiangsi railway, along which the Chinese hitherto have scored their chief gains in a remarkable comeback campaign.

Chuhsien, a Chekiang air base which was the principal objective of the Japanese summer campaign, and Juihung, only 30 miles east of their main Kiangsi base of Nanchang, were menaced by dual Chinese offensives today.

Under heavy pressure the Japanese were reported hastily withdrawing along the Chekiang-Kiangsi railway, which they gained at heavy cost, and Chinese press dispatches said the fall of Juihung was expected shortly.

RAIL CITY IN RUINS

Chinese correspondents entering Shangjao, one of the railway cities vacated by the Japanese, found it reduced to a heap of blackened ruins as the result of a three-day fire set by Japanese incendiary bombs and grenades.

Chinese forces were fighting fiercely with the Japanese today near Suichang, about 45 miles west of Lishui in Southwestern Chekiang Province, after other units had widened the Chinese hold on the Chekiang-Kiangsi railway to 110 miles, the Chinese Central News Agency reported.

CHINESE PUSH EASTWARD

The fighting near Suichang has raged for two days as Chinese troops drove eastward toward Lishui, to which the main Japanese force was reported withdrawn, the agency said.

In the fighting for the Chekiang-Kiangsi railway, the Chinese said three of their columns drove eastward into Chekiang Province and forced the Japanese to withdraw from Kiangshan, 20 miles from Chuhsien.

IN THE NEWS-POST TODAY

Amusements — 11
Annette — 11
"Bugs" Baer — 16
Classified Ads — 22-23
Comics — 18
Editorial — 16
Fashions — 8
Financial — 21-22
Gif-Ted Club — 17
Horoscope — 7
Local News — 13-14
Louella O. Parsons — 11
Louis Azrael — 17
Mr. Fixit — 7
Norman Clark — 11
Outdoors — 17
Radio — 24
Rodger Pippen — 19
Society — 9
Sports — 19-20-21
Walter Winchell — 11

Largest U. S. Convoy In Britain

A BRITISH PORT, Aug. 24—(U. P.). — American pilots, ground crews, troops, nurses, planes, tanks, guns and assorted equipment were distributed to United States Army depots throughout the British Isles today from the greatest Atlantic convoy of this war and one of the greatest of all time.

The convoy was so big that it was necessary to land it at several ports, where special buses, trucks, trains and even street cars were waiting to start the fighting men and the Army nurses to their destinations.

Men in the gigantic convoy came from all parts of the United States.

POWERFUL U. S. ESCORT

They were escorted by a powerful force of United States Navy ships. On the American side, Army planes shepherded the convoy far out to sea, and British planes picked it up on this side.

Once during the voyage, the convoy veered sharply to a new course when submarine activity was reported nearby.

Soon after the convoy left the United States there was a moment of excitement when a destroyer dropped depth charges.

But a derelict merchantman wreck had been mistaken for a submarine, and the only result of the bombing was that a "slic "

Continued on Page 2, Column 7.

Australia To Get Turkeys From U. S.

MELBOURNE, Australia, Aug. 24—(A. P.). — The "long-range view" of this global war already is focused on the Thanksgiving turkey situation for United States troops in Australia. The turkey population of Australia has been found inadequate and arrangements have been made to have a refrigerated cargo shipped here from the United States.

1,079 Arrested In Liquor Violations

WASHINGTON, Aug. 24—(A. P.). The Internal Revenue Bureau today announced the arrest of 1,079 persons and the seizure of property valued at $115,002 in connection with liquor violation cases during July.

Both figures represented a decline from the comparative period in 1941, when arrests totaled 1,904 and seized property was valued at $182,66_.

Allied Fliers Bag 13 Jap Planes

GENERAL MacARTHUR'S HEADQUARTERS, Australia, Aug. 24—(U. P.).—Allied figher pilots using new secret battle tactics shot down at least 13 Japanese planes and probably 15 or more out of an enemy fleet of 47, which attacked the great Australian base of Darwin, it was announced today.

Not a single Allied plane was downed.

Curtiss P-40D planes, in what Gen. Douglas MacArthur himself called brilliant tactical interception, dived at all angles on a powerful force of 20 new Japanese Zero fighters and 27 heavy bombing planes.

JAP ATTACK SMASHED

Holding their fire until the last, the Allied pilots smashed the Japanese attack completely.

They shot down at least nine Zeros and four bombers, saw two other bombers struggling off jettisoning their bombs and trailing smoke and damaged others so severely that it seemed highly unlikely they reached the nearest enemy bases.

So devastating was the Allied attack, the enemy bombers never had a chance to drop their bombs on military targets.

Such bombs as were not jettisoned in wild flight struck in the bush outside the Darwin defense zone and started a few grass fires.

The fires were the only damage in one of the biggest Japanese raids.

LAST RAID JULY 30

It was the first enemy attack on Darwin since July 30. Then

Continued on Page 2, Column 6.

Von Clemm Given 2 Yrs. In Jail, Fine

NEW YORK, Aug. 24—(A. P.).—Werner von Clemm, forty-four, former German artillery officer, was sentenced today in Federal Court to two years' imprisonment and a $10,000 fine for conspiring to sell Dutch and Belgian diamonds in this country in violation of President Roosevelt's freezing order of 1940.

Nelson Asks Busy Plants Labor Day

WASHINGTON, Aug. 24—(A. P.). Chairman Donald M. Nelson of the War Production Board, called upon American labor today to arrange its annual Labor Day observance this year so there might be operation of all mines, industries and plants in which a shut down would be injurious to the war effort.

Nelson wrote to President William Green of the A. F. of L. and President Philip Murray of the C. I. O. saying that there were many plants in which it would be possible to rearrange schedules in such a way that Labor Day might be celebrated as a holiday.

Local representatives of the armed services, Nelson wrote, will be prepared to tell management and labor which plants and mines should operate throughout the holiday September 7. In these places, he suggested, brief celebrations should be planned within the shops.

Gibbons, Flying Ace In China, Killed

SEATTLE, Aug. 24—(A. P.).—Elwyn Gibbon, Seattle's flying soldier of fortune who was shooting down Japanese planes over China as early as 1937, was killed four days ago in Karachi, India, his brother, W. L. Gibbon, an attorney, learned today. News of the flyer's death came from the American Aircraft Company, for which he was flying in India.

R. A. F. Raids Axis Base At Tobruk

LONDON, Aug. 24—(I. N. S.).—Winging over the desert in bright moonlight Saturday night, U. S. Army medium bombers pounded Axis workshops in the Egyptian battlefront area, the News-Chronicle said today in a dispatch from Cairo.

CAIRO, Aug. 24—(A. P.).—Heavy British bombers made a successful attack on the Axis supply base of Tobruk at dusk yesterday to bring to a climax a week-end of aerial activity over the Egyptian front in which United States Army planes again were active, a British communique announced today.

American fliers were reported to have attacked enemy workshops in the western desert in bright moonlight Saturday night, scoring numerous hits.

R. A. F. fighter-bombers continued their attacks on Axis overland communications yesterday, and numerous dogfights developed with indecisive results, the bulletin said.

One enemy transport plane was reported destroyed by British long-range fighters northwest of Derna and at least one Axis bomber was destroyed during an attempted attack on a British airdrome.

Except for British night patrol operations no activity was reported on land.

THE WEATHER

Quite cool tonight, with lowest temperature around 52 degrees in northern and western suburbs and 62 degrees in center of city; moderate humidity, gentle winds, no rain.

Detailed Weather report on Page 24

Read The Baltimore News-Post for complete, accurate war coverage. It is the only Baltimore newspaper possessing the three great wire services—
ASSOCIATED PRESS
INTERNATIONAL NEWS SERVICE
UNITED PRESS

When the Princess put on a magic ring strange things happened. You'll read what they were in "Canece and the Talking Falcon," interpreted by John Erskine, and illustrated by Edmund Dulac. See the front page of The American Weekly, the magazine distributed with next Sunday's Baltimore American.—adv.

Argentina To Clarify War Position

BUENOS AIRES, Aug. 24—(A. P.).—South American diplomats awaited with undisguised interest today a statement by the Argentine Government clarifying its position in the new international situation created by Brazil's entry into the war against Germany and Italy.

While the Foreign Office, which announced last night that such a statement would be forthcoming, gave no indication of its attitude, there was general belief the Government would grant Brazil non-belligerent status, thu enabling her ships to use Argentine ports as in peace times.

BOLD RELIEF

The position of Argentina—one of two Western Hemisphere nations still maintaining relations with the Axis Powers—was thrown into bold relief by an expression of solidarity with Brazil which came from their joint neighbor, Uruguay.

In a message to President Vargas of Brazil, President Baldomir of Uruguay declared his nation was ready to carry out the Havana agreement which he said "makes the continent a single nation against aggressions of a non-American state."

AGREE ON TERMS

Some observers took this statement as an indication that Uruguay might follow Brazil into the war.

An official announcement issued in Montevideo last night by Foreign Minister Alberto Guani after a series of conferences with the Brazilian and United States Ambassadors said the Uruguayan Government had decided on the terms of a decree fixing its position, but details were not immediately disclosed.

It was expected that the decree

Continued on Page 2, Column 1.

Temperatures

12 Midn't.,	68	6 A. M.,	64
1 A. M.,	68	7 A. M.,	65
2 A. M.,	67	8 A. M.,	67
3 A. M.,	65	9 A. M.,	68
4 A. M.,	64	10 A. M.,	70
5 A. M.,	63	11 A. M.,	73

War At A Glance

MOSCOW—
Hand-to-hand battle rages as Nazis strike out for Stalingrad.

AUSTRALIA—
13 Jap planes shot down in dog fight over Darwin.

LONDON—
Largest U. S. convoy arrives in British Isles.

BUENOS AIRES—
Argentina to take stand today on Brazil's war declaration.

CAIRO—
R. A. F. bombers attack Axis supply base at Tob

Baltimore Girls Take Exams For WAACS

Jobs Open As Stenographers; Women Anxious To Don Uniforms And Be Secretaries

Ready to trade good paying jobs in civilian life for Army pay and uniforms of the Women's Army Auxiliary Corps, these young women were among those taking a stenographic test here for posts in WAAC headquarters, Fort Des Moines, Iowa. In the rear row, left to right, are Miss Florence Matchar and Mrs. Maxine Fielding. Front row (left to right) Miss Bernice Skolnik, Miss Marie Gerlach and Miss Betty Snyder. Giving the test is Lieut. Evan A. McNear.

BALTIMORE NEWS-POST

2ND FRONT PAGE — NEWS-POST HAS TWO FRONT PAGES DAILY

MONDAY EVENING, AUGUST 24, 1942 — 13

Cites Draft Benefits Limit

O'Conor Praises Navy Spirit Of State

Recruiting Drive To Start On August 30

By ALDINE R. BIRD

Maryland has always meant "Navy" to the nation, and its up to the people of the State to give that traditional "additional lustre" in the Navy's recruiting drive for 4,000 additional volunteers, Governor O'Conor said today.

The Governor heads a list of Legionnaires appointed to the general committee along with a number of other officials and prominent individuals which will conduct the American Legion - sponsored Navy recruiting campaign beginning August 30.

His appointment, along with those of Mayor Jackson, Judge J. Craig McLanahan and Judge W. Conwell Smith, of the Supreme Bench of Baltimore, were announced yesterday by Legionnaire W. Allan Rhynhart, general chairman and chief judge of the People's Court.

LEADS NATION

In accepting, the Chief Executive noted with "supreme satisfaction" that, consistently, Maryland has led the nation proportionately in the naval enlistments since Pearl Harbor. He said:

"It is hardly necessary to state that the campaign inaugurated by a little belated at the request of the American Legion to speed up enlistments in the United States Navy has my hearty approval.

"I shall be very happy to do everything possible, both personally and on behalf of the State, to further the efforts of Judge Rhynhart and those Legion officials who are assisting him.

NAVY TO NATION

"Maryland has always meant 'Navy' to the nation, and it has been a supreme satisfaction to note that consistently Maryland has led the nation, proportionately, in naval enlistments since Pearl Harbor.

"I sincerely hope the splendid record established to date will not only be continued, but given additional lustre."

The general, or steering committee, has not been fully organized and additional appointments will be made as soon as possible, Judge Rhynhart pointed out in announcing a partial list of those who have accepted.

Members assigned to special sub-committees are to be considered members of the steering committee, he added, and listed the personnel of the first seven such committees to be formulated.

SPECIAL EVENT

These are the speakers, radio, church, publicity, finance and special events.

The special events committee is headed by John H. Threadgill, Maryland chairman for "Navy Day" by appointment of the Navy League of the United States.

Its function will be to arrange the presence of the Navy and Marine Bands for concerts, mass ceremonies in connection with the swearing in of recruits, and similar activities. Of particular importance will be the arrangement by this committee of an appropriate program for the observance of "Navy Day" on October 27.

(Other Story on Page 14)

TODAY'S TIDES	
High tide	5.58 A. M., 6.02 P. M.
Low tide	12.31 P. M.

Bananas Save Child

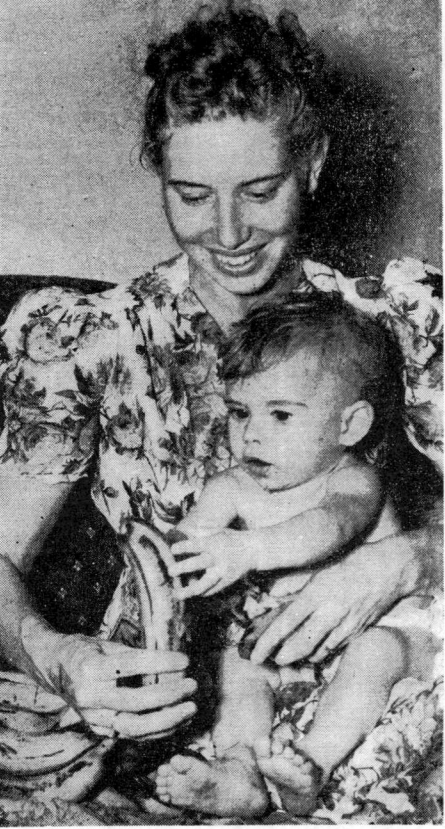

Two dozen bananas, rushed 80 miles, from Washington to Piney Point, Md., saved, or at least prolonged the life of Roni Lee Scroggins, one, shown with her mother, Mrs. Lee Scroggins. The child was stricken with the dreaded disease, celiaca, according to Dr. G. H. Gouze, a naval physician, and the bananas, rare now because of war conditions, were ordered for her.

Woman's $145 Loss Cost Of 'Blessing'

Mysterious incantations, added to a little sleight-of-hand artistry yesterday, changed Mrs. Rushie Mallett's savings of $145 to slips of blank paper, she reported to the Detective Bureau.

Mrs. Mallett said an attractive gypsy girl in her early twenties came to her home in the 1000 block Sumwalt court seeking a donation for a church.

According to Mrs. Mallett, she gave the girl 25 cents.

'SPIRIT' MESSAGE

Then the gypsy said:

"The spirits tell me you have more upstairs."

Mrs. Mallett revealed she had $145, police said. The gypsy departed, but soon returned, and said: "It would be best for you if I blessed the money."

MONEY WRAPPED UP

Mrs. Mallett said she got the money and the gypsy wrapped it in a handkerchief, went through a series of incantations, handed the package back to Mrs. Mallett, but instructed her not to open it for several days.

Soon after the gypsy left Mrs. Mallett said she grew suspicious, opened the handkerchief and found only blank slips of paper instead of her savings.

Two similar thefts have been reported to detectives during the past few weeks.

CAA Office To Open At Hagerstown

HAGERSTOWN, Md., Aug. 24.— (A. P.).—A district office of the Civil Aeronautics Authority—taking in a range of about 75 miles and including Cumberland, Frederick and Chambersburg, Pa., soon will be located at Hagerstown airport.

The Hagerstown field was described by C. A. A. officials as one of the finest small airports in the East, with an excellent civilian pilot training school.

Dispute Halts Brick Plants

MT. SAVAGE, Md., Aug. 24.—(A. P.).—Six brick plants and fire clay mines of the Union Mining Company in this section were closed today by a work stoppage called after a series of differences between the United Construction Workers' Local No. 193 and the management.

Union labor officials said about 425 workers were on a "holiday" and charged that the dispute reached a climax Saturday when several union members at Ellerslie were furloughed and others hired in their place. The local is an affiliate of District No. 50, United Mine Workers' of America.

The properties, employing more than 600 persons, are the four brick plants and a fire clay mine here, a fire clay mine at Barrellville and a brick plant at Ellerslie.

Probe Gas 'Chiseling' With Extra-Size Tanks

Reports that traveling salesmen operating out of Maryland are having special 100-gallon gasoline tanks installed in their automobiles, to be filled in the unrationed area in Pennsylvania, will be checked by investigators of the Office of Price Administration, it was learned today.

Gasoline retailers in the nearby unrationed areas report "our big business" is filling the extra-size tanks and selling cans filled with gasoline to motorists from the "drought" area of Maryland.

CITES 'LOOPHOLE'

A spokesman for the local office of the OPA, revealing that the alleged situation will be investigated immediately, said:

"It is against the law for a motorist to bring gasoline in cans from the unrationed area into the rationed area, and the dealer who knowingly sells gasoline for such a purpose is just as guilty as the buyer.

TANKS IN DEMAND

Salesmen traveling through the rationed South are said to be able to secure enough gasoline to carry them through their territory and return.

The demand for the oversized tanks is reported to far exceed the supply.

"While there so far as we know there has been no case testing the legality of the special oversized tanks in automobiles, this appears to be an attempt to 'beat the law' and is, in my opinion, either illegal now, or constitutes a loophole in the law that should be corrected."

Another curious result of the rationing situation in Maryland was revealed when it was learned that gasoline shipped to Cumberland from Baltimore in tank cars is being hauled into the unrationed areas by trucks. The motorists who are unable to secure the gasoline in the Cumberland drive over the State line and buy all they please.

CALLED UNAVOIDABLE

This seeming inconsistency was explained by the OPA as unavoidable, because gasoline for the nearby unrationed areas must be refined in Baltimore. An OPA official, who declined to allow his name to be used, said:

"Of course, this requires tank cars that could be used in hauling gasoline from the West. It simply points to the need for rationing scheme that will work on a nation-wide basis."

KILLED IN CRASH

CUMBERLAND, Aug. 24.—Clement B. Huntsman, sixty-seven, of Cumberland, a retired railroad engineer, was killed instantly yesterday when his automobile collided with a truck near Frostburg.

GAS STORING FINE

Charged with storing gasoline in his garage, James R. Plowman, 4900 block Belair road, was fined $50 and costs at a hearing before Magistrate Samuel M. Campanaro in Northeastern Police Court.

Tydings Cites U. S. Gains In Pacific

Capture by the Marines of three of the Solomon Island groups is the "most far-reaching achievement since Pearl Harbor," Senator Millard E. Tydings, outlining the progress of the war, told Marylanders in a broadcast address.

He asserted that the islands would be valuable principally as air fields from which land-based planes can harass the Japanese and protect the supply lines between the United States and Australia.

"STEPPING STONES"

Senator Tydings went on to say:

"In time, attacks on Japanese-held territory will be launched from our air fields in the group. The many islands lying between the Solomons and Japan must be conquered and used as stepping stones to carry our forces gradually northward toward the Philippines as well as northwestward to the continent of Asia, and finally to the islands of Japan.

TIME REQUIRED

"It will, of course, take time. One island after another will have to be conquered. The point is that we have made a fine start, that we have established a firm foothold. We now have air fields for land-based planes and protected harbors for ships. With these we can change from defense to attack."

Bottles Aid Navy Drive

Milk bottles in Baltimore have enlisted for the duration on behalf of the Navy. Estimated anywhere from 80,000 to 200,000 in daily output in the local area, the bottles are now bearing "Join the Navy" tags as shown here by John A. Jean, chief specialist of the United States Naval Reserve, attached to the local recruiting office of the Navy. The tags tell that Navy needs men from seventeen to fifty.

Hershey Warns Wives Of Cash Law Allows

Wives of men about to be inducted into the armed forces under the Army's expansion program may expect no benefits beyond those already provided by law, Major General Lewis B. Hershey, National Draft Director, warned from Washington today.

These benefits include payment of $50 monthly allotment to a wife, $62 a month to a wife and one child, and $10 additional for other children.

HERSHEY'S WARNING

General Hershey has warned the nation that able-bodied married men within the age limits will be called for military service "certainly before Christmas," and today added that individual family problems will have to be handled without Government assistance.

For instance, he said, a wife who moves to another home after her husband's induction, or goes back to her parents, can't expect the Government to pay moving expenses.

WOMEN'S EMPLOYMENT

Anticipating the time when married men would be called, Army and draft officials have urged wives without children to obtain employment for themselves, especially in the light of the country's need for women in war industry.

Commenting on the Army's new call for married men, since Congress refused to give authority for drafting of youths of eighteen and nineteen, a War Department spokesman said:

"We would rather have these youths than the married men. Physically they are young, mentally they are pliant. They haven't any strong home ties to cause emotional upsets. They make the best possible soldiers."

County Seeks Curb On Raid Sirens

Baltimore county Civilian Defense leaders Wednesday night will put their heads together to try to determine what to do about fire engine and air-raid alarm sirens which sound alike.

The conference, to be held at 8 o'clock in the Towson Police Station, was inspired by protests from wardens who early Saturday morning (4 o'clock, to be exact) responded to what they thought was the air-raid alarm, only to discover it was only a fire after all.

FORTY PROTEST

It was the second such experience the county wardens had been through, and some forty of them have written letters, a few threatening to resign, J. Kemp Bartlett, Jr., deputy director of Civilian Defense, announced.

Only solution so far offered has come from both H. Streett Baldwin, president of the Board of County Commissioners, and Col. H. S. Barrett, head of the State air-raid precaution services in the State.

Both suggest that the fire engines depend on their bells instead of their sirens, though Col. Barrett goes further and declares that he would like to see all but Civilian Defense sirens silenced in Maryland for the duration.

Mr. Baldwin said today that the fire department in Towson has been asked not to use the siren except "in emergency," and that he learned why it was used at 4 A.M.

Fritz Maisel has indicated his willingness to go along with any plan adopted.

Car Hits Woman In Safety Zone

Struck by an automobile as she was standing in a safety zone at Broadway and Gough streets last night, Mrs. Nell Frederick, fifty-six, 1900 block Harlem avenue, suffered head injuries. She was treated at Johns Hopkins Hospital.

Mrs. Frederick was thrown against Mrs. Ethel Bruck, fifty, 600 block Cokesbury street, according to police, and they both fell to the street. Mrs. Bruck was uninjured.

Win Cash For News Tips And Amateur Photographs

Do you want money for being alert? The Baltimore News-Post and Sunday American are offering cash prizes each week for news tips and amateur photographs. Total awards of $50 are distributed weekly for news tips, $25 for the best, $10 for the next best and $1 prizes for the next fifteen. For each amateur photograph published $3 will be paid, with special bonuses for outstanding pictures. Spot-news pictures are preferred, but candid camera shots that pull at the heartstrings are acceptable. Avoid pictures of ordinary scenes. Telephone The News-Tip Editor at Lexington 0100 for news tips and rush spot-news photographs in to the Picture Editor.

BOOGIE WOOGIE — By Michael Berry

AFTER HIS DUEL WITH THE COBRA SHARK, VICTOR EMERGES JUST IN TIME TO SAVE GLORIA FROM DROWNING.

TYING THE HELPLESS GIRL TO THE FLOATING HARPOON KEG—

—AND THE KEG TO HIMSELF HE HEADS FOR THE SHORE.

LOOK, JIM! HERE COMES ANOTHER SWIMMER WITH TRAILER! / I WONDER IF THEY COULD BE ENEMY SPIES TRYING TO INVADE BOOGIE WOOGIE. WE'LL GIVE THEM A HOT RECEPTION!

RACING AT MARLBORO
8 RACES Aug. 19 thru Aug. 29, incl.
Aug. 25 Chesapeake Beach Purse
Purse $700—3-Yr.-Olds & Up
Daily Double Closes 2.15 P. M.
ADM. $1.10 incl. Tax $2.30 BUY WAR BONDS AND STAMPS

VACATION GOLF
Play on a fine, sporty, 18-hole course that is in the pink of condition. Greens 60c Before 11.30 A. M. or After 4 P. M. $1.00 from 11.30 A. M. to 4 P. M. Mon. BONNIE VIEW—Mt. Washington, Smith Ave., between Falls & Park Heights.

Ruth Belts Two Homers; Runs On Foul One

THE BALTIMORE NEWS-POST SPORTS

MONDAY EVENING, AUGUST 24, 1942

Old Rivals Shake

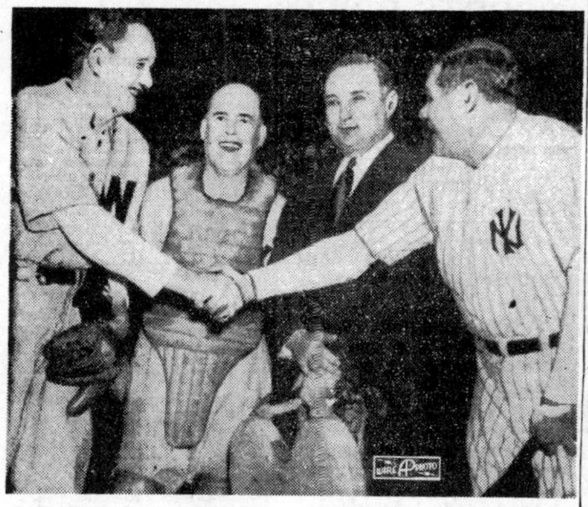

HAD FUN—Walter Johnson, Babe Ruth and 69,000 baseball fans had a high old time at Yankee Stadium yesterday as the Big Train pitched to the Bambino, who parked two slams in the bleachers. The exhibition was part of an Army-Navy Relief program. Benny Bengough caught for them and Billy Evans umpired. Left to right above: Johnson, Bengough, Evans and Ruth. Associated Press Wirephoto.

BROTHER ACT

OTTAWA, Aug. 24—(A. P.).—They'll soon have to build an ext[...]sion to the mantel piece in the Falkenburg home in Hollywood, Cal.

Tom, seventeen, won the singles title of the Junior Davis C[...] tennis tourney between the best young players in the United Sta[...] and Canada, by defeating brother Bob, sixteen, in the final, 11—9, 2–[...] 6—2. Then they combined to take the doubles crown.

FACE JERSEY CITY, NEWARK IN PLAYOFF SCRAMBLE

Birds Open Important Trip

Rodger H. Pippen Sports Editor Says

KEEP YOUR CHIN UP

If Tommy Thomas can pilot four Orioles into the International League play-offs, he should be hailed as the miracle manager of the year.

The pitching is O. K. and Bob Repass, at short, has soldered the weak point in the infield.

But the general picture isn't one about which to do much cheering.

Hank Edwards' all-around slump is probably the most discouraging factor as you study Baltimore's chances. Although he made three hits Saturday, he went hitless in both games yesterday. His body and arms appeared to lack co-ordination yesterday and he was pushing at the ball. In the field he hasn't been covering as much ground as usual. I wouldn't say that Edwards is loafing or has quit, but from a distance he gives one the idea he is fussing at himself. A day or two of mental and physical rest might put him back in stride. For the Birds to finish as high as fourth Hank must be at his best.

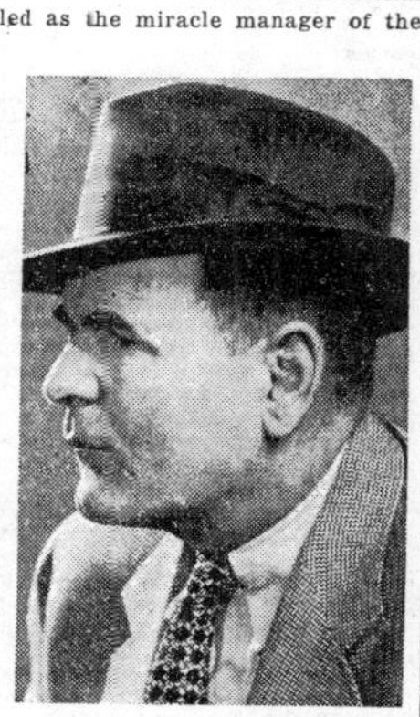

RODGER H. PIPPEN

The batting of the team as a whole must improve. If Ed Robinson's injured knee does not bother him, his return to the line-up will help. But ten such hits as the locals made in two tests yesterday would not suffice against a club like Newark. The boys were rather futile at the plate against Hallett in the opening clash.

It is well to remember, however, that the Birds appeared even more helpless when they left on the last road trip. They rallied sensationally, however, and with Ted Sczepkowski doing the best and most timely clubbing, fought their way into third place for a day. Ted is ready to return to action and here's hoping he once more supplies the spark. Bell, not overlooking his three blows in the final game yesterday, has been most disappointing at the plate. Out for a long time, he hasn't been able to find the range.

* * *

Robertson Is Most Valuable

If left to a vote of the customers, Bob Lemon, at third and Ed Robinson, at first, would be named Baltimore's most popular as well as most valuable players. Both have been consistent and at times, actually sensational. Lemon, I believe, would win in a poll by a narrow margin.

Sherry Robertson, the utility man, would get my vote as having done the most for the Birds. He has played six positions—four in the infield and two in the outfield. He has won half a dozen games with homers. He has hustled every minute he has been on the field. Subbing at first for Robinson yesterday he made two great plays, throwing out a man at second on a force and cutting off a run at home after Repass had made a thrilling stop back of second. His homer in the second game made victory certain.

* * *

Trinkle's Sudden Reversal In Form

Ken Trinkle, Baltimore's first pitcher in yesterday's game, had perfect control when he started.

He used nine pitches in the first inning, and all were over the plate.

In the second inning seven out of his eight pitches were across the dish. That means he threw only one ball in seventeen attempts.

After three innings he had thrown only four balls in 24 tries.

Then, for some unknown reason, he lost control, hit a couple of batsmen and had trouble in finding the range.

* * *

Is It the Ball or the Pitching?

Merwin Jacobson, graceful Oriole outfielder of other days, watched yesterday's games from the press box. He commented on the fact that the baseballs appeared lifeless and had a punk or hollow sound when hit. The manufacturers have sought to prove with facts and figures that the balls in use today have not lost their "zing" and are just as lively as ever. The batsmen say it isn't so and point to the lower averages in all leagues. The pitchers just laugh and say they have improved.

The sixteen games played yesterday in the majors might be used both ways in the argument. Seven were shutouts and six were six-hit jobs. There was one two-hitter, a three-hitter, four four-hitters and a five-hitter. The others were a seven-hit job, a nine-hit performance and an 11-hit affair.

Only 11 homers were hit, four in the American League, the sluggers' circuit. Was it the ball? Or was it great pitching?

Tex Hughson, baseball's hottest pitcher, provided one of the best jobs, racking up his seventeenth victory and eleventh in a row, 2-0, on four hits, in the first game of a double-header that the Red Sox won from Philadelhpia. Joe Dobson equalled his teammate's performance with a four-hit, 7-0 triumph in the nightcap. It was Dobson's eighth victory. The Sox made six hits in the first game and 11 in the first game and 11 in the second.

Venerable Ted Lyons checked in with a three-hit masterpiece—perhaps his last performance before entering the Army—as the White

Continued on Page 20, Column 4.

Ruth Hits Two Homers; Runs On Foul One

By JACK CUDDY

NEW YORK, Aug 24—(U. P.).—Babe Ruth swung with all his power, his bat met the ball, and it sailed toward the distant right-field stands.

The forty-seven-year-old Bambino never looked to see where that ball went. As soon as he felt the decisive thud of ash against horsehide, he started to run—not trot—and he ran around the bases there in the same Yankee Stadium that his booming bat helped to build back in 1923.

As Ruth ran the bases, the ball that he hit so hard swerved outside the white pole and landed in foul territory. It fell in the upper right field stands—a foul—by the margin of six scant feet. But Ruth kept running the bases for a homer, and when he wound up at the dugout, perspiring like a human shower, everyone congratulated him just as if he had achieved one of his greatest homers of 1927—the year he blasted 60 and set an all-time record for four-baggers in one season.

DIDN'T LIKE FIRST

Walter Johnson, the big train who at fifty-five had come out of retirement to pitch to Ruth in this historic exhibition before 69,136 fans at the Senators-Yankee double-header, looked askance at Ruth's foul "home run," and then meandered in from the mound.

Johnson, who had allowed Ruth only 10 home runs in the 14 seasons they opposed each other, was touched for a bona fide run on his fifth pitch, when the Bambino sent a lusty drive sailing into the lower right field stands. Ruth wasn't satisfied with that. He didn't consider that home run well hit—and he wanted to show the young players on the Yanks, and the younger generation of sports fans what a real home run is like. Thus it was that he still was swinging on Johnson's nineteenth pitch.

Ruth, the all-time home run king and baseball's greatest showman, shrugged off his first homer into the lower stands, and didn't even trot around the bases. But when he got the feel of that foul "homer" on his last swing, he knew it was well hit, and started running. On this particular blow, Ruth didn't trot—as one usually does in case of a home run. Instead, he put his head down and started to sprint—with all the speed that the muffin-faced, barrel-bodied, splindly-legged old-timer could achieve. And the huge crowd—who had contributed $85,000 to service relief funds—didn't know and didn't care if the final wallop had gone fair or foul as it bellowed approval.

HAND SWOLLEN

In the dressing-room, Ruth sat on a rubbing table and said, "I never looked to see where that ball went. I knew it was the first ball I hit properly and I started running. I knew it was hit for a home run. My hands told me that—particularly my left hand, which is so swollen between the thumb and forefinger that I couldn't have hit many more."

The demonstration of Ruth's prowess was staged between games in yesterday's double-header between the Yanks and Senators.

Between these contests Ruth—in his white home uniform with his old No. 3 on the back, strode to the plate against tall, lean Johnson, probably the fastest pitcher baseball ever knew. Bald Benny Bengough, formerly of the Yanks but now a Washington coach, was catching, and Billy Evans, former American League umpire, officiated.

SPUN AT CURVE

"Johnson can pitch, although he's fifty-five years old," Ruth enthused. "The old buzzard threw me a curve once and I almost broke myself in two swinging at it." He was fererring to the Big Train's sixteenth pitch, on which he whirled to a foul tip.

Ruth's towering foul "homer" gave him such a kick that he said:

"I wish I could get out there every day, but I can't at forty-seven and weighing 237 and not being able to run the outfield or on the basepaths. But I hope the gounger generation—the kids who never saw me or Johnson do our stuff—can get a rough idea of how this game of baseball used to be played."

PACIFIC COAST LEAGUE

Los Angeles, 4-4; San Francisco, 2-5.
Sacramento, 6-2; San Diego, 2-1.
Portland, 4-6; Seattle, 3-4.
Hollywood, 5-1; Oakland, 4-7.

The Babe Sends A Homer On Its Way

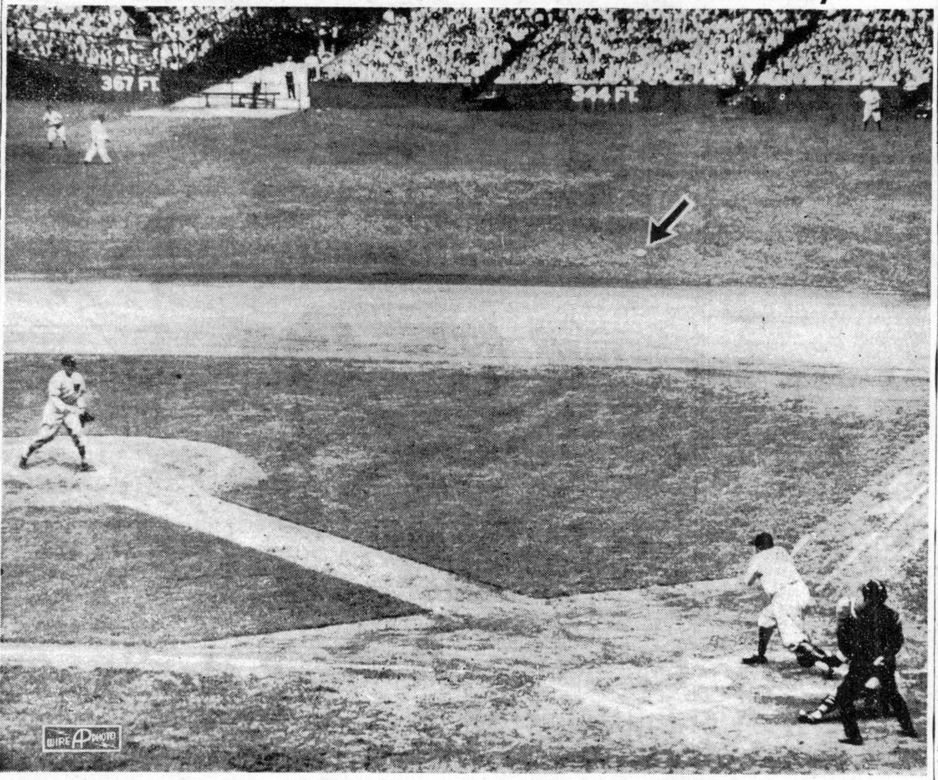

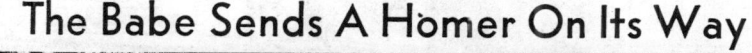

THERE IT GOES—Babe Ruth (at bat) sends a home run lofting toward the "Ruthville" section of the Yankee Stadium bleachers, with Walter Johnson pitching in an exhibition between the games of a Yankee-Washington double-header at New York yesterday for Army-Navy Relief Funds. The ball (arrow) dropped in the stands for a homer, but the Babe didn't think it was well hit and didn't run. He hit another one harder later on that he considered worthwhile, so he raced around the bases. The ball celared the fence, but curved foul—the Babe kept right on going. The catcher above is Benny Bengough and Billy Evans is umpiring. Associated Press Wirephoto.

Grid All-Stars Train Furiously

By H. C. WARREN

CHICAGO, Aug. 24—(I. N. S.).—A hard-fighting collegiate All-Star equad keyed to a high pitch of enthusiasm by a corps of the outstanding coaches of the nation promised today to give the World Champion Chicago Bears a real battle in the ninth annual All-Star football game Friday night in Soldier Field.

While thousands of gridiron fans feel that the aggregation of college stars hardly can cope with the powerful, smooth-working machine that Owner-Coach George Halas of the Bears has trained, the All-Star squad of 63 and the six coaches have nothing but confidence.

And if confidence, team-work, the hardest kind of gruelling practice and a sheer desire to win can turn the trick, it looks bad for the world champions Friday night.

The head coach of the All-Stars, Bob Zuppke, who for 29 years directed the gridiron destinies of the University of Illinois, had planned to give his charges a rest yesterday, but suddenly changed his mind. Instead of the promised day of rest, the entire squad was sent through the roughest, toughest workout since the team was assembled.

It is possible that yesterday's workout may be a costly one for the All-Stars. Four men came up with serious injuries. Bill Dudley of Virginia suffered a broken finger on his left hand; Dick Erdlitz of Northwestern had a twisted ankle; Steve Lach of Duke got a broken nose, and Vic Lindskog of Stanford received a cut on the chin that required two stitches.

HAGERSTOWN WINS

HARRISBURG, Pa., Aug. 24.—Behind the six-hit hurling of Stratton, the Hagerstown Owls scored a 4-0 Interstate Baseball League victory over Harrisburg yesterday. The second game was postponed.

SOUTHERN ASSOCIATION

Atlanta, 18-8; New Orleans, 4-1.
Nashville, 11-2; Memphis, 4-1.
Birmingham-Chattanooga, postponed.
Little Rock-Knoxville, postpones.

Dodgers, Cards Come To Grips

NEW YORK, Aug. 24—(I. N. S.).—Brooklyn's knock-'em-down, step-on-'em Dodgers roared into St. Louis today to await their opening tussle with the dogged Cardinals tonight. The Durochermen hit the sultry banks of the Mississippi 7½ games ahead of the Red Birds in the race for the National League flag and dead set on settling the issue with their rivals during the coming four-game series.

If Brooklyn can hold the upper hand for the four contests, they would be harder to stop than a river boat in a Mississippi flood. The Cards are playing hot ball, too, having won eight straight before being knocked by Pittsburgh in the opening game yesterday's twin bill, 5 to 3. Undaunted the Southworth peons came right back to take the nightcap, 5 to 2.

BLAST BY CAMILLI

The Dodgers clubbed the Giants, 6 to 4, in ten innings and 7 to 5 in the nightcap that was halted after the winning run was scored in the fifth frame. Dolph Camilli blasted out a rousing warning of things to come in St. Louis when he belted a homer with the bases loaded in the extra frame to win the opener.

Billy Herman's two-run single won the nightcap, the game being abbreviated by agreement to allow both teams to entrain for the West. The Giants open Tuesday in Cincinnati.

Philadelphia beat Boston, 2 to 0, in the first stanza of a twin bill, then lost the finale to the resurgent Braves, 3 to 1.

REDS REELING

Chicago whipped Cincinnati twice, Claude Passeau hurling nine-hit ball to take the opener, 3 to 0, and Lon Warneke allowing only two safeties to win the nightcap by the same score. The double defeats left the Reds reeling under the impact of ten losses in their last 11 games.

Big doings of the day in the American League were the Army and Navy relief games played between New York and Washington, Philadelphia and Boston and Detroit and St. Louis.

With the immortal Babe Ruth coming out of retirement to smack an exhibition home run off the equally immortal and retired Walter Johnson, the Yankees split a double-header with the Senators, losing the first game, 7 to 6, and winning the second contest which was halted after five and a half innings on account of darkness, 3 to 0.

YANKS' LEAD CUT

The Red Sox cut the Yankees lead to nine games by blanking the Athletics twice, 2 to 0 and 7 to 0. Tex Hughson allowed the A's only four hits in winning the opener. For his eleventh straight victory and seventeenth of the season, Hughson, as a result, became the first A. L. hurler to reach that mark.

Joe Dobson duplicated Hughson's performance in the nightcap by yielding only four bingles.

The Browns beat the Tigers, 2 to 1, and 4 to 2, and Cleveland and Chicago split a twin bill, the White Sox winning the opener, 3 to 1, with the Indians taking the second contest, 1 to 0, in ten frames.

WILLARD'S SON IN ARMY

MIAMI BEACH, Fla., Aug. 24—(A. P.).—Jess Willard, Jr., twenty-eight, son of the former heavyweight boxing champion, is a student at the Army Air Force Officer Training School here.

Chiefs' Sluggers Blast Newark

SYRACUSE, N. Y., Aug. 24—(A. P.). — Members of the Syracuse Chiefs evidently were tired of being referred to as the "hitless wonders." Practically all successes enjoyed by the Chiefs until last weekend were because of their hurlers.

The Chiefs went on the warpath Saturday night when they lambasted the Montreal Royals, 19-2. Then they ambushed the Newark Bears yesterday, scalping the International League leaders in both ends of a double-header, 8-3 and 6-2.

In the opener, Clayton Lambelt of the Chiefs and Randy Gumpert of the Bears dueled on even terms until the sixth, where Syracuse tallied five times to seal the contest.

Newark jumped off to a two-run lead in the second game, but the Indians halved the margin in the next inning and clinched the game with another five-run sortie in the fourth. The victories boosted Manager Jewel Ens' crew to third place as Jersey City lost a pair. The last-place Rochester Red Wings pulled the surprise of the day by twice defeating the Giants, 5-2 and 6-4.

TRACK RECORD

OESTERSUN, Sweden, Aug. 24—(A. P.).—Gunder Hegg, Swedish fireman, ran 2,000 meters in the record breaking time of 5.11.8, five full seconds faster than Archie san Romani's accepted world standard.

Shut Out, Alsab To Meet In Chicago Race

CHICAGO, Aug. 24—(I. N. S.).—Shut Out, the three-year-old king at this stage of the racing season, and Alsab will renew their duel for supremacy Saturday in the $50,000-added American Derby at Washington Park.

While these two are regarded the outstanding colts of the three-year-old crop, they may encounter some stiff opposition from other possible starters, notably Rounders, the Valdina Farm's newest threat for top honors, and T. D. Grimes' With Regards, an in-and-outer.

Aletern, a recent graduate from the claiming ranks, and King's Abbey, also are entered for the big race which may gross $80,000. Col. E. R. Bradley's Bless Me, an easy winner at Saratoga last week, is eligible, but it was not known whether the colt would be shipped here.

Ailing Player Returning For Hard Drive

By HUGH TRADER, JR.

What are the Orioles' play-[...] chances now as they open a fi[...] eight-game swing through Jers[...] City and Newark this afternoo[...] against the Little Giants?

I should say that the Birds a[...] a fifty-fifty proposition for the fi[...] division from here on out. Partic[...]larly does this opinion apply wi[...] the news that Eddie Robin[...] Teddy Sczepkowski and Hal Sie[...] all will be available the latter [...] of this week, though Sczepkov[...] won't join the club on the [...] until Wednesday.

Let's analyze the scramble.

THREE-WAY FIGHT

Apparently it's a three-corne[...] fight among Baltimore, Jersey C[...] and Syracuse. Toronto is fadi[...] and so is Buffalo. Montreal, [...] sounder club and with a percent[...] margin to fall back on in trou[...] has a softer schedule in finishi[...] up with Buffalo, Toronto a[...] Rochester. Newark is a cinch, a[...] the Royals are 8 to 5 to make t[...] play-offs.

On that deduction, two play-[...] places are left for the Oriol[...] the Giants and the Chiefs. The[...] is nothing in the schedule now [...] favor any of the three clubs, sin[...] they're playing each other, a[...] each must oppose Newark in o[...] or more series. Jersey City hol[...] an edge, in that it is present[...] three games over .500, but, with [...] more game to play with the O[...]oles before the finish, the Gi[...] could be snuffed out in one seri[...] the same as the Birds.

FINAL SERIES

Finally, there's the extreme po[...]sibility that the duel will narro[...] down between the Birds and th[...] Chiefs in the final series of th[...] season in Oriole Park next wee[...] when the Flock returns for [...] games with Jersey City and Syr[...]cuse.

So, no matter how you look at i[...] the Orioles have just as good [...] chance as the next club. The pitc[...]ing is holding up, Repass and Be[...] are clicking around the keyston[...] sack and the power is sufficient [...] Robinson can get back in there i[...] two or three more days. Dr. Be[...]nett says Eddie will be ready b[...] Wednesday, that his knee injur[...] isn't serious, only troublesome.

Begining today, this is the fin[...] trip and, simultaneously, the mos[...] important, as every game is vita[...]

BIG DRIVE HERE

The Birds must play .500 ball o[...] the swing, win at least four out o[...] eight, to hold their ground for th[...] big push next week in Oriole Par[...]

Anything under .500 on this tr[...] will make the Birds' task th[...] much tougher later.

Anything over .500 will put th[...] pressure on the other guy.

HOWELL TO PLAY

What makes the series in Jers[...] City even fuller at this point [...] the race is the presence of R[...] Howell, the big slugger who help[...]

Continued on Page 20, Column

17 Wins

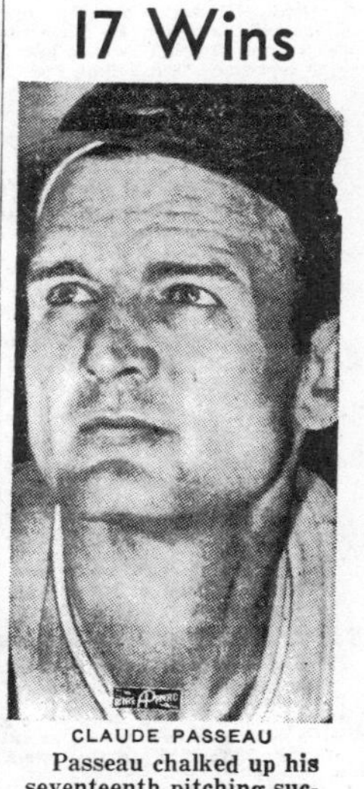

CLAUDE PASSEAU

Passeau chalked up his seventeenth pitching success of the season for the Chicago Cubs yesterday when he beat the Cincinnati Reds.

Packers Boast Of New Speed In Backfield

The Corner On Baseball

By Hugh Trader, Jr.

There are always a lot of base-
ll stories untold for a season.
me are personal, of course, which
ve no place in print; a ball play-
's private life should not be for
blic consumption, anymore than
urs or mine. Other stories are
nored or avoided, because there
no point in deliberately knocking
player down in his profession.

At least, that's the column policy.
he facts are printed always. I
ave never attempted to pull any
unches nor to "cover up" for any
ayer or manager. If honest and
served criticism is warranted, it's
ritten herein.

Few players, however, appreciate
hat is not written about them—
d that goes for managers, too.
hey "beef" about a scolding now
d then, not realizing what might
written during the course of a
ason.

I think the story can be told now
out Pooch Puccinelli to illustrate
e point.

POOCH'S "YEAR"

It was back in 1935. Puccinelli
d a spectacular year here with
e Orioles. He led the circuit in
out every batting department in-
ented. He slammed out 209 hits
hich included 49 doubles, 53 home
ns, 172 runs batted in. He drew
bases on balls, scored 135 runs
d topped the loop with a percent-
ge of .359.

That was quite a year, wasn't it?
ans daily asked how could a slug-
er like that in double-A ball, even

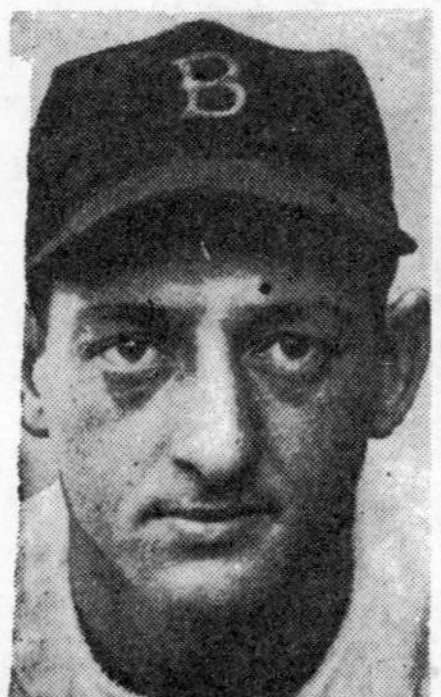

GEORGE PUCCINELLI

hough Pooch was a poor fielder,
e passed up by the majors. Surely,
hey argued, Puccinelli could hit
in the big show and with his
ower help any club at the plate.

Well, that sounds good but there's
sually a lot more behind it than
he average fan sees. For instance,
ny qualified observer could have
een in time that Pooch had some-
hing of a "blind" spot around his
etters against a pitcher with a
igh, hard one that hopped. Pooch
idn't like that pitch. That's why
e consistently struck out against
ven a pitcher like Tom Dela Cruz.

Anyhow, the writer thought he'd
o a yarn on Puccinelli for the
porting News, baseball weekly.
o, seeking some extra facts and a
ifferent angle, I poured over
Pooch's record for the season. I
ecided, for example, to see what
he big fellow had hit against the
eague's ten best bitchers.

END OF STORY

That was the end of that story.
When I finished the figuring, it was
evealed that Puccinelli had hit
bout .275 against the top hurlers
nd about .400 against the loop's
nediocre pitchers. That's how he
ot to .359 for the year.

So, you see, there was no point
writing that story. It would only
hrow the cold shoulder on Puc-
nelli's great season and popular-
y here. So the story was unwrit-
n, and the Philadelphia Athletics
afted Pooch in the fall. He got
f to a great start, but eventually
owed up and finished hitting .278
the American League.

Pooch never realized or appreci-
ed what was not written about
m. When he returned to the
ioles and began to slip and not
stle, I criticized him in the col-
n and that was the end of a
easant friendship between the
och and the writer. He left with-
a farewell and I haven't heard
m him since. But I liked Pooch.
ope he isn't still peeved at me.

Bringing Fleet Ball Carriers To Baltimore

GREEN BAY, Wis., Aug. 24—"The fastest backfield in the history of the Green Bay Packers," is the way that Coach E. L. (Curly) Lambeau regards the ball-carriers he is grooming for a pre-season invasion of the east. The Bays are scheduled to play the Brooklyn Dodgers in Brooklyn August 29, and the Washington Redskins in Baltimore under the lights on Labor Day night, September 7.

In the veteran Cecil Isbell and a pro-league sophomore, Tony Canadeo, Lambeau has a pair of left halfbacks that provide triple-threat scoring punch for anybody's backfield, and the supply of veterans also includes Lou Brock, a Purdue teammate of Isbell's who has been converted to fullback; Larry Craig, a blocking back who plays end on defense; Joe Laws, one of the league's finest field generals from the right half position; and Andy Uram, one of the many Minnesota gridders on the squad.

COUNT ON KAHLER

One acquisition expected to strengthen the Packer offensive is Bob Kahler, recalled from the Long Island Indians. He was sent there last season after reporting to the Packers, provided plenty of trouble for Indian opponents, and earned himself a great deal of glory in the Long Island team's championship campaign.

The fullback corps has 205-pound Ted Fritsch, a bulky ball-carrier that Backfield Coach Eddie Kotal brought along with him from near-Stevens Point, Wis., State Teachers, when Kotel, himself a former Packer, joined the Bays' coaching corps. Another Wisconsin native is Charles (Chuck) Sample, from Appleton, who played under Doc Spears at Toledo U. He tips the scales at 202.

PAIR OF NEW BACKS

Tom Bushby, Kansas State, and Ben Starrett, St. Mary's, are a pair of new backs and both of them go well over 200 pounds. But it's speed, and not size, that the Bay mentor likes about his new backfield combinations and the conversion of Lou Brock to fullback is greatly credited for the increased swiftness.

Still another prospect is Babe Webb, a Hawaiian signed by cable, who has not yet reported from his Honolulu home. He was an all-Border conference back at New Mexico State.

21,000 See Baugh Star In Intra-Squad Game

SAN DIEGO, Cal., Aug. 24—(I. N. S.).—The Washington Redskins today intensified training for their game next Sunday in Los Angeles with the Army All-Stars following an intra-squad warm-up game in which Sammy Baugh sparked the East to a 31-to-21 win over the West.

San Diegos' largest football crowd, estimated at 21,000 customers, witnessed yesterday's game.

Baugh tossed two touchdown passes to Wilbur Moore, former Minnesota star, another to Bob Masterson and set up the East's fourth with two passes. The ball was carried over from the 1-yard line by Andy Farkas.

Slingin' Sammy's third pass broke a 21-21 deadlock in the fourth quarter. Masterson boosted the score with a field goal.

Runs For Week

(Week Ending August 23)

NATIONAL LEAGUE

	M.	T.	W.	T.	F.	S.	S.	Tl.
Philadelphia	..	3	..	..	..	6	3	12
Boston	2	2	1	..	..	5	3	13
Chicago	..	0	1	..	6	5	6	18
New York	3	10	..	1	..	5	9	28
Brooklyn	..	1	11	2	..	10	13	37
St. Louis	5	5	4	..	10	7	8	39
Cincinnati	2	0	2	5	3	4	0	16
Pittsburgh	..	3	9	3	2	6	7	30

AMERICAN LEAGUE

	M.	T.	W.	T.	F.	S.	S.	Tl.
Boston	..	8	7	7	7	22	9	60
Chicago	..	0	..	8	2	3	3	16
Washington	..	2	0	3	7	0	7	19
St. Louis	5	7	..	5	1	..	6	24
New York	15	7	6	4	17	1	9	59
Detroit	..	..	6	..	4	..	3	13
Philadelphia	0	1	8	15	5	8	0	37
Cleveland	2	..	1	..	3	1	2	9

Believe It Or Not :-: By Ripley

On request, sent with stamped, addressed envelope, Mr. Ripley will furnish proof of anything depicted by him.

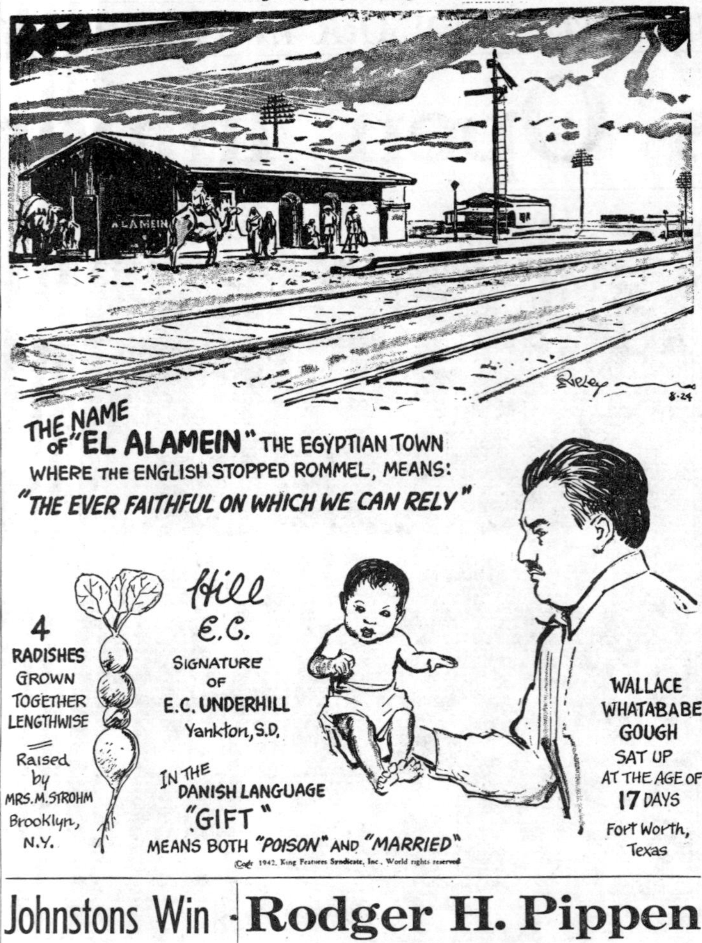

AL AMEIN
Ripley
8-24
THE NAME of "EL ALAMEIN" THE EGYPTIAN TOWN WHERE THE ENGLISH STOPPED ROMMEL, MEANS:
"THE EVER FAITHFUL ON WHICH WE CAN RELY"
4 RADISHES GROWN TOGETHER LENGTHWISE
Raised by MRS. M. STROHM Brooklyn, N.Y.
Hill E.C.
SIGNATURE OF E.C. UNDERHILL Yankton, S.D.
IN THE DANISH LANGUAGE "GIFT" MEANS BOTH "POISON" AND "MARRIED"
WALLACE WHATABAE GOUGH SAT UP AT THE AGE OF 17 DAYS Fort Worth, Texas

© 1942, King Features Syndicate, Inc., World rights reserved

Johnstons Win Father-Son Golf

The team of Bill and Eddie Johnston toured the Country Club of Maryland links in 78 strokes to win their third State father-and-son golf championship yesterday.

Bill Johnston and his son, Eddie, put together tunes of 38-40 for their winning 78. Runners-up to the Johnstons were J. V. and Bobby Brownell, former titleholders from Washington, who scored an 83.

John Weare, Sr., and John Weare, Jr., of the Country Club of Maryland, won the low net prize, posting 94-25—69.

Rodger H. Pippen Says:

(Continued from Page 19)

Sox beat the Indians, 3-1, in the first game of a double-header. It was Lyons' eleventh win.

Sixteen Runs After Two Were Out

In the last inning of the first game, with the Birds trailing, 3 to 0, the gamblers were betting 5 to 1 the locals wouldn't tie the score. While admitting that the chances were slim, Jacobson, mentionad above, recalled how the St. Paul Club of the American Association made 16 runs after two were out back in 1930. Jake was with that club for about a month.

• • •

Timely Golf Suggestion

Don Kirwan, some years ago a member of Walbrook's roller polo club and now a golfer, makes a worthwhile suggestion to help soldiers and sailors get in a little golf while visiting here. He suggests that all golfers contribute balls and extra clubs to the pros at the public courses, to be loaned free of charge to the boys in uniform.

• • •

Case Beats Keller by a Foot

Washington's George Case, as expected, proved the running star in the field events held at the Yankee Stadium yesterday. Case easily won a 60-yard dash, outfooting Johnny Sullivan. Tuck Stainback and Johnny Lindell along a course laid down in the infield.

Case came right back to anchor a Washington relay quartet in an Australian type pursuit race around the bases, beating the Yankee anchorman, Charley Keller, by a step.

"That Case can run," said one of the Yankee players when Twinkle Toes Selkirk chirped up, "Yes, but they ought to make him keep his feet on the ground when he is doing it."

Coliseum Fight Card Tonight

Following is the complete program of boxing which the Century Club will offer tonight at the Coliseum, probable winners printed in capitals:

TWELVE ROUNDS

LEO RODAK, Chicago, vs. Slugger White. Lightweights. 6 to 5 on Rodak.

SIX ROUNDS

BABE SCOTT vs. Eddie Finazzo. Middleweights. 6 to 5 on Scott.

MANUEL ROSA vs. Phil Enzenga. Welterweights. 7 to 5 on Rosa.

BOBBY GARCIA vs. Benny Sciliato. Lightweights. 6 to 5 on Garcia.

FOUR ROUNDS

TOD COLE vs. Dan Biggers. Heavyweights. 6 to 5 on Cole.

First Bout: 8.45 P. M.

State M.P.'s Win Softball Title

The State Military Police softball team of the Maryland State Guard has been presented the pennant for the Baltimore asea championship and next month will oppose three battalion teams for the State championship.

The military team was coached by Capt. James Lutz, and its captain was First Sergt. Ben Kershman. In addition to the pennant each member of the team won a silver softball.

The State championships will be held in the Fifth Regiment Armory, and the opposing teams for the Brig. Gen. Dwight H. Mohr Trophy, in addition to the S. M. P., will be the First, Second and Fifth Battalions.

Members of the Baltimore area military police championship team are Corp. Albert Stretcher, pitcher; Corp. Roland Etzler, pitcher-first baseman; Sergt. William Gillingham, catcher; Sergt. Ben Kershman, first base; Pvt. Richard Plage, second base; Corp. Ralph Daily, third base; Sergt. Mike Norton, third base-sub; Sergt. Melvin Harris, short stop; Pvt. Roger Graft, shortstop-center; Sergt. Sylvester Sandy, left field; Pvt. Maurice Gillingham, center field; Pvt. Reed Haman, right field; Pvt. Sam Brinsfield, right field-sub.

Hot Springs Golf To Open Sept. 5

HOT SPRINGS, Va., April 24—(A. P.).—The Cascades Golf Club is going ahead with plans to hold its Fairacre tournament despite the war. The threeday event will open September 5 with Don O'Brien, Richmond, defending champion, seeking another leg on the Fairacre Bowl.

EASTERN LEAGUE

Elmira, 7-3; Springfield, 1-0.
Binghamton, 7-1; Albany, 1-6.
Williamsport, 3-0; Hartford, 2-1.
Scranton-Wilkes-Barre, postponed.

Oriole Batting; Hurling Records

BATTING

	AB.	H.	2b.	3b.	HR.	Rbi.	Pct.
Repass	39	12	4	0	1	4	.308
Robinson	480	146	20	6	22	93	.304
Brightman	14	4	0	0	0	1	.286
Staller	398	113	13	2	17	65	.284
Lemon	521	141	22	7	19	69	.270
Edwards	437	118	15	4	16	64	.270
Sieling	246	66	9	0	7	26	.268
Becker	308	81	14	1	3	26	.263
Langood	8	2	0	0	0	0	.250
Sczepkowski	303	74	11	3	3	30	.244
Jones	280	68	5	3	0	31	.243
Rabe	66	15	3	0	4	15	.227
Bell	143	32	4	0	0	7	.224
Robertson	235	49	6	1	14	37	.209
Burkart	34	7	1	2	0	1	.206
Waldt	5	1	0	0	0	0	.200
McGarity	77	15	1	0	0	7	.195
Krakauskas	31	6	1	0	0	2	.194
Center	59	7	0	0	0	2	.119
Flanigan	52	5	0	0	0	1	.096
Niller	31	3	0	0	0	1	.097
Gromek	21	2	1	0	0	1	.095
Smoll	33	3	1	0	1	2	.090
Trinkle	40	3	0	0	0	1	.075

PITCHING

	G.	CG.	IP.	R.	H.	SO.	W.	L.
Smoll	31	8	121 1-3	61	115	62	9	6
Krakau'as	20	6	97 2-3	57	106	59	7	4
Center	28	13	183	86	160	114	11	10
Niller	27	2	69	48	68	15	3	2
Trinkle	42	11	145 2-3	79	170	51	12	12
Burkart	30	4	104 1-3	52	99	39	5	6
Gromek	12	2	48 1-3	37	54	44	3	5
Flanigan	32	5	150 2-3	81	157	76	9	14
Waldt	11	0	22	27	34	9	0	0

TEXAS LEAGUE

Fort Worth, 4-3; Oklahoma City, 2-1.
Tulsa, 7-4; Dallas, 4-0.
San Antonio, 6-2; Beaumont, 0-1.
Shreveport-Houston, postponed.

Segura Has Eye On National Tennis Title

CHESTNUT HILL, Mass., Aug. 24—(U. P.).—Francisco Segura of Ecuador prepared for the national singles tournament beginning Thursday at Forest Hills, N. Y., by capturing the Longwood Bowl tennis tournament yesterday.

Segura, two-handed stylist and top-seeded foreign player, defeated Lieut. Gardnar Mulloy of Miami, 6—3, 6—4, 7—9, 3—6, 6—1. Then he teamed with Alejo Russell of Argentina and won the men's doubles title, 6—2, 10—8, from the favored team of Mulloy and Dick McKee of Miami.

In the women's final, nineteen-year-old Louise Brough of Beverly Hills, Cal., won her fifth straight major title, defeating third-seeded Margaret Osborne of San Francisco, 6—2, 6—1. Miss Brough, national junior girls' titlist, is undefeated this season.

'Olympic' Games Resume Today

The East-West Olympics, revived at Easterwood Park on Saturday, will be resumed today with softball games on the program. The competition will continue through Friday.

The West took the lead in Saturday's field events at Easterwood. Over 200 boys and girls competed.

In today's featured softball contest, the Poplar Grove team, representing the West, will meet the Long Hats, representing the East, at 6.15 P. M. at Easterwood Park. However, other games are listed in four divisions, starting at 1.30 P. M. when the 80-pounders clash on the softball diamond. Ninety-five pounders, 115-pounders and junior unlimited teams will follow in that order, with the seniors providing the 6.15 feature.

Sandlot Baseball

BALTIMORE MAJOR LEAGUE PLAY-OFFS

Brooklyn A. A., 3-3; Arbutus, 2-2.

NORTH BALTIMORE MAJOR LEAGUE

Bloomingdale, 5; Mt. Washington, 0.
St. Ambrose, 2-4; Hanlon, 1-3.
Stone P. C., 6-7; Rustless, 5-2.

BELAIR-HARFORD ROAD LEAGUE

De Molay, 5; Grace, 2.
Belair Road A. A., 7; Overlea, 3.

MARYLAND AMATEUR LEAGUE

Barclay, 13; Rosedale, 0.

WEST BALTIMORE INTERMEDIATE LEAGUE

Sioux Eagles, 8; Universal, 4.
Arbutus, 2; Calverton Juniors, 0.
Beckers, 9; Ravens, 0.
Western Trojans, 5; Kenwood, 1.

WESTERN CATHOLIC INTERMEDIATE LEAGUE

St. Cecilia, 6; Monastery, 4.
St. Rose, 11; Ascension, 4.

EASTERN CATHOLIC INTERMEDIATE LEAGUE

St. James, 6; St. Francis, 5.
St. Elizabeth, 3; St. Ambrose, 2.

WESTERN JUNIOR CATHOLIC LEAGUE

St. Bernardine, 4; Monastery, 2.
St. Peter's, 10; St. Rose, 3.

NORTHEASTERN JUNIOR LEAGUE PLAY-OFFS

Evergreen, 6; Highland Club, 1.

BALTIMORE MAJOR LEAGUE CONSOLATION SERIES

Odenton, 9-5; American Hammer, 0-0.

Elites Play Sandlot Champs Here Tonight

The Baltimore Elite Giants, one of the pace-setting teams of the Negro National League, will meet the Brooklyn Athletic Association team, one of the powerhouses of local sandlot baseball, tonight at Bugle Field at 8.45.

The Brooklyn A. A. nine is the newly-crowned champion of the Baltimore Major League and already has qualified for the State sandlot championship tournament which opens next Sunday.

The Elites are currently engaged in a nip-and-tuck battle with the Homestead Grays for the second-round title in the Negro National League. The Elites will use Harvey or Glover on the hillock tonight against the vaunted power of the Brooklyn A. A. Manager Harry Booth of the Brooklyn team is expected to send Fick or Weatherow, aces of the Brooklyn pitching corps, against the hard-hitting Elites.

Probable line-ups for tonight:

ELITE GIANTS	BROOKLYN A. A.
Kimbro,cf	Squillace,ss
Hughes, 2b	Arvin,cf
Wright,rf	Matecki,2b
Campanella,c	Lombardi,lf
Hoskins,lf	Tiedeman,3b
Scales,1b	Rolf,1b
Butts,ss	Koenig,rf
Snow,3b	Lowman,c
Harvey,p	Weatherow,p
Glover,p.	Fick,p

Joe Louis Opens Game; Kansas City Triumphs

KANSAS CITY, Aug. 24—(A.P.). The Kansas City Monarchs Negro baseball team received tight pitch-

DR. N. B. GWYNN
SURGEON-DENTIST
WYETH BLDG.
36-38 W. Lexington St.
SAratoga 3039
Office Hours:
Daily 9 A. M. to 8 P. M.
Sundays 10 A. M. to 2 P. M.

SPORTS BRIEFS

LOCAL

The Calvert Hall football team held its first drills today at Walbrook Oval. Coach Ray Bahr has lost only six players through graduation. Tomorrow Forest Park High starts practice.

TENNIS FINALS

Al Borleis and Dan Sullivan yesterday won the Mount Washington men's double tennis crown. They beat Arthur Simmons and Ed Higgins in the finals, 6—2, 8—6, 6—8, 6—2.

TITLE TO BROOKLYN

The Brooklyn A. A. nine won the Baltimore Major League baseball title by trimming Arbutus twice yesterday, 3 to 2. Fick pitched the opener, allowing only five hits. Brooklyn will play in the State title series, which opens next Sunday.

Orioles Start Important Trip

(Continued from Page 19)

drive the Birds into the 1940 play-offs, Howell will be in there blasting against the Flock now, and later here in Baltimore, and the burly redhead looms large in Jersey City's stretch run.

Clyde Smoll was the gent who loomed large for the Birds yesterday, however, as he pitched a 7-to-0 victory over Toronto after Jack Hallett had stopped our side, 3 to 0, on three hits in the opener. A crowd of nearly 10,000 sat in on the games to cheer the Birds and brought the local attendance totall to over 150,000 for the season.

Smoll's victory yesterday can't be underestimated. It gave the Birds a split for the day and saved them the ground they had picked up off the Leafs. So for the series the Birds beat Toronto in five out of six and for the season, 13 out of 22. Indeed, Baltimore won 49, lost 39, in its play with the four Northern clubs this year, beating Buffalo, Toronto and Rochester, and splitting even with Montreal.

SMOLL'S NINTH WIN

Smoll gave up only five hits for his ninth win of the campaign and Sherry Robertson, subbing for Robinson, slashed his fourteenth homer to salt the game away. Staller and Bell also contributed important hits and Repass flashed afield at short. In fact, Repass supplied the defensive gem in the nightcap on a play back of second on Handley.

Hallett was simply too much in the opener, and only Staller, who is doing a good job in the clean-up spot, hit him. Trinkle started and was charged with the loss, as Center and Krakauskas finished it up strongly.

Elmer Burkart is the flipper this afternoon. Every pitch means something now, pal!

Wakefield Named 'Most Valuable'

BEAUMONT, Texas, Aug. 24—(A. P.).—Dick Wakefield, young Beaumont rightfielder who was paid a purported $50,000 for signing with Detroit, entered illustrious company in winning the title of the most valuable player in the Texas League. Among the Tiger farm star's predecessors were such diamond notables as Dizzy Dean, Hank Greenberg, Zeke Bonura and Rudy York.

N. J. Gets $513,850 From Race Betting

TRENTON, N. J., Aug. 24—(A. P.).—New Jersey's income from pari-mutuel betting at the new Garden State race track near Camden passed the half-million-dollar mark last week, the State Racing Commission reported today.

Secretary Fred H. Ryan announced that for the secen-day period ended last Wednesday the State's 4 per cent. cut of wagers totaled $132,859, bringing to $513,850.80 the amount turned into the State treasury since the horses began racing there July 18.

Blood, Nerve, Skin Stomach, Gland
and CHRONIC AILMENTS
Successfully Treated
Men—Women Are You Ill?
You are invited to call for an EXAMINATION—$1.00
Central Medical Offices
408 E. Baltimore St.
Office Hours: 9 A. M. to 12 Noon, 1 P. M. to 6 P. M. Thursday, 9 A. M. to 1 P. M. Only Sunday, 10 A. M. to 1 P. M.

The Standings

INTERNATIONAL LEAGUE

YESTERDAY'S SCORES

Toronto, 3-0; Baltimore, 0-7.
Montreal, 5-3; Buffalo, 2-0.

STANDINGS

	W.	L.	P. C.
Newark	83	52	.615
Montreal	70	65	.519
Syracuse	69	66	.511
Jersey City	66	64	.508
Baltimore	66	67	.496
Buffalo	67	71	.486
Toronto	65	70	.481
Rochester	53	84	.387

TODAY'S GAMES

Baltimore at Jersey City, 3.15 P. M.
Newark at Syracuse, 8.30 P. M.
Rochester at Toronto (2), 7 and 8 P. M.
Buffalo at Montreal, 8.30 P. M.

NATIONAL LEAGUE

YESTERDAY'S SCORES

Boston, 3-0; Philadelphia, 1-2.
Brooklyn, 6-7; New York, 4-5 (first game, 10 innings; second game 5 innings).
Chicago, 3-3; Cincinnati, 0-0
Pittsburgh, 5-2; St. Louis, 3-5.

STANDINGS

	W.	L.	P. C.
Brooklyn	84	35	.706
St. Louis	77	43	.642
New York	65	57	.533
Cincinnati	59	61	.492
Pittsburgh	55	63	.466
Chicago	58	68	.460
Boston	50	74	.403
Philadelphia	34	81	.296

GAMES TODAY PITCHERS

Brooklyn at St. Louis (French vs. Lanier), 9.30. P. M.
(Only game scheduled.)

GAME TOMORROW

Philadelphia at Chicago.
Boston at Pittsburgh (night).
New York at Cincinnati (night).
Brooklyn at St. Louis (night).

AMERICAN LEAGUE

YESTERDAY'S SCORES

Washington, 7-0; New York, 6-3 (second game, 6 innings).
Boston, 2-7; Philadelphia, 0-0.
St. Louis, 2-4; Detroit, 1-2 (second game, 10 innings).
Chicago, 3-0; Cleveland, 1-1.

STANDINGS

	W.	L.	P. C.
New York	8[illegible]	42	.659
Boston	7[illegible]	51	.585
Cleveland	6[illegible]	58	.525
St. Louis	6[illegible]	59	.520
Detroit	6[illegible]	64	.488
Chicago	5[illegible]	64	.4[illegible]
Washington	4[illegible]	71	.403
Philadelphia	4[illegible]	82	.369

TODAY

Open date.

GAMES TOMORROW

Cleveland at Boston (2).
St. Louis at Washington (night).
Chicago at New York.
(Only games scheduled.)

INTERSTATE LEAGUE

YESTERDAY'S SCORES

Hagerstown, 4; Harrisburg, 0.
Allentown, 5-3; Trenton, 3-4.
Lancaster, 4-5; Wilmington, 1-4.

STANDINGS

	W.	L.	P. C.
Wilmington	68	50	.576
Hagerstown	64	52	.552
Harrisburg	60	59	.504
Allentown	58	60	.492
Lancaster	54	65	.454
Trenton	49	67	.422

AMERICAN ASSOCIATION

YESTERDAY'S SCORES

Toledo, 5-0; Indianapolis, 1-1.
St. Paul, 3-2; Kansas City, 1-7.
Milwaukee, 6-3; Minneapolis, 5-6.
Louisville, 7-7; Columbus, 2-3.

STANDINGS

	W.	L.	P. C.
Milwaukee	73	62	.541
Columbus	73	63	.537
Kansas City	73	65	.529
Louisville	69	66	.511
Toledo	68	65	.511
Minneapolis	70	69	.504
Indianapolis	68	69	.496
St. Paul	52	87	.374

Golfers Raise $116 For Army Relief

Suburban Club contributed $116 to the Army Emergency Relief Fund yesterday by the means of a golf handicap tournament.

Certificates in the event were won by Isaac Strouse and Mrs. Albert Rich. Strause won the men's class with 88-22—66. Mrs. Rich scored 105-27—78 to win the women's event.

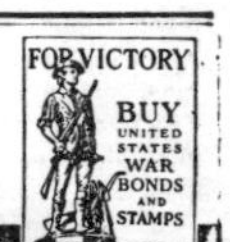

FOR VICTORY
BUY
UNITED STATES
WAR BONDS
AND STAMPS

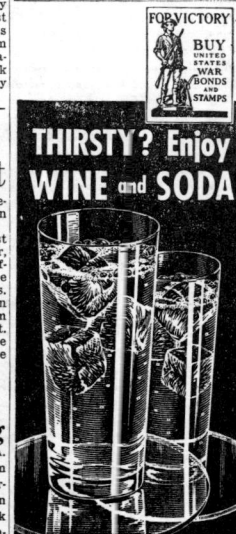

THIRSTY? Enjoy
WINE and SODA
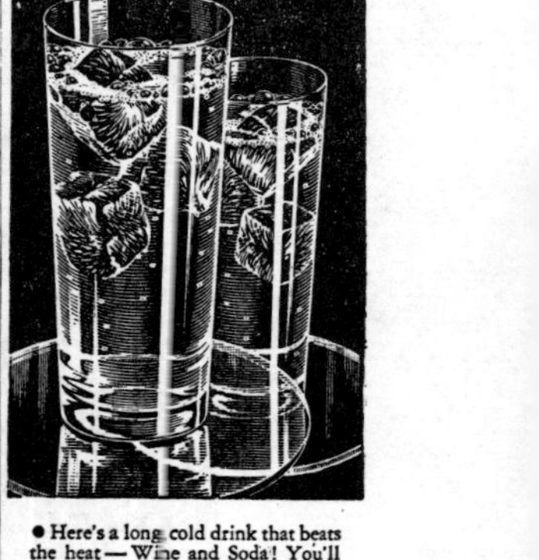
• Here's a long cold drink that beats the heat—Wine and Soda! You'll find it the just-right refreshment for any afternoon or evening occasion. To make one, or two (or three!): Half-fill a tall glass with your favorite California red or white wine, add ice cubes and sparkling water. Wine Advisory Board, 85 Second St., San Francisco.
EVERYBODY 10%
SHOOT STRAIGHT
With Our Boys!
BUY WAR BONDS

Sports Roundup:

NEW ANGLES ON SERVICE FOOTBALL

By HUGH FULLERTON, JR.

NEW YORK, Aug. 24 — (Wide World).—Here are a couple of new angles on the football-for-soldiers' business, presented by a guy who was closely connected with the college game before he went into the Army Air Force . . . His idea is that the only service men who can get ready to play tough schedules are the cadets who have regular hours set aside for athletics. The ones who work with planes (or make it machine guns, tanks, etc.) for 12 or 14 hours a day are too tired for serious athletics.

"As you know, football is pretty tough," he remarks, "and the boys will not go for it in a big way unless some provision is made to give them some practice. The boys in khaki have another big battle and they will not be as interested in football as they were in college."

Still, if they can run a big-time program and not interfere with training—and some say they can—we don't see the purposes in calling it off. . . . A winning team is a handy way to build up the old collitch—or we got the best damn outfit in this man's Army—spirit!

MONDAY MATINEE

When Jimmie Hitchcock reports to the Chappel Hill Navy Pre-Flight School Thursday Head Coach Jack Meagher of Auburn will be fresh out of assistants to help him start football practice September 1 . . . Hitchcock is the seventh Auburn coach to enter the service . . . Glad note for suburbanites: When his Milwaukee Brewers are playing at home Manager Cholly Grimm goes to the park early every afternoon and helps cut the grass in the outfield with a hand mower. He says it is a great conditioner.

When a sailor thumbed a ride on a truck in Detroit the other day the result was the sale of $27,500 worth of tickets for the Amateur Softball Association world championships. . . . The sailor was Chief Petty Officer Max Gail, who has been working with the Association because his year's profits will go to the Detroit Navy Recreational Fund . . . He told the truck driver, who was Bill Barnett, athletic director of the Teamsters' Union. . . . Barnett got a bright idea, and the eventual result was that the union bought out the U. of Detroit Stadium for the night of the tournament semi-finals.

SERVICE DEPT.

Rene Choteau of St. Louis and Yale, intercollegiate 1,500-meter champion last year, still is one of the fastest swimmers at the North Carolina naval pre-flight school, but he's slowing down. The intensive physical fitness program the cadets go through has developed a lot of muscles Choteau never used in swimming . . . Branch Rickey reports that the St. Louis Cardinals' organization has sent 124 players to the armed forces, including 17 from the Columbus (Ga.) farm club . . . And the latest P. G. A. checkup shows 148 pro golfers in uniform.

Leading Hitters

NATIONAL LEAGUE

	G.	AB.	R.	H.	P. C.
Reiser, Brooklyn	99	383	82	129	.337
Slaughter, St. Louis	119	466	80	152	.326
Lombardi, Boston	83	231	23	74	.320
Medwick, Brooklyn	115	443	57	141	.318
Musial, St. Louis	108	355	71	113	.318

AMERICAN LEAGUE

	G.	AB.	R.	H.	P. C.
Williams, Boston	121	422	107	146	.346
Gordon, New York	116	424	69	143	.337
Spence, Washington	117	489	72	163	.333
Wright, Chicago	83	292	42	97	.332
Pesky, Boston	118	493	81	161	.327

Potomac Rises 50 Feet

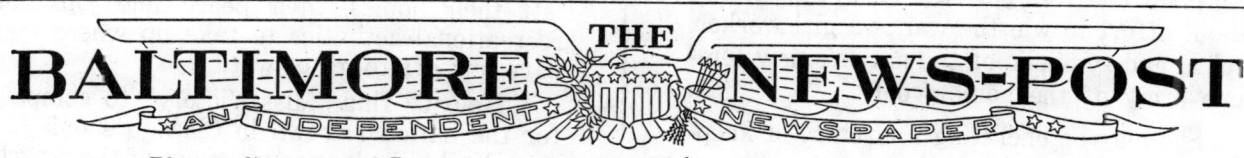

THE WEATHER
Rain likely ending by noon today. Little change in temperature. High humidity and moderate winds.

Read The Baltimore News-Post for complete accurate war coverage. It is the only Baltimore newspaper possessing the three great wire services—
ASSOCIATED PRESS
INTERNATIONAL NEWS SERVICE
UNITED PRESS

THE BALTIMORE NEWS-POST
AN INDEPENDENT NEWSPAPER
The Largest Evening Circulation in the Entire South

COMPLETE FINAL

VOL. CXLI.—NO. 142 | Entered as second-class matter at Baltimore Postoffice. | SATURDAY, OCTOBER 17, 1942 | PRICE 3 CENTS

HUGE JAP FLEET OFF GUADALCANAL ISLAND

House Vote Set Today On 18-19 Draft Bill; Limit Debate To 2 Hours

WASHINGTON, Oct. 16—(A. P.).—Halting of voluntary enlistments in the Army and Navy was revived as an issue today. Informed officials said they understood the proposal to ban volunteers, long opposed by the War and Navy Departments, had been renewed and urged on President Roosevelt.

By ROBERT HUMPHREYS
International News Service Staff Correspondent.

WASHINGTON, Oct. 16.—Draft of eighteen and nineteen year old youths moved another step towards actuality today when the Senate Military Affairs Committee unanimously recommended passage of such an amendment to the Selective Service Act.

Earlier the House Rules Committee, by a unanimous vote, had approved legislation calling for the draft of 'teen-agers and sent it to the floor for a vote tomorrow.

APPROVES BILL

The Senate committee approved the bill sponsored by Senator Chan Gurney (Republican) of South Dakota and the House group reported the measure written by Representative James Wadsworth (Republican) of New York. The Gurney measure is almost identical with the Wadsworth bill and carried two amendments recommended by the War Department.

The first provides that no draftee be rejected because he has been convicted of an offense that is not a felony; the second prohibits the discharge of men eighteen to twenty-one who entered service originally by falsifying their ages.

AMENDMENT OUT

An amendment offered by Senator Josh Lee (Democrat) of Oklahoma to prohibit the sale of beer, wine and liquor in the vicinity of military establishments was voted down.

The House rule limited debate to two hours.

Speaker Rayburn announced that

Continued on Page 2, Column 2.

Successor For Byrnes Unchosen

WASHINGTON, Oct. 16—(I. N. S.).—President Roosevelt disclosed today he had reached no decision on a successor to James F. Byrnes, who resigned from the Supreme Court to become Economic Stabilization Director.

Mr. Roosevelt was asked at his press conference if he had decided upon a successor to Mr. Byrnes. He replied, no.

When A Terrible Burglar Turns Out To Be a Female Raffles What Do You Do? By All Means Refer to "Instantaneous Etiquette." Don't Miss It On the Front Page of The American Weekly, the Magazine Distributed With Next Sunday's Baltimore American.—Adv.

Outbreaks In Unoccupied France

BERN, Switzerland, Oct. 16—(A. P.).—Violent disorders have broken out in the unoccupied zone of France as the Nazis increased their pressure to get French workers to go to Germany, dispatches to the Swiss press reported today.

Lyon, Chambery and Annecy were mentioned as trouble centers in a dispatch to the Tribune De Lausanne, which said that "violent outbreaks occurred and that public forces (whether police, gendarmes or army units was not specified) had to intervene, and that blood flowed."

This dispatch said there were unconfirmed reports "that bombs were thrown, that the public forces had used weapons, chiefly hand grenades, that railway stations and other strategic points were occupied by troops."

Defer A. P. Reply To U. S. Plaint

NEW YORK, Oct. 16—(A. P.).—Remarking that "the complaint, as I see it, is a library in itself," Federal Judge Samuel Mandelbaum today extended to November 2 the time for the Associated Press to answer a Government Anti-Trust Law complaint filed August 28.

Opposing the extension, John Henry Lewin, special assistant U. S. Attorney General, argued that the Government had been "very generous" in allowing additional time for filing the answer.

Timothy N. Pfeiffer, defense attorney, asserted that the complaint represented a multiplicity of complaints since about 1,400 members of the Associated Press ewer named co-defendants.

Potomac Flood Rises 50 Ft. Above Normal

Departure Of Terps Delayed

COLLEGE PARK, Md., Oct. 16—(A. P.).—The University of Maryland's football squad, which was scheduled to leave Washington shortly before noon today for the V. M. I. game at Lexington, Va., tomorrow, still was awaiting means of getting to the scene this afternoon.

Floods overflowing west and south railroad tracks prevented the Old Liners from leaving as planned, and officials held little hope that the team would be able to get away even tonight.

The officials said that even if trains could get through, the question remained of obtaining buses to Lexington from points along either of the available railways.

Duke, Florida U. Gridders Stranded

RICHMOND, Va., Oct. 16—(A.P.). Two college football teams were stranded in Richmond today, unable to obtain transportation North.

They were Duke, which is scheduled to play Colgate at Buffalo, N. Y., tomorrow, and Florida, which had a game scheduled with Villanova in Philadelphia tonight.

(The Villanova-Florida game has been postponed until tomorrow.)

Duquesne Gridders Stranded In Va.

CHAPEL HILL, N. C., Oct. 16—(A. P.).—Word was received here this afternoon that Duquesne's football team, scheduled to play North Carolina here tomorrow, was stranded between Washington and Richmond because of flooded rivers.

Wall Street Has Casualty Station

NEW YORK, Oct. 16—(I. N. S.). Wall Street today has its first bomb-proof casualty station.

The station, equipped with 24 cots and other hospital equipment is on the ground floor of a steel skyscraper in the heart of the financial district.

—For Salvage Information
(1) Iron and Steel
(2) Kitchen Fats
(3) Tin Cans
Call PLaza 6877

Flood Closes Main Road To Md. Track

By JACK CARPENTER

LAUREL, Md., Oct. 16.—Maryland's race fans, who have undergone any number of inconveniences of late to witness their favorite sport, were forced to overcome a new obstacle to reach the Laurel track today.

Flood waters backing up from the nearby Patuxent river forced authorities to close the main road leading to the track's entrance. Motor traffic was diverted to two back roads, which, fortunately, remained high and dry. State policemen were stationed at the two alternate routes to facilitate traffic.

UNDERPASS OPEN

For the first time the underpass from the new parking area across the railroad tracks was opened to automobile traffic, and several hundred fans drove through the narrow tunnel to the otherwise isolated main parking area.

SEA OF MUD

The track was more conductive to boating than racing when a limit field of two-year-old Maryland-breds paraded in the six-furlong opener. At the end of the muddy spin it was Briar Knoll Farm's Briarchal by four lengths.

Briarchal came with a belated rush through the last sixteenth

Continued on Page 33, Column 7.

President O. K.'s Willkie's Report

WASHINGTON, Oct. 16—(I. N. S.). — President Roosevelt today said that his conference with Wendell Willkie, White House envoy to the war fronts, was exceedingly successful and interesting.

Willkie conferred with the President Wednesday, reporting to him on his 31,000-mile globe-girdling trip. Following his meeting with the Chief Executive Willkie said that any Presidential expression on the success of his mission would have to come from Mr. Roosevelt.

At his press conference today the President was asked if as a result of Willkie's visit any change was to be made in war startegy. He replied that all he could say was that he had had an exceedingly successful and interesting talk with Willkie and that, of course, he could not disclose military secrets.

Daily Double (Briarchal Abrupt) Paid $119.00

LAUREL CHARTS

Copyright, 1942, by Triangle Publications, Inc. (Daily Racing Form.)
TRACK MUDDY.

FIRST RACE—SIX FURLONGS. CHUTE. FOR TWO-YEAR-OLDS. CLAIMING. Purse $1,100. Value to winner $800, second $150, third $100, fourth $50. Went to post at 2.04½. Off at 2.05. Start good from gate. Won easily, place driving. Winner ch f 2, by Challenger II.-Parabola. Owned by BRIAR KNOLLS FARM. Trained by N. RAY. Time 23 3-5, 48 3-5, 1.16 2-5.

	Wt.	Post	St.	¼	½	Str.	Fin.	Jockeys	Odds
Briarchal	109	11	11	6^h	4½	2^h	1^4	J. Berger	$11.65
Romney Rex	112	3	9	10^3	10^3	$3^{1½}$	2^n	R. Root	2.45
Go Wes.	115	12	1	$2^{1½}$	1^3	1^2	3^2	L. Knapp	4.05
June Quest	112	6	10	$8^{1½}$	8^1	6^3	4^3	F. Zufelt	6.85
Bowsprit	115	9	2	1^h	2^1	4^h	5½	R. Howell	7.80
Toy-Quay	109	8	4	3^h	5^h	5½	6^2	H. Claggett	25.95
Lord Bart	112	4	7	9½	9^1	8^3	7^6	J. nBoyle	57.20
Ship Signal	118	5	3	7½	6^2	7½	8½	G. Acosta	7.50
The Duck	110	10	5	$5^{1½}$	$7^{1½}$	$9^{1½}$	9^1	H. Trent	8.65
Darting Orphan	112	1	8	4^h	3^2	10'	10^3	F. Remerscheid	104.30
Yankee Victory	112	2	12	12	12	11^3	11^5	M. Fator	122.75
Latest	115	7	6	11^6	11^3	12	12	W. Balzaretti	78.20

$2 Mutuels Paid—Briarchal, $25.30 straight, $9.70 place, $6.20 show. Romney Rex, $5.50 place, $3.70 show. Go Wes, $4.40 show. Total mutuels...... $54.80

Briarchal at home in the going and never far back, was forced to lose ground when improving her position, bumped Romney Rex in the stretch wore down the leaders swiftly and won with something left. Romney Rex slow to begin and well back early moved forward through the field, met interference in the drive, recovered quickly and finished strongly. Go Wes raced Bowsprit into submission during the opening five sixteenths, established a big advantage swiftly and stopped badly under pressure. June Quest raced through the field. Bowsprit tired. Toyquay was unable to keep up. Lord Bart had no misshaps. Ship Signal and Darting Orphan could not keep up. The Duck showed little.

SECOND—SIX FURLONGS. CHUTE. FOR THREE-YEAR-OLDS AND UP. Claiming. Purse $1,200. Value to winner $850, second $200, third $100, fourth $50. Went to post at 2.34. Off at 2.34½. Start good from gate. Won driving, place same. Winner b g 3, by Brevity-Pantica. Owned by J. KELLY. Trained by G. KELLEY. Time 23 1-5, 48 2-5, 1.15.

	Wt.	Post	St.	¼	½	Str.	Fin.	Jockeys	Odds
Abrupt	110	5	7	5^2	5^3	3^3	1^1	H. Claggett	$5.05
Little Bolo	120	2	9	7^3	6^3	$4^{1½}$	2^n	F. Zufelt	1.50
La Reinette	112	6	6	2^h	$1^{1½}$	1^h	3^4	T. Luther	5.70
The Thane	111	9	2	4^1	3^1	2^2	4^h	P. Keiper	5.05
Walter Haight	116	10	3	$8^{1½}$	7^2	7^6	5^3	D. Scocca	14.15
Pal	110	11	1	$3^{1½}$	$4^{1½}$	5^2	6^6	J. Breen	10.70
All Whims	105	3	4	1^h	2^h	6½	7^1	W. Rudert	35.45
Wintime	103½	1	11	11	10^1	9^2	$8^{1½}$	J. Tammaro	100.05
Praetor	114	7	10	10^4	9^4	10^6	9^2	R. Sisto	108.10

Continued on Page 33, Column 4.

Inundation Of D. C. Is Feared

(Picture on Page 3.)

The worst flood in the history of the Potomac river valley was raging through Maryland river towns and smashing down toward Washington yesterday, with the crest of swirling water 50 feet above normal at one point.

Scores of families have been driven from their homes in the lowlands as the Potomac and the Shenandoah river, which flows into the Potomac, burst through their banks at many places.

RAIL TRAFFIC HALTED

Rail traffic is halted, highways are blocked and the flood is battering at four major bridges over the Potomac.

Near Point of Rocks, Md., the family of Harry Smallwood, consisting of the father, mother and six small children, was rescued from their home on Heather Island, in the middle of the Potomac, by State Patrolman Harry A. Holsinger, Jr., and a civilian, Ralph G. Kline. The two men made three trips to the island in a canoe to bring the marooned family to safety.

40 COTTAGES WRECKED

At Harper's Ferry, W. Va., two houses were swept away by the flood and 40 small cottages at a summer resort on the Shenandoah river near Harper's Ferry were reported destroyed.

Crest of the river still was to reach the Maryland towns on the lower Potomac as the flood-swollen Shenandoah poured a mighty cataract of water into the Potomac.

In Washington, preparations were made for coping with the highest water in years—higher than the record floods of 1936 and 1937.

50 FEET ABOVE NORMAL

Officials of the Weather Bureau's river and flood division said the flood was the worst in history on the Shenandoah. At Riverton, Va., the highest water ever recorded was in March, 1936, when the record was 37.5 feet above normal.

Yesterday, at Riverton, the water stood at 50 feet above normal.

This torrent had made a vast

Continued on Page 2, Column 7.

The Baltimore News-Post today is printed in
3 Sections
Be sure you get the complete newspaper.

U. S. Positions On Isle Shelled By Artillery; Foe Lands New Troops

By JOSEPH A. BORS
International News Service Staff Correspondent.

WASHINGTON, Oct. 16.—Striking an ominous note, the Navy today announced that American positions on Guadalcanal "are now being shelled by enemy artillery," and disclosed that a large group of Nipponese warships are poised to strike from the Northern Solomons.

At the same time the Navy stated that U. S. motor torpedo boats have joined in the furious battle for the Southern Solomons and have reported one probable hit on an enemy cruiser.

SITUATION GRAVER

In view of the shelling, the situation appeared grave because until to date Nipponese forces have been unable to move in heavy weapons.

The communique said:

"A large number of enemy troops with equipment have been landed on Guadalcanal and our positions are now being shelled by enemy artillery on the island."

According to latest battle reports, however, the American forces as late as October 14 still were using their shelled airfield on the island to blast the oncoming Japanese land, sea and air forces. The Navy said:

JAP SHIPS MASSING

"During the same afternoon (October 14) Navy and Marine Corps dive bombers, with fighter escort, left Guadalcanal and made two attacks on the enemy transports which were approaching the island. Minor damage was reported and one U. S. fighter was lost."

In addition to the shelling and the landing of large enemy forces, the following paragraph in the communique appeared very ominous:

"A large group of enemy ships has been observed in the Buin-Faisi area near Shortland Island, in addition to the various units in the Southeastern Solomons."

Since Shortland Island is roughly 260 miles northwest of Guadalcanal, these ships could move quickly into the battle area to support forces now blasting U. S. Marines and Army troops on the vital Southern Solomons.

U. S. REINFORCING ISLE

Mention of U. S. torpedo boats in action for the first time indicated that American forces are moving in more reinforcements, but there was no mention of possible support by the U. S. Pacific fleet.

A second night shelling by Japanese vessels of American positions on the island was reported by the Navy. It was this attack on the night of October 14-15 that torpedo

Continued on Page 2, Column 1.

Russ Fall Back In North Stalingrad

MOSCOW, Oct. 16—(U. P.).—Soviet troops today fell back in the battered streets of a North Stalingrad industrial section under crushing Nazi pressure applied in the third day of what the Red Army organ, Red Star, called the "decisive battle of Stalingrad."

(BACKGROUND NOTE: The German high command claimed a Nazi tank division broke through to the Volga on a two-mile front in a smashing night attack on the Dzerzhinsky tractor factory.)

'SEVERAL STREETS' YIELD

Reports from Stalingrad said that "several streets" in the Northern industrial section had been yielded to the Nazis and that the Germans were rapidly sending more men and armored machines "into the gap."

The German Luftwaffe was said to be supporting the Nazi attack with a block-by-block bombardment described by Soviet reports as even heavier than the famous Nazi dive-bombing attack which obliterated the heart of Rotterdam during the campaign in the west.

Russian fighter planes, heavily outnumbered, shot down 14 German planes in an attempt to protect the Red Army ground forces.

EVERY TWO HOURS

The German attacks were coming over in waves about every two hours, front dispatches said. Between sunrise and sunset yesterday seven major land thrusts were repulsed, but the Russian troops were forced to fall back under the pressure of admittedly superior enemy forces.

HELP US FIND 'MISS VICTORY' OF BALTIMORE

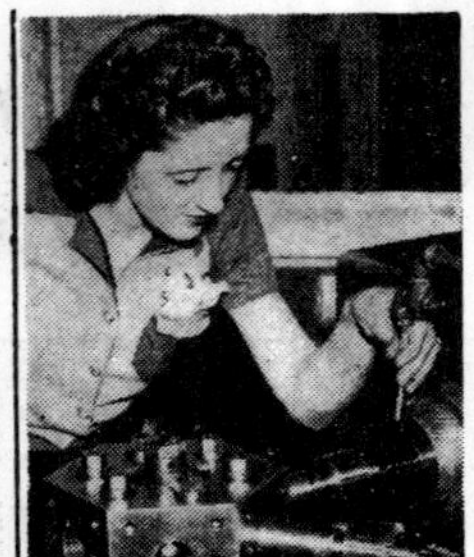

MINNIE DELLAMALVA
Operating a turret lathe is a cinch to girls who try it.

Somewhere in a Baltimore war-production plant and filling a vital role in America's all-out effort to win the war is a girl worker, typical and symbolic of the nation's new feminine army of the home front.

She may be operating a machine or keeping records of other workers.

We want to find her, single her out as typical of all those young women who have left their homes, their peace-time jobs and recreational activities to take up where men have left off to go to war.

Help us find "Miss Victory" to compete for the national crown in Chicago soon!

Read today's announcement of the search.

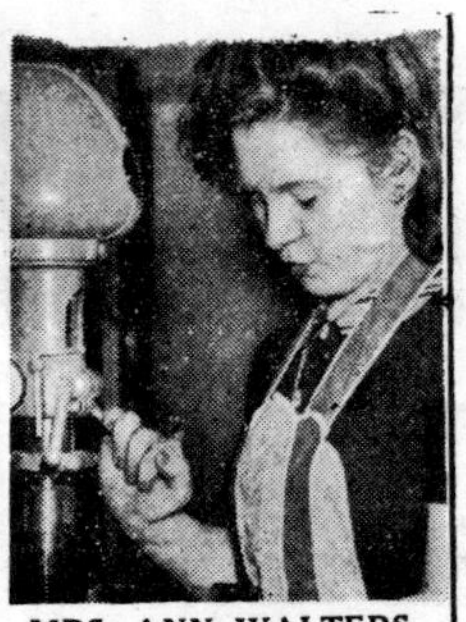

MRS. ANN WALTERS
Electric drills make tools of war, she handles one.

The News-Post Has the Largest Circulation of Any Evening Newspaper in the South

THE BALTIMORE NEWS-POST
AN INDEPENDENT NEWSPAPER

2ND FRONT PAGE
NEWS-POST HAS TWO FRONT PAGES DAILY

SATURDAY, OCTOBER 17, 1942

Girls Inspect Monster Tank

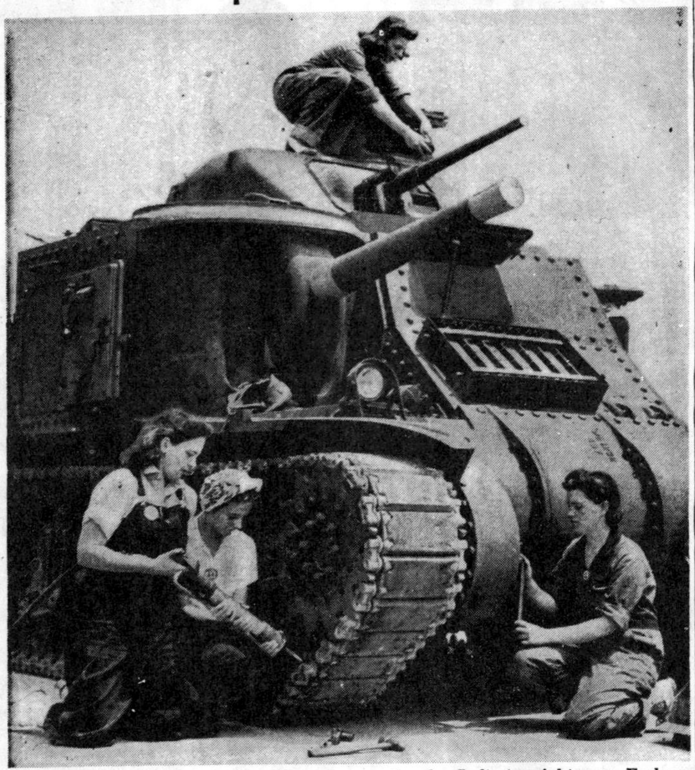

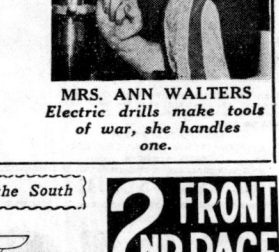

These powerful tanks look ponderous enough to the laymen, but trained girl war workers find their operation simple enough. Here are some "Miss Victory" girls putting final touches to a tank at the Aberdeen Proving Ground where more than 1,000 young women now are employed. Left to right are Earlye Brinkman, Havre de Grace; Ruth Gibson, Savage; Jean McMullen, Perryville, and perched on top inspecting the tank's cannon is Dorothy Chapin, of Richmond. Who will be Baltimore's typical worker—"Miss Victory."

'Miss Victory' Gets Crown December 7

Will Select Typical War-Plant Girl In Chicago

By ALDINE R. BIRD

Remembrance of Pearl Harbor on the anniversary of that treacherous attack will be the presentation of a typical American girl working in a war-production plant to the American people and their Axis enemies symbolic of the new spirit of victory.

She will be "Miss Victory of America" and will be crowned in Chicago on December 7.

In that nation-wide competition, a typical war worker from a Baltimore plant will take part with an equal chance to win the national crown and a coveted trip to the National Capital to meet high Government offidials.

TEST HERE NOV. 27

We're looking for "Miss Victory of Baltimore" right now!

Announcement of the date of the Chicago national finals was made here, coincident with the further announcement that the Baltimore winner will be chosen in a city wide contest among scores of war-production plants on Friday night, November 27.

Every girl who has gone into a war plant to help her country win the war is eligible to compete for the local crown and a $500 war bond.

Every war-production plant in the Baltimore area is eligible to stage its own contest among the girl and women employes and select its own candidates for the crown.

One candidate may be chosen for each 100 feminine workers in each plant, although this is a maximum figure allowed under the general rules and not a minimum requirement.

WAYS TO SELECT

The selections may be made on the basis of outright selection of the most typical worker in a plant by a board of judges chosen by the personnel management and employes' group, or by direct balloting, either with or without the sale of war stamps, as some plants will follow.

Where war stamps are to be sold to aid Uncle Sam's treasury, a voter would be required to buy a ten or twenty-five cent stamp in order to get one ballot. As many ballots could be obtained by each individual as stamps purchased.

POSTERS TO AID

The Baltimore competitions are expected to get seriously under way next week when attractive posters, patriotically designed and printed in the national colors, are distributed to the war plant bulletin boards.

They will contain the rules and directions for the contest within the plant.

Personnel managers are invited to write the Miss Victory Contest Editor for a supply of these posters if they have not already been contacted and arrangements made to obtain them.

Come on—let's find "Miss Victory of Baltimore!"

Excess Tire Sales Increase

Will Keep 'Em Rolling

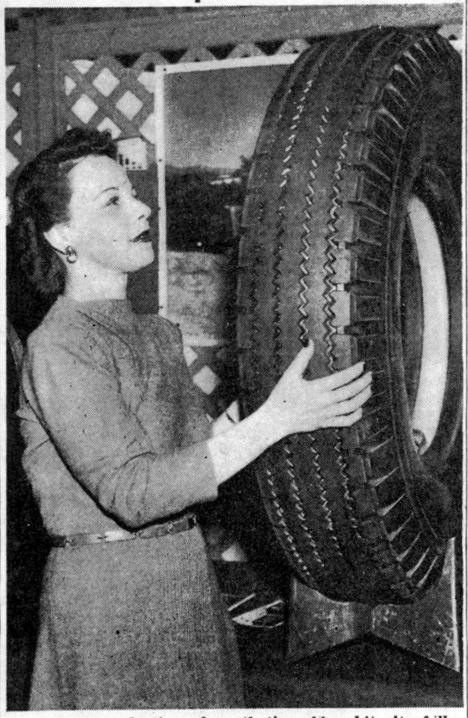

Once production of synthetic rubber hits its full stride, tires such as Miss Verna A. Lane, 4900 block Haddon avenue, is shown admiring, will keep vehicular traffic rolling, transportation experts said at a meeting held in the Emerson Hotel under auspices of the Baltimore Association of Commerce. This big tire was one of several synthetics shown at an exhibit set up in the hotel.

Movement Gaining Momentum After Slow Start On Thursday

Used-Tire Prices Announced By U. S.

WASHINGTON, Oct. 15—(I. N. S.).—Used tire ceiling prices in effect as the Government started buying all excess passenger-car tires today are as follows:

Size.	Maximum New Price.	First Category.	Second Category.	Third Category.	Fourth Category.
6.00-16	$14.75	$8.10	$6.65	$4.45	$1.50
6.25-16	$16.60	$9.15	$7.45	$5.00	$1.50
6.50-16	$17.90	$9.85	$8.05	$5.35	$1.50
7.00-16	$20.30	$11.15	$9.15	$6.10	$1.50
5.25-17	$13.55	$6.55	$5.35	$3.55	$1.50
5.50-17	$13.55	$7.45	$6.10	$4.05	$1.50

First category includes tires that retain 7/32 of an inch or more of tread design depth; second category, more than 3/32 inch but less than 7/32 inch of tread design depth; third category, all regrooved tires and tires that retain 3/32 inch or less of tread design depth; fourth category, worn smooth and usable as basic carcases for retreading or recapping.

Business in the sale of excess automobile tires to the Government tripled in volume in Baltimore yesterday, as collectors from the Railway Express Agency made between 25 and 30 calls for the tires, as against the collection of fewer than a dozen Thursday.

In addition, about a dozen motorists with more than five tires for each vehicle brought their own offers to the collection center at 208 East Franklin street and thirty-five calls offering the tires today were on file at the agency headquarters.

FIVE-TIRE LIMIT

Under the rubber conservation program each automobile owner is limited to five tires per car,. with the privilege of selling the excess equipment to the Government.

After November 22, when gasoline rationing becomes effective all over the nation, holders of more than five tires per car will become ineligible for rationing allotments, it was pointed out.

Under the general plans the Railway Express Agency has been empowered to accept the surplus tires for sale to the Government.

The tires acquired Thursday were shipped to a warehouse in Wilmington, Del., Mr. Dorsey said, because the Government so far has failed to find storage facilities here.

MUST REG'STER TIRES

Before the November dead line each motorist will be required to certify to the number of tires in his possession and to give the tire serial numbers, Office of Price Ad ministration officials have pointed out.

This certification will be necessary before the driver is allowed gasoline rations. Punishment for making false statements to the Government involves a possible $10,000 fine, or ten years' imprisonment, or both.

(Picture on Page 28)

Fine Boy, 18, For Ration Books

A second eighteen-year-old youth was sentenced here in Federal Court in connection with the recent illegal disposition of gasoline ration books at a local defense plant.

Milton Ecolono admitted having received two books, admittedly stolen by another boy previously sentenced, with the intention of selling them.

Ecolono was fined $200 and costs by Judge William C. Coleman, the money to be paid in installments from his own earnings. He was put on probation until he is twenty-one.

Richard F. Curley, Jr., a co-defendant, recently was fined $300 on similar conditions.

Visit Baltimore's Newest and Coziest
Chinese-American Restaurant
Good Food—Courteous Service
LUNCHEON 11 A. M. to 2.30 P. M. 45c | DINNER 5 P. M. to 8.30 P. M. 55c
K-K Chinese American Restaurant
525 N. Howard St.
Opposite Stanley Theatre

RED STAR BUSES
To EASTERN SHORE AND DEL-MAR-VA
Leave 7.50 A. M., 12.50 P. M., 5.50 P. M.
Howard & Lombard Sts. PLaza 4008

KEITH'S ROOF— SPECIAL DANCE MONDAY
Charlie Spivak & Band
BUY TICKETS IN ADVANCE & SAVE 25c EACH!

Newcomers—You Are Invited To Hear
MISS LETITIA STOCKETT
Speak on "Baltimore Town"—YWCA
Saturday, Oct. 17—10:30 A. M.

Jr. Army Still Faces Scrap Problem

ATTENTION—JUNIOR VICTORY ARMY!

Baltimore's 20,000,000 pounds of scrap metal and rubber which recently you were instrumental in having collected isn't a drop in the bucket compared with the tonnage still available here—and, more important, what our war plants need.

Even the huge collection didn't compare favorably with a lot of other cities on the basis of population—for instance, Lynchburg, Va., collected nearly 13,000,000 pounds and they have only 44,541 persons living there.

KEEP BALL ROLLING

That means we have got to keep the ball rolling here in Baltimore!

It also means that you boys and girls have another job to do—help bring in some more.

We're not going to wait for another city-wide collection arrangement, because transportation is a big problem. What we're going to do is to get it in small lots to the filling stations and automobile agencies displaying "Official Salvage Depot" posters.

'SPOTTER' PROCEDURE

If you find some scrap metal or rubber and you are unable to move it, or if there is an iron fence or some other emplacement you think is no longer needed and might be turned in by the owner, fill in the "Scrap Spotter" report blank and notify the Chief Adjutant.

In turn, the War Production Board will be notified to get it!

Miss Victory Of Baltimore Rules

Here are the rules for the MISS VICTORY OF BALTIMORE contest, the time of which will be announced later:

1. Each plant engaged in war work, which employs 100 or more girls, is eligible to compete. The maximum number of entrants selected from each plant will be at the ratio of one to each 100 girls employed. The number of entrants is to be determined by the plant, provided it does not exceed the maximum allowed.

2. Contestants shall include girls and women of any age, single or married, working in war industries, who are regularly employed. They must have good attendance records and must be approved for honesty and efficiency by their employers.

3. Each plant may select its candidates in any manner the management and employes choose, so long as candidates qualify in accordance with Paragraph 2. The manner of selection may be by ballot within the shop or by a jury of executives and workers.

4. Contestants from each qualified plant shall be eligible to participate in finals for the selection of MISS VICTORY of BALTIMORE. The jury will be made up of important Government and war production officials, women interested in patriotic activities, and possibly an artist.

5. Selections are to be made on the basis of the candidate's record, including the quality of her work, and secondarily on her activity in outside patriotic programs such as the Red Cross, USO, civilian defense, service men's canteen work. The sacrifices she has made in giving up normal life for war work will also count.

6. Decisions of the judges in plant contests and in the final shall stand. In case of ties, duplicate awards will be given.

How To Get Your 'Key Kans' For Metal Drive

A number of attractive "Key Kans" for use in collecting keys for the war effort are available to members of the Junior Victory Army.

If you want to do your part in this big nation-wide key salvage campaign, call at the office of the Chief Adjutant, Hearst Production Building, Pratt and Commerce streets.

Keys contain nickel and other vital metal to make guns, ships and other war machinery. Do your part to help arm the boys on the fighting fronts.

Get your "Key Kans" today!

10 Get Terms In Relief Fund Cases

Ten persons were sentenced to six months, each, in the House of Correction yesterday after pleading guilty before Judge J. Abner Sayler in Criminal Court to indictments charging them with obtaining money from the Maryland Unemployment Commission through misstatements. Assistant State's Attorney Morton E. Rome, told the court they obtained funds varying from $1 to $124 last March.

Warns Of Gamble On Synthetic Tire Output

A warning to motorists not to gamble on rapid production of synthetic rubber to meet their need for tires in 1942 or 1943 was sounded here by Edward K. Atkinson, addressing a meeting of transportation co-ordinators, Maryland Committee on Wartime Transportation, and the Baltimore Association of Commerce in the Emerson Hotel.

After reviewing all angles of the current tire situation, he declared:

"If we meet our production schedule on Buna S and Butyl, there will be a total of 369,000 tons of rubber available for passenger cars sometime in 1944. Then and only then will we be able to relax our restriction on speed limits, mileage and driving habits.

WAY TO CONSERVE

"In the interim, if we are wise we will conserve. We will attempt to make three-year-tires out of one-year tires, and this can be done."

And the way to conserve tires, Mr. Atkinson said, is to drive not more than 30 miles an hour; beware of under-inflation and have tires "cross-switched" every 2,500 miles.

'BUTYL' TIRES

Exhibits included products of the major oil and rubber companies. Attracting unusual attention were the tires made of the synthetic rubber "buna S" and "butyl."

The transportation experts, through motion pictures and exhibitions of actual tires were shown the condition of a synthetic tire after 10,000 miles and one after 19,000 miles of service.

The grooves were still visible in both tires, but the one with 19,000 miles service was almost smooth.

TIRES OF WOOD

Wooden tires, made of layers of oak, bolted together and assembled on steel centers, attracted considerable attention. These tires, however, the experts were told, may be good for emergencies.

Pupils' Defense Work In Survey

School officials have decided to make a survey to determine the number of students in junior and senior high schools of the city who are working in defense industries and other plants, it was announced today.

The survey is to be made by the Board of School Commissioners in co-operation with the Child Bureau of the Federal Department of Labor.

The purpose of the survey is to ascertain how many hours the students are devoting to school work and how much time to employment in industry. Also, it is planned to determine the effect of outside employment on the students' school work.

Jail Sentence For Too Much Voting

Convicted on charges of unlawfully representing himself as an employe of the Board of Supervisors of Elections and of voting more than once in the primary election September 8, George Parsons, 500 block Scott street, yesterday was sentenced to 10 days in jail by Judge W. Conwell Smith in Criminal Court. Parsons was identified as a South Baltimore Democratic executive.

The Baltimore News-Post and Sunday American are offering weekly cash prizes for news tips and amateur photos. Best tip gets $25, the next best gets $10, and the next 15 get $1 each. For each amateur photo published $3 will be paid. Phone news-tip editor, Lexington 0100 (Lex. 4165 midnight to 6.30 A. M.). Rush news photos to picture editor.

BOOGIE WOOGIE — By Michael Berry

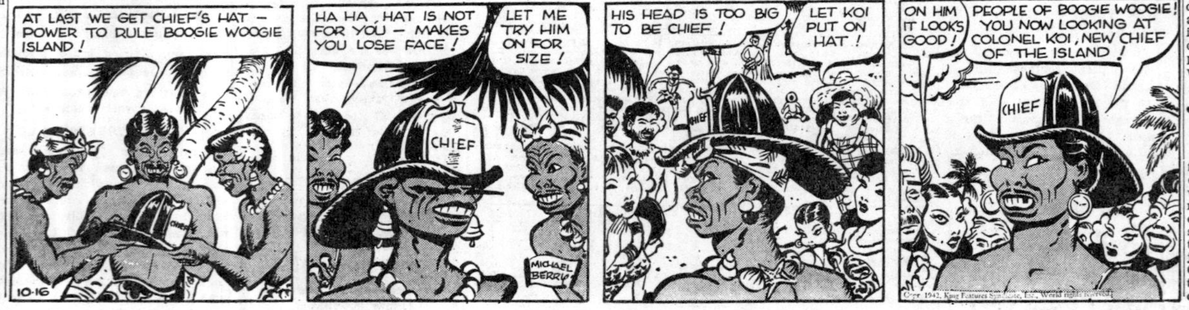

Starts Monday!
Meet the War's Outstanding Soldier-Cartoonist
PRIVATE BREGER ABROAD
The war's funniest soldier—the artist whose cartoons have made millions laugh—now sends you sketches from overseas where he is an army sergeant traveling with the United States fighting forces. Don't miss this new feature!
Starts Monday *In The* NEWS-POST

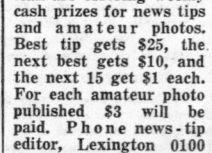

Yale Grid Team Arrives For Navy Game

ON THE LINE

Sports Heroes Bolster Technical Training Force | **Physical Fitness Of Men Important**

By BOB CONSIDINE

NEW YORK, October 16.

FOR EVERY PILOT trained by the United States Army, the Technical Training Command must turn out from 10 to 20 mechanics and technicians.

To "sustain the wings," as the Technical Training Command motto goes, these men must perform their difficult duties under tremendous pressure in theatres of war ranging from fog-shrouded Alaska and ice-bound Iceland to the metal-blistering heat of Egypt and India.

The training of many of them, including the radio men, is a confining task calling for bewildering precision. Their physical condition is an important part of the story. They must be kept fit physically to remain sharp mentally.

"Alertness is the reflection of a sound mind in a sound body," Major General Walter R. Weaver, commanding general, has said. And the gargantuan job of achieving mass alertness was turned over to Lieut. Col. C. L. Brownell, a World War I, flier who became one of the country's outstanding physical education authorities during the years of peace.

Colonel Brownell authored or co-authored 21 books on health and physical education, taught at Columbia and lectured all over the world. But the "genial man is as far from a classroom theorist as you could find. He wanted to become

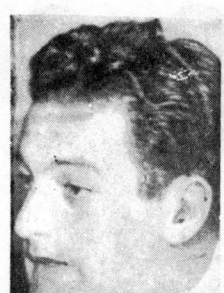

SID LUCKMAN

a big league ball player and got as far as Class AA. Among his products in physical education are Ethan Allan, Big Bill Edwards, Sid Luckman and Al Baggett, who later coached the skyscraping West Texas State basket ball team.

As late as 1938 we had only one technical training school. It was at Chanute Field, Illinois, and taught only three subjects. A year ago we had about a dozen. Now there are more than 100 schools all over the country turning out scores of mechanics and technicians who'll keep the pilots flying and the myriad of nautical gadgets working. We cannot say how many men are involved, but we can tell you that the Technical Training Command now is the largest educational system in the country. Its food bill, by the bye, is a half a million dollars a day.

Baseball And Football Aces Do Bit

Into this work has gone a vast number of the country's sports heroes. Baseball has contributed Lieut. Hank Greenberg and Lieut. Hugh Mulcahy; Lieut. Billy Hitchcock, Corporal Uhle and Jimmy Walkup, all former Detroit Tigers; Pvt. Milt Galatzer, formerly of the Indians and Reds; Pvt. Davey Short, White Sox rookie, and Pvt. Ray Poole, who was just getting started with Connie Mack. The sons of George Sisler and Jess Willard are also present.

The Technical Training Command could not put an elegant football team on the field—if Colonel Brownell did not believe it is more important to foster a rounded program than stress and glorify a few top men. Headquarters has Lieut. Paul Christman, the Bears' great end, is en route to a lieutenancy, via Officers' Candidate School; and also present are Pvt. Archie Kodros, of the 1939 Michigan team; Lieut. Derace Moser, Texas A. and M.; Lieut. Jim Purvis, Purdue's All-America; Lieut. Banks McFadden, Clemson's and Brooklyn's pride; Pvt. Tarzan White, of Alabama and the Giants Pvt. Park Myers, captain of Texas' 1940 team, and many others.

Track has provided Lieut. Ray Barbuti, Lieut Chuck Fenske and Lieut. Allan Tomlich. Basket ball: Capt. Al Jaggert; Lieut. Sid Glickman, Brooklyn College's 10-letter man, and Chuck Hyatt, who was an All-America at Pitt and later star and coach of the crack Phillips 66 team.

Capt. Jeff Dickson, "the Tex Rickard of Europe," and Lieut. Steve Hamas are boxing's main contributions, and from the highly important, but generally overlooked, field of swimming have come Lieut. Marshall Wayne, Carmine Orsini and Hy Schwartz. Lieut. Col. Fred W. Siebert, of the Command, is a former national fencing champion. Golf has provided Lieut. Bud Ward and Dick Chapman and Private Abbott. Tennis has come through with men like Lieut. Frank Shields and Pvt. Bitsy Grant.

Cogs In Machinery Of Great Air Force

These stars work, of course, and they work hard. Some will be detailed to physical education work at scattered schools; most of them will go into the multitude of technical posts that have sprung up in and around the makings of the greatest air force in history. Like the flabbiest civilian admitted to this training, the star athletes must be rebuilt on a rounded sports basis. In the Command it is more important to be able to swim 10 feet under a batch of blazing oil, with full equipment, than it is to be able to hit a 430-foot home run...

It is the feeling of General Weaver that a "technical wizard without the stamina to demonstrate his skill is scarcely more valuable than the physical giant who is a technical moron." Colonel Brownell's resulting program won't make the sports page headlines. He declined, for instance, to release Plazman to play with the All-Army football team. But he is building men, fine men. He is building well the whole astounding groundwork without which we could have no fliers.

Returns

GIL SCHUERHOLZ

This veteran soccer player will swing back into action Sunday when the Baltimore Americans face the New York Americans in an American League game at Bugle Field.

Suggests Boxing Titles Be Frozen

LOS ANGELES, Oct. 16—(A.P.)—Jerry Giesler, as chairman of the California Boxing Commission, has established something of a reputation for espousing the cause of the underdog, but today he finds himself going to bat for the champions.

Giesler, in private life a prominent lawyer, sees no reason why a fighting man, when he swaps the padded mitt for a rifle and goes off to the wars, should find himself in danger of being deprived of whatever championship boxing baubles he may have picked up along the way.

So Giesler has proposed to Abe J. Green, New Jersey, president of the National Boxing Association, that the titles of any champions now in the armed services or who enter them subsequently, be "frozen" for the duration.

Obviously, Giesler is fearful of promotional skullduggeries to take advantage of the boxing champs who enter the services and so are unable to defend their crowns.

Kansas Teams Try Eight-Man Football

LECOMPTON, Kan., Oct. 16—(A.P.)—And now it's eight-man football. Rossville and Lecompton High School teams will try it tonight. The 11-man variety was originally scheduled, but injuries forced Lecompton to forfeit. The eight-man idea will be used as an experiment. The line-up will include a center, two guards, two ends and three backs.

BALTIMORE NEWS-POST SPORTS

SATURDAY, OCTOBER 17, 1942   33

Yale Backfield In Action

BLUE ROMPERS—With one exception this is the backfield that Yale will start against Navy today at the Stadium. From left to right above are Ed Taylor, left halfback; Jim Potts, quarterback; Tim Hoopes, right halfback, and John Ferguson, fullback. Potts is injured and his place in the starting line-up will be taken by Sam Scovil. Associated Press Photo.

Phila. Grid Fans Get Army-Navy Priorities

By N. P. CLARK

As far as Philadelphia is concerned, you can stop worrying about where the Army-Navy football game might be moved to this year. The Quaker City insists the classic will stay put where scheduled—in its Municipal Stadium.

According to the Philadelphia Chamber of Commerce, it has been assured by both Annapolis and West Point that the service academies' authorities are going right ahead with their plans with no thought of being forced to shift the site due to transportation difficulties.

There is to be a change in disposition of the tickets, however. Priorities on the precious pasteboards are being given Philadelphians and an attempt will be made to sell out the vast Stadium's 102,000 seats in the home town alone.

The Philly Chamber of Commerce has announced that it has been notified by Army and Navy officials that all requests for tickets from Philadelphians will be filled before any applications will be considered from other localities. If the Quakertown citizens can fill their own bowl, therefore, every one else in other cities will get left.

Gophers Use Soph Gridmen

MINNEAPOLIS, Oct. 16—(I.N.S.)—Three sophomores were listed today for starting positions in the Minnesota backfield against Nebraska tomorrow. They are: Joe Silovich, at left half for Bill Daley; Dick Luckemeyr, at right half for Herman Frickey, and Bob Sandberg, at quarterback for Bill Garnaas. The three regulars were benched by injuries.

Injuries Hit Tiger Eleven

PRINCETON, N. J., Oct. 16—(I.N.S.)—Princeton's coach, Tad Wieman, was chanting the "infirmary blues" today after being informed that three of his players will be unable to start against Penn tomorrow and that a fourth is available only for limited duty.

Men out because of injuries are: Dave Marshall and John Heath, halfbacks, and Charley Brown, center. Slated for light duty is George Franke, freshman fullback from Baltimore who made the Princeton touchdown against Navy.

LAUREL CHARTS

Continued from Page 1.

	Wt.	Post	St.	¼	½	¾	Fin.	Jockeys	Odds
San Stefana	112	3	8	6h	9	8½	10h	W. Balzaretti	53.90
Conduct	111	4	5	11	11	11	11	M. Fator	45.60

$2 Mutuels Paid—Abrupt, $12.10 straight, $5.50 place, $3.40 show. Little Bolo, $3.60 place, $2.70 show. La Reinette, $4.10 show. Total mutuels..........$31.50. Abrupt slow to reach his best stride, improved his position on the outside, responded to strong urging when wearing down the leaders and drew clear at the end. Little Bolo well back early, raced forward through the field and finished strongly. La Reinette was rushed forward between horses to subdue All Whims and attained a clear lead, was put to strong urging when challenged and tired. The Thane was caught in hand when outrun, came fast when called upon and weakened under pressure. Walter Haight lost much ground. All Whims had good speed for a half mile. Pal quit.

THIRD—ABOUT TWO MILES. FOR THREE-YEAR-OLDS AND UP. CLAIMING. Steeplechase. Purse $1,000. Value to winner $700, second $150, third $100, fourth $50. Went to post at 3:00½. Off at 3:00½. Start good from flag. Won easily, place driving. Winner, b. g. 7, by Exeter-Tantarn. Owned and trained by F. BOSLEY, JR. Time 4.26 2-5.

	Wt.	Post	St.	6	8	12	13	Fin.	Jockeys	Odds
Rougemount	146	1	1	1½	1½	1h	1m	Mr. J. Bosley	77.25
aGreenwich Time	141	4	2	2h	2½	2½	2½	W. Leonard	6.50
Baris	141	7	9	7h	5½	3m	3½	W. Owens	12.55
Star Bramble	137	10	10	5h	4½	4½	4½	E. A. Russell	11.35
African Boy	138	9	5	4h	7m	5½	5m	S. O'Neill	5.10
Speed Demon	151	5	7	6h	2½	7m	6h	Mr. J. R. Harrison	8.30
Brown Prince III	145	3	6	10	10	9	7m	F. C. McKay	16.55
Lone Gallant	148	8	4	2m	6h	6m	8	A. Greco	23.85
Massa	151	2	3	3½	3h	2m	8h	fell	G. Walker	24.60
Black Ned	148	6	5	4m	4½	pulled up		J. Penrod		9.50

aJack Grabosky and Mrs. Frank M. Gould entry.

$2 Mutuels Paid—Rougemount, $16.50 straight, $6.20 place, $5.60 show. Greenwich Time, $4.50 place, $4.00 show. Baris, $6.80 show. Total mutuels............$43.60. Rougemount took command at the start, held away steadying restraint, increased his advantage when roused and was eased up while holding a decisive advantage. Greenwich Time never far back, moved forward after the eighth brush and responded well. Baris moved forward in steady fashion. Star Bramble came from well back. African Boy finished under strong pressure. Speed Demon tired after improving his position. Lone Gallant was done after six furlongs. Massa fell at the thirteenth brush. Black Ned was pulled up after the eleventh brush.

FOURTH—SIX FURLONGS. CHUTE. FOR TWO-YEAR-OLDS. ALLOWANCES. Purse $1,500. Value to winner $1,000, second $300, third $150, fourth $50. Went to post at 3:31½. Off at 3:32. Start good from gate. Won driving, place same. Winner, c. 2, by Chance Sun-Hildrum. Owned by M. MARMORSTEIN. Trained by J. McGEE. Time 23, 47 4-5, 1.14 2-5.

	Wt.	Post	St.	¼	½	Str.	Fin.	Jockeys	Odds
Castleman	118	3	5	1½	1½	1½	1½	S. Young	$7.55
Little Wizard	115	4	3	5	4½	3h	2n	R. Siatt	6.50
Alacyon	115	2	7	7	6½	4½	3½	F. Zufelt	7.50
Halberd	118	1	1	1½h	1½	3½	4n	G. Woolf	11.44
Blenhour	107	6	6	6	4½	5h	5½	St. Claggett	20.85
Gallant Witch	115	7	2	3½	5	6½	6n	A. Greco	29.10
Jamesborough	115	5	4	2n	7	7	7	W. Mann	2.10

$2 Mutuels Paid—Castleman, $17.10 straight, $6.10 place, $4.50 show. Little Wizard, $7.00 place, $4.60 show. Alacyon, $4.90 show. Castleman slow to begin and attended early, came to the inside approaching the stretch, responded to strong urging when wearing down Little Wizard and drew clear near the end. Little Wizard factor from the start and under steading restraint for three eighths, moved to the front when Halberd drifted out entering the stretch, alternated a clear lead swiftly was unable to hold the winner back. Alacyon safe. Latter came from well back and on the outside. Halberd opened up a clear lead rapidly and tired after drifting out entering the stretch. Blenhour and Gallant Witch were outrun. Jamesborough had speed.

FIFTH—MILE AND A SIXTEENTH. FOR THREE-YEAR-OLDS AND UP. CLAIMING. Purse $1,500. Value to winner $1,000, second $300, third $150, fourth $50. Went to post at 3.58. Off at 3:58½. Start good from gate. Won driving, place same. Winner, ch. c. 3, by American Flag-Traumerete. Owned by C. R. WATKINS. Trained by R. NIXON. Time 24 2-5, 49 3-5, 1.16 2-5, 1.43, 1.49 2-5.

	Wt.	Post	St.	¼	½	¾	Str.	Fin.	Jockeys	Odds
Flag Trumpeter	107	5	2	1½	1½	1½	1½	1m	Ross	$10.05
Get Off	120	(B. Thompson)$28.80	$15.30	$6.80						
Flying Double	120	(J. Westrope)			6.50	3.40				
Recap	120	(J. Westrope)				2.40				
Also Ran—Penn Royal, Nainsook, Tiptoes Tower, Valjohn, Third Rail, Smart Hombre, Fire Box, Ule, fEtf Queen, fAcquaintance and Henry Shot. tFeld.										

Daily Double—Single and Single paid $164.90 for $2.

SIXTH—MILE AND A SIXTEENTH. FOR FOUR-YEAR-OLDS AND UPWARD. CLAIMING. Purse $1,500. Value to winner $1,000, second $300, third $150, fourth $50. Went to post at 4.24½. Off at 4.24½. Start good from gate. Won driving. Place driving. Winner br g 7, by Mad Hatter-Brown Kill. Owned by A. C. BOSTWICK. Trained by M. DUPUT. Time, 23 4-5, 48, 1.13 2-5, 1.44 2-5, 1.51.

	Wt.	Post	St.	¼	½	¾	Str.	Fin.	Jockeys	Odds
Cacodemon	104	1	2	4h	3½	1h	1½	1m	W. Balzaretti	$7.60
Ginoca		111	3	4	3½	2½	A. Shelhamer	3.90		
Woodvale Lass	117	4	5	4½	4m	3½	3m	S. Young	3.75
Haste Back	116	5	1	1h	1½	2½	4	J. Berger	2.00
Busy Fingers	117	6	6	6½	6m	6h	6	C. Cardoza	7.90
Detroit Bull	117	2	3	2½	2m	4h	6	R. Risto	14.95
Yarn Spinner	112	7	7	7	7	7	7	R. Keiper	15.25

$2 Mutuels Paid—Cacodemon, $17.20 straight, $7.60 place, $5.90 show. Ginoca, $6.40 place, $4.10 show. Woodvale Lass, $3.60 show. Cacodemon opened up a commanding lead swiftly, held away under light restraint, responded to strong hand riding when tiring and held Ginoca safe. Latter never far back and steadied early, saved ground to the stretch and held on gamely. Woodvale Lass improved her position when ready and hung at the end. Haste Back had no mishaps. Busy Fingers was outrun.

SEVENTH—One mile and a sixteenth. Off at 4.51½. Time, 1.51.
Conquer, 107 (B. Thompson)........ $6.40 $4.20 $3.10
Justice Nap, 109 (H. Claggett)........   11.00   4.50
Nosy, 109 (P. Keiper)...............   4.50
Also Ran—Purport, Guerrilla, Indian Sea, James, Grand Court, Chaldar and Wire Me.

Keeneland Results

FIRST RACE—Six furlongs. Off at 3.29½. Time, 1.13 4-5.
Another Rules, 110
(D. Gorman)........ $2.80 $2.40 $2.40
Uncle Otho, 115 (F.A.Smith).. 2.80   3.40
Madwenz, 112 (F. Farrell)....   2.40
Also Ran—Shifting Wind, Blondie Jayne, Borsch and I Am In.

SECOND—Six furlongs. Off at 3.59. Time, 1.14 1-5.
Vay, 108 (G. Basham)..... $21.00 $8.20 $5.80
Gold Mike, 113 (J. Delucia) 4.40   4.20
Ackwell, 105 (D. Gorman)....   4.40
Also Ran—Bold Lucy, Hometown, Pairfort, Canigo, Lady Roulette.

THIRD—Six furlongs. Off at 4.30. Time, 1.14 2-5.
Lady Romery, 106
Sonny Casey, 111 (D. Scurlock) $5.20 $3.80 $3.80
Sidonia, 104 (D. Gorman).....   3.20 2.40
Also Ran—Mr. Nam, Loretta Rito, Dark Witch, Epola, Superose, Gay Kit, Daden.

FOURTH—Six furlongs. Off at 5.01¼. Time, 1.14.
Valdina Spiros, 105 (D. Scurlock).
Valdina Spiros, 105 (L. Barney) $6.40 $2.80 $2.85
War Gleam, 108 (D. Gorman)....   4.80
Also Ran—Mr. Eboney Bee, War Way, Miami Springs, fCoy Damsel, Ballie Star, Devil Dancer, Lady Salle and O K. Sugar, t—Field.

Daily Double Chart

Briarchal-Wintime........ $3,729.00
Little Bolo............. 77.60
All Whims...............1,398.30
Conduct..................2,237.40
Abrupt..................119.00
La Reinette............149.10
Praetor...............1,017.00
San Stefana..........1,243.00
The Thane...........233.00
Walter Haight.......588.70
Pal.................210.00

Elis Limber Up In Drill At Stadium

By N. P. CLARK

October 16.

Yale's football team arrived in Baltimore today and immediately took over the Stadium for a final workout in preparation for its game with Navy tomorrow on the same field.

Limbering-up exercises and signal drill were on the schedule. Following the workout Howie Odell, the new Eli head coach, took his squad to Gilman School, where the boys are to be quartered while in the city.

The Navy team, of course, will not come to town until time to dress for the game, as always.

Weighing the interest shown by the early ticket sales, and praying for good weather for the cautious fans who have waited to see what the day is going to be like, Naval Academy authorities see reason to anticipate a crowd of better than 40,000. If they reach it, that will double the attendance which turned out in New York's Yankee Stadium last week-end for the Navy-Princeton game.

MIDDIES TO MARCH

For one thing, the attractiveness of the game is enhanced by the fact that this will be one of the few times during the season that the Midshipmen will parade on a football field before the game. Some 2,000 Middies are to be brought from Annapolis by boat, railroad transportation being what it is. They will march from the dock to the Stadium and form on the field as in the past.

Not even the Army-Navy battle will have that this year, because of the travel difficulties. In fact, the service classic may be just another football game this time, as far as the public is concerned. It seems pretty certain by now that the game will not be played in Philadelphia's giant bowl and reports from Washington yesterday hinted that the big tiff would probably be played on Navy's field at Annapolis, cutting out all display.

To get back to tomorrow's rumpus, for closer followers this game represents a turning point in the season for somebody. Whether it will be the Yales or the Sailors is the item that's causing the commotion.

The Elis romped late in the game against Lehigh in their first game, then ran into a complete stone wall against powerful Penn. If sunk by the Navy, Odell's first season with the Blue will begin to take on a dismal hue.

ATTACK ERRATIC

The same goes double for Commander Johnny Whelchel and the Middies. Navy's attack has been highly erratic. Against William and Mary it could find no scoring punch. The next week it hit pay dirt almost at will to swamp Virginia. Last Saturday it short-circuited again against Princeton.

Whelchel and his assistants have been laboring mightily with that offense this week. The hope is that the boys show decided improvement tomorrow, what with Georgia Tech, Notre Dame and Penn coming up in the next three successive Saturdays. The result of all the work at Annapolis will get its tryout against Yale.

Along this line, Whelchel has dug down into the plebe ranks and promoted one Monty Johnson to varsity ranking during the week. Monty, it seems, has been exhibiting marked ability as a forward passer, or just why, the doctor ordered for the Sailors.

This newcomer stands as an uncertain quantity at best, of course, but his arm is almost sure to get its test if Yale gets too tough and that Navy attack bogs down again.

PLAYERS MISSING

Navy will not exactly be at full strength for the contest. Gene Goudie and Bob Wilcox, the two regular starting ends, are due to miss the game. Goudie is sidelined with an injury and Wilcox was called home by the unfortunate death of his father. Laboon and Channell or Strong may be the starters.

Yale, likewise, is not without its troubles. It is unlikely that its first-string center and captain, Spence Moseley, who has been a bulwark of the Blue line, will be able to play. And bother yet, Steve Stack, bulky tackle who has been another mainstay among the forwards.

Moseley's absence gives a chance to John "Wally" Warfield of Baltimore to operate before the home folks as Yale's starting center. Marion Deitrich, a large junior who won his way up from last fall's junior varsity, will replace Stack.

Something of a surprise in the starting backfield will be the presence of Ed Taylor at left half instead of the spectacular sophomore passer, Hugh Knowlton. Odell says that Taylor, a junior who was a regular tailback last year and not a bad passer himself, would add steadiness to the starting machine.

As a feature of the recruiting drive by the Baltimore Naval Recruiting Office, a large group of men will be sworn into the Navy in a ceremony on the field between the halves. The recruits will see the game as guests of the Navy Athletic Association and leave immediately after to go into service.

FEARS OVERCONFIDENCE

PHILADELPHIA, Oct. 16—(I.N.S.)—Penn's gridiron mentor, George Munger, is attempting to combat a feeling of overconfidence in his squad, top-heavy favorites over Princeton in their clash tomorrow.

PLUNGING TAR

Hume Ready To Face Yale Today

LINE BUCKER—Navy has been getting some fine running and plunging this season from Fullback Hillis Hume (above). And the Sailors expect him to furnish a lot more of it when they tackle Yale today at Baltimore Stadium. Hume, one of the stars of last year's hard-hitting plebe eleven, is also an expert faker in the ball-handling department.

Flood Closes Main Road To Laurel

Continued from Page 1.

moved to overhaul Romney Rex and Go'Wes. Joe Berger rode Briarchal. Briarchal was neglected in the wagering and was returned $25.30 straight. Needless to say, The Duck was a bunch but wound up ninth. The time was 1.16 2-5.

$119 DOUBLE

The hard-pressed form players suffered another reverse in the six furlongs second race when the 3-to-2 choice, Little Bolo, could do no better than second to Janet Kelly's Abrupt. La Reinette was third.

Abrupt kept the ball rolling for the longshot players, paying $12.10 straight and completing a $119 daily double payoff.

FIFTH—Six and one-half furlongs (chute). Off at 4.17. Time, 1.48.
Rebbina, 107 (C. Chaflin)..... $12.80 $5.40 $4.20
Sparrow Chirp, 102 (J. Gabriel)....   3.40 2.20
Apropos, 116 (E. Durando).....   4.20
Also Ran—Wanna Hypo, Valdina Zeel, Textile, Heddle Lass and Lady Lyonors.

SEVENTH—One mile and one-eighth. Off at 4.43. Time, 1.57.
Take It, 114 (A. Daniels)....$7.40 $3.80 $2.80
Hard Heart, 120 (J. D. Jeffords)...   4.20   3.00
Parfait Ann our, 115 (H. Adair)....   2.60
Also Ran—Warbridge, Gigi, Impressioniste, Whichaway, Sweepa, Knight's Duchess.

Rougemont Romps

The two-mile steeplechase, third race, was little more than a romp for John Bosley, Jr.'s, Rougemont. The seven-year-old gelding led all the way to beat Greenwich Time by about 50 lengths. Baris was third. Rougemont, sent into the lead immediately by Jackie Bosley, widened his lead as he went along. Rougemont was neglected in the betting and paid $77.25 straight after completing the two miles in 4.26 2-5.

Massa was the seventh but fell with G. Walker at the last jump. The gelding was dead-tired and well shaken when he came a cropper. Walker was uninjured.

The infield odds board again flashed a telephone number payoff after Max Marmorstein's Castleman had dashed to an easy score in the six furlongs fourth race. Castleman paid $17.10 to run the number of longshot winners here to 12 straight.

Runner-up to Castleman was Little Wizard, which set the pace but weakened badly through the sixteenth. Little Wizard beat Alacyon by a length and a half for the place. Mrs. Walter M. Jeffords highly regarded juvenile Halberd joined the beaten favorites when he finished far back at odds of 7 to 5.

KUZMA TO PLAY

ANN ARBOR, Mich., Oct. 16—(I.N.S.)—Michigan fans were assured today that the Wolverine ace, Tom Kuzma, will be in action against Northwestern tomorrow.

Rockingham Results

FIRST RACE—Six furlongs (chute). Off at 2.02. Time, 1.14.
(E. Robart)..... $48.60 $43.20 $15.80
Journey On, 116 (K. Dattilo).... 5.80   4.80
Bagrave, 116 (J. Dattilo)....   4.60
Also Ran—Sawbreaker, Carnarvon, Paul Scarlet, Buckets, Unionmill, Ketengea, My Lawyer, Bonifield, Alkyon.

SECOND—Six furlongs (chute). Off at 2.27½. Time, 1.14 1-5.
Ned's Guess, 113
(G. Seabo).......... $4.40 $3.20 $2.60
Merry Glow, 116 (J. Dattilo)....   4.80 3.20
Valdina Luster, 113 (G. McMullen)...   3.80
Also Ran—Free Boy, Miss Martha, Field Thoughts, Ho Hum, Ghost Hunt, Wild Javelin.

Daily Double—Don Pecos and Ned's Queen paid $334.80 for $2.00.

THIRD—Six furlongs (chute). Off at 2.54. Time, 1.14.
Keene Advice, 113
(G. Seabo).......... $32.20 $12.80 $6.00
Scarcity, 113 (W. Turnbull)..... 4.00 3.40
Desert Brush, 103 (E. Crowther)....   3.40
Also Ran—Ring Leader, Pneumatique, Valdina Caper, Tiara, Accuse Me, Caesar B. and Oleivick.

FOURTH—Six furlongs (chute). Off at 3.18½. Time, 1.13.
Equitation, 108 (C. Bates)$10.00 $5.20 $3.60
Foust Lance, 112 (G. Mara)....   7.00 4.20
dhLeroi Minn, 113 (A. Lynch)....   5.40
Also Ran—Shakey-Minn, Flaming Night, d-Madelite, 104 (E. Crowther)...
dAndwelle, 108 (D. Gorman)....
d—Field heat for third place.

FIFTH—Six and one-eighth miles. Off at 3.46. Time, 1.13.
Tetra Rock, 115
(J. Spanich)..... $9.60 $2.60 $2.40
Prairie Dog, 112 (G. Moore)...   2.20 2.20
Victory Bound, 115 (F. Millman)....   2.40
Also Ran—Billy Siker, Maemay, Daly Mischief and Bit o' Green.

SIXTH—One and one-sixteenth miles. Off at 4.17. Time, 1.48.
Rebbina, 107
(E. Chaflin).... $12.80 $5.40 $4.20
Sparrow Chirp, 102 (J. Gabriel)....   3.40   2.20
Apropos, 116 (E. Durando)....   4.20
Also Ran—Wanna Hypo, Valdina Zeel, Textile, Heddle Lass and Lady Lyonors.

SEVENTH—One mile and one-eighth. Off at 4.43. Time, 1.57.
Take It, 114 (A. Daniels)....$7.40 $3.80 $2.80
Hard Heart, 120 (J. D. Jeffords)...   4.20   3.00
Parfait Amour, 115 (H. Adair)....   2.60
Also Ran—Warbridge, Gigi, Impressioniste, Whichaway, Sweepa, Knight's Duchess.

Hawthorne Results

FIRST RACE—Six and one-half furlongs (chute). Off at 3.17½. Time, 1.22 2-5.
Bolle Servant, 110
(F. Grin).......... $32.20 $14.00 $7.00
Elms Kerry, 110
(C. MacAndrews)...   16.60   7.20
Bolina, 108 (R. Henson)....   3.40
Also Ran—Little Fluid, Blinky Ray, Alpine Mountaire, Cushing, Treecla and Gloroff.

SECOND—Six furlongs (chute). Off at 3.43. Time, 1.14.
Suprafage, 103 (R. Reeves)$15.60 $7.60 $4.20
Red Bud, 105 (R. Fragetti)....   4.60 3.40
Tedtel Call, 105 (J. Adair)....   4.20
Also Ran—Yourot, Ralph Deer, Bloesom Queen, Tecco, Calcutator, Dusty Miner, Seattle, Sumatra II and Grandee Boy.

Daily Double—Bolo Servant and Suprafage paid $208.40 for $2.00.

THIRD—Six furlongs (chute). Off at 4.07. Time, 1.13.
Scarlet Insco, 108
(R. Adair)..... $16.20 $7.00 $5.00
Darby Dallas, 108 (E. Guerin)..... 3.40 2.80
Rugged Rock, 109 (J. Wood)....   2.80
Also Ran—Sun Archer, Gallant Sew, Princely Gift, Comex, Auld Lang Syne, Brave Chance, Bezique, Monothra, Hasty Star.

FOURTH—Six and one-half furlongs. Off at 4.35½. Time, 1.20 4-5.
Cloudy Weather, 115
(E. Higley).......$6.40 $3.80 $2.80
Lady Ballet, 113 (H. Chinn)....   3.80 2.60
Brilliant Jr., Good Set, 112 (E. Guerin).....   3.00
Also Ran—Van Waxfield, Stray Chord, Post Ram-Wolville, Crumpet, Meadville and King Star.

FIFTH—Six and one-half furlongs (chute). Off at 4.58½. Time, 1.20 1-5.
Liberty Lad, 108
(J. Adair)......$18.40 $19.20 $7.40
Ann Glare, 111 (W. Reeves)....   3.60 3.20
Post Laureate, 110 (E. Guerin)...   3.20
Also Ran—Gummed Up, New Glory, Captain Fury, 100 (E. Reeves)....
Captain Fury, 100 (E. Reeves)....
boy.

5,000 Japanese Killed In Solomons

THE WEATHER

Slightly colder tonight, with lowest temperatures around 40 degrees in Northern and Western suburbs

Detailed Weather Report on Page 11

Read The Baltimore News-Post for complete, accurate war coverage. It is the only Baltimore newspaper possessing the three great wire services—

UNITED PRESS
INTERNATIONAL NEWS SERVICE
ASSOCIATED PRESS

THE BALTIMORE NEWS-POST

AN INDEPENDENT NEWSPAPER

The Largest Evening Circulation in the Entire South

10

VOL. CXLII.—NO. 3 | Entered as second-class matter at Baltimore Postoffice. | SATURDAY EVENING, NOVEMBER 7, 1942 | PRICE 3 CENTS

NAVY CONQUERS PENN, 7 TO 0

NOTRE DAME DEFEATS ARMY, 13-0

AXIS RETREATS 240 MILES

Navy Whips Penn By 7 To 0

Navy	7	0	0	0	7
Penn	0	0	0	0	0

PHILADELPHIA, Pa., Nov. 7—(A. P.).—Scoring on an 11-yard pass play, H. A. Hamberg to Ben Martin, in the first period, and staging two stirring goal-line stands in the final seconds of the game to protect its lead, Navy turned in one of the day's major football upsets today by defeating Penn before 74,000 spectators at Franklin Field, 7 to 0.

FIRST PERIOD

Navy was unable to make headway after taking the kickoff on its 32, and Odell ran Hume's punt back 11 yards to the Penn 41. Penn started a steady drive, with stiff hammering the line and Odell slanting off the tackles. The march reached the Navy 24 before bogging. Two pass plays being incom-

Continued on Page 13, Column 7.

Notre Dame Beats Army, 13 To 0

Army	0	0	0	0	0
Notre Dame	0	0	7	6	13

YANKEE STADIUM, New York, Nov. 7—(A. P.).—Held in check for two periods by an underdog Army team that failed to give ground when backed into its own territory, Notre Dame finally battered down the defense in the second half and defeated the Cadets, 13-0, in their twenty-ninth annual grid clash before a sellout crowd of 76,000 here today.

FIRST PERIOD

Army took the ball on its 35 when the opening kickoff went out of bounds and on the first play Woods fumbled and Dove recovered for Notre Dar on the Cadet 32. Bertelli entered the Irish lineup and after one incomplete pass he tossed a good one to Ashbaugh for

Continued on Page 13, Column 3.

Bertelli's Pass Fails Against Army

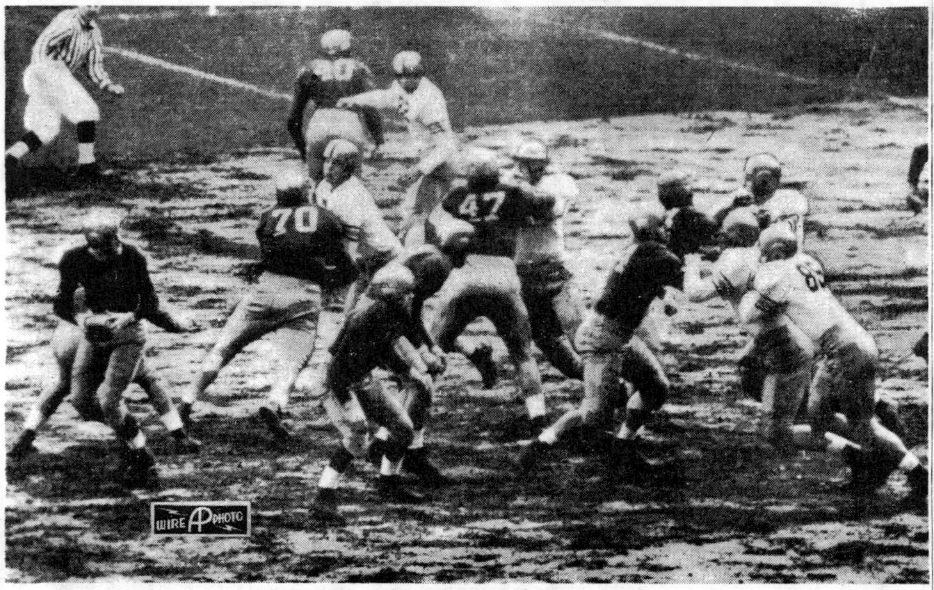

The Cadets were wide awake to Angelo Bertelli's forward passing in their game against Notre Dame in New York today. Here Army is shown breaking up a Bertelli toss in the first half. After faking a reverse play, Bertelli (48) tried to pass as the Irish threatened the Cadet goal line, only to have it knocked down by the alert West Pointers. Identifiable Notre Dame players are Rymkus (70), Livingstone (40), McBride (47). Army players, Crowell (83). Kelleher (85).

25,000 Left Of Army Braces For Stand At Libya Frontier Pass

LONDON, Nov. 7—(U. P.).—Berlin radio pointed out that Field Marshal Erwin Rommel, commander of the Axis North African armies, might have been taken prisoner. There were no Allied reports substantiating this German speculation which suggested that Germany was uncertain of his whereabouts.

CAIRO, Nov. 7—(U. P.).—The Imperial Eighth Army hurled armored forces, motorized infantry and swarms of planes tonight at the remnants of Marshal Erwin Rommel's once-proud Afrika Korps—possibly only 25,000 out of an original 140,000 now trying to brace for a stand at the Halfaya (Hellfire) Pass on the Libyan frontier, 240 miles west of the Alamein battle ground.

How many men Rommel had left in the Halfaya area could not be established. Already 20,000 prisoners have been counted in British hands. Rommel's desert casualties were estimated at something like another 20,000, and 75,000 Italian troops had been left far behind the swirling battleground, ready to surrender when the British can find time and men to round them up.

MAY NOT EVEN STOP

Rommel entered the desert battle with a maximum of 140,000 troops in the forward area. Unless he has been able to rush up reinforcements from the rear in large numbers, it was doubted that he had more than a division or two left to attempt another stand at Halfaya.

It appeared possible tonight that the bruised and beaten Axis forces might not even attempt to stand at Halfaya but would instead continue their headlong flight as deeply as possible into Libya in an effort to open up a gap between themselves and the pursuing Eighth Army.

Such a maneuver, however, may already be doomed to failure.

BRITISH PLAN CUT-OFF

Lieutenant General Bernard L. Montgomery has ordered that every attempt be made to cut off Rommel's retreat and it was believed he may have sent a hard-

Continued on Page 2, Column 1.

The Man the Japs Most Want to Kill, Bill Moran Now Has a Price On His Head Because He Pokes Fun at the Enemy. See His Cartoons and Read How They Make the Jap War Lords Squirm, In The American Weekly, the Magazine Distributed With Tomorrow's Baltimore American.—Adv.

Football Scores

STATE					
Hopkins	6	0			
Susquehanna	6	0			
W. Maryland	0	6			
Dickinson	0	0			
EAST					
Boston Coll.	7	7	7		
Temple U.	0	0	0		
Brown U.	0	7	7		
Holy Cross	14	0	0		
Bucknell	0	0	7	0	7
Gettysburg	0	0	6	0	6
Colgate	7	21			
Columbia	13	13			
Cornell	0	0	6		
Yale	0	7	0		
Delaware	0	12	0		
Swarthmore	7	0	0		
Duquesne	7	0	0	0	7
St. Mary's	0	7	0	0	7
Fordham	7	0	0	6	13
L. S. U.	0	0	6	20	26
Lehigh	7	6	0		
Muhlenberg	0	6	0		
Penn State	6	0	12	0	18
Syracuse	7	0	6	0	13
Rutgers	0	0	6		
Lafayette	0	6	6		
Princeton	0	0			
Dartmouth	6	0			

MIDWEST			
Pitt	0	0	7
Ohio State	21	20	6
Illinois	0	7	
Northwestern	0	0	
Indiana	0	0	
Minnesota	0	0	
Iowa	0	6	
Wisconsin	0	0	
Michigan	7	21	
Harvard	0	0	
Purdue	0	0	
Great Lakes	7	14	
SOUTH			
Davidson	0	0	7
N. Carolina	14	6	7
Georgia	28	7	27
Florida	0	0	0
Virginia	0	20	
W. & L.	0	7	
V. M. I.	0	0	0
Wake Forest	14	7	0
W. & M.	0	19	14
Randolph-M.	0	0	0
Auburn	7	7	
Ga. Pre-Fl.	41	6	
Citadel	0	0	
Furman	0	7	
Clemson	0	0	
George Wash.	0	0	

Continued on Page 13, Column 4.

Duke In Big Lead Over Maryland

Maryland	0	0	0
Duke U.	14	7	7

DURHAM, N. C., Nov. 7—(A. P.). Duke's thrice-beaten Blue Devils went against Maryland in a Southern Conference football game here today before 5,000 fans. The Old Liners had lost but one game in six starts.

FIRS TPERIOD

Duke got two breaks in the first period and quickly manufactured two touchdowns. Carver intercepted a long pass by Mont at midfield and returned to the Maryland 17. Two running plays got seven yards and Storer sprinted 10 yards at left end for the first score. Gantt kicked the point. Wright fumbled on his 29 to give the Dukes their second chance. Luper recovered and the first play went 15 yards. Davis went the rest of the way in two tries of four and ten yards over right tackle. Gantt again place-kicked the point and Duke led, 14 to 0.

SECOND PERIOD

On the second play of the second period Luper took a punt from Mont and scampered 72 yards behind excellent blocking across the goal line, but a clipping penalty

Continued on Page 13, Column 4.

Daily Double (Boy Soldier / Rough Honey) Paid $121.90

PIMLICO CHARTS

Copyright, 1942, by Triangle Publications, Inc. (Daily Racing Form.)

TRACK FAST.

FIRST RACE—MILE AND SEVENTY YARDS. FOR TWO-YEAR-OLDS. ALLOWANCES. Purse $1,000. Value to winner $700, second $150, third $100, fourth $50. Went to post at 1.27. Off at 1.27½. Start good from gate. Won handily, place driving. Winner b c 2, by Jamestown-Bird Flower. Owned by FLAMINGO FARM. Trained by W. C. KENNEDY. Time 23 2-5, 48, 1.13 4-5, 1.41 3-5, 1.45 4-5.

	Wt.	Post	St.	¼	½	¾	Str.	Fin.	Jockeys	Odds
Boy Soldier	115	10	8	7h	8²	7²	5¹	1¹½	S. Young	$3.60
Reigh Star	112	8	2	2²	2²	2¹	4h	2⅔	L. Ensor	16.05
Star Bien	115	1	3	3h	3h	3h	1h	3¹½	P. Keiper	4.40
Uncle Billies	115	4	4	8²	5½	4½	2h	4nº	F. Remerscheid	1.80
aKanlast	112	2	11	10½	10½	10¹	7½	5nº	R. Sisto	45.60
Tracelette	112	11	6	1²	1¹	1¹½	3h	6½	J. Deering	107.55
In the Night	107	6	5	5½	4h	5½	6¹	7¹	J. Tammaro	8.35
Far Sight	115	7	7	6¹	7½	6h	9¹	8²	L. Knapp	35.20
Camille	107	9	12	12	9h	9½	8¹½	9½	L. Barney	11.10
Dizzy Heights	115	5	1	4h	6h	8h	10⁶	10⁶	C. Rollins	22.50
aStop Harping	112	12	10	9¹	11³	11¹	11³	11³	D. Scocca	45.60
Yankee Victory	112	3	9	11²	12	12	12	12	H. Claggett	102.35

aMrs. W. W. Vaughan and W. W. Vaughan entry.

$2 Mutuels Paid—Boy Soldier, $9.20 straight, $5.90 place, $4.10 show. Reigh Star, $11.50 place, $6.50 show. Star Bien, $4.70 show. Total mutuels......$41.90

Boy Soldier steadied early, lost ground when racing forward, responded to strong urging when wearing down the leaders and drew clear swiftly to win with something left. Reigh Star, strong factor from the start and under steadying restraint until nearing the stretch, was carried wide by Tracelette came fast when straight and finished strongly. Star Bien saved ground early, was forced wide approaching the stretch, came fast to reach the lead midway of the drive and tired. Uncle Billies saved ground and tired. Kanlast raced through the field. In the Night and Dizzy Heights had speed.

SECOND—SIX FURLONGS. CHUTE. FOR TWO-YEAR-OLDS. CLAIMING. Purse $1,000. Value to winner $700, second $150, third $100, fourth $50. Went to post at 1.57. Off at 1.57½. Start good from gate. Won driving, place same. Winner br f 2, by Duel-Bay Ordy. Owned by MRS. J. Y. CHRISTMAS. Trained by J. Y. CHRISTMAS. Time 22 4-5, 46 4-5, 1.13 4-5.

	Wt.	Post	St.	¼	½	Str.	Fin.	Jockeys	Odds
Rough Honey	112	2	4	1¹	1h	1¹	1½	H. Mora	$6.20
Two Timer	115	9	1	2¹	2¹½	2½	2½	J. Deering	2.90
Rocky Craig	113	6	7	5¹	5³	3¹	3¹½	D. Scocca	11.40
Budgeteer	110	12	3	4¹½	3½	4³	4¹½	W. Mann	14.10
Parachutist	111	8	12	12	10²	6½	5h	M. Berg	2.80
Tangelo	107	7	10	9½	7½	5h	6¹½	J. Tammaro	6.40
Pickwick Arms	105	5	6	6h	8¹	7¹	7½	H. Trent	36.00
Huina Loo	107	3	11	11¹½	11³	9½	8²	H. Claggett	180.55
Pious Display	115	10	9	10¹½	6h	10½	9½	F. Zufelt	11.35
Four Stars	110	4	8	8h	9½	11³	10²	C. Erickson	47.45
Bowsprit	110	11	2	3h	4¹½	8¹½	11²	L. Ensor	54.10
Go West	111½	1	5	7h	12	12	12	L. Knapp	41.90

$2 Mutuels Paid—Rough Honey, $14.40 straight, $6.50 place, $4.70 show. Two Timer, $4.50 place, $3.40 show. Rocky Craig, $7.10 show. Total mutuels $40.60

Rough Honey took command under energetic handling, responded well when repeatedly challenged and withstood Two Timer. Latter strong factor from the start, held on gamely. Rocky Craig raced forwardly under pressure and was sent to the inside in the drive. Budgeteer lost much ground and tired. Parachutist broke slowest of all, lost much ground and finished well. Tangelo raced through the field and tired near the end. Bowsprit had speed.

THIRD—TWO MILES. FOR THREE-YEAR-OLDS AND UP. ALLOWANCES. Steeplechase. Purse $1,200. Value to winner $850, second $200, third $100, fourth $50. Went to post at 2.25½. Off at 2.25½. Start good from flag. Won driving.

Continued on Page 13, Column 5.

Aonbarr Beats Riverland At Pimlico

By JACK CARPENTER

PIMLICO, Nov. 7.—Miss Helen Hickman's Kentucky-bred Aonbarr engineered a major upset today when he drove to a nose decision over Louisiana Farm's Riverland in the fifth running of the mile and a half Grayson Stakes.

Hal Price Headley's Equinox was third, six length back of Riverland and five lengths before H. M. Babylon's Abbe Pierre, which brought up the rear.

$12.50 MUTUEL

Backed into the almost prohibitive odds of 1-4 by the overflow crowd of 18,000. Riverland was showing the way at the sixteenth pole, but could not withstand Aonbarr's last-ditch challenge through the final seventy yards. Aonbarr paid $12.50 and completed the long route in 2.33 1-5.

The heavy impost and the exact-

Continued on Page 13, Column 8.

—For Salvage Information

(1) Iron and Steel
(2) Kitchen Fats
(3) Tin Cans

Call PLaza 6877

VERY LATEST NEWS

(Race Results From Howard Sports Daily, Inc.)

5,000 JAPS KILLED IN SOLOMONS CAMPAIGN

WASHINGTON, Nov. 7—(A. P.).—At least $5,188 Japanese have been killed by United States forces in the Solomon Islands land fighting since the American invasion of those islands began August 7, the Navy announced today.

AT PIMLICO

Eighth—Supreme Speed, 1st; Conquer, 2d; Quiz Kid, 3.

AT BELMONT PARK

Seventh—The Rhymer, 1; Yankee Dandy, 2; Bon Jour, 3.

AT ROCKINGHAM

Seventh—Veris, $19.60, $10.80, $5.20; Sun Town, $7.60, $4.40; Knight's Duchess, $2.80.

AT CHURCHILL DOWNS

Fifth—Gingall, $16.20, $6.60, $5.80; Surprise Party, $4. $3.80; Orlando Girl, $14.00.

AT SPORTSMAN'S PARK

Fifth—xWayriel, xSam Houston, won; Earlian, 3d.
xDead heat.

FOOTBALL SCORES

At Homewood—City, 18; Mercersburg, 0; final.
Colgate, 28; Columbia, 26; end 3rd period.
Lehigh, 22; Muhlenberg, 6; final.
Layfayette, 19; Rutgers, 13; final.

HOURLY TEMPERATURES

Midnight, 55	3 A. M., 54	6 A. M., 51	9 A. M., 49
1 A. M., 56	4 A. M., 54	7 A. M., 50	10 A. M., 50
2 A. M., 56	5 A. M., 54	8 A. M., 49	11 A. M., 52

167th ANNIVERSARY OF U. S. MARINES---4 Pages of Vivid Pictures in TOMORROW'S SUNDAY AMERICAN

HELP US FIND 'MISS VICTORY' OF BALTIMORE

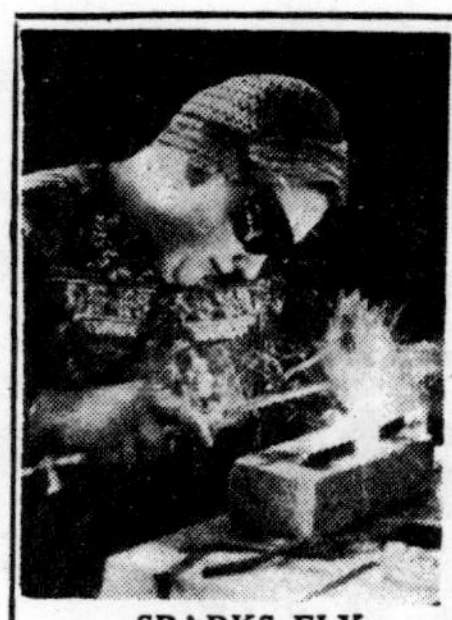

SPARKS FLY
Welding to this girl war worker is 'duck soup.'

Somewhere in a Baltimore war-production plant and filling a vital role in America's all-out effort to win the war is a girl worker, typical and symbolic of the nation's new feminine army of the home front.

She may be operating a machine or keeping records of other workers.

We want to find her, single her out as typical of all those young women who have left their homes, their peace-time jobs and recreational activities to take up where men have left off to go to war.

Help us find "Miss Victory" to compete for the national crown in Chicago soon!

Read today's announcement of the search.

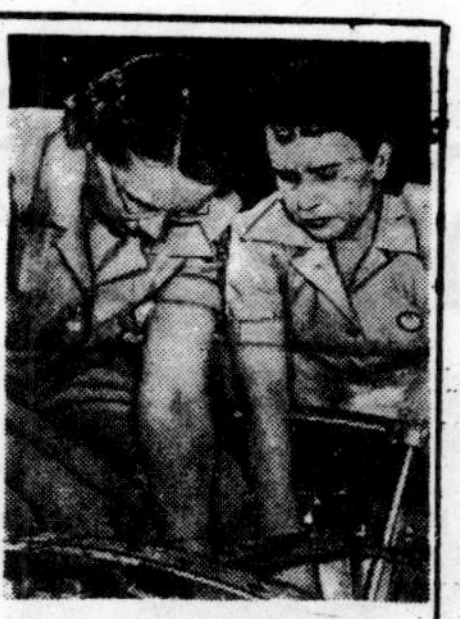

MAKING WARBIRDS
This young lady helps turn out Consolidated B-24's.

Famous Names In Army Show

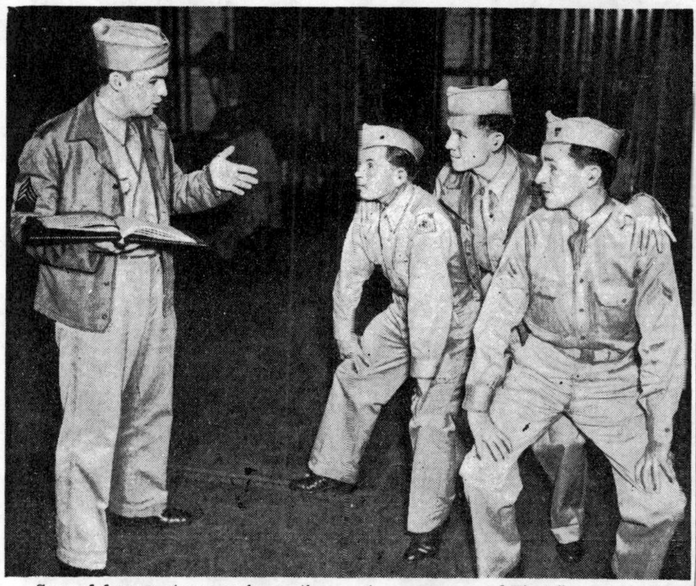

Sons of famous stage people are the four young men of Uncle Sam's Army in the scene above from Irving Berlin's "This Is The Army," which opens at Ford's Theatre next Monday. They are (left to right) Sergeant Alan Anderson, stage manager and First Sergeant in the show, who is a son of Maxwell Anderson, playwright; Private Robert Moore, son of Victor Moore; Private Joe Cook, Jr., and Sergeant Philip Truex, son of Ernest Truex.

The Baltimore News-Post Has the Largest Circulation of Any Evening Newspaper in the South

THE BALTIMORE NEWS-POST
AN INDEPENDENT NEWSPAPER

2ND FRONT PAGE
NEWS-POST HAS TWO FRONT PAGES DAILY

SATURDAY EVENING, NOVEMBER 7, 1942

Bandits Kidnap Manager, Rob Store

$2,465 Stolen From Safe After 'Ride' Through Streets

Three bandits kidnaped a chain store manager last night, held guns against his side as they rode about the northern section of the city for an hour, used him as a decoy to lure another employe from the chain store, and finally forced the manager to open the store safe almost within sight of nine other employes.

After scooping up cash and checks totaling $2,465.59, the bandits fled.

Herbert C. Cox, the chain store manager, said he left the store in the 600 block Gorsuch avenue about 11 P. M. and was driving toward his home in the 2100 block Woodbourne avenue when his car was forced to the curb by another machine.

WORE UNIFORM CAPS

He said one of the men in the other car wore a hat which resembled a policeman's cap.

As Cox, in the belief that the man was a policeman, was arguing that he had not been speeding, another man opened the door of Cox's car and thrust a pistol against him. A third man, also armed with a gun, appeared a moment later, Cox told Detectice Lieut. Frederick Harbourne and Detective Sergeants Robert Menendez and Frank Waltman.

DRIVE ABOUT CITY

The three men abandoned their car, Cox said, climbed into his machine and with guns against his side drove about the city until after midnight. He said they forced him to don spectacles from which the lenses had been removed and pieces of cardboard substituted.

When Harry J. Weaver, 2800 block Presbury street, appeared at the door, the bandits forced Cox to call Weaver, who was seized by the bandits when he approached the machine.

Cox, coached by the bandits, said he told Weaver:

"This is a hold-up. Better do what they say."

Then, Cox said, he was forced from the car and was taken into the store where he was instructed to open the safe. Cox said one of the bandits crouched in a telephone booth, covering the manager with his gun, as Cox opened the safe.

More Surprise Alerts To Be Arranged

Maryland may expect more surprise air-raid alerts and blackouts over an indefinite period, Col. H. S. Barrett, chief of the air-raid precaution services of the State, announced today in repeating his general gratification over yesterday's first unannounced drill.

Colonel Barrett already had warned that at least one blackout may be expected this month, but today he added:

"I'm going to hold as many as I can, both at night and in the daytime. I may have one in the morning and another at night of the same day. I am not going to say whether another daylight alert may be expected before the first surprise blackout."

Although traffic continued to move for a time in some outlying sections during the 20-minute alert, downtown Baltimore stopped dead in its tracks between 2.25 and 2.45 P. M. In many instances, outside the business area, the alarm either was not heard or not recognized, and wardens had to warn drivers.

In commenting on this situation, Adrian Hughes, chairman of planning for the Baltimore Committee on Civilian Defense, made this statement:

"It is realized that all sections of the city are not fully covered by the air-raid warning signal system. That is because the committee was unable to obtain priorities from the War Production Board last March for all of the equipment which it requested.

NEED PRIORITIES

"It has continued its efforts to obtain priorities for additional equipment, and is hopeful, but unsuccessful so far.

"The money for this additional equipment is available if priorities can be obtained. Less than three-quarters of the amount of money appropriated for the purchase of the equipment has been spent.

"The important war production industrial areas, the waterfront areas and the downtown business area, which would be the principal objectives of active air raids are thoroughly covered, but in some of the outlying residential sections, it was necessary to spread the available equipment further apart than was planned.

ORGANIZED WARDENS

"However, the warden organization is best organized in those residential areas, so that even where the signals are only faintly heard it should not take long for the wardens to spread the alarm.

"The weekly 11 A. M. Saturday tests have been the opportunity to discover such areas and make provision for spreading the alarm.

MORE VOLUNTEERS

"The committee is doing everything possible to obtain additional signals, but obviously is limited to the equipment for which WPB will issue priorities, and, of course, WPB has to consider the relatively greater importance of equipment for our armed forces.

"However, the present signal system can be made to give reasonably adequate warning everywhere as soon as more volunteers are obtained for those sectors which are undermanned."

'Mollie' Performs For Pupils

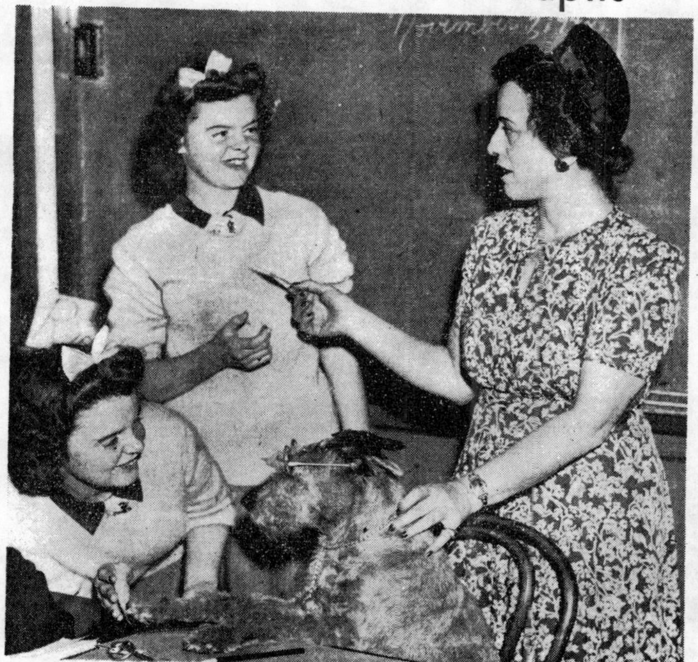

"Mollie", aristocratic Irish terrier owned by Roslyn Terhune (right) dog editor of the Baltimore News-Post and Sunday American, demonstrated how a well-trained canine obeys orders, before the Pet Club of the Gwynn's Fall Junior High School yesterday. At the conclusion of the demonstration Mrs. Terhune presented each member of the club a pass for "War Dogs," film which opens at the Times Theatre on Armistice Day. Catherine (left) and Thelma Hasloop, twins, are receiving their tickets as "Mollie" plays "schoolteacher." *(Story on Page 4.)*

Shipyards Seek 'Miss Victory'

By ALDINE R. BIRD
(Full Page Fairfield Shipyard Girls On Page 5)

Girls and women who do the work behind the work of building the nation's victory cargo fleet today are balloting with increasing enthusiasm at the Fairfield shipyards for potential "Miss Victory" winners.

Although they are not riveting the huge steel plates into position for the freighters or operating giant hoisting machines these war workers are keeping intricate records of men who are doing the heavy jobs and that's their contribution toward victory.

INCLUDED IN SEARCH

No sooner had they received announcement from their personnel department that they would be included in the city-wide search for a typical war worker than they began casting about for favorite candidates.

From the large force of feminine workers will emerge contenders for the crown of "Miss Victory of Baltimore" and a $500 war bond, which has been posted by The Baltimore News-Post and Sunday American as a companion top prize to the titular crown.

FINALS ON NOV. 27

The finals will be held on Friday, November 27, and "Miss Victory" will be chosen from among plant winners by a board of impartial judges. In addition to her $500 war bond she will receive a free trip to Chicago to compete for the national crown and a trip to Washington to meet high Government officials.

PLANTS IN RIVALRY

Numerous other war plants in Baltimore are conducting competitions in search of their most typical war workers—all as a movement to encourage more women to enter war industries and to give public recognition to their roles in helping win the war of production.

Each plant conducts its own contest in any form it deems best suited to its needs, and there is still time for others who have not yet launched their competitions to do so.

Ballots and posters will be furnished on request to The News-Post.

If no notices have been posted on your bulletin boards about a "Miss Victory" contest in your war plant see your foreman or personnel representative immediately. Let it be known that the girls want a chance to compete in this competition.

Come on, join the fun, let's find "Miss Victory!"

Happy Hills Aided By Fund

Thanks to careful nursing and medical care received at Happy Hills Convalescent Home for Children, many boys and girls have been returned to their parents in radiant health.

Happy Hills, located in a wooded section of Mount Washington, provides convalescent care for children no longer acutely ill, but who still require special care which their parents cannot give.

80 BEDS

The institution maintains 80 beds for youngsters between two months and twelve years. Contributors to the Baltimore War and Community Fund help to support the home.

Elsewhere in today's Baltimore News-Post is a picture of a young patient at Happy Hills. Write a short caption for the picture and mail your entry to the Contest Editor of The Baltimore News-Post.

$5 PRIZE

Entries received by next Wednesday will be considered for a prize of $5. The winner's name will be printed on Friday.

Mrs. Kathryn Sparks, 1813 Riggs avenue, won $5 for submitting the winning caption for the picture in The Baltimore News-Post last Monday.

Thousands To Help Yule-Time Movies

With interest running at fever-pitch, thousands of mothers, wives, sisters and sweethearts of Maryland troops now in England are expected to turn out tomorrow to send their soldier boys sound-movie greetings for Christmas.

The filming will take place on a lot in front of the Preston street entrance to the Fifth Regiment Armory at 3 P. M., and later these movies will be shown to the former Fort Meade trainees during the Yule season.

FEATURED SPEAKERS

Featuring the cinematic greetings will be those from Governor O'Conor, commander-in-chief of Maryland's home military forces; Maj. Gen. Milton A. Reckord, who commanded the troops in the early training at Meade; Col. John A. Cutchins, former chief of staff there, and a score of other ranking officers.

In event of rain, the movie-taking will be postponed until the following Sunday, with the exception of the army officers, who will be photographed inside the Armory under artificial lights.

MOTHERS OF THREE

Mothers who have three sons or more in the armed forces, and at least one in the Maryland outfit in England, will be brought before the sound-camera for a close-up greeting to their sons, providing they have registered in advance.

Others will be photographed in groups but close enough to be easily recognized on the screen. Tentative plans to record greetings individually by all relatives of the boys had to be abandoned due to the large number expected to turn out—far in excess of the film allowance for transportation and exhibition overseas.

AT ARMORY SUNDAY

Here are your directions:

Go to the Preston street entrance of the Armory shortly after 2.30 P. M. Sunday and await instructions which will be given over loud speakers.

In case of rain, wait until next Sunday.

If you have three sons in the armed forces and have registered your name with The Baltimore News-Post, you will be called to the front for individual greetings. Be prepared to say about a dozen words to him.

The films are not intended for relatives of Maryland troops anywhere else in the service other than England, and will not be shown in any other place.

Help get the best recordings possible for the fellows who soon may be on their way across the continent to Berlin. Co-operate fully and the cameramen will do the rest!

The Baltimore News-Post and Sunday American are offering weekly cash prizes for news tips and amateur photos. Best tip gets $25, the next best gets $10, and the next 15 get $1 each. For each amateur photo published $3 will be paid. Phone news-tip editor, Lexington 0100 (Lex. 4165 midnight to 6.30 A. M.) Rush news photos to picture editor.

Cash For A Caption

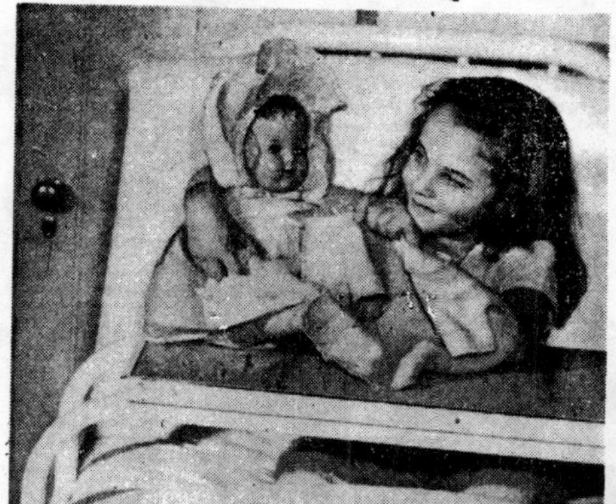

Happy Hills Convalescent Home for Children in Mount Washington, care for youngsters no longer acutely ill, but who still require nursing and medical attention. Above is a little patient at the home who is well on the road to recovery. Happy Hills is an agency of the Baltimore War and Community Fund. Write a snappy caption for the picture and you may win $5.

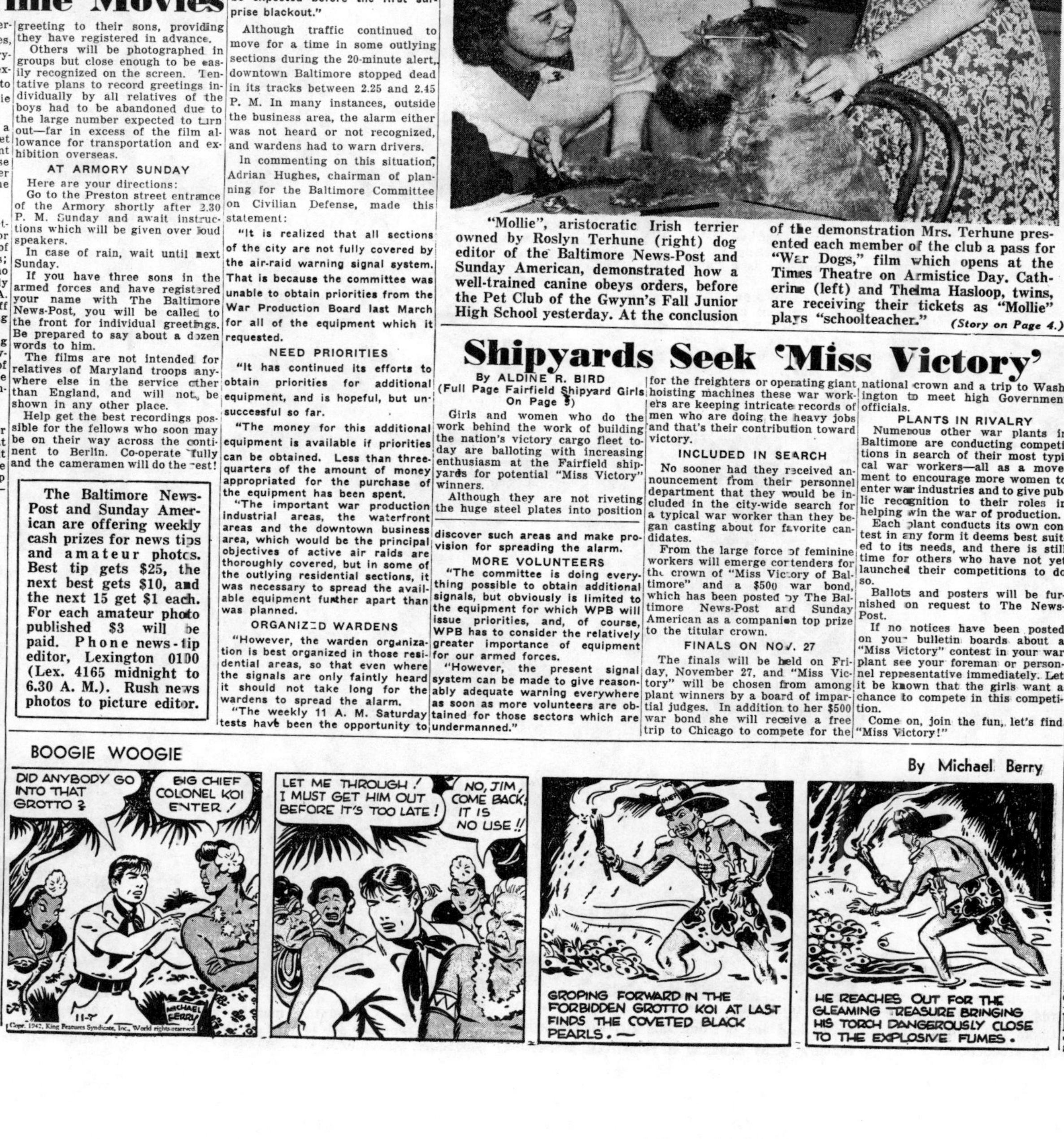
BOOGIE WOOGIE
By Michael Berry
DID ANYBODY GO INTO THAT GROTTO ?
BIG CHIEF COLONEL KOI ENTER !
LET ME THROUGH ! I MUST GET HIM OUT BEFORE IT'S TOO LATE !
NO, JIM, COME BACK! IT IS NO USE !!
GROPING FORWARD IN THE FORBIDDEN GROTTO KOI AT LAST FINDS THE COVETED BLACK PEARLS. —
HE REACHES OUT FOR THE GLEAMING TREASURE BRINGING HIS TORCH DANGEROUSLY CLOSE TO THE EXPLOSIVE FUMES.

RACING AT PIMLICO
DAILY TO NOVEMBER 11
A Stake Race Every Day
TODAY—THE GRAYSON HANDICAP
FIRST RACE 1.15 P. M.
DAILY DOUBLE CLOSES 1 P. M.
Admission (with tax) $1.65
Street Cars Nos. 5, 25, 31, 33
Direct to Pimlico Gates
Buy War Bonds and Stamps

A. F. of L.
Members and Friends
Will commemorate the anniversary of the death of their late President of the Baltimore Federation of Labor Henry F. Broening on Sunday, November 8th, 10 A. M., St. Bernardine's Catholic Church, Edmondson Ave. and Mt. Holly St.
Special Services
You Are Invited To Attend

DANCING TONIGHT
JOE DOWLING'S MUSIC
ALCAZAR
Cathedral and Madison Sts.
Couples, $1.15
Singles: Ladies, 45c. Gentlemen, 85c
Tax Included

DANCING
This Sunday and each Friday and Sunday
9 P. M. to 1 85c a couple
DON AINSLE'S MELODYMASTERS
New Mt. Holly. North Av. & Poplar Grove
No. 13 or No. 31 Cars Direct

THERE'S FUN AT THE VILLA
Music and dancing plus 3 gala Floor Shows nitely make the GREEN VILLA one of Baltimore's most sought-after spots! 5423 O'Donnell St. No cover, no minimum.

KEITHS ROOF
Ladies 30c
Gentlemen 40c
(Plus Tax)
TONITE—SEAMON ELDRIDGE and BAND
SUNDAY—BOB CRAIG & SHIRLEY DULO

Ship Plant Girls Aim At 'Miss Victory' Title

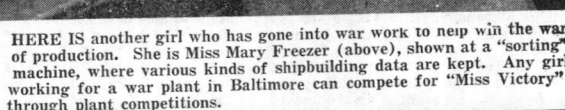

HERE IS another girl who has gone into war work to help win the war of production. She is Miss Mary Freezer (above), shown at a "sorting" machine, where various kinds of shipbuilding data are kept. Any girl working for a war plant in Baltimore can compete for "Miss Victory" through plant competitions.

KEEPING records of shipbuilding work is also a vital war job and Fairfield-Bethlehem girls are competing for "Miss Victory" crown and public recognition. Above, Miss Dorothy Germershausen is shown adding man hours spent in building "Victory" cargo vessels in the vast plant here.

THIS war worker isn't welding or riveting cargo vessels but she is a "machine operator." Miss Jean Fleishell is shown operating a numerical key punching machine which helps keep records of how fast Fairfield is turning out Liberty ships. Like others in her office, she's thrilled at chance to win "Miss Victory" crown.

"HELLO, THERE!" Mrs. Alice Marshall, one of several hundred girls at Fairfield shipyards, is doing her part for Uncle Sam by working efficiently in the offices there, keeping records of ships-for-victory production!

NOW, this looks a bit more complicated, and might lead one to think this girl worker is in a foundry plant handling a monstrous production machine. Really, Miss Margaret Sorensen (above) is operating an accounting machine at Fairfield shipyards, but her job is vital to the success of production schedules in the shipways.

ORDINARILY, you might say Miss Pauline Faust (above) is a "Toiling Tillie" in a modern office, but right now she's a typical girl war worker who is out to help win the shipping war anyhow! She's shown operating a wide-carriage typewriter, keeping war records. Baltimore's "Miss Victory" will be chosen Friday, November 27.

Aonbarr Whips Riverland In Grayson Stakes

Rodger H. Pippen Sports Editor Says

KEEP YOUR CHIN UP

Very justly, Commissioner Landis has suspended Frankie Crosetti of the Yanks for the first 30 days of the 1943 season. With the Baseball Commissioner among those present, the New York infielder shoved Umpire William Summers in the third game of the 1942 World Series. The Judge didn't need any testimony from the official. He saw with his own eyes. For that reason it was a foregone conclusion that Crosetti would be spanked.

Both the player and the Yanks will suffer by the verdict. Phil Rizzuto, the regular shortstop, has joined the Navy and Frankie had been expected to fill his shoes. With players very, very scarce, the Yanks will have to go to one of their farm clubs to dig up a sub for the first month of the race.

It probably is fortunate for the Baltimore Club that Landis delayed his announcement about Crosetti until after the closing date for drafting players. The Yanks, looking around for talent, might have focussed upon Bob Repass, Oriole shortstop.

RODGER H. PIPPEN

Two Were Fined

Crosetti's punishment didn't stop with the suspension. He and Joe Gordon, second baseman, were both fined $250.

Both clashes occurred in the third game of the Series, October 3, in which the Yankees were shut out, 2-0, at New York. Crosetti's penalties were for "pushing and shoving Umpire Bill Summers and for language in connection therewith." Gordon was fined for "language addressed to Umpire George Magerkurth."

Following the Cardinals at bat in the ninth inning, Magerkurth called Jimmy Brown out at second on Terry Moore's sacrifice, then reversed himself and Gordon protested. Crosetti's fist with Summers came a few minutes later after Enos Slaughter singled, scoring Brown and sending Moore to third. The play on Moore as Joe DiMaggio threw to Crosetti, was close and Crosetti objected when Summers ruled Moore was safe.

Hassett To Enlist

Indeed, the Yanks will be in dire straits for infielders next spring. Buddy Hassett, first baseman, has announced that he will enlist. Red Rolfe, veteran third sacker, says he has retired to coach at Yale.

Hassett will become the second successive first baseman lost to the Yankees because of the war. A year ago Johnny Sturm, who had covered first for McCarthy through 1941, was inducted into military service. The job fell to Hassett, who, after having spent all his major league career in the National circuit playing for the Dodgers and the Braves, had gone to the Yanks during the winter in a deal which sent Tommy Holmes of Newark to Boston.

Following an unimpressive spring training start, Hassett, who had been waived in by all clubs in the National, made sparkling comeback for the Yanks and finished the season as the American League's top-ranking first baseman. He promised to continue his fine efforts in the World Series, but after some timely hitting in the first two games he broke a thumb in his first turn at bat in the third game.

Nova Should Forget Comeback Idea

Lou Nova should forget that come-back idea he is nursing today after knocking out an unknown in four rounds. He hasn't a chance to get to the top and will wind up cutting out paper dolls. The human brain can stand only so much pounding. Joe Louis pounded Nova to

Continued on Page 14, Column 6.

Belmont Park Results

FIRST RACE—One mile. Off at 1.36½.
Time, 1.39 3-5.
Spare Room, 106 ....$23.40 $10.70 $6.70
(J. Rienzi)
Auletta, 103 (D. Dodson) 7.40 4.40
Stature, 117 (V. Nodarse) 3.60
Also Ran—Flange, Dian, Be Impudent, Only Porter, War Master, Libertyile and Isolation.
SECOND—Six furlongs. Off at 2.11½.
Time, 1.12 1-5.
Paper's Blade, 121 ....$11.20 $4.20 $3.00
(A. Kirkland)
I. Secretary, 121 (J. Longden) 3.40 2.40
scap, 121 (C. McCreary) 2.60
Also Ran—Mr. Turnbull, Fortune Cookie, Byrd Boy, Bowling Green, Ishnocks Win, ars, Baalet and Ufe.
(Christmas and Gilsen entry.
Daily Double—Venture Cap and Reaper's Blade paid $153.30 for $2.
THIRD—Six furlongs. Off at 2.39½.
Time, 4.00 1-5.
Knight's Quest, 144
(M. Passmore) $4.90 $3.60 $3.00
Bavarian, 113 (J. Rich) ....3.30 out
Strolling On, 140 (H. Brooks) .... out
Also Ran—Benekkar.
FOURTH—One and a half miles. Off at 3.14½.
Time, 2.31 3-5.
Seven Hills, 115
(J. Rienzi) $3.80 $2.90 $2.20
Resolute II., 117 (D. Dodson) 3.10 2.90
Bonnie Goles, 98 (V. Contenero) 2.70
Also Ran—Slade Smith, Ripcats.
FIFTH—Six furlongs. Off at 3.49.
Time, 1.09 3-5.
Rowstown, 113 (N. Coule) ..$9.40 $4.00 $2.90
Mime Mo, 116 (L. Haas) 3.30 2.70
Margoy, 105 (B. Thompson) 2.80
Also Ran—Enthrall, Imperatrice, Happy Warrior and Roney.
SIXTH—One mile. Off at 4.21½. Time, 1.37 4-5.
Good Morning, 119 ....$5.80 $3.10 $2.50
Too Timely, 109 (M. Mehrtens) 3.20 2.60
La Reigh, 115 (J. Longden) 2.80
Also Ran—Bridlevor, Regimental, Navigating, Royal Flush and alhedd.
(Mr. and Mrs. H. Barrett entry.

Churchill Downs Results

FIRST RACE—One mile. Off at 1.33. Time 1.42 2-5.
Big Boss, 115
(M. Caffarella) $20.20 $7.80 $5.00
Shuckles, 112 (C. Swaim) 7.40 4.60
Modwana, 112 (N. Jemas) 3.40
Also Ran—Great Book, Chromeleel, Herio Limited, Okabena, Thoth, Magnelium, Flamin, Baby Joies, Count Fearless, if Field.
SECOND—Six furlongs. Off at 2.07.
Time, 1.29 3-5.
Star Whiz, 115
(C. Robinson) $4.60 $4.60 $3.20
Linger On, 106 (S. Murphy) 8.20 6.00
Patrol Flight, 106 (M. Duhon) 6.60
Also Ran—Betty, Uncle Walter, Ar-rowtraction, Charting, Hand Jester, Black Brummell, thipsu, Countess Abbot and Badly.
THIRD—Six and one half furlongs. Off at 2.30½. Time, 1.21.
Mr. Howelll, ...$20.20 $2.40 $2.20
Allquest, 119 (M. Caffarella) 3.20 2.80
Queen's Risk, 110 (C. Bierman) 3.40
Remote Control, 103 (E. Robert) 7.60
Also Ran—Alar, Van Greenock, Carbon-ado.
FOURTH—One and sixteenth miles. Off at 4.01½. Time, 1.53.
Pimlico Polly, 106
(B. Vandergrift) $15.20 $5.80 $3.80
My Myri, 107 (O. Scurlock) 3.80 2.80
Millie, 110 (K. McCombs) 2.40
Also Ran—Tiptotate, Aridelcal, More Re, finest, Sabemla, Alumont, tWork Shop, Lumber Queen, fMagaloy and fBall and Chain.

Rockingham Results

FIRST RACE—Six furlongs (chute). Off at 2.07½. Time, 1.14.
Bonnie Rue, 110 (C. Stevenson) 7.60 4.00
Also Ran—Tex Clipper, Ghost Hunt, Turnabout, Cabinle, Acrid, Neva's Queen and Fair Evelyn.
SECOND—Six furlongs (chute). Off at 2.31. Time, 1.14.
Hunting Home, 111 (W. Turnbull)
..............$10.20 $4.80 $2.80
Castine, 112 (A. Daniels) $3.20 2.60
Also Ran—Blue Leons, Witness Stand, Hittle, Paul Scarlet.
Daily Double—Spare Room and Northbound paid $35.20 for $2.
THIRD—Six furlongs (chute). Off at 3.01. Time, 1.13.
Wise Decision, 113
(J. Dattilo) $7.40 $4.00 $3.20
Guile, 112 (C. Burando) 5.20 4.40
Flying Adversary, 113
(J. Dattilo) 5.40
Also Ran—Daddy Ford, Sir Lyr, Elsie, Range Dust, Whiscendent, Stimulate Last-pass, Athelhidia.
FOURTH (Original Fifth)—One and one sixteenth. Off at 3.33½. Time, 1.47 3-5.
Dense Path, 102 (Dattilo) $5.00 $3.40 $3.00
Irene Hope, 106 (Shuffit) 7.00 6.00
Centuple, 111 (Grass) 3.00
Also Ran—Pavillion, Klelg Light, Dinsen and Head Sea.
FIFTH (Origina Fourth)—One mile and seventy yards (chute). Off at 3.51. Time, 1.12 3-5.
Bill's Sister, 104
(M. Shuflitt) $14.60 $4.40 $3.20
Frontier Jane, 105 (J. Finnegan) 3.00 2.40
Ballast Reef, 111 (E. Gross) 2.00
Also Ran—Bramtown, Dark Mischief, La Scala and Bit of Juvene.
SIXTH—Six furlongs (chute). Off at 4.16½. Time, 1.13 3-5.
Easy Blend, 113 (E. Gross)
..............$3.60 $6.00 $4.20
Victory Bound, 113 (K. Craig) 3.80 3.00
Remote Control, 103 (E. Robert) 7.60
Also Ran—Altegero, Lou O'Neill, Taking Ways, Wake Robin and Ack-Ack.

Sportsman's Pk. Results

FIRST RACE—Seven furlongs. Off at 2.36½. Time, 1.32 2-5.
Float Away, 119
(W. Warren) $3.40 $2.80 $2.40
Darby Dallas, 112 (J. Higley) 4.00 3.00
Doctor Reder, 106 (A. Skoronski) 4.00
Also Ran—Gaylie F., Gipsy M, Shirley G., Copper Heels, Future Winning.
SECOND and one-half furlongs. Off at 4.21½. Time, 1.54.
Tip Your Hat, 104
(Beverly) $8.00 $4.00 $3.10
Ann O'Vision, 109 (Taylor) 4.60 3.80
Black Fire, 98 (Skoronski) 7.00
Also Ran—Reggo Silver, Be Sweet, Burnin Chips, Valordor, Keep Flying, Dabitem, Dallas King.
Daily Double — Float Away and Tip Your Hat paid $18.80 for $2.00.
THIRD—One mile and seventy yards. Off at 3.53½. Time, 1.52 4-5.
Lactose, 109
(B. Vandergrift) $12.00 $5.20 $3.20
Devil's Frolic, 107 (T. Tower) 3.40 2.80
Busa, 110 (E. Piesz) 3.40
Also Ran—Miss Yip, Sweet Suse, G.C. Hav. Fly. Mr. Bobble, Holly, Wooden In.
FOURTH—One mile and seventy yards. Off at 4.21½. Time, 1.54 3-5.
Mazur pocketed $4.00 ....$15.00 $5.80 $3.20
Extrems, 100 (K. Piesz) 10.80 4.60
Valdin Marg, 101 (A. Beverly) 3.40
Also Ran—Golden Gable, Bill Lane, Scarlet Omen, Brush Brush, Bessie Girl, Jump Bid, Tournade and Minotra.

Irish Win Over Army Eleven By 13-0

Continued from Page 1.

9, then Clatt plunged to a first down on the 17.

Two of Bertelli's passes were knocked down and Creevey returned to try a field goal from the 21 which was blocked and recovered by Crowell of Army on the Cadet 17. Army lost two on three tries by Anderson, who then kicked on fourth down to Ashbaugh, and the latter was downed on his 40.

CLATT GAINS

Clatt clattered six yards in two thrusts, but Ashbaugh failed to smash to a first down and Ashbaugh kicked out on the Army 37. Woods fought off tackle for three yards and after Troxell failed at the line, Anderson punted to Army's 49 where the ball was grounded.

A 21-yard sprint by Ashbaugh was nullified by a clipping penalty, setting the Irish back to the Army 43. Ashbaugh picked up a first down at the 39 and then took a six-yard pass from Bertelli. A long pass by Bertelli was knocked down by Anderson.

Jarrell batted down another Bertelli toss and Army took the ball on downs at its 22. Woods hit center for 9, but an incomplete plunge by Troxell failed to gain a first down and Anderson kicked to Ashbaugh who was run out on his 24.

Two short shovel passes from Bertelli to Clatt barely made a first down as Capt. Hanz Mazur entered the Army line-up. Short thrusts by Ashbaugh and Livingstone picked up another first down at the Irish 42.

Livingstone and Ashbaugh pounded 5, but Bertelli's pass was no good and Bertelli kicked to Mazur, who handed the ball to Hill and the latter returned only 5. However, a clipping penalty set the Cadets back to their 1. Mazur kicked out on his 27 as the period ended without score.

SECOND PERIOD

Two plays gained only two and two passes by Bertilli were incomplete, the last knocked down by Mazur in the end zone to give Army the ball at its 25. Hill rambled eight down the middle but Army went no further and Mazur kicked out on the Irish 34. Cowhig skirted end for a first down at his 49 and went the same way again for another first down on Army's 38. Bertelli passed to Livingstone for eight and the latter was hurt on the play but remained in the game.

Cowhig lost two and a penalty for too much time in the huddle set Notre Dame back 5 more. A pass Bertelli to Ashbaugh was good for only two and Army took the ball on downs at its 37. Hill carried three straight times but made only eight and Mazur kicked to Ashbaugh, who returned 16 before being run out on his 34. Cowhig picked up a yard and than smashed eight. Limont dropped a Bertelli pass, so Bertilli punted to Mazur who was dropped in his tracks on his 24.

PASS INTERCEPTED

Two plays lost 5 before Mazur punted to Ashbaugh, who returned 17 to Army's 48. Two slants by Cowhig gained 9 and the Irish smashed to a first down at the 34. Again Cowhig carried, gaining 5, but a long pass by Bertelli was intercepted by Hill in the end zone and Army took over on its 20. Hill failed to gain and Mazur hit center for three as the half ended without score.

THIRD PERIOD

Woods took the kickoff and returned 8 to his 17. Mazur ripped off tackle for 14, but a holding penalty set the Cadets back to their five. Woods gained six before Mazur punted dead at Army's 47. Two plays lost two and after Bertelli failed to connect with a long pass, he punted over the goal and Army took the ball at its 20. Mazur lost five and kicked dead to Army's 47.

HILL PICKS UP 15

Bertelli had two long passes batted down before completing one to Clatt for a two-yard loss and Bertilli punted over the Irish goal on the first play from his 20, Hill rambled to the 35, where he fumbled and Ashbaugh recovered for Notre Dame.

Clatt made five and R. Creevy picked up six for a first down. Ashbaugh circled end for four and then Clatt drilled the middle for five. R. Creevy took the ball from Bertilli and went straight through the middle for 15 yards and a touchdown. Bertelli kicked the extra point and Notre Dame led, 7 to 0.

Army started at its 35 following an out-of-bounds kickoff, but three plays gained only 8 and Mazur punted to the Irish 25. On the second play, Bertelli tossed a long pass that was intercepted by Hill, who was stopped in his tracks by Dove at the Army 45.

Mazur tossed a long pass which Hennessy took off the finger tips of two defenders and rambled 19 yards to the Irish 14. Mazur then passed to Troxell for 5 but a penalty set the Cadets back to the 10. Mazur had two passes knocked down and the Irish took the ball at their 10. Three plays carried to a first down at the 21 as the period ended with the Irish leading.

FOURTH PERIOD

The Irish couldn't gain and Bertelli kicked to Anderson, who returned 8 to his 49. When two plays failed, Hall tried a long pass that was intercepted by Ashbaugh, who was stopped in his tracks on the 17. Clatt rammed 10 and Ashbaugh made seven in two tries, but Clatt was stopped cold on third down and Bertilli booted to Anderson, who was stopped on his 27 without advancing.

Anderson shot through the line for 29 yards on the first play, but the next three missed a first down by two yards. On fourth down Anderson passed to Crowel for seven and a first down at the 30.

Livingstone intercepted Anderson's pass and returned four to the Irish 20. After two short jabs, Cowhig skirted right end for 14 yards. Clatt banged five yards and again smacked off tackle for seven and a touchdown on the Notre Dame 48. C. Killer picked up four and then took a backward pass from Bertilli which was barely good for first down at the Army 42.

PASS COUNTS

Two more tries by Clatt brought a first down at the 25, with the big Irish freshman simply running over the tiring Army squad. Tim Miller went around his right end on an end-around play and Earley picked up three. When Bertelli passed into the end zone, with Murphy making the ball batted into the air by two Army backs. It was a 16-yard pass. Bertilli missed the extra point, but Notre Dame led, 13-0.

DIMAGGIOS ACCURATE

All three DiMaggios are free throwing arms and are noted for accuracy, but Joe's arm is perhaps the strongest.

BRIEF GLORY—Ossabaw, with Jackie Bosley up, is shown above leading the field in today's steeplechase event, third race, at Pimlico. Trailing the lepper over the first jump are Mad Policy and Himmel. However, Ossabaw became a cropper at the thirteenth fence and Frederic II, not shown above, hit the finish line a winner over Compasse Rose and Mad Policy.

BALTIMORE NEWS-POST SPORTS

SATURDAY EVENING, NOVEMBER 7, 1942

Ossabaw Leads In Pimlico 'Chase

Duke Gridders Lead Liners At Durham

Continued from Page 1.

nullified the play. After a punt exchange the Blue Devils rolled again to a touchdown from the two. Gantt added the point. On the kick-off Rigby ran from his five to the 44, but the Terps could not gain consistently.

SECOND PERIOD

Woods took the kickoff and returned 8 to his 17. Mazur ripped off tackle for 14, but a holding penalty set the Cadets back to their five.

Football

Continued from Page 1.

SOUTH

Georgia Tech	7	20
Kentucky		0
Mississippi		0
Vanderbilt		6
Richmond		0
V. P. I.	6	7
Tennessee	7	20
Cincinnati		0
Tulane		0
Miss. State		0

SOUTHWEST

Texas C.		0
Texas Tech		0
Texas U.		0
Baylor		0
Rice		0
Arkansas		0
S. M. U.		0
Texas Aggies	13	

Suspend, Fine Frank Crosetti

CHICAGO, Nov. 7—(A. P.)—Frankie Crosetti can sit out 30 days and go away with it. But it wasn't the New York Yankee infielder's idea. Commissioner K. M. Landis yesterday suspended him for that period starting next season because he pushed Umpire William Summers in the third game of the 1942 World Series.

Landis also fined Crosetti $250. Teammate Joe Gordon was assessed a similar fine "for language addressed to Umpire George Magerkurth" in the same game.

JAYS' FINAL GAME

Hopkins closes its grid season next Saturday, meeting Swarthmore at Homewood Field.

PIMLICO CHARTS

Continued from Page 1.

place same. Winner b g 5, by Lacken-Fanglia. Owned by L. Bieber. Trained by J. T. SKINNER. Time 4.12 1-5. Turf course fast.

	Wt.	Post. St.	¼	½	¾	Str.	Fin.	Jockeys	Odds
Frederic II	145	6	5	4½	5	4	1	K. Roberts	$2.30
Compass Rose	140	1	4	3	4½	2½	2nk	J. Penrod	3.50
Mad Policy	145	3	2	2	2	3	3	W. Gallaher	2.70
Himmel	143	2	1	3	3	5	4	S. Kies	19.90
Ossabaw	152	4	2	1	1	lost rider	Mr. John Bosley III	7.40

$2 Mutuels Paid—Frederic II., $6.60 straight, $3.80 place, $2.90 show. Compass Rose, $4.70 place, $2.90 show. Mad Policy, $2.70 show. Total mutuels....$23.50

Frederic II., crowned to begin, and steadied for more than a mile, moved forward with a rush, took command after the fourteenth jump, drew clear rapidly, tired in the last stages and withstood Compass Rose's late effort. Compass Rose swung steadily after a bad landing at the ninth brush and finished under strong pressure. Mad Policy used up in the front when inside the final furlong and drew clear under strong pressure. Marksman misstepped forward to the start, wore down Clyde Tolson and was unable to hold the winner. Clyde Tolson, going in improved form and showing fine speed, took command soon after the start, was unable to draw clear and tired after five eighths. Visiting Nurse was rushed forward after a slow beginning, came to the inside for the drive and tired. Bostoff was taken back when in close quarters, was blocked at the turn and showed little thereafter. Spare Man was outrun. Twink had speed.

FOURTH—SIX FURLONGS. CHUTE. FOR THREE-YEAR-OLDS AND UP. Claiming. Purse $1,200. Value to winner $850, second $200, third $100, fourth $50. Went to post at 2.56½. Off at 2.56½. Start good from gate. Won driving, place same. Winner br g 7, by Queen's Guild-Little Star. Owned by ROKEBY STABLES. Trained by J. E. RYAN. Time 23 4-5. 46 4-5. 1.11 4-5.

	Wt.	Post. St.	¼	½	Str.	Fin.	Jockeys	Odds
Enterprise	117	7	7	7	3½	1½	K. Bowman	$2.00
Markman	107	6	3	3	1½	2½	H. Trent	9.60
Clyde Tolson	109	4	5	1h	1h	3	J. Deering	14.65
Visiting Nurse	108	3	4	4	3h	4	J. Zoffer	2.35
Bostoff	110½	2	2	5½	5	5	P. Keiper	4.25
Spare Man	114	5	1	5h	4h	6	S. Young	10.00
Twink	106½	1	4	5	7	7	J. Tammaro	53.75

$2 Mutuels Paid—Enterprise, $6.00 straight, $4.00 place, $2.90 show. Markman, $4.70 place, $4.70 show. Clyde Tolson, $6.50 show.

Enterprise slowest to begin and reserved until ready, moved forward on the extreme outside, forced to the front when inside the final furlong and drew clear under strong pressure. Marksman misstepped forward from the start, wore down Clyde Tolson and was unable to hold the winner. Clyde Tolson, going in improved form and showing fine speed, took command soon after the start, was unable to draw clear and tired after five eighths. Visiting Nurse was rushed forward after a slow beginning, came to the inside for the drive and tired. Bostoff was taken back when in close quarters, was blocked at the turn and showed little thereafter. Spare Man was outrun. Twink had speed.

FIFTH—MILE AND ONE-SIXTEENTH. FOR THREE-YEAR-OLDS AND UP. Fillies and mares. Handicap. Purse $1,300. Value to winner $950, second $200, third $100, fourth $50. Went to post at 3.26½. Off at 3.26½. Start good from gate. Won handily, place driving. Winner b f 3, by Trace Call-San Etoile. Owned by H. P. METCALF. Trained by T. BONHAM. Time 23 4-5. 47 5-5. 1.12 1-5. 1.38. 1.44 2-5.

	Wt.	Post. St.	¼	½	¾	Str.	Fin.	Jockeys	Odds
Star Copy	120	2	1	1	1	1	1	F. Zufelt	$1.80
Mar-Kell	120	3	2	2½	2	2	2	P. Keiper	4.00
Night Glow	120	1	4	4	4	4	3	M. Cloggett	4.10
Chalomine	107	5	5	3	3	3	4	J. Tammaro	13.65
Lotopolse	108	4	2	3½	4	4	5	L. Barrey	21.20

$2 Mutuels Paid—Star Copy, $5.60 straight, $2.80 place, $2.60 show. Mar-Kell, $2.80 place, $2.30 show. Night Glow, $2.60 show.

Star Copy opened up a commanding lead swiftly, held away under steadying restraint, responded when roused and won with something to spare. Mar-Kell strong factor from the start, offered a strong bid approaching the stretch, failed to menace the winner and was much the best of the others. Night Glow was rated along and finished well. Chalomine was outrun. Lotopoise was unable to keep up.

SIXTH—MILE AND A HALF. FOR THREE-YEAR-OLDS AND UPWARD. Grayson Stakes. $5,000 added. Value to winner $4,130, second $1,000, third $500, fourth $250. Went to post at 3.56. Off at 3.56. Start good from gate. Won driving, place same. Winner b f 4, by Boatswain-Hedemora. Owned by HELEN HICK MAX. Trained by J. F. HARRAN. Time 25 1-5. 51 2-5. 1.16 4-5. 1.42 4-5. 2.07.

	Wt.	Post. St.	¼	½	¾	Str.	Fin.	Jockeys	Odds
Aonbarr	116	4	3	3	3	2	1	G. Woolf	$2.30
Riverland	125	5	1	1	1	1	2½	E. Gilbert	out
Equinox	110	3	4	4	4	3	3	F. Zufelt	11.65
Abbe Pierre	118	2	2	2	2	4	4	P. Keiper	out

$2 Mutuels Paid—Aonbarr, $12.50 straight, $2.80 place, out for show. Riverland, $2.30 place, out for show. Equinox, out for show.

Aonbarr, correctly handled and rated from the start, kept Riverland from being out during the opening half mile, moved forward with Riverland, responded to strong urging in the stretch, slowly drew down Riverland in the final stages and was drawing away. Riverland was inclined to bear out early, took command when ready, drew clear rapidly and weakened in the last stages. Abbe Pierre was outrun and passed the tiring Abbe Pierre in the drive. Abbe Pierre opened up a clear lead under light restraint, was put to pressure after a mile and gave way steadily in the drive.

SEVENTH—MILE AND A HALF. FOR THREE-YEAR-OLDS AND UPWARD. Claiming. Purse $1,200. Value to winner $850, second $200, third $100, fourth $50. Went to post at 4.26½. Off at 4.27. Start good from gate. Won driving, place same. Winner b f 4, by Questionnaire-Fancy Feathers. Owned by MRS. V. FLANNERY. Trained by J. H. C. FORBES. Time 23 2-5. 46 4-5. 1.11 4-5. 1.40 3-5. 2.08 1-5. 2.34 1-5.

Navy Conquers Penn In Grid Upset, 7-0

Continued from Page 1.

plete and two running plays stymied. The Middies took the ball on downs at that point.

Again the Navy offense was offensive, but the Middies gained more than 20 yards on an exchange of punts when Stiff's weak kick went outside of the Navy 41. The Middies opened up on passes and from the stripe, Cameron passing on Martin on the Penn 26. On a lateral pass, Cameron to Hume, the ball was carried to the Penn seven. After a five-yard penalty and two running plays had lost four yards, Hamberg shot a pass to Martin in the end zone for a touchdown. Crepen's placekick was good to put Navy ahead, 7-0. After Stiff had run back the next kick-off to the Penn 35, the Quakers drove to the Navy 46 before the Middies dug in. Two running plays and an attempted pass lost four yards. Pletz's punt carried to the Navy 18, but Hume got away a beautiful kick to the Penn 36 as the first period ended, with the score Navy 7; Penn, 0.

SECOND PERIOD

A fine quick kick by Pletz, Penn back, set the Navy back to its six-yard line as the second period opened, and Navy's return punt carried only to the Middie 40. With Stiff doing the heavy work, Penn advanced to the Navy 22, but again the Middies dug in, taking the ball on downs on their 23. Studer away for a nice 13-yard gain before the Navy offense fizzled and was punted out of the danger zone. The Quakers started another determined drive and with a 24-yard gallop by Pletz, the major factor, advanced to the Navy nine. A five-yard penalty set Penn back to the 14 and the Quakers' offense, suddenly interrupted, faltered and after running plays had failed and two passes had been knocked down, Navy took the ball on downs on its 25.

Studer picked up eight yards on an off-tackle drive before the Middies panted out of the danger zone, the ball rolling dead on the Penn 48. Abandoning their ground attack after a five-yard gain by Odell, the Quakers opened up with passes. None were completed and Penn punted to the Navy 15 as the half ended with Navy still in front, 7-0.

THIRD PERIOD

Hume ran the Penn kickoff from behind his own goal to the Navy 28, where the Middies, spearheaded by Studer, started driving. Again the Quakers launched an offensive, with Miller advancing the load this time on slashing drives.

Penn advanced to the Navy 41 this time, and again the Middies dug in, forcing the Quakers back on downs on the Navy 36. Hamberg, taking a punt, galloped around his left end for nine yards before Hamberg punted to the Navy 31, where again the Quakers started marching.

This time it appeared the Quakers would make good. Aided by a 15-yard penalty against the Middies, they advanced to the Navy 27. Here Kane broke away around his left end to the five-yard line, but four drives at the line found the ball with a yard from the goal and it was Navy's ball on downs. Hamberg's punt out was weak, going outside on the Navy 14. Odell went to the six on the seventh play, and Ferrell. Another running play was piled up and a pass intercepted by Martin in the end zone and run out on the seven. The Middies froze the ball with line plays the remaining seconds to end the game, 7 to 0.

18,000 See Upset At Pimlico Track

Continued from Page 1.

ing mile, and a half journey combined to bring about the downfall of Riverland. The strapping son of Cold Stream, whose recent victories over Whirlaway and Alsab had sent his stock soaring to dizzy heights, conceded Oonbarr a nine-pound pull in the weights at 125 to 116. It was his initial effort over the long route.

WOOLF ON WINNER

Aonbarr, who had been holding his own with the top-notchers of the handicap division all season, was given a sterling ride by George Woolf. The gelding son of Boatswain and Hedemora was restrained off the pace cut out by Abbe Pierre and Riverland for almost a mile of the journey, then came on with amazing reserve speed to outgame the favorite in a desperate duel through the last sixteenth.

Equinox was a trailer through the first mile of the journey and although he was far outdistanced by the one, two horses, he, too, turned on with a gallant charge to earn the show award.

ANOTHER FOR STAR COPY

H. P. Metcalfe's Star Copy nailed it four in a row when he earned a length and a half decision over Mar-Kell in the mile and a sixteenth Con Amore Handicap, fifth race and secondary feature.

Star Copy, with Farril Zufelt up, took the lead just beyond the half mile pole and, although he was challenged repeatedly by Mar-Kell, he managed to cling to his advantage down to the wire. Night Glow was third.

Both Star Copy and Mar-Kell closed 8-5 choices. Star Copy paid $5.60 and was timed in 1.44 2-5.

ENTERPRISE WINS

Rokeby Stable's versatile gelding Enterprise, who can jump, competed with equal ability and sped three-quarters of a mile in the good time of 1.11 4-5 to record a length and a half victory over Marksman in the fourth race. Clyde Tolson was third.

Top weight in the seven-horse field under 117 pounds, Enterprise came around horses on the stretch turn to gain command from the pacemaking Marksman approaching the sixteenth pole. Only Clyde Tolson, showing a return to his best form, made a fast run through the stretch to be third.

Flamingo Farm's Boy Soldier, easy winner of his last sprint race, was tried at a mile and 70 yards in the opener and the bay son of Jamestown made good at odds of $9.20 to $2.00.

FAVORITE RUNS FOURTH

Boy Soldier, under Sterling Young, saved many lengths on the rail turning for home and at the finish was showing the way to Reigh Star by a length. Dan Bien was third and Uncle Billies was 9-5 choice, wound up fourth.

Tracellette went out to set the pace and the gelding was closely attended by Reigh Star and Star Bien. All three swung wide turning for home and with Boy Soldier and Uncle Billies saved ground on the rail. Uncle Billies began shortening his stride through the last sixteenth.

$121.90 DOUBLE

Rough Honey carried the silks of Mrs. J. F. Y. Christmas to an upset victory in the six-furlong second race to pay $14.40 and complete a $121.90 daily double.

Getting to the front under heavy Mora just beyond the eighth pole, Rough Honey outgamed Two Timer in a sizzling stretch duel to gain a half-length victory. Two Timer and Rough Honey swept into the stretch only heads apart. Rocky Craig was third in the field of 12. The running time was 1.13⅘.

Parachutist, the favorite, broke very slowly, trailed far out of it for a half mile then closed a big gap while running on the outside through the stretch.

up five yards before Hume punted on the Penn 40, Pletz making a flashy return of nine yards to the 49. Again the Quakers launched an offensive, with Miller advancing the load this time on slashing drives.

Penn advanced to the Navy 41 this time, and again the Middies dug in, forcing the Quakers back on downs on the Navy 36. Hamberg, taking a punt, galloped around his left end for nine yards before Hamberg punted to the Navy 31, where again the Quakers started marching.

This time it appeared the Quakers would make good. Aided by a 15-yard penalty against the Middies, they advanced to the Navy 27. Here Kane broke away around his left end to the five-yard line, but four drives at the line found the ball with a yard from the goal and it was Navy's ball on downs. Hamberg's punt out was weak, going outside on the Navy 14. Odell went to the six on the seventh play, and Ferrell. Another running play was piled up and a pass intercepted by Martin in the end zone and run out on the seven. The Middies froze the ball with line plays the remaining seconds to end the game, 7 to 0.

Nova Scores K.O. In Comeback

PORTLAND, Ore., Nov. 6—(A. P.)—Lou Nova, the heavyweight Yogi man, launched a comeback attempt tonight by knocking out Ernie Nordman, Goddard, Kan, in the fourth round of a scheduled 10-round bout.

Nova, 208, whose self-styled Yogi punch failed against Champion Joe Louis, opened cautiously. He caught Nordman, 195, with a few hard rights in the second, tagged him frequently in the third and floored him twice in the fourth before putting the Kansan out for keeps in 2:02 of the round.

Nova's home is Sacramento.

GAME MOVED

Princeton and Yale have shifted their November 14 grid tussle from Princeton, N. J. to New York City.

NITE LIFE -:- By LOU and KEN CALVERT

Comedy seems to be the order of the week at local niteries, with a particularly fine brand on tap at many of the better spots. The perennially popular Ralph Lewis, opening at 21 Club Wednesday; Douglas Brothers and Peck & Peck, comedy sepia jitterbug teams at Club Charles and Beachcomber respectively; Arthur Blake and the Band Box all come in for their share of receptions due really fine performers. Belly-laughs-of-the-week most certainly go to Dude Kimball, Madison's country plumber. If Bob Burns could play thirty or so bazooka-type instruments, if he was gifted with an even smoother patter and more genial personality, and if he had a stock of original routines and stories to go with it all, he'd be the performer that Dude Kimball is. Kimball, veterinarian and turkey farm proprietor on the side, is on his first tour East in years and is definitely a treat.

WELCOME NEWS is the return of Dick Abbott and his orchestra tomorrow night to the Chesapeake Lounge of the Emerson Hotel. Abbott comes direct from Washington's swank Mayfair. His smoothly relaxing rhythms will be remembered by many Baltimore lounge-lovers.

WORTH YOUR WHILE: A visit to Kibby's for a look-see at Ruth Brewer, whose playing of five different musical instruments is real solid entertainment . . . a whirl at Kay's girlie revue, emceed by genial Willie Gray . . . a session with Scott and Davis, with Kay Gardner and Mary De Angelus at New Hotel Broadway . . . Clemmy's piano work at Club Bar . . John Shuey's tall tales, Mom Shuey's genuine home-style and thoroughly enjoyable meals at Shuey's down on Stoney Creek . . . the playing of Danny's Rhythm Boys at Benny Benjamin's Fayette Street lounge . . . De Luca's new trio, Jack Weber and his boys, with Dell Hardy at the piano.

EDDIE BROWN NIGHT AT CLUB CHARLES on Tuesday will pay tribute to Eddie "Curley" Brown, ace of clubs manager, slated to leave for the armed forces shortly. Eddie will be honored with a presentation by the Club Charles staff and a host of friends will be on hand to bid him God speed.

THE WORD HAS IT that one of Charles street's most popular lounges is dickering for the services of Ann Starr, talented Manhattan pianist and composer who has indicated a willingness to locate in Baltimore. The swell elegant Owens Sisters who scored heavily during a recent engagement at Doc's Lounge are spotlighted at Herb Sachs' Del Rio in Washington, now, with Nat Brandywine's Orchestra and June Robbins. They are scheduled for an early return to Doc's. Jack Grant, vocalizing pianist fresh from a successful run at Florida's Royal Palms, has made quite a hit at the Band Box. Ditto Les Timmons, slapping bass with Nat Conway and doing vocals in the Madison show.

HIGHLIGHTS ABOUT TOWN: Kathleen's Five Dukes of Rhythm . . . evenings of chatting with Pat at Pat's Bar . . . Nolan's popular musicrew, Rudy's Reveters . . . 2 O'Clock Club's new merry-go-round bar, making a total of three available for service . . . Green Villa's Doris White and her novelty tapping atop a high silk hat; Virginia Wayne and Leroy the Frog Man at the Asner's spot as well . . . Whitey Keith's merrymakers at Mac's Walnut Grove in Brooklyn . . . Cerilla Mitchell's casual entertaining at Frank Crosbie's Sportsman . . . the capable manner in which Genial Jack, Sweeney's new major-domo, has taken over operations . . . Teddy Reichhart's pleasant banter and the swell food his chef turns out . . . Golden Ring Inn's genial hostess, Laura . . . Bill Higgs' smooth Hawaiianizing at Crystal Ball Inn . . . the weekend barndancing at Keystone Nite Club in Dundalk. Real country atmosphere with genuine hillbilly rhythms makes these Saturday and Sunday parties loads of fun.

SUBWAY'S OPENING on Wednesday proved a gala occasion, with exclamations of "oh" and "ah" prevailing as hundreds poured in for a squint at Roy Helms' latest spot. Tex LeGrange, Helms' manager, will have his hands full trying to accommodate all who will make this cleverly appointed room their rendezvous.

EL PATIO'S EXPANSION is virtually complete and the newly constructed balcony should be ready for formal induction into service on or about Wednesday of next week. Complete redecorating has added a lot to the spot.

DUTCH MILL'S Babe La Tour goes into her sixth week tomorrow. Those who haven't seen her, should. Ditto Cora Walsh in a series of new arrangements at the Kolker's Blue Room. Her alternate work with Milt Lyons and his orchestra has built a rapid and consistent following.

BLUE MIRROR

Eileen George, popular D. C. vocalist well known for her club and radio work, is heard nightly at Charles street's Blue Mirror. George Yeatman and his WBAL Quartet play for dancing; Margie Wood handles vocals with the unit.

Star Studded Revues Boast These Headliners

RALPH LEWIS
Merry master of mirth opening with laughs-a-minute at 21 Club.

ARTHUR BLAKE
Satirical reflections his forte . . . topping Band Box presentation

FAYE MERYL
Earle Club's pert and talented tap stylist

TEDDY BLACK
Club Charles' new and capable maestro whose band is heard nightly

MARY MARTIN
Spotlighted dance in current 2 o'Clock Club Revue

DUDE KIMBALL
Madison's hysterical country plumber

GRETA VAN KIRK
The vocal side of Doc's new team, Jerry & Greta

ZIGGY TVORANOS
Talented pianist with Blue Mirror quartet

BABE LA TOUR
Still "Whoopee-ing" to capacity houses at Dutch Mill

Additional news of night clubs and cocktail lounges will be found on Page 11.

New Team Seen At Doc's Lounge

Jerry and Greta, piano and song duo, is the latest unit to handle entertainment at Doc's, popular Charles street rendezvous, and the two girls have been received nicely. Greta Van Kirk, vocalist of the duo, has appeared in many of the local spots as headline attraction.

Also on the revolving music stand at Doc's are the Groverneers, quartet of sepia song and instrumentalists specializing in clever lyrical arrangements and smooth harmony.

Mallory and Grue continue to draw nightly applause for their musical offerings. Paul Mallory's solo piano number have become a demand item.

STRICKLER'S

Music par excellence is on tap nightly at Strickler's popular Harford road lounge, where Lynne Corrine and her all-girl orchestra turn out unusual and well-arranged dance rhythms. Miss Corrinne's piano solos are drawing considerable interest, as is the work of featured musicians Frances Quinn, Betty Dey and Lou Hart.

Carl's Vocalist

SAUNDRA PHILLIPS
Popular and personable young vocalist, comedienne and M. C. appearing currently at Carl's.

ALGERIAN ROOM

Play what your patrons request and they're bound to be satisfied. That's the philosophy of Ivan Frank, genial host of the New Algerian Room in the Mount Royal Hotel, and both on his electric organ and in the policy of Ruth Gehlert's all-girl orchestra patron's requests get first call.

OPENING NOV. 11th ALL HEADLINER SHOW! RALPH LEWIS · MARGO GOOD · CRAIG MATHEWS · ANDREWS SISTERS · SUNDAY COCKTAIL DANCE With Complete Floor Show 4 to 8 P. M. No Cov. No Min. · 1ST SHOW TONITE 10 P. M. · 21 Club · NO COVER · RESERVATIONS SAr. 5552 · 21 W. BALTIMORE ST. · LAST 4 DAYS—TONI LANE—JAN MURRAY · LISTEN TO LARRY LONDON'S ORCH. NITELY W-I-T-H 10:15 P. M.

Held Over! FRANCES FAYE America's Swingsational Queen of Jive Heading An ALL-NEW Show . . . with DOUGLAS BROS. · CLIFF CONRAD · CHIQUITA · Elaine & Glenn · WALLY WANGER GIRLS · NEW! TEDDY BLACK & His N. B. C. Orch. · club charles · CHARLES at PRESTON · VERNON 8020-21

Frank Morgan, Boyer, Hepburn, Edna May Oliver All Rolled Up In One! MARGIE TAYLOR, M. C. Presents ARTHUR BLAKE SATIRICAL REFLECTIONS · SHIRLEY DULOW DYNAMIC SONGSTRESS · With EDITH DELANEY, Sweetheart of Taps; JACK GRANT, Piano & Songs · CHARLIE FRANZ'S BAND BOX ORCHESTRA · COCKTAIL JAMBOREE EVERY SUNDAY 4 TO 7 WITH COMPLETE FLOOR SHOW · BAND BOX 1309-11 N. CHARLES ST. VERNON 6795

Helms' NAUTICAL LOUNGE featuring BARBARA GREY & THE ADMIRALS nitely · EVERYBODY RAVED · SUBWAY · Balto's Smartest, Newest, Most Intimate Lounge! · 112-120 PATAPSCO AVE., Brooklyn · Reservations: CURTIS 1007

What Jitterbugs! Not a Bone in Their Bodies! PECK & PECK · JUNE BROOKS · JOE CAMPO · Gracie Collins · Beachcomberettes · 2 ORCHESTRAS · Continuous Entertainment · BEACHCOMBER · 110 N. LIBERTY ST. PL. 5049

POSITIVELY NONE LIKE HER! 6TH AND FINAL WEEK! BABE LA TOUR · HOST OF OTHERS · Mike Traill's Orchestra · DUTCH MILL · SUPPER CLUB HAM. 9703 · 6615 HARFORD ROAD · NO COVER NO MINIMUM

Algerian Room · MT. ROYAL HOTEL · RUTH GEHLERT'S ALL-GIRL ORCHESTRA · UNDER THE PERSONAL MANAGEMENT OF IVAN FRANK at the Electric Organ · MT. ROYAL and CALVERT ST.

Get In The Groove With The Grooverneers MALLORY & GRUE TOPS IN SONGS Jerry & Greta · COCKTAIL HOUR DAILY 4 to 7 P.M. · DOC'S COCKTAIL LOUNGE 1817 N. CHARLES ST.

LEO BATEMAN HILARIOUS M. C. presenting BOB STANLEY & CO. His Wire Work, His Trained Dogs · KAY WAYNE SPARKLING PERFORMER · JACK DECKER'S ORCHESTRA with FREDDIE FLEISCHMANN'S · WARREN'S UPTOWN NITE CLUB · Fulton Near Pennsylvania Ave.

Homespun Hilarity Like You Never Heard Before! DUDE KIMBALL Turning "Everything But the Kitchen Sink" into a Musical Instrument · LES TIMMONS · BETH MORRIS · Madison NITE CLUB · MADISON at CHESTER Res. WOlfe 8677

A Grand Show With VALDEZ & PEGGY · RUTH BREWER & VIETTE · CLIFF & MORRIS · SAM VINCI & FRANK YOUNG · A COMPLETE JAMBOREE OF JUMPIN' JIVE ENTERTAINMENT with AL MAGIN'S ORCHESTRA · KIBBY'S NITE CLUB

A Double Musical Treat Nitely! CORA WALSH Her Accordion, Her Vocalizing · MILT LYONS His Piano, His Orchestra · Arundel BLUE ROOM · MT. ROYAL at CHARLES · LEXINGTON 7640

"WHERE IT'S SMART TO BE SEEN" DANCING NITELY TO GEORGE YEATMAN and his famous WBAL QUARTET · Margie Wood · EILEEN GEORGE · COCKTAIL HOUR 4 to 7 DAILY · NO COVER NO MINIMUM · Blue Mirror · 929 N. CHARLES ST.

Earle CLUB · What's Gonna Happen? · FAY MERYL · MARCOS & ODETTE · June Hurley · Jackie Hill · Sunday Cocktail Matinee 4 to 7 with Complete Floor Show · 12 S. PATTERSON PARK AVE. WOLFE 9223

SWINGSATIONAL! LYNNE CORRINNE'S All-Girl ORCHESTRA · STRICKLERS · RESTAURANT · BAR · LOUNGE · 6800-10 HARFORD RD.

FUN! NITE CLUB CARLS · 3316 KEYSTONE ROAD at 33rd St. · A SCOOP! SAUNDRA PHILLIPS Plus HELENE CHARELLE · KAYANAUGH & RAYMOND · Jimmie Nichols' Orch. · 2 SHOWS NITELY 10:30-12:30

NEW STARS · 2 O'CLOCK CLUB · 414 E. BALTIMORE ST. · CALVERT 0704

PAN-AMERICAN REVUE · El Patio · ST. PAUL AT MADISON · DON CASANOVA, Emcee · Hermanos Contreras · Dancing Dolores · Caesar & Rosita · RHUMBA SUNDAY 4-7 P. M.

Chesapeake Lounge · Return Engagement! Beginning Tomorrow · DICK ABBOTT AND HIS BAND · Their down-beat makes your heart beat! · HOTEL EMERSON · G. C. CLEMENTS, Mgr.

MATUSKY'S SUPPER CLUB · Eddie COOK'S ORCHESTRA · DINNERS FROM 50c UP · RIVIERA BEACH, MD.

Benjamin's BAR and LOUNGE PRESENTS DANNY and his RHYTHM BOYS · 12 W. FAYETTE ST.

The One and Only WILLIE GRAY · KAY'S CABARET Baltimore & Frederick Sts.

STONY CREEK TAVERN · SHUEY'S · Fun for All · CHARLEY MOORE'S MUSIC SATURDAY AND SUNDAY

GAYETY NITE CLUB · COMPLETE NEW SHOW EVERY WEEK ALL STAR ACTS

CLUB BAR

NEW HOTEL BROADWAY · NEW FLOOR SHOW · KAY GARDNER · Scott & Davis, Dancers · Mary De Angelus · CHARLEY DEGELE'S ORCHESTRA · Reservations, WOlfe 0602 · BROADWAY AT ORLEANS ST.

BUY WAR BONDS AND STAMPS

DINING DANCING GAIETY

AIR PORT GRILL	6500 Riverview Ave., Dundalk. Music Fri., Sat. and Sun. Dine and Dance to Bill Yaeger and His Yanks of Rhythm—Al "Abe" Shaeffer, Emcee. No cover, no minimum.
CATON TAVERN	Edmondson & Dutton Aves. Featuring the Caton Rhythm Rousers! Good food at all hours. Liquors. Cars 14 & 8 go by door at Catonsville Junc. Phone Caton. 317.
CRYSTAL BALL INN	Buck Jones Orchestra Fri. and Sat. Bill Higgs' Hawaiian Trio Sunday, 8.30 to 12.30. New Philadelphia Road at Race Road.
CRYSTAL BAR	417 E. BALTO. ST., next door to EMBASSY THEATRE, featuring LUCILLE ENGLE and BILL TAYLOR. Continuous entertainment nitely. Delicious food and tempting drinks. No cover or minimum ever.
DE LUCA'S	62 WILLOW SPRING ROAD, DUNDALK FEATURING JACK WEBER'S ENTERTAINING TRIO WITH DELL HARDY AT THE PIANO.
GOLDEN RING INN	Golden Ring Road and Old Phila. Road. Three Ambassadors Trio. Sat. and Sun. Delicious Food, Drinks, Never a Cov. or Min.
Green Villa Nite Club	3 Floor Shows Nitely. Continuous Entertainment. 3 Fine Acts plus Music, Dancing. 5423 O'DONNELL ST. First Show at 9 P. M.
KATHLEEN'S	EAT, DRINK AND MAKE MERRY. 2 BIG FLOOR SHOWS NITELY. NO COVER OR MINIMUM. 612 EAST BALTIMORE ST.
KEYSTONE NITE CLUB	Barn Dancing Sat. nite and Sundays beginning 2 P. M. Chicken and Spaghetti Dinner Sunday. Turn left from Dundalk Ave. to Keystone sign. 7018 Holabird Ave.
LA RICCI	RESTAURANT, 1119 N. CHARLES, SERVING THE FINEST ITALIAN AND AMERICAN LUNCHEONS, DINNERS. SPECIAL CHICKEN AND SPAGHETTI, 85c. OPEN 24 HOURS DAILY.
LEON'S	MERRY-GO-ROUND BAR—BALTIMORE'S NEWEST RESTAURANT—LOUNGE—BAR. 870 PARK AVENUE. UNDER PERSONAL DIRECTION OF LEON LAMPE
(Mac's) Walnut Grove	3612 Hanover St., Brooklyn. Dancing to Whitey Keith's Orchestra. Music 9 to 2. Take Car No 6. Get Off at Patapsco Avenue.
NATE & LEON'S	DELICATESSEN. Stop in after the show for a Midnight Snack. Delicious Sandwiches. OPEN ALL NIGHT. 850 WEST NORTH AVENUE.
NOLAN'S NITE CLUB	Wilkens & Monroe. Mixed Drinks. The finest food. Music of Rudy's Revelers. Dancing, 9 P. M. 'Til 2 A. M.
PAT'S BAR	116 N. LIBERTY ST. "THE MOST TALKED ABOUT PLACE IN BALTIMORE." NIGHT CLUB ATMOSPHERE. FEATURING HALF FRIED CHICKEN—60c.
SAM'S RAIL INN	2630 W. NORTH AVE. Dancing tonite and every Fri., Sat. and Sun. to Charlie Sipes' Orchestra. No cover. No minimum. Moroccan atmosphere.
SPORTSMAN	Cocktail Lounge & Bar. 1429 N. Charles St. Cerilla Mitchell, piano; Kay Gardner, songs. Cocktail Hour 4-8 Sunday. Open 7 A. M. to 2 A. M. Daily. No Cov. or Min.
SWEENEY'S	3128 GREENMOUNT AVE. Dance to Jerry Kaufman's Trio. Continuous Entertainment Nitely. Pleasantly AIR-CONDITIONED always. Plenty of fun at all times!
TEDDY REICHHART	2208 HARFORD RD. A cordial welcome and plenty of fun for everyone. Best Food and Drink. No COVER. No MINIMUM.

BUY WAR STAMPS & BONDS

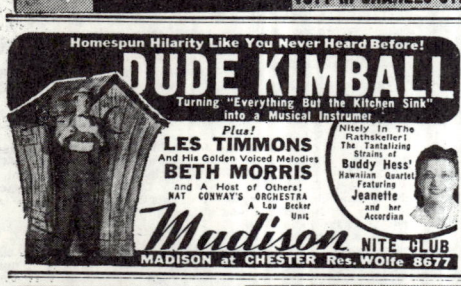

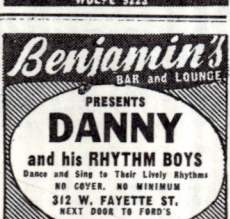

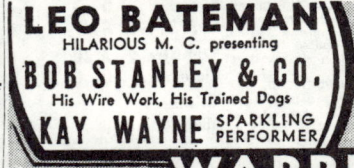

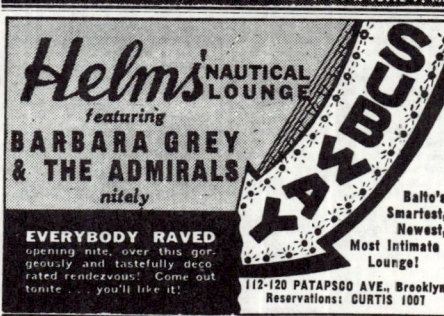

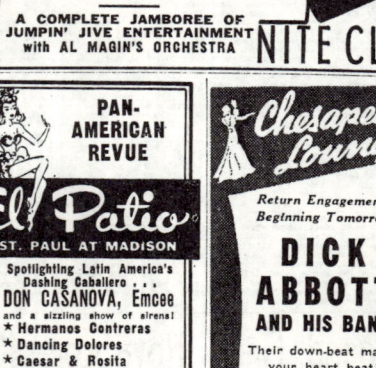

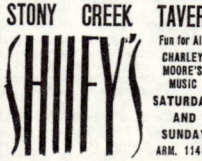

EIGHTH ARMY BATTLES NAZIS INSIDE TUNISIA

Baltimore News-Post

THE WEATHER
Colder today, with low humidity, moderate winds.

The Largest Evening Circulation in the Entire South

VOL. CXLII—NO. 74   MONDAY, FEBRUARY 1, 1943   PRICE 3 CENTS

COMPLETE FINAL

Axis Supply Dumps Burn At Tripoli

A heavy black cloud of smoke rises from Axis supply dumps after the war material was set afire by Marshal Erwin Rommel's fleeing Africa Corps troops. This official British picture was radioed from Cairo to New York.

Russian Armies Aim At Two Anchor Cities

MOSCOW, Jan. 31—(U. P.).—Two Russian armies intensified offensives against Kursk and Kharkov, great anchor cities of the entire German defense system in the south, and in the North Caucasus a third army advanced up the Caucasus railroad on Rostov.

West of Voronezh, where the Red Army yesterday reached a point only 63 miles from Kursk, the Russians during the night captured 40 inhabited localities, the noon communique reported, after freeing 200 towns and villages, killing 12,000 Germans, capturing 14,000 Germans and 11,000 Italians and routing seven German divisions, two German regiments and an Italian Alpine Corps in three days.

100,000 CAPTIVES

The prisoners on the Voronezh front, after a night in which 600 more were taken, totaled more than 100,000 since the Russians started that offensive two weeks ago, special dispatches said.

At Stalingrad, dispatches revealed that a total of 6,000 prisoners had been taken up yesterday, 450 more were taken during the night. As many had been taken yesterday.

The noon communique reported that the mutinous troops, remnants of 220,000 left by Adolf Hitler to die to his glory, were abandoning their units at Stalingrad and, led by their officers, trying to escape in little groups.

GUISE OF PRISONERS

Red Army sentries caught German officers, dressed as soldiers, trying to escape in the guise of prisoners, led by a German soldier wearing a Russian uniform.

One general was made prisoner yesterday. In addition it was confirmed that German Major General Trebber had surrendered several days ago with what remained of his Two Hundred and Ninety-seventh Infantry Division.

In the North Caucasus several inhabited localities fell to the Russians this morning the noon communique reported, after the capture yesterday of the great Kropotkin railroad junction 128 miles southeast of Rostov. One strongly fortified base was captured against fierce resistance and the Germans were put to flight.

Fish Cakes For Two

Far from the comforts of their homes, these two tommies are shown cooking fish cakes in Egypt in a pause in their pursuit of Rommel. One of problems of the Allied forces is that of keeping forces moving at the rapid pace set by the Rommel.

MD. SUPPLY OF OIL AMPLE FOR RATIONS

British Fight Nazis Inside Tunis Border

LONDON, Jan. 31—(U. P.).—The British Eighth Army battled the retreating Africa Corps inside Tunisia, 150 miles or less from American forces on the western side of the rapidly contracting African front.

The Middle Eastern Command announced that forward elements of the Eighth Army crossed the border on the middle sector.

It was not made clear whether all of the Africa Corps had gotten out of Tripolitania, ending in fact the Italian Empire. Presumably some rear guards were still a trifle short of the border on the southern and northern (coastal) sectors.

SFAX IS LEVELED

The harbor of Sfax had already been leveled by wave upon wave of Flying Fortresses and medium bombers in the greatest air attack the Allies have made to date in Tunisia. Observers in London believed Axis ships now were unable to get in or out of Sfax harbor.

WRECKING AXIS PORTS

The Middle Eastern Command said bad weather still interfered with its air operations, but that all planes returned yesterday from limited missions.

American bombers based in North Africa were believed embarking on a program to systematically devastate every Axis-held port in Tunisia so the German and Italians would be cut off from sea-borne aid when the nearing-zero hour of the supreme Allied offensive strikes.

GERMANS ALARMED

The German official news agency, in a dispatch broadcast by Radio Berlin, said of American Lieutenant General Dwight D. Eisenhower:

"He is about to throw in... new forces taken from the British First Army and from the American Army group concentrated on the Algerian-Tunisian border.

"He seems to have the intention to take the offensive and push toward the Tunisian east coast."

Eisenhower, the dispatch said, intended to strike on the Central

U-Boat Nest At Lorient RAF Target

LONDON, Jan. 31—(A. P.).—British bombers attacked the German submarine base at Lorient in Western France again the Air Ministry announced. Four bombers are missing from the raid, it said.

It was the sixth raid on the Bay of Biscay U-boat nest in 16 days. The R. A. F. struck at it last on the night of January 26 after a lull of two days.

The raid of January 23 was described as a major attack and in it five bombers were reported lost. The four reported missing in last night's assault indicated that the raid was made in force.

In an early morning retaliatory raid, a flight of four German planes bombed a town on the southeast coast of England demolishing two private dwellings, killing three persons.

Italy Choice Of Diners For Invasion

CHICAGO, Jan. 31—(I. N. S.).—Italy is the American public's favorite site for an Allied landing in Europe, according to the military doodling on restaurant tablecloths.

The Linen Supply Association of America, which handles 90 per cent. of the nation's hotel and restaurant napery, declared that amateur strategists are displaying unusual agreement in the maps they draw on their favorite medium—the dinner table linen.

Since the American landing in Morocco, the linen suppliers say, the African coastline has taken precedence over all others in the doodlers' interest. Next in order are Italy and its neighboring islands, the southern coast of Europe, the Russian front, the West coast of Europe, the Solomon Islands, the China and Siberian coast, Alaska and Japan.

"The imagination of the average citizen," a linen supply dealer said, "gets its greatest exercise when he sits down to eat. All he needs, in a good restaurant, is a sharp pencil and someone to listen and look."

Brazilians Laud Accord With U. S.

RIO DE JANEIRO, Jan. 31—(A. P.).—Brazilians applauded the "complete accord" reached by President Getulio Vargas and President Roosevelt in their surprise conference at Natal and it was even hinted that the "co-operation without restrictions" promised by President Vargas might include sending Brazilian soldiers to the African battle front.

Smiling and optimistic after his meetings with President Roosevelt aboard a U. S. destroyer in the harbor at Natal, President Vargas told a press conference that complete agreement had been reached on war operations and other points we discussed."

HINT TROOPS TO SEE LONG WAR

Vargas said:
"United nations are preparing war, not wishing to be optimistic because war has crises.

"German military power evidently is declining. There may be a collapse one moment or the other. But, generally, we are preparing for the emergency and are considering a long war.

"I found the President of the United States fully satisfied with the results of the Casablanca conference, one of the purposes of which was to achieve unity of the French people."

Vargas said he found Roosevelt "in the best of body and spirits, his intense demonstrating a firm decision to carry forward the crusade in which we all are engaged." He added:

"President Roosevelt was frankly optimistic over the outcome of the battle."

The Brazilian press, splurging the biggest Brazilian story since this nation entered the war on August 22, 1942, hinted that the meeting of the two Presidents might bring fulfillment of the wishes of many Government leaders to send Brazilian troops to the African and later the European battlefields.

Vichy Recalls Ecuador Envoy

QUITO, Ecuador, Jan. 31—(A. P.).—French Ambassador Andre Boissier said he had received orders from Vichy to return to France with his staff and all French consular officials.

(Earlier dispatches from Rio de Janeiro said French Ambassador Rene de Saint Quentin had received similar orders, but had announced his intention to ignore them.)

Let It Rain

Nobody is going to advise this outfit for a sleet storm like Baltimore experienced a few days ago, but it appears O. K. for Hollywood. Actress Gail Russell is shown heading for a movie set fully outfitted to cope with rain.

Chinese Woman Sponsors Warship

MARE ISLAND NAVY YARD, Feb. 1—(U. P.).—Mrs. Emma Yam, fifty-one, was granted the honor of being the first Chinese woman to launch an American warship here. She works in the Navy yard as an electrician's helper.

To Redeem All Coupons Issued

There is enough fuel oil in Maryland to cover all outstanding ration coupons, E. S. Ferguson, regional rationing executive for the Office of Price Administration, declared in a statement in New York.

Maryland, one of five States under the regional direction, was included in Ferguson's declaration that there is enough oil in the 17 Eastern States to redeem coupons issued.

The executive said he had no figures as to the gallonage of oil or of the number of coupons, but added that "they have a pretty close approximation in Washington."

Although he affirmed his belief that general stocks are adequate to cover coupons in the 17 States, Mr. Ferguson declared that, in distribution snarls, it might be necessary for the OPA to invoke its recently granted right to establish priorities in emergencies.

Resigns Union Post To Go Into Army

WASHINGTON, Jan. 31—(A. P.).—The Maryland and District of Columbia Industrial Union Council (C. I. O.) announces the resignation of its president, George A. Meyers, who has been inducted into the Army.

Meyers' unexpired term will be filled by Boyd E. Payton, who was elected by the council's executive board.

Air Pilots Come From 35 States

SAN ANTONIO, Jan. 31—(I. N. S.).—Most cadet pilot classes at Randolph Field, Texas, have representatives from at least 35 States.

Red Guardsmen Cross Don

Guardsmen of the Red Army are shown crossing to the western bank of the Don river as counter-attacks are pressed against the Nazi invaders. Buoyancy of the small craft permits movement of many troops as the Russians go forward with reports of many Nazis killed and others taken prisoner. These valiant fighters are adequately clothed and equipped to meet the hardships of Russian winter. Every day brings news of further conquests by the Soviets.

'Cat People' Is Chiller At Hipp; 'Ghost' At Times

SIMONE SIMON KENT SMITH

By NORMAN CLARK

IF YOU SHOULD get mad with a girl like Irene Dubrovna and call her a cat, you'd probably receive the surprise of your life. She'd be mighty apt to turn into a panther right before your very eyes and claw your heart out.

It seems—at least there's a legend to that effect—that the women of a certain tribe in the Balkans have to suffer for the sins of their ancestors. If they should happen to become greatly enraged, or indulge in a bit of romance, they are liable to turn into wild cats or tigers or panthers.

Irene Dubrovna, a sketch artist in New York, believes she is a descendant of the cat people. She tries to keep calm and unromantic, but Oliver Reed thinks she's a cute kitten and asks her to marry him. She gives in. It isn't long before a psych 'trist and a woman, who loves Irene's husband, are making her as mad as a hornet.

Who's that sneaking up with soft tread but harsh snarls? Right-o. Irene—mad as a hornet but looking and acting like a panther.

"Cat People" is odd and weird. It's for the chiller fans. Kent Smith, who once acted here with the University Players, portrays the harassed husband with manly strength and charm. Simone Simon and Tom Conway are satisfactory in their roles.

"Cat People"

"CAT PEOPLE," at the Hippodrome. Story by De Witt Bodeen. Directed by Jacques Tourneur. An RKO picture.

THE CAST

Irene Dubrovna.......Simone Simon
Oliver Reed.............Kent Smith
The Psychiatrist.......Tom Conway
Alice Moore.........Jane Randolph
Commodore ....Jack Holt
Carver ....Alan Napier
Miss Plunkett......Elizabeth Dunne
The Cat Woman...Elizabeth Russell

AT TIMES

"TOMORROW WE LIVE," starring Ricardo Cortez and Jean Parker. Story and screen play by Bart Lytton. Directed by Edgar Ulmer. A PRC picture, presented at the Times.

THE CAST

The Ghost..........Ricardo Cortez
Julie ....Jean Parker
Pop Bronson.........Emmett Lynn
Lieut. Bob Lord...William Marshall
Melba ....Rosemary Stevens
Chick ....Ray Miller
Kohler ....Frank S. Hagney

THE GHOST in "Tomorrow We Live" doesn't belong to the cat people of the Balkans, but it would appear as if he had almost as many lives as a cat.

A couple of times vengeful persons almost smack this wicked gangster into his grave, but he comes up sneering and eager to murder a few more citizens. An extremely mean man is The Ghost. He tries to force Julie, a good girl, into marrying him, even though she is bethrothed to a handsome young officer in the U. S. Army.

The Ghost has a lot of lead in him—a bullet here and a bullet there. In fact, he'd be a rich haul in a scrap-metal collection. Justice and the undertaker finally catch up with him.

"Tomorrow We Live" is vigorous melodrama. Ricardo Cortez, Jean Parker, Emmett Lynn and William Marshall play the main parts with confidence.

RECONCILED

The Don Barrys, who have been having marital troubles, are reconciled again. Mrs. Barry was staying with Maureen O'Hara, but has moved home.

FEMININE Voice Of BROADWAY

By DOROTHY KILGALLEN

How Do You Get Those Items?

He came over to the table and sat down without saying anything first, without being asked. He just slid into the banquette and made himself comfortable.

He was wearing lieutenant's bars on his shoulders, silver ones that looked gold under the gleaming lights of the Stork Club, and the sleeve of his uniform carried the emblem of the Signal Corps. His voice was thick and a little combative, as though he were expecting an argument. He said:

"Do you know what you ought to write about? Those guys on Guadalcanal. Those guys haven't seen a woman in months. I'm not saying where I've been, but I've seen action. Plenty of action. I've been where it's hot. I know what those guys on Guadalcanal want. Do you know what they want?"

He paused. His eyes remained fixed on his audience but his right hand moved toward a bottle of Scotch on the table.

"They want to come home and ride in a taxicab."

He poured himself a drink.

"I know that. That's the truth. Do you know what I've just been doing? I've been riding around in a cab with my girl. That's what I'd been dreaming of doing and now I've done it and it doesn't mean a thing and now I'm in the Stork Club that those guys on Guadalcanal are dreaming about and it doesn't mean a thing either. Now I'm ready to go back."

He tilted the glass high and drank half of what was in it. He said:

"I've been bombed 270 times and I've been over the target 23 times.

"Do you know what it's like to go over the target? Well, it's like this. You write yourself off the books every time you go over the target.

"That's why I rode in that taxicab tonight and that's why I'm here and that's why I'm going to marry my girl Ruth before I leave again. She doesn't know it, but I am."

He finished his drink and got up.

"I'm going to marry her before I go over the target again, and then if I don't come back she'll get $5,000. She's a nice kid."

He said goodbye and turned and went back to his own table and to his girl whose name was Ruth.

MONTY WOOLLEY IN CENTRE'S FEATURE

Monty Woolley and Ida Lupino are starred in "Life Begins at Eight-Thirty," film feature at Centre from tomorrow through Wednesday.

Cornel Wilde, Sara Allgood, Melville Cooper, J. Edward Bromberg and Edward Demarest have the principal roles. It was produced and written by Nunnally Johnson from a play by Emlyn Williams, and directed by Irving Pichel.

JULIE BRYAN TO STAR AT GAYETY

Julie Bryan heads the cast of the burlesque show, "Heart Breakers," which opens at the Gayety tomorrow afternoon.

Supporting Miss Bryan are Comedians George Murray and Eddie Lloyd, Wade and Wade, Lew Denny, Ben Bernard, Eileen Hubert, Betty Coette, Julie Ruthe and a nobby chorus of "Heart Breakers."

UP FROM COLLEGE

Joyce Reynolds, who makes her motion picture debut in "George Washington Slept Here," was discovered in a college production of "Snow White."

DYED HIS HAIR

Oscar Homolka made his hair blond to win the role of Maxim Litvinov in the filmization of ex-Ambassador Joseph E. Davies' book, "Mission to Moscow."

Would Cast Marlene Dietrich In 'Seven Deadly Sins' Movie

Edward Small Reveals Biblical Epic Plans

By LOUELLA O. PARSONS
Motion Picture Editor International News Service.

HOLLYWOOD, Jan. 30.—If Marlene Dietrich doesn't want to accept that Broadway offer to play in "One Man's Venus," Edward Small has a motion picture for her. He told me he plans to do a Biblical epic called "The Seven Deadly Sins." He will make it along the lines of some of the Cecil B. De Mille spectacles that were so impressive several years ago. He wants Marlene for the siren, a character embodying all the seven sins, and he explains it's a terrific role.

These sins, as listed by Eddie, are pride, covetousness, lust, anger, gluttony, envy, sloth. The settings will be both modern and Biblical and Arthur Sheekman, who has returned to Hollywood with his wife, Gloria Stuart, is preparing the script.

Billy Rose blew into town, and out, so fast that all I could get was his forwarding address when I tried to catch up with him at the Beverly Wilshire Hotel. But Broadway's dynamo showman didn't come all the way to Hollywood for the train ride.

Billy closed a deal with Metro-Goldwyn-Mayer selling them the movie rights to "Jumbo," his big hit of several years ago. And the Rogers and Hart musical score goes along with the deal. "Jumbo" was a great stage success. It is the story about two rival circus shows and M.-G.-M. plans to make it on a scale as elaborate as was Billy's musical.

Chatter in Hollywood: The Karen Morley divorce from Charles Vidor is no surprise since they have been separated two years, with Karen living in New York and Charles directing movies here. He is now in New York, having gone there by train, and Evelyn Keyes, whom he will wed when his divorce is final, flew there to join him.

The ovation Ethel Barrymore received at the Biltmore theatre on her opening night brought a lump in the throats of all her old friends. She looks so radiant on the stage and her performance in "The Corn Is Green" is a triumph. I went back stage to see my old friend and I could hardly believe my eyes.

She hasn't looked as well in years. She said Lionel had called her three times and was coming later in the week to see her performance. I was sorry he wasn't there opening night for he would have been so happy if he could have seen the reception she received.

She was called back again and again. I am going to have tea with her and find out what she has done to herself to look so marvelous. For my money Ethel Barrymore is still the first lady of the theatre.

A Line or Two: Irving Berlin, who was born in Russia and came to this country at the age of four, said to Fred Astaire a few days ago he hoped when "This Is the Army" goes abroad to play for the soldiers that Russia would be included in their itinerary.

Margaret Sullavan is so enthusiastic about the lead in "The Outward Room" that she may even consider stepping out of her announced retirement, although it is by no means definite.

Snapshots of Hollywood Collected at Random: Hal Peary (the Great Gildersleeve) broke a glass signing an autograph and cut his hand so badly he was taken to Hollywood Hospital.

Lieutenant Van Heflin and Mrs. Van, the former Frances Neal, really having fun in our big city. They have been living in San Luis Obispo, where Van is stationed. Must say Army life agrees with him, he looks so well.

Eddie Bracken showing his mother-in-law and father-in-law the sights of our town. Sheila Ryan, who was very sick with flu, now has, of all things, the measles.

Carl Esmond is the first slice-your-own-bread victim. He sliced right through Mrs. Esmond's best lace tablecloth.

Lois Andrews is heading for New York and a tour of the Army camps. You can't eat alfalfa, but the cows and chickens can. So Bill Gargan is raising sixty acres. Catherine Craig leaves to join Bob Preston, who graduates from officers' training school. Mike Whelan and Simone Simon dancing at the Mocambo.

Alan Curtis, in spite of his lameness, gets around. Now it's Louise Albritton he has been seeing. Judy Garland and her sister slipping into the darkened theatre to see the sneak preview of "Madame Du Barry."

Hollywood advices are that Lois Andrews (above) is heading for New York and a tour of the Army camps.

Behind Scenes In Hollywood Studios

By HARRISON CARROLL
King Feature Syndicate Writer.

HOLLYWOOD, Jan. 30.—After sub-leasing her Westwood home and taking an apartment near the Columbia studio, where she'll be working in "My Client Curly," Rita Hayworth now is in one fine mess.

The manager at the apartment house took a look at "Genius," the bulldog that Victor Mature gave to Rita, and said, sorry, but no pooches allowed and she couldn't make an exception, not even for the star.

So poor Rita hasn't a roof over her head.

De Mille's latest worry on "The Story of Dr. Wassell" is how Gary Cooper's long, lanky legs will look in shorts. Seems as the doctor wore them often during his early career in the Orient.

To get around the difficulty, the studio actually is assigning Stylist Natalie Besart to whip up a special type of shorts that will show the Cooper gams off to advantage.

Providing, of course, that Gary doesn't refuse absolutely to wear them.

A gag by Susan Peters had the Hollywood reporters working overtime. From the Brown Derby, Susan phoned her agent that she and Richard Quine were eloping to Las Vegas and nothing could stop them.

Somebody overheard the conversation and it was all over town in an hour. As a matter of fact, the kids say they have no wedding plans at all. Quine would be a crippled bridegroom right now anyway. He tore several shoulder muscles in a screen fight with Noah Berry, Jr., and the "We've Never Been Licked" company may have to shoot around him for a week.

The Air Corps let John Payne return to Hollywood for one day's added scenes on "Hello, Frisco, Hello." The first person John called was June Havoc.

By coming down to work in "Girl Crazy" with a temperature of 102. Mickey Rooney saved 100 extras part of a day's paycheck. He arrived all bundled up in a raccoon coat.

Gayety

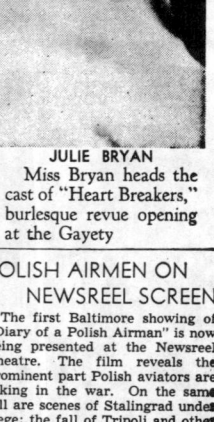

JULIE BRYAN

Miss Bryan heads the cast of "Heart Breakers," burlesque revue opening at the Gayety

POLISH AIRMEN ON NEWSREEL SCREEN

The first Baltimore showing of "Diary of a Polish Airman" is now being presented at the Newsreel Theatre. The film reveals the prominent part Polish aviators are taking in the war. On the same bill are scenes of Stalingrad under siege; the fall of Tripoli and other camera accounts of the European battlefronts and an analysis of President Roosevelt's African conference.

Latest Report From Broadway

NEW YORK, Jan. 30.—Ed Wynn is now tied up with "The Big Time," it was announced by Paul Small, who will be associated with Fred F. Finklehoffe in the sponsorship of the vaudeville show. Mr. Wynn confirmed the engagement and admitted that he was no longer connected with Peter Arno's much-postponed revue. Others mentioned for "The Big Time" aggregation opening in San Francisco on March 1 are Paul Draper and Jane Pickens.

The reunion of the team of Clayton, Jackson & Durante will take place in a subsequent variety bill, according to Mr. Small, who added that he was making arrangements for Frank Fay and Bill Robinson to be in it, too.

A stranger to Broadway since 1930 when he tarried for 11 performances in "Roadside," Ralph Bellamy, the film actor, has been persuaded by Theron Bamberger to return in "Follow the Leader," the James Gow-Arnaud d'Usseau collaboration until recently known as "Suffer Little Children." Mr. Bellamy's role will be that of a Midwestern college professor who is the guardian of a twelve-year-old German refugee. Elliott Nugent will direct. Mr. Bamberger is planning to unveil the production here some time in March.

The Theatre Guild has relinquished the Zoe Akins comedy, "Plans For Tomorrow." Ina Claire was to have appeared in it. According to Miss Claire, the play was started before the war and has had to be switched around a lot, and although Miss Akins "has a good idea in it, history keeps passing you by."

The premiere of "The Moon Vine" at the Morosco has been deferred a night to February 9.

Movie CLOCK

CENTURY—"In Which We Serve," 10.45 A. M., 12.55, 3.05, 5.15, 7.25, 9.48 P. M.
MARYLAND—"Secrets of a Co-Ed," 11.30 A. M., 1.43, 3.56, 6.09, 8.30, 10.35 P. M.
NEW—"The Black Swan." 10 A. M., 12, 2, 4, 6, 8, 10 P. M.
STANLEY—"Now Voyager," 11.15 A. M., 1.55, 4.30, 7.05, 9.40 P. M.
KEITHS—"Palm Beach Story," 10.21 A. M., 12.17, 2.13, 4.09, 6.05, 8.01, 9.57 P. M.
HIPPODROME—"The Cat People," 10 A. M., 12.25, 3.00, 5.30, 7.50, 10.20 P. M.
VALENCIA—"Andy Hardy's Double Life," 1.32, 3.36, 5.40, 7.44, 9.48 P. M.
PARKWAY—"Standby For Action," 12.45, 2.52, 5.08, 7.24, 9.41 P. M.
MAYFAIR—"Silver Queen," 10.30 A. M., 12.30, 2.30, 4.30, 6.30, 8.30, 10.30 P. M.
LITTLE—"Under Two Flags," 11.30 A.M., 1.40, 3.50, 5.50, 7.50, 9.50 P. M.
ROSLYN—"Men of Boys Town," 12.03, 2.34, 5.05, 7.36, 10.07 P. M.
TIMES—"Tomorrow We Live," 12.30, 2.33, 4.36, 6.39, 8.42, 10.45 P. M.

HIPPODROME EUTAW NEAR BALTO. ST.
ON STAGE IN PERSON! POPULAR PRICES
EARL CARROLL'S "VANITIES OF 1943"
A CAST OF 90 STARS
MOST BEAUTIFUL GIRLS IN THE WORLD
SCREEN "CAT PEOPLE" SIMONE SIMON
TOM CONWAY—JANE RANDOLPH
LAST COMPLETE STAGE & SCREEN SHOW TONITE AT 9:30 P. M.

Tomorrow, Lyric at 8.30
BALTIMORE SYMPHONY
Reginald Stewart, Conductor
★ ★ Favorite works by Rossini, Mozart and Rimsky-Korsakoff ★ ★
Seats 25c, 55c and 85c at Albaugh's, 11 E. Lexington and at Lyric after 1 P. M. tomorrow. C. C. Cappel, Manager.

KEITHS Children 15c Plus Tax
PRESTON STURGES' GREATEST CAST... IN HIS BIGGEST HIT SINCE "LADY EVE"!
CLAUDETTE COLBERT · JOEL McCREA · MARY ASTOR · RUDY VALLEE
in THE PALM BEACH STORY
Your Ticket To Keith's Tonite Also Admits To Dance Free!

MARYLAND THEATRE FRANKLIN NEAR HOWARD ST.
PERF. CONTINUOUS FROM 11 A.M. DAILY 28c UNTIL 12 NOON
IN PERSON ● ON STAGE: CROSS & DUNN · HAL LE ROY · SHARKEY the SEAL · THE MAXELLOS ● NASH & EVANS
SCREEN: TINA THAYER IN "SECRETS OF A CO-ED"

ALL CARS and BUSSES lead to LOEW'S
CENTURY LEXINGTON & CHARLES
It Stands Alone! NOEL COWARD'S IN WHICH WE SERVE
STARTS THURSDAY Paulette Goddard ● Ray Milland "THE CRYSTAL BALL"
VALENCIA ATOP THE CENTURY
Now! MICKEY ROONEY in "Andy Hardy's Double Life"
PARKWAY NORTH & CHARLES
TAYLOR-DONLEVY-LAUGHTON "Stand By For Action"

MAYFAIR HOWARD & FRANKLIN
Silver Queen
starring George BRENT ★ Priscilla LANE

LITTLE SECOND WEEK!
CLAUDETTE COLBERT
RONALD COLMAN
ROSALIND RUSSELL
"UNDER 2 FLAGS"

Gayety ONLY BURLESK IN BALTIMORE
"MIKE SACKS' OWN BIG SHOW"
WINNIE GARRETT
"SENSATIONALLY DIFFERENT"
Plus
BERNARD—WHITE—GOLDEN, JR.
Cast of 35. Vaudeville Acts, Etc.

WARNER BROS STANLEY HOWARD NEAR FRANKLIN ST DOORS OPEN 10 30 A M
3rd. WEEK!
BETTE DAVIS
more radiant, more exciting than ever—in love with
PAUL HENREID
who matches her every emotion, in
"Now, Voyager"
with CLAUDE RAINS
GLADYS COOPER · BONITA GRANVILLE · ILKA CHASE
BUY WAR BONDS AND STAMPS

SPENCER TRACY · MICKEY ROONEY
MEN OF BOYS TOWN
ROSLYN 800 Blk. N. Howard St.
Plus GIANT NEWSREEL Show

Ricardo CORTEZ Jean PARKER in Tomorrow WE LIVE
TIMES Plus BIG NEWSREEL Show

RIVOLI
Sonja Henie · John Payne "ICELAND"
Jeanette M'Donald · Robert Young "CAIRO"
DOUBLE SHOW DAILY

Tyrone POWER · Maureen O'HARA in Rafael Sabatini's THE Black Swan in TECHNICOLOR
NEW THEATRE LEX. ST. AT PARK
POSITIVELY FINAL WEEK!

Today's Movie Calendar

Theatres advertised in this column belong to the Motion Picture Theatre Owners of Maryland.

Buy War Savings Bonds and Stamps at Your Favorite Theatre. Immediate Delivery.

Aero Middle River, Md. Bing Crosby in "ROAD TO MOROCCO" News.

Alpha Catonsville. Hedy Lamarr in "WHITE CARGO" Comedy.

Ambassador 4604 Liberty Heights. Monty Woolley in "LIFE BEGINS AT 8.30" "Conquer by the Clock."

Apollo 1500 Harford Ave. Ginger Rogers in "ONCE UPON A HONEYMOON" 2 Carlines to Apollo—19—27.

Arcade Harford Rd. & Hamilton Ave. Monty Woolley in "LIFE BEGINS AT 8.30" "Man Power."

Astor Poplar Grove at Edmondson. Ginger Rogers in "ONCE UPON A HONEYMOON" 3 Carlines to Astor—4—14—9.

Aurora 7 East North Ave. James Craig in "NORTHWEST RANGERS" "March of Time."

Avalon 4300 Park Heights Ave. Bing Crosby in "ROAD TO MOROCCO" Cartoon.

Avenue Milton Ave. & Hoffman St. Judy Garland in "FOR ME AND MY GAL" Comedy.

Avon 3019 Hamilton Ave. OPEN SATURDAYS AND SUNDAYS ONLY

Belnord 2700 Philadelphia Ave. Monty Woolley in "LIFE BEGINS AT 8.30" "Keep 'Em Sailing."

Boulevard 33rd at Greenmount. Monty Woolley in "LIFE BEGINS AT 8.30" "Boogie Woogie Sioux."

Bridge Edmondson Ave. & Pulaski St. Monty Woolley in "LIFE BEGINS AT 8.30" Comedy.

Broadway Bela Lugosi in James Craig in "NORTHWEST RANGERS" 4 Carlines to Broadway—16—18—10—21.

Cameo 4705 Harford Road. Van Hefling in "SEVEN SWEETHEARTS" Take 19 Carline to Cameo.

Capitol 1518 W. Baltimore St. Ginger Rogers in "ONCE UPON A HONEYMOON" Carlines 15—8—1—11—Q Bus.

Casino 1118 Light St. John Howard in "ISLE OF MISSING MEN" "Overland Mail."

Cluster 303 S. Broadway. Margie Hart in "LURE OF THE ISLANDS" "Spirit of West Point."

Columbia 709 Washington Blvd. Bob Hope in "ROAD TO MOROCCO" "Boogie Woogie Sioux."

Earle Belair Rd. at Woodlea Ave. Bob Hope in "ROAD TO MOROCCO" With Bing Crosby.

Edgewood 3500 Edmondson Ave. Monty Woolley in "LIFE BEGINS AT 8.30" "Keep 'Em Sailing."

Eureka 404 S. Fremont Ave. Roy Rogers in "RIDIN' DOWN THE CANYON" "G-Men vs. Black Dragon."

Forest Garrison & Liberty Heights. Hedy Lamarr in "WHITE CARGO" Symphony Hour.

Fulton Fulton Ave. & Baker St. Gene Tierney in "THUNDER BIRDS" "Keep 'Em Sailing."

Garden Charles at Cross. Fay Bainter in 'Mrs. Wiggs of the Cabbage Patch' "Tale of Two Kitties."

Glen Glen Burnie. Walter Pidgeon in "DARK COMMAND" Comedy.

Grand 511 S. Conkling St. Ginger Rogers in "ONCE UPON A HONEYMOON" "Jivin' Jam Session."

Gwynn 4609 Liberty Heights Ave. John Beal in "STAND BY, ALL NETWORK" "Keep Shooting."

Hampden 911 W. 36th St. Brian Donlevy in "NIGHTMARE" Comedy.

Harford 2610 Harford Ave. Judy Garland in "FOR ME AND MY GAL" "Magic Alphabet."

Hilton 3117 W. North Ave. Henry King and Orchestra in "THE YANKS ARE CONING" "Between Showers."

Horn 2014 West Pratt St. Ellen Drew in "ICE CAPADES REVUE" "Jasper and the Haunted House."

Howard 115 N. Howard St. Bing Crosby in "ROAD TO MOROCCO" Comedy.

Ideal 903 W. Thirty-sixth St. Ginger Rogers in "ONCE UPON A HONEYMOON" With Cary Grant.

Irvington 4113 Frederick Ave. Hedy Lamarr in "WHITE CARGO" Comedy.

Lane Dundalk, Md. Jerry Colonna in "PRIORITIES ON PARADE" With Ann Miller.

Leader 248 S. Broadway. James Ellison in "UNDYING MONSTER" 5 Carlines to Leader—16—10—18—21—5.

Linwood 908 S. Linwood Ave. Brian Donlevy in "NIGHTMARE" "Serenade in Swin."

Little 523 North Howard St. Claudette Colbert in "UNDER TWO FLAGS" With Ronald Colman (Second Week).

Lord Baltimore 1110 West Baltimore St. Richard Denning in "ICE-CAPADES REVUE" With Ellen Drew.

Lord Calvert 2244 Washington Boulevard. Hedy Lamarr in "WHITE CARGO" Comedy.

Lyceum Sparrows Point, Md. Judy Garland in "FOR ME AND MY GAL" Comedy.

McHenry 1037 Light St. Ginger Rogers in "ONCE UPON A HONEYMOON" "Swing Is the Thing."

Maryland Franklin St. nr. Howard. Tina Thayer in "SECRETS OF A CO-ED" Plus 5 Acts of Vaudeville.

Mayfair 508 N. Howard St. Priscilla Lane in "SILVER QUEEN" With George Brent.

Met Pennsylvania & North Aves. Gingers Rogers in "ONCE UPON A HONEYMOON" Cars 13—2—18—1—11—21—5—33.

New Reisterstown, Md. Ginger Rogers in 'THE MAJOR AND THE MINOR' "Scrap the Japs."

New Essex Essex, Md. Brian Donlevy in "WAKE ISLAND" Short Subjects.

New Glen Glen Burnie. Cary Grant in "ONCE UPON A HONEYMOON" Feature Starts at 7 and 9 P. M.

Northway Harford & North. Pky. Ellen Drew in "ICE CAPADES REUE" "Women at Arms."

Overlea Belair Rd., End of Car Line. Betty Grable in "Springtime in the Rockies" "Hep Cat."

Palace Gay and Hoffman Sts. Brian Aherne in "A NIGHT TO REMEMBER" With Loretta Young.

Patterson Eastern and East Aves. Ellen Drew in "ICE CAPADES REVUE" "Keep 'Em Sailing."

Pikes Pikesville, Md. Bob Hope in "ROAD TO MOROCCO" Cartoon.

Pimlico Park Heights & Belvedere. Ellen Drew in "ICE CAPADES REVUE" "A Letter From Bataan."

Preston 1108 E. Preston St. Ginger Rogers in 'THE MAJOR AND THE MINOR' 3 Carlines to Preston—19—27—21.

Red Wing 2241 E. Monument St. James Craig in "Seven Miles From Alcatraz" "Chasin' the Blues."

Rex 4600 York Road. Fred MacMurray in "FOREST RANGERS" "You're a Sap, Mr. Jap."

Rialto 845 W. North Ave. Monty Woolley in "LIFE BEGINS AT 8.30" Cars 13—32—31—15—B Bus.

Ritz 1607 N. Washington St. Cary Grant in "ONCE UPON A HONEYMOON" With Ginger Rogers.

Senator 5904 York Rd. Ellen Drew in "ICE CAPADES REVUE" "Jivin' Jam Session."

State Monument and Castle Sts. Monty Wooley in "LISE BEGINS AT 8.30" Vaudeville.

Strand Dundalk, Md. Bob Hope in "ROAD TO MOROCCO" With Bing Crosby.

Towson Towson, Md. Fay Bainter in 'WAR AGAINSTMRS. HADLEY' Comedy.

Uptown 5010 Park Heights Ave. Monty Woolley in "LIFE BEGINS AT 8.30" News of the Day.

Vilma Belair Rd. and Mayfield Aves. Cary Grant in "ONCE UPON A HONEYMOON" With Ginger Rogers.

Walbrook 3100 W. North Ave. Hedy Lamarr in "WHITE CARGO" "Showdown."

Waverly Greenmount at Gorsuch. James Craig in "Seven Miles From Alcatraz" "Chasin' the Blues."

Westport 2205 Russell St. James Craig in "OMAHA TRAIL" Comedy.

Westway 5300 Edmondson Ave. Fay Bainter in 'Mrs. Wiggs of the Cabbage Patch' Comedy.

THE WEATHER

Continued humid, with scattered thundershowers this afternoon and evening; gentle winds, except for thundergusts.

Detailed Weather Report on Page 21

Read The Baltimore News-Post for complete, accurate war coverage. It is the only Baltimore newspaper possessing the three great wire services—
ASSOCIATED PRESS
INTERNATIONAL NEWS SERVICE
UNITED PRESS

THE BALTIMORE NEWS-POST

AN INDEPENDENT NEWSPAPER

The Largest Evening Circulation in the Entire South

10

VOL. CXLIII.—NO. 71 | Entered as second-class matter at Baltimore Postoffice. | MONDAY EVENING, JULY 26, 1943 | PRICE 3 CENTS

DUCE HELD, 22 DIVISIONS ORDERED HOME, REPORT

Italy Jubilant; Shout For King

BERN, Switzerland, July 26—(A. P.).—Italian people went wild with joy on hearing of the downfall of Mussolini and the end of more than 20 years of Fascism and years of preparation for war, reports reaching Bern said today.

The only Italian newspaper arriving at Chiasso on the Swiss frontier, the Gazzetta del Sport published in Milan, declared that cheering throngs had burst into the streets as soon as they heard the radio announcement, and despite the blackout paraded through the streets of Rome and invaded the empty halls of the Palazzo Venezia from whose balcony Il Duce had harangued them for a score of years.

ACCLAIM KING, ARMY

An impromptu parade formed and there were demonstrations against Fascism with shouts of long life to Italy's King, to Marshal Pietro Badoglio and the army.

The throngs carried Italian flags and sang.

One parade went to the Quirinal where the people shouted for the king. Others demonstrated at the War Ministry, acclaiming the army, and in various other parts of the city in front of newspaper offices. The Gazetta Del Sport reported similar demonstrations at Milan and Bologna.

NAZIS GLOOMY

Reports that trucks and railways had been commandeered for the withdrawal of German troops could not be confirmed. The first Nazi reaction privately was that there now was no chance of their withdrawal even if it had been intended.

Mussolini's whereabouts were not established, and one diplomat said he still was in Italy this morning, and if not under arrest was at least under police protection.

Reports from the Swiss-Italian frontier said there was a brawl at Como when non-party members spit at Blackshirts and tore their uniforms from their backs.

OFFICERS STONED

A mob was said to have hurled stones and smashed doors and windows at offices of Mussolini's Il Popolo d'Italia, which another report said had been partly burned.

The Fascist salute was abolished and signs erected throughout the country in the last two decades were being erased. Locomotives of Italian trains arrived at the frontier stripped of their Fasces decorations. Throughout the day the Italian radio broadcast only official communiques and music.

Russ Advancing On Orel Regain Over 70 Villages

LONDON, July 26—(A. P.).—Russian troops gained from three to five and a half miles today and captured more than 70 villages in their drive to encircle Orel, a special Moscow communique announced tonight. The broadcast was recorded by the Soviet monitor.

Two of the villages captured were southeast of Zhizdra, in the Red army drive to cut off Orel from the rear. Zhizdra is 38 miles east of Bryansk, another big German base lying 75 miles northwest of Orel.

Rome Radio Ends German Lessons

ALGIERS, July 26—(U. P.).—Radio Rome announced today that it was discontinuing, effective now, its daily morning lesson in the German language.

VERY LATEST NEWS

(Race Results From Howard Sports Daily, Inc.)

EXEMPLIFY WINS EIGHTH AT SARATOGA

SARATOGA RESULTS

Eighth—Exemplify, $4.20, $3.10, $2.40; George Lamaze, $4.20, $2.80; Marmeduke, $2.90.

LATEST BASEBALL SCORES

(A) Aa Boston—St. Louis, 7; Boston, 1; end 8½.
(N) At Pittsburgh—Brooklyn, 5; Pitts., 5; end 5½.
(N) At St. Louis—Boston, 3; St. Louis, 2; end 5½.
(N) At Chicago—New York, 4; Chicago, 0; end 3½.

DUCE MADE STATEMENT ON EVE OF QUITTING

LONDON, July 26—(A. P.).—Benito Mussolini made a statement on the political and military situation before an extraordinary meeting of the Fascist Grand Council Saturday night, on the eve of his resignation, the Italian Stefani News Agency announced over the Rome radio tonight. It was the first meeting of the council since December 7, 1939, six months before Italy entered the war.

NANTUCKET BOAT STRIKE ENDS

NEW BEDFORD, Mass., July 26—(I. N. S.).—A strike of steamboat crews ended today and service between the mainland and the islands of Martha's Vineyard and Nantncket was resumed.

British Eager To Get Hands On Mussolini

LONDON, July 26—(I. N. S.)—The cry of "We want Mussolini" was raised in the London press today as the hours passed with no solution of the mystery surrounding his "resignation."

The London News summed up the average feeling with these words:

"We want Mussolini: He must be handed over."

CANBERRA, July 26—(I.N.S.). Prime Minister John Curtin of Australia today declared the repercussions in Axis-occupied countries resulting from Italian Premier Mussolini's resignation cannot be overestimated. Said Curtin:

"Hitler sees in the fate of his ally the handwriting on the wall for himself."

LONDON, July 26—(I.N.S.).—A Swiss news broadcast heard in London today reported the resignation of Benito Mussolini as Premier was received with calm in Milan, Turin and Venice.

MADRID, July 26—(I. N. S.).—The fall of Mussolini was regarded today in Spain as an extremely sensational development.

It particularly was noted that his retirement from political power closely follows his rumored talk with Adolf Hitler, when Spanish correspondents anticipated energetic Axis measures to change the course of the war.

ANKARA, July 28—(I. N. S.).—The sudden eclipse of Ben to Mussolini caused a sensation in Turkey today. The expression 'Italy is done for" was heard on all sides.

ZURICH, July 26—(I. N. S.).—Mussolini's fall was due to his badly shaken political regime and Italy's precarious military situation, the Swiss newspaper Neue Zuericher Zeitung said today.

NEW YORK, July 26—(I.N.S.). Count Carlo Sforza, former Italian Foreign Minister and chief of the Free Italian Movement, today expressed doubts as to the sincerity of King Victor Emmanuel's ouster of Mussolini. Count Sforza said:

"The removal of Mussolini may be an honest change—or it may be a trick; we must wait and see what concrete developments will follow."

Temperatures

12 Midn't, 75	9 A. M., 73
1 A. M., 74	10 A. M., 73
2 A. M., 73	11 A. M., 75
3 A. M., 73	12 Noon, 80
4 A. M., 72	1 P. M., 85
5 A. M., 73	2 P. M., 85
6 A. M., 72	3 P. M., 86
7 A. M., 73	4 P. M., 86
8 A. M., 74	5 P. M., 86

The Scientist Who Was Twisted To Death By His Pet Whirlpool. This Curious Tragedy Happened In the Brazilian Jungles. Read This Unusual Story In The American Weekly, the Magazine Distributed With Next Sunday's Baltimore American.—Adv.

Yanks Closing Pincers Upon Axis' Final Stand In Northeastern Sicily

ALLIED HEADQUARTERS IN NORTH AFRICA, July 26—(A. P.).—Allied troops are squeezing tighter upon Axis last-stand defenses in Northeastern Sicily against bitter resistance, it was announced today, and American troops mopping up Western Sicily have captured Termini, 20 miles east of Palermo, and taken 7,000 more prisoners, including six Italian generals and an admiral.

"Further pressure on the enemy was maintained in all sectors" by American, Canadian and British forces closing in on the Catania-Etna-Messina area, the Allied communique declared.

CONTINUE TO ADVANCE

Canadians striking east from Central Sicily "continued to advance, but their progress was slowed in the face of bitter resistance," it added.

Some units of the U. S. Seventh Army driving toward Messina are far to the east of Termini, and its capture consolidates the grasp upon the northern coastal area of the island.

More than 70,000 prisoners now are in Allied hands of whom 56,000 were taken by Americans. The six Italian generals and the admiral were not immediately identified.

To date, ten generals and two admirals have surrendered.

AXIS PORT BLASTED

It was officially estimated that three and a half German divisions and three Italian divisions were bottled up in the northeastern corner of Sicily. One of the Nazi units in the Messina bridgehead was identified as the Twenty-ninth Division, named for the German unit destroyed by the Russians at Stalingrad.

Allied planes kept up their incessant hammering, and the Axis supply port of Milazo west of Messina was blasted. Saturday night with many fires started. Road objectives near Orlando also were hit.

Three Axis aircraft were destroyed against loss of one Allied plane.

ORIOLE PARK LINE-UPS

ORIOLES	ROYALS
5—Jones, lf.	1—Barnh't, 2b.
7—Monaco, 1b.	9—Howell, c.
23—Honoc'k, cf.	27—Brack, cf.
10—Staller, rf.	24—Ortiz, rf.
24—Tiede'n, 3b.	x—Hooks, 1b.
8—Becker, c.	19—Badke, lf.
4—Sczepk'i, ss.	11—Kimball, 3b.
11—Bell, 2b.	3—Campa's, ss.
14—Smoll, p.	18—Chipman, p.
17—Swift, p.	14—DeForge, p.
12—Van Sl'e, p.	12—Webb, p.
15—Ecker, p.	15—Spauldi'g, p.
16—Klieman, p.	16—Flowers, p.
18—Calvert, p.	20—Collins, p.
19—Gromek, p.	21—Sherer, p.
20—Hueser, p.	22—Gregg, p.
21—Burkart, p.	x—Washb'n, p.
2—Rabe, outf.	4—Castro, c.
9—Pare, c.	8—Roch'i, outf.
25—Mac'z, outf.	10—Corr'n, outf.
26—McGarity, c.	5—Tho'n, mgr.
22—Tho's, mgr.	

Time—6.15 P. M.

Umpires—Soladare and Kennedy.

Keep your own box score of tonight's game—Page 10.

Kiska Is Raided By U. S. Planes 10 Times In Day

By The Associated Pess.

A Tokyo dispatch broadcast by the Berlin radio said eight B-24 Liberator bombers attacked Japanese-held Wake island early Sunday.

WASHINGTON, July 26—(A. P.).—Ten battering aerial assaults on Kiska, carrying on the campaign to soften that Japanese base for occupation by ground troops, were reported today by the Navy.

Army Warhawk fighter planes made the assaults in a speedy series of raids Saturday, bombing and strafing the Japanese on the rocky Aleutian Island.

Numerous hits, the Navy reported, were scored on the runway at the Japanese air field there. In addition, other bombs struck among gun emplacements of the enemy.

One United States plane failed to return from the attacks which brought to 30 the number of times that Kiska has been bombed this month.

Surface units also have turned their big guns on the island seven times since the first of the month.

Upshur, Paddock Burial In Alaska

SAN FRANCISCO, July 26—(A. P.).—The bodies of Maj. Gen. William P. Upshur and of Capt. Charles Paddock will be buried in Alaska, where the two were killed in a plane crash last week.

Badoglio Order Sets Martial Law

BULLETINS

LONDON, July 26—(A. P.).—Wladyslaw Banaczyk, Minister of Home Affairs of the Polish Government-in-Exile, said today he had information that the Germans were preparing defense lines in Lublin Province in Poland, roughly 400 miles behind their present line in Russia. He learned all road, rail and telephone communication had been suspended and that mass murders were being committed by the Germans to rid the area of its Polish population.

ALLIED HEADQUARTERS IN NORTH AFRICA, July 26—(A. P.).—"It is entirely too early to form a competent opinion on what Mussolini's dismissal will do to the Italian war effort," an Allied general officer declared today. He pointed out that if the Germans began pulling out of Sicily, that could be taken as evidence they feared that Italy would try to quit the war.

NEW YORK, July 26—(A. P.).—Stocks of companies engaged in or connected with armament activities tumbled $1 to around $5 a share in today's market as Wall Street construed the ousting of Mussolini and other Italian developments as another broad step toward ultimate Allied victory.

By United Press.

The London radio today quoted a report form Bern that there were clashes between German and Italian soldiers in Italy. The report was not otherwise confirmed.

(Page of Pictures on Page 8).

ALGIERS, July 26—(A. P.).—Marshal Pietro Badoglio was reported today to have ordered 22 Italian divisions home from Yugoslavia and Greece, and to have recalled three or four more from France.

LONDON, July 26—(A. P.).—Reuter's reported from Stockholm today that Benito Mussolini had been captured by officers while trying to escape from Italy to Germany. Other reports from Bern, Switzerland, indicated that Mussolini and several of his Fascist ministers were under arrest. These reports were without confirmation.

MADRID, July 26—(U. P.).—Usually reliable sources said today that Benito Mussolini and other Fascist leaders and ministers now are under police protection at a villa believed to be in the Rome area.

LONDON, July 26—(I. N. S.).—Two entirely uncorroborated but separate rumors circulated in the press room of the Ministry of Information today said Mussolini already is dead.

LONDON, July 26—(A. P.).—Martial law was proclaimed throughout harassed Italy today in swift succession to a government shake-up which eliminated Benito Mussolini and his Fascist cabinet and installed the conservative Marshal Pietro Badoglio as Premier.

King Vittorio Emanuele made the change in the war leadership, the first major break on the Axis front and a possible prelude to an Italian bid for peace.

FORBIDS GATHERINGS

Badoglio ordered the army to take over the preservation of public order throughout the nation, forbade gatherings of more than three persons, directed the people to remain at their work and empowered the troops to fire on any one who violated the instructions.

Hour by hour, developments in the situation which may hasten the end to the struggle into which Mussolini plunged Italy with the attack, as Germany's ally, upon France, June 10, 1940, were broadcast by the Rome radio and recorded by listening posts throughout the world.

Dispatches from both Switzerland and Sweden said Mussolini had been arrested. These were without confirmation from Axis quarters.

"WAR CONTINUES"

Confronted by some of the gravest problems that the commander of a beaten and dispirited army ever faced, with the bulk of Sicily overrun by Allied armies, with German troops and German police on Italian soil, and with mainland cities beset by bombings

Continued on Page 2, Column 1

NEWS-POST

Amusements	19	Horoscope	15
N. Clark	19	McLemore, Henry	17
Bugs Baer	16	Movies	19
Classified Ads	21, 22, 23	Parsons, Loella	19
Comics	18	Pippen, R. H.	10
Crossword	23	Radio	24
Dulaney	17	Robinson, Elsie	16
Durling	16	Society	7
Editorials	16	Sports	10, 11, 12
Financial	20	Rukeyser	20
Health	4		

RACING RESULTS AT SARATOGA

FIRST RACE—Five and a half furlongs. Off at 1.18½. Time, 1.04 1-5.

Faro Queen, 115 (W. Mehrtens)	$22.10	$9.60	$5.90
Bee Mac, 115 (S. Young)		6.20	4.40
Music Hall, 115 (S. Brooks)			3.70
Total mutuels			$51.90

Also Ran—fQuatre Measure, Penomp, aFairy Bee, bBriarhone, cGaltown, bJohn's Dear, Vienna, Vitamin, f—Sun Victory, fCavellena, aPeace Dust, cStarend, iFery Ruler, fModest One, fHigh Legend, Surf. aM. Van Beuren and C. V. Whitney entry; bLazy F Ranch entry; cFox catcher Farm entry. fiFeld.

SECOND RACE—Six furlongs. Off at 1.48. Time, 1.12 4-5.

Sarge, 118 (W. D Wright)	$9.60	$4.80	$3.60
Liquid Lunch, 108 (C. Givens)		4.60	3.40
Hianne, 113 (A. Pascuma)			8.70
Total mutuels			$33.70

Also Ran—Xam, Wuskenin, Joe Burger, Adventurous, Peace Eagle, Tindell, Diggie, Phar blaze.

Daily Double—Faro Queen and Sarge paid $260.70

THIRD—About two miles. Off at 2.17½. Time, 3.50 2-5.

Bank Note, 156 (Roberts)	$11.50	$5.60	$4.30
Royal Archer, 141 (Merriweather)		5.90	4.40
Winged Hoofs, 154 (Brown)			7.30
Total Mutuels			$39.00

Also Ran—Bavarian, Kennebunk, Frederic II and Free State II.

FOURTH—Five and a half furlongs; Widener course. Off at 2.48½. Time, 1.05.

Tropea, 114 (G. Woolf)	$13.00	$6.90	$5.20
Plucky Maud, 111 (C. McCreary)		5.60	4.50
Free Lance, 114 (J. Gilbert)			4.30

Also Ran—Vim, Ringaway, Great Ripple, Morani, Autocrat.

FIFTH—Six furlongs. Off at 3.16½. Time, 1.10 3-5.

Light Lady, 102 (Mehrtens)	$4.30	$3.20	$2.80
Best Risk, 102 (C. McCreary)		5.50	3.50
Generous, 105 (C. Givens)			3.80

Also Ran—aTwin Lakes, Sparkling Maid; aBrittany, Jaquita. aJ. M. Roebling entry.

SIXTH—Seven furlongs. Off at 3.47½. Time, 1.23.

With Regards, 126 (J. Longden)	$7.40	$4.90	$3.60
Water Pearl, 108 (T. Atkinson)		7.00	4.10
Pompion, 113 (J. Gilbert)			3.10

Also Ran—Kingfisher, Bossuet, Wait a Bit, Flaught and Woolford Lad.

SEVENTH—One mile. Off at 4.17½. Time, 1.38 1-5.

Meneither, 110 (C. Erickson)	$33.10	$11.50	$8.20
Top Reward, 117 (T. Atkinson)		4.90	3.70
Golden Thorn, 121 (J. Gilbert)			5.90

Also Ran—Shannon, Cincus, Accord, Best Irish, This Freedom, The Watch.

Duce Seized In Italy, Is Report

Continued from Page 1.

which threaten ever-increasing force, Badoglio said "the war continues."

In addition to his instructions to the people, the new Premier issued a special order of the day stating that the voluntary Fascist militia "is an integral part of the armed forces of the nation and with them, as always, co-operates in the common work and intentions for the defense of the fatherland."

TACIT WARNING

The 250,000 Blackshirts — once Mussolini's private army—are the best equipped group among Italy's military forces of about 2,000,000 men.

(The broadcast did not bring out why Badoglio considered such a special order necessary, but it may have been a tacit warning to the militiamen that they would remain under his control to the end, despite the withdrawal of Mussolini and the Fascist ministers.)

The Berlin radio said Badoglio had appointed Baron Raffaele Guariglia, fifty-four, Italian Ambassador to Turkey for the last six months, as Foreign Minister in Italy's new Government. The Foreign Ministry was among the portfolios formerly held by Mussolini. With 30 years experience in diplomacy, Baron Guariglia could have been a go-between in any negotiations for a separate peace during his residence in neutral Ankara.

One Italian political source in London, who cannot be further identified, predicted that Italy would be out of the war against the Allies within a week. Others were not so optimistic.

This source credited the bombing of Rome and related events, particularly the Vatican radio's denial of Axis propaganda concerning the raid, for the announced "resignation" of Mussolini and his replacement by a veteran, seventy-one-year-old soldier who was one of the dictator's critics and a close friend of the King.

PEACE IS POPULAR

Andrea Simoni, secretary of the Free Italian movement in London, said:

"The King certainly rallied many people to his side, some of whom did not like him. Getting Italy out of the war is naturally extremely popular with the people."

Badoglio's orders placing Italy under siege conditions and stressing that the Fascist militia is an "integral part" of the King's forces—not political Storm Troops—may be preliminary measures looking toward the utter elimination of the Fascist party.

The new Premier strictly barred all public meetings and parades, which, obviously, includes Fascist party functions. He banned the posting of bills, except in Catholic churches, which presumably will prevent the Fascists from hanging any more of their bombastic slogans and exhortations on Italian walls and fences.

GUNMEN OUTLAWED

Firearms permits were canceled, thus outlawing Fascist gunmen who had helped Mussolini terrorize political enemies.

The Fascist militia, when formed in the early 1920's, owed allegiance only to Mussolini. In 1923 it was incorporated into the army, but still took oath to Il Duce and not to the King, as did the rest of the armed forces. In 1940 the militiamen began taking oath to serve the King as well as the dictator.

The militia now includes Italy's lone armored division.

In a royal proclamation to Italians last night the King announced that he had accepted Mussolini's "resignation" and had installed seventy-one-year-old Badoglio — bitter foe of Il Duce and Fascism —as head of a military government "to stand against those who have wounded the sacred soil of Italy."

RALLIES ALL ITALIANS

"The war continues," the aged Marshal told the people in a proclamation announcing that he had assumed supreme command of all Italian armies and calling on Italians to rally around the King.

But the conviction grew that Italy, her cities shattered, her empire vanished, internal unrest and violence growing, and a mighty Allied army pounding at her threshold—had taken the "guilty hierarchy" of Fascism and had taken a necessary step toward eventual peace.

The immediate effect on Germany and Italy of the end to Mussolini's 21-year reign as dictator international bully could not be estimated immediately.

World Reaction To Duce's Ouster

By Associated Press.

From around the world today came speculation and assertion that the exit of Benito Mussolini as Premier of Italy had spelled out the prelude of a separate peace for Germany's Axis partner.

In capital after capital the reaction, although frequently only semi-official, was the same. It was that a tottering Italy had moved one step nearer to an exit from the war, whether through early armistice or easier capitulation to marching Allied armies.

Some of the reaction follows:

LONDON—There was quick unofficial speculation that, since Italy had moved toward fulfillment of the Allies' initial condition of surrender, the British and American Governments might soon present terms for "honorable capitulation" to King Vittorio Emanuele and Marshal Badoglio. At the same time, however, there was evidence of an attitude not to relax and wait for Italy to quit, but rather to "pour it on" for a smash finish.

WASHINGTON — Despite initial official silence, there was wide speculation that in choosing Marshal Badoglio to head the military government, the King had more than nodded at the Roosevelt-Churchill invitation to the Italian people to rid themselves of their Fascist government. Since Badoglio is a royalist and anti-Fascist, it was regarded in many quarters that his appointment might well be followed by dissolution of the Fascist party and a bid for separate peace.

MOSCOW: The Russian people were electrified by the news of Mussolini's downfall. The immediate reaction, as heard in homes and on street cars and subways, was that Germany had suffered a severe blow. Some said they felt this might mean that Italy would drop out of the war in a few weeks, and that even if she carried on, her resistance would be only half-hearted.

ALGIERS: A Frenchman who reflects French feeling, but who would not permit his name to be used said the appointment of Badoglio may portend Italy's withdrawal from the war. In this event, he said France would be one of the United Nations most vitally affected and should have a voice in whatever arrangements might be made with the new Italian Government.

GERMANY: German propagandists asserted in press radio reports that Mussolini's exit was "among developments running counter to the Allies' wishes." Their makeshift line apparently was that the appointment of Badoglio's military government "means Italy's will to resist continues unchanged." One dispatch declared that "the change of government brings no visible change in the German-Italian relationship."

Badoglio Shuns The Fascist Salute

Benito Mussolini (left), current whereabouts not definitely known, gives the Fascist salute after laying a wreath at the German Cenotaph in Berlin during a visit there September 29, 1937. Behind him stands Marshal Pietro Badoglio—who replaced him as Premier of Italy yesterday—not saluting.

Air Raiders Blast Essen, Saint-Omer

LONDON, July 26—(A. P.).—U. S. heavy bombers attacked Northern Germany and medium bombers hit Saint-Omer, France, by daylight today after a 2,000-ton night raid by the R. A. F. on the German industrial city of Essen.

No details were given in the first announcement from headquarters of the European theatre of operations of the United States Army.

Besides the concentrated night attack on Essen by heavy bombers, R. A. F. Mosquito bombers struck at Hamburg and Cologne and swept over Northwest Germany, the Low Countries and France last night.

The Essen raid proper took 50 minutes. Smoke rose to 20,000 feet, the Air Ministry said.

NOTED DOCTOR DIES

ARCADIA, Cal., July 26—(A. P.).—Dr. Orville Harry Brown, sixty-eight, noted allergy specialist who formerly taught at the University of Chicago and St. Louis University, died here last night.

Writer In Hunt For Sicily Sniper

By CLARK LEE

International News Service Staff Correspondent.

CALTANISSETTA, Sicily, July 20—(Delayed)—I went on a sniper hunt through the moonlit streets of Caltanissetta tonight for a hidden machine-gunner who had lain doggo for three days before firing on our troop convoy en route to the front.

We had just entered the city and were passing a modernistic apartment building and rounded a corner when a burst of fire and a sudden shout came from a jeep beneath a tree.

PINNED BY FIRE

We jumped from our car and ran over to find three military policemen pinned to the ground under a parked jeep by fire, apparently from the third floor of the apartment house across the street.

We opened with 50-caliber machine guns and Springfields and plastered the building. Meanwhile a long convoy of trucks halted down the street to await the outcome.

CLEAN-UP CONTINUES

Despite occasional sniping, the work of cleaning up and restoring Caltanissetta continues. Soldiers are digging up bodies buried in bomb debris. They found 50 in one building.

The populace is returning in increasing numbers. They are hungry but not resentful of the bombings, saying they had been given warnings and admitting a German headquarters was located there. I found these headquarters four miles outside the town. They had not been hit.

The bombing here could not compare in intensity with Coventry or Guernica, but it proved conclusively the entire city could have been levelled if we had continued the attacks. As it was, nearly every building is shrapnel scarred, but only about one-tenth received direct hits and was completely ruined.

Scenes of farewell, which I have seen in dozens of towns were repeated here. Women and children gathered in the prisoners' enclosures to bid a tearful farewell to soldier relatives and weep copiously when told their men are being sent to the United States. They wailed:

"All will be drowned. It is impossible for an Allied ship to cross the Atlantic controlled by German submarines."

The job of trying to cover various fronts daily as the Army moved forward faster than its press relations office communications system, necessitating traveling up to 125 miles a day and hitch-hiking rides on jeeps to take "copy" back to a Southern coast port does not allow much time for sleeping.

AUTO WON'T RUN

I finally located an Italian automobile, spent several hours fixing it to run sweetly and got new tires. Now it won't run and the Army's mechanics are too busy to repair it, so it's back to the jeeps.

Incidentally, the men who made Army maps showing first-class highways in Sicily should be made to traverse them in jeeps and swallow tons of white limestone dust that goes along with it.

Final Drive In Sicily Under Way

Allied forces in Sicily today turned their full attention to a final drive to crack the 65-mile Axis line (broken line) barring their way to Messina and the Italian mainland. British troops (arrow, flag symbol) were within three miles of Catania; Canadian forces (arrow, flag symbol) were in the vicinity of Regalbuto and American units (arrow, flag symbol) were in the neighborhood of San Stefano Di Camastra. Germans (flag symbol) hold the eastern part of the line while Italians (flag symbol) hold the northwestern sector. Naval units blasted Axis land positions at the port of Taormina (A).

Allied Planes Rip Munda In Record Raid

ALLIED HEADQUARTERS IN THE SOUTHWEST PACIFIC, July 26—(A. P.). — American bombers, in the mightiest aerial assault of the Southwest Pacific war, dropped 186 tons of bombs on Japanese positions at Munda, New Georgia, yesterday.

More than 200 planes—Liberators, Flying Fortresses, Mitchells, Avengers and Dauntless bombers with strong fighter escort—participated in the attack, and only one failed to return.

The communique from Gen. Douglas MacArthur's headquarters made no comment on the results of the raid beyond saying that "the area was thoroughly bombed."

Six hundred miles to the west the Royal Australian Air Force executed the heaviest attack yet made on the Gasmata airdrome on the south coast of New Britain. Roaring in at dawn, Beaufords, Beaufighters and Bostons, with Kittyhawks as cover, destroyed the radio station and grounded aircraft.

"The runway and dump areas and enemy personnel were thoroughly strafed," the communique said. "Anti-aircraft positions were silenced."

Governor Is Delighted Over Italy

WASHINGTON, July 26—(A. P.).—Governor Herbert R. O'Conor of Maryland issued the following statement today following a conference with U. S. State Department officials:

"The news of Premier Mussolini's overthrow was most gratifying to every American, but particularly so, I am sure, to those many loyal citizens of Italian birth or extraction, such a large number of whom reside in Maryland. These fine citizens have given continued evidence of their loyalty and love for America.

"Unquestionably this latest development constitutes a far step toward that historic hour which our many Italian-American friends have long desired—namely, the cessation of hostilities between this country and Italy.

"Certainly no national group has given greater evidence of its uncompromising support to the nation's war activities than Maryland's Italian-American colony . . .

"Actually all of us are apprehensive of what Italy has done in the cultural and religious advancement of civilization. While false leadership in recent years has directed Italian efforts to wrong purposes, the success of present American efforts will mean ultimately the preservation of these ideals and principles which characterized the Italy of former days."

Sugar Stamp No. 14, Good For 5 Lbs., Is Valid Aug. 16

WASHINGTON, July 26—(A. P.).—Sugar stamp No. 14 in ration book No. 1 will become valid Aug. 16 and will be good for five pounds of sugar through October, the Office of Price Administration announced today. This is on the same basis of previous rations—about one-half pound per person per week.

The presently valid stamp No. 13 will expire August 15.

OPA said it made the early announcement to enable the trade to plan packaging.

Hull Sees Harder Drive On Italy

WASHINGTON, July 26—(A. P.).—Secretary of State Hull indicated today that increased military pressure to insure Italian capitulation to the Allied demand for unconditional surrender would be this country's response to the downfall of Benito Mussolini.

He termed very timely and appropriate the ending of the Italian Premier's regime and said it was the first major step in the early and complete eradication of Fascism. But Hull emphasized repeatedly that chief reliance is on military developments.

The State Department head, making the first official American comment on the displacement of the Italian dictator, told a press conference that the Allies were fighting like the devil, when asked what the United States was doing in the face of the Italian internal developments.

Hull indicated no change in the unconditional surrender policy laid down by President Roosevelt and Prime Minister Churchill, and said if all minds are kept on fighting, like the devil the Allies will win the war much sooner.

He emphasized that all attention now is on military developments.

Hull said in response to another question that he believed Japan will take due notice of what has occurred in Italy.

At the outset of the press conference, Hull was asked whether he anticipated any change in the unconditional surrender terms fixed by the United States and Great Britain for capitulation by the Axis. He said he had no information to that effect from the President and War Department and did not anticipate anything.

DUCE'S END 'TIMELY'

Asked to comment generally on the Mussolini shift he said that he has been convinced that Fascism carries with it the seeds of its own destruction. He added that the very timely and appropriate ending of Mussolini's regime was the first major step in the complete destruction and eradication of every vestige of Fascism both nationally and internationally.

Asked whether the United States would negotiate with King Vittorio Emmanuel or whether he regarded the King in the same class as the Fascists, said he had not conferred with the President.

He said there was no truth in reports that the United States had contacted the new Italian premier, Marshal Pietro Badoglio, a few months back.

RULE APPLIES TO ALL

When asked whether the no-surrender terms applied to Hungary, Bulgaria and Rumania, Hull first referred his questioner to President Roosevelt and the War Department, but then remarked that he imagined the same terms applying to the Axis would apply to all other countries which had declared war against the Allies.

He would not undertake, however, to discuss what he termed marginal cases such as Finland.

Another question was whether Hull considered the House of Savoy a faction of the Fascist party. He replied that as far as the State Department is concerned the war is still on in Italy and it has not as yet reached that question.

Little Italy Happy Over Duce's Fall

Joy, hope and gratitude filled the hearts of Baltimore's Little Italy with the news of the crumbling of Mussolini's power in their former homeland, and celebrations started with the first word of the Duce's downfall, continued today.

Leaders in the colony here were quick to declare that the recent campaign conducted by The Baltimore News-Post and other Hearst newspapers, appealing directly to the Italian people, had had telling effect in speeding the debacle.

Under the Hearst program, prominent Americans of Italian descent have been beaming short wave radio messages to their friends and kinsmen in the old country, calling upon them to free themselves of the Fascist and German shackles and save Italy's honor by quitting the war.

D'ALESANDRO MESSAGE

Another such message, prepared by Representative Thomas D'Alesandro after the good news came, was to be directed to Italy by the Office of War Information.

It is as follows:

"You must not be too jubilant over Mussolini's signing out. He is just one individual. Fascism of 21 years brought nothing but destruction to the Italian nation. The fight is still going on under Fascist leadership. You are fighting for a lost cause. For the honor of Italy and yourselves, I call upon you to quit in a war you cannot win because it is too late.

"You must make an unconditional surrender. I warned you before, time and time again that the United States is a mighty nation. They do not wish to destroy Italy but you will make it possible unless you quit now for the honor of yourselves and Italy."

COMMENT BY SODARO

From Anselm Sodaro, Assistant State's Attorney, and a leader in the committee which arranged the local broadcasts, came this statement:

"We in America have no doubt but that the short-wave messages of the Hearst papers, sent to Italy had their effect upon the Italian populace who were reported at different points within the last few days as clamoring for peace.

"The Italians have got rid of Mussolini who has hoodwinked them for more than 20 years. Now they will have to also drive every German from their midst, if they wish to survive as a nation.

"Until that is done there can be no peace between the Allies and Italy. But I am hoping that further short-wave messages by the Hearst papers, with our pleas that they give up the fight, will quickly bring about a withdrawal of Italy from the war."

Forts Get Nazis Far From Base

AT A U. S. BOMBER BASE, Somewhere In England, July 26—(A. P.).—U. S. Eighth Air Force Flying Fortresses from this station caught Nazi defenses far off base when they hit North Germany today for the second successive day.

Major William R. Calhoun, twenty-three, pilot of the Eight Ball, which led the attack on Nazi industrial targets, said:

"It was an easy one. Bombing looked pretty good. I saw one hell of a big explosion."

FEW FLIERS APPEAR

"There were only about 20 or 25 fighters and they only made three passes at use," said Sergt. Frank Mathews of Watsonville, Cal., ball turret gunner on the bomber Charlie Horse, piloted by Flight Officer Elmo Clark of Pasadena, Cal.

Tail Gunner Sergeant Goudie Hoover, who has a fourteen-year-old son back in Ambridge, Pa., and who says with a wink that his official age is thirty-five, observed:

"Yesterday I shot about 1,500 rounds—today not more than 500 or 600, just keeping them off.

"Yesterday you could shake hands with them. Today none came closer to me than 600 yards."

RIGHT ON TARGET

It looked like bombs were right on the target, said Photographer Sergeant Martin Kagey of Cleveland Heights, Ohio, who was photographing bomb bursts. It was his twentieth raid.

Lieut. Howard Ness of Galion, Ohio, co-pilot of the Thumper Again, piloted by Lieut. Jacob James of Valliant, Okla., was sure a group of warehouses was knocked out.

The crew of the Thumper Again, which claimed five German planes yesterday, claimed one today—by Top Turret Gunner Sergeant Jake Good of Indianapolis, Ind., who yesterday was knocked out of his turret and slightly burned by a German 13-millimeter bullet which later was found in his underwear. Good was on his twenty-second raid today.

Bowles Promises New OPA Policy

HARTFORD, Conn., July 26—(A. P.).—Chester Bowles, newly appointed general manager of the national Office of Price Administration, today promised a down-to-earth policy of rationing and price control as he prepared to leave for Washington to assume his new duties under OPA Director Prentiss M. Brown.

26 HURT IN BUS CRASH

TRENTON, N. J., July 26—(U. P.).—Twenty-six passengers were injured last night when a Trenton-bound bus skidded into an electric light pole.

Founder Of Fascism Played Many Parts

BENITO, the bombastic, was on top of his career in 1938 when this picture was made, with Il Duce taking part with (left to right) Chamberlain, Daladier and Hitler, in the famous Munich appeasement conference now credited with having started the World War II.

KING VITTORIO EMANUELE and Mussolini were "just like that" in 1938, shown here during Army maneuvers. But now, with Italy's entire empire shattered, her fleet shackled and bombs falling on Rome, the King said just two words to Mussolini—"You're fired!"

BETWEEN his brave bellowings over microphones to his controlled audiences Mussolini put on the usual show of big-heartedness. Here he is giving a medal and a kiss to a little girl whose father died in the "noble war" against Ethiopia, where Haile Selassie now rules again.

MUSSOLINI, in this picture, is shown in his army helmet and uniform in 1940, just as Italy pulled the great "stab in the back," entered the war with France tottering, and opened a 120-mile front on the south of France while Hitler slammed at the north and east. This was the pose Il Duce loved.

BUT OH! Scandal! Oh, terror! Here's the now famous picture of Mussolini in 1915, when he was just "an anarchist who gets grabbed." Two hefty detectives have Benito in the bag, and are hauling him off to the hoosegow. Which is he? The one with his mouth open, of course. The Duce, who was ducking in those days, went on to win many a political race. Now he's believed "on the lam" somewhere, who knows?

ITALIAN soldiers, famous for back-pedaling on the double, are shown here being led in a peace-time trot by Musso himself. Many believe that Benito is bounding through the foothills of the Alps seeking a job as a Swiss goatherder and hoping to escape the fate that awaits dictators responsible for World War II. The Italian leader had this gay photo of himself made some time in 1940, on maneuvers.

Henry Cotton Invited To Play Golf In U.S.

Rodger H. Pippen
Sports Editor Says
KEEP YOUR CHIN UP

The impression is general today that the Yanks and Cards will once more be foes in this year's World Series.

Both clubs are so far in front in their respective leagues that you would naturally assume that Billy Southworth and Joe McCarthy, the managers, would be in a cheerful frame of mind.

For different reasons you would be wrong about both leaders.

McCarthy is of the worrying type. He was born a pessimist. He doesn't relax in a ball game until his Yanks are six or eight runs out in front. And it's the same thing so far as the league race is concerned. You couldn't coax him into claiming the flag.

A change has come over Southworth. Time was when Billy, no matter how aggravating things might be, was cool and and pleasant and smiling. He took the bad breaks with the good. Today, for perhaps the first time in his diamond career, Southworth is more or less of a gloom. The war and a plague of sore arms have gotten on his nerves. He is plainly jittery and admits it.

RODGER H. PIPPEN

Within two weeks Billy has seen two of his aces change into service clothes. He cannot hope to replace Jimmy Brown and Howie Pollett.

By the middle of next month two more will be gone. They are Harry Walker and Harry Brechen.

And that isn't all. Max Lanier, Ernie White and Harry Gumbert, pitching dependables, have arm miseries. A sore finger worries Slats Marion. Danny Litwhiler has a sprained ankle. George Follan and Lou Klein have other things to bother them.

Do you blame the usually placid Southworth for not cheering when he glances at the standings and sees that the Dodgers have lost twelve more games than his Cards? As you probably know, the lost column, where the leaders are concerned, is more important than the won figures, and it does seem silly for Billy to be perturbed. Time will tell whether he is right.

When you look at the American League standings the position of the Yanks recalls some predictions made some weeks ago by Hal Newhouser of Detroit and Lou Boudreau of the Indians. Hal, a pitcher, had just fanned fourteen of the Yankees.

Flushed with victory, Newhouser said:

"Those Yanks beat me every time I faced them last year. But his year they are just another bunch of guys. Those letters across their shirts used to mean something. Now all we see is a bunch of young guys trying too hard, like every other young fellow in the league.

"The Tigers will win the pennant this year if Rudy York begins to hit. We've got swell pitching and good fielding and our hitting is bound to get better."

Incidentally, Hal is 4F in the draft. He has a leaking heart.

Boudreau, of Cleveland, was just as confident his Indians would finish ahead of the Yanks. He figured he would get more opposition from Washington.

Three Cheers For Donald Barnes

While on the subject of baseball, President Donald Barnes, of St. Louis Browns, is to be congratulated for having resigned Luke Sewell as manager for 1944 and 1945.

His announcement proves that he feels confident that baseball will carry on.

Some of his fellow magnates in the major leagues, showing less judgment and betraying a weakness that isn't necessary, have openly expressed doubt about 1944.

There are many reasons why baseball should continue. The only important one is this: Our soldiers in other lands are always asking for baseball, fight and other results.

To Keep Jones In Oriole Line-Up

Del Jones is hitting .205 for the Orioles. Until a few days ago he was under the .200 mark. Judged by that figure, Del would be warming the bench. But Manager Tommy Thomas hasn't any idea of removing Jones from the line-up. Indeed, unless he should secure some new outfielder who can hit, he expects to keep Del in the game every day. This decision is the result of Di's spirit and the fact that he never ceases to hustle.

Bass Sees Murray As Winner

Lee Q. Murray, is seen by Sylvan Bass, matchmaker of the Century Athletic Club, as the winner over Harry Bobo in their fifteenth round battle at Oriole Park on the night of August 9. Bass bases his selection on these claims:

Murray is the harder puncher.
Murray has a tougher defensive style.
Murray has more endurance.

The only concession Sylvan makes about Bobo is that he is the better boxer.

What do you think?

Jeffra Starts Comeback Thursday

Harry Jeffra, who believes that he is the exception to the rule "they never come back," makes his promised return to the ring wars Thursday night at the Fort Hamilton arena in New York. The former bantamweight and featherweight champion takes on Frankie Rubino of New York in an eight-round main bout.

Bombers Get Baseball Offers

Four members of the Martin Bombers, playing in the War Industrial League, have attracted attention of pro clubs.

Our Orioles would like to try out Herman Deviney, Martin shortstop. He played with Kingsport in the Appalachian League for a season before taking a war job. Deviney is married, with a five-year-old youngster, but wouldn't give up his work for baseball. It is possible he might get a furlough to help out the Birds for a month.

Frank Gibson, the star southpaw of the Martins, got a call from Clark Griffith of the Senators and went over last Saturday to show his stuff on the mound.

Griff is also interested in Earle Bellew, the big left-handed first baseman of the Bombers, and Red Betz, the slugging outfielder. None of these boys, however, will consider playing professional baseball until after the war.

Peckinpaugh's Eight Errors

Henry Harnek, Maryland avenue, writes in to ask about errors made by Roger Peckinpaugh in a World Series.

That shortstop, playing for Washington, made eight errors during the World Series of 1925, to establish a new record.

BALTIMORE NEWS-POST SPORTS

10   MONDAY EVENING, JULY 26, 1943

Birds Open Vital Home Stand

By HUGH TRADER, JR.

There's really no cause for criticism, nor any reason for surprise, in the case of the Birds' slump to seventh place. Having lost a large chunk of double-A power and defense in the persons of Bob Repass and Hal Sieling, and finding replacements an impossibility for love or money, the Flock is simply skidding along on three wheels.

In short, the club has neither the hitting nor the fielding to move consistently and the Birds' chances now of recovering are wrapped up almost entirely in airtight pitching.

Players are tied up tighter than a Scotchman's purse. Skippe Thomas has tried a dozen or more leads and met with the same blank answer in each instance, including a conference yesterday with George Weiss in Newark. The Birds' offer to buy Jim McLeod, even though he's classified 1-A in the draft, has been rejected and the Yankees have for sale only a couple of guys who couldn't improve the locals.

INDIANS NO HELP

Baltimore's one out should be through Cleveland in such a baseball year as this, but the Indians are as silent as the cigar store model. The only club in our circuit which is blessed with reserves is Toronto and consequently the Leafs are on top. Pittsburgh has helped the Toronto plenty.

Of course, while the Birds are perceptibly weaker with young Teddy Sczepkowski gallantly trying to fill Repass' shoes at short and failing yesterday when they dropped a pair of 4-3 decisions to Newark, the situation has been aggravated by the sudden slump of George Staller.

In the last 10 games Staller has hit an anemic .108 average and batted in just four runs. This has served to pull Staller down to the borderline of an even .300, and checkmate the Birds' run-making considerably after George had been going like a house afire to top the circuit with .333.

Some relief should be realized as the Flock opens a two-week home stand, beginning with a double-header tonight with Montreal. The hitting should pick up and whatever chance the Birds have of climbing back into the playoff race should be evidenced here in the next two weeks.

MONACO RETURNS

Likewise, providing a ray of sunshine is the expected return to first base of Blas Monaco, who
Continued on Page 12, Column 4.

166,904 Watch Major Games

Eight double-headers in the major leagues drew a total of 166,904 yesterday. The Chicago-Yankee game at New York was witnessed by the largest crowd, 34,164. The crowds:

NATIONAL LEAGUE
New York at Chicago 32,192
Brooklyn at Pittsburgh 30,309
Boston at St. Louis 14,089
Phillies at Cincinnati 10,346
Total 86,936

AMERICAN LEAGUE
Chicago at New York 34,164
St. Louis at Boston 16,860
Cleveland at Washington ... 14,800
Detroit at Philadelphia ... 14,144
Total 79,968
Grand Total 166,904

Army Calls Braves' Catcher For Exam

BOSTON, July 26.—(A. P.)—The Army may strike a heavy blow at the first division hopes of the Boston Braves today when Catcher Clyde Kluttz undergoes a pre-induction physical examination.

How About Mussolini And Galento Match?

PORTLAND, Ore., July 26.—(A. P.)—Benito Mussolini can start his comeback right away.

Advised of the Italian dictator's resignation, Fight Promoter Joe Waterman wise-cracked:
"I'd like to match him with Tony Galento."

Held The Ball But Not His Balance

[WIRE PHOTO]

THE HARD WAY—Ellis Clary, third baseman for the Washington Senators, goes heels over head after making a catch the hard way. He is shown as he crashed into the field boxes yesterday at Griffith Stadium as he caught a foul fly in the second game of a double-header against the Cleveland Indians. But he held the ball for the putout. Associated Press Wirephoto.

Gentry Earns 12th Victory

BUFFALO, July 26.—(A. P.)—Buffalo scored 22 runs to Montreal's six, but the Bisons had to be satisfied with a spit of their twin bill with the Royals yesterday. Montreal took the opener, 5 to 2, but was outclassed in the afterpiece when the Bisons pounded out a 20-1 victory as Rufe Gentry notched his twelfth triumph of the season.

Mueller's Homers Help Reds Win

CINCINNATI, July 26.—(A. P.)—Two home runs by Catcher Ray Mueller, each with two men on base, helped Ray Starr and Cincinnati's Reds to an 8-2 victory over Philadelphia today in an 8 o'clock game played before a crowd of 3,839 war-work swing-shifters, knothole club members and service men.

PHILADELPHIA					CINCINNATI			
	ab	r	h	o		ab	r	h	o
Murth,2b	3	0	1	3	Frey,2b	5	0	2	1
Northey,rf	5	0	1	2	Clay,cf	4	0	1	2
Triplett,lf	5	0	1	4	Walker,rf	3	0	1	1
Wadell,rf	3	0	0	1	Marshall,rf	1	0	0	1
Adams,cf	1	0	0	1	McCor,1b	3	1	2	6
Dhlg'n,1b	3	0	0	6	Haas,1b	1	0	0	0
May,3b	3	0	1	2	Mesner,3b	2	1	1	3
Stewart,ss	2	1	1	1	Williams,3b	1	2	2	0
Kimbell,p	0	0	0	0	Tipton,lf	3	1	2	3
1 Moore	1	0	0	0	Crabtree,lf	0	0	0	0
Kraus,p	0	0	0	0	Mueller,c	4	2	2	6
Eyrich,p	1	0	0	0	Miller,ss	2	2	0	1
Livin'ton,c	3	1	1	4	Mueller,c	4	3	3	6
Finley,c	1	0	0	1	Starr,p	3	0	0	0
Kraus,p	1	0	0	0	Etarr,p	3	0	0	2
Brew'er,ss	2	0	0	1					
Totals	34	2	7	24		32	8	12	27

1 Batted for Kimbell in sixth inning.

SCORE BY INNINGS
Philadelphia .... 0 1 0 0 0 1 0 0 0—2
Cincinnati ..... 0 1 4 0 3 0 0 0 x—8

Errors — Livingston, McCormick. Runs — Mueller (2). Sacrifices — Mesner, Starr. Double plays—Miller, Frey and Mc-Cormick. Left on bases—Philadelphia, 11; Cincinnati, 5. Base on balls—Off Kraus, 2; off Kimbell, 1; off Starr, 6. Struck out—By Kimbell, 1; by Eyrich, 1; by Starr, 4. Hits—Off Kraus, 6 in 3 innings; off Kimbell, 2 in 2; off Eyrich, 1 in 3. Losing pitcher—Kraus. (Umpires—Ballantant, Reardon and Gomez.)

Brink Triumphs In Del. Tennis

WILMINGTON, Del., July 26 (A. P.)—James Brink of Seattle, Wash., captured the Delaware and Middle Atlantic States clay court tennis championship yesterday by downing Gene Garrett of San Diego, Cal., 6—1, 6—1, 6—3.

Aberdeen Soldiers Watch Tennis Stars

ABERDEEN, Md., July 26.— Capt. A. C. Nielsen, former Wisconsin tennis captain, beat Mary Hardwick, former British Wightman Cup star, in an exhibition match for the soldiers here yesterday.

The weather halted a match between Corp. Charley Hare and Johnny Faunce, from the Bainbridge Naval Training Station. Other exhibition matches are scheduled at Fort Meade today.

HURLS THREE-HITTER

The Red Shield Boys' Club scored a 9-2 baseball victory over St. Mary's of Govans in a Saturday Junior League game. Swayko, Red Shield hurler, allowed only three hits.

GAELS STOPPED

The Park A. C. of Havre de Grace stopped the Schoolboy Gaels, 4 to 3, in a Maryland Amateur League baseball game. O'Brien held the Gaels to five hits. Park scored all four runs in the seventh inning.

YESTERDAY'S STARS

By Associated Press.

Thurman Tucker, White Sox, and Bill Johnson, Yankees—Tucker's ninth inning homer won opener 2-1; Johnson drove in three runs in Yanks' 6-3 nightcap win.

Bob Klinger and Wally Hebert—Pitched two-hitter and four-hitter, respectively; let down Brooklyn twice by 7-1.

Dizzy Trout, Tigers, and Luman Harris, Athletics—Trout blanked A's, 5-0, in opener with five hits; Harris pitched six-hitter for 3-1 nightcap win.

Alpha Brazle and Stan Musial, Cardinals—Brazle came back to big leagues with seven-hit performance for 5-1 opener win over Braves; Musial hit double and three singles, driving in three runs, in 7-3 nightcap victory.

Injuries Force English Star To Stop RAF Flying

CHICAGO, July 26— (U. P.).—Henry Cotton, former British open golf champion and for the past three years a member of the Royal Air Force, was invited today to come to the United States for a series of exhibition matches with American stars.

The invitation to Cotton, who has been forced to abandon his war career as a flier because of injuries, was called by Fred Cochran, tournament manager of the Professional Golfers' Association.

Cochran discussed the proposition with Cotton when he was in England as a representative of the Red Cross.

If Cotton accepts the invitation it is hoped he will be able to arrive in the United States in time to participate in the Ryder Cup-Hagen Challenger matches at Detroit August 7-8. He has been asked to play with the Challenger team captained by the veteran Walter Hagen. The matches are for war relief.

Cochran, here for the final round of the All-American Open tournament, also announced the playing personnel of the Ryder Cup and Challenger teams.

The Ryder Cup members will be Craig Wood, Jimmy Demaret, Byron Nelson, Lloyd Mangrum, Vic Ghezzi, Harold (Jug) McSpaden and Gene Sarazen. The Challengers will be Hagen, Sam Byrd, Bob Cruikshank, Melvin (Chick) Harbert, Willie Goggin, Clayton Heafner, Jimmy Thomson and Joe Kirkland, Sr.

Ed Dudley, president of the P. G. A., has been invited to play and will be allowed to choose his team.

Patty Berg Joins Marines

CHICAGO, July 26—(U. P.)— Red-haired Patty Berg, twenty-five-year-old Minneapolis pro-fessional, was sworn into the Marine Corps Women's Reserve today less than 24 hours after she had won the All-American women's golf championship.

Limping slightly from the leg injury suffered 18 months ago, she entered the Marine Corps recruiting office to stand at earnest attention as she was sworn in by Capt. Arthur J. Murphy.

"I am a very happy and very lucky girl," she said. "And very honored, too."

Patty explained that she was joining the service which is her favorite because two of her "heroes" are marines. They are Lieutenant Colonel Bernie Bierman, formerly head football coach at the University of Minnesota, and her cousin, Paul Kennedy, who is resting at his Minneapolis home after seeing combat duty at Guadalcanal.

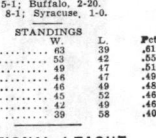

The Standings

INTERNATIONAL LEAGUE
YESTERDAY'S SCORES
Toronto, 9-3; Jersey City, 2-1.
Newark, 4-4; Baltimore, 3-3.
Montreal, 5-1; Buffalo, 2-20.
Rochester, 8-1; Syracuse, 1-0.

STANDINGS
	Won	Lost	Pct.
Toronto	63	39	.618
Newark	53	42	.558
Montreal	49	47	.510
Syracuse	48	47	.495
Rochester	46	49	.484
Buffalo	45	52	.464
Baltimore	42	49	.462
Jersey City	39	55	.402

GAMES TOMORROW
New York at Pittsburgh.
Boston at Cincinnati.
Philadelphia at St. Louis (two).
(Only games scheduled.)

NATIONAL LEAGUE
YESTERDAY'S SCORES
Cincinnati, 7-1; Philadelphia, 3-2.
Pittsburgh, 7-7; Brooklyn, 1-1.
Chicago, 3-2; New York, 0-6.
St. Louis, 5-7; Boston, 1-3.

STANDINGS
	Won	Lost	Pct.
St. Louis	56	28	.667
Brooklyn	51	40	.560
Pittsburgh	48	43	.558
Cincinnati	44	43	.506
Chicago	41	46	.471
Philadelphia	39	50	.438
Boston	35	47	.427
New York	28	55	.375

GAMES TOMORROW
New York at Pittsburgh.
Boston at Cincinnati.
Philadelphia at St. Louis (two).
(Only games scheduled.)

AMERICAN LEAGUE
YESTERDAY'S SCORES
Chicago, 2-3; New York, 1-6.
Cleveland, 8-2; Washington, 3-7.
Detroit, 5-1; Philadelphia, 0-3.
Boston, 7-6; St. Louis, 0-4.

STANDINGS
	Won	Lost	Pct.
New York	51	33	.607
Detroit	44	40	.524
Washington	44	43	.517
Chicago	42	42	.500
Cleveland	42	45	.500
Boston	41	45	.477
St. Louis	39	44	.470
Philadelphia	36	52	.409

GAMES TOMORROW
Chicago at Washington (night).
St. Louis at Philadelphia (night).
Cleveland at New York.
(Only games scheduled.)

AMERICAN ASSOCIATION
YESTERDAY'S SCORES
Louisville, 9-2; Minneapolis, 5-3.
Indianapolis, 5-4; St. Paul, 2-5.
Columbus, 2-5; Milwaukee, 1-2.
Kansas City, 4-2; Toledo, 3-4.

STANDINGS
	Won	Lost	Pct.
Milwaukee	59	33	.593
Indianapolis	48	38	.585
Columbus	49	38	.524
Toledo	43	44	.494
Minneapolis	43	45	.489
Louisville	43	46	.483
St. Paul	39	48	.448
Kansas City	31	52	.415

INTERSTATE LEAGUE
Lancaster, 5-3; Hagerstown, 2-3.
Trenton, 16-9; Allentown, 4-2.
Wilmington, 3-0; York, 0-1.

STANDINGS
	Won	Lost	Pct.
Lancaster	69	33	.598
Wilmington	59	38	.585
Hagerstown	50	40	.541
Trenton	41	42	.506
York	28	60	.328
Allentown	22	60	.268

KEEP YOUR OWN SCORE TONIGHT

No.	ORIOLES	Pos.	1	2	3	4	5	6	7	8	9	10	R.	H.	P.O.
5	Jones	LF													
7	Monaco	1B													
23	Honochick	CF													
10	Staller	RF													
24	Tiedemann	3B													
8	Becker	C													
15	Sczepkowski	SS													
11	Bell	2B													
14	Smoll	P													
17	Swift	P													
	Totals														
12	Van Slate	P	19	Gromek	P	25	Mackiewicz	CF
15	Ecker	P	20	Burkart	P	9	Pare	C
16	Klieman	P	21	Heiser	P	26	McGarity	C
18	Calvert	P	2	Rabe	OUTF	22	Thomas	MGR

No.	ROYALS	Pos.	1	2	3	4	5	6	7	8	9	10	R.	H.	P.O.
1	Barnhart	2B													
3	Howell	C													
27	Brack	CF													
24	Ortiz	RF													
x	Hooks	1B													
19	Badke	LF													
11	Kimball	3B													
2	Campanis	SS													
18	Chipman	P													
14	DeForge	P													
	Totals														
12	Webb	P	21	Sherer	P	8	Rochelli	2B
15	Spaulding	P	22	Gregg	P	10	Corriden	OUTF
16	Flowers	P	x	Washburn	P			
20	Collins	P	4	Castro	C	5	Thompson	MGR

Time of First Game—6.15 P. M.

Baltimore Day By Day

IF FISH ARE BASHFUL, USE GAS TO GET 'EM

By Carroll Dulaney

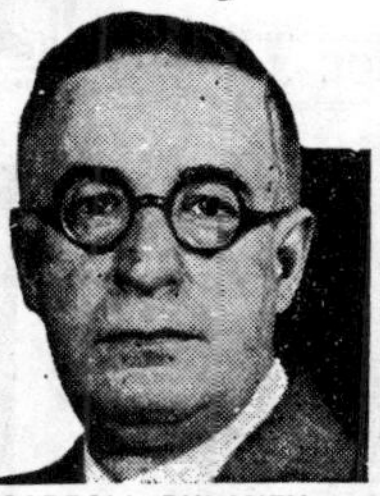
CARROLL DULANEY

Did you motorboat men know that if the fish do not come to you, you can use your motorboat to go to them?

Well, I did not, either, but the idea is not mine. It comes from a high official of the OPA.

And here's the story:

Commander William B. Matthews, Jr., of the Patapsco River Power Squadron, which is made up of motorboat owners who have placed their motorboats in the service of our Government for the duration of the war, wrote to the OPA asking for some definite ruling on the use of gasoline in power boats.

In reply Commander Matthews received the following letter which he has had copied and sent to all members of the squadron:

Dear Sir:

Mr. Haddon has referred to this department your recent letter inquiring about the use of gasoline in power boats. We regret very much not having had an opportunity to answer your letter sooner, but this office has been under extremely heavy pressure for the past two weeks and that accounts for the delay.

You inquire particularly under the ban on pleasure driving the conditions under which boats may be used for fishing purposes.

Under the regulations neither the possession of a commercial fishing license nor the fact that the catch is sold upon return from fishing trips will of itself establish eligibility for an occupational allowance of gasoline for use in a boat used for fishing. The regulations provide that a non-occupational ration of gasoline may not be issued for pleasure cruising, sight-seeing, conducing pleasure parties or conducting fishing parties. A ration may be used in a boat, however, if the applicant is regularly engaged in fishing as a business.

Similarly under the pleasure driving ban it is permissible to use gasoline to obtain fish as a food upon which a person customarily relies as a principal part of his diet and which cannot reasonably be secured without the use of a boat.

You inquire whether it is permissible to use gasoline which was already in the tank prior to the ban, but this question must be answered in the negative.

If the boat owner is actually engaged in commercial fishing, he will not be denied the gasoline he needs for this purpose merely because he takes with him some fishermen who accompany him purely for sport; but on the other hand he will not be able to establish that he is a commercial fisherman if his activities are limited to disposing of the catch procured by persons who engage in amateur fishing.

In conclusion, therefore, we wish to advise that gasoline may not be used in boats except by persons actually engaged in commercial fishing or by those persons who depend upon gasoline to obtain fish as a food which cannot reasonably be secured without using a boat.

Very truly your,
WILLIAM A. GRAHAM,
Chief Rationing Attorney.

Please note the repetition of the amazing statement: that gasoline MAY be used "by those who depend upon gasoline to obtain fish as a food which cannot reasonably be secured without using a boat."

In other words, if you are at the shore, or your home by the water's edge and want some fish, and the fish refuse to come to you, you can go to them, using gasoline to carry you there.

CAR FARE SIX CENTS

A group of passengers were boarding a trolley car the other day. The motorman placed his hand over the fare box and said to each passenger as he or she reached for the box to deposit a fare:

"Show your money, please."

After the people had boarded the car, one man asked the motorman why he made them show their money.

The motorman explained that the new pennies which have just been placed in circulation here have a silvery look and resemble a nickel at first glance. Some of his passengers, it seems, have made the mistake of dropping a nickel and one of the new pennies into the fare box.

And said the motorman:

"I lost 60 cents that way yesterday. I'm not going to have it happen to me today."

McLemore

AMERICANS PRAISED BY ENGLISH PEOPLE

By Henry McLemore

NEW YORK.—Since New York suffered that staggering blow—my return from England—I have been asked the same questions by many different people. They all seemed to be sincerely interested in what answers I could give them, and so, on the off-chance that you'll be interested, too, here are a few samples of them:

Do the English people really appreciate what the United States is doing in this war, or are they smug about having won the Battle of Britain and feel that we came in after the tide had turned?

The answer is no, a thousand times no. The English will tell you that our food saved them from starvation, to begin with. And they are as high in their praise of our soldiers, fliers, sailors and armament as they are of their own.

TROOPS FRIENDLY

Actually, how do our soldiers get along with the English troops?

Despite all the handbooks that have been printed on both sides telling the boys now to get along with one another, they are remarkably friendly. You see them buddying around together, sightseeing together, dating together, drinking together and generally behaving as if they hadn'e been advised that they were likely not to get along at all. Of course, there have been some fair country fights up and down the United Kingdom between the boys of the two countries, but not any more than there have been between our own troops scrapping it out among themselves.

IMPRESSED BY YANKS

How do the English citizens feel about our soldiers?

They are tremendously impressed by them. If the American fighting men abroad today aren't the best behaved expeditionary force that ever went anywhere, then I have been badly misinformed. The English people are impressed by their good manners, their cleanliness and neatness, and they all agree that the average G. I. Joe is a better behaved person than the average tourist who went to England in pre-war times.

How long do the people over there think it will take to finish off Germany?

Opinion varies as much as it does in this country. For every person who thinks the conquest of Germany is a matter of months away, there is one who feels it will take years. I'd say that the general feeling is that Hitler won't be done in before sometime in 1945.

WILL FIGHT JAPS

How do the English feel about the Japanese? We know that Churchill said all England's resources would be thrown against the Japs when the Nazis were licked, but is the talk in the street in agreement with that?

Yes. Not only do the people know how much England has at stake in the Pacific, but they want to make a real-clean-up of the war before they put down their arms.

(Distributed by McNaught Syndicate, Inc.)

Paul Mallon is on vacation for two weeks. His column will be resumed when he returns.

What Do You Know?

By DR. SABINA H. CONNOLLY

(Reg. U. S. Patent Office)

Score yourself on each question. THREE, you're perfect; TWO, you're good; ONE, you're fair.

1. Do you know—
   (a) how many States Australia has?
   (b) how long Belgium has been an occupied country?
   (c) how to translate the name Costa Rica?
2. Fill the blank—
   (a) Eider is a kind of ....
   (b) Thrush is a kind of ....
   (c) Chalcedony is a kind of ....
3. How did they die—
   (a) Madame DuBarry?
   (b) Holofernes?
   (c) Sir Walter Raleigh?

Decide the answer—
   (a) Is treacle molasses or mucilage?
   (b) Is a vendetta a fanfare or a feud?
   (c) Is a drone a bee or a bird?

5. What are the three main branches of the United States Government?
6. Who said—
   (a) "Wise men learn much from their enemies"?
   (b) "Love your enemies"?
   (c) "There is no little enemy?"

(ANSWERS ELSEWHERE ON THIS PAGE)

(Copyright, 1943, King Features Syndicate, Inc.)

A Library In Miniature

A psychological checkup of mental power, based on intelligence and aptitude test formulae used in officer candidate schools, universities and business organizations. Single tests are inconclusive. Compile your daily scores and try for an average of 65. Over 80 is excellent, over 90 is A1. Starred questions count 20; others 10.

**1. Quickly, please: How can you cash a check for $11 without using any $1 bills or any coins?
2. What President was defeated for Vice-President in 1920?
3. Edward M. House, who bore the courtesy title of Colonel, was born 85 years ago today in Austin, Texas. Of what other war President could he be called the Harry Hopkins?
4. This is the calendar day of St. Anne, according to tradition was the Mother of Who?
5. Which island is bigger—New Guinea, where the Allies are fighting the Japs; or Sicily where a much larger Allied force has been battling the Axis?
6. The adage, "an apple a day keeps the doctor away," is often reversed this time of the year when there are green apples to tempt little Johnny, but is the actual reason (a) greenness of the apples; (b) Johnny's improper mastication of them; (c) Johnny's habit of eating too many apples; (d) worms in the apples?
7. Lieut. Comdr. John D. Bulkeley, now commanding PT boats in the Southwest Pacific campaign, inspired the best-selling book called (a) "They Call It Pacific"; (b) They Were Expendable'; (c) "30 Seconds Over Tokyo"; (d) "John D., Portrait in Oil"?
**8. If removal of a growth on the throat is called a tonsilectomy, and removal of a growth on the intestine is called an appendectomy, what's removal of a growth upon the head called?

Answers Elsewhere on this Page.

(Copyright, 1943, King Features Syndicate, Incorporated.)

PRIVATE BREGER ABROAD

By Lt. Dave Breger

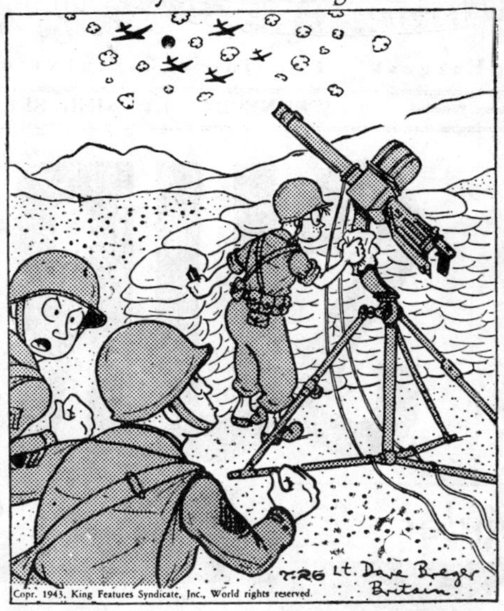

"He knows they're enemy planes, but there's an inspection by the General scheduled today!"

Answers to Library Miniature.

1. With one $5 bill, three $2 bills.
2. Franklin D. Roosevelt.
3. Woodrow Wilson.
4. Of Mary the Mother of Christ.
5. New Guinea. It is the second largest island in the world—1,000 miles long.
6. B. Because green apples are no more likely to cause stomach ache than others when properly chewed. But their tartness often causes them to be improperly masticated, and indigestion results.
7. "They were Expendable."
8. A haircut.

(Take other "What's the Answer?" tests this week and average your score, to get a rating.)

What Do You Know? Answers To Today's Test

1. (a) six States and two territories, (b) since May, 1940; (c) rich coast.
2. (a) duck, (b) bird, (c) quartz.
3. (a) guillotined in Reign of Terror, (b) killed in his sleep by Judith, (c) executed on charge of treason.
4. (a) molasses, (b) feud, (c) bee.
5. executive, legislative, judicial.
6. (a) Aristophanes, "The Birds"; (b) Bible, (c) Benjamin Franklin, "Poor Richard's Almanac."

PRIVATE BUCK .·. By Clyde Lewis

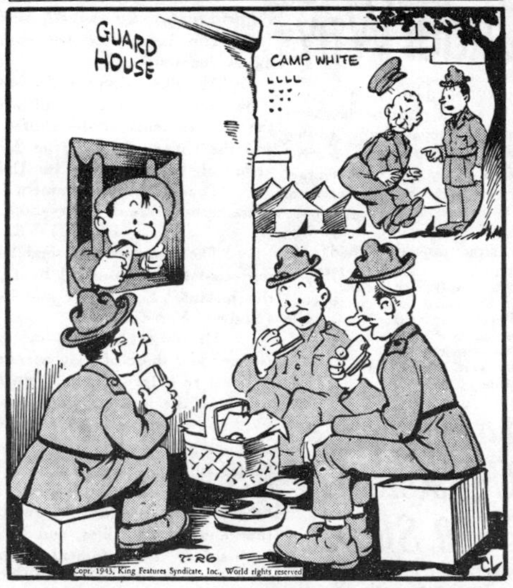

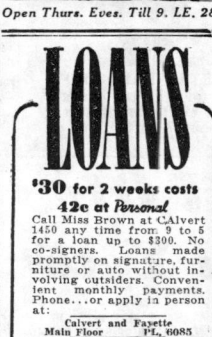

"Buck's throwing a little house-warming, Sir. This is his first time in the new guard-house!"

G. NORMAN MEDINGER
"Creative Jeweler"
DIAMOND SPECIALIST
206 W. Saratoga, Near Park.

Kool-Aid
Makes 10 BIG, COOL Drinks!
KOOL-AID 5¢
7 FLAVORS

PRECAUTION AGAINST
BALDNESS
STIMULATE HEALTHY HAIR GROWTH AND BANISH
FALLING HAIR
WE STOP IT Or We Won't Take Your Money
Start Our Scientific Treatment
FREE CONSULTATION
AMBASSADOR
Scalp Specialists
604 KATZ BLDG.
111 N. CHARLES ST.
Open Thurs. Eves. Till 9. LE. 2815

LOANS
$30 for 2 weeks costs 42c at Personal
Call Miss Brown at CAlvert 1450 any time from 9 to 5 for a loan up to $300. No co-signers. Loans made promptly on signature, furniture or auto without involving outsiders. Convenient monthly payments. Phone...or apply in person at:
Calvert and Fayette Main Floor PL. 6085
204 N. Liberty, Cor. Lex. 3rd Floor PL. 2696
Corner Charles and Fayette Sts. Above Read's PL. 1254
Highlandtown, 3501 Eastern Av. Broadway 1780
Waverly, 3212 Greenmount Ave. 2nd Floor BElmont 3650
Personal
FINANCE COMPANY OF BALTIMORE

Thirty Seconds Over Tokyo -:- BASED ON THE FORTHCOMING Book-of-the-Month

By CAPT. TED W. LAWSON
EDITED BY BOB CONSIDINE

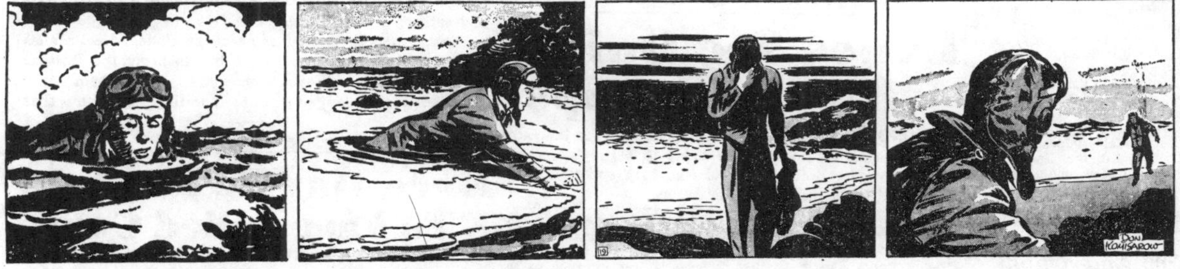

I couldn't swim; I was paralyzed — *Finally I reached shallow water* — *I must have been punch-drunk . . .* — *Davenport was walking toward me*

MY PNEUMATIC LIFEBELT brought me from the seat of the wrecked plane to the surface. Through some streak of luck the shock of the crash had broken the dioxide capsule that inflates the belt. I came up into the driving rain that beat down out of the blackening sky. I couldn't swim. I was paralyzed.

The waves lifted me and dropped me. I struggled feebly against them, but they'd pick me up and roll me under with their punishing roar in my ears and I'd roll around on the bottom until my belt brought me to the top again. Finally I reached shallow water. I stood up and my legs felt very numb. I thought that if I walked around a little bit it would bring circulation back to them. So I walked around in little circles on the beach in the rain. I was all alone. That didn't impress me much when I first thought of it. When I did comprehend what it meant I started to curse in a muffled voice I couldn't recognize. I cursed myself for the loss of my men and the loss of that ship.

My voice sounded so strange to me, and the words came so thickly, that I vaguely reached up to my mouth and felt it. The bottom lip had been cut through and torn down to the cleft of my chin, so that the skin flapped over and down. My upper teeth were bent in. I reached into my mouth with both thumbs and put my thumbs behind the teeth and tried to push them out straight again. They bent out straight again, then broke off in my hands. I did the same with the bottom teeth and they broke off too, bringing with them pieces of my lower gum. I stood in the rain with that wet handful of teeth and gum for a while trying to think. Then I dropped the stuff on the beach. I guess I must have been punch-drunk because I remember saying to myself that now I'd have to go to a dentist.

For some reason I can't explain I started to stagger up the beach. I didn't know where I was going. After a bit I thought I heard someone behind me and when I looked around there was Davenport walking toward me.

Davenport came up to me. We didn't say anything. He took my head in his hands and held it back so he could see it a little better. I tried to say how glad I was to see him, but he said, "Damn! You're really bashed open. Your whole face is pushed in!" Somehow, his words meant nothing to me.

(Continued tomorrow)

Drawings copyright, 1943, by King Features Syndicate, Inc. Text copyright, 1943, by Random House, Inc. A Book-of-the-Month Club selection.

★ What You Buy With ★
WAR BONDS
Pontoon Bridges

Every bridge in occupied Europe has been mined by Hitler's corps of destruction, ready for immediate dynamiting when our troops approach, so our Army Engineers have in readiness thousands of pontoon sections to replace the ruined spans. One short span costs $15,000.

How many we'll need to get to Berlin we don't know, but we do know it will require a great surge of War Bond purchases.

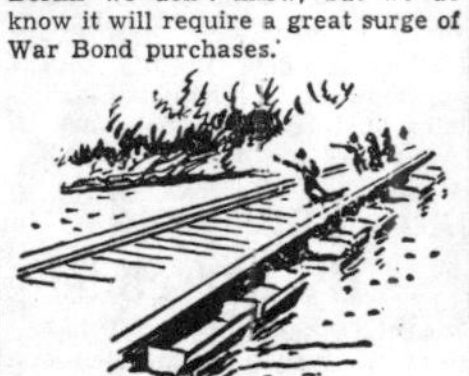

There'll be many bridges to cross before our soldiers hold their watch on the Rhine, and all of us will have to redouble our efforts on the War Bond front. "Figure It Out Yourself." U. S. Treasury Department

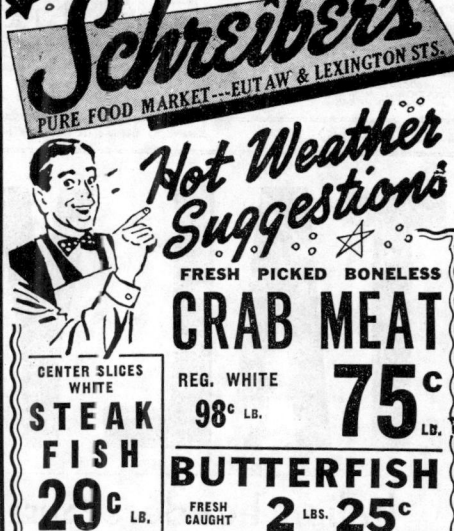

Schreiber's
PURE FOOD MARKET---EUTAW & LEXINGTON STS.
Hot Weather Suggestions
FRESH PICKED BONELESS CRAB MEAT REG. WHITE 98c LB. 75c LB.
CENTER SLICES WHITE STEAK FISH 29c LB.
BUTTERFISH FRESH CAUGHT 2 LBS. 25c
QUALITY MEATS
FRESH DRESSED FRYING CHICKENS NOT RATIONED 44c LB.
SLICED BACON ½ LB. 4 PTS. 16c
MEATY RIB END PORK CHOPS (7 PTS.) 30c LB.
BRAUNSWEIGER (2 PTS.) ¼ LB. SLICED 10c
PHILA. CREAM CHEESE PKG. (1 PT.) 11c
SHARP CHEESE NEW YORK STATE (8 PTS.) LB. 43c
MACARONI SALAD NOT RATIONED LB. 17c
PRODUCE
ANNE ARUNDEL SLICING TOMATOES FULL POUND 10c
FANCY NEW POTATOES 5 LBS. 15c
BAKERY
ALMOND TOPPED COFFEE RINGS FRESH BAKED 12c
ASSORTED FRESH DO-NUTS 25c DOZ.
These Items NOT RATIONED
GOLDEN HARVEST MARMALADE BIG 2-LB. JAR 29c
LANG'S SWEET PICKLES FULL QUART 25c
GRAPE-NUTS FLAKES 2 LGE. PKGS. 25c
NEW PACK APPLE JUICE 9-OZ. CAN 5c
WHEAT PUFFS 4-OZ. PKG. 4c
PEANUT BUTTER 16-OZ. JAR 23c
MIRACLE WHIP FULL PINT 24c
LIBBY'S MUSTARD 6-OZ. JAR 7c
• THESE ITEMS REQUIRE POINTS •
FLORIDA NEW PACK (4 PTS.) GRAPEFRUIT JUICE HUGE 46-OZ. CAN 23c
10 PTS. GIBBS CARROTS NO. 2 CAN 5c
4 PTS. TOMATO JUICE NEW PACK 46-OZ. CAN 17c
16 PTS. SUGAR CORN CREAM STYLE NO. 2 CAN 10c
18 PTS. RED RIPE TOMATOES NO. 2 CAN 10c
11 PTS. TENDER GREEN BEANS NO. 2 CAN 10c
PATENT MEDICINES
BATHING & RUBBING ALCOHOL 70% COMP. ISOPROPYL 15c PT.
Phillips Tooth Paste 25c SIZE 16c
Pebeco Tooth Powder PKG. 10c
Alka-Seltzer 60c SIZE 49c
Seidlitz Powders PKG. OF 9 17c
5-Grain Aspirin BOTTLE OF 100 12c
LIBBY'S EVAP. MILK 3 TALL CANS 28c 1 RED POINT EACH
CALIF. (23 PTS.) PEACHES 2½ CAN 22c
SUNSWEET (3 PTS.) PRUNE JUICE QT. 23c
FELS NAPTHA SOAP 5 FOR 24c
On Sale Monday, Tuesday, Wednesday In Our Advertised Food and Economy Depts. We reserve the right to limit quantities.

THE WEATHE
Moderate temperature, with no showers this afternoon; somewhat cooler tonight and Thursday morning, with moderate humidity
Detailed Weather Report on Page 37.

Read The Baltimore News-Post for complete, accurate war coverage. It is the only Baltimore newspaper possessing the three great wire services—
ASSOCIATED PRESS
INTERNATIONAL NEWS SERVICE
UNITED PRESS

THE BALTIMORE NEWS-POST
AN INDEPENDENT NEWSPAPER
The Largest Evening Circulation in the Entire South

10

VOL. CXLIII.—NO. 108 | Entered as second-class matter at Baltimore Postoffice. | WEDNESDAY EVENING, SEPTEMBER 8, 1943 | PRICE 3 CENTS

ITALY SURRENDERS

Italian Leaders Surrender

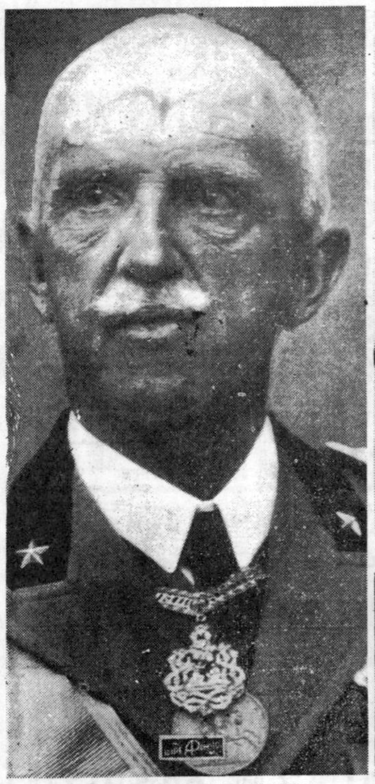

KING VITTORIO EMANUELE

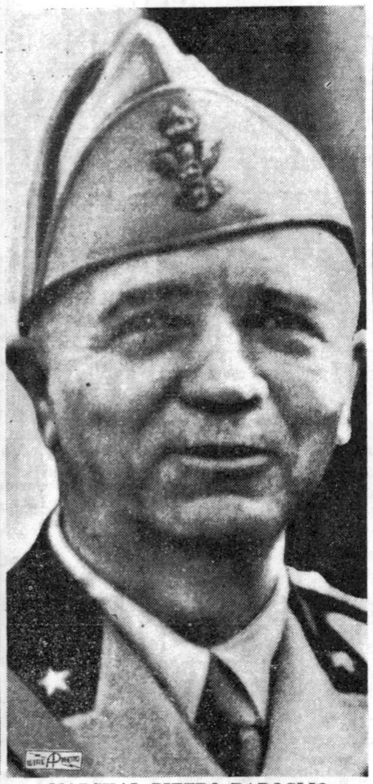

MARSHAL PIETRO BADOGLIO

Italy slipped out of the war today with the unconditional surrender of her armed forces to Gen. Dwight D. Eisenhower. The surrender came from the Government of Marshal Pietro Badoglio, placed at the head of Italian affairs by King Vittorio Emanuele after the collapse of Mussolini.

Armistice Backed By Britain, Russia, Eisenhower Reveals

ALLIED HEADQUARTERS IN NORTH AFRICA, Sept. 8 --- (A. P.) --- Gen. Dwight D. Eisenhower today announced the unconditional surrender of Italy in the greatest knockout victory for Allied arms in four years of war. Simultaneously, the Italian Government ordered its troops to drop the fight against Allied forces, but to "oppose attacks from any other quarter." Russia, as well as the United States and Britain, approved the granting of the armistice, Eisenhower announced.

It was signed in Sicily last Friday—on the very day that Italy was invaded—and Italy, accepting all the terms, agreed that it would become effective "at a moment most favorable for the Allies."

"That moment has now arrived," an official statement declared.

Italy will be obliged to "comply with political, economic and financial conditions" which the Allies will impose later.

Simultaneous announcement by the Allies and the Italian Government was agreed upon in view of "the possibility of a German move to forestall publication of the armistice" by the Italians, headquarters said.

Hitler's "European Fortress" was cracked, the way was opened for new offensives, the course of World War II. immeasurably shortened.

Italy To Help Rout Germans

Eisenhower called on the Italians to join the Allies in helping to eject the Germans from their country, and promised that all who do so will have the "assistance and support of the United Nations."

Marshal Pietro Badoglio's proclamation for the Italian armed forces to cease fighting, but oppose attacks "from any other quarter," was closely related to this.

Surrender of Italian armed forces "unconditionally" was made by the government of Marshal Pietro Badoglio, successor of Benito Mussolini, the architect of Fascism.

There still are sizeable German armed forces in Italy.

Events may continue to move swiftly in the coming hours and days.

Planes Carry News To People

Italy's main contribution to Germany in the war was her geographical position, and this is now lost to the Germans except in so far as they may be able to hold on to part of Northern Italy themselves.

As soon as the announcement was made, Allied planes roared over Italy—not to bomb but to bring the Italians the news that the Allies no longer are fighting them.

The planes dropped pamphlets telling the Italians that

Contiuued on Page 2, Column 1.

Text Of Statements On Italy's Surrender

Announcing the brilliant news of Italy's surrender, General Eisenhower, who led the Allied triumph in Tunisia and Sicily as well, declared:

"The Italian Government has surrendered its armed forces unconditionally.

"As Allied Commander-in-Chief, I have granted a military armistice, the terms of which have been approved by the Governments of the United Kingdom, the United States and the Union of the Soviet Socialist Republics. Thus I am acting in the interests of the United Nations.

"The Italian Government has bound itself to abide by these terms without reservation.

EFFECTIVE AT ONCE

"The armistice was signed by my representative and the representative of Marshal Badoglio, and it becomes effective this instant," Eisenhower said in a broadcast at 12.30 P. M. (Eastern War Time).

"Hostilities between the armed forces of the United Nations and those of Italy terminate at once. All Italians who now act to help eject the German aggressors from Italian soil will have the assistance and support of the United Nations."

The truce actually was reached last Friday at Allied advance headquarters in Sicily—the very day that British and Canadian troops swept across Messina Strait to invade the Italian toe—but it was agreed, a special announcement said, "that the armistice should come into force at a moment most favorable to the Allies, and be simultaneously announced by both sides. That moment has now arrived.

HOLD ITALIAN HOSTAGE

"The possibility of a German move to forestall publication of the armistice by the Italian Government was discussed during the negotiations.

"To meet this eventuality, it was agreed that one of

Continued on Page 2, Column 3.

Reports 200 Allied Ships Under Way

LONDON, Sept. 8—(U. P.).—The German Transocean News Service said today that Allied ship movements had been observed north of Sicily and concluded that "further landings" were planned.

The German agency's radio transmission asserted there were two large convoys totaling 200 freighters and transports, strongly escorted by fighter planes.

Large Allied ship movements also were reported to have been observed at North African ports.

The convoys moving north of Sicily were believed to come from Palermo, Transocean said.

Italy Fleet Consists Of 190 Ships

WASHINGTON, Sept. 8—(U. P.).—The Italian fleet consists of about 190 warships, only a portion of which are believed fit for sea duty.

The whereabouts of the fleet was not immediately made clear. European reports earlier this week said units had sailed from the naval base at Taranto, in the instep of the Italian "foot," for an unknown destination.

Presumably, however, the fleet was included in the terms exacted by Gen. Dwight D. Eisenhower, who reported surrender of all Italian "armed forces."

Best available information here indicated that the Italians had seven battleships, one of which—the Impero—is probably incomplete. The Littorio, the Vittoria and the Veneto are comparatively new.

Capital Sees End Of Europe War In Year

By KINGSBURY SMITH
International News Service Staff Correspondent.

WASHINGTON, Sept. 8.—Italy's unconditional surrender today greatly increased the hopes of an electrified Washington that the European war may be won within the next 12 months.

As jubilation swept the national capital over the news of Italy's surrender to Gen. Dwight D. Eisenhower's victorious Allied armies, a meeting of the supreme Anglo-American High Command was held in the White House to consider the next immediate move against Hitler's crumbling European fortress.

President Roosevelt and British Prime Minister Winston Churchill presided over the White House victory conference, which was attended by Gen. George C. Marshall, Army chief of staff; Admiral Ernest J. King, commander-in-chief of U. S. Fleet; high British military officials and Harry L. Hopkins, chairman of the Munitions Assignment Board.

SEE NEW INVASION

The view prevailed in diplomatic circles that the Anglo-American victory in Italy may be swiftly followed by a powerful invasion move at some new point in the Mediterranean area, possibly the Balkans or Southern France.

Complete capitulation of Italy's armed forces to the Allied armies with the apparent approval of King Victor Emmanuel by the direction of Premier Pietro Badoglio was seen as dealing a staggering psychological as well as military blow to Nazi Germany's continued prosecution of the war.

Coming on top of the defeat of the German armies on the Russian front, the Allied aerial destruction of Germany's cities, the withdrawal from the war of Hitler's original partner was considered likely to undermine the morale of the German people almost to the breaking point.

INSPIRES NEW HOPE

It also was seen likely to inspire new hope of early liberation in the people of the conquered territories of Europe, and probably lead to widespread up-

Continued on Page 3, Column 4.

VERY LATEST NEWS

(Race Results From Howard Sports Daily, Inc.)

GOLD TINT WINS EIGHTH AT AQUEDUCT

Eighth — Gold Tint, $10.80, $4.90, $4.10; Jacomina, $8.30, $5.90; Topless Tower, $4.80.

AT CAMDEN

Fifth—Love o' Maud, $8.70, $4.30, $3.00; Miss Gosling, $6.20, $3.80; Quillon, $3.20.

AT HAWTHORNE

Third—Epola, $18.00, $7.20, $5.40; Highthorne, $4.80, $3.40; Electrical, $7.70.

AT DETROIT

Second — Hogan, $4.80, $3.00, $2.40; Call to Colors, $3.80, $2.60; Through Train, $3.20.

Daily Double — Darby Donna and Hogan paid $27.80.

LATEST BASEBALL SCORES

(N) At St. Louis—St. Louis, 5; Pittsburgh, 1; end 7th.

ITALIANS IN BALKANS MUST OBEY GEN. WILSON

CAIRO, Sept. 8—(U. P).—Gen. Sir Henry Maitland Wilson, British Middle East commander, declared in a broadcast tonight that "Italian troops in the Balkans must not obey German orders; they must obey my orders."

Italy Surrender Pleases Willkie

PROVIDENCE, R. I., Sept. 8—(U. P.).—Wendell Willkie said today that the unconditional surrender of Italy was "not unexpected but a magnificent result."

Spain Impressed By Surrender

MADRID, Sept. 8—(U. P.).—News of Italy's unconditional surrender created a great impression in all official quarters when it was received tonight.

Racing Results On Page 34.

1,200 Americans Italy Prisoners

WASHINGTON, Sept. 8—(U. P.).—Only about 1,200 Americans are held as prisoners of war in Italy according to figures reaching the International Red Cross from the Italian Government. Presumably, officials here said, these will bereleased as the Allies gain control of the areas where the men are interned.

Do You Know How To Sleep Right? Do You Toss and Turn? If You Don't Get All the Best Sleep You Should Read An Amusing Illustrated Feature With Plenty of Helpful Hints. In The American Weekly, the Magazine Distributed With Next Sunday's Baltimore American.—Adv.

Exiles See Quick Hitler Collapse

LONDON, Sept. 8—(U. P.).—Spokesmen for the European Governments-in-exile said today that Italy's unconditional surrender probably would lead to a speedy collapse of Adolf Hitler's entire satellite empire.

Hungary and Bulgaria were expected to seek peace immediately.

One spokesman said:

"With Italy's Eastern coast in Allied hands, Germany cannot expect to hold the Balkans."

BLOW TO AXIS

Other observers described the Italian capitulation as "a tremendous blow to the whole united European Axis structure—like a great building rocked and tumbled by an earthquake."

Greek and Yugoslav officials said they expected an immediate surge of anti-German activity by nearly 300,000 guerrillas in their countries. They pointed out that guerrilla leaders recently conferred with Allied Middle Eastern staff members, presumably in anticipation of just such a development.

WATCH BULGARIA

Bulgaria was expected to sue for peace and withdraw her divisions from Greece and Yugoslavia unless the Germans were able to take over total control of the country.

Temperatures

Midnight, 72	9 A. M., 70
1 A. M., 72	10 A. M., 72
2 A. M., 71	11 A. M., 74
3 A. M., 70	12 Noon, 76
4 A. M., 69	1 P. M., 76
5 A. M., 69	2 P. M., 77
6 A. M., 69	3 P. M., 78
7 A. M., 69	4 P. M., 80
8 A. M., 68	5 P. M., 81

Duce May Be First To Face Allied Court

By International News Service.

Possibility Benito Mussolini may be handed over to the United Nations as the first of the Axis war criminals to meet justice arose today in the wake of Italy's surrender.

Announcement was made by the Rome radio on July 25 that Mussolini had "resigned" his office and had been replaced by a military government under Marshal Pietro Badoglio.

President Roosevelt immediately countered with an official warning that the "expedient of resignation" would not spare the Axis leaders just punishment for their crimes when the war has ended.

Mussolini's whereabouts since his unceremonious departure from the Palazzo Venezia where for 18 years he had held out in bombast and state comprise the war's No. 1 mystery.

He has been reported in custody at various places and jails in the Italian kingdom.

NEWS-POST

Classified Ads	37, 38, 39	Mallon, Paul	11
Clark, Norman	18	Movies	[illegible]
Comics	32	Parson, Louella	18
Crossword	39	Pippen, R. H.	34
Dulaney	29	Radio	33
Editorials	28	Robinson, Elsie	25
Financial	36, 37	Society	[illegible]
Kilgallen, Dor.	18	Sports	34, 35, 36

City's Little Italy Jubilant At Surrender

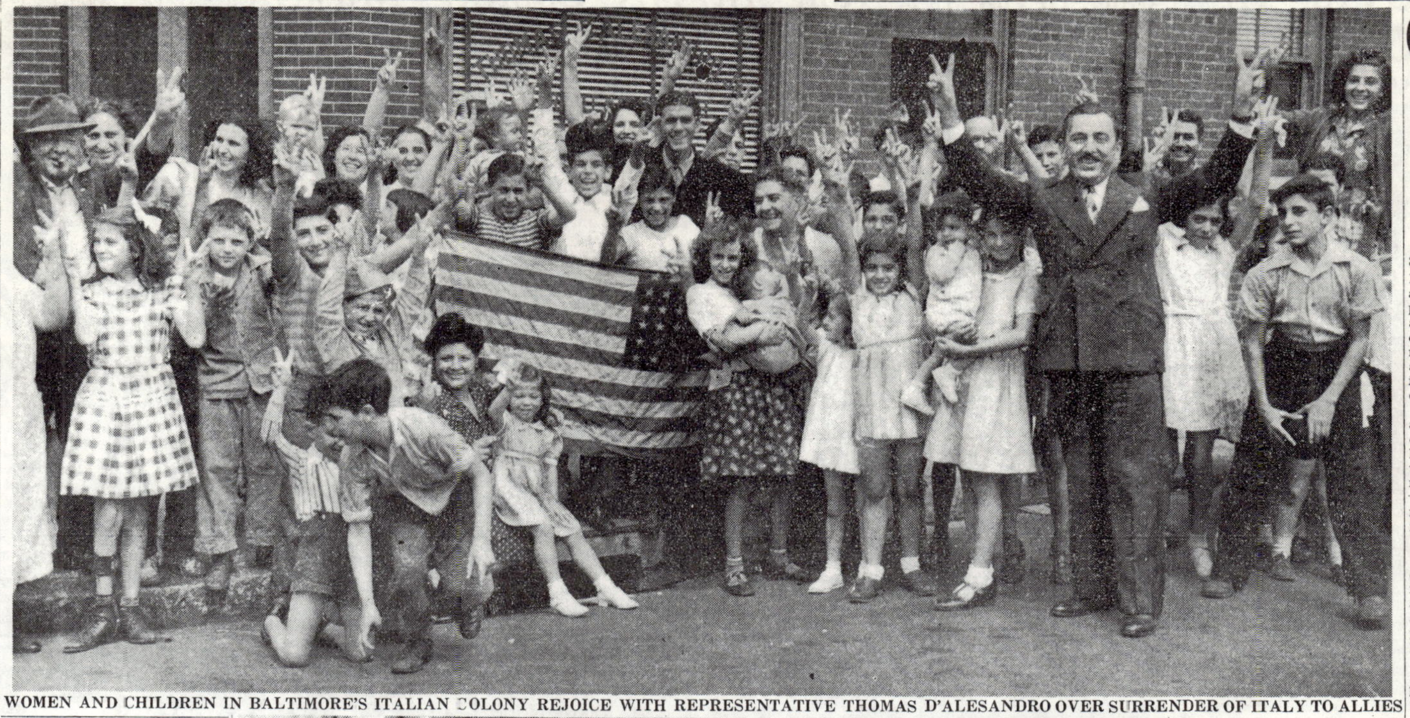

WOMEN AND CHILDREN IN BALTIMORE'S ITALIAN COLONY REJOICE WITH REPRESENTATIVE THOMAS D'ALESANDRO OVER SURRENDER OF ITALY TO ALLIES

News Received With Cries Of Welcome

Baltimoreans received the news of Italy's unconditional surrender placidly, although there was widespread jubilation in "Little Italy."

Newsboys had a booming business as shoppers and business men crowded street-corner stands to read Gen. Dwight D. Eisenhower's official announcement that Italy had given up.

The first thoughts of Baltimoreans upon receiving the news seemed to be that many American lives would be saved and that victory was one step closer.

Mrs. Robert B. Coleburn, 2011 West Baltimore street, said:

"I think Italy knew this was coming because of the fine work our boys over there have been doing. The Italian people themselves never seem to have been really in this war—they just didn't have their hearts in it."

A downtown shopper, Mrs. Albert Remke, 700 block Wyndhurst avenue, remarked that "it brings peace that much nearer."

She added:

"I'm certainly glad Italy finally decided to give up. Now it will be easier to knock out Germany and Japan."

"IT'S MARVELOUS"

Miss Elizabeth Cook, 3412 Gwynn's Falls parkway, commented:

"I think the news of Italy's surrender is marvelous. It will certainly save a lot of our boys' lives and help bring them home sooner. This is the beginning of the end for the Axis."

Baltimore's Italian coloney received the news with high jubilation, mingled with tears of joy. In private homes, retsaurants, taverns and stores of all description it seemed that serious work for the day was at an end.

As the true meaning of Italy's surrender was comprehended, informal celebrations began throughout the city. There were indications that before nightfall there would be many formal assemblages to celebrate the beginning of the liberation of Europe.

D'ALESANDRO THANKFUL

Representative Thomas J. D'Alesandro, leader of the Italian colony, said, on hearing the news:

"Thank God. I always knew the Italian people had no enmity against the United States. We can be thankful because so many lives will be saved.

"The favorable results will be incalculable."

The proprietress of one of "Little Italy's" well-known restaurants, Mrs. Emma Macciocca, said with a cry of joy:

"Tonight I'm going to cook Mussolini and make the Japs and Hitler eat him. I'm going to sharpen my best knife and cut him into fine chops. This is the happiest day of my life."

'NOTHING ELSE TO DO'

Vincent Miligoce, 314 South Eden street, added a serious touch to the conversation when he said:

"Italy couldn't do anything else. They had Lucifer on their side. What else could they do? Mussolini brought nothing but strife to his people. Now Italy is paying the penalty."

Tears streamed down the face of Anthony Sergi and sobs shook him as he was told of the news of Italy's surrender. His daughter Pauline is in Messin and he hasn't heard from her for many weeks. His son, Private Dominic Sergi, is in the Army. Sergi's home is at 248 Albemarle street.

NEWS "WONDERFUL"

His daughter-in-law, Mrs. Benny Sergi, whose husband is in the Army, said:

"The news is wonderful. I can't wait to tell my sister Jean."

Mrs. Jean Kidwell, the sister, is a defense worker whose husband is also in the Army.

With eyes filled with tears Mrs. Mary Tana of 311 High street came to see Mrs. Marias Allori, 300 Albemarle street. She talked in Italian and Mrs. Allori translating, said:

"She says she's glad that her nephew; he's an orphan—and she raised him—will be coming home now. He's just gone to camp, and it nearly broke her heart to part with him."

Yank Fliers Sink Jap River Craft

FOURTEENTH U. S. A. A. F. HEADQUARTERS IN CHINA, Sept. 8—(A. P.)—American Lightnings and Warhawks took further toll of Japanese transport facilities in the area south of Hankow Monday in dive-bombing and strafing sweeps, a communique announced today. Four Yangtze River boats, two tugs and two barges were sunk and five other river boats were burned or damaged. One Japanese plane was shot down.

Roosevelt Will Open Bond Drive

WASHINGTON, Sept. 8—(A. P.). — President Roosevelt will open the $15,000,000,000 third war loan drive tonight with a 10-minute radio address as part of an hour-long program, beginning at 9 P. M.

The broadcast, originating in Washington and Hollywood, will include an all-star cast of motion picture and radio headliners. Mr. Roosevelt will speak at about 9.40 P. M.

'SOLID FRONT LINE'

The Treasury's war finance division meanwhile paid tribute today to the manner in which it said the nation's press is "forming a solid front line for the record-breaking bond-selling" campaign.

Despite the handicap of a newsprint shortage and other wartime problems, the division reported that "a barrage of front-page news coverage, plus millions of lines of advertising, is being laid down by the publishers and editors of the nation."

Hundreds of editorials have appeared, keynoting the drive's aim to sell 50,000,000 individual war bonds in September.

In many cities publishers and editors are serving on war finance committees, members of newspaper staffs have been loaned as volunteers and cartoonists and comic-strip artists have enlisted in the drive, the division said.

GASTON TO SPEAK

In Chicago the annual meeting of the Associated Press Managing Editors' Association will devote one session to a forum on the third war loan. Herbert E. Gaston, assistant secretary of the Treasury, will be among the speakers.

12 Billion In Tax Revenues Sought

WASHINGTON, Sept. 8—(A. P.).—Wanted: $12,000,000,000.

With that staggering sum as its challenge, the House Ways and Means Committee called an executive huddle today to map plans for measuring John Taxpayer's ability to meet more and more of war's cost out of current income.

Most of the session probably will be devoted to setting the procedure for public hearings on a new revenue bill and on a more immediate review of the war contract renegotiation law, which permits the Government to recoup "excessive" profits.

—For Salvage Information

(1) Iron and Steel
(2) Kitchen Fats
(3) Tin Cans
(4) Waste Paper

Call PLaza 6877

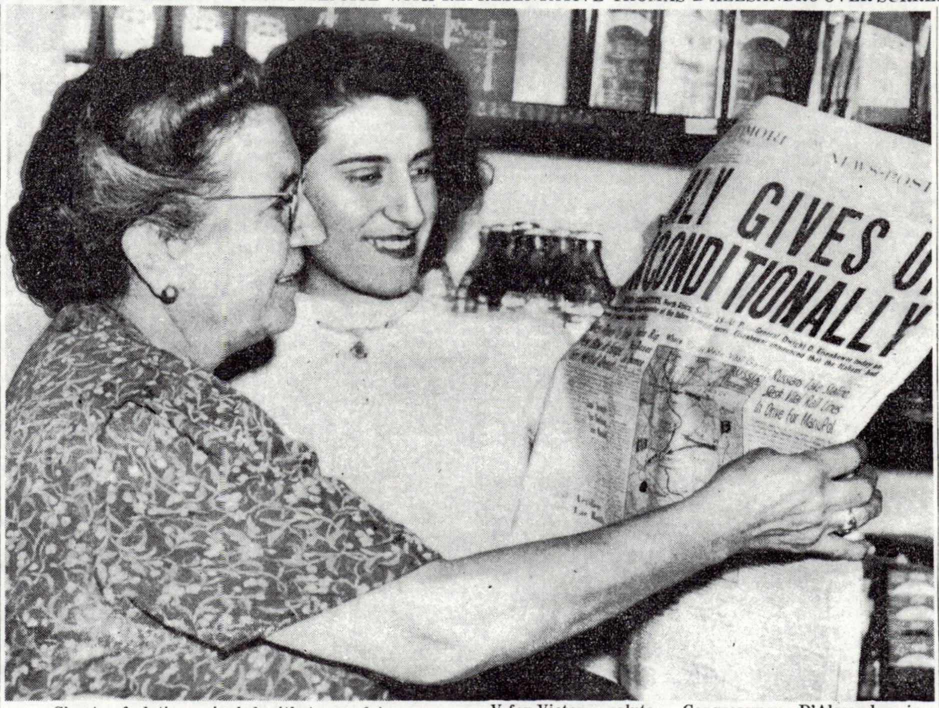

Shouts of elation, mingled with tears of joy, were let loose today in Baltimore's Italian colony as word of Italy's unconditional surrender spread like a prairie fire. Men, women and children dashed in and out doorways spreading the news with hands upraised in the V-for-Victory salute. Congressman D'Alesandro is shown in top picture in a typical street scene. At left, Mrs. Elvira Lancelotta, mother of four sons in the U. S. armed services, and her daughter, Eleanor, read about Gen. Dwight D. Eisenhower's announcement in The News-Post Extra.

Yanks Rip Nazi Bases In France

LONDON, Sept. 8—(A. P.).—American twin-engined Marauders blasted two enemy airfields near Lille in France today, rounding out a full week of non-stop assaults by Allied air units based in Britain to support the Mediterranean campaign and pave the way for the invasion of Western Europe.

At the same time Thunderbolt fighters of the U. S. Eighth Air Force augmented the drive with sweeps over Belgium and Northern France.

RAKE NAZI BASES

The targets of the medium Marauders in their seventh consecutive day of operations were the Nazi airbases at Lille-Nord and Lille-Vandeville, both of which had been hit previously in recent days. The announcement, from the U. S. Army's European theatre headquarters, said R. A. F., Dominion and Allied Spitfires escorted the bomber fleets.

The Nazi-controlled Paris radio declared that American bombers had struck in "violent attack" at Amiens and had pounded Abbeville twice more, but there was no announcement from Allied air officials of new raids against these oft-battered objectives.

D. C. Jubilant Over Italy

Continued from Page 1.

risings against the German occupational forces.

Official Washington immediately hailed Badoglio's capitulation as complete justification of the Anglo-American policy of insisting on unconditional surrender — a policy that has been subject to recent attack by critics as unlikely to have satisfactory results in Italy.

It is expected that President Roosevelt and Churchill will soon issue a joint statement concerning this first total surrender of one of the leading Axis powers. The President and Churchill are believed likely to tell the Italian people that they may rest assured they will be granted a just peace.

MILITARY UNITY

General Eisenhower's announcement that Russia will be associated with the United States and Britain in connection with Italy's formal surrender was regarded by American officials as a gratifying sign of political as well as military unity between the three major Allied nations.

Disclosure that the armistice was granted Italy on September 3 confirmed the general belief in Washington that Churchill had been remaining in the Capital in order that he and the President could deal jointly with the anticipated capitulation of the Italian nation.

KNOWN FOR DAYS

It is now obvious that the President and Churchill have been aware for some days that Italy was about to accept the Allied terms of unconditional surrender. This is considered responsible for the buoyant spirit which both leaders are known to have displayed in recent days.

The big question in the mind of official and diplomatic Washington now was how the Italians were going to get rid of the Germans who are still in Italy.

Extreme gratification was expressed on all sides at Marshal Badoglio's order to the Italian armed forces to oppose attack from any quarter except the Allied side.

This was seen as an indication that Italy's armed forces would resist any attempt by the Germans to maintain their position in Italy by force.

Greeks, Italians Cheer At News

LONDON, Sept. 8—(A. P.).—News of Italy's surrender was greeted happily by the free Italian organization here and by the Greeks, who called it the biggest step yet toward liberation of their countries.

Andrea Simoni, head of the free Italian movement, said "it is perhaps too soon to talk, but it is a happy thing that Italy is out of the war."

Awaiting word from the Government seat in Cairo, Greek sources were cautious, but stressed that the Axis would be unable to continue domination of the Balkans with the east coast of Italy occupied by the Allies.

Mrs. Roosevelt Visits Hospitals

SYDNEY, Australia, Sept. 8—(A. P.).—Making friends with Australian service groups and "meeting as many Americans as I can," Mrs. Eleanor Roosevelt spent two hours at One Hundred and Eighteenth General Hospital and then made brief visits today to Australian hospitals.

She visited many battle casualties from the Pacific campaign, which now is gaining full momentum in the Lae and Salamaua area.

America's First Lady ate dinner at the regular mess and autographed a white chef's cap for Pfc. John Mourey, Johnstown, Pa. She was serenaded by the Fourth Replacement Depot Band, led by Corporal John Waide, 121 Rose street, Jackson, Miss.

Opinion Split On Dewey Plan For Alliance

By GEORGE ROTHWELL BROWN

Special to News-Post.

MACKINAC ISLAND, Mich., Sept. 8. — Governor Thomas E. Dewey took off for New York ahead of time last night, leaving party opinion here sharply divided as to the probable effect his advocacy of a "continuing" post-war military alliance with Great Britain would have upon his availability as Republican Presidential candidate in 1944.

Criticism of the Governor's advanced stand, taken at a press conference on Sunday, centered largely in Republicans attending the party's policy council from the mid-Continent States.

Spokesmen from the East minimized the unfavorable effect the incident might have.

REITERATES STAND

Far from softening the straight-out indorsement he gave, upon first arriving here, to a British alliance, the New York Governor at an impromptu press conference yesterday afternoon in a hotel lobby virtually reiterated it.

When questioned about the unfavorable criticism arising from his alliance stand, Governor Dewey laughed off the suggestion that he could be read out of the Republican party. He said:

"As for a military alliance with Great Britain, upon calm reflection the inevitability of it will be realized."

RESENTMENT STOPS

Today much of the resentment among Republicans here against the Governor, for his alliance statement, had worn off. It had been rather caustic.

Nevertheless, the resolutions on foreign policy adopted late yesterday by the Republican council outlined a position as to post-war foreign relationships completely at variance with the alliance views previously expressed by the man who is, as of today, recognized as the principal contender for the Republican Presidential nomination.

Pleads Insanity To Kidnap Charge

ALBANY, Ore., Sept. 8—(U. P.).—Mrs. Catherine Wright, twenty-six, confessed kidnaper of two-day-old Judith Gurney, pleaded innocent to a baby-stealing charge today on grounds she "was insane at the time the act was committed."

Seattle In Unique Bond Drive Plan

SEATTLE, Wash., Sept. 8—(A. P.).—Seattle has its own plan to increase bond sales. To the 500 highest bidders in a bond auction will go 500 pairs of nylon hose.

Ann Lewis's
LEXINGTON AT PARK

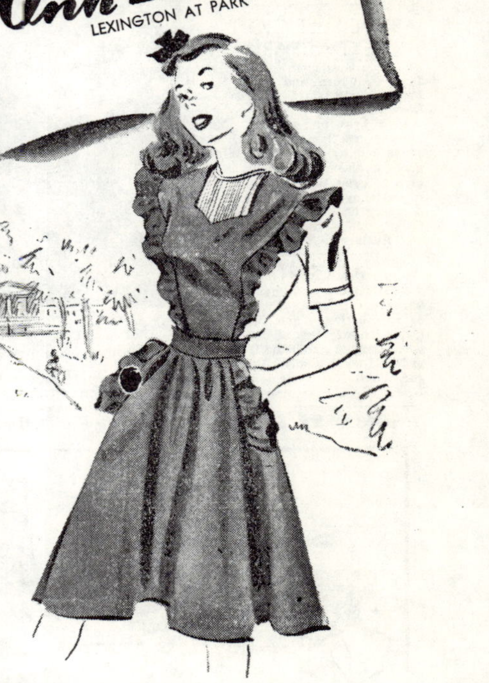

fashion's darling of the hour

JUMPERS . . . 5.99

Have you seen our lovely new selection? Styles galore in classic tailored models, gay novelties and colorful peasant types . . . all-wool jersey and flannel, shetland, rayon gabardine and twill. New colors. Junior's and Misses' sizes.

BLOUSES 2.99

STORE HOURS THURS.: 10 A. M. 'TIL 9 P. M.!

Shop in Air-Cooled Comfort

Paul Lukas And Bette Davis In 'Watch On Rhine'

By NORMAN CLARK

"WATCH ON THE RHINE" is a distinguished film drama—even more distinguished than it was as a stage play.

We think this is in a measure due to the superior portrayal Paul Lukas gives as the anti-Nazi. Here is a truly magnificant figure of a man, a gentle, loving father and husband—but also a heroic figure in whom burns a democratic flame, who hates Fascism so much, who understands so well that this disease must be stamped out if the world is to live in healthful peace that he is willing to leave his beloved family and die for his beliefs.

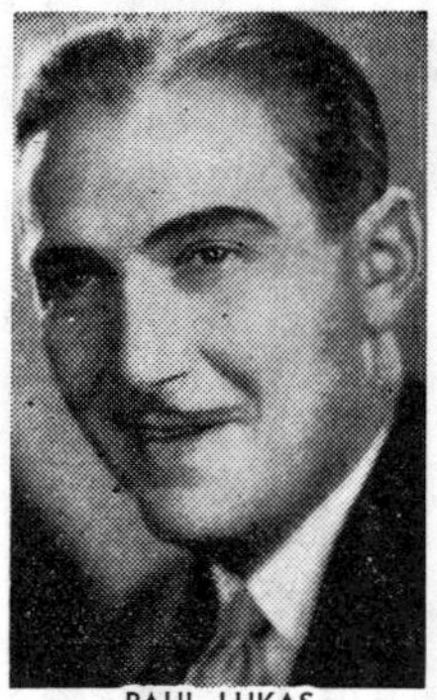

PAUL LUKAS

Lillian Hellman's play is as pertinent today as it was when it was produced here in 1941 before going on to great success in New York. Nazism still remains to be crushed, there are still ratty opportunists willing to gamble in human lives, and there are still some people blind to the constant vigilance needed to keep freedom alive.

Perhaps Fanny Farelly's beautiful country home outside Washington, D. C., wouldn't be the soft and happily indifferent place today that it was in 1941. There would certainly be a greater awareness of the danger America has been facing for a long time. But Miss Hellman needed just as an American home and atmosphere in which to contrast the stinking fever of Fascism with the fat happiness of contented democracy.

We also found Lucille Watson even more incisive and brilliant in this film at the Stanley than she was in the original piece. Bette Davis is excellent as the devoted wife of Kurt Muller—a woman who knows the meaning of true love—and there is colorful acting by George Coulouris and Geraldine Fitzgerald.

"Watch on the Rhine" is somewhat static in its early passages, but presently there comes enough sturdy drama, even melodrama, to satisfy the most demanding of action fans.

Hollywood may well be proud of "Watch on the Rhine."

"Watch On Rhine"

"WATCH ON THE RHINE," co-starring Bette Davis and Paul Lukas. Screen play by Dashiell Hammett, from the stage play of Lillian Hellman. Directed by Herman Shumlin. A Warner Brothers' picture, presented at the Stanley.

THE CAST

Sara Muller............Bette Davis
Kurt Muller............Paul Lukas
Mathe de Brancovis.
Geraldine Fitzgerald
Fanny Farrelly......Lucille Watson
Anise ....Beulah Bondi
Teck de Brancovis.George Coulouris
David Farrelly.......Donald Woods
Bodo ....Eric Roberts
Babette ....Janis Wilson
Joshua ....Donal Buka

'ABOVE SUSPICION' NEXT AT PARKWAY

"Above Suspicion," starring Joan Crawford and Fred MacMurray, will start Saturday at Loew's Parkway.

Miss Crawford and Mr. MacMurray are honeymooners, who are asked by the British Intelligence to discover the whereabouts of a missing British agent while in Germany. They lead the Nazis a merry chase all over the continent, finally escaping into neutral Switzerland.

AT CENTRE

A story of war-time America, with counterfeiting as the basis of a situation which finally attracts the attention of the F. B. I., is "I Escaped From the Gestapo," at the Centre today. Dean Jagger, John Carradine and Mary Brian play the featured roles.

2nd Week For Success At New

"Claudia," starring Dorothy McGuire and Robert Young, will remain at the New.

The story concerns a young architect and his child wife. The girl has yet to learn to be a woman. And there is where the husband's job lies. His attempt to break her of her slavish attachment to her mother and teach her the responsibilities of a wife and a sane, mature and realistic outlook on life inspires a variety of emotions, with a laugh here and a tear there.

Other Dramatic News on Pages 19 and 21.

Comedian

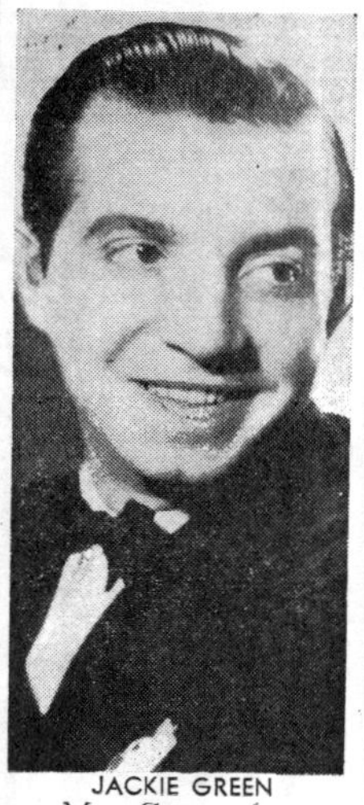

JACKIE GREEN

Mr. Green, funster and mimic, is a top act on the current stage bill at the Hippodrome.

ANCHORS AWEIGH Wig Wag For A Wave

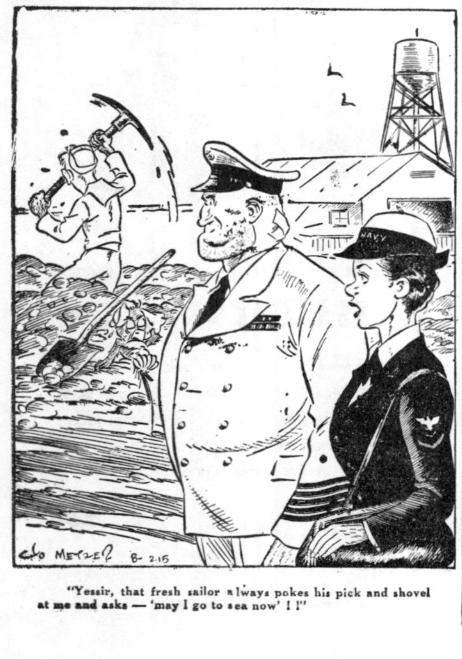

"Yessir, that fresh sailor always pokes his pick and shovel at me and asks — 'may I go to sea now' ! !"

The Feminine Voice Of Old Broadway

By DOROTHY KILGALLEN

Hi'Ya, Stranger!

(Continuing last week's daytime quick-see of Manhattan with a tour of the night shift.)

So you want to catch all the high spots, and never mind the expense? Then let's make the bar at 21 the first stop.

We'll walk there, because W. 52nd st. is New York's Montmartre, and you mustn't miss it—the gaudy banners outside the little basement jive joints, the neon signs, the come-on pictures of floor-show strippers, the musicians "taking five" in little groups on the sidewalk, the sound of jazz coming from every open door and now and then the melodic whimper of a torch singer wailing about love.

It would take you and your girl a week of nights and at least a $100 to see everything on this noisy, rowdy street.

You want to see a ballplayer or a prizefighter? Okay, finish your cocktail and we'll go to Toots Shor's around the corner. Looks like a Hollywood place, doesn't it, with all the wood paneling and red leather.

While you eat you can watch a girlie show, if you like. The Diamond Horseshoe and the Latin Quarter are both good and both a lot of entertainment for your money.

Let's just take a look in so you can get a rough idea of what they're like and decide which one you want to see first when you have plenty of time; then we'll have dinner at Leone's, where you can get a table alongside a trout stream and look at a genuine tree.

You like this town, and you like this kind of life? I'll take you to another kind of night spot and show you another kind of night life, something you'll remember a long time. That is W. 54th st.—and that's night court. Come in and listen for a while.

This sort of thing goes on 24 hours a day in this great, tall, beautiful, shining city. It is the low, sorrowful, dirty side of our town, and it never changes.

Want to call it quits now? Had a good time? Well, so long, stranger—glad you liked our town. We'll do it again some time!

'Crime School' Now At Times

Starring Humphrey Bogart, the Dead End Kids, and Gale Page, "Crime School," now at the Times, tells a story of schools of correction, that are really schools of corruptions.

Directed by Lewis Seiler from a screen play by Crane Wilbur and Vincent Sherman, "Crime School" shows classrooms with barbed wire, teachers with clubs and whips, pupils with scarred bodies.

The Times also features a showing of latest news films.

Movie CLOCK

CENTURY—"Best Foot Forward," 10.45 A. M., 12.58, 3.11, 5.24, 7 37, 9.50 P. M.

NEW—"Claudia," 10 A. M., 12, 2, 4. 6, 8, 10 P. M.

KEITH'S—"So Proudly We Hail," 10.05 A. M., 12.27, 2.49, 5.11, 7.33, 9.55 P. M.

VALENCIA—"Hi Diddle Diddle," 12.45, 2.29, 4.20, 6.11, 8.02, 9.53 P. M.

TIMES—"Crime School," 1.47, 3.55, 6.03, 8.11, 10.19 P. M., 12.27, 2.35 A. M.

STANLEY—"Watch on Rhine," 10.45 A. M., 12.57, 3.09, 5.21, 7.33, 9.45 P. M.

PARKWAY—"Du Barry Was a Lady," 1, 3.12, 5.24, 7.36, 9.49 P. M.

HIPPODROME—"Sky's the Limit," 11 A. M., 1.50, 4.40, 7.30, 10.10 P. M.

LITTLE—"They Died With Their Boots On," 10.45 A. M., 1, 3.15, 5.30, 7.45, 10 P. M.

MAYFAIR—"Souls at Sea," 10.30 A. M., 12.30, 2.30, 4.30, 6.30, 8.30, 10.30 P. M.

ROSLYN—"I Was a Spy," 1, 2.53, 4.46, 6.39, 8.32, 10.25 P. M.

WARNER BROS. STANLEY HOWARD NEAR FRANKLIN ST. DOORS OPEN 10:30 A. M.
BETTE DAVIS ★ PAUL LUKAS "WATCH on the RHINE"
BUY WAR BONDS AND STAMPS

RIVOLI
Lena Horne "STORMY WEATHER" — Rochester "What's Buzzin' Cousin"
DOUBLE SHOW DAILY DOORS OPEN 9 A. M.

Gayety ONLY BURLESK BALTIMORE
Winnie Garrett
Billy "Cheese & Crackers" Hagan
Lou Powers—Carole King

Red Skelton Has Politician's Role In His Coming Musical

Runs For Alderman In The Hectic Days Around 1880

By LOUELLA O. PARSONS
Motion Picture Editor International News Service.

HOLLYWOOD, Sept. 8.—Red Skelton runs for alderman—but hold everything! It's only for the laughs in his next musical, "Hot Time in the Old Town Tonight." Red's fling into politics will be coming up just about the time the real politicos start tuning up for the 1944 excitement — which is nice timing, if you ask me. Jack McGowan's original story utilizes all the color, slang and Police Gazette antics of the hectic days around 1880—at least they tell me they were hectic. I wasn't around, myself.

Speaking of Red, he still holds the all-time record for maintaining diplomatic relations with his ex-wife, Edna. The marvel of this relationship is that his present fiancee, Muriel Morris, seems just as friendly with Edna as does Red. The three of them often dine together. He still thinks Edna is his best "gag" writer.

Ever since Beryl Wallace was signed to play Louella O. Parsons (me) in "Gunmaster," the movie about Bat Masterson, she tells me the gang has rechristened her Beryl O. Wallace. Beryl, the pulchritudinous Earl Carroll star, looks about as much like I did in the days when I knew Bat as I look like Shirley Temple—not that I wouldn't like to be as beautiful as Beryl. Now Beryl O. has settled down into a permanent screen career. She is at the General Service Studios to play Goebbels' girl friend in "Dr. Paul Joseph Goebbels, his Life and Loves." Sigrid Gurie plays Goebbels' wife, with Donald Woods, H. B. Warner and others completing the cast.

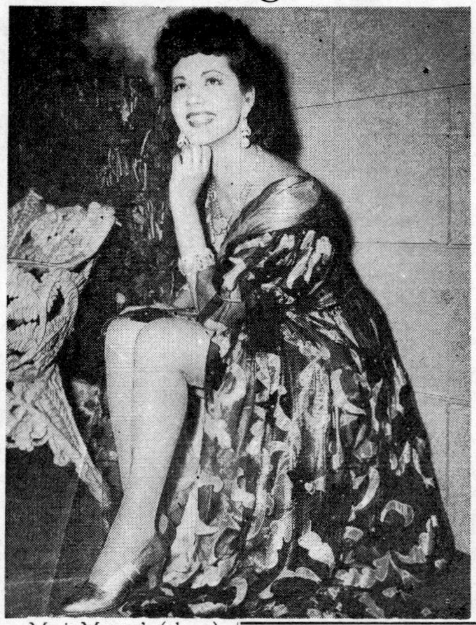

Maria Montez's (above) popularity is so great that many important plans are being made for her, one of them "Queen of the Nile" in technicolor.

The popularity of Maria Montez is one of those Hollywood stories that is almost stranger than fiction. I used to see her about, and didn't even know that she had movie aspirations. When Universal signed her I wondered, like everyone else, why the sudden interest? Whoever had the idea apparently knew what he was doing, because she is so popular at the box office that many important plans are being made for her future pictures. One of them is "Queen of the Nile" in Technicolor, which Paul Malvern will produce with the handsome Turhan Bey in the leading role.

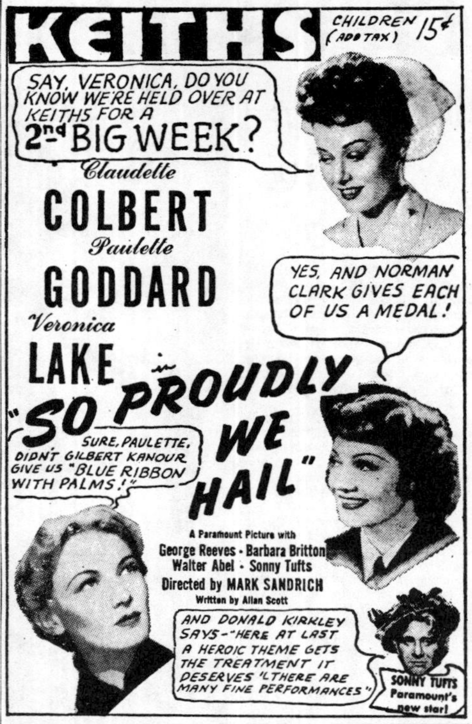

Cool LOEW'S
CENTURY LEXINGTON NR. CHARLES — 2nd GAY WEEK! "BEST FOOT FORWARD" in TECHNICOLOR — SEE AD PAGE 19
VALENCIA ATOP THE CENTURY — LAST DAY · HI DIDDLE DIDDLE
STARTS TOMORROW First Baltimore Showing: WALT DISNEY'S VICTORY THROUGH AIR POWER IN TECHNICOLOR SEE AD PAGE 19
PARKWAY NORTH AT CHARLES — ★ IN TECHNICOLOR ★ "DuBARRY WAS A LADY" Red Skelton · Lucille Ball

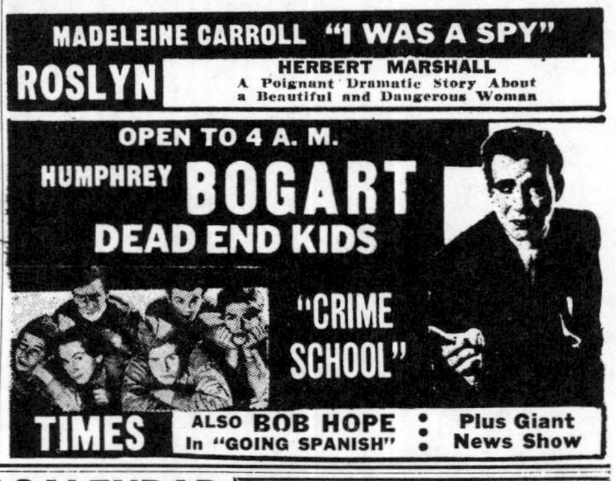

★ ★ BACK THE ATTACK—BUY BONDS! ★

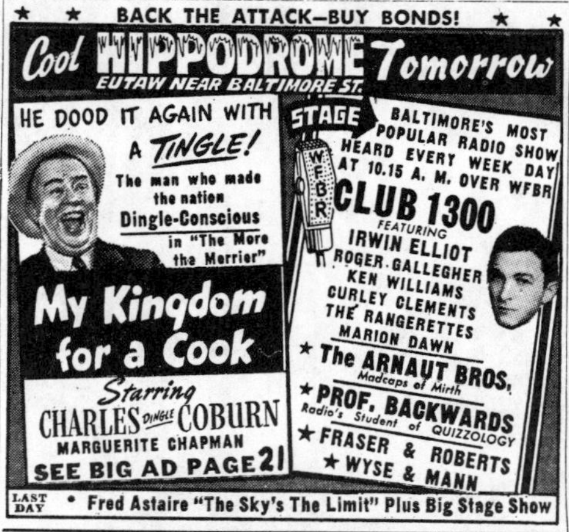

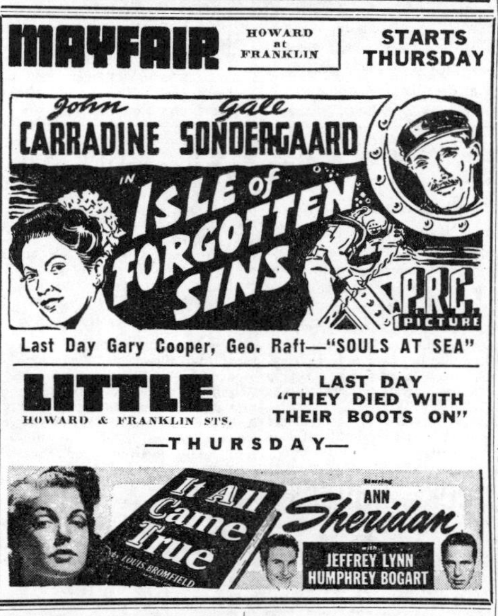

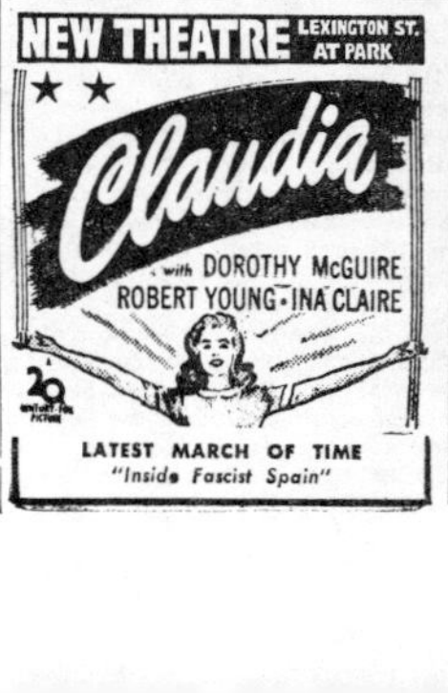

FORD'S—Tonight at 8:30 Mat. Today & Sat. 2:30
BORIS KARLOFF IN PERSON
IN ARSENIC AND OLD LACE
Wed. & Sat. Mats.—56c, $1.11, $1.66
FORD'S—Next Week—Seats Thurs.
BROADWAY'S GAY COMEDY HIT— "JUNIOR MISS"
MORE THAN 700 TIMES IN NEW YORK!
By The Authors of "MY SISTER EILEEN"
Eves.—56c, $1.11, $1.66, $2.21
Wed. & Sat. Mats.—56c, $1.11, $1.66

TODAY'S MOVIE CALENDAR

Theatres advertised in this column belong to the Motion Picture Theatre Owners of Maryland

Back the Attack--- Buy War Bonds

Aero Middle River, Md. Ann Miller in "WHAT'S BUZZIN' COUSIN" With John Hubbard.

Alpha Catonsville. Walter Huston in "MISSION TO MOSCOW" Comedy.

Ambassador 4604 Liberty Heights. Cheryl Walker in "STAGE DOOR CANTEEN" "Night Life in the Army."

Apollo 1500 Harford Ave. John Carradine in "HITLER'S MADMEN" 2 Carlines to Apollo—19, 27.

Arcade Harford Rd. & Hamilton Ave. All-Star Cast in "STAGE DOOR CANTEEN" "Black Marketing."

Astor Poplar Grove at Edmondson. Robert Paige in "COWBOY IN MANHATTAN" 3 Carlines to Astor—4, 14, 9.

Aurora 7 East North Ave. George Sanders in "APPOINTMENT IN BERLIN" "Gem Jams."

Avalon 4300 Park Heights Ave. Virginia Weidler in "THE YOUNGEST PROFESSION" "Heavenly Music."

Avenue Milton Ave. & Hoffman St. Barbara Stanwyck in "LADY OF BURLESQUE" News.

Avon 3019 Hamilton Ave. Evelyn Ankers in "CAPTIVE WILD WOMAN" "Doing Their Bit."

Belnord 2700 Philadelphia Ave. George Sanders in "APPOINTMENT IN BERLIN" "Two Sapplings."

Boulevard 33rd at Greenmount. All-Star Cast in "STAGE DOOR CANTEEN" "Slay It With Flowers."

Bridge Edmondson Ave. & Pulaski St. Brian Donlevy in "HANGMEN ALSO DIE" Comedy.

Broadway 509 S. Broadway. All-Star Cast in "STAGE DOOR CANTEEN" 4 Carlines to Broadway—16, 18, 10, 21.

Cameo 4705 Harford Road. Ronald Colman in "THE LOST HORIZON" Take 19 Carline to Cameo.

Capitol 1518 W. Baltimore St. All-Star Cast in "STAGE DOOR CANTEEN" Carlines 15, 8, 1, 11—Q Bus.

Casino 1118 Light St. Errol Flynn in "THE SEA HAWK" "G-Men vs. the Black Dragon."

Cluster 303 S. Broadway. Tom Conway in "THE FALCON STRIKES BACK" "Hot Foot."

Columbia 709 Washington Blvd. All-Star Cast in "STAGE DOOR CANTEEN" "He Dood It Again."

Earle Belair Rd. at Woodlea Ave. George Raft in "BACKGROUND TO DANGER" Comedy.

Edgewood 3500 Edmondson Ave. All-Star Cast in "STAGE DOOR CANTEEN" "School Daze."

Eureka 404 S. Fremont Ave. Mabel Paige in "SOMEONE TO REMEMBER" "The Batman."

Forest Garrison & Liberty Heights. Lena Horne in "STORMY WEATHER" "Royal Araby."

Fulton Fulton Ave. & Baker St. Betty Grable in "CONEY ISLAND" Comedy.

Garden Charles at Cross. Evelyn Ankers in "CAPTIVE WILD WOMAN" "Gay Rio."

Glen Glen Burnie. Richard Travis in "SPY TRAIN" "The Batman."

Grand 511 S. Conkling St. Grace McDonald in "GET GOING" "Climbing the Peaks."

Gwynn 4609 Liberty Heights Ave. Laurel and Hardy in "JITTERBUGS" "Higher Than a Kite."

Hampden 911 W. 36th St. All-Star Cast in "STAGE DOOR CANTEEN" Comedy.

Harford 2610 Harford Ave. Donald O'Connor in "MISTER BIG" "Climbing the Peaks."

Hilton 3117 W. North Ave. All-Star Cast in "HER CARDBOARD LOVER" "Ben Franklin, Jr."

Horn 2014 West Pratt St. Mable Paige in "SOMEONE TO REMEMBER" "Yankee Doodle Daffy."

Howard 115 N. Howard St. All-Star Cast in "VIRGINIA CITY" Comedy.

Ideal 903 W. Thirty-sixth St. Tom Conway in "THE FALCON STRIKES BACK" Comedy.

Irvington 4113 Frederick Ave. George Sanders in "They Came To Blow Up America" Comedy.

Lane Dundalk, Md. John Carradine in "I Escaped from the Gestapo" With Dean Jagger.

Leader 248 S. Broadway. Jinx Falkenburg in "Two Senoritas From Chicago" 5 Carlines to Leader—16, 10, 18, 21, 5.

Linwood 908 S. Linwood Ave. MacDonald Carey in "SALUTE FOR THREE" "The Vanishing Private."

Little 523 North Howard St. Errol Flynn in "They Died With Their Boots On" Held Over Second Week.

Lord Baltimore 1110 West Baltimore St. Donald Barry in "WEST SIDE KID" With Dale Evans.

Lord Calvert 2244 Washington Boulevard. Walter Huston in "MISSION TO MOSCOW" Comedy.

Lyceum Sparrows Point, Md. Arline Judge in "GIRLS IN CHAINS" Comedy.

McHenry 1037 Light St. All-Star Cast in "STAGE DOOR CANTEEN" "Tin Pan Alley Cat."

Mayfair 508 N. Howard St. Gary Cooper in "SOULS AT SEA" With George Raft.

Met Pennsylvania & North Aves. George Sanders in "APPOINTMENT IN BERLIN" Cars—13, 2, 18, 1, 11, 31, 5, 33.

Nemo 4815 Eastern Ave. Otto Kruger in "SECRETS OF A CO-ED" "The Batman."

New Reisterstown, Md. Cary Grant in "MR. LUCKY" "Confusion in India."

New Essex Essex, Md. Basil Rathbone in "Sherlock Holmes in Washington" With Nigel Bruce.

New Glen Glen Burnie. Charles Boyer in "THE CONSTANCE NYMPH" Feature Starts 3.30, 5.30, 7.30, 9.30.

Northway Harford & North. Pky. Cary Grant in "MR. LUCKY" "Frankenstein's Cat."

Overlea Belair Rd., End of Car Line. Humphrey Bogart in "Action in the North Atlantic" "Tin Pan Alley Cat."

Palace Gay and Hoffman Sts. Patricia Morison in "HITLER'S MADMEN" Comedy.

Patterson Eastern and East Aves. All-Star Cast in "STAGE DOOR CANTEEN" "Night Life in the Army."

Pikes Pikesville, Md. Donald O'Connor in "IT COMES UP LOVE" News.

Pimlico Park Heights & Belvedere. Leon Errol in "GALS, INC." News.

Preston 1108 E. Preston St. Constance Cummings in "SOMEWHERE IN FRANCE" 3 Carlines to Preston—19, 27, 21.

Red Wing 2241 E. Monument St. Cary Grant in "MR. LUCKY" "Barnyard WAAC."

Rex 4600 York Road. Brian Aherne in "FOREVER AND A DAY" "First Aid."

Rialto 845 W. North Ave. Bob Hope in "THE CAT AND THE CANARY" Cars—13, 32, 31, 16, B Bus.

Ritz 1607 N. Washington St. All-Star Cast in "STAGE DOOR CANTEEN" Comedy.

Senator 5904 York Road. George Sanders in "APPOINTMENT IN BERLIN" "Mouse of Tomorrow."

State Monument and Castle Sts. All-Star Cast in "STAGE DOOR CANTEEN" Vaudeville.

Strand Dundalk, Md. Chester Morris in "AERIAL GUNNER" With Richard Arlen.

Uptown 5010 Park Heights Ave. All-Star Cast in "STAGE DOOR CANTEEN" Feature Starts 1.30, 4.02, 6.39, 9.12.

Vilma Belair Rd. and Mayfield Ave. All-Star Cast in "STAGE DOOR CANTEEN" Comedy.

Walbrook 3100 W. North Ave. Deanna Durbin in "HERS TO HOLD" "Ration Bored."

Waverly Greenmount at Gorsuch. Tom Conway in "THE FALCON STRIKES BACK" "Gay Rio."

Westport 2205 Russell St. Humphrey Bogart in "Action in the North Atlantic" Comedy.

Westway 5300 Edmondson Ave. Walter Huston in "MISSION TO MOSCOW" Comedy.

FIGHTING MARYLANDERS ON ALL FRONTS IN GLOBAL WAR

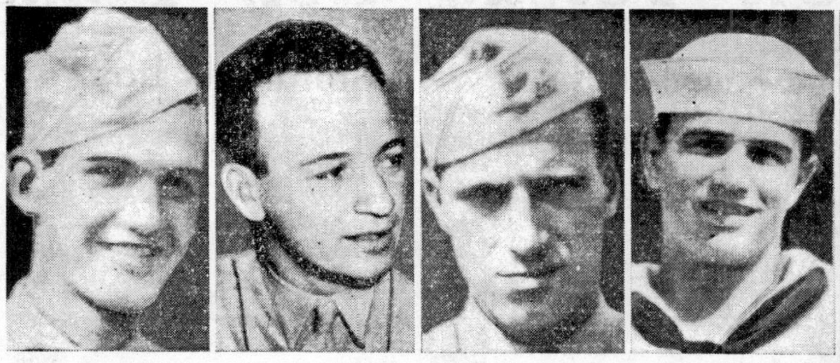

Now overseas, Pvt. H. H. Luehrs, Jr., 2639 East Biddle st. Graduate of City College. He is in Medical Corps.

Living at Fort Belvoir, Va., with his wife, Tech. Sgt. Louis Bengermino, 349 East 27th st. City College grad.

Doing good work overseas, Corp. Wm. Helmick, 4 E. York st., whose mother is Mrs. Belle Helmick.

Just through with "boot" training, Walter R. Schisler, 2004 W. Lexington st. Brother, Howard E., overseas.

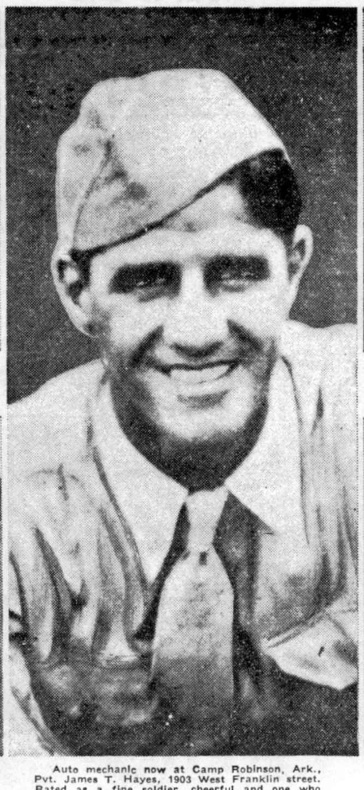

Auto mechanic now at Camp Robinson, Ark., Pvt. James T. Hayes, 1903 West Franklin street. Rated as a fine soldier, cheerful and one who knows every angle of his job.

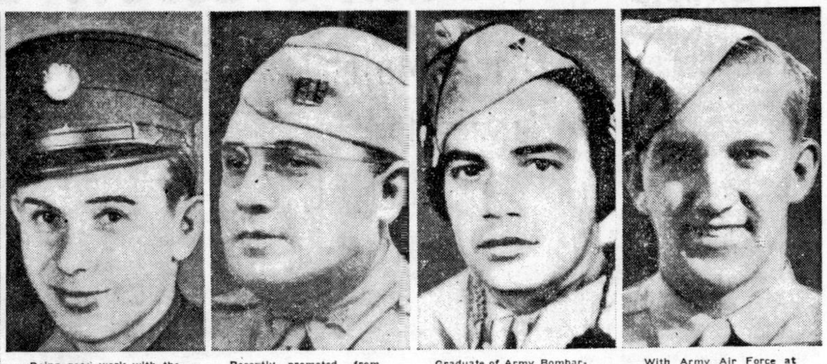

Doing good work with the Army in San Francisco, Pvt. Lee Kaufman, Chester, Md. Says Army life suits him.

Recently promoted from First Lieut., Capt. Charles Wollak, 2217 Eutaw pl. He is at Indiantown Gap, Pa.

Graduate of Army Bombardier School, Albuquerque, N. M., Second Lieut. Chester S. Jerrell, of Hyattsville, Md.

With Army Air Force at Fairmont Field, Geneva, Neb., Pvt. Earle Klemer, 3127 Clearview ave.

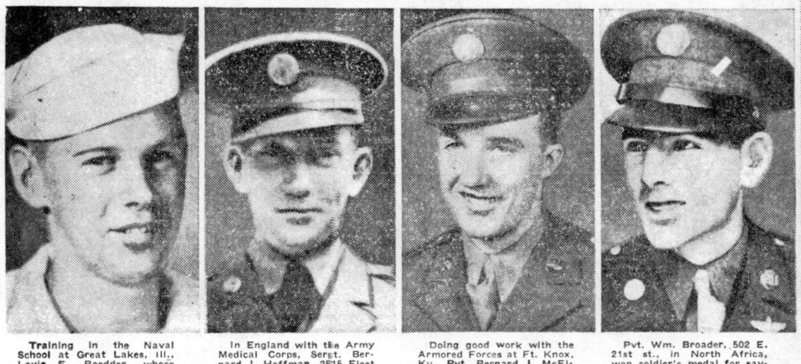

Training in the Naval School at Great Lakes, Ill., Louis E. Roedder, whose home is at Fort Howard.

In England with the Army Medical Corps, Sergt. Bernard J. Hoffman, 2515 Fleet street. Good soldier.

Doing good work with the Armored Forces at Ft. Knox, Ky., Pvt. Bernard J. McElroy, 2114 Harford road.

Pvt. Wm. Broader, 502 E. 21st st., in North Africa, won soldier's medal for saving three from burns.

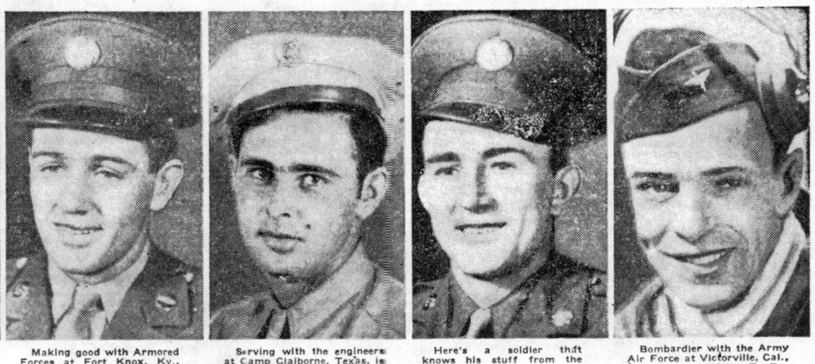

Making good with Armored Forces at Fort Knox, Ky., Pvt. George Hauser, 518 E. 23d st. Ready for combat.

Serving with the engineers at Camp Claiborne, Texas, is Private James R. Gibson, 3902 West Garrison ave.

Here's a soldier that knows his stuff from the ground up—Private August Zimmerman. Making good.

Bombardier with the Army Air Force at Victorville, Cal., Second Lieut. John E. Bacon, 5100 Whiteford ave.

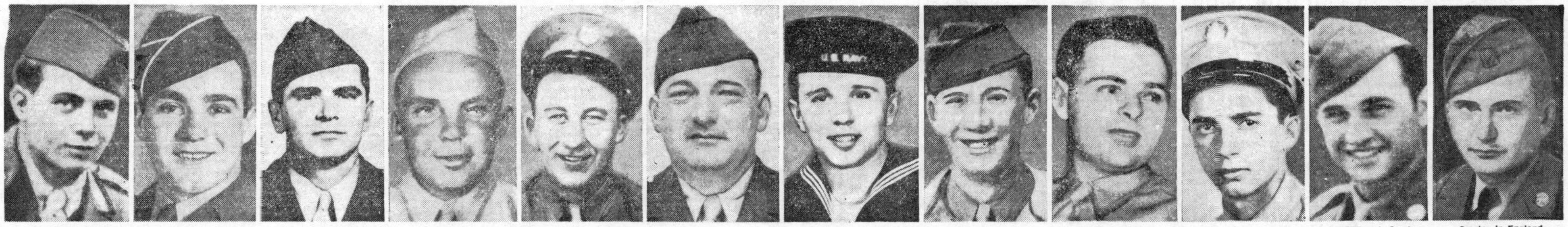

With armored forces in Africa, Pvt. Herman J. Davis, Jr., Old York road.

At Fort Brown, Texas, Pvt. Charles E. Campbell, 4805 Snader avenue.

Recently here on furlough, Pvt. Richard D. Marshall, 1906 West Mulberry street.

At Fort Bliss, Tex., Private Louis R. Kotowski, 822 South Bond street.

Serving in England, Pvt. Vernon F. Brick, 220 N. Ellwood ave.

Training at Westover Field, Mass., Pvt. Herman L. Pennell, 1822 Raynor av.

With Navy at Berkley, Va., Louis J. Memphis, S3c, 210 N. Patterson Park ave.

H. Maurice Boettinger, 114 S. Loudon ave., with Army Air Corps, Univ. of Mich.

Handling documents at Ft. Belvoir, Va., Pvt. Melvin Pierce, 2512 Cold Spring la.

Recently made corporal, Camp Shelby, Miss., S. J. Avara, 44 S. Carrollton ave.

In Officers' Cand. School, England, Staff Sergeant B. J. Romeo, 104 S. High st.

Serving in England, Corp. John Badonic, son of Mr. and Mrs. Thomas Badonic.

STATE'S SONS UPHOLD TRADITIONS OF COURAGE, GALLANTRY

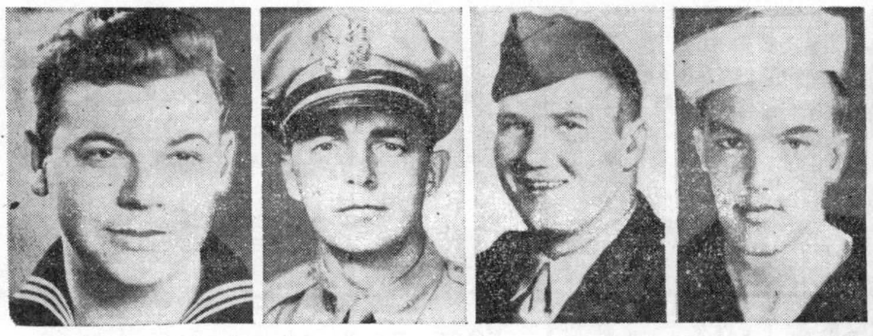

Serving overseas with Navy (his third voyage) Henry V. Wetters, 2137 W. Fayette st. Wife awaits return.

Recently promoted at Seymour Johnson Field, N. C., Capt. Luther S. Williams, 4408 Sedgewick road.

Driving M-10 tank destroyer, Kenneth G. Venzke, former Baltimore News-Post carrier.

Training for U. S. Maritime Service, Earl G. Taylor, 3125 Abel avenue.

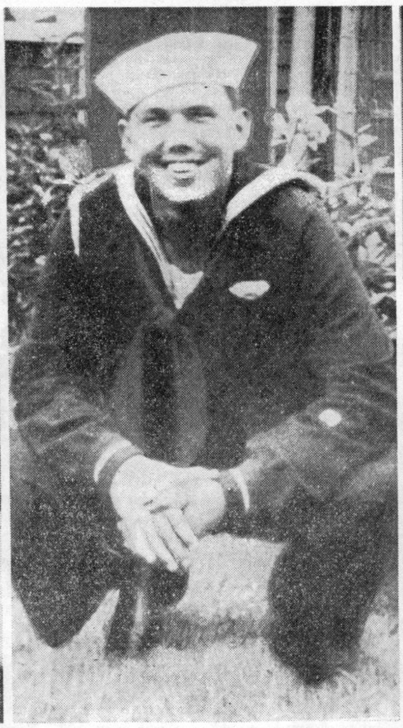

Smiling Seabee stationed at Camp Parks, Cal., John H. Baumgart, Jr., F2c., son of John H. Baumgart, Sr., 129 South Clinton street. Another brother, Charles, serving in Army, and their Dad is mighty proud of them.

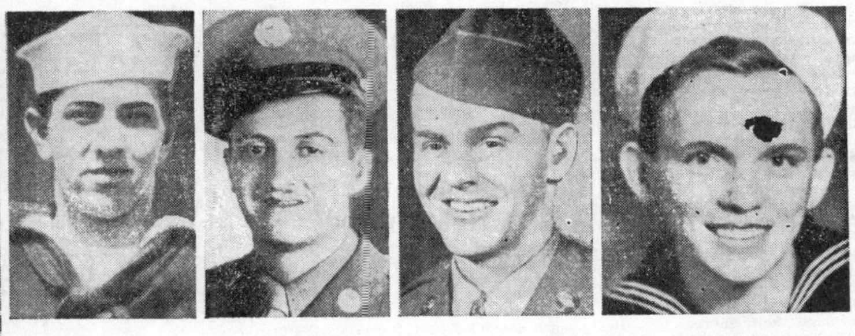

Somewhere at sea is Charles H. Keim, S2c, of 1726 Wilmington avenue.

Pfc. George T. Davis, 2044 Braddish avenue, serving valiantly in N. Africa.

At Fort Knox, Ky., with Armored Forces, Pvt. Charles Moran, 3703 Old York road.

Charles M. Bosse, F3c, of Rosedale, Md., graduate Kenwood H. S., is training with Navy, Great Lakes, Ill.

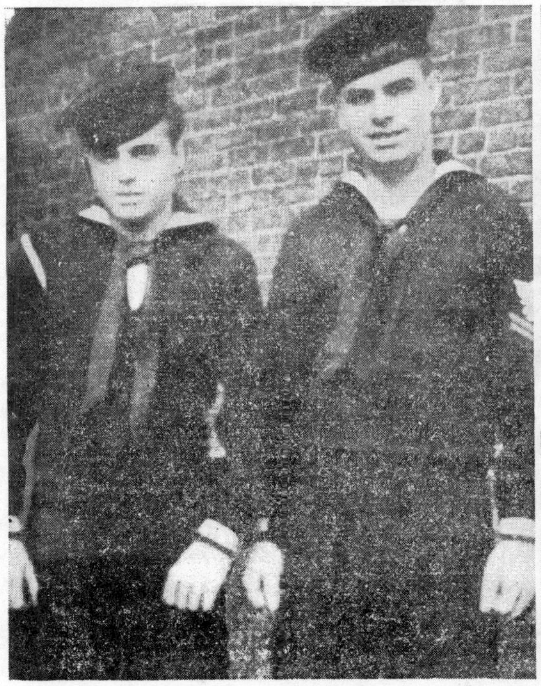

Two jolly sailors here, yet always ready to fight the Axis, are James Tiburzi (left) and brother, Michael, of 3402 Claremont street. Michael is overseas in a war zone. James, just ending a 10-day furlough, has returned to his Navy training at Jacksonville, Fla.

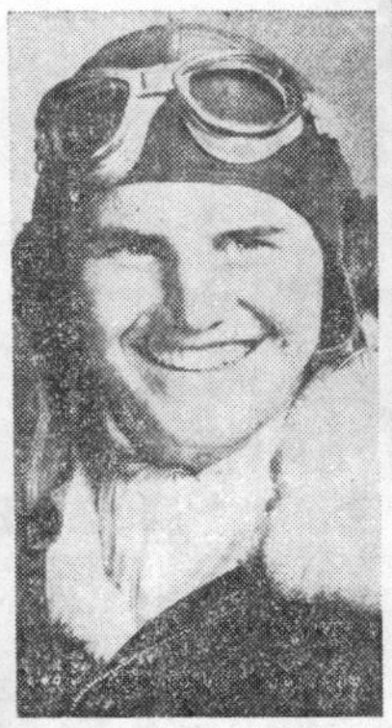

Recently appointed Naval Aviation Cadet and now at Pensacola, Fla., Richard C. Aldrich, 1820 Overland ave.

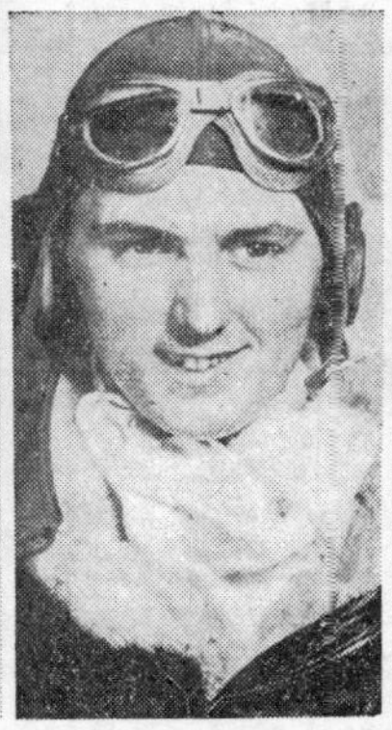

George A. Heinmiller, 608 East 33d st., is another Naval Aviation Cadet who is training at Pensacola.

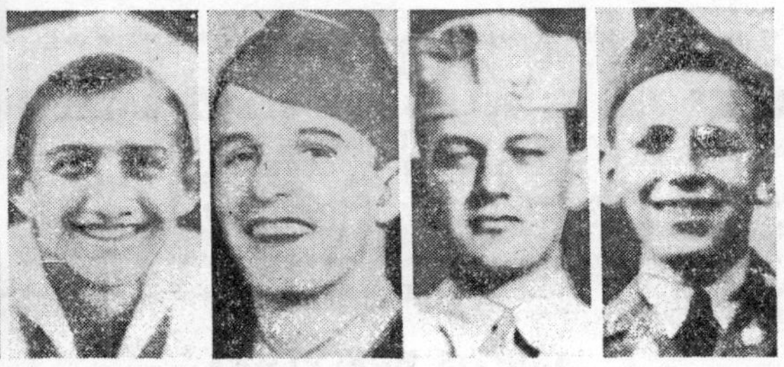

Training with the Navy at Norfolk is Michael Szczesniak, S2c, 804 S. Linwood.

Private Gordon C. Thompson, at Fort Knox, Ky., ready for combat service.

In aviation at Lincoln, Neb., Pfc. Bernard R. Burns, 1146 West Cross street.

Serving well in N. Africa, Pfc. Carroll E. Hughes, 3430 Elm avenue.

Relatives or others sending pictures of those serving in the Armed Forces can help in the correct printing of names, addresses, etc., by using the typewriter, or carefully printing with pen or pencil, all details. Also, please do not send pictures that are not perfectly clear. Photos that are blurred in the slightest cannot be used. —EDITOR.

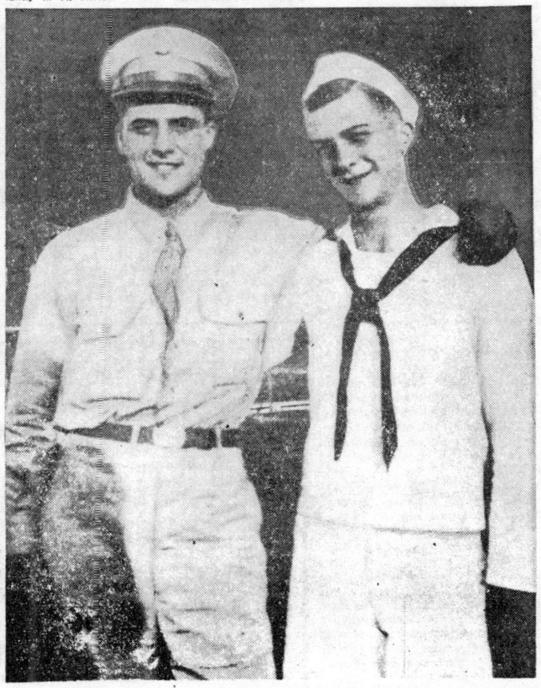

These fine-looking Baltimore brothers represent the Army and Navy—and how! They are Pvt. William Edward Knisley (left) training at Camp McCain, Miss., and Brother Jack, going over the jumps at Bainbridge, Md. Their parents, Mr. and Mrs. Arden Knisley, take pride in their progress.

Wood, Nelson To Meet On Toledo Golf Links

Racing Gossip

By GABY

Early indications point to a small field competing for the $15,000 added Edgemere Handicap prize at Aqueduct Saturday.

Originally 30 had been nominated for the one mile and a furlong Edgemere, but declarations reduced the list until Handicapper Jack Campbell had to assign weights to only 14.

Campbell honored Alsab and Market Wise by giving each 126 pounds to carry. Neither will start. The topweight very likely will be Shut Out, leading money winning thoroughbred last year and the handicapper's headache this season. Shut Out will work under 123 pounds.

Of course, Shut Out must have a fast track or he will remain in his stall this week-end. The Green tree Stable colt must have looked all over a champion to work watchers at Aqueduct yesterday morning when he stepped one mile and a quarter in the very good time of 2.05 2-5.

Shut Out had the veteran Eddie Arcaro up. He went the first quarter in .23 2-5, three-eights in .35 2-5, half mile in .47 4-5, five-eighths in 1.00 2-5, three-quarters in 1.13 1-5, seven-eighths in 1.25 3-5, mile in 1.38 2-5 and eased up the 10 furlongs in 2.05 2-5.

The Rhymer may be a running mate with Shut Out Saturday. The 1942 Widener Stakes winner was given a package of 110 pounds. Other weights are Boysy, 110; First Fiddle, 117; Apache, 120; Plantagenet, 110; Pictor, 110; Vagrancy, 108; Royal Nap, 106; Salto, 106; Water Pearl, 105, and Bonnet Ann, 105.

With the long Detroit meeting scheduled to close Saturday some of the stables will move east to await the opening of the Maryland fall season at Pimlico on October 9 . . . Trainer R. E. Potts will bring the entire Bomar Stable string, consisting of Seebeebee, Peemar, Scot's Bill, Hi Neighbor, Love Pact, Biscayne Blue, Detroit Bull, Cal's Pet, Little Wizard, Brass King, Blue and Gray and Silk . . . W. G. Wilson is going to ship 10 of B. Wark's runners to the Baltimore track and in the same car will be two trained by Whitey Abel.

George D. Widener's Lucky Draw, top juvenile of the early New York season and inactive since he placed in the Myles Standish Stakes at Aqueduct on July 3, is back in training at Belmont Park . . . Being a gelding Lucky Draw cannot start in the Belmont Futurity, richest race in America for two-year-olds.

Hirsch Jacobs, now pacing the American trainers in number of winners saddled, was the leading conditioner of the recent Saratoga meeting . . . Jacobs tightened the girths on 11 victorious runners during the 30-day session . . . Ted Atkinson was the leading flat jockey with 35 winners, a little better than one a day, and Howard Cruz topped the steeplechase riders with a total of seven winners . . . Bee Mac, the fleet two-year-old filly which Col. E. R. Bradley presented to Miss Beatrice MacGuire, daughter of Dr. Phillip MacGuire, vice-president of the Empire City track and general manager of Laurel, was the leading money winning thoroughbred . . . Her earnings totaled $44,360 . . . By virtue of Bee Mac's important triumphs, Miss MacGuire was the leading money winning owner with the same total her only horse, Bee Mac, earned.

72-Hole Match Arranged For Sept. 18-19

CHICAGO, Sept. 8—(I. N. S.). Golf fans were looking forward today to a challenge match between two great professional stars, Craig Wood, National Open champion, and Byron Nelson, Masters' king and players' No. 1 choice in American golf.

The match, which originated in a challenge thrown out by Wood at the Golden Valley tournament in Minneapolis, will be played on September 18 and 19 at the Inverness Club in Toledo, Ohio, Nelson's home course, over a 72-hole route for the benefit of a war relief agency.

News of the special encounter between the two stars came as they returned to Chicago from Minneapolis, where Wood and Jim Demaret won the Golden Valley four-ball title and Nelson and Harold McSpaden took second.

The last meeting of the two pros was in the 1939 National Open playoff in Philadelphia, where Nelson beat Wood by three strokes.

Nelson was voted the No. 1 man in American golf by the 16 standout golfers who participated in the Golden Valley tournament.

Sugar Hill Nine To Play Vipers

An outstanding attraction is carded for Bugle Field this evening at 8.15 P. M. when Odell Culleys' Sugar Hill team, runner-up in the Colored Baltimore Amateur Athletic League, play the Annapolis Vipers, the 1943 champions of the Anne Arundel Baseball League.

The Vipers have an outstanding comic star in Raspberry Davis, the colored Nick Altrock of baseball. Davis' comic antics have been the feature of the Anne Arundel Baseball League and a large following is expected to turn out to witness the funny man from Annapolis.

The Vipers are piloted by the veteran star Bobby (Ace) Green.

The line-ups:

VIPERS	SUGAR HILL
J. Watkins, ss.	Patterson, 1b.
R. Green, c.	S. McKay, cf.
J. Gross, lf.	Tucker, lf.
E. Watkins, 3b.	Kelley, 2b.
J. Hastey, cf.	"Babe," ss.
J. Atkins, rf.	White, rf.
R. Davis, 2b.	Attoy, 3b.
W. Bryant, 1b	Cann, c.
S. Carr, p.	Green, p.
D. Booze, p.	Clayton, p.
S. Sykes, p.	Saunders, p.
W. Wright, p.	Snowden, p.
J. Cole, p.	Tarrant, p.
Smell, ss.	McCoy, 3b.
J. Cole, 2b.	Roach, rf.

Donald Mockett Gets Hole In One

Forest Park's caddy champion, Donald Mockett, is Baltimore's most recent member of the hole-in-one club. The young golfer scored an ace on the 180-yard twelfth hole with a No. 2 iron.

Playing with Mockett at the time was Paul Downey, Rodger Faulkner and Clyde Smoll.

Believe It Or Not :-: By Ripley

On request, sent with stamped, addressed envelope, Mr. Ripley will furnish proof of anything depicted by him.

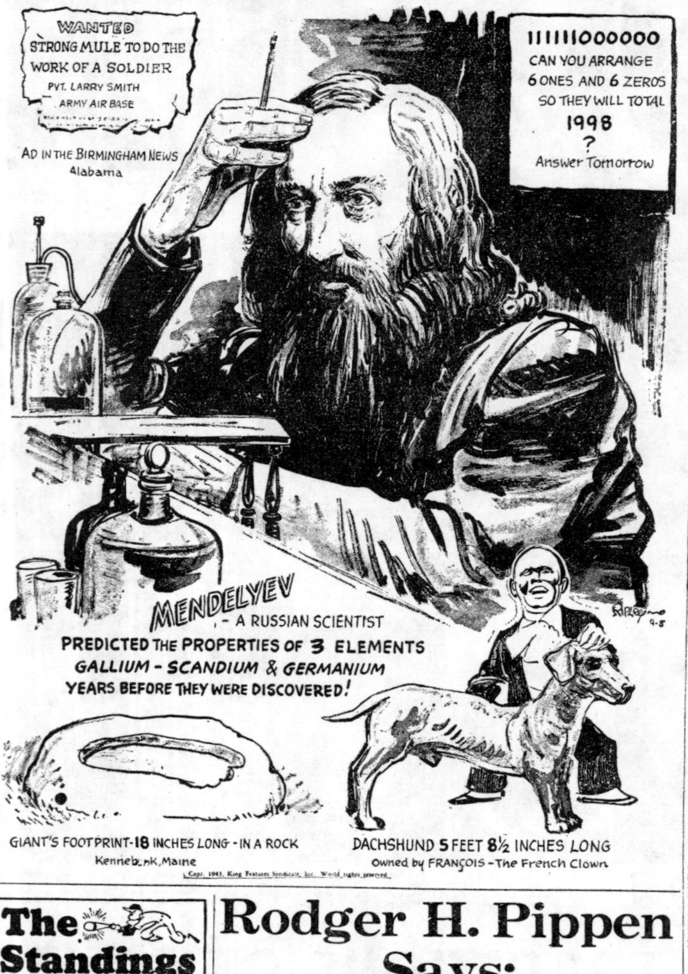

WANTED
STRONG MULE TO DO THE WORK OF A SOLDIER
PVT. LARRY SMITH
ARMY AIR BASE
AD IN THE BIRMINGHAM NEWS
Alabama
11111000000
CAN YOU ARRANGE 6 ONES AND 6 ZEROS SO THEY WILL TOTAL 1998 ?
Answer Tomorrow
MENDELYEV
- A RUSSIAN SCIENTIST
PREDICTED THE PROPERTIES OF 3 ELEMENTS
GALLIUM - SCANDIUM & GERMANIUM
YEARS BEFORE THEY WERE DISCOVERED!
GIANT'S FOOTPRINT-18 INCHES LONG - IN A ROCK
Kennebunk, Maine
DACHSHUND 5 FEET 8½ INCHES LONG
Owned by FRANÇOIS - The French Clown

Copr. 1943, King Features Syndicate, Inc. World rights reserved.

The Standings

INTERNATIONAL LEAGUE

YESTERDAY'S SCORES

Baltimore, 7; Syracuse, 5.
Toronto, 5; Buffalo, 4.
Newark, 2; Jersey City, 1.
Only games scheduled.

STANDINGS

	W.	L.	Pct.
Toronto	91	55	.623
Newark	81	67	.547
Syracuse	77	71	.520
Rochester	73	74	.497
Montreal	72	74	.493
Baltimore	72	77	.483
Buffalo	64	84	.432
Jersey City	60	88	.405

AMERICAN LEAGUE

YESTERDAY'S SCORES

Detroit, 5-6; Chicago, 0-5.
Only games scheduled.

STANDINGS

	W.	L.	Pct.
New York	80	49	.620
Cleveland	68	59	.535
Washington	71	62	.534
Detroit	68	60	.531
Chicago	66	63	.512
Boston	62	69	.473
St. Louis	58	71	.450
Philadelphia	44	84	.344

EASTERN LEAGUE

Open date.

NATIONAL LEAGUE

YESTERDAY'S SCORES

Open date.

STANDINGS

	W.	L.	Pct.
St. Louis	87	44	.644
Cincinnati	72	58	.554
Brooklyn	70	59	.543
Pittsburgh	70	65	.519
Chicago	61	69	.469
Boston	56	68	.452
Philadelphia	57	72	.442
New York	45	83	.352

Grid Players Have No Coach

SALT LAKE CITY, Sept. 8—(A. P.).—Fort Douglas has plenty of experienced football players, but—

Capt. M. R. Williamson, special service director at the fort, said they've been looking everywhere—vainly—for a coach.

Rodger H. Pippen Says:

Continued from Page 34.

fighters, Cecil Hudson, has been matched here with Jackie Cooper. Armstrong paid $3,500 for Hudson's contract.

The commission made its decision after the veteran Negro fighter testified yesterday that he was "tired of fighting" but denied it was eye trouble that had discouraged him.

The members, apparently unconvinced about Armstrong's eyes, called off the White bout, but they declined to rule on his future efforts.

"We don't feel the commission should retire Armstrong," Jules Covey, chairman, said. "That is something he should do himself."

Armstrong, asserting he is in better condition than at any time since his comeback, denied making statements attributed to him after he lost to Ray Robinson at New York two weeks ago.

"I told reporters before the fight I was quitting, but I never said I was retiring on account of my eyesight," he said. "And I had forgotten about my contract with White."

Staller Keeps Birds In Play-Off Fight

Continued from Page 34.

held the Chiefs scoreless and got credit for the victory.

Lollar led off the ninth and fanned on a bad pitch, being Schultz's eleventh strikeout victim, but the ball got away from Catcher Dick West and Lollar reached first. Rookie Johnny Blum, pinching for Burkart, drew a walk and so did Jones to load the bases.

At this point, Nelson replaced Schultz and Monaco popped out. With a count of two strikes and no balls, the improved Tiedemann fouled off five pitches and drew another pass to force in Lollar, Staller then blasted the only hit of the inning, a shot to the right of the box which Harrington couldn't field but knocked down and the ball rolled away ten feet. Blum and Jones scored, Phillips recovering the ball but his throw hit the dirt in front of the plate and bounded away. Tiedemann raced on to third and West heaved wildly, the ball bouncing into left field and Ab sprinting home with the winning run. Staller went all the way to third during this wild action and scored on a fly by Mackiewicz who had fanned four previous times up.

That was it, like a bolt of lightning. Gromek flipped the last inning without allowing a hit. For **Staller, it was his ninety-ninth run** batted in for the year and he and Ortiz of Montreal are the only players likely to drive in 100 or more tallies for the season.

But the two runs Staller batted in last night in the ninth may mean the difference of ten thousand dollars and up.

You never know.

Naval Nines Set For Big Series

NORFOLK, Va., Sept. 8—(A. P.).—Dont be asking a sailor around this naval base whether he thinks the St. Louis Cardinals or the New York Yankees will win the World Series because you won't get a satisfactory answer.

These sailors are much more concerned about the Navy's "World Series" which opens Sunday between the rival Norfolk Naval Training Station and the Norfolk Naval Air Station.

The two rivals of the Navy will play a seven-game series—both clubs say it won't last beyond four contests—and from a squint at their respective rosters, you'd think they might be playing the classic which comes off every autumn between the champions of the National and American Leagues.

Camden Entries

FIRST RACE—Purse $1,100; claiming; three-year-olds and up; six furlongs (chute).

Mr. Goose	114	Sir Mowlee	114
Caesar B	114	Bell Bottom	111
Miss Addie	106	xShip Signal	107
xMary Schulz	106	Slow Motion	120
aPilates Dream	114	New Life	114
bChance Sord	111	bDomkin	114
Galful	106	xWar Smoke	106
aSpikery	112	Amperage	117

aJ. York & Mrs. W. Whitney entry.
bJ. J. Hanley & Mrs. J. Alexander entry.

SECOND — Purse $1,200; claiming; maidens; three-year-olds and up; six furlongs (chute).

xOak Queen	107	xSir Talbot	115
Touring Lady	117	Good Dream	117
aDedham	120	xStar Flag	112
aJumping Bean	120	xVirginia Girl	112
War Boat	120	Cinema Queen	112
Free Spender	115	Moalee	115
Carlatera	112	xBlicky Boy	115
Strange Play	117	Satiation	120

aMrs. E. D. Weir & G. Garrett entry.

THIRD—Purse $1,400; claiming; two-year-olds; six furlongs (chute).

George Case	118	Nibble	118
Army Belle	115	Elcan	111
Canee	111	Free Dutch	118
Amalka	107		

FOURTH—Purse $1,200; maidens; special weights; 2-year-olds; six furlongs (chute).

xMachere	110	Voyageur	118
Quick Draw	118	Record March	118
Outside Pair	118	xJunior's Pet	110
Royal Display	118	xaArch McDo'ald	113
Cactus Foot	118	xaMolliann	110
Fleet Hat	118	xAfter Time	110
Art Brown	118		

aB. B. Jones and Mrs. E. Trueman entry.

FIFTH—Purse $1,300; claiming; 4-year-olds and upward; six furlongs (chute).

Sir Echo	117	Mar d'Esprit	117
Blue Steel	115	xBola Mowlee	107
Marogay	117	Layaway	112
Smart Bet	117		

SIXTH—Purse $1,400; claiming; 3-year-olds and up; one and one-sixteenth miles.

Sobriquet	112	xRingle	109
xThorino	115	Rubicon	111
Still Pond	114		

SEVENTH—Purse $1,200; claiming; 3-year-olds; one mile and seventy yards.

Sure Fire	115	xGingerman	105
xHy Kerry	110	xChance Cross	110
Buzzie Jr.	112	Toy Quay	110

EIGHTH — Purse $1,200; claiming; 3-year-olds and up; one and one-sixteenth miles.

Saran	117	Jim Wallace	114
Dinsen	120	Panther Creek	117
xWoodvale Lass	109	xBloodhound	109
xOff Guard	109		

xApprentice allowance claimed.
First race, 2.30 P. M. Track fast.

WANTED PIN BOYS!

Afternoon or evening! Make $25 or more. Enjoyable work. Bring your friends. Come in today . . . and start at once.

CHARLES BOWLING
1700 Blk. N. Charles

Bimmie Is Lost

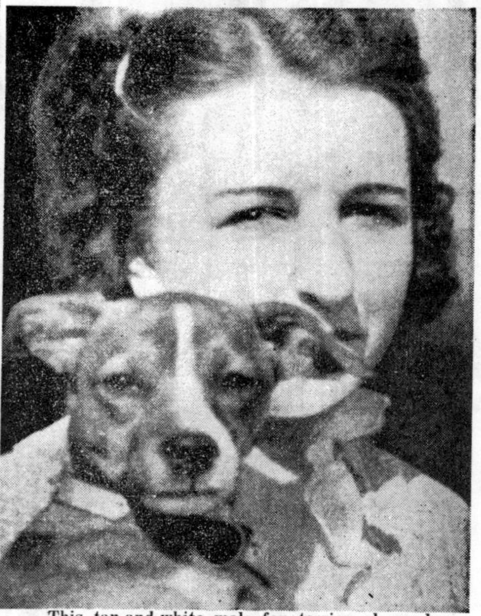

This tan-and-white male fox terrier, shown here with his owner, Mrs. Emily Colvin, was lost in the vicinity of South Hanover street and Cherry Hill road last Thursday night. He is a small, slim dog, shaped somewhat like a whippet. He is friendly and gentle. When lost, he was wearing a collar with two gold-plated bands. Please phone Curtis 0364 or get in touch with Mrs. Colvin at 2914 South Hanover street.

Detroit Entries

FIRST RACE—Purse $1,200; claiming; 3-year-olds; six furlongs (chute).

xBrilliant Ann	105	Gold Betty	114
Hi Murt	114	Epigal	109
Miss Flyer	108	xPoojo	109
xImp's Way	107	Semper Ego	116
Purple Magic	112	Homeward	114
xTop Class	107	Silver Ace	112

SECOND — Purse $1,200; claiming; 2-year-olds; six furlongs (chute).

Nancy Sweep	102	Sug Mae	110
xBaby Advice	102	xMary Rene	102
Patsy T	102	Betty Van	102
Sway	110	xQuick Kick	100
Helm's Pride	105	Gay Flag	102
Bursweep	110	Miss Julie Y.	110

THIRD—Purse $1,400; claiming; 2-year-olds; six furlongs (chute).

xBozie	105	Dodo's Girl	107
Hi Henry	111	Gallahue	110
Houghton	110	Duolc	105
xPlay Hands	105	Deckhand	116

FOURTH — Purse $1,500; claiming; 3-year-olds; six furlongs (chute).

Camp Town	111	xThe Duck	109
Flying King	117	xAmble Tint	109
Good Daughter	108	Kind Sir	102
Lady Rebecca	115		

FIFTH — Purse $1,300; allowances; 3-year-olds; one and one-sixteenth miles.

Time Was	105	Celosia	99
Singing Satin	111	xFiddler's Bit	106
O. K. Sugar	111	Take Courage	102

SIXTH — Purse $3,000; allowances; 3-year-olds and up; one and one-sixteenth miles.

Boom On	102	Here She Is	99
Trelawny	111	Buttermilk	106
Spanish Duke	111		

SEVENTH—Purse $1,500; claiming; 3-year-olds; mile and a sixteenth.

Contemplation	110	Junior Easton	113
Greenock Image	110	Air Corps	110
Queen Justice	107	Darby Diavolo	110
Air Beauty	113		

EIGHTH—Purse $1,200; claiming; 3-year-olds and upward; mile and a sixteenth.

Off Key	112	Jacotot	108
Honey Bee	106	Here She Comes	106
xColorado Ore	101	Bosky Dell	106
Ambo	106		

xApprentice allowance claimed.
First Race, 4.15 P. M.
Track fast.

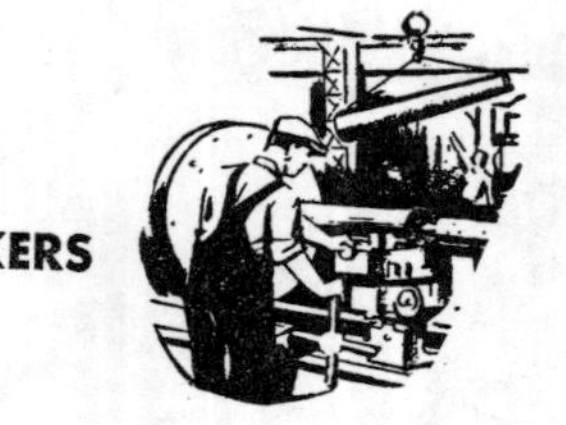

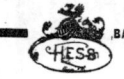

BACK THE ATTACK WITH WAR BONDS

WAR WORKERS

You can't break production records with aching feet!

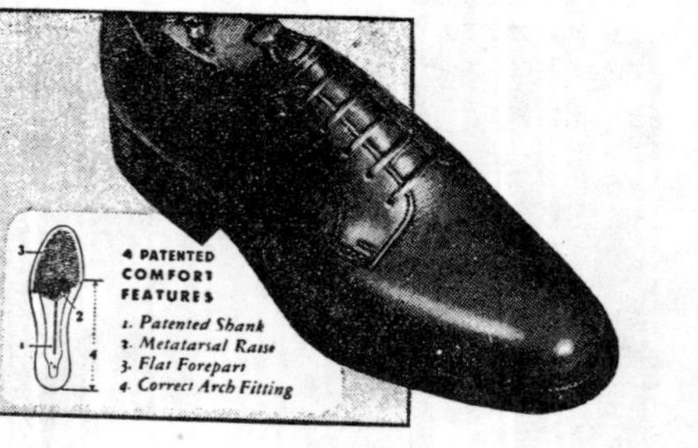

4 PATENTED COMFORT FEATURES
1. Patented Shank
2. Metatarsal Raise
3. Flat Forepart
4. Correct Arch Fitting

Change to HESS ARCH PRESERVERS

—Scientifically designed to prevent fatigue by E. T. WRIGHT & CO.

Keep on the job . . . comfortable and efficient! Hundreds of your fellow workers can testify that ARCH PRESERVERS mean relief from aching feet. Hess expert fitting insures comfort and longer wear.

OPEN THURSDAY NIGHT

HESS
8 E. BALTIMORE STREET
312 N. HOWARD ST.

WE'LL PREPARE THE PAPERS . . .

We will prepare all the necessary papers for you to present to the Rationing Board when you need new tires or tubes.

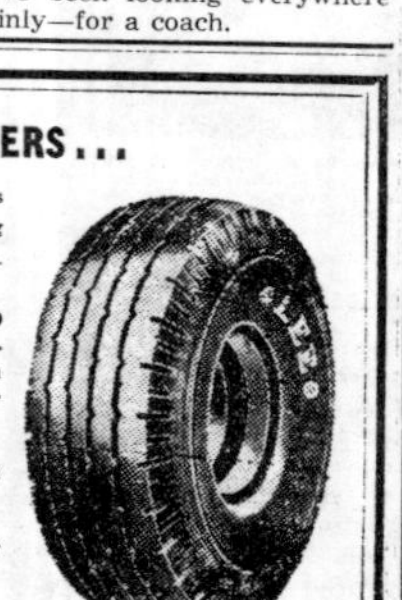

GRADE 111 TIRES INCLUDE FINISHED RECAPS. We recommend them for economy and mileage. Certificates for them are easy to get and we have an ample stock.

TIRE AND TUBE REPAIRING. Prompt and at reasonable prices.

RECAPPING. Truck and Passenger Car Tires done promptly.

Buy Now: Batteries, Chains, Antifreeze

LEE TIRE SERVICE
Authorized Inspection Station
1101 CATHEDRAL ST.
BALTIMORE Phone MUlberry 4770

HERE'S THAT ESSENTIAL JOB YOU'RE LOOKING FOR

★

DAVISON

NEEDS MEN—PLANT LABORERS

NO EXPERIENCE REQUIRED! NO SPECIAL SKILL NEEDED!

GOOD PAY . . . GOOD WORKING CONDITIONS . . . GOOD FOOD IN A RESTAURANT THAT SERVES GENEROUS PORTIONS AT STANDARD PRICES!

The work is steady . . . and the pay good to start, with an increase after 300 hours of employment! . . . Drop in at 1313 Pennsylvania Ave. or 242 North Exeter St., where our Special Employment Offices are open daily except Sunday from 8 A. M. to 9 P. M.

Or . . . better still . . . apply at the Curtis Bay Plant ready to go to work, and save yourself a trip.

HERE'S HOW TO GET TO OUR CURTIS BAY PLANT

TAKE NO. 6 CURTIS BAY STREET CAR TO END OF LINE AT CURTIS BAY.

FREE B. T. C. BUSSES leave car line every 5 minutes from 6 A. M. to 8 A. M. and 2 P. M. to 6 P. M.

Curtis Bay Employment Office open 24 hours a day, including Sunday.

WORKERS NOW ENGAGED IN ESSENTIAL WORK SHOULD NOT APPLY, AND WILL NOT BE HIRED!

CURTIS BAY PLANT
THE DAVISON CHEMICAL CORP.

THE WEATHER

Slightly warmer, with decreasing humidity this afternoon; cooler, with low humidity tonight; nc showers, gentle to moderate winds.

Read The Baltimore News-Post for complete, accurate war coverage. It is the only Baltimore newspaper possessing the three great wire services—
ASSOCIATED PRESS
INTERNATIONAL NEWS SERVICE
UNITED PRESS

THE BALTIMORE NEWS-POST
AN INDEPENDENT NEWSPAPER
The Largest Evening Circulation in the Entire South

NIGHT
Wall St. Opening

VOL. CXLIII.—NO. 120 Entered as second-class matter at Baltimore Postoffice. WEDNESDAY EVENING, SEPTEMBER 22, 1943 PRICE 3 CENTS

GERMANS TURN NAPLES INTO CITY OF FIRE, RUINS

5th And 8th Armies Continue Advances

Marshall, MacArthur To Be 'Kicked Upstairs' Say Rumors In Capital

Capital sources reported today that Gen. George C. Marshall is slated to become chief of all American and British forces throughout the world, a move regarded in some quarters as a "demotion" rather than "promotion." In the South Pacific, rumor is afloat that Gen. Douglas MacArthur's command will be subordinated to that of Lord Mountbatten.

Gen. M'Arthur Expects To Be Shelved

By LEE VAN ATTA
International News Service Staff Correspondent.

GENERAL MacARTHUR'S HEADQUARTERS IN NEW GUINEA, Sept. 22—Gen. Douglas MacArthur, supreme commander in the Southwest Pacific, admitted frankly today that he expects to be shelved as the dominant leader in the Allied campaign against Japan.

The four-star general released from his headquarters in the New Guinea battle area a sharply-worded statement in answer to "press reports from the United States and England implying" his part in the war was to be progressively curtailed and his com-

Contiuued on Page 2, Column 8.

Friends Rap Plan To Shift Marshall

By WILLIAM K. HUTCHINSON
International News Service Staff Correspondent.

WASHINGTON, Sept. 22.—Friends of Gen. George C. Marshall are resigned today to his ouster as Chief of Staff of the United States Army and transfer to a glorified field command, which may carry the title of commander-in-chief of all American and British forces throughout the world.

A White House announcement of the change in Marshall's status is expected Friday.

LEADING FIGURE

Marshall's friends regard the impending transfer as a "demotion" rather than a "promotion." They say that Marshall today is

Continued on Page 2, Column 6.

Aussies Seize Base Above Lae

ALLIED HEADQUARTERS IN THE SOUTHWEST PACIFIC, Sept. 22—(A. P.).—Only two days after the fall of Lae, New Guinea, airborne troops of Gen. Douglas MacArthur seized a village 60 miles to the northwest while waves of American bombers wrecked airdromes, bridges, trucks and roads along a path of future conquest for 350 miles north.

The seizure of Kaiapit by transport-flown Australians last Saturday night, following quickly the overrunning of Lae the previous Thursday, was disclosed in a communique today.

QUICK DIVIDENDS

The new stroke, which the Japanese futilely tried to erase by counter-attacks, and the latest air strikes with 97 tons of bombs and 120,000 rounds of ammunition all the way from south of Madang up to Wewak, clearly indicated the determination of MacArthur that his victories at Lae and Salamaua shall yield quick dividends.

Captured Kaiapit is inland on the Huon peninsula behind the Markham valley positions which airborne troops seized September 5 to set in motion a pincers movement which swallowed up Lae in less than two weeks. It is not far from Bena Bena which, some time ago, was raided repeatedly by Japanese planes. These raids never have been explained but indicated the presence of Allied forces at Bena Bena.

CLEAR JAPS OUT

The Australians who were landed on a grassy field at Kaiapit Saturday night and Sunday now have driven Japanese out of that immediate area.

On Monday, more than 50 Mitchells and Flying Fortresses without a loss, strewed 54 tons of bombs and 120,000 rounds of strafing bullets among the communication areas around Astrolabe bay, some 70 miles above Kaiapit. Four important bridges on Japan's costal supply road were blown to bits. On the same day, fighters escorted Liberators in a 43-ton bombing of airdromes at Wewak, more than 300 miles above Lae.

Treasury Plans Big Tax Hike

WASHINGTON, Sept. 22—(A. P.).—A tax program that would take at least another dime out of every dollar of taxable individual income—but refund about 13 cents after the war—has been presented by the Treasury to President Roosevelt for his opinion.

To keep lower bracket taxpayers on a pay-as-they-earn basis under such a program, the 20 per cent. withholding levy would have to be hiked to at least 30 per cent.

The Treasury's plan calls for individual income taxes to yield at least $8,000,000,000 of the $12,000,000,000 in new 1944 revenue demanded by Mr. Roosevelt. The remainder would be accounted for from equal increases in corporation and excise levies.

The income tax phase entails increases in all brackets, but most notably a 100 per cent. jump in the present 13 per cent. bracket surtax.

However, the present 3 per cent. (net) Victory Tax would be integrated in that levy, together with provision for a 50 per cent. post-war refund.

BASIC RATES

Thus the basic rate—now 6 per cent. normal, plus 13 per cent. first bracket surtax, plus 3 per cent. net Victory Tax, a total of 22 per cent.—would be 6 per cent. plus 26 per cent., a total of 32 per cent. Of that amount, however, 13 per cent. would be paid back after the war.

Although opposed to a broad compulsory savings plan, the Secretary is reported to favor the idea of a refundable tax because it would ease any inflationary threat and at the same time provide a backlog of post-war buying power.

Minnesota Labor Opposes 4th Term

MINNEAPOLIS, Sept. 22—(I. N. S.).—The Minnesota State Federation of Labor today refused to indorse a fourth term for President Roosevelt and spurned sanction of a proposal to call for readmission of John L. Lewis and his United Mine Workers into the A. F. of L. The fourth-term resolution was ruled out of order under a federation provision against indorsing political candidates.

Reindeers Provide Nome With Meat

NOME, Alaska, Sept. 22—(U. P.).—Nome was saved from a meat shortage today by 21 Eskimo reindeer herdsmen who brought back 74,000 pounds of meat from the annual autumn deer round-up on the plains bordering Bering Strait. Meat and skins, valued at more than $30,000, were delivered as residents faced their first real meat shortage.

A Weird Jinx Carves Still Another Gravestone. The Heritage of Violent Death Bequeathed By a Ruthless Old Millionaire To His Descendants Strikes at the Third Generation. Don't Miss This Revealing Account In The American Weekly, the Magazine Distributed With Next Sunday's Baltimore American.—Adv.

Where Reds Gained

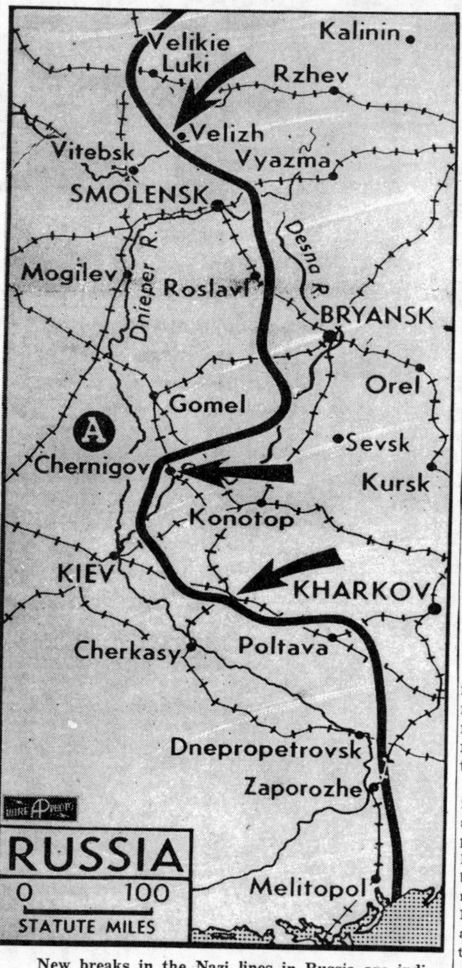

New breaks in the Nazi lines in Russia are indicated in the map above, showing the Red Army's capture of Chernigov (A), cracking the German Desna river winter defense positions. The solid line is the approximate battle line, with arrows indicating major Soviet drives.

Lion 'Mugger' Kills Twin In Zoo Fight

(Picture on Page 2)

NEW YORK, Sept. 22—(I. N. S.).—Death came to the Bronx Zoo in what officials today described as one of the most unusual accidents in the history of the institution—an animal mugging.

Principals in the incident were Harry and Johnnie, five-year-old twin lions, with Johnnie the victim.

It was feeding time, and William Dalton, the keeper, mounted the feeding platform in the outdoor "natural habitat" enclosure to throw the first of a number of eight-pound chunks of horse meat to the five beasts quartered there.

Harry and Johnnie, the twins, reached the first tidbit simultaneously and a brief scuffle ensued, in which Harry snapped at his twin's throat. Within five seconds Johnnie was dead.

Lee S. Crandall, general curator of the zoo, said that an examination of the carcass, strangely enough, failed to disclose a single mark on the throat. Johnnie, he said, had died of a ruptured larynx, similar to that suffered by victims of street hold-ups in which so-called "muggers" come from behind and put their arm around the throat, causing injuries to the windpipe.

Allies Take 4 More Towns

ALLIED HEADQUARTERS IN NORTH AFRICA, Sept. 22—(A. P.).—Huge fires and demolitions scarred Naples today as the Germans hastily threw a defensive ring around the city to retard Allied armies steadily pressing outward from the Salerno bridgehead. The great metropolis of nearly a million persons in Southern Italy was described officially as overhung with smoke.

A military spokesman said the enemy was estalishing a strong de line on the approac Naples from the south. east, but the extent demolitions in and near the city appeared evidence that the Germans hoped to hold back Allied attack toward the city from the Salerno area.

The Fifth Army, meanwhile, fought its way steadily east and northeast from Salerno, with American troops capturing the towns of Campagna and Montecorvino-Rovella, while the British chased fleeing Germans from the town of San Cipriano.

On Corsica French soldiers and native patrols pursued a German garrison estimated at 12,000 men toward the eastern shores while American Liberator bombers blasted at the principal avenue of German evacuation from the island—the Corsican harbor of Bastia and the Italian port of Leghorn.

The military spokesman said he had "nothing to add" to Winston Churchill's statement yesterday that American troops had landed on Sardinia, but the belief prevailed here that whatever units were sent to that island intended only to co-operate with an Italian division which already at Premier Pietro Badoglio's command took control and compelled the Germans to flee.

COTENZA OCCUPIED

Another menace to the Germans on the Italian mainland, Gen. Sir Bernard L. Montgomery's Eighth Army, drove northward and inland and occupied the key highway and rail center of Potenza.

Occupation of Potenza, which

Continued on Page 2, Column 1.

War At A Glance

By United Press.

ITALY—Allies straighten line across Italy while Liberators bomb Leghorn and Germans put torch to Naples.

CORSICA—French regulars and guerrillas drive Nazis from half of Corsica and push them toward east coast after eight days of fighting; Liberators attack Bastia.

RUSSIA—Red Army pounds at gates of Smolensk and Kiev.

EUROPE—Allied air formations fly against Continent in resumption of offensive from Britain.

PACIFIC—Airborne Australian troops seize Japanese strong point of Kaiapit, 60 miles inland from Lae and on road to Madang base.

Nazis Reeling Back:

Russ Offensive Rolls Unchecked

LONDON, Sept. 22—(A. P.).—Adolf Hitler's badly-mauled German divisions, cracking under the terrific punishment meted out to them by the powerful Russian offensive, reeled back to their eastern defense wall on the Dnieper river today as the Red Army scored new advances along the whole length of a 750-mile front.

Dangerously weakened by the incessant hammer blows of Russian artillery, tanks, infantry and planes, the once invincible German legions apparently were being broken up into isolated units and nowhere, according to the latest Moscow war bulletin, were they able to halt the surging Red Army tide.

SLASHES ACROSS RIVER

The last formidable barrier before the Dnieper on the central front was battered down yesterday when a savage Soviet drive slashed across the Desna river line between Bryansk and Kiev. With the capture of Chernigov, most important German base on the lower reaches of this river the way was open for Red Army forces to strike directly at Kiev and Gomel. The latter, 80 miles northwest of Chernigov, is the gateway to White Russia.

At Chernigov, the Russians were 30 miles from the Dnieper, 25 miles from the southern border of White Russia while the old Polish border was less than 160 miles to the west. Stalingrad, high water mark of the German advance, is more than 600 miles southeast of Chernigov.

7,000 NAZIS SLAIN

Another thousand-odd towns and villages were liberated by Russian advances yesterday, while upwards of 7,000 Nazi troops were slain and many more captured, the Russian communique said. Soviet guns destroyed 80 enemy tanks and 34 more were listed in the enormous quantities of war equipment said to have been left by the Germans in their precipitous retreat.

In addition, the Soviet Air Force, credited with 63 Nazi planes destroped over the front yesterday, blasted concentrations of railway trains at Gomel, Vitebsk and Dzhankoi on the central front last night, setting many of the mafire.

In their drive to push the invaders from Russian soil, the Red Army spearheads were withing 18 miles of Smolensk, which was slowly bein flanked on the north and south.

Scratches At Belmont

First Race—Surf, Stolen Kiss, Gallant Rose, Flaming Top.
Second—Swish, Dog Show, Umbril.
Fourth—Dr. Johnson.
Fifth—Aloraye, Seeing Eye, Sweeping Time, Spheric, Kuvta.
Seventh—Menex, Pig Tails, Lady Flame.
Eighth—Histrionic, Woodsaw, Chickore.
Track fast.

Edge And Murphy Nominated In N. J.

TRENTON, N. J., Sept. 22—(U. P.).—Mayor Vincent J. Murphy, Democrat of Newark, and former Governor Walter E. Edge, Republican of Ventnor, were nominated as Gubernatorial candidates yesterday, in a quiet New Jersey primary.

Temperatures

12 Midn't,	64	6 A. M.,	63
1 A. M.,	64	7 A. M.,	63
2 A. M.,	63	8 A. M.,	64
3 A. M.,	63	9 A. M.,	68
4 A. M.,	63	10 A. M.,	70
5 A. M.,	63	11 A. M.,	72

NEWS-POST

Amusements	22	Haney, Dr. Lewis	39
Bugs Baer	15	Kilgallen, Dor.	23
Classified Ads	39, 40, 41	Mallon, Paul	31
Comics	34	Movies	22
Crossword	41	Parsons, Louella	22
Dulaney	31	Pippen, R. H.	35
Durling	6	Radio	20
Editorials	20	Robinson, Elsie	11
Financial	38, 39	Society	33
Health	7	Sports	35, 36, 37, 38
Horoscope	8		

Gloria Hallward Hies To Broadway And Gets Big Role

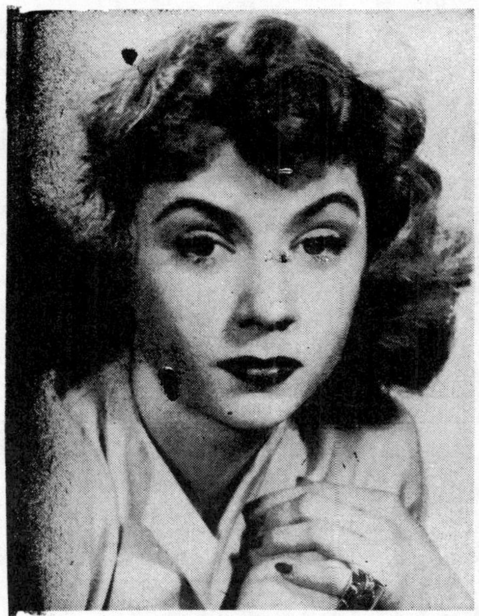

GLORIA HALLWARD

By NORMAN CLARK

[TH]IS COLUMN has a weakness for Cinderella stories and we [come] upon them from time to time, with some movie starlet usually [the] heroine. Today we have a Cinderella tale and it is about a young [a]ctress. Gloria Hallward is her name and she will have a lead[ing role] in the new comedy, "Star Dust," which begins a ten-day en[gagem]ent at the Maryland tomorrow night.

[Accor]ding to Publicity Director [...] Maney, Gloria, young and [ambit]ive, decided to quit the in[genue] lead in "Good Night [Ladies]" in Chicago—she had been [playin]g it for a year—and strike [out for] Broadway.

[As] a youngster in California, [Miss] Hallward had seen enough [...] pictures to know that the [first] impression you make on a [Broad]way impresario is the most [impor]tant. Being well endowed [by na]ture, she didn't have much [trouble] making herself into an [allur]ing glamour girl. The first [one] she tackled was Michael [Myer]berg's. While waiting in the [outer] office she heard his secre[tary te]ll an actress they were [looking] for a fifteen-year-old girl. [Glori]a scooted for home to [transfor]m herself into a moppet. [Removin]g her exotic costume jew[elry, do]nning a two-dollar ging[ham fr]ock and letting down her [upswept] hair-do, she returned to [Myerb]erg's domain. The producer [took o]ne look at her and said:

[...]y, you're a glamour girl. [Go ho]me and get into some ap[propri]ate clothes, and then come [back he]re. I may have a part for [you."]

[The u]pshot of it was that Miss [Hallw]ard, who never before [ha]d a producer, was signed [for th]e comedy lead of "Star [Dust."] She will portray Adrianne [...], movie idol of the male [...]rs, who admire her physi-cal endowments to the exclusion of her histrionic talents.

Gloria's mother, the former Jean Graham, was a member of the Stratford-on-Avon Players and a popular London actress. Her father, Michael Hallward, is a director of the American Institute of Design. She was born and raised in Pasadena, Cal., and attended schools in San Diego, Pasadena and Hollywood. Two years ago she won the first prize at the Hollywood High School for the National Forensic League declamation contest.

While entertaining with a U. S. O. unit at a veterans' hospital in Hollywood, Myron Selznick, the agent, saw Gloria and recommended her to the sponsors of "Good Night Ladies." Fresh from high school and a scholarship at Guy Bates Post's drama school, Gloria was signed as general understudy for the Al Woods' farce while it was still on the West Coast. By the time it had moved to Chicago, she was playing the ingenue lead, Dodie Carleton, opposite Buddy Ebsen.

Marquand's 'So Little Time' To Be Offered In Movie Form

Resemblance To Author's Former Success Appears

By LOUELLA O. PARSONS
Motion Picture Editor International News Service.

HOLLYWOOD, Sept. 22.—When J. P. Marquand's novel, "So Little Time," reaches the screen you'll see Joseph Cotten as Jeff Wilson. Cotten is certainly hitting the high spots with choice assignments, and no matter what your private opinion on the possibilities of this book as a movie, it will be an important one because of the sensational sales and all the publicity.

Having David Selznick at the production helm won't hurt either. Of course it is only one person's opinion (mine), but I think David has his work cut out making "So Little Time" sufficiently different in plot from Marquand's former hit, "H. M. Pulham, Esquire."

Take away some of the grand satirical passages from "So Little Time" and the plots are very similar.

Big business looms ahead for Anita Loos who is in New York to confer with Arthur Hopkins. She'll discuss the play she and Lionel Barrymore wrote, "Old Buddha," which Hopkins is producing, and she will also talk with Zoe Akins about another stage play they wrote together. The Theatre Guild has already nodded its head in approval of the latter, which is, up to this writing, nameless.

Anita will probably stay in New York until winter. She is no longer under contract to M.-G.-M., and her interests this year are with the stage.

John Payne flew out to see Elsye Knox before he is transferred to Carson City for three or four months of additional flight training. Just when these two plan to get married is still pretty much up in the air. You can get some bets that the wedding will never come off, the lady herself says it won't be until after the war.

Elyse is just back from a highly successful bond tour, and she is so pretty she broke records everywhere, equaling the high-water marks set by stars much more famous than she is.

A Line or Two: Neither Col. James Roosevelt nor Col. Elliott Roosevelt knew the other was in town and when they met unexpectedly Saturday they fell on each other's necks. It was a short reunion for the brothers, however, because Jimmy pulled out for Washington the next day.

Four new mothers—Lana Turner Crane, Frances Neal Heflin, Peggy Moran Koster and Dorothy Darrell Pasternak stole all the thunder away from Joe Pasternak at his own birthday party by talking constantly about their bambinos.

Eva Gabor got so wound up selling bonds at the Victory House that she couldn't stop talking when she got home and the result is she sold a $10,000 bond to her brother-in-law, Conrad Hilton, the hotel magnate.

Snapshots of Hollywood Collected at Random: John Wayne goes into the Army when he finishes "Fighting Seabees." Carmen Miranda has been ordered back to bed and again to cease all social and business activity. Her M. D. feels she needs a longer rest.

Sally Eilers has gone to Chicago to join her bridegroom, Lieut. Howard Barney, who is stationed there. Mrs. Eddie Sutherland gave a shower and farewell luncheon for her Saturday.

Ella and Billy Gilbert have arrived safely overseas where they went to entertain at camps. Jane Wyatt is home from the hospital, but her twin boys are remaining in an incubator for two more weeks.

Mrs. Bing Crosby has bought a house at Malibu, and she and her youngsters have moved there for the months of September and October.

That's all today. See you tomorrow!

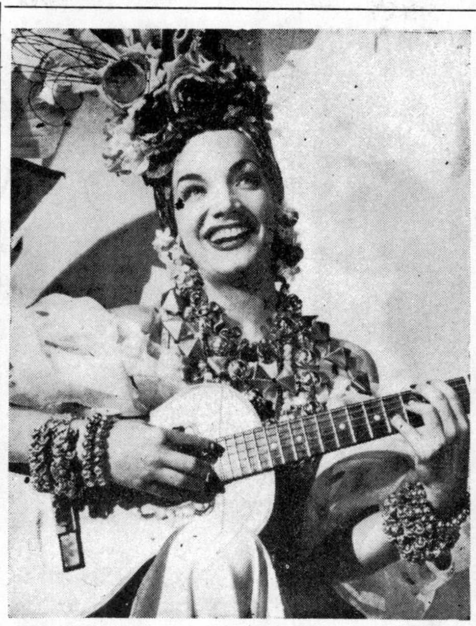

Hollywood advices are that the physician of Carmen Miranda has ordered her back to bed for a longer rest.

Movie CLOCK

CENTURY—"Swing Shift Maisie," 11.39 A. M., 1.39, 3.39, 5.39, 7.39, 9.39, 11.55 P. M., 2.13 A. M.

NEW—"Claudia," 10 A. M., 12, 2, 4, 6, 8, 10 P. M.

KEITHS—"Fired Wife," 10.01, 11.40 A. M., 1.28, 3.07, 4.55, 6.34, 8.22, 10.11 P. M.

VALENCIA — "Best Foot Forward," 1, 3.12, 5.24, 7.34, 9.46 P. M.

TIMES—"Henry Aldrich Swings It," 1.30, 3.43, 5.56, 8.09, 10.22 P. M. 12.35, 2.48 A. M.

STANLEY—"Watch on Rhine," 10.45 A. M., 12.57, 3.09, 5.21, 7.33, 9.45 P. M.

PARKWAY — "Hi Diddle Diddle," 1.33, 3.39, 5.45, 7.51, 9.58 P. M.

HIPPODROME—"Falcon in Danger," 10.45 A. M., 1, 3.30, 5.40, 8, 10.15 P. M.

LITTLE—"It All Came True," 11 A. M., 12.50, 2.40, 4.30, 6.20, 8.10, 10 P. M.

MAYFAIR—"All By Myself," 11.32 A. M., 1.22, 3.12, 5.02, 6.52, 8.45, 10.30 P. M.

ROSLYN—"Oklahoma Kid," 1.32, 3.19, 5.06, 6.53, 8.40, 10.27 P. M.

FORD'S—TONIGHT 8.30
Mat. Today at 2:30
BROADWAY'S GAY COMEDY HIT—
"JUNIOR MISS"
By The Authors of "MY SISTER EILEEN"
MORE THAN 700 TIMES IN NEW YORK!
Eves.—56c, $1.11, $1.66, $2.21
Today & Sat. Mats.—56c, $1.11, $1.66
FORD'S Next Week, Seats Thurs.
The Boston Comic Opera Co. in
GILBERT & SULLIVAN OPERAS with an ALL-STAR NEW YORK CAST
Mon., "The Mikado"; Tues., "The Pirates of Penzance"; Wed. Mat., "Trial By Jury" and "Pinafore"; Wed. Eve., "Patience"; Thurs., "Iolanthe"; Fri., "The Gondoliers"; Sat. Mat., "The Mikado"; Sat. Eve., "The Pirates of Penzance."
EVES., $2.77-$2.21; Bal., $1.66-$1.11; 2d Bal., 56c. Mats. Wed. & Sat.: Orch., $1.66; Bal., $1.66-$1.11; 2d Bal., 56c.

LITTLE HOWARD & FRANKLIN
3rd WEEK
It All Came True
ANN Sheridan
JEFFREY LYNN
HUMPHREY BOGART
A WARNER BROS.—First Nat'l Picture

ROSLYN 2ND BIG WEEK JAS. CAGNEY HUMPHREY BOGART "OKLAHOMA KID"
Donald Crisp ROSEMARY LANE

OPEN to 4 A. M. • TIMES Theater
IT'S A JAM SESSION! And Henry's in the jam... AS USUAL!
"HENRY ALDRICH SWINGS IT"
First Balto. Showing
A Paramount Picture with JIMMY LYDON as Henry Aldrich
Charles Smith • John Litel • Olive Blakeney • Mimi Chandler
PLUS
Truly Great... I beg you to see it! WANDA HALE N.Y. DAILY NEWS
AN ARTKINO PRODUCTION
MOSCOW STRIKES BACK
"Magnificent!"—N. Y. Times
EDWARD G. ROBINSON (NARRATOR)
Plus News Show
TIMES 1700 BLOCK N. CHARLES
OPEN TO 4 A. M.

CENTURY LEXINGTON NR. CHARLES
HELD OVER FOR A 2nd WEEK
She's doubled production on laffs...
Swing Shift Maisie
M-G-M Romantic Hit Starring ANN SOTHERN JAMES CRAIG JEAN ROGERS
Back the Attack Buy BONDS
LOEW'S
VALENCIA ATOP THE CENTURY
LAST DAY "Best Foot Forward"
STARTS TOMORROW
1st. Baltimore Showing
ALIVE WITH THRILLS, ACTION AND ROMANCE!
"The KANSAN"
RICHARD DIX
JANE WYATT
PARKWAY NORTH AT CHARLES
Adolphe MENJOU
Martha SCOTT
hi diddle diddle

STARTS TOMORROW
NEW THEATRE LEXINGTON ST. at PARK
They're made for laughing... and for each other!
AND THEY'RE MAKING ENTERTAINMENT HISTORY TOGETHER!
SEE AD ON PAGE 23
Monty WOOLLEY Gracie FIELDS
in HOLY MATRIMONY
with LAIRD CREGAR
20th CENTURY-FOX PICTURE
Directed by JOHN STAHL
Last Day "CLAUDIA"

MAYFAIR Howard & Franklin
Last Day "ALL BY MYSELF"
TOMORROW
[...]IED CONVOY SAILS....
SUBMARINE READY
TO ST[...]
SUBMARINE ALERT
WITH
RICHARD ARLEN
WENDY BARRIE
Nils Asther • Roger Pryor
Marc Lawrence • Ralph Sanford

Gayety ONLY BURLESK IN BALTIMORE
INGA BORG
SUZANNE
BOZO SNYDER

BUY BONDS HIPPODROME EUTAW NEAR BALTIMORE ST.
Starts TOMORROW
THE PICTURE THAT MAKES YOU MAD ENOUGH TO FIGHT!
BEHIND THE RISING SUN
Based on the Book by James R. Young
MARGO • TOM NEAL • J. CARROL NAISH
ROBERT RYAN • GLORIA HOLDEN
SEE BIG AD PAGE 23
On Stage
Radio's Famous Sweethearts of Songland!
IN PERSON!
Lee SIMS & Ilomay BAILEY
LADD LYON A Lesson in Brevity
ARTHUR BLAKE Satirical Impressions
BILLY WELLS & 4 FAYS The Acme of Versatility
LAFLEUR & MANNERS Thrills Galore
LAST DAY — Stage, SAMMY KAYE & ORCH. • Screen, THE FALCON IN DANGER

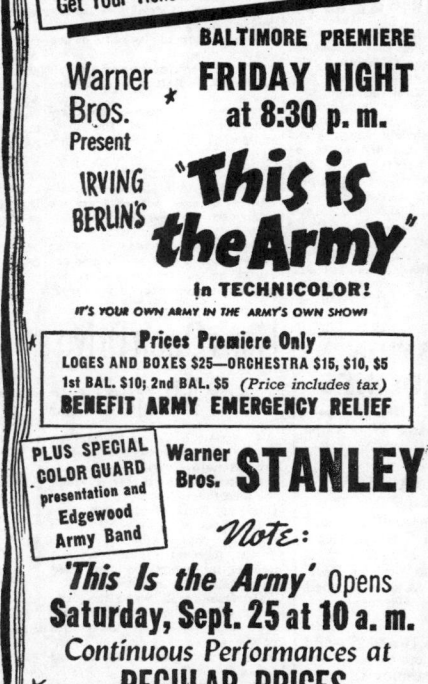

CHOICE SEATS Available!
Get Your Tickets TODAY
BALTIMORE PREMIERE
FRIDAY NIGHT at 8:30 p. m.
Warner Bros. Present
IRVING BERLIN'S
"This is the Army"
In TECHNICOLOR!
IT'S YOUR OWN ARMY IN THE ARMY'S OWN SHOW!
Prices Premiere Only
LOGES AND BOXES $25—ORCHESTRA $15, $10, $5
1st BAL. $10; 2nd BAL. $5 (Price includes tax)
BENEFIT ARMY EMERGENCY RELIEF
PLUS SPECIAL COLOR GUARD presentation and Edgewood Army Band
Warner Bros. STANLEY
Note:
'This Is the Army' Opens Saturday, Sept. 25 at 10 a. m.
Continuous Performances at REGULAR PRICES
LAST 3 DAYS BETTE DAVIS • PAUL LUKAS In "WATCH ON THE RHINE"

MARYLAND, Thurs., Sept. 23
Seats Now
Michael Myerberg Presents
"Star Dust"
A New Comedy by Walter Kerr
Eves. & Sun. Mat.—$2.21, $1.66, $1.11
84c. Sept. 22 & Sat. Mats.—$1.66, $1.11, 84c, 56c.
2 Performances Sun., Sept. 26

RIVOLI
Geo. Sanders "Appointment in Berlin"
John Carroll "HIT PARADE OF 1943"
DOUBLE SHOW DAILY DOORS OPEN 9 A. M.

KEITHS
ROBERT PAIGE LOUISE ALLBRITTON
Fired Wife
with DIANA BARRYMORE WALTER ABEL
WALTER CATLETT ERNEST TRUEX
ALAN DINEHART GEORGE DOLENZ
RICHARD LANE REX INGRAM
AT LAST IT'S COMING TO KEITHS!
ERNEST HEMINGWAY'S
"FOR WHOM THE BELL TOLLS"
IN TECHNICOLOR
WITH GARY COOPER & INGRID BERGMAN

TODAY'S MOVIE CALENDAR

Theatres advertised in this column belong to the Motion Picture Theatre Owners of Maryland

Back the Attack--- Buy War Bonds

Aero Middle River, Md. Lee Tracy in "THE PAYOFF" With Tina Thayer.

Alpha Catonsville. Betty Rhodes in "SALUTE FOR THREE" Comedy.

Ambassador 4604 Liberty Heights. Richard Quine in "WE'VE NEVER BEEN LICKED" "Pluto at the Zoo."

Apollo 1500 Harford Ave. Merle Oberon in "FIRST COMES COURAGE" 2 Carlines to Apollo—19-27

Arcade Harford Rd. & Hamilton Ave. Franchot Tone in "PILOT NO. 5" "Neptune's Daughter."

Astor Poplar Grove at Edmondson. East Side Kids in "GHOSTS ON THE LOOSE" 3 Carlines to Astor—4-14-9

Aurora 7 East North Ave. Brian Aherne in "FIRST COMES COURAGE" "I Spied for You."

Avalon 4300 Park Heights Ave. Merle Oberon in "FIRST COMES COURAGE" Comedy.

Avenue Milton Ave. & Hoffman St. Tyrone Power in "CRASH DIVE" News.

Avon 3019 Hamilton Ave. Gloria Jean in "IT COMES UP LOVE" "Report From the Aleutians."

Belnord 2700 Philadelphia Ave. Franchot Tone in "PILOT NO. 5" "Climbing the Peaks."

Boulevard 33rd at Greenmount. Merle Oberon in "FIRST COMES COURAGE" "He Dood It Again."

Bridge Edmondson Ave. & Pulaski St. All Star Cast in "STAGE DOOR CANTEEN" Comedy.

Broadway 509 S. Broadway. Merle Oberon in "FIRST COMES COURAGE" 4 Carlines to Broadway—16-18-10-21.

Cameo 4705 Harford Road. Constance Cummings in "SOMEWHERE IN FRANCE" Take 19 Car to Cameo.

Capitol 1518 W. Baltimore St. John Carradine in "I Escaped from the Gestapo" Carlines—15-8-1-11—Q Bus.

Casino 1118 Light St. Lloyd Nolan in "MANILA CALLING" "G-Men vs. the Black Dragon."

Cluster 303 S. Broadway. Humphrey Bogart in "ACROSS THE PACIFIC" News.

Columbia 709 Washington Blvd. Merle Oberon in "FIRST COMES COURAGE" "Smoke Rings."

Earle Belair Rd. at Woodlea Ave. Brian Aherne in "FIRST COMES COURAGE" Comedy.

Edgewood 3500 Edmondson Ave. George Montgomery in "BOMBER'S MOON" Comedy.

Eureka 404 S. Fremont Ave. Patricia Morison in "HITLER'S MADMEN" "The Batman."

Forest Garrison & Liberty Heights. Leon Errol in "FOLLOW THE BAND" "Report from the Aleutians."

Fulton Fulton Ave. & Baker St. Cheryl Walker in "STAGE DOOR CANTEEN" With William Terry.

Garden Charles at Cross. Grace McDonald in "GET GOING" "Vanishing Private."

Glen Glen Burnie. Alan Curtis in "TWO TICKETS TO LONDON" "The Batman."

Grand 511 S. Conkling St. Claire Trevor in "GOOD LUCK, MR. YATES" "Yankee Doodle Daffy."

Gwynn 4609 Liberty Heights Ave. Betty Grable in "CONEY ISLAND" "Smoke Island."

Hampden 911 W. 36th St. Merle Oberon in "FIRST COMES COURAGE" Comedy.

Harford 2610 Harford Ave. Chester Morris in "AERIAL GUNNER" "Popular Science."

Hilton 3117 W. North Ave. Wallace Beery in "JACKASS MAIL" "First Aid."

Horn 2014 West Pratt St. William Lundigan in "Heading For God's Country" "Sing, Helen, Sing."

Howard 115 N. Howard St. Richard Quine in "WE'VE NEVER BEEN LICKED" Comedy.

Ideal 903 W. Thirty-sixth St. Franchot Tone in "PILOT NO. 5" With George Murphy.

Irvington 4113 Frederick Ave. Richard Quine in "WE'VE NEVER BEEN LICKED" Comedy.

Lane Dundalk, Md. James Cagney in "CAPTAINS OF THE CLOUDS" Comedy.

Leader 248 S. Broadway. Lupe Velez in "Redhead from Manhattan" 5 Carlines to Leader—16-10-21-18-5

Linwood 908 S. Linwood Ave. Jimmy Lydon in 'Henry Aldrich Gets Glamour" "Dancing On the Stars."

Little 523 North Howard St. Ann Sheridan in "IT ALL CAME TRUE" With Jeffrey Lynn.

Lord Baltimore 1110 West Baltimore St. Robert Lowery in "A SCREAM IN THE DARK" Comedy.

Lord Calvert 2244 Washington Boulevard. Lena Horne in "STORMY WEATHER" Comedy.

Lyceum Sparrows Point, Md. All Star Cast in "BOSS OF BIG TOWN" Comedy.

McHenry 1037 Light St. Richard Quine in 'WE'VE NEVER BEEN LICKED" "Shipyard Symphony."

Mayfair 508 N. Howard St. Rosemary Lane in "ALL BY MYSELF" With Patrick Knowles.

Met Pennsylvania & North Aves. Sidney Blackmer in "PRISON GIRLS" Cars—13, 2, 18, 1, 11, 31, 5, 33.

Nemo 4815 Eastern Ave. Dennis O'Keefe in "MOONLIGHT MASQUERADE" "The Batman."

New Reisterstown, Md. Charles Boyer in "THE CONSTANT NYMPH" News.

New Essex Essex, Md. Donald O'Connor in "MISTER BIG" With Gloria Jean.

New Glen Glen Burnie. Leslie Howard in "SPITFIRE" Feature Starts 3.30, 5.30, 7.30, 9.30.

Northway Harford & North. Pky. Patricia Morrison in "HITLER'S MADMEN" Comedy.

Overlea Belair Rd., End of Car Line. Warner Baxter in "CRIME DOCTOR' "Jamboree."

Palace Gay and Hoffman Sts. Leon Errol in "STRICTLY IN THE GROOVE" Comedy.

Patterson Eastern and East Aves. Richard Quine in "WE'VE NEVER BEEN LICKED" "Somewhere in the Pacific."

Pikes Pikesville, Md. George Montgomery in "BOMBER'S MOON" Comedy.

Pimlico Park Heights & Belvedere. Leon Errol in "FOLLOW THE BAND" "Rear Gunner."

Preston 1108 E. Preston St. Chester Morris in "AERIAL GUNNER" 3 Carlines to Preston—19-27-21

Red Wing 2241 E. Monument St. Evelyn Ankers in "CAPTIVE WILD WOMAN" "Tin Pan Alley Cat."

Rex 4600 York Road. MacDonald Carey in "SALUTE FOR THREE" "Information, Please."

Rialto 845 W. North Ave. Ginger Rogers in "STAGE DOOR" Cars—13-32-31-16—B Bus.

Ritz 1607 N. Washington St. Brian Aherne in "FIRST COMES COURAGE" With Merle Oberon.

Senator 5904 York Road. Richard Quine in "WE'VE NEVER BEEN LICKED" "Scrap for Victory."

State Monument and Castle Sts. Ann Gwynne in "WE'VE NEVER BEEN LICKED" Vaudeville.

Strand Dundalk, Md. Franchot Tone in "PILOT NO. 5" Comedy.

Towson Towson, Md. Charles Boyer in "THE CONSTANT NYMPH" "Dizzy Acrobats."

Uptown 5010 Park Heights Ave. Franchot Tone in "PILOT NO. 5" Comedy.

Vilma Belair Rd. and Mayfield Ave. Robert Paige in "COWBOY IN MANHATTAN" With Frances Langford.

Walbrook 3100 W. North Ave. Cheryl Walker in "STAGE DOOR CANTEEN" "Black Marketing."

Waverly Greenmount at Gorsuch. Dead End Kids in "MUG TOWN" "Three Cheers for the Girls."

Westport 2205 Russell St. Red Skelton in "DU BARRY WAS A LADY" Comedy.

Westway 5300 Edmondson Ave. George Sanders in "They Came To Blow Up America" Comedy.

Youth In This Changing World

Boys Sew A Fine (?) Seam In School Classes While Girls Learn Mechanical Arts Under New 2-Sided Education Program Here

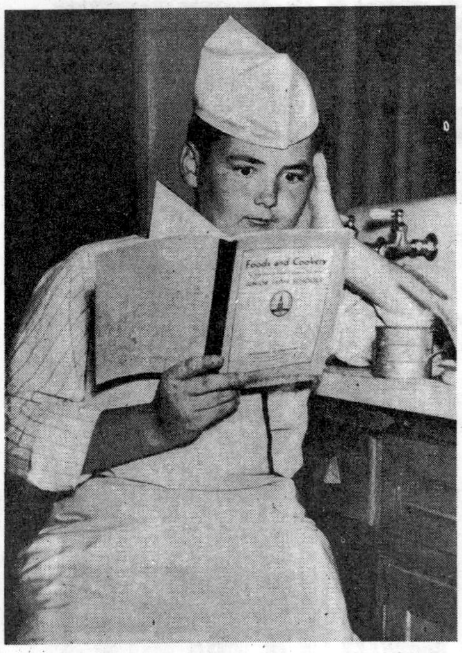

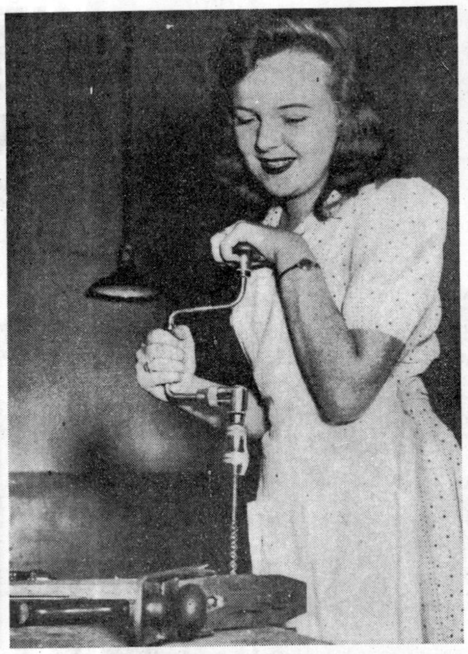

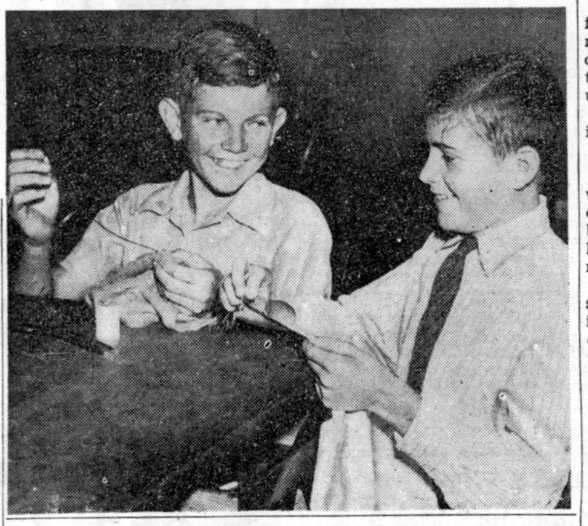

There is no such thing as "one-sided" training in schools of today. The girls learn how to wield the tools of trade and the boys learn homely arts like cooking and sewing. The proof? School No. 41, at Hamilton, showed some activities, and the pictures are of Charles Burnett and his book on cookery; Dorothy Blugis with brace and bit; while in the lower picture James Gummick (left) and Roland Kummer are much amused with themselves as they ply needle and thread.

Test Waste Paper Here For Army Use

A waste-paper collection test, whereby the paper will be reconverted to military uses, will be carried out in a large section of Baltimore on Saturday, Robert O. Bonnell, chairman of the Baltimore Civilian Mobilization Committee, announced today.

The collection will be made by the boys and girls of the Youth Mobilization division, who will get the paper from housewives in the district and take it to collection centers.

The householders in the area were being visited today and urged to have the paper ready for the boys and girls when they call.

The area, bounded by the city line on the north, Green Spring avenue on the east and Baker and Laurens streets on the south and west, contains about 650 blocks, 22,000 homes and an estimated 75,000 persons.

If the plan is successfully carried out here, other districts will be visited, Mr. Bonnell said.

Water Shortage Hits Low Level

Baltimore's water supply today had been reduced to 85.8 per cent. of the total storage capacity of the city's two big dams, with 66.67 per cent. fixed as the danger point, according to J. S. Strohmeyer, assistant city water engineer.

The assistant engineer said that consumption is now from two and one-half to three and one-half times the replenishment rate. The water level at Loch Raven is two feet nine inches below the dam crest, and seven feet eight inches below the crest at Prettyboy Dam.

Loch Raven was reported to have 21,700,000,000 gallons stored in its capacity of 23,700,000,000, according to the last check. At Prettyboy, where th ecapacity is 19,650,000,000 gallons, the latest check showed 16,200,000 000, the latest check revealed.

Air-Raid Talks At School Church

"Fire Protection in Air Raids" will be the topic of a talk by Hamilton A. Hooper, chairman of the Baltimore Committee on Civilian Defense Speakers' Committee, today at 8.30 P. M. in Public School No. 61, Linden avenue and Koenig street. Tomorrow at 7.30 P. M. Miss Florence Hooper will talk on "Protecting Your Home Against Air Raids" at a meeting in the Homestead Methodist Church, Gorsuch and Kirk avenues.

The Baltimore News-Post and Sunday American are offering weekly cash prizes for news tips and amateur photos. Best tip gets $25, the next best gets $10, and the next 15 get $1 each. For each amateur photo published $3 will be paid. Phone News-Tip Editor, Lexington 0100 (Lexington 4165 midnight to 6.30 A. M.). Rush news photos to Picture Editor.

Beth Tfiloh Plans Its 20th Opening

Enrollment of more than 500 members of Beth Tfiloh Brotherhood will mark the opening of the twentieth season of that organization tomorrow evening in the auditorium at 3202 Garrison avenue. Combined brotherhood and sisterhood of the congregation are approaching a $2,000,000 war bond goal in conjunction with Menorah Lodge of B'nai Brith. Maurice Samuel, author, traveler and publicist, will speak September 28 at a meeting of the brotherhood.

Promoted

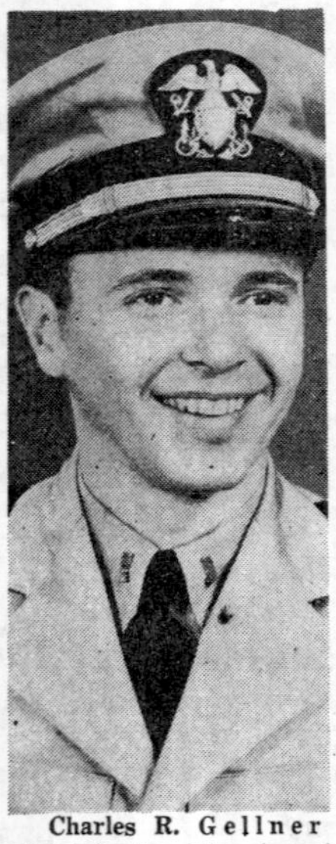

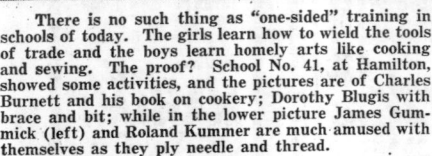

Charles R. Gellner (above) has been promoted from Naval Ensign to Lieutenant (j. g.). Honor man in his class at Loyola College and winner of a fellowship at Washington University, he is a son of Mr. and Mrs. Raymond A. Gellner.

Liberty Ship Honors Late John J. McGraw

The late John J. McGraw, Mr. Baseball himself during the golden era of the New York Giants, is slated to receive an honor today usually reserved for statesmen, war heroes, the great in science and kindred professions.

McGraw started on his road to baseball fame as third baseman for the three-time National League pennant winning Baltimore Orioles in the mid-nineties.

The beloved "Muggsy"—and it was all your life was worth to call him that to his face—will have his name emblazoned on a Liberty ship, marking the second time in this war that a baseball figure has been so honored. The first was Lou Gehrig, late New York Yankee first baseman.

McGraw's widow will sponsor the vessel in ceremonies at the Bethlehem-Fairfield shipyard and among those expected to be on hand to do honors to the only man to win ten major league pennants for a single club are:

Edward T. Mulrooney, former baseball commissioner; Horace Stoneham, owner of the Giants, Mrs. T. B. Cagnew, sister of Christy Mathewson, one of McGraw's brightest stars, and ex-mayor Howard W. Jackson of Baltimore.

Snake Greets Lawyer From Bureau

"Snakes in the boots" are legendary. A "snake in the grass" can happen.

But whoever heard of a snake in a bureau drawer? Well, it came to pass, all right, out at Lawyer's Hill, Relay.

Two Orphans' Court appraisers, John P. McElgunn and Samuel C. Williams, went to the home of the late J. Seymour Waters, attorney, who died February 18 last, to appraise 65 acres of land at Lawyer's Hill as well as the home, outbuildings and their contents.

In going over tangible assets Mr. McElgunn opened a bureau drawer in the presence of Miss Lindsay T. Waters.

Coiled there, evidently for the winter months, was a 30-inch blacksnake. Like blacksnakes generally do, it pretended to fight at first, then changed its mind and was scurrying away when Mr. Williams picked up an ice chopper and beheaded it. Then he heaved a sigh and said:

"It was real, all right."

CAPT. GINSBERG ASSIGNED

Capt. Joseph Ginsberg, 3509 Sequoia avenue, Baltimore, has been assigned to the Army Exchange Branch at Third Service Command headquarters for duty as a uniform specialist, inspecting and supervising operations in Army exchanges of the Maryland, Pennsylvania and Virginia area. Maj. Gen. Milton A. Reckord, commanding general, announced today.

RATION DEADLINES

CANNED GOODS—
U, V and W stamps valid through October 20.

MEAT, BUTTER, OILS—
Red stamps X, Y and Z valid through October 2. Brown stamps "A" and "B" in Book 3, now valid, are good through October 2.

SUGAR
Stamps 15 and 16 valid for 5 pounds each for home canning through October 31. Last day for No. 14, good for 5 pounds—October 31.

GASOLINE—
Last day for use of No. 6 "A" gasoline ration stamp — November 21.

SHOES—
Shoe stamp 18 valid until October 31.

FUEL OIL—
No. 5 coupons from last year's ration valid through September 30. Period 1 coupons in new fuel-oil rations valid through January 3, 1944.

TIRES—
Last day for second tire inspection for A drivers—September 30.

The News-Post Has the Largest Circulation of Any Evening Newspaper in the South

THE BALTIMORE NEWS-POST
AN INDEPENDENT NEWSPAPER

2ND FRONT PAGE
NEWS-POST HAS TWO FRONT PAGES DAILY

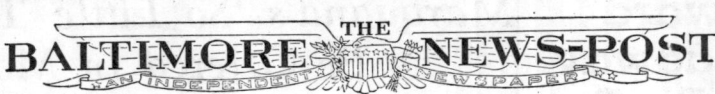

WEDNESDAY EVENING, SEPTEMBER 22, 1943 — 27

Baltimore Faces Coal Famine

Dealers Short And Supply Rapidly Decreasing

Baltimore's hard coal coal shortage was called so severe today that dealers were urging users of anthracite to change to soft coal, but with a warning that unless conditions improve rapidly, the city's needs may not be met.

The situation was this:

Instead of a normal supply of about 10,000 tons of hard coal in the bins of dealers, there was something less than 1,000 tons.

Many dealers who normally handled only anthracite were making frantic efforts to get soft coal to fill the orders of their customers.

URGES CHANGE OVER

Arthur H. Hendley, secretary of the Baltimore Coal Exchange, in a public statement, urged all users of hard coal to accept soft in substitute, wherever the furnace equipment would permit its use.

Many factors entered into the shortage:

The individual truckers of coal from Western Maryland, who annually brought thousands of tons of fuel into Baltimore have either turned to other work or other uses for their trucks.

There is a labor shortage in the industry generally.

NEW DEMANDS

Because of the oil shortage last winter, many users converted to coal, and many of the new houses being constructed for war workers here installed coal-burning equipment, thus increasing the demand.

Buyers of coal from "bootleg" sources in other years also were increasing the calls on coal dealers, now that the "bootleg" trucks are out of business.

While none of the dealers mentioned the mine strike as a contributing factor, this was seen indirectly, as some reported that coal normally sent to Baltimore was now being shipped to Canada and Northern New York State.

RAP GOVERNMENT

Several dealers complained that the Government was apparently intent on increasing the dealers' "headaches" from paper work and the filling out of forms instead of being intent on getting a proper coal supply into Baltimore.

Brief statements by some of the dealers were:

"There won't be nearly enough hard coal in Baltimore this winter."

"I have 1,600 tons of back orders and cannot get the men, equipment or coal to fill new orders."

NEW BUSINESS

"We have our 90 per cent. allotment of coal, but what are we to do with the new business cropping up?"

"With deliveries held to one ton or two tons, many people are going to be out of coal before we get around to a second delivery."

War Scribe Arrives

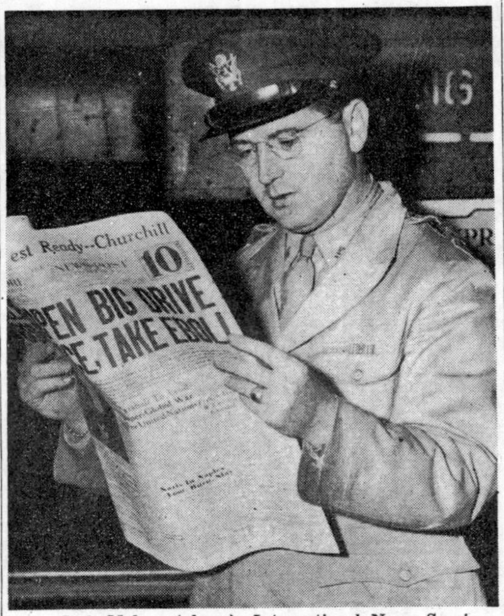

Jack Mahon (above), International News Service correspondent, who was injured in the Southwest Pacific war zone, is scheduled to address the Advertising Club of Baltimore today in the Hotel Emerson. Mr. Mahon has just returned from the battle front and will give a first-hand report of the progress of the war against the Japanese.

10 Coast Guards Working In War Plant Here

Ten yeomen of the United States Coast Guard Port Security Training School at Fort McHenry took up jobs last night in the plant of the American Hammered Piston Ring Division of the Koppers Company, inaugurating what is claimed to be the first appearance of service men at work or war contracts in industry.

They will continue at the work daily on a shift from 5.30 P. M. to 10.30 P. M. for seven days a week during their hours of leave from the Coast Guard post, it was announced at the plant.

They are to receive pay on the same basis provided for civilian beginners at the plant.

In order to qualify as "civilian war workers" it was necessary for the yeomen, who already had helped in emercency at canning plants, to obtain permission from their commanding officer.

Plant officials said the movement promises to spread among men of the other armed services. They said that many have already applied for permission to work at the plant, and soldiers and sailors are being allowed to go to work in hours of leave from duty.

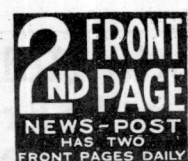

'Ad' Men To Hear Mahon, War Writer

Just back from the South Pacific battle front, Jack Mahon, International News Service war correspondent, arrived today in Baltimore for a talk before the Advertising Club at its weekly meeting in the Emerson Hotel.

Mahon, who experienced the rigors of jungle warfare with the American troops fighting the Japs, was injured during the landing operations on New Georgia, near Munda, in the Solomon Islands.

He is one of the few correspondents to receive a military award, having been given the Service Decoration by Gen. Douglas MacArthur.

Mahon is all too familiar with the life of soldiers in the foxholes of the South Pacific islands, Japanese snipers and other horrors of warfare in the Pacific theatre of operations.

Church Group Will Hear Missionary

A missionary convention will open at the First Church of the Nazarene, on Whitmore avenue, tonight and continue through Sunday. The Rev. Geoffrey W. Royall will speak. He recently returned from China.

Gaston
214 N. Charles St.

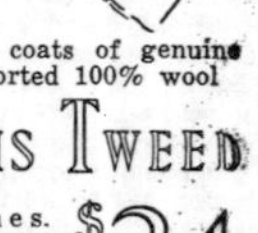

A Can't-Be-Beat Value!

Much-wanted coats of genuine British imported 100% wool

HARRIS TWEED

Heather tones. Classic styles. All sizes. 2nd floor. $24

OPEN THURS. 12 to 9 P. M.

ARMY-NAVY WIVES

If your husband is stationed in the area and you expect to be here for at least 60 days, we cordially invite you to come in and discuss your opportunity to fill in your spare hours doing interesting

Full or Part-Time Work

We have open a number of jobs that are safe, clean and enjoyable. Hours can be arranged to suit your convenience. Apply

4th Floor Employment Office

"Those now employed in war industry will not be considered."

MONTGOMERY WARD

Washington Blvd. at Monroe St.
or stop in at our convenient Downtown Office.
124 W. Fayette St.

Sherwood's Say

Please Mail Us Your Fuel Oil Ration Coupons Right Away

We are busy filling tanks, arranging for fuel oil supplies, setting up Automatic Delivery schedules. If you are a user of Sherwood Fuel Oil we want to include your requirements—so please mail us your Ration Coupons as soon as they arrive from the Ration Board.

SHERWOOD BROTHERS INCORPORATED

DANCING TONIGHT
THE PAUL JONES
ALCAZAR
Cathedral & Madison Sts.
Joe Dowling's Music
A Thos. L. Keating Presentation
No Intoxicating Beverages Sold or Permitted on the Premises

Lions Open Drive For Music Discs

A city-wide campaign for the collection of phonograph records for ultimate distribution by the Red Cross has been started under the direction of the Uptown Lions' Club of Baltimore, it was announced today.

Civic organizations, church groups, mercantile establishments and service groups are being lined up to take part in the drive.

On October 15, when the campaign will end, the collected records will be taken to central points, wheer they will be transported to headquarters by the Red Cross oMtor Corps.

Even broken records will be accpetable, as they can be traded in for new ones by the Red Cross.

Desk Set Given To Judge Moylan

Baltimore's newest jurist, Judge Charles E. Moylan, today was possessor of a desk set, the gift of officials and employes of the State Industrial Accident Commission. Judge Moylan, who served two years as chairman of the commission, was appointed to the Supreme Bench by oGvernor O'Conor last week.

SPECIAL NOTICES

ATTENTION, LADIES
Permanent Wave and Hair Tint Problems Wanted. We Can Help You!
LOVELY BEAUTY SHOP
Call WO. 6266

Safety For Sale
Tires Recapped—Factory Method
O'Toole General Tire Co.
10 E. Mount Royal Ave.
Official Tire Inspectors

QUESTION:
"What must I do to arrange a funeral"?
ANSWER:
Call Mulberry 8080 day or night to secure the services of Baltimore's largest undertakers. Select a suitable casket at the price you wish to pay from our plainly marked display. Then leave all details to our capable staff. You may be sure that Wm. Cook, Inc., will arrange a complete, dignified funeral . . . that everything will be exactly as you wish.
Wm. Cook
INCORPORATED
Baltimore's Largest Undertakers
St. Paul Street at Preston
Call MUlberry 8080 Day or Night

ARLINGTON FEDERAL
SAVINGS & LOAN ASSOCIATION
104 St. Paul St.
Are You SAVING Regularly?
Open An Account TODAY!
"BACK THE ATTACK"
BUY WAR BONDS
Accounts Insured up to $5,000

First Baltimore Showing!
ALIVE WITH ROMANCE ACTION AND ADVENTURE
"THE KANSAN"
With
RICHARD DIX
STARTS TOMORROW
LOEW'S VALENCIA

BATTERIES EVERY SIZE & TYPE
24-HOUR SERVICE
MOTOR REPAIRS—EASY TERMS
MARTIN J. BARRY
1700 N. CHARLES ST. SA. 4180

FRATERNITY
has helped thousands of Marylanders to become home owners or owners of the ground under their homes by its patient and careful analysis of their problems.
and
by effecting the best loan plan in keeping with the income of the borrower.
See
FRATERNITY FEDERAL
SAVINGS & LOAN ASSN.
788 Washington Blvd.
at Scott St.
before financing the purchase of a home or the ground under your home.
Open Daily Lex. 4710

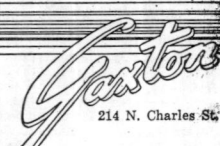

RENTED

PARKVILLE—2707 Aldan Rd., single or double room; hot water. Boulevard 1131-M.

THROUGH A
NEWS-POST & SUNDAY AMERICAN
CLASSIFIED WANT AD

Next Time You Have a Vacant Room Use This Quick Result Medium
PHONE
LExington 0100

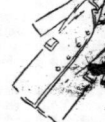

NAZIS MOVE TO EVACUATE BERLIN REPORT, AS 3D RAID JOLTS CITY

THE WEATHER

Fair with mild temperature this afternoon; moderately coid tonight.

Detailed Weather Report on Page 28

Read The Baltimore News-Post for complete, accurate war coverage. It is the only Baltimore newspaper possessing the three great wire services—
ASSOCIATED PRESS
INTERNATIONAL NEWS SERVICE
UNITED PRESS

THE BALTIMORE NEWS-POST

AN INDEPENDENT NEWSPAPER

The Largest Evening Circulation in the Entire South

7 HOME FINAL

VOL. CXLIV.—NO. 18 Entered as second-class matter at Baltimore Postoffice. THURSDAY EVENING, NOVEMBER 25, 1943 PRICE 3 CENTS

Russ Smother Kiev Thrust, Hint Yanks Slay 4,000 Japs In 4 Days

Take Key Isle In Conquest Of Gilberts

PEARL HARBOR, Nov. 25—(A. P.).—In a bloody four-day battle Americans have annihilated all but a few of the Japanese on the Gilbert Islands, climaxing their conquest with the capture of Betio and its strategic airfield, from where new thrusts may come soon. Betio fell to Maj. Gen. Julian C. Smith's second marine division at dusk Tuesday, most of its 4,000 defenders dead or dying on its sandy battlefield.

ALLIED HEADQUARTERS, SOUTHWEST PACIFIC, Nov. 25. (U. P.).—An outnumbered American naval flotilla sank four Japanese destroyers and damaged a fifth in a two-hour battle almost under the guns of the big enemy base at Rabaul, New Britain, today, and official sources indicated the Japanese were trying to evacuate key personnel from the Northern Solomons.

The night battle, fought midway between Rabaul and Buka Island, northernmost of the Solomons, began shortly before 2 A. M. and ended just before dawn without loss to the American warships, a communique said.

ONE SHIP ESCAPES

Only one of the six Japanese destroyers engaged escaped undamaged from the hail of American gunfire and torpedoes.

The destroyers were intercepted in an apparent attempt to slip through the American blockade into Buka, and two were sunk almost immediately by torpedoes. The rest turned tail and fled back at high speed toward Rabaul.

In the running gun battle that followed two other destroyers were riddled with shellfire and sunk, and another was heavily damaged.

ENEMY IN TRAP

A spokesman at Gen. Douglas MacArthur's headquarters said

Continued on Page 2, Column 3.

Dyke Breaks, Scores Marooned

SYRACUSE, N. Y., Nov. 25—(I. N. S.).—Scores of persons were marooned in the State Fair Hotel today when a dyke retaining huge limestone waste water broke, flooding the surrounding area with a clay-like ooze.

Some of the victims were rescued from their homes opposite the entrance to the New York State Fairgrounds. Syracuse Red Cross disaster units were summoned to the scene to seek methods of bringing the State Fair Hotel guests across the flood to safety.

The Baltimore News-Post today is printed in

3 Sections

Be sure you get the complete newspaper.

Yugoslavians Fight Nazis To Standstill

LONDON, Nov. 25—(A. P.).—Fought to a standstill by partisan forces in Serbia Bosnia and Croatia, the Germans are rushing up reinforcements preparatory to launching new attempts to break through in those areas, headquarters of the Yugoslav liberation army said in a broadcast today.

On the Dalmation coast the partisans are battling superior German forces attempting to gain possession of the entire coast line.

Hurled back near the town of Kremen in Serbia, the Germans, strengthened by fresh troops from Uzice, resumed their attack and heavy fighting was still going on, the communique declared.

In Bosnia, Germans and Bulgarian troops were said to be continuing their drive in the direction of Pryepolte. They, too, were forced to call for reinforcements.

Two Nazi motorized columns were reputed driven back in Croatia.

Sues Mother Of Sonja Henie

INDIANAPOLIS, Ind., Nov. 25. (U. P.).—A hotel maid sought $50,000 damages today from Sonja Henie's mother and from the hotel management on grounds ring, which later was found beneath the skating star's bed. Police denied that they made an arrest. They said Mrs. Gerran was "picked up for questioning and released."

Thanksgiving Day Service For Troops

CAIRO, Nov. 25—(A. P.).—The Thanksgiving Day proclamation of President Roosevelt was read at a special service in the American mission church today in advance of a big turkey dinner served to all United States troops in the Middle East.

Ex-President Of France Is Ill

MADRID, Nov. 25—(A. P.).—Former President Albert Lebrun of France is seriously ill in the village of Vizille near Grenoble, a Paris dispatch to the Spanish press said today.

Reds Hold As Nazis Batter Kiev Front

MOSCOW, Nov. 25—(A. P.).—The Red Army appeared today to be overcoming successfully the German "last gasp" attack 45 miles west of Kiev. After a dozen days of violent battle along the edge of the Kiev bulge in the Western Ukraine, the Russians reported they not only were repulsing enemy assaults against the Brusilov and Chernyakhov sector but improving their own positions. (Berlin claimed both towns captured.)

LONDON, Nov. 25—(A. P.).—German infantry, tanks and planes still battered furiously today against a stiffening Red Army line 45 miles west of Kiev as a Russian communique, first in 12 days to indicate that Field Marshal Fritz von Mannstein's desperate drive to recapture the Ukrainian capital had been halted, declared:

"All attempts of the Germans to penetrate our defenses met with failures. Our gunners, infantry and tankmen inflicted heavy losses on the Germans and improved their positions."

GERMAN CLAIMS

Earlier the Berlin radio had claimed the capture of Brusilov, midway between Zhitomir and Kiev, and Chernyakhov, a railroad town 13 miles north of Zhitomir, while the Russians have admitted the loss of some towns and villages in this sector of the Kiev bulge, today's bulletin indicated the German drive had been halted short of those two cities.

Whether Von Mannstein had exhausted his strength in the bitter fighting of the past 12 days was problematical, but previous report said he had been ordered to break the Russian lines before Kiev at all costs.

START COUNTERDRIVE

The German-controlled Paris radio, in a broadcast recorded by the Associated Press, claimed that the German counter-offensive at Zhitomir, had not yet reached its height, but admitted that Vatutin had brought up reinforcements and had launched a series of counter drives.

8th Crosses Sangro, Rips Nazi Line

ALLIED HEADQUARTERS, ALGIERS, Nov. 25—(A. P.).—Gen. Sir Bernard L. Montgomery's Eighth Army has battered its way across the swollen Sangro river, the toughest obstacle yet encountered in the march up the Italian peninsula, in the face of ferocious fire and thereby has cracked a piece out of Adolf Hitler's winter defense line, Allied headquarters announced today.

A bridgehead 9,000 yards wide and 2,000 yards deep has been firmly established and held against furious counter-attacks, it was stated.

In this first full-scale dent carved by Montgomery's troops in the so-called winter line set up by the Germans the enemy put up the strongest resistance.

"HOLD AT ALL COSTS"

Reports reaching headquarters said Nazi prisoners said they had been ordered to hold their positions at all costs.

The onslaught across the river on a front of a little more than five miles was made "during the past few days," official reports said.

DESPERATE ATTACKS

Official sources announced that the German Sixty-fifth Infantry Division was thrown against the British in desperate counter-attacks to prevent a breach in the river line.

American P-40 Warhawks, A-20 Bostons and B-25 Mitchells teamed up with R. A. F. Baltimores in forays against enemy positions near Lanciano and Fossacessia, a few miles beyond the Sangro along the coast. Their bombs touched off a big explosion and also hit a crossroads and railway station.

French See Lebanon Incident Closed

ALGIERS, Nov. 25—(A. P.).—The French Committee of National Liberation has been complimented by the French consultative assembly for "having settled the recent incident" relating to Lebanon without harming French collaboration with the Allies or French interests. The assembly also expressed France's adherence to the principles of the Atlantic Charter.

Samos Officials Make Their Escape

ISTANBUL, Nov. 23—(Delayed) (A. P.).—Irineo, metropol of Samos, and members of the provisional Government formed on the Aegean Island after its first capture by the Allies, have escaped to Turkey, advices from Izmir said today.

Army To Reveal Stand On Patton

WASHINGTON, Nov. 25—(A. P.).—The responsibility for disciplining Lieut. Gen. George S. Patton, Jr., for striking an enlisted man in a fit of anger was placed on Gen. Dwight D. Eisenhower by Secretary of War Stimson today. Stimson said until a full report has been received from Eisenhower he had nothing to say about the case.

WASHINGTON, Nov. 25—(U. P.).—The War Department may make public today its stand in the much-publicized slapping by Lieut. Gen. George S. Patton, Jr., of a shell-shocked American soldier in a Sicilian field hospital.

(BACKGROUND NOTE: At Allied headquarters in Algiers today it was said that while the name of the soldier involved in the hospital slapping by Lieut. Gen. George S. Patton, Jr., has not been disclosed, it can be stated definitely he was not Charles H. Kuhl of Mishawaka, Ind., who entered service after Pearl Harbor. The man in the hospital incident was from the Carolinas, and joined the Army before Pearl Harbor.)

The question whether there will be any official censure of the colorful Seventh Army commander,

Continued on Page 2, Column 1.

Temperatures

12 Mid't,	48	6 A. M.,	45
1 A. M.,	47	7 A. M.,	43
2 A. M.,	46	8 A. M.,	42
3 A. M.,	47	9 A. M.,	47
4 A. M.,	46	10 A. M.,	50
5 A. M.,	46	11 A. M.,	52

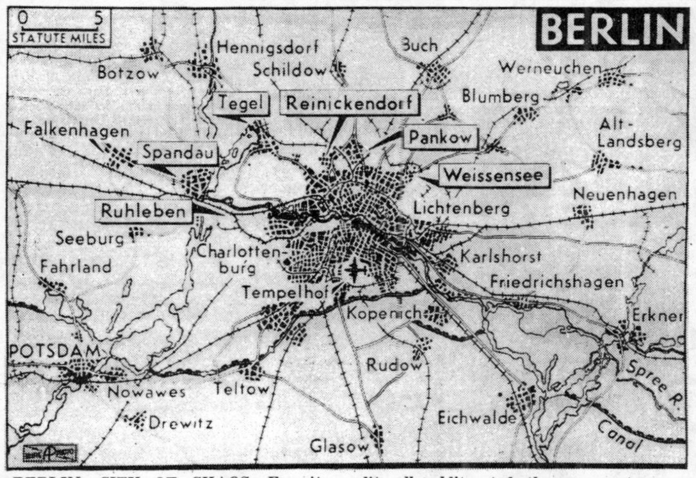

BERLIN, CITY OF CHAOS—Eyewitness accounts of Berlin bombings, relayed through neutral Sweden, reveal almost unbelievable destruction wrought by successive nights of Allied assault from the air. Vast areas have been literally obliterated, these accounts say. Boxes in map above show six suburbs which were reported hardest hit. Damage was described as secondary only to that in the Tiergarten area in the center of the German capital.

2-Billion New Tax Bill Up To Senate

WASHINGTON, Nov. 25—(A. P.).—A new tax bill, which would dip $2,140,000,000 deeper into American pocketbooks and hoist the Government's income to an estimated $43,500,000,000 a year, moved over to the Senate today, where its rapid approval was indicated.

Chairman George (Democrat) of Georgia announced the Finance Committee would open hearings Monday and try to complete them by the end of next week.

$4 MORE PER CAPITA

The bill clips an average of less than $4 more from the 44,000,000 individual income taxpayers, hits corporations for $616,000,000 additional in excess profits rates, increases postal rates by $166,800,000, and comes down heaviest—to the extent of $1,201,700,000—on purchasers of such items as liquor, furs and jewelry.

Secretary of the Treasury Morgenthau got little encouragement that he would receive anything more than a courteous reception when he poses the $10,500,000,000 question again Monday morning.

GEORGE SILENT

While Chairman George would not comment on the private conversations between Morgenthau and the Senators, he told reporters later he considered the two-billion-dollar bill "a considerable increase."

Report Nazi Force In Jutland Area

LONDON, Nov. 25—(I. N. S.). The Danish underground newspaper Frie Danske reported that the Nazis have massed 250,000 troops in the Jutland area "in anticipation of an Allied invasion," according to a Reuter's dispatch today from Stockholm.

Move For Army Jap Camp Control

By RAY RICHARDS

News-Post Washington Bureau.

WASHINGTON, Nov. 25.—Representative Clair Engle, California Democrat, today introduced a House resolution to have the United States Army take over the actual administration of the rebellious Tule Lake segregation camp for Japanese subversives.

At present troops are merely policing the camp after a four-day uprising there early this month, and the procedure and policy of the War Relocation Authority still prevail.

Before he introduced the resolution, Engle talked by telephone with an observer at Tule Lake and was informed that "as of today" disorders of increasing severity are still occurring as the Japanese continue their habitual campaign of work stoppages and other covert sabotage.

ARMY BETTERS CONDITIONS

Engle said the mere presence of the military inside the camp is a distinct advance over former conditions, and reassuring to the population of the district. His resolution, he said, is to consolidate the military step, preliminary to direct Congressional action to substitute a far firmer form of control than the WRA for the entire national problem.

With the Tule Lake camp completely under Army administration, Engle said, it may be easier to convince Congress that the War Department, or at least the Department of Justice, should be placed in administrative control of nine other centers where 82,000 evacuated West Coast Japanese are still located.

25,000 TURNED LOOSE

The WRA has turned about 25,000 of the Japanese loose, including many listed as members of Japanese patriotic societies by the Dies House Committee on Un-American Activities.

A sequence of events in the Capital today indicated the shadows of official oblivion are gathering about Dillon S. Myer, the WRA director, but there were no indications that the New Deal is as yet willing to admit a serious blunder has been committed and yield to West Coast demand that the WRA be wiped out entirely.

On the floor of the House, Representative Norris Poulson, California Republican, declared that if the Myer "appeasement program" continues, the country can expect Japanese camp outbreaks much more serious even than the one at Tule Lake.

Engle told the Senate sub-com-

Continued on Page 2, Column 5.

–For Salvage Information
1—Waste Paper
2—Used Fats
3—Tin Cans
4—Scrap Metal
Call PLaza 6877

Pope In Mediation Move, Swiss Hear

BERN, Switzerland, Nov. 25—(A. P.).—The Basler Nachrichten said in a dispatch from the Swiss border town of Chiasso today that Pope Pius XII. had undertaken a mission of mediation between Germany and the Allies. No independent confirmation was obtainable from diplomatic or church sources, although the dispatch quoted "Italian Catholic circles" as the basis of its information.

Romance Is a Racket With the Cold-Blooded Japs. Most of the Marriages Are Arranged Through Matrimonial Brokers. Read This Enlightening Sidelight On One of Our Enemies In The American Weekly, the Magazine Distributed With Next Sunday's Baltimore American.—Adv.

Report Nazi Move To Quit Berlin Area

STOCKHOLM, Nov. 25—(U. P.).—Nazi leaders were reported setting in motion today a wholesale evacuation of Berlin, where raging fires were kindled by British bombardment. The Nazi-controlled Scandinavian telegraph bureau reported that Martin Bormann, deputy party leader, had notified the leaders of so-called bomb-free cities to prepare accommodations for 3,000,000 to 4,000,000 evacuees soon.

LONDON, Nov. 25—(A. P. Swift R. A. F. Mosquito bombers set the air-raid sirens howling in Berlin for the third successive night by stabbing at the German capital again last night as smoke still rose skyward from conflagrations set by Britain's heavy bomber fleets.

The purpose of the attack, from which only one of the raiders failed to return, obviously was to harass and confuse the battered defenses of the city, which already had been burned and devastated on a scale hitherto unknown.

THICK PALL OF SMOKE

A thick, yellow pall of smoke spread 300 miles from the German capital—far as the Swedish east coast — as the speedy all-wood bombers attacked.

The effect of the Mosquito raid must have been to put a new strain on the morale of dazed Berliners, who were unable to tell whether to expect another new blow from the great forces of heavy bombers which struck Monday and Tuesday nights.

Only one Mosquito of a force of undisclosed size failed to return from the "Berlin run" which in recent months was a familiar trail for the twin-engined aircraft.

The bomber version of the Mosquito is capable of carrying four 500-pound bombs — relatively small change compared with the great two and four-ton blockbusters deposited by Britain's four-engined heavies on the previous two nights.

SEA OF FIRE

The Mosquitos have been over Berlin 17 times since the middle of August.

By all accounts the heart of Nazidom still was sea of fire. A report from Stockholm said a blanket of yellow haze over Oeland Island off the Swedish east coast covered the island for three hours yesterday.

(BACKGROUND NOTE: Observers along the Channel coast today that a large formation of bombers accompanied by fighter

Continued on Page 2, Column 4.

NEWS-POST

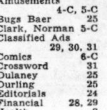

Amusements	4-C, 5-C	Horoscope	15
Bugs Baer	25	Kilgallen, Dor.	5-C
Clark, Norman	5-C	Mallon, Paul	25
Classified Ads	29, 30, 31	Movies	4-C, 5-C
Comics	6-C	Parsons, Louella	4-C
Crossword	31	Pippen, R. H.	26
Dulaney	25	Radio	23
Durling	25	Robinson, Elsie	24
Editorials	24	Society	3-C
Financial	28, 29	Sports	26, 27, 28
Health	8	Women's Clubs	3-C

Eleanor Boardman Plans Return To Screen

By LOUELLA O. PARSONS
Motion Picture Editor, International News Service.

HOLLYWOOD, Nov. 25.—Good morning! Happy Thanksgiving! Over your Thanksgiving turkey you may be interested in knowing that the chances are most favorable for Eleanor Boardman's return to the screen. Do you remember Eleanor when she was one of Metro-Goldwyn-Mayer's reigning beauties and most popular stars? Well, Darryl Zanuck had an inspiration and made a silent test of her for Mrs. Woodrow Wilson in the "Wilson" movie.

It was so good that Darryl has asked her to make a voice test Friday. If the voice test is what they expect, well, you'll see Eleanor Boardman back in movies as Mrs. Wilson. I like the way Darryl Zanuck works. He trusts his own judgment and he knew that Eleanor would be valuable once she was given a suitable role.

AVA GARDNER
Ava Gardner, above, glamorous M.-G.-M. actress and ex-wife of Mickey Rooney, says she is not going to marry again. She just wants a career.

Why Ricardo Cortez has been off the screen for over two years is a mystery to me. He's just as good looking as he was in the days when Jesse Lasky was promoting him as another Rudy Valentino. Well, Ric is resuming his acting career after a long "time out" as the light comedy villian in "Make Your Own Bed" at Warners with Jane Wyman and Jack Carson. When I ran into him on the lot he told me it seemed good to get back in front of the camera after a fling at directing for the past few years.

The glamorous Ava Gardner—and again I say she is glamorous—was aparently serious when she told me a few weeks ago that she wasn't going to marry anybody and that all she wanted was a career. She's again on the M.-G.-M. lot where her ex, Mickey Rooney, is one of the top stars. This time she is not there as a star's wife but as an actress. She has the leading femme role in "Three Men In White," the next Lionel Barrymore "Dr. Gillespie" series.

Snapshots of Hollywood Collected at Random: Norman Millen, one of Hollywood's favorite praise agents, is to marry Mady Lawrence, stage actress. She arrived in Hollywood ten days ago on a vacation after leaving the Skeets Gallagher "Good Night Ladies" show in Chicago; Slapsie Maxie's new heart is Dorothy Merritt.

Olivia De Havilland might have been a ghost the way everyone stared at her when she walked into the Warner commissary to lunch with Bette Davis. Olivia and Warners battle is still on; Kim Hunter and Lieut. Billy Bakewell an attractive Valley Lodge dinner duo.

Lieut. Tyrone Power arrives tomorrow to spend Thanksgiving with Annabella. He'll make an infantile paralysis short for the Government while he is in town.

Veronica Lake hostess at a kitchen party with Lana Turner as one of her chief assistants. That's one of Hollywood's favorite ways of entertaining these war-time days; Constance Bennett's black velvet dress in "Without Love" brought forth spontaneous applause in the second act, it is so eye-filling. Connie, who had a temperature of 101, looked stunning.

Barbara Hutton Grant, Virginia Zanuck, Joan Bennett, Joseph Schenck, the Lew Schreibers, Jean Feldman and many others were in the audience and all of them thrilled with Connie's performance in a play that leaves much to be desired. That's all today. See you tomorrow!

SHAKESPEARE'S PLAYS

Holinshed's *Chronicles* were one of the sources used by Shakespeare for his plays.

MUSEUM WAR FILM

The second sound film in the current "Path of War Series" will be screened at P. M. Snuday in the Baltimore Museum of Art without admission charge.

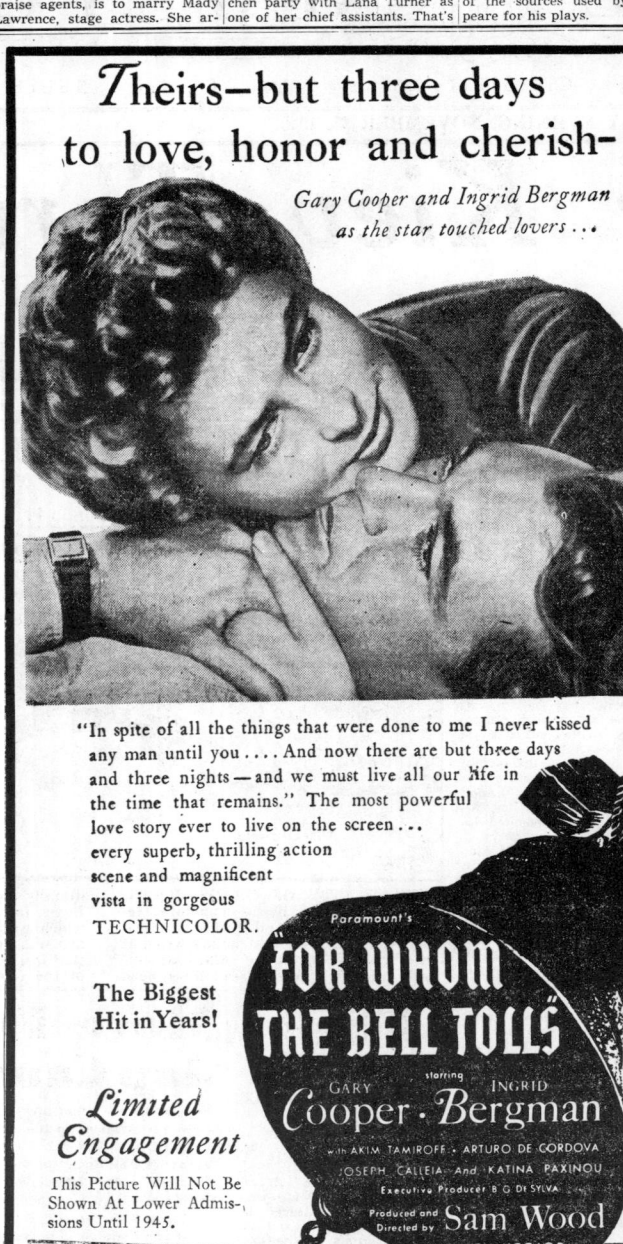

Theirs—but three days to love, honor and cherish—
Gary Cooper and Ingrid Bergman as the star touched lovers . . .
"In spite of all the things that were done to me I never kissed any man until you . . . . And now there are but three days and three nights—and we must live all our life in the time that remains." The most powerful love story ever to live on the screen . . . every superb, thrilling action scene and magnificent vista in gorgeous TECHNICOLOR.
The Biggest Hit in Years!
Limited Engagement
This Picture Will Not Be Shown At Lower Admissions Until 1945.
Paramount's FOR WHOM THE BELL TOLLS starring Gary Cooper · Ingrid Bergman
with Akim Tamiroff · Arturo de Cordova · Joseph Calleia · and Katina Paxinou
Executive Producer B. G. De Sylva
Produced and Directed by Sam Wood
IN TECHNICOLOR
SHOWS START 10 A. M., 1 P. M., 4 P. M., 7 P. M. & 10 P. M.
MAYFAIR HOWARD & FRANKLIN
PRICES: 75c 'til 6 P. M.—$1.10 after 6 P. M. Holiday Prices Today—$1.10

THIS THANKSGIVING DAY
You Want All the Laughs and Music and Happiness You Can Find . . . And Folks . . .
THAT'S WHAT WE'VE GOT!
HIPPODROME EUTAW NEAR BALTO. ST. NOW
Some seek glory . . . a hero makes it!
Football, love or war, Frank Cavanaugh played to win! . . . His genius for making men winners on gridiron and battlefield make the exciting, fighting story of a great American!
Pat O'Brien
The IRON MAJOR
with Ruth Warrick · Robert Ryan
Leon Ames · Russell Wade · Bruce Edwards · Richard Martin
Produced by Robert Fellows · Directed by Ray Enright
Screen Play by Aben Kandel and Warren Duff
RKO Radio
ON STAGE · ANOTHER All in Person SHOW!
"America's Foremost Table Tennis Wizard" · "National Jr. Table Tennis Champion"
Coleman CLARK vs. Allan THOMAS
SEE THEM PLAY A COMPLETE MATCH AT EACH SHOW
MAYSY & BRACH WORLD'S GREATEST UNICYCLISTS
The 6 DEBUTONES A HARMONY TREAT
The CAPPY BARRA BOYS HARMONICA STARS OF THE AIR WAVES
Extra Added! JERRY MANN PUBLIC NUISANCE NO. 1—HE'S A ONE MAN RIOT

LOEW'S Happy Shows for HOLIDAY FUN
CENTURY LEXINGTON NR. CHARLES
NOW THE TERRIFIC TWOSOME.. TOGETHER AGAIN... YOU'LL LOVE THEM BOTH
Mickey ROONEY Judy GARLAND in GERSHWIN'S "GIRL CRAZY"
M-G-M'S MUSICALULU With RAGS RAGLAND Tommy DORSEY and his Orchestra
VALENCIA ATOP THE CENTURY
STARTS TODAY! Doors Open 12.45 P. M.
YOU'LL HOWL YOUR HEAD OFF AT RED SKELTON IN M-G-M'S HILARIOUS "WHISTLING IN BROOKLYN"
ANN RUTHERFORD · JEAN ROGERS and THE BROOKLYN DODGERS
PARKWAY NORTH AT CHARLES
STARTS TODAY YOUNG IDEAS
SUSAN PETERS · HERBERT MARSHALL · MARY ASTOR

WARNER BROS. STANLEY HOWARD NEAR FRANKLIN ST. DOORS OPEN 10:30 A. M.
The story of the hidden love of a woman of the world....
Bette Davis AND MIRIAM HOPKINS
The co-stars of 'THE OLD MAID' in "OLD ACQUAINTANCE"
A NEW WARNER BROS. HIT
with GIG YOUNG
JOHN LODER · DOLORES MORAN
BUY WAR BONDS AND STAMPS

FORD'S • Last 4 Times
"The Most Satisfying Drama of the Season." —Donald Kirkley, The Sun
N.Y. CRITICS' PRIZE PLAY 1943
WALTER HAMPDEN in THE PATRIOTS by SIDNEY KINGSLEY
with CECIL HUMPHREYS · MARK HAYDON · GUY SOREL

Celebrate Our 31st anniversary.
THANKSGIVING PARTY TONITE (Thursday)
Music and Dancing
Chicken or Turkey Dinner $1.00
NOLAN'S Monroe St. and Wilkens. Ave.

KAY'S Nite Club
Presents WILLIE GRAY, M. C.
Plus TINA ★ ROSE & DIXIE LOVELY SINGING HARMONISTS
10—DANCING DOLLS—10
Balto. At Frederick Sts.

LITTLE HOWARD & FRANKLIN
HELD OVER!
CARY GRANT · JEAN ARTHUR AND RONALD COLMAN
The Talk of the Town
A GEORGE STEVENS PRODUCTION
with EDGAR BUCHANAN
A COLUMBIA PICTURE

RIVOLI
Wallace Beery "SALUTE TO THE MARINES" · Leo Carrillo "FOLLOW THE BAND"
DOUBLE SHOW DAILY DOORS OPEN 9 A. M.

EL PATIO
Have a real cause for Thanksgiving—celebrate tonight amid authentic tropical surroundings and see a real Cuban show with rhumba music.
ST. PAUL AT MADISON

Tonight—Lyric—8 P. M.
PHILADELPHIA LA SCALA OPERA CO.
I Pagliacci
Cavalleria Rusticana
Martinelli, Ercole, Rayner Kirsten, Pilotto, Frigerio
Conductor, Carlo Peroni
Prices 3.87, 3.32, 2.77
BONNEY CONCERT BUREAU
327 N. Charles Street LExington 6829
ON SALE AT LYRIC BOX OFFICE AFTER 1 P. M. TODAY—LEx. 9253

Next Sunday • Lyric • 8.30
Baltimore Symphony
REGINALD STEWART, Conductor
Overture "Euryanthe" ....Weber
Symphony in D ("The Clock") . Haydn
Lincoln Portrait ....Copland
Narrator: Wm. G. Horn
Prelude in E Major......Bach-Wood
Overture "1812" ....Tchaikovsky
Tickets: 25c, 55c, 85c, $1.10, $1.65
On sale at Cappel Concert Bureau, Stieff Hall, 315 N. Howard St., Vernon 1343, and Albaugh's, 11 E. Lexington St.
First Young People's Concert
Saturday morning, Dec. 4 • Lyric • 11 o'clock

Linden
North Ave. at Linden
Now Playing
All-Star Musical Hit of 1943
MELODY PARADE
With Betty Jane Rhodes

KEITHS
She's worth $1000 a week to each of them!
CHILDREN 15c (plus tax)
SHE'S A HONEY... SHE'S THE MONEY!
The Year's Top Comedy Romance ... With Four Great Stars! Dick and Mary sing 3 Hit Tunes!
MARY MARTIN · FRANCHOT TONE · DICK POWELL · VICTOR MOORE in "TRUE to LIFE" —and twice as funny!
A Paramount Picture with Mabel Paige · William Demarest
Your Ticket to Keiths Tonite Also Admits to Dance Free To Bob Craig and Band

NEW THEATRE LEX. ST. NEAR PARK 2nd. BIG WEEK
"Flaming, powerful, realistic drama . . . Episodes are almost overpoweringly tense . . . Story is convincing all the way."
Norman Clark, News-Post
RICHARD Tregaskis' GUADALCANAL DIARY
with Preston FOSTER · Lloyd NOLAN · William BENDIX
The most thrillingly human picture to come blazing out of the smoke of Victory!

A GREAT ROMANCE 1.41 P. M., 3.59 P. M., 6.07 P. M., 8.15 P. M. 10.23 P. M. ROSLYN
HUMPHREY Bogart · INGRID Bergman · PAUL Henreid "CASABLANCA"
A HAL B. WALLIS PROD'N.
A WARNER BROS. HIT
800 N. Howard

FIRST BALTO. SHOWING TIMES OPEN to 4 A. M.
HI 'YA SAILOR with Donald WOODS · Elyse KNOX · Eddie QUILLAN · Jerome COWAN
RAY EBERLE and His Orchestra · DELTA RHYTHM BOYS · WINGY MANONE and His Orchestra · and MAYRIS CHANEY Dance Trio
PLUS 3 Sergeants—1 Girl 1000 LAUGHS
Wm. Tracy · Joe Sawyer
HAY FOOT

Phone: Cal. 2669
GAYETY ★ BALT. THEATRE OF BURLESK
Baltimore & Holiday Sts.
Starring
STARTS TOMORROW NOON
MYRNA DEAN
"She's Blonde & Daringly Different"
JACK DIAMOND
JACK LAMONT
"The Two Comedy Jacks"
Ethel Deveaux—Arnolds Comedy Dogs
Pat Morgan—Joe Kelso—Bea Hayden
LAST TIMES TODAY
Eleanor Sheridan—Kenny Brenna
Cont. Matinees 12 to 5 P. M. Eves. 8:30 Res.

TODAY'S MOVIE CALENDAR

Theatres advertised in this column belong to the Motion Picture Theatre Owners of Maryland

Back the Attack---
Buy War Bonds

Aero Middle River, Md. John Garfield in "THE FALLEN SPARROW" With Maureen O'Hara.

Alpha Catonsville James Cagney in "JOHNNY COME LATELY" Comedy.

Ambassador 4604 Liberty Heights Sonja Henie in "WINTERTIME" "War for Men's Minds."

Apollo 1500 Harford Ave. James Cagney in "JOHNNY COME LATELY" 2 Carlines to Apollo—19, 27.

Arcade Harford Rd. & Hamilton Ave. Jean Arthur in "A LADY TAKES A CHANCE" "Inside Fascist Spain."

Astor Poplar Grove at Edmondson Basil Rathbone in "Sherlock Holmes Faces Death" 3 Carlines to Astor—4, 14, 9.

Aurora 7. East North Ave. Jean Arthur in "A LADY TAKES A CHANCE" "This Is America."

Avalon 4300 Park Heights Ave. Eddie Cantor in "THANK YOUR LUCKY STARS" "Private Pluto."

Avenue Milton Ave. & Hoffman St. Penny Singleton in "FOOTLIGHT GLAMOUR" "Three Stooges."

Avon 3019 Hamilton Ave. Andrew Sisters in "ALWAYS A BRIDESMAID" "Sleep Walker."

Belnord 2700 Philadelphia Ave. James Cagney in "JOHNNY COME LATELY" Comedy.

Boulevard 33rd at Greenmount Sonja Henie in "WINTERTIME" "War for Men's Minds."

Bridge Edmondson Ave. & Pulaski St. Pat O'Brien in "BOMBARDIER" Comedy.

Broadway 509 S. Broadway James Cagney in "JOHNNY COME LATELY" 4 Carlines to Broadway—16, 18, 10, 21.

Cameo 4705 Harford Road Dead End Kids in "KEEP 'EM SLUGGING" Take 19 Carline to Cameo.

Capitol 1518 W. Baltimore St. James Cagney in "JOHNNY COME LATELY" Carlines 15, 8, 1, 11, Q Bus.

Casino 1118 Light St. Red Skelton in "WHISTLING IN DIXIE" "Dizzy Acrobat."

Cluster 303 S. Broadway Humphrey Bogart in "THANK YOUR LUCKY STARS" Comedy.

Columbia 709 Washington Blvd. Jean Arthur in "A LADY TAKES A CHANCE" "Kiss and Make Up."

Earle Belair Rd. at Woodlea Ave. Basil Rathbone in "Sherlock Holmes Faces Death" With Nigel Bruce.

Edgewood 3500 Edmondson Ave. Sonja Henie in "WINTERTIME" Comedy.

Eureka 404 S. Fremont Ave. Allan Jones in "LARCENY WITH MUSIC" "Three Stooges."

Forest Garrison & Liberty Heights Edward G. Robinson in "DESTROYER" "Education for Death."

Fulton Fulton Ave. & Baker St. Lionel Barrymore in "Dr. Gillespie's Criminal Case" With Donna Reed.

Garden Charles at Cross Andrew Sisters in "ALWAYS A BRIDESMAID" "Quack Service."

Glen Glen Burnie Wallace Beery in "THE BUGLE SOUNDS" News.

Grand 511 S. Conkling St. Allan Jones in "LARCENY WITH MUSIC" "And Then Japan."

Gwynn 4609 Liberty Heights Ave. Basil Rathbone in "Sherlock Holmes Faces Death" "Women at War."

Hampden 911 W. 36th St. Andrews Sisters in "ALWAYS A BRIDESMAID" Comedy.

Harford 2610 Harford Ave. Douglas Fairbanks in "CORSICAN BROTHERS" News.

Hilton 3117 W. North Ave. Louis Hayward in "DUKE OF WEST POINT" "Suggestion Box."

Horn 2014 West Pratt St. Humphrey Bogart in "THANK YOUR LUCKY STARS" "Corny Concerto."

Howard 115 N. Howard St. Jean Arthur in "A LADY TAKES A CHANCE" Comedy.

Ideal 903 W. Thirty-sixth St. John Garfield in "THE FALLEN SPARROW" With Maureen O'Hara.

Irvington 4113 Frederick Ave. Jean Arthur in "A LADY TAKES A CHANCE" Comedy.

Lane Dundalk, Md. Andrews Sisters in "ALWAYS A BRIDESMAID" With Patric Knowles.

Leader 248 S. Broadway Kenny Baker in "DOUGHBOYS IN IRELAND" 5 Carlines to Leader—16, 10, 18, 21, 5.

Linwood 908 S. Linwood Ave. Lana Turner in "SLIGHTLY DANGEROUS" "A Maid Made Mad."

Little 523 North Howard St. Jean Arthur in "THE TALK OF THE TOWN" Held Over Second Week.

Lord Baltimore 1110 West Baltimore St. All-Star Cast in "THANK YOUR LUCKY STARS" Comedy.

Lord Calvert 2244 Washington Boulevard Wallace Beery in "SALUTE TO THE MARINES" Comedy.

Lyceum Sparrows Point, Md. Diana Barymore in "FRONTIER BADMEN" Comedy.

McHenry 1037 Light St. Jean Arthur in "A LADY TAKES A CHANCE" "Inside Fascist Spain."

Mayfair 508 N. Howard St. Gary Cooper in "FOR WHOM THE BELL TOLLS" With Ingrid Bergman.

Met Pennsylvania & North Aves. Eddie Cantor in "THANK YOUR LUCKY STARS" Cars 13, 2, 18, 1, 11, 31, 5, 33.

Nemo 4815 Eastern Ave. Billy Conn in "PITTSBURGH KID" "Streamline and Stamina."

New Reisterstown, Md. Edward G. Robinson in "DESTROYER" News.

New Essex Essex, Md. Cary Grant in "MR. LUCKY" With Laraine Day.

New Glen Glen Burnie Bob Hope in "LET'S FACE IT" Feature Starts 2.30, 4.15, 6.00, 7.45, 9.30.

Northway Harford & North. Pky. Lionel Barrymore in "Dr. Gillespie's Criminal Case" "My Wife's An Angel."

Overlea Belair Rd., End of Car Line Robert Paige in "FRONTIER BADMEN" "Our Gang."

Palace Gay and Hoffman Sts. Basil Rathbone in "Sherlock Holmes Faces Death" With Nigel Bruce.

Patterson Eastern and East Aves. Jean Arthur in 'THE LADY TAKES A CHANCE' "Dizzy Pilots."

Pikes Pikesville, Md. Lionel Barrymore in "Dr. Gillespie's Criminal Case" "March of Time."

Pimlico Park Heights & Belvedere William Ludigan in "Heading for God's Country" Comedy.

Preston 1108 E. Preston St. Johnny Mack Brown in "Outlaws of Stampede Pass" 3 Carlines to Preston—19, 27, 21.

Red Wing 2241 E. Monument St. Ann Sothern in "SWING SHIFT MAISIE" "Two Saplings."

Rex 4600 York Road Walt Disney's "DUMBO" "Fighting Spirit."

Rialto 845 W. North Ave. Clark Gable in "SOMEWHERE I'LL FIND YOU" Cars, 13, 32, 31, 16, B Bus.

Ritz 1607 N. Washington St. James Cagney in "JOHNNY COME LATELY" Comedy.

Senator 5904 York Road Jean Arthur in "A LADY TAKES A CHANCE" Comedy.

State Monument and Castle Sts. Sonja Henie in "WINTERTIME" Vaudeville.

Strand Dundalk, Md. James Cagney in "JOHNNY COME LATELY" Comedy.

Towson Towson, Md. Wallace Beery in "SALUTE TO THE MARINES" "Pandora's Box."

Uptown 5010 Park Heights Ave. James Cagney in "JOHNNY COME LATELY" News.

Vilma Belair Rd. and Mayfield Ave. Sonja Henie in "WINTERTIME" With Jack Oakie.

Walbrook 3100 W. North Ave. James Cagney in "JOHNNY COME LATELY" Comedy.

Waverly Greenmount at Gorsuch James Cagney in "JOHNNY COME LATELY" "Victory Vehicle."

Westport 2205 Russell St. Richard Dix in "THE KANSAN" Comedy.

Westway 5300 Edmondson Ave. Leslie Howard in "SPITFIRE" Comedy.

U. S. ESCORT CARRIER SUNK

Admiral, Captain Missing In Pacific

THE WEATHER

Light showers this evening. Colder late tonight with lowest temperature 30 degrees in the suburbs. Fair and cold Friday.

Detailed Weather Report on Page 29

Read The Baltimore News-Post for complete, accurate war coverage. It is the only Baltimore newspaper possessing the three great vire services—
ASSOCIATED PRESS
INTERNATIONAL NEWS SERVICE
UNITED PRESS

THE BALTIMORE NEWS-POST
AN INDEPENDENT NEWSPAPER
The Largest Evening Circulation in the Entire South

WALL ST. CLOSE 9

VOL. CXLIV.—NO. 24 Entered as second-class matter at Baltimore Postoffice. THURSDAY EVENING, DECEMBER 2, 1943 PRICE 3 CENTS

ROOSEVELT, STALIN IN TEHERAN, REPORT

Carrier Sunk With Captain And Admiral

WASHINGTON, Dec. 2—(U. P.).—The Navy announced today that the escort aircraft carrier Liscome Bay was sunk by a Japanese submarine in the Gilberts Islands and that this was the only American ship lost in the conquest of the islands.

The skipper of the carrier, Capt. Irving D. Wiltsie of New York city, and Rear Admiral Henry M. Mullinix, who was aboard as commander of a task force, were reported as missing in action.

FIRST ESCORT CARRIER

It was the first escort carrier lost by the Navy in this war and the first U. S. carrier of any type to be sunk since the Hornet went down in the South Pacific in October, 1942.

The Navy gave no details on the sinking except to say that the Liscome Bay went down after being torpedoed by a submarine on November 24.

Denying grossly exaggerated Japanese claims of American ship losses in the Gilberts, the Navy stated:

"This is the only ship lost in the Gilbert Islands operations."

The Liscome Bay was the one hundred and thirty-first U. S. naval vessel lost in this war.

COMPARATIVE SMALL

Escort carriers, comparatively small craft built on merchant ship hulls, normally provide air protection for convoys against submarines and planes, but they have been used for combat purposes as well.

The Navy gave no details of the size of the ship or its complement. Because these are a newly developed type of craft, the Navy

Continued on Page 2, Column 7.

"The Daisy!" Henry Clive Paints His Interpretation of the Kind of Girl Who Represents This Popular Wild Flower. Don't Miss This Beautiful Front Color Page In The American Weekly, the Magazine Distributed With Next Sunday's Baltimore American.—Adv.

BERLIN AFTER RAIDS—Caption accompanying this picture, radioed from neutral Sweden, described it as first photo to show any bomb damage after last week's Allied raids on the German capital—with military band marching in Unter den Linden. Scene was typical, Stockholm caption said, of Nazi efforts to hide bomb damage, with little damage shown except ruins of one building at left and some shattered windows in building in background. Parade of military band was resumed after streets were cleared of debris, caption continued, to help morale. Picture apparently was taken at the corner of Unter den Linden and Friedrichstrasse, with Krantzler Coffee House, familiar to tourists, on corner in background.

Germans In Full Retreat In Italy

LONDON, Dec. 2—(A. P.).—The American Fifth Army has launched large-scale attacks in Italy, supported by three destroyers, the Berlin radio said today.

ALLIED HEADQUARTERS, ALGIERS, Dec. 2—(A. P.).—The Germans are in full retreat from their ponderously fortified winter line in Italy near the Adriatic, leaving the battleground littered with dead, wounded and wrecked equipment, Allied headquarters announced today.

At the same time the Nazis apparently were making preparations to abandon Cassino on the Via Casilina, the main inland road up a broad valley to Rome, in the face of rising pressure from Lieut. General Mark W. Clark's Fifth Army—supported yesterday by a terrific aerial bombardment, one of the heaviest seen in the Italian campaign.

REPORT DEMOLITIONS

Spitfire pilots reported heavy German demolitions were taking place at Cassino, approximately 12 miles northwest of the Allied front at Mignano, shortly after fighter-bombers, Warhawks and A-36 dive bombers had pounded the German defenses along a 20-mile front for three hours.

Sweeping over at 10-minute in-

Continued on Page 2, Column 8.

Red Army Leaders With Stalin At Parley

LONDON, Dec. 2—(I. N. S.).—High military and political chiefs of the Soviet Union are accompanying Premier Marshal Josef Stalin for a conference with President Roosevelt and Prime Minister Winston Churchill in Persia, the German overseas radio said today, according to a Reuter's dispatch from Stockholm.

Quoting the newspaper Svenska Dagbladet, the dispatch said that Soviet Marshal Vassilevsk is traveling with Stalin, as well as former Foreign Commissar Maxim Litvinov.

Temperatures

12 Mid., 41	8 A. M., 38
1 A. M., 40	9 A. M., 41
2 A. M., 40	10 A. M., 44
3 A. M., 40	11 A. M., 44
4 A. M., 39	12 Noon 48
5 A. M., 39	1 P. M., 50
6 A. M., 39	2 P. M., 56
7 A. M., 37	3 P. M., 62

U. S. War Toll To Date 126,969

WASHINGTON, Dec. 2—(A. P.).—Secretary of War Stimson reported today that American Army casualties from the beginning of the war to November 15 were 94,918, bringing the total announced casualties for all branches of the armed forces to 126,969.

Casualties reported by the Navy Department for the Navy, Marine Corps and Coast Guard to date—except for the preliminary reports announced yesterday from the recent operations in the Gilbert Islands—total 32,051, of which 13,160 were killed, 5,740 wounded, 8,926 missing and 4,225 prisoners of war.

14,321 ARE KILLED

Stimson told a news conference that the Army total included 14,321 killed, 32,690 wounded, 23,417 prisoners of war and 24,490 missing in action. Of the Americans officially listed as prisoners, 1,610 have died in prison camps, mostly in Japanese-occupied territory, he reported.

Stimson announced that American Army casualties in Lieut. Gen. Mark W. Clark's Fifth Army from the beginning of operations on the Italian mainland to date total 11,572, of whom 1,811 were killed, 7,091 wounded and 2,670 missing. Casualties of British elements in the Fifth Army have been somewhat smaller, he said.

NAVY BREAKDOWN

The Navy supplied these figures making up the 32,051 total in the Navy-Marine Corps-Coast Guard:

Navy — 10,663 killed, 3,001 wounded, 8,248 missing and 2,276 prisoners of war; total, 24,188.

Marine Corps — 2,181 killed, 2,666 wounded, 637 missing and 1,948 prisoners of war; total, 7,427.

Coast Guard—316 killed, 78 wounded, 41 missing and one prisoner of war; total, 436.

Ultimatum To Germany Reported Due As Drive At Early Date Is Set

By United Press.

Josef Stalin, President Roosevelt and Winston Churchill were reported drafting the obituary of Nazi Germany at Teheran today in a conference paralleling that at Cairo where plans were agreed upon for stripping Japan of her empire and forcing her unconditional surrender.

Unofficial reports circulated that the leaders of Russia, the United States and Great Britain were framing an ultimatum to Germany, demanding immediate capitulation on pain of progressively severe terms.

Congressional quarters in Washington accepted as completely factual the reports that Mr. Roosevelt and Churchill had proceeded to Teheran to meet Stalin after their meeting in Cairo with Generalissimo Chiang Kai-Shek of China.

LONDON, Dec. 2—(U. P.).—The Ankara radio reported today that Premier Josef Stalin and President Roosevelt had arrived in Teheran.

Plan German Quarantine After War

LONDON, Dec. 2—(U. P.).—President Roosevelt, Prime Minister Churchill and Premier Stalin were reported conferring in Teheran today and observers believed they were mapping a post-war program to "quarantine" Germany and saddle her manpower, raw materials and production for rebuilding stricken Europe.

Through such a program, observers were convinced, the "big three" Allied Western Powers plan to punish Germany and smash her ability to make future wars as completely as Mr. Roosevelt, Churchill and Generalissimo Chiang Kai-shek plotted the crushing of Japan at Cairo.

NO OFFICIAL WORD

There was no official confirmation of the whereabouts of Mr. Roosevelt and Churchill since their departure from Cairo for an "unknown destination" following the Anglo-American-Chinese conference, but a dispatch published in a Lisbon newspaper reported they already had begun conversations with Stalin in Teheran, capital of Iran (Persia).

(American Congressional circles accepted reports of a Roosevelt-Churchill conference with Stalin as completely factual.)

Laurence Steinhardt, U. S. Ambassador to Turkey, was reported by Lisbon also to have flown to Teheran. There has been wide-

Continued on Page 2, Column 5.

Parley Maps Crush-Jap Strategy

CAIRO, Dec. 2—(A. P.)—Britain and the United States agreed on details for a new invasion of Europe and perhaps discussed a strike into the Balkans, it was reported on good authority today, at the epic tri-Power conference, where, with China, they pledged unrelenting war to thrash Japan into unconditional surrender and tear away the whole empire she has won in 50 years of conquest.

There was a feeling here that big developments would come from the five-day meeting of President Roosevelt, Prime Minister Churchill and Generalissimo Chiang Kai-shek, who left for unannounced destinations last Friday after completing their talks.

(A Reuters' dispatch from Lisbon said they had gone to Iran to meet Premier Josef Stalin, and Berlin declared a four-Power meeting already was underway in Teheran.)

WILL STRIP JAPAN

For Japan the three war leaders promised "unrelenting pressure . . . by sea, land and air," and declared they would strip her of all her empire stolen in five wars since 1894—reducing Japan virtually to the same territorial status as before Commodore Perry opened up that Oriental land of the Shoguns in 1853. Only her home islands would remain.

Major decisions were reported reached for brilliant developments in World War Two, and while the official announcement dealt only

(Continued on Page 2, Column 1.)

Honolulu Hails Fate Set For Japs

HONOLULU, Dec. 2—(U. P.).—The Cairo pronouncement of what is in store for Japan was received enthusiastically in Honolulu where the bombing of Pearl Harbor resulted in U. S. entrance into the war.

VERY LATEST NEWS

(Race Results From Howard Sports Daily, Inc.)

RACING RESULTS

AT CHARLES TOWN

Fifth—Heloria, $4.20, $2.60, $2.40; Canto Gallo, $3.40, $2.60; Royal Fleet, $3.80.

AT FAIR GROUNDS

First — Heel Call, $9.20, $5.60, $4.00; Victory Play, $18.20, $9.40; Five A. M., $3.80.

BERLIN RADIO GOES OFF AIR

LONDON, Dec. 2.—(I. N. S.).—Wireless transmitters in the Berlin area went off the air early tonight as Allied warplanes were believed striking once again at Continental Europe and possibly the German capital.

NEW YORK STOCK EXCHANGE TOTAL SALES

NEW YORK, Dec. 2.—(A. P.).—Total sales on the New York Stock Exchange today were 715,280 shares.

RACING RESULTS AT CHARLES TOWN TRACK

FIRST RACE—About seven fur longs. Time, 1.28 3-5.

Miss Louise, 107 (Florio)	$7.60	$4.20	$2.20
Leaping Moose, 105 (Pannell)		5.80	2.80
Bonnie Ina, 107 (Scocca)			2.20

Also Ran—Ecolita, Wee Tam, Bellclapper and Black Slave.

SECOND—Charles Town course. Off 2.06½. Time, ..17.

White Sea, 115 (L. Knapp)	$6.80	$4.00	$2.20
Miss Beeville, 106 (A. Florio)		4.60	2.20
Gay Elf, 113 (C. Kirk)			2.20

Also Ran—Propose, Lady All, Pneumatique, Grouchy, Donarose.

Daily Double—Miss Louise and White Sea paid $39.60

THIRD—Charles Town Course. Off at 2.36. Time, 1.16 2-5.

Remolee, 118 (Daugherty)	$6.60	$3.20	$2.80
Double B., 118 (Wholey)		3.20	2.80
Lady Mascara, 108 (Pannell)			5.60

Also Ran—Bright 'n' Happy, Seven Seas, Clock Time, Meysah, Wabaunsee.

FOURTH—About four and one-half furlongs (Chute). Off at 3.07½. Time, 1.49 1-5.

Roman Boy, 116 (C. Kirk)	$5.20	$3.00	$2.20
Pilot Boat, 119 (Bracciale)		3.00	2.20
Happy Hannah, 114 (Sheaffer)			2.20

Also Ran—Courlander, Incentor, Ohio Lady and Baby Dismay.

NEWS-POST

Bugs Baer	21	Horoscope	7
Clark, Norman	14	Movies	14
Classified Ads	29, 30, 31	Parsons, Louella	14
Comics	24	Pippen, R. H.	25
Crossword	31	Radio	9
Dulaney	21	Robinson, Elsie	20
Durling	21	Society	22
Editorials	20	Sports	25, 26, 27, 28
Financial	28, 29	Women's Clubs	22
Health	21		

21 Liberty Ships Launched Here; New Record

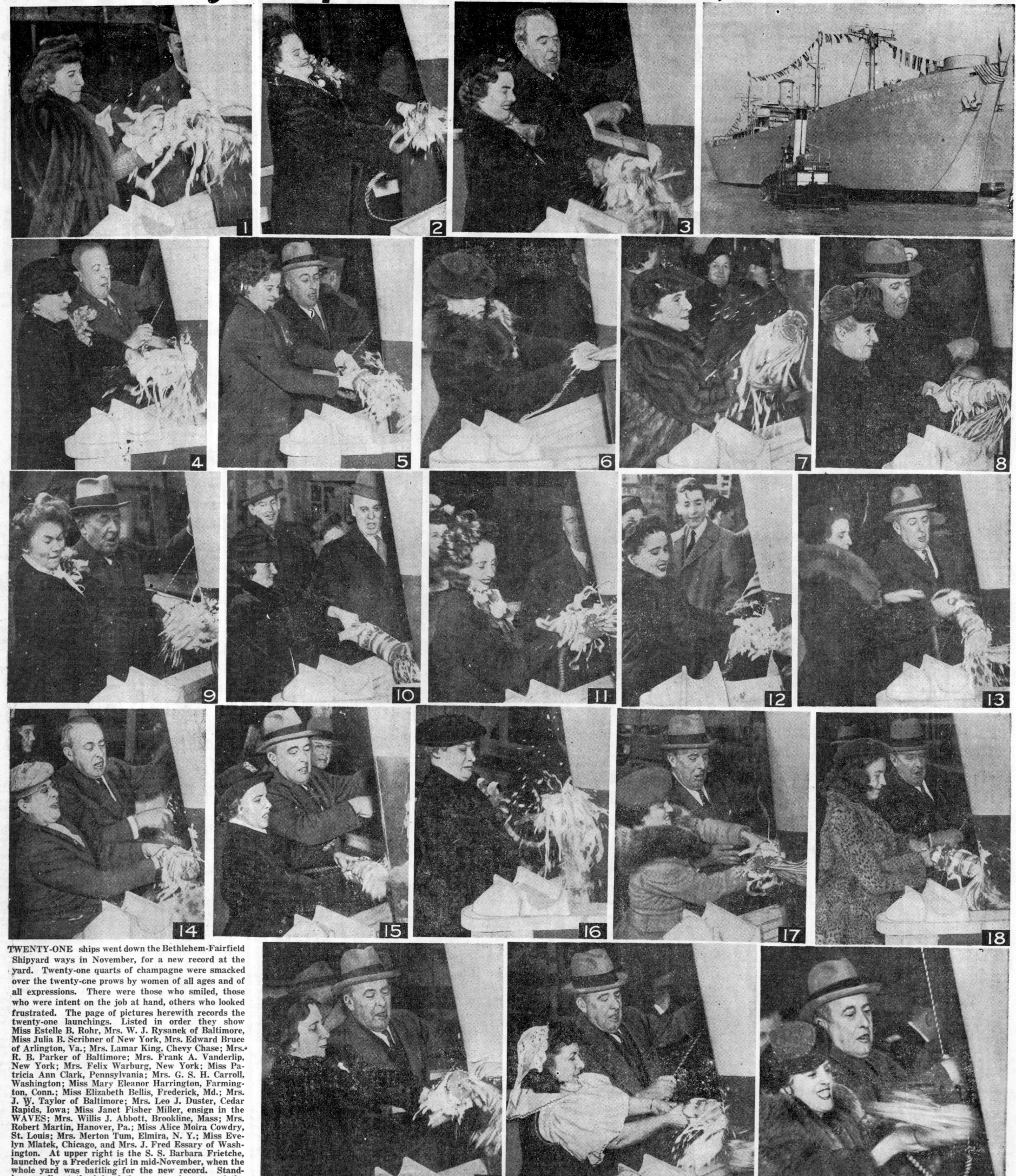

TWENTY-ONE ships went down the Bethlehem-Fairfield Shipyard ways in November, for a new record at the yard. Twenty-one quarts of champagne were smacked over the twenty-one prows by women of all ages and of all expressions. There were those who smiled, those who were intent on the job at hand, others who looked frustrated. The page of pictures herewith records the twenty-one launchings. Listed in order they show Miss Estelle B. Rohr, Mrs. W. J. Rysanek of Baltimore, Miss Julia B. Scribner of New York, Mrs. Edward Bruce of Arlington, Va.; Mrs. Lamar King, Chevy Chase; Mrs. R. B. Parker of Baltimore; Mrs. Frank A. Vanderlip, New York; Mrs. Felix Warburg, New York; Miss Patricia Ann Clark, Pennsylvania; Mrs. G. S. H. Carroll, Washington; Miss Mary Eleanor Harrington, Farmington, Conn.; Miss Elizabeth Bellis, Frederick, Md.; Mrs. J. W. Taylor of Baltimore; Mrs. Leo J. Duster, Cedar Rapids, Iowa; Miss Janet Fisher Miller, ensign in the WAVES; Mrs. Willis J. Abbott, Brookline, Mass; Mrs. Robert Martin, Hanover, Pa.; Miss Alice Moira Cowdry, St. Louis; Mrs. Merton Turn, Elmira, N. Y.; Miss Evelyn Mlatek, Chicago, and Mrs. J. Fred Essary of Washington. At upper right is the S. S. Barbara Frietche, launched by a Frederick girl in mid-November, when the whole yard was battling for the new record. Standing usually at the left of the sponsor in many of the pictures is John M. Willis, head of the shipyard.

CHARLES DUCKPIN TEST DRAWS LEADING BOWLERS

THE BALTIMORE NEWS-POST SPORTS
THURSDAY EVENING, DECEMBER 2, 1943

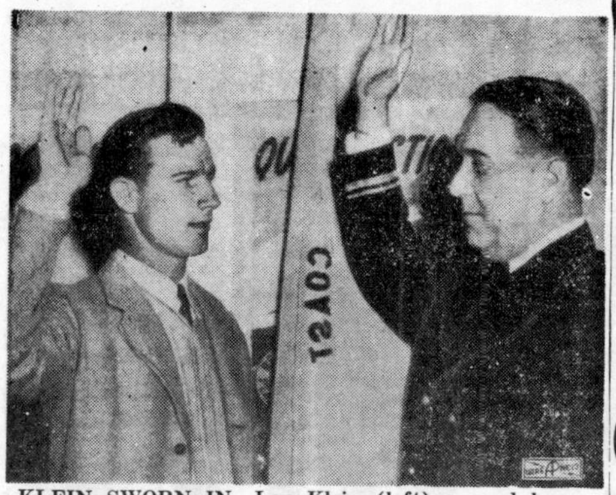

KLEIN SWORN IN—Lou Klein (left), second baseman for the St. Louis Cardinals, decided he would "rather ride a boat than walk"—and so he chose the Coast Guard as his favorite service. He enlisted at New Orleans and is shown as he was sworn into the service by Lieut. F. Legendre (right), recruiting officer. Associated Press Wirephoto.

RODGER H. PIPPEN

SPORTS EDITOR, SAYS:

As is its custom every December, the Associated Press again asks the sports editors to co-operate in the annual poll dealing with competitive athletic developments during 1943. The questions which were asked and the answers I am sending follow:

1—Who was the outstanding male athlete of the year, amateur or professional? (Name three in the order of preference.)

Gunder Hagg, Swedish runner.
Luke Appling, Chicago White Sox shortstop.
Stan Musial, Cards' outfielder.

2—Who was the leading woman athlete? (Name three in order of preference.)

Patty Berg, golf.
Pauline Betz, tennis.
Stella Walsh, track.

3—What was the outstanding team, amateur or professional? (Name three.)

Notre Dame, football.
Detroit Red Wings, ice hockey.
New York Yankees, baseball.

4—What was the outstanding comeback of the year, amateur or professional? (Name three.)

Patty Berg, golf.
Harry Jeffra, boxing.
Bronko Nagurski, pro football.

5—What was the biggest sports surprise of the year, team or individual? (Name three.)

Notre Dame's defeat by Great Lakes in the final game of the season.
Bobby Ruffin's defeat of Beau Jack in New York.
Redskins' defeat of Chicago Bears, especially with Baugh on the sidelines for practically the whole game.

6—Who or what was the biggest disappointment of the year, team or individual? (Name three.)

Bobo Newsom, big league pitcher.
Cards' showing in World Series.
Shut Out's failure on turf.

7—What were the oddest happenings in sports during the season, any sport?

Water boy of a Texas college being used in three games to kick goals after touchdowns.

8—What were the principal effects of the war on sports?

Quality lowered in most pro sports and attendance increased. Amateur sports almost knocked out, especially golf and college football. Scarcity of talent gave kids a chance and kept veterans in action.

* * *

Cutters May Win Argument

While no recent developments have been reported on the local hockey front, and the Coast Guard Cutters still are "out" of the Eastern League, the impression prevails that this is one argument Baltimore eventually will win from Messrs. Thomas F. Lockhart & Co., and that it won't be long before the Curtis Bay pucksters are again battling New York, Boston, Philadelphia and New Haven in league competition.

For years, Baltimore was given pretty much of a pushing-around by the Eastern loop officials, so far as dates and other considerations were concerned, but in the days of the Orioles, nothing much could be done about it. The situation happens to have a somewhat different complexion now. The Cutters don't have to "take it and like it." They are not a "commercial" organization, in hockey for their livelihoods. They play the game chiefly for their own amusement and recreation—and on their own time, when their regular chores at Curtis Bay are done for the day. They don't "need" the Eastern League—but the Eastern League DOES need them.

The Cutters have proved themselves the finest attractions in the circuit, and, as such, they are vital to the box offices of the Rovers, Olympics, Falcons and Eagles.

And they certainly are entitled to more consideration than they have received from the schedule-makers in the matter of home dates, particularly Sundays.

Until the controversy finally is settled, the Cutters are going ahead with plans to import prominent Canadian service teams for tussles at Iceland. Already, one of the finest club in the Dominion—the Toronto Navy sextet, coached by our old favorite, Bill (Pick) Hines, and boasting a brilliant array of ex-professional and amateur stars—is booked for a two-game series here two weeks hence. There also is a possibility of professional major and minor league clubs dropping in for occasional battles with the Coast Guardsmen.

Meanwhile, an intrasquad "play-off" between the Cutters and the Clippers is scheduled for Sunday night at Iceland. The two clubs split the honors in their three-game pre-season series, the Cutters winning the first clash, the Clippers the second, and the third meeting resulting in an overtime tie.

* * *

Dogs Being Poisoned In Homestead Neighborhood

Harry Schuchman reports that animal lovers in the neighborhood of Homestead and Montpelier streets are greatly disturbed over the poisoning of seven pet dogs. Detectives have been hired to watch for the inhuman wretch who is placing the poison for three or four blocks in that neighborhood. A reward has been offered for his apprehension.

* * *

Says Iowa Pre-Flight Team Was Best

J. H. Webb, seaman, second class, of Bainbridge, Md., offers this football comment:

"The Iowa Pre-Flight team played just as tough a schedule as Notre Dame and outplayed the Irish even though losing by a single point.

"Meanwhile, Iowa came back last week to whip Minnesota, 36 to 0, while Notre Dame was again outplayed for the second straight week, this time to lose their only game. On the basis of this it is my belief that Iowa Pre-Flight should be the No. 1 team in the country, and not the Irish. However, unless I miss my guess, the so-called experts will probably keep Notre Dame on top.

"If you agree with them, perhaps you can give me an explanation why."

Yes, I still think the Irish were tops. Their record speaks for itself.

Landis Turns Down Minors' Protest Against Defeat

Orioles Sell Johnny Pare To Richmond

Catcher Johnny Pare has been sold to the Richmond club, Tommy Thomas, manager of the Orioles, announced today. It was a straight cash transaction.

NEW YORK, Dec. 2—(A. P.).—Commissioner Kenesaw M. Landis today turned down the protest of six "rebel" minor leagues against the action of the minor league convention yesterday in defeating a rebellion aimed at ending the commissioner's control over the minors.

After receiving the protest from a committee representing the insurgents, whose revolution collapsed on the floor of the meeting of the National Association of Professional Baseball Leagues, Landis made the simple announcement that he had "overruled" the protestants.

The insurrectionists' aims were (1) Defeat of William G. Bramham, who, as president of the National Association, is the Minor League czar, and (2) to throw out the major-minor league agreement by having the convention vote against its renewal. This agreement is the pact by which Landis has power over the minors.

BOTH AIMS DEFEATED

They were defeated in both of these aims, for Bramham, who has been president of the National Association since 1932 was reelected for another five-year term at a $25,000 annual salary and the major-minor agreement was renewed for another year.

The National Association convention, which recessed yesterday to await the commissioner's decision, had to take two more recesses this morning before the verdict was brought to the winter baseball meetings by Landis' secretary, Leslie O'Connor.

As a result of Landis' decision, it was reported that some sentiment had been expressed for the three double-A leagues — The American Association, and the International and Pacific Coast loops—to pull out of the National Association, form a group by themselves and ask to be placed directly under the commissioner's jurisdiction, rather than to be bound by the major-minor league agreement, with which they are dissatisfied.

TRADE TALK PICKS UP

Meantime, major league trade talk, which has been playing second fiddle to the minor league scramble, picked up a bit. On the heels of continued rumors that the Washington Senators and Cleveland Indians were trying to make a deal involving Pitcher Jim Bagby and Infielder Russ Peters of the Tribe and Outfielder Stan Spence and old Bobo Newsom of the Nats, came whispers that the Philadelphia Phillies and Chicago Cubs were talking.

The Cubs probably have more available playing talent and extras than any club in either league and the Phillies are rather short of catcher and outfielder—of which the Cubs have several of each. Talk of this trade indicated that Herb Pennock isn't wasting any time on his new job, since he became general manager of the Phils only yesterday.

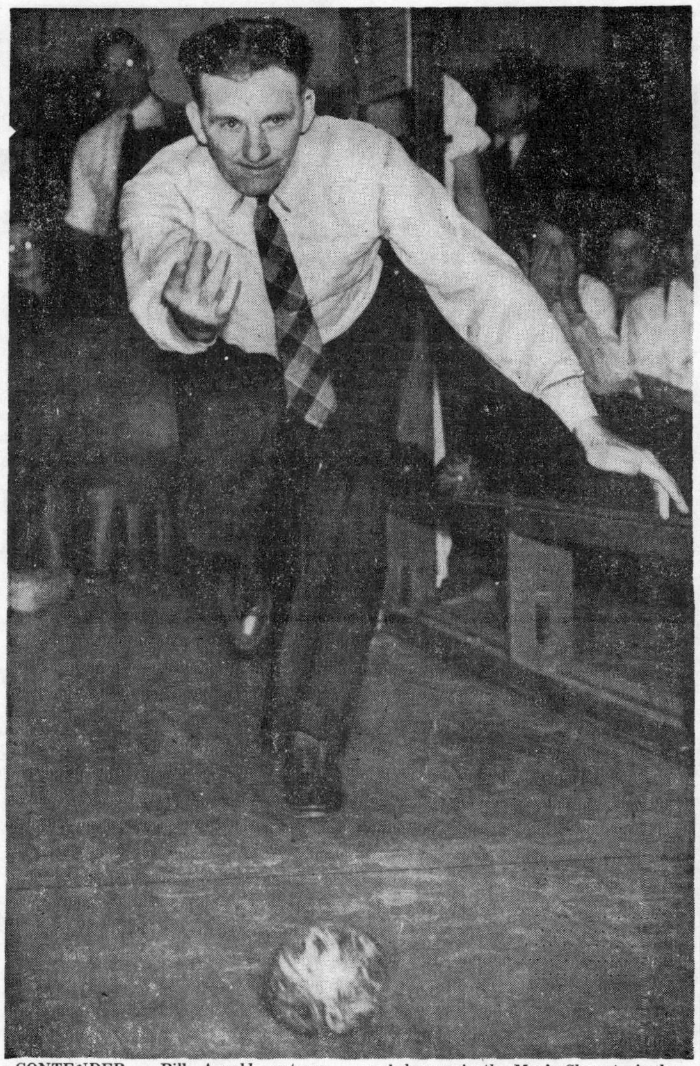

CONTENDER — Bill Arnold, veteran Annapolis roller, is included in the star-studded field of contestants which will seek honors in the Men's Class A singles event in the annual Charles Duckpin championships, opening Saturday evening over the Charles Center alleys.

Tentative Winter Golf Dates Set

NEW YORK, Dec. 2—(I. N. S.).—Tentative dates for the first half of the professional winter golf tour were set today by Freddie Cochrane, tournament manager of the Professional Golf Association.

The tour will open in Miami December 16-19 and move to Los Angeles January 7-10. San Francisco is next, with a aJnuary 14-16 date. After playing other unannounced dates on the Coast the pros will meet in Phoenix, Ariz., in February, then move into the South.

The highest prize money will be $12,500 at the Los Angeles Open, and all prize money in this tour will be paid in war bonds.

HOCKEY TONIGHT

NATIONAL LEAGUE

Chicago at Montreal.
Detroit at Toronto.

SPORTS BRIEFS

OAKLAND, Cal., Dec. 2—(U. P.).—Dolph Camilli, former first baseman for the Brooklyn Dodgers and now the property of the New York Giants, was free today to negotiate for the managerial post of the Oakland Baseball Club in the Pacific Coast League. Oakland president, C. L. Laws, wired from the major-minor league baseball meeting yesterday that Horace Stoneham, president of the Giants, had given his permission for the club to seek Camilli's services.

PLAN EASTERN TRIP

CHICAGO, Dec. 2—(I. N. S.).—St. George High School's football players, city-wide prep champions, started drills today in preparation for their game December 12 at Baker Field with Mount St. Michael, New York City titleholder. Coach Max Burnell, announcing acceptance of Mount St. Michael's invitation, said the entire squad of 35 would leave for the East next Thursday.

ALSAB AT N. O.

NEW ORLEANS, Dec. 2—(A. P.).—The mighty Alsab has been shipped here where he will run in the $15,000 Louisiana Handicap, December 13. Trainer Sarge Swenke said the colt was in good condition and might run once before the handicap.

MARTIN SIGNED

NEW YORK, Dec. 2—(A. P.). Frank Martin, former Alabama U. baseball and football star, was signed by the Columbus Red Birds of the American Association. Martin has been a halfback this season with the Brooklyn Professional Dodgers.

LIDDY MOST VALUABLE

IOWA CITY, Dec. 2—(I. N. S.). Bob Liddy was announced today as Iowa's most valuable football player during the 1943 season.

Liddy is a veteran guard and co-captain of the Hawkeyes.

PITTSBURGH GETS GAME

NEW YORK, Dec. 2—(I. N. S.). The All-Star baseball game of 1944 will be held in Pittsburgh, July 11, it was announced at the annual major league meetings.

DODGERS KEEP COACH

BROOKLYN, Dec. 2—(A. P.).—Pete Cawthon will be retained as coach of the Brooklyn Dodgers of the National Football League, Club President Jack Davies said.

HOCKEY Scores

EASTERN LEAGUE

Philadelphia, 4; N. Y. Rovers, 2.

AMERICAN LEAGUE

Hershey, 2; Pittsburgh, 1.
Providence, 3; Indianapolis, 3 (tie).

Navy Team Wins Lambert Trophy

NEW YORK, Dec. 2—(U. P.). The August V. Lambert memorial trophy, significant of football supremacy in the East, today was awarded to the United States Naval Academy's grid team.

Defeated only by Notre Dame in nine games, the Middies polled 56 votes to two for Army, the only other team given consideration by the voting sports writers.

The trophy will be awarded to representatives of the Navy team in special ceremonies here next Tuesday, December 7.

A's To Train At Frederick

FREDERICK, Md., Dec. 2—(A. P.).—Maryland was assured today of at least one major league baseball club training within her boundaries next spring with the announcement that the Philadelphia Athletics would work out at Frederick.

Roger B. Wolfe, president of the Frederick Chamber of Commerce, disclosed he had been notified by Connie Mack, veteran leader of the Athletics, that the club would come to Frederick about March 11 and practice at McCurdy Field, a municipally-owned recreation park.

The Toronto Maple Leafs of the International League also have been reported interested in coming to this Maryland town, in which case they probably would train at the high school field and play frequent games with their major league neighbors.

Colorado Rejects Post-Season Games

COLORADO SPRINGS, Colo., Dec. 2—(A. P.).—Colorado College's football team—undefeated and untied—will play no post-season games, college officials announced.

The Tigers rejected several bowl invitations, principally because the team's Navy personnel could not obtain sufficient leave.

Howell Sold

NEW YORK, Dec. 2—(A. P.).—The Atlanta Crackers of the Southern Association today purchased Outfielder Murray Howell from the Jersey City Giants.

Class A Singles To Feature Saturday's Opening Program

By JACK CARPENTER

Entries having closed last night at midnight, a check reveals that the field which will participate in this year's annual Charles Duckpin Championships, opening Saturday at the Charles Center in co-operation with The Baltimore News-Post and Sunday American, is far and away the strongest in years.

This is particularly true of the men's Class A singles, an event which consistently highlights the affair and which will officially open the annual classic at 7.15 P. M. Saturday.

STRONG FIELD

With few exceptions, every name bowler in the city and State will toe the firing line for a shot at the singles title and a share of the $410 in war bonds and stamps which will be awarded the various winners.

Heading the Class A singles field, of course, is Buck Koenig, the "dark horse" who spreadeagled a star-studded field to garner the 1942-43 crown. Koenig has bowled with a high degree of perfection this season and if one is to establish an early favorite he must be accorded that distinction.

Koenig's chief opposition, and it will be formidable to say the least, is expected to be furnished by Bob Fisher, who won the championship two years ago with a record-smashing 2,020; and such top-flight major leaguers as Bill Arnold, Lee Seim, Fish Campbell, Dick Arthur, Bill Brozey, Tony Petro, Ray Florentino, Nick Paye, Wilmer Robey and a host of others.

QUALIFYING ROUNDS

Manager Sol Shecter, director of the huge tourney, has announced that foul-line judges will be employed for the Class A singles event. The Class A singles takes on additional importance in that the scores will be used as a yardstick in determining each bowler's national ranking.

In contrast to previous years when total pinfalls determined the various winners, each individual or team must bowl ten qualifying games to earn a starting place in the finals, slated for the week-end of December 18-19. This week-end and the week-end of December 11-12 will be given over to the qualifying rounds of five-game sets. As has been pointed out previously, the finals will begin from scratch, with the championships being decided on the final five-game sets.

In addition to the men's Class A singles, the mixed 220 doubles event will be staged on Saturday. Sunday's schedule lists the men's Class B singles, at 2.15 P. M.; the Class C and D singles and Open Handicap doubles.

Following are the entries:

MEN'S CLASS A SINGLES

John R. Johnson, Eddie Bornscheuber, Charles Clabaugh, Jr., Forrest Kirchenbauer, Bill Arnold, Sam Gentile, William Walkling, Homer W. Snyder, Don Stewart, Lee Seim, Fish Campbell, Cliff Kidd, Dick Arthur, Hal Tucker, Bill Brozey, Lou Pohl, Red Sheppard, Lou Crocetti, Tony Petro, Ray Florentino, Bob Fisher, Buck Koenig, Nick Paye, Wilmer Robey, Walter O'Brien, Marion Staylor, Teddy Weinberger.

MEN'S CLASS B SINGLES

Ray Callery, Joseph Bahnline, Rudolph Serra, Sidney Ducat, Jack Palmer, William Dieter, Lloyd Hahn, John Delaney, Jr., Edwin Linthicum, Fred Smith, John Despeaux, Arthur Johnson, Edward Mazerski, William Fink.

MEN'S CLASS C SINGLES

Joseph Liberto, Carl Freitag, Reason Wareheim, Jack Gross, Victor Mullin, Earl Sabiston, E. P. Shanahan, Joseph E. Pfeiler, Joseph Glick, Maurice Byan, Marvin Anderson, James Vogel, Bernard Weberm, Howard Patone, Frank Reinhardt, Leroy Heath, Carl Martin, John Scheck, Joseph Armetta, Frank Armetta, John Kildnoff, John Bizon, Chester Borowski, Joseph Fulco, William Clipper, Darwin Morton, W. R. Cosgrove, David Atkinson, Carroll Whitely, Louis Kowalewski, Sergt. Jules Bernard, Alvin G. Ward, Robert M. Sylvia, Charles Lanahan, John Spawn, Earl Crage, Rex Chesonia, William Miller, Albert Miller, Bill McFarlane, Ercel W. Ensley, Kenneth McDonald, Norman Chelf, Frank Stickline, John G. Bizon, Chester Ciborowski, John Despeaux, Fred Smith, John Trimp, Lloyd S. Hahn.

MEN'S CLASS D SINGLES

David Kneller, Charles Citrard, Alton E. Fouch, Bernard Waxman, Joseph De Sota, Nick Chinquina, Roger Hans, Chips Keller, James E. Silk, Charles S. Komin, Alex Soroka, Chester A. Chalk, George Maxwell, George Roessler, George Baker, John T. Halberstadt, Bill Tucker.

OPEN-HANDICAP DOUBLES

John G. Bizon and Chester Ciborowski, Elizabeth Marks and Don Stewart, Darwin Morton and William Freimiller, Robert M. Sylvia and Alvin Ward, Albert Maufer and Carroll Rackensperger, Marion Lesniewski and William Wenger, John R. Johnson and Carl T. Freitag, George Roessler and George Baker.

MIXED DOUBLES

Carolyn McGinn and Frank Stickline, A. Porter and Morrison Smith, Lillian Peterson and Forrest Dirchenbauer, William Hafey and Dorothy Prodoehl, Norman Almony and Levola Almony.

Service Gridders Get Equipment

NEW YORK, Dec. 2—(A. P.).—After all these years Fordham and Columbia will get together on a football field at Bermuda on January 2, when the uniforms of the two New York city universities will be worn by teams representing the U. S. Army and Navy units stationed on the island. The complete outfits were shipped by plane.

BASKETBALL SCORES

Indiana 40; Camp Atterbury, 28.
Notre Dame, 56; Alma, 32.
Hamline, 49; Carleton, 26.
George Williams, 50; Chicago, 27.
Newark, 35; Panzer, 29.
Norfolk Navy, 62; Camp Peary, 40.
Kansas 40; Herington Air Base, 27.
Monmouth, 38; Cornell (Iowa), 27.

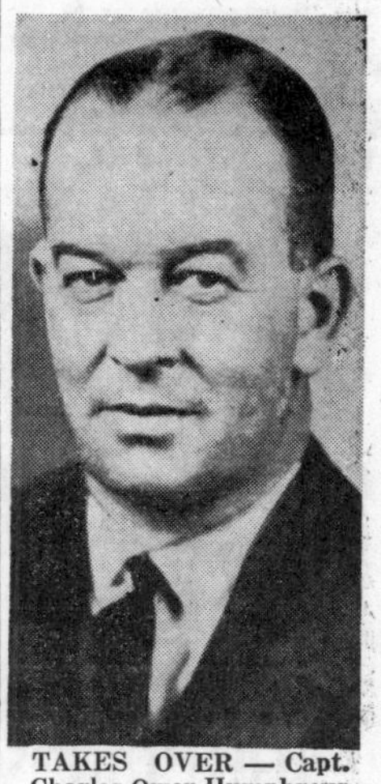

TAKES OVER — Capt. Charles Owen Humphreys (above) is the new director of athletics at the Naval Academy, according to an announcement by Rear Admiral J. R. Beardall, Academy superintendent. He will take over his duties in the near future, succeeding Capt. John Whelchel, who is going to sea. Associated Press Wirephoto.

Mate Of Harmon Describes Tom's Fall In China

By JERRY LISKA

ANN ARBOR, Mich., Dec. 2—(A. P.). — A flight of Jap Zeros roaring out of the sun knocked down Army Pilot Tommy Harmon and three flying mates "before they knew what hit them."

So began a story the rescued former Michigan All-America football player's parents heard from an officer in Harmon's squadron who seven days ago left China.

The officer, who declined to have his identity disclosed, said that long before it was announced officially this week that Harmon was rescued by Chinese after being missing in action since October 30, his safety was rumored through a "wonderful grapevine" existing among Chinese guerrillas.

FLEW IN 'GRIEF SPOT'

Louis Harmon, Tom's seventy-year-old father, said the officer, over long-distance telephone, gave this version of Harmon's disappearance.

Tom was flying in a squadron of eight Lightning fighters, four acting as low-level bombers and four as escorts, which raided Jap-held Kiukiang on October 30.

Harmon flew the "tail" position, described by the officer as the "grief spot," in a top cover of fighters at between 6,000 and 7,000 feet.

DOWN IN FLAMES

After successfully plastering the Jap base, the squadron headed for home, but five minutes away from the objective, a flight of Zeros zoomed down on the escort from behind, using the sun for cover. On their first run, they knocked four P-38s out of the formation. Harmon's plane went down in flames.

Other Lightnings drove off the Japs, bagging two, and then protected the parachute jump of a "husky" flyer, who, presumably was Harmon, circling until he reached ground.

This occurred several hundred miles behind Jap lines, but Chinese guerrillas found Harmon and hid him for 10 days while gradually working back towards advance American bases.

Falcons Rally To Stop Rovers

PHILADELPHIA, Dec. 2—(A. P.).—A third-period rally gained the Philadelphia Falcons a 4-2 Eastern Hockey League victory over the New York Rovers last night.

Goals by Stu Jud Cousins and Ted Garvin in the final session gave the Falcons a win after Roger Leger, sent down by the New York Rangers, had knotted the count at two-all early in the period.

2,100 PLANES RAID EUROPE IN NON-STOP DAYLIGHT ATTACK

THE WEATHER

Fair and colder tonight; lowest temperature around 32 degrees in the suburbs and 38 degrees in the city tomorrow; Sunday fair.
Detailed Weather Report Page 10

Read The Baltimore News-Post for complete, accurate war coverage. It is the only Baltimore newspaper possessing the three great wire services—
ASSOCIATED PRESS
INTERNATIONAL NEWS SERVICE
UNITED PRESS

THE BALTIMORE NEWS-POST
AN INDEPENDENT NEWSPAPER
The Largest Evening Circulation in the Entire South

9

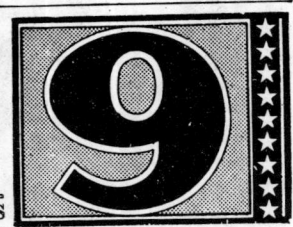

VOL. CXLIV.—NO. 72 Entered as second-class matter at Baltimore Postoffice. SATURDAY EVENING, JANUARY 29, 1944 PRICE 3 CENTS

SPEED-UP OF JAP WAR DEMANDED IN CONGRESS

MIAMI, Fla., Jan. 29—(U. P.).—Two Filipino prisoners at the Davao penal colony assisted in the escape of three American officers on whose sworn statements the account of Japanese prison camp atrocities was based, according to Philippines President Manuel Quezon. The American officers were the late Lieut. Col. William E. Dyess, Comdr. Melvyn H. McCoy and Lieut. Col. S. M. Mellnik. Whether the aides escaped, too, Quezon did not say. Quezon, who came here for his health, issued this statement:

"The escape of Col. Dyess, Col. Mellnik and Comdr. McCoy was made possible with the help of two Filipinos who had been sentenced to many years' imprisonment and were confined in the penal colony wherein these three officers were kept as prisoners of war. Upon learning of what they did I granted these prisoners absolute pardon."

2,100 Planes Raid Europe All Day

LONDON, Jan. 29—(A. P.).—German long-range transmitters at Berlin went off the air early tonight, suggesting new Allied air raids against the Reich and perhaps the third in a row against Berlin.

LONDON, Jan. 29—(U. P.).—Ppward of 1,600 Allied bombers struck two staggering blows at Germany today when well over 800 Fortresses and Liberators dropped probably more than 2,000 tons of explosive on Frankfurt after the Royal Air Force hammered home one of its most successful raids on Berlin.

Maj. Gen. James H. Doolittle's Eight Air Force hit Frankfurt, the "German Chicago," with the biggest fleet of four-motored bombers ever sent against a single target by daylight.

United States fighters in unannounced numbers shepherded the bombers, with probably 1,500 American planes in action against Frankfurt as the pre-invasion assault through the roof of "the Fortress Europe" climbed to an unprecedented peak of intensity.

NON-STOP OFFENSIVE

Hundreds of Allied Marauders, Spitfires, Typhoons and other planes carried the non-stop offensive through the day with an intense attack on the French coast, boosting to perhaps 2,100 the number of raiders over the Continent in a single day.

Heavy clouds over Europe kept the bulk of the German air force grounded and gave the American heavies an almost unmolested run over Frankfurt, where 30 per cent. of the German aircraft propellers and other plane parts are turned out.

Returning crewmen said only a few sections of the miles-long procession of bombers were attacked by German fighters, and the escorts soon drove them off.

Probably fewer than 200 Nazi planes rose to challenge the Americans, and they arrived too late to hinder the bombing.

FIND NEW DEFENSE

One group ran into "strange" anti-aircraft fire—waht looked

Continued on Page 2, Column 7.

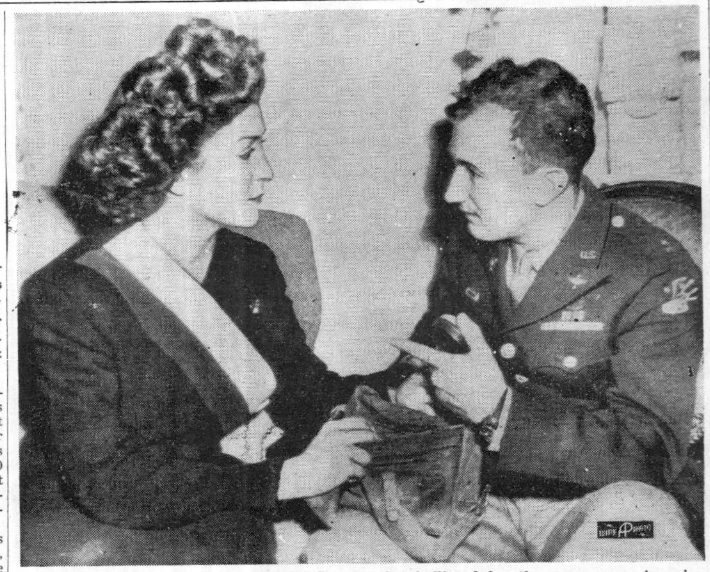

WIDOW HEARS OF ATROCITIES—Capt. Samuel Grashio of Spokane, Wash., who escaped from a Jap prison camp in the Philippines to report atrocities inflicted by the enemy on American and Filipino prisoners, is shown in Los Angeles as he described his experience to Mrs. Marajen Dyess, widow of Lieut. Col. William E. Dyess.

Himmler Reported Executed

NEW YORK, Jan. 29—(I. N. S.) Heinrich Himmler, chief of the Nazi Gestapo, possibly has been executed because of ambitions to replace Adolf Hitler, according to the Journal de Geneve, quoted today by N. B. C. Correspondent Paul Archinard in Bern, Switzerland.

Himmler has been replaced as Interior Minister by Martin Bormann, chief of Hitler's private chancellory, the Swiss paper says. Reports of his execution "agree with recent rumors that a brutal elimination of the Fuehrer was being planned," according to the Swiss paper.

Himmler's plot came to light through a series of German postage stamps bearing his picture, which the would-be dictator apparently had prepared for future use, the broadcast said.

West Coast Vows Revenge On Japs

SAN FRANCISCO, Jan. 29—(A. P.).—Vows of vengance and demands for retribution swept the war-conscious Pacific coast today as the reaction of horror to the stories of Japanese atrocities mounted to new heights.

So acute was the feeling in many localities on the West coast, home of more than 100,000 persons of Japanese ancestry prior to Pearl Harbor, that Lieut. Gen. Delos C. Emmons, commanding general of the Western Defense Command, cautioned against individual retaliation in this country. He said:

"It would do us more harm than good."

DEMAND U. S. RULE

Angry citizens gathered on street corners at Tule Lake, Cal., six miles from the segregation center housing 15,000 proven, potential or suspected disloyalists, and muttered renewed demands that the military again resume control over the center. The War Department recently relinquished control to the War Relocation Authority.

At the Manzanar center in Southern California, R. P. Merritt, project director, said the evacuees were "very much disturbed," while in the Arizona relocation centers guards were tightened and evacuees were forbidden to leave the grounds. In the Rivers (Arizona) center Japanese condemned the atrocities, saying "we have 200 men out in the Pacific and if they fall into Japanese hands they will be treated worse than the Americans."

CALLS JAPS "SAVAGES"

Representative Carl Hinshaw demanded that the Japanese be "wiped off the map" for such "brutal savagery."

In Salinas, Cal., home of 150 captured Bataan heroes, Mayor E. G. Ohomas declared that nothing less than "complete subjugation" of Japanese "savages" would erase the memories of such inhuman treatment.

5 CHILDREN DIE IN FIRE

CHICAGO, Jan. 29—(I. N. S.). Five children, ranging from two months to eleven years in age, died today when fire destroyed their frame home while the parents, Lawrence and Caroline Porter, were at work in a defense plant.

Spinach Can Be Popular! Adults and Youngsters Both Will Demand More of This Healthful Vegetable If It Is Prepared in Some of the Unusual and Appetizing Ways Suggested in The Housewife's Food Almanack, That Popular Feature in The American Weekly, the Magazine Distributed With Tomorrow's Baltimore American.—Adv.

HIALEAH RESULTS

FIRST RACE—Six and one-half furlongs. Off, 2.31½. Time, 1.20.

Air Supremacy, 118 (T. Atkinson)	$9.70	$4.20	$3.10
Vim, 110 (H. Pratt)		3.40	2.50
Cactus Foot, 115 (S. Young)			3.60
Total mutuels			$26.50

Also Ran—Dansation, Shined Up, Tidy Reward, Jamoke, Busy Nine, Swift Marine, Expose, High Clock, King of Castle.

SECOND—Purse, $1,600; allowances; 3-year-olds; 6½ furlongs. Off, 3.01½. Time, 1.20 3-5.

Rene B, 110 (C. McCreary)	$10.30	$5.90	$5.20
Double Feature, 115 (G. Moore)		79.70	24.90
Lawrinson, 115 (S. Young)			9.00
Total mutuels			$135.00

Also Ran—Hindu Prince, Roman Red, Clansman, Edemgee, Jean Buttons, Vain Pursuit, Hayai Tinty.

Daily Double—Air Supremacy and Rene B. paid $70.30

VERY LATEST NEWS

(Race Results From Howard Sports Daily, Inc.)

AT HIALEAH

Third — Sweepalot, $5.80, $4.20, $3.20; Belfry Chimes, $5.80, $4.10; Rest Awhile, $4.80. T. M., $27.90.

AT FAIR GROUNDS

First—Albino, $9.80, $5.20, $4.00; Stop Harping, $5.00, $4.40; Ebon Flag, $28.20.

ICKES DIRECTS SUNDAY ANTHRACITE MINING

WASHINGTON, Jan. 29.—(A. P.).—Secretary of the Interior Harold L. Ickes today directed managers to operate mines in the anthracite region on Sundays in February and asked workers to show up on the job.

ESCAPED YANKS AIDING ITALIAN UNDERGROUND

STOCKHOLM, Jan. 29.—(A. P.).—Numerous escaped American and British prisoners of war a[illegible] hiding in Rome and working with the Italian underground[illegible] a campaign of sabotage since Allied troops landed south [illegible] the Italian capital, it was reported today.

Planned Torture By Japs Is Shown

By JULIAN HARTT
International News Service Staff Correspondent.

LOS ANGELES, Jan. 29.—New and shocking details of Japan's unbridled reign of brutality in the Philippines were recounted today by another survivor of Bataan's hellish "march of death."

The grim story was unfolded by Capt. Samuel C. Grashio, Spokane (Wash.) Army flier who was reduced from 150 pounds to a living skeleton of 90 under Japan's program of calculated torture, yet survived the ordeal, escaped and finally made his way back to Allied territory, a year after the fall of Bataan.

An American soldier deliberately run over and crushed to death by a Japanese tank—

An American boy of nineteen, lying nude in filth as flies swarmed about his open sores, pleading pitifully that he be carried away to die:

"So the others won't see me like this."

OFFICERS BRUTALIZED

American officers, forced to stand at attention while Japanese enlisted men beat them unmercifully, and then forced to bow to their tormentors when the beating was over—

An American soldier bayoneted to death for the "offense" of having fallen exhausted in the road.

These are among the unspeakably barbaric incidents seen by Captain Grashio with his own eyes during his seven-day march, without food and with very little water, from fallen Bataan to the prison camp at San Fernando, 140 miles away.

These are among the tragic incidents he experienced later at Camp O'Donnell, where he said:

"They buried 1,100 Americans and 14,000 Filipinos in the two months I was there."

Captain Grashio shared the tortuous treatment with his commanding officer, the late Lieut. Col. William E. Dyess, upon whose account the joint Army-Navy report of Japanese atrocities was principally based.

He and Colonel Dyess, who died in the crash of his P-38 at Burbank, Cal., last December 22, were vainly seeking means of escape from the doomed peninsula on April 9, 1942, when they were trapped by two Japanese tanks on a Bataan roadway.

At a news conference Captain Grashio related:

"They gave us hell in Japanese and took our 45's.

"Jap planes were still dive-bombing and strafing Americans even though the white flags were up."

In the nightmare of marching under the tropical sun which followed, times and places became "a bloody haze," but through that haze Captain Grashio's mind was stamped with sights and sounds and shells which time never will erase.

"SPORT A LA JAPS

He recalled, grimly:

"We came upon Americans and Filipinos dead in the ditches, and definite evidence of their being killed after the surrender.

"You can't forget it. It's in my nostrils now."

At one point, Japanese soldiers in trucks passing in the opposite direction made grim sport by sud-

Continued on Page 2, Column 1.

Nazis Slay 13,000 In Polish Town

LONDON, Jan. 29—(A. P.).—More than 13,000 citizens of Sarny, a town in Old Poland recently recaptured by the Red Army, were slain by the Germans, the Moscow radio said today.

The broadcast, recorded by the Soviet monitor, said the atrocities included:

"Twenty-three men killed in a Gestapo torture chamber, two orthodox priests smothered with tar and burned to death on a bonfire, 1,000 youths driven away to slavery in Germany and 400 houses burned."

NEW QUAKES IN SAN JUAN

BUENOS AIRES, Jan. 29—(A. P.).—The city of San Juan which was virtually destroyed by an earthquake January 15 experienced four new temblors late yesterday but no additional damage was reported.

Speed Jap War, Congress Urges

By KINGSBURY SMITH
International News Service Staff Correspondent.

WASHINGTON, Jan. 29.—A mounting wave of turious indignation swept the nation today as a result of official revelation of the Japanese torture, starvation and murder of thousands of American war prisoners in the Philippines.

Throughout Congress there was a growing demand for intensification of the war in the Pacific. Several members of Congress, led by Senator Clark (Democrat) of Missouri, urged a new "Doolittle" raid on Tokyo and bomb it "out of existence."

Chairman Andrew May (Democrat) of Kentucky of the House Military Affairs Committee proposed that President Roosevelt proclaim a "Remember War Prisoners' Day" to give America's answer to Japan for the barbaric treatment accorded the American and Filipino soldiers captured on Bataan and Corregidor. He said:

"I strongly favor having the President set aside a day on which the American people can show their indignation for the fiendish treatment of our war prisoners by the Japanese.

WOULD SPEED PACIFIC WAR

"I would suggest on this 'Remember War Prisoners' Day' attention be devoted to the importance of intensifying our war effort in order to assure the complete and utter destruction of Japanese militarism.

"Management, labor and the farmers might co-operate in working two extra hours that day as their special answer to Japan for the mistreatment of our boys. The general public might be asked to dedicate a special contribution to the Fourth War Loan as America's warning to Japan that the day of retribution is surely coming."

Adding fuel to the nation's flaming hatred of the Japanese was the charge by Palmer Hoyt, former director of the OWI's domestic branch, the enemy actually had "brutally murdered most of the 50,000 prisoners taken at Bataan."

In their official statement, the War and Navy Departments said more than 5,200 American soldiers and thousands of Filipinos were wantonly murdered, tortured and starved to death.

Convinced further diplomatic protests to the Japanese Government through the Swiss would be futile, the State Department concentrated its attention on compiling all available evidence on Japanese war crimes and criminals so that swift punishment can be meted out when victory has been achieved over Japan.

DEMAND CRIMINALS

There were strong indications one of the main points of the armistice terms which eventually are imposed on Japan will be a demand that all military war criminals be handed over to the Allies for trial and punishment.

The revelation of Japanese mistreatment of war prisoners also strengthened the belief Japan must be completely and permanently disarmed after this war. The view prevails in official circles that Japan is a half-savage urchin in the family of nations, too immature in the ways of civilization to be trusted with the modern weapons of warfare.

Meanwhile, diplomatic representatives of the conquered countries of Europe joined in expressing their sympathy with the American people over the disclosures of Japanese brutality.

Nation Calls For New Jap Blows

By JOSEPH A. BORS
International News Service Staff Correspondent.

WASHINGTON, Jan. 29.—Pulverizing revenge blows against the entire Japanese nation undoubtedly were in the making today as the result of the revelation that enemy forces tortured and starved to death countless thousands of American and Filipino war prisoners.

The revelation by the Army and Navy that at least 5,200 and possibly many hundreds or thousands more Americans were starved to death or killed by Japs paved the way for a merciless bombing of the enemy homeland which spawned such brutality and horror and condoned it.

The coming new blows against the enemy in the Pacific assuredly will take on a new meaning for American fighting men in that war zone and for civilians in war plants turning out equipment for the Army, Navy, marines and air forces.

PLAN NO NEW STRATEGY

Military and naval experts warned that no immediate change in strategy may be expected in the near future due to the fact that plans already have been formulated for new offensive operations which may explode along the Pacific battlefront at any time.

The long-promised bombing of Tokyo and other Japanese cities may not be too long in coming, and any possible enemy cries of American brutality are expected to fall on deaf ears throughout the world.

KING'S PREDICTION

It must be remembered Admiral Ernest J. King, commander in chief of the U. S. fleet and chief of naval operations, recently predicted that Allied power would be shifted from the European to the Pacific war theatre even before the collapse of Germany.

Thus the disclosure of Jap atrocities in the Philippines caused a sharp shift of public interest from the European to the Pacific war,

Temperatures

Midnight, 61	8 A. M., 45
1 A. M., 59	9 A. M., 45
2 A. M., 55	10 A. M., 46
3 A. M., 53	11 A. M., 47
4 A. M., 50	12 Noon, 48
5 A. M., 48	1 P. M., 50
6 A. M., 47	2 P. M., 46
7 A. M., 46	3 P. M., 47

NEWS-POST

Amusements	5	Health	7
Bugs Baer	7	Haney, Dr. Lewis	7
Clark, Norman	5	Horoscope	4
Classified Ads	11-12-13	Movies	5
Comics	8	Parsons, Louella	5
Crossword	13	Radio	11
Dulaney	7	Robinson, Elsie	6
Durling	7	Society	5
Editorials	6	Sports	9-10
Financial	11	Women's Clubs	5

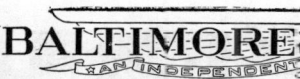

THE BALTIMORE NEWS-POST
AN INDEPENDENT NEWSPAPER
SATURDAY EVENING, JANUARY 29, 1944

$4,250 Penalty In Rent Case Refused

Judge Eugene O'Dunne, in the Baltimore City Court, today refused Elmer Gibbs a hundredfold penalty against his landlord, McKinley Gibbs, said not to be a relative.

Elmer Gibbs had sought $4,250 at the rate of $50 a week on the charge of a 50-cent-a-week rent violation over a period of 85 weeks for his apartment at 1703 East Chase street. Judge O'Dunne finally awarded him damages of $126, a counsel fee of $25 and court costs of $13.25.

COURT'S COMMENT

When told that Gibbs was entitled to the $50 maximum for each violation, under a Congressional ruling, Judge O'Dunne said that he could not construe the Congressional Rent Control Act as stripping the State courts of their rights to apply common sense in the administration of law.

In refusing to impose the $50 maximum for each penalty in this case, Judge O'Dunne said he was not taking into account any case of this nature which might come before him in the future.

'COMMON-SENSE' RULE

Judge O'Dunne said:

"This claim is out of proportion to all common sense, and it could result in an absolute racket by tenants who would court violations and let them run on until the limitation date was near an end and then seize the landlord's property."

Following the ruling by Judge O'Dunne, Acting Chief Rent Attorney Thomas E. Barrett told the court that the Gibbs claim was excessive from its inception because the Office of Price Administration regulation permits recovery for one year only before the date of filing suit.

Launches 13th Of Tanker Series

The 16,000-ton oil tanker Duquesne, last of a special series of 13 built for the Maritime Commission, was christened at the Bethlehem-Sparrows Point shipyard today by Miss Mabel T. Boardman, American Red Cross secretary since 1919.

Miss Boardman, associated with the Red Cross since 1900, was accompanied by Mrs. C. O. Port, wife of Admiral Pott, naval attache at the British Embassy in Washington.

Daily Fashion

TODAY'S PATTERN

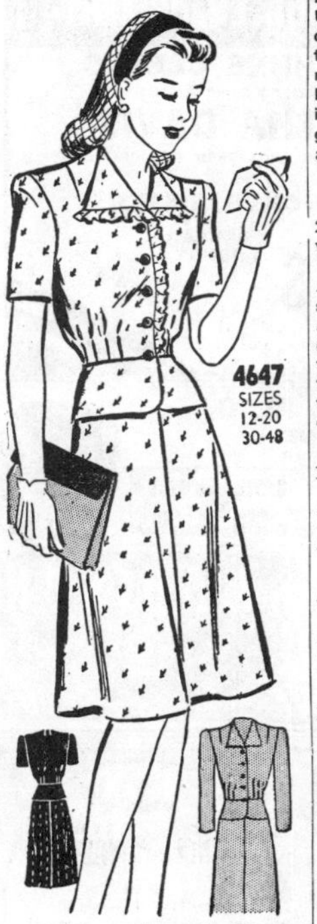
4647
SIZES
12-20
30-48
by Anne Adams

A trim, efficient two-piecer designed to flatter the mature woman's figure as well as that of the slim misses'. Pattern 4647 is equally chic and well-fitting in both size ranges . . . 12 to 20 and 30 to 48. Be sure to choose from the range that suits you.

Pattern 4647 is available in misses' sizes 12 to 20 and women's sizes 30 to 48. Size 36 requires 3½ yards 35-inch.

This pattern, together with a needlework pattern of useful and decorative motifs for linens and garments, TWENTY CENTS.

Send TWENTY CENTS in coins for these patterns to The Baltimore News-Post, Pattern Department, P. O. Box 141, Station 0, New York 11, N. Y.

TEN CENTS more brings our 1944 Anne Adams Spring Pattern Book. New, easy-to-make styles. Free Pattern printed in book.

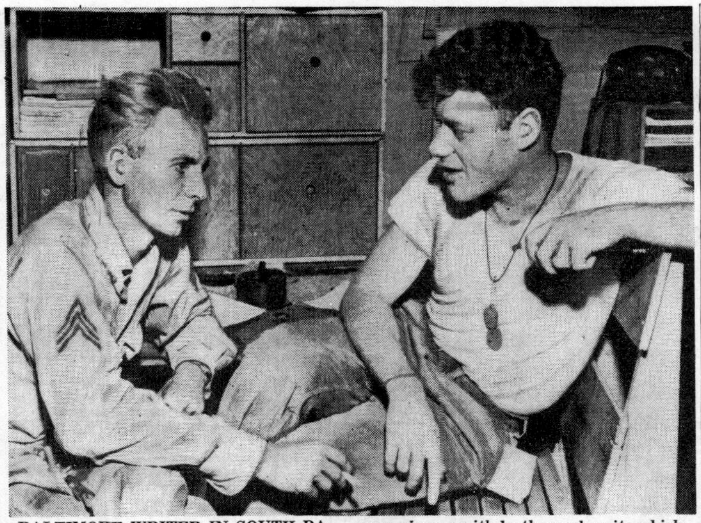

BALTIMORE WRITER IN SOUTH PACIFIC—Marine Corps combat correspondents Technical Sergt. Harold Azine of Baltimore (right) and Sergt. Roy A. Maypole of Summit, N. J., are shown relaxing at a base as they discuss their experiences with leatherneck units which landed at Empress Augusta bay, Bougainville. The Baltimore writer was among those who participated in the early fighting against Japanese defenders. International News Photo.

Horror At Jap Atrocities Voiced By Baltimoreans

"Savage," "cruel," "harsh," "atrocious."

These were the words Baltimoreans used to express their feelings over revelations of Jap treatment of American soldiers and Marines in the Philippines.

On the street in their home, everywhere, parents with sons in the armed forces, wives of fighting men, sisters, brothers, sweethearts shuddered in horror at the tales, torture, suffering and death at the hands of the Japanese.

Their comments were:

HAROLD B. MOTTERN, 3621 Park Heights avenue, store manager:

"There's no reason why we shouldn't retaliate with the Jap internees in this country instead of giving them so many privileges like playing golf and eating other Americans' food."

ANNETTA FREUND, 3401 East Baltimore street office worker:

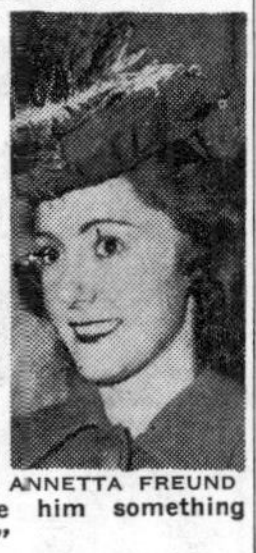
ANNETTA FREUND

"I'm in favor of giving the Japs back even more than they've given our boys. My fiance, Capt. Jack Cronin, is with the University of Maryland Hospital Unit and of course he can't tell me what's really going on but I think this is one time I'm going to write him something about the war."

TYPE OF ENEMY

MRS. ROBERT B. COLEBURN, 2011 West Baltimore street, housewife:

"The barbaric treatment of American prisoners by the Japs should make this country realize at last the kind of enemy we're dealing with. I don't think anything we could do to the Japs in this country could ever make up for what they've already done to our boys."

FRANK T. FOOS, 2801 Silver Hill avenue:

"We ought to give them back some of their own medicine. What I really think about the Japs isn't what you'd call printable."

PEARL GEARE, 4814 Reisterstown road, salesgirl:

"I'd like to beat the hell out of them—and I don't mind if they know it."

HENRY H. DUTROW, 4626 Park Heights avenue, war worker:

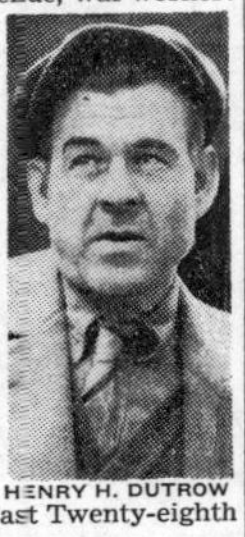
HENRY H. DUTROW

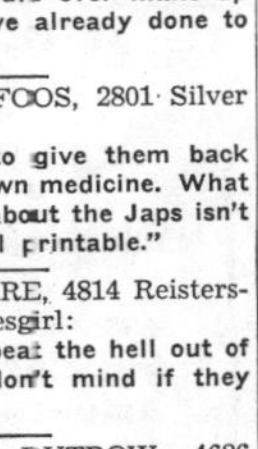

"The sooner we wipe the Japs out from the Emperor on down, the better off we will be. My son is in the Navy. So I really dread to think that he and other boys will be treated that way, if they are captured."

JOHN A. POWERS, 301 East Twenty-eighth street, clerk:

"Naturally, we all are incensed at reading the reports of Jap cruelty, but it will do us no good to treat the Japs likewise. We will be destroying what we are fighting for if we treat them that way."

WHAT WAR MEANS

ELEANOR BUDACZ, 2532 East Baltimore street, Government clerk:

"The reports of such cruel treatment of our men make us realize more fully what war means."

MRS. K. B. SPENCE, 1427 Linden avenue, clerk:

"My husband is fighting in the Pacific, and I think that anything we give the Japs in the way of harsh treatment will be no more than they deserve."

LORETTA LOVE, 404 East Preston street, Government typist:

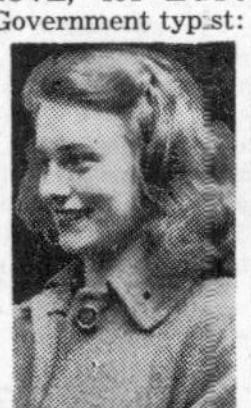
LORETTA LOVE

"Such reports of these atrocities make you feel that you should try to buy more war bonds."

SOL BLANK, 1675 Ruxton avenue, accountant:

"I think we should treat the Japs the same way that they have treated our men."

DORIS CLARK, 4205 Arizona avenue, student:

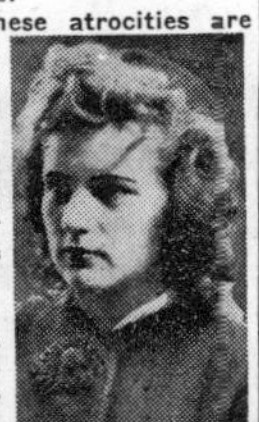
DORIS CLARK

"Although these atrocities are horrible to us, I do not think that we should treat them likewise. We would be destroying part of our democratic ideals."

WIFE OF A NAVAL OFFICER who made her home in Japan eight years, but who feared to disclose her name because of possible reprisal:

"Knowing the Japs as I do, this report does not surprise me. Their outlook is entirely different from ours. With them there is no such thing as honor or a gentleman's code. Naturally then, we will not be able to fight a clean, aboveboard type of war."

ANNE COHEN, 424 West Camden street, salesgirl:

"I have a brother in the service and a boy friend in North Africa, but I'd just like to meet one Jap that didn't know jiu jitsu. These Jap crimes should certainly be an incentive for everyone to put the Fourth War Loan over the top."

MRS. ISABELLE NIESSNER, 240 North Hilton street, elevator operator:

"We will get no place by being fair with the Japs. We should give them what they are giving us."

JOSEPH L. GRIGGS, 10 North Lakewood avenue, Draft Board No. 26:

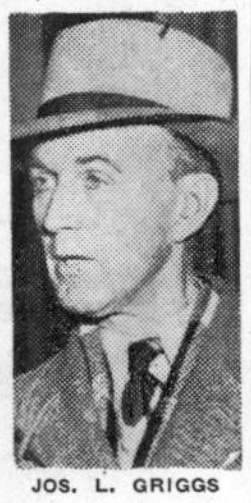
JOS. L. GRIGGS

"I helped to send boys over to fight the Japs. When I read of these atrocities, I felt that I signed death warrants for the boys from our draft board. We must fight fire with fire. Such treatment is the only thing that the Japs will understand."

JOHN M. HARTLINE, 2009 West Saratoga street, former printer:

"We ought to kill everyone we catch. The Japs expect us to treat the men we capture in the friendliest manner possible while they commit such atrocities as beheading our officers."

ALL OUGHT TO ENLIST

SUMNER SLOBODKIN, 3916 Garrison boulevard, assistant store manager:

"Everybody ought to enlist in this war effort instead of being dragged into it. The very least we can do to hit back at the Japs for the crimes they have committed against our boys is to put every penny in excess of our actual needs into War Bonds."

C. W. JENNISON, 741 North Fulton avenue, war worker:

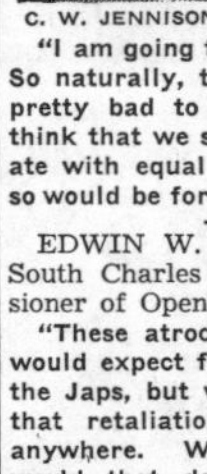
C. W. JENNISON

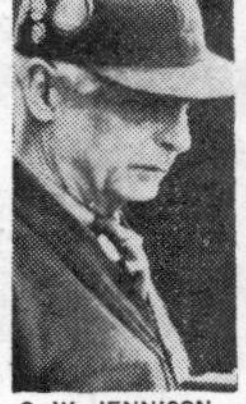

"We should not return such treatment with equally cruel action. We can't make savages out of Americans. The only way we can deal with the Japs is to overcome evil with good."

MORRIS POTLOCK, 2005 North Pulaski street, cab driver:

"I am going to be inducted soon. So naturally, these reports sound pretty bad to me, but I do not think that we should try to retaliate with equal treatment. To do so would be forsaking democracy."

EDWIN W. WINDLE, 1629 South Charles street, a Commissioner of Opening Streets:

"These atrocities are what you would expect from such people as the Japs, but we must remember that retaliation never gets you anywhere. We must show the world that democracy does not work that way."

WIN WAR QUICKLY

I. W. NEAL, 839 Power street, head porter at Emerson Hotel:

"The only thing for us to do is to try to win the war as quickly as possible. We should remember that such savages as the Japs know nothing of humane treatment. My boy is at Bougainville. So, naturally, such atrocities as those reported make all fathers such as I hate the Japs with all our hearts."

RATION DEADLINES

CANNED GOODS—
Green stamps G, H and J expire February 20.

MEAT, BUTTER, OILS—
Brown stamps R, S, T, and U valid through January 29. V expires February 26.

SUGAR—
Sugar stamp 30, in Book 4, valid through March 31 for five pounds.

GASOLINE—
Last day for use of No. 8 A gasoline ration stamp — February 8, 1944. License number and State must be written on face of all coupons in ink immediately upon receipt.

SHOES—
Shoe stamp 18, in Book 1, and Airplane stamp No. 1, in Book 3, valid indefinitely.

FUEL OIL—
Period 2 coupons expire February 7, 1944. Period 3 coupons expire March 13.

MOTHERS' UNIT INSTALLS

New officers were installed last night by Unit No. 2, Mothers of Men and Women in Service at the home of Mrs. Grace H. Betz, 5217 Eastern avenue. The unit is working for establishment of a recreation center in the eastern section of the city, according to Mrs. Margaret Hansen, State president.

Tax Assistance Bureau Opens Monday

For the benefit of perplexed taxpayers the Collector of Internal Revenue will establish a bureau of assistance, beginning Monday, at 8 South street, where citizens may obtain the free assistance of tax experts in the preparation of their income tax returns.

The purpose of the office, in view of the greatly increased number of new taxpayers occasioned by the lowering of exemptions, George Hofferbert, collector for the Maryland district, said, is to aid the public and expedite the filing of tax returns.

He gave notice also that cash, money orders, certified checks and, in connection with certain taxes, bank checks, will be accepted in payment of income and other tax returns and should be mailed to the Collector of Internal Revenue, Custom House, Baltimore.

Plan For New Recreation Centers

Another meeting of the youth club composed of teen-agers living in the vicinity of North and Patterson Park avenues will be held tonight in Sears Community Hall, North and Harford avenues, at 8 o'clock.

Further discussion concerning the location of the proposed recreation center will be one of the features of the program.

Youths of Southwest Baltimore, meeting in the branch library at Barre and Carroll streets, have chosen Donald Riesett as president; Lambert Neimur, secretary; George Nazerenus, Betty Taylor and Leah Robertson as co-chairmen.

This club will hold another meeting Thursday night in the library to further plans for locating a recreation center in the community.

Ticket sales for the President's Birthday Ball to be held from 9 o'clock tonight to 2 A. M. in the Fifth Regiment Armory have been "brisk," the committee for the ball reported today. The tickets are on sale at all department stores, Read Drug Stores and at the Mile-O-Dimes stand at Charles and Lexington streets.

Needle Craft

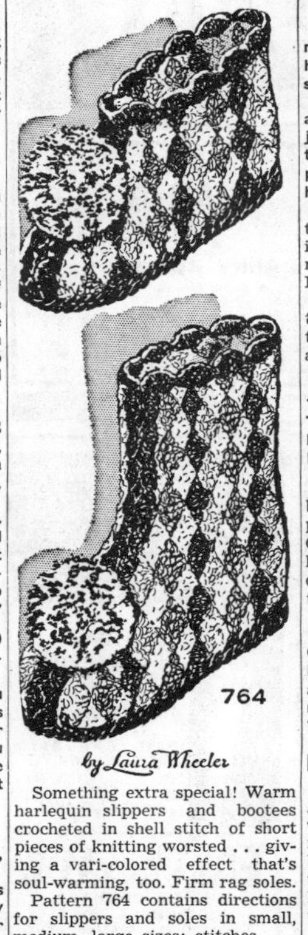

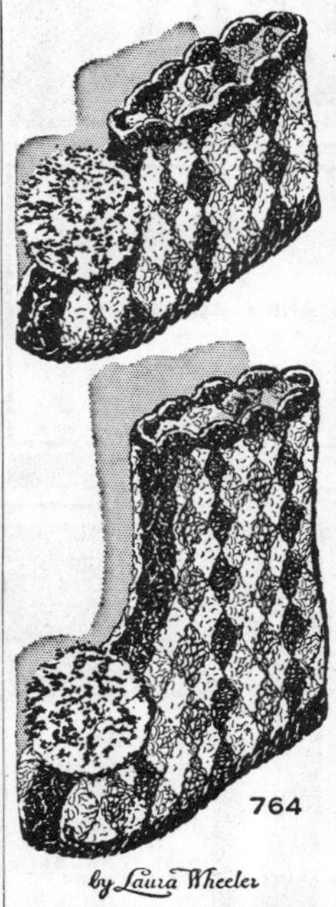
764
by Laura Wheeler

Something extra special! Warm harlequin slippers and bootees crocheted in shell stitch of short pieces of knitting worsted . . . giving a vari-colored effect that's soul-warming, too. Firm rag soles.

Pattern 764 contains directions for slippers and soles in small, medium, large sizes; stitches.

This pattern, together with a transfer pattern of tasteful embroidery motifs that you can use on many articles, FIFTEEN CENTS.

Send FIFTEEN CENTS in coins for these patterns to The Baltimore News-Post Needlecraft Dept., 82 Eighth Avenue, New York 11, N. Y. Write plainly PATTERN NUMBER, your NAME and ADDRESS.

Fifteen cents more brings you our New 32-page Needlecraft Catalog . . . 133 illustrations of designs for embroidery, knitting, crochet, quilts, home decoration, toys.

Jap Cruelty Brings Jump In Bond Sales

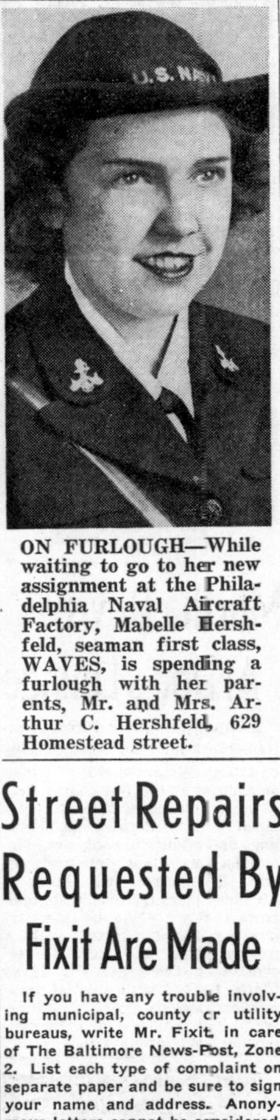

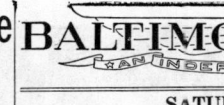

ON FURLOUGH—While waiting to go to her new assignment at the Philadelphia Naval Aircraft Factory, Mabelle Hershfeld, seaman first class, WAVES, is spending a furlough with her parents, Mr. and Mrs. Arthur C. Hershfeld, 629 Homestead street.

$5,000,000 Taken By Provident Savings Bank, Many Double Purchases

Public reaction to the news of Jap atrocities in the Philippines was indicated today in reports of yesterday's sales of war bonds in Baltimore.

Although figures for the day have not yet cleared through the Federal Reserve Bank, according to Walter N. Ruth, executive manager of the War Finance Committee, all indications at rallies and at banks and other issuing agencies were of "vast increases" in sales.

DOUBLE PURCHASES

At Stanley Theatre, where Mr. Ruth, former Mayor Jackson and James M. Hepbron, director of the War and Community Fund, conducted bond sales, bond buyers, according to Mr. Ruth, declared they were doubling, and in some cases tripling, their purchases because of the news.

Total sales there, he said, amounted to $70,000, of which $30,000 was for the purchase of bonds for admission and $40,000 represented sales from the floor.

Baltimore's Fourth War Loan was boosted by $5,000,000 late yesterday with the announcement by Frank W. Wrightson, president of the Provident Savings Bank of Baltimore and chairman of the Baltimore City Committee in the Fourth War Loan Campaign, that the figure represented his bank's initial subscription in this campaign.

TWO FIRMS GIVE $225,000

John H. Threadgill, Baltimore manager of the U. S. Lines, reported that the company has allocated $200,000 to Baltimore's quota. Howard W. Jackson, State chairman of the War Finance Committee, announced that the Milcor Steel Co. has purchased $25,000 in war bonds to be credited to Baltimore area.

Louis Miglioretti, war bond chairman of the Italian-American group, reports sales to date totaling $306,000, and Samuel Salit, chairman of the Hashimer Zionists, reports sales amounting to $200,000.

Anne Baxter, movie star, and Thomas Campbell, veteran of several Pacific campaigns against the Japs as a member of the United States Army and now a welder at the Bethlehem-Key Highway plant of the Bethlehem Shipbuilding Company, spoke at a lunch time bond rally at the Bethlehem-Fairfield Shipyard.

WEEKLY RALLIES

Campbell, who was mustered out of the service after being injured on New Guinea, told of his experiences in the Pacific war theatre. The rally is the first of a series which will be held each Saturday at the yard between 11.30 A. M. and noon. The Bethlehem-Fairfield 30-piece band furnished music.

Tonight Miss Baxter, who has been in Baltimore all week in the interest of the Fourth War Loan, will make a bond appeal at the President's birthday ball.

PLAN BOND PREMIERE

Chairman Jackson urges Baltimoreans to get their tickets for the third bond premiere, which will be "A Guy Named Joe," with Spencer Tracy and Irene Dunne. Admission is by a $25 to $100 bond and tickets may be had at all local theatres. The premiere will be on February 9 at 8.30 P. M. The U. S. Coast Guard Training Station Band will furnish music for the opening.

Father Held In Burning Of Daughter

Charged by the Family and Children's Society with placing the hands of his ten-year-old daughter, Helen, on a hot stove when he accused her of taking candy from his wares, William Huber, fifty-eight, a storekeeper, 1200 block Glyndon avenue, was under $500 bail today awaiting Grand Jury action.

The child appeared in Southwestern Police Court with bandaged hands when her father was given a hearing before Magistrate Edward Daugherty, but she was asked to give no other evidence than show her injuries.

George Harwood of the Family and Children's Society obtained a warrant for Huber's arrest. The welfare worker said he had been informed Huber burned his daughter's hands after accusing her of taking the candy from a room where he stored the confection for sale at a stand near the Curtis Bay Coast Guard Station.

The witness said the girl was treated at home by her mother, Mrs. Agnes Huber, who has had nursing training.

DR. WINSLOW RE-ELECTED

Dr. C. I. Winslow has been reelected president of the Citizens' League of Baltimore and James H. Richardson succeeded himself as secretary-treasurer, it was announced today.

Street Repairs Requested By Fixit Are Made

If you have any trouble involving municipal, county or utility bureaus, write Mr. Fixit in care of The Baltimore News-Post, Zone 2. List each type of complaint on separate paper and be sure to sign your name and address. Anonymous letters cannot be considered.

By MR. FIXIT

The street hole in front of the residence of Mrs. Francis Romero, 3100 block Pinewood avenue, was a regular house-wrecker.

Her home was already beginning to show the effects of the vibrations caused by vehicles passing over the rut.

Her letter stated:

"On Sefton avenue near the corner of Pinewood avenue there is a hole in the street which is on the side of my property.

"This hole has been there over a year, and I believe the thud and jolt cars and trucks make in going through it are responsible for the plaster cracking on this side of my house."

Wishing to correct this condition as soon as possible, Mr. Fixit immediately forwarded Mrs. Romero's complaint to the Bureau of Highways.

That department has written that repairs have been made to the street and the annoyance has abated.

MRS. MILDRED COOPER, 1100 block West Lanvale street: The street light in your block has been fixed, the Bureau of Street Lighting tells me.

JOHN E. DREWANZ, 2100 block Hawkins Point road: A report from the Bureau of Street Cleaning states that the materials have been removed and that Tuesday is collection day for garbage, trash and ashes in your area.

JULIUS MANDL, 2500 block Oswego avenue: Repairs have been made to the light in your alley, according to the City Illuminating Engineer, Walter C. Tome.

PLAN SHOW FOR ORPHANS

Theta Epsilon Chapter of Sigma Alpha Rho Fraternity of America will give an entertainment tomorrow for the children of St. Elizabeth's Orphanage. Motion pictures, a magician's show by William N. Smith, and refreshments will be on the program.

The Baltimore News-Post and Sunday American are offering weekly cash prizes for news tips and amateur photos. Best tip gets $25, the next best gets $10, and the next 15 get $1 each. For each amateur photo published $3 will be paid. Phone News-Tip Editor, Lexington 0100 (Lexington 4165 midnight to 6.30 A. M.). Rush news photos to Picture Editor.

Select a WAR JOB now!

A well-paid job is waiting for you at the Bethlehem-Sparrows Point shipyard. This yard, which has been operating for 55 years, is turning out vessels that are so urgently needed to smash the enemy.

No experience is necessary. Pick out a job, and you'll be paid while learning. Average wages at the yard are $75.95 a week. Beginners earn $44 to $50.

Help keep the ships moving down the ways to Victory!

☆ ☆ ☆

BETHLEHEM EMPLOYMENT OFFICES:
Howard and Lombard Streets
Weekdays, 7 A. M. to 10 P. M.
Sundays, 10 A. M. to 5 P. M.
and
3811 Eastern Avenue
Weekdays, 8.30 A. M. to 6 P. M.

☆ ☆ ☆

Bethlehem Steel Company
Sparrows Point Shipyard

"Be a Satisfied Tire Buyer—
Buy U. S. Tires from Kimmel"
C. E. Kimmel & Co.
Direct Factory Distributors
U. S. Tires
TUBES BATTERIES
Mt. Royal at Guilford. MU. 8444

Splendid Opening For
MAN WITH CAR
Full time employment as district manager for Home Delivery Department of newspaper. Good salary, plus liberal car allowance.
Apply Room 305
HEARST PRODUCTION BLDG.
Pratt and Commerce Sts.

KEITHS ROOF--DANCE
Sat. and Sun. BOB CRAIG & BAND
ADM., 50c, SOLDIERS, 40c (ADD TAX)
Theatre Ticket Does Not Admit to Dance

'37 Buick Club Coupe
A-1 Condition, $395
LANDAY'S EAST END AUTO SALES
6507 Philadelphia Rd. WOlfe 1074

DANCING TONIGHT
ALCAZAR
Joe Dowling's Music

Begins Monday
Read
GEORGE E. SOKOLSKY'S
Brilliant Column
"THESE DAYS"
A vigilant observer and keen analyst of public affairs, George E. Sokolsky will write his column, "These Days," six times a week for readers of The Baltimore News-Post. Sokolsky will not only bring you timely comment but add greatly to your store of necessary information.
Begins Monday
in the
NEWS-POST

NITE LIFE
By LOU and JUDD CALVERT

If we can use anything so final as the phrase "at last," then let us say at last this town's rockin' with good old fashioned humor again. The spot is the ace of clubs, Club Charles at Charles and Preston where a top comic buffoon, Alan Gale is nightly bringing the house down with laughter and applause. So for an hour and twenty minutes of gay excitement and laughter make it Club Charles with funster Alan Gale.

NOTHIN' TRIVIAL ... the sweet swing singing of Anne Brower, "queen of swing," heard currently in the gay new 21 Club revue ... a new sepia addition to Doc's lounge, the Three Cleffs, smooth melody hits ... smooth interludes by Enzio and Lonia, hold overs in the beautiful Blue Mirror ... new Algerian Room's smart interior and continuous entertainment bill a sterling drawing card ... a grand dance duo, Doyle and O'Donnell, one of Dutch Mill's many entertainment hits this week ... food entree or a la carte—but delicious—to be had anytime at Patapsco House ... Baltimore street's new playground the 408 Bar, has a fine entertainment star in Lou, her songs and piano ... that swell band of George Finister's and the Kay Gardner revue current Duke's bistro hits.

DIS 'N' DATA ... the fact that Hooper's 32nd and Greenmount avenue restaurant is now open all night should bring all you after dark fun lovers here for some of the most delicious foods about ... it's a fine trio nightly at the Crystal Bar for your dancing and listening enjoyment ... there's an awful lot of class in the voice of beautiful Margaret Phelan heard at the Beachcomber ... Club Madison has held over Jerry Niles, mimic ... lovely Evelyn Demer is singing over to Hotel Broadway currently ... Leo Bateman says that "you'll be sorry" was not originated on the Phil Baker program, he heard it in church the day he was married.

Pat of Pat's Bar who once was employed in a bank, quips, "He resigned 'cause there were bars all 'round but nothing to drink" ... those tasty sea food platters at the Govans Grill are truly a gourmet's delight ... Crystal Roller Rink is donating half of Sunday nights proceeds to the Infantile Paralysis Fund, which we think might be followed by quite a few spots ... for dancing and refined atmosphere make it Baltimore's most beautiful Strickler's lounge any night except Monday closed for the duration ... that's all 'cept ... BUY, BUY BONDS OR BYE, BYE FREEDOM!!!

Richards Closing At Beachcomber

"Little Red Book" fans who consistently enjoy a night of dancing and fun sparked by Danny Richards, tonight and tomorrow night have their last two opportunities to see him during his current engagement at the Beachcomber.

Richards will be replaced by Ted Blake, popular comic with a well stocked larder of gags and situations, on Tuesday when a new revue featuring the held-over Margaret Phelan will get under way.

Miss Phelan is enjoying splendid success in her current engagement and never fails to incite numerous encores.

Bill Stoos' Orchestra plays for shows and dancing, with interludes furnished by the well-received Aubrey Lee Trio.

Barney Long Is Kibby's Comic

One of Baltimore's favorite night life personalities of humor and such, Barney Long, current at Kibby's lucky number spot at 711 Poplar Grove street, held over by popular demand, is making quite a name for himself in laugh circles. Others that fill the entertainment bill here are Ruth Mason with her acrobatic sensations and Sheila Dawn, vivid dance characterizer. Of course your hosts, Sam Vinci and Frank Young, are always on tap to assure you and yours a "full house" in enjoyment. Jimmy Nichols' Orchestra for dancing.

New Show Bill Carl's Hit

3316 Keswick road sports the Neon sign, Carl's, and within its portals one can always find a galaxy of fun and entertainment at a most moderate prix fixe. Yes, it's one of Baltimore's neighborly spots that gives you fine music and equally as fine entertainment. This week's personalities include the master juggling on the comic side with Billy Dale, plus exotic Xandra in her dance portrayals and the song hit, Frances Doyle, colleen of melody. Dancing to George Decker's music.

JERRI KEEVER — Pert song attraction nightly Bandbox feature

THAREEN AUROAAA — El Patio's smart song addition

Jerri Blanchard — Broadway's sophisticated vocalark at Club Charles

EARL KAHN — Major domo of the Earle Club now in army

Larry LONDON — And his orchestra enjoyed at 21 Club

CORA WALSH — Intimate song and accordion in the Blue Room

BARRY SMALL — Fine vocal addition to Helms' lounge

LOIS BYRON — Staccato in taps in new Club Madison revue

Martha Davis At Doc's Lounge

Another hit musical revue extravaganza for rendezvous patrons on tap at celebrated Doc's Lounge on Charles street. For charm, personality and showmanship combined with modern tempos, stylings and a touch of boogie-woogie, Martha Davis is a stellar attraction. This sepia star builds a Steinway from the pedals up, then tears it down again in fine harmonious fashion mixed with a mellow voice. A bunch of newcomers to Doc's are the Three Cleffs, packed with musical madness and melody styles. The lovely Tucker Sisters, with their melody in song are a treat.

Alan Gale Riot at Club Charles

Alan Gale, by virtue of his current engagement at Club Charles, has definitely established himself as America's No. 1 soap-box orator. He is seen at the ace of clubs leading an all-around fine production with Jerri Blanchard, song stylist of note.

Patricia King contributes sparkling tap routines, Mildred and Maurice perform complex adagio numbers, the Club Charles debs round out the production with colorful precision routines.

Eddie Wald's Orchestra, plays for shows and dancing, which starts tonite at 8.30.

ARUNDEL BLUE ROOM

A new policy has been installed in the Blue Room of the Arundel Hotel at Charles and Mount Royal. That of closing Tuesday's for the duration, but still open as usual for your fun and enjoyment, Monday and the rest of the week. Current attractions are Milt Lyons orchestra and the accordion with Miss Cora Walsh.

New Song Star At Helms' Lounge

Helms' nautical lounge in suburban Brooklyn, just a few minutes from downtown Baltimore, currently boasts the singing talents of handsome Barry Small in their swagger musical entertainment bill. Along the lines of melody and dancing rhythms comes the well-balanced trio with Lois Butler and her violin for your listening and dancing pleasures.

laugh. His style suggests a composite of Bob Hope, Willie Howard and ... yes, Alan Gale.

Bandbox Spot For Frivolity

Charles street's Bandbox is the smart rendezvous bubbling with frivolity nightly. Those of you looking for musical entertainment include this swell spot on your sundogding adventures. For your melodic entertainment try a heaping portion of the Pete Frasier Trio of native Hawaiian music. Fine rhythms for smooth dancing. The modern vein is socko with Danny Teagarden's swing trio and lovely songstar Jeri Keever tops this surefire entertainment fest. Matinee cocktail from 4 to 7 every Saturday and Sunday afternoon.

SILVER DOLLAR

Hurry, hurry, hurry—get in to see the biggest show in town at those low prices—no cover, no minimum, no nuthin' but the finest of beverages, the bestest of entertainment features and all 'round good time for all. The place you've heard so much about, the Silver Dollar, full of colorful person-oddities. Two floor shows nightly and a Saturday and Sunday matinee.

21 Club Sports Big Hit Revue

Tonight's another all-star parade of entertainment stars at Club 21 for your enjoyment time. That comic cuss from Mars, Sunny Mars, in person tops this gay showbill with humor and antics that have labeled him the season's outstanding funnyboy. Sunny's pleasure in presenting the balance this four-star showbill is in the talents of fascinating Anne Brower, queen of swing. The torrid taps of sepia Sammy Campbell and the novelty act of Two Bobbies and Company round out a fine floor show. Larry London's orchestra and Sunday matinee time from 5 to 8.

WARREN'S NITE CLUB

The guy who's launched "a thousand quips," Leo Bateman, is the dynamic fun purveyor of Warren's brighterie these nights. Leo's knack for new material makes this spot one to continually return to for laughs. Others are Charlie Howard, Ann Carroll and Agnes Kasper. The Jack Decker gang dish out your dancing rhythms.

HOOPER'S restaurants
John A. Burke, mgr.

415 E. 32nd St. at Greenmount Ave. (Open All Night)

511 Goruach Ave.

3 W. Chesapeake Ave. TOWSON

"nite life's biggest showbill" starring **SUNNY MARS** this season's comic star Anne Brower Queen of Swing SAMMY CAMPBELL 2 Bobbies and Co. tops in taps

Larry London Orchestra with Al Speldock, drums — Sunday Matinee 5 to 8 — NO COVER

21 CLUB
21 W. BALTO. ST. Res. SAr. 5552

FOR YOUR ENJOYMENT—
THE THREE CLEFFS
Nationally Known Artists
MARTHA DAVIS
Her Songs and Piano Rhythms
Plus
THE TUCKER SISTERS

DOC'S COCKTAIL LOUNGE
Lexington 5785
Cocktail Session 4 to 7 Daily
1817 N. CHARLES ST.

JERRY NILES, M. C.
JEWELL PAIGE SEPIA SONG STAR
LOIS BYRON Tapstress
CARL NUBER and his Trio In Our Rathskeller
MARIE LOPEZ
IVAN FRANK at the Hammond Organ
RUTH GEHLERT'S All-Girl Orchestra
WOlfe 8677

MADISON
NITE CLUB RESTAURANT RATHSKELLER
Madison & Chester

LUCKY NUMBER NITE CLUB
711 POPLAR GROVE ST.
Two Shows Nightly

headlining **Sam VINCI** ★ **Frank YOUNG**
plus
Barney Long — comic hit
Ruth Mason — acrobatic
Sheila Dawn — dance hit
Jimmy Nichols Orch.

kibby's
2 SHOWS NITELY
MADISON 1098

AT EL PATIO
STAR-STUDDED SHOW
THAREEN AUROAAA
Featured Songstress of all the leading clubs and hotels on the Pacific Coast ★ starred over the Orpheum Circuit.
★ BEVERLY & MARJORIE Sister Song and Dance Act
★ DIAZ & VILLA ★ NIELDA RAMOS
Dance to Music By **OSCAR CALVET** And His Thrilling Orchestra

Reservations & Aratoga 2035
ST. PAUL AT MADISON
RHUMBA MATINEE Sunday 4 to 7 P. M. Learn FREE. Complete Floor Show

New! Tuesday! — Hold Over! Golden-Voiced
TED BLAKE, M. C. — **MARGARET PHELAN**
LAST 2 DAYS: DANNY RICHARDS
Plus a Vast Array of Other Important Stars!
BILL STOOS' ORCHESTRA — AUDREY LEE TRIO

the BEACHCOMBER
110 N. LIBERTY — PLAZA 5049 — 3 SHOWS TONITE—1st at 9 P. M.

DANNY TEAGARDEN MUSICAL THREESOME
PETE FRASIER ALL HAWAIIAN TRIO PLUS
JERRI KEEVER—Charming Song Star
COCKTAIL JAMBOREE SAT. & SUN.—MATINEE 4 to 7 P. M.

BAND BOX
1309 N. CHARLES ST. — VE. 6795

THE ACE COMIC
ALAN GALE
raising the roof nitely in a sizzling revue with
JERRI BLANCHARD Songstress Supreme
PATRICIA KING
MILDRED & MAURICE
CLUB CHARLES DEBS
ELAINE PFEIFFER ★ EDDIE WALD'S ORCH.
Sunday Matinee from 4 P. M.
Fun Tonite from 8.30

club charles
CHARLES & PRESTON ★ VERNON 8020-21

112-120 PATAPSCO AVE., BROOKLYN
presenting
BARRY SMALL song star
Lois Butler her violin and trio
Tex Lagrange Mgr.

HELMS
Nautical Cocktail Lounge
CU. 1007

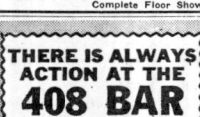

CARL'S nite club
the most congenial spot in town...
presents
BILLY DALE comic juggler
XANDRA exotic dancer
FRANCIS DOYLE lovely song star
music by geo. decker's orchestra
3316 KESWICK RD.

THERE IS ALWAYS ACTION AT THE 408 BAR
Presenting...
"LOU" Her Piano and Songs
PLUS... **DICK DASHIELL** and his debs...
CONTINUOUS ENTERTAINMENT
Extra Added—**"SUNDRA"** Exotic Starlet
408 E. BALTIMORE ST.

new revue!
Cody and Cody ★ Novelty
Doyle & O'Donnell ★ Dance Duo
Kay Crandall ★ Vocalark
and a host of others!

DUTCH MILL SUPPER CLUB
6615 HARFORD RD.

Enjoy the best with the rest!
HENRY LEE TRIO with Leo & Lena Fielding — Songs and Guitar
Requests and Community Singing played on our new Solovox.
★★★★★★★★★★★★
SIR WALTER SCOTTY Accordion Stylist

NEW ALGERIAN ROOM
Mt. Royal Ave. & Calvert St.
HAmilton 1570

THE NEW FUN-CONDITIONED
SILVER DOLLAR
2 FLOOR SHOWS NIGHTLY SAT. & SUNDAY MATINEE 4 TO 7 P. M.
NO COVER CHARGE MINIMUM CHARGE OVER CHARGE
Balto. St. at Howard

Calling all Fun Lovers!
EXCITING!!!
NO TRIP TO BALTO. IS COMPLETE WITHOUT A VISIT TO THIS WONDER CLUB ... YOU'LL SEE THE MOST UNUSUAL SHOW IN TOWN!!
2 Shows Nitely in the Gayest Spot in Town
SIGNED **MICKEY STRAUSS**

EARLE CLUB
SUNDAY COCKTAIL MATINEE 4 TO 7
WITH COMPLETE FLOOR SHOW
12 S. PATTERSON PARK AVE. — WOLFE 9223

enjoyment time plus smooth dancing
Carroll Kelly's orchestra
Closed Mondays
HAmilton 9744

STRICKLER'S
BALTIMORE'S SMARTEST LOUNGE
6800-10 HARFORD ROAD

Warren's
UP-TOWN Nite Club
CLOTHESLINE NITE EVERY WED. — PRIZES! LAUGHS!
presenting
LEO BATEMAN comic guy
Ann Carroll song bird
Charlie Howard taphappy
Jack Decker's Orchestra
Fulton near Pennsylvania
1st Show Tonite 10.30 — Res. MA. 9368

"WHERE IT'S SMART TO BE SEEN"
929 NORTH CHARLES
Blue MIRROR
NAT CONWAY and his FOURSOME
PLUS
ENZIO & LONIA Song Stars
MICKEY STRAUSS
PENNY MALONE
DANCING SAT. & SUN. 2–5, for details
COCKTAIL HOUR DAILY 4 to 7 — Closed Mondays

ENJOY THE music of **MILT LYONS** orchestra
plus musical interludes
with the charming lady of accordion and song
CORA WALSH
a perfect combination for an enjoyable evening...
ARUNDEL Blue Room
charles at mt. royal

DINING ★ DANCING ★ GAIETY

AIR PORT GRILL	6500 Riverview Ave., Dundalk. Music Fri., Sat. and Sun. Dine and Dance to Bill Yeager and His Yanks of Rhythm to "Abe" Shaeffer, Emcee. No cover... no minimum.	**LEON'S**	MERRY-GO-ROUND BAR—BALTIMORE'S NEWEST RESTAURANT—LOUNGE—BAR. 870 PARK AVENUE UNDER PERSONAL DIRECTION OF LEON LAMPE.
CRYSTAL BAR	AND COCKTAIL LOUNGE ★ 417 E. BALTO. ST., next door to Embassy Theatre. Featuring Four of Glamorous Bar Maids. The home of those folks. No cover or minimum charge.	**NATE & LEON'S**	DELICATESSEN. Stop in after the show for a Midnight Snack. Delicious Sandwiches. OPEN ALL NIGHT. 500 WEST NORTH AVENUE.
CRYSTAL ROLLER RINK	5400-11 Harford Rd. Open Every Evening, 8-11; Sunday Afternoons, 2-5, for children at Reduced Prices.	**NOLAN'S NITE CLUB**	Wilkens & Monroe. Mixed Drinks. The finest food. Charlie Moore's Orchestra. Dancing—9 P. M. till closing. Finest Whiskeys.
DE LUCA'S	62 WILLOW SPRING ROAD, DUNDALK FEATURING JACK WEBER'S ENTERTAINING TRIO	**PAT'S BAR**	116 N. Liberty St. "The Most Talked About Place in Baltimore." No more Night Club Atmosphere.
GOVANS GRILL	restaurant, lounge and bar serving the finest liquors and luncheons in a smart atmosphere 5744-46 York Rd. J. M. Adams, owner.	**SAM'S RAIL INN**	2630 W. NORTH AVE. HARVEY ROCKS ORCH. No cover. Moroccan atmosphere. Low Down Prices.
KATHLEEN'S	EAT, DRINK AND MAKE MERRY 2 BIG FLOOR SHOWS NITELY. NO COVER OR MINIMUM. 602 EAST BALTIMORE ST.	**SPORTSMAN**	MINIMUM ALWAYS A GREAT TIME! Continuous Entertainment and Dancing. SLIM STAPLETON'S Orch.
KEYSTONE NITE CLUB	Dance to our own lovely every Saturday, Sunday nite. Take No. 26 car, walk short distance to Keystone Sign. 2018 Holabird Ave. Lou Mellon's orchestra.	**SWEENEY'S**	3128 GREENMOUNT AVE. NEVER A COVER, NEVER A MINIMUM. COME 7 A. M. to 2 A. M. daily, 1429 E. CHARLES STREET. FINEST IN BEERS AND LIQUORS.

Served with Golden Brown Potatoes 'N A Jug Of Honey PLUS—HOT ROLLS

PATAPSCO HOUSE
Hammonds Ferry Rd. at Patapsco River
½ mi. Drive from West Blvd. and Eaton Ave.
Phone ARbutus 332 — Lansdowne, Md.

CLUB BAR
Marion Dawn — Joe Miller's Trio
SWEDE ANDERSON—IRVIN CLAS
FREDDY WEISSAL BOOGIE WOOGIE PIANO
McCLELLAN PLACE AT 2 BALTIMORE ST.
Half Block West of Lord Balto. Hotel

Jose Martinez
GAYETY NITE CLUB
COMPLETE NEW BROW EVERY WEEK ALL STAR ACTS

RAY MADDOX at **MAC'S WALNUT GROVE**
3612 HANOVER ST. Reservations, CURTIS 1424

Fun and Entertainment at
MAC'S WALNUT GROVE
3612 HANOVER ST. Reservations, CURTIS 1424

ANDY THUMSER JUGGLER — **HELEN NORRIS** & Orch.

DUKES
nite club ★ ★ ★
geo. finister's orchestra
Kay Gardney's revue!!!
continuous entertainment
two floor shows
3302-7 PHILADELPHIA RD.

CURLEY MILLER nightly at **MAC'S WALNUT GROVE**
3612 HANOVER ST. Reservations, CURTIS 1424

Hotel BROADWAY
Reservations, WOlfe 0602
BROADWAY AT ORLEANS

THE WEATHER
Fair with moderate temperature today; clear and cooler tonight; Thursday clear, cool in morning and warmer in afternoon.
Detailed Weather Report Page 25

Read The Baltimore News-Post for complete, accurate war coverage. It is the only Baltimore newspaper possessing the three great wire services—
ASSOCIATED PRESS
INTERNATIONAL NEWS SERVICE
UNITED PRESS

Baltimore News-Post
AN INDEPENDENT NEWSPAPER

The Largest Evening Circulation in the Entire South

VOL. CXLV.—NO. 29   Entered as second-class matter at Baltimore Postoffice.   **WEDNESDAY EVENING, JUNE 7, 1944**   PRICE **3** CENTS

ALLIES CRUSH FIERCE NAZI COUNTER-ATTACKS

SUPREME ADVANCE COMMAND POST, ALLIED EXPEDITIONARY FORCE, June 7 -- (A. P.).-- German armored counterthrusts have been thrown back near Caen and Allied forces are striking forward on a broad front, which heavy air-borne reinforcements have been thrown into heavy fighting, Allied Headquarters said tonight. At the same time German accounts told of new air-borne landings, not confirmed by headquarters. The Germans indicated a bold attempt to cut off the Cherbourg peninsula and seize the vital Transatlantic port might be in progress.

YANKS WADE ASHORE TO OPEN SECOND FRONT. American infantrymen wade ashore through the surf under cover of naval shellfire to make the first landings on the Normandy coast of France and open the Allied invasion of Fortress Europe. The ship from which the soldiers disembarked is at right, firing a gun. A shell hits the beach in front of them, bursting in a terrific ball of flame. This is the first picture of landing operations in France. U. S. Signal Corps Radiophoto.

With the enemy cleared from their landing beaches, many of which had been linked into a solid front, the Allies sent from 250 to 500 Flying Fortresses and Liberators — part of a day-long aerial parade—to bomb the road intersections south of Caen and block off German reinforcements rolling northward.

German radio announcements declared a new Allied sea-borne landing off Le Havre, where a hundred or more Allied warships had been previously reported, had been beaten back by coastal guns.

This report was not confirmed here, nor were other German reports that an entire Allied air division had been landed on the west coast of the Normandy peninsula and other air-borne forces dropped at Lessay and Coutance, 30 and 44 miles below Cherbourg.

(The British Information Service, in a cable from London, said air reconnaissance showed all railroad bridges between Paris and Rouen were down and that only two highway bridges remained. Only one railroad bridge and five highway bridges over the Seine between Paris and Le Havre were said to be intact.)

Reports from the Cherbourg peninsula invasion front showed "decided improvement" at midday, and the Allies are making "considerable progress on the whole front" despite bad weather and stiffening resistance, a headquarters officer said.

BOTH USE AIR-BORNE TROOPS
Both sides dropped air-borne troops into the flaming battle front, with Allied parachutists and glider troops pouring down early today from a 50-mile-long reinforcement sky train.

Caen is at the base of the Cherbourg peninsula and southwest of Le Havre.

Headquarters said front reports showed improvement by midday after being "disappointing" early this morning.

BEACHHEADS UNDER FIRE
Though the initial beachheads—which the Germans said extended over more than a 50-mile stretch—have been cleared and some linked with those near by, a few may still be under German artillery fire.

Air headquarters declared the Allied air forces in mammoth support of the invasion thrust had flown more than 31,000 sorties between June 1 and last night.

The huge numbers of air-borne Allied troops seized key positions and helped throw back Nazi tank-led counter-blows. The Germans likewise rushed in parachutists.

NEW YORK, June 7—(A. P.).—A German broadcast heard by N. B. C. said today Nazi forces had given up the town of Bayeux, six miles inland on the Cherbourg peninsula and 16 miles northwest of Caen, after a night battle with the Allies.

REPORT 12-MILE PENETRATION
Wholly unconfirmed reports said penetrations as deep as 12 miles had been made.

Headquarters said reports early this morning indicated

Continued on Page 2, Column 1.

---

2 SOLDIERS KILLED
FORT KNOX, Ky., June 7—(U. P.).—Two soldiers were killed and 11 injured yesterday by an explosion shell—a dud which had been picked up on the range by one of the men and brought to where a group of men were receiving instructions, officials announced today.

VERY LATEST NEWS
(Race Results From Howard Sports Daily, Inc.)

RACING RESULTS
AT CHARLES TOWN
Seventh—Bill K., $11.40, $7, $4.80; Marandan, $6.80, $3.80; Seven Seas, $3.40.
AT DELAWARE PARK
Third—Beneva, $94.70, $35.10, $16.70; Royal Display, $13.10, $9.50; Navy Nurse, $6.40.
Fourth—Gallant Witch, 1; Hadawin, 2; Jay Jay, 3rd.
AT AQUEDUCT
Seventh—Topsy Sue, won; Hutch, 2d; Gunflash, 3d.
AT HAWTHORNE
Fourth—Alfa, $8.00, $3.60, $3.40; Wise Admiral, $2.80, $2.40; Fox Rime, $8.40.

LATEST BASEBALL SCORES
(N) At At Brook.—Phila., 6; Brooklyn, 5; final.
(A) At Boston—Boston, 8; N. Y., 1; final.

U. S. PLANES HIT GUAM, OTHER TARGETS
PEARL HARBOR, June 7—(U. P.).—American warplanes bombed Guam, Nauru, Ponape and Mili in separate attacks over the vast Central Pacific front Sunday and Monday, Admiral Chester W. Nimitz announced today.

Allied Tanks Rout Nazis In Italy

ALLIED HEADQUARTERS, NAPLES, June 7—(U. P.).—Allied Fifth Army columns drove more than 10 miles north and 12 miles west of Rome today, beating down disorganized Nazi rear guards in their path, and Gen. Sir Harold R. L. G. Alexander confidently declared that the strength of the German armies in Central Italy has been broken.

British and American armored forces raced northward along Highway 2 toward Lake Bracciano, 15 miles above Rome, while infantry units swung out to the west over the Aurelian way to within sight of the Tyrrhenian sea, almost 15 miles north of the Tiber estuary.

REAR-GUARD BATTLES
Scattered German rear guards were battling to stem the advance with anti-tank guns and tank destroyers, but front reports said most of these troops were stragglers left behind by the fleeing Fourteenth Army and rounded up for a suicide stand by their officers.

Low-flying Allied attack planes bombed and machine gunned the retreating enemy and heavier bombers ranged on ahead to blast

Continued on Page 4, Column 3.

ORIOLE PARK LINE-UPS
Following are line-ups for tonight's games at Oriole Park at 6.30 P. M. between the Orioles and Rochester Red Wings.

ROCHESTER	ORIOLES
26 Hazen, rf	7 Monaco, 2b.
4 Burnett, ss.	24 Tiedemann, ss.
11 Sturdy, 1b.	23 Benjamin, lf.
4 Heid, 3b.	17 Moss, cf.
12 Rausch, 2b.	11 Roby, rf.
14 Astbury, cf.	4 Mackiewicz, 1b.
5 Overman, lf.	11 Skaff, 3b.
2 Malone, c.	8 Lollar, c.
..69 Wicker, p.	12 Van Slate, p.
10 Rice, c.	6 Devlin, c.
17 Mizerak, lf.	x Imhoff, c.
7 Davis, out.	16 Pfeifer, inf.
5 Emmerich, p.	29 Shaefer, outf.
6 Sumey, p.	13 Latshaw, 1b.
4 Kuipers, p.	12 Van Slate, p.
9 Roy, p.	15 Lowry, p.
24 Strohmeyer, p.	14 Rochevot, p.
7 Sakus, p.	18 Embree, p.
2 Gardner, p.	27 Burkart, p.
25 Byerly, p.	21 Hooks, p.
6 Hanrahan, p.	26 West, p.
29 Trotter, p.	20 Kieckky, p.
1 Penner, mgr.	22 Thomas, mgr.

Time of first game, 6.30 P. M.

Education By the Comic Strip. The Chicago Natural History Museum, Introducing Joe Elk, Turns to the Cartoonists to Increase our Knowledge of Our Prehistoric Ancestors. Read It In The American Weekly, the Magazine Distributed With Next Sunday's Baltimore American.—Adv.

DELAWARE PARK RESULTS
FIRST RACE—Five furlongs. Off at 3.31. Time, 1.00 3-5.
Service Ribbon, 117 (D. Dodson) $5.60 $4.00 $2.90
Miss War, 117 (W. Balzaretti) 11.50 7.80
Contrary Mary, 112 (K. Scawthorn) 3.70
Also Ran—Display Flight, Jono ra, Flying Past, Tacaro Identy, Picardy Rose, Ellsilver, Pre possessing, Relheub Kay, Constance V.

SECOND—Five furlongs. Off at 3.58. Time, 1.00 4-5.
Apropiado, 113 (W. Nall) $20.90 $11.30 $3.20
Agate, 113 (J. Breen) 7.70 3.00
Forward, 113 (D. Dodson) 2.30
Also Ran—Our Candidate and Dolly Varden.

Baltimorean First To Invade Europe
(Pictures on Page 22.)
By B. J. McQUAID
Representing the Combined United States Press.
(Distributed by International News Service.)

ABOARD COMBAT TRANSPORT U. S. S. BARNETT IN THE TRANSPORT AREA—(Delayed).—Lieut. Abe Condiotti, U. S. N. R., a twenty-three-year-old Spanish-Jewish American boy from Brooklyn, today commanded the first wave of small assault boats which set troops ashore in this section of Adolf Hitler's Europe.

Condiotti's own boat actually was the first to touch on the beaches of this assault area between Cherbourg and Le Havre. Condiotti's boat hit the beach within fewer than 60 seconds of H-Hour, so it may well have been the first ashore of the entire cross-channel invasion.

The boat carried members of an infantry company commanded by Capt. Leonard T. Schroeder, Jr., twenty-five, who comes from Baltimore, Md., and is of old German-American stock.

Just as Condiotti's was the first boat to hit the beach, Schroeder may have been the first American or even Allied soldier, to invade Europe. He and his men were

Continued on Page 2, Column 6.

Kimmel, Short Trials Delayed
WASHINGTON, June 7—(A. P.).—The House and Senate approved today a compromise bill which would extend for six months—until after the elections —the time in which Rear Admiral Husband E. Kimmel and Major Gen. Walter C. Short could be court martialed in connection with the Pearl Harbor disaster.

NEWS-POST
Amusements	16, 17	Haney, Dr. Lewis	23
Bugs Baer	25	Kilgallen, Dorothy	23
Classified Ads	29, 30, 31	Mallon, Paul	23
Clark, Norman	16	Movies	16, 17
Comics	14	Parsons, Louella	17
Crossword	31	Pippen, R. H.	25
Dixon, George	23	Radio	15
Dulaney	25	Robinson, Elsie	23
Editorials	26	Society	13
Financial	24	Sports	25, 27
Horoscope	2	Women's Clubs	13

Bulletin
WASHINGTON, June 7—(I. N. S.).—Maj. Gen. Henry J. F. Miller, commanding general of the Ninth Air Force Service Command was identified today by the War Department as the high-ranking officer who was demoted and sent home for indicating in advance the date of the invasion. Miller is a native of Salem county, New Jersey, and is a graduate of West Point.

He is alleged to have remarked at a social gathering in London that the European invasion would take place before June 15. He was reported to Gen. Dwight Eisenhower, who reprimanded him, demoted him to his permanent rank of lieutenant colonel and sent him back to the States.

In March, 1942, Miller was commanding general of the Air Service Command in Washington, and was assigned as commander of the Air Service Command of the A. A. F. in the European theatre of operations before assuming the Ninth Air Force post.

UPSET STOMACH

"Pepto-Bismol is good for that"

Never upset an upset stomach with overdoses of antacids or harsh physics. Be gentle with it. Take soothing PEPTO-BISMOL. Not a laxative. Not an antacid. It calms and soothes your upset stomach. Pleasant to the taste — children love it. Ask your druggist for PEPTO-BISMOL when your stomach is upset.

A NORWICH PRODUCT

Dr. E. J. LESLIE
Surgeon Dentist
HOURS: 9 A.M. TO 8 P.M.
SUNDAYS: 9 A.M. TO 1 P.M.
201 N. Liberty St.
Over Read's Drug Store
SAratoga 4173

Advertisement.

Tired Husbands! Rundown Wives!
Want New Pep, Vim, Energy?

Thousands of men and women, weak, rundown, peppy-less because blood needs iron, positively amazed at results of Ostrex. Supplies thorapeutic doses of iron for pep, vitality; prophylactic doses of vitamin B1 (TWICE minimum daily adult requirement) to protect against deficiency lack of vital, plus calcium, phosphorus. Try this famous tonic for listless, exhausted, iron-poor condition that makes you feel weak, tired-out, older than your years. No introductory size now only 35c. Get Ostrex Tonic Tablets today.
AT READ'S DRUG STORES

---

100 Years Of YMCA Being Celebrated

To celebrate the one-hundredth anniversary of the founding of the Young Men's Christian Association, on June 6, 1844, service clubs, churches and local organizations of the "Y" are sponsoring special programs throughout this week.

Special services in more than 60 Baltimore churches began last Sunday to commemorate the founding of the organization which now has more than 10,000 "Y's" throughout the world. Services will continue this Sunday in many of the churches.

Civic organizations in the city also are recognizing the anniversary of the association. The Rotary Club of Baltimore yesterday dedicated its weekly meeting to the "Y's" anniversary. At the meeting, Carlton Harrison, general secretary of the Baltimore Y. M. C. A., discussed "Y" activities.

At a dinner meeting last night at "Y" headquarters, more than 100 members and friends of the organization were addressed by Charles D. Hurrey, Y. M. C. A. secretary, who has served in China, the Near East and Europe. Stewart Cort, Baltimore president of the "Y," also spoke. Hamilton Davis, chairman of the Metropolitan Community Branch of Y. M. C. A., presided.

DIARY OF A MARYLAND HORSEWOMAN
By Elizabeth Ober

Haying time is here! A new way to cure hay so it will be green, leafy and contain more carotene, the source of vitamin A, has caught the attention of horsemen. It is cured largely in the barn independently of the weather.

Curing hay in the barn is not particularly new, but the method I am going to describe is new, as it requires a device installed in the hay loft which is different and not nearly as expensive as the ones formerly used.

The device I have seen and which I understand is similar to the one which has been completely tested in Virginia, looks something like the backbone of a fish after the cat has finished with it.

CHIEF AIR DUCT

It consists of a principal air duct which is 21 inches high and six feet wide at the large end, running down the center of a hay loft 44 by 39 foot.

From each side of this air duct run smaller ducts, 8½ inches high and 10 inches wide, extending out to within five feet of the walls, and they are closed at the end. They are built five feet apart.

These ducts are closed on the top and both sides but the bottom is open and they are mounted on little crosswise boards an inch high, so there is an inch opening along the floor.

MOTOR OPERATES FAN

At the large end of the main duct a fan is mounted, operated by an electric motor. The air is drawn up through a hole in the floor and forced out through the secondary ducts by the fan.

It has been found you need ten cubic feet of air per minute for each square foot of floor space, so your fan and power of your motor depend on the size of the loft. Motors, of course, are almost impossible to buy now, but many farms already have motors which are used for other purposes.

BECKER'S PRETZELS
BAKED FROM BETTER BATTER
THE PRETZEL WITH THE REAL TASTE TWIST

Reisinger Siehler Co.
FURNITURE
612-14-16 WASHINGTON BLVD.   Near Greene St.
Phone LE. 9578   Open Late Friday and Saturday Nights

5-Pc. MAPLE BEDROOM OUTFIT — $95
Complete outfit in attractive maple pieces consisting of double bed, dresser and mirror, chest, comfortable tufted mattress and coil springs. See it — a real value!
Terms If Desired

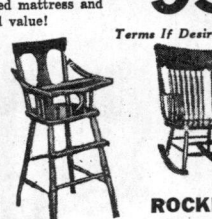

3x5 FLAG SET Complete **$1.59**
Sewed stripe. Fast colors. 2-section pole complete with bracket.

High Chair $4.75
Maple finish. Very sturdy. Nicely designed.

ROCKER $7.95
Walnut finish. Sturdy and very comfortable saddle seat.

CLEAN-RITE VACUUM STORES
Vacuum Cleaner Specialists! We Sell Nothing Else!
16 N. Howard Street
OPEN DAILY 9 A. M. TO 6 P. M.
THURSDAY 9 A. M. TO 9 P. M.
FREE PARKING—Palace Garage

FAMOUS—REBUILT EUREKA
$11.95 FULL CASH PRICE

Owing to conditions beyond our control these cleaners are sold only with a trade-in.

Backed by our GUARANTEE BOND for the same length of time as a new machine—one full year!

Liberal Allowance for Your Old Cleaner

IF YOU CANNOT COME IN PHONE PLAZA 0688-89 OR WRITE FOR FREE HOME DEMONSTRATION.

Advertisement.

The Voice gives the eye to eye-catching Jane Wyman. "Name and hobby?" asks Sinatra. "Wyman," replies Jane. "Well, men are a nice hobby, but what's your *name*?" gags our Frank. Learn on Frank Sinatra's own radio show tonight how Jane Wyman jumped from stage and radio to become a Warner Brothers' star. You'll hear Frank's inimitable singing, Jerry Lester's inimitable heckling, and Axel Stordahl's inimitable music ... all brought to you by Vimms, the best-known name in vitamins. Tune in tonight. WCAO 9 P.M.

De Luxe Saddlery Co.

FIRE SALE

Still a good selection in:

- SUITS
- COATS
- DRESSES
- SWEATERS
- BLOUSES
- SKIRTS
- JACKETS
- HANDBAGS
- LUGGAGE
- LEATHER GOODS
- COSTUME JEWELRY
- SHORTS
- SLACKS
- PLAY CLOTHES
- RIDING APPAREL

Special Items
MEN'S SPORT SHIRTS
CAMP TRUNKS

Sorry—All sales final. No charges
No alterations. No C. O. D's
No telephone orders. No deliveries.

STORE HOURS: Thursday—12 noon to 9 P. M.
Daily 10.30 A. M. to 5.30 P. M.

De Luxe Saddlery Co.
336 North Charles Street

Borden's ICE CREAM
If it's Borden's—it's GOT to be good!

All Ways—Always

Borden's Ice Cream deserves all the nice things said about it. It's an excellent food—delicious as can be. For home serving, it's Borden's Golden Crest Ice Cream in the handy pint pail.

Borden's ICE CREAM
First of All—Buy War Bonds

Julius GUTMAN & Co.
LEXINGTON AND PARK

FASHION FIRSTS IN OUR DOWNSTAIRS THRIFT DEPARTMENT

SUIT DRESSES
5.98

Put your money on these fashion favorites—Bemberg sheers, smart cottons, rayon seersuckers, jersey gabardines in 2-piece tailored styles! At this low price your budget will probably allow more than one. They're cool, comfortable and charming!

Sizes 9 to 17, 12 to 20

Also women's dresses in sheer bemberg and spun rayon. Sizes 38 to 44, 46 to 52.

Gutman's Thrift Dresses, Downstairs.

Applause for These Non Rationed
Saddle Oxfords
2.99

Brown and white with good wearing soles. Your ten little toes will thank you for the comfort. You'll adore wearing them! Sizes 4 to 9.

Other Ration-Free Casuals
2.99, 3.99, 4.99

Mail and Phone Orders—Call Mulberry 6400

Gutman's Shoes, Second Floor.

Clothes Harmony for Dad's Summer!

Sport Shirts
1.39

Comfortably cut with 2-way collar, short sleeves and 2 pockets. Green, tan, blue and white. Well tailored! Sizes small, medium and large.

Men's Pajamas 1.94
Broadcloth pajamas in fancy patterns. Popular middy style. Sizes A, B, C and D.

Men's Straw Hats 1.49
Great variety of straws in light, medium and dark shades. Snap brims, leather sweat bands. Sizes 6⅝ to 7½.

Gutman's Men's Furnishings, Street Floor.

THE CASH STORE OPEN 'TIL 9 THURSDAY

Thursday 'til 9 P. M.
REGAL SHOP
613 W. BALTIMORE STREET

For Smart Summer Wear!
PINAFORES
SHORT ALLS
SLACKS
$2.88
At The Regal Shop

Choose your play clothes from this grand selection. Pinafores are dotted with embroidered trim, sailor styles are in navy blue with nautical design, short Alls are in maize, kelly, powder, navy and white.

REGAL SHOP
613 W. Baltimore St.

You'll See Yourself At Your Loveliest In This
"SWEET HEART"
A Dress With Excitement In Every Detail!
$5.99
THURSDAY 'Til 9 P. M.
At The Regal Shop

- Smartly styled ... low waisted.
- Checked skirt and collar with plain bodice and sleeves.
- Applique on collar ... button down the front.
- Sizes 9 to 17.

"Sweet Heart" Dress, $5.99

The Kind of A Dress You'll Feel Your Best In
"STARLET CLASSIC"
$2.99
At The Regal Shop

The very practical two-piecer ... checked skirt and plain jacket with checked trim on flap pockets and front.
Large buttons down the front.
Choice of summer shades.

EVENING GOWNS
Graduation Dresses
7.99
Choose from this fine selection of glamorous gowns and graduation dresses.

Starlet Classic $2.99

Joyce Reynolds Wins Title Role

By LOUELLA O. PARSONS
Motion Picture Editor International News Service

HOLLYWOOD, June 7.—Well, all the guessing is over about "Junior Miss." The winner is not Shirley Temple, as often rumored, but little Joyce Reynolds, who blossoms like a flower in "Janie." Honestly, this Reynolds girl is a honey. She is a younger Teresa Wright with a freshness and verve all her own and when the younger generation get a look at her as "Janie," I agree with Jack Warner that she will be the next big league star.

Warners paid the record price of $425,000 for "Junior Miss," which gives an even better idea of what her studio thinks of Joyce. She is also the choice of Sally Benson, the author, who saw a rough cut of "Janie" and was captivated by the little star.

Marc Connolly has an interesting and different writing assignment. He is taking a sentiment on a birthday card, written by Richard Stern, and converting it into a script for Gary Cooper. Marc won't talk about it because he doesn't know how it will work out. If he gets the story written the way he wants it, it will be Gary Cooper's first independent picture for International Pictures and my guess is that that is probably well on the way.

I hear that M-G-M wants very much to buy Marion Hargrove's sequel to "See Here Private Hargrove," but the young author is asking $200,000, which Boss Louis B. Mayer said was too much for an original story. Maybe a compromise can be effected since "See Here Private Hargrove," with Robert Walker, has been one of M-G-M.'s most successful movies and certainly one of the best war comedies of the year.

Snapshots of Hollywood collected at random: The Richard Englishes are happy in the expectation of a visit from the stork in October. Papa is the well known writer; Jeanette MacDonald and Gene Raymond will be married seven years June 17 and, of course, that calls for a celebration; Alice Faye, looking unusually well, came in town with Phil Harris on Saturday, her first visit from her ranch since the new baby arrived.

Pola Negri is visiting friends in Santa Barbara but will go East when her lawyer calls her; Mary Hay Barthelmess, Dick's actress daughter, has written a song titled "So Long"; Major Clark Gable will take a month rest or longer before he even talks pictures at the studio; Nancy Kelly and her former husband, Sergt. Edward O'Brien, here with the "Winged Victory" company, have been doing the town.

Martha Raye turned down a $10,000 offer from Bob Burns to go on the radio for four shows because of the stork's arrival; Steve Crane, who has admired Betty Hutton from afar, finally met her and bought her luncheon; Fred Allen gets here July 6 to start his picture; Sonny Tufts has bought the Billy Wilder house, chickens and all.

Amusing idea—Don O'Connor gave his bride a diamond ring for her graduation; Martha Kemp and Al Bloomingdale danced the evening away at the Mocambo; Gloria de Haven, who sang with Jan Savitt's band a year ago in New Orleans, will be Jan's guest when his band opens here tonight; Eddie Norris has received his medical discharge from the Army; Al Rockett proudly tossed a party in honor of his son, Chief Petty Officer Norman Rockett, one of the heroes at Pearl Harbor. That's all today. See you tomorrow!

Jeanette MacDonald, above, will have been married to Gene Raymond seven years on June 17, which, Louella Parsons says, calls for a celebration.

'Make Your Own Bed' At Stanley

Jack Carson, Jane Wyman and Irene Manning are stars of the farce, "Make Your Own Bed," coming to the Stanley Saturday.

The supporting cast includes George Tobias, Alan Hale, Robert Shayne, Tala Birell, Ricardo Cortez, Marjorie Hoshelle and Kurt Katch.

ONCE SCHOOL

Selena Royal, who plays Greer Garson's Swedish housekeeper and confidante in "Mrs. Parkington," has a home in Bucks County, Pa., which was converted from a one-room schoolhouse.

NIGHT SCHOOL

Since her motion picture career keeps her busy during the daytime, Marilyn Maxwell, who enacts the feminine lead in "Lost in a Harem," has been attending night school the past year, studying psychology, French and sculpturing.

Advertisement:

STUBBORN CASE OF CONSTIPATION GONE

"No more salts, oils, every day," writes ex-sufferer.

Want to stop dosing—and yet keep regular? Then read this unsolicited letter from Mr. Lowe.

"I am 71 years old. Today I'm in the best of health. But, for 15 years I had a stubborn case of constipation—had to rely on salts or castor oil every day. Got so weak I could hardly walk. Five months ago I read one of your ads and my wife advised me to try your ALL-BRAN. After first week my passage was normal. For 5 months I have been eating KELLOGG'S ALL-BRAN regularly and haven't taken a laxative. Thanks for ALL-BRAN'S grand relief." Frank Lowe, 4505 S. W. 9th St. Des Moines, Iowa.

You'll be interested in knowing exactly how KELLOGG'S ALL-BRAN helps so many people—how this wholesome cereal *gets at* a common cause of constipation—lack of certain dietary cellulosic elements. You see ALL-BRAN is one of Nature's most effective sources of these elements—which help the friendly colonic flora to fluff up and prepare wastes for easy elimination. KELLOGG'S ALL-BRAN is not a purgative, it is a "regulating" food.

If your constipation is this kind, eat KELLOGG'S ALL-BRAN regularly—and drink plenty of water. See if it doesn't help. Insist on *genuine* KELLOGG'S ALL-BRAN, made *only* by Kellogg's in Battle Creek.

When kids are bad, Mothers scold— But when they're good, Ah-h! Meadow Gold!

Meadow Gold ICE CREAM

IN HOME... OR AT THE FOUNTAIN

Cheer your friend in the service—and him

Your Photograph

Have it taken now in our Photo Studio!

- Large 8x10-inch size
- No appointment necessary
- Satisfaction guaranteed

49c

Gutman's Photo Studio, Second Floor.

Julius Gutman & Co.
Lexington Street and Park Avenue

KERR'S KELL-A-KOUGH
(for coughs due to colds)
MONEY-BACK GUARANTEE **35c**
A few swear AT it for its bad taste; many swear BY it for its goodness. So, "It's bad, but it's good."
MYRTLE AVE. AND GEORGE ST.

HESS
312 N. Howard St.

OPEN THURSDAY, 10 A. M. TO 9 P. M.

WHITE SPECTATORS

5.95

HESS THRIFTY ... All white doeskin—the freshest, coolest accent you will find for your summer costumes. A classic spectator that is right with everything from cottons to dressy sheers.

THRIFTY SHOP

Ring up the Curtain... ON THE CAVALCADE OF SHOWS AND SHOW-FOLKS!

Singing, clowning, dancing, romancing... MAKING Broadway... from Burlesque to the Big Time!

SHOW BUSINESS

starring
EDDIE CANTOR
GEORGE MURPHY
JOAN DAVIS
NANCY KELLY
CONSTANCE MOORE
with Don Douglas

Directed by Edwin L. Marin

Produced by **Eddie Cantor**

Another of the great RKO RADIO

Screen play by Joseph Quillan & Dorothy Bennett

SONGS YOU CAN'T FORGET!
"It Had to Be You,"
"Whoopee," "I Don't Want to Get Well," "Dinah,"
"I Want a Girl," "Alabamy Bound," "They're Wearing 'Em Higher in Hawaii" and that new hit! "You May Not Remember"

N. Y. CRITICS Acclaim This Picture!
"a success"	N. Y. MIRROR
"lively, amusing"	N. Y. NEWS
"bound to click"	HER.-TRIBUNE
"a swell show"	JOUR. AMER.

Starts TOMORROW THE Cool **HIPPODROME** and BIG STAGE SHOW
EUTAW Near BALTO. ST.

M-G-M'S BIG BEAUTIFUL ROMANTIC MUSICAL!

IT'S SHIP-SHAPELY!

Joy ahoy! "See the world" of entertainment in this mighty musical launched for your delight!

TWO GIRLS AND A SAILOR

VAN JOHNSON
JUNE ALLYSON — **GLORIA DeHAVEN**
JOSE ITURBI
JIMMY DURANTE
GRACIE ALLEN — **LENA HORNE**
HARRY JAMES — **XAVIER CUGAT**
AND HIS MUSIC MAKERS WITH HELEN FORREST AND HIS ORCHESTRA WITH LINA ROMAY

Hear these song-hits "Take It Easy" • "In A Moment Of Madness" • "A Love Like Ours" • "Young Man With A Horn" • "My Mother Told Me"

★ TOM DRAKE ★ HENRY STEPHENSON ★ HENRY O'NEILL
★ BEN BLUE ★ CARLOS RAMIREZ ★ FRANK SULLY
★ ALBERT COATES ★ DONALD MEEK ★ AMPARO NOVARRO
★ VIRGINIA O'BRIEN ★ WILDE TWINS

Original Screen Play by Richard Connell and Gladys Lehman
A METRO-GOLDWYN-MAYER PICTURE
Directed by Richard Thorpe — Produced by JOE PASTERNAK

★ **STARTS MIDNIGHT TONIGHT** ★

COOL **LOEW'S CENTURY**
18 WEST LEXINGTON STREET

CONTINUOUS ALL NITE SHOW TONIGHT ONLY

Baltimore Day By Day
GWYNN'S FALLS PARK, ONCE GEM; NOW EYESORE
By CARROLL DULANEY

From Sherman Lee Pruitt, 3123 Belmont avenue, comes an appeal for Gwynn's Falls Park—the latest of several received by me recently.

A visit to the park shows that the complaints are justified. The once beautiful park, where countless people have spent carefree hours in days gone by, is now in a sad state. The Falls, once clear and sparkling, is little more than an open sewer.

Certainly, the city must have the authority to stop the pollution of the Falls. There must be some way to end this abuse of public property.

Thirteen years ago, in the summer of 1931, I received similar complaints about the condition of Gwynn's Falls and went there to investigate. I found the one-time lovely stream the color of dark mud and from it arose a fearful stench. Residents whose homes bordered on the Falls told me that life was made almost unbearable for them by the odor from the stream.

At that time the city was using the stream as an open sewer. As a result of the outcry, however, conditions were improved—for a while. Now they are as bad as ever, if not worse.

If our city is using one of its prettiest parks as a sewer, the situation defies adequate words to describe. If private individuals or corporations are polluting the stream, then the city should stop it.

Baltimore never made a more favorable purchase than Gwynn's Falls Park. Its 390 acres are an area of great natural beauty, with towering hills, steep bluffs, mighty rocks and streams that delight the eye. It is, I believe, the very finest of Baltimore's equipment of natural parks.

That such disgraceful conditions should be permitted there is outrageous.

THE LARGEST BUS
Mrs. Irvin Sweeting, 3116 Woodhome avenue, Hamilton, writes to say that the largest bus in Baltimore in 1904 was the "Pride of Baltimore," which was hauled by 10 horses and carried 54 persons seated.

Mrs. Sweeting has a photograph of the bus taken at Rose Bank Shore, June 22, 1904, when the Washington Pleasure Social held its annual outing. She and her husband were among the guests.

REALLY!
Sign in a Charles street night club window!
"Buddy Mack. Chock full of fun. Air conditioned."

MORE ABOUT D'ANMOUR
Apropos my recent articles about the Columbus Monument at North and Harford avenues, erected by the Chevalier D'Anmour, a reader calls by attention to this item in the Maryland Journal of December 17, 1782:
"Married, the Honourable L'Chevalier d'Anmour, his Most Christian Majesty's Consul for the Middle District of the United States, to Miss Julia de Rocour, a young lady arrived here from the West Indies."

SCRAP BOOK CLUB
The suggestion of Alfred J. O'Ferrall that what Baltimore needs is more hobby clubs and that our Municipal Museum should foster these clubs and provide them with quarters, brings me an inquiry.
Miss Sophie W. Stewart, 429 East North avenue, wants to know if there is a Scrap Book Club in Baltimore. Miss Stewart says she had been interested in scrap books and has kept them since she was a child. And she wonders if other persons in Baltimore have a similar hobby.

CUTIES :: By E. Simms Campbell

"It's just some homework from the factory, dear!"

PRIVATE BUCK

"I don't want to be caught short on Armistice Day, Sir!"

One Word Led To Another
By ARTHUR (BUGS) BAER

My car has been up on blocks so long I will have to teach it to skid all over again.

But I don't mind after I took a trip through one of those high-octane plants.

When the Wrights buzzed Kitty Hawk they used a fluid the Standard Oil used to dump out at sea because it exploded in parlor lamps.

Its monicker was gasoline. It was okay, but it didn't have the zipper to produce steady power in a light engine. There was a fluid available at the time in 1903 called iso-octane. It was a combination of carbon and hydrogen atoms that cost twenty-five smackers a gallon.

It was too expensive for commercial use. But it could be utilized as a yardstick against new fuels. Along about 1924 the petroleum experts were mixing a gasoline reaching 70 on the octane scale.

They added tetraethyl of lead and boosted the octane to 87 in 1931.

Along about 1934 California scientists tore the oil molecule into shreds and got iso-butylene. They learned to cement the atoms with cold acid polymerization. When they added hydrogen they had iso-octane, 1934 style.

And iso-octane reached the perfect hundred mark. It cost one-tenth of the original twenty-five smackers. But it was still higher than a giraffe's cud.

With catalytic cracking and other gadgets they finnally got iso-octane down to the price of motor gasoline. That's the stuff that conquered Africa and Sicily and will the war.

(Copyright, 1944, King Features Syndicate, Incorporated.)

Washington Scene
EMINENT VISITOR AT BLAIR HOUSE
By GEORGE DIXON

WASHINGTON, June 7.—Across Pennsylvania avenue from the State Department is a very high-class joint named Blair House. This is the famous mansion in which distinguished visitors are bedded down while in our fair city, thereby saving wear and tear on White House linen.

Blair House has a long and interesting history, which I am going to skip, because of a grim suspicion that you do not like long and interesting histories.

I will report, however, that the historic trap was completely redecorated some time ago and there was so much talk about the beauties of Blair House that a certain fairly permanent resident of Washington expressed a desire to see it. Inasmuch as I am no good at maintaining suspense, the name of this fairly permanent resident is Franklin Delano Roosevelt.

GRACIOUS HOUSEKEEPER
Now, the housekeeper of Blair House is a very gracious lady named Mrs. Victoria Geaney. She likes the place so well she seldom leaves, meaning that there is nearly always somebody on hand. Recently, however, we happened to have a nice, bright, Sunday and Mrs. Geaney decided to take a walk. And it happened that this was the day the President made known his wish to visit Blair House.

He made known his pleasure to Howell G. Crim, head White House usher. Crim went to Blair House and found it locked.

He came back to the White House and began demanding who might have the keys. Nobody knew.

STALLING IN VAIN
Crim went to the President and tried to stall. He suggested that a week day might be a nicer time to view Blair House. The President retorted he was too busy week days.

Well, the White House staff and half the Secret Service began scurrying around for the keys. Finally somebody suggested it might be an idea to consult the watch officer at the State Department.

"Sure, I know where they are!" said the watch officer. "They are where they're always kept. In the safe of the protocol division!"

An exalted protocol officer had to be routed out and do a Jimmy Valentine on the safe. But the President got to see Blair House! And while I am on the subject, I would like to report a very strange thing that befell Steve Early, the White House press secretary.

Mr. Early rose early (no pun, confound it!) the other day and reached the White House betimes. All was silent, or, at least it was until Mr. Early started walking across the flagstones.

Soon he noted a weird phenomenon. One of his feet made a sharp, clicking, sound as he put it down, but the other was soundless!

"My goodness!" said Mr. Early to himself. "This is indeed eerie! Do you suppose I have been hoodooed and that one of my feet has gone Republican?"

SIGH OF RELIEF
He became so concerned over the uncanny incompatibility of his dogs that he sat down on the flagstones and examined his shoes. He heaved a sigh of relief.
He had on odd shoes. One had a rubber heel; the other, not! Early said:
"You have my full permission to publish this. I would like somebody to know that I have two pairs of shoes."

(Distributed by King Features Syndicate. Reproduction in whole or in part prohibited.)

Let's Explore Your Mind
MARRIAGES TO CONTINUE
By ALBERT EDWARD WIGGAM, D. Sc.

Answer to Question No. 1
1. Not on your wedding march. About 90% of the women in the United States and Canada now marry at some time in life; and they are about the most "emancipated" women in the world. Yet the most married women in the world. One of the worst results of war is that it leaves more marriageable women than marriageable men. The result is not only much unhappiness and even an increase of illicit relations, but the splendid heredity of the brave men who have died on the battlefield, as well as that of their potential wives, is lost forever from the human blood stream. What Hitler and Japan have done to the best blood of the human race, both in their own and their enemy countries, is beyond calculation.

Answer to Question No. 2
2. It's a grand thing to resolve to reform this or that bad habit, but to reform all your bad habits at once is too big a job. Better take Benjamin Franklin's plan of forming three good habits each week. This makes 156 per year—enough to make a start.

Answer to Question No. 3
3. Only a fool thinks he is always right. The wise man compromises his opinions all the time. He knows if he sticks to the idea that he cannot be wrong, he cannot even keep his friends, not to mention his enemies. This does not mean he has to sacrifice his fundamental principles of right and wrong; but principles are themselves made up of numerous compromises with other people's ideas and personalities. Morality is getting the highest good out of life. This means you must compromise with other people's ideas of the highest good.

The News Behind The News
ISSUES CLOUDED IN DIXIE POLITICS
By PAUL MALLON

WASHINGTON, June 7.—The participants are shouting "Fascism," "Communism" and even direr things, if there are any, concerning the Democratic political rebellions in Texas, South Carolina, and elsewhere.

Great moral issues are being whetted. But the specific news behind those situations heads far away from morals into tough, smart political jockeying by both sides.

The tie-up of the Texas delegation beyond Mr. Roosevelt's reach—for the time being at any rate—is attributed in the Senate cloakroom to quiet Senator "Pappy" O'Daniel.

As the story is told, he went into the counties where the delegates to the State convention were elected several weeks in advance, with this idea of how to handle the matter.

JOHNSON TOO LATE
When the New Deal's leading Texas representative, Lyndon Johnson, arrived, it was apparently too late, although Johnson may not have realized it until after the votes came out in the open on the convention floor—refusing the delegation to Mr. Roosevelt, leaving it uninstructed with subtle orders not to support any candidate unless certain things were done.

The New Dealers were quite angry and have been circulating stories that it was Jesse Jones, the Commerce Secretary, who failed to note the rebellion in time to stop it. They are always glad to hurl stones at Jones, even the left-over ones thrown at themselves.

In any event, it would be too much to surmise what the Texas delegation is going to do about Mr. Roosevelt until you see what the convention does about the Texas delegation and its viewpoint.

The jockeying does not violate sharp political custom and does not ordinarily lead to either Fascism or Communism.

So also in South Carolina, where the prevailing Democratic authorities decided (in a different way) to hold back what electoral or other power they have as long as possible, and keep it away from Mr. Roosevelt until they see what Mr. Roosevelt does about their matters. Such tactics has as often led to harmony in the end as to discord.

BAD NEWS FOR SMITH
Consequently, the furore now sweeping up on the news about the situation may not necessarily prove painful except, perhaps, for one person. South Carolina's Senator "Cotton Ed" Smith, who considered himself "roped in" at the Philadelphia convention eight years ago and has advocated "withholding" tactics—uninstructed delegations—ever since, got bad news last Friday.

He has always had some opposition, but when the Friday filing date closed, he had five opponents. The leading one is Gov. Olin Johnson, a Rooseveltian, beaten by Smith last time. Johnson had indicated he did not intend to run, but someone apparently cured his reluctance fast.

Smith thinks it was Mr. Roosevelt himself, because the President sunned recently at the Baruch plantation.

(Distributed by King Features Syndicate, Inc. Reproduction in whole or in part strictly prohibited.)

Dr. Haney Says
GOVERNMENT MONOPOLY MENACE TO DEMOCRACY
By LEWIS HANEY
Professor of Economics, New York University.

A recent speech by the assistant U. S. attorney general in charge of the anti-trust division much attracted much attention. Obviously, the Berge address was designed to carry on in the Thurman Arnold manner, by advocating competition as the basis of democracy, but also injecting so much Government and politics that it would be doubtful if competition could work.

Some very true things are said. For example, Mr. Berge makes the point that we have to contend against two enemies of free private enterprise.

These are (1) the "mirage of self-governing monopoly" and (2) the "mirage of Government control over business." In other words, in order to preserve competition we have to fight both private monopoly and Government monopoly.

But how are we to do this? The direct way to deal with the problem would be to prevent both kinds of monopoly wherever it is possible to do so. What the attorney general's office proposes, however, is to fight private monopoly by subjecting it to public monopoly. It would break up private monopoly, but encourage Government monopoly.

For example, few things are more important in the competitive system than credit. Ours is sometimes called the age of credit. But the proposal now before us is to give the Government control over credit.

It is stated that "credit must be made available to small business," and the idea is that the Government should provide. This is a thoroughly dangerous approach.

No business, big or little, deserves credit unless it is sound and productive. The Government as a monopolist of bank credit is one of the greatest menaces to democracy.

Again, it is proposed to use taxation as a device for stimulating business—another thoroughly bad suggestion. Says Mr. Berge, "taxation incentives should be given for the launching of new enterprises." But the power to stimulate is also the power to retard. This use of taxation would give the state complete control over business.

Taxes should be used only to raise revenue for Government. Their effect upon business should be considered, but this should be purely incidental.

Another example of the thought of the competition wing of the New Deal Administration is the tendency to favor active Government participation in industry. They propose to expand Government "public works," not merely as emergency measures. Also, they would hang on to Government plants constructed in war times, even though they are uneconomically located and would be scrapped by any private enterpriser.

These proposals spell competition by Government with its own citizens. Such competition is not the life of trade. Indeed, it is a mirage. Mr. Berge should add to his list of "mirages" the mirage of the Federal Government as a business man!

These Days
MIRACLES VISIONED IN ROME'S HISTORY
By GEORGE E. SOKOLSKY

The fact that Rome is intact, that its historic magnificence has not been reduced to rubble, that the symbols of Western civilization blossoming in the religion of our various peoples still stand—that is a triumph that speaks of the miracles that for thousands of years have saved the city on the Tiber. And today this city is important to us not for its Caesars, ancient or modern, but for its association with the religion of God.

One need not be a Roman Catholic to appreciate the importance of Rome. We live in an age of ugly, base materialism, an age in which morals have been debased to the principle that if you can get away with it, it is right.

We live at a time when even the ideal of God has been subjected to a degenerate whittling away from a glorious leadership toward the heavenly life to a doctrine that there is no absolute truth at all and that what is one day provable is on that day right, and that what is right today may be everlastingly wrong tomorrow.

CAUSES OF DECAY
The industrialization of vast multitudes, the shifting of population from one part of the earth to another, the swiftness of transportation are a few of the causes for the uprooting of individuals from their traditional moorings.

But even more, these and other forces have assumed a leadership in destroying the one instrument of civilization which is wholly conceived in love, the family as the central unit of society, the core of everything we are and everything we have.

Against these destructive forces making for the enslavement of the spirit of man, poisoning the wells of civilization, reducing man to a statistical entity, a dot on a chart, a thing to be used and moved about and even destroyed in the interest of force and power, stands the symbol of the instrument of God's good.

AMERICAN'S PRIDE
I am proud, as an American, that it was my people and my flag that marched into Rome to liberate it.

And I am prouder still that those who commanded our troops restrained an impulse to an easier victory by bombing the eternal city into a mass of unidentifiable rubbish.

The instruments with which this war is being fought are so horrible in their effectiveness that one cannot be human who does not dread in each day's news the accounts not of what is being conquered but of the irreplaceable that is being destroyed.

Only the railroad yards in Rome were completely demolished and they can be built anew in little time.

But who could begin to dream of restoring the walls upon which Raphael and Leonardo Da Vinci and Michelangelo spent their souls to the glory of God and man? The Eternal City stands—to remind the world that their wisdom and genius in this age of efficiency and statistics has yet to reach the beauty and truth of its spirit.

(Copyright, 1944, King Features Syndicate, Incorporated.)

OH, YEAH?

"American Youth Is Without Ideals and Without Leadership."
BALDUR von SCHIRACH
September 4, 1942

Betrayal From The East
Based on the new best-seller unmasking the Jap network of espionage and treachery in America
BY ALAN HYND
ILLUSTRATIONS BY WM. SHARP

Aboard ship the Japs or Germans trailed Blake.

Blake helped the old man to his cabin...

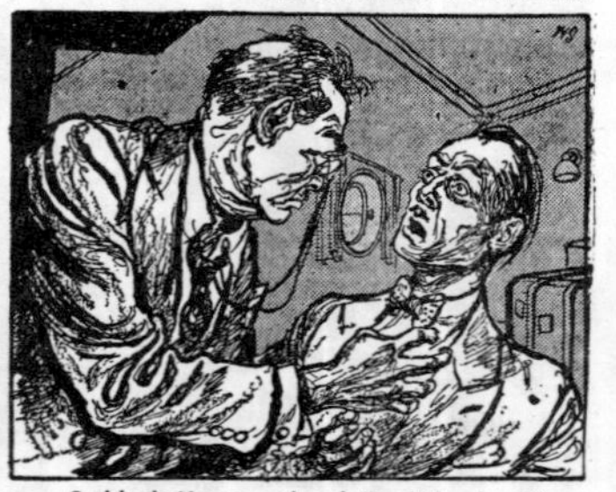

Suddenly Horner ordered: "Lock the door!"

THE President Garfield had hardly passed through the Golden Gate when Al Blake realized he was to be spied upon during the trip to Honolulu. Two gentlemen of distinctly Teutonic appearance shared a cabin on one side of Blake's and two Japs occupied the cabin on the other side.

No matter where the King of the Robots went aboard ship, the Germans, or the Japanese, or all four, were always near. Blake learned that both Germans were named Mueller, which didn't mean much, and, of course, the Japanese names meant nothing to him either. All four names were obviously phoney.

The Office of Naval Information could have given Blake some information about his "shadows." But, while they hadn't had time before the sailing to contact Blake, they did do something about his ship-board predicament.

In the ship's bar, Blake became friendly with an elderly American tourist named Horner, and his wife. Horner, a garrulous old man, played the bar heavily. He let it be known to all that he was expecting a radiogram — his daughter was to have a baby.

It came, on the last night out. It was a boy, and the radiogram gave complete details about weight, coloring, etc. Horner promptly began celebrating and soon was roaring drunk, Mrs. Horner appealed to Blake for assistance in getting the old boy to his cabin. Horner, resenting the interruption to his gaiety, struck Blake under the eye, inflicting a nasty cut. Blake wanted nothing further to do with Horner, but Mrs. Horner pleaded. He finally managed to get the old man to his cabin. There Horner bellowed that he wanted his radiogram, dropped in the scuffle in the bar, and insisted that his wife get it. When she left, Blake was startled by a now apparently cold-sober Horner, who whispered under, "Lock the door!"

The door locked, Horner continued in a low voice: "That radiogram contained your instructions." He told Blake he was to contact "Yeoman Jimmy Campbell" on the Pennsylvania as soon as he reached his hotel. He said the Japs had already planted a dictograph in the hotel room reserved for Blake and told the latter exactly where it had been placed. "Be sure," he whispered, "when Campbell calls on you, that you converse near that spot."

"How will I know Campbell?" interrupted Blake.

"There will be a torn spot on the left breast of his uniform," said Horner. "Now get back to the bar or they'll get suspicious!"
(Continued tomorrow)

Drawings Copyright, 1944, by King Features Syndicate, Inc. Text Copyright, 1943, by Robert M. McBride & Company.

"I think we better transfer Easterly back to the mattress department!"

The Baltimore News-Post
Wednesday, June 7, 1944—25

BARKLEY NOMINATES ROOSEVELT

THE WEATHER

Mostly cloudy, with moderate temperature this afternoon; showers and thunderstorms this evening and tonight.
Detailed Weather Report Page 19

Read The Baltimore News-Post for complete, accurate war coverage. It is the only Baltimore newspaper possessing the three great wire services—
ASSOCIATED PRESS
INTERNATIONAL NEWS SERVICE
UNITED PRESS

THE BALTIMORE NEWS-POST
AN INDEPENDENT NEWSPAPER
The Largest Evening Circulation in the Entire South

10

VOL. CXLV.—NO. 66 | Entered as second-class matter at Baltimore Postoffice. | THURSDAY EVENING, JULY 20, 1944 | PRICE 3 CENTS

HITLER ESCAPES ASSASSIN BURNED, BRUISED BY BOMB

Reds Take 2 Outposts Of Lwow

LONDON, July 20—(U. P.).—Premier Josef Stalin announced tonight that Red armies had advanced 31 miles on a 93-mile front in a new offensive in Lower Poland, and to the south had captured the big rail junctions of Rawa Ruska, 30 miles northwest of Lwow, and Wlodzimierz, 52 miles to the northeast.

Stalin issued two orders of the day in quick succession reporting the offensive aimed from the Kowel area toward Brest-Litovsk and later the fall to the First Ukrainian Army of Rawa Ruska and Wlodzimierz, major outposts of Lwow against which the Russians were closing.

STORM TWO JUNCTIONS

Marshal Ivan S. Konev's army stormed and captured the two rail junctions which Stalin described as "important strongholds of the German defenses in the Western Ukraine." Moscow regards that area of pre-war Poland as a part of the Ukraine.

The first order of the day said:

"Troops of the first White Russian front, having launched an offensive from the area of Kowel, broke through the heavily fortified German defenses and in three days of offensive battles advanced 31 miles, widening their breach to 93 miles."

LINKS BATTLE ZONES

Among the captured towns were Ratno, 46 miles southeast of Brest Litovsk, and Lyuboml, 30 miles west of Kowel.

The new drive linked Rokossovsky's battle zone with that of Marshal Ivan S. Konev, whose First Army of the Ukraine was pushing across the Bug river directly to the south and closing against Lwow.

At the other end of the front Berlin reported heavy fighting only eight miles from the frontier of East Prussia.

British Drive Beyond Caen Toward Paris

SUPREME H. Q., A. E. F., July 20 — (U. P.).—The British Second Army, hammering out a steadily expanding Normandy break-through arc, drove through nine more towns today, stormed into the streets of Troarn and Bourguebus, and sent a spearhead down the Paris road to Vimont, eight miles southeast of Caen.

Many scores of Allied Sherman tanks were smashing through the network of German fortifications on the Caen plain in wild battles of armor against the Nazis who now had massed at least five and a half divisions in frantic effort to stem the march inland.

United Press Correspondent Richard D. McMillan reported that British and Canadian assault forces stormed six more villages in the area of the break-through. Whether they supplemented or duplicated the nine announced at Supreme Headquarters was not certain.

The German Transocean News Agency said American and Canadian Army forces under Lieut. Gen. George S. Patton had gone into action on the Normandy front. Gen. Dwight D. Eisenhower's headquarters had no comment.

CAPTURE MORE TOWNS

Inside the battle arc, lying an average of four miles from Caen—with advanced positions at Troarn, seven miles to the east, and Vimont, eight miles to the southeast—the British and Canadian troops captured Ifs, Cormelles, Bras, Hubert-Folie, Soliers, Four, Le Poirier, Cagny and Grentheville.

(BACKGROUND NOTE: The German DNB news agency asserted today that British and Canadian troops have opened a new offensive "from Colombelles, in the Touffreville and Sannerville area" of Western France. The enemy outlet said in their thrust the Allies took Emieville, Frenouville, Soliers and Bourguebus.)

A headquarters' spokesman said

Continued on Page 2, Column 7.

STADIUM LINE-UPS

Following are the line-ups for tonight's game at 8.30 P. M. between the Orioles and Newark Bears at Baltimore Stadium.

NEWARK	ORIOLES
6 Kuk, c.f.	7 Monaco, 2b.
16 Rhabe, r.f.	24 Tiedemann, ss.
23 Zimmerman, 1b.	23 Benjamin, lf.
5 Rabe, l.f.	18 Moss, cf.
9 Drescher, c.	9 Latshaw, 1b.
2 Buzas, 2b.	4 Mackiewicz, cf.
3 Portner, 3b.	35 Skaff, 3b.
4 Reynolds, s.s.	8 Lollar, c.
17 Holcombe, p.	25 Palica, p.
11 Hiller, p.	1 Brann, inf.
22 Bevans, p.	5 Riley, outf.
15 Maldovan, p.	6 Devlin, c.
21 Hiller, p.	29 Shaefer, outf.
14 Page, p.	x Imhoff, c.
10 Marleau, p.	x Holton, c.
18 Queen, p.	12 Van Slate, p.
8 Van Grofsky, c.	14 Rochevot, p.
7 Dwyer, o. f.	15 Lowry, p.
19 Flick, o. f.	20 Embree, p.
12 Crosby, inf.	21 Hooks, p.
1 Meyers, mgr.	26 West, p.
28 Kahn, c.	27 Burkart, p.
	28 Kleckley, p.
	18 Kleine, p.
	16 Pfiefer, inf.
	22 Thomas, mgr.

Time of game, 8.30 P. M.

7 DIE OF POLIO

LOUISVILLE, Ky., July 20—(A. P.). — The State Board of Health reported today the seventh death this year in Kentucky from poliomyelitis and said the number of cases now totals 202.

Sen. Barkley Nominates Roosevelt

CHICAGO STADIUM, July 20 (A. P.).—The name of Franklin D. Roosevelt was placed in nomination for a fourth term today by Senator Alben W. Barkley of Kentucky and the Democratic National Convention moved toward speedy nomination and an acceptance speech by radio from the President tonight.

By WILLIAM K. HUTCHINSON
International News Service Staff Correspondent.

CHICAGO, July 20.—Vice-President Henry A. Wallace was within 48 votes of renomination in the Democratic National Convention this afternoon as chances of Senator Harry S. Truman winning were dimmed by action of Illinois in deciding to cast its 58 votes for its own Senator, Scott Lucas.

The Illinois caucus was accepted generally as indicating Mayor Edward J. Kelly of Chicago had given up hope of nominating Truman.

Wallace was out in front at 1.15 P. M. (C. W. T.) today with a total of 539 votes, according to an International News Service poll of delegations.

TRUMAN LAGS

Truman, the President's second personal choice as a running mate, lagged far behind with but 258½ votes. His chances were badly hit when Illinois failed to give him its 58 votes.

Senator Alben W. Barkley of Kentucky was in third place with but eighty-one votes. Fourteen other possibilities had scattered support.

If Truman fails of nomination it means this convention will have rejected both the President's first and second choices. Earlier the

Continued on Page 2, Column 1.

"Mind Reading Is The Bunk." It's Nothing But Old-Fashioned Hocus-Pocus In Modern Dress, Says Richard Himber, in the First of a Series of Articles, Beginning in The American Weekly, the Magazine with Next Sunday's Baltimore American.—Adv.

ADOLF HITLER
Fuehrer in Belligerent Mood.

Louis Bromfield Says:

Feudin' Enlivens Chicago Conclave

By LOUIS BROMFIELD
Author and Lecturer.
(Written Expressly for the Hearst Newspapers.)

CHICAGO, July 20.—Although outwardly all appears to be serene and under control, there is no such unity at the Democratic Convention as made the Republican gathering seem a dull affair.

Under cover there exists every sort of feud, division and even enmity between groups and even inside State delegations.

You have only to circulate through the corridors of hotels or drop into hotel bedrooms to find what is going on.

I have seen more out-and-out fights and more insults exchanged in a few hours than I heard during the whole Republican convention.

GREAT FEUD THERE

There is, of course, the great feud between the New Dealers and the Old Line Democrats, a fierce and bitter feud which flares up at the most unexpected moments.

And there is a feud that has developed at the last moment between the C. I. O. Political Action Committee and the organization bosses.

It has flared up suddenly when Philip Murray and Sidney Hillman showed their intention to dictate not only policies but who would be acceptable to them as Vice-Presidential candidate.

ARROGANCE IN TACTICS

There was clearly a kind of arrogance in their tactics which the political bosses found hard to swallow from these newcomers in the political game.

Far deeper and more profound is the resentment and hostility toward Murray and Hillman of scores of delegates from the Mississippi basin, the South, the Southwest and the Northwest.

These are the delegates from the small towns, the ranches, the farms, who, in one sense at least,

Continued on Page 2, Column 5.

Jackson Escorted By Gov. O'Conor

STADIUM CHICAGO, Ill., July 20.—Governor Herbert R. O'Conor of Maryland was named to the committee which escorted Senator Samuel D. Jackson of Indiana, the permanent chairman of the Democratic Convention, to the speakers' platform at the second day's session today.

Governor O'Conor got a big hand as he was presented to the audience in the vast hall and the organ and band played "Maryland, My Maryland."

The Governor's associates in the State delegation arose and raised the Maryland standard as O'Conor was presented.

West Coast Blast Death Toll At 322

PORT CHICAGO, Cal., July 20—(A. P.).—The death toll of the explosion of two ammunition-laden ships here Monday night stood at 322 today with a Navy announcement of 213 names of men known to be dead or missing.

Temperatures

Midnight, 68	9 A. M., 70
1 A. M., 69	10 A. M., 72
2 A. M., 70	11 A. M., 76
3 A. M., 69	12 Noon, 79
4 A. M., 70	1 P. M., 80
5 A. M., 70	2 P. M., 80
6 A. M., 70	3 P. M., 81
7 A. M., 69	4 P. M., 80
8 A. M., 70	5 P. M., 75

7 Generals Are Injured In Explosion

LONDON, July 20—(A. P.).—Adolf Hitler was slightly burned and bruised by a bomb in an attempt on his life today while he was surrounded by closest personal military advisers, an announcement from his headquarters said.

Seven generals and two admirals were injured by the blast, Berlin added.

(One broadcast attributed the blast to dynamite while another said "explosives" were used. An account recorded by N. B. C. said the unnamed perpetrators escaped, but that police were "on their trail.")

NEW YORK, July 20—(A. P.).—The Berlin home radio said today "the would-be perpetrators of Hitler's assassination have escaped, but the police are on their trail," N. B. C. reported.

Closely controlled official announcements gave no inkling of the nature of the originators of the attempt, but London contacts with the German underground suggested that the sensational development was the result of serious feuds within the military hierarchy in Germany.

These sources said the attempt might have occurred at Breda, Holland, where Hitler was reported to have gone yesterday for a conference with Marshal Erwin Rommel, his commander in Normandy.

There was speculation that a general brawl may have resulted when Rommel demanded more divisions to prop his front and met with refusal.

SEES MUSSOLINI

Quick to stress the minor nature of the fifty-five-year-old dictator's injuries, the radio announcement said he conferred immediately afterward with Benito Mussolini and also received Reichsmarshal Hermann Goering, who was en route to the headquarters at the time of the atack.

By strange coincidence the attack took place only about 16 hours after Hideki Tojo, the third of the ill-starred Axis leaders who led their countries into war, had been shelved in Tokyo.

Among the seriously injured, Berlin said, was Lieutenant General Schmundt, chief of the German Army's personnel department and chief military aide de camp to Hitler for several years.

OTHERS INJURED

Two lieutenant colonels named Brandt and Borgmann and a "collaborator" named Berger also were listed as seriously injured.

Slightly injured were these:

Generals Jodl, Hitler's personal military aide; Karl Bodenschatz, aide to Hitler; Guenther Korten, chief of staff of the German Air

Continued on Page 2, Column 3.

Baltimoreans Sorry That Hitler's Safe

Prominent Baltimoreans gnashed their teeth in helpless rage today at an unkind fate that, apparently, had spared Herr Hitler when an assassin's bomb missed its target.

Their comment on the incident follows:

Mayor McKeldin:

"What I think about Skunk Hitler can't be printed. My best wish for him right now is that his injuries may take a decided turn for the worse."

G. H. Pouder, executive vice-president, Baltimore Association of Commerce:

"Hitler has bruised and burned the rest of the world. I certainly hope his injuries are nothing trivial."

City Solicitor Simon E. Sobeloff:

"Too bad it didn't succeed. Better luck next time."

State's Attorney J. Bernard Wells:

"It's a shame the assassin didn't take better aim. There ought to be a law in Germany to punish bad marksmanship."

Bernard J. Flynn, U. S. District Attorney:

"If Hitler were permanently out of the way I feel certain the war would be over a lot more quickly."

Col. Henry S. Barrett, State Commander, U. S. Citizens' Defense Corps:

"It's a damn pity they haven't assassinated him long ago."

NEWS-POST

Amusements	10	Financial	19
Azrael, Louis	15	Haney, Dr. Lewis	15
Bugs Baer	15	Horoscope	13
Classified Ads	19, 20, 21	Mallon, Paul	14
Clark, Norman	10	Movies	10
Comics	16	Parsons, Louella	10
Crossword	21	Pippen, R. H.	17
Dixon, George	15	Radio	9
Dulaney	15	Robinson, Elsie	14
Durling	14	Society	12
Editorials	14	Sports	17, 18

VERY LATEST NEWS

(Race Results From Howard Sports Daily, Inc.)

RACING RESULTS

AT EMPIRE CITY

Seventh—Dit, $11.40, $4.00, $3.00; Boston Man, $3.20, $2.50; Eire, $3.40.

AT GARDEN STATE

Fifth—Adelphia, $3.30, $2.70, $2.50; Viva Teddy, $4.70, $3.30; Morning Choice, $5.50.

AT SUFFOLK DOWNS

Fifth—Due Sport, $22.80, $8.20, $3.20; Red Ted, $3.80, $2.60; City Bred, $2.40.

AT HAGERSTOWN

Third—Famas Time, $8.40, $3.90, $2.70; Semper Ego, $5.00, $4.10; Ler-Lin, $3.40.

Fourth — Worries, $16.40, $8.70, $5.60; Maroc, $3.90, $3.00; Myrtle M., $4.10.

AT ARLINGTON PARK

Second—Linger Along, $5.60, $3.40, $3.20; Stage Door, $6.00, $5.60; Big Bubble, $8.80.

Daily Double—Special Pet & Linger Along paid $165.00.

LATEST BASEBALL SCORES

(A) At Detroit—Detroit, 7; Wash., 5; end 8th.
(A) At Cleveland—Phila., 1; Cleve., 0; end 6½.
(A) At Chicago—Boston, 7; Chicago, 0; end 2½.
(N) At New York—St. Louis, 2; New York, 0; end 3d.

GARDEN STATE RESULTS

FIRST RACE—Five and one-half furlongs. Off 2.31½. Time, 1.06 2-5.

Leystan, 118 (J. Gilbert)	$67.20	$22.90	$13.20
Split The Wind, 118 (C. Kirk)		6.50	4.10
British Buddy, 118 (J. Breen)			5.10

Also Ran—Tellmenow, Sunredgra, Quatre Call, Royal Gem, Geronimo, Brookfield, Romanicus, Linza and War Archives.

SECOND—Five and one-half furlongs. Off 3.11½. Time, 1.06 3-5.

Lucky Aunt, 118 (L. Knapp)	$20.50	$11.40	8.10
In the Purple, 118 (A. Kirkland)		11.10	7.90
Bride's Biscuit, 113 (K. Scawthorn)			6.70

Also Ran—Beau's Nurse, Panacea, Guernsey Isle, bWar Hysteria, Ginokum, Four Queens, Center Stage, Santa Candida, bPolly Warden. bGlen Riddle Farms entry.

Daily Double—Leystan and Lucky Aunt paid $903.40

THIRD—Six furlongs (chute). Off at 3.41. Time, 1.12 1-5.

Pat O'See, 120 (J. Gilbert)	$11.90	$5.00	$4.40
dhFlying Tartar, 109 (R. Meade)		5.90	7.40
dhSir Echo, 114 (T. Luther)		3.10	3.60

Also Ran—Sunset Boy, Alatamo, Post War Style, High North, Miss Ada J., War Art, Dick Manners, Wise Decision, Nanny Bones. dhDead heat for place.

FOURTH—Six furlongs (chute). Off at 4.15½. Time, 1.11 2-5.

Hornbeam, 113 (N. Wall)	$41.90	$15.00	$9.20
Dawn Attack, 113 (L. Knapp)		4.00	3.20
Gallant Witch, 109 (W. Gerlock)			6.00

Also Ran—Picket Line, Wise Up, Fairy Trace, Dark Danger, Sir Counsellor, Blue Steel, Maecase, Gondalina and Boy Angler.

The Baltimore News-Post
Thursday, July 20, 1944

What Do You Know?

By DR. SABINA H. CONNOLLY
(Registered U. S. Patent Office)

Score yourself on each question: ONE for each of the first five questions and FIVE for the last question.
Score: 9-10, brilliant; 7-8, bright; 4-6, average; 0-3, dull.

1. The word amphibious, sometimes applied to soldiers, really means: (a) having a double life; (b) living in water; (c) having a backbone.
2. Poi is native Hawaiian. Is it: (a) a drink; (b) a food; (c) a dance.
3. A man who wanted to kill a whale would use: (a) a heavy fish line; (b) a harpoon; (c) a stiletto.
4. The national dance of Scotland is: (a) Scottish waltz; (b) Highland fling; (c) Lowland reel.
5. Can you guess to within 10,000 square miles the area of Alaska? (a) 586,400 square miles; (b) 497,342 square miles; (c) 901,375 square miles.
6. Fill each blank with the name of a girl: (a) "———— with the light brown hair;"
(b) "I'll take you home again, ————;" (c) "When you and I were young, ————;" (d) "Santa ————;" (e) "Sweet ————."

ANSWERS TO TODAY'S TEST
1. (a) both water and land; 2. (b); 3. (b); 4. (b); 5. (a); 6. (a) Jeannie; (b) Kathleen; (c) Maggie; (d) Lucia; (e) Adeline.
(Copyright, 1944, King Features Syndicate, Incorporated.)

Kerr's SPAGHETTI DINNER — No Ration Points — 15¢

LORD CALVERT COFFEE
One of the finest coffees you can buy... and it costs you less than ONE CENT A CUP
Another Fine Levering Product

LADY CALVERT TEA

NO WONDER IT'S RATIONED
• Tons of Pride, of the Farm are being sent to our armed forces. That's why the home-front supply is limited.
PRIDE OF THE FARM TOMATO CATSUP
ONE OF THE PRITCHARD FINE FOODS

COOL OFF with Iced Coffee
Make it double strength... pour hot over ice.
HAVE ANOTHER GLASS!
The friendly drink — from good neighbors
PAN-AMERICAN COFFEE BUREAU
Brazil Colombia Costa Rica Cuba Dominican Republic El Salvador Mexico Venezuela

Dari-Rich Syrup
MAKES MILK A REAL TREAT!
CHOCOLATE FLAVOR CHILDREN LOVE!
★ A&P SUPER MARKETS ★ ACME SUPER MARKETS and other leading food stores

Delicious Hot MUFFINS
EASY TO MAKE WITH DUFF'S
PERFECT... served with a crisp salad and iced tea on a summer eve.
just add WATER **Duff's** FULLY-PREPARED HOT MUFFIN MIX

Schreiber's
COMPLETE FOOD MARKET — EUTAW-LEXINGTON STS.

REAL SUGAR CURED SMOKED HAMS
SHANK END 31¢ LB.

FRYING CHICKENS BALTO. KILLED **35¢ LB.**	CUT-UP POULTRY Ready To Fry! BREAST....LB. 69¢ / LEGS....LB. 65¢ / WINGS....LB. 35¢

FRESH GROUND HAMBURG STEAK	LB. 25¢
FRESH SHOULDERS	LB. 25¢
LAMB SHOULDERS	LB. 23¢
SMOKED PICNIC HAMS	LB. 29¢
BEEF CUBES BONELESS BRISKET	LB. 29¢
BEST PURE LARD	1-LB. PKG. 15¢

RICH CREAMY CHEESE (10-Pts.) **35¢ LB.**
WAFER SLICED CHIPPED HAM **13¢ ¼-LB.**
SKINLESS FRANKS LB. 33¢
CORNED BEEF LOAF ¼-LB. SLICED 12¢

SLICED FRESHLY MADE BRAUNSWEIGER ¼ LB. **10¢**

RIB-END PORK CHOPS **25¢ LB.**
SUGAR CURED SLAB BACON BY THE PIECE **19¢ LB.**
FRESH CRISPY COLE SLAW **23¢ LB.**

Garden Fresh Produce

TOMATOES FULL POUND **10¢**	
FRESH GREEN LIMA BEANS	2 LBS. 25¢
CALIFORNIA SWEET PLUMS	LB. 15¢
CALIFORNIA SEEDLESS GRAPES	LB. 29¢
OPEN-STONE GEORGIA PEACHES	2 LBS. 25¢
ICEBERG LETTUCE LGE. HEAD 9¢	CRISP CELERY LGE. BUNCH 9¢

Seafood Dept.
FRESH PICKED CRAB MEAT
BONELESS CLAW **89¢ LB.**

BAY CROAKERS LB. 15¢

HADDOCK FILLETS **37¢ LB.**
FRESH FLOUNDER FILLETS **39¢ LB.**

NO POINTS REQUIRED
PEANUT BUTTER 1-LB. JAR 17¢

• SWEET MIXED PICKLES	FULL QUART 24¢
• FRENCH STYLE GREEN BEANS	NO. 2 CAN 14¢
• VAN CAMP TENDERONI	PKG. 5¢
• MAXWELL HOUSE TEA BAGS	PKG. OF 16 15¢
• RAISIN BRAN CEREAL	PKG. 10¢

SCHIMMEL'S JELLIES ASSTD. FLAVORS 12-OZ. GLASS (3 PTS.) **15¢**

LITTLE DARLING EXTRA SIFTED PEAS NO. 2 CAN (5 PTS.) **15¢**

SOUR PITTED CHERRIES NO. 2 CAN (25 PTS.) **26¢**

CHESAPEAKE BAY SHAD STEAKS TALL CAN **21¢**
CHESAPEAKE BAY HERRING ROE 17-OZ. CAN **25¢**

McCORMICK'S MUSTARD 2 8-OZ. JARS 17¢

Staley's CUBE Laundry Starch 1¢ SALE STOCK UP TODAY! 2 Regular Size Packages 15¢ / 1 Regular Size Package 1¢ / Total 16¢

MASON JARS PINT SIZE 49¢ DOZ. / QUART SIZE 59¢ DOZ.
KEEBLER'S SALTINES PKG. 10¢
GRAPEFRUIT JUICE 46-OZ. Can 25¢

BIRDS EYE FROSTED FOODS NO POINTS!
BAKED BEANS PKG. **15¢**
BIRDS EYE PEAS .... PKG. 26¢
BIRDS EYE CORN .... PKG. 23¢
BIRDS EYE SPINACH .... PKG. 30¢
ASPARAGUS SPEARS .... PKG. 45¢

FRESH FRUIT BLUEBERRY PIES
Golden Flaky Crusts Freshly Made **39¢ EACH**

FRESH BAKED COFFEE RINGS .... EA. 12¢
SANDWICH CREAMS LB. 22¢
LAYER CAKES .... EA. 33¢

TOMATO JUICE LIBBY'S (6-Pts. Each) 2 NO. 2 CANS **17¢**	DUZ LGE. PKG. **23¢**	IVORY SOAP 3 LGE. BARS **29¢**

On Sale Friday and Saturday in Our Advertised Foods and Economy Departments. We Reserve the Right to Limit Quantities.

YANKS, FRENCH ENTER PARIS
BATTLE OF LIBERATION RAGING

THE WEATHER

Sunny and cool today. Highest temperature 77 degrees this afternoon. Clear and cool tonight. Tomorrow, sunny and warmer.
Detailed Weather Report Page 29

Read The Baltimore News-Post for complete, accurate war coverage. It is the only Baltimore newspaper possessing the three great wire services—
ASSOCIATED PRESS
INTERNATIONAL NEWS SERVICE
UNITED PRESS

THE BALTIMORE NEWS-POST
AN INDEPENDENT NEWSPAPER
The Largest Evening Circulation in the Entire South
7 HOME FINAL
VOL. CXLV.—NO. 97 Entered as second-class matter at Baltimore Postoffice. FRIDAY EVENING, AUGUST 25, 1944 PRICE 3 CENTS

NAZIS QUITTING ROMANIA---BERLIN ABANDONING BULGARIA, CAIRO HEARS

Balkans Are Reported In Turmoil; Hungary's Government Reshuffled

LONDON, Aug. 25—(I. N. S.).—A Reuter's dispatch from Cairo today quoted "authentic reports" as saying that the situation in Romania is disintegrating rapidly with the Russians said to be in control of all of Romania to the Danube.

LONDON, Aug. 25—(U. P.).—The Hungarian Government is now being "reshuffled," a German Foreign Office statement broadcast by the DNB news agency said today.

LONDON, Aug. 25—(U. P.).—A Berlin broadcast said today that German forces had begun a withdrawal from Romania, and Cairo heard they also were abandoning Bulgaria as the result of Romania's capitulation to Russia.

The entire Balkans were reported in a turmoil over Germany's setback in Romania and the growing Red Army threat to Southeastern Europe. Slovakia was reported to have proclaimed martial law and an underground radio called on the Hungarian army to revolt against the Germans.

Wilfred von Oven, German home service radio commentator, acknowledged in a Berlin broadcast that German troops were pulling out of Romania, where the front was "disintegrating under the impact of troubles and treason."

NAZIS REFUSE AID

Diplomatic circles in Ankara said Romania's surrender followed the failure of Germany to promise military help against the Russian offensive.

When Premier Marshal Ion Antonescu, since ousted, returned empty-handed from a six-day talk with Adolf Hitler, Ankara said, unrest spread through the army and peace demonstrations broke out in Bucharest.

Faced with military chaos, the army prevailed upon King Mihai to seek an armistice, these sources said.

A United Press Moscow dispatch said Russian and Romanian authorities were believed to have begun formal peace negotiations on the basis of King Mihai's announcement that Romania had decided to accept a Soviet armistice offer.

REDS CONTINUE DRIVE

The Red Army was continuing its advance through Northern Romania toward Bucharest, however, and the Soviet Foreign Commissariat said in its first formal statement on the Romanian situation that military operations would continue until the Germans had been driven from Romanian soil.

Romanian and German troops already were fighting one another in Northern Romania, the Soviets said, while other reports reaching

Continued on Page 2, Column 4.

Russ Capture 47,000 In 5 Days

MOSCOW, Aug. 25—(A. P.).—Two Red armies, slashing deeper into Romania against an apparently tottering enemy from whom 47,000 men have been taken as prisoners in five days, today were within 35 miles of the Galati gap defenses guarding the Danube gateway to Bucharest and the Ploesti oil fields.

The armies of Gen. Rodio Y. Malinovsky and Gen. Feodor Tolbukhin, obviously taking no chances on the outcome of Romania's peace bid through King Mihai, swept up more than 550 cities, towns and villages yesterday, including the Bessarabian capital of Chisinau.

MAKE LIGHTNING STAB

In a lightning attempt to get a firm grasp on Romania before her Nazi overlords can complete plans for counter measures, the armies took 25,000 German and Romanian prisoners in a single day and sent spearheads to less than 100 miles from Ploesti and slightly more than that from Bucharest.

Front dispatches said Red Army tankmen, as liberators and not conquerors, cruised through hundreds of Northern Romanian towns and villages, followed by sweaty, dusty columns of singing infantry.

Red Army political officers, carrying out the official Russian position, explained to Romanian soldiers and civilians that liquidation of German forces in the

Continued on Page 2, Column 1.

Dewey, Hull In Accord On Peace Policy

WASHINGTON, Aug. 25—(I. N. S.).—John Foster Dulles, foreign affairs adviser to Gov. Thomas E. Dewey, is scheduled to meet with Secretary of State Hull for the third straight day today as delegates to the International Security Conference continued their secret talks at Dumbarton Oaks.

After two days of foreign policy talks with Hull, Dulles described the meetings as "something novel in American political life" and said "we are breaking ground and making progress slowly and carefully."

NO DIFFERENCES

G. O. P. members of Congress, who also have been conferring with Dulles, said there was virtually no fundamental difference of views between Dewey and Secretary Hull.

Senator Taft (Republican) of Ohio said "all Republicans in the House and Senate have kept in touch with Secretary Hull's plan" for an international organization to keep the peace.

Taft added:

"Both parties are very much in accord on the general details, but there are many details—important ones—to be considered. These are nothing to cause a political issue, however."

JOINT COMMUNIQUES

Following a protest by State Department correspondents, Edward R. Stettinius, Jr., Under Secretary of State and chief American delegate at Dumbarton Oaks conference, promised there would be a periodical release of joint communiques on the secret talks.

Stettinius re-emphasized that the world security deliberations were "informal conversations and exchanges of views."

The report on Thursday's meeting said:

"The subcommittee on international organization continued its discussions at a meeting this morning. The legal subcommittee met this afternoon and began its discussions on the subject of an international court."

Japs Decline To Evacuate Paris

NEW YORK, Aug. 25—(I. N. S.).—Some 40 Japanese residents of Paris declined to be evacuated with other Japanese nationals from the French capital, according to a Tokyo broadcast reported by United States Government monitors.

Pope Holds Private Churchill Audience

ROME, Aug. 25—(I. N. S.).—Pope Pius XII. gave a private audience to British Prime Minister Winston Churchill on Wednesday, an official announcement disclosed today.

"Fly Traps For Germs." Robert D. Potter Tells How a New Invisible Oil Baits and Destroys Invisible Bugs That Give Us Colds, Pneumonia and Other Diseases. In The American Weekly, the Magazine Distributed with Next Sunday's Baltimore American.—Adv.

FLORENTINES RETURN HOME — A clergyman balances himself precariously with other Florentines as they pick their way home across the Ponte Allegrozie, which spanned the Arno river until destroyed by the Germans, who fled when the ancient city was liberated by Allied forces. U. S. Signal Corps Photo.

Planes Renew Record Attacks On Reich

LONDON, Aug. 25—(U. P.).—American bombers from Britain and Italy delivered another double attack on Germany and her satellites for the second consecutive day today, Berlin radio reported.

The enemy broadcast said one force had swept over Northwestern Germany and the Baltic area, while the other ranged over Austria.

The raids, apparently aimed at sources of vital materials for the German war machine, followed yesterday's record attack in which more than 1,900 heavy bombers blasted oil refineries in Germany and Czechoslovakia.

RECORD NUMBER

The co-ordinated attack, which involved the greatest number of planes ever dispatched by the U.

Continued on Page 2, Column 2.

Temperatures

Midnight, 66	6 A. M., 58
1 A. M., 63	7 A. M., 59
2 A. M., 62	8 A. M., 62
3 A. M., 62	9 A. M., 65
4 A. M., 61	10 A. M., 68
5 A. M., 59	11 A. M., 72

Yanks Capture Cannes, Grasse

MARSEILLE, France, Aug. 25—(A. P.).—The Allies launched a smashing attack on the four remaining enemy strongpoints in Marseille today after capturing two German generals and 5,000 prisoners in this area in the last 72 hours.

ROME, Aug. 25—(U. P.).—American forces captured the Riviera resort city of Cannes today and were reported battling the Germans only 15 miles below Lyon, the big Rhone valley industrial center, 170 miles inland from the Mediterranean coast.

A United Press dispatch from Annecy, capital of Haute Sovoie Province, said an American flying column was expected there momentarily from Grenoble, 53 miles to the south.

Liberated by French Maquis, Annecy was draped with American and French flags in anticipation of the arrival.

The fact that the Americans had not yet arrived at Annecy appeared to disprove earlier reports that they already had reached the Swiss border at St. Julien, 16 miles farther north, and Evian, 25 miles northeast of St. Julien.

YANKS MAKE ADVANCE

The Rome newspaper Il Tempo said an American armored column had engaged the Germans 15 miles south of Lyon after an advance from Grenoble, 58 miles to the southeast.

French Maquis were said to be in control of Lyon, long a resistance center, but the Germans appeared in be fighting to prolong the American advance as long as possible.

The fall of Lyon would cut all the main escape routes for Ger-

Continued on Page 2, Column 6.

Mountbatten Back After London Talks

LONDON, Aug. 25—(A. P.).—Admiral Lord Louis Mountbatten has returned to his post as head of the Allied command in Southeast Asia after a series of conferences in London with British and American leaders, during which plans were made to step up the war against Japan, it was disclosed today.

Admiral Fraser Arrives In Ceylon

COLOMBO, Ceylon, Aug. 25—(A. P.).—Admiral Sir Bruce Austin Fraser has arrived here by plane to assume his new post as commander of the British Far Eastern fleet. He succeeds Admiral Sir James Somerville.

Yank, French Troops Enter Paris; Battle For City Raging In Street

NEW YORK, Aug. 25—(I. N. S.).—Liberation of Paris by French and American forces now "is a fact," an N. B. C. correspondent at headquarters of Gen. Dwight D. Eisenhower reported today.

LONDON, Aug. 25—(A. P.).—French armored forces burst into Paris this morning, the Allied Supreme Command announced, to relieve French Forces of the Interior which had been battling the Germans almost a week for possession of the French capital.

Nazis Retreat Along Line Of Seine

SUPREME HEADQUARTERS ALLIED EXPEDITIONARY FORCE, Aug. 25—(A. P.).—Disorganized and battered German forces made a last-ditch attempt today to flee across the last few miles of the Seine adjoining the sea in Northern France, but front dispatches said this battle already was virtually over.

"The enemy is leaving bits and pieces to try and delay us, but there is no major stand all the way back to the Seine," a field headquarters officer said last night after a sharp Canadian advance of 20 miles had driven the Germans into an area about 25 miles long and 15 miles wide.

THOUSANDS LEFT

As the Germans fell back before this enveloping attack, managing to get many of their troops beyond the Seine but leaving thousands of others and a great bulk of equipment behind, the first Allied force—the Second French Armored Division—finally entered Paris.

The supreme command still remained largely silent about the activities of Lieut. Gen. George S. Patton's armored forces southeast of Paris.

The only news was that Montereau, near Fontainebleau, and Montargis, further south, had been occupied, with an advance east of the latter city.

SILENT ON POSITION

There was no report on the Americans who two days ago penetrated 15 miles beyond Sens, approaching to within 150 miles of the German frontier.

The present speed of advance indicated that the Lower Seine pocket, which extends from Elbeuf to Bernay then roughly to the coast at a point four miles from Honfleur, may be wiped out in another 24 hours.

Beyond the Seine on the ap-

Continued on Page 2, Column 5.

French Army Storms Into Paris

LONDON, Aug. 25—(U. P.).—French armored columns rode down Nazi troops at the gates of Paris and stormed in to relieve the embattled Parisian street army today and headquarters spokesmen indicated that the final liberation of the historic capital may be only a matter of hours.

Allied headquarters said tough veterans of the French Second Armored Division under the legendary desert warrior, Brig. Gen. Jacques Leclerc, spearheaded the relief column and unconfirmed reports said Lieut. Gen. Omar N. Bradley had ordered his American tanks and infantrymen to follow the Poilus into the city.

CRUSH SCREENING

United Press War Correspondent Robert Miller reported from the Paris environs that Gen. Charles DeGaulle, president of the French Committee for National Liberation, personally commanded the French forces entering the city.

The French armor swept in from the western suburb of Versailles at 2.30 A. M., crushing a light German screening force, and by mid-morning was reported to have reached the Latin quarter, on the left bank of the Seine.

LOUVRE BATTLE SCENE

The German DNB news agency said the historic Louvre, treasure house of the world's greatest art, was the scene of bloody fighting and asserted that a force of patriots had seized the building and

Continued on Page 2, Column 1.

News-Post Directory

Amusements	18	Financial	28, 29
Bugs Baer	25	Health	17
Classified Ads	29, 30, 31	Horoscope	6
Clark, Norman	18	Mallon, Paul	25
Comics	14	Movies	18
Crossword	31	Parsons, Louella	18
Dixon, George	25	Pippen, R. H.	26
Dulaney	25	Radio	23
Durling	25	Robinson, Elsie	24
Editorials	24	Society	16
		Sports	26, 27, 28

Morrell Park 'Rek' Proving Big Success

When there's a will, there's a "Rek," and the Morrell Park Youth Club has one of the best independent places of fun in Baltimore.

Teen-agers of the Washington boulevard area had no outside help in securing a modern "Moline Plan" recreation center, but they were determined to have one.

CLUB ORGANIZED

The former police sub-station offered a likely solution and getting on the youth movement band wagon of The Baltimore News-Post, boys and girls of Morrell Park called a mass meeting, organized a club, elected officers and pinned down parents and other adults for aid.

They obtained use of the building from Mayor McKeldin and the Board of Estimates, solicited enough funds around the neighborhood to clean and remodel the interior and are now enjoying all kinds of fun four nights a week.

MANY ATTRACTIONS

They have a pingpong set, dance floor, their own "juke box" and gay decorations.

Recently, they staged a barn dance and members attended in farm attire.

Next Tuesday, they will hold a watermelon party at the home of Robert Baxter, chairman of the Adult Advisory Committee at 1922 Breitwert avenue, "admission" being 50 cents.

HAS OWN ORCHESTRA

The "Rek" also has its own orchestra and it will make its debut August 31 at a special dance for members.

The center is open on Wednesday, Thursday and Friday from 7.30 P. M. to 11 P. M., and Saturdays from 7.30 P. M. to 11.30 P. M. It is closed on the other nights.

One of its few headaches right now is a heating system for the winter, although it is still in need of a good piano. Several have been offered but found to be in need of extensive repairs. Can any one donate a piano in playable condition for the orchestra debut?

GARIBALDI SOCIETY

The Garibaldi American Fraternal Society, International Workers' Order, Inc., will hold a celebration at 3 P. M. Sunday, in Finnish Hall, 700 block South Ponca street.

"HAYSEEDS" SWING OUT AT "REK"—One of the ways Baltimore's juvenile delinquency rate has been reduced to pre-Pearl Harbor days is by absorbing idle time among youths in gainful play. The Baltimore Youth Commission, set up at the instigation of The Baltimore News-Post and American, established a modern "Rek" center at Morrell Park. At left, "hayseeds" swing out at a barn dance held in the "Rek," 2800 Washington boulevard, while, at right, Joe Mory and Jean Given take time out for refreshments.

Roaming Boy Returns Home After 6 Hours

Three-year-old Donald Reed, is back home at 3134 Presstman street, again after being AWOL from that address for six hours yesterday on a jaunt that caused search of parked automobiles, police radio broadcast, and a twilight search by a neighbor through Gwynns Falls Park.

Donald was missed at 3 P. M. by his mother, Mrs. Warren J. Reed, and when a hunt through the neighborhood and Gwynns Falls Park failed to locate him, she called police. When told that the boy had a weakness for climbing into parked cars, patrolmen searched all in the vicinity, then broadcast a description.

Harry E. Niles, 3023 Clifton avenue, heard the broadcast while in bed. Recalling that he had seen and talked with a boy of that description in the park shortly before five, he got up and with Mrs. Niles searched the locality without success. As they arrived at the Reed home to report that at least they had seen Donald earlier, the boy was brought in by Mrs. Eileen Barth of the Walbrook Apartments, who had found him crying. The climax of Donald's busy day occurred when he was connected by telephone with Capt. John Carey, night commander of police, and promised to be a good boy in the future.

Crump Picked To Head Cheltenham

ANNAPOLIS, Md., Aug. 25—(A. P.)—Royal A. B. Crump will become superintendent of the Cheltenham School for Boys September 1, bringing the institution under supervision of an all-Negro management. Crump, whose appointment was announced by Governor O'Conor yesterday, formerly was assistant superintendent of the Hanover (Va.) training school for Negro boys.

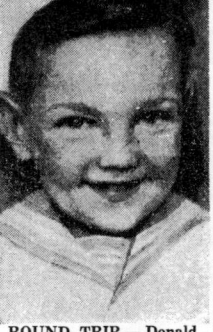

ROUND TRIP — Donald Reed, three, is back home at 3134 Presstman street after alarming six-hour absence, police broadcasts and extensive search.

OPA Warns Landlords In Bay Resort Area

Complaints that landlords have been seeking to evict tenants from resort communities along the western shore of the Chesapeake bay in order to qualify for exemption from rent control next summer have been received at the State OPA office, it was learned today.

Lucien E. D. Gaudreau, district rent executive, disclosed that landlords will not qualify for any future exemption of seasonal housing from rent control by keeping properties vacant during the winter of 1944-45.

Since the present exemption of summer properties not rented during the past winter applies only during the present summer season, which ends September 30, resort housing will not be exempt next summer unless present rent regulations are amended, Mr. Gaudreau said.

Landlords holding properties vacant this winter to qualify for the exemption applicable to resort housing this season will merely have lost the income from winter occupancy they might otherwise have had, the rent executive declared.

Drive Tomorrow For Waste Paper

Wastepaper collections will be made tomorrow in the eastern section, beginning at Charles street and including Curtis Bay, Brooklyn, Masonville, Canton and Highlandtown.

Newspapers, magazines, corrugated boxes, brown paper bags, wrapping paper and wastebasket paper are to be placed in bundles at curbs for collection and assembling by collectors later at street intersections. Trucks will carry the waste away.

If the waste paper is not picked up householders and business representatives are requested to telephone the War Production Board's salvage office, Lexington 6260.

PLAN TO ATTEND PARLEY

Joseph A. Giammateo, chief of the Glen Echo Fire Department, will attend the annual conference of fire chiefs, to be held in Grand Rapids, Mich., August 28 to 31. He will be accompanied by David Tuohey of the Cabin John Fire Department and Irving W. Johnson, former chief at Takoma Park.

Girl 'Crashes Gate' At Boys' Club Opening

The "open house" at the Boys' Club of the Southwestern District Police Station drew a capacity crowd last night, sponsors of the organization expressing the belief that the entire membership of 920 was present.

There was, in fact, even a "gate-crasher," a seven-year-old girl who dressed herself up in a pair of overalls and a khaki shirt and came into the male precincts with her two boy cousins.

The party, complete with ice cream and cake, was furnished by the Baltimore Variety Club, organization of theatre men, which provided the club with its furnishings and equipment.

Both Police Commissioner Atkinson and Inspector John R. Schueler expressed pride in the organization, which started out with 400 members less than two months ago, and already has more than doubled in membership.

Send him a lovely Photograph of you!

Have it taken now in our Photo Studio, Second Floor

49c

Large 8x10 inch size
No appointment necessary
Satisfaction guaranteed

Overseas mailing date for Christmas packages — Sept. 15th to Oct. 15.

Julius Gutman & Co.
Lexington Street & Park Avenue

SHARE THE RIDE TODAY
...and You Give Uncle Sam a Lift

Where would we be today if our forefathers had gone their separate ways at their own convenience? When this nation was in its infancy, neighbor gave neighbor a helping hand. That spirit expanded 13 struggling colonies into a vast, united nation.

Today our country is calling upon every one of us to enlist in a great awakening of that early American creed of helping ourselves by helping our neighbors. Sharing our automobiles is as easy as it is helpful. Wherever we go, there's somebody going our way. When we give him a lift, we give Uncle Sam a lift on the way to Victory.

*   *   *

In addition to supplying the armed forces with glider and bomber fuselage frames, wing parts, gun turret parts and foodstuffs, Anheuser-Busch produces materials which go into the manufacture of: Rubber • Aluminum • Munitions • Medicines • B Complex Vitamins • Hospital Diets • Baby Foods • Bread and other Bakery products • Vitamin-fortified cattle feeds • Batteries • Paper • Soap and Textiles—to name a few.

It is in those moments of well-earned relaxation that a beverage of moderation proves a welcome companion. Budweiser matches your mood for a friendly chat or your mood for repose. It is considerate of tomorrow's obligations.

Budweiser
ANHEUSER-BUSCH ... SAINT LOUIS

Many may have to stand
THESE 5 DAYS!

In addition to heavy Labor Day travel, the railroads will as usual be carrying a peak load of essential business and military furlough traffic.

For your own comfort and convenience, we suggest you plan to go before and return after the five days indicated.

PENNSYLVANIA RAILROAD
Serving the Nation

★ 48,537 in the Armed Forces   ☆ 294 have given their lives for their Country

1,250 U. S. PLANES BATTER FORTS IN REICH

THE WEATHER

Sunny, with moderate breezes; highest temperature 88 degrees; clear and cooler tonight; Wednesday fair and cooler.

Detailed weather report Page 13.

Read The Baltimore News-Post for complete, accurate war coverage. It is the only Baltimore newspaper possessing the three great wire services—

ASSOCIATED PRESS
INTERNATIONAL NEWS SERVICE
UNITED PRESS

THE BALTIMORE NEWS-POST

AN INDEPENDENT NEWSPAPER

The Largest Evening Circulation in the Entire South

8

VOL. CXLV.—NO. 105 | Entered as second-class matter at Baltimore Postoffice. | TUESDAY EVENING, SEPTEMBER 5, 1944 | PRICE 3 CENTS

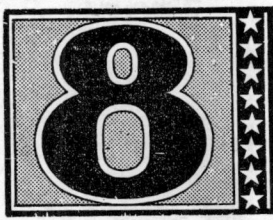

PATTON'S TROOPS IN BATTLE WITH FLEEING GERMANS NEAR METZ

YANKS FIGHTING ON NAZI SOIL, REPORT

21 Jap Ships, 85 Planes Blasted

By RICHARD V. HALLER

PEARL HARBOR, Sept. 5—(I. N. S.).—A powerful United States carrier task force threatened further smashes against Japanese island defenses today after executing a devastating three-day raid on the Volcano and Bonin groups at the southern approaches to the enemy homeland, which left destroyed or damaged 21 Jap ships and barges and 85 Jap aircraft.

Pacific fleet headquarters, in disclosing the raid, revealed that 13 enemy vessels were definitely sunk. They were: Five small cargo ships, one landing barge, one small tanker and six barges. One cargo ship and three sub chasers were probably sunk and three sub chasers and a sampan were damaged.

KEY TARGETS BLASTED

Targets for the assault by the carrier force were Iwo Jima, in the Volcanos, about 750 miles south of Tokyo, and Chichi Jima and Haha Jima, in the Bonins, about 650 miles south of Tokyo.

The raids included sweeping carrier-based aircraft strikes in which 196 tons of explosives were unloaded and 490 rockets launched, and were executed August 30, 31 and September 1.

American cruisers and destroyers joined in the attacks on Chichi Jima and Iwo Jima on August 31 and September 1.

Not a single American vessel was damaged. Losses in aerial operations were five planes and four men.

WAKE DAMAGE HEAVY

Pacific fleet headquarters also announced that on September 3 U. S. cruisers and destroyers bombarded Wake Island, causing extensive damage in the harbor and shooting up three small craft.

The carrier strikes and warship bombardments caused extensive damage to Jap installations in the Bonins and Volcanos. Several gun emplacements were destroyed and hangars, fuel dumps, shops and warehouses were severely damaged.

1,250 U. S. Planes Hit Reich Forts

LONDON, Sept. 5—(U. P.).—More than 1,250 American war planes swept ahead of the Germany-bound Allied armies today and hammered Karlsruhe, Stuttgart and Ludwigshafen, great Rhineland bastions anchoring the first line of defense of the Reich proper.

Upwards of 750 Flying Fortresses and Liberators were escorted by some 500 Mustangs of the Eighth Air Force Fighter Command in the three-pronged assault on the Rhineland area bordering the northeastern tip of France.

MAJOR-SCALE ACTION

Improving weather enabled Allied air forces to resume action on a major scale. Coastal observers reported intense activity this afternoon, with all types of planes shuttling to and from Europe.

The attack on the Rhineland cities was described as a combination strategic-tactical assautl, labeling it as at least partially in direct support of the Allied forces striking Germany.

The bombing of Karlsruhe, big rail center only a few miles from the tip of France, which British Mosquitoes hit last night ,was the most spectacular of the daylight attacks.

BLAST OIL RESOURCES

The Ludwigshafen assault was aimed primarily at synthetic oil and chemical resources in a renewal of the effort to constrict the Nazis' oil potential.

At Stuttgart the Daimler-Benz aerial engine and medium motor truck plant was the chief target. This parent plant of the Daimler-Benz chain was believed to be the center of experimental work.

Jap Merger Aims To Ease Oil Crisis

By Associated Press.

A Tokyo broadcast said today that Japan's Munitions Ministry had effected two large-scale mergers of the country's synthetic oil producers to meet "a crying need for urgent action regarding the production of synthetic oil." The broadcast was recorded by the Federal Communications Commission.

Bulgarians Break Ties With Reich

LONDON, Sept. 5—(U. P.).—Bulgaria broke her last ties with Germany today and ordered her peace emissaries in Cairo to conclude an armistice with the United States and Great Britain as quickly as possible.

Bowing to powerful Red armies massed along the Bulgarian-Romanian frontier, Premier Constantin Muraviev broadcast a proclamation to the Bulgarian people announcing that his Government had repuliated the Axis tri-partite and anti-comintern pacts and was ready to make peace with the Allies.

PROCLAIMS NEUTRALITY

Muraviev, a veteran peasant party leader who formed a new cabinet last Saturday night to replace that of ex-Premier Ivan Bargianov, proclaimed his country's full neutrality in the Soviet-German war and promised that any German troops attempting to escape into Bulgaria would be disarmed.

Radio Moscow re-broadcast Muraview's declaration and followed it almost immediately with a semi-official statement from the Soviet Tass News Agency denouncing the Bulgarian stand as unsatisfactory.

Tass said bluntly that the new Bulgarian Government was incapable of abandoning neutrality and joining the anti-German coalition.

ACTS TO AVOID BREAK

Muraviev, apparently still struggling to avert a declaration of war against the Reich, said only that his Government would break diplo-

Continued on Page 2, Column 3.

Exchange Of 5,000 Internees Slated

STOCKHOLM, Sept. 5—(U. P.). An exchange of nearly 5,000 Allied and Axis prisoners of war and civilian internees will be made for a three-day period starting tomorrow at Goteborg and Trelleborg, Count Bernadotte of Wisborg, vice-chairman of the Swedish Red Cross, announced today.

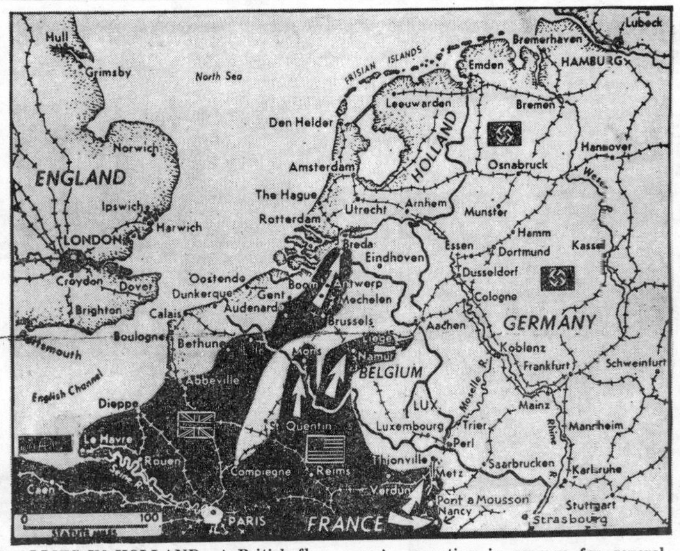

ALLIES IN HOLLAND—A British flying column, which captured Brussels and Antwerp in sweep across Belgium, is reported to have reached Breda, five miles inside Holland. General Patton's tank columh, operating in secrecy for several days, is fighting at Pont-a-Mousson, near Metz. Reported crossing of the German border in several places is unconfirmed.

Nazi Soldier Says:

Only Hitler Holds Reich Together

By LOUIS AZRAEL
News-Post War Correspondent.

WITH U. S. FORCES IN BRITTANY, Aug. 29 (Delayed).—An American sergeant and a blindfolded German sergeant sat on the ground in this camp last night and until the early hours of this morning and calmly discussed war, Nazism and many other things.

Both boys were German-born and reared, but Sergt. Lawrence Brandon, whose family now lives at 3 St. John's road, Baltimore, left Germany seven years ago because he hated Nazism.

The other boy, slightly older, felt differently. It never occurred to him to leave when Nazism rose to power. Leaving his orthopedic practice, he served as a medical aide in a German parachute unit in Russia, Crete, Italy and now in France.

ASK FOR TRUCE

Last night he came as one of a three-man delegation under a white flag to ask the Americans for a three-hour truce to evacuate civilians from besieged Brest.

While officers discussed the proposition in a nearby tent, the two sergeants and I sat outside and talked, with Brandon doing most of the questioning.

The German soldier does not believe the Nazis can win the war, and he thinks it will be over this year. Most of the other soldiers feel the same way, he said.

SEES MILITARY VICTORY

It will be a military victory, he says, not internal German collapse. Of the latter he has no hope, despite the fact that four out of every five soldiers have lost all faith in the Hitler regime.

The chief hatred, he says, is centered on the Gestapo. The blindfolded German said bitterly:

"There are not enough lampposts in Berlin on which to hang all the Gestapo members if the German populace gets a chance at them."

Sergeant Brandon asked:

"But if four out of five of the soldiers and civilians oppose the

Continued on Page 2, Column 4.

All Nazis In South France Wiped Out

LONDON, Sept. 5—(I. N. S.).—The Algiers radio said today that all remaining German forces isolated in Southwestern France, numbering about 11,000, have been encircled or captured by French Forces of the Interior. There was no confirmation of the report from any official source.

NAZIS FACE TRIAL

ROME, Sept. 5—(A. P.).—Declaring that 800 to 1,000 Romans were shot or beaten to death and that 1,000 more were severely injured during the Nazi occupation of Rome, the Allied Control Commissioi has promised that the Germans responsible will be tried before a military court if they are ever found alive.

Finn, Soviet Pact Ends 4 War Years

LONDON, Sept. 5—(U. P.).—Soviet troops on the Finnish front ceased firing today, ending four years of war.

The Russian Supreme Command ordered the halt of military operations against Finland effective at 8 A. M. today in view of the Finns' acceptance of preliminary conditions to an armistice offered by the Soviet Government.

The Soviet terms were believed similar to previous proposals, based on the restoration of frontiers and reparations. Russia did not demand unconditional surrender of the Finns.

A Moscow dispatch said there was no grounds for belief that the Russians would be excessively harsh and foreign observers believed Finland would retain its independence.

A Helsinki dispatch said the Finnish Parliament held two secret sessions last night believed preparatory to the sending of a peace delegation to Moscow.

(A Helsinki broadcast, recorded by FCC monitors, said Premier Anders Hacksell's Cabinet was given a vote of confidence by Parliament at the close of the sessions.)

The Stockholm Morgon Tidningen reported from Helsinki that German civilians and soldiers were leaving Southern Finland in compliance with the government's order that they must be out of the country by September 15.

Worst News for Germs Since Penicillin. Gobind Behari Lal, Tells of Streptothricin, Which Takes Up the Precision Massacre of Our Bacteriological Foes Where the Magic Mold Extract Leaves Off. In The American Weekly, the Magazine Distributed with Next Sunday's Baltimore American.—Adv.

Allies Capture Aachen, Saarbrucken In Reich, Frontier Reports Assert

AT THE SWISS-FRENCH FRONTIER, Sept. 5—(A. P.).—Reports reaching this frontier tonight said the Allies had captured Aachen and Saarbrucken in Germany.

WITH U. S. THIRD ARMY ON MOSELLE RIVER, Sept. 4—(U. P.).—Lieut. Gen. George S. Patton's battle-grimed fighters came to grips tonight with the Germans in the tiny village of Pont-a-Mousson, astride the Moselle between Metz and Nancy.

(This dispatch was the first word direct from the Third Army front in several days.)

LONDON, Sept. 5—(A. P.).—American troops were believed to be stabbing into the Rhine valley beyond the German border in a secrecy-shrouded offensive today. Perhaps they are well into the Siegfried Line defense zone.

This drive, which Supreme Headquarters has kept under a security silence for three days, has had time enough to have penetrated anywhere up to 75 miles.

A dispatch from the French frontier said it was reliably reported tanks had reached the outskirts of the French border city of Strasbourg, on the Rhine, 70 miles east of Nancy, and that fighting was in progress on German soil around Saarbrucken.

Other unofficial reports said the Americans had crossed the German frontier at three places on a 100-mile front.

RACE THROUGH BREDA

To the north a British flying column which captured Brussels and Antwerp in a 48-hour border-to-border sweep across Belgium was reported to have raced through Breda, five miles inside Holland, and to be pushing down the last 28 miles to the important port of Rotterdam.

Breda, with a population of 50,792, is the twentieth city of the Netherlands.

Behind these advances German forces estimated all the way from 50,000 to 100,000 men were caught in a cauldron along the Channel coast—a Dunkirk in reverse. The

Continued on Page 2, Column 1

Allies In France Forging New Link

By JAMES L. KILGALLEN

ROME, Sept. 5—(I. N. S.).—The American Seventh Army, continuing its rapid advance up the Saone river valley against ineffectual resistance by the Germans, moved steadily today toward a junction with Allied forces in Northern France, now believed little more than 100 miles away.

French troops have reached Macon, 38 miles north of Lyon, and Sanbonnet de Bruyeres, while on the east bank of the Saone the Americans have driven past Montrevel, 42 miles northeast of Lyon.

65,000 NAZIS BAGGED

Since the Allied landings in Southern France August 8 a total of 65,000 enemy troops have been taken prisoner.

(The Brazzaville radio reported that American columns had reached Petit St. Bernard pass leading through the Alps into Northwestern Italy from the Haute Savoie region of France.)

Evidence is piling up to indicate that the Germans are speeding up their withdrawal in Southern France in an effort to escape entrapment. French forces pushing northward on the west bank of the Saone lost contact with the enemy Sunday and Monday.

OPPOSITION SLIGHT

Likewise, the American advance farther to the east is not meeting serious opposition following a stiff battle at Montrevel Monday.

French troops that captured Ville Franche, north of Lyon, rounded up 2,400 Nazi prisoners.

VERY LATEST NEWS

(Race Results From Howard Sports Daily, Inc.)

RACING RESULTS

AT AQUEDUCT

First — Insolate, $25.90, $6.90, $4.20; Reason, $3.00, $2.60; Fire High, $4.10.

'IKE' ASKS REFUGEES NOT TO MOVE INTO LOWLANDS

NEW YORK, Sept. 5—(I. N. S.)—Gen. Eisenhower appealed today to Belgian and Dutch refugees and homeless nationals of other countries who might be in the lowland countries to "stand fast" and not attempt to reach their homes immediately, the OWI reported.

THE WAR STILL ON!

LONDON, Sept. 5—(A.P.). The Brussels radio caused a flurry of excitement in radio listening stations today by denying a report of a German capitulation, which, it said, was broadcast by an otherwise unidentified "foreign station."

No official listening station in London reported having heard the broadcast, which the Belgian National Radio denied.

"We regret to announce that Germany has not capitulated as was announced this morning wrongly," Brussels said. "The war continues."

Temperatures

Midnight	81	7 A. M.	77
1 A. M.	80	8 A. M.	78
2 A. M.	79	9 A. M.	79
3 A. M.	77	10 A. M.	83
4 A. M.	78	11 A. M.	84
5 A. M.	78	12 Noon	85
6 A. M.	77		

NEWS-POST

Amusements	8	Health	6
Bugs Baer	15	Haney, Dr. Lewis	15
Classified Ads	19-20-21	Horoscope	9
Clark, Norman	8	Mallon, Paul	15
Comics	10	Movies	8
Crossword	21	Parsons, Louella	8
Dixon, George	15	Pippen, R. H.	16
Dulaney	15	Radio	12
Editorials	14	Robinson, Elsie	14
Financial	18-19	Society	11
		Sports	16-17-18

"Seventh Cross," At Century, Has Tracy As Its Star

SPENCER TRACY—SIGNE HASSO

By NORMAN CLARK

"THE SEVENTH CROSS" is a grim drama that will make one even happier in the knowledge that the Nazis are running for home and that the doom of Hitler and his brutal followers is sealed.

Seven men escape from a concentration camp, to which they were sent because they were liberals and couldn't stomach the bestiality of the Hitlerites. The irate commandant of the camp has seven crosses erected and vows that the seven fugitives will be caught and hanged upon them. Six of the hapless men are allowed to die on these crosses but the seventh—George Heisler—eludes his would-be captors. The man-hunt goes relentlessly on, with Heisler trying to contact the underground. He cannot make the necessary connections and through failure to reach him—and the Gestapo continues to press at his heels.

Heisler has harrowing experiences indeed in his determined effort to keep off that "seventh cross."

Such a realistic story is bound to be full of suspense. A gilt-edged cast and admirable direction add to the strength of this film now at Loew's Century.

Spencer Tracy, playing as usual in a subdued key, is excellent as Heisler and a portrayal equally as good as the star's is that of Hume Cronyn, in the role of the loyal friend of the hunted liberal.

There is a brief interlude of romance between Tracy and Signe Hasso, with the lady carrying out her task prettily. Others who do well in secondary roles are Jessica Tandy, Ray Collins, Agnes Moorehead, Herbert Rudley and Felix Bressart.

Anna Seghers, who wrote the novel on which the film is based, is, we understand, a refugee herself from Germany, and is now living in Mexico City.

"Seventh Cross"

"THE SEVENTH CROSS," starring Spencer Tracy. Screen play by Helen Deutsch from the novel by Anna Seghers. Directed by Fred Zinneman. A Metro-Goldwyn-Mayer picture, presented at Loew's Century.

THE CAST
George Heisler .... Spencer Tracy
Toni .... Signe Hasso
Paul Roeder .... Hume Cronyn
Liesel Roeder .... Jessica Tandy
Mme. Marelli .... Agnes Moorehead
Franz Marnet .... Hubert Rudley
Feidl Schlamm .... Felix Bressart
Wallau .... Ray Collins
Zillich .... Alexander Granach
Mrs. Sauer .... Katherine Locke

Marylanders In Armed Forces

Sergt. JOSEPH P. KRUL, JR., 311 South Wolfe street, is now at an Army camp in England after having landed in France on D-Day; fighting there for 30 days.

Sergeant Krul, who now wears the Purple Heart for wounds received in action, explains an exciting incident:

"My buddies and I were fighting the Germans when we got right at the edge of woods about 70 yards away from us. We were firing on the enemy and found out later that the rest of our outfit had pulled out. In the rear our own troops kept firing on us, thinking that we had moved out to join the rest of my company.

"We were up front, as I am a mortar squad leader. We never realized that our company had pulled out until we ran out of ammunition. Then we had to withdraw 150 yards to catch up to our outfit. In the meantime our own paratroops were driving the enemy toward us. We got them in the open field and wiped them all out."

September 11 will mark the return of one bluejacket who will be mighty glad to get home. ANTHONY A. BUTNER, apprentice seaman, will finish his boot training at Bainbridge and merit a ten-day leave at 1623 Filbert street, Curtis Bay. He is the son of Mrs. John Butner.

A. A. BUTNER

There was a happy reunion at 6223 Brown avenue recently. CLIFFORD R. McINTEE, petty officer, second class, came home from the South Pacific to see his mother, Mrs. Mary McIntee. Another son, Lieut. JAMES McINTEE, is a pilot at Keesler Field, Mississippi. RUTH McINTEE, wife of a lieutenant, is a member of the WAVES.

Two Baltimore men were recently awarded sharpshooter's medals for proficiency in firing the .45-caliber automatic pistol at Maxwell Field, Alabama. They are PHILIP T. DUESBERRY, son of Mr. and Mrs. Charters Duesberry, 911 Mt. Holly street, and ROBERT L. RENNER, son of Mr. and Mrs. Cleveland Renner, 300 East University parkway.

The recent promotion of WILLIAM W. RENNER from the grade of corporal to sergeant has been announced at an Eighth Air Force Bomber Station in England. B-17 Flying Fortress base, by his squadron commander. Sergeant Renner is a top turret gunner on a Fort which is participating in the air offensive against military targets deep within Nazi Europe. He is the son of Mr. and Mrs. William W. Renner, 618 East Fort avenue.

To get on the dean's list of distinguished students at Franklin and Marshall College, Lancaster, Pa., a student must have completed his academic work in the previous term with an average of "B" and no grade below "C."

Three Baltimoreans, all apprentice seamen, have attained this honor. They are LEONARD BACHMAN, 2512 Liberty Heights avenue; LEO W. LATHROUM, 2935 Walbrook avenue, and JOHN A. SPITTEL, JR., 612 Tunbridge road.

ROBERT A. PROPF

ROBERT A. PROPF, JR., aviation cadet, is now completing his instruction as pilot at Frederick Army Air Field, Frederick, Okla. Before entering the service on June 1, 1943, he was employed at Martin's. His home is at 716 North Montford avenue and he is the son of Robert A. Propf, 1010 Franklintown road.

Corporal FRANK W. BURKE, son of Mr. and Mrs. Andrew W. Burke, 201 North Monroe street, has reported to the A. A. F. Redistribution Station at Atlantic City, N. J., after 18 months of service overseas in the European theatre of war. He was a mechanic on a B-24 Liberator and a B-17 Fortress while overseas.

Mary Pickford Buys 'Venus' Film Rights

By LOUELLA O. PARSONS
Motion Picture Editor
International News Service

HOLLYWOOD, Sept. 5.—"One Touch of Venus" has been sold to the movies, according to word from New York. Mary Pickford has bought it through Victor Orsatti, who represents John Wildberg and Cheryl Crawford, the producers, as well as Ogden Nash and the other authors.

Every company in Hollywood has been bidding for it. Mary, who finally obtained the rights, goes East today to sign the papers.

It is possible that Mary Martin, who created the star role on the New York stage, will be brought here for the part. If Mary isn't available then a top motion picture actress will get it. I know at least six young ladies who, after seeing the play in New York, wish they might do the movie version.

This is just the beginning of things Mary Pickford has planned. Sam Coslow will work with Mary as co-producer. He has just obtained a cancellation of his contract with Paramount.

Friends of Lois Wilson are going to be pleased to hear her name is in electric lights on Broadway in "Chicken Every Sunday."

Lois is a pioneer movie star and received her acting training on the screen. She has been on the stage about three years, but this is the first time she's had a break in the big town.

I saw her in "Junior Miss" and she was excellent. According to New York critics she's even better in the Epstein play.

I was much interested in meeting red-haired Jane Farrar, who comes from my home town, Chicago. She's a vivacious young lady who is extremely ambitious to make a big name on the screen. She started very well in "Phantom of the Opera," with Susanna Foster. She had a lot of nice things to say about Susanna.

Jane has just finished a couple of pictures at Universal and I have an idea, given the chance, you'll hear from her.

Snapshots of Hollywood Collected at Random: Marjorie Johnson, Nunnally's daughter, is marrying Gene Fowler, Jr., Gene's son, next Sunday in New York, where Gene, Jr., is stationed.

The Joseph Browns have welcomed a baby. He is the hotel magnate who married the former Elizabeth Avery, movie actress.

The first call Shirley Temple gets in New York will be a big one from Lon McCallister. He's fallen hard for our Shirley.

Come September 19 Paulette Goddard choochoos east to visit her husband, Capt. Buzz Meredith, in Indiana. She'll go on to her farm in New York.

Lotta Lehman has been the house guest of Jeanette MacDonald, who has been working very hard for her comic appearances.

James Francis Crow, former newspaper man, has moved to RKO to be editorial assistant to William Dozier.

On land or sea no girl will ever have a better wardrobe than Maria Montez when she leaves for the East.

That's all today. See you tomorrow!

KEEPING HOUSE

Dorothy Lamour has finished her role in "A Medal for Benny" and returned to her role as housewife—to Major William Howard III, who is stationed at the Army air base in San Bernardino, Cal.

Movie CLOCK

CENTURY—"Seventh Cross," 10.50 A. M., 1.01, 3.12, 5.23, 7.34, 9.45 P. M.
NEW—"Greenwich Village," 10 A. M., 12, 2, 4, 6, 8, 10 P. M.
KEITH'S—"Going My Way," 10.01 A. M., 12.24, 2.47, 5.10, 7.33, 9.56 P. M.
VALENCIA—"Canterville Ghost," 12.55, 3.01, 5.17, 7.33, 9.49 P. M.
MAYFAIR—"Ghost Catchers," 10.40 A. M., 1.02, 3.24, 5.46, 8.08, 10.30 P. M.
STANLEY—"Janie," 11.05 A. M., 1.10, 3.10, 5.10, 7.20, 9.30 P. M.
ROSLYN—"I Married a Murderer," 1, 3.15, 5.42, 8.10, 10.37 P. M.
TIMES—"Block Busters," 1.50, 3.59, 6.08, 8.17, 10.26 P. M., 12.35, 2.44 A. M.
PARKWAY—"Bathing Beauty," 1, 3.18, 5.26, 7.34, 9.42 P. M.
HIPPODROME—"Casanova Brown," 11 A. M., 1.46, 4.30, 7.15, 10 P. M.
LITTLE—"When You're in Love," 11 A. M., 12.50, 2.40, 4.30, 6.20, 8.10, 10 P. M.

Mary Martin (above) is mentioned as probably to be cast to star in the "One Touch of Venus" film, the rights to which have been bought by Mary Pickford.

Latest Report From Broadway

NEW YORK, Sept. 5. When Michael Todd took Jeanette MacDonald to dinner at Mike Romanoff's on his last trip to Hollywood local scouts began to wonder if the New York producer was trying to lure the singing star back to Broadway. Now it is known that Mr. Todd's efforts were not in vain and that Miss MacDonald will return in January to star in his new production of a Victor Herbert operetta. The show will go into rehearsal immediately after the Sigmund Romberg-Herbert and Dorothy Fields musical, "Way Up In Central Park," reaches the boards.

It will mark the first time that Miss MacDonald has appeared in a Broadway musical since 1928. In that year she appeared in the Shuberts' comedy with music, "Angela," at the Ambassador Theatre, where Ernst Lubitsch saw her and decided that she was the girl to play opposite Maurice Chevalier in "The Love Parade." Since that time she has starred in a succession of successful screen musicals.

Josephine Hull has been signed by Brock Pemberton for one of the leading roles in the Mary Coyle Chase comedy, "The Pooka," which is scheduled to go into rehearsal in two weeks. Antoinette Perry will direct the production which will have settings by John Root. Miss Hull made her last appearance here as Abby Brewster in the Howard Lindsay and Russel Crouse production of "Arsenic and Old Lace."

Phil Waxman has left the office of Dave Wolper and will become co-producer this season with Albert Johnson. Their first venture will be Ben Martin's "Bonanza," a comedy which takes place in a Western ghost town. Margaret Lindsay and Alan Hale are said to have been approached by the producers for important roles in the play.

In preparation for their forthcoming musical, "Holiday for Girls," Harry Delmar, Al Borde and Emil Friedlander have opened offices at the St. James Theatre.

Oliver Smith, who designed the scenery for "Rosalinda," has been commissioned to perform a similar chore for "The Perfect Marriage," Samson Raphaelson's new play.

Dick Himber has departed for the West Coast to sign a film comedian, whose identity the producer refused to disclose at the moment, for the leading male role in "Abracadabra," the magic show due here later in October.

ONCE FIGHTER

Denis Hoey, huge Scotsman featured in "Kitty" with Paulette Goddard, once was sparring partner of Bombardier Wells, British heavyweight champion.

CAROLE LORD

Miss Lord is the leading dancer with the burlesque revue now occupying the stage at the Gayety.

New Musical Is Hilltop Bill

"Keep It Clean For the Boys," a new musical comedy, will be the closing production of the Hilltop Theatre. It will have its first performance at the Mt. Washington Casino next Friday evening and will play there through Saturday, September 16, every night except Sunday. Curtain time is 8.45 P. M.

The book and music for "Keep It Clean For the Boys" were written by Lieut. (j. g.) Edward N. Heghinian, U. S. N. R., and Al Moritz. "Slice the Ham Thin" and "Yesterday Is Tomorrow" are two plays by this pair of Baltimoreans which were produced earlier in the season at Hilltop.

The leading role of the new musical is in the hands of Clara Cedrone, one of the original Hilltoppers. Others in the cast include: Bob Scheck, Bill Mullikin, Joan Field, Mary Jane Stockham Swann, Jane Strahan, Sue Thomas, Neal Miller, Josephine Shyers, Betty Ann Sagle and Gertrude Mund.

ABE MARTIN

It don't look like we'd ever have t' double track th' straight an' narrow path. There's lots o' honest people who never had a good chance t' be an'thing else.

(Copyright, John F. Dille Co.)

John Payne Plans Return To Movies

HOLLYWOOD, Sept. 5—(I. N. S.).—John Payne, Hollywood film actor, was back in civvies today following an Army discharge and will be resuming his movie career in the near future. Payne formerly was married to actress Anne Shirley. They share custody of their daughter.

ROSLYN 850 N. Howard — STARTS WEDNESDAY! 4 GREAT COMICS
BUD ABBOTT LOU COSTELLO — RIO RITA — WORLD'S FUNNIEST COMEDIANS — In the daffy-dilly jubilee of mirth and music!
ROSLYN! LAST DAY "I MARRIED A MURDERER" PLUS "WESTLAND CASE"
PLUS LAUREL & HARDY "A-HAUNTING WE WILL GO"

Last Day! DEAD END KIDS "BLOCK BUSTERS"
MIDNIGHT TONIGHT
Balto. Premiere TIMES
1700 Blk. N. Charles Pls NEWS Show
1st Howling Hit From A Screaming New Comedy Combination!
LAUGH HAPPY!
MONOGRAM PICTURES presents BILLY GILBERT SHEMP HOWARD MAXIE ROSENBLOOM in "THREE OF A KIND" with HELEN GILBERT JUNE LANG

EXTRA ADDED!
THE ADVENTURE KING IN HIS MOST THRILLING FILM!...TOPS IN ACTION, MUSIC, DANGER-PACKED EXCITEMENT!...
GENE AUTRY in BELLS of CAPISTRANO
SMILEY BURNETTE
OPEN TO 4 A. M. TIMES

NEW THEATRE BEGINNING SEPTEMBER 14th
EVERYTHING YOU EVER DREAMED OF SEEING IN A PICTURE!
Darryl F. Zanuck's WILSON in Technicolor
A 20th CENTURY-FOX PICTURE
DIRECTED BY HENRY KING — WRITTEN FOR THE SCREEN BY LAMAR TROTTI

NOW PLAYING — 2ND BIG WEEK!
Carmen Miranda Don Ameche William Bendix with Vivian Blaine
GREENWICH VILLAGE IN TECHNICOLOR
20 CENTURY-FOX PICTURE

KEITHS LEXINGTON AT PARK
It's Bing at his all-time Best
Doors Open at 9:45 A. M.
Prices Today: 35c Until 12.30 — 44c Until 5 P. M. — 60c 5 P. M. Until Close — All Tax Incl.
"Going my way"
A Paramount Picture with BING CROSBY RISE STEVENS Barry Fitzgerald

WARNER BROS. STANLEY HOWARD AVENUE FRANKLIN — DOORS OPEN 10:30 A. M.
WARNERS' NATIONAL JOY SHOW!
JANIE
She's the gleam in the eye of every G.I.
Joyce Reynolds — Robert Hutton — Edward Arnold — Ann Harding — Robert Benchley — Alan Hale
BUY WAR BONDS AND STAMPS

Now CENTURY LEXINGTON
SPENCER TRACY in M-G-M's THE SEVENTH CROSS
NEXT ATTRACTION RETURN ENGAGEMENT of Rob't TAYLOR — Vivien LEIGH "WATERLOO BRIDGE"

LAUREL Races
DAILY THRU OCT. 31st
FIRST RACE 1:45 P. M.
DAILY DOUBLE 4 CLOSES 1:30 P. M.
GENERAL ADMISSION $1.80 tax incl.
JOINT MEETING, BOWIE HAVRE DE GRACE, LAUREL & PIMLICO

2nd Hit VALENCIA "THE CANTERVILLE GHOST" CHAS. LAUGHTON ROB'T YOUNG

2nd Hit PARKWAY "BATHING BEAUTY" Red Skelton Esther Williams

RIVOLI Otto Kruger "THEY LIVE IN FEAR" Allan Lane "SILVER CITY KID"
DOUBLE SHOW DAILY
DOORS OPEN 9 A. M.

MAYFAIR HOWARD at FRANKLIN
FIRST BALTIMORE SHOWING
OLSEN and JOHNSON
GHOST CATCHERS
LEO CARRILLO ANDY DEVINE LON CHANEY GLORIA JEAN MARTHA O'DRISCOLL WALTER CATLETT MORTON DOWNEY ELLA MAE MORSE
SPECIAL ADDED ATTRACTION "THE ATTACK" in Southwest Pacific

COOL AIR CONDITIONED LITTLE HOWARD FRANKLIN
6th WK.
CARY GRANT When You're in Love with GRACE MOORE

COOL AIR CONDITIONED HIPPODROME
Most Hilarious Comedy of All Time
Gary COOPER TERESA WRIGHT in Casanova Brown FRANK MORGAN
ON STAGE! Danny KAYE The Daffy Auctioneer in "THE ATTACK" PETER CHAN WALLY WARD & THE FONTAINES

FORDS • NEXT WEEK • SEATS NOW
ROBERT REUD presents OUR FANNY
A new farce by HARRY SEGALL With JOY HODGES
JOHN ARCHER — LOU POLAN
N. T. NUGENT, JR.

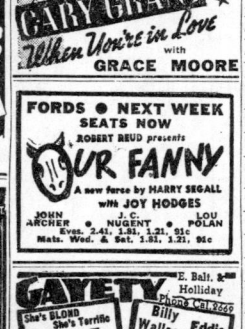

E. Balt. St. Holliday
GAYETY
She's Terrific!
CAROLE LORD 3 Cont. Balls. in "Hour of Love"
Billy Wallace Eddie Lloyd
BURLESQUE

TODAY'S MOVIE CALENDAR

Theatres advertised in this column belong to the Motion Picture Theatre Owners of Maryland.

Aero Middle River. "The Bridge of San Luis Rey."	**Fulton** Fulton & Baker. Leon Errol in "Slightly Terrific."		
Alpha Catonsville. Peter Lorre in "Mask of Dimitrios."	**Garden** Charles & Cross. Gloria Jean in "Pardon My Rhythm."		
Ambassador 4604 Lib. Hts. F. Sinatra in "Step Lively."	**Glen** Glen Burnie. Tex O'Brien in "Spook Town."		
Apollo 1500 Harford. Phil Baker in "Take It or Leave It."	**Grand** 511 S. Conkling. William Bendix in "The Hairy Ape."		
Arcade Harford & Hamilton. Frank Sinatra in "Step Lively."	**Gwynn** 4600 Liberty Hts. Jean Parker in "Detective Kitty O'Day."		
Astor Poplar Grove at Edmondson. P. O'Brien in "Marine Raiders."	**Hampden** 911 W. 36th. Wm. Bendix in "Step Lively."		
Aurora 7 E. North. Frank Sinatra in "Step Lively."	**Harford** 2620 Harford. D. O'Connor in "This Is the Life."		
Avalon 4300 Park Hts. F. March in "Adventures of Mark Twain."	**Hilton** 3117 W. North. Gene Kelly in "Thousands Cheer."		
Avenue Milton and Holbrook. Joel McCrea in "Buffalo Bill."	**Horn** 2016 W. Pratt. John Garfield in "They Made Me a Criminal."		
Avon 3019 Hamilton. Lee Gorcy in "Mr. Mugg Steps Out." Short.	**Howard** 115 N. Howard. A. Gwynne in "South of Dixie."		
Belnord 2700 Phila. Frank Sinatra in "Step Lively."	**Ideal** 906 W. 26th. Frank Sinatra in "Step Lively."		
Boulevard 33rd at Greenmount F. Sinatra in "Step Lively."	**Irvington** 4113 Frederick. F. March in "Adventures of Mark Twain."		
Bridge Edmond. at Pulaski. P. Lorre in "Mask of Dimitrios."	**Lane** Dundalk. Chester Morris in "Gambler's Choice."		
Broadway 905 S. Broadway. Johnny Weissmuller in "Tarzan's New York Adventure."	**Leader** 248 S. Linwood. Alan Ladd in "The Glass Key."		
Cameo 4400 Harford. Dan Dailey, Jr. in "Mokey."	**Linwood** 908 S. Linwood. Barbara Stanwyck in "Double Indemnity."		
Capitol 1515 W. Balto. Frank Sinatra in "Step Lively."	**Little** 523 N. Howard. Cary Grant in "When You're in Love."		
Casino 1118 Light. Robert Paige in "Her Primitive Man."	**Lord Baltimore** 1108 E. Preston. Bela Lugosi in "Gambler's Choice."		
Century 709 Wash. Blvd. F. Sinatra in "Step Lively."	**Lord Calvert** 2544 Wash. Blvd. F. Tone in "Hour for Love."		
Columbia 709 Wash. Blvd. F. Sinatra in "Christmas Holiday."	**Mayfair** 508 N. Howard. Lon Chaney in "The Hairy Ape."		
Cluster 303 S. Broadway. P. Lorre in "Mask of Dimitrios."	**McHenry** 1017 Light. Wm. Bendix in "The Hairy Ape."		
Earle Belair at Woodlee. Irving Berlin's "This Is the Army."	**Met** Pennsyl. at North. Wm. Bendix in "The Hairy Ape."		
Edgewood 3500 Edmond. W. Bendix in "The Hairy Ape."	**Nemo** 4921 Eastern. John Garfield in "Destination Tokyo."		
Eureka 401 S. Fremont. Irving Berlin's "This Is the Army."	**New** Reisterstown. Peter Lorre in "Mask of Dimitrios."		
Forest Garrison & Lib. Hts. William Bendix in "The Hairy Ape."			

New Essex Essex. Anne Baxter in "Five of St. Mark."	
New Glen Glen Burnie. Red Skelton in "Bathing Beauty."	
Northway Harford & Northern. Ed. G. Robinson in "Mr. Winkle Goes to War."	
Overlea Belair Rd. Gregory Peck in "Days of Glory."	
Palace Gay & Wolfe. Basil Rathbone in "The Scarlet Claw."	
Patterson Eastern & East. Ed. G. Robinson in "Mr. Winkle Goes to War."	
Pikes Pikesville. Deanna Durbin in "Christmas Holiday."	
Pimlico Park Hts. & Bel. Gene Kelly in "Thousands Cheer."	
Preston 1106 E. Preston. Bela Lugosi in "Voodoo Man."	
Red Wing 2241 E. Monument. Gary Cooper in "Story of Dr. Wassell."	
Rex 4617 York. Francis Lederer in "Voice in the Wind."	
Rialto 948 W. North. Ed. G. Robinson in "Mr. Winkle Goes to War."	
Ritz 1607 N. Washington. Wm. Bendix in "The Hairy Ape."	
Senator 5904 York. Wm. Bendix in "The Hairy Ape."	
State Monument & Chester. Frank Sinatra in "Step Lively."	
Strand Dundalk. Fredric March in "Adventures of Mark Twain."	
Towson Towson. Barbara Stanwyck in "Double Indemnity."	
Uptown 5010 Park Hts. Ed. G. Robinson in "Mr. Winkle Goes to War."	
Vilma Belair & Mayfield. Phil Baker in "Take It or Leave It."	
Walbrook 3100 W. North. Wm. Bendix in "The Hairy Ape."	
Waverly Greenmount & 32nd. "The Hairy Ape."	
Westport 2305 Russell. Eddie Cantor in "Show Business."	
Westway 5200 Edmond. Irene Dunne in "White Cliffs of Dover."	

BACK THE ATTACK—BUY WAR BONDS

50,000 NAZIS FLEEING BRITISH IN HOLLAND

THE WEATHER
Sunny today; clear and cooler tonight. Friday fair and cooler.

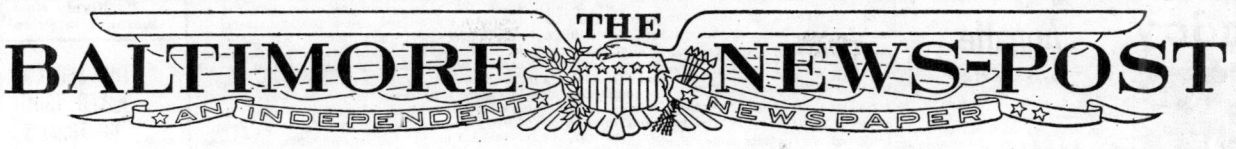

Read The Baltimore News-Post for complete, accurate war coverage. It is the only Baltimore newspaper possessing the three great wire services—
ASSOCIATED PRESS
INTERNATIONAL NEWS SERVICE
UNITED PRESS

THE BALTIMORE NEWS-POST
AN INDEPENDENT NEWSPAPER
The Largest Evening Circulation in the Entire South

8

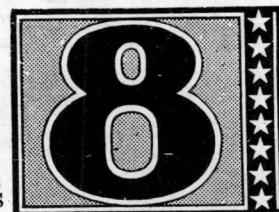

VOL. CXLV.—NO. 149 | Entered as second-class matter at Baltimore Postoffice. | THURSDAY EVENING, OCTOBER 26, 1944 | PRICE 3 CENTS

U. S. NAVY SANK, DAMAGED 26 JAP WARSHIPS IN PHILIPPINES BATTLE

DEFEAT MAY MARK END OF ENEMY FLEET

Nazis Flee British Army In Holland

ON THE BRITISH SECOND ARMY FRONT, Oct. 26—(A. P.). Lieutenant General Miles C. Dempsey's troops have captured Fort Orten, one mile north of 'S Hertogenbosch and have reached Zorgen, less than a half mile from Tilberg, 12 miles southwest of 'S Hertogenbosch on a vital Nazi supply line.

SUPREME HEADQUARTERS, A. E. F., Paris, Oct. 26—(U. P.).—More than 50,000 Germans were on the run in a general retreat along a 100-mile front in Southwest Holland today before British and Canadian armies closing swiftly against every major stronghold in a shrinking pocket below the lower Maas (Meuse) river.

Berlin reported that Allied amphibious forces were trying to land on the south coast of Walcheren Island, the westernmost of the Dutch islands above the Schelde estuary, where German guns contributed heavily to preventing the Allies from using the port of Antwerp.

RESISTANCE SLOWED

Front dispatches and Supreme Headquarters spokesmen said Marshal Sir Bernard L. Montgomery's troops were wheeling forward over the Dutch flatlands as much as eight miles in two hours against steadily diminishing resistance.

Only at 'S Hertogenbosch, vital northeastern anchor of the imperiled German pocket, was the enemy making a fight of it in a desperate bid to hold open the secondary bridge across the Maas, the only practical escape channels.

The Germans clung to a tottering foothold in the southwest cor-

Continued on Page 2, Column 4.

YANK WRITER KILLED

WITH THE U. S. SEVENTH ARMY IN FRANCE, Oct. 25 (Delayed)—(A. P.).—Sergt. Alfred O. Kohn of Miami Beach, Fla., Stars and Stripes combat correspondent, was killed by German machine-gun fire recently in the Rhone valley.

WASHINGTON, Oct. 26—(U.P.).—Officially announced American combat casualties in this war reached 472,779 today.

Secretary of War Henry L. Stimson said Army casualties through October 14 totaled 403,074, including 78,522 killed, 220,529 wounded, 51,009 missing and 53,014 prisoners of war.

Navy, Marine Corps and Coast Guard casualties reported as of today totaled 69,705, including 27,831 dead, 27,857 wounded, 9,537 missing and 4,480 prisoners of war.

Azrael Sees:

Baltimorean Greet New Units

By LOUIS AZRAEL
(News-Post War Correspondent)

SOMEWHERE IN GERMANY, Oct. 13—(Delayed).—Several hundred replacements arrived at an infantry unit here today to take the places of men who have been killed, injured or otherwise removed from combat duty.

To these men it was, of course, a fateful day. But arrival of the units was important to the unit they joined. For these men, hardly any of whom ever before had been in combat, must be fitted almost overnight into an organization requiring perfect team-work, an organization which, like most Army units, has developed its own tactics, methods and standards.

GREETED BY BALTIMOREAN

The unit these replacements joined has developed a unique method of integrating them.

Assembled on a field, the new men were greeted by a tall, sturdy young major from Baltimore, Grat B. Hankins, 21 North Wickham road, who has commanded a battalion in combat.

On a large map Major Hankins

Continued on Page 2, Column 7.

Contest closes November 15! Get your contest blank from your dealer today! Yes, $10,000 in War Bonds . . . 299 prizes in the big $10,000 contest on Mrs. Filbert's Margarine closes November 15. Mrs. Filbert's Margarine is so new—so fresh tasting—so different that Mrs. Filbert is putting up $10,000 in War Bonds—299 prizes in all—to get the women of America to try this sensational new fresh tasting Mrs. Filbert's Margarine. Get your contest blank from your dealer today, for Mrs. Filbert's Margarine $10,000 contest closes November 15.—Adv.

Dewey Links Roosevelt To '1,000 Club'

(Text of Governor Dewey's speech in Chicago last night will be found on Page 5.)

By LEO W. O'BRIEN

ABOARD DEWEY CAMPAIGN TRAIN EN ROUTE TO ALBANY, N. Y., Oct. 26—(I. N. S.).—Gov. Thomas E. Dewey returned to the East today for the climactic phase of his campaign after accusing President Roosevelt of "sponsoring an idea to sell special privileges and a voice in the formulation of Administration policies for one thousand dollars on the barrel-head."

The Republican Presidential nominee, by the stinging tone of his Chicago speech last night, indicated he has unmasked his heaviest guns for the closing days of the campaign.

NEW SPEAKING SITES

From now until November 7 Governor Dewey will confine his speaking activities to New York and New England, with talks presently scheduled in Syracuse, Buffalo, Boston and New York city.

Twenty-five thousand persons jammed into the huge Chicago Stadium heard the Republican nominee r e p e a t e d l y challenge President Roosevelt's "veracity" and heard him read a letter which, he asserted, revealed a Democratic plot to sell "special privilege" to 1,000 persons "for $1,000 laid on the line to finance the fourth-term drive."

Governor Dewey pulled no

Continued on Page 2, Column 5.

A. P. Correspondent Is Killed On Leyte

SAN FRANCISCO, Oct. 26—(A. P.).—Asahel (Ace) Bush's luck ran out yesterday. The thirty-one year old Associated Press war correspondent was killed by a Japanese bomb at Tacloban, liberated capital of Leyte Island in the Philippines. Bush was the tenth civilian newsman killed in the Pacific theatres.

Cruiser Australia Damaged In Action

CANBERRA, Australia, Oct. 26—(A.P.).—Prime Minister John Curtin announced today that H. M. S. Australia suffered superficial damage October 20 during the early stages of the Philippines invasion, and that Capt. E. F. V. Dechaineux, the ship's commander, was fatally wounded.

Jap Fleet Smashed In Huge U. S. Naval Victory In Pacific

By FRANK ROBERTSON

ABOARD ADMIRAL KINKAID'S FLAGSHIP, PHILIPPINES, Oct. 26—(I. N. S.).—Almost all of Japan's Imperial fleet battleships and cruisers were sunk or damaged by Vice-Admiral Thomas C. Kinkaid's Seventh Fleet during 24 hours of two flaming actions off Leyte and Samar Islands, in the Central Philippines.

Smashing a desperate Japanese attempt to annihilate Gen. Douglas MacArthur's invasion forces on Leyte and Samar, Kinkaid's naval forces sank at least one enemy battleship, severely damaged four others, destroyed an unknown number of cruisers and crippled six more. In addition, many Jap destroyers were sunk and damaged.

JAP FLEET SPLIT

Split as it was into separate forces, the Japanese fleet was engaged by Seventh Fleet ships and planes only 40 miles south of MacArthur's Leyte beachhead and little more than 60 miles from this flagship's position off Samar.

The southerly Japanese naval force, consisting of two battleships, three cruisers and six destroyers, was sighted by PT boats at 1.23 A. M. Wednesday in Surigao strait between Southern Leyte and Northern Mindanao.

Rear Admiral Jesse D. Olendorf's battleship formation roared into action against this force in Leyte gulf at 3.05 A. M. The battle lasted an hour and a half, but the Jap flotilla, utterly defeated, had turned tail and begun to flee after 40 minutes of action.

ALL JAP SHIPS HIT

Carrier-based planes, pursuing remnants of the shattered enemy battle force into the Mindanao sea, broke off action at 9 A. M. after all 11 of the enemy ships had been blasted to the bottom or severely crippled. One of the two battleships in this formation was last observed dead in the water and burning fiercely.

The second thunderous engagement began at 7.30 A. M. Wednesday, when Japanese battleships and cruisers, moving south in the Pacific about 30 miles off Samar's east coast, opened fire on Rear Admiral Thomas L. Sprague's lightly escorted force of baby flat-tops.

This Japanese naval force, obviously intending to sweep everything before it and join up with the other, but already beaten, Japanese force in Leyte gulf, con-

Continued on Page 2, Column 1.

Churchill Balks Service Releases

LONDON, Oct. 26—(A. P.).—Prime Minister Churchill, observing "we are at a most grim moment in the war," declined in Commons today to discuss the return of soldiers who have long been overseas. Releases from the Army on a large scale are not possible now, he stated.

NAZI GENERAL KILLED

LONDON, Oct. 26—(A. P.).—The Berlin radio reported today that General Schneckenburger, commander of a German army corps, was killed by Russian planes in a low-level attack on an advanced trench position at Belgrade.

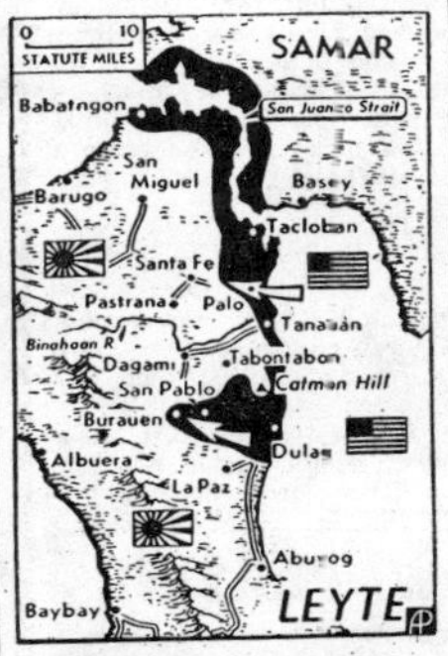

PHILIPPINE GAINS—Driving north of Tacloban, U. S. forces have seized control of San Juanico strait by capturing Babatngon, on Leyte, and the southern coast of Samar Island. On Leyte Americans also advanced westward from Palo and to the south took Burauen (see arrows).

Yanks Advance On Leyte And Samar Isles

GENERAL MacARTHUR'S HEADQUARTERS, LEYTE, Oct. 26—(U. P.).—American troops have landed on Samar and seized the southern coast of the island, last barrier in the Philippines before Luzon, while other forces extended their gains on Leyte to bring 31 towns and villages and six airfields under U. S. control, Gen. Douglas MacArthur announced today.

MacArthur also disclosed that American troops had driven 10 miles inland to capture the road junction of Burauen splitting the Japanese forces on Northern Leyte. He reported that Field Marshal Count Juichi Terauchi's forces in that sector were "disintegrating."

STAGE 17-MILE DRIVE

The invasion of Samar, third largest island in the Philippines, was made by Maj. Gen. Verne D. Mudge's First Dismounted Cavalry Division, which made a 17-mile amphibious drive up the eastern coast of Leyte and crossed over the narrow San Juanica strait.

Although MacArthur's communique said the landing was made on the southern coast of Samar, which gave the Americans control of the eastern shore of the strait, the cavalrymen apparently landed at a point about 90 miles southeast of Luzon.

The northeastern tip of Samar, an island of 5,124 square miles, is separated from Luzon by the 12-mile-wide San Bernardino strait.

CLIMAX OF DRIVE

The landing on Samar was a culmination of amphibious jumps

Continued on Page 2, Column 2.

Roosevelt vs. Dewey—which one for a sound national administration? Hear both sides, as Secretary Harold Ickes and Republican Senator Homer Ferguson fight it out verbally tonight on America's Town Meeting of the Air. Sponsored by The Reader's Digest. WCBM, 8:30—Advt.

U. S. Fleet Victory Will Shorten War

By ARTHUR F. HERMANN

WASHINGTON, Oct. 26—(I. N. S.).—The crushing defeat of the Japanese Navy in Philippine waters was viewed today as serving to hasten by months the projected United States thrust to the China coast and heralded the probability of early smashing assaults on the Pacific enemy's home islands.

Naval officials in Washington felt that the Japanese Navy may never again be able to face American sea forces in any all-out battle, prompting optimistic forecasts that the Pacific phase of World War II. has been shortened by months at an incalculable saving of American lives.

HASTEN NEW ATTACKS

Another probable outcome of the terrific battle, naval circles believe, is an early strike at Japan's strategic bastions on Formosa, which would serve to minimize or remove the ever-present danger of air attacks to the projected United States sea road between that island and the Northern Philippines on the route to the China coast.

While a final capitulation of the damage wrought on the once proud Japanese Imperial Navy has not been tabulated completely, there was no doubt in any official mind, from President Roosevelt

Continued on Page 2, Column 5.

"Zodiac Girls"—Don't Miss Scorpio, Another in the Series of Novel Interpretations of the Signs of the Zodiac. Watch for the Painting by Willy Pogany, Reproduced in Full Color on the Front Page of The American Weekly, the Magazine Distributed with Next Sunday's Baltimore American.—Adv.

Yank Force Pursues Fleeing Injured Nips; Declare Toll To Grow

U. S. PACIFIC FLEET HEADQUARTERS, PEARL HARBOR, Oct. 26—(A. P.).—More than 26 Japanes warships were sunk or heavily damaged in the three-pronged battle of the Philippines, incomplete reports on the most crushing defeat ever administered the modern Nipponese navy disclosed today.

Wreckage-strewn waters marked the possible end of the Imperial fleet as a major obstacle in the path to the coasts of Japan and China, and probably shortened the Pacific war by months.

Combined reports of Admiral Chester W. Nimitz and Gen. Doughlas MacArthur on the three major engagements involving the bulk of the Japenes fleet listed these known results:

Eight Japanese ships sunk—two carriers, one battleship, five cruisers.

Three probably sunk—two battleships, one carrier.

More than 14 damaged—seven battleships, four cruisers, four destroyers and "several" more destroyers.

Both commanders made it clear that their final reports will show heavier Japanese losses, particularly in ships sunk.

Today's combined total compared with Nimitz' first report of the three-way action listing one carrier sunk, two damaged and five or six battleships and a cruiser torpedoed. All of these, with the possible exception of two battleships, are included in the combined total.

ABOARD ADMIRAL KINKAID'S FLAGSHIP OFF LEYTE, PHILIPPINES, Oct. 26—(I. N. S.).—Remaining units of two Japanese naval forces which for a time seriously threatened Gen. Douglas MacArthur's invasion of Leyte Island are being pursued and attacked today by American carrier planes ranging over inland Philippine waters.

One cruiser and five destroyers were all that remained of the original force of 14 battleships, cruisers and destroyers.

STIMSON ISSUES WARNING

Secretary of War Henry L. Stimson in Washington warned today that increasingly stubborn Japanese resistance must be anticipated in the Philippines, despite the brilliant American naval victory.

He told a news conference landing of Gen. Douglas MacArthur's forces in Leyte was a challenge which the Japanese could not refuse, and that the landings represented the complete materialization of the increasing, suffocating pressure which is being brought to bear on the stolen Japanese Empire.

American forces entered the Philippines anticipating that the Japanese would strike back in force, he said.

JAP NAVY HIT VITAL BLOW

The crushing three-fold defeat stripped Emperor Hirohito's navy of the greater part of its known carrier, battleship and cruiser power, necessary to engage the U. S. fleet in another major action or seriously check its further incursions into the Western Pacific.

During the three-day battles the fate of MacArthur's invasion hung in the balance.

This was the touchstone that brought the Japanese fleet out of hiding and precipitated one of the greatest engagements in naval history, involving almost every type of warship from battleships to PT boats and submarines, and seaborne and land-based planes.

By comparison, in the greatest previous Nipponese de-

Continued on Page 2, Column 1.

VERY LATEST NEWS

NAZI RADIO HAS RAID WARNING

NEW YORK, Oct. 26—(I. N. S.).—Allied air raids on Hannover and Brunswick were indicated today by German home radio warnings. The bombers were over the two cities for close to two hours, the German network reported.

STIMSON SILENT ON PEARL HARBOR REPORT

WASHINGTON, Oct. 26—I. N. S.). — Secretary of War Stimson declined to comment today on how soon he might make public the War Department report on the Pearl Harbor attack.

NEWS-POST

Temperatures

12 Midn't, 57	7 A. M., 54
1 A. M., 55	8 A. M., 55
2 A. M., 54	9 A. M., 56
3 A. M., 53	10 A. M. 56
4 A. M., 53	11 A. M., 57
5 A. M., 54	12 Noon, 61
6 A. M., 55	1 P. M., 63

Marquand's Story "Late George Apley" At Ford's Monday

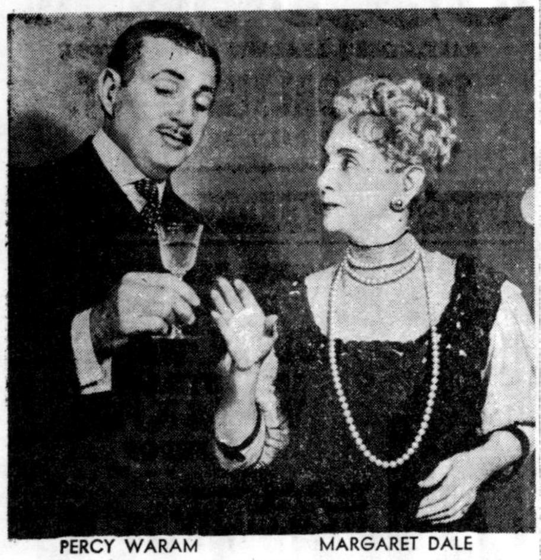
PERCY WARAM MARGARET DALE

By NORMAN CLARK

TALL, DIGNIFIED John Peter Toohey, who has won renown in the literary as well as the publicity field, is the advance agent for the new play, "The Late George Apley," which is based on the John P. Marquand novel and is coming to Ford's next Monday night, Mr. Toohey avows that the story we are unfolding in this space today truly happened in Boston.

Readers of "The Late George Apley," will recall that it is a satire on the Boston Brahmins, those insular persons say Mr. Toohey, who move in the upper social brackets of society in the "Athens of America." They look down with condscending superiority on anyone who is not of their own "class," or who happens to have been born in any other part of the country.

When the well known actor, Leo G. Carroll, was engaged to play the title role in the comedy, Mr. Marquand thought it would be interesting if he journeyed over to Boston and spent a couple of days absorbing something of the atmosphere and feeling of the play. Mr. Marquand agreed to act as his cicerone. The two met by appointment at the office of the novelist's publishers one afternoon a few weeks ago.

"Perhaps we might start by a visit to the Somerset Club," suggested Mr. Marquand. "I happen to be a member. It's over on Beacon street and it's very like the club shown in the epilogue of the play."

The two strolled over to the club which proved to be deserted at that time of the day. The attendant on the door didn't recognize Mr. Marquand at first, but was finally persuaded that the noted author was a bona-fide member.

"I have a visitor with me" said Mr. Marquand, reaching for the book in which members are required to register the names of their guests.

The attendant caught his arm and inquired:

"Is your visitor from Boston?"

"Why, no, he isn't," replied Mr. Marquand. "He happens to be from New York."

A look of something approximating mild distaste spread over the attendant's face as he indicated a small book on the desk adjoining the regular guests' register.

"This is for outside guests," he said snappily.

And thus did Mr. Carroll, within two hours after his arrival in Boston, find himself immersed in the authentic atmosphere of the play.

In the cast at Ford's next week, besides Mr. Carroll, there will be such notable players as Janet Beecher, Percy Waram and Margaret Dale. Geoorge S. Kaufman collaborated with Mr. Marquand on the dramatization of the book and is directing the play.

Needle Craft

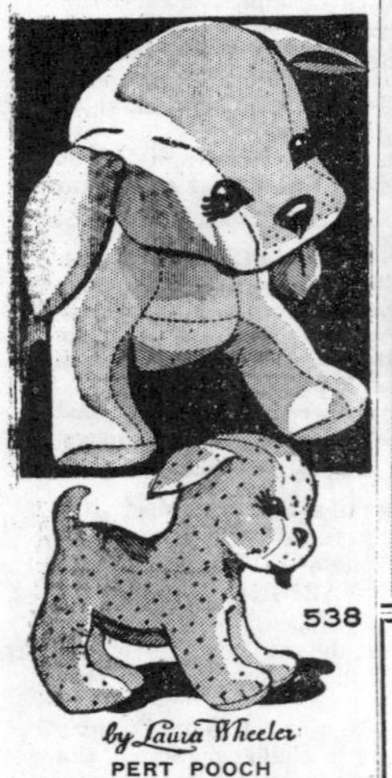
538
by Laura Wheeler

PERT POOCH

This pert and playful pooch will make an instant hit when he's spied under the Christmas tree. Use up odd pieces of colorful material.

This pup with his mischievous and curious eyes is put together like magic. Pattern 538 has transfer pattern; directions for dog.

This pattern, together with a needlework pattern for personal or household decoration, FIFTEEN CENTS.

Send FIFTEEN CENTS in coins for these patterns to The Baltimore News-Post, Needlecraft Dept., P. O. Box 147, Station O, New York 11, N. Y.

Fifteen cents more brings you our new 1945 Needlecraft Catalogue . . . 95 illustrations of designs for embroidery, toys, knitting, crochet, quilts, handicraft, . . . a free doll pattern printed right in catalogue.

GIs Young Wife Given Advice By Annette

By ANNETTE

Dear Annette: I have been divorced and now I am married again and my husband is overseas. He has been there now 17 months and I haven't seen him for 18 months. I also have a son fourteen months old, whom he has never seen. My husband and I are about twenty and he treats me good and sends me all his money. Until here lately I've been receiving letters from him that have me worried.

I'm a true wife and I work, too. Now I have just received a letter from him stating that it has been bothering him ever since he married me about my being divorced. He also says that he loves me deeply, except that when he comes home he will like to straighten this bother out without causing him or myself unhappiness.

Now he knew before he married me I was divorced. Don't you think it is a little late for him to tell me after he has a son? I don't understand him; he has never before written me such a letter. Please advise me.

MARRIED PARTY.

My dear, I think you have misunderstood the letter from your husband, who obviously loves you a great deal. My interpretation of his remarks is that he is preparing you for his request that you join his church. When a man is close to war, as your husband is, he begins to think about such things as religion and the values of life with far more seriousness than before.

This accounts for his having mentioned it to you at this time. His obvious tenderness for you indicates that he is very much in love with you, and yours, that you love him. Keep on being a "true wife" and good luck to you!

HIS 65TH

"Without Love," Spencer Tracy-Katharine Hepburn starrer, will be veteran character actor Felix Bressart's sixty-fifth motion picture.

Bressart has been cast as a scientist, in the picturization of Philip Barry's Broadway stage hit.

Berlin To Write Crosby Film Music

By DOROTHY MANNERS
Staff Writer International News Service.

HOLLYWOOD, Oct. 26.—I can hardly wait! Irving Berlin has made a deal with Mark Sandrich a Paramount to whip up the next big Bing Crosby musical. Remembering the previous get-together of Berlin and Crosby in "Holiday Inn" and the unforgettable "I'm Dreaming of a White Christmas"—this is news to set the box office jumping for joy—and me, too. The new picture is tentatively titled "Blue Skies," and in addition to the new Berlin numbers there will be many of the old hits, including the title song.

First, however, Berlin wants to spend a couple of months in the South Pacific entertaining the heroes, and he plans to leave in December. So far, Bing isn't afflicted with the wanderlust of his sidekick, Bob Hope. Crosby wants to make pictures, believing they reach a bigger service audience than he could cover even if he were triplets.

There's nothing much duller than listening to a producer tell the plot of his next picture—but Walter Morosco's really got an unusual idea in "Enchanted Voyage." It's about a man who wants to go to sea so much that he builds a boat in his backyard. Then along comes a storm that carries both the man and the boat off on an unexpected and enchanting voyage. Oddly enough, this charming story, written by Robert Nathan, has been reposing on the Twentieth Century-Fox shelf since it was published in 1936. Morosco's enthusiasm has carried right up to Head Man Darryl Zanuck, who has promised him Monty Woolley and Pegy Ann Garner for the star spots.

Myrna Loy isn't going to be in any hurry to make another picture. She's up to her neck in hospital work in New York and likes it. She's also learned to like New York better than Hollywood for a permanent address—could be because Capt. Gene Markey is so close by in Washington, D. C. Once before Myrna said she was through with the screen. Maybe she means it this time.

Hollywood in shorts: Carole Landis and Woolie Donahue dancing the nights away in New York; Alf Vanderbilt's new heart interest is a beauty named Florence Pritchard; Dare Harris, eighteen-year-old beau of Shirley Temple, is being inducted into the airborne infantry as a paratrooper tomorrow morning; it's a seven-pound-four-ounce girl for the Richard Dennings (Evelyn Ankers); the Matty Malneck rift looks permanent. Ken Murray and Harold Lloyd tossed a party congratulating themselves on their new air shows for the same sponsor.

The real reason that top band leader wants to break with the company that has been making his records for years is that they refused him a $50,000 advance—and he's broke. Are Dolores Moran and Major Gus Daymond secretly welded? He's living at the home of her parents while he's on leave here. Mary Martin tossed a birthday party back stage of "One Touch of Venus" for her daughter who was three year old Tuesday; with Robert Walker these nights it's Shirley Patterson—and vice versa.

Jackie Coogan went straight to Ciro's to meet Ramsay Ames for a pre-arranged date after he flew in tonight. The "Winged Victory" troupe leaves Sunday night for San Francisco on the start of a tour that will wind up in Washington for a special performance for F. D. R. Betty Jane Graham, one of the cover girls brought out by Columbia, has been secretly married for three months to Bob Desiel, civil engineer with the Navy; personal to Lop: You got a V-letter from Jean Pierre Aumont but he wrote so small I can't read a word of it—darn it. That's all today.

ACTING SNAKE

Hollywood's first acting snake, a 25-foot python, made its debut in "Objective, Burma," acting on cue from its trainer, Albert Schloess.

Movie CLOCK

CENTURY—"Marriage Is a Private Affair, 11.44 A. M., 2.14, 4.44, 7.14, 9.44 P. M.

NEW—"Irish Eyes Are Smiling," 10 A. M., 12, 2, 4, 6, 8, 10 P. M

KEITHS—"San Diego, I Love You." 10.10 A. M., 12.09, 2.08, 4.08, 6.08, 8.08, 10.08 P. M.

VALENCIA—"Since You Went Away," 12.30, 3.30, 6.30, 9.30 P. M.

MAYFAIR—"Ladies of Washington," 11.21 A. M., 1.13, 3.04, 4.56,. 6.47, 8.39, 10.30 P. M.

STANLEY—"The Conspirators," 11.15 A. M., 1.15, 3.15, 5.15, 7.25, 9.35 P. M.

ROSLYN—"Are These Our Parents," 1.45, 3.58, 6.11, 8.24, 10.37 P. M.

TIMES—"Machine Gun Mama," 1.59, 4.39, 7.09, 9.39 P. M., 12.09, 2.39 A. M.

PARKWAY—"Soul of Monster," 1.24, 3.06, 4.48, 6.30, 8.12, 9.55 P. M.

HIPPODROME — "None But the Lonely Heart," 10.50 A. M., 1.35, 4.20, 7.05, 10 P. M

LITTLE—"Mr. Deeds Goes to Town," 11 A. M., 1.12, 3.24, 5.36, 7.48, 10 P. M.

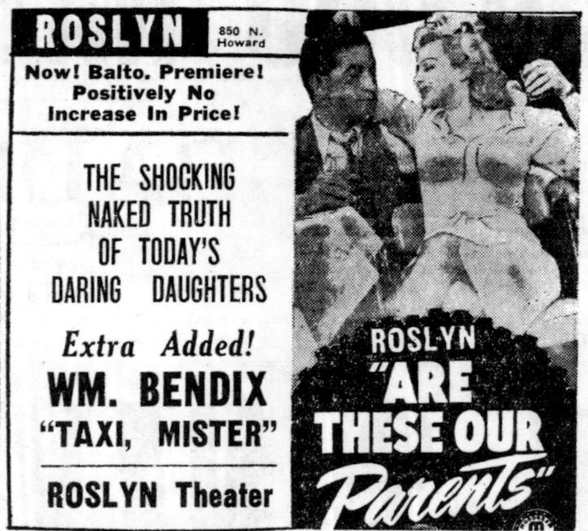
ROSLYN 850 N. Howard
Now! Balto. Premiere! Positively No Increase In Price!
THE SHOCKING NAKED TRUTH OF TODAY'S DARING DAUGHTERS
Extra Added!
WM. BENDIX
"TAXI, MISTER"
ROSLYN Theater
ROSLYN "ARE THESE OUR Parents"

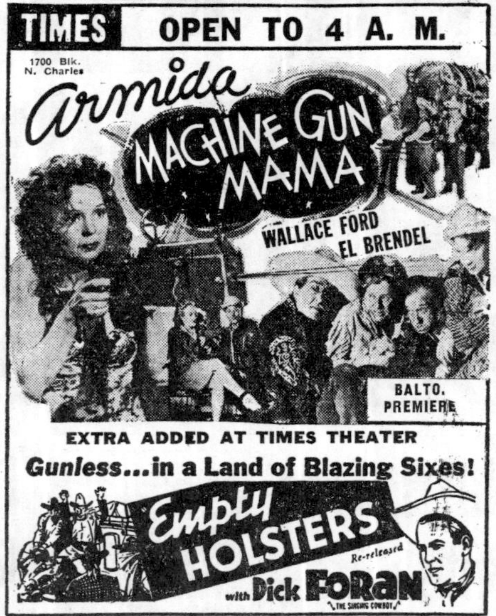
TIMES OPEN TO 4 A. M.
1700 Blk. N. Charles
Armida
MACHINE GUN MAMA
WALLACE FORD
EL BRENDEL
BALTO. PREMIERE
EXTRA ADDED AT TIMES THEATER
Gunless...in a Land of Blazing Sixes!
Empty HOLSTERS
Re-released
with Dick FORAN

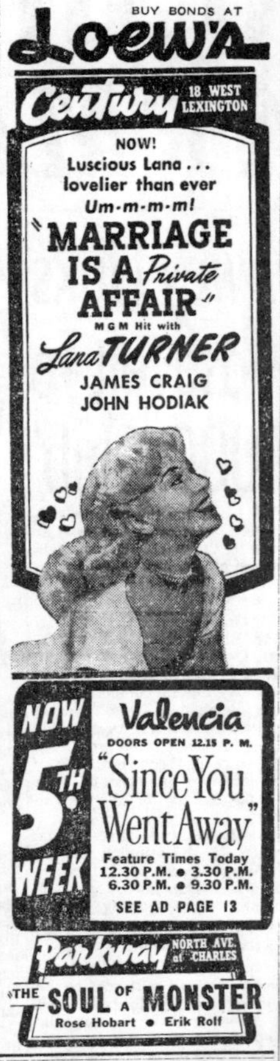
BUY BONDS AT
Loew's
Century 18 WEST LEXINGTON
NOW!
Luscious Lana... lovelier than ever
Um-m-m-m!
"MARRIAGE IS A Private AFFAIR"
MGM Hit with
Lana TURNER
JAMES CRAIG
JOHN HODIAK
NOW 5th WEEK
Valencia
DOORS OPEN 12.15 P. M.
"Since You Went Away"
Feature Times Today
12.30 P.M. ● 3.30 P.M.
6.30 P.M. ● 9.30 P.M.
SEE AD PAGE 13
Parkway NORTH AVE. AT CHARLES
THE SOUL OF A MONSTER
Rose Hobart ● Erik Rolf

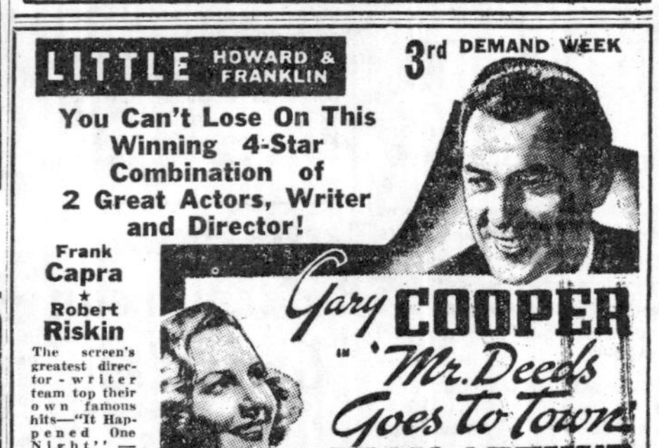
LITTLE HOWARD & FRANKLIN
3rd DEMAND WEEK
You Can't Lose On This Winning 4-Star Combination of 2 Great Actors, Writer and Director!
Frank Capra
Robert Riskin
The screen's greatest director-writer team top their own famous hits—"It Happened One Night"—"Lady for a Day"—"Broadway Bill"!
Gary COOPER
in "Mr. Deeds Goes to Town"
JEAN ARTHUR

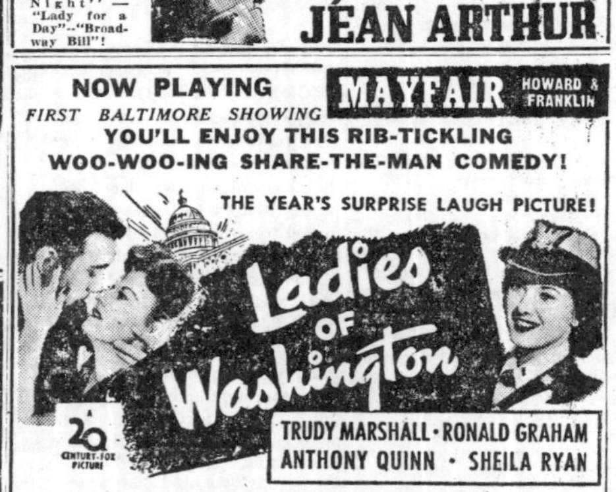
NOW PLAYING
FIRST BALTIMORE SHOWING
MAYFAIR HOWARD & FRANKLIN
YOU'LL ENJOY THIS RIB-TICKLING WOO-WOO-ING SHARE-THE-MAN COMEDY!
THE YEAR'S SURPRISE LAUGH PICTURE!
Ladies of Washington
A 20 CENTURY-FOX PICTURE
TRUDY MARSHALL • RONALD GRAHAM
ANTHONY QUINN • SHEILA RYAN

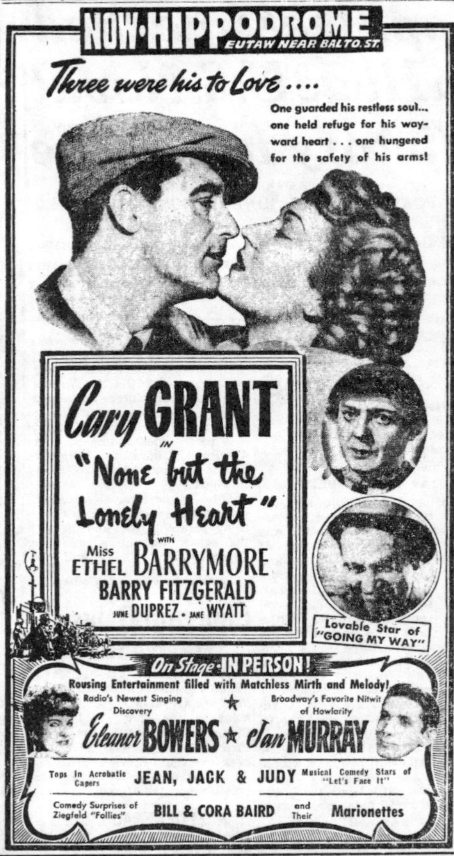
NOW • HIPPODROME EUTAW NEAR BALTO. ST.
Three were his to Love....
One guarded his restless soul... one held refuge for his wayward heart... one hungered for the safety of his arms!
Cary GRANT
in "None but the Lonely Heart"
with Miss ETHEL BARRYMORE
BARRY FITZGERALD
JUNE DUPREZ • JANE WYATT
Lovable Star of "GOING MY WAY"
On Stage - IN PERSON!
Rousing Entertainment filled with Matchless Mirth and Melody!
Radio's Newest Singing Discovery
Broadway's Favorite Nitwit of Howlarity
Eleanor BOWERS ★ Jan MURRAY
Tops in Acrobatic Capers JEAN, JACK & JUDY Musical Comedy Stars of "Let's Face It"
Comedy Surprises of Ziegfeld "Follies" BILL & CORA BAIRD and Their Marionettes

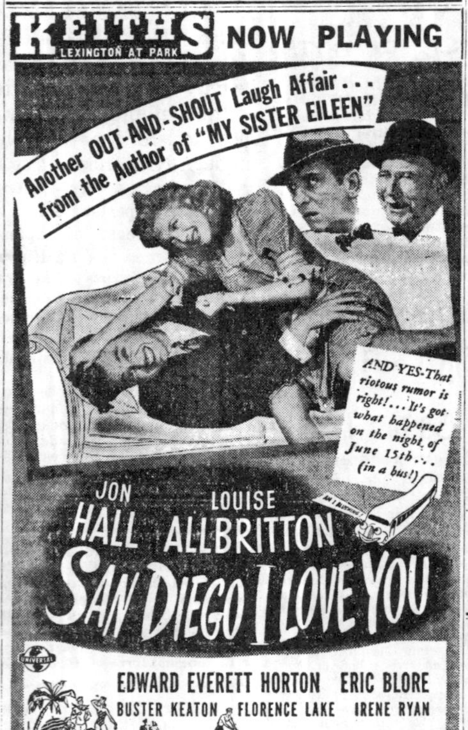
KEITHS LEXINGTON AT PARK
NOW PLAYING
Another OUT-AND-SHOUT Laugh Affair... from the Author of "MY SISTER EILEEN"
AND YES-That riotous rumor is right!... It's got what happened on the night of June 15th! (in a bus!)
JON HALL
LOUISE ALLBRITTON
SAN DIEGO I LOVE YOU
EDWARD EVERETT HORTON ERIC BLORE
BUSTER KEATON FLORENCE LAKE IRENE RYAN

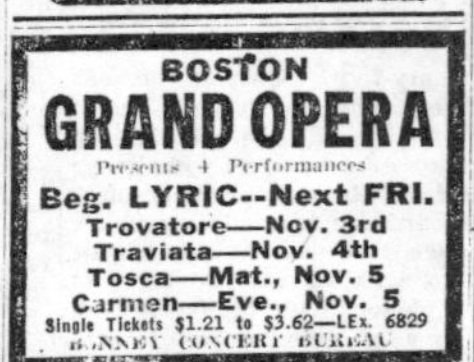
BOSTON
GRAND OPERA
Presents 4 Performances
Beg. LYRIC--Next FRI.
Trovatore—Nov. 3rd
Traviata—Nov. 4th
Tosca—Mat., Nov. 5
Carmen—Eve., Nov. 5
Single Tickets $1.21 to $3.62—LEx. 6829
BONNEY CONCERT BUREAU

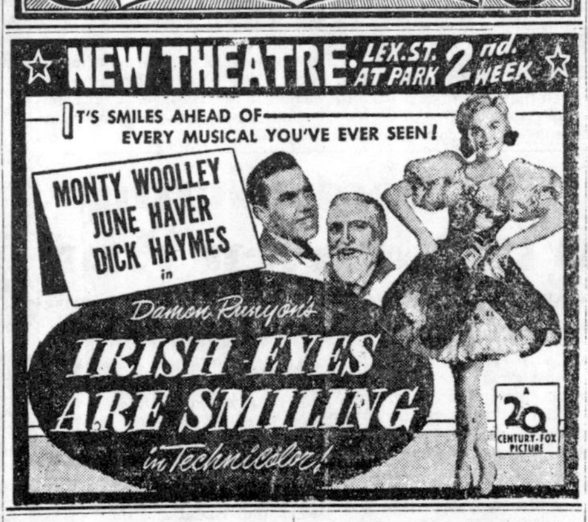
NEW THEATRE LEX. ST. AT PARK 2nd WEEK
IT'S SMILES AHEAD OF EVERY MUSICAL YOU'VE EVER SEEN!
MONTY WOOLLEY
JUNE HAVER
DICK HAYMES
Damon Runyon's
IRISH EYES ARE SMILING
in Technicolor!
A 20 CENTURY-FOX PICTURE

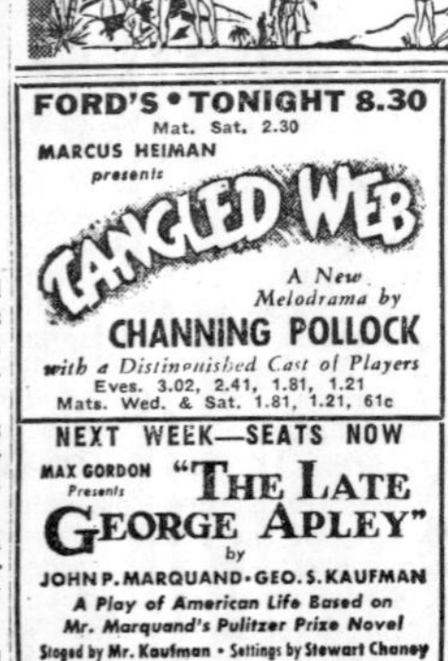
FORD'S • TONIGHT 8.30
Mat. Sat. 2.30
MARCUS HEIMAN presents
TANGLED WEB
A New Melodrama by
CHANNING POLLOCK
with a Distinguished Cast of Players
Eves. 3.02, 2.41, 1.81, 1.21
Mats. Wed. & Sat. 1.81, 1.21, 61c
NEXT WEEK—SEATS NOW
MAX GORDON Presents
"THE LATE GEORGE APLEY"
by JOHN P. MARQUAND • GEO. S. KAUFMAN
A Play of American Life Based on Mr. Marquand's Pulitzer Prize Novel
Staged by Mr. Kaufman • Settings by Stewart Chaney
Eves. 3.02, 2.41, 1.81, 1.21
Mats. Wed. & Sat. 2.41, 1.81, 1.21, 61c

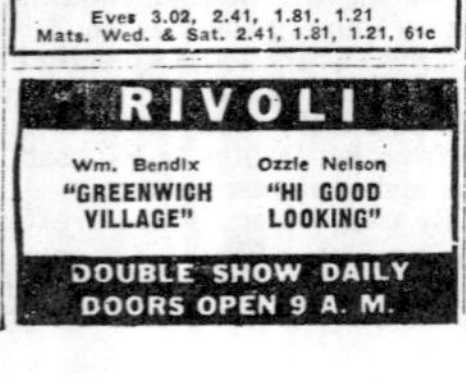
RIVOLI
Wm. Bendix "GREENWICH VILLAGE"
Ozzie Nelson "HI GOOD LOOKING"
DOUBLE SHOW DAILY
DOORS OPEN 9 A. M.

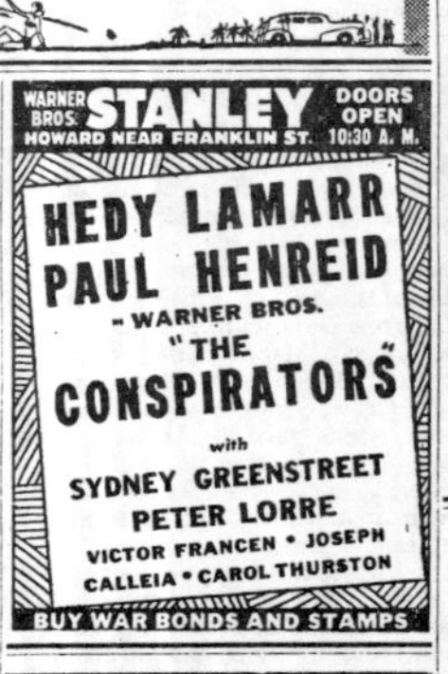
WARNER BROS. STANLEY HOWARD NEAR FRANKLIN ST.
DOORS OPEN 10:30 A. M.
HEDY LAMARR
PAUL HENREID
WARNER BROS.
"THE CONSPIRATORS"
with
SYDNEY GREENSTREET
PETER LORRE
VICTOR FRANCEN • JOSEPH CALLEIA • CAROL THURSTON
BUY WAR BONDS AND STAMPS

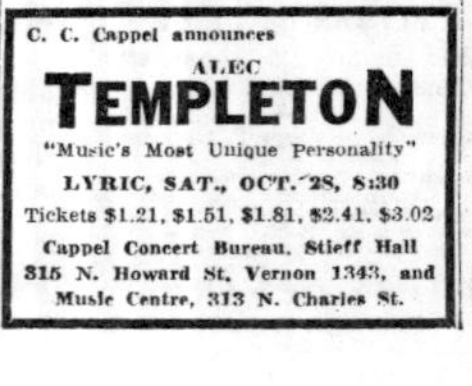
C. C. Cappel announces
ALEC
TEMPLETON
"Music's Most Unique Personality"
LYRIC, SAT., OCT. 28, 8:30
Tickets $1.21, $1.51, $1.81, $2.41, $3.02
Cappel Concert Bureau, Stieff Hall
315 N. Howard St, Vernon 1343, and
Music Centre, 313 N. Charles St.

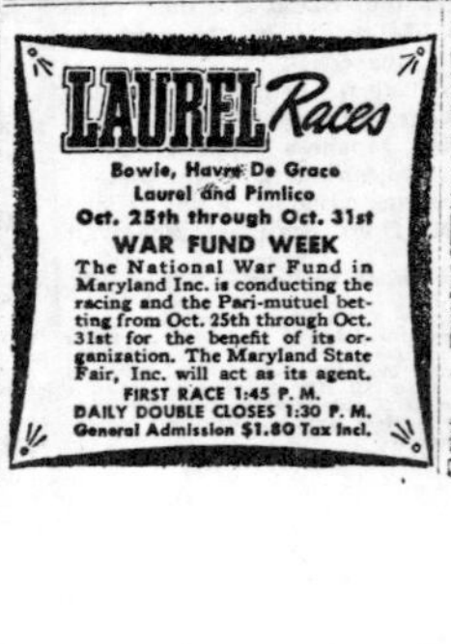
LAUREL Races
Bowie, Havre De Grace
Laurel and Pimlico
Oct. 25th through Oct. 31st
WAR FUND WEEK
The National War Fund in Maryland Inc. is conducting the racing and the Pari-mutuel betting from Oct. 25th through Oct. 31st for the benefit of its organization. The Maryland State Fair, Inc. will act as its agent.
FIRST RACE 1:45 P. M.
DAILY DOUBLE CLOSES 1:30 P. M.
General Admission $1.80 Tax Incl.

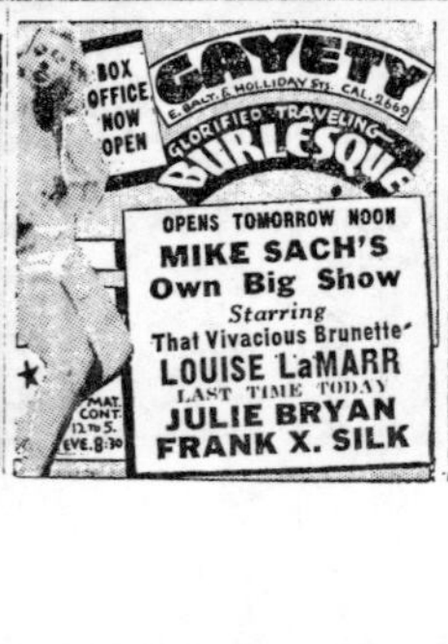
GAYETY
BURLESQUE
BOX OFFICE NOW OPEN
OPENS TOMORROW NOON
MIKE SACH'S Own Big Show
Starring
That Vivacious Brunette
LOUISE LaMARR
LAST TIME TODAY
JULIE BRYAN
FRANK X. SILK

TODAY'S MOVIE CALENDAR

Theatres advertised in this column belong to the Motion Picture Theatre Owners of Maryland.

Aero Middle River. Tom Conway in "Night of Adventure."

Alpha Catonsville. Wally Brown in "Seven Days Ashore."

Ambassador 4604 Liberty Heights. Fibber McGee and Molly in "Heavenly Days."

Apollo 1500 Harford. Acquanetta in "Jungle Woman."

Arcade Harford & Ham. Laraine Day in "Bride by Mistake."

Astor Poplar Grove & Edmondson. Acquanetta in "Jungle Woman."

Aurora 7 E. North. Laraine Day in "Bride by Mistake."

Avalon 4300 Park Hts. Fibber McGee and Molly in "Heavenly Days."

Avenue Milton & Hoffman. R. Watson in "The Hitler Gang."

Avon 3029 Hamilton. Van Johnson in "Two Girls and a Sailor."

Belnord 2700 Phila. Fibber McGee & Molly in "Heavenly Days."

Boulevard 33rd at Greenmount. S. Tracy in "Seventh Cross."

Bridge Edmond. at Pulaski. K. Hepburn in "Dragon Seed."

Broadway 509 S. Broadway. C. Moore in 'Atlantic City.'

Cameo 4705 Harford. Robert Taylor in "Stand By for Action."

Capitol 1518 W. Balto. Acquanetta in "Jungle Woman."

Casino 1118 Light. Thomas Mitchell in "The Sullivans."

Cluster 303 S. Broadway. E. Knox in "A Wave, a Wac, a Marine."

Columbia 709 Wash. Blvd. Evelyn Ankers in 'Jungle Woman.'

Earle Belair Rd. & Woodlea. L. Bari in "Sweet and Low Down."

Edgewood. 5200 Edmond. V. Leigh in "Waterloo Bridge."

Eureka 401 S Fremont. Elsa Lanchester in "Passport to Destiny."

Forest Gar. & Lib. Hts. Jack Haley in "Take It Big."

Fulton Fulton & Baker. R. Young in "Canterville Ghost."

Garden Charles & Cross. Fibber McGee and Molly in "Heavenly Days."

Glen Glen Burnie. Judy Canova in "Louisiana Hayride."

Grand 511 S. Conkling. Jack Haley in "Take It Big."

Gwynn 4600 Liberty Hts. V. Johnson in "Two Girls and a Sailor."

Hampden 911 W. 36th. Judy Canova in "Louisiana Hayride."

Harford 2620 Harford. Abbott and Costello in "In Society."

Hilton 3117 W. North. Chas. Laughton in "The Private Life of Henry VIII."

Horn 2016 W. Pratt. Jack Haley in "Take It Big."

Howard 115 N. Howard. S. Tracy in "Seventh Cross."

Ideal 906 W. 36th. Tom Conway in "A Night of Adventure."

Irvington 4113 Frederick. Jack Haley in "Take It Big."

Lane Dundalk. Grace MacDonald in "Hat-Check Honey."

Leader 218 S. Broadway. All-Polish Talking Picture "Pan-Twardowski."

Linwood 908 S. Linwood. E. Knox in "A Wave, a Wac ang a Marine."

Little 523 N. Howard. G. Cooper in "Mr. Deeds Goes to Town."

Lord Baltimore 1110 W. Balto. Jack Haley in "Take It Big."

Lord Calvert 2444 Wash. Blvd. Joel McCrae in "The Great Moment."

Lyceum Sparrows Point. Anne Baxter in "Eve of St. Mark."

Mayfair 508 N. Howard. T. Marshall in "Ladies of Washington."

McHenry 1037 Light. Spencer Tracy in "Seventh Cross."

Met Penn. at North. Fibber McGee and Molly in "Heavenly Days."

Nemo 4921 Eastern. Robert Watson in "The Hitler Gang."

New Reisterstown. Phil Baker in "Take it or Leave It."

BACK THE ATTACK— BUY WAR BONDS

New Essex Essex. Bette Davis in "Mr. Skeffington."

New Glen Glen Burnie. Joel McCrea in "The Great Moment."

Northway Harford & North. Pkwy. H. Bogart in 'Dead End.'

Overlea Belair Rd. J. Reynolds in "Janie."

Palace Gay & Hoffman. S. Craie in "Cry of Werewolf."

Patterson Eastern & East. S. Tracy in "Seventh Cross."

Pikes Pikesville. D Ameche in "Greenwich Village."

Pimlico Park Hts. & Belvd. J. Haley in "Take It Big."

Preston 1108 E. Preston. Judy Canova in "Sleepy Lagoon."

Red Wing 2231 E. Monument. Gary Cooper in "Casanova Brown."

Rex 4617 York. Red Skelton in 'Bathing Beauty.'

Rialto 816 W. North. Joan Crawford in "They All Kissed the Bride."

Ritz 1607 N. Wash. Evelyn Ankers in "Jungle Woman."

Senator 5904 York. Laraine Day in "Bride by Mistake."

State Monument & Castle. Laraine Day in "Bride by Mistake."

Strand Dundalk. Fibber McGee and Molly in "Heavenly Days."

Towson Towson. Ann Harding in "Janie."

Uptown 5010 Park Hts. Larane Day in "Bride by Mistake"

Vilma Belair & Mayfield. E. Ankers in "Jungle Woman."

Walbrook 3100 W. North. J Reynolds in "Janie."

Waverly Greenmount & Gorsch. J. Haley in "Take It Big."

Westport 3305 Russell. Linda Darnell in "Sweet and Low Down."

Westway 5200 Edmond. Jimmy Lydon in "Henry Aldrich, Boy Scout."

CASH OR CREDIT
USE OUR BUDGET SYSTEM
JACOB SUGAR
OFFERS
MEN'S OR LADIES' ALL-WOOL
TOPCOATS OR OVERCOATS
FOR
$5.00
WITH THE PURCHASE OF A MAN'S SUIT FROM $25 TO $45
SIZES UP TO 52
NATIONAL FAMOUS MAKES
- 2—$25 GARMENTS FOR $30
- 2—$30 GARMENTS FOR $35
- 2—$35 GARMENTS FOR $40
- 2—$40 GARMENTS FOR $45

BOYS' ALL WOOL OVERCOATS
$5
WITH THE PURCHASE OF A BOY'S SUIT
FROM $10 TO $17
SIZES UP TO 18
MEN'S AND BOYS' RAINCOATS & TRENCH COATS FROM $3.95 TO $12.95
JACOB SUGAR'S SAMPLE CLOTHING HOUSE
1314-16 W. NORTH AVE.
NEAR DRUID HILL AVE.
LOOK FOR THE WHITE HOUSE

CURRENT DIVIDEND 3% PER ANNUM
Each account insured up to $5,000 by the Federal Savings & Loan Insurance Corporation.
OCCIDENT FEDERAL
Savings & Loan Ass'n.
1201 W. Fayette St. Open Daily

How To Relieve Bronchitis

Creomulsion relieves promptly because it goes right to the seat of the trouble to help loosen and expel germ laden phlegm, and aid nature to soothe and heal raw, tender, inflamed bronchial mucous membranes. Tell your druggist to sell you a bottle of Creomulsion with the understanding you must like the way it quickly allays the cough or you are to have your money back.
CREOMULSION
for Coughs, Chest Colds, Bronchitis

FALSE TEETH FIT LIKE NEW WITH DENTUR-EZE
ONE APPLICATION makes loose plates fit comfortably for weeks. *Not a powder—not a paste.* Thousands delighted. Economical; tubes 59c and 98c at all good drug stores.
MONEY-BACK GUARANTEE
READ'S DRUG STORES

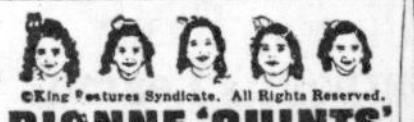
©King Features Syndicate. All Rights Reserved.
DIONNE 'QUINTS'
promptly relieve coughing of
CHEST COLDS
WITH MUSTEROLE

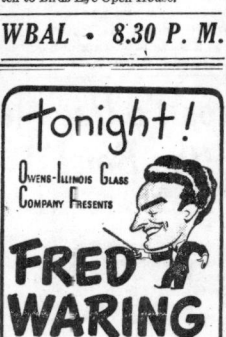

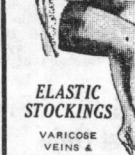

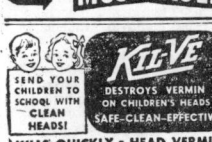

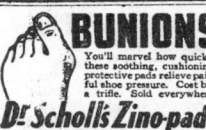

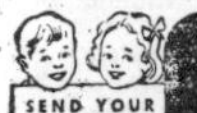
SEND YOUR CHILDREN TO SCHOOL WITH CLEAN HEADS!
KIL-VE
DESTROYS VERMIN ON CHILDREN'S HEADS
SAFE—CLEAN—EFFECTIVE
KILLS QUICKLY • HEAD VERMIN—BODY LICE. For Sale at Read's and other drug stores.

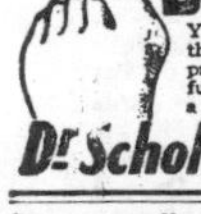
BUNIONS
You'll marvel how quickly these soothing, cushioning, protective pads relieve painful shoe pressure. Cost but a trifle. Sold everywhere.
Dr Scholl's Zino-pads

Hands That ITCH and BURN
and are rough or dry, often find longed-for relief in the bland, comforting action of
RESINOL OINTMENT AND SOAP

Exterminate Bedbugs ! !
WITH "GETRIDOFTHEM"
Clean out Bedbugs in 1 or 2 sprayings a year. Stainless and odorless. Kills roaches at once. Pint size, $1.25; quart size, $1.45; half gal., $1.85; one gal., $2.50. Buy the gallon size and save money. Shipped C. O. D. PAINT PRODUCTS CO., 30 Church St., New York City.
"IT'S WORTH THE PRICE BECAUSE IT DOES THE JOB"

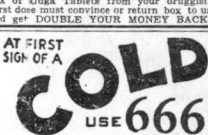

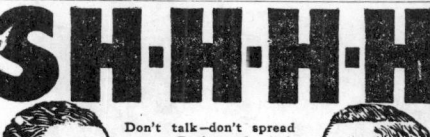

SH-H-H-H
Don't talk—don't spread rumors, Don't cough—don't spread germs. Smith Bros. Cough Drops, Black or Menthol, are still as soothing and delicious as ever—and they still cost only a nickel.
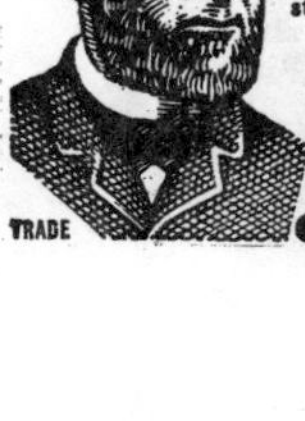
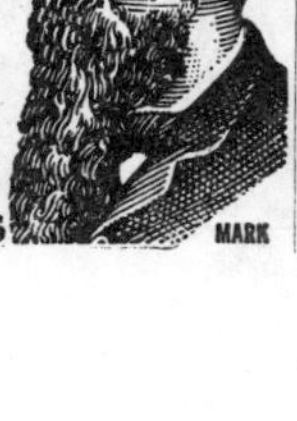
SMITH BROS.
TRADE COUGH DROPS MARK

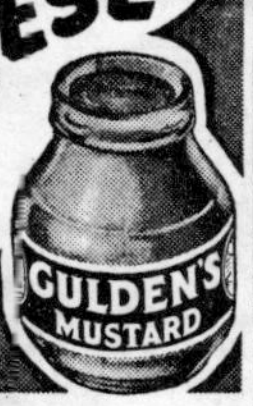
SERVE WITH CHEESE
GULDEN'S MUSTARD

Advertisement.

How Many Hearts?

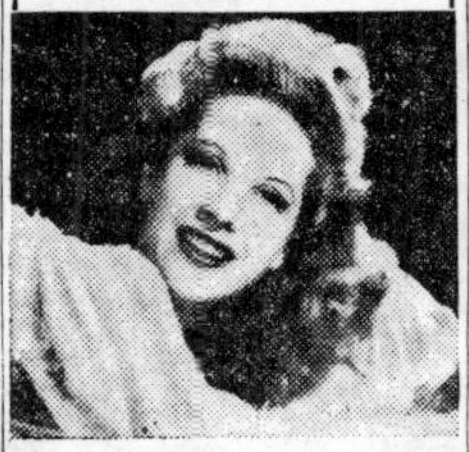

DINAH SHORE who flippety-flops nation's hearts, is top-liner in her own fast-moving musical and comedy ½ hour on coast-to-coast NBC network. Chuckle-provider Eddie Cantor guests it with Robert Emmett Dolan providing well-paced orchestra spots and 12-male chorus under Joe Lilley. Harry Von Zell carries commercials as well as part opposite de-beautiful Dinah. Listen to Birds Eye Open House.

WBAL • 8.30 P. M.

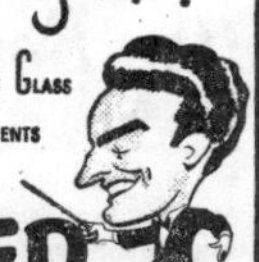
tonight!
OWENS-ILLINOIS GLASS COMPANY PRESENTS
FRED WARING
AND HIS PENNSYLVANIANS!
WCBM-7 PM

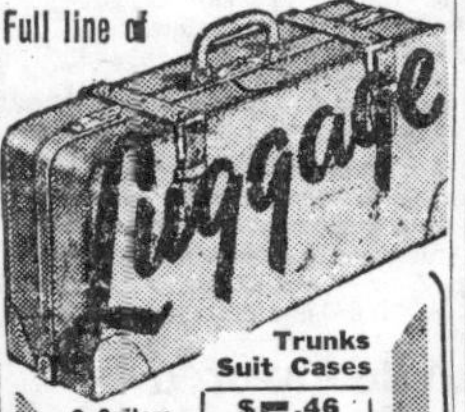
Full line of Luggage
Trunks
Suit Cases
2 Suiters—Gladstones—Overnight
$5.46 UP Tax Incl.
CAPITAL LOAN CO.
531 N. Eutaw, Cor. Franklin
Est. 1904

DR. N. B. GWYNN
SURGEON-DENTIST
WYETH BLDG.
36-38 W. Lexington St.
Phone SAratoga 3039
Office Hours:
Daily 9 A. M. to 8 P. M.
Sundays 10 A. M. to 2 P. M.

Advertisement.

Could Cleopatra Drink a Pearl with Stomach Ulcer Pains?

An intriguing story of Cleopatra is the one where an admirer praised the beauty of two of her pearls, whereupon she dropped one into a glass of wine and drank it. She would hardly have done this had she suffered after-eating pains. Those who are distressed with stomach or ulcer pains, indigestion, gas pains, heartburn, burning sensation, bloat and other conditions caused by excess acid should try Udga. Get a 25c box of Udga Tablets from your druggist. First dose must convince or return box to us and get DOUBLE YOUR MONEY BACK.

AT FIRST SIGN OF A
COLD
USE 666
Cold Preparations as directed

Programs This Evening

Thursday, October 26

	WBAL 1090 KC	WFBR 1300 KC	WCAO 600 KC	WCBM 1400 KC	WITH 1230 KC
3.00	†Woman of Amer.	‡News; Tune Shop	†Mary Marlin	*Morton Downey	*Jimmy Dorsey
3.15	†Ma Perkins	*Tune Shop	†Tina and Tim	‡Star Time	" "
3.30	†Pepper Young	" "	‡Md. Women's Cl.	*Czechoslov. Pgm.	‡I. R. MacFarlane
3.45	†Right to Happin	" "	‡Bob Trout	*Echoes of Poland	*Club Time
4.00	†Back Stage Wife	‡News	§Service Time	" "	‡News; Spt. Spec.
4.15	†Stella Dallas	‡Laurel Races	" "	‡Jewish Comment	‡Sports Special
4.30	†Lorenzo Jones	*Tune Shop	*Varieties	‡Roslyn Terhune	" "
4.45	†Widder Brown	" "	"	†Hop Harrigan	" "
5.00	†A Girl Marries	‡Race Resume	*Varieties	†Terry & Pirates	§News, Spt. Spec.
5.15	†Portia	†Chick Carter	*Sing Club	†Dick Tracy	§Sports Special
5.30	†Plain Bill	†Superman	*Bob Iula	†Jack Armstrong	" "
5.45	†Front Pg. Farrell	†Tom Mix Show	*Pioneers' Sons	†Capt. Midnight	" "
6.00	‡News, Sports	*Dinner Rhythms	‡Calmer & Eliot	*Tune Time	*Twilight Tunes
6.15	*Dinner Table	‡Stewart Kennard	‡Don Riley	‡Eddie Fenton	*Better Music
6.30	" "	‡News	*Lyn Murray	§Carroll Dulaney	‡Richard Eaton
6.45	‡Lowell Thomas	§Dottie Gibson	‡World Today	‡Henry J. Taylor	*Sugar Bill
7.00	‡Jos. A. Cantrell	‡Fulton Lewis, Jr.	†I Love a Mystery	*Fred Waring	*Enjoyment Time
7.15	‡World News	‡Amer. Action	*Music Satisfies	" "	" "
7.30	§Bob Burns	‡Judge L. Sloan	†Mr. Keene	†It's Murder	*Swing Class
7.45	" "	‡World Tonight	" "	‡Chester Bowles	" "
8.00	§Frank Morgan	‡Frank Singiser	†Suspense	‡Clifford Prevost	§News, Jackpot
8.15	" "	‡Dem. Nat'l Com.	"	†Lum and Abner	§Let's Fly
8.30	*Dinah Shore	§Kaye's Varieties	†Death Valley	‡Town Meeting	‡News, Crosby.
8.45	" "	" "	" "	" "	‡Red Cross Show
9.00	*Music Hall	‡Gabriel Heatter	§Major Bowes	‡Town Meeting	*Velvetunes
9.15	" "	§Screen Test	"	" "	*Symphony Hall
9.30	§Village Store	*Starlight Serenade	‡Corliss Archer	*Dance Orch.	" "
9.45	" "	" "	" "	" "	" "
10.00	§Abbott & Costello	‡Henry Gladstone	†First Line	‡Senator Ball	[illegible]mentator
10.15	" "	‡Rep. Natl. Com.	" "	‡I. L. G. U. Talk	[illegible]ral Agent
10.30	‡Gov. Dewey	*M. Piastro	§Here's to Romance	‡Sen. Truman	‡Time for News
10.45	and March of Time	" "	" " "	" "	*Alvina Rey
11.00	‡News; Sports	‡News; Races	‡News	‡Journal of Air	*Dick Haymes.
11.15	‡Open Bible	*Cyril Mansfield	*Joan Brooks	*Music You Want	*Music a la Carte
11.30	" "	*Guy Lombardo	*Viva America	*Norman Gordon	*Concert Miniature
11.45	*Dance Time	" "	" "	" "	"
12.00	*Dave Minor	‡News, Sign Off	*News, Nocturne	*Harry James	*Memory Tunes
12.15	*Design for Listen		"	" "	" "
12.30	*Modern Moods		*Woody Herman	*George Paxton	" "
12.45	*Fairfield Four		" "	" "	" "
1.00	‡Open Bible		‡News, Sign Off	‡News, Sign Off	‡Amer. School
1.15	" "				*Recreation Time
1.30	Sign Off				" "

Friday, October 27

	WBAL 1090 KC	WFBR 1300 KC	WCAO 600 KC	WCBM 1400 KC	WITH 1230 KC
6.00	§Happy Johnny	*Morn. in Md.	*Musical Clock		*Wake Up Balto.
6.15	" "	" "	" "		" "
6.30	*Fairfield Four	" "	" "	*Morning Melody	" "
6.45	*Bob Ellis	" "	" "	" "	" "
7.00	*News, Bob Ellis	‡News	*Musical Clock	" "	‡News Scout
7.15	" "	*Morn. in Md.	" "	" "	*Wake Up Balto.
7.30	" "	‡News	‡News	" "	" "
7.45	" "	*Clock Capers	*Musical Clock	" "	" "
8.00	‡Headline Stories	*Morn. in Md.	‡World Today	‡Martin Agronsky	‡News
8.15	*Bob Ellis	‡News	*Musical Clock	*Morning Glories	*Wake Up Balto.
8.30	‡Bonnie Gay	*Time to Shine	" "	‡Points & Prizes	*Headline News
8.45	‡News	*Morn. in Md.	" "	‡Timely Tips	*Wake Up Balto.
9.00	§Break. Table	‡Every Wom. Hour	‡Friendly Neighbor	§Breakfast Club	‡Good Neighbor
9.15	‡Molly Martin	" "	‡School of Air	‡News	" "
9.30	§Galen Fromme	" "	" "	§Breakfast Club	§All the Family
9.45	‡Victor Lindlahr	*Here's Music	†Life is Mine	§Dial for Dollars	*Sinatra Sings
10.00	†Lora Lawton	*News, Music	†Valiant Lady	†True Story	*Princess of Song
10.15	‡Robt. St. John	§Club 1300	†Light of World	" "	*Crooners' Battle
10.30	§Finders Keepers	"	†Changing World	*Cliff Edwards	§Housewives Pgm.
10.45	†Betty & Bob	" "	*Morning Melodies	‡Listening Post	" "
11.00	†Road of Life	‡Club 1300	†Honeymoon Hill	§Sardi's	‡Race Scratches
11.15	†Rosemary	" "	†Second Husband	"	*Voices You Love
11.30	†Playhouse	‡Fun to Cook	†Bright Horizon	‡Gilbert Martyn	‡I. R. MacFarlane
11.45	†David Harum	‡Your Idea	†Aunt Jenny	*Jack Berch	*Songs of Romance
12.00	‡News	‡Boake Carter	‡Kate Smith	§Glamour Manor	§Charles St. Shop
12.15	‡Sen. O'Daniel	*Music Interlude	†Big Sister	" "	" "
12.30	*Musical Express	‡News	†Helen Trent	*Music Box	*Noonday Novelties
12.45	*Fairfield Four	*392nd Army Band	†Gal Sunday	*Melody Mix	*Musical Shows
1.00	‡News	‡Ray Dady	†Life Beautiful	‡Baukage	§Blocks of Luck
1.15	*Bob Ellis	§House Party	†Ma Perkins	*Varieties	*Blue Barron
1.30	*Piano Lessons	*Lunch with Lopez	‡Bernardine Flynn	*Italian Pgm.	‡Commentary
1.45	‡Morgan Beatty	*Tune Shop	†Goldbergs	" "	‡Voice of Exper.
2.00	†Guiding Light	‡Cedric Foster	†Joyce Jordan	‡Kiernan News	*Enric Madriguera
2.15	†Today's Children	*Tune Shop	†Two on Clue	‡Mystery Chef	*Footlight Parade
2.30	†Wom. in White	" "	†Dr. Malone	§Ladies Be Seated	§Housewives Pgm.
2.45	‡Betty Crocker	" "	†Perry Mason	" "	" "

§Variety *Music †Drama ‡Talk

For ROOSEVELT
WCBM Tonight 10:15
Vice-President WALLACE
FRANK SINATRA
Authority Wm. Preston Lane, Jr.

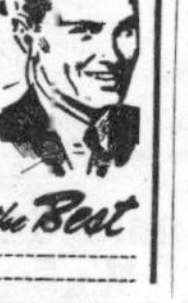
NEW LOW PRICES
Western Electric
HEARING AIDS
Designed by Bell Telephone Laboratories
Phone, Mail Coupon or Visit Office
204 W. SARATOGA
VErnon 2420
Hours 9-5,
Thurs. 'til 9 P. M.
Rent and Test the Best
Name ______
Address ______

JARMAN JOURNAL OF THE AIR
COMPLETE COVERAGE OF NATIONAL—INTERNATIONAL AND LOCAL NEWS
The only
15 MINUTES OF LATE NEWS
At 11 to 11.15 P. M.
Monday thru Friday
Presented by
JARMAN MOTORS
on
WCBM
1400 ON YOUR DIAL

RUPTURE STOPPED!
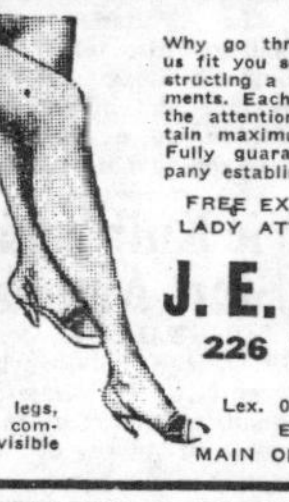
ELASTIC STOCKINGS
VARICOSE VEINS & SWOLLEN LIMB SUFFERERS
Beautify your legs, with light, cool, comfortable and invisible under-hose.
Why go through life feeling miserable? Let us fit you scientifically. We specialize in constructing a truss best suited to your requirements. Each case is individual and must have the attention of an experienced fitter to obtain maximum comfort.
Fully guaranteed and backed by our company established over 80 years.
FREE EXAMINATION, NO OBLIGATION
LADY ATTENDANT BY APPOINTMENT
J. E. HANGER, Inc.
226 W. Monument St.
Balto. 1, Md.
Lex. 0170. Open Mon. and Thurs. Evenings Until 9 P. M.
MAIN OFFICE WASHINGTON, D. C.

Advertisement.

Roosevelt or Dewey?

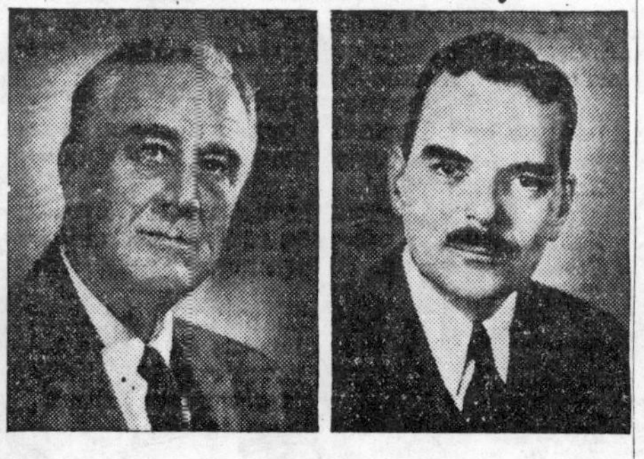

Tonight Secretary Ickes and Senator Ferguson, a couple of two-fisted spokesmen for the major political parties, discuss the question of the year—in the verbal battle of the week! America's Town Meeting of the Air brings you this exciting radio program just 12 days before election. Secretary Harold Ickes will tell why you should vote for Roosevelt. Republican Senator Homer Ferguson will tell why you should vote for Dewey. Then *both* will face cross-questioning from a typical American audience. A unique opportunity to hear *both* sides on the same program! Don't fail to listen tonight!

TONIGHT! WCBM 8:30—AMERICA'S TOWN MEETING OF THE AIR

Sponsored by The Reader's Digest

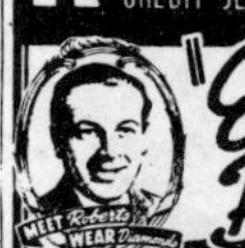
ROBERTS CREDIT JEWELERS
"Early Bird"
MEET Roberts WEAR Diamonds
SPECIAL for TODAY!
HANDSOME WALLETS
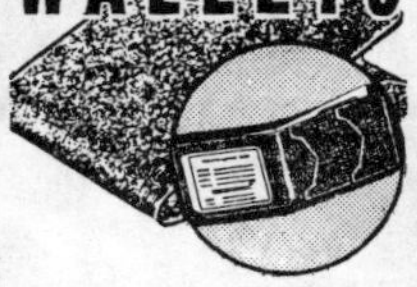
Choice of leathers from a large selection. Use your Credit—Inc. 20% Fed. Tax.
Priced From $1.95
AMERICA'S EASIEST CREDIT TERMS!
402 N. HOWARD Open Thurs., Sat. Nites
2110 E. MONUMENT Open Mon., Fri., Sat. Nites

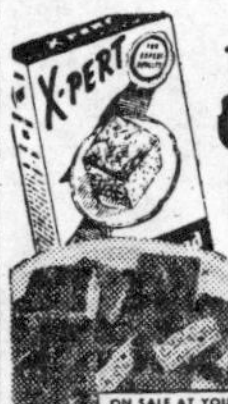
X-PERT
THE BEST GINGER BREAD YOU EVER ATE!
ADD ONLY WATER MIX AND BAKE
ON SALE AT YOUR FAVORITE GROCER ASK FOR IT TODAY
X-PERT GINGER BREAD MIX

For ROOSEVELT
WCBM Tonight 10.00
AUSPICES INDEPENDENT REPUBLICAN COM. FOR ROOSEVELT
SEN. JOS. H. BALL
By Authority Wm. Preston Lane, Jr.

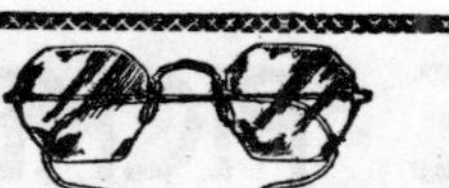
COMPLETE GLASSES
THIS INCLUDES
- Examination
- Single Vision or Bifocals
- Choice of 40 styles of Frames and Mountings
WHY PAY MORE?
$8.50 No Higher
THE ORIGINAL New Deal Optical
23 N. Liberty 845 N. Howard 3703 Eastern Ave.
BIFOCALS SAME PRICE

Christmas Cards
FOR ALL PURPOSES
NOW ON DISPLAY
MEYER & THALHEIMER
Stationers, 10 N. Howard St.
50 Years of Service

... SPEAKING OF Loans ON YOUR OWN SIGNATURE

We advertise "Simplified Loan Service" which means just what it says. It eliminates red tape and makes the borrowing of money a truly simple procedure.

The prime bases of obtaining a loan from us are ability to repay and personal character and credit reputation. We never ask for either co-makers or security unless absolutely necessary and we gladly and freely make, on a liberal credit basis, loans on one name, without co-makers or security to anyone—married or single—who has a steady job and the same sort of good record which any credit house would expect.

We frankly state that we never have made and cannot make so-called "single signature" loans to every person coming into our office... nor can any other organization do so.

To us, every application represents a special and individual case and we gladly make that type of loan which is best suited to individual necessity, depending upon the amount, etc. *WE ALWAYS CONSIDER THE SIMPLEST AND BEST METHOD FIRST.*

We give an attentive and considerate ear to personal problems and endeavor to complete each loan as quickly as possible. We feel that every customer has a right to expect courtesy, confidence, speed and fair and reasonable charges. He should NOT be subjected to unnecessary red tape, unnecessary guarantees or security and embarrassing investigations which might disclose private affairs to employers.

In making loans our aim is to render only that kind of service which is certain to foster lasting mutual friendship.

FAMILY FINANCE CORPORATION
DOWNTOWN: 1 Light St., Cor. Baltimore, 2nd Fl., Thomas Building, Tel. PLaza 1730
HIGHLANDTOWN: 507 South Conkling St., next to Grand Theatre, Tel. BRoadway 3020
WAVERLY: 3204 Greenmount Ave., 2nd Floor, Tel. UNiversity 3660
SOUTH BALTIMORE: 1037 Light Street, near Cross Street, Telephone SOuth 2640
HAMILTON: 5440 Harford Rd., Ent. on Hamilton Ave., 2nd Floor, Tel. HAmilton 1424

FREE WIN $5.00 IN GROCERIES
$5000.00 worth of prizes

THIS OFFER MADE SOLELY TO INDUCE YOU TO TRY ZERO, THE MODERN LIQUID HOUSEHOLD CLEANER

No Soap! No Water! No Mess! Zips Dirt from Surfaces the Quicker, Easier, Better Way!

First, we'd like you to do us a favor. Thousands of women who have tried Zero have written us hundreds of uses for it. We want YOU to try Zero ... and help us find the ten most important uses for Zero in your home.

Look at the coupon to the right. Read the Zero uses listed. Select any ten uses shown under the three important rooms in the home. Number your selections from 1 to 10, in the order of their importance to you, on the blank spaces provided. **Mail us the coupon properly filled in and we will send you a certificate good for two bottles of Zero, FREE!**

HERE'S HOW TO WIN THE $5.00 GROCERY ORDER

Here's all you do. Tell us in 20 words or less why you selected your No. 1 use as the most important. Write your 20 words or less in the space at the bottom of the coupon.

Then fill in your name and address, and the name and address of your grocer, then mail to the Beacon Chemical Corporation, 1 Porter Street, Philadelphia 48, Pa. If your answer is among the 1000 chosen as best by the judges you will receive a check for a $5.000 Grocery Order, absolutely FREE.

Prizes will be awarded on the basis of clearness of thought, logic and neatness, and the judges' decisions will be final. In case of ties, duplicate prizes will be awarded. Offer closes at midnight, December 31, 1944. All entries become the property of the Beacon Chemical Corporation.

Get a bottle of Zero at your grocer's today ... less than 20c a quart.

ZERO
"Reduces Dirt to Nothing"
Liquid HOUSEHOLD CLEANER
Guaranteed by Good Housekeeping
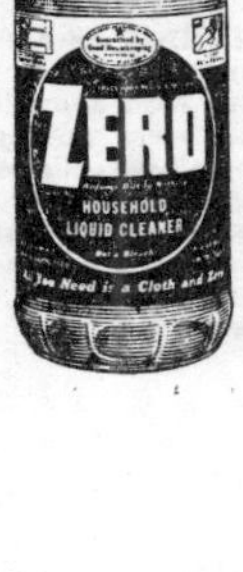

Here are my choices, numbered from 1 to 10, of the 10 best cleaning uses for ZERO Liquid Household Cleaner
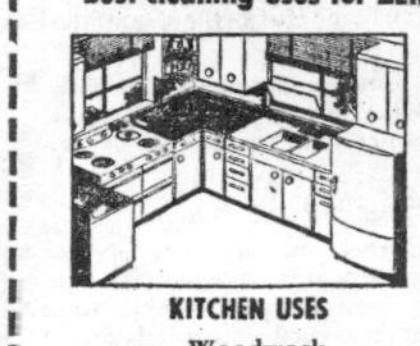
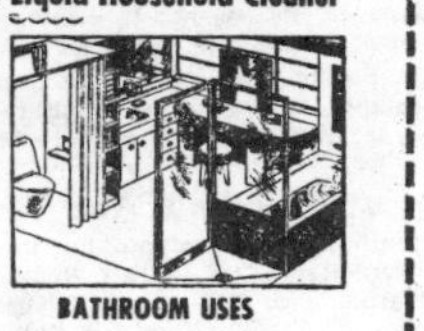
KITCHEN USES
.......Woodwork
.......Floors
.......Painted Walls
.......Stoves
.......Sinks
.......Refrigerators
.......Windows
.......Tile

BATHROOM USES
.......Fixtures
.......Tile
.......Windows
.......Woodwork
.......Floors
.......Painted Walls
.......Mirrors
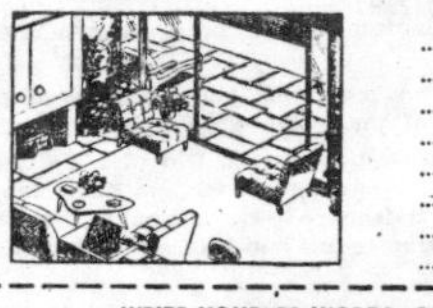
LIVING ROOM USES
.......Venetian Blinds
.......Floors
.......Painted Walls
.......Woodwork
.......Furniture
.......Rugs
.......Windows
.......Mirrors

WRITE YOUR 20 WORDS, OR LESS, BELOW:
(EXAMPLE: "I like to clean my woodwork with Zero because it doesn't take the gloss off the paint.")

MY NAME
MY STREET
MY GROCER'S NAME
MY GROCER'S ADDRESS
TOWN STATE
MAIL TO BEACON CHEMICAL CORP., P. O. BOX 537, PHILA. 5, PA.

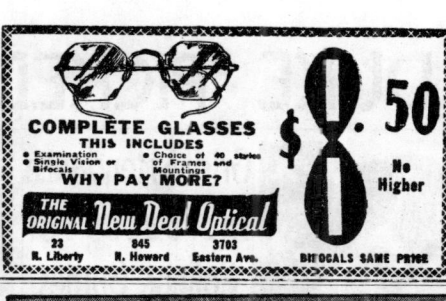

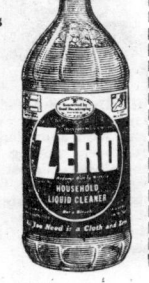

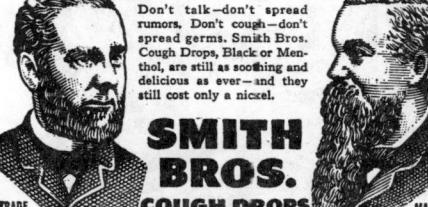

NAVY, DUKE PICKED TO WIN ON GRID BY CUDDY

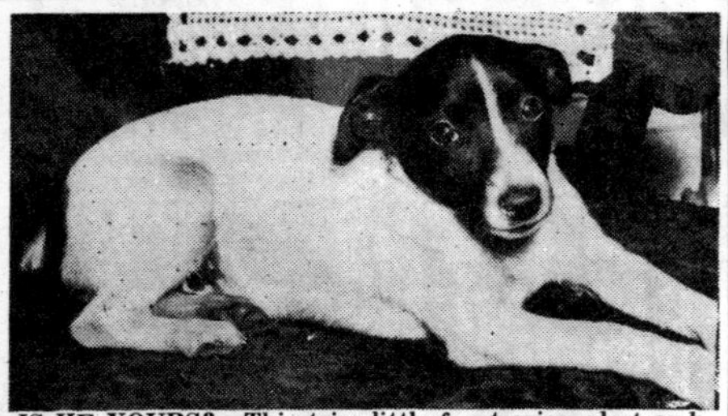

IS HE YOURS?—This trim little fox terrier, alert and friendly, is being cared for by Mrs. Mary Merson, 1305 West Cold Spring lane, near the Falls road. You can recover this fine animal by proving ownership.

RODGER H. PIPPEN

SPORTS EDITOR, SAYS:

Leroy Goldsworthy, Baltimore's new ice hockey coach, played 17 years of league ice hockey. That's a long career for baseball or any other sport and particularly long for the slam-bang game played on skates. With so much experience, Leroy should know his business. It is said of him that he was a dashing player and that's the type of team he is expected to turn out here, starting next Wednesday night at Carlin's.

Eleven years ago Goldsworthy broke his shoulder in a mix-up in front of the net and that injury introduced him to a game in which he had never taken any interest. While on the mend, he began to pitch and putt on a course near his home and now he is a regular bug about golf. He shoots in the low and middle seventies and several summers ago acted as pro at Jasper Peak Lodge at Alberta, in the Canadian Rockies. He says he is best with the short irons.

When he was thirty-five years old, Leroy played for Dallas, Texas, in the American Association. Minneapolis was in the league and the players made that long, long jump in buses. At home, in Dallas, the hockey players representing that city would go around in their shirt sleeves. Two days later, in Minneapolis, they would be struggling through two feet of snow.

Baltimore's ice hockey players this year will be a gay gang, adorned in red and white sweaters and with blue trousers.

* * *

What Navy Scouts Think Of Penn

In the opinion of Navy scouts, Penn's eleven this year is somewhat stronger than the 1943 team. Although somewhat younger, it is more alert. The Quakers are rated as powerful down-field blockers, deceptive and untiring. One scout summed it up by saying: **"Penn is a smart team with good quarterbacking and a clever offense. An average punting team, but good-to-excellent in all other departments of playing."**

Navy won last year, 24 to 7. For Navy, Vic Finos (Everett, Mass.) became a "dark horse" hero of the game, making two touchdowns and leading several long drives that scored. Hal Hamberg (Lonoke, Ark.) was Navy's other star, largely through passing and running back punts. Both players are again in the Navy line-up this season. For Penn, Bob Odell (now graduated) was outstanding.

Here are the records:

NAVY		PENN		NAVY-PENN SERIES	
14 N. C. Pre-Flt.	21	18 Duke	7	Total games	28
55 Penn State	14	20 Dartmouth	6	Won by Penn	14
7 Duke	0	46 Wm. & Mary.	0	Won by Navy	12
15 Georgia Tech.	17	— Navy	—	Tied	2
— Penn	—			Series began	1888

* * *

English Setter Lost On West Fayette Street

A two-year-old English setter, white body, black head, named Chappy, has been lost from the home of Mrs. George Chapman, 1814 West Fayette street. The dog belongs to a soldier on the other side, so please look out for him. He is very gentle and has not been trained for hunting. When he jumped the fence and got away he didn't have on his collar or license.

* * *

Shiney, A Black Spaniel, Still Lost

You can do a soldier a great favor and make a family mighty happy if you can return Shiney, a seven-month-old male black spaniel, to Mrs. G. O. Whitaker. This dog, lost Monday morning from 5 East Biddle street, belongs to Mrs. Whitaker's husband, Capt. Glenn O. Whitaker, who is stationed at Camp Ritchie. Mrs. Whitaker is anxious to get the dog back before her husband comes home on leave.

When he wandered away Shiney was wearing a brown leather hobnailed collar with the name Whitaker stamped on it. Attached to the collar was an Oklahoma vaccine tag. Shiney has a close coat of black hair, floppy ears, a bob tail, a white spot on his breast and one single white hair on his back. If you have any information on his whereabouts, please contact Mrs. Whitaker, 5 East Biddle street, or phone Vernon 1549-M.

* * *

Ruth Played With Braves In 1935

Inquiring about Babe Ruth's career, Robert Legore, 201 Broadway, Hanover, Pa., wants to know for which clubs the Bambino played after leaving the Yankees.

Ruth played for only one club, the Boston Nationals, in 1935, after leaving the Yanks, although he later served as coach with Brooklyn in 1938. Babe appeared in 28 games with the Braves in '35.

* * *

Baseball And Boxing Quiz

Appealing to this column for the correct answers in a sports debate, Paul Revene, of the Mt. Royal Hotel, wants to know (1) the Orioles' attendance this season at Oriole Park before the club was forced into the Stadium, and (2) Baltimore's record gate for boxing.

In 26 playing days, the Orioles had drawn approximately 99,000 paid admissions at Oriole Park before the plant caught fire and burned to the ground on the morning of July 4.

And the record boxing gate was approximately $30,000 for the Lee Murray-Harry Bobo fight at Oriole Park in August of 1943.

* * *

Talks Of Old And New Stadium

From Mrs. Aileen E. Turner, 1413 Poplar Grove street, comes the following letter about the old Stadium and the proposed new one:

Dear Mr. Pippen:

Just a few lines of comment on the letter you were dared to print in your column. My opinion of the letter is as follows:

First, you were told to stick to writing sports. Did Mr. Waltjen stop to think of the good you and several sports writers have done for the sports-minded people of Baltimore? He probably hasn't. Such people as he is the reason Baltimore has had this white elephant on its hands.

He says you don't own any property in this so-called residential area. Why didn't he protest when they were building this so-called worm-eaten stadium. If his excuse is it was there when he bought his property, then why did he buy? He wasn't compelled to do so.

Suppose we would protest things we didn't like in our neighborhood? What kind of town would this be? We don't like railroad tracks almost in our back yards. They have to be some place. In Mr. Waltjen's mind we would probably be terrible people if we would protest about anything like this.

Just such people as Mr. Waltjen will be the reason our Orioles will have to find a new home.

Has the committee ever thought of Bloomingdale Oval? Plenty of natural scenery, plenty of parking space where people will appreciate having it.

Grid Attendance Increases For College Games

NEW YORK, Oct. 26—(U. P.). Competition, the factor that is keeping college football alive in its third war-time season, also is turning the turnstiles over at an increased pace over last year in every section of the country but the East and Midwest, a United Press attendance survey of major schools revealed today.

A check of attendance at 39 key colleges and universities throughout the nation revealed that their games thus far have attracted a total of 1,799,996 spectators as compared with 1,733,745 in 1943, an increase of 66,251.

ROCKIES GAIN

The Rocky Mountain, Pacific Coast, South and Southwestern areas all showed gains, with the Rockies offering the biggest percentage of increase and the South the largest actual number of additional fans. The Midwest, where gasoline rationing has reduced crowds at many colleges, showed the biggest decline, with the East only slightly less than last year. Major games yet to be played in both areas were expected to bring the 1944 total above that of 1943.

The comparative attendance by sections:

Section	1944 Attendance	1943 Attendance
East	403,175	412,250
Midwest	561,022	630,037
Pacific Coast	374,812	313,398
South	273,932	210,119
Rocky Mountain	62,200	44,996
Southwest	124,855	122,945
Totals	1,799,996	1,733,745

The 39 teams have played a total of 101 home games, with an average crowd of 17,820 as compared with 17,066, the average 1943 turnout.

In the East five schools, Pittsburgh, Pennsylvania, Dartmouth, Brown and Yale, showed increases; Colgate showed no change, while Navy, Holy Cross, Columbia and Army showed decreases. The largest decrease was Navy's, 25,486 for three games, while Pittsburgh's oft-trounced Panthers had the largest gain, 14,400 for four games. The Navy decrease was attributable to the fact that in 1943 it played two of its first three games at the big Baltimore Municipal Stadium, whereas only one has been played there this year, probably creating enough difference to have put the East ahead of 1943.

MIDWEST TRAILS

In the Midwest and midlands decreases at such major institutions as Minnesota, Michigan, Oklahoma A. & M., Ohio State and Iowa State were the principal factor in the decline with all others polled, Illinois, Notre Game, Purdue, Indiana, Oklahoma, Tulsa and Kansas showing increases. Notre Dame had the biggest gain, 25,000 for two games. Surprisingly, Ohio State's unbeaten Buckeyes had a loss of 48,500 for three games, while Michigan was off 66,274 for the same number.

California, Southern California and U. C. L. A. all showed substantial gains on the Coast, while Washington, playing only minor neighboring schools in the Northwest, showed a decrease of 15,000.

Georgia Tech's increase of 21,000 for four games was the biggest in the South, and all other schools polled, Tennessee, Tulane, Louisiana State, Duke and North Carolina, showed gains.

Both Denver and Colorado College, the only schools with representative schedules, showed gains in the Rocky Mountain region.

The Southwest schools, Texas A. & M., Texas and Rice, showed increases, while Southern Methodist and Texas Christian, reporting decreases, have had less attractive schedules than in 1943.

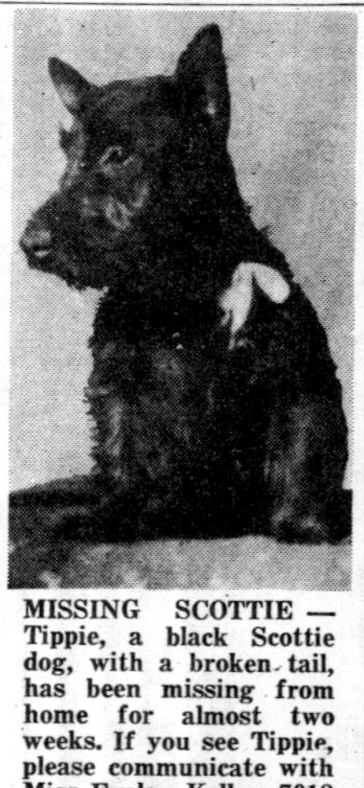

MISSING SCOTTIE — Tippie, a black Scottie dog, with a broken tail, has been missing from home for almost two weeks. If you see Tippie, please communicate with Miss Evelyn Keller, 7018 Holabird avenue, Baltimore (22).

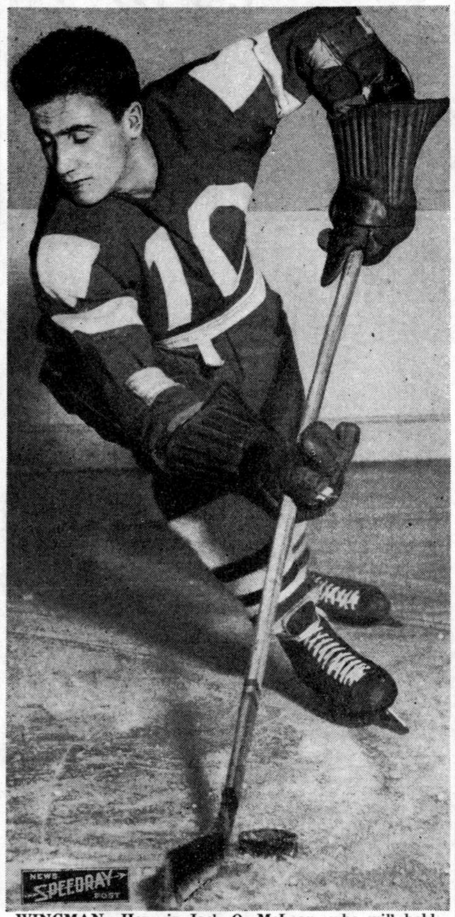

WINGMAN—Here is Jack O. McLean, who will hold down a wing position for the Baltimore Ice Hockey Club in this year's Eastern Amateur Hockey League campaign. The locals have been practicing at Carlin's Iceland for next Wednesday's league opener with the New York Rovers.

Alert Penn Team Set For Navy

ANNAPOLIS, Oct. 26.—Navy has returned from a "razzle-dazzle" battle against Georgia Tech in the South to face an entrenched Penn in the North this Saturday. According to popular acclaim everything known to football thrilled the spectators in the game last week. Navy should continue the same kind of football from that point on.

Navy will arrive in Philadelphia with a tall and a short backfield, two good lines, the Navy goat and a loud-cheering contingent of midshipmen.

The tall backfield, designed as pass stoppers, consists of: Dick Duden at quarterback, Bob Jenkins at left half, Ralph Ellsworth at right half, Clyde Scott at fullback. The alternate backfield generally consists of Barksdale at quarterback, Hamberg and Pettit, halfbacks, and Walton, fullback.

These are not first and second string back fields but alternate combinations of about equal strength, used to meet different situations.

Navy scouts have followed George Munger's Penn team with unusual interest. They consider it somewhat stronger than the one of last year and decidedly more alert, though somewhat younger.

The probable line-up:

NAVY		PENN
87 Bramlett	L. E.	Helman 14
70 Whitmire	L. T.	Savitsky 5
61 Deramee	L. G.	Kurtz 37
50 Martin, J.	C	Mostertz 4
75 Chase	R. G.	Sanft 17
73 Gilliam	R. T.	Stickel 7
19 Martin, B.	R. E.	Rosenthal 2
43 Duden or 29 Barksdale	Q. B.	Lawless 33
18 Jenkins or 49 Hamberg	L. H.	Sica 10
21 Barron or 12 Pettit	R. H.	Minisi 11
33 Sullivan or 47 Scott	F. B.	Edenborn 12

Referee— J. H. Williams (Bucknell). Umpire—C. L. Bolster. Linesman—J. J. Allinger (Buffalo). F. Judge—J. C. French (Penn State).

Cuts N. Y. U. Cage Squad To 15

NEW YORK, Oct. 26—(A. P.). Coach Howard G. Cann today cut his New York U. all-civilian basket ball squad to 15 men, including seven veterans of last year's team and one discharged service man who played two years with the Violets. Cann is in his twenty-second year of basket ball coaching at the university.

BUD MILLS RECUPERATING

JAMAICA, L. I., Oct. 26—(A. P.).—Apprentice Bud Ivan Mills fractured three small bones in his left foot in a recent accident here and has gone to his Omaha, Neb., home with assurances he will be able to ride again in Florida.

SPORT NEWS IN BRIEF

NEW YORK, Oct. 26—(A. P.). War Prisoners' Aid of the Y. M. C. A. announced today it had sent 500 golf balls to Geneva, for transfer to American prisoners of war in German camps. Clubs for 100 players also were in the shipment. The announcement said:

"Lest anyone think American war prisoners in Germany lead a country club life, War Prisoners' Aid points out that the golf courses in prison camps are miniatures, that boundary lines are marked by barbed wire, and that there is a permanent 'gallery' of guards armed with machine guns."

28,000 TO SEE GAME

HOUSTON, Texas, Oct. 26—(A. P.).—The largest crowd in the history of Rice Stadium—a capacity 28,000—will see Rice play Texas Saturday for the Southwest Football Conference lead.

TO RESUME BASKET BALL

PROVO, Utah, Oct. 26—(A. P.). Brigham Young University, which fielded a basket ball team to start the 1943-44 season, but dropped out after the Christmas vacation, will return to the sport this season, Basket Ball Coach Floyd Millet said today

CLIFTON GOLF PAIRINGS

Pairings for the fifth annual Red and Blue dinner match at the Clifton links Sunday:

11.30 A. M.—Henry J. Miller and S. J. Doukas, Reds, vs. Ray Plecker and Frank Kopp, Blues.

11.37 A. M.—Mike Fiore and Larry Di Pasquale, Reds, vs. Ed Harrison and Jerry Hunt, Blues.

11.44 A. M.—C. Balling and G. E. White, Reds, vs. J. J. Schultz and Jack Dixon, Blues.

11.51 A. M.—C. J. Berknes and Frank Kelly, Reds, vs. Frank Bucharewicz and E. G. Morwood, Blues.

11.58 A. M.—Bud Cunningham and John E. Wessels, Reds, vs. Richard Mullen and Charles Kreider, Blues.

12.05 P. M.—Bill Allen and Walter Corcelius, Reds, vs. Ray Heins and Tommy Tinker, Blues.

12.12 P. M.—Bob Brill and Henry Eser, Reds, vs. Lefty Russel and John Heath, Blues.

12.19 P. M.—James Burrows and Jerry Hunt, Reds, vs. Bob Wheely and J. T. Smith, Blues.

12.26 P. M.—Edward McAllister and Robert Canby, Reds, vs. E. W. Enright and Milt Kraut, Blues.

12.33 P. M.—Jerry Simms and Herb Vivell, Reds, vs. Harvey Hall and Willard G. Waters, Blues.

12.40 P. M.—Joe McLeary and Charles Appling, Reds, vs. Mike D'Arciprete and Mike Martin, Blues.

12.47 P. M.—Lester Peltzer and Ed Clark, Reds, vs. Joe Castini and Harry O'Donnell, Blues.

1.04 P. M.—Ed Taylor and Otto Guertler, Reds, vs. C. W. Treadwell and Ed Dietrich, Blues.

1.11 P. M.—George Zumbrun and Phil Minderlein, Reds, vs. John Tornabene and Austin Dietrich, Blues.

1.18 P. M.—Al Laur and Ken Scales, Reds vs. Eddie Meyer and Cliff Melton, Blues.

1.25 P. M.—Gus Hook and Irvin Schloss (pro.) Reds, vs. Joe Vaeth and Johnny Bass (pro.), Blues.

1.32 P. M.—Walter Gaynor and L. Page.

Selects Devils To Hand Army First Defeat

By JACK CUDDY

NEW YORK, Oct. 26—(U. P.). Picking the football winners—maybe:

EAST

Navy over Pennsylvania—mysterious weapon ready to explode.

Duke over Army—Cadets flunk first big test.

Bucknell over Temple—came up heads.

Dartmouth over Brown—graspin' for straws.

Colgate over Columbia—lathering the Lions.

Also Syracuse over Boston College, New York U. over City College of N. Y., Holy Cross over Coast Guard, Chatham Field over Pittsburgh.

MIDWEST

Notre Dame over Illinois—much closer than it looks.

Indiana over Iowa—Hoosier line now?

Purdue over Michigan—Bartender Ned favors Boilermakers.

Ohio State over Minnesota—speed's the thing.

Great Lakes over Wisconsin—or we'll be badgered.

Also Iowa Pre-Flight over Marquette; Tulsa over Oklahoma A. and M., Oklahoma over Texas Christian, Iowa State over Kansas State, Missouri over Nebraska.

SOUTH

Georgia Tech. over Georgia Pre-Flight—after tough fight.

Georgia over Louisiana State—should be free-scoring affair.

Tennessee over Clemson — volunteered information.

Mississippi over Arkansas—don't give points.

Also Tulane over Southern Methodist, Florida over Maryland, Mississippi over Arkansas, Mississippi State over Jackson Airbase.

SOUTHWEST

Texas over Rice—that's the way we're steered.

Oklahoma over Texas Christian—could be a tie.

Also Randolph Field over Third South Air Force; Texas Aggies over North Texas Aggies.

FAR WEST

California over Washington—whinny from Trojan horse.

Southern California over St. Mary's—just a breeze.

Denver over Utah State—why not?

Also Coast Guard over U. C. L. A., El Toro Marines over Fleet City, Second Air Force over Norman Training, Ft. Warren over Lincoln Air, Utah over Nevada.

(Last week—43 right, 8 wrong, 4 ties for .843. Season, .805.)

Connie Mack Lauds Walker Cooper

PHILADELPHIA, Oct. 26—(A. P.). — Walker Cooper, St. Louis Cardinal backstop, rates as the greatest catcher in baseball today, says Connie Mack.

The Philadelphia Athletics' manager also told the Main Line Baseball League last night that Walker and his brother, Pitcher Morton, form one of baseball's outstanding batteries.

Vic Kulbitski To Start Against Ohio

MINNEAPOLIS, Oct. 26—(I. N. S.).—Vic Kulbitski, who returned recently to the Minnesota football squad, will start at fullback Saturday in place of Tom Cates against Ohio State. Thirty-seven players were named by Coach George Hauser to make the trip to Columbus.

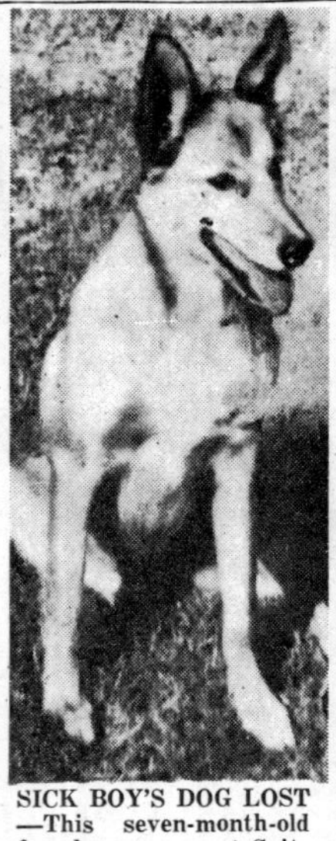

SICK BOY'S DOG LOST —This seven-month-old female puppy, part Spitz and part police, belonging to a little sick boy has been lost since Monday from the home Mrs. Mary Stephens, 3705 Hillsdale road, Forest Park. The dog is brown and answers to the name of Tippy. If you have seen this dog please call Forest 5761.

Pros To Use Cotton Bowl

NEW YORK, Oct. 26—(U. P.). John F. (Chick) Meehan, president of the newly organized Trans-America Professional Football League, announced today arrangements had been completed for the Dallas (Texas) team to play its home games in the famous Cotton Bowl there, with plans under way for its seating capacity to be increased to 100,000.

The bowl, which is packed annually for the New Year's Day Cotton Bowl football game now holds about 46,600 fans. Meehan said the Dallas franchise, owned by George Schepps, also a director of the Dallas (Texas) League baseball team, has completed the structure of the organization and that a nationally-famous coach will take over when the war is over.

The Trans-America circuit, scheduled to begin operations as soon as possible after the war also has franchises in Boston, Baltimore, New York, Houston, Los Angeles, Miami and Philadelphia.

Temple Favored Over Bucknell

PHILADELPHIA, Oct. 26—(I. N. S.). — Temple University's youthful but spirited grid squad today was considered as the favorite for its meeting with Bucknell University's service squad on the Temple grounds Friday night.

Bucknell will go through an all-day workout in Philadelphia today to make up for time lost by service players on leave.

Francis, Shans Box Tomorrow

NEW YORK, Oct. 26—(A. P.). With the rodeo still using Madison Square Garden, New York's fight activity remains at St. Nicholas Arena this week, with Leo Francis, twenty-five-year-old Panama lightweight, meeting Cleo Shans of Los Angeles, in Friday night's eight-round headliner.

Louis-Conn Bout Unlikely Until War Is Over

PITTSBURGH, Oct. 26—(I. N. S.). — Without explanation the tour of Pittsburgh district war plants, which had been scheduled for World's Heavyweight Champion Staff Sergt. Joe Louis, today had been cancelled. Louis, it was announced, has been ordered to report to New York.

PHILADELPHIA, Oct. 26—(I. N. S.).—Sergt. Joe Louis intimated today that he won't defend his heavyweight championship against Billy Conn—or anyone else—until the war is over.

Louis, who returned from overseas Monday, toured four Philadelphia and Chester war plants on a War Manpower Commission anti-absenteeism drive.

When queried on reports that Mike Jacobs would promote a Louis-Conn bout next summer if both fighters are out of the service, Louis commented:

"I don't think I can discuss such a bout now. Certainly, I'm thinking about the future, but let's get this war over first."

Louis, weighing 10 pounds more than his fighting weight of 205, said he fought a total of 90 exhibitions in England, Africa and Italy during his six months overseas. Conn refereed one of the English bouts, he said.

Terps Off For Florida Tilt

COLLEGE PARK, Md., Oct. 26 (A. P.).—The University of Maryland football team, hoping for its first win of the season, left today for Gainesville, Fla., for Saturday's game with the Florida Gators.

The Old Liners have dropped three and tied one, mustering a season total of six points in their 6-to-6 deadlock with West Virginia.

The Maryland gridmen ran through their final workout on home soil last night, with Coach Clarence E. (Doc) Spears still undecided as to a replacement for crack tailback Jack Love, injured in the Michigan State game. With the exception of Love, he was expected to start the same line-up that began last Friday's contest with M. S. C.

Willie Pep Easily Outpoints Leamus

MONTREAL, Oct. 26—(U. P.). Featherweight Champion Willie Pep of Hartford, Conn., added another decision to his long record today, a 10-round verdict over Jackie Leamus, boxer from New York, which he gained unanimously from Montreal Athletic Commission judges last night.

Pep was credited with six rounds on the score sheet after a slow beginning. The first three rounds were rated even, with both fighters devoting their efforts to sparring. Leamus gained only one round.

Illini Ace Ready For Irish Tilt

CHAMPAIGN, Ill., Oct. 26—(I. N. S.).—Bill Heiss, Illinois fullback, who has been out of the game because of injuries, was back in the line-up today. His return strengthened the team's hopes of slowing up Notre Dame's running attack next Saturday on the Illini home grounds.

They'll Do It Every Time —:— By Jimmy Hatlo

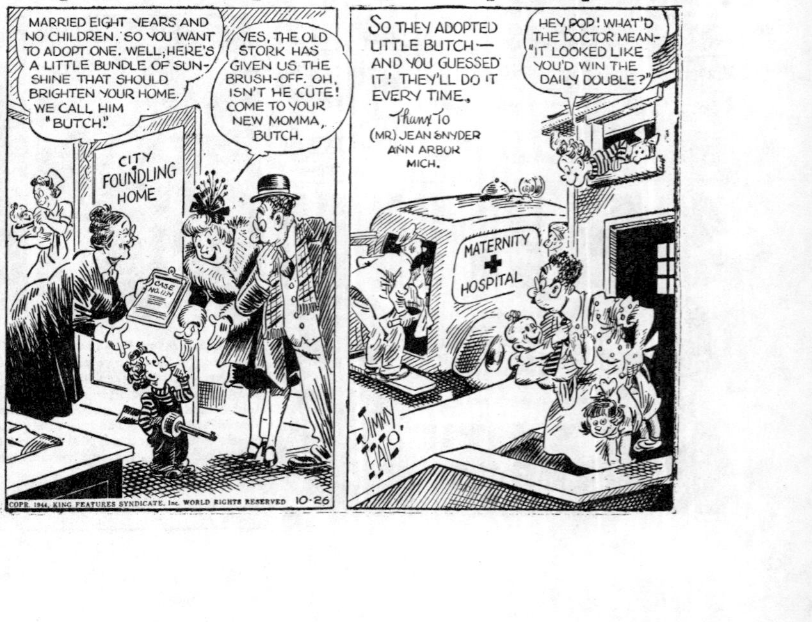

Baltimore Officer Captures Nazi General

THE WEATHER

Sunny, warmer this afternoon; increasing cloudiness, warmer tonight. Thursday occasional rain.

Read The Baltimore News-Post for complete, accurate war coverage. It is the only Baltimore newspaper possessing the three great wire services—
ASSOCIATED PRESS
INTERNATIONAL NEWS SERVICE
UNITED PRESS

THE BALTIMORE NEWS-POST
AN INDEPENDENT NEWSPAPER
The Largest Evening Circulation in the Entire South

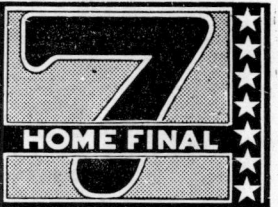

7 HOME FINAL

VOL. CXLVI.—NO. 3 | Entered as second-class matter at Baltimore Postoffice. | WEDNESDAY EVENING, NOVEMBER 8, 1944 | PRICE 3 CENTS

ROOSEVELT RE-ELECTED FOR 4TH TERM, WINS 34 STATES WITH 407 VOTES, CONGRESS IS DEMOCRATIC

Lieut. Walter Berlin, Baltimore Officer, Captures Nazi General

By LOUIS AZRAEL
News-Post War Correspondent.

WITH U. S. FORCES IN GERMANY, Nov. 8.—Capture of German Major General Von Aulock, brother of the "mad colonel of Saint Malo," and the man who was to have defended Paris, was accomplished by a Baltimore soldier, it was learned today.

Lieut. Walter Berlin, 643 West Redwood street, commanded the platoon which captured Von Aulock, and with Pfc. Salvatore Battalo, Sacramento, Cal., personally took the Nazi general prisoner.

It occurred during the battle of Mons, where Berlin commanded a platoon of the Third Armored Division.

HELD ROAD JUNCTION

He was assigned to hold a road intersection to prevent the enemy's passage.

For two days, Berlin and his men remained in the vicinity of the intersection capturing German soldiers who were trying to escape from the American forces then closing around them.

In two days the single platoon took 134 prisoners and killed a large number of Germans, including a full colonel.

Von Aulock was caught when his sports model automobile leading 10 German military vehicles suddenly wung from a side road to the road Berlin's men were guarding.

FIRE ON GERMANS

The Germans apparently did not know of the American's presence there. As the platoon opened fire on the German vehicles, knocking out eight out of nine of them, an elaborately uniformed general leaped out of a car and tried to enter a civilian home.

A French householder, however, pushed the officer back into the street as Lieutenant Berlin and Pfc. Battalo came up.

It was later learned he was attempting to take his battle group, which was named after him, to protect Paris.

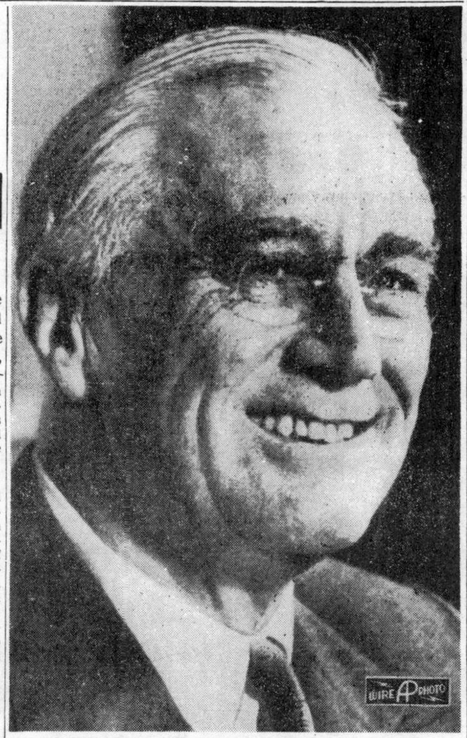

WINS FOURTH TERM—Flashing this victory smile, President Roosevelt told his neighbors, as Governor Dewey early today conceded his defeat in the election: "Well, it looks as though I'll be taking the train from Washington to Hyde Park for another four years."

By WILLIAM K. HUTCHINSON

NEW YORK, Nov. 8—(I. N. S.).—President Roosevelt held a fourth term mandate from the American people today to win the global wars, bring our armed services home promptly and to secure the future peace of the world. Mr. Roosevelt was overwhelmingly re-elected to another term in the White House in a smashing victory over Gov. Thomas E. Dewey that was mounting hourly and may even surpass his 1940 defeat of Wendell Willkie.

The President either carried or led in 34 States an electoral vote of 407.

(BACKGROUND NOTE: Other political surveys gave President Roosevelt the additional States of North Dakota, with four electoral votes, and Michigan, with 19.)

Governor Dewey lagged far behind, carrying or leading in only fourteen States, having 124 electoral votes. Dewey may even lose three more States in which he is leading. These were Indiana, where his lead was cut to 14,000; in Ohio, where he was ahead by 27,000, and in Wisconsin, where he was out in front by 16,000.

MAY WIN 39 STATES

The President may well win 39 States, having 480 electoral votes, leaving Dewey with nine States, with 51 electoral votes. If he does, it will surpass his victory over Willkie, who carried 10 States, with 82 electoral votes, and even his slaughter of former President Hoover, who carried but six States, with 59 electoral votes, in 1932.

It was a decisive victory as fully 50,000,000 people voted. Dewey, though badly beaten in the Electoral College, ran well in popular votes. He should get close to 23,000,000 votes against Roosevelt's 27,000,000 as the President carried many States by quite small margins. Roosevelt's biggest triumph was in New York State, which he won by 325,000.

Dewey conceded his defeat graciously in a little speech to newsmen at his Hotel Roosevelt headquarters at 3.14 A. M. (E. W. T.).

The President heard the broadcast and telegraphed his thanks to the Governor.

Although the campaign was waged furiously and the rival nominees hurled bitter charges at each other at times, it ended on a solemn note of unity.

DEWEY ASKS FOR UNITY

It was Dewey who called for this unity and he invoked Divine aid to guide and protect the President in his efforts to win the global war and secure peace for future generations.

After asserting that "every good citizen will accept the will of the people" and expressing hope that "the President's term will lead to victory, to the establishment of a lasting peace and a return to tranquility," Dewey added:

"I am confident that all Americans join me in the hope that in the years ahead Divine Providence will guide and protect the President of the United States."

The President heard the broadcasted message and telegraphed Dewey in reply:

"I thank you for your statement which I heard over the radio a few minutes ago."

Dewey had used the radio to give his message to the American people, rather than sending a formal telegram to the President, because he had been informed that Mr. Roosevelt had retired earlier for the night.

TRUMAN PRAISES DEWEY

The Vice-President-elect, from Kansas City, issued a statement, declaring:

"It was a grand statement by Governor Dewey and it shows American sportsmanship. It is up to the people to make good the Dewey statement by winning both the war and the peace."

The outcome of the election showed the world that the

Continued on Page 2, Column 1.

Roosevelt 407 Elector Vote

By Associated Press.

Tabulation of returns from yesterday's war-time election showed these results:

Presidential: Roosevelt led in 34 States with 407 electoral votes (141 more than a majority); Dewey was in front in 14 with 124.

Senate: Democrats elected 15, including Barkley, Wagner, Tydings, McMahon, Hayden, Thomas (Okla.), Thomas (Utah), and Lucas outside the solid South. Brien McMahon, former assistant attorney general, upset Republican Senator John Danaher in Connecticut. Republicans had elected seven, including two in Oregon and one each in Kansas, South Dakota, Vermont, Iowa and Colorado.

House: Democrats elected 182, including 16 seats now held by Republicans. Republicans elected 99, including one seat now held by a Democrat. Representative Clare Luce (Republican) of Connecticut was re-elected. Representative Hamilton Fish (Republican) of New York was defeated after 12 terms.

Governors: Democrats elected 10 (Arizona, Arkansas, Florida, Idaho, Missouri, North Carolina, Rhode Island, Tennessee, Texas and West Virginia); led in six other States. Republicans elected seven (Connecticut, Iowa, Kansas, Maine on September 11, Nebraska South Dakota and Vermont); were ahead in eight others.

Democrats Clinch Congress Control

WASHINGTON, Nov. 8—(A. P.).—The Democratic party bored ahead today toward an electoral triumph at the Capitol, as well as at the White House.

Smashing yesterday's Republican prediction that the Administration would lose control of both houses of Congress, the Democrats made certain of a Senate majority with votes to spare and snatched 16 seats from the Republicans in the House, while losing only two of their own.

With 12 Senate races still to be decided, Democrats counted 51 certain Senate seats compared with 58 they hold in the present session. The Republicans tallied up 30, counting holdovers, contrasted with the 37 they now occupy. The Senate's lone minor-party member was not up for election this time.

LINE-UP IN HOUSE

In the House forenoon totals showed 187 Democrats elected, 104 Republicans.

Eleven incumbent Democratic Senators already had been returned: George of Georgia, Overton of Louisiana, Hil of Alabama, Pepper of Florida, majority leader Barkley of Kentucky, Thomas of Oklahoma, Tydings of Maryland, Hayden of Arizona, Thomas of Utah, Wagner of New York and Lucas of Illinois.

New Democratic Senators-elect included J. William Fulbright of Arkansas, Olin D. Johnston of South Carolina, Clyde R. Hoey of North Carolina and Brien McMahon of Connecticut, who upset Republican Senator John Danaher.

GILLETTE UNSEATED

The Republicans unseated a Democrat, too—Senator Guy M.

Continued on Page 2, Column 4.

Third U. S. Army Launches New Drive In West

LONDON, Nov. 8—(A. P.).—U. S. Third Army troops charged in a dawn offensive today at points along a 25-mile front between Metz and Nancy, seized four lightly contested villages and scored advances up to a mile.

To the north, doughboys of the First Army still battled strongly reinforced Germans in the town of Vossenack, 13 miles southeast of Aachen.

Bloody and as yet inconclusive fighting continued throughout the Hurtgen forest area.

Two Nazi counterattacks near Schmidt were broken.

The Third Army "substantially improved" its line between Nancy and Metz, a front dispatch said. Midway between the two French cities, the Americans crossed the Seille river. Resistance ranged from light to moderate.

In Holland the Germans re-

Continued on Page 2, Column 6.

Wings for the Dead! The Eskimos of Greenland Believe There Are Such Things and More Than One Yank Soldier Is Ready to Accept the Legend. Read This Unusual Story in The American Weekly, the Magazine Distributed With Next Sunday's Baltimore American.—Adv.

Roosevelt Wins Maryland By 17,000 Votes

For the fourth time President Roosevelt stood today as the winner of Maryland's eight electoral votes, but the narrow margin of under 17,000 by which he triumphed over Gov. Thomas E. Dewey was in decided contrast to the runaway victories he has enjoyed in his three previous elections.

With all but 12 of the State's 1,328 polling places reporting, including Baltimore city's 471 precincts, the Presidential vote stood:

Roosevelt, 294,653; Dewey, 278,100.

It was Baltimore city, always the Roosevelt stronghold, which tilted the scales in his favor, although the vote in the counties was adverse to extending the Roosevelt White House tenure to 16 years.

Returns from the counties pared down the Roosevelt majority of 42,775 in the city, but it seemed impossible that they could reverse the result.

Roosevelt's Maryland victory was conceded in a statement is-

Continued on Page 2, Column 8.

Dewey Admits His Defeat, Asks Unity

NEW YORK, Nov. 8—(A. P.). Gov. Thomas E. Dewey took it on the chin with a smile today, conceding at 3.15 A. M., Eastern war time that President Roosevelt had been re-elected for a fourth term.

He expressed confidence that "all Americans will join me in the hope that Divine Providence will guide and protect the President of the United States."

With Mrs. Dewey standing behind him, the Republican Presidential nominee said simply in a nation-wide radio broadcast that "it's clear that Mr. Roosevelt has been re-elected for a fourth term and every good American will wholeheartedly accept the will of the people."

300 REPORTERS PRESENT

Nearly 300 reporters, cameramen and employes of the Republican National Committee jammed

Continued on Page 2, Column 3.

Roosevelt Happy Over Smashing Fourth Victory

By ROBERT G. NIXON

HYDE PARK, N. Y., Nov. 8—(I. N. S.).—President Franklin D. Roosevelt, tired but happy over his smashing fourth term victory, retired at 3.50 A. M. today after replying to the statement of Governor Thomas E. Dewey conceding defeat.

"I thank you for your statement which I heard over the air a few minutes ago," the President said in a telegram to his defeated opponent.

The President, who remained at his work table in the dining room of the Hyde Park Manor throughout the evening as election returns filtered in, was still wide awake when Mr. Dewey made his statement.

SPREADS CONGRATULATIONS

The President also sent telegrams to Senator Harry S. Tru-

Continued on Page 2, Column 1.

Temperatures

Midnight, 49	7 A. M., 51
1 A. M., 48	8 A. M., 51
2 A. M., 46	9 A. M., 52
3 A. M., 47	10 A. M., 54
4 A. M., 47	11 A. M., 57
5 A. M., 48	12 Noon, 59
6 A. M., 49	1 P. M., 61

NEWS-POST

Amusements	28, 29	Haney, Dr. Lewis	33
Bugs Baer	27	Horoscope	13
Clark, Norman	29	Mallon, Paul	27
Classified Ads	33, 34, 35	Movies	28, 29
Comics	30	Parsons, Louella	28
Crossword	35	Pegler	27
Dixon, George	27	Pippen, R. H.	31
Durling	26	Radio	19
Dulaney	27	Robinson, Elsie	26
Editorials	26	Society	20
Financial	33	Sports	31, 32, 33
Health	14	Women's Clubs	20

The Baltimore News-Post, Wednesday, Nov. 8, 1944

YOUR INDIVIDUAL HOROSCOPE
By Frances Drake

Look in the section in which your birthday comes and find what your outlook is, according to the stars.

FOR THURSDAY, NOVEMBER 9, 1944

MARCH 21 to APRIL 20 (Aries)—Most encouraging for money, business contracts and intimate personal matters. Sane thinking, healthy living and avoiding overcaution will bring fine results.

APRIL 21 to MAY 20 (Taurus)—With your fortunes on the upswing, with planetary vibrations ringing with good cheer, what better could one ask? You can stay on top.

MAY 21 to JUNE 21 (Gemini)—You've been waiting for just such a day to show those Doubting Thomases. Friendly aspects. What are we waiting for? Day loaded with possibilities.

JUNE 22 to JULY 23 (Cancer)—And still the good days keep coming! Don't let lack of co-operation freeze your chances. Open up with all you have, especially in matters important to your family's and country's welfare.

JULY 24 to AUGUST 22 (Leo)—Flexibility, that's it. Be mobile, ready to shift to sounder daily plans and propositions. And there are many uses really favorable day. Oh, yes, Romance also benefits.

AUGUST 23 to SEPTEMBER 23 (Virgo)—No time to waste! So many fine openings this generous day. In your speed, don't forget to promote harmony between associates, friends, and don't forget loved ones' wishes.

SEPTEMBER 24 to OCTOBER 23 (Libra)—It's a toss-up which has the count. Hearts or Business—but both are highly sponsored. So you be the judge, and don't neglect obligations or family interests.

OCTOBER 24 to NOVEMBER 22 (Scorpio)—Will probably experience some agreeable surprises today. A definite signal for better conditions indicated for investments, Romance, domesticity raises high.

NOVEMBER 23 to DECEMBER 22 (Sagittarius)—Excellent influence. Expect benefits through associates, acquaintances; new issues can be started now. But get sufficient outdoor exercise and sleep.

DECEMBER 24 to JANUARY 21 (Capricorn)—Be grateful for this stimulating day. Your every-day life can be enhanced, made happier by turning in a brisker day's job. You have the ability.

JANUARY 22 to FEBRUARY 20 (Aquarius)—A sort of checkmate day. Pull in your reins, there are some difficult problems you may encounter. When your patrol clears you can proceed confidently.

FEBRUARY 21 to MARCH 20 (Pisces)—Your advantages are in the upper brackets. Your stars favorable, be sure to do the right thing at the right time. No gloomy moods. Be demonstrative, with reservations.

YOU BORN ON THIS DAY: An individual of great possibilities if you seek the truth and education. Can hold high position of trust; are keen, astute. Would make a good detective, writer. Try for-getting self, and don't waste time on waste, people of uncertain character. Birthdays: Mark Akenside, English poet, physician; Marie Dressler, famed comedienne.

(Copyright, 1944, King Features Syndicate, Incorporated.)

Art Museum Will Show Films Sunday

The Baltimore Museum of Art will show two films Sunday at 3.30 P. M. in the museum auditorium. The films, "The New Earth" and "The Dutch Tradition," make up the second program in the current series of "Three Decades of Peace and War" sound pictures.

AUXILIARY TO MEET

The regular monthly meeting of the Ladies' Auxiliary of the Hamilton Improvement Association will be held Monday, November 13, in the lecture hall of Enoch Pratt Free Library, 3006 Hamilton avenue, at 8.30 P. M.

High Quality! Low Cost! Valuable Coupon!
(Redeemable at all Octagon Premium Stores)

HEARTH CLUB BAKING POWDER — MADE BY RUMFORD

GRANTS FOR SPORTSWEAR
SCOOP! All Wool SWEATERS

Grants has exactly what you want in 9 mouth-watering colors.

pullover 3.98

matching cardigan 3.98

Cherry	Dusty Pink	Lime
Spice	Fireman Red	Maize
Purple	Light Blue	Lilac

Heavy rib-knit! 100% pure wool!
Long boxy torso! Sizes 34 to 40.

W. T. GRANT CO.   216 W. LEXINGTON ST.

REGAL SHOP — 613 W. Baltimore St.
THURSDAY 'TIL 9! DON'T MISS THIS CHANCE TO SAVE
$59 to $69 FUR COATS AT THIS LOW PRICE

$33 At The Regal Shop

Don't fail to be here early for this Fur Coat Sensation! Beaverette Coney in brown only! No more when these are gone at this price.
TAX INCLUDED
USE OUR LIBERAL CREDIT TERMS

Values Extraordinary! DRESS CLEARANCE!
$2.99 — $4.99 to $6.99 Values — At The Regal Shop

A thrilling assortment to select from. One and two piece styles ... lace embroidered and fancy trims. Many worth many times this low price. Be here early for best selection. Sizes 9 to 20 and 38 to 44 in the group

You'll Look Lovely in This "Magic Charmer" $5.99 At The Regal Shop

You'll see yourself at your loveliest in this smart fashion. Charming black net with white embroidery. Princess styled. Shirred skirt. Full of the sparkle and charm that only a fashion like this can give you. Newest shades. Sizes 9 to 17.

Fur Chubbies $12.95 At The Regal Shop
Add that luxurious touch to your new suit or coat with this beautiful fur chubby. Outstanding at this low price.

Juke Suits $21.95 At The Regal Shop
In choice of Blue, Green and Gold with the popular slit back. Velvet collar and cuffs. New 3/4-length coat. Sizes 10 to 20.

Girls' Plaid COATS! Tots' Legging SETS $9.95 each

Coats are lined and interlined: Sizes 7 to 14. Tots' legging sets. Sizes 3 to 6x. Velvet trim coat, zipper leggings.

SWEATERS SKIRTS BLOUSES $2.99 At The Regal Shop
Blouses in chartreuse and melon and other shades. Sweaters in pullover and cardigan style, in gold, red, blue, pink, maize, white, lilac, mint green and rust. Sizes 34 to 40. New 8-gore gabardine skirts in solids. Others in plaids. Sizes 22 to 32 for Juniors and Misses.

Julius GUTMAN & Co. — LEXINGTON AND PARK
Thursday --- a Thrifty Day for Cash Shoppers
No Mail, Phone or C. O. D. Orders
OPEN UNTIL 9 P. M.

Lace Tablecloths Irregulars!	**3.98**	**Satin Face Damask** 36 Inches Wide!	**89c**	**Lovely Fur Coats** Tax Included	**$54**
Homespun and Cretonne Drapes	**6.94**	**Acetate Rayon Crepes** For Your Best Dress!	**1.49** yd.	**Smart Chesterfields** 100% Wool!	**19.00**
Organdy Curtains Permanent Finish!	**4.94**	**Blended Dress Woolens** 54 Inches Wide!	**1.98** yd.	**Attractive Dresses** Many Lovely Styles!	**3.00**
Christmas Wreaths Sizes 14 to 19 Inch!	**89c to 3.99**	**Bareleg Hose** Irregulars!	**47c**	**Cotton Blouses** For Tots and Girls!	**59c**
Crystal Vanity Lamps Sparkling Brighteners!	**2.94**	**Girls' Double Duty Sets** Sizes 7 to 12!	**12.88**	**Boys' Cloth Longies** Full Cut!	**2.88**
25% Wool Blankets Solid Colors!	**3.99**	**Flannelette Gowns** Well Made!	**2.29**	**Reversible Fingertip Coats** All Weather Coats!	**8.77**
Four-Year Sheets 81x99 Inch Size!	**1.19**	**Honey Lou Doll** 18 Inch Size!	**1.94**	**Original Shortee Skirt** Well-Tailored!	**2.99**
All Steel Spring Platform Top!	**11.88**	**Table and Chair Set** Maple Finished Hardwood!	**9.97**	**Men's Union Suits** Heavy Weight!	**1.29**
Fibre Rugs Typically Cash Priced!	**10.98**	**Cotton Plaid Blankets** Size 70x80 Inches!	**97c**	**Men's Dress Shirts** Sizes 14 to 17!	**1.88**

Get the Cash Store Habit---You'll Save!

Pope Pius Raps Totalitarianism

THE WEATHER

Snow, not so cold tonight; snow changing to freezing rain or rain and warmer Tuesday.

Detailed Weather Report Page 16

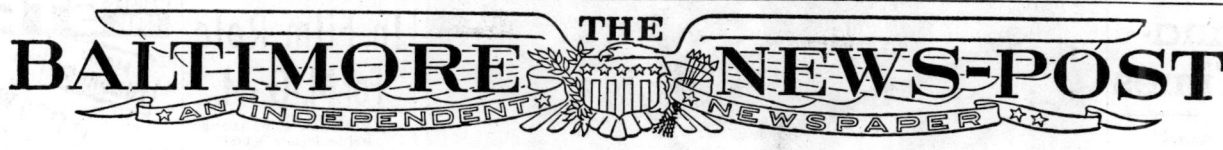

Read The Baltimore News-Post for complete, accurate news coverage. It is the only Baltimore newspaper possessing the three great wire services—
ASSOCIATED PRESS
INTERNATIONAL NEWS SERVICE
UNITED PRESS

THE BALTIMORE NEWS-POST

AN INDEPENDENT NEWSPAPER

The Largest Evening Circulation in the Entire South

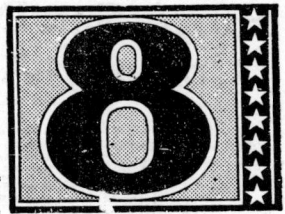

8

VOL. CXLVIII.—NO. 43 | Entered as second-class matter at Baltimore Postoffice. | MONDAY EVENING, DECEMBER 24, 1945 | PRICE 3 CENTS

Woman Found Dead; Murder Theory Probed

Patton Rests With GIs

Travel Rush Ends; New Jam Seen

By JACK VINCENT
International News Service Staff Correspondent.

Railway officials said the nation's worst railroad traffic jam in history appeared broken today.

However, railroad officials warned that post-holiday travel might see an even greater jam than that which clogged the rail lines Friday, Saturday and Sunday.

More than 150,000 Pacific veterans were stranded on the West Coast with not even a hope of getting home for Yuletide.

MEDAL FOR 'BATTLE'

Persons who make it home for Christmas deserve it, according to one GI who suggested that all persons who were caught in the week-end travel jam be awarded a campaign ribbon with battle star.

Chicago, East-West railroad junction, was hard hit. Gov. Dwight Green ordered out part of the militia with more than 100 trucks and jeeps to help break the jam.

OFFICIALS STAND BY

Governors of Michigan and Indiana had State officials standing by because of jams in stations at Detroit and Indianapolis.

In Washington, the demand for accomodation on trains, airplanes and buses slumped sharply to a near-normal level today after three days during which nearly 400,000 persons taxed every transportation facility leaving the city.

An official at the Trailways bus depot summed up the situation by saying:

"There's no one left in Washington now."

George Earle To Wed In Turkey

ISTANBUL, Dec. 22 — (U. P.). Official Turkish sources said today that Commander George Earle, former Governor of Pennsylvania, will be married December 28 or 29. Reports had circulated persistently in Istanbul for some time that Earle and Jacqueline Sacre, daughter of a Belgian adviser to Turkish railroad interests, would wed.

Temperatures

12 midn't, 20	7 A. M., 17
1 A. M., 19	8 A. M., 17
2 A. M., 18	9 A. M., 19
3 A. M., 17	10 A. M., 21
4 A. M., 16	11 A. M., 23
5 A. M., 17	12 Noon, 29
6 A. M., 17	1 P. M., 31

Pope Selects 32 Cardinals; 4 From U. S.

VATICAN CITY, Dec. 24—(A. P.).—Thirty-two new cardinals, including four from the United States, six from Latin America and one from Canada, have been named by Pope Pius XII. They will receive the red hats emblematic of their office in Rome February 18 at a consistory of the Sacred College of Cardinals, which now will number 70 members.

The four new United States members will be Archbishop Francis J. Spellman of New York, Archbishop John J. Glennon of St. Louis, Archbishop Samuel A. Stritch of Chicago and Archbishop Edward Mooney of Detroit, a Vatican announcement said yesterday.

At present the only living U. S. cardinal is Dennis Cardinal Dougherty of Philadelphia.

U. S. WILL HAVE FIVE

The four new United States cardinals, together with Cardinal Dougherty will give that country its largest representation on the college. The United States has never before had more than four members.

Archbishop Spellman has been reported to be a probable choice for secretary of state at the Vatican.

An unusual aspect of the Pope's appointments was the comparative youth of some of the new members. The youngest, Msgr. Bernard Griffin, Archbishop of Westminster, England, is only forty-six, and Msgr. Norman Gilroy, Archbishop of Sydney, Australia, is only forty-nine.

Archbishop Glennon, eighty-three, is the oldest of the new appointees.

LAST ONE IN 1936

Because of the war the calling of a consistory had been long delayed. The last consistory was called June 15, 1936, by Pope Pius XI, when he brought the membership of the college to 69, the customary figure.

Precedent was shattered by the naming of a Chinese prelate, Msgr. Tomaso Tien, titular bishop of Ruspe and apostolic vicar of Tsingtao, will be the first non-Caucasian cardinal.

The new appointees, in addition to those already named, include three each from Germany and France, two from Brazil and one apiece from Canada, Cuba, Chile, Peru, Argentina, Hungary, The Netherlands, Poland, Turkish Armenia and Mozambique.

Chinese Is Victim Of Hammer Slayer

CHICAGO, Dec. 24—(I. N. S.). The hammer slaying of a Chinese laundryman confronted police today with Chicago's sixteenth murder this month. Police identified the latest victim as Sam Wing, sixty-seven. A neighbor told police he saw Wing's slayer, another Chinese, beat the laundryman with a hammer and then escape.

Pope Pius XII Asks End Of Totalitarians

VATICAN CITY, Dec. 24—(A. P.).—Pope Pius XII, replying to the Cardinal's Christmas message, said today that the hatred and devastation of war would long remain impressed on the world.

By MICHAEL CHINIGO

VATICAN CITY, Dec. 24—(I. N. S.).—Pope Pius XII, calling for the end of totalitarian systems, today laid down three basic principles for world peace.

In a world-wide pre-Christmas broadcast, His Holiness denounced totalitarianism "which the whole world decries as tyranny," and urged totalitarian states to "return to God and true Christianity."

Declaring that "true peace" had not yet arrived, the pontiff called on all nations interested in post-war order to end their private conflicts and limit their demands for reparations from the defeated enemy nations. Reparation demands must be made on a moral basis, he said.

His second principle was "renunciation everywhere" of efforts to influence public opinion through such devices as censorship and propaganda.

MUST RESPECT OPINIONS

The pontiff declared true value must be given to the opinions expressed by true majorities.

Pope Pius declared banishment of totalitarianism was the third step to bring true peace.

The Pontiff said international leaders entrusted with responsibility for world peace shouldered unprecedented responsibility. His Holiness asked

"How long will it take to heal the scars of this terrible war?

"Now mankind is awakening to the realization of how much wisdom, patience and good-will

Continued on Page 2, Column 6.

Gen. Short Patient At Army Hospital

WASHINGTON, Dec. 24 — (A. P.).—Maj. Gen. Walter C. Short, U. S. A., retired, Army commander of the Hawaiian Department when the Japanese attacked Pearl Harbor, is a patient at Walter Reed Hospital. It was reported that he was threatened with pneumonia. Short has been in almost daily attendance at the Congressional hearings on Pearl Harbor.

Britons Rebel At Yule Eve Sailing

LIVERPOOL, Dec. 24—(A. P.). Three hundred angry British soldiers walked off the troopship Orion today in protest against living conditions aboard. They battled military police who tried to force them back for a Christmas Eve sailing to the Middle East. Several were injured. Officials were pelted with tin cans and other small objects.

FRENCH TO RECOGNIZE TITO

PARIS, Dec. 24—(A. P.).—The French Government has decided to recognize Marshal Tito's Yugoslav regime, but formal recognition has not yet been extended.

Doomed to Wither Away! There Is Still Hope That a New Treatment For Muscular Dystrophy May Save the Little Boy's Life. Read Gobind Behari Lal's Story of How Science is Striving to Solve the Old Puzzle, in The American Weekly, the Magazine Distributed With Next Sunday's Baltimore American.—Adv.

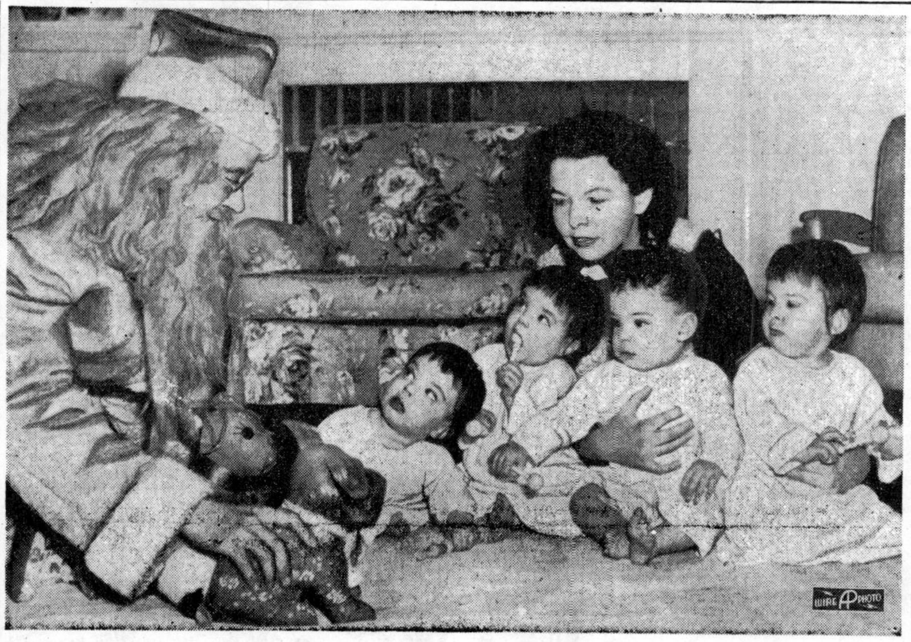

SANTA VISITS QUADS — Philadelphia's Cirminello Quadruplets, first ever born by Caesarean section, seem pleased with the gifts Santa Claus (their father) has brought them. That is with the possible exception of Eileen (left). There's a flicker of a doubt in her eye. Mrs. Cirminello sits with her children, a year old.

Soldier Held In Mich. Kidnap, Murder

WASHINGTON, Dec. 24—(A. P.).—The Federal Bureau of Investigation said today it has captured Robert Frederic Smith, twenty-one, wanted in connection with the death of Ray Gordon Beh, Grosse Point, Mich.

FBI Chief J. Edgar Hoover said Smith and a companion, Boleslas Walter Czajkowski, eighteen, were captured at Blue Island, Ill., Saturday.

Beh was a neighbor of Henry Ford II.

BOTH HELD IN CHICAGO

Both men are now being held in Chicago, and later today, Hoover said, will be charged with kidnaping. He added that "prosecutive action for the other offenses is under consideration."

Hoover gave this version of how Beh met his death on December 20:

Beh picked up Smith in Chicago, where Smith was attempting to hitch-hike a ride. Near Holland, Mich., Smith pulled a gun on Beh and told him to turn over his money.

Beh tried to talk Smith out of robbing him. That started a scuffle, and Beh was shot in the side with a .45-caliber revolver which Smith had stolen at Camp Robinson, Ark.

CLEARS ONE IN MURDER

Hoover said Czajkowski was not involved in Beh's death.

But, he said, both Smith and Czajkowski had confessed to a busy seven days during which they

Continued on Page 2, Column 7.

'American And Soldier':

General Patton Man Without Fear

(EDITOR'S NOTE: Larry Newman, veteran International News Service war correspondent, spent more than nine months covering the activities of Gen. George S. Patton, Jr., and his famed Third Army. Out of this constant association and from biographical material of the general's earlier days, Newman has culled a rich, anecdotal biography of Gen. George S. Patton, Jr., soldier and American. In the following first chapter, Newman paints a vivid word-portrait of the man who became one of the greatest generals in the history of the American Army.)

Chapter One.

By LARRY NEWMAN
International News Service Staff Correspondent.

NEW YORK, Dec. 24.—When the epitaph is written only these words will be needed:

"Gen. George S. Patton, Jr., American and soldier."

There are a thousand stories of Patton as a soldier, of his audacity, disregard for personal injury, indomitable spirit.

But too often in his tempestuous career, the real Patton was ignored.

GOES TO FRONT LINE

There was an afternoon at about this time a year ago in the Ardennes when the Germans were giving us a pretty good going over.

The general, surrounded by many of his underlings, went to the front to get a first-hand look at the situation because reports coming back to his headquarters in Luxembourg were meagre.

Just east of Bastogne is a little town called Wardin. The Germans fought bitterly there. Our casualties were heavy but for the moment, at least, we held the town.

The debris of battle still cluttered the streets and the smell of cordite filled the air when General Patton arrived.

Some of us were sitting on the steps of a battered hotel—just sitting, not talking, not thinking, because after battle there are no thoughts, just exhaustion.

DOUGHBOY IN GUTTER

Lying in the gutter a few yards away was a young doughboy. He was sprawled like all war dead are sprawled. Usually with the hand clutching the rifle. The helmet a few feet away.

Patton's jeep entered the dog-leg street about 50 yards from us; unconsciously we all knew who it was and everyone stood up and waited.

We thought he would go on, but when he saw the body he motioned to his driver to stop.

He got out of the jeep, and the other officers also stepped down from the little battlewagons and walked up to where Patton was standing.

For a long time the great gen-

Continued on Page 2. Column 3.

Yamashita Defense Flies To Capital

WASHINGTON, Dec. 24—(I. N. S.).—Attorney for the defense and for the Government prepared today to argue a last ditch appeal for the life of Lieut. Gen. Tomoyuki Yamashita, convicted Japanese commander in the Philippines. Word came from Tokyo that three members of Yamashita's defense counsel were being flown to Washington to get set for oral arguments on the appeal, directed by the Supreme Court for January 7, 1946.

The Baltimore News-Post Will Not Be Published On Christmas Day

Woman Found Dead; Hint Murder

Mrs. Dorothy Davis, twenty-seven, a comely brunette, was found dead today in her locked apartment at 1124 North Eutaw street by her mother, who had gone to accompany her on a shopping trip. Police said bruises about her head indicated she might have been murdered.

On the kitchen table the mother found a note addressed to her

"Dear Mother

"See you on Christmas Day.
"DOROTHY."

The body was found by Mrs. Davis' mother, Mrs. Clinton Smith of Brooklyn, Md.

HEARD CAT CRYING

Mrs. Smith became alarmed when her knocks received no answer, and she heard her daughter's cat crying on the other side of the locked door.

Using her key to the apartment, Mrs. Smith entered and found her daughter's body, covered with blood, sprawled on the dining room floor within two feet of the doorway.

Mrs. Smith said her daughter had been badly wounded in the head, and that there were other bruises on her hips and legs.

TELLS OF THREAT

She said:

"I know who did this. My daughter told me a man had been threatening her life!"

Police said as far as they could learn, Mrs. Smith was the last person to see Mrs. Davis alive. That was on Saturday.

The apartment is on the second floor of the building.

Mrs. Smith said her daughter was estranged from her husband, who is living in Louisiana.

GALE LASHES ENGLAND

LONDON, Dec. 24—(I. N. S.). England was lashed by a Christmas Eve gale today and the Channel was littered with drifting mines. Tremendous seas were stirred up by heavy wind and rain squalls.

11 Nations At Funeral Of Warrior

HAMM, Luxembourg, Dec. 24—(U. P.).—Gen. George S. Patton was buried on a bluff beneath wind-swept pines today, surrounded by white crosses above the graves of soldiers who fell along his Third Army's victory road.

Raw blasts of wind swirled across the U. S. Military Cemetery and snapped the khaki canvas canopy over the grave as the casket was lowered.

TAPS FOR A WARRIOR

Three rounds of salutes from 12-man firing squad rattled against the leaden sky. Then a lone bugler, his back to the wind, sounded taps.

The general's wife, Beatrice, stood quietly through the committal service, but almost broke down when Patton's Negro orderly, Sgt. William G. Meeks, Junction City, Kan., handed her the American flag that had covered the casket.

ORDERLY IN TEARS

There were tears in Meeks' eyes and his face was strained as he bowed slowly and handed her the folded flag. He saluted with a gloved hand and peered directly into her eyes, exchanging a final message of condolence.

Like the 7,933 crosses around it, Patton's simple white marker held only his name and metal serial number tag. Just "George S. Patton, Jr." The American Army knows no rank in death.

The burial ceremony, attended by military dignitaries of 11 nations, was brief. It was executed as the "spit and polish" general would have wanted, in perfect discipline. Mrs. Patton stood to the left of Lt. Gen. Geoffrey Keyes, commander of the U. S. Seventh Army.

LUXEMBOURG IN BLACK

The body was lowered at 10.15 A. M. after it had been borne in a half-track armored car through the black-draped streets of Luxembourg. Rain had been falling all night, but stopped as soldier pallbearers lifted the casket from the train on which it had been brought from Heidelberg.

Along a narrow road over the Ardennes Hills the procession of military and civilian vehicles wound its way toward the cemetery. Somewhere in the hills a French artillery battery of 105-mm. cannon rolled out a 17-gun salute.

HIS RIDERLESS HORSE

Soldiers lined both sides of the road from the cemetery entrance. The general's saddled brown charger, riderless and forlorn, stood at the head of a 50-foot path leading through the white crosses to Patton's grave.

The general's gleaming riding boots hung backwards in the stirrups, in the tradition of the cavalry he loved.

Mrs. Patton glanced at the horse and turned quickly away.

The casket was lifted from the

Continued on Page 2, Column 5.

VERY LATEST NEWS

(Race Results From Howard Sports Daily, Inc.)

AT GULFSTREAM

First—Unitran, won; Hemboss, 2d; Bobtown, 3d.

POLISH PRESIDENT CONFERS WITH U. S. DELEGATION

NEW YORK, Dec. 24—(A. P.). — The Polish Press agency reported from Warsaw today that President Boleslaw Bierut had held a long conference with a Polish-American delegation headed by Catholic Bishop Stefan Woznicki of Detroit.

JUSTICE JACKSON IN JERUSALEM

JERUSALEM, Dec. 24—(A. P.).—Justice Robert H. Jackson, chief United States prosecutor at the Nuernberg War Crimes trial, arrived today from Europe accompanied by his son and six other persons.

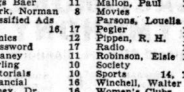

NEWS-POST

At Your Service	13	Horoscope	5
Bugs Baer	11	Mallon, Paul	11
Clark, Norman	8	Movies	8
Classified Ads	16, 17	Parsons, Louella	9
Comics	12	Pegler	11
Crossword	17	Pippen, R. H.	14
Dulaney	11	Radio	18
Durling	10	Robinson, Elsie	10
Editorials	10	Society	6
Financial	16	Sports	14, 15
Haney, Dr.	16	Winchell, Walter	8
Health	5	Women's Clubs	6

Three Stars In Hipp's Sea Drama— Comedy At Times

By NORMAN CLARK

JOHNNY MAY BE an Angel by name but he isn't by nature. No sir, he's a two-fisted sea captain and he doesn't shrink from a fight in which guns are brought into play.

Neither is Johnny averse to making a little bit of love to a couple of girls, especially when he thinks that one, or both, of them, might help him run down the murderers of his father, who was also a sea captain.

The elder Angel's ship is found floating in the Gulf of Mexico with nobody on board and it is taken into the port of New Orleans. Johnny gets right to work to find out who it was that killed his father. A lot of people try to prevent the captain from discovering the truth but Johnny is the sort of man who sits down everytime somebody shoves a comfortable chair in his direction.

George Raft in the title role of this moderately interested drama of the seas is—well, the usual frowning, tight-lipped Mr. Raft. Claire Trevor and Signe Hasso are the luscious peppermint sticks. A highlight of the tale is Songwriter Hoagy Carmichael, in the role of a taxi driver singing a ditty called "Memphis in June."

AT TIMES

"BLONDE FROM BROOKLYN," at the Times. Screen play by Erna Lazarus. Directed by Del Lord. A Columbia picture, presented at the Times.

THE CAST
Susan Parker............Lynn Merrick
Dixon Harper............Robert Stanton
"Col." Hubert Farnsworth
 ....Thurston Hall
Diane Peabody............Mary Treen
W. W. Wilbur............Walter Soderling
Daniel Frazier............Arthur Loft
Mrs. Frazier............Regina Wallace
Harvey Branson............Bryon Foulger

THIS TOWN of Brooklyn gets its name into screen comedies quite often, it seems to us. However there's a heap of "you-all" stuff—you know, Dixie accent—in the "Blonde From Brooklyn."

Susan and Dixon—he's a singer who has been in the Army—team up and to help land a radio spot advertising coffee adopt a Southern accent. When Susie gets her chance before the mike, of course, she makes the usual big hit, but she becomes frightened and takes it on the lam, as the saying goes, when the sponsors pick her up as the heiress to a fortune and an old plantation.

Lynn Merrick and Robert Stanton—he's Dick Haymes' brother and has appeared on the screen under his own name of Bob Haymes—are pleasant folk and they sing some songs nicely. Thurston Hall as a phoney Southern colonel, and round-faced Mary Treen indulge in comedy antics.

BONNIE LEE IN SHOW AT GAYETY

Bonnie Lee, a newcomer, has the starring role in the burlesque revue opening at the Gayety Theater today. At the comedy counter will be Walter Brown and Bert Berry.

Also in the cast are Fred Nerret, Agnes Dean, Louise Sharee, Bea Hayden, Claire Cain and Herb Leighton.

AT REX

The Pine-Thomas team has produced another murder thriller, with William Gargan and Ann Savage courting bullets in "Midnight Manhunt," showing tomorrow at the Rex Theater, 4600 York road.

Movie CLOCK

CENTURY—"House on 92nd Street," 10.45 A. M., 1.01, 3.17, 5.26, 7.42, 9.58 P. M.
STANLEY—"Rhapsody in Blue," 10.40 A. M., 1.15, 4, 6.45, 7.30, 10 P. M.
HIPPODROME—"Johnny Angel," 11 A. M., 1.45, 4.30, 7.10, 10 P. M.
NEW—"State Fair," 10 A. M., 12, 2, 4, 6, 8, 10 P. M.
TIMES—"Blonde From Brooklyn," 1.28, 4.07, 6.46, 9.25 P. M.
KEITHS—"That Night With You," 10.40 A. M., 12.05, 2.05, 4.05, 6.05, 8.05, 10.05 P. M.
MAYFAIR—"Men in Her Diary," 11.18 A. M., 1.10, 3.02, 5.54, 6.46, 8.38, 10.30 P. M.
VALENCIA—"Abbott and Costello in Hollywood," 1.40, 3.42, 5.44, 7.46, 9.48 P. M.
ROSLYN—"Strange Case of Dr. Rx," 2.42, 5.32, 8.10, 10.48 P. M.
LITTLE—"Arrowsmith," 11 A. M., 12.48, 2.36, 4.36, 6.15, 8, 9.48 P. M.
PARKWAY—"Incendiary Blonde," 12.45, 2.57, 5.09, 7.21, 9.34 P. M.

BAMPTON! SPALDING! HEINZ! STERN! BRAILOWSKY! MARCUS! MALSUZYNSKI! SCHKOLNIK! TRAUBEL! PIATIGORSKY! TALLARICO! MENUHIN! All Soloists with

BALTIMORE SYMPHONY
Reginald Stewart, Conductor
14 Midweek | 5 Sunday
Concerts | Concerts
Opening Concerts Oct. 31 and Nov. 4
Season Tickets at reduced rates now at Cappel Concert Bureau; Music Centre, N. Charles St., and Stieff Hall, 315 N. Howard St.

"Johnny Angel"

"JOHNNY ANGEL," starring George Raft, Signe Hasso, Claire Trevor. Screen play by Steve Fisher, based on a story by Charles Gordon Booth. Directed by Edwin L. Marin. An RKO picture, presented at the Hippodrome.

THE CAST
Johnny Angel............George Raft
Lilah..................Claire Trevor
Paulette...............Signe Hasso
Sam Jewell.............Lowell Gilmore
Celestial O'Brien....Hoagy Carmichael
Gustafson..............Marvin Miller
Miss Drumm..........Margaret Wycherly
Captain Angel......J. Farrell Macdonald
Bartender...............Mack Gray

Walter Winchell
All Around the Town

Parks autographed with autumn's colorful signature . . . A foghorn's melancholy wail—loneliness carved in sound . . . Script-wrecked playwrights stranded on an island of hope making the rounds of producers' offices. The private park at Tudor City exhibiting well-manicured lawns. At one time it was a hideaway for criminals . . . Twilight wrapping itself in the gaudy toga of a vanishing day and moving into infinity.

The stylish subway guard wearing his cap at a jaunty MacArthur angle . . . Sidewalk Romeos attempting to defrost passing gals with a wink, while scanning the horizon for skirted craft.

Uppity Park Ave. shops catering to a cosmopolitan trade. Many of the clerks are linguists . . . The delight-eyeful Riverside Drive waterfront sector. Most arresting at this time of year when the sky is a rhapsody in blue and cool breezes herald the approach of winter . . . A bonfire of sunset spreading its glow across the morning sky as silence stands guard over the fabulous town.

Broadwayites planted on street corners straining conversation through cigars, idly fishing in an ocean of small talk . . . A waddle of womanhood entering a Fifth Ave. reducing salon which features this query in its show-window: "What have you got to lose?"

A pert-cupcake of a smile balanced on the pretty faces of hostesses in swanky eateries . . . Derelicts strolling along Tenth Ave. wearing faces scribbled with sordid autobiographies.

Sprawling Madison Sq. Garden which can be emptied of a capacity crowd (20,000) within five minutes . . . Radio City's buildings staggered both as to height and location, in order to shade each other as little as possible.

The RCA building entrance surmounted by a glass mosaic. It is made of a million pieces of glass in various shades of color . . . The million-candlepower beacon atop the George Washington Bridge sweeping its reassuring light across fifty miles of darkened sky.

KEITHS ROOF

Keiths Roof will present dancing tomorrow and Sunday nights. Bob Craig and his band will furnish the musical program and Ronnie Taylor will be the vocalist both nights.

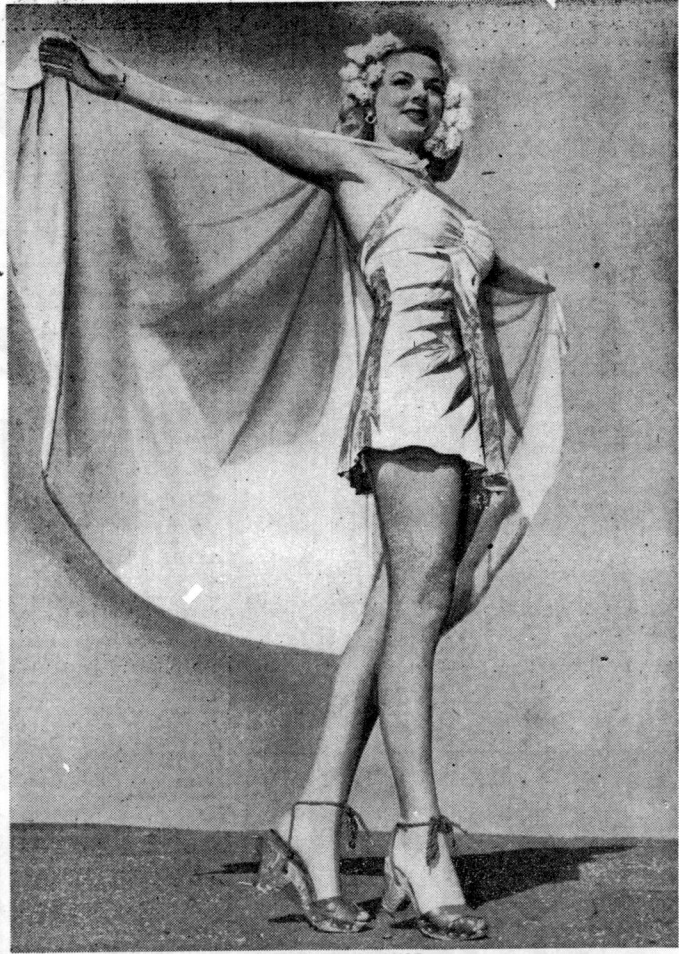

VIRGINIA DE LUCE

Looks are certainly deceiving. Dainty Virginia is a jui-jitsu expert. Before making her film debut in "The Dolly Sisters" she taught the ancient Oriental art to a Hollywood class of 15 girls. Five feet four inches in height and weighing 115 pounds, Virginia experiences no difficulty in throwing a 220-pound male over either of her pretty shoulders. Learned jui-jitsu from a boy friend in the Marine Corps.

Jean Carroll On Hipp Stage

The stage show at the Hippodrome this week is headed by the stage and radio comedienne, Jean Carroll.

Well known to Hippodrome audiences, clever Miss Carroll clicks solidly with her adroit "emceeing" and her comedy material.

Miriam Burroughs, pretty young violinist, proves to be one of the highlights on the bill.

Ben Yost's Mimic Men register soundly with their singing and imitations of stage, screen and radio celebrities. The Three Reddingtons offer eccentric acrobatic tricks.

Sterling Is Back In Film Role For M.-G.-M.

By LOUELLA O. PARSONS
Motion Picture Editor
International News Service.

HOLLYWOOD, Oct. 19.—Bob Sterling, just out of uniform, gets right back into one for "The Last Time I Saw Paris," his first movie for his old alma mammy in three years.

Yes, that's the Elliott Paul novel title, all right, but M.-G.-M. is throwing away the story and working a brand-new idea based just on the title. It's about a paratrooper who bails out in France and meets some old and fascinating characters. Later, after he's mustered out he returns to Paris to find them not so fascinating in civilian clothes.

I know one fan who will be mighty glad to have Bob back on the screen and that's Ann Sothern, his bride. She thinks he has Van Johnson, Clark Gable, Frank Sinatra and Mike Mazurka all lashed to the mast.

Producer Sam Marx hasn't yet found the gal to emote opposite Bob—fact is, he is the only member of the cast so far.

Snapshots of Hollywood collected at random: Betsy Blair, Gene Kelly's pretty wife, may do a picture at Twentieth.

Heard from New York that Spencer Tracy is leaving the cast of "The Rugged Path."

Verbena Hebbard flies to Mexico City today and flies right back Tuesday. That's a long way, I'd say, to spend a week end. She's taking the Hernando Courtrights there to introduce them.

Col. Jimmie Stewart attended a party tonight with pretty Margo Stevens on his arm. He seems to be playing the field.

Cesar Romero and John Weissmuller, arm in arm, were doing the town with Cesar introducing Johnny as Victor Mature.

Joe Schenck has so perfected his Spanish that he ordered a complete dinner at the Beverly Hills Club in Spanish.

Dick Foran has changed his name to Richard for dramas. He'll keep Dick for Westerns.

Capt. Bud Lesser, Sol's son, is back after 39 months in the marines.

That's all today. See you tomorrow!

TODAY'S MOVIE CALENDAR

Theaters advertised in this column belong to the Motion Picture Theater Owners of Maryland.

Message From F.D.R.

Wainwright Discloses Text Of 2 Notes From President

Subs Arrive, Too Late For Bataan

Mine Sweeper Runs Nip Fire To Bring In Cargo

Continued from Preceding Page

"Go back and tell him not to do it," I shouted.

But it was done, I soon learned. Let me say here that I have no criticism of Gen. King for accepting the situation and surrendering. It was a decision which required great courage and mental fortitude. I was soon to find out that it is not easy for an American to surrender.

But I had my orders from MacArthur not to surrender on Bataan, and therefore I could not authorize King to do it. But King was on the ground and confronted by a situation in which he had either to surrender or have his people captured or killed piecemeal. This would most certainly have happened to him within two or three days.

TERRIBLE SILENCE

A terrible silence settled over Bataan about noon on April 9. It deepened with the coming of the night, even though Corregidor itself was under bombardment and shelling. Bataan was something dead that lay up there two miles across the dark water.

If there is anything worse than a battlefield that shakes with explosions and the cries of men it is one that becomes mute and dead and just sprawls there broken and exhausted. That was Bataan on the night of April 9, 1942.

In the last hours of Bataan I knew, at least, that I had the support of my Commander in Chief. President Roosevelt radioed MacArthur asking him to relay to me an expression of his (Roosevelt's) support, ". . . if you (MacArthur) concur both as to substance and timing."

The message, which we received simultaneously on Corregidor, read:

"I am keenly aware of the difficulties under which you are waging your great battle. The exhaustion of your troops obviously precludes the possibility of a major counter-stroke unless our efforts to get food to you should quickly prove successful.

"Because of conditions over which your forces have no control I am modifying my orders to you as contained in my telegram to General MacArthur February 9 and repeated March 23. (The no-surrender note.)

FUTURE OF BATAAN

"I shall leave to your own best judgment any decisions affecting the future of the Bataan garrison.

"I have only admiration for your soldierly conduct and your performance of your difficult mission and have every confidence that whatever decision you may sooner or later make will be dictated by the best interests of the country and of your splendid troops.

"I am still hopeful that the efforts of the Navy to supply you by submarine will be successful and in time, and that at least one or more of the surface vessels trying to run the blockade will reach you soon.

"I deem it proper and necessary that you should be assured of complete freedom of action and of my full confidence in the wisdom of whatever decision you may be compelled to make."

FREEDOM OF ACTION

Just before I received the above message from Mr. Roosevelt I had transmitted to him the dreadful news that Bataan had fallen. He promptly radioed back, in part:

"I am hopeful you will be able to hold Corregidor. However, you are assured of freedom of action and my confidence in your wisdom in whatever decision you may make.—Franklin D. Roosevelt."

I radioed back the following message from Corregidor to the White House:

"Your confidence in my judgment in this desperate situation as well as the kindness of your message have my heartfelt gratitude.

"I have done all that could have been done to hold Bataan, but starving men without air and with inadequate artillery can not endure the terrific aerial and artillery bombardment to which my troops were subjected.

"The Japanese have emplaced heavy artillery on south shore of Bataan and now keep Corregidor under constant artillery fire as well as air bombing.

MORE JAP TROOPS

"This morning we have been informed that enemy is now landing in considerable force on Cebu. Due to communication difficulties I have no further information on the progress of this landing.

"Obviously if the enemy takes Cebu it will be impracticable to ship the supplies which have been assembled there.

"An unusually large number of hostile warships and transports have been operating in waters close to southern islands during the past 48 hours. The enemy next will direct his attention to other islands of the Visayan group.

"Communication with Bataan troops is cut so I have no knowledge of terms arranged by General King . . ."

And I finished the message from Corregidor with this:

"The American flag still flies on this beleaguered island fortress."

I meant to see that it kept flying.

(Tomorrow: The Battle of Corregidor begins.)

SURRENDER OF BATAAN—Maj. Gen. Edward P. King (center, rear) is shown surrendering on Bataan, with Lt. Col. E. P. Williams holding the white flag. Photograph of this scene, one of the darkest in American history, was printed in the Japanese propaganda magazine, Freedom, published in Shanghai. As General Wainwright explains today, he had ordered General King, pursuant to General MacArthur's instructions, not to give up, but the situation on Bataan was hopeless.

THIS LITTLE EXTRA TOUCH adds a lot to waffles!

SIMPLY SPREAD the right margarine on them and m-m-m, how much *better* those waffles will taste.

The *right* margarine? Is there really a *difference* between margarines? You bet there is—just try new GOOD LUCK and see!

This delicious margarine is a *new blend* of fresh pasteurized skim milk absorbed in choice food oils made from wholesome products of American farms. And the *fresh country flavor* this new blend gives new GOOD LUCK really does wonders for food!

Try it on waffles—rolls or bread—hot vegetables. See how its fresh country flavor *steps up* any food you serve it with. And GOOD LUCK never lets you down—every pound is deliciously the same.

Get new GOOD LUCK! Use it at the table —in recipes, too. Try this tempting

GOOD LUCK PECAN PIE
(Makes one 8-inch pie)

½ recipe pastry
½ cup GOOD LUCK Margarine
2 eggs, well beaten
Dash of salt
1 cup dark corn syrup
1 teaspoon vanilla
1 cup chopped pecans

Line 8-inch pie pan with pastry; chill. Have GOOD LUCK Margarine at room temperature. Cream margarine. (Compare new GOOD LUCK Margarine—for freshness and flavor—with any spread at any price. Its fresh country flavor does wonders for the recipes you use it in—the foods you serve it with!) Add eggs; beat well. Add rest of ingredients. Mix well. Pour into pie shell. Bake in moderate oven (375° F.) 45 minutes or until knife inserted in center comes out clean.

For FRESH COUNTRY FLAVOR ... get New GOOD LUCK margarine
—THE GRAND ENERGY FOOD THAT'S RICH IN HEALTHFUL VITAMIN A!

JELKE'S GOOD LUCK VEGETABLE OLEOMARGARINE RICH IN VITAMIN A

Dramatic Details Of Bataan Fall Told By Wainwright

Turn To Page 18

THE WEATHER

Some cloudiness, mild tonight; sunny, cooler Saturday; clear, cooler Saturday night and Sunday.

Detailed Weather Revort Page 34

Read The Baltimore News-Post for complete, accurate news coverage. It is the only Baltimore newspaper possessing the three great wire services—
ASSOCIATED PRESS
INTERNATIONAL NEWS SERVICE
UNITED PRESS

THE BALTIMORE NEWS-POST

AN INDEPENDENT NEWSPAPER

The Largest Evening Circulation in the Entire South

7 HOME FINAL

VOL. CXLVII.—NO. 142 Entered as second-class matter at Baltimore Postoffice. FRIDAY EVENING, OCTOBER 19, 1945 PRICE 3 CENTS

MAN LASHED IN WIFE BEATING

Move In Parliament To Curb Attlee

NAZI WAR CRIMINALS GO ON TRIAL NOV. 20

Japan Balks At Busting Its Trusts

TOKYO, Oct. 19—(A. P.).—Japanese Communist leaders asked the Socialist Party today to join in a united front against the Shidehara Government, which they said "has no ability to cope with the present situation."

TOKYO, Oct. 19—(U. P.).—The Japanese Cabinet today balked at immediate action on Gen. Douglas MacArthur's demand that industrial monopolies be broken up.

A Japanese source said the Cabinet discussed the demand for some time at today's meeting, but failed to reach a decision.

"The issue concerns the very foundation of the Japanese industrial slstem and has immediate, far-reaching effects on the people's livelihood," the informant said in explaining the Government's apparent reluctance to take immediate action.

SEES NO BENEFIT

Even before the Cabinet meeting, Foreign Minister Shigeru Yoshida told a press conference he doubted that dissolution of the

TOKYO, Oct. 19—(A. P.).—The man in Tokyo's streets glances with scant favor on President Truman's proposal that the Japanese should be permitted to vote on whether Emperor Hirohito keeps his throne. Of 21 persons interviewed at random, only seven favored such a ballot. The others thought either Hirohito or another of the imperial line should remain enthroned and the Emperor system be retained.

old "Zaibatsu"—such family industrial trusts as Mitsui, Mitsubishi and Sumitomo — would benefit Japan in the long run.

He contended it was mainly through the efforts of these established monopolies that Japan's trade originally was built up to a point where the nation prospered. He said:

"The old Zaibatsu built up their enterprises in times of peace and they were the first

Continued on Page 2, Column 5.

19 D. C. Hotels Facing Strike

WASHINGTON, Oct. 19—(I. N. S.).—Managements of 19 Washington hotels were confronted today with a strike threat involving about 8,000 employees.

Sam Levine, general counsel for the Hotel and Restaurant International Union and Bartenders' Alliance, said those organizations have done all they could to avoid a walkout. He reported that negotiations for a new contract had collapsed.

Golden Crop for New Lady Novelists. Some People Find Gold Mines, Some Invest in Them—and Some Women Write Them. How Your Modern Authoresses Are Cleaning Up in the Writing Field Is Given an Interesting Analysis in The American Weekly, the Magazine Distributed With Next Sunday's Baltimore American.—Adv.

Seek To Block Socialist Powers Of Attlee Party

By KINGSBURY SMITH

LONDON, Oct. 19—(I. N. S.).—Conservative members of Parliament made a final effort in the House of Commons today to curb the drastic Socialist powers which the Government is demanding for its five-year controlled economy plan.

During a report on the state services, supplies and transitional powers bill, the Conservatives moved a series of amendments designed to limit the powers of Prime Minister Clement Attlee's Government. Limits were sought especially in respect to the control of prices.

Sir David Maxwell, Conservative, said that the only reason he could see for the controls the Government demanded was to discriminate against private enterprise.

He said:

"If that is the reason it is a reason capable of very sinister manifestation, and if it is not the only reason then we are left with a bankrupt, nauseating idea of controls for control's sake."

AMENDMENT KILLED

The first amendment put forth by the Conservatives was defeated, 212 to 83.

The five-year program was attacked by the Recorder, weekly Conservative organ, as "subjugation" of the British nation by "bureaucracy."

The Recorder said:

"Under this bill of Government can command the services, property and wealth of any citizen in the country. It can enter into competition with industry and dictate the price at which industry must sell its products.

CAN TAKE BUSINESS

"It can take over business if it dislikes the looks or political complexion of the directors.

"And, since the life of the measure will be five years after it has been placed on the statute book it will still be law when the next general election is fought."

Asserting that the Government of Prime Minister Clement Attlee managed to get this unprecedentedly drastic peace-time measure through the House of Commons Monday night, "not by argument, but by sheer weight of numbers," under the iron discipline of the Labor Government whips, the Recorder said:

"As a demonstration of democracy, the action was pitiful.

"Not even Hitler's Reichstag was more subservient."

PREDICTS APPROVAL

The Conservative mouthpiece pointed out that the bill still has to pass through the House of Lords and predicted a rough passage, but final approval.

The Recorder went on:

"The position of the Lords is not an enviable one.

"They are rather like the American Cabinet at the threatened outbreak of the Civil War when Lincoln said to his ministers: *'Neither by your significance nor your insignificance can you now escape history.'* ".

The Oxford Union Society, at its first debate of the term last night defeated, 306 to 200, a motion welcoming the prospect of five years of Labor Government in Britain.

Move For New Anti-Strike Law

WASHINGTON, Oct. 19—(A. P.).—The Labor Department today urged repeal of the strike-notice section of the War Labor Disputes Act. The Department said this section is "h[illegible]ing rather than helping the cause of industrial peace."

DETROIT, Oct. 19—(A. P.).—Emergency crews strove today to maintain electric power service to more than 2,000,000 Michigan residents while Federal and State officials sought an end to a strike of 2,000 Consumers Power Company employees which began Thursday.

Foremen and other nonstrikers remained on duty in the company's power plants and substations in a score of communities in heavily industrialized lower Michigan in an effort to keep the area provided with electricity. Detroit was not affected.

NO VIOLENCE

Company spokesmen said the situation was "normal," but union officials said they believed it unlikely the supervisory employees could maintain regular service for long.

Picket lines were maintained at most of the points, but State police said there had been no reports of violence.

State police said they planned no arrests unless company officials swore out warrants under provisions of a law making it a felony to interfere with operation of a public utility.

John W. Gibson, special assistant to Secretary of Labor Schwellenbach, was en route from Washington to attend a meeting at the State capital in Lansing today, which was to include presidents

Continued on Page 2, Column 7.

New York Arrives In N. Y. Harbor

NEW YORK, Oct. 19—(U.P.).—The 34-000-ton New York, third oldest battleship in the U. S. Navy, docked here today to be shined up for her role in the Navy Day celebration October 27. Aboard her were 1,064 Navy and Coast Guard passengers an da crew of 1,500.

Marylander Lashed As Wife Beater

UPPER MARLBORO, Oct. 19.—In the corridor on the second floor of the two-story brick county jail, Sheriff R. Earle Sheriff wielded a plaited brown leather whip and laid ten lashes on the back of brawny Lloyd O. Busching, convicted of assaulting his wife.

The man's arms were thrust through the bars of a cell and were handcuffed to the bars, as he stood unclosed to receive the lash.

As about 20 official witnesses looked on, the sheriff, without removing his coat, swung the whip and brought it down across the man's buttocks, raising a series of welts, but not breaking the skin.

HANDCUFFS REMOVED

As soon as he had counted the tenth lash, the handcuffs were unlocked, the man was led to his cell and put on his clothing.

Throughout the entire proceeding, except for the sheriff, no one spoke a word.

The sheriff, as the man was led from his cell, spoke to him as follows:

"Lloyd Busching, you have been sentenced by the court to receive ten lashes upon you for beating your wife..

"As I am the sheriff of Prince George's county, it is my duty to carry out that sentence, which I will now proceed to do."

Busching then removed his clothes, had his hands cuffed to the cell bar and was whipped.

SLIGHT FLINCHING

The only reaction the convicted man showed, witnesses said, was a slight flinching as the leather made contact with his flesh.

Afterward, when he had resumed his clothes, he conversed privately with his attorney, George Burroughs. The lawyer did not divulge what his client had said.

Shortly after 10.30 A. M. the sheriff, Chief of Police Ralph Brown, several other policemen and the members of the jury which had found Busching guilty of "brutal assault," walked the distance of one block from the courthouse to the jail. They were let into the building by the jailer, Ellis Middleton, the owner of the whip used in carrying out the sentence.

Then the doors of the jail were closed, but opened a few minutes later for the sheriff and the chief

Continued on Page 2, Column 6.

Halsey Resting In New Castle

NEW CASTLE, Del., Oct. 19—(I. N. S.).—Admiral William F. ("Bull") Halsey, commander of the victorious Third Fleet, rested today after a flight from the Pacific Coast. He will make no engagements until Navy Day, October 27, when he will take part in ceremonies at Indianapolis, following which he will make a three-week tour with the Eighth War Loan drive.

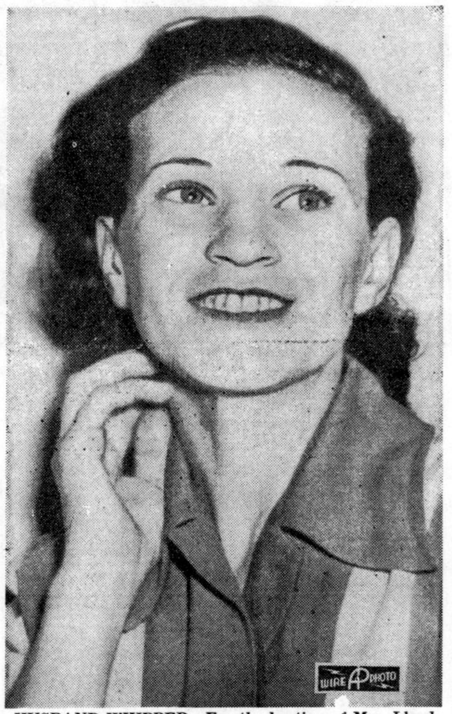

HUSBAND WHIPPED—For the beating of Mrs. Lloyd O. Busching (above) of Dillon Park, Md., her husband, thirty-two-year-old electrical worker, received 10 lashes by whip from a sheriff in Upper Marlboro Jail today. Busching weighs 175 pounds, his wife 98.

Butter Cost Up, Points To Drop

WASHINGTON, Oct. 19—(A. P.).—Butter may cost fewer red points next month. But housewives probably will shell out more cold cash for it.

They are likely to pay five or six cents more a pound, beginning November 8. That's because cancellation of a Government subsidy to butter processors will push up retail ceiling prices that much.

On the other hand there is a good possibility that the current butter ration value of 12 points a pound may be cut to eight, effective October 28.

One reason, said food officials who asked anonymity, is the recent release by the Army of 80,000,000 pounds of butter.

At the same time there was an indication that the better cuts of meat will continue to be rationed in November; OPA already is printing meat point charts for next month.

Temperatures

12 Mid.,	61	7 A. M.,	57
1 A. M.,	60	8 A. M.,	59
2 A. M.,	59	9 A. M.,	63
3 A. M.,	59	10 A. M.,	67
4 A. M.,	58	11 A. M.,	70
5 A. M.,	57	12 Noon,	73
6 A. M.,	55	1 P. M.,	75

5 Hungary Parties Agree On Slate

BUDAPEST, Oct. 19—(A. P.). The five major parties which make up Hungary's coalition government reached complete agreement yesterday on presenting a single slate to the voters for the parliamentary elections. The step was taken to avoid violence which has been threatening between Communists and the Smallholders party ever since the latter won the Budapest city election.

U. S. Plane Crew, 50 Chinese Killed

PEIPING, Oct. 17—(Delayed). More than 50 Chinese troops and an American crew were killed today when a troopship crashed attempting to land at Nanyuan Airfield, near here. The plane was one of the first arriving with Chinese Government troops on a schedule under which 29 planes began bringing soldiers from Shanghai to Nanyuan.

Army Dentists Pull 16,500,000 Teeth

WASHINGTON, Oct. 19—(U. P.).—Army life may have been a headache to some, but it was a toothache to plenty of others. The War Department reported today that the Army Dental Corps made 71,700,000 fillings and 16,500,000 extractions for GIs during the war.

23 Top Ringleaders Of Hitler's Gangsters Receive Indictments

NUERNBERG, Oct. 19—(U. P.).—The trial of Nazism's foremost surviving war criminals will open November 20 in this one-time shrine city of the party which started the second World War, it was announced officially today.

The four-Power Allied military tribunal which will conduct the Nuernberg trial announced that the date of its opening had been set for four weeks and four days from today.

The trial date was set soon after the Allied war crimes indictment was served on the bulk of the defendants—a who's who of the remainder of the Nazi hierarchy—in the Nuernberg Prison.

SERVICE ON 23

Today's service of the indictment here and elsewhere in the American Occupation Zone completed notification of the 24 defendants save for Martin Bormann, former Nazi party deputy whose whereabouts are unknown.

Grand Admiral Reich Raeder and propagandist, Hans Fritzsche were notified in Berlin yesterday. Gustav Krupp von Bohlen, head of Krupp, was served in an Army hospital, and former Reichsbank President Walther Funk in another prison.

SERVED IN CELLS

A special clerk of the international tribunal which will try the Nazis, Maj. Anthony Neave, made the rounds of the cells in Nuernberg Prison and slipped copies of the bulky indictment through the doors.

Harold Willey, general secretary of the tribunal, accompanied Neave and passed out copies of an article in the tribunal charter setting forth the rights of the defendants and listing civilian lawyers known to be alive in Germany.

Article 16 of the charter guarantees the defendants full particulars of the charges against them, the right to give any explanation relevant to the charges either at thetrial or preliminary hearings, and that the trial wil be conducted in a language the defedant understands.

TWO IN BERLIN

Raeder and Fritzsche, the first defendants upon whom the indictments were served, were in Russian custody at Berlin. They were expected to be moved to Nuernberg soon.

Krupp is recovering from a par-

Continued on Page 2, Column 6

Church Training For Pupils Asked

Baltimore's School Board today was studying a proposal made by a committee of Protestant and Catholic churchmen asking that pupils of the third, fourth, fifth and sixth grades be released an hour weekly for religious education during school hours.

The request was made with the authority of the Council of Churches and Christian Education and by the Catholic Archdiocese of Baltimore. If granted it would bring Baltimore into a system now being tried in 1,500 other communities in the United States.

STUDY OF PLAN

John R. Sherwood, member of the School Board, said:

"I think we should have a plan submitted to us so that we may study this realistically. We are told that many of these schools have failed. We should not enter into anything that is going to fail."

The absence of Jewish representation on the committee was not to be construed as an objection to the plan, it was stated by Dr. Louis L. Kaplan, executive director of the Board of Jewish Education, who explained that weekday religious schools have been developed with an enrollment of about 2,000 Jewish children.

SEVEN POINTS

The plan, as submitted by the committee included seven points:

1. Only children with signed cards from parents or guardians would be released to attend the classes.
2. The classes to be held at co-operating churches or other sites outside the schools.
3. The Council of Churches would direct Protestant teaching, the Archdiocese of Baltimore the Catholic instruction.
4. The Baltimore Week-day Religious Education Committee to supervise standards.
5. The plan to be run the first year on a small scale as an experiment.
6. Teachers to be professionally trained.
7. Pupils' work to be graded.

NEWS-POST

Your Service	17	Haney, Dr. Lewis	34
Ezrael, Louis	27	Horoscope	9
Bugs Baer	27	Movies	28
Clark, Norman	28	Parsons, Louella	28
Classified Ads	35, 36, 37	Pegler	27
Comics	30	Pippen, R.H.	32
Crossword	37	Radio	25
Dulaney	27	Robinson, Elsie	26
Durling	26	Society	20
Editorials	26	Sports	33, 33, 34
Financial	34, 35	Winchell, Walter	28
Health	7	Women's Clubs	20

Mighty Atomic Bomb Hastened End Of War

FIRST ATOMIC PILOT—Capt. Paul W. Tibbets, pilot of the Army's first atomic bomber, waves good-by before taking off on a mission that cut short the Japanese conflict and revolutionized all conception of future wars.

AREA OF BOMB'S EFFECTIVENESS—Approximate area of an atomic bomb's effectiveness is encompassed in this photo-diagram of downtown Baltimore. Assuming the bomb dropped near the B. & O. Mount Clare yards, the city would vanish to its eastern limits.

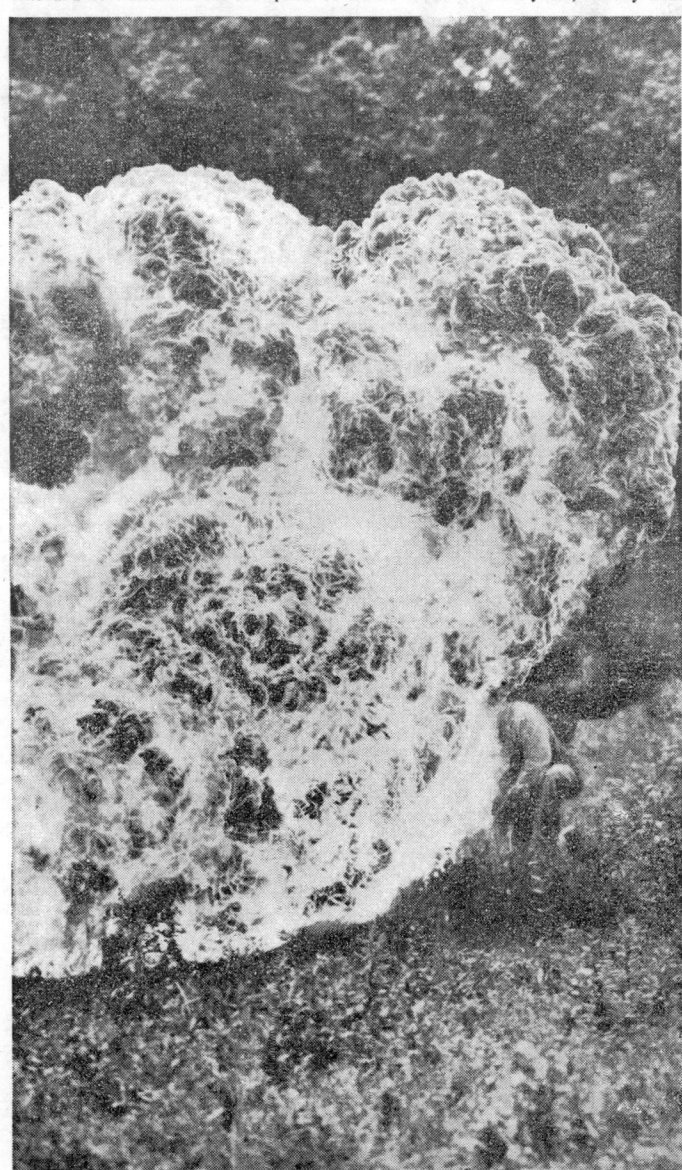

BALL OF FIRE—Japs report the first atomic bomb disintegrated the city of Hiroshima, killing more than 100,000 persons. A searing flame engulfed a four-square-mile area, disintegrating everything in its path. Deadly flame throwers such as the one in operation above, have a similar effect on humans, but heat from the atomic bomb is so terrific that all matter disappears in a cloud of dust.

DROPPED BOMB—Maj. Thomas W. Ferebee was bombardier aboard the B-29 that dropped the first atomic bomb on Japan. His effort hastened the end of the war.

ATOM SMASHER—Long before development of the atom bomb scientists had perfected the Cyclotron—or atom-smashing machine—shown being examined by Dr. E. O. Lawrence, one of the principal atomic pioneers. Control of unlimited power generated by unlocking the atom's energy was the next step. Scientists throughout the world sought this elusive clue. We won.

TWO THOUSAND TO ONE—British troops direct the lifting of one of their 11-ton "Grand Slam" bombs, considered the greatest instrument of destruction ever known until the American atomic bomb brought Japan to its knees. The new revolutionary weapons have such tremendous energy that one atomic bomb is equal to 2,000 of the 11-ton missiles which sowed destruction on Germany before its defeat.

THE WEATHER
Warm and humid, with some chance of thundershowers, and highest temperature 85 degrees this afternoon. Fair, with lowest temperature around 70 degrees.

Read The Baltimore News-Post for complete, accurate war coverage. It is the only Baltimore newspaper possessing the three great wire services—
ASSOCIATED PRESS
INTERNATIONAL NEWS SERVICE
UNITED PRESS

The Baltimore News-Post
AN INDEPENDENT NEWSPAPER

The Largest Evening Circulation in the Entire South

VOL. CXLVII.—NO. 86   Entered as second-class matter at Baltimore Postoffice.   TUESDAY EVENING, AUGUST 14, 1945   PRICE 3 CENTS

NIGHT
Wall St. Opening

TOKYO RADIO SAYS JAPS SURRENDER
White House Expects Reply Today

By J. LYNN LEONARD, International News Service Foreign Writer.

Acceptance by Japan of the Allied terms of surrender was reported today by the Japanese Domei agency. Domei said in further dispatches that at 9 P. M. tonight Jap time, (8 A. M., E. W. T.) "there probably will be something important." Another Domei transmission said, however, that the important word to be disclosed would come an hour later, or at 9 A. M., E. W. T. Immediately thereafter monitors in America and in Europe reported that a Tokyo code station had been sending long code messages to Switzerland which has acted as go-between for Tokyo and Washington. These monitors said the Tokyo transmissions to Switzerland had been in progress since 12.48 A. M., E. W. T.

Washington did not immediately confirm the Japanese report, nor was it substantiated for the time being in any other quarter.

From Washington came word of the arrival of Capt. James K. Vardaman, President Truman's Naval aide, at the White House shortly after 2.15 A. M. There was no official announcement on the reason for the early morning visit.

The Domei account, recorded by the F. C. C., said that the Japanese Government had agreed to the surrender formula as transmitted to Tokyo by the U. S. State Department.

The announcement, although coming only from the Japanese, had all the authoritative ring of the first reports from Tokyo last week that Japan was ready to capitulate.

Domei is the agency for transmission of official information, and throughout the war was the principal propaganda outlet of Nippon.

The first word from Tokyo on the momentous decision by the Japs was brief. Domei said:

"It is learned that an imperial message accepting the Potsdam proclamation is forthcoming soon."

The Domei dispatch was recorded at 1.49 A. M., EWT., that is 2.49 P. M. Japanese time.

CALLS FOR FULL SURRENDER

The Potsdam declaration, issued by the U. S., Britain and China and later subscribed to by Russia after Soviet entry into the Far East conflict, calls for unconditional surrender of Japan.

The Japanese last Friday announced to the Allies, through the Swiss Government, their willingness to accept the terms of Potsdam but requested that Emperor Hirohito be permitted to remain on the throne.

In the answer dispatched to Nippon by U. S. Secretary of State James F. Byrnes with the approval of the three other principal Allies it was agreed that Hirohito might remain as the figurehead in Japan, subject to the directives of an American Allied commander-in-chief.

INSIST ON ELECTIONS

The Allies stipulated also that subsequent democratic elections must be held in the Japanese Empire to give the

Continued on Page 2, Column 1.

White House Expects To Release Big News Same Time As Allies

WASHINGTON, Aug. 14— (A. P.).—The White House definitely expects Japan's surrender reply during the day and Presidential Secretary Charles G. Ross commented "it looks as if we're at last nearing the end of our long vigil."

Ross announced to newsmen at 9.50 A. M. (Eastern war time) that the Japanese reply to the latest Allied surrender note "is now in the hands of the Swiss."

It probably will take several hours, he added, for it to reach Washington.

By PHILLIPS J. PECK

WASHINGTON, Aug. 14 — (I. N. S.).—The fourth day of tense waiting for the Japanese surrender began for official Washington today with a 20-minute conference at the White House between President Truman and Secretary of State Byrnes.

The conference began at 8.20 A. M. (Eastern war time) and ended at 8.40. As he left the White House, a reporter asked Byrnes if he expected any news today.

"Yes," was Byrnes' one-word reply.

Soon after 7 A. M., E. W. T., Presidential press secretary Charles Ross arrived at the White House and told reporters:

"The President is up. He is fully aware of what is going on and I expect to see him shortly."

FIRST OFFICIAL WORDS

Ross' words were the first official statement that President Truman had been informed of Tokyo radio reports that Japan had accepted surrender, which had flooded the air waves and spread through the world since shortly before 2 A. M., E. W. T.

Minutes after the first Jap flash was broadcast, a handful of reporters and photographers appeared at the White House to begin a night-long vigil, despite assurances there would be no news between midnight and 9 A. M. E. W. T.

At intervals throughout the night, reporters would stroll casu-

Continued on Page 2, Column 3.

Fleet Cheers Jap Radio's Peace News

GUAM, Aug. 14—(A. P.).—American Superfortresses will continue their attacks on Japan until the final official announcement of surrender is received from Washington, it was indicated tonight at the Strategic Air Forces Headquarters.

By JOHN R. HENRY

GUAM, Aug. 14—(I. N. S.).—America's victorious ocean and air fleets rang with cheers and emotional rejoicing today when radio Tokyo's report that Japan had surrendered was flashed throughout the Pacific area.

Pilots of Admr. William F. Halsey's famous Third Fleet, their floating bases still lying on Japanese waters, hardly had rested up from Monday's great attack on the Tokio area—probably their last blow of the war—when the report came through from Tokyo.

Some 200,000 servicemen, who have wiped out the Jap fleet and, with other commands, reduced the Nipponese air force to impotency,

Continued on Page 2, Column 4.

Temperatures
12 Mid.,	77	7 A. M.,	75
1 A. M.,	76	8 A. M.,	74
2 A. M.,	76	9 A. M.,	74
3 A. M.,	75	10 A. M.,	77
4 A. M.,	75	11 A. M.,	80
5 A. M.,	75	12 Noon,	82
6 A. M.,	74		

NEWS-POST
At Your Service	8	Health	
Azrael, Louis	11	Horoscope	9
Bugs Baer	11	Mallon, Paul	11
Clark, Norman	9	Movies	
Classified Ads	15, 16, 17	Parsons, Louella	9
Comics	12	Pippen, R. H.	13
Crossword	17	Radio	18
Dixon, George	11	Ration Points	10
During	10	Robinson, Elsie	7
Editorials	6	Society	
Financial	10	Sports	13, 14
		Thomas, Lowell	11

GEN. DOUGLAS MacARTHUR   ADMIRAL CHESTER W. NIMITZ
Pacific war chiefs who are expected to accept Japanese surrender.

WAC Heroine Puts Up At 'Shangri-La' Hotel

THE WEATHER

Mostly cloudy and humid, with occasional showers today, tonight and Tuesday morning; warmer; temperature in low 70s tonight.

Detailed Weather Report Page 13

Read The Baltimore News-Post for complete, accurate war coverage. It is the only Baltimore newspaper possessing the three great wire services—
ASSOCIATED PRESS
INTERNATIONAL NEWS SERVICE
UNITED PRESS

THE BALTIMORE NEWS-POST

AN INDEPENDENT NEWSPAPER

The Largest Evening Circulation in the Entire South

7 HOME FINAL

VOL. CXLVII.—NO. 79 Entered as second-class matter at Baltimore Postoffice. MONDAY EVENING, AUGUST 6, 1945 PRICE 3 CENTS

Hawaii Mars Crashes In Bay Off Love Point

Prepare To Salvage Plane

Glenn L. Martin Company engineers prepared today to raise the 72½-ton Hawaii Mars, world's largest flying boat, which crashed and sank in Chesapeake Bay off Love Point yesterday afternoon in what was officially described as a "semicontrolled rough landing."

An investigation was also under way.

The crash, in which one member of the crew of ten was injured, followed the breaking of a vertical fin when the ship was cruising at 6,000 feet, according to one of the men aboard.

The injured man is R. S. Nobles of the Latrobe Apartments, a flight test engineer.

SHIP SHUDDERED

According to a statement from the Martin Company, he suffered "cuts and contusions and possible internal injuries."

As the giant craft, destined for the Navy and launched July 21, shuddered, Lt. Cmdr. William E. Coney, the pilot, gave the order:

"'Prepare to abandon ship.'

The crew attached their parachutes, got set to jump.

Commander Coney issued another order:

"Stand by for crash."

The pilot then nosed the huge

Continued on Page 2, Column 5.

AFTER YESTERDAY'S CRASH—ONLY WING AND TAIL SHOW
World's largest flying boat sinks off Love Point
—Crash Picture by Lt. Ace Rosner.

HAWAII MARS JUST BEFORE LAUNCHING TWO WEEKS AGO

(Other Pictures on Page 3.)

"Whereabouts Unknown," Tragic Stories from the files of New York's Bureau of Missing Persons, starts in The American Weekly with Sunday's Baltimore American. —Adv.

Truman Announces:

ATOMIC BOMB

Has 2,000 Times TNT Power

Weapon Tried On Japs Result Of Secret Work In Big Gov't Gamble

WASHINGTON, Aug. 6—(A. P.).—The United States Army Air Force has released on the Japanese an atomic bomb containing more power than 20,000 tons of TNT.

It produces more than 2,000 times the blast of the largest bomb ever used before.

The announcement of the development was made in a statement by President Truman released by the White House today.

The bomb was dropped 16 hours ago on Hiro Shima, an important Japanese Army base.

The President said that the bomb has "added a new and revolutionary increase in destruction" on the Japenese. The President's statement said:

"It is an atomic bomb. It is a harnessing of the basic power of the universe. The force from which the sun draws its power has been loosed against those who brought war to the Far East."

TRIED ON JAPS

The base that was hit is a major quartermaster depot and has large ordnance, machine tool and aircraft plants.

The city of 318,000 also contains a principal port.

The President declared that the Germans "worked feverishly" in search of a way to use atomic energy in their war effort, but failed. Meantime American and British scientists studied the problem and developed two principal plants and some lesser factries for the production of tomoc power.

TOOK GREAT GAMBLE

The President disclosed that more than 65,000 persons now are working in great secrecy in these plants, adding:

"We have spent $2,000,000,000 on the greatest scientific gamble in history—and won.

"We are now prepared to obliterate more rapidly and completely every productive enterprise the Japanese have above ground in any city. We shall completely destroy Japan's power to make war."

The President noted that the Big Three ultimatum issued July 26 at Potsdam was intended "to spare the Japanese people from utter destruction" and the Japanese leaders rejected it. The atomic bomb now is the answer to that rejection and the President said:

"They may expect a rain of ruin from the air, the like of which has never been seen on this earth."

Mr. Truman forecast that sea

Continued on Page 2, Column 4.

50,000 Chinese Missing As Japs Sack Two Cities

CHUNGKING, Aug. 6—(A. P.). The once-beautiful city of Kweilin was sacked by the Japanese with a thoroughness comparable to the Roman sacking of Carthage, it was reported today, while at recently liberated Kanhsien officials listed 50,000 of the Chinese population dead or missing.

Kweilin, once a city of 500,000, was ravaged with a fury reminiscent of Lidice, said a dispatch from the former provisional capital of Kwangsi, written by O. W. I. Correspondent David Chandler.

The Kahnsien report asserted that 50,000 Chinese residents of that Southern Kiangsi province city were killed or disappeared during six months of Japanese occupation. No details were given.

Says Petain Favored Patriots

By THURSTON MacCAULEY

PARIS, Aug. 6—(I. N. S.).—Marshal Henri Philippe Petain was pictured today as having worked closely with the French underground during the time he was chief of state under Adolf Hitler.

Petain's co-operation with the resistance movement was described by Prince Xavier de Bourbon-Parme, a defense witness at the marshal's treason trial.

Parme, a resistance worker, recently freed from a German concentration camp, told of meetings he had with Petain in 1942, dealing with the underground.

He said Petain told him:

"Continue the resistance plot. My door is open to any Frenchman. I am trying to save what is left to be saved and as soon as peace is signed the republic will return."

COMMUTED SENTENCES

Parme told the court Petain had commuted 231 death sentences passed on resistance workers.

In 1943, Parme continued, Petain told him:

"I am certain of an Allied victory."

Another witness, Gen. Henri Lacaille, disclosed an attempt by Petain to return to France after the liberation of Paris.

The general related the day after the liberation of Paris Admiral Auphan had contacted him with instructions from Petain to attempt to reach Gen. Charles de Gaulle and thus unite France.

JUROR INTERRUPTS

A juryman interrupted the general to remark that Petain wanted to return as chief of state with De Gaulle as his prime minister.

A cable from Pierre Merillon, French consul at San Francisco, praising Petain's "perfect loyalty and patriotism" was read at the opening of the trial today.

The trial took a Hollywood twist today with the revelation that the jurors have been receiving threatening letters daily.

SEN. HIRAM W. JOHNSON
Dies in Bethesda Hospital

Hiram Johnson, Veteran Senator, Dies At Age Of 79

WASHINGTON, Aug. 6—(I. N. S.).—Senator Hiram W. Johnson of California whose long and colorful career in the United States Senate made American history, died today in Bethesda, (Md.) Naval Hospital.

Senator Johnson died at 6.40 A. M. Death was caused by thrombosis of the cerebral artery. He was in his seventy-ninth year.

The California statesman was stricken during Senate debate on American ratification of the United Nations charter last minth. He was admitted to the hospital at that time and failed rapidly.

The Senator is survived by his widow, who was at his bedside when eh died, and one son, Hiram W. Johnson, Jr.

OPPOSED JOHNSON

An insurgent to the end Senator Johnson cast the lone dissenting vote in the Senate Foreign Relations Committee against recommending ratification of the United Nations charter.

Although he was in the hospital when the Senate voted on ratification he still held out and although not casting a ballot against

Continued on Page 2, Column 3.

'Forts' Batter 6 More Jap Cities

GUAM, Aug. 6—(A.P.).—Striking savagely for the second time in five days, 680 Superfortresses and Mustang fighters spread fire and destruction through six Japanese war centers stretching almost from the Imperial Palace in Tokyo to the southern home island of Kyushu yesterday and today.

Once again an all but helpless Japan—forewarned that the big bombers were coming on a mission of death—was unable to offer effective resistance while the industrial areas of Nishinomiya, Imabari, Maebashi and Saga and Ube Coal Liquefaction Company burned and fell apart from 3,850 tons of incendiary and high explosive bombs dropped by a fleet of 580 Superforts.

TOKYO SIRENS SCREAM

Yesterday air raid sirens screamed throughout Tokyo in a warning that 100 P-51 Mustangs had returned to strike terror with rockets and machine guns against anything they could find in the Tokyo area.

Radio Tokyo said 150 Mustangs carried the assault into the daylight today with an attack on the Tokyo area.

A single Japanese fighter watched them come yesterday and then fled from the skies.

10,500 TONS BOMBS

The B-29s in two raids August 2 and today have sown 10,500 tons of dreaded fire and demolition bombs on Japanese cities in warnings to the people of Japan to surrender unconditionally.

They have burned out approximately 160 square miles of war-

Continued on Page 2, Column 1.

Shangri-La Diary:

Trio Enters Glider Camp

(In the following chapter of her exciting story, Margaret Hastings describes life in the larger of the two valleys of Shangri-La, and tells of her chance to become a queen of the land that time forgot.)

"SHANGRI-LA DIARY"
CHAPTER SIXTEEN
By CORP. MARGARET HASTINGS, WAC
(Written Exclusively for International Special Service.)
(World Copyright and All Rights Reserved.)

OWEGO, N. Y., Aug. 6.—Surely the followers of Moses when they came upon the Promised Land saw a sight no more fair than that which unrolled before Lieutenant McCollom, Sergeant Decker and myself when we stood upon the last height overlooking the big valley of Shangri-La.

It was a beautiful, fertile land, ringed by the giant peaks of the Oranje Mountains. A copper-colored river wound through the valley's green length. It was our promised land, too. There below us, clearly marked, was the glider strip.

Below us, too, was a small, neat U. S. Army camp, ready and waiting for us. The three paratroopers who had stayed behind in the big valley to prepare the glider strip obviously had worked like beavers.

Captain Walters made a brave entry into the camp, truckin' every inch of the way.

For this special occasion, the radio operator in the Army plane hovering over us had brought along a small

Continued on Page 7, Column 1.

Detroit Orphanage Fire Kills Five

DETROIT, Aug. 6—(A. P.).—Five persons, including two seven-year-old twin brothers, lost their lives and another inmate was in critical condition after a Sunday night explosion and fire at a Detroit orphanage and old people's home. More than 120 other persons were led or carried to safety by orphanage employees and firemen.

Truman, Advisers Meet On Augusta

ABOARD U. S. S. AUGUSTA WITH PRESIDENT TRUMAN, Aug. 6—(U. P.).—President Truman continued to hold frequent conferences with his top advisers today as this warship carried him steadily closer to the United States. The President was expected to be back at the White House by midweek. He will report to the nation by radio on the recent Big Three meeting.

Temperatures

12 Midn't, 74	6 A. M., 72
1 A. M., 74	7 A. M., 71
2 A. M., 74	8 A. M., 72
3 A. M., 74	9 A. M., 72
4 A. M., 73	10 A. M., 73
5 A. M., 72	11 A. M., 74

"THE SECRET WAR OF SANTO TOMAS"

Such is the title of a thrilling, authentic inside story of how a small group of American businessmen at the Jap prison camp at Santo Tomas University in Manila organized a secret underground and outwits their heartless, death-dealing Jap captors.

The first installment of this dramatic "Now It Can Be Told" story of the war, revealed for the first time by the leader of the underground, Earl Carroll, will appear in the Baltimore Sunday American next Sunday, August 12.

Mr. Carroll brought back to America with him the complete log book of the underground's dealings with the Japs during more than three years of horror at Santo Tomas.

Jap Burma Army Almost Destroyed

CALCUTTA, Aug. 6—(A. P.).—British Empire troop patrols have crossed the Sittang River channel in the advance toward Thailand, Admiral Lord Louis Mountbatten's Headquarters announced today, after almost complete destruction of the Japanese Twenty-eighth Army. The crossing was made south of Abya, 22 miles northeast of Pegu, on the Pegu-Martaban railway, which curves around the Sittang estuary.

NEWS-POST

At Your Service	4	Health	4
Azrael, Louis	9	Horoscope	6
Bugs Baer	9	Mallon, Paul	9
Clark, Norman	6	Movies	6
Classified Ads	13, 14, 15	Parsons, Louella	6
Comics	10	Pippen, R. H.	11
Crossword	15	Radio	16
Dixon, George	9	Ration Points	3
Dulaney	9	Robinson, Elsie	8
Durling	9	Society	5
Editorials	8	Sports	11, 12
Financial	12, 13	Winchell, Walter	6

NITE LIFE

By LOU and JUDD CALVERT

Just a year and a few months old, but already one of the top-ranking cocktail lounges and musical bars of the country, that's Eddie Leonard's Spa at Charles and Preston. Eddie has done much to improve the entertainment standards of Baltimore. Currenly starring are the Piccadilly Pipers with Bonnie Davis. And now one can find also summer entertainment 'cause the Spa is all decked out in brand-new air-conditioning . . . Another Charles street cocktail lounge that enjoys rightful popularity is Doc's, where, too, one continually finds the veribest in continuous entertainment to take the heat out of summer and put the blues back in the closet.

WHATTA SHOW . . . was the gala farewell party to comic star Sonny Mars last night at the **Club Charles.** If you weren't there you missed some of the greatest fun stars of our time. To say the least, the **Chanticleer** certainly tuned up with the current Miss Maryland Beauty contest, with a fast-moving revue starring melody funstar Marty Drake, with a finale topper of all time, bringing to light a true picture of a Miss America pageant that meets with wonderful applause—and by the way those June Taylor gals shine like a 10-dollar bill in those creaative bathing suits.

One of the finest song duos to hit town in a long time is the one of Ruth Cruz on vocals and Bob Chapman at the console, starring in the **Bandbox** . . . a reminder of the great Bunny Berigan, listening to youngster Freddie Erlich on trumpet, out at the **Summit** with Jimmy Kestler's musicrew . . . looking for steaks or big jucy steamed crabs . . . just make your dining place the **Charles Sea Food Restaurant** and say no more . . . **Leon's** on Park will be closed July 29 to August 12 reopening.

A new song tunesmith at the **Arundel Blue Room,** Renee Ross and a bit good to add . . . the exotic dancing of Toni Barton is the hit at **Kibby's** . . . that boy Larry Lee has been held over at the **Dutch Mill,** sorta got the whole town listenin' to his songs . . . for a family touch in foods it's **Hughes** on East Preston street . . . learn the rhumba and just about every other Latin American dance by being a habitue of the **Pan American Casino,** where your host Ralph Diaz is always more than willing to show you the right steps . . . it isn't far from the center of town and listening to tenor star Tony Lanasa is worth it, **Helms' Lounge** in Brooklyn.

Say, those Contonese dishes or American, too, for that matter, are certainly some of the best we've ever had, thanks to the **Chungking,** where you can always enjoy the best in food plus a bright Broadway revue twice nightly . . . we can't understand it either—why **Nate** winks at **Leon** . . . in case you've forgotten where Nat Conway and crew are, it's the smart **Casa Blanca** out Gwynn Oak . . . **Baker's** on North Broadway now features Slim Stapleton and his novachord . . . Justine Wayne not only looks good but sounds better with her Dwight Fiske sophistication in song at the **Rio** . . . Johnny and George, the Rudy Vale stars, the hit of the **21 Club** . . . that's all 'cept . . . **KEEP BUYING THOSE BONDS TILL IT'S REALLY OVER ! ! !**

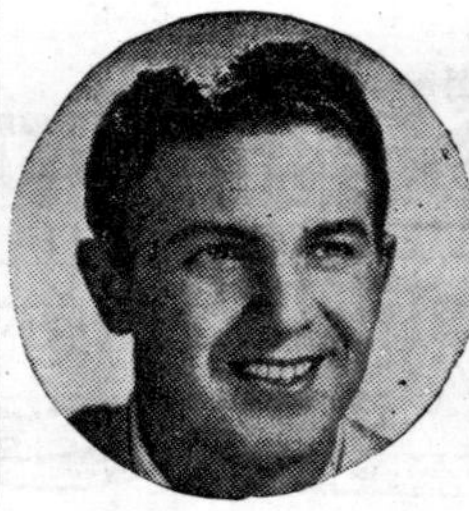
MARTY DRAKE
Melody Funstar of the new Chanticleer revusical

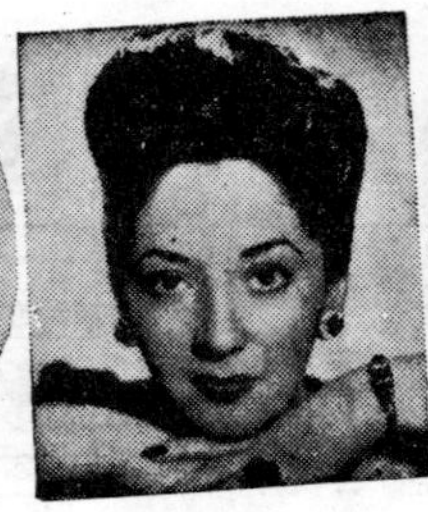
JUSTINE WAYNE
Miss sophisticate of song at the Beautiful Rio

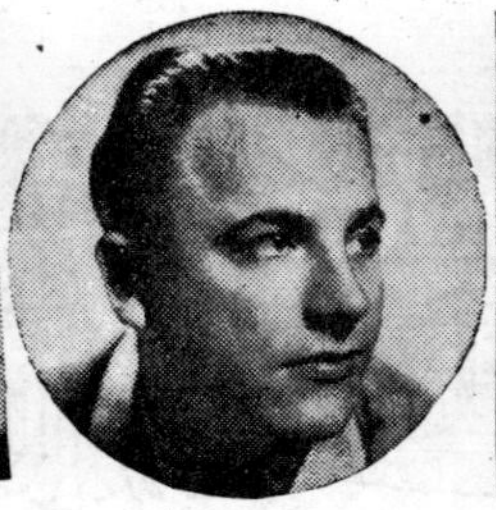
TED SMITH
America's newest comedy find starring at 21 Club

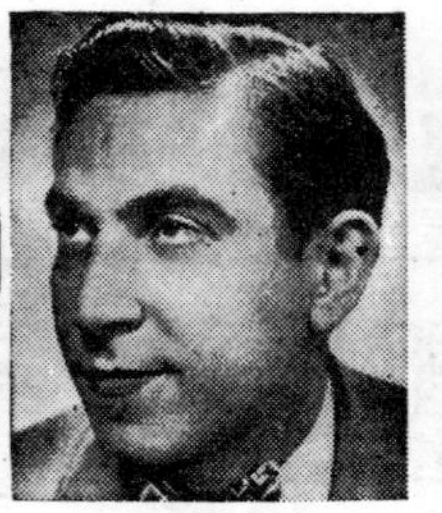
LARRY KENT
The laugh sensation of the bright Club Charles showbill

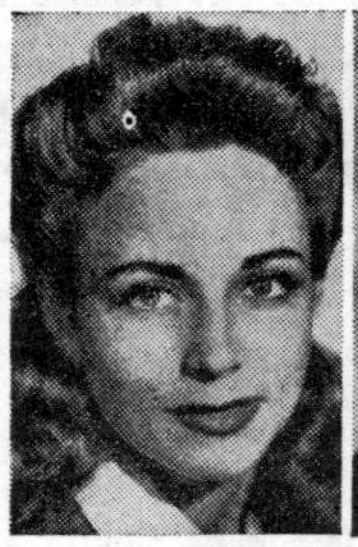
'ADELINE'
of the new song duo heard at Doc's cocktail lounge

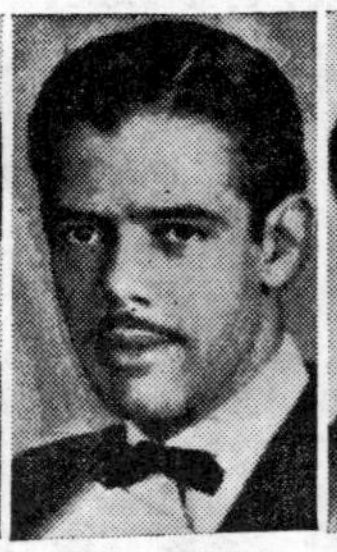
ISMAEL UGARTE
Featured with the Melodians at the smart Bandbox

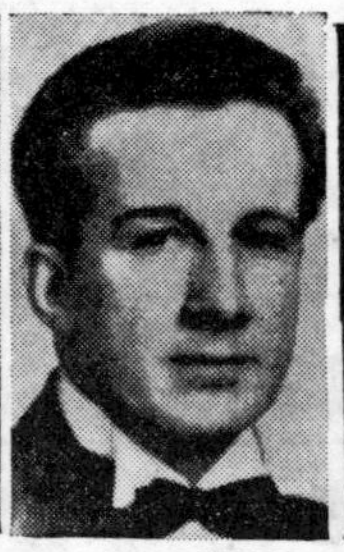
DICK LEUTNER
Vocal hit with Jimmy Kestler's music at the Summit

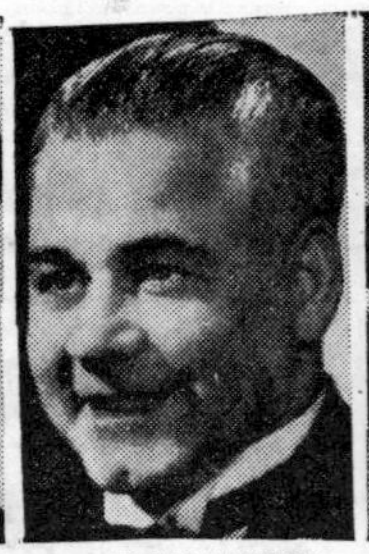
TONY LANASA
International tenor starring at Helms' lounge

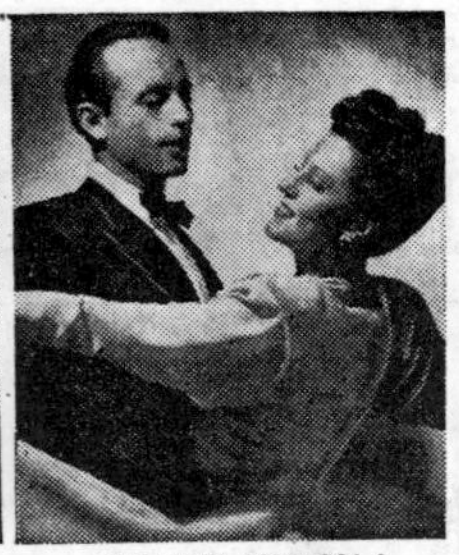
ARTHUR AND IOLA
Dancing stars of the bright new Chungking revue

EVERGREEN 501
TUXEDO 0103
TONITE & EVERY NITE! except MONDAYS
JIMMIE KESTLER AND HIS ORCHESTRA
DANCING 9 TILL 2
TO REACH THE SUMMIT . . . drive right out Old Pimlico Rd. 1 mile beyond the race track, or out Falls Rd. and follow the signs! Just 19 minutes from the heart of the city!
SUMMIT
Overlooking the Gorgeous Greenspring Valley TUxedo 0103
OLD PIMLICO ROAD AT SMITH AVENUE
10 Minutes from the Heart of the City! Reservations: EVERGREEN 501

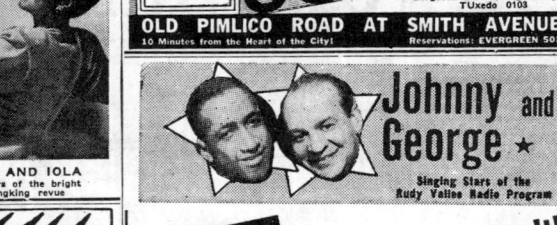

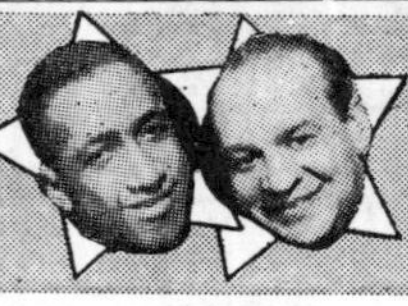
Johnny and George
Singing Stars of the Rudy Vallee Radio Program

The CHANTICLEER Presents
1ST SHOW TONITE 10 P. M.
ZIGGY TRAVERS MUSIC and RICARDO'S RHUMBA BAND
MASTER OF MELODY AND WIT
MARTY DRAKE
the unparalled dance styles of JERRY LEWIS
the satirical impressions of RENEE & ROOT
THE JUNE TAYLOR LOVELIES
ALWAYS AIR-CONDITIONED
COCKTAILS DAILY FROM 4 P. M.
The CHANTICLEER Charles at Eager LExington 0234

New Revue
HOME OF CELEBRITIES
CLUB CHARLES
LARRY KENT comedian of ceremonies
THE MASTER KEYS • Song Harmony
HUDSON and SHARAE • Adagio Stars
CHIQUITICA • Latin-American Songs
THE SIX GORGEOUS MAUREEN HALL GIRLS
EDDIE WALD'S MUSIC • ELAINE PFEIFER SONG HITS
• CELEBRITY SHOWTIME every SUNDAY at 4
Charles at Preston VE. 8020-21
SCIENTIFICALLY AIR-CONDITIONED

21 CLUB 21 W. Balto. St.
Air-Conditioned
Plus --- Ted Smith
America's Greatest Comedy Find!
And Other Star Attractions
LARRY LONDON and his Londonaires
Continuous Entertainment
Terrace Bar Open 1 P. M. till 2 A. M. Res. Phone SA. 5552 Never a Cover Charge

The Rio AIR-CONDITIONED THRU-OUT . . . Presents
IT'S NEW AND DIFFERENT
LES FIELDING & His All String Orchestra Direct from the Copacabana, Miami.
JUSTINE WAYNE Feminine Dwight Fiske Song Star
ARTHUR PRINZ at the Concert Grand and Accordion. WEST COAST SENSATION
All Food Prepared By Mrs. Gertrude Becker World Famous
SMORGASBORD Dinner & Cocktails From 4.30 P. M.
Continuous Entertainment
Summer Policy—Closed Mondays
JACK TRENT—Your host & mgr.
RESERVATIONS PHONE LEX. 0663
Visit Our Leather Bar—No Tax
NO MINIMUM OR COVER EVER
306 W. FRANKLIN ST. Entrance at Md. Theatre

MUSICAL BAR ★
PICCADILLY PIPERS and BONNIE DAVIS
THE THREE CLEFS
JACK DUPREE at the piano
GALA MATINEE Sat., 5 to 7 Sun., 3 to 7
Come and join our gala radio show every Sunday via W-I-T-H, 3.05 to 3.30 P. M.
NOW!!! COMPLETELY AIR CONDITIONED FOR YOUR COMFORT
EDDIE LEONARD'S SPA
1308 N. CHARLES ST. LE. 9552

Featuring the Piano of COL NEMETH and his Gypsy Melodians plus Ken Nealy Trio
Ruth Cruz Vocal Star
Bob Chapman Piano & Solo-Vox
BALTIMORE'S BIGGEST LITTLE MADHOUSE VE. 6795
BAND BOX
1309-11 NORTH CHARLES STREET
Cocktail Jamboree Every Saturday & Sunday 4 to 7 P. M.

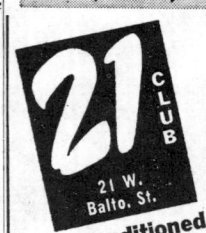

The DOLLODIANS Singing Instrumentalists
MARTHA DAVIS her Songs and Piano Rhy'
Entertainment and Music Starts at 9 P. M. till 2 A. M.
LARRY & ADELINE Piano and Songs
DOC'S
Cocktail Hour SAT. and SUNDAY 3 to 6 P. M.
1817 N. CHARLES ST.

CHUNGKING
Chinese-American Restaurant and Supper Club
110 N. LIBERTY STREET PLaza 5049
重慶
THE SHOW PLACE OF DIGNITY
IMP SMITH Gay Deceptionist
DOT GARCY Impressionist
JUNE BOWEN Vocal Star
ARTHUR & IOLA Darlings of the Dance
AIR-CONDITIONED THRU-OUT
THREE SHOWS 7:30, 10:30 and 12:30
BOB BARBER AND HIS ORCHESTRA For Your Dancing Pleasure
FOR RESERVATIONS PHONE PL. 5049

112-120 PATAPSCO AVE.
Helms' Cocktail Lounge
NOW APPEARING . . .
TONY LANASA
INTERNATIONAL TENOR STAR

"Where It's Smart To Be Seen"
"BERNIE" His Violin & Quartet Featuring Carroll Warington
Lucille Cunningham Piano and Songs
AIR-CONDITIONED
MUSIC AND DANCING BEGINS 9 P. M. till 2 A. M. Including Sat. & Sun. from 5 to 7 P. M.
Cocktail Hr. Daily 5 to 7
CLOSED MONDAYS
Blue Mirror
929 N. Charles St.

BALTIMORE'S OWN COMICLOWN
LEO BATEMAN
LOUISE WRIGHT ★ songs ★ JUANITA ★ dancer
MUSIC AND DANCING STARTS AT 9 P. M. to JACK DECKER, his Solo-Vox & Orch.
Two Shows Friday, Saturday, Sunday 10:30 and 1 A. M.
CARL'S
TAKE CAR #25 OR #10 BUS TO DOOR
RES. CH. 9605
3316 KESWICK RD.
COMPLETELY AIR-CONDITIONED

Rafael Diaz says "Saludos Amigos" to Balto.'s Only Spanish Nite Club in Town
Featuring Los Ojedas
Mexican Folk Dancing Stars of Stage—Screen
Eleanor Kade—Song Star
Ruth Haney Danseuse
Floor Shows 10:30 & 12:30
AIR-CONDITIONED
PAN-AMERICAN CASINO
In The Mount Royal Hotel—Formerly Algerian Room
DON GILBERTO and his Latin American Orchestra Direct from Copacabana, Brazil
Continuous Entertainment from 8.30 till 2 A. M.
Rhumba Matinee Every Sunday 4 till 6 P. M.
No Cover or Minimum . . .
Mt. Royal at Calvert
Res.-Phone Mu. 1570 Ext. 15
delightfully cool

Steamed Crabs
You've tried the rest now try the best!
Imperial Crabs, Hard Fries, Crab Cakes, Delicious Home Made Crab Soup.
TAKE-OUT DEPT. Beer, Wines & Liquors
Phone VE. 0786 or SA. 5241
Charles Sea Food Restaurant
1724 N. Charles St.
Closed Every Thursday

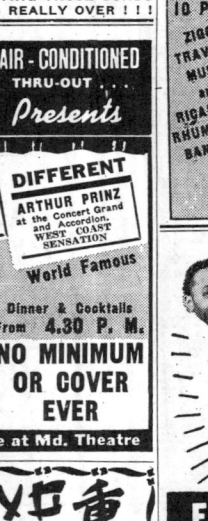

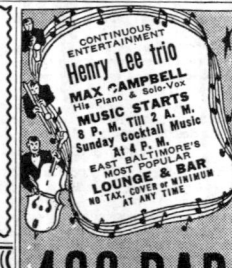

starring
SAM VINCI & FRANK YOUNG
BEALE and FLETCHER BALLROOM STARS
TONI BARTON ★ dance darling
JIMMY NICHOLS' MUSIC
COME EARLY! MA. 1098
KIBBY'S 711 POPLAR GROVE ST.
LUCKY NUMBER NITE CLUB

Open Tuesday Thru Sunday!
RATHSKELLER—Sir Walter Scotty Trio
Dancing from 9 P. M. till 2 A. M.
BAR OPEN from 5.30 P. M. Till 2 A. M.
—Ladies Invited—
Restaurant Exclusive— Weddings, Banquets, etc.
AIR-CONDITIONED Thru-Out
NITE CLUB RE-OPENING AUG. 14
MADISON Rathskeller Bar & Restaurant
Madison & Chester Sts. Phone WO. 8677

Full Course DINNERS
SOFT & IMPERIAL CRABS
COCKTAILS
Delightful Music
OPEN DAILY EXCEPT MONDAY
NO 20% TAX
DICKMAN'S RESTAURANT Cor. Mt. Royal & Maryland Ave.

SWEENEY'S
MUSIC & ENTERTAINMENT
Begins at 9 P. M.
BUDDY MONROE
Baltimore's Favorite M. C. Song Star
WANDA LEACH
CHARMING VOCAL HIT!
IRVIN CLAS AND HIS TRIO
Continuous entertainment and dancing. No cover or minimum ever. Completely air-conditioned.
3128 Greenmount Ave.

Slim Stappelton and his NOVACHORD at BAKER'S
TAVERN-RESTAURANT
BROADWAY and OLIVER
Reservations Phone—Broadway 9640

CONTINUOUS ENTERTAINMENT
Henry Lee trio
MAX CAMPBELL His Piano & Solo-Vox
MUSIC STARTS 8 P. M. Till 2 A. M.
Sunday Cocktail Music 3 to 4 P. M.
EAST BALTIMORE'S MOST POPULAR LOUNGE & BAR
NO TAX, COVER or MINIMUM AT ANY TIME
408 BAR
408 E. BALTIMORE ST.

NAT CONWAY
POSITIVELY BALTO.'S DANCIEST OUTFIT
ENTERTAINS NITELY AT THE
CASABLANCA
MARIAN DAWN—WFBR Singing Star
WE SERVE DELICIOUS CHICKEN & SEA FOOD DINNERS AT ALL TIMES
AIR-CONDITIONED
NO COVER
CONTINUOUS ENTERTAINMENT
Take Number 32 or 33 Cars—Direct to Door
Reservations Phone Forest 9838
NO MINIMUM
GWYNN OAK AVE. AT LIBERTY HEIGHTS

Blue Room presents ★ dancing rhythms
from 9 P. M. nitely with
MILT LYONS Orchestra
dante FIOCCHI piano wizard
RENEE ROSS song lovely
★ in the ARUNDEL HOTEL
Charles at Mt. Royal

Open Daily 9 A. M. till 2 A. M.
The Most Enchanting Cocktail Lounge
WITH AN ATMOSPHERE THAT SPORTSMEN PREFER!
JOCKEY Manny Berg
Says: "No Cover, Tax or Minimum at Any Time"
TURF BAR & LOUNGE
102 WATER ST., at LIGHT
1 BLK. S. OF SOUTHERN HOTEL. LE. 4333

CLUB BAR
COCKTAIL LOUNGE
Continuous Entertainment. No Cover or Minimum ★
Vacation Time, Closing Monday, July 23, Re-opening Tues., July 31
ELMER BARROWS, H. HERZ, LE ROY GROLL, MARTHA LEE
McClellan Place at Balto. St.
Half Block West of Lord Baltimore Hotel

NEW HOTEL BROADWAY
MUSIC STARTS AT 9 P. M.
CARROLL'S ORCHESTRA
plus a host of others
BROADWAY AT ORLEANS

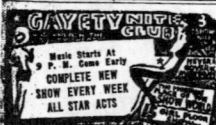

DUKES Nite Club
Presents a Sparkling Week-End Revusical For Your Pleasure.
starring DORIS BARRY, CARROLL CAYNE, BETTY GAY
Dance To The Tunes Of Geo. Finster's Orchestra
3303-7 PHILADELPHIA ROAD

GAYETY NITE CLUB
Music Starts at 9 P. M. Come Early
COMPLETE NEW SHOW EVERY WEEK
ALL STAR ACTS

NOTICE
MEET YOUR FRIENDS
Tonite, July 28
AT THE MOOSE
First Big Party . . .
MUSIC & DANCING 9—1
410 W. FAYETTE ST. Carley Pannell Chairman

"Relax In Your Slax"
"HAMILTON'S PLAYGROUND"
Presents LARRY LEE, DALLAS BROWN, JOE LUSK
DANCING FROM 9 P. M.
MIKE TRALIK'S MUSIC
DUTCH MILL
6615 HARFORD ROAD
No Cover Ever

STRICKLER'S
6800-10 Harford Rd. HA. 9744
Dancing to Carroll Kelly's Orchestra
Dancing nightly
Baltimore's Most Beautiful Lounge

FOOD ★ FUN ★ FRIVOLITY

DE LUCA'S — 62 Willow Spring Road, Dundalk. Dance to JACK WEBER'S Orchestra
GREEN VILLA — Open Nitely—Dancing Tues. thru to Sun. Two Floor Shows. All-Star Cast. Cocktail Matinee Sun. 3 till 6 P. M. 5423 O'DONNELL ST. UNDER NEW MANAGEMENT.
HUGHES — Restaurant-Bar & Lounge, 2443 Preston St. at Milton Ave. Serving the finest food—Beer & mixed drinks in town. Moderately Priced. ● Open 8 A. M. till 2 A. M. including Sundays. J. MURRAY HUGHES, Prop.
KATHLEEN'S — BERNIE RANDOLPH'S ORCHESTRA STARTS AT 9 P. M. 3 BIG SHOWS NITELY. NO COVER OR MINIMUM. 612 EAST BALTIMORE ST.
KEYSTONE — Dance to your heart's content—9 till 2 A. M. No. 26 Car. CHICKEN DINNERS A SPECIALTY. 7018 Holabird Ave. Lou Mellon's orchestra.
LEON'S — MERRY-GO-ROUND BAR—BALTIMORE'S NEWEST RESTAURANT—LOUNGE—BAR. 870 PARK AVENUE "VACATION TIME" CLOSING JULY 29 RE-OPENING AUGUST 12
NATE & LEON'S — DELICATESSEN. Stop in after the show for a Midnight Snack. Delicious Sandwiches. OPEN ALL NIGHT. 850 WEST NORTH AVENUE.
NOLAN'S NITE CLUB — Wilkens & Monroe. Mixed Drinks. The finest food. SAMMY LEBOWE & his Sisters Orchestra. Dancing—7 P. M. till 2, FRI., SAT. and SUN.
SLOPPY JOE'S — "Pick-A-Rib." Under New Management. All Foods Are Charcoal Broiled. Delicious Full-Course Luncheon-Dinners Served Daily. Open all night. 1218 N. Charles St.
SPORTSMAN — BAR & LOUNGE. See the Finest Collection of Action Sporting Events in the World. No cover, no tax, no minimum. SAM LAMPE, 1429 N. Charles St.
Ye Old Caton Tavern — Catonsville Junction, Edmondson & Dutton Aves. Tom Perry & his Singing Strings, Fri. & Sat. 9 P. M. to 2 A. M. Sun. cocktail matinee 4 to 8. Take Cars No. 14 or 8 to door. Phone CAT. 317.

WAC'S "Shangri-La" Diary

THE WEATHER
Mostly cloudy, moderate temperatures, humid, occasional showers and thunderstorms this afternoon, tonight and Sunday.

Read The Baltimore News-Post for complete, accurate war coverage. It is the only Baltimore newspaper possessing the three great wire services—
ASSOCIATED PRESS
INTERNATIONAL NEWS SERVICE
UNITED PRESS

THE BALTIMORE NEWS-POST
AN INDEPENDENT NEWSPAPER
The Largest Evening Circulation in the Entire South

NIGHT
Wall St. Opening

VOL. CXLVII.—NO. 72 | Entered as second-class matter at Baltimore Postoffice. | SATURDAY EVENING, JULY 28, 1945 | PRICE 3 CENTS

PLANE HITS EMPIRE STATE BUILDING, 5 DIE

Jap Battleship Sunk In 1,500-Plane Raid On Last Of Nip Fleet

SAN FRANCISCO, July 28—(A. P.).—The unconditional surrender ultimatum of the United States, Britain and China was rejected today by the president of Japan's mass totalitarian political party, first identified enemy official to speak out.

GUAM, July 28—(U. P.).—The Japanese cities of Fukui, Tsuruga and Kuwana suffered damage ranging from 68 to 85 per cent of their total area as the result of Superfortress raids in recent weeks, reconnaissance photographs disclosed today. The total raised to 150 the number of square miles damaged in 46 Japanese cities.

GUAM, July 29—(A. P.).—A Japanese battleship was reported sunk today as nearly 1,500 U. S. and British carrier-planes battled through heavy flak and fighter screens, and dealt the third heavy blow of the week on the broken and bleeding enemy fleet in the Inland Sea.

Pilots reported that the 29,990-ton battleship Hyuga, a converted warship with a flight deck for catapulting planes, had been sunk in the great Japanese naval base of Kure, where the remnants of the Mikado's fleet took futile refuge under extensive camouflage.

In order to bore into their targets along the inland sea, the swarms of Allied carrier planes knocked down scores of Japanese planes which came out of hiding and tried to ward off the pre-invasion blows.

The Hyuga had been reported damaged in strikes earlier this week. An Associated Press dispatch from the fleet did not make clear whether it had been sunk today or in the previous raids.

PLUMB ON TARGETS

Three of the first four naval planes that roared in through a heavy curtain of flak landed their half ton bombs squarely on warships already hard hit by raids Tuesday and Wednesday, Associated Press correspondent Richard O'Malley reported from the U. S. Third Fleet.

After the third attack within a week, Japan was left without a single heavy warship fit for action.

Admiral Halsey's hard-hitting carrier planes knocked out 26 warships, including three battle-

Continued on Page 2, Column 1.

Inland Sea Raids Wreck 26 Warships

GUAM, July 28—(A. P.).— Admiral Nimitz' box score of Japanese shipping and planes hit in the inland sea carrier raids of July 24-25:

WARSHIPS

Damaged — Twenty-six ships totaling more than 258,000 tons, including:

Seriously Damaged — One Ise class battleship, aircraft carrier Amagi; an unidentified aircraft carrier; heavy cruiser Aoba, light cruisers Oyodo and Kuma, gunboat Settsu, two destroyers.

Moderately Damaged—One Ise class battleship, the aircraft carrier Katsuragi, one destroyer, one destroyer transport.

Damaged — One destroyer and two corvettes.

Slightly Damaged—The battleship Haruna, small aircraft car-

Continued on Page 2, Column 4.

Air, Sea Battle Rages Off Malaya

MANILA, July 28—(U. P.).—Radio Tokyo said today a fierce air-sea battle was raging off the Malayan Peninsula as Allied troops for the fifth day persisted in their attempts to invade Puket Island.

The Japanese Domei Agency claimed enemy suicide planes had sunk "one Allied cruiser and heavily damaged another which was probably a converted aircraft carrier."

Domei said the Allied naval task force had pushed up in close support of a second landing on Thursday and today its heavy guns were raking shore installations on Puket with a tremendous bombardment.

Domei said "fierce fighting"

FIGHTING CONTINUES

continued in the island's coastal areas. The agency declared

Continued on Page 2, Column 4.

Attlee Goes To Potsdam As Premier

LONDON, July 28—(A. P.).—Prime Minister Clement R. Attlee went to Potsdam today as the freshman member of the Big Three. Herbert Morrison, new Lord President of the Council and Attlee's principal understudy, was left in charge of the country.

Attlee departed after the six senior members of his Cabinet, named last night, took the oath from King George VI. With Attlee away, it seemed unlikely that other members of the new Labor Party Cabinet would be announced over the week-end.

WORK FOR MINISTERS

Morrison and Ernest Bevin, longtime trade union leader who is the new Foretign Secretary, are destined to play principal roles in Winston Churchill. Morrison will devote most of his time to leading Labor's 2-to1 majority in Commons. He also will be responsible for the Parliamentary timetable and will preside over the Cabinet in Attlee's absence.

Bevin was expected to follow Attlee to Potsdam, along with Sir Edward Bridges, Secretary to the Cabinet, and Gen. Sir Hastings Ismay, Chief of Staff to the Ministry of Defense.

MEET LABOR MEMBERS

After the oath-taking at Buckingham Palace Attlee and his Cabinet confreres appeared before the 388 Labor members of the new 640-man House of Commons and received an ovation. Bevin moved a vote of appreciation for Attlee's leadership in the election compaign, and this passed unanimously.

Attlee addressed the meeting, which was held in private.

The new government leaders

Continued on Page 2, Column 3.

Reds Revive Old Party; Ask Action

NEW YORK, July 28—(U. P.).—The Communist Political Association became the Communist party again today and opened its doors to anyone willing to support the party's principles and pay dues.

A statement issued from a special national convention now in session indicated that control of the party would remain in the hands of a three-member secretariat which two months ago replaced Earl Browder, American Communist leader for the last 16 years.

TURN TO 'ACTION'

The convention repudiated Browder's policy of labor-capital co-operation and announced a new "vigorous policy of action."

The leaders demanded that every member "fight with all his strength against any and every effort, whether it comes from abroad or within our country, to

Continued on Page 2, Column 7.

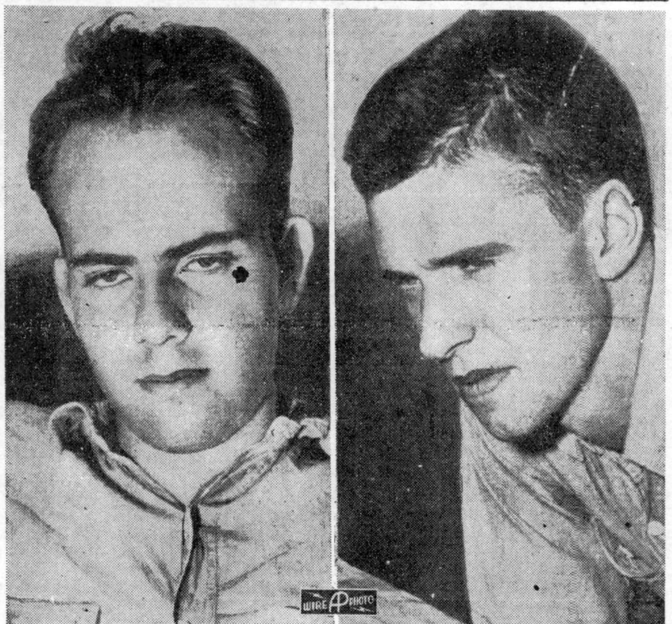

END SLEEPLESS TEST—Tom Lovering (left) and Ed Flaccus presented this haggard appearance as they and 10 other youths, all conscientious objectors, entered the home stretch in the California Institute of Technology's fatigue experiment. Shortly after picture was taken the "guinea pigs" ended their test and fell into a sound slumber, the first since last Monday.

Shangri-La Diary:

Tells How Plane Sighted Party

"SHANGRI-LA DIARY"
CHAPTER SEVEN
By CORP. MARGARET HASTINGS, WAC
(Written Exclusively for International News Special Service.)

(World Copyright And All Rights Reserved.)

Her burns and wounds festering, her body so bruised she could barely walk, WAC Corp. Margaret Hastings staggered down the New Guinea mountainside with Lt. John McCollom and Sgt. Kenneth Decker. They were the only three survivors from a plane load of sightseers that had crashed high on the rim of Hidden Valley. After terrible hardship and a precarious night on the bank of a mountain stream they resumed their tortuous descent into the mysterious valley.

OWEGO, N. Y., July 28—(I. N. S.).—At the end of what seemed a year this aching, miserable night came to a close. After yesterday's excruciating journey we were at least part way down the mountain.

How far we had traveled from the scene of the crash we could not tell. How much further we had to go before we reached the clearing Lieutenant McCollom had spotted, we could not estimate.

But we had to reach that clearing if the Army search planes were ever to spot us. We had to force ourselves to get back into that icy stream. We were shaking with cold in the dim morning light. I realized that Sergeant Decker and McCollom must ache in every joint, muscle and nerve even as I did.

I tried to stand up and I was scared. My legs were so stiff they wouldn't seem to work. I looked at them and then I looked away. They were a sickening sight. I

Continued on Page 6, Column 1.

Temperatures

Midnight, 74	6 A. M., 72
1 A. M., 73	7 A. M., 72
2 A. M., 72	8 A. M., 72
3 A. M., 72	9 A. M., 73
4 A. M., 71	10 A. M., 73
5 A. M., 72	11 A. M., 74

12 Men Sleep After 112 Hrs. Awake

PASADENA, Cal., July 28—(A. P.).—Twelve young men slept the sleep of utter exhaustion today after staying awake nearly five days—a total of 112 hours.

Volunteers from a nearby conscientious objectors' camp, they had participated in a fatigue test conducted by California Institute of Technology. Spokesmen said it was for the armed services and that it will take some time to develop the data obtained.

The youths were steady on their feet but wearily silent as they emerged from a Cal-Tech laboratory shortly after 10 o'clock last night for a ride to a hospital for their first shut-eye since 5.45 A. M. last Monday.

The four meals which the subjects received daily were "very good." Each was allowed only one cup of coffee each 24 hours.

The test will continue during the hours the youths are asleep. During the experiment the volunteers chopped wood, did gardening work and played volley ball, basketball and ping pong.

NEWS-POST

Azrael, Louis	9	Health	9
Bugs Baer	9	Horoscope	9
Clark, Norman	5	Movies	5
Classified Ads	14 15	Parsons, Louella	5
Comics	10	Pippen, R. H.	11
Crossword	15	Radio	7
Dixon, George	9	Ration Point	3
Durling	9	Robinson, Elsie	8
Dulaney	9	Society	5
Editorials	8	Sports	11, 12
Financial	12, 14	Thomas, Lowell	9

Bulletin

NEW YORK, July 28—(A. P.).—An Army bomber crashed through fog into an upper floor of the 102-story Empire State Building today, set the tower of the building afire and scattered debris over a wide area, killing at least five persons in the building.2 At least two persons in the building were badly burned.

Eleven floors of the building above and below the 86th floor of the towering structure were in flames and the spire of the building soon was enveloped in a vast smoky, foggy screen.

NEW YORK, July 28—(U. P.).—A low-flying plane crashed into the 102-story Empire State Building today, police reported, and exploded.

A four-alarm fire broke out through five floors of the building, from approximately the 80th to the 86th. Emergency fire-fighting equipment and a fleet of ambulances from city hospitals raced to Fifth Avenue and Thirty-fourth street, site of the world's tallest building.

Immediately on contact with the fog-shrouded tower, the plane burst into a mass of flames. An apron of fire licked out 300 feet from the tower and Midtown New York shook with the blast.

SMOKE, FOG BLEND

The crash occurred at approximately 10 A. M., and moments later smoke rolled from the tower, blending into thick fog that hid the spire.

Flames swept upward from the eightieth to the eighty-sixth floors.

At 10.10 A. M. the fog began slowly to lift, but the fire-stricken section of the tower still was invisible to thousands who huddled on the streets to watch the most sensational fire in recent years.

PLANE EXPLODES

The plane struck the east side of the building. The resulting explosion was deafening.

In a blanket of flames the plane bounced off the tower and fell to the roof of a building on Thirty-third street.

Occupant Describes Scene In Building

NEW YORK, July 28—(A. P.).—When the Empire State Building, James W. Irwin, management consultant and former managing editor of the Chicago Herald-Examiner, who has offices on the seventy-fifth floor of the building, said he heard the plane coming through the fog.

It struck the north side of the building, above Thirty-fourth street, about the seventy-seventh or seventy-eighth floor.

GASOLINE FILLS HALL

Irwin said that the hall on the seventy-fifth floor was filled with flaming gasoline and fumes and that the tall elevator bank in the building was put out of commission so that people served by that bank could not leave.

Irwin said he could not say whether anyone in the building

Continued on Page 2, Column 1.

Scratches At Bel Air

First Race—Patch Party, Careless Knight, Todcan, Walter Light.
Eighth—Mr. Jim.
Weather cloudy; track heavy.

Nature Played Strange Trick On Year Old Baby That Gave Him Unique Food Problem. How Science Came to the Rescue Makes an Interesting Story Which You May Read In the Pages of The American Weekly, the Magazine Distributed With tomorrow's Baltimore American.—Adv.

Baltimorean At Kure:

Planes Set Fire To Jap Warships

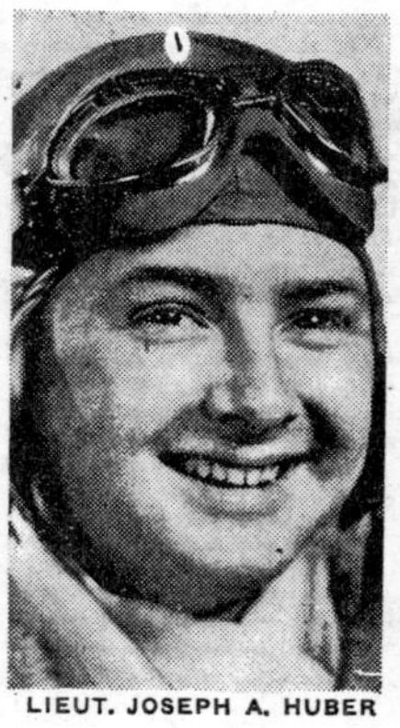

LIEUT. JOSEPH A. HUBER

ABOARD ADMIRAL McCAIN'S FLAGSHIP, Off Japan, July 28—(A. P.).—"All hell broke loose" when American carrier planes roared down on the great Japanese naval base at Kure today, but when they left warships in the harbor were burning, the air group commander aboard this carrier said.

Declared Comdr. W. A. Herrell of West Newton, Mass.:

"We did a beautiful job. We really smacked 'em."

Herrell said the Japanese changed their antiaircraft tactics today from their Wednesday defense and made the going rough for the American pilots.

ACK-ACK IS ACTIVE

"On Wednesday they started firing before we got into the target. Today they waited until we got over the shipping and then gave it to us.

"We had no air-borne opposi-

Continued on Page 2, Column 2.

JAPS CONCEDE LOSS OF OKINAWA, REPORT

THE WEATHER

Cloudy, moderate temperatures tonight and Thursday; warmer Thursday afternoon.
Detailed Weather Report Page 24

Read The Baltimore News-Post for complete, accurate war coverage. It is the only Baltimore newspaper possessing the three great wire services—
ASSOCIATED PRESS
INTERNATIONAL NEWS SERVICE
UNITED PRESS

THE BALTIMORE NEWS-POST
AN INDEPENDENT NEWSPAPER
The Largest Evening Circulation in the Entire South

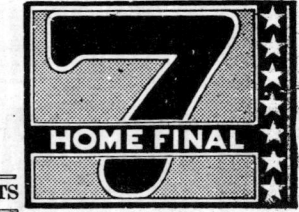

7 HOME FINAL

VOL. CXLVII.—NO. 40 Entered as second-class matter at Baltimore Postoffice. WEDNESDAY EVENING, JUNE 20, 1945 PRICE 3 CENTS

Franco Spain Barred From World League

Tokyo Fears Invasion Of New Island

3 Jap Cities Afire After B-29 Raids

NEW YORK, June 20—(I. N. S.).—The Tokyo radio reported that approximately 30 American fighter planes based on Okinawa attacked the Japanese home island of Kyushu today at 8.20 A. M., Japanese time.

By KENNETH McCALEB
International News Service Staff Correspondent.

GUAM, June 20.—Sprawling industrial target areas in three Japanese cities with populations of from 200,000 to more than 300,000 were left raging infernos today by about 450 B-29 Superforts.

The three-pronged fire strike touched off gigantic blazes in Shizuoka and Toyohashi, on Japan's main home island of Honshu, and in Fukuoka, on the southernmost home island of Kyushu.

Approximately 3,000 tons of the latest type of incendiary bombs were poured on the three cities which never before had felt the mighty fiery lash of the Superforts.

FIRES SPREAD

Returning pilots reported they had observed towering and spreading fires as far as 75 miles away after they had unloaded huge clusters of fire bombs that probably obliterated the industrial and military value of the three cities.

Radio Tokyo acknowledged the predawn raids, saying about 260 Marianas-based B-29s appeared over Fukuoka, Shizuoka and Toyohashi, while about 60 others laid mines in waters off Western Honshu and in the Kanmon strait between Honshu and Kyushu.

Tokyo admitted fires had broken out in "a number of places" but claimed that "most" of them had been extinguished within two hours after the attacks ended.

USING 'NEW TACTICS'

The enemy broadcast made no mention of damage and did not claim any planes shot down or damaged. It added that the B-29s were using "new tactics," changing "from the former raids on the large cities to the medium and small cities as well as dropping mines in waters near our mainland."

Returning airmen of the Seventy-third Wing based on Saipan described Fukuoka as being "clear as a bell" when the B-29s swept in at altitudes as low as 5,000 feet.

When they left it, the city was ablaze with a path of fire two miles wide and 10 miles long, extending inland from the dock area where several ships were burning.

U. S. Warns 20,000 On Strike

By Associated Press.

The Government, headed by President Truman, waved big sticks at thousands of the nation's idle workers today, prodding them to go back to jobs they had left over labor disputes.

More than 20,000 employes in vital war work were the targets for directives from the President, as well as from the War Labor Board and the Office of Defense Transportation. Meanwhile, an estimated 18,000 glass workers in four States threatened to stop work tomorrow.

Transportation facilities in several areas appeared the hardest hit by the work stoppages in the East, South and Midwest. The WLB acted to end five strikes while President Truman ordered Army seizure of one war plant.

In Chicago some 1,200 soldiers manned trucks as the ODT sought to restore normal operations for the 1,700 Government-seized trucking lines. Speedy drafting of union truck drivers remaining away from the jobs was being prepared by ODT officials.

Tri-State Company officials in Jackson, Miss., estimated 60,000 passengers in nine States were affected by a strike of more than 400 bus drivers and mechanics.

Army seizure and operation of plants of the Diamond Alkali Company at Painesville, Ohio, was ordered yesterday by President Truman.

Gen. Spaatz Gets Cross From King

LONDON, June 20—(U. P.).—King George today received in audience Gen. Carl A. Spaatz and invested him with the Knight Grand Cross of the British Empire.

SIGN OCCUPATION PACT

ROME, June 20—(A. P.).—Allied Headquarters announced today that a program for implementing the Allied-Yugoslav agreement on the occupation of Venezia Giulia had been signed.

29th Division Band Plays U. S. Concert For Germans

VEGESACK, Germany, June 20 (U. P.).—The Twenty-ninth Division band gave an "Americanization" concert for German civilians last night. After the last scheduled number an officer took the microphone and announced:

"Next comes the American national anthem."

Every German in the audience rose and stood with bared head while "The Star-Spangled Banner" was played.

Story Of Hero; Buy War Bond

(The News-Post Washington Bureau.)

WASHINGTON, June 20.—Hurdling the hedge with fixed bayonet, Pvt. Ernest Prussman disappeared from view. Seconds later, he was back in sight, motioning his squad onward and passing two prisoners back.

After leading his squad across an open field to the next hedgerow, Prussman advanced to a machine-gun position, destroyed the gun, captured its crew and two riflemar

Again advancing ahead of his squad in the assault, Prussman was mortally wounded by a Nazi rifeman.

As he fell to the ground he threw a hand grenade, killing the enemy rifleman.

At least we can buy another war bond.

Nations Bar Spain Entry In League

SAN FRANCISCO, June 20—(A. P.).—The United States joined 49 other nations today in a blunt notice that a Franco regime in Spain cannot join their world league.

They said, in plain words: Generalissimo Franco's Government would not be a fit companion because it was set up with the aid of the Nazi-Fascist Axis.

Diplomats crowding this conference city looked toward Madrid for possible effects of their action.

The vote to blackball Spain so long as its present Government remains in power was unanimous. It came last night to loud acclaim in an open meeting of the conference commission handling the membership problem of the new world organization.

It was touched off by tall, vigorous Luis Quintanilla of Mexico, an eloquent man in English, Spanish and French, his speech condemning Franco as a willing worker behind Hitler and Mussolini drew supporting talks by France, Belgium, the Ukraine, White Russia, Australia, Uruguay, Chile, Guatemala and this statement by James C. Dunn, U. S. assistant Secretary of State:

"The United States delegation is in complete accord with the statement on interpretation by Mexico and desires to associate itself with that declaration."

Admiral Royal Dies In Pacific

WASHINGTON, June 20—(I. N. S.).—The Navy announced today that Rear Admiral Forrest B. Royal, fifty-two, commander of an amphibious force, died in the Pacific area June 18, of natural causes. Admiral Royal, a native of New York, was in command of the amphibious operation in the Brunei bay area on the northwest coast of Borneo, June 10 and 11.

Rule By Decree Approved In Tokyo

SAN FRANCISCO, June 20—(A. P.).—The law giving Japanese Premier Kantaro Suzuki's Cabinet power to rule by decree, previously passed by the Diet, was approved today by the Privy Council, Domei agency reported in a broadcast heard by the Federal Communications Commission.

QUISLING TRIAL IN JULY

OSLO, June 20—(U. P.).—Annaeus Schjoedt, the prosecuting attorney, said today that former puppet Premier Vidkun Quisling probably would go to trial for treason in late July.

Temperatures

12 Midn't	69	7 A. M.,	70
1 A. M.,	69	8 A. M.,	72
2 A. M.,	68	9 A. M.,	74
3 A. M.,	69	10 A. M.,	76
4 A. M.,	68	11 A. M.,	78
5 A. M.,	68	12 Noon,	80
6 A. M.,	67	1 P. M.,	82

"Servants in Paradise"—Two of Them Have a 14-Room Apartment on Park Avenue With No One to Serve But Themselves. How This Strange Situation Came About Is Explained in The American Weekly, the Magazine Distributed With Next Sunday's Baltimore American.—Adv.

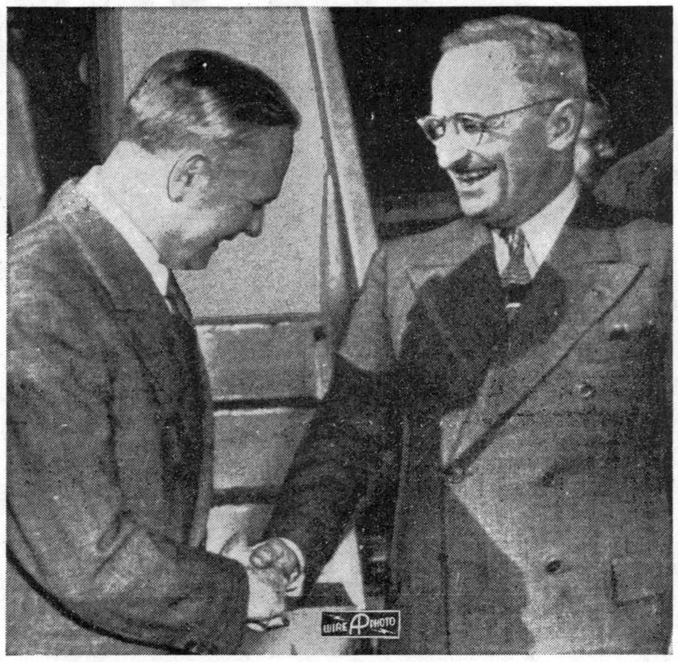

PRESIDENT ON COAST—Governor Mon Wallgren (left) of Washington State greets President Truman as he arrives at McChord Field, near Olympia, for a brief vacation. Later the President will fly to San Francisco, where he will speak at the closing session of the World Security Conference.

Returns To Alma Mater:

Gen. Eisenhower Visits West Point

By SAUL PETT
International News Service Staff Correspondent.

WEST POINT, N. Y., June 20. Gen. Dwight D. Eisenhower returned to West Point today on a sentimental journey to the shaded, ivy-clad beauty of his alma mater.

The general and his official entourage reached the U. S. Military Academy located high above the Hudson river in the scenic Catskill mountains at 10.30 this morning. They were greeted with a 17-gun salute at Washington gate.

There, too, the general reviewed a mounted honor guard of Negro cacalrymen. Standing beside him during the brief and colorful ceremonies was Maj. Gen. Francis B. Wilby, superintendent of the Academy, and his entourage.

IN NEW DRESS

Unlike his New York and Washington appearances when he wore a summer dress uniform, the Supreme Allied commander in chief wore an overseas cap and a battlejacket on the triu up the historic Hudson valley to West Point.

Only scattered receptions greeted the motorcade on its journey, apparently because few persons knew the route and the time. A small handful of greeters cheered the general when he swept through Highland Falls, a little village south of West Point.

Rain and mist filled the morning hours. Less than 15 minutes [illegible] General reached Wash[illegible] the skies cleared and [illegible] down with a genial welcome equalling Ike's famed and infectious grin.

THOSE IN PARTY

Preceding the motorcade were four military policemen mounted on motorcycles. A staff car came next, and then followed the general's sedan. Accompanying the general were his mother and father-inlaw, Mr. and Mrs. John Shelton Doud of Denver.

After his review of the mounted guard of honor, Ike went to the superintendent's office.

He was graduated from West

Continued on Page 2, Column 1.

Bulletin

WASHINGTON, June 20—(A. P.).—Brig. Gen. Claudius M. Easley, assistant commander of the Ninety-sixth Infantry Division, was killed in action on Okinawa Tuesday, his wife was notified by the War Department today.

'FLYING GRANDMA' HURT

WASHINGTON, Pa., June 20—(U. P.).—Mrs. Maude Rufus, sometimes known as the "flying grandma," and Mrs. Louella O. Gillen, both of Ann Arbor, Mich., were in serious condition today at Washington Hospital following a plane crash.

SOONG IN CHUNGKING

CHUNGKING, June 20—(U. P.).—T. V. Soong, Premier and Foreign Minister, returned to Chungking from the San Francisco conference today.

Truman Eyes Progress Of Parley

OLYMPIA, Wash., June 20—(A. P.).—President Truman started a holiday today in the Pacific Northwest but his thoughts were centered on the postwar security conference at San Francisco.

Associates said the Chief Executive's plans for the immediate future were predicated upon hope of quick action on the final form of the projected international peace charter.

A delay in the closing of the San Francisco meeting beyond this week, they asserted, may force the rearrangement of Mr. Truman's schedule for the period leading up to his departure next month for his first "Big Three" meeting, at Berlin.

The President already has all but abandoned thought of being able to attend the Governor's conference in Michigan.

Churchill Rival Quits Election

LONDON, June 20—(U. P.).—William Douglas-Home, rival of Prime Minister Churchill for a Parliament seat in the forthcoming general election, withdrew from the race today in favor of a trooper serving in the Mediterranean theater.

JACKSON IN LONDON

LONDON, June 20—(U. P.).—Supreme Court Justice Robert H. Jackson, chief American prosecutor of war criminals, arrived in London today for conferences with the United Nations War Crimes Commission.

Political, Military Change Seen In Japan As Result Of Defeat Near Homeland

SAN FRANCISCO, June 20—(I. N. S.).—Tokyo radio commentator today conceded the loss of Okinawa to American forces, according to an Australian broadcast heard by ABC monitor. The Tokyo radio commentator added that loss the island will result "in serious repercussion both military and political, in the Japanese capital."

GUAM, June 20—(U. P.).—The Tenth Army hacked the last 2,000 or more Japanese into tiny, isolated pockets on the southern tip of Okinawa today. Final victory was at hand.

Admiral Chester W. Nimitz announced the enemy's last defenses were collapsing and resistance steadily was weakening.

But even as the bloody campaign was nearing a triumphant end, American forces were preparing for the next amphibious leap toward Japan.

100 TRANSPORTS NEAR

Radio Tokyo reported more than 100 American transports were riding at anchor in the American-held Kerama Islands, 20 miles southwest of Okinawa, ready for new operations.

Two Allied task forces also were sighted near Miyako Island, 200 miles southwest of Okinawa, Tokyo said. One was built around five aircraft carriers and a battleship, while the other included three battleships, the enemy account said.

Scores of the trapped enemy leaped to their deaths from the southern cliffs. Others were surrendering in such numbers that no accurate count could be kept. Even more were being slain in their caves and foxholes.

AT MOPUP STAGE

The 81-day campaign reached the mopup stage with a marine break-through to the south coast on a wide front. Marines and doughboys then knifed out in all directions, carving up the enemy survivors into helpless groups of only 10 to 100 soldiers each.

The Americans were advancing so rapidly on the southern tip of Okinawa that there were as many Japanese behind them as in front, a field dispatch said.

Land artillery and naval guns offshore were ordered to cease fire for fear of hitting marines and doughboys in the tiny remaining battlefield.

The Eighth Regiment of the veteran Second Marine Division paved the way for final victory with a three-mile thrust through disorganized enemy resistance to

Continued on Page 2, Column 1.

'Japs Insects—Kill Them':

Gen. Slim Calls For All-Out War

LONDON, June 20—(U. P.).—The Pacific war will last "a hell of a long time" unless the Allies throw everything they have against the Japanese, Lt. Gen. Sir William Slim, commander of the British Fourteenth Army in Burma, said.

The veteran British jungle commander, just back from the Burma front, told a press conference the campaign against the Japanese is a war of extermination. He said:

"The Japanese is a stupid little man, but he will fight to the end. Other armies say they will fight to the last man, but it's only the Japanese Army that does it."

Slim said the only way to defeat the Japanese, "like all insects," was to kill them, and he revealed his Fourteenth Army had killed 100,000 of them since its formation in October, 1943. He continued:

"War is killing, especially when you're fighting a Jap. If we tell you in the Fourteenth Army we have killed a Jap we have killed him. I won't allow my men to count anything unless they have the body."

Slim characterized the Japanese soldier as "neither man nor animal," but something like a soldier ant, adding:

"You can stamp on them, but still they come on. If you do something to disturb their plan they run in circles and get very confused indeed, but they can be a most damnable nuisance."

As for the campaign in Burma, Slim said, he believed the worst of the fighting there was past.

NEWS-POST

At Your Service	11	Horoscope	7
Azrael, Louis	21	Mallon, Paul	21
Bugs Baer	21	Movies	14, 15
Clark, Norman	14	Parsons, Louella	15
Classified Ads	25, 26, 27	Pegler	21
Comics	10	Pippen, R. H.	22
Crossword	27	Radio	19
Dixon, George	21	Ration Points	18
Dulaney	21	Robinson, Elsie	20
Editorials	20	Society	12
Financial	24, 25	Sports	22, 23, 24
Haney, Dr. Lewis	24	Thomas, Lowell	21
Health	13	Winchell, Walter	14
		Women's Clubs	12

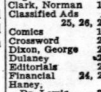

ALL STAR THE EVENING SUN SPORTS
BALTIMORE, TUESDAY, MAY 8, 1945

ORIOLES SCORE 9 RUNS IN THIRD INNING

KEN RAFFENSBERGER LT. (jg) ALOISIUS RYKACZEWSKI
The Phillies' big pitcher is sworn into Navy at Philadelphia, preparatory to leaving for Bainbridge

It's All In The Viewpoint

Schott Won Another, But Was Unimpressive

By PAUL MENTON
[Sports Editor, The Evening Sun]

Freddie Schott, the young, hopeful heavyweight from Akron, Ohio, goes marching along successfully today as a result of his thirty-ninth straight victory last night at the Coliseum over Jimmy Bell.

But he doesn't march with his head held very high. Or, at least, he shouldn't.

His lighter opponent from near-by Washington, no better than a good club fighter, even in these nights of wartime fighters, messed up Freddie's face no end in the ten rounds.

One of Schott's eyes was cut and the other badly puffed before hostilities ceased and the Akron lad's hand was raised in victory. Whether he deserved the decision is a matter of opinion and hardly worth getting excited about.

The referee and two judges thought he did. The majority of the ringsiders thought Bell won. And the latter undoubtedly would have gotten the official decision also had he not taken a short count after slipping in the tenth round, when he obviously was tired.

The important point to me is if Schott is now the sixth best heavyweight in the land, all rankings should be discontinued until the real fighters return to the ring. Granted that he is only a youngster and can improve during the next few years, Freddie certainly did not look the part of a prospective heavyweight challenger last night.

Evidently his opponents have been carefully handpicked to roll up 39 victories in a row.

Arena Club Has Trouble About Armory

Evidently the Arena Club hasn't yet reached the end of its year-old fight for the doubtful and expensive honor of staging boxing shows in Baltimore.

After two programs at the Fifth Regiment Armory, the second of which drew the largest crowd Fred Squires and company has enticed to a show since its inaugural offering last August, the club doesn't know whether it has a home for the future.

Request for use of the Fifth Regiment for May 18 has not yet been granted. There seems to be some mystery now whether jurisdictiton over the big hall belongs to the military or the State.

I should think the time to settle this point, as well as the armory policy regarding its use for sports, would have been before the Arena Club was allowed to move in.

The troubles of the Arena Club started last summer when Squires sought to renew an old license he once held to promote boxing in Baltimore. The commission refused on the ground there were not sufficient fighters to enable two clubs to run steadily in Baltimore. Squires went to court and lost, but Judge Eugene O'Dunne suggested the commission reconsider the application. Later the commission granted the Arena Club the right to conduct boxing monthly, then increased it finally to semi-monthly. The club opened at Carlin's, shifted last month to the Fifth Regiment Armory.

Should Be Racing At Pimlico Next Week

With the war in Europe over, the Eastern race tracks are simply waiting at the barrier for word from the Government that the ban on thoroughbred racing has been lifted

New England, New York, New Jersey and Delaware Park have announced their plans.

Narragansett, which normally would be bringing its spring meeting to a close the middle of this month, will open the instant the ban is lifted. It may be running by Saturday. New York will be away from the barrier almost as quickly.

Garden State will use its usual summer dates following the close of Delaware Park on July 4. Opening for Delaware will be May 29.

Therefore, there's no reason why Maryland shouldn't have racing next week at Pimlico if the ban is lifted immediately, as is expected. That would give us 12 days this spring, plus one, June 9, for the Preakness. Seventy-five at Pimlico and Laurel in the fall, beginning September 1, would give the State 88 of its 100 days.

There will be adjustments and curtailments throughout the country because of the ban which has kept the tracks closed; but, as far as is practical, most tracks will run on the dates they normally use.

Sports Leaders Await Word

Washington, May 8 (AP)—Athletic leaders waited expectantly today for definite Government word affecting sports as the result of Germany's unconditional surrender.

They were eager to learn, first, when the racing ban will be lifted, and, next, if the War Department will take action on congressional contentions that 4-F professional athletes have been discriminated against in the draft.

Government officials in positions to know what plans are being made remained silent about racing, but turf spokesmen said they had learned the ban will be removed on or about V-E day.

The War Department has been investigating for some time complaints that professional athletes who could not meet physical requirements were being inducted into service.

An announcement was expected yesterday but the War Department said "it still is being cased. You'll just have to coast along until it's ready."

Cochrane-Greco Bout Is Sought

Augusta, Ga., May 8 (AP)—Promoter Jack Laken is seeking to arrange a bout in Jacksonville, Fla., June 22 between Welterweight Champion Freddie Cochrane and Johnny Greco, the Canadian titleholder.

Olmo, Cuccinello Leading Major Loop Hitters

New York, May 8 (AP)—Two surprise-package hitters, Luis Olmo, of Brooklyn, and Tony Cuccinello, of the Chicago White Sox, led the major league batsmen today at the end of the first three weeks of competition.

Olmo picked up 123 points for himself by collecting eight hits in nine at bats against the Phillies last Sunday, boosting his average from .286 to a lofty .409. The Puerto Rican was riding the Dodgers' bench for ten days because of "weak hitting."

Started With Bang

Cuccinello, who spent most of his fifteen big-league years in the National loop, started the season with a bang by working the old hidden-ball play on Manager Lou Boudreau, of Cleveland, and continued to hit so hard even Skipper Jimmy Dykes was amazed. A .395 mark for eleven games was one reason the Sox were in first place.

Last year's champions were bringing up the rear, far removed from the top ten hitters. Brooklyn's Dixie Walker was still trying to get under way and hitting only .192. Boudreau, who nosed out Bob Johnson last day of the 1944 season, was batting .250.

Nieman Is Second

Olmo's closest competitor was Butch Nieman, of the Braves, at .400, one of the most improved hitters in the circuit. Tommy O'Brien, of Pittsburgh, followed at .377, two degrees higher than Mel Ott, of New York. Vance Dinges, standout Phill rookie, was fifth at .369.

Vern Stephens, of the St. Louis Browns, was a close second to Cuccinello in the American at .389. Eddie Mayo, of Detroit, was clubbing at .352 for third honors, followed by the two base-stealing "champs," George Case, of Washington, .339, and George Stirnweiss, of New York, .333.

The leaders:

NATIONAL LEAGUE

Player, Club	G.	AB.	R.	H.	P.C.
Olmo, Brooklyn	13	44	7	18	.409
Nieman, Boston	15	50	15	20	.400
O'Brien, Pittsburgh	14	53	6	20	.377
Ott, New York	17	56	20	21	.375
Dinges, Philadelphia	16	65	9	24	.369
Holmes, Boston	16	68	15	25	.368
Kurowski, St. Louis	14	49	7	17	.347
Weintraub, New York	17	55	16	19	.345
Rucker, New York	17	79	14	27	.342
Stanky, Brooklyn	14	50	9	17	.340

AMERICAN LEAGUE

Player, Club	G.	AB.	R.	H.	P.C.
Cuccinello, Chicago	11	38	8	15	.395
Stephens, St. Louis	11	36	10	14	.389
Mayo, Detroit	14	54	10	19	.352
Case, Washington	16	62	14	21	.339
Stirnweiss, New York	15	54	13	18	.333
Dickshot, Chicago	12	46	11	15	.326
Etten, New York	15	56	9	18	.321
Hall, Philadelphia	16	64	7	20	.313
Hockett, Chicago	12	48	8	15	.313
Newsome, Boston	16	62	5	19	.306

Looking Ahead

New York, May 8 (AP)—Surrender day means baseball will play its World Series this fall and may reinstate its All-Star game, but no great influx of returning GI athletes is to be expected.

Of about 500 major leaguers now on the national defense service lists, a majority are believed overseas, many in the Pacific theater. War Department estimates are that more than 12 months may be required to return the European armies to this nation, giving little hope for any familiar names returning to the 1945 box scores.

After three weeks of play, both circuits appear to be in such delicate balance that reappearance of a star player in the lineup of any team could make it a pennant contender. The 1944 experience of Dick Wakefield and the Detroit Tigers was proof enough it could happen.

The New York Giants and Chicago White Sox are the big surprises of the new season, but the intersectional tests are just beginning. Chicago polished off some unfinished business with Cleveland today before opening a series with the Philadelphia Athletics tomorrow.

70 In Service Ring Tilts

Fort Story, Va., May 8 (AP)—Seventy boxers, representing nine service teams from Virginia, Pennsylvania and Maryland, arrived here today to participate in the annual 3d Service Command boxing tourneys, which begin tomorrow night and run through Friday.

The ringmen, both professionals and amateurs, will clash in all weight divisions from 118 pounds to the unlimited-weight class and will bid for individual and team trophies. Preliminary and semifinal rounds are scheduled for tomorrow night, with the finals Friday.

Hundreds of war veterans from the convalescent hospital here at Fort Story will be guests at the opening bouts as well as several notables in the fight game.

Tony Zale, middleweight champion, now in the Navy; Petey Scalzo, former welterweight champion in 1934 and 1940, and Nicky Jerome, ex-welterweight contender, will alternate in the ring as referee.

The tourney, conducted by the 3d Service Command athletic department, is under the direction of Lieut. Col. Medford G. Ramay, former V.M.I. athlete.

Service Roundup

By Hugh Fullerton, Jr.

New York, May 8 (AP)—The news of Germany's surrender had just come over the cable and in the comparatively quiet corner where the sports department functions there was some speculation as to when horse racing would be resumed, when real big league baseball players would be rejoining their clubs and whether football will be better next fall.

One opinion was offered that hockey, the first major sport to feel the war's effect, will be the first to recover—apart from racing, which is ready to go at a moment's notice. When the discussion simmered down the day's sports news still came from the armed forces. Here are a few samples:

Lipon Flies Casualties

John Rigney, former White Sox pitcher, sends word from the Marianas, where he manages a ball team, that his best man, ex-Tiger Johnny Lipon, misses a lot of games while flying casualties from the Okinawa region. Rigney says that riding a B-29 bomber is "just like a trip on the Chicago 'L' except the ride isn't so jerky and it doesn't cost a dime."

In England, six soldier boxers speaking on a radio program, picked Billy Conn as the one most likely to succeed Sergt. Joe Louis as heavyweight champion. Pfc. Ben Schurr, in civilian life, Referee Patty Ryan, named Pete Morelli, of Stockton, Cal., as his candidate. Morelli agreed with Schurr.

A note from the University of Arkansas points out that three former razorbacks have been awarded the Congressional Medal of Honor—Capt. Maurice L. (Footsie) Britt, Lieut. Nathan Gordon and, posthumously, Lieut. Harold (Buck) Lloyd.

Net Title To Patty

In Italy, Private Edward J. (Budge) Patty, of Hollywood, Cal., former national junior tennis champion, won the Florence Allied area singles championship last week end, beating Capt. Edward Minch, of New York, 6-1, 6-1, 6-0. Minch holds the North African title.

In a letter written from a German prison camp last January, Capt. Hal Van Every, ex-Minnesota and Green Bay Packers back, commented: "Just heard Green Bay won the Western division title. I'm a scatback now." Apparently he lost a lot of weight.

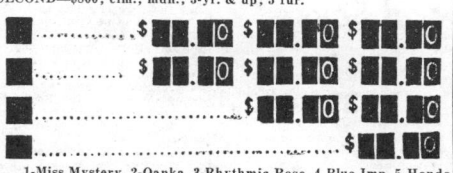

BOB STEVENS
He's reserve on Poly ten

IN STICK BATTLE—Poly and Friends lacrosse teams clash tomorrow afternoon, 4 o'clock, on the latter's field and Stevens is due to see action.

Sun Stream Wins At Newmarket

Newmarket, England, May 8 (AP). Lord Derby's Sun Stream, a five-to-two favorite, won the One Thousand Guineas over the Bunbury mile today in the first classic race of Britain's racing season.

Lord Roseberry's Blue Smoke was second and Mrs. Dorothy Paget's Mrs. Father ran third.

Sun Stream came from behind to win by three lengths in the classic race for 3-year-old fillies. Ridden by Harry Wragg, Britain's second best-known jockey, Sun Stream waited her turn and finished strong.

Lawson Signs As 'Frisco Coach

San Francisco, May 8 (AP)—Lieut. Com. James Lawson, former Stanford football coach, has signed a contract to serve on the coaching staff of the San Francisco club of the All-America Conference when the professional football league begins operations after the war, according to A. J. (Tony) Morabito, owner of the club franchise.

Lawson had been expected to return to Stanford as head football coach, a position he received appointment to and was unable to fill in 1942 due to his commissioning in the Navy.

Mexico City Results

[By the Associated Press]

FIRST—$800; clm.; mdn.; 2-yr.; 3½ fur.

Don Penalo, 117 (H. S. Jones)............$4.00, $3.40, $2.20
Gergar, 112 (M. Diaz)............$9.80, $2.80
Sun Vine, 114 (F. Fernandez)............$2.60

Time—.41. Mi Chata, Crystal Mile, Bank Club, Blue Chance also ran.

SECOND—$800; clm.; mdn.; 3-yr. & up; 5 fur.

[redacted]............$[redacted].[redacted]0 $[redacted].[redacted]0 $[redacted].[redacted]0
[redacted]............$[redacted].[redacted]0 $[redacted].[redacted]0 $[redacted].[redacted]0
[redacted]............$[redacted].[redacted]0 $[redacted].[redacted]0
[redacted]............$[redacted].[redacted]0

1-Miss Mystery. 2-Oanka. 3-Rhythmic Rose. 4-Blue Imp. 5-Hondo Boss. 6-Low Heels. 7-Valhat. 8-Tormentor. 9-Jessie's Girl. 10-Jimmie Gray. 11-Tia Maria. 12-Sky Quest. 13-March Showers. 14-Nancy Carroll. 15-Chatplay. 16-Miss Adare.

Havana Results

FIRST—$225; clm.; 3-yr. & up; 6 fur.

[redacted]............$[redacted].[redacted]0 $[redacted].[redacted]0 $[redacted].[redacted]0
[redacted]............$[redacted].[redacted]0 $[redacted].[redacted]0 $[redacted].[redacted]0
[redacted]............$[redacted].[redacted]0 $[redacted].[redacted]0
[redacted]............$[redacted].[redacted]0

1-Ron. 2-Pattie Donna. 3-Palina Real. 4-Computer. 5-Bombing. 6-Witchswall. 7-Chilly Mac. 8-Azorado. 9-Maebeau. 10-Jimmy H. 11-Blondkin. 12-Mumble. 13-Nananina. 14-Leopoldina.

5 Days, 5 Tilts For Poly Nine

Polytechnic's pennant push in the Maryland Scholastic Association's two-division baseball league is fast becoming as much a wearing test of stamina and endurance as a test of diamond skill.

Due in part to a pileup of postponments forced by rainy weather, the Engineers have embarked on a program of five games in five days in an effort to catch up on their schedule and not delay the interdivision series.

Score Sixth Win

Tech got off to a fast start on this marathon menu yesterday by tripping Patterson Park, 2 to 1, for its sixth straight league victory, a win that kept its record inviolate in the public school sector.

No breathing spell was planned in sight until Saturday, for Poly today was to face Forest Park, then tomorrow go against Southern, Thursday meet City College in a game postponed from last week and Friday test Southern again.

Fortunately, the Engineer mound corps is well rested and in good shape physically for the week's grind. Main reliance, is being placed in Cal Barnes, who beat Patterson yesterday, and Jack Shanahan, but it may be there also will be plenty of work for Charlie Rappazzo, Bill Gable and Otto Lebron, who round out the staff.

Loyola, beaten just once in five starts—by Mount St. Joe, 1-0—has a lighter bill of fare ahead of it in the private-school division it heads. Its Thursday interdivision tilt with Poly has been canceled, so its lone outing was to be today's contest with Calvert Hall, running third in its section, half a game behind St. Joe

Prep Meeting

The Maryland Scholastic Association will hold its regular May meeting tonight. The session is set for the Department of Recreation offices on North Calvert street, at 8 o'clock, according to Secretary Ad Hausman.

Tennis Standing

City College and Forest Park are fast becoming the giants of the schoolboy tennis league. Each racked another victory yesterday to remain tied with Polytechnic atop the wheel.

The Collegians have won four, the Foresters three and the Engineers two straight matches.

The new standing:

	W.	L.	P.C.		W.	L.	P.C.
City	4	0	1.000	Mt. St. Joe	1	2	.333
Forest Pk.	3	0	1.000	Friends	1	3	.250
Poly	2	0	1.000	Calvert H.	0	2	.000
Gilman	2	2	.500	Southern	0	3	.000
Loyola	2	3	.400				

Prep Schools

Tomorrow

BASEBALL
Southern vs. Poly, Bloomingdale, 4 P.M.
Forest Park vs. McDonogh, Hanlon Park, 4.15 P.M.
Kenwood at Catonsville, 2.45 P.M.
Vocational vs. City, Clifton Park, 4.15 P.M.
Calvert Hall at St. Joe, 4 P.M.

TRACK
Mount St. Joseph at Forest Park, 4 P.M.
Poly vs. Patterson, Patterson Park, 4 P.M.

LACROSSE
Poly at Friends, 4 P.M.
McDonogh at City, 4 P.M.

Thursday

BASEBALL
Poly vs. City, Bloomingdale, 4.30 P.M.

LACROSSE
Park at St. Paul's, 4 P.M.

TENNIS
Friends at Mount St. Joseph, 4 P.M.
Poly at Gilman, 4 P.M.
City at Forest Park, 4 P.M.
Southern at Calvert Hall, 4 P.M.

Friday

BASEBALL
Catonsville at Towson, 2.45 P.M.
Franklin at Kenwood, 2.45 P.M.
McDonogh vs. Calvert Hall, Bloomingdale, 4 P.M.
Gilman at Mt. St. Joseph, 4 P.M.
Patterson vs. City, Clifton Park, 4.30 P.M.
Forest Park vs. Vocational, Clifton Park, 4.30 P.M.
Poly vs. Southern, Carroll Park, 4.30 P.M.

LACROSSE
Boys' Latin at City, 3.45 P.M.
Forest Park at McDonogh, 4 P.M.
Poly at Gilman, 4 P.M.
Severn at Mount St. Joseph, 4 P.M.

Saturday

LACROSSE
Poly vs. Navy Plebes, Annapolis, 3 P.M.
St. Paul's vs. Army Plebes, West Point.

TRACK
Loyola College Invitation Meet, Evergreen.

TENNIS
City at Woodberry Forest.
Forest Park vs. Navy Plebes, Annapolis, 2 P.M.

GOLF
Forest Park vs. Navy Plebes, Annapolis, 1.30 P.M.
Scholastic championships, first and second rounds, Mount Pleasant.

Scratches

Mexico City

SECOND RACE—March Showers, Nancy Carroll, Chatplay, Miss Adare.
THIRD—Hy Lieutenant.
EIGHTH—Zac's Gal.
NINTH—Stem Winder, Ella Gal, Maestro Shasta.
Track fast.

Havana

THIRD—(To be run as the fourth race)—No scratches.
FOURTH—(To run as the third race)—Stadium, Jawar, B. P. Greenock.
SIXTH—Opportunity.
SEVENTH—Martiano, Ivory Tip, Rollsona, Chicken Lady, Humdrum.
Track fast.

M. Skaff Hits Homer With Bases Loaded

Buffalo, May 8—Idle yesterday, after copping a double-header from the Bisons on Sunday, the Orioles swung back into action here this afternoon seeking their third straight win over Buffalo.

Johnny Podgajny, the Birds' 3-and-0 winner who gained all his victories through relief work, drew the hill assignment for the Flock and was opposed by Frank (Bull) Hammons.

Ralph (Red) Kress was back in the Oriole lineup and stationed in left field. He replaced Jim Tropea, who has a sore arm. Kress has been bothered by a groin muscle injury.

Less than 2,500 fans were on hand when the game began.

The lineup:

BALTIMORE	BUFFALO
Braun, ss.	McNabb, 2b.
Riley, rf.	Held, 3b.
Kress, lf.	Mierkowicz, cf.
Mellendick, cf.	Boland, rf.
Latshaw, 1b.	Butka, 1b.
F. Skaff, 3b.	Wright, lf.
M. Skaff, 2b.	Gomez, ss.
Devlin, c.	Radakovich, c.
Podgajny, p.	Hammons, p.

Umpires—Tighe, Felerski and Tobin.

First Inning

ORIOLES—Braun singled over second. Riley doubled to right center, Braun stopping at third. Kress hit to Held, who threw wild to first, and both runners scored, Kress going to second. Mellendick lined to Mierkowicz, who made a shoestring catch. Latshaw doubled off the left-field wall, Kress scoring. F. Skaff hit a home run over the left-field fence, at the 340-foot mark, Latshaw scoring ahead of him. M. Skaff singled over second. That was enough for Hammons, and Bob Callan, also a right-hander, came in. Devlin forced M. Skaff at second, Callan to Gomez. Podgajny flied to Mierkowicz. Five runs; five hits; one error.

BUFFALO — McNabb walked. Held forced McNabb, Braun to M. Skaff. Mierkowicz sent Mellendick against the wall for his hard smash. Boland grounded out to Latshaw, unassisted. No runs; no hits; no errors.

Second Inning

ORIOLES—Braun doubled to right. Riley flied to Wright. Kress singled to center, Braun scoring. Mellendick fouled to Radakovich. Latshaw grounded out, McNabb to Butka. One run; two hits; no errors.

BUFFALO—Butka doubled down the third-base line. Podgajny took Wright's foul. Gomez doubled over Kress's head, scoring Butka. F. Skaff threw out Radakovich, Gomez holding second. Podgajny threw out Callan. One run; two hits; no errors.

Third Inning

ORIOLES—F. Skaff popped an easy one to Butka, but the wind allowed it to drop safely for a one-base hit. M. Skaff doubled to left-center, his brother pulling up at third. Devlin doubled to the same spot, both of the Skaffs scoring. Podgajny bunted toward the mound and Callan threw to third, but Devlin remained on second and both runners were safe. Braun sacrificed, Callan to Carl McNabb, who covered the bag. That was all for Callan and Woody Wheaton, a southpaw, came in. Riley walked, filling the bases. Kress hit to Gomez, whose throw was dropped by McNabb, Devlin scoring. Mellendick was hit by a pitched ball, Podgajny scoring. Latshaw walked, scoring Riley. F. Skaff popped to Held. M. Skaff hit a home run over the left-field wall, at the 330-foot mark, Kress, Mellendick and Latshaw scoring before him. Devlin singled to right, but was out trying for a double, Boland to Gomez. Nine runs; five hits; one error

BUFFALO — McNabb walked. Held hit to Latshaw, who touched first, then got McNabb with a throw to Braun. Mierkowicz singled to center. M. Skaff threw out Boland. No runs; one hit; no errors.

Fourth Inning

ORIOLES—Bob Gillespie, another right hander, went to the mound for Buffalo. Podgajny popped to Held. Braun beat out a hit to Gomez. Riley hit to Gillespie, whose throw to Gomez was dropped by the latter for an error. Kress walked, filling the bases. Tropea, batting for Mellendick, doubled down the third-base line, scoring Braun and Riley. Latshaw walked, again filling the bases. F. Skaff walked, forcing in Kress. M. Skaff walked, forcing in Tropea. Parkhurst, a southpaw, came in for Buffalo. Devlin walked, Latshaw scoring. Podgajny struck out. Braun walked, F. Skaff scoring. Riley grounded out to Butka unassisted. Six runs; two hits; one error.

BUFFALO—Tropea went to center for the Orioles. Butka grounded out to Braun. Wright fouled to F. Skaff. Podgajny threw out Gomez. No runs; no hits; no errors.

Fifth Inning

ORIOLES—Kress singled off the left center fence. Tropea hit into a double play, Butka to Gomez. Latshaw flied to Mierkowicz in deep center. No runs; one hit; no errors.

BUFFALO — Radakovich was thrown out by F. Skaff. F. Skaff threw Parkhurst out at first. McNabb was safe when F Skaff threw low to first, but Latshaw tagged him out when McNabb started for second. No runs; no hits; one error.

Sixth Inning

ORIOLES—Mierkowicz took F. Skaff's long fly in center. M. Skaff hit his second home run over the left-field wall. Devlin fanned. McNabb threw out Podgajny. One run; one hit; no errors.

BUFFALO—Held singled to right center. Mierkowicz hit a home run over the center-field wall, scoring Held ahead of him. M. Skaff threw out Boland. Butka hit short bouncer to Podgajny, who threw him out. Two runs; two hits; no errors

Standings

INTERNATIONAL LEAGUE

	W.	L.	P.C.	
Jersey City	10	2	.833	
ORIOLES	9	5	.643	2
Montreal	7	6	.538	3½
Toronto	6	7	.462	4½
Newark	5	7	.417	5
Syracuse	4	7	.364	[illegible]
Rochester	4	7	.364	[illegible]
Buffalo	4	8	.333	[illegible]

Games Tomorrow
ORIOLES at Buffalo (3 P.M.).
Jersey City at Montreal.
Syracuse at Toronto.
Newark at Rochester.

AMERICAN LEAGUE

	W	L.	P.C.	G.B.
Chicago	9	3	.750	
New York	10	5	.667	½
Detroit	9	5	.643	1
Washington	9	8	.529	2½
Philadelphia	7	9	.438	4
St. Louis	5	8	.385	[illegible]
Boston	6	10	.375	[illegible]
Cleveland	3	10	.300	[illegible]

Games Tomorrow
Washington at St. Louis (night).
Philadelphia at Chicago.
Boston at Cleveland.
New York at Detroit.

NATIONAL LEAGUE

	W.	L.	P.C.	G.B.
New York	12	4	.750	
Brooklyn	9	6	.600	2½
Chicago	8	6	.571	3
St. Louis	8	6	.571	3
Boston	7	8	.467	4½
Cincinnati	6	7	.462	[illegible]
Pittsburgh	6	9	.400	[illegible]
Philadelphia	3	13	.188	9

Games Tomorrow
Pittsburgh at Boston.
St. Louis at Brooklyn.
Chicago at Philadelphia.
Cincinnati at New York (night).

BASEBALL SCORES

International League

At Buffalo
Orioles .... 5 1 9 6 0 1 1 [redacted]
Buffalo ..... 0 1 0 0 0 2 [redacted]
Baltimore—Podogany and Devlin. Buffalo—Hamons and Radakovich.

At Toronto — First Game
Syracuse .... 0 0 1 0 0 3 0 0 1—5 10 2
Toronto ..... 1 0 0 0 0 1 4 3 x—9 9 4
Syracuse—Kalski and Kerns. Toronto—Crowson and George.

At Toronto — Second Game
Syracuse .... 2 0 [redacted]
Toronto ..... 0 0 [redacted]
Syracuse—Krall and Kerns. Toronto—Stein and George.

At Rochester — First Game
Newark ..... 0 2 0 0 0 0 0 0 0—2 10 0
Rochester ... 0 0 0 0 0 0 0 0 0—0 3 0
Newark—Houtz and Taylor. Rochester—Trotter and Martin.

At Rochester — Second Game
Newark ..... 0 0 [redacted]
Rochester ... 1 0 [redacted]
Newark—Suckey and Vangrofsky. Rochester Radler and Pratt.

Jersey City at Montreal, both games postponed.

National League

Cincinnati at New York, postponed.
Only game scheduled.

American League

At Chicago
Cleveland ... 0 0 0 0 0 2 2 3 0—7 12 0
Chicago ..... 1 0 0 0 0 0 0 0 0—1 7 0
Cleveland—Embree and McDonnell. Chicago—Grove and Tresh.

Washington at St. Louis, 9.30 P.M.
Only games scheduled.

ALL STAR
THE EVENING SUN
FINAL

Vol. 71—No. 18 | PAID CIRCULATION APRIL MORNING, 168,851 EVENING, 192,089 360,940 ‖ SUNDAY 275,260 | BALTIMORE, TUESDAY, MAY 8, 1945 | Entered as second-class matter at Baltimore Post Office | Zone 3 | 26 Pages | 3 Cents

VICTORY PROCLAIMED STORY OF SURRENDER

Scene At Signing Of Surrender By Nazis At Reims Is Depicted

Reims, France, May 7 [*AP—Delayed*]—Through an iron-faced Prussian general, speaking after he had finished signing the unconditional surrender of the Nazis, Germany pleaded today for mercy for the German people. On the wall behind his back was a huge chart tabulating Allied casualties.

He was Col. Gen. Gustaf Jodl, chief of staff of the German Army.

17 Correspondents There

On a big wooden table in front of him lay four identical documents to which he had just affixed his signature. There was one each for the United States, Britain, France and Russia. Each bore the words first written by President Roosevelt and Prime Minister Churchill at Casablanca: "Unconditional surrender."

Seventeen correspondents, including Edward Kennedy, of the Associated Press, were present at the signing and heard Jodl's plea.

Continues In German

General Jodl snapped to attention after signing the documents and said: "I want to say a word."

He spoke in English, but then continued in German saying:

"General, with this signature, the people and German armed forces are, for better or worse, delivered into the victor's hands.

"In this war, which has lasted more than five years, both have achieved and suffered more than perhaps any other people in the world. In this hour I can only express the hope that the victor will treat them with generosity."

After Jodl finished speaking and sat down, a moment passed in dead silence and then the German representatives were taken down the hall to meet General Eisenhower.

Eisenhower Behind Desk

Eisenhower and his deputy, Air Chief Marshal Sir Arthur Tedder, were waiting, standing behind Eisenhower's small desk.

Jodl entered first, followed by Gen. Admiral Hans George Friedeburg and then by Colonel Poleck, a supply expert.

Poleck glanced once at the Allied officers and then studied the floor. Friedeburg looked out the windows. Only Jodl, his bald head gleaming beneath naked electric light bulbs, looked the American and British commanders in the face.

Another Moment Of Silence

Again there was a moment of heavy silence.

Then Eisenhower spoke. He was brief and terse as always. His voice was cold and stern and his steel blue eyes were hard.

In a few clipped sentences, he made it plain that Germany was a defeated nation and that henceforth orders to the German people would come from the Allies. He said they would be obeyed.

Then the Germans filed out. It was over.

Nazi Germany had ceased to exist.

The war had ended.

Two Days Of Negotiations

The signatures of the document of surrender climaxed two days of negotiations in the cathedral city, scene of many dramatic events in European history. Possibly what was born here today will be known as the "Peace of Reims."

The doom of the Third Reich was sealed in the war room of the Allied supreme command's advanced headquarters in the big brick Ecole Professionelle, which in peacetime was a co-educational industrial school.

The signatories sat at a wooden table twenty feet long and ten feet wide, with its top painted black. The war room itself is L-shaped, about 30 feet long and 30 wide on the outer sides of the "L."

How Delegates Were Seated

Its walls are Nile green beaverboard covered with battle maps.

The delegates were seated as follows:

LIEUT. GEN. SIR FREDERICK E.

[Continued On Page 2, Column 3]

'Heil Hitler' Is Banned For German Forces

New York, May 8 (AP)—A communiqué issued by the German high command today and broadcast over the radio identifying itself as Flensburg announced that henceforth the greeting "Heil Hitler" would be banned within the German armed forces.

The broadcast communiqué was reported by the FCC.

FIRST PICTURES OF GERMAN SURRENDER—This was the scene at General Eisenhower's headquarters at Reims, France, yesterday when the unconditional surrender of all German forces was signed. From left are: Front, with backs to camera: General Admiral Freideburg, German Navy commander in chief; General Jodl, German chief of staff; General Oxenius, aide to Jodl. Rear, seated at table and facing camera: Lieut. Gen. Sir F. E. Morgan, staff deputy; General Sevez, of France; Admiral Burroughs, commanding general of Allied naval expeditionary forces; General Smith, chief of staff to Eisenhower; General Chermiaeff, of Russia; General Susloparoff, of Russia; American General Spaatz; Air Marshal Robb (or General Bull—not definite which), and Colonel Zenkovitch, interpreter (at end of table). [AP wirephoto from Signal Corps radiophoto.] [For other surrender pictures, see Page 2.]

Sunday To Be Day Of Thanksgiving

London, May 8 (AP)—The guns fell silent on the Western Front tonight and President Truman and Prime Minister Churchill proclaimed the victory to the world.

All hostilities were ordered ended by 6.01 P.M. (E.W.T.). The cease-fire orders had gone out earlier from supreme headquarters. The United States 3d Army, it was disclosed, had been ordered to hold its fire at 2 A.M. (E.W.T.) yesterday, six hours after Germany's representatives had acknowledged their defeat to General Eisenhower.

Premier Stalin was yet to proclaim full victory, but he announced two triumphs by his Red Army virtually eliminating the last resistance on the Russian sector. These were the capture of Dresden in Germany and Olmuetz in Czechoslovakia. The Czech-controlled radio at Prague said cease-fire orders had gone out there both to the Germans and Czechoslovak forces.

Terms Being Ratified In Berlin

Churchill announced Russia's Marshal Gregory Zhukov and other Allied representatives were ratifying and confirming the peace at Berlin today.

Eisenhower said his victory had been made possible by "teamwork not only among all the Allies participating, but among all the services, land, sea and air."

Both Churchill and Truman summoned their nations to a battle to the finish against Japan.

Eisenhower observed:

"The victory bells of Europe are sounding Japan's doom."

Supreme Allied Headquarters in a special communiqué said: "Allied expeditionary forces have been ordered to cease offensive operations, but will maintain their present position until the surrender becomes effective."

Germany's unconditional capitulation to the Western Allies and Russia was signed at 2.41 A.M. (French time) Monday (8.41 P.M., E.W.T., Sunday), this communiqué announced.

Surrender Terms Are Listed

Supreme headquarters announced the Germans agreed to:

Order all resistance halted.

Yield all ships and aircraft unscuttled and undamaged.

Insure compliance with all further orders from the Allied Supreme Commander and the Soviet High Command.

The surrender document specified that nothing it contained limited or restricted any terms which might later be imposed on the Reich.

"In the event of the German High Command or any of the forces under their control failing to act in accordance with this act of surrender," it warned, "the Supreme Commander . . . and the Soviet High Command will take such punitive or other action as they deem appropriate."

Thus was effected the uncompromising dictate of unconditional surrender laid down by Churchill and the late President Roosevelt at Casablanca.

Churchill Cautions Britain On Jap War

London, May 8 (AP)—Prime Minister Churchill, proclaiming the victory in Europe, said today that the unconditional surrender of Germany "will be ratified and confirmed at Berlin" and that hostilities will cease one minute after midnight, British time.

(This will be 6.01 P.M., E.W.T.)

Churchill, officially bearing out yesterday's dispatch of Edward Kennedy, of the Associated Press, said the German capitulation occurred at General Eisenhower's headquarters at Reims at 2.41 A.M. Monday.

The capitulation was made simultaneously to the Allies and the Soviet high command, with General Jodl, representative of the German high command and of Grand Admiral Doenitz, signing the pact for Germany.

Warns Nazis Still Fighting

"Today," Churchill said, "this agreement will be ratified and confirmed at Berlin, where Air Chief Marshal Tedder, deputy supreme commander of the Allied Expeditionary Force, and General Tassigny will sign on behalf of General Eisenhower."

He said the Germans are "still in places resisting the Russians," but added that if resistance continued after midnight "they will, of course, deprive themselves of the protection of the laws of war and will be attacked from all quarters by the Allied troops."

He said it was not surprising that commands of the German high command should not be obeyed immediately, because of disorganization.

Cautions On Jap War

But he added immediately that—as a result of information furnished by Eisenhower—it should not prevent "us from celebrating today and tomorrow as Victory-in-Europe days."

"The German war is therefore at an end," he said.

He reminded Britain at the same time that "we may allow ourselves a brief period of rejoicing, but let us not forget for a moment the toil and efforts that lie ahead."

"Japan, with all her treachery and greed," he declared, "remains unsubdued. The injury she has inflicted on the United States and other countries and her detestable cruelties call for justice and retribution.

Palace Area Packed

"We must now devote all our strength and resources to the completion of our task both at home and abroad."

Churchill closed his historic message with these words:

"Advance Britannia! Long live the cause of freedom! God save the King!"

As he ended, buglers from the Scots Guard blew their ceremonial sign of victory.

At Buckingham Palace, packed thousands cheered in exultation as the King and Queen with the two

[Continued On Page 2, Column 7]

Teamwork Led To Victory, Ike Says

Paris, May 8 (AP)—General Eisenhower in a Victory Order of the Day told members of the Allied Expeditionary Force today that their great triumph was achieved by "working and fighting together in a single and indestructible partnership" and by a "unification of air, ground and naval power that will stand as a model in our time."

The Supreme Allied Commander said:

"The crusade on which we embarked in the early summer of 1944 has reached its glorious conclusion. It is my especial privilege, in the name of all nations represented in this theater of war, to commend each of you for the valiant performance of duty.

"Heart Overflowing"

"Though these words are feeble, they come from the bottom of a heart overflowing with pride in your loyal service and admiration for you as warriors. Your accomplishments at sea, in the air, on the ground and in the field of supply have astonished the world.

"Even before the final week of the conflict you had put 5,000,000 of the enemy permanently out of the war. You have taken in stride military tasks so difficult as to be classed by many doubters as impossible. You have confused, defeated and destroyed your savagely fighting foe.

"On the road to victory you have endured every discomfort and privation and have surmounted every obstacle ingenuity and desperation could throw in your path. You did not pause until our front was firmly joined up with the great Red Army coming from the East and other Allied forces coming from the South.

Model Of Unification

"Full victory in Europe has been attained. Working and fighting together in single and indestructible partnership you have achieved a perfection in the unification of air,

[Continued On Page 2, Column 7]

Great Power To Hit Japs, Truman Warns

By Joseph H. Short
[Sunpapers Staff Correspondent]

Washington, May 8—President Truman announced to the people of America today the "glorious hour" of Germany's unconditional surrender and warned the Japanese that the United Nations could now turn loose on them the greatest war machine in the history of the world.

The President called upon the Japanese to surrender unconditionally, too, and advised them that "does not mean the extermination or enslavement of the Japanese people."

In announcing victory in Europe, Mr. Truman carefully avoided any use of the popular term "V-E Day," and White House sources later made it clear that for the United States no formal V-E day was proclaimed.

Instead, the President—in keeping with his announced wish that the European victory should not be made the occasion for unrestrained celebration—set aside next Sunday as "a day of prayer."

Promptly at 9 A.M. (E.W.T.), the Chief Executive went on the radio to confirm the widely-heralded capitulation of the German army and to call upon "every American," in his rejoicing, "to stick to his post until the last battle is won."

"Let No Man Abandon Post"

"Until that day, let no man abandon his post or slacken his efforts," he urged.

Then, in a proclamation which he personally read, the President fixed Sunday, May 13—Mother's Day—as a day of prayer, calling on "the people of the United States, whatever their faith, to unite in offering joyful thanks to God for the victory we have won and to pray that He will support us to the end of our present struggle and guide us into the way of peace."

"I also call upon my countrymen," he said, "to dedicate this day of prayer to the memory of those who have given their lives to make possible our victory."

The proclamation reminded that "the victory won in the West must now be won in the East."

The President also released telegrams of congratulation which he dispatched to Prime Minister Churchill,

[Continued On Page 3, Column 1]

Surrender Communique Issued By SHAEF

Allied Headquarters, Paris, May 8 (AP)—Special Supreme Headquarters Communique No. 8:

All German land, sea and air forces in Europe were unconditionally surrendered to the Allied Expeditionary Force and simultaneously to the Soviet high command at 0141 hours, central European time, May 7 (2.41 A.M., summer time).

The surrender terms, which will become effective at 2301 hours, central European time, May 8 (11.01 P.M., central European time, or 12.01 A.M. summer time), were signed by an officer of the German command.

Allied expeditionary forces have been ordered to cease offensive operations, but will maintain their present position until the surrender becomes effective.

WPB Revokes Its Order Against 'Brown-Out'

Washington, May 8 (AP)—The "brown-out" is ended.

The War Production Board today revoked its order against unnecessary lighting immediately after President Truman's proclamation of victory in Europe.

It was the first lifting of the so-called "morale" curbs on civilian activity imposed during last winter's military setbacks.

The midnight curfew and the prohibition against horse racing are expected to be dissolved shortly, but no action has been taken yet.

Ends Ban On Electric Power

The revocation signed by Edward Falck, director of WPB's Office of War Utilities, ends the ban on the use of electric power for advertising, promotional, decorative, ornamental or sign lighting.

It was imposed as a coal-saving measure, although its effect on fuel conservation was not great, being estimated by Falck at 500,000 tons in the more than three months of its effectiveness.

Urges Conservation

"Now that we can shift from a two-front to a one-front war," Falck said, "it is felt that a mandatory order is no longer required, although all-out conservation of fuel

[Continued On Page 6, Column 5]

Flashes

Seyss-Inquart Arrested

With the Canadian 1st Army, Holland, May 8 (AP) — Arthur Seyss-Inquart, German Commissioner for the Netherlands, was placed under arrest today by the Canadian 1st Army. He faces war crimes charges.

Tydings To Leave Soon

Washington, May 8 (AP)—Senator Millard E. Tydings (D., Md.) today disclosed he would leave for the Philippines some time next week with the special nine-man committee appointed by President Truman.

No News Agency Faces Penalty, General Says

Paris, May 8 (AP)—General Eisenhower informed correspondents at supreme headquarters today that no action could be taken against a news agency or organization for the act of any individual correspondent or correspondents.

For nearly seven hours yesterday afternoon, after the surrender story was published, all Associated Press filing facilities from the European theater were suspended, but later this was lifted for all the Associated Press staff except Edward Kennedy, chief of the Associated Press' Western front staff.

Another Man Suspended

This afternoon the suspension order was imposed also on Morton Gudebrod, member of the Associated Press Paris staff, whose assignment is to supervise the distribution of AP service to the French press. This service supplied Kennedy's story to Paris newspapers with the approval of French censorship.

The AP was informed that Gudebrod was suspended, as in the case of Kennedy, pending the outcome of Supreme Headquarters' investigation.

54 Sign Request

Eisenhower replied by telephone through his deputy chief of staff, Major General Sir Frederick E. Morgan, to a letter signed by 54 correspondents at SHAEF which asked that all Associated Press correspondents in this theater be suspended until 24 hours after the official announcement of Germany's surrender.

The correspondents made the request as a result of what supreme headquarters described as an "unauthorized" transmission of Kennedy's story yesterday of the Reims surrender.

General Is Checking

Brig. Gen. Frank A. Allen, Jr., director of Supreme Headquarters' public relations division, told a meeting summoned by correspondents that the original suspension was imposed at his own order "so that I might check SHAEF communications to determine if there had been any violation by the Associ-

[Continued On Page 4, Column 6]

The Weather

Fair, cooler tonight; Wednesday, sunny, cool.

Detailed report on Page 21

BARILLARI WINS BIRD HILL JOB; PFEIFER HURT

RODGER H. PIPPEN

SPORTS EDITOR, SAYS:

Unless some badly needed pitching help is secured for our Orioles from Cleveland or elsewhere before they open their first northern trip in Montreal next Thursday, Manager Tommy Thomas faces many unpleasant hours.

With the present pitching staff our 1944 champs won't finish in the first division. The Birds were in front in three of the four lost games and the mound men faltered. Hooks' wildness was responsible for the fourth defeat.

So far, twenty-year-old Guy Coleman has turned in the best hurling job. He shut out Buffalo last Wednesday, 2 to 0, allowing only two hits. For three innings of the first game yesterday he looked like a ten thousand dollar beauty. Only nine men faced him in those first three innings, and his knuckle ball was behaving so beautifully for him that Davis and Drake took third strikes with their bats on their shoulders. His knuckler is a fadeaway or drop, and is a most effective pitch when it breaks. Carl Hubbell of the Giants southpawed his way to fame and fortune with a screw ball, which is a somewhat similar pitch. All star hurlers have one pet pitch and it is possible that this pint-sized youngster will be Baltimore's surprise package this summer. Coleman is fairly fast, and what is more important, has good control to go along with his knuckler.

The Canucks got to Guy for three runs in the fourth, but his troubles started with a scratch single to short. The batsman, hitting a knuckler, got only a piece of the ball and the result was a slow, twisting roller to Slugger Braun. Later the visitors hit Coleman hard and he was relieved. And it might well be said here that the Canucks gave every indication that they will make trouble and plenty of it for opposing pitchers this year. They have three or four real good hitters, including Ira Houck, the right fielder, from Woodsboro, Md.

* * *

Skaff Gets Two Homers

As the Birds split with Toronto, Baltimore's batting stars yesterday were Ralph Kress, Frankie Skaff and Ken Braun. Five hits, including two homers, were pounded out by Skaff. A triple by Braun in the fifth inning with three on bases really won that game. Kress also made five hits. Another bingle worth mentioning was a run-producing single over second by Coleman in the fifth. With the infield in, this young hurler placed the hit by reaching out for an outside ball. In the first inning he also dropped a perfect bunt down third, beating it out. This boy has a lot of natural ability and he may gain in stature.

All ball players have off days occasionally and the same thing goes for umpires. For that reason, no violent adjectives will be hurled from this column today in the general direction of Felerski and Tobin, who did the guessing in yesterday's game. They were in hot water all afternoon with players of both clubs. Tobin even got mixed up once on the count on a Toronto batsman on balls and strikes.

* * *

Has Washington Uncovered A Star?

Speaking of small pitchers, Lawton Carver, sports editor of the International News Service, is out with a prediction that the Washington Americans have come up with a real budding star in Parino Pieretti. He says all this twenty-three-year-old right-hander needs is experience.

When on Saturday afternon he toiled 13 innings against the Yankees a couple of Washington veterans greeted him as he came off the hill and slapped him on the back. Some of the fans clutched at his hands. The story would be much better if he had won the game. He lost it finally by 2 to 1, but in the meantime had gone the route where Ernie Bonham had failed for the Yankees and he lost decision to the veteran Jim Turner, who finished for the winners.

Pieretti won 26 games in the Pacific Coast League last season and was bought immediately thereafter by the Senators. They must be running out of pitchers in Cuba.

In his only previous major league start he had to go 12 innings to beat the Philadelphia Athletics, which gives you an indication of how a guy can break in the hard way.

Twelve innings to win from the A's, then 13 to lose to the Yanks is what might be called doing it over the long haul, not once but twice.

He stands only five feet, eight inches. But he showed how to go about doing a man-sized job, especially against the Yanks in that defeat. He allowed 10 hits and toyed around with the hitters to walk 11 of them, but he offset all that in the clutch by leaving 17 Yankees stranded on the bases, seven of these in the tenth, eleventh and twelfth frames.

In the eleventh, for instance, the Yanks loaded up the sacks on him with one out and couldn't get a man home. In all the Yanks had runners on the bases in 11 of the 13 innings. They still had to go all out to finally win it in the fourth extra frame.

This from a kid who had never been to New York before. Either he is one of the best in the clutch the game has seen or the Yankees are the worst. Perhaps it is a little of both.

* * *

Kochan Promises Real Fistic Fireworks

You can look for real action when Georgie Kochan, middleweight, climbs into the ring, and this former Coast Guardsman should draw a big house when he tackles Johnny Carter at the Coliseum tonight. As was the case with Jack Dempsey, Kochan's defense is his offense, and he is always willing to slug it out. He will be a six-to-five favorite tonight, although Carter is coming here with a recent victory over Cocoa Kid.

Oriole Pitching Bogs, But Punch Is Picking Up

By HUGH TRADER, JR.

As the Orioles close out their first home stand of the season tonight, holding third place in the derby with a five-and-four record after yesterday's split with Toronto before 11,020 partisans, the club has won the stamp of approval from the city's baseball fandom in all but the pitching.

Newcomers like Red Kress, Joe Mellendick, Jimmy Tropea and Al Barillari all have gained favor, and the vast improvement of little Kenny Braun (who, believe it or not, tops the club in runs batted in with 10) makes for even more optimism and interest.

But the pitching has proved inadequate, especially over the past week end.

TAKES EXAM TODAY

That was recognized during the early stages of spring camp, for no club can lose three hurlers like Embree, West and Lowry, who won 47 games among them, and Manager Tommy Thomas was the first to see and admit that the Birds' greatest need was for pitching help from Cleveland. At least two more experienced hurlers are a necessity for a winner, and you can make that three if Bobo Palica, scheduled to do the elbowing tonight, passes his physical induction exam today and is accepted for military duty.

But, even so, we don't think the pitching is as bad as it has shown in the last four games. What has hurt, but can't be helped, are the sore arms of both Lefty Ed Henry and Yock Smith, who took brief turns yesterday, but had to retire. Henry, a southpaw with good speed and control, would have been particularly helpful against such left-handed power as displayed by the Royals and Leafs.

Along these lines, handy-man Barillari has won himself a starting job on the mound. Al showed enough stuff in his one-inning relief role in the nightcap yesterday as the Orioles lost, 8-5, after winning the opener, 8-7, to indicate to Skipper Two-T that the lad will be of aid on the hill.

Others news concerns the injuries Sherman Lollar and Freddy Pfeifer, both of whom will be sidelined until the Birds open in Montreal Thursday.

KRESS AT SECOND

Lollar sprained his ankle in a slide in the first game. While he rests Jimmy Devlin will get his chance, and Devlin is capable of the job. He's a good receiver and a dangerous sticker. Pfeifer may be out longer. Fred has been troubled with a sore back all spring, playing well in spite of it, though he wasn't hitting, and yesterday wrenched it painfully as he pivoted on a double play.

That brought Kress in on second base from the outfield, Tropea taking over the left pasture, and the redhead had himself quite a time yesterday. He poked in five hits, one his third homer of the year; drove in three runs and hoisted his average to a leading .395 figure. He figured in one double play at second, handled two other chances and got involved in a verbal brawl with Greek George, Toronto catcher, when the latter protested so vehemently over Frankie Skaff's homer in the nightcap that he was ejected by Ump Tobin. The incident created a turbulent scene as the Leafs stormed Tobin and one fan made threatening gestures at Harry Davis, Toronto manager.

So Kress will stay at second base for the time being, his punch giving the Birds five .300 or better hitters. Tropea has a mark of .429, Skaff .367, Mellendick .333 and Lollar .300. Braun is rapping .273.

SKAFF STARS

Little Guy Coleman, shut-out winner in his first start, came back yesterday with another good effort, though he didn't finish. He chucked seven and two-third innings, allowing seven hits and three earned runs and had a 6-to-3 lead going into the seventh mainly through Skaff's second-ining homer and Braun's fifth-inning triple with the bases full. But Guy faded in the eighth and Johnny Podgajny took over to gain credit for the victory as he held the Leafs in the pinch and the Birds got the winning runs in the eighth off Crowson on Riley's walk, Kress' single, a walk to Mellendick, Latshaw's long fly to right and Skaff's double.

Skaff, indeed, went right along with Kress at the plate and also slammed five hits for the day. Frankie homered and doubled in the nightcap, and, along with Red, who poled a three-run homer, helped mightily to hold the Birds in the ball game. But the Leafs bombarded George Hooks for six runs in the opening two rounds and picked up another pair off Smith in the fifth on Lady's hit and an error. Jim Gruzdis stole home with the Leafs' eighth run, an art in which the little outfielder is proficient.

"WHY, YOU BLASTED . . ."—Excited? Who's excited? Well, you can see for yourself and almost hear Umpire Jim Tobin and Charley (Greek) George, Toronto catcher, as they exchange thunderous opinions of each other while battling over whether Frankie Skaff's homer was fair or foul in the fourth inning of the nightcap game yesterday at the Stadium between the Orioles and Leafs. At any rate, they're getting a good look at each other's tonsils. They both appear to be slightly hard of hearing but George heard Ump Tobin clearly enough when he told him to scram from the field. And Skaff's homer is still fair, even though the Birds lost the game, 8-5, after winning the opener, 8 to 7.

KERPLUNK, RIGHT IN THE BREAD-BASKET!—Jimmy Tropea, Oriole outfielder, tries to race from first to third on Red Kress' single in the first inning of the second game yesterday at the Stadium, but George Souter, Toronto third-sacker, takes the peg from the outfield and tags Tropea smack-dab in the pantry. The Leafs got a big early lead and went on to win the nightcap, 8 to 5, after the Birds had copped the opener, 8 to 7, before 11,020 fans.

Major Leagues Flag Winners Hit Stride

By LES CONKLIN

NEW YORK, April 30—(I. N. S.).—The major league pennant races began to assume a semblance of normalcy today with both of last year's flag winners, the Cardinals and the Browns, making a clean sweep of their double-headers in Sunday's twin bills.

The Cards' two triumprs over Cincinnati, 2 to 1 and 8 to 3, put the champion Red Birds only a game and a half behind the New York Giants in the National League race.

GIANTS IN FRONT

The Giants eased back into first place by weird process of losing their single game to Brooklyn, 4 to 3, while the Chicago Cubs slipped back into the second notch by dropping both ends of their twin bill with Pittsburgh, 6 to 2 and 5 to 4.

While the Browns are still wallowing in the depths of sixth place in the American League scramble, they are not far off the pace. The Brownies are only two games behind the Chicago White Sox, who managed to hold on to first place by a gnat's whisker despite the loss of two games to St. Louis, 3 to 2 and 10 to 4. Hot on the heels of the White Sox are the Detroit Tigers, who split a twin bill with the Cleveland, and the New York Yankees, who divided honors with Washington.

HURLS FIVE-HITTER

The Cards took the Reds over the rapids in the first game behind in the five-hit pitching of Max Lanier. A double by Rookie Jim Mallory of the Cards was the pay-off blow in the nightcap.

Elwood Roe and Nick Strincevich were the Pittsburgh hurlers who made the Cubs bite the dust twice.

The Giants bowed to the four-hit pitching of Hal Gregg of Brooklyn and a three-run homer by the veteran Dixie Walker.

JAVERY BLANKS PHILS

Big Al Javery of the Boston Braves forgot all about his alleged sore arm as he blanked the Phillies, 1 to 0, and scored the only run of the game after hitting a single. In the opener of the twin bill the Phils beat Jim Tobin, 5-to-3.

The St. Louis Browns racked up their third straight win the American League in beating the White Sox twice. Frank Mancuso's triple and a long fly by pinch hitter Gene Moore won the opener. In the nightcap the Sox handed a two-run lead to their veteran southpaw, Thornton Lee, but he couldn't hold it. Previously, Chicago was undefeated this season.

Steve Gromek of Cleveland blanked Detroit, 4 to 0, with five hits, and Detroit then won the second game by the same score with Dizzy Trout racking up his third win. Trout yielded only four hits, allowed no Cleveland runner to advance past second base, and helped himself to a home run.

YANKEES LOSE

Roger Wolff of Washington again beat the Yankees, 2 to 1, on Myatt's triple and Kuhel's single. It was a heart-breaking loss for the losing hurler, Atley Donald, who accounted for his team's only run with a homer. The Yanks took the opened, 13 to 4, when Rookie outfielder Russ Derry duplicated his opening-day feat of hitting two homers.

Rookies led the luckless Boston Red Sox to a double triumph over the Athletics, 2 to 0 and 6 to 3, the second game going 13 innings. In the opener Dave Ferriss, recently discharged from the Army Air Force, held the A's to five hits and made three himself. The nightcap was broken up when Walters doubled, Steiner and Metkovich singled and Johnson hit a fly. Johnson had tied the score in the ninth with a two-run homer with two out.

IS THIS YOUR PET?—Jean Groin, 3303 Edmondson avenue, is shown above with the young male dog, part chow, which followed her home from near the Astor Theater on Popular Grove street last Friday night. The pet was wearing a small leather collar. If you can make proper identification, phone Gilmor 7735.

Didrikson Golf Victor

SAN ANTONIO, April 30—(U. P.).—San Antonio golf fans grudgingly conceded today that Babe Didrickson Zaharias probably is the nation's top-ranking woman golfer.

The Babe defeated the home-town favorite, Betty Jameson, by ten strokes in yesterday's wind-up of their 72-hole challenge match. Mrs. Zaharias closed out the math on the sixty-fourth hole after Miss Jameson missed a six-foot putt, but they played out the remaining eight holes in deference to the 3,000 onlookers.

Mrs. Zaharias held a four-stroke lead after the first 36 holes at Los Angeles two weeks ago. At the end of 18 holes in the second round, which was played on Miss Jameson's home course, San Antonio Country Club, Mrs. Zaharias said they would stage a shorter match in the near future for wounded soldiers at McCloskey General Hospital in Texas.

Kochan Favored To Trim Carter

Despite the fact he holds a smart victory over the formidable Cocoa Kid, young Johnny Carter, Philadelphia middleweight, appears destined to be cast in the underdog role when he squares off with Georgie Kochan, New York in the ten-round windup on the Century Club's weekly fight card tonight at the Coliseum. Pre-fight spectators are quoting the shifty Kochan a 6-to-5 choice.

Carter, principal in a number of stirring bouts before Century Club audiences, can cut himself a huge chunk of fame if he follows up the Cocoa victory with a clean-cut triumph over Kochan tonight. Johnny's win over Cocoa moved him right to the front rank of the middleweight class and he will further strengthen his lofty position if he puts the skids under Kochan.

Kochan, ex-Coast Guardsman and one of the most feared operatives in the 160-pound division, is a prime favorite with local fans who fully appreciate the thunder he carries in each fist. Georgie's superior punching power and his wide edge in experience qualify him to be favored over the less experienced, but ambitious Carter.

The Kochan-Carter bout is expected to prove a fitting climax to a 32-round card that shapes up as one of the finest programs of the new season. Slated to tangle in the eight-round semiwindup is Johnny Pappas from Reading, and the ever-dangerous Howard Bennett, local star. Pappas will be gunning for his third straight win in the Coliseum ring, but in the more experienced Bennett, the young Greek light heavyweight encounters the toughest of his brief, but meteoric career.

A newcomer will appear on the card in Leon Szymurski of Philadelphia, who will meet Charley Pope of Washington in a special six. Two fours complete the fine program.

SPORT NEWS IN BRIEF

LONG BEACH, Cal., April 30—(U. P.).—Red Ruffing, former New York Yankee pitching star and coach of the Sixth Ferrying Group Army baseball team, left today for a new assignment at Camp Lee, Va.

BASEBALL TRADE

CLEVELAND, Ohio, April 30—(I. N. S.).—Three Detroit and Cleveland players exchanged uniforms today as the result of a deal in which Outfielder Roy Cullenbine went to the Tigers in exchange for Outfielder Don Ross and Second Baseman Lambert Meyer

CABECILLA WINS

HAVANA, April 30—(A. P.).—Cabecilla, owned by R. F. Crusellas and ridden by Jose Marrero, took command at the half-mile post to win the $1,500 Camaguey Stakes by a length at Oriental Park yesterday. Tesoro was second and Serapio third.

STADIUM LINE-UPS

Following are the probable line-ups for tonight's game at the Stadium at 8.30 o'clock between the Orioles and Toronto Leafs:

ORIOLES		LEAFS	
6	Tropea, lf.	1	Theole, ss.
5	Riley, rf.	14	Riggio, cf.
23	Kress, 2b.	2	Davis, 1b.
7	Mell'ndick, cf.	11	Houck, rf.
3	Latshaw, 1b.	8	George, c.
25	Skaff, 3b.	15	Drake, lf.
9	Devlin, c.	10	Souter, 3b.
1	Braun, ss.	3	Ogorek, 2b,
19	Palica, p.	22	Stein, p.
10	Smith, p.	17	Hamlin, p.
11	Coleman, p.	18	Martin, p.
12	Van Slate, p.	19	Snavely, p.
14	Rochevot, p.	20	Smole, p.
15	Henry, p.	23	Jordan, p.
17	Jamison, p.	21	Cronin, p.
16	Hooks, p.	26	Johnson, p.
21	Skinner, p.	5	Richard, inf.
24	Podgajny, p.	7	Kratzer, c.
2	Barillari, utl.	9	Lady, c.
8	Lollar, c.	12	Gruzdis, outf.
27	Pfeifer, inf.	4	Castana, inf.
20	Sudol, 1b.		
22	Thomas, mgr.		

Time—8.30 P. M. Place—Stadium.

DOGS

Mrs. M. Batton, 1733 Lamont avenue, has appealed to The News-Post for assistance in recovering a female spitz, gray and white, which has been missing from the above address since last Wednesday. The pet is wearing a collar with license No. 11792, and was last seen in the vicinity of Lamont avenue and Holbrook street. If you have seen this dog please contact Mrs. Batton at the above address.

W. Cooper To Be Inducted Tomorrow

ST. LOUIS, April 30—(U. P.). Catcher Walker Cooper, receiver end of the Cardinals' famous brother act, is slated for induction at Jefferson barracks tomorrow.

Cooper, originally scheduled for induction today, said transfer board papers reset his appearance.

CAROLINA LEAGUE

Danville, 7; Durham, 6.
Raleigh, 5; Burlington, 4.
Greensboro, 8; Leaksville, 7.
Winston-Salem at Martinsville; rain.

Ed McKeever Here Friday

Ed McKeever, newly appointed football coach at Cornell University, will be the guest of honor at a dinner given by the Cornell Club of Maryland Friday evening at the Engineers' Club.

After the dinner McKeever will discuss the football prospects at Ithaca.

COLISEUM RING CARD

Following is the complete program of boxing which the Century Club will present tonight at the Coliseum. Probable winners are indicated by capitals, and probable odds follow:

TEN ROUNDS

GEORGIE KOCHAN vs. Johnny Carter; 6 to 5 on Kochan.

EIGHT ROUNDS

JOHNNY PAPPAS vs. Howard Bennett; 6 to 5 on Bennett.

SIX ROUNDS

ERNIE POPE vs. Leon Szymurski; even money.

FOUR ROUNDS

EDGAR POE vs. Kid Lewis; even money.

EDDIE DAVIS vs. Jim Driscoll; even money.

Time of First Bout—8.45 P. M.

MUSSOLINI WITH REICHSMARSHAL GOERING DURING LAST VISIT TO GERMANY
Ex-Premier of Italy was shadow of former self when executed by Partisan troops.

PAYS PENALTY FOR DICTATOR'S LOVE
Clara Petacci, young mistress, among those executed.

TYPICAL STUDY OF FASCIST DICTATOR ADDRESSING HIS FOLLOWERS
Mussolini loved balconies, ceremonies, crowds and intrigue.

BENITO VISITS HITLER AT RUSSIAN FRONT IN 1941
Studies war map as Der Fuehrer outlines plan of Soviet campaign.

Mussolini Roared Way To Fame, Died A Traitor

By Associated Press.

Benito Mussolini, whose disfigured body lay last night in a Milan square on display before jeering, spitting crowds, was just a skinny, wrinkled caricature of the one-time chest-thumping dictator of Italy, who in 21 flamboyant years helped to plunge the world into its bloodiest and most destructive war.

The sixty-one-year-old former poor man's son and one-time country schoolmaster, who knew what it was to beg in the streets for his daily bread, reached heights of glory, but died a traitor's death—an international buffoon despised and hated. He had brought ruin to the Italy he had dreamed of building to a chief world power.

TOO RADICAL AS TEACHER

Mussolini was born July 29, 1883, in the province of Forli (Romagna), the son of a blacksmith. Poverty was his lot through boyhood. Expelled from one school because he was rebellious, he attended a normal school, was graduated and became a rural school teacher, but his radical political theories clashed with his profession and he abandoned it.

He went to Switzerland, where he did odd jobs, lived in the parks, and frequently had to beg for food, but there he attended night school. Bern and Geneva expelled him, and he returned to Italy, where he was jailed seven times as a dangerous Socialist.

LED REVOLT IN MILAN

Once the government concentrated the entire Italian army about Milan to quell a revolutionary movement led by Mussolini.

Mussolini saw much service in the First World War, and bragged of 98 wounds he suffered from a bursting hand grenade. Typically, he refused an anesthetic while the surgeons worked on him.

He divorced himself from the Socialists after the war, and Fascism was born—his Fascism, in which he adjured his countrymen that "it is better to live a day as a lion than 100 years as a sheep."

Followers flocked at his standard, impressed by his colorful strongman posing, his roaring nationalist speech-making and his editorial effervescences.

SEIZES POWER

Fascism and Socialism became powerful opposing forces. There were street fighting, rioting, ambushes of leaders of both sides. A sort of political creeping paralysis gripped all Italy.

This Mussilini broke up with his march on Rome, completed October 28, 1922, the fateful day he skyrocketed to power. King Victor Emmanuel summoned him to form a new government and the self-styled "Il Duce" rode high until, on July 25, 1943, his former lieutenants forced him to resign as Premier and immured him on a lonely Apennine mountain top from which German paratroopers rescued him the following September 12.

PEOPLE LOVED BLUSTER

In this span of years the stocky dictator became a dramatic world figure, a sword rattler, whose word swayed the fate of millions in many lands.

Mussolini shouted and blustered and strutted and bluffed and most of his people loved it. His Blackshirts took care of those who didn't through an almost perfect system of espionage.

He defied the world and conquered Ethiopia, proclaimed the new Roman Empire, of which he had spoken for so many years, tendered the Ethiopian crown to Italy's king, and spoke with scorn of Great Britain and 51 other nations that opposed the Ethiopian conquest with economic sanctions. He withdrew Italy from the League of Nations.

FRIENDSHIP WITH HITLER

About this time his friendship with Adolf Hitler grew, and Il Duce led his nation down the road to disaster in 1937 and 1938 by cementing the friendship.

He backed Hitler's claims to the Sudeten section of Czechoslovakia. Hitler then gobbled up all of Bohemia and Moravia and established a protectorate over Slovakia.

To save face at home, Mussolini took over Albania for Italy in a surprise armed movement, and Il Duce and Der Fuehrer considered themselves a great team. They were the Axis, linked in May, 1939, in military and political treaty.

STABS FRANCE IN BACK

Mussolini took to the sidelines when Hitler and Great Britain came to grips, then stunned the world on June 10, 1940, with his "stab-in-the-back" declaration of war on France, when Britain seemed doomed.

He extended the war to Greece, and the Germans had to rescue him. He really began to lose face with the Libyan reverses.

His fleet dwindling under the growing might of Britain's and America's forces, Sicily, the invasion of the Italian mainland and a rain of Allied bombs on Italian soil and finally on Rome itself made clear his doom.

He rushed to Hitler in Berlin for help, but it was too late for help—his lieutenants had recognized their country was in ruins owing to his reckless conduct, and they forced him to resign, then they surrendered to the Allies.

After his rescue by German forces he was spirited to Northern Italy, where set up a puppet "neo-Fascist" government.

ABANDONED BY ALL

At the last, when Mussolini fled for his life before an uprising of patriots against his new government, he was reported to have lamented that "even Hitler" had bereft him and that he had no friends.

These are the last reported words of this one-time man of lust and many loves.

Italy knew little of his wife, Donna, because he believed a woman's place was in the home. She bore him three sons and two daughters, Edda, Vittorio, Bruno, Romano and Anna Maria. Bruno, an aviation captain, was killed in a bomber wreck in 1941.

Russians Charge U. S. With Cruelty

LONDON, April 30—(A. P.).—Russia asserted today that Soviet citizens liberated by the British-American Armies in the west have been held in Allied camps behind barbed wire "in absolutely intolerable conditions" and—in some cases—forced to work 10 or 12 hours daily.

The assertion was made in a Moscow broadcast quoting Col. Gen. S. I. Golikov, commissar for the repatriation of Soviet prisoners of war, who cited specificially an American-controlled camp in Britain and a British camp in Egypt.

Golikov, in an interview with the official Tass News Agency, maintained that in some instances Soviet officers had been transferred to the United States, "often without knowledge of our representatives." This, he said, constituted a violation of the Crimea Conference agreement on questions of repatriation.

The broadcast said Russia had been assured by a representative of the American administration that "all these violations and disorders would be eliminated."

The broadcast said the Allies had liberated about 150,000 Russians, but asserted only 35,000 had been returned home.

Execute Duce In North Italy

Continued from Page 1.

placed on a metal slab in the morgue courtyard.

Someone tilted the death slab upward so the bodies were visible to hundreds of persons still milling about the morgue, peering over the stone and plaster wall.

JACKET WAS TORN

In contrast to Mussolini's disfigured features, his mistress' face remained youthful and beautiful even in death. Her even, white teeth, now splotched with blood, were visible through her parted lips and her dark-brown, curly hair still hung in tidy ringlets.

Her slim torso was covered with an old pair of men's trousers tossed carelessly over her body. A pink silk garter belt and frilly blue underclothes were exposed.

By the time Mussolin's body reached the morgue his jacket had been torn away, revealing his barrel chest encased in a short-sleeved undershirt.

Sahring the morgue with Il Duce and Clara were the bodies of 16 of his henchmen, executed like them by Italian patriots after a "people's trial." They shared his final disgrace as they had the infamy of his life.

MET PARTISANS

One of Mussolini's final appearances in a leader's role occurred last week when he met with Italian Partisans, who had sponsored an uprising in Milan.

The committee told the Fascists that their terms for Milan were unconditional surrender, but Marshal Rodolfo Graziani said they must consult the Germans first.

Mussolini interrupted the conversation to say the Germans had betrayed them.

He asked for one hour's time to consider the surrender request and to communicate with the Germans. At the end of the hour he sent word that the terms had been rejected and he would leave Milan. He had already left the city on his final flight.

"Mussolini died badly," said Edouardo, leader of the 10-man firing squad which sent the dictator to his death.

When he was sentenced to death the man who had ruined his career through illusions of empire ironically cried:

"Let me save my life and I will give you an empire."

KILLED IN VILLA

The execution took place at 4.20 P. M. Saturday near the town of Dongo, on Lake Como. Mussolini was killed at the villa where he had been living since their arrest last Friday night with Clara Petacci, the Rome doctor's daughter who wanted to be a movie star.

(BACKGROUND NOTE: The Italian Government has condoned the summary execution of Benito Mussolini and other top-flight Fascists by northern patriots, and the Rome press hailed the deed as paving the way for the establishment of real democracy in Italy.)

Mussolini, the "jackal" to the last, was caught as he attempted to flee to Switzerland in a 30-car convoy, his bulky frame cloaked in a German military overcoat to escape detection.

Edouardo, who commands all the Partisan forces south of the Po, said:

"I heard Mussolini was arrested and taken to a villa near Dongo. None of us wanted Mussolini to be freed or escape to Switzerland so I sent ten men with an officer to Dongo.

"Mussolini was in the cottage on the hill with Signorina Petacci. When he saw Italian officers coming to him, he thought they had come to free him and he embraced his sweetheart.

"When he understood he was going to be tried he was shocked. But our men gave them both a trial and condemned them to death."

Edouardo said the 16 others were examined later and shot in the town square at Dongo. They included the brother of Signorina Petacci, who tried to escape. He was shot down as he ran.

The others, whose bodies were piled here with Mussolini's, included:

Alessandro Pavolini, former propaganda minister and secretary of state in Mussolini's Fascist puppet government.

Francesco Maria Barracu, under secretary to the Premier.

Dr. Paola Zerbino, Minister of the Interior.

Fernando Messazoma, Minister of Popular Culture.

Ruggero Romano, Minister of Public Works.

Augusto Liverrani, Undersecretary of State for Communications.

Goffredo Coppola, rector of the University of Bologna.

Paolo Porta, a Fascist party inspector.

Luigi Gatti, a prefect.

Ernesto Daquanno, editor of Stefani News Agency.

Mario Nudi, president of the Fascist Agricultural Association.

Nicola Bombacci, former Communist.

Italian Patriots Nab John Amery

LONDON, April 30—(U. P.).—Radio Milan said today that Italian patriots have arrested John Amery, thirty-three-year-old Briton, who denounced his British Cabinet Minister father to broadcast for the Nazi and Fascist radios. The elder Amery declined comment on his son's arrest.

CURTIN IN HOSPITAL

CANBERRA, April 30—(U. P.). Prime Minister John Curtin was admitted to a hospital today suffering from a congestion of the lungs.

CHICAGO
Cincinnati · Dayton

Swift air service is provided daily for Passengers, Air Mail and Air Express to Cincinnati, Dayton, Indianapolis and Chicago. Also to Nashville, Dallas, Fort Worth, San Antonio and Mexico City; El Paso, San Diego, Los Angeles and San Francisco. And via New York to Hartford, Providence and Boston. *Ticket Office:* 1014 O'Sullivan Bldg. Please make reservations well in advance.

Phone RIverside 2000

AMERICAN AIRLINES Inc.
ROUTE OF THE FLAGSHIPS

LIMIT YOUR LUGGAGE IN WARTIME. TRAVEL LIGHT!
★ BACK OUR BOYS WITH WAR BONDS ★

Join me at lunch... Have a Coke

...adding refreshment to the noon hour

You see them all over America at the lunch hour. Happy groups of girls enjoying wholesome food with ice-cold Coca-Cola. At the office, in your home, or at your favorite luncheon place, Coca-Cola makes good food taste better... makes lunch time refreshment time.

BOTTLED UNDER AUTHORITY OF THE COCA-COLA COMPANY BY

COCA-COLA BOTTLING COMPANY OF BALTIMORE

Coca-Cola — the global high-sign

"Coke" = Coca-Cola
You naturally hear Coca-Cola called by its friendly abbreviation "Coke". Both mean the quality product of The Coca-Cola Company.

© 1945 The C-C Co.

Mussolini Executed, Trampled, Spat Upon

THE BALTIMORE NEWS-POST
AN INDEPENDENT NEWSPAPER
The Largest Evening Circulation in the Entire South
7 HOME FINAL

THE WEATHER

Clear, cool tonight. Tuesday, sunny, little warmer.

Detailed Weather Report Page 19

Read The Baltimore News-Post for complete, accurate war coverage. It is the only Baltimore newspaper possessing the three great wire services—
ASSOCIATED PRESS
INTERNATIONAL NEWS SERVICE
UNITED PRESS

VOL. CXLVI.—NO. 147 Entered as second-class matter at Baltimore Postoffice. MONDAY EVENING, APRIL 30, 1945 PRICE 3 CENTS

Report New Nazi Peace Offer

FALL OF BERLIN NEAR, REDS SAY

Hearst Newspapers Give Scholarship To U. Of Maryland

(Pictures On Page 11)

By ALDINE R. BIRD

Responsibility of American citizenship "invites and insures disaster" without knowledge of America's great past, William Randolph Hearst yesterday declared upon the establishment of a four-year scholarship and three-year fellowship in the American Civilization Studies of the University of Maryland by The Baltimore News-Post and Sunday American.

The noted publisher declared that it is the duty of the schools and colleges of the nation to teach American citizens the history of American civilzation, and added:

"With full information and sincere purpose, the obligation of good citizenship can be successfully exercised."

PRESENTED $50,000 FUND

The scholarship, for high school graduates, and the fellowship for college graduates, of the United States, were established through the presentation of $50,000 to the University of Maryland by C. Dorsey Warfield, publisher of the Hearst newspapers in Baltimore, on the occasion of the eighty-second birthday of Mr. Hearst, and each will bear Mr. Hearst's name.

In presenting the fund at College Park, Mr. Warfield read the following message from Mr. Hearst:

SAN FRANCISCO, CALIFORNIA
April 26, 1945

W. M. BASKERVILL AND C. DORSEY WARFIELD

I am very happy that The Baltimore News-Post and Sunday American has devoted a part of its available funds to the presentation of a scholarship and a fellowship to the University of Maryland for its admirable course in the History of American Civilization.

This offering by The News-Post and Sunday American is a fine practical expression of the deep and earnest interest which the Hearst Newspapers have shown for many years in support of comprehensive courses in American History in the schools and colleges.

It has always seemed to me that in a democracy where the citizen is the rightful and final source of all power in government, his most essential study should be the history of his own country,—the country he is privileged to govern and obligated to govern wisely and well.

And since that country has developed from a trackless wilderness to become the greatest and the richest and happiest of all civilized nations in the short space of 150 years, it is his especial duty to learn and know what fundamental principles and sustained policies have made it great and prosperous, and to make sure in his labors of government that these principles and policies shall not be neglected nor forgotten, but shall continue to be faithfully applied in order that the liberties of his great country shall continue to exist and the prosperity and happiness of himself and of his fellow citizens shall continue to increase.

With full information and sincere purpose the obligation of good citizenship can be successfully exercised.

But responsibility without knowledge invites and, in fact, insures disaster.

Consequently it would seem that the first duty of the schools and colleges of this American Republic is to teach American citizens the History of American Civilization.

And the first duty of the American Press is to support the schools and colleges in the education and graduation of good American citizens, and to continue to inform and aid the citizen in after-life in the performance of his vital democratic obligations.

WILLIAM RANDOLPH HEARST.

In accepting the gift, Dr. Byrd, president of the university, paid high tribute to the Hearst newspapers and to their publisher in the following telegram to Mr. Hearst at his home in California:

"In accepting the gift of The Baltimore News-Post and Sunday American to establish a fellowship and scholarship in your honor the University of Maryland is proud to play its part in rediscovering and perpetuating the ideals on which our Government has become powerful in world councils and has provided for the American people rights and liberties and economic advantages such as are enjoyed nowhere else on earth.

"May I congratulate you on your birthday for your significant contribution to our national welfare because your efforts to preserve the foundation of America's greatness will always be remembered in the grateful hearts of your people."

IN PIONEER FIELD

Presentation of the fund, a history-making event in the institutions of higher learning, launched the University of Maryland upon a pioneering field to indoctrinate young America with a deeper sense of Americanism through intimate knowledge of American history, with emphasis, Dr. Byrd pointed out, "upon American culture rather than European culture."

In setting up the new curriculum Dr. Byrd looked over the field of qualifed American teachers for a director and finally chose "a true American scholar," Dr. Guy A. Cardwell, acting chairman of the English department at Tulane University.

The university faculty will decide upon the requirements for the fellowship and the scholarship, the president said, adding that each will be available for the beginning of the September term.

FAVORABLE COMMENT

Announcement several weeks ago of the establishment of a school for American Civilization Studies at the university, Dr. Byrd continued, at first was viewed with skepticism and doubt

Continued on Page 2, Column 7.

MUSSOLINI EXECUTED—The bullet-riddled body of Italy's ex-Fascist Premier, Benito Mussolini, lies in the Plaza Loretto in Milan as Italians struggle with Partisan executioners to view it. The bald head of the fallen dictator rests on the body of his mistress, Clara Petacci, one of his 17 followers given a hasty trial, then shot after being caught trying to flee the country.
—Photo courtesy New York Times.

Mutiny In Fleet Is Reported

NEW YORK, April 30—(I. N. S.).—Whole companies of German marines have mutinied at Kiel and Nazi Elite Guards thrown against them failed to establish control, the Stockholm Dagens Nyheter reported today.

LONDON, April 30—(A. P.).—Russian tanks have smashed into the Tiergarten, Berlin's central park converted into an underground fortress, the Nazi-controlled Oslo radio said today, and Moscow reports said the fall of the capital was imminent.

Earlier Moscow dispatches said the Russians were approaching the spacious park.

The Hamburg radio, chief Nazi transmitter still broadcasting in Germanq, proclaimed that "the hard battle for Berlin reached its climax today."

Moscow dispatches said Marshals Gregory K. Zhukov and Ivan S. Konev, commanding Red Armies at Berlin, were going all-out for a May Day victory and had thrown in maximum artillery

MOSCOW, April 30—(I. N. S.).—Battlefront reports from Berlin said today that Nazi parachutists were being dropped down into the stricken German capital as last-ditch reserve forces.

and air power to reduce the Nazis' strongholds in the center of the city.

Soviet dispatches from Berlin said the Nazis hemmed in a very small area made up roughly of the Tiergarten, the Reichstag district just to its north, the Wilhelmstrasse administrative quarter and most of the crowded commercial district centered on Unter den Linden running east from the Tiergarten.

WAVE OF SUICIDES

A wave of suicides and desertions whittled the ranks of the capital's defenders and the Russians squeezed the mauled German garrison into a flame-swept 18-square-mile pocket — all that

Continued on Page 2, Column 1.

Argentina, Poles Force Showdown In Parley

SAN FRANCISCO, April 30—(A. P.). — British-American-Russian relations teetered on the rim of another crisis today, with the Polish issue again building up behind the scenes of the United Nations conference.

Efforts of Latin American nations to have an invitation issued for Argentina to join the conference appeared to be forcing the showdown this time. Some conference leaders were privately fearful of a deadlock.

Soviet Foreign Commissar Molotov was reported to have told his big-power colleagues—Stettinius of the United States, Eden of Britain and Soong of China—that he is willing to have Argentina invited if the Warsaw Government

Continued on Page 2, Column 4.

The Lovely, Blue-Eyed Brunette Who Graces the Cover of The American Weekly, the Magazine Distributed With Next Sunday's Baltimore American, Is the Glamorous Creation of Willy Pogany. Her Beauty Is Accentuated With Emeralds, the Birthstone of All Girls Who Were Born In the Month of May.—Adv.

Mussolini Slain By Italy Patriots

MILAN, April 30—(U. P.)—The broken body of Benito Mussolini lay unclaimed beside his slain mistress in the Milan morgue today. Dishonored in death by the people he led to empire aid ruin.

The fallen Duce died badly in the sight of the Partisan executioners who killed him and his paramour, Clara Petacci, in their hideout on Lake Como last Saturday.

And the people he rules for two decades paid him their last tribute by hanging his remains head down from the rafters of a gasoline station in Milan's Loreto square.

SHOT HIS BODY

There, for a night and day they spat upon their fallen leader, shot his body in the back and kicked his face into a toothless, pulpy mass.

For hours after the body of the executed dictator was brought to Milan with that of his mistress and 16 other slain Fascist leaders, Mussolini lay in a filthy pile of dirt in the center of the square. Then the mob tied wire about the ankles of Il Duce and Clara Petacci and suspended them upside down from the roof of the gasoline station.

His mistress' skirth was torn off and people spat upon both bodies.

When the mob tired of its ghastly sport the bodies were takn down and dumped into an open truck. They were carted to the city morgue and the pair were

Continued on Page 3, Column 4.

Temperatures

12 Midn't, 53	7 A. M., 49
1 A. M., 52	8 A. M., 50
2 A. M., 51	9 A. M., 52
3 A. M., 51	10 A. M., 54
4 A. M., 50	11 A. M., 56
5 A. M., 50	12 Noon, 59
6 A. M., 48	1 P. M., 61

Say 'Higher' Nazis Have Ended Life

NEW YORK, April 30—(I. N. S.).—The Stockholm newspaper Svenka Dabbladet said today that Xaver Franz Schwarz, Reich treasurer of the Nazi party, and several other "higher Nazis" had committed suicide.

Ninth Contacts Russians, Making New Nazi Pocket

PARIS, April 30—(A. P.).—The American Ninth Army established another contact with the Russians three miles west of Wittenberg today, creating a small new untenable German pocket between their diminishing northern and southern redoubts.

A hard battle was in progress in the south for Munich, birthplace of the Nazi party and largest German city ket entered by the Americans.

The new junction was east of Dressau at Apolendorf, 51 ciles northwest of Reisa in the Dresden-Leipzig area where the Russians and American First Army met and cut Germany in two. American forces were released for other duties by the new meeting.

BATTLING IN MUNICH

Five divisions of the Seventh Army, probably 70,000 men in all, were engaged in a stiff battle in the fringes of Munich, where the beer hall from which Hitler start-

Continued on Page 2, Column 5.

New Peace Offer By Germans Reported

STOCKHOLM, April 30—The Stockholm radio reported today that a new surrender offer from Heinrich Himmler, addressed to the United States, Great Britain and Soviet Russia, will be communicated "within the next few hours." The intermediary again will be Count Folke Bernadotte.

LONDON, April 30—(A. P.).—A new surrender offer from Heinrich Himmler, presumably to all three major powers, was understood to be "on its way" today.

British cabinet ministers were ordered to stand by as swiftly moving developments pointed to Germany's collapse.

EXPECT ANNOUNCEMENT

Prime Minister Churchill was reported preparing a statement for Commons tomorrow—May

Continued on Page 2, Column 6.

BULLETIN

WASHINGTON, April 30. (A. P.). — The White House said today that President Truman will report on any end of European hostilities "whenever anything can be released officially and with proper authority." Press Secretary Jonathan Daniels made this comment at a news conference. He said he had nothing to report along that line at present.

NEWS-POST

At Your Service	6	Horoscope	6
Bugs Baer	15	Mallon, Paul	15
Clark, Norman	6	Movies	6
Classified Ads	19, 20, 21	Parsons, Louella	6
Comics	8	Pegler	15
Crossword	21	Pippen, R. H.	16
Dixon, George	15	Radio	10
Durling	14	Ration Points	12
Dulaney	15	Robinson, Elsie	14
Editorials	14	Society	9
Financial	18, 19	Sports	16, 17, 18
Haney, Dr.	18	Winchell, Walter	6
Health	22	Women's Clubs	9

3 ALLIED ARMIES NEAR MUNICH
REVOLT BREAKS OUT IN CITY

THE WEATHER
Rain late tonight and Sunday, ending late Sunday night. Monday partly cloudy, moderate temperature.
Detailed Weather Report Page 11

Baltimore News-Post
An Independent Newspaper

The Largest Evening Circulation in the Entire South

VOL. CXLVI—NO. 146 — SATURDAY EVENING, APRIL 28, 1945 — PRICE 3 CENTS

BERLIN BATTLE NEAR END
9TH ARMY LINK-UP READY

Russ Cossack Divisions Reach Elbe River For Fresh Yank Juncture

LONDON, April 28—(U.P.)—A Moscow dispatch said Soviet Cossack divisions swept nearly 50 miles west of Berlin and reached the Elbe river opposite the American Ninth Army. The Russians were awaiting an "imminent junction" with the Ninth Army, Moscow said.

PARIS, April 28—(U.P.)—The American-Russian junction south of Berlin linked 13,000,000 Allied troops for the final act of the battle of Europe, military observers said today.

Though superficially the armies of the east and west became a mighty combined force, no change in the command setup was believed contemplated.

Premier Marshal Stalin was expected to remain in command of his seven Russian armies and Gen. Dwight D. Eisenhower in command of the five American, one British, one French and one Canadian Army of the Western Allies.

Neither was any change likely in the supplying of the Red Army despite the opening of the east-west corridor.

VAST SUPPLIES BY AIR

The American lines alone in the west were so extended that in the first two weeks of this month 35,000 tons of supplies had to be sent east of the Rhine by air.

(BACKGROUND NOTE: A battle flag that flew over Stalingrad during the battle which changed the course of world history symbolized the brotherhood of American and Russian armies. The flag was presented to a Russian corps commander to Maj.

Continued on Page 2, Column 1.

Report Munich Swept By Revolt

ZURICH, Switzerland, April 28 — (I.N.S.) — Reports reaching Switzerland today said Gen. Franz Ritter von Epp, leader of the German revolt inside menaced Munich, had declared the Bavarian capital an open city.

PARIS, April 28—(A.P.)—The American Seventh Army closed today within 25 miles of Munich and broadcasts from that Nazi citadel said a revolt was seething in the city.

Augsburg, third city of Bavaria, fell to Lt. Gen. Alexander M. Patch's troops. The Seventh Army reached the Austrian frontier at

Continued on Page 2, Column 6.

Say Redoubt Push Bogged By French

PARIS, April 28—(A.P.)—A Supreme Headquarters statement today declared that the French First Army was obstructing the Allies drive southeast against the Nazi redoubt by its persistence in continuing to occupy Stuttgart.

The statement said Sixth Army group headquarters had asked the French First Army to move out of the city, capital of Wuerttemberg, which the French captured.

At latest reports the French still were there—backed by the French Council of Ministers which voiced disapproval of the request on grounds that the Big Three had not taken any action on France's postwar occupation zone claims in Southwest Germany.

HANDS ACROSS GERMANY—U. S. First Army infantrymen (left) extend hands to Russian troops (right) on a broken bridge over the Elbe river at Torgau, Germany, as soldiers of the two Allied armies meet to cut the Reich in two after 2,100 miles of bitter fighting. The Yanks traveled 700 miles across Europe to make the junction, while their Soviet Allies fought 1,400 bloody miles from Stalingrad. A. P. Wirephoto.

U.S. Hopes Russia Will Make Good On Vote Deal

SAN FRANCISCO, April 28—(A.P.)—The American portion of the Yalta agreement was marked paid in full today, and to the United States delegates here it now looks like Russia's turn.

There was no mistaking what America wants—a Russian declaration of war against Japan. No one, however, was saying out loud that she expects this right away.

As the United States delegates completed their work on preliminary revisions of the Dumbarton Oaks peace-keeping formula, the belief was general that some action may be forthcoming soon from Russia in return for support of the Soviet's successful bid for three votes in the proposed league's general assembly.

That support was given in recognition of a pledge made by President Roosevelt at Yalta—reaffirmed by President Truman in a letter to the delegation dated

Continued on Page 2, Column 7.

Western Allies Firm:
Report Himmler Offers Surrender

LONDON, April 28—(A.P.)—Heinrich Himmler was reported today to have offered unconditional surrender to Great Britain and the United States, but Prime Minister Churchill said in a special statement declared that only unconditional surrender to all three big Powers would be accepted by the Allies.

The Prime Minister neither confirmed nor denied reports that surrender had been offered to the two Western Allies, but not to Russia.

FITS FOE'S PLIGHT

Churchill declared:

"It has been reported by Reuters

der was offered by Himmler to Britain and the United States only. Further that Britain and the United States have replied saying they will not accept unconditional surrender except on behalf of all the Allies including Russia.

"No doubt at a time like this all kinds of reports of proposals for German surrender from various parts of the Reich are rife, as these are in harmony with the enemy's desperate situation.

"His Majesty's Government have no information to give about any of them at this moment. But it must be emphasized that only unconditional surrender to the three major Powers will be entertained, and that the closest accord prevails between the three Powers."

Unofficial reports of a German unconditional surrender offer to Britain and the United States were

Continued on Page 2, Column 7.

Fifth Reported At Swiss Line, Halving Italy

ROME, April 28—(U.P.)—A Zurich dispatch said today that the American Fifth Army had reached the Swiss border in a spectacular 60-mile dash that cut Northern Italy in two, trapped tens of thousands of Germans and isolated Milan and Turin.

The dispatch said the Americans entered Como, on the Italian side of the frontier, last night after an advance from their last reported positions west of Lake Garda.

The patriot-controlled Milan radio reported that the Americans also had entered Milan, Italy's second city, but this was not confirmed. The radio said patriot forces already had liberated the city.

Turin, the other great industrial center of Northern Italy, was isolated by the advance which cut the last roads to Austria from Northwest Italy.

Reds At Brandenburg Gate, Alexanderplatz In Center Of Capital

LONDON, April 28 — (A.P.). — The German High Command declared today that Soviet troops had crashed through Berlin's inner defense ring and were fighting on Alexanderplatz, site of Gestapo headquarters. Nazi planes were flying in reinforcements, food and ammunition to the fanatical garrison, the German communique said.

LONDON, April 28 — (U.P.) — The German High Command admitted today that Russian siege forces had slashed to the Brandenburg Gate and Alexanderplatz in the heart of Berlin.

Moscow dispatches said the suicide garrison of the ruined capital virtually had been wiped out with the killing or capture of 19,500 Nazi troops yesterday. Only relatively small units of fanatical elite guards and Volkssturmers remained to fight the last hours of the nearly ended battle.

A Nazi communique said German troops on the Elbe "have turned their backs on the Americans in order to relieve the defenders of Berlin by attacks from outside." But it sounded like a pep talk.

Bulletin

ST. MARGRETHEN, Switzerland, April 28 — (U.P.) — A high diplomat who has just arrived at the Swiss border from Germany said today that Adolf Hitler and Propaganda Minister Paul Joseph Goebbels were shot three days ago.

BARRIER MILES WIDE

The Russian barrier around the capital was miles wide, and two American Armies were ready to pounce from the rear on any army turning toward Berlin.

Admitting Russian penetrations inside the inner defense ring to Charlottenburg, to the Brandenburg gate where Unter Den Linden reaches the Tiergarten, and to Alexanderplatz, the Nazi com-

Continued on Page 2, Column 2.

Louis Azrael Reports:
Gen. Dittmar Sees Reich Crash Near

By LOUIS AZRAEL
News-Post War Correspondent

MAGDEBURG, Germany, April 25 (Delayed).—Berlin will fall in a "couple of days" and German resistance will collapse completely a few days later, Lt. Gen. Kurt Dittmar of the German Army said today a few minutes after he surrendered.

Dittmar, a Prussian Junker, retired from active combat command about two years ago and since then has been the foremost military analyst on the German radio.

TALKS WITH BALTIMOREAN

Dittmar came across the Elbe river today under a white flag, in a rowboat. His first contact was with American infantry under the command of Lt. Col. Samuel T. McDowell of Rock Hall, S. C.

One of the unit's staff officers,

Continued on Page 2, Column 4.

doubt" area in the South German mountains.

Goering is now an inconsequential figure in Germany, rarely even mentioned.

SAYS HITLER IS IN BERLIN

Dittmar also made the following assertions:

He knows Hitler is now in Berlin and will die in Berlin. So will Goebbels.

Himmler is in "the national re-

NEWS-POST

Azrael, Louis 7	Haney.........
Buge Baer	Dr. Lewis
Clark, Norman 8	Horoscope 5
Classified Ads 14	Movies
	Parsons, Louella 5
Comics 12, 13	Pippen, R. H.
Crossword 7	Radio
Dixon, George 7	Ration Points 7
Dulaney 7	Robinson, Elsie 7
Editorial	Society
Financial	Sports 9, 10
Health	Women's Clubs

Temperatures

12 Mid., 45		7 A. M., 42	
1 A. M., 44		8 A. M., 45	
2 A. M., 43		9 A. M., 48	
3 A. M., 43		10 A. M., 51	
4 A. M., 42		11 A. M., 55	
5 A. M., 41		12 Noon, 55	
6 A. M., 41		1 P. M., 57	

THE BALTIMORE NEWS-POST

The Largest Evening Circulation in the Entire South

THE WEATHER
Clear, cooler, frost in suburbs tonight. Saturday sunny, warmer in afternoon.

Detailed Weather Report Page 36

Read The Baltimore News-Post for complete, accurate war coverage. It is the only Baltimore newspaper possessing the three great wire services—
ASSOCIATED PRESS
INTERNATIONAL NEWS SERVICE
UNITED PRESS

VOL. CXLVI.—NO. 145

Entered as second-class matter at Baltimore Postoffice

FRIDAY EVENING, APRIL 27, 1945

PRICE 3 CENTS

HOME FINAL

YANK, RED ARMIES JOIN IN GERMANY

WASHINGTON, April 27—(A. P.).—President Truman announced today the junction of Soviet and American forces in Germany. Press Secretary Jonathan Daniels said the junction officially took place yesterday at Torgau, a town on the Elbe river, 75 miles south of Berlin. Patrols, he said, met a day earlier. The President said that, as a result of the meeting, "the enemy has been cut in two," and added: "This is not the hour of final victory in Europe, but the hour draws near, the hour for which all the American people, all the British people and all the Soviet people have toiled and prayed so long."

Third Within 25 Miles Of Munich

PARIS, April 27—(U. P.).—American armies invaded Austria today and smashed into the western fringe of the Bavarian redoubt in a general breakthrough that carried within 25 miles of Munich, birthplace of the dying Nazi regime.

PARIS, April 27—(A. P.).—General Patton's Third Army invaded Austria and established radio contact with the Russians west of Vienna today in a swift advance nearly sealing off Czechoslovakia and shutting the front door to Hitler's Alpine redoubt.

The French closed to within 31 miles of Munich and 78 of the Brenner Pass, toward which the rampaging American Fifth Army in Italy was striking from the south. The Seventh Army approached Munich from 35 miles northwest of that cradle of the Nazi party.

IN RADIO CONTACT

At last reports, many hours behind the action, the Third Army and the Russians west of Vienna were 85 miles apart, but A. P. Correspondent Edward D. Ball messaged:

"The two armies are in radio contact and a physical junction appears likely soon."

The ordinary range of Russian radio tanks is 25 miles.

Ball's dispatch was heavily censored, but he was allowed to say that:

"The impending line-up would mean that all Southern Germany, with its so-called national redoubt, and the Germans forces in Italy would be trapped."

While the "doubtful redoubt" in the south was shivering under combined blows from all directions, the British in the north plunged beyond conquered Bremen in a maneuver to split the northern redoubt and seal off Denmark and Schleswig Holstein.

SMASH KUSTEN CANAL

The Canadians broke the Kusten canal line west of the port and advanced on Emden, Bremenhaven and Wilhelmshaven—still workable submarine bases on the North sea.

Marshal Feodor I. Tolbukhin's Third Ukrainian Army Group last

Continued on Page 2, Column 5.

Temperatures

12 Midn't, 60		7 A. M., 48	
1 A. M., 58		8 A. M., 49	
2 A. M., 57		9 A. M., 51	
3 A. M., 55		10 A. M., 53	
4 A. M., 52		11 A. M., 55	
5 A. M., 50		12 Noon, 56	
6 A. M., 49		1 P. M., 58	

GENERAL EISENHOWER   MARSHAL ZHUKOV

WHERE AMERICAN AND RUSSIAN ARMIES JOIN IN GERMANY
Final link in armored chain cutting country in two forged at Torgau, north of Leipzig.

Parley Will Reach Agreement, Belief

By WILLIAM K. HUTCHINSON
International News Service Staff Correspondent

SAN FRANCISCO, April 27.—The United Nations conference presented the strange paradox today of moving swiftly toward complete agreement on the momentous issues of future world peace, while bickering over the minor point of electing a presiding officer.

A steering committee of Foreign Ministers from the 46 participating nations were called into session again to solve the dispute yesterday when they agreed to rotate the presidency among American Secretary of State Edward R. Stettinius, British Foreign Secretary Anthony Eden, Russian Foreign Commissar V. M. Molotov and China's famed T. V. Soong.

PRESSURE FOR STETTINIUS

However, the American delegation—which wanted to name Stett-

Continued on Page 2, Column 1.

Conference Schedule

SAN FRANCISCO, April 27 (U. P.)—Here is today's schedule for the United Nations Conference:

12.30 P. M. (E. W. T.)—Meeting of the U. S. delegation.
1.30 P. M. (E. W. T.)—Meeting of the conference steering committee.
7.30 P. M. (E. W. T.)—Third plenary session of the conference to hear report of steering committee and addresses by heads of delegations.

Yanks In Italy Enter Genoa, Report

ROME, April 27—(A. P.).—Troops of the United States Fifth Army smashed to within 35 miles or less of Milan today as the entire Italian Front surged toward a sealoff of the Nazis' Alpine redoubt on the south.

(On the Ligurian coast in the west, said a "free Milan" radio reported recorded in London, a swift Allied advance penetrated Genoa, a big North Italian city, where partisans reportedly had been reported unofficially in control after driving out the German garrison.)

Swiss dispatches cited mounting indications that the Nazis were abandoning Mussolini's Blackshirt troops to their fate and withdrawing rapidly toward the German

Continued on Page 2, Column 7.

Louis Azrael Says:

Chaos Reigns As Nazis Flee Reds

By LOUIS AZRAEL
News-Post War Correspondent

SANDAU, Germany, April 27.—In the thin and punctured slice of Germany between the American and Russian Armies, chaos and stark terror lived today.

Filled with horror at prospect of falling into Russian hands, thousands of fanatic Germans sought the comparative refuge of surrender to the Americans. But 300 feet of water—the Elbe river—was between them and the American lines. And American Army officials, in this region at least, would not let them cross.

Early in the afternoon the unit commander ordered that the patrol—

This village, just west of the Elbe—Russian side—was the focal point for the drama which ensued. For this is where American patrols crossed in hopes of meeting the oncoming Russians.

MISTAKEN FOR REDS

The meeting did not take place. What was thought to be a Russian unit turned out to be Germans. There was a nasty little series of skirmishes which continued well into today.

(BACKGROUND NOTE: On official announcement from Washington today told of the junction of the Russians and Americans at Torgau, 75 miles due south of Berlin.)

While it was going on many hundreds of German civilians and many hundreds of liberated Russian, Polish and other Allied soldiers came across the river on outboard-motored boats, on which our patrols had crossed.

Continued on Page 6, Column 5.

69th Made Juncture

By United Press.

The Sixty-ninth U. S. Infantry Division, made the first juncture with Russian troops 75 miles south of Berlin on Thursday, is a part of Gen. Courtney H. Hodges First Army. The Sixty-ninth at last reports was commanded by Maj. Gen. E. F. Reinhardt.

people have toiled and prayed so long."

MEANING IN UNION

"The union of our arms in the heart of Germany has a meaning for the world which the world will not miss. It means first, that the last faint, desperate hope of Hitler and his gangster government has been extinguished."

"The common front and the common cause of the Powers allied in this war against tyranny

Continued on Page 2, Column 6.

Fall Of Berlin Believed Near

LONDON, April 27—(U. P.).—Russian siege forces clamped the German defenders of Berlin into a fast shrinking death pocket around the Tiergarten today and a Swedish report said the fall of the razed capital was "only a matter of hours." Tiergarten is Berlin's famous central park west of Unter Den Linden boulevard.

Fanatical Nazi diehards, purportedly led by Adolf Hitler, were reported falling back into the Tiergarten at the heart of Berlin for a last hopeless stand against the constricting ring of Soviet steel and troops.

Red Army assault forces plunging for the Tiergarten from the north were reported to have overrun the Moabit district, a workers' area adjoining the central business district reaching within half a mile of the Brandenburg gate.

(BACKGROUND NOTE: At Moabit the Russians were in the area of the biggest prison in Berlin. The district adjoins the Tiergarten on the northwest.)

The most optimistic of a flood of reports indicating that the Nazis were beaten in Berlin came from Stockholm, the nearest neutral listening post.

'A MATTER OF HOURS'

A Mutual Broadcasting correspondent reported:

"It is only a matter of hours before the Russian High Command can announce that Berlin is ours... Eyewitness reporters say that all resistance outside

the fortress (in the Tiergarten) is unorganized and sporadic, and that by nightfall Friday, today, Berlin will be considered liquidated."

United Press Correspondent Henry Shapiro reported from Moscow that Marshal Gregory K. Zhukov's assault battalions storming through Siemensstadt broke into Charlottenburg and linked up with Marshal Ivan S. Konev's troops battling northward from the botanical gardens.

He said:

"A circle is drawn around the heart of Berlin, with spearheads thrusting from the Goerlitzer station northwestward and the Pankow district southwestward

Continued on Page 2, Column 8.

NEWS-POST

At Your Service	18	Health	31
Bugs Baer	29	Horoscope	32
Clark, Norman	32	Movies	22
Classified Ads		Parsons, Louella	22
27, 28, 29		Pegler	23
Comics	30	Pippen, R. H.	24
Crossword	29	Radio	32
Duluney	26	Robinson, Elsie	23
Durling	25	Society	20
Editorials	23	Sports	24, 25, 26
Financial	27	Winchell, Walter	24
Haney	22	Women's Clubs	22
Dr. Lewis	31		

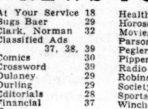

BIRD-NAT GAME OFF IN RESPECT TO ROOSEVELT

RODGER H PIPPEN

SPORTS EDITOR, SAYS:

Two letters arrived today touching upon the Chalky Wright-Jackie Wilson fight, which Referee Lee Halfpenny stopped after the seventh round because, as he saw it, Wright was stalling and not doing his best. The opinion expressed in both letters is that the referee was right and that the purse to be taken from Wright should be given to the Red Cross or some other worthy charity. Most fight fans will agree with that sentiment.

Bentley Thomas, of the Kemper-Thomas Company of Cincinnati, who has been in this city for several months on business, had this to say:

I have not had the pleasure of meeting you personally and during my 56 years of happy life this is the first time I have ever felt it my duty to write a sports editor and compliment him upon his splendid article. After witnessing the terrible fiasco at the Coliseum Monday night between Ex-Champions Chalky Wright and Jackie Wilson, and after reading your splendid article in the Tuesday News-Post I just cannot, in justice to myself and the sports game, refrain from writing you and complimenting you upon your excellent article and your awfully good judgment and the fact you had enough guts to write your article plain enough so that any New York gambler or average Baltimore fan could understand exactly what you meant.

I am definitely a sports fan and in my younger days I thought nothing of traveling thousands of miles to witness a fight between top contestants. I had a ringside seat at Toledo when little Jack Dempsey pulverized big Jess Willard and I have tried to witness most of the top contests since that exciting day in Toledo. As I have lived at the Emerson Hotel here in Baltimore three months and as I expect to remain here three months or longer, I have been patronizing the fights at the Coliseum and never, absolutely never, in all my experience, have I seen such a poor and such a miserable showing as Chalky Wright put up at the Coliseum Monday night. And I also want to compliment Referee Lee Halfpenny who proved as a referee he knows what the fight situation is all about and who also has the courage of his convictions and the guts to use his head in spite of the New York gamblers and the howling mob present.

Frankly, I did not have one dime bet on the fight, therefore, I am not a sorehead squawking I was robbed, but, Mr. Pippen, that was a terrible fiasco and, according to my way of thinking, Chalky Wright's purse should be held up and donated to the Red Cross or some other worthy charity organization. And Chalky Wright should be suspended from Maryland fight rings for the balance of his life, because to even the novice it was very plainly evident Monday night that Chalky Wright was stalling and was also pulling his punches and not trying. I want to compliment you upon your very truthful and frank article in The News-Post, and if you should happen around the Emerson Hotel any afternoon after 5 o'clock I would be glad for you to telephone room 836, and if I do not answer, then have me paged and I would like to meet you and buy you a drink.

The other letter was from Harry F. Klinefelter, well-known local insurance man. He wrote as follows:

When Referee Lee Halfpenny pronounced the Chalky Wright-Jackie Wilson fight no contest with all bets off, the State Boxing Commission should give the money that won't be paid to Chalky Wright to charity and also give rain checks to the customers who had paid as high as $6 for ringside seats—to see what? Governor O'Conor should put Lee Halfpenny on the Boxing Commission. Men of Lee's caliber are very rare these days. They are badly needed now. Due to the stoppage of racing, boxing seems flooded with the boys who love to bet on rather than witness horse racing and boxing conducted on the level. Halfpenny seems to have their measure.

* * *

Says Fifth Is Ideal Place For Fights

Here is another letter about the local fight situation:

**Mr. Rodger H. Pippen, Sports Editor,
The Baltimore News-Post,
Baltimore, Md.
Dear Sir:**

In moving from their small and uncomfortable quarters to the huge Fifth Regiment Armory the Arena A. C. has served notice to all who are interested in fights that they mean business. The Fifth is by far the best building in Baltimore in which to hold fights; it is well located and offers the customers comforts comparable to some of the best fight arenas.

Most of the fight fans like the idea of fights in the big Fifth and I think I talk for most of them when I say I hope the Maryland Boxing Commission permits the Arena A. C. to hold weekly fights there. Both fight clubs should be given equal rights and I feel certain they can secure the services of enough good fighters to operate properly.

The bringing to Baltimore of undefeated Elmer Ray, the world's fourth best ranking heavyweight, to box Vince Pimpinelli tonight at the Fifth proves you can obtain the services of good fighters if you are willing to pay them their price. Then, too, the fact that two fight clubs are operating in Baltimore weekly will boost this city's sport stock no end.

With the Orioles playing in the huge Stadium and weekly fights at the big Fifth Regiment Armory (the Boxing Commission permitting), we sport fans will enjoy our sports like never before because never before have they been served to us in such big-time surroundings. Yours for better sports,

**NICHOLAS J. ABATE,
5205 Reisterstown road,
Baltimore 15, Md.**

* * *

Eagle At Bonnie View

Thomas W. King, 751 McCabe avenue, is just an ordinary golfer, but he can visualize what it is to be a big-time linksman.

King got the thrill of his life the other day at Bonnie View. While playing the 322-yard fifteenth hole he scored an eagle two. The ninety shooter hit a good drive to the left of the fairway, pulled out a spoon for his second shot and rammed it right into the hole for a deuce. This hole, although short in distance, is quite difficult. It is a dog-leg to the right and is lined on both sides with trees.

Playing in the foursome with King at the time of his golf thrill was Otto Muller, Carl Brittingham and Bill McWilliams.

Duke Trackmen Prep For Navy

DURHAM, N. C., April 13—(A. P.).—The Duke U. track team, victim of a 73-57 beating at the hands of North Carolina Pre-Flight last Saturd- is setting its sights on the Naval Academy with hopes of throwing a surprise or two when the squads meet at Annapolis April 21. It is Duke's next major test and two weeks of concentrated work will have gone into the preparations.

Counted on heavily to score points will be Jim LaRue, who took two firsts and a second in dash events against Pre-Flight, Frank Irwin, who took firsts in discus and shotput and a one-two-three punch in the javelin which topped anything Pre-Flight had to offer.

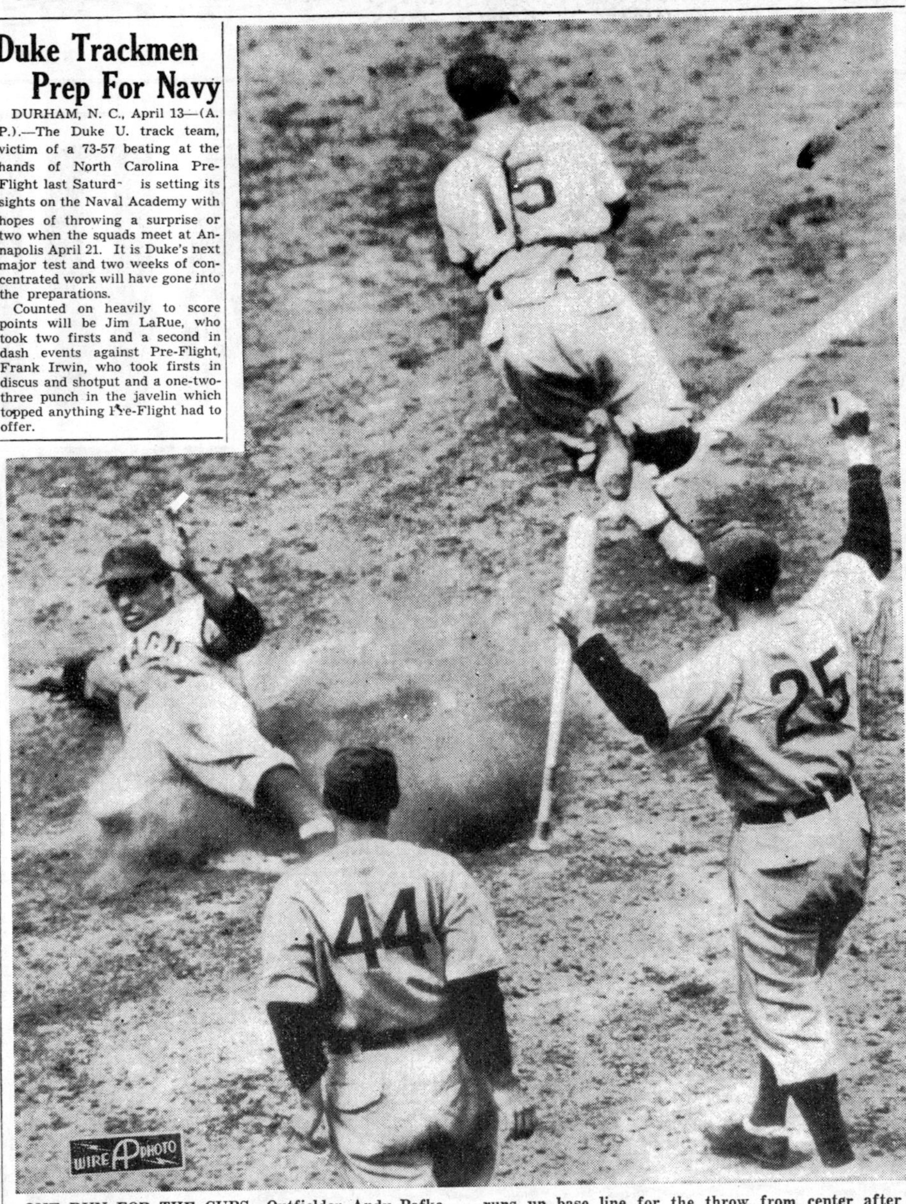

ONE RUN FOR THE CUBS—Outfielder Andy Pafko of the Chicago Cubs slides safely across home plate in the fourth inning for a score in yesterday's game with the White Sox. White Sox Catcher Mike Tresh (15) runs up base line for the throw from center after Mickey Livingston singled. Watching are Cubs' First Baseman Phil Cavaretta (44) and Third Baseman Stan Hack (25). Cubs won, 15-3. A. P. Wirephoto.

Name Van Slate As Choice To Hurl Opener

Manager Tommy Thomas, after a phone conversation today with Clark Griffith, president of the Washington club, announced that Sunday's game here between the Orioles and Senators has been cancelled out of respect to President Roosevelt, who died yesterday. Griffith, greatly affected by the President's death, has called off all of Washington's games this week-end.

The Orioles will hold a squad game Sunday. Today's practice was called off as the Birds are well-conditioned after a strenuous and fast training season and Manager Thomas wants to guard against his clug being overtrained.

By HUGH TRADER, JR.

Any hurler who can breeze through 18 innings against Bainbridge and the Phils like Rollie Van Slate did, holding such clouters as Musial, Wakefield, Spence, DiMaggio, etc., to a total of five runs over that distance, certainly figures to be capable of handling the Orioles' International League opener next Thursday against Montreal.

And Manager Tommy Thomas puts the official stamp on Rollie as his inaugural hurler, barring the unexpected. The assignment carries with it more than the customary and traditional honor this 1945 season, since the champion Orioles will be formally and ceremoniously beginning defense of their proud title.

Incidentally, there's still a strong possibility that the Oriole-Royal opener will be staged at night, marking the first arc-light inaugural in baseball history. The reason is that several defense plant leaders have suggested this innovation for the benefit of their workers, who wouldn't be able to attend in force the usual afternoon opening.

LINE-UP IN DOUBT

The rest of the Birds' official starting line-up is still subject to revision, for, as we mentioned a couple of days ago, Joe Mellendick is the logical candidate for the fourth place, or clean-up, hitting job. And Manager Thomas, from the beginning, has asserted that he wants Jimmy Tropea somewhere in the batting order. Jimmy is a promising sticker, but he hasn't been able to show his best yet because of injuries.

Red Kress, too, can be a valuable man for the Birds, particularly for the home games and for a fast get-away next week. Now is the time to utilize his hitting. Red can still poke that ball with any hitter on the club, with the present exception of Mellendick, who looks like he'll be the Birds' big gun.

OUTSTANDING IN CAMP

Joe's slugging is outstanding in camp now and he appears to be reaching his peak for the opener. He got off several more powerful drives in yesterday's camp game and he looked okay running, too. If he clicks the Birds will be able to hold their own in the power department until any additional help arrives from Cleveland. Mellendick, Tropea, Lollar, Kress, Skaff and Latshaw represent a fairly tough batting order in these times. And Jimmy Devlin is a pretty good sticker, too.

The pitching staff needs help badly to carry through a 154-game grind, but Van Slate, Palica, Hooks, Podgajny and Henry appear ready and capable of holding the fort at the start until the Indians send along a couple like Bonness and Kleine.

Young Pete Taylor further impressed Manager Thomas yesterday and he plans to ship Pete and Shortstop Whitey Sybert, along with Paul Harris, out for the proper seasoning, possibly to Batavia in a Class B loop. A lad like Bill Kostiuk, husky first sacker, probably will be farmed to Wilkes-Barre.

Thomas will continue his squad game tomorrow as the best means of conditioning his athletes, though he has scheduled a final tune-up game with the Navy nine at Annapolis next Tuesday.

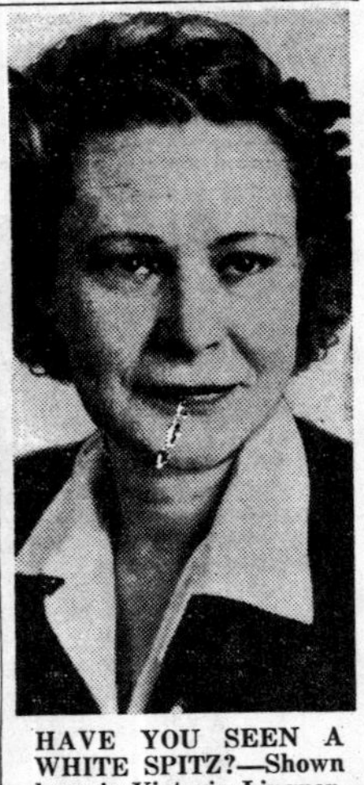

HAVE YOU SEEN A WHITE SPITZ?—Shown here is Victoria Lingner, 317 East Twenty-eighth street, who asks for aid in the search for her male Eskimo spitz, who got away from a doctor's office on Greenmount avenue. The pet's name is Ambrose and he has been gone ten days. If you have seen this pet, please phone Tuxedo 8497 or Tuxedo 3149.

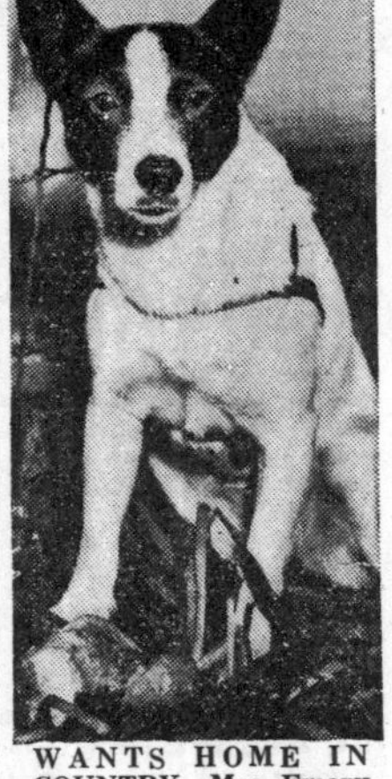

WANTS HOME IN COUNTRY—Mrs. Emory Collins, 709 McCabe avenue, Govans, is endeavoring to find a nice home for this friendly female fox terrier. Mrs. Collins prefers to give the pet to someone residing in the suburbs because the animal is very active and likes to run. If you would like to adopt this pet, phone Mrs. Collins at Chesapeake 7017.

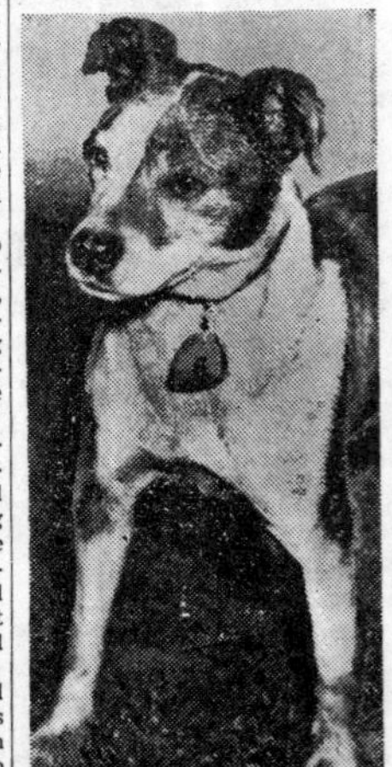

WANTS OWNER OR A NEW HOME—This fellow, a male brindle bull terrier, medium sized, was found in Baltimore and sent to the Baltimore County Humane Society on Park Heights avenue, where he is receiving the usual gentle care. He is friendly and affectionate and well behaved and will make a fine pet for someone if his owner does not claim him. He is in good condition.

Martin Boxing Test Postponed

The Glenn L. Martin boxing tourney, scheduled for tonight, and other Martin athletic events today have been postponed because of President Roosevelt's death. The boxing tourney will be held next Wednesday night at Vill-Nar gym, it was announced.

The entries:

118-Pound Class—Joe Holland, Louis Apicella, Charles Liberto.

126-Pound Class—Harry Trageser, John Schaefer, George Zeun.

135-Pound Class—Kenneth Hutchinson, William Vogel, Lee Brosius, Loren Maquet.

147-Pound Class—Eddie Dixon, Paul Wilson, Morris Gaver.

160-Pound Class—Harry Dodson, Melvin Espy, John Dixon, William Kern.

175-Pound Class—Gene Alger, Horace Hall.

Heavyweights—Jerry Keene, William Jimeson, Tom McLewee.

SOUTHPAW HOPEFUL

BEAR MOUNTAIN, N. Y., April 13—(A. P.).—Vic Lombardi, twenty-two-year-old 150-pounder, was the only southpaw pitcher in the Brooklyn Dodger camp this spring. In 1941, Lombardi, five feet seven, struck out 204 batters for Johnstown in the Penn State League. His earned-run average was 1.85.

ARMORY FIGHT CARD

Following is the complete card of boxing to be presented by the Arena Athletic Club at the Fifth Regiment Armory tonight. Probable winners are indicated in capitals, with probable odds following:

TEN ROUNDS

ELMER RAY, Florida, vs. Vince Pimpinelli, New York. 8-5 on Ray.

JIMMY McALLISTER, Baltimore, vs. Charley (Cabey) Lewis, Havana. 7-5 on Lewis.

BILLY MORRIS, Baltimore, vs. Johnny Lawler, Cleveland, 6-5 on Lawler.

SIX ROUNDS

ODELL POLEE, California, vs. Joe Golembeck, Fort Meade. 7-5 on Polee.

FOUR ROUNDS

NICK LONGO, Baltimore, vs. George Junior, Baltimore. Even money

BOWLING TEST

Bowling championships of the Third Service Command will be held heer over the week-end with 18 Army posts in Pennsylvania, Maryland and Virginia due to compete.

Ray Choice Over Vince Pimpinelli

Elmer Ray, the fourth-ranking heavyweight in the country, will step into a local ring for the first time tonight and rule the choice to make his debut a successful one when he faces Vince Pimpinelli, the New York heavy, in one of the Arena Club's three 10-round bouts at the Fifth Regiment Armory.

In the other two tens, the local entrants, Jimmy McAllister and Billy Morris, will be underdogs to their respective opponents, Charlie (Caby) Lewis and Johnny Lawer.

Ray packs dynamite in both fists, and his string of 26 consecutive wins, in which are included 24 knockouts, justifies his being installed the favorite tonight, but the other two bouts definitely belong in the pick 'em class.

McAllister is Benny Trotta's hope for the featherweight championship, and the clever 126-pounder has been going great guns of late, all of which leads Trotta to believe that the youngster packs title possibilities. A victory over Lewis this evening would be a feather in Jimmy's cap and leave him in a position to dicker for more lucrative bouts.

As for Morris, the young Trotta-owned welterweight has been unbeaten for three years and faces one of his most formidable opponents to date in Lawer. Lawer, who is a Cleveland product, trounced Danny Aldridge in an eight-rounder in New York several weeks ago, and this bout shapes up to be an interesting affair.

Also on the card will be a six-rounder and a four. In the six, Odell (Jack) Polee, a heavy from the West coast, meets Joe Golembeck, popular local club fighter, and in the other fight Nick Longo, returning to the fistic wars after a nine-year lapse, meets George Junior.

HOCKEY SCORES

STANLEY CUP PLAYOFFS

Toronto, 1; Detroit, 0.

Majors Call Off Tilts As Token Of Respect

By United Press.

Baseball, preparing for its fourth wartime season, called a halt today to its final tune-up activities in respect to the death of President Roosevelt, who more than any other one man had been responsible for the perpetuation of the sport since Pearl Harbor.

The game between the New York Yankees and the Brooklyn Dodgers, scheduled for tomorrow at Ebbets Field, was called off. Sponsors of the city series between the Chicago Cubs and White Sox announced that all games had been postponed until after the President's funeral.

RED CROSS GAME

In yesterday's Red Cross game between Brooklyn and the Yanks, the Dodgers were 3-to-1 winners, getting to Hank Borowy, ace of the New York staff, for two runs in the first inning and protecting the margin all the way. Curt Davis, pitching for Brooklyn, gave up six hits.

At Chicago, the Cubs opened up with a 22-hit attack to defeat the White Sox, 15 to 3, in the opener of the Windy City preseason series. Veteran Paul Derringer and Hank Wyse shared Cub pitching duty and yielded seven hits.

The Philadelphia Athletics made two runs in the ninth to defeat the Washington Senators, 7 to 6, at Fort Meade, Md., before 7,500 fans, mostly soldiers. Manager Connie Mack of the A's announced he had purchased rangy Charley Gassaway, six-foot three-inch left-hander, from the Milwaukee Brewers for $15,000. Gassaway recently was released to Milwaukee by the Cubs after a prolonged hold-out.

STREAK SNAPPED

The Pittsburgh Pirates ended Cleveland's winning streak of exhibition games at six straight at Muncie, Ind., Fritz Ostermueller giving up only five hits in a 5-to-2 victory.

The Boston Braves won their fifth straight game in the late innings, scoring two runs in the last of the ninth to top the Red Sox at Boston, 12 to 11.

PREP BASEBALL

McDonogh, 13; Franklin High, 0.

Roosevelt's Death Blow To Baseball

WASHINGTON, April 13—(U. P.).—President Clark Griffith of the Washington Senators said today that the death of President Roosevelt would make no change in plans for the season's opening game here Monday with the New York Yankees.

By CARL LUNDQUIST

NEW YORK, April 13—(U. P.). When President Roosevelt, early in his first term, answered critics of his policies with the words, "I don't expect to make a home run every time I come to bat," the sports world knew it had a friend in the White House.

Without the provisional "green light" for baseball which he issued in one of his last press conferences there would have been little hope for continuation of the sport into its fourth wartime season.

Because few persons knew of his fatal illness, there had been hope to the last that he might follow up the "green light" declaration by throwing out the first ball at the Presidential opener between the Senators and Yanks at Washington next Monday.

Mr. Roosevelt in urging the continuation of baseball for 1945 said he did not think the sport should use perfectly healthy men who could do something more useful in the war effort. The teams probably would be a little older and maybe not as proficient, he said.

LOYOLA SCORES

Loyola defeated McDonogh, 10-4, in a junior varsity lacrosse game yesterday at Pikesville.

DOGS

Mrs. Barbara Kraus, 33 South Decker avenue, has befriended a young female fox terrier. The pet is black and white and was wearing a collar with a bell and string attached. If this is your pet, contact Mrs. Kraus at the above address.

Frank Schmidt, 441 South Fulton avenue, requests residents of that neighborhood to be on the lookout for a medium-sized male dog, part chow and part collie. The pet should be easy to identify because he has a white breast and his right ear hangs down as the result of an old injury. The dog is about eight years old and answers to the name of Bis.

Joseph Paulus, 3322 Foster avenue, in the Highland section, has befriended a male Boston bull. The pet is brindle and white and appears to be about two years old. If you can make proper identification, you can recover the pet at the above address.

William J. Kane, 3609 Hicks avenue, sends in another appeal for assistance in recovering a small brown and white dog, part cocker spaniel and part spitz. The pet was wearing a brown collar when he strayed last Friday morning. If you have seen this dog, please phone Forest 6647.

Frank L. Mohler, 13 Somerset road, requests residents of the Catonsville area to be on the lookout for a male toy terrier. The pet strayed from the above address last Tuesday. If you have seen this small dog, please phone Catonsville 2163-W.

Dolores Klina, 922 North Luzerne avenue, has appealed to The News-Post for assistance in recovering a black and white female Boston terrier. The pet, which answers to the name of Boots, strayed from the above address on Good Friday. If you have seen this dog, please phone Broadway 6752.

HOMER FOR HOLMES

Tommy Holmes of the Boston Braves was the only player to homer off Rube Melton of the Brooklyn Dodgers in 1944.

SPORTS BRIEFS

MERCERSBURG, Pa., April 13. The Mercersburg Academy baseball team will open its season here tomorrow against a team representing the Koppers Company of Baltimore. The second game of the season will be played with Valley Forge Military Academy here next Wednesday.

LEE JOINS PHILS

WILMINGTON, April 13—(U. P.).—Bill Lee, the bespectacled thirty-five-year-old righthander, joined the Phillies and in his first workout was initiated by being hit on the arm from a line drive off Coaker Triplett's bat. The injury proved slight and Lee continued on the mound.

SECOND 8 TIMES

A short nose cost Alex Barth, Millbrook Stable five-year-old, a total of $164,040 during 1944. The hardy campaigner finished second in eight stake races last season.

Our Thirty-Second President

BOY OF FOUR—President Harry S. Truman, at the age of four, is shown with his brother, J. Vivian Truman (right), when they were youngsters on a Missouri farm.

ELEVEN YEARS LATER—Former Senator and Vice-President Harry S. Truman at the age of fifteen. The thirty-second President of the United States has a conservative Southern background. President Truman has pledged himself to carry out the immediate international policies of his predecessor.

TRUMAN AS OFFICER—As a first lieutenant in Battery F, 129th Field Artillery, Harry S. Truman chalked up an enviable record in World War I. Outstanding characteristics of this unpretentious man, now President of the mightiest nation on earth, are loyalty and fidelity.

ADDRESSED LEGION—While Democratic nominee for Vice-President, War Vet Harry S. Truman spoke to delegates at American Legion convention in Chicago.

WITH MILITARY AIDE—This is an informal picture of Harry Truman and Col. Harry Vaughan, his military aide, during another of his visits to Baltimore.

KEY TO BALTIMORE—Shortly after being sworn into the second highest office in the nation, Vice-President Truman was guest speaker at a Rotary Club luncheon in Baltimore. Mayor McKeldin presents the nation's new President with the key to the city.

32ND PRESIDENT—Grief-stricken by news of President Roosevelt's sudden death, Vice-President Harry S. Truman, the Missouri farm boy who did not want to be President, prepares to take the oath of office making him the Commander-in-Chief of the United States. By his side is the saddened new First Lady.

NOVEMBER, 1944—Helping his aged mother to the polls at Grandview, Mo., last November, as Sister Martha watches, the man selected by destiny to lead the nation in war and peace — Harry S. Truman.

—Pictures from A. P. Wirephoto and INP Soundphoto.

Historic Events In Roosevelt's Life

FIRST INAUGURATION—Franklin Delano Roosevelt began his distinguished career as President of the United States on March 4, 1933, when he was sworn into office by Chief Justice Charles E. Hughes, now retired, of the Supreme Court. Standing near his father for the White House ceremony is James D. Roosevelt.

FOURTH "PEACE" TERM—When he ran for his unprecedented fourth term in the nation's highest office, the President's avowed purpose was to achieve final victory over the Axis and establish a lasting peace. He took the oath on January 20, 1945, from Chief Justice Harlan F. Stone (behind the flag).

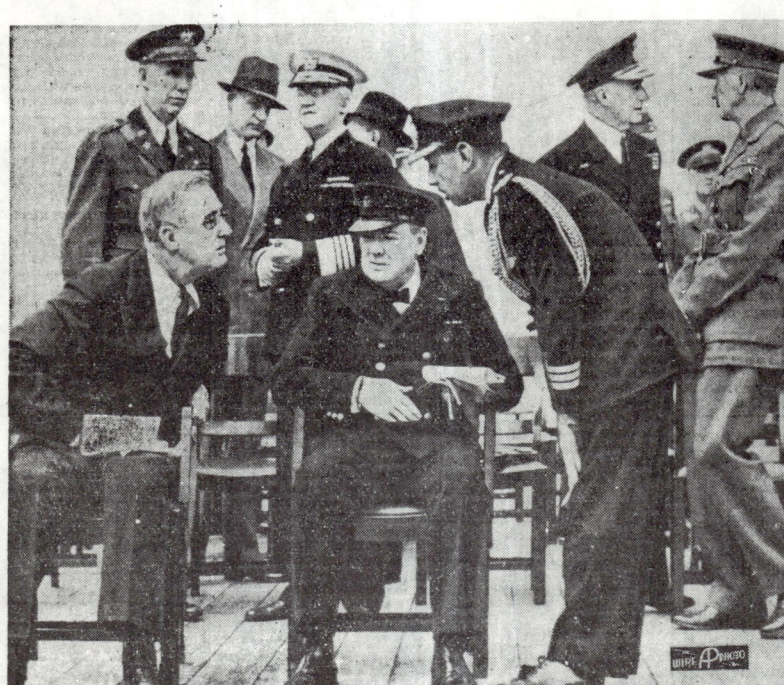

ATLANTIC CHARTER BORN—President Roosevelt's star as a world statesman was on the ascendancy when he and Prime Minister Churchill, shown during their historic meeting at sea in August, 1941, proclaimed the four freedoms as the peace aims of the United Nations.

CASABLANCA—The President and Churchill, with Generals Giraud and de Gaulle, mapped United Nations' offensive for "unconditional surrender" of Axis in 1943.

LAST MEETING AT YALTA—Plans for final victory and permanent peace were drawn by the Big Three last February but the strain of leading the nation through its stormiest history was taking its toll.

SUPREME SACRIFICE—The White House flag flies at half staff in mute tribute to the man whose death symbolizes war's high cost—Franklin Delano Roosevelt.
—Pictures from A. P. Wirephoto and INP Soundphoto.

FAMILY ALBUM
From Boyhood to Presidency

THE BEGINNING—One of the earliest photos of our late President, Franklin Delano Roosevelt, shows him in swaddling clothes. At left is another portrait made in 1892 at the age of ten years.

SAILOR AND SPORTSMAN—The portrait above was made in 1889 when young Franklin was aged seven. Sailor suit was the style of the day. At right he is pictured a few years later as a young sportsman in riding togs, crop, and checkered vest. The part in the center of his hair graduated in later years to one side. Other photos on this page show later stages of his life.

IN HIS STUDENT DAYS—Dressed in the style of the times, the future President of the United States is shown on the campus in his early college days. He was educated at Groton School and Harvard University.

EARLY IN PUBLIC LIFE—At the age of thirty-four Mr. Roosevelt was well on his way in public life. He became Assistant Secretary of the Navy and helped direct Naval operations in World War I.

AS NAVY SECRETARY—In his job as Assistant Secretary of the Navy, which he held from 1913 to 1920, Mr. Roosevelt gained national prominence. He is shown here at his desk in the Navy Department at Washington.

VICE-PRESIDENTIAL NOMINEE—In 1920, when this photo was taken, President Roosevelt was acknowledging the congratulations called to him from the windows of the Navy Department following his nomination in San Francisco for the Vice-Presidency on the James Cox ticket.

FIRST YEAR AS PRESIDENT—The above picture of the late President was made during the first year of his first term as Chief Executive of the nation, shortly after his inauguration on March 4, 1933. This healthy, hardy countenance showed worn lines of the stress of war before his death yesterday. After more than twelve difficult years at the helm of the country's Government, the fourth-term President's utter disregard of his own well-being took its fatal toll.

—Pictures from A. P. Wirephoto and INP Soundphoto.

BALTIMORE THE NEWS-POST

AN INDEPENDENT NEWSPAPER

7 ★★★★★

The Largest Evening Circulation in the Entire South

VOL. CXLVI.—NO. 133   FRIDAY EVENING, APRIL 13, 1945   Entered as second-class matter at Baltimore Postoffice   PRICE 3 CENTS

NATION MOURNS

1882---Franklin Delano Roosevelt---1945

NITE LIFE
By LOU and JUDD CALVERT

HOTELS are so crowded anybody who hits town without a room reservation had better bring a sleeping bag. However, if he or she is a member of the armed forces, the Travelers' Aid in Union Station or B. & O. will get a billet for them somehow ... the superb New Chanticleer, where Chanticletts are on the hoof, has held over the song-terrific Dean Martin for an indefinite stay and, boy, the customers are taking him in ... Baltimoreans who think this town is theirs are kidding themselves as they discover it belongs to the whole country when they try to elbow into Club Charles with Joey Adams on the bill.

THE BANDBOX'S lordly-rafted "little madhouse" is athrob to the rhythm of the Grooveneers ... blithe bloomer belle Jeri Keever is singing while you sip at the smart 21 Club ... the forte in musical rhythm comes in a la carte from Eddie Leonard's Spa with the Three Aces and a Queen on tap ... Amigos and the like go well with Carlos-Melisa and Ramon on the podium at Doc's lounge ... a sixth anniversary is in order beginning Tuesday at Club Madison and lovely song star Joyce Evans comes in to add melody ... chow traffic as usual is smacko-colossal at Dickman's steak house (Mt. Royal avenue) ... and for beverages that attain ocean proportions the Blue Room with lovely Tess Harry ... a terrific skating act is feature billing at Kibby's, Art and Margie Brooks ... something nothing short of sensational are the rhythms, electric organ and guitar of George Menen and his musical aggregations heard in the beautiful Club Rio ... the Twain shall meet and has with pert lotus blossom, Ruth Chin, headlining the Earle Club extravaganza.

ICECAPADE ... The many friends of Betty Collier of Pat's Bar will be sorry to learn the ice is one of the hardest of the Lord's creation and that she is recupin' at home.

In her fourteenth week and still going strong Comic Clown Ducky Rhoades at Carl's Keswick road spot ... Blue Mirror still boasts the talented music of Nat Conway and his Foursome ... Curley Miller in his third year at Mac's Walnut Grove calls for real celebration ... that sensational study in balance out to the Dutch Mill has been held over again, the reason—the Manshinos ... thanks to Bob Marsching it's always a pleasure to make the Algerian Room a stopping place and particularly with lovely Rita Nagle on tap with her piano and songs ... that's all 'cept' ... BUY U.S. WAR BONDS!!!

CHAMPIONS OF FUN
Adams, Canzoneri and Plant starring at Club Charles

JIMMY HUSSON
New comic find of the 21 Club revue

DEAN MARTIN
Nation's latest singing star held over at New Chanticleer

CARLOS, RAMON & MELISA
Latin American Trio of Doc's Lounge

GEORGE MENEN
And his music held over at the Club Rio

RUTH CHIN
Singing lotus blossom of the Earle Club

KEN NEALY
His voice and trio nightly in the Bandbox

JOYCE EVANS
Lovely radio songstar opening Tuesday at the Club Madison

Gala New Revue At Chanticleer

It's an all new sparkling revusical at the beautiful New Chanticleer as of last Thursday night with the exception of Dean Martin, latest song star, who was held over by popular demand.

New faces are the All Time Lucky Strike Hit Parade favorite Lulu Bates; direct from the West Coast and USO abroad, Barney Grant for a switch in comedy that should take Baltimore by storm; lovely Helen Osborne, ballet, and the tap-terrific Jimmy Byrnes.

For beauty in production it's the lovely Chanticletts and, of course, your music is a fine point sincerely with Ziggy Travers and his society orchestra. "Orchid" matinee each and every Sunday from 4 P.M. Cocktails daily 'round the same hour.

Joey Adams Star Of Club Charles

America's Ace of Clubs currently stars Joey Adams, Tony Canzoneri and Mark Plant and a host of other hits for your entertainment pleasure. For solid humor one can't go wrong with such a trio as the above and for songs from another world Mark Plant's voice is the answer.

Rounding out this top bill are Lucille Finlay, the six Guy Martin Adorables plus the fine rhythms of Eddie Wald and his orchestra, and, last but not least, the extra added attraction of the Appletons, whose Apache dance is breathtaking.

Gala Sunday matinee, "Celebrity Showtime," starting at 4 P.M. every Sunday.

The Rio
RESTAURANT BAR & LOUNGE
NO COVER NO MINIMUM EXCEPT—SAT. & SUN.
Everybody's Talkin' and Raving About America's Newest Food Craze...
SMORGASBORD
DINNER SERVED from 5:30 to 8:30 P.M.
After Theatre Snacks Until 2 A.M.
Held over by Popular Demand!!
★ GEORGE MENEN
His Electric Organ Guitar and Orchestra
★ Henry Day & his Society Orchestra
★ Marian Weis—Vocalark
OPEN MONDAYS—No Food Served
JACK TRENT, Mgr.
Reservations LEx. 0663—
Visit Our LEATHER BAR ★ NO TAX
306 W. FRANKLIN ST. Entrance at Md. Theatre

6th Year Anniversary Celebration!
STARTING TUESDAY, FEB. 20TH...
Our New Policy
3 SWING SHIFT SHOWS
9.30 P.M., 11.30 P.M. & 1 A.M.
Presenting—The Most Outstanding Floor Show Ever Presented
Last 2 days LEE WARWICK — FLORENCE YOUNG — JACK & SALLY TAYLOR
MADISON NITE CLUB WO. 8677
Madison and Chester Sts.

"Where It's Smart To Be Seen"
NAT CONWAY
And his musical foursome featuring
MARIAN DAWN — CORA WALSH
WFBR Song Star — ACCORDION and SONGS
DANCING NITELY, INCLUDING SAT. & SUN. FROM 8 to 2
Cocktail Hr. Daily 5-7—Closed Mondays
Blue Mirror
929 N. CHARLES ST.

FREDDY WEISGAL & his RHYTHM KINGS
★★★★★
"LILYON"
And Her Solo-Vox
Plus Continuous Action
EAST BALTIMORE'S MOST POPULAR BAR & LOUNGE
No tax, cover or minimum at any time
Presenting the finest in ENTERTAINMENT
408 BAR
408 E. BALTIMORE ST.

Full Course DINNERS LOBSTERS-OYSTERS COCKTAILS
Delightful Music
OPEN DAILY EXCEPT MONDAY
NO 20% TAX
DICKMAN'S Cor. Mt. Royal and Maryland Ave.

CLUB BAR COCKTAIL LOUNGE
THE FINEST LIKE HERE AT THE FISHO

"baltimore's biggest little madhouse" presents
The BAND BOX
1309 NORTH CHARLES
COCKTAIL HOUR 4 to 7 SUNDAY
VE. 6795
GROOVERNEERS
SENSATIONAL SEPIA QUARTET
KEN NEALY TRIO
WITH VOCALOVELY RUTH CRUZ

EDDIE LEONARD PRESENTS
THREE ACES AND A QUEEN
DEE LLOYD McKAYE
FOUR MEN OF RHYTHM
SPA MUSICAL BAR
charles and preston sts.
ON THE AIR! W-I-T-H
MAT. SAT. 5-7 SUN. 3-7 LE. 9552
SUNDAY 3:05 3:30

STARTING TUES.
RIFF ROBBINS Trio
Sepia Musical Sensation
Carlos-Melisa and Ramon
Latin America's Favorite Trio
Kirby Walker
Sepia Boogie Woogie Piano Star
Last 3 Days—The 4 Bits
Cocktail Hour Sat. & Sun. 4 to 7 P.M.
DOC'S COCKTAIL LOUNGE
1817 N. CHARLES ST. LE. 6786

ALL STAR COMEDY REVUE!
DUCKY RHOADES
FOURTEENTH WEEK! STILL GOING STRONG!
HOWARD FOE'S music ★ VIETTE WINGO exotic dancer
CARL'S
2 SHOWS NITELY NO COV.—MIN.
RES. CH. 9476
3316 KESWICK RD.

ALL BALTIMORE WELCOMES "HIS HILARIOUS FUNSTER AND M.C."
LEO BATEMAN The Comiclown
Jack DECKER and his orchestra
UPTOWN NITE CLUB
MARIE WYATT ★ VICKI GALLO
2 Shows Nightly. All the Beer you can drink and food from 9-2 A.M. Tues., Feb. 20. $1.50 per person, incl. tax.
FULTON NEAR PENNSYLVANIA
CLOTHESLINE NITE EVERY WEDNESDAY

GORDON WHARRAN
and his swinging strings
CURLEY MILLER
his songs and piano nitely
plus
RAY MADDOX
and his orchestra
MAC'S WALNUT GROVE
3612 HANOVER ST.

BIGGEST SHOW IN TOWN
Baltimore's Favorite Hosts
SAM VINCI and FRANK YOUNG
Art & Margie Brooks
clever skating duo
COBY YEE ★ **RUTH HANEY**
Jimmy Nichols' orchestra
KIBBY'S LUCKY NUMBER NITE CLUB
711 Poplar Grove Rd.
MAdison 1098

Club Charles
BETTER COME IN EARLY
BECAUSE proudly we present the GREATEST SHOW ON ANY NITE CLUB FLOOR
Joey ADAMS World's Laff Weight CHAMP
Tony CANZONERI 7 Times World's Champ "Punches to Punch Lines"

EVERY SUNDAY AT 4 P.M.
"Celebrity Showtime"
Stars from Baltimore Clubs will appear as our guests for your pleasure. Dancing and complete show with celebrated entertainers every Sunday afternoon from 4 to 7.30 P.M.
Never A Cover or Minimum on Sunday Afternoons

MARK PLANT ★ **THE APPLETONS**
LUCILLE FINLAY
SIX GUY MARTIN ADORABLES
EDDIE WALD'S ORCHESTRA
SONGS BY ELAINE PFEIFER
1ST SHOW TONITE 10 P.M.
Club Charles
charles at preston ve. 8020-21

The Most Enchanting
COCKTAIL LOUNGE
SOUTH OF N.Y.
WITH AN ATMOSPHERE THAT SPORTSMEN PREFER!
Entertainment Nightly!
JOCKEY **Manny Berg**
Says: "No Cover, Tax or Minimum at Any Time"
TURF BAR & LOUNGE
102 WATER ST., at Light
1 BLK. S. OF SOUTHERN HOTEL. LE. 4333

STRICKLER'S
6800-10 Harford Rd. HA. 9744
Dancing to Carroll Kelly's Orchestra
Fine foods served daily and Sunday. Reservations for dinner parties invited.
Baltimore's Most Beautiful Lounge

GAYETY NITE CLUB
PLENTY OF ACTION
FOR COMPLETE NEW SHOW EVERY WEEK ALL STAR ACTS

A HOST OF HITS CARROLL'S ORCHESTRA plus a host of others
Reservations, WOlfe 0602
NEW HOTEL BROADWAY
BROADWAY at ORLEANS

FOOD ★ FUN ★ FRIVOLITY

AIR PORT GRILL — 6500 Riverview Ave., Dundalk. Music Fri., Sat. and Sun. Dine and Dance to Rhythm Boys Orchestra—Al "Abe" Shaeffer, Emcee. No cover, no minimum.

DE LUCA'S — 4009 Wilson Spring Road, Dundalk. Dance to WES WARREN and His Musical Trio

GREEN VILLA — 5423 O'Donnell St.

KATHLEEN'S — EAT, DRINK AND MAKE MERRY 2 BIG FLOOR SHOWS NITELY. NO COVER OR MINIMUM. 612 EAST BALTIMORE ST.

KEYSTONE — Dance to your heart's content at Dundalk's Top Spot. Take No. 26 car, walk short distance to Keystone Sign. 7018 Holabird Ave. Lou Mellon's orchestra.

LEON'S — MERRY-GO-ROUND BAR—BALTIMORE'S NEWEST RESTAURANT—LOUNGE—BAR 870 PARK AVENUE UNDER PERSONAL DIRECTION OF LEON LAMPE

MUELLER'S — Dancing to Charlie Blair's Rhythmakers Friday and Saturday. Sunday Featuring "Chester" and his Piano Accordion. GI. 0837. 7200-11 WASHINGTON BLVD. AT DESOTO RD. No cover or Minimum at any time.

NATE & LEON'S — DELICATESSEN. Stop in after the show for a Midnight Snack. Delicious Sandwiches. OPEN ALL NIGHT. 850 WEST NORTH AVENUE.

Gala New Revue Ad — CHANTICLEER

THE SECOND EDITION OF
"SPRING TONIC"
STARRING
DEAN MARTIN — **LULU BATES** — **BARNEY GRANT**
and a host of 25 other stars
"Orchid" Matinee Sunday
Starting at 4 P.M.
SIX GORGEOUS CHANTICLETTS ★ TWO ORCHESTRAS NITELY
ZIGGY TRAVERS' SOCIETY MUSIC ★ MARIO'S RHUMBA RHYTHMS
THE GLASS AND INTIMATE BARS FOR COCKTAILS DAILY FROM 4
TWO REVUES NITELY AT 10 AND 1 A.M.
NEW **CHANTICLEER**
OPEN MONDAYS
Charles at Eager
LExington 0234

CRAIG MATHUES
Singing Star of Geo. White's Scandals
JIMMY HUSSON
The Nation's Sensation M.C.
Plus other Star Attractions
1st Show Tonite 10 P.M.
21 Club
COCKTAIL MATINEE TODAY
WITH COMPLETE FLOOR SHOW
FROM 5.30 to 8.30 P.M.
FIRST SHOW TONIGHT 10 P.M.
21 W. Balto. St.
LARRY LONDON'S ORCH. Alvin Spieldock at the Drums Bella Caffero—Piano & Songs
SA. 5552—Never A Cover Charge
Saratoga 5552

Brown Out or Black Out!
THE EARLE CLUB IS A Knockout
MICKEY STRAUSS Presents—
Ruth Chin Singing Lotus Blossom
Dixie Fenton—Tap & Character Dancer
Plus—"Donnetta"—Vocalovely
EARLE CLUB
Sunday Cocktail Jamboree 4 to 7 P.M.
LOW DOWN PRICES
12 S. Patterson Park Ave. WO. 9223

"WHERE THE SMART SET MEETS"
Rita Nagle
America's Star of Radio & Stage in Songs And Impressions At The Piano
Plus Bill Stoos' Orchestra
DANCING NIGHTLY
Algerian Room
at the Mount Royal Hotel
MT. ROYAL AT CALVERT ST. MU. 1570

"HAMILTON'S PLAYGROUND"
Two Shows Nitely
THE MANSHINO'S
study in balance
PAUL and PAULETTE
and a host of others
MIKE TRALIK'S MUSIC
Continuous entertainment and dancing. No cover or minimum at any time. Completely air-conditioned.
DUTCH MILL
6615 HARFORD ROAD

SWEENEY'S presents
BUDDY MONROE
Baltimore's Favorite M.C. Song Star
LOUISE WRIGHT
Charming Vocal Hit!
SLIM STAPLETON
HIS NOVACHORD AND TRIO
3128 Greenmount Ave.

NOLAN'S NITE CLUB — Wilkens & Monroe. Mixed Drinks. The finest foods. Dance to SAMMY LEDOWE & his Sisters Orchestra. Dancing—9 P.M. till 2 A.M. Fri., Sat. and Sun.

PAT'S BAR — 116 N. LIBERTY ST. "THE MOST TALKED ABOUT PLACE IN BALTIMORE." TIMES SQUARE ATMOSPHERE.

SLOPPY JOE'S — "Pick-A-Rib." Under New Management. All Foods Are Charcoal Broiled. Delicious Full-Course Luncheons-Dinners Served Daily. Open all night. 1218 N. Charles.

SPORTSMAN — BAR & LOUNGE. NO MINIMUM, NO COVER NO TAX. SAM LAMPE, 1429 N. CHARLES ST.

Ye Old Caton Tavern — Formerly Willoughs. Catonsville Junction, Edmondson & Bolton Aves. Presenting Bud Witt and his Sextette, featuring the "Palos" in Song. Lime Cart No. 14 of 8 to door. Phone CAT. 317.

ZEBELEANS CAFE — Friday, Saturday and Sunday, "Romanian Style." Mixed drinks. Dance to the "Cavaliers"

BUY U.S. WAR BONDS AND STAMPS

MISSED SHORT PUTT KEEPS SNEAD FROM RECORD

RODGER H. PIPPEN

SPORTS EDITOR, SAYS:

Although one of the most unpleasant memories of his baseball career was engraved by Fred Merkle back in 1925, Tommy Thomas, Oriole leader, declared this morning he would like nothing better than to have a player as capable as this former first sacker in his line-up for 1945.

Merkle, as Tommy saw him, was a great hitter in the pinches, a smart base runner and a fine team player. Thomas' thoughts reverted to Fred when he read in his column how Merkle, now in business in Daytona Beach, Fla., was still being hounded by reporters because of his failure to touch second base years ago, an oversight which cost the New York Giants a National League pennant.

Tommy never will forget how close Merkle came to driving him right away from Oriole Park and to another baseball club.

It was late in the season of 1925 and the Birds, fighting for their seventh consecutive flag, were leading by a game or two. Rochester, with Merkle as the first sacker, was playing here. Lefty Grove developed a wild spell in the seventh inning and Thomas was rushed to the rescue. Tommy got by the seventh and eighth, but in the ninth, with two out, Boley made a low throw of a grounder and Jimmy Walsh, subbing at first, let the bounce get away. Miljus singled and this brought up Merkle. Tommy, who was a fast-ball pitcher, with little or no curve, blazed one high on the outside. Fred, a big man, took an easy swing and Tommy turned to watch the ball sail into the bleachers in right.

The hit cost Baltimore the game and when Thomas returned to the bench, Jack Dunn, the manager, was raving.

"Take off that uniform," he shouted, "and don't ever come back. If I can get waivers, you'll be pitching in South Carolina as soon as a train can get you there. Who do you think you are, Walter Johnson? You haven't got enough speed to throw one past Merkle."

The present Oriole leader had no answer to that tirade, but the very next day he was back in uniform and, before the afternoon was over, he was back on the rubber. And that will give you a good idea of the managerial tactics of the man who established a record of seven straight flags. The late owner of the local club was a firebrand, but he was just as loud in his praise when the players earned it.

* * *

Tommy Was His "Cousin"

Merkle didn't mention that particular hit when I talked to him in Florida recently, but he did mention Tommy.

"I was delighted," declared Fred, "to read about Tommy's success with the Orioles. As a pitcher, he was my 'cousin.' All I had to do was to stick out the bat and out would go a base hit. His fast ball just suited my swing."

Thomas recalled another incident which spikes the general belief that Merkle was a slow thinker because of the one bad play of his career. The Birds were playing in Rochester and Gonzales was on third and Griffin on second for the home club. Two were out and Merkle was at bat. When Cowboy Tomlin, pitching for the Orioles, wound up, Griffin got confused and started to steal third with a runner already occupying that bag. At the plate, Merkle, always alert, saw Griffin's mistake and, although the pitch was outside, he reached far out and in some manner pulled the ball to left-center and over the fence. The homer, however, didn't save the situation. Griffin, running with his head down, rounded third and passed Gonzales, who had stopped momentarily to see the ball soar over the fence. Griffin, of course, was called out for passing another runner and, as that was the third out Merkle's homer was reduced to a single.

In those days, according to the present Oriole manager, the two batsmen most feared on the Rochester Club were Merkle and Fothergill.

* * *

Sailor's Hound Dog Lost In Lansdowne

A female dog, who belongs to a young man serving his country in the Navy in the South Pacific, has been lost at Lansdowne, Md. She is a rabbit hound about four years old. When lost, she had on her collar with license number 25278. She is white with two black spots on her back and a brown head. Her name is Blue and she is to have puppies the first of next month. Was last seen near Lansdown last Sunday afternoon. Please contact Mrs. Anna Schatz, 111 Clyde avenue, Lansdowne 27, or phone Arbutus 533-J.

* * *

South Baltimore Boys Should Be Helped

A plan of much merit, and worth great consideration, is explained in a letter to this writer by William J. Hesse, president of the South Baltimore Improvement Association, 337 Warren avehue. Here is Hesse's letter in full:

**Mr. Rodger H. Pippen,
Sports Editor, News-Post,
Pratt and Commerce streets,
City.**

Dear Sir:

Knowing of your great interest and of your many efforts to obtain proper recreation for the children of our city we are turning to you for help and advice.

We in South Baltimore have, as you already know, very inadequate recreational facilities for the great number of children in this section. To supplement our meager facilities we have been endeavoring to have established a Police Department boys' club at the little-used Cross Street Market Hall. Inspector Schueler who has charge of these clubs knew of our plans and was very encouraging to their successful conclusion.

The Cross Street Market Hall was chosen because of the extreme demand for floor space, due to war work, the Cross Street Market Hall was the only suitable site available. Now then, the Cross Street Market Hall is under the jurisdiction of the Department of Recreation. They at first denied us its use for this important recreational purpose for the reason that it would interfere with their three-nights-a-week basketball schedule.

Inasmuch as a boys' club would supply additional recreational activities for a much greater number of boys, we took the matter up with the Mayor and other interested persons. But in order to keep down any feelings of animosity between the Department of Recreation and the Police Department, Commissioner Atkinson called in Inspector Schueler, and instructed him to publicly reject the Cross Street Market Hall as unsuitable. This leaves the boys of South Baltimore sacrificed on the altar of selfish interest, by our youth leaders. If they do not use the Cross Street Market Hall for this purpose then we will lose the club at least until after the war.

We feel that the boys' club is too important a project to pass off so lightly and we are turning to you for help. Any effort you can make in our behalf will be greatly appreciated by this Association to say nothing of the many boys who will benefit by its establishment. With kindest personal regards I am,

Very truly yours,
(Signed) WILLIAM J. HESSE,
President, S. B. I. A.

SPORTS MIRROR

Today A Year Ago—Clarence Rowland named president of the Pacific Coast Baseball League.

Three Years Ago—Marty Servo defeats Lew Jenkins in a 10-round lightweight match at Philadelphia.

Five Years Ago—Heirs of J. Louis Comiskey began fight to block sale of Chicago White Sox, proposed by bank, the executor of the estate.

Ten Years Ago—New York Rangers, climaxing great comeback, take lead in American division of the National Hockey League.

Kenwood Captures Girls' Cage Title

The Kenwood High School girls' basketball team hung up its fifth straight triumph of the season by defeating Franklin, 51 to 7, and with the win clinched the championship of the Baltimore County League.

Sills and Kidd battled for top scoring honors with the former clicking with 11 baskets and one foul shot for 23 tallies. Kidd was close behind with nine field goals and four foul shots for 22 points.

Southworth, Sr., Stunned By Boy's Death

By JACK CUDDY

NEW YORK, Feb. 17—(U. P.). Sam Breadon, owner of the St. Louis Cardinals, spoke hesitantly. He seemed uncertain about confiding his "obsession" to a reporter. In the long pauses between his words the wintry wind could be heard gusting past windows of his room, high in the Hotel New Yorker.

Breadon and the reporter were alone in the room that night last December. Manager Billy Southworth of the champion Cardinals and a couple of St. Louis newspapermen had just gone out the door after a lengthy gabfest. Apparently it was this conversation that had primed Breadon for his intimate talk with the reporter. Much of the conversation had been about Southworth's son an Army aviator.

CLOSELY ATTACHED

Breadon—middle-sized, slightly florid, and gray-haired—nervously adjusted his blue bathrobe about his pajama-clad body and leaned forward in his chair. He said:

"Maybe I shouldn't talk about this—but it's becoming and obsession with me. It's on my mind, more and more. You know—Southworth and his son.

"In my long years of dealing with human beings I have never seen two persons so attached to one another as Billy and young Billy. Their lives are so wrapped together that they seem to live not only for each other but through each other. I mean that each seems to get his inspiration—his drive from the other.

"When young Billy first went overseas—in '42, I believe—I began thinking about this close father-son tie, because I noticed the strain on his dad—a tenseness he always tried to hide. And then I began wondering: What will become of Billy, Sr., if anything happens to his boy?

DEEP CONCERN

"Thoughts are peculiar things. Some times they start small like a snowball and run down the hill of your brain, getting bigger and bigger, until they crowd out almost everything else in your head. Well, that's what happened to me. For the past year this concern over Billy and his boy has been on my mind constantly, like a dreadful load.

"I've been fearful of the newspapers; fearful of the telephone, and particularly afraid of reading the bad news in Billy's face. I've kept hoping and even praying—don't let anything happen to young Billy—don't let anything happen to young Billy——."

Yesterday Manager Billy Southworth stood on the shore of Rikers Island channel, just north of New York's LaGuardia field. He gazed sadly out over the windswept waters to an area marked by four tossing buoys. He had been informed that 30 feet below the surface lay the wreckage of the B-29 Superfortress that young Billy—Major William Brooks Southworth—had piloted to his death.

Manager Southworth seemed stunned. He acted like a man in a daze. And a reporter standing near him remembered what Breadon had asked in December:

"What will become of Pilot Southworth if his co-pilot goes?"

NEEDS A MASTER'S CARE—This gentle female dog, about 6 months old, would like to be adopted into a nice, comfortable home. She is thoroughly house-broken and will make someone a splendid pet. Interested parties should write Mrs. Howard C. Wooden, 1308 South Hanover street, or phone Saratoga 1385.

Louis Denies New Romance

PHILADELPHIA, Feb. 17—(I. N. S.).—Staff Sergeant Joe Louis, heavyweight ring king, was in Philadelphia today on a two-day pass from Camp Shanks, N. Y., with a flat denial that he has a new romance lined up.

"People!" Joe exclaimed. "They're trying to get me all hooked up with a romance and here I am not even unhooked yet."

When asked if he was trying to get "unhooked," he grinned and said, "Sure," but denied that he was romantically interested in anyone else.

VOLS COACH STILL 4-F

KNOXVILLE, Tenn., Feb. 17—(A. P.).—The Knoxville Vols have no worries over a line coach this fall—he is still 4-F.

Ray Craves, a former Vol captain, said after an examination at Fort Oglethorpe, Ga., he had been rejected for service a fourth time because of a bad ear.

Vines Reports For Army Exam

DENVER, Feb. 17—(I. N. S.).—Ellsworth Vines, former national singles tennis champion and Davis Cup star, reports to Fort Logan, Col., today for a pre-induction physical examination.

HERE'S ICE IN YOUR EYE—Harold Hursley, rugged defenseman of the Baltimore hockey team, is shown putting on the brakes in a practice drill yesterday at the Carlin's rink. The action-minded Birds will lock horns with the Washington Lions tonight in a regular Eastern League tilt at Iceland. The contest will be a revival of one of the bitterest hockey rivalries in the league.

Ice Birds Test Lions Here Tonight

By GEORGE TAYLOR

The bitter inter-city hockey rivalry between Baltimore and Washington will flare anew tonight at Carlin's Iceland.

Tonight will mark the sixth time of the season these two Eastern League rivals have locked horns here and if past performances are any indication local fans will pass through the turnstiles expecting nothing less than general bedlam to break loose. And they probably will be right.

The battle gets under way at 8.30 o'clock and hold your hats.

OLD FEUD

It seems this hatred between the two neighboring cities started back in the days of the old Washington Eagles and the Baltimore Orioles. They were at each others throats in those days and apparently the feud has grown worse with age.

Coach Leroy Goldsworthy's hard-skating Birds have been very successful against their rivals from the capital this season. However, they are presently forced to bow their heads to the Lions.

Washington nipped the locals in a close one the last time they met. The setback was handed to the Birds on their home ice, too.

LOCALS READY

Goldsworthy has his club in its best shape of the season right now. All hands are on deck and anxious to supply plenty of fireworks in the final few weeks.

Bill Meloche, the newcomer to the team, worked out with the second line of Frank Eizenzoph and Jerry Lubeck during yesterday's practice. He will probably play on this line in place of Lou Smrke tonight.

Melpche, a former Oriole, played his first game with the new Baltimore Hockey Club last Wednesday and helped himself to the hat trick by scoring three goals.

The line-ups:

BALTIMORE		WASHINGTON
1 Pisodney..	G......	Francis 1
2 Currie....	D..	McClelland. 3
3 Hurlsey...	D........	Dorn 9
6 Powell....	C....	A. Smith 5
9 Carlson...	W......	G. Kelly 8
15 Bedard...	W.....	Percival 12

Alternates: Baltimore, 10 McLean, 5 Waldner, 11 Eizenzoph, 16 Meloche, Lubeck, 8 Smrke; Washington: 11 Phillips, 14 Long, 15 Nicowski, 16 Kusmaski, 20 P. Long.

PREP CAGE RESULTS

Poly, 27; City, 25.
Southern, 36; Forest Park, 23.
St. Paul's, 35; Calvert Hall, 25.
Loyola, 37; McDonogh, 29.
Mt. St. Joe, 42; Gilman, 36.

Zavala To Get Return Bout

NEW YORK, Feb. 17—(U. P.). Danny Bartfield, New York lightweight, won a unanimous 10-round decision over Humberto Zavala of Mexico at Madison Square Garden last night. However, Zavala made such a hit with the 11,680 fans that they will be rematched later for 12 rounds.

Bartfield floored his man twice and won the bout by a clear margin. The United Press scored six rounds for the New Yorker, three for Zavala and one even.

AWAITING OWNER—This small female dog, part collie, has been given temporary refuge by Mrs. Daisy Brown, 938 North Gilmor street. The dog is light tan and white and is very friendly.

DOGS

Billy, a rather large male wire-haired terrier, has been missing from his home at 1006 Cathedral street since early yesterday. Billy has long, white with two tan ears. He is about nine years old and is rather stout. He is very friendly. If you have seen this pet please contact Mrs. Bertie Welch at the above address or phone Saratoga 3499.

Residents of Lansdowne, Md., are requested to be on the lookout for a large black and white male St. Bernard, which has strayed from his home at 128 American avenue, Lansdowne. This dog answers to the name of Chubby. If you have seen this pet, please write Charles Leake at the above address or phone Arbutus 2-J.

A small female rabbit hound, who is due to have puppies next month, has become lost from her home at 111 Clyde avenue, Lansdowne, Md. The dog answers to the name of Blue and was wearing a collar bearing license No. 25278. She is mostly white with two black spots on her back and an all-brown head. If you have seen this dog please contact Mrs. Anna Schatz at the above address or phone Arbutus 533-J.

Mrs. Harry W. Burkhardt, 7235 Hughes avenue, Sparrows Point, phoned in this morning to report the loss of a black and brown female Scottie, about a year old. The pet, which answers to the name of Charky, was last seen on the ice at Jones creek, opposite the Sparrows Point Golf Club. This dog is the pet of a small girl who is away at school. The phone at the above address is Sparrows Point 443-W.

PATTERSON MATMEN WIN

Patterson Park's wrestling team won their eighth victory yesterday when they downed Gilman, 20 to 18.

Sammy 6 Under Par In Test At Gulfport

By SKIPPER PATRICK

GULFPORT, Miss., Feb. 17—(A. P.).—Slammin' Sammy Snead steps back on professional golf's gold path today after leading a talented field of 71 pros and amateurs with a six-under-par 65 in the opening round of the $5,000 Gulfport Open tournament yesterday.

The stocky Hot Springs naruball hitter, who has won $3,846.67 in war bonds this year, gave the favorites Byron Nelson, Toledo, Ohio, and Harold (Jug) McSpaden, Sanford, Maine, a golfing lesson in the initial round here by tying the great Southern Country Club course record set by Jim Wilson, Gulfport pro, in 1923.

MISSED RECORD

He was on the verge of a new course record when he reached the eighteenth green, but missed a three-foot putt.

Snead was just about perfect yesterday, shooting both nines in three under par. He had one eagle, four birdies and 13 pars, and was off the green in par only on the second green.

Sammy said he was in the best physical condition since a back ailment forced a temporary two-tournament retirement after the Tucson Open.

Claude Harmon, Grosse Point, Mich., who finished third at New Orleans, and Ky Laffoon, Chicago, start today as Snead's closest rivals. Both had four under par 67s yesterday

NELSON, McSPADEN CLOSE

The gold dust twins, Byron Nelson and Jug McSpaden, are in good position to catch up, should Sammy falter. McSpaden was three under par 68 yesterday and Nelson two under 69.

Leonard Dodson, San Francisco, and Frank Strazza, Chicago, tied the first round with McSpaden at 68.

Fourteen others start the second 18 holes today with par or better scored for their first round. They include Chick Rutan, Birmingham, Mich.; Jimmy Gauntt, Ardmore, Okla., and ~~Ed Fargo~~, Detroit, amateur (69); Mike Turnesa, White Plains, N. Y.; Milton Demaret, Houston, Texas; Bob Hamilton, Evanston, Ill.; George McAllister, Dayton, Ohio, and Bob Stupple, Chicago (70); Willie Goggin, New York; Sammy Byrd, Detroit; Craig Wood, Mamaroneck, N. Y.; Joe Zarhardt, Norristown, Pa.; George Kunes, Hollywood, Fla., and Sam Schneider, Corpus Christi, Texas (71).

BASKETBALL RESULTS

Illinois, 56; Ohio State, 41.
St. Francis, 42; Fordham, 41.
Citadel, 41; Clemson, 39.
Xavier of New Orleans, 45; Sam Houston, 25.
Kansas, 33; Kansas City, 31.
Michigan, 46; Northwestern, 45.
Davidson, 39; Furman, 32.
Washburn, 64; St. Benedicts, 40.
Warrensburg (Mo.) Teachers, 30; Drury, 29.
Arkansas, 59; Southern Methodist, 52.
Loyola of New Orleans, 49; Millsaps, 47.
Anthonians, 33; Hofstra, 32.
Great Lakes Naval, 64; DePaul, 56.
Wright Field Air Techs, 62; San Antonio Service League All-Stars, 44
Washington, 37; Gonzaga, 30.

Poly Rallies To Nip City Five

With Charley Kreis, lanky forward, sparking a final half rally the Poly basketball team upset City last night at Evergreen, 27 to 25. Kreis tallied the final nine points scored by Poly, which brought the Engineers from a six-point deficit to a two-point upset victory. For his night's work Kreis hit the cords for four field goals and four out of five foul shots.

PALS SEPARATED—Young Bobby Poole of 111 Clyde avenue, Lansdowne, Md., is shown above with the pet rabbit hound which strayed from the above address almost a week ago. The little dog is a female and is due to have puppies next month. Answering to the name of Blue, she is white with brown spots on her back and a brown head, and was wearing a collar with license number 25278. If you have seen this pet, please contact Mrs. Schatz at the above address or phone Arbutus 533-J.

Places to Dine SUNDAY

HARRY L. HASSLINGER CO., INC.
NORTH AVE. & ST. PAUL ST.
DELICIOUS Raw, Padded and Fried OYSTERS
Imperial Crabs—Crab Cakes
Fried Chicken • Steaks • Chops
Choice Wines and Liquors
VISIT OUR TAKE-OUT DEPT.
CLOSED TUESDAYS

WHITE RICE INN
Chinese-American Restaurant
320 Park Ave.—Baltimore 1, Md.
156 Main St., White Plains, N. Y.
Air Conditioned ★ Phone VE. 3428
Real Cantonese Family Dinners
OPEN 11 A. M. TO 4 A. M.
ROBERT LEW, Proprietor

OYSTERS
RAW BAR SPECIALS
OYSTERS AND CLAMS On the Half Shell
Delicious Oyster PLATTERS And OYSTER SANDWICHES
FRESH LOBSTERS Prepared in All Styles
Volkmer's Seafood RESTAURANT Closed Tues.
700 WASHINGTON BLVD., Cor. Fremont

OUTSTANDING FOR FINE FOOD!
Baltimore's Smartest RESTAURANT COCKTAIL LOUNGE
Luncheon • Dinner After-Theatre Supper
Johnson's MECCA Open Daily and Sundays!
32 S. CALVERT ST. • NO TAX
SA. 6691 for Reservations

In the Smartest Circles People Consider the 2 CHINA INNS
Baltimore's Finest Chinese-American Restaurants
• New China Inn, 2430 N. Charles St. Open Daily From 11 A. M. to 3 A. M.
• Original China Inn, 406 Park Ave. Open Daily 'Til 4 A. M. ● James Wu, Mgr.

MANDELL'S 118 EAST BALTIMORE ST. Near Covert
A Restaurant that realizes our customers' memory will last longer than the war!
Continuous Music by Muzak

COME TO THE Penn Hotel
TOWSON—BALTIMORE COUNTY
(Directly on No. 8 Car Line)
Specializing in Fried Golden Brown Chicken
Delicious Broiled Steaks
Dinners $1.00 Up
Catering to Parties and Banquets For Reservations Call Towson 905
Mrs. Edna C. Wells, Mgr.
Formerly Wellsmore Inn, Cape Cod, Mass.

PIK ★ CHICK
FRIED Chicken DINNER
Open Daily 11 A. M. to 12 P. M. Closed Monday
SERVED WITHOUT SILVER 95¢
Prepared to eat and enjoy just as you do at home, with delicious French Fries and Hot Rolls. It's Really Good!
PIK ★ CHICK RESTAURANT
3607 Fleet St. at Conkling
In The Center of Highlandtown

HOME COOKED DINNERS
Open every Sunday, and Every day Except Tuesday
Fresh Poultry From Nearby Farms Served Daily
WESTWOOD RESTAURANT
101 W. 22nd St.

Two Marriages Are Arranged For Today

Kinsley-Dorsey Wedding To Be In Evening

Two weddings are on today's calendar, one in the afternoon and another in the evening.

The evening event will be the marriage of Betsy Hillen Dorsey and Reuben Clark Kinsley, Jr., son of Mr. and Mrs. Kinsley of Baltimore and it will be performed at Corpus Christi Rectory at 7 o'clock this evening by the Rev. Joseph J. Lilly of the Catholic University of America.

Only the two families have been invited, and Mr. J. Marshall Dorsey is giving his daughter in marriage, her sole attendant being her sister, Deborah. William Kinsley will be his brother's best man.

A small reception will follow at the house of Mr. and Mrs. Dorsey on Bolton street.

IN MEETING HOUSE

The wedding of Phebe Elizabeth Martenet, daughter of Mrs. Joseph Burden Mitchell, to Arnold Evert Look, Jr., son of Mr. and Mrs. Look of Newton Square, Pa., is taking place at 3 o'clock this afternoon at Friends Meeting House.

A reception follows.

Mrs. Mitchell is entertaining at luncheon before the ceremony.

The marriage of Mrs. Julian Van Buren, daughter of Mr. and Mrs. Edward McKinney Hunt of Washington and New York, to Van Rensselaer Schuyler, son of Mrs. J. Ramsay Speer of Easton, Md., and the late Sidney Schuyler, took place on February 10 in New York. There were four attendants.

Lieutenant Van Buren, A. U. S., died in Norfolk two years ago.

The Mount Royal Garden Club, of which Mrs. Emmett R. Ewell is president, will meet next Tuesday afternoon, February 20, at 3, at the house of Miss Anne G. Turnbull, a vice-president; Mrs. Albert Baker being the other.

Other officers include Mrs. William Caulk, Miss Elise Ingle, Mrs. Louis Passano and Mrs. George R. Vickers IV.

Mrs. Richard H. R. Toland has returned to Philadelphia after a brief visit to her cousin, Mrs. L. Wilkin Boynton.

WINTER COTILLON TONIGHT

The Winter Cotillon, under the auspices of Mrs. Brent H. Farber, Jr., is taking place this evening, preceded by the meeting of the Saturday evening dancing class for a younger group both at Cadoa Hall.

The Victory Cotillon was held last night, at the same place, and the closing dance will take place on March 9.

Gough Winn Thompson, Jr., and William M. Passano, Jr., will be joint hosts at a dance for the school set this evening at the Gough Thompson residence.

Mr. and Mrs. Charles Buckner Ray are passing part of the late winter visiting relatives in North Carolina.

Mr. and Mrs. Edward Voss have returned to their estate in Harford county, after spending some time in New York. Their son, Edward Voss, Jr., has joined the Merchant Marine, and is in training at Sheepshead Bay.

Lieutenant and Mrs. Joseph J. Dockman have announced the birth of a son, to be named for his father. Mrs. Dockman was Jean Riley.

Mrs. Cadwalader Kelsey is returning this week-end after a fortnight in New York, to rejoin her mother, Mrs. W. Graham Boyce, at Bacon Hall Farm.

John Taylor Arms, American etcher, will be the guest of honor and speaker at a meeting of the Three Arts Club of Homeland at the Baltimore Museum of Art on Monday. He will give a demonstration lecture on "Making An Etching." Mrs. Edward V. Milholland is president of the club. Tea will be served. Two others taking part in the program planning are Mrs. John W. Lewis and Mrs. H. Leary Taylor.

Billy Bachelor

SEE IT MADE WHILE YOU WAIT
POINTLESS CHOWMEIN for DINNER TONIGHT
Complete with crisp noodles and sauce! Pick it up on your way home.
Service for 4 $1.10
VEr. 8193
ASIA BAKING CO.
917 Linden Ave.

The Smart Set — Women in Wartime

VIRGINIA WHITE PENNIMAN MARGARET HILGARTNER

When serving as bridesmaids at the Boyden-Offutt wedding, Miss Penniman wore a frock of peach faille, while Miss Hilgartner was in blue, of the same material and model. Evidently the reception was a very jolly affair, to judge from the merry faces of the two attendants.

M.-G.-M. Refuses To Allow Another Boys' Town Film

By LOUELLA O. PARSONS
Motion Picture Editor
International News Service.

HOLLYWOOD, Feb. 17.—John Considine's plan to film another version of "Boys Town" has been hit on the head by M.-G.-M. Today John, who has been in bed a week with the flu, received a telegram from Father Flanagan saying M.-G.-M. had informed him that because of the contract the film company holds on the rights to the stories of Father Flanagan's Boy Town, they wouldn't permit another version to be made. Father Flanagan had previously asked for permission to make it.

Johnny produced the other two "Boys Town" pictures when he was at M.-G.-M. He brought Bob Considine out from New York to write the story. He says he hasn't any grievance against the studio, but Father Flanagan, being an honorable man, wants to live up to terms of his contract. Now John has to start again from scratch and find another story.

Taking my dog for a walk around the block I ran into Constance Moore who had her small daughter, Gina, out for an airing. Connie was happy. She had just signed a long-term contract at Republic. She'll make three pictures a year and she said with Frank Borzage there and the possibility of John Ford signing a contract. She felt her prospects had never been better. She isn't going to New York. She never was very keen about it but she'll report at Republic for a musical called "Mexicana," in which Tito Guizar has a role. I was interested to hear Alfred Santell, who directed such stars as Marion Davies and Richard Barthelmess and many others, will direct "Mexicana." Al has a new long term contract.

Snapshots of Hollywood Collected at Random: Sylvia Sidney is laid up with a torn ligament in her right foot. She won't be able to walk for at least two weeks; Susan Hayward and Jess Barker, who had no place for the expected twins, have located a home in Bel-Air. It's the one formerly occupied by Sonny Tufts; Capt. Eddie Hillman is home on a 21-day leave. He looks wonderful and did a great job overseas. Maybe you think June—Mrs. Hillman to you—wasn't glad to see him.

Eleanor Parker's brother, Charles, is here on furlough after two years in the Pacific. And, by the way, I hear Eleanor is going to have a date with Robert Cummins very soon—it's mutual admiration; Barbara Whiting, age thirteen, knocked her teacher cold when she put the name of Errol Flynn opposite the word "virile" in a definition test.

Agnes Moorehead, Academy Award candidate, is learning to ride a motorcycle. She gave it to her husband, Jack Lee, for a present, and she's getting more fun out of it than he is; Judy Garland parts with a wisdom tooth this week-end. She and Alan Ladd come back February 26 from their hospital tour; Bonita Granville has bought a beauty parlor in the valley. Not only will she be in business but will get all her work done free; Stanley Clements, who has had so much favorable comment on his "Salty O'Rourke" performance, is undergoing a tonsillectomy. That's all today. See you tomorrow!

Fred ASTAIRE Rita HAYWORTH in You Were Never Lovelier with ADOLPHE MENJOU Music by JEROME KERN

2 BIG HITS
HENRY FONDA JOAN BENNETT in STEWART EDWARD WHITE'S WILD GEESE CALLING
800 Blk. N. Howard ROSLYN

2ND BIG WEEK TIMES 2 CHILLERS!
SIDNEY TOLER as CHARLIE CHAN in "THE JADE MASK"
EXTRA ADDED "LISBON CLIPPER MYSTERY" Anna LEE John LODER
MURDER in Mid-Air A Powerhouse of SUSPENSE!

COMING! ROSLYN & TIMES!
ALAN LADD The DASHIELL HAMMETT'S GLASS KEY

DELICIOUS DINING
Best Chicken Chow Mein In Town
Our Kitchen Is Always Open For Inspection
CHUNG HING
CHINESE-AMERICAN RESTAURANT
3312 GREENMOUNT AVE.

Murder Mystery On Hip Screen— Drama At Mayfair

By NORMAN CLARK

THE SCREEN ADDS to its detective force, also its killers, in the chiller-diller, "I Love a Mystery."

Like quite a few of the yarns popping up in the movies these days, this comes from the radio, where, we understand, the original series is popular. The new sleuths that you will meet at the Hippodrome are Jack Packard and Doc Long, portrayed, respectively, by Jim Bannon and Barton Yarborough. The latter, we are told, plays the same part that he originated on the air.

"I Love a Mystery" has an Oriental tinge—a strange doom that stalks through American streets. There is a guy, a peg-legged killer, with a face that should give a scary person 18 brands of creeps. There are strange messages from the Far East, mystic rites, knives, murders.

Of course, there is also feminine decoration, furnished by Nina Foch and Carole Mathews. George Macready helps supply some of the frightened looks, while Lester Mathews also turns in a good job, too.

"I Love a Mystery" should furnish the fans who go for this type of entertainment with an hour of shivery pleasure.

"I Love Mystery"

"I LOVE A MYSTERY," at the Hippodrome. Screen play by Charles O'Neal. Directed by Henry Levin. A Columbia picture.

THE CAST

Jack Packard..........Jim Bannon
Ellen Monk..........Nina Foch
Jefferson Monk...George Macready
Doc Long.......Barton Yarborough
Jean Anderson.....Carole Matthews
Justin Reeves.....Lester Matthews
Dr. Han..............Gregory Gay
Vovaritch..........Leo Mostovoy

AT MAYFAIR

"SERGEANT MIKE," at the Mayfair. Screen play by Robert Lee Johnson. Directed by Harry Levin. A Columbia picture.

THE CAST

Allen..................Larry Parks
Terry..................Jeanne Bates
Sims...................Loren Tindall
Patrick Henry..........Jim Bannon
Sergeant Rankin...Robert Williams
Reed...............Richard Powers
S. K. Arno.........Larry Joe Olsen
Monahan..............Eddie Acuff
Mike.....................Himself
Pearl.....................Herself

MIKE, HANDSOME shepherd dog, who gets up to be a sergeant is the hero of the drama called "Sergeant Mike," which shows dogs in training for war and also in battle.

At first Larry Parks is good and sore when he is transferred from a machine-gun outfit to the K9 Corps and he doesn't take any interest in the training of Mike, who has been given to the Army by his eight-year-old master, Larry Joe Olsen, whose father died on the battlefield.

"Mike" comes near being washed out, too, until Larry learns about the great sacrifice that his little master had made. Then does he make a scout out of that animal! There's another dog in the story, too—Pearl, and she's good, too.

"Sergeant Mike" has patiently been whipped up for the juvenile film-goers.

GASHED BY GUITAR

After eight weeks of dodging fists, bullets, knives, flying bottles and chairs for "San Antonio," Errol Flynn was gashed by a steel guitar string which snapped when he was tuning the instrument for a scene.

Women's Club Calendar

TOMORROW

Maryland Branch, National Woman's Party, 3 to 6 P. M., in home of Mrs. Theodore Weems Forbes, 1432 Park avenue. Tea honoring the one hundred and twenty-fifth anniversary of the birth of Susan B. Anthony. Mrs. Alma Harrison Ambrose in charge. Miss Carola Bell Williams to give impersonation of Miss Anthony.

Queen Anne Juniors, 3 P. M., in Parochial School, 3701 Cottage avenue. Memorial service for members, Faye Nachman and Fay Cutler.

Goucher Club of Baltimore, 4.15 P. M., in home of Mrs. H. Elmer Singewald, 4404 Atwick road. Board meeting.

Baltimore Council of Navy League, 6 P. M. Dinner at 806 St. Paul street.

Altrua Guild, at 307 West Fayette street. Celebration of sixth anniversary with banquet and dance. Mrs. Theodore A. Baum and Mrs. Harry Eisenstein in charge.

Movie Clock

CENTURY—"Dark Waters," 11.33 A. M., 1.35, 3.37, 5.39, 7.41, 9.43 P. M.
STANLEY — "To Have and Have Not," 11.15 A. M., 1.20, 3.30, 5.35, 7.40, 9.50 P. M.
NEW—"Keys of the Kingdom," 10 A. M., 12.21, 2.42, 5.03, 7.24, 9.45 P. M.
MAYFAIR — "Sergeant Mike," 11.24 A. M., 1.15, 3.06, 4.57, 6.48, 8.39, 10.30 P. M.
ROSLYN — "You Were Never Lovelier," 1.16, 4.12, 7.14, 10.16 P. M.
VALENCIA — "Meet Me In St. Louis," 12.55, 3.06, 5.17, 7.28, 9.39 P. M.
TIMES — "Charlie Chan in Jade Mask," 12.24, 3.01, 5.38, 8.15, 10.52 P. M.
LITTLE—"Bluebeard," 11.18 A. M., 1.05, 2.52, 4.39, 6.26, 8.13, 10 P. M.
KEITHS—"House of Frankenstein," 10.57 A. M., 12.49, 2.41, 4.33, 6.25, 8.17, 10.09 P. M.
PARKWAY—"Blonde Fever," 2.02, 3.58, 5.54, 7.50, 9.47 P. M.
HIPPODROME — "I Love a Mystery," 10.15 A. M., 12.35, 3.10, 5.40, 8.05, 10.30 P. M.

LOEW'S
CENTURY OPENS 10.45 A.M. Mystery! Suspense! Romance! "DARK WATERS" Merle OBERON Franchot TONE. STARTS WEDS. MIDNITE "MUSIC FOR MILLIONS" Margaret O'Brien & Jimmy Durante
VALENCIA OPENS 12.45 P.M. 4th WEEK! IN TECHNICOLOR "MEET ME IN ST. LOUIS" JUDY GARLAND-MARGARET O'BRIEN
PARKWAY OPENS 12.45 P.M. "BLONDE FEVER" Mary ASTOR • Philip DORN

MAYFAIR HOWARD & FRANKLIN
FIRST BALTIMORE RUN! Meet the Bravest War-Dog of Them All!
MIKE TAUGHT HIM TO LOVE! MIKE TAUGHT HER TO LIVE! MIKE TAUGHT HIM TO BE BRAVE!
No Wonder They Loved COLUMBIA'S SERGEANT MIKE
LARRY PARKS • JEANNE BATES • LOREN TINDALL • JIM BANNON "MIKE" and "PEARL"

A. J. Cronin's THE KEYS OF THE KINGDOM
NEW THEATRE LEX. ST. at PARK AVE.

HIPPODROME
Stage IN PERSON ALL-NEW 1945 EDITION! EARL CARROLL'S VANITIES CAST OF 50 STARS
Screen "I LOVE A MYSTERY"

KEITH'S LEXINGTON AT PARK
HOUSE OF FRANKENSTEIN Starring BORIS KARLOFF LON CHANEY JOHN CARRADINE J. CARROL NAISH ANNE GWYNNE ELENA VERDUGO PETER COE LIONEL ATWILL
KEITHS ROOF—Dance SAT. SUN. BOB CRAIG & BAND

FORD'S—NEXT WEEK SEATS NOW ON SALE
The THEATRE GUILD presents Tallulah BANKHEAD in PHILIP BARRY'S New Comedy FOOLISH NOTION
HENRY HULL • DONALD COOK
Directed by JOHN C. WILSON

RIVOLI
GARY COOPER JEAN PARKER
"The Cowboy and the Lady" "Adventures of Kitty O'Day"
DOUBLE SHOW DAILY DOORS OPEN 9 A. M.

VAGABOND THEATRE 3 W. Read St. LEx. 9865
Tonight—8.30—Seats $1.20 Inc. Tax
"THE DOUGH GIRLS"

GAYETY ONLY REAL BURLESK IN BALTO.
She's Daringly Different! GLORIA LOVE
Charlie Robinson
Lou Devine

LITTLE HOWARD & FRANKLIN
2nd SMASH WEEK
John CARRADINE in "BLUEBEARD" JEAN PARKER • NILS ASTHER

WARNER BROS. STANLEY HOWARD NEAR FRANKLIN ST. DOORS OPEN 10:30 A. M.
3rd and FINAL WEEK!
HUMPHREY BOGART in ERNEST HEMINGWAY'S "TO HAVE AND HAVE NOT"
with LAUREN BACALL
WALTER BRENNAN • DOLORES MORAN • HOAGY CARMICHAEL
A HOWARD HAWKS Production
BUY WAR BONDS AND STAMPS

Tomorrow—The Lyric—8:30 P. M.
BALTIMORE SYMPHONY
Reginald Stewart, Conductor
Bach Concert For Three Pianos
SKLAVERSKI, TALLARICO, CONRADI Soloists
PEABODY CHORUS
IFOR JONES
150 Voices Under the Direction of
TCHAIKOVSKY'S "Pathetique" Symphony
Popular Prices, 25c to $1.80
Tickets at the Cappel Concert Bureau, Stieff Hall, 315 N. Howard St., VErnon 1343; the Music Center, 313 N. Charles St., LExington 6040.

TODAY'S MOVIE CALENDAR

Theatres advertised in this column belong to the Motion Picture Theatre Owners of Maryland.

Let's Finish the Job
BUY WAR BONDS

Aero Middle River. Tim Holt in "Red River Robin Hood."
Alpha Catonsville. John Garfield in "Hollywood Canteen."
Ambassador 4606 Lib. Hts. D. Durbin in "Can't Help Singing."
Apollo 1500 Harford. Claudette Colbert in "Under Two Flags."
Arcade Harford & Ham. J. Leslie in "Hollywood Canteen."
Astor Pop. Grove. & Edmond. Carmen Miranda in "Something for the Boys."
Aurora 1 E. North. Roy Rogers in "Lights of Old Santa Fe."
Avalon 4300 Park Hts. Richard Travis in "The Last Ride."
Avenue Milton & Hoffman. East Side Kids in "Bowery Champs."
Avon 3039 Hamilton.. Allan Lane in "Silver City Kid."
Belnord 2600 Phila. Deanna Durbin in "Can't Help Singing."
Boulevard 33rd at Greenmount. D. Durbin in "Can't Help Singing."
Bridge 2100 Edmond. Roy Rogers in "Yellow Rose of Texas."
Broadway 509 S. Bdway. R. Dix in "Mark of the Whistler."
Cameo 4700 Harford. Dead End Kids in "Block Busters."
Capitol 1518 W. Balto. Bob Hope in "Nothing But the Truth."
Casino 1118 Light. Roy Rogers in "Song of Texas."
Cluster 303 S. Bdway. Priscilla Lane in "Brother Rat."
Columbia 709 Wash. Blvd. B. Hope in "The Princess and the Pirate."
Earle Belair & Woodlea. Richard Dix in "Mark of the Whistler."
Edgewood 5200 Edmond. Kent Taylor in "Alaska."
Eureka 404 S. Fremont. S. Burnette in "Firebrands of Arizona."
Forest Garrison & Lib. Hts. Bob Hope in 'The Princess and the Pirate.'
Fulton Fulton & Baker. Abbott and Costello in "Lost in a Harem."
Garden Charles & Cross. Gene Autry in "Ride, Ranger, Ride."
Glen Glen Burnie. Billy Gilbert in "Crazy Knights."
Grand 511 S. Conkling. C. Starrett in "Cyclone Prairie Rangers."
Gwynn 4600 Liberty Hts. C. Starrett in "Cyclone Prairie Rangers."
Hampden 911 W. 36th. Fuzzy Knight in "Trail to Gunsight."
Harford 2620 Harford. Richard Arlen in "Storm Over Lisbon."
Hilton 3117 W. North. Jerry Colona in "Priorities On Parade."
Horn 2016 W. Pratt. Jean Heather in "The National Barn Dance."
Howard 115 N. Howard. V. H. Ralston in "Lake Placid Serenade."
Ideal 906 W. 36th. J. Mack Brown in "Land of the Outlaws."
Irvington 4118 Frederick. J. Heather in "The National Barn Dance."
Lane Dundalk. Eddie Dew in "Trail to Gunsight."
Leader 348 S. Bdway. Dead-End Kids in "Mob Town."
Linwood 908 S. Linwood. All-Star Cast in "Ride, Ranger, Ride."
Little 523 N Howard. Jean Parker in "Blue Beard."
Lord Baltimore 1110 W. Balto. Smiley Burnette in "Firebrands of Arizona."
Lord Calvert 2444 Wash. Boulvd. Virginia Bruce in "Brazil."
Lyceum Sparrows Point. Ruth Terry in "Jamboree."
Mayfair 508 N. Howard. Larry Parks in "Sergeant Mike."
McHenry 1037 Light. D. Durbin in "Can't Help Singing."
Met Penn. at North. Robert Henry in "The Great Mike."
Nemo 4921 Eastern. Gene Autry in "Gaucho Serenade."
New Reisterstown. Charles Starrett in "Sagebrush Heroes."
New Essex Essex. June Carlson in "Delinquent Daughters."
New Glen Glen Burnie. Ronald Colman in "Kismet."
Northway Harford & North. Pkway. V. H. Ralston in "Lake Placid Serenade."
Overlea Belair Rd. Ann Savage in "Unwritten Code."
Palace Gay & Hoffman. Allan Lane in "Sheriff of Sundown."
Patterson Eastern & East. J. Leslie in "Hollywood Canteen."
Pikes Pikesville. Virginia Bruce in "Brazil."
Pimlico Park Hts. & Belvd. A. Gwynn in 'Murder in the Blue Room.'
Preston 1108 E. Preston. B. Crabbe in "Rustlers Hide-Out."
Red Wing 2241 E. Monument. Chas. Starrett in "Saddle Leather Law."
Rex 4617 York Rd. Leo Gorcey in "Bowery Champs."
Rialto 846 W. North. Evelyn Keyes in "Strange Affair."
Ritz 1607 N. Wash. Joan Leslie in "Hollywood Canteen."
Senator 5904 York. Joan Leslie in "Hollywood Canteen."
State Monument & Castle. D. Durbin in "Can't Help Singing."
Strand Dundalk. Deanna Durbin in "Can't Help Singing."
Towson Towson. Charles Starrett in "Sagebrush Heroes."
Uptown 5010 Park Hts. Evelyn Keyes in "Strange Affair."
Vilma Belair & Mayfield. Joan Leslie in "Hollywood Canteen."
Walbrook 3100 W. North. N. Eddy in "Naughty Marietta."
Waverly Greenmount & Gorsuch. J. Frazee in "Swing in the Saddle."
Westport 3305 Russell. Vera Hruba Ralston in "Lake Placid Serenade."
Westway 5300 Edmond. Vivien Leigh in "Waterloo Bridge."

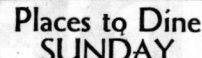

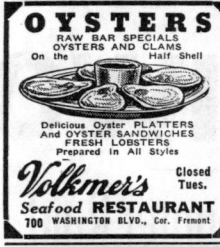

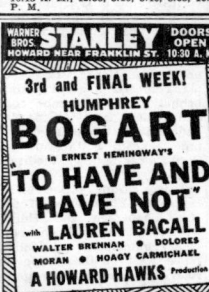

U. S. TROOPS INVADE CORREGIDOR, REPORT

THE WEATHER
Snow, cold tonight; Sunday mostly cloudy, continued cold.
Detailed Weather Report Page 11

Read The Baltimore News-Post for complete, accurate war coverage. It is the only Baltimore newspaper possessing the three great wire services—
ASSOCIATED PRESS
INTERNATIONAL NEWS SERVICE
UNITED PRESS

THE BALTIMORE NEWS-POST
AN INDEPENDENT NEWSPAPER
The Largest Evening Circulation in the Entire South

7 HOME FINAL

VOL. CXLVI.—NO. 87 | Entered as second-class matter at Baltimore Postoffice. | SATURDAY EVENING, FEBRUARY 17, 1945 | PRICE 3 CENTS

RUSS BREAK INTO BRESLAU, NAZIS SAY

YANKS ALSO LAND ON IWO

Reports Red Break Into Breslau

NEW YORK, Feb. 17—(A. P.). An NBC broadcast from Moscow today said Marshal Ivan Konev had swept to within three miles of Cottbus, rail center 47 miles southeast of Berlin.

LONDON, Feb. 17—(U. P.).—The German High Command said today that a Russian siege army had broken into Breslau, encircled capital of Silesia.

A Berlin communique acknowledged Soviet penetrations in attacks on the fortress of Breslau and other reports indicated that the industrial city of more than 600,000 on the Oder was doomed.

ADMITS LOSS OF SAGAN

The Nazi command admitted the loss of Sagan, key city on the Berlin-Breslau railway and on the Bober river, to the First Ukrainian Army driving west toward Dresden and northwest toward Berlin.

Moscow dispatches said the Red Air Force was carrying out one of

(The Nazi DNP agency admitted today Russian forces have broken into Klettendorf, southern suburb of the encircled Silesian capital of Breslau, after „massive artillery preparation.)

its greatest campaigns of the war over the Oder, Neisse and Spree valleys.

Fighting off German planes shifted from the western front, Soviet reports said, the Russian airmen blasted German air fields, spread havoc through their communications and scattered troop concentrations along and behind the front.

FLY 10,000 SORTIES

Red Star, the Soviet military journal, said that for three successive days the Russians flew 10,000 sorties a day.

A front dispatch to the Communist party organ Pravda said Rus-

Continued on Page 2, Column 5.

Oil Substitutes Urged By Japs

By Associated Press.

Domei, the Japanese news agency, today broadcast an article by a high Army officer in which he urged development of substitutes for oil and other imports in anticipation of possible loss of the occupied southern regions.

NUNCIO QUITS BERLIN

VATICAN CITY, Feb. 17—(A. P.).—The Papal Nuncio to Berlin has transferred his residence from Berlin to Eichstaett in Bavaria, the Vatican said today. He is the guest of the bishop of Eichstaett.

Temperatures

12 Mid.,	43	7 A. M.,	34
1 A. M.,	43	8 A. M.,	33
2 A. M.,	42	9 A. M.,	33
3 A. M.,	41	10 A. M.,	33
4 A. M.,	41	11 A. M.,	33
5 A. M.,	40	12 Noon,	33
6 A. M.,	35	1 P. M.,	33

Allies Push On Goch, Calcar

PARIS, Feb. 17 — (U. P.).—Canadian First Army troops plunged forward more than two miles in the northern section of the Siegfried Line today, cut the Goch-Galcar highway and closed within a little more than a mile of both Goch and Calcar.

PARIS, Feb. 17—(A. P.).—Allied troops of the Canadian First Army battled today to within 1½ miles or less of the shell-ripped Nazi bastions of Goch and Calcar, southeast of Kleve in a sudden, resurgent push over mired battlefields.

Britons, Scots and Canadians under Gen. Henry Crerar's command lunged forward yesterday behind a wall of bombs, rockets and bullets from Allied planes, and British troops speared 2¼ miles ahead, cutting the main Goch-Calcar highway at two points. points.

Troops closing on Goch and Calcar gained 2,500 yards. They entered Asperden and Hervorst, within 1½ miles of Goch, and toppled Hommersum and Mull, five miles west of the strongly-held road center seven miles south of Kleve.

CANADIANS PUSH ON

Canadian tanks and infantry troops fought a mile and a half from Calcar, southeast of Kleve, and 17 miles from bomb-wrecked

Continued on Page 2, Column 7.

PIT BULLDOG

A "pit" bulldog belongs to a strain of dogs which have been trained for centuries to fight each other in bloody battle to the death in a dog pit.

Around this pit, or arena, inhuman humans, more brutal than the brutes that they brutalized, assembled to gratify an evil lust for blood and rejoice in the suffering and death of the wretched animals they had trained to cruelty and ferocity.

Today dog fighting is forbidden by law, but its sadism and evil blood lust still persist in various forms.

Indeed, dog fights are still held secretly in hidden cellars.

And other equally sadistic crimes against miserable animals are still perpetrated behind the closed doors of laboratories into which the public is never allowed to look.

Small wonder that pit bulldogs have inherited the ferocity of their masters, who trained them to brutality.

No pit bulldog should ever be made the companion of a child.

Parents should heed this warning.

There are plenty of dogs trained by gentleness and kindness to protect children and which will sacrifice their own lives in their loyalty to their humane masters.

U. S. LANDING ON IWO JIMA REPORTED—American Liberator planes fly over the tiny island of Iwo, 750 miles south of Tokyo, in this Air Force photo made several months ago. Today Japanese radio broadcasts claim that American assault forces have landed on Iwo following a two-day naval bombardment.

Congress Clears Way For O. K. Of Wallace

WASHINGTON, Feb. 17 — (A. P.).—Only time, a stroke of the President's pen and some debate in the Senate today appeared to separate Henry A. Wallace from a coveted Cabinet post.

Congress let down the last practical bar to his confirmation as Secretary of Commerce when the House passed and sent to the White House the George bill shearing the multi-billion-dollar lending agencies from the Commerce Department.

President Roosevelt has promised to let the bill become law—an action without which the former Vice-President admittedly could not be confirmed. With that accomplished, effective Senate opposition appeared almost certain to collapse.

Threat To Close Plant Defies WLB

NEW YORK, Feb. 17.—Rather than abide by a War Labor Board order to rehire three union officials convicted of extortion, John M. Alfiero today said he would close the war plant of which he is president, the E. A. Laboratories, Brooklyn. Stabilization Director Vinson directed the War and Navy Departments to cancel contracts with Alfiero's company and ordered denial of priorities to the firm.

Convoy Raid Cost Foe 7 Planes--Berlin

LONDON, Feb. 17—(A. P.).—The Berlin radio said today that German fighters shot down seven British bombers which attempted unsuccessfully to attack a Nazi surface convoy off the Norwegian coast north of Bergen.

Nazi Withdrawal In Italy Seen By Gen. Clark

ROME, Feb. 17—(A. P.).—Lieut. Gen. Mark W. Clark warned the people of Northern Italy today that "the full might of Allied air power is being turned against supply and communications routes of the enemy leading out of Northern Italy in order that any attempt at a German withdrawal may be made as costly as possible."

This was the first official mention here of the possibility of German withdrawal of some 27 divisions that have faced the British Eighth and U. S. Fifth Armies.

The Allied command in Italy told patriots in the north that "attempts by the Germans to withdraw in Italy become increasingly likely," particularly "in this phase of the war when in the east the Russian armies are sweeping on to Berlin and in the west the British and Americans are smashing through the Siegfried Line defenses."

He added:

"Your main task will also be to attack lines of communication, take all freedom of movement from the enemy. The efforts of the patriots must be coordinated with those of the Allied air forces.

"Keep away from roads, railways, communications centers, bridges and also all industrial targets to the fullest extent possible. Restrict all civilian travel and traffic to an absolute minimum because the enemy's use of the Italian communications system makes it impossible to distinguish between military and civilian transport."

The Water Wizard of the Mojave. Neither Julius Gobar Nor the Experts Know How He Does It, But California's Champion Water Witcher Finds Water Even in the Desert. Read Dr. Harold O. Whitnall's Story in The American Weekly, the Magazine Distributed With Tomorrow's Baltimore American.—Adv.

Discharged Veterans "Badge of Honor"

Get acquainted with this badge that bespeaks honor for the wearer!

It is the tiny gold medal issued by the Government to men and women who have been discharged from military service after honorably serving their country.

Whenever and wherever you see it worn, render tribute to it. Let the wearer know that you recognize his or her faithful service!

Veterans who failed to receive their buttons upon discharge may obtain one by calling in person with discharge papers at the induction center, Fifth Regiment Armory, for Army, and the Navy, Marine and Coast Guard recruiting offices, Post Office Building.

Nazis Hold 300,000 Women Of France

LONDON, Feb. 17—(A. P.).—A total of 300,000 French women are among prisoners of war and deportees in Germany, the Paris radio estimated today in announcing that a special reception camp had been set up to receive women repatriated after Germany's defeat.

Yanks Hit Villages West Of Mandalay

SOUTHEAST ASIA COMMAND HEADQUARTERS, KANDY, Ceylon, Feb. 17—(A. P.).—Allied ground forces driving through Burma got heavy aerial support again yesterday as U. S. medium and heavy fighter bombers attacked villages south and west of Mandalay.

U. S. Bombers In 4th Day Of Raids On Germany

LONDON, Feb. 17—(A. P.).—U. S. heavy bombers, carrying the mighty air offensive against Germany into its fourth day, smashed at the Reich from the west today and Berlin indicated Mediterranean-based squadrons were striking from the south again.

Another flurry of German "Achtung!" warnings placed the British-based bombers' attack on an arc close behind the western front. Coblenz, big German supply base on the Rhine, was in the path of the bombers, the Nazi radio said.

Three hundred and fifty Flying Fortresses attacked the great freight yards at Frankfurt behind the western front today, escored by 150 Mustang fighters which strafed German troops on the return flight.

About 1,700 U. S. and British heavies, including a force of Italian-based Fortresses, which struck the Regensburg factory where German jet-propelled planes are turned out, ranged unmolested over a wide area of Germany yesterday.

The Regensburg assault cost the enemy a number of the jet fighters which were caught on the ground, the Mediterranean Air force announced. U. S. Fifteenth Air Force Liberators also hit a jet plant at Neuburg, 50 miles north of Munich, and Landsburg Field, 35 miles west of Munich, where the Nazi twin-engined Messerschmitts are based.

SLAVS TAKE 5 TOWNS

LONDON, Feb. 17—(I. N. S.). Yugoslav Partisans, in their northward drive, captured five more German occupied towns and were within six miles of Sarajevo, the capital of Bosnia, the communique from Marshal Tito's headquarters said today.

Big Scale Counter Raid Launched On Luzon, Jap Agency Declares

LONDON, Feb. 17—(I. N. S.).—Japanese forces on Luzon have launched a large-scale counteroffensive, the Japanese Domei Agency asserted today.

WASHINGTON, Feb. 17—(U. P.).—American troops invaded the fortress island of Corregidor at the entrance to Manila bay by air and sea today, Radio Tokyo reported.

A Tokyo domestic broadcast said:

"Fierce battles now are raging on the southern shores of the island."

Paratroops opened the assault, swarming down on the island from transport planes, and soon afterward seaborne forces stormed ashore from assault-landing barges, Tokyo said.

BATAAN RECAPTURED

The reported combined operation followed by only a few hours Gen. Douglas MacArthur's announcement of the re-conquest of Bataan in an amphibious landing Thursday on the tip of the peninsula, five miles north of Corregidor.

No further details of the Corregidor fighting were given in the broadcast, which was recorded by the FCC. However, it opened the final phase of an offensive to unlock Manila bay to American shipping and to avenge the bloody defeats of 1941 and 1942.

Corregidor's giant batteries, which held off Japanese assaults on the island for months in 1942, had been all but neutralized by a terrific air and sea bombardment earlier this week.

FORT GUNS SILENCED

They fired a few rounds at the convoy carrying troops to Bataan Thursday, but were silenced quickly by salvos from American cruisers and destroyers, dispatches from Manila said.

Tokyo said American minesweepers began clearing the channel between Bataan and Corregidor Tuesday, followed by 10 troop-jammed transports.

After Corregidor has been captured American shipping safely can enter the bay. Once inside the bay American warships could lend their support to the annihilation of the last pockets of enemy troops holding out along the Manila waterfront. Newly captured Cavite naval base south of Manila also could be restored to use.

It was on May 6, 1942, that American forces on Corregidor surrendered to the Japanese, ending organized American resistance in the Philippines. Bataan had fallen a month earlier.

TEXT OF COMMUNIQUE

Meanwhile, Gen. Douglas MacArthur announced in a triumphant communique:

"We have captured Bataan."

Less than 48 hours after landing all the peninsula's militarily important objectives were in Ameri-

Continued on Page 2, Column 1.

Tells Nips To Yield

MANLIA, Feb. 17—(I. N. S.).—Maj. Gen. Oscar Griswold, Fourteenth Corps commander, in an endeavor to save the lives of Filipinos and other civilians trapped with the Japs in the Intramuros, today broadcast an ultimatum to the Nips defending the walled city.

Griswold told the Japs their position was hopeless and offered them honorable surrender.

Nips Report Yank Landings On Iwo

LONDON, Feb. 17—(I. N. S.). The Tokyo radio reported today that the unprecedented American aerial assault now pounding the Japanese homeland and reputedly-invaded Iwo Jima Island has been

ADMIRAL NIMITZ'S HEADQUARTERS, Guam, Feb. 17—(U. P.).—American troops stormed ashore today on Iwo Island, only 750 miles south of Tokyo, enemy broadcasts reported, while carrier planes hit the burning Japanese capital itself for the second straight day.

Invasion forces swarmed over the southwest and southeast beaches of Iwo in twin landings only 10 minutes apart, a Tokyo Domei broadcast said. It added the customary claim that the troops had been "repulsed" after fierce fighting.

SHORE BATTERIES OUT

The report of the invasion came on the second day of an earth-shaking bombardment of Iwo by

Continued on Page 2, Column 3.

NEWS-POST

Amusements	5	Haney, Dr. Lewis	11
Bugs Baer	7	Horoscope	[illegible]
Clark, Norman	5	Movies	[illegible]
Classified Ads	12, 13	Parsons, Louella	[illegible]
Comics	8	Pippen, R. H.	[illegible]
Crossword	13	Radio	11
Dixon, George	7	Robinson, Elsie	[illegible]
Durling	7	Society	[illegible]
Dulaney	7	Sports	9, 1[illegible]
Editorials	6	Women's Clubs	[illegible]
Financial	11		

BIG RED REALLY DESERVED A SHUTOUT—The Cornell Ithacans, who play Navy here next Saturday, had little trouble defeating Columbia in New York, 25 to 7. A recovered fumble gave the Lions their only score in the first period. The photos taken with the International News Service "magic eye" camera shows the Lions' left end, Gilbert as he made a 55-yard run for the touchdown. 1—Russell (35) of Cornell receives ball from center and fumbles. 2—Gilbert (83) of Columbia comes in to pick up the ball. 3—Gilbert (83) and Murchison (85) both of Columbia fall on the ball. 4—Gilbert (83) races away with the ball under his arm as Heller (7) runs interference. 5—Heller precedes Gilbert here and prepares to tackle Dekdebrun (43) of Cornell. 6—Heller halts the Cornell man and Gilbert continues on. 7—Heller made a leap for Gilbert and fell flat as Gilbert goes on. 8—Gilbert crosses the goal line for a touchdown. Sniadack (50) of Columbia blocks Golden (53) of Cornell.

HAGBERG OF NAVY NAMED 'COACH OF WEEK'

RODGER H. PIPPEN

SPORTS EDITOR, SAYS:

When Navy and Cornell meet in the Stadium here Saturday they will play under the new Eastern intercollegiate rules. This permits a recovered fumble to be run for a touchdown and requires kick-offs to be within bounds for runbacks. These same rules were used in the Navy-North Carolina Pre-Flight game and contributed materially to the thrills of that game; in fact, were very much responsible for the deciding score.

Cornell, in contrast with the "razzle dazzle" of Georgia Tech, is known as America's No. 1 "mouse-trapping" team. Coach Snavely has devised a baffling system of reverse teasers, end around and trap plays that often bewilder an opponent. Such was the case last Saturday in the Cornell 25-to-7 victory over Columbia.

George Trevor, writing of Cornell's strategy and stars in the New York Sun, stated:

"Young Paul Robeson, Jr., rangy son of the actor-singer who brought Othello to life on the stage, circled the Orange flanks on the same end-around maneuver that made Brud Holland famous. Young Robeson smeared every Syracuse sweep in the emphatic manner which made his dad an all-American picket at Rutgers in 1918 . . . What an end! That goes for both father and son . . . Paul carrying the ball at arm's length in one hand as he feinted Syracuse tacklers dizzy . . . Robeson, Senior, while a play-smashing end, never ran with the ball as his 190-pound son does."

* * *

Praise For Baltimorean

Commenting further on Cornell's tricky style of play, Trevor states:

"Among the legitimate backs in Cornell livery, the most elusive was Nate Scherr from Baltimore (Nathan Scherr, 185 pounds, six feet), who darted inside guard on Snavely's mouse-trap play in a manner that recalled Whit Baker of 1938-39 memory. John Cullen, a transfer from Northwestern . . . bore the Big Ten stamp."

* * *

About Last Year's Game

Playing the first night game in their history, the Middies beat the Big Red in the local Stadium on October 2, 1943, 46 to 7. Navy scored in every quarter, the touchdowns being made by Ben Martin, Sullivan, Hume, Barron, Pettit, Jenkins and Murray. In the third quarter Jenkins (Navy) caught a Cornell punt on Navy 20 and ran 71 yards to a touchdown.

* * *

Wants Nursing Mother For Six Puppies

If you have a mother dog who has been nursing puppies, you can save the lives of six little dogs whose mother died two hours after her babies were born. Please contact Mrs. Louis Linn, 1915 Greenmount avenue, or phone Chesapeake 2895.

* * *

Calls Baltimore Big-League Town

With the pleasant comment that Baltimore is ripe for big league sports, Vincent H. Flaherty, in his daily column in the Washington Times-Herald, says that a previous story he wrote about this city was misconstrued. Here is his article:

"The biggest baseball game in America (on Oct. 9) wasn't the one in which the St. Louis Cardinals won the world championship in St. Louis. It was in Baltimore, where 52,883 fans watched the Baltimore Orioles battle Louisville in the Junior World Series.

"Out in St. Louis less than a capacity crowd of 31-odd thousand people saw the Cardinals and Browns in the final game of 'big' World Series. Even as the St. Louis series was coming to a close, thousands of sportsgoers were flooding into the big Baltimore Municipal Stadium.

* * *

Drew Rebuke

"All of which reminds me to make a friendly reply to a recent notice I drew in the column of Rodger Pippen, the veteran Baltimore sports editor. It seems some Baltimore fan stumbled over a recent piece I wrote in which I said Baltimore was a big-league town in everything except sports. He penned a mild rebuke and sent it to Pippen.

"Apparently, the gentleman who wrote to Pippen misconstrued the meaning somewhere along the line. I've always said Baltimore rated the best in sports—a big league, not minor league, baseball franchise; a big league football franchise, and all else that goes toward the best in sports attractions.

"Baltimore, because of the availability of its big Stadium, is also a city that has been too long overlooked as a profitable spot for a world heavyweight championship prize fight. Give Baltimore Joe Louis against a first-flight contender and, in my humble opin-

Continued on Second Sports Page.

Stormy Minor Loop Confab Looms

By JACK HAND

NEW YORK, Nov. 8—(A. P.).—Minor league baseball appears to be heading toward another stormy session at its December 6-8 annual conclave in Buffalo, where a revolt of the higher classification circuits may develop into an open split with the national association.

If President Frank Shaughnessy of the International League can attract the support of the American Asociation and the Pacific Coast League, which has major-league ambitions, a new Double A bloc will be organized, acting independertly, but in co-operation with the big show and other minors.

LANDIS' RULE

The most important result of such a revolt would be to make the three circuits directly accountable to Commissioner K. M. Landis instead of President W. G. Bramham of the Association.

American Association support appears unlikely, although President George M. Trautman has reserved an opinion until after the meeting of his league's board of directors December 3. Trautman has been mentioned as a possible successor to Bramham, along with Presidents Thomas K. Richardson of the Eastern League;, William G. (Billy) Evans of the Southern Association, Clarence Rowland of the Pacific Coast League and Shaughnessy.

WANT MAJOR STATUS

Pacific Coast League directors insist upon major-league status, a stand that has not drawn the support of the International or Association.

A key plank in the platform President Rowland will put before the convention is an increase in the major-league draft price from $7,500 to $15,000. Failing in this, the prosperous circuit has threatened to refuse to give up players selected in the annual draft grab ba. Such a stand would involve breaking away from all organized ball.

KEY FACTOR

In the final estimate the physical condition of Bramham may be the key factor. The Durham (N. C.) executive was re-elected for a five-year term at $25,000 per last December at New York's highly controversial "battle of the proxies." Although he recently was confined to a hospital, Bramham has resumed his work and is reported ready to have charge of the Buffalo convention.

If Braham's health should make it impossible for him to attend Richardson, as chairman of the executive committee, would preside until a new leader could be named.

HAVE YOU SEEN SNOWBALL? — Snowball, the laughing dog pictured above, has been missing from his home for a week, and his owner, Elaine Paska, 402 Cornwall street, is very much concerned over his disappearance. He is a two-year-old Samoyed, and is very gentle. If you have seen Snowball, please contact his owner at the above address.

SPORT NEWS IN BRIEF

CHICAGO, Nov. 8—(A. P.).—Lee Savold, ranked among boxing's first 10 heavyweight contenders, tonight will attempt to redeem himself for his defeat by Joe Baksi three months ago in a 10-round main event bout against Larry Lane here. Lane suffered a leg injury in training, but was okayed for the bout by State Athlectic Commission physicians.

POLY TAKES TITLE

Poly took the Maryland scholastic soccer title yesterday at Clifton Park by beating Mount St. Joe, last year's champion, 4 to 2. Al Kondor and Gene Tyler each scored twice for the Engineers.

DETROIT BOWLER LEADS

CHICAGO, Nov. 8—(A. P.).—Chet Bukowski, thirty-year-old Detroit war plant machinist, fired a sensational 1,772 total for eight games to take a commanding lead in the Bomar Diamond Diamond Medal Individual Bowling Classic.

Hershey Icers Play Pittsburgh Tonight

NEW YORK, Nov. 8—(A. P.).—Action in the American Hockey League tonight will see a clash of the loop leaders at Hershey, where the Pittsburgh Hornets at the top of the Western Division will face off against the Bears, tied for the lead in the East.

Notre Dame To Test Army's Grid Line

By LAWTON CARVER
International News Service Sports Editor.

NEW YORK, Nov. 8.—In running wild against fair to middlin' opponents this season Army indicated very strongly that it possesses a good, tough, rugged and alert line.

If it's ability hasn't been overestimated the Cadets should remain undefeated against Notre Dame on Saturday at Yankee Stadium. There is nothing unusual about a situation in which the line is thus regarded as the key to touchdowns, except that in this particular case the Army forwards are brought more prominently into the picture by virtue of what Navy did to Notre Dame last Saturday.

NAVY LINE STRONG

The Irish had been having pretty much their own way all season until they ran into forwards who opened great gaping holes on the offense and stopped the Irish running game as cold as a deceased fish on the defense. The Navy line stole the show.

The Army line doesn't figure to be quite as tough as Navy's mature and unshaken forwards, but generally is given an edge over Notre Dame by observers who have followed them both. Coach Red Blaik of Army is pinning all his hopes on the chance that his line is not far behind Navy's.

He points out, however, the all-important facts that this Navy line is the same one that played last year, thus is mature and seasoned, while Army has only one hold-over up front, the rest being second-stringers of 1943.

If Notre Dame beats Army to the surprise of everybody, except possibly Notre Dame, you can attribute it to Army weaknesses up front that weren't apparent in the games to date.

IRISH HAVE CHANCE

I was among the few who thought Notre Dame would defeat Navy. Now I'm among the few who give Notre Dame a chance against Army, which can accomplish that which has never happened before, make it a year in which both Navy and Army beat Notre Dame.

The Irish have dropped a scattered few games to the service teams in the past—a total of so few that it looks actually like poor rivalry—but never in any one season have the Irish bit the dirt against both of those elevens. Everybody seems insistent that this will be the year.

CITY BOOTERS WIN

City College turned back Vocational in a 3-0 soccer game yesterday. Johnny Cooper scored all three goals.

Tennessee Seen Rose Bowl Choice

By TED ME ER

NEW YORK, Nov. 8—(A. P.). College football took a back seat to the Presidential election, but within the next few weeks the air probably will be filled with guesses on what teams will play in the various bowl games on New Year's Day.

While nothing official has been announced, the various committees in charge of the Rose Bowl, Sugar Bowl, Orange Bowl, Sun Bowl, Cotton Bowl and all the other bowls no doubt have been maneuvering backstage for some time.

This is the way things shape up now according to information from unofficial sources:

Rose Bowl (Pasadena)—The November 25 game between Southern California and University of California at Los Angeles (U. C. L. A.) is expected to decide the Pacific Coast representative. The winner will invite an Eastern team, with Tennessee reported as the likely choice. Last year U. S. C. trimmed Washington, 29 to 0, before 68,000.

Sugar Bowl (New Orleans)—Tulane, Georgia Tech, Mississippi State and Tennessee being considered as Southern representative. Committee would like a Western Conference eleven as opponent. Last year Georgia Tech nipped Tulsa, 20 to 18, in thriller before 69,000.

Orange Bowl (Miami)—Tennessee, Alabama, Mississippi State or Georgia Tech most likely choices to meet either Wake Forest, Duke, Holy Cross, Tulsa, or perhaps second ranking team in Southwest Conference. Last year Louisiana State beat the Texas Aggies, 19 to 14, before 27,000.

Cotton Bowl (Dallas)—Oklahoma Aggies, Mississippi State, Wake Forest and Georgia Tech most prominently mentioned as opponents for champions of Southwest Conference. Rice now tops conference, but Texas, Texas Christian and Arkansas still are in race. Last year Texas and Randolph Field tied, 7-7, before 15,000.

Sun Bowl (El Paso)—Sports writers are booming the Second Air Force of Colorado Springs, Col., and mighty Randolph Field as opponents. Last year Southwestern of Texas beat New Mexico, 7 to 0.

The East-West game will be played as usual at San Francisco, but nothing as yet has been heard from the Oil Bowl at Houston; Vulcan Bowl at Birmingham, Ala., and the Flower Bowl at Jacksonville, Fla.

Then, too, there probably will be, as last year, an Arab Bowl game at Oran, a Potato Bowl at Belfast, a Lily Bowl in Bermuda and a Tea Bowl in London.

MISSING—Duke, a black and white Lewellyn setter, has been missing from home about a week. His owner, Col. Randolph Coyle of Montgomery road (Elkridge 27) has been searching the countryside in an effort to find Duke. The dog has not been trained to hunt and it is hoped that anybody finding him does not hurt him if he fails to obey orders. If you know of Duke's whereabouts please notify Colonel Coyle at the above address or call Elkridge 89.

Local Booters In Derby Test

The Baltimore Americans and the Baltimore Soccer Club clash in their first Derby Day game of the American League season Sunday afternoon at Bugle Field at 3.15 o'clock. The league designates as Derby Day the Sunday when the teams of the same city face each other.

As far as the local clubs are concerned these Derby Day clashes have always been hard fought battles. Records or past performances mean nothing when the Amerks and Clubmen get together. In a majority of the instances the "underdog" has come up the winner.

Both teams are primed for this Sunday's test. The Amerks last week handed the Kearny Scots their first defeat of the season and will take the field favored to beat their rivals. However, Coach Millard Lang believes he has straightened out his forward line and that Goalie Gil Schuerholz of the Amerks will face one of his busiest Sundays.

Manager Ed Hanson has arranged for the Martin Bombers and British Overseas Airways to play their War Industrial League game as a preliminary test to the American League battle.

PREP SOCCER

Poly, 4; Mt. St. Joe, 2.
City, 3; Vocational, 0.

Middies To Face Corneil Here Saturday

By JOE JAMES CUSTER

NEW YORK, Nov. 8—(U. P.). It's a military secret how many tons of Japanese shipping he sent to the bottom as skipper of submarine S-16, but his work with the football is out in the open for all the gridiron world to see.

For his exploits in the Pacific, he'd be the coach of the year even if his team didn't win a single game all season, but for Navy's smashing victory last Saturday over previously unbeaten Notre Dame, Comdr. Oscar E. (Swede) Hagberg is the United Press choice for the nation's coach of the week.

The Middies face Cornell in Baltimore Stadium on Saturday.

KEEPS BALANCE

The 13 years since his graduation from Annapolis have strengthened the lasting impression Hagberg made upon his classmates, who wrote of him in their year book:

"He has a strong, likeable personality, with a sparkling sense of humor."

The sparkling humor enabled him to keep his balance as the sky-touted Middies blew two games because they "couldn't get rid of the fumble play," and to claim responsibility for the setbacks.

"I am an incurable optimist," he chuckled today, "and I should never say anything to anybody. When the season started I heartily agreed with the press notices and completely forgot to turn to page two of the high school coaches' manual which says to "never underestimate an opponent." So when, against North Carolina we found ourselves third down and six to go, our quarterback didn't know what to do, because I'd never thought we'd ever find ourselves third down and six to go."

BORN IN WEST VIRGINIA

The tall, wavy-haired, dark and handsome commander is "pure Swede." His father emigrated from Stockholm in 1906, met the future Mrs. Hagberg in Pennsylvania, where they were married.

Oscar was born in West Virginia and distinguished himself in football, basket ball and baseball throughout his grammar and high school days at Follansbee, carrying on for Bethany College in 1926 before entering the Naval Academy the following year.

As versatile as he was valuable, Hagberg served as tackle, end and fullback under "Navy Bill" Ingram, an all-around experience that was to mark his coaching in the future.

STADIUM TUSSLE

The Forest Park and City College grid teams tangle Saturday night at the Stadium. In its last start Forest Park upset Poly.

Another Drama Based On Novel To Be Seen Here

By NORMAN CLARK

BALTIMORE HAS seen two new plays by well-known writers already this season and we are to have a third before the bells of Christmas begin to ring.

We refer to "A Bell for Adano," the dramatization of John Hersey's novel of the same title by Paul Osborn. The new drama, with Fredric March starred in the role of Major Joppolo and with Margot in the leading feminine part of Tina, will have its first performance on any stage in New Haven tomorrow night. It will then go to Boston for a fortnight's stay and will be seen here at Ford's for the week beginning November 27. Its New York opening will take place at the Cort Theatre on December 6.

Mr. Hersey's novel was published last February by Alfred Knopf and has been rated by some reviewers as the finest novel to come out of the war. Its plot has to do with the difficulties encountered by a major with the American military government of occupied territory as he attempts to rehabilitate an invasion-swept Italian town, after the Nazis have fled. Mr. Hersey was with the American Army of Occupation in the Sicilian and Italian campaigns, wrote his novel from first-hand observation and experience. Paul Osborn was last represented on the New York stage by "The Innocent Voyage," and is best known for his "On Borrowed Time" and "The Vinegar Tree."

Prominent in "A Bell for Adano" are Alexander Granach, Everett Sloane, Leon Rothier, Bruce MacFarlane, Le Roi Operti, J. Harold Stone, Tito Vuolo, Silvio Minciotti, Rolfe Sedan, Harry Selby and Joseph Verdi.

"A Bell for Adano" is the first production of Leland Hayward, long an actors' and playwrights' representative.

Those two new plays mentioned in our first paragraph are, of course, Rose Franken's "Soldier's Wife," now a hit on Broadway, and the J. P. Marquand-George S. Kaufman comedy, "The Late George Apley," which certainly seems headed for Manhattan acclaim.

Before we get around to "A Bell for Adano" there will come to Ford's next week another presentation of "Blossom Time," to be followed the week of November 20, by R. H. Burnside's Gilbert and Sullivan operas. The only booking for December at Ford's thus far is the Theatre Guild's offering of "The Cherry Orchard," the week of the eleventh.

To our desk the other day came a long, important looking envelope from across the Atlantic. Inside was a small piece of paper, evidently torn from a scratch pad. It read:

"Here's 'mud in your eye' from a gay bar in Paris from a couple of guys from Baltimore. Best to you—our friend—"Ben Lyon and Koffy Katz."

The former is the stage and screen star—now a lieutenant colonel in the U. S. Army—the latter, Capt. Kaufman Ray Katz, who is also with our forces in Europe. "Koffy" is the son of the late A. Ray Katz and a grandson of Jacob Epstein.

Movie CLOCK

CENTURY—"American Romance," 11.36 A. M., 2.07, 4.38, 7.09, 9.40 P. M. "Abroad With Two Yanks," 12.47, 2.49, 4.51 P. M.
NEW—"Irish Eyes Are Smiling," 10 A. M., 12, 2, 4, 6, 8, 10 P. M.
KEITHS—"I Love a Soldier," 10.01 A. M., 12.01, 2.01, 4.01, 6.01, 8.01, 10 P. M.
VALENCIA—"Marriage Is Private Affair," 1.53, 4.27, 7.01, 9.35 P. M.
MAYFAIR—"Sing, Neighbor, Sing," 10.30 A. M., 12.13, 1.56, 3.39, 5.22, 7.05, 8.48, 10.31 P. M.
STANLEY—"Rainbow Island," 10.50 A. M., 12.45, 3, 5.15, 7.30, 9.50 P. M.
ROSLYN—"Rise and Shine," 1.01, 4.05, 7.09, 10.13 P. M.
TIMES—"Gildersleeve's Ghost," 2, 4.38, 7.16, 9.44 P. M., 12.12, 2.40 A. M.
PARKWAY—"Going My Way," 1.39, 4.23, 7.07, 9.52 P. M.
HIPPODROME—"Tall in the Saddle," 11 A. M., 1.50, 4.40, 7.30, 10.10 P. M.
LITTLE—"48 Hours," 11.05 A. M., 12.54, 2.43, 4.32, 6.21, 8.10, 9.59 P. M.
MARYLAND—"Free Combat Movies," 7 and 8 P. M.

'Master Race' Is Film At Hipp

"The Master Race" comes to the Hippodrome screen tomorrow. An Edward A. Golden Production, the producer, who presented "Hitler's Children," the film features George Coulouris, Stanley Ridges, Eric Feldary, Jason Robards, Osa Massen, Nancy Gates and Gavin Muir.

The theme treats of the dangerous real leaders of Germany, and their post-war activities. It reveals how Colonel Von Beck, a fanatical Nazi, makes plans with many of his associates to infiltrate the conquered areas and create disunity. He comes to the town of Kolar in the guise of a Belgian patriot endeavoring to aid Belgian patriots and British forces in the tasks of reconstruction.

2nd Week For Hit At Keiths

Sonny Tufts is another of the tall boys of the movies who is having stand-in difficulties. He is six feet, four and there just aren't any stand-ins that tall around the place. However, the situation was solved for Mark Sandrich's I Love a Soldier.

A six-footer was hired and given four-inch wooden sandals to strap to his feet when standing in for the big fellow who appears opposite Paulette Goddard in this Paramount film which will spend a second week at Keiths.

'RISE AND SHINE' NOW AT ROSLYN

Jack Oakie, George Murphy, Walter Brennan, Linda Darnell and Milton Berle are the stars of Mark Hellinger's "Rise and Shine," the musical comedy now at the Roslyn.

Set on a college campus at the height of the football season, "Rise and Shine" offers songs, dances, girls, comedy. The story is taken from James Thurber's "My Life and Hard Times."

The Roslyn also presents an added feature, "Smith of Minnesota," a football drama.

'SINCE YOU WENT AWAY,' PARKWAY

"Since You Went Away," starring Claudette Colbert, Jennifer Jones, Joseph Cotton, Shirley Temple, Monty Woolley, Lionel Barrymore and Robert Walker, will start Saturday at Loew's Parkway.

Neil Hamilton asserts that he has the nearest thing to a title role in "Since You Went Away." But, as Hamilton points out, he plays the soldier husband of Miss Colbert, the "You" who went away.

Gene Tierney In New Drama

When a screen star winds up on a lonely prairie keeping house for her Army husband and manages at the same time to become a competent, though brand new mother — that's news. Therefore, the fact that Gene Tierney has returned from her temporary retirement to star in "Laura," the new 20th Century-Fox murder mystery film, is news, too.

"Laura," which opens at the New tomorrow, is Gene's first screen assignment since she left Beverly Hills almost a year ago to follow her husband's fortunes while he attempted to become an officer at Fort Riley, Kan. By the time Count Oleg Cassini had a "Lieut." tacked to his name, he was a proud father, and Gene Tierney found herself in the novel position of having received as much, if not more, attention from newspapers and fan magazines than when she was on active duty at the 20th lot.

WILLIAM BENDIX in his first starring comedy role!

EDWARD SMALL presents
WILLIAM BENDIX
HELEN WALKER
DENNIS O'KEEFE

THIS IS NOT A WAR PICTURE for laffs only

ABROAD with TWO YANKS

with JOHN LODER • JANET LAMBERT • GEORGE CLEVELAND

Based on an original story by Fred Guiol • Adaptation by Edward E. Seabrook and Tedwell Chapman
Screen Play by Charles Rogers, Wilkie Mahoney, Ted Sills • Directed by ALLAN DWAN
Released thru United Artists

★ ★ **STARTS MIDNIGHT TONIGHT!** ★ ★

LAST FEATURE Starts 5.00 A. M.

LOEW'S CENTURY
18 WEST LEXINGTON STREET

Gildersleeve Is Hero At Times

The efforts of Throckmorton P. Gildersleeve to unmask a couple of scientists who are using a kidnaped girl and a vicious gorilla for their experiments, provide the plot of "Gildersleeve's Ghost," now having its first Baltimore showing at the Times.

In a cemetery two of Gildy's ancestors are interred. Their ghosts plot to help "Gildy" win the election for chief of police by having him unmask the scientists, rescue the girl and become a hero.

In addition, the Times presents on the same bill "Drums of the Desert."

'48 HOURS' WILL STAY AT LITTLE

"Forty-eight Hours" will spend a second week at the Little.

It starts calmly in the pastoral setting of a typical rural English village, but begins accumulating speed and suspense almost immediately and ends up in a blaze of shootin' and killin' the likes of which haven't been seen since Jack Dalton and his Horse Marines gave the Indians what for.

Calling all smart students!

$22.50

■ Leed's prep suits need no pep talks... they speak for themselves! And they're at Leed's in regulars as well as huskies... ages 12 to 22. ALSO boys' new overcoats, sizes 12-22. Brown, blue and tan cameltone effects.. **$20.95**

Leed's
A Store Worth Knowing
15 W. BALTIMORE ST.
Regular Charge or Budget Accounts

Open Thurs. & Mon. to 9 P. M.

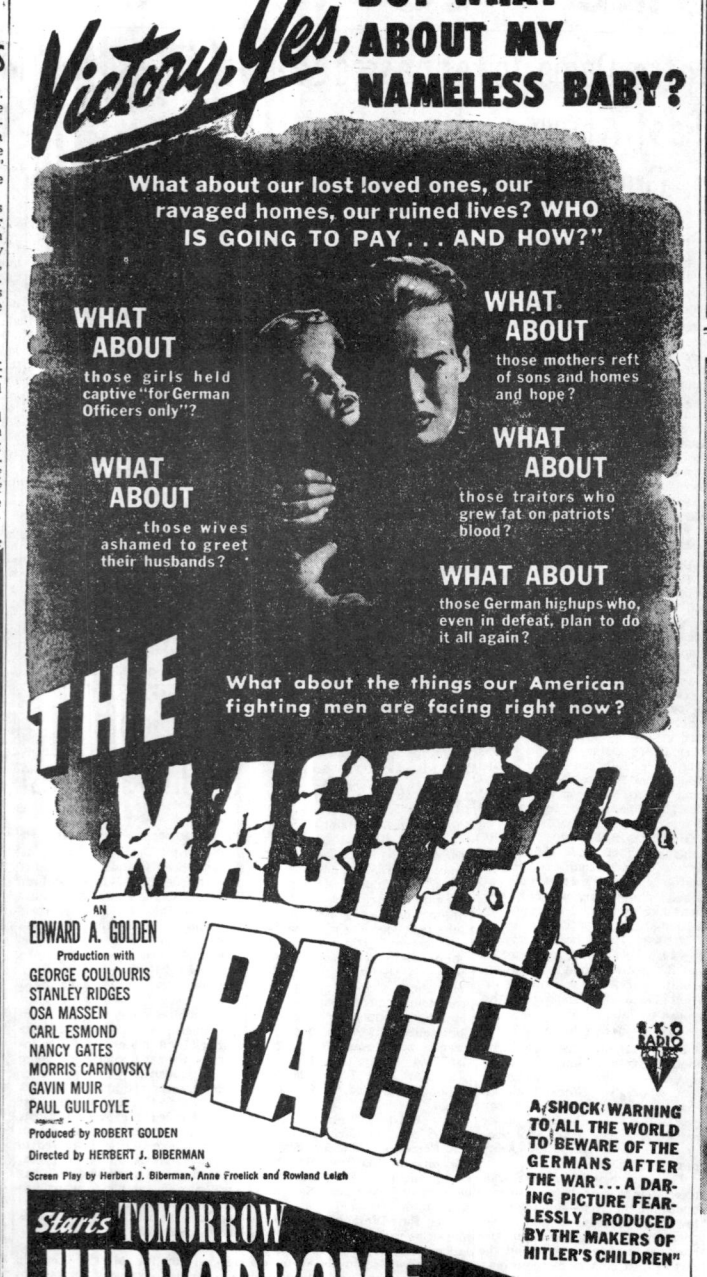

Victory, Yes, BUT WHAT ABOUT MY NAMELESS BABY?

What about our lost loved ones, our ravaged homes, our ruined lives? WHO IS GOING TO PAY... AND HOW?"

WHAT ABOUT those girls held captive "for German Officers only"?

WHAT ABOUT those mothers reft of sons and homes and hope?

WHAT ABOUT those wives ashamed to greet their husbands?

WHAT ABOUT those traitors who grew fat on patriots' blood?

WHAT ABOUT those German highups who, even in defeat, plan to do it all again?

What about the things our American fighting men are facing right now?

THE MASTER RACE

AN EDWARD A. GOLDEN Production with
GEORGE COULOURIS
STANLEY RIDGES
OSA MASSEN
CARL ESMOND
NANCY GATES
MORRIS CARNOVSKY
GAVIN MUIR
PAUL GUILFOYLE

Produced by ROBERT GOLDEN
Directed by HERBERT J. BIBERMAN
Screen Play by Herbert J. Biberman, Anne Froelick and Rowland Leigh

A SHOCK WARNING TO ALL THE WORLD TO BEWARE OF THE GERMANS AFTER THE WAR... A DARING PICTURE FEARLESSLY PRODUCED BY THE MAKERS OF "HITLER'S CHILDREN"

Starts **TOMORROW**
HIPPODROME
Plus A BIG STAGE SHOW

GRACE MOORE
Star of the Metropolitan Opera says:
"I have used Arrid for years and like it immensely... and I notice that Arrid is used by many of my friends in the stage, screen and radio world."

New Cream Deodorant
Safely helps **Stop Perspiration**

1. Does not irritate skin. Does not rot dresses or men's shirts.
2. Prevents under-arm odor. Helps stop perspiration safely.
3. A pure, white, antiseptic, stainless vanishing cream.
4. No waiting to dry. Can be used right after shaving.
5. Awarded Approval Seal of American Institute of Laundering — harmless to fabric. Use Arrid regularly.

39¢ Plus tax Also 59¢ jars
Guaranteed by Good Housekeeping
ARRID
THE LARGEST SELLING DEODORANT

...unattainable...she became desirable beyond all desire!

Men were ready to die for her smile... to kill for her kiss!

GENE TIERNEY • DANA ANDREWS • CLIFTON WEBB

Laura

Never a woman so irresistible — or a picture so haunting!

ANOTHER HIT FROM **20th CENTURY-FOX**

VINCENT PRICE • JUDITH ANDERSON • PRODUCED AND DIRECTED BY OTTO PREMINGER
SCREEN PLAY BY JAY DRATLER, SAMUEL HOFFENSTEIN AND BETTY REINHARDT

STARTS TOMORROW

NEW THEATRE
Lexington St. Near Park Ave.

LATEST MARCH OF TIME "Uncle Sam, Mariner"